MEDAL OF HONOR RECIPIENTS 1863–1994

Volume I
Civil War to 2nd Nicaraguan Campaign

MEDAL OF HONOR RECIPIENTS 1863–1994

Volume I
Civil War to 2nd Nicaraguan Campaign

Compiled by George Lang, M.H.,
Raymond L. Collins and
Gerard F. White

Facts On File, Inc.
AN INFOBASE HOLDINGS COMPANY

Medal of Honor Recipients 1863–1994

Facts On File, Inc.
460 Park Avenue South
New York, NY 10016

Library of Congress Cataloging-in-Publication Data

Lang, George.
    Medal of Honor recipients, 1863–1994 / compiled by George Lang,
Raymond L. Collins, and Gerard F. White
        p. cm.
    Includes bibliographical references and index.
    ISBN 0-8160-3259-9 (set)
    ISBN 0-8160-3260-2 (vol. 1)
    ISBN 0-8160-3261-0 (vol. 2)
    1. Medal of Honor. 2. United States—Armed Forces—Biography.
I. Collins, Raymond L. (Raymond Luther) II. White, Gerard F.
III. Title.
UB433.L36 1995
355.1'342—dc20   95-12529

Facts On File books are available at special discounts when purchased in bulk quantities
for businesses, associations, institutions or sales promotions. Please call our Special Sales
Department in New York at 212/683-2244 or 800/322-8755.

This book is printed on acid-free paper.

Printed in the United States of America

VB CC 10 9 8 7 6 5 4 3 2 1

TABLE OF CONTENTS

BATTLE IS THE SENSATION OF LIFE.

"A human being is never so alive as he is in combat. He may feel terror or he may not, but the prospect of losing his life makes it surge and flare within him. At no other time do his senses more acutely perceive the world. At no other time does his nerve fire with such spark. Never again will he weld as tight an emotional bond to others around him . . . ."

Philip Edwards, in *Soldier of Fortune* magazine

ACKNOWLEDGMENTS

Assistance has been received from the following individuals or organizations:

Jerry Lucino, Director, Institute of Heraldry, Washington, D.C.; Andrew Woods, First Infantry Division Museum, Wheaton, IL; Chuck Lafferty, Irish Brigade, Ft. Schyler, NY; Ron Gough, USAF (Ret), Dover, DE; Joseph L. Murphy, 1st Marine Raiders, Ashland, MA; Albert Lerner, Jewish War Veterans National Museum, Washington, D.C.; Marine Corps Historical Center, Washington Naval Yard; Scott Armstrong, Spring City, PA; Joseph Kralich, Sante Fe, NM; Naval Historical Society, Washington, D.C.; Terrence L. Adkins, USA (Ret), Portland, OR; Wilson Smith, Wilmington, DE; Transportation Museum, Ft. Eustis, VA; Quartermaster Museum, Ft. Lee, VA; U.S. News & World Report, New York City and Washington, D.C.; Rudi Williams, Armed Forces Information Service, Alexandria, VA; Mr. Ednor, United States Navy Still Photo Branch, Washington, D.C.; U.S. Naval Academy Alumni Association, Annapolis, MD; Bernard F. Cavalcante, Naval Historical Center, Washington, D.C.; Johnny Concannon, National Historian, Ancient Order of Hibernians, Flushing, NY; Jerry Anderson, Department of Defense, Indian Affairs, Arlington, VA; Fred Anthony, United States Marine Corps Decorations and Awards Branch & Staff, Washington, D.C.; Robert Aquilina, United States Marine Corps History Department, Washington, D.C.; Rick Arndt, Department of Veterans Affairs, Public Affairs Office, Washington, D.C.; Fred Bauer, Queens, NY; Stan Bozich, Michigan's Own, Inc., Frankenmuth, MI; James Cappadanno, Staten Island, NY; Jack Conway, Woodside, NY; Dave Erbstoesser, Bismarck, ND; John Neilson, Ft. Concho Museum, San Angelo, TX; Judy Van Ben Thuysen, Chief, Public Liaison Branch, Navy Dept., Washington, D.C.; Tom Hennesey, Latham, NY; Frank Lynch, Oneonta, NY; Kenneth Smith-Christmas, USMC History Museum, Quantico, VA; Dr. Robert Morris, National Archives & Records Section, New York, NY; Bill Pierce, 6th Marine Div., Mt. Pleasant, SC; Herb Rosenbleeth, Jewish War Veterans, Washington, D.C.; Military History Institute, Carlisle Barracks, PA; William Linn, National Archives and Records Administration, Washington, D.C.; Charles E. Chambers, Houston, TX; Leonard Close, Saco, ME; Raymond R. Davis, USMC (Ret), CMH, Stockbridge, GA; Francis S. Currey, CMH, Bonneau, SC; Thomas F. Durning, North Haven, CT; John Barry Kelly, Philadelphia, PA; James W. Kenney, San Antonio, TX; Gary F. Lettow, Cedar Falls, IA; Glade H. Lyon, Ashton, ID; Charles A. MacGillivary, CMH, Past President, Congressional Medal of Honor Society, Braintree, MA; Benedict R. Mayrniak, Buffalo, NY; Hank Morris, USA (Ret), Portsmouth, VA; Edward F. Murphy, President, Medal of Honor Historical Society, Mesa, AZ; Michael Robert Patterson, Wantagh, NY; Charles E. Sharrock, Denver, CO; Wes Slusher, McKeesport, PA; Richard Straight, Rensselaer, NY; Timothy M. Touchette, Niagara Falls, NY; all Veteran Service Officers, State of North Carolina; Dan Cole Younger, N., Richland Hills, TX; D. E. Tex Powell, Fullerton, CA; Charles Worman, Curator, Wright-Patterson Air Force Base Museum, Dayton, OH; Stan Smith, Potomac, MD; John and Joyce Davidson, Middletown, RI; Jack McMullen, Seaford, NY; and Sharon Vance Kiernan, Poway, CA.

The generous donation by the Atari Corporation of the Mega4 ST computer on which the original database was created is deeply appreciated as is the technical assistance from Paul Heckel, Producer/Director, of Zoomracks, the database originally used to input the information.

The legal assistance given by Cravath, Swaine & Moore (CS&M), New York, NY is gratefully acknowledged. Our thanks to David O. Brownwood, Philip J. Boeckman, Peter N. Flocos and Douglas J. Kepple (formerly with CS&M).

A special note of thanks to Jean Kirk, Chief, Navy Department, Decorations and Awards Branch, Washington, D.C.; Roger D. Hunt, Bethesda, MD, author of *Brevet Brigadier Generals in Blue;* and many thanks to Harold "Sonny" Wells, Liberty, MO.

We gratefully acknowledge the words of encouragement from Rep. Wendell H. Ford and Sen. Guy V. S. "Sonny" Montgomery.

The Congressional Medal of Honor Society members and the many families of deceased members rendered their encouragement and assistance in our research.

We cannot forget the encouragement and assistance from our families, especially our wives, Grace, Jackie and Pat. The assistance in proofreading this book by Charles and Cathy White and Jackie Lang is deeply appreciated.

Needless to say, we hope that we did not forget anyone that assisted in making this project possible. For those that we may have omitted we apologize for the oversight and wish to thank them here and now.

The authors would like to also acknowledge and thank the "expeditors" for their assistance in getting the copy back and forth from the publisher: Kevin Egan, Seaford, NY and Joseph Williams, Farmingdale, NY.

INTRODUCTION

This history of the Medal of Honor is an attempt to write a systematic account of the decoration's creation and to bring together the stories of the award and its recipients. In the process, it is our hope to uncover, collect and record past events and bring to light new facts. Since the beginning of this massive project we have known that the information previously recorded was incomplete and only partly correct. It required hours of cross checking on our part to uncover the historically correct versions of events.

Since we became a nation, American fighting men have demonstrated a great bravery without regard for personal safety. The history of the United States abounds with stories of the valor of our servicemen. Yet prior to the American Civil war, very little recognition was given to members of the armed forces.

The Medal of Honor was not the idea of any one American. Like most ideas that consolidate into institutions, it was the result of a coordinated effort evolved during the Civil War, in response to the needs of the times. During the first 56 years of the history of the Medal of Honor many changes were made in both the design and the regulations governing its award; and in 1918 additional medals were authorized for acts of bravery that did not merit the Medal of Honor.

The keeping of a Medal of Honor Roll was approved by an act of Congress in 1916. When a recipient reached the age of 65 he was eligible for a pension of $10.00 a month for life. In 1917, to protect the integrity of the Medal, a military board was convened to review all the awards to date, and those who did not meet certain criteria were removed from the Medal of Honor Roll.

These measures may appear to be extremely restrictive, but in reality they are the only means of maintaining the high standards as prescribed by the regulations that govern the award of the Medal. For the same reasons it is imperative that the history of the Medal recipients be preserved. These recipients represent the highest traditions of the armed forces. The many unknown heroes who also give their lives for this nation, and their deeds, just as great, must be preserved as an integral part of our history.

It has been said: "Poor is the Nation that has no heroes, but beggared is that Nation that has and forgets them."

The legacy of the Medal of Honor and the story of its recipients is very much a part of the history of this nation. A handful of 3,401 have been chosen to represent all who have worn the uniform of the armed forces of the United States. Today, we have only 185 recipients living, but they are still to be seen at parades and on patriotic occasions. They will forever keep that flag waving. They have been, and still are, defending our nation, but now it is with words, not guns. They have never let us down and we cannot let their history, which is in essence our history, fade away.

METHODOLOGY

Citation number: To facilitate searching, the entries are indexed to a citation number rather than a page.

Name: The name following the citation number is that under which the recipient served in the armed forces and received the Medal of Honor. Those who received the Medal posthumously are indicated by an asterisk before the name. A double awardee is indicated by a ✢ following his name.

True Name: Many members of the armed forces elected not to use their "given name" in the military. They served under an alias or, as in the case of the foreign born, their names were Americanized or misspelled. Frequently they revealed their true names at the time that they applied for the Medal of Honor pension. In some cases the true name was not known until the recipient died and his family revealed the name.

Rank: Rank is that at time of action for which the individual received the award. If the rank and receipt of award differ from that at time of action, rank at time of action is given in parentheses. The individual's highest rank in the military is also given in parentheses.

Service: Lists the branch of the armed forces in which the individual served.

Birthday: Lists the day, month and year of birth, where known.

Place of Birth: Lists the city, county, and state, territory or country of birth, where known.

Date of Death: Lists the day, month and year of death, where known.

Place of Death: Lists the city, county, and state, territory or country of death, where known.

Cemetery: Lists the name of the cemetery and the city and state in which the cemetery is located. Location of the burial plot is also given where known. If the recipient was cremated or buried at sea, the fact is indicated in this field.

Entered Service at: Lists the city, county and state in which the recipient entered the armed forces.

Unit: Lists the unit to which the recipient was assigned at the time of the action for which he was awarded the Medal of Honor.

Served as: Indicates the job the recipient had at the time of the action for which he received the Medal of Honor.

Battle or Place of Action: Lists the name of the battle for which the recipient received the Medal of Honor. If the action had no commonly known name, the city and state or country of action is given.

Date of Action: Lists the day, month and year of the action for which the recipient won the Medal of Honor

G.O. Number, Date: Lists the general order number and the date of the order under which the recipient received the Medal of Honor.

Date of Issue or Presentation: Lists the day, month and year the Medal of Honor was issued. If the Medal was presented to the recipient, the field gives the date of presentation rather than issue.

Place of Issue or Presentation: Lists the place of issue or presentation. If the Medal was not presented to the individual, the field indicates to whom the Medal was given, if known.

Citation: This field contains the exact wording of the congressional citation. In several cases, the wording contains phrases that contemporary Americans will consider offensive. However, the compilers have chosen to keep the original wording so that readers will have a better understanding of the social and political milieu in which the Medal was awarded.

Notes: Indicates whether the recipient was a prisoner of war or a double awardee.

THE HISTORY OF THE MEDAL OF HONOR

Military leaders have long recognized that awards for valor and extraordinary conduct were a way to recognize good soldiers and inspire others to deeds of greatness. The Greeks and Romans gave laurel wreaths to their best and bravest citizens. Medieval barons gave titles and land. Napoleon created the Legion d'Honneur for soldiers and citizens. This award further inspired loyalty and bravery among the ranks, and Napoleon once remarked that he could conquer Europe with a bolt of ribbon.

It was George Washington who established the first American military award for the enlisted soldier. With the creation of the Badge of Military Merit on August 7, 1782, he had found a way to reward soldiers for "singularly meritorious action." Although it was only awarded to three men, it was a step in recognizing the enlisted man for his military accomplishments. In 1932, the badge was resurrected as the Purple Heart, which is still in existence.

In the days of the American Revolution, Congress awarded specially struck medals for various accomplishments, General Washington being awarded a medal for driving the British from Boston in 1776. General Horatio Gates received a specially struck medal for his victory in the battle of Saratoga, as did General Anthony Wayne for the capture of Stony Point, New York; General Daniel Morgan for the victory at Cowpens, South Carolina; General Nathaniel Greer for victory at Eutaw Springs, South Carolina; General Henry Lee for his attack on Paulus Hook, New Jersey; and Captain John Paul Jones for defeating the British warship HMS *Serapis*. In 1780, Congress created the "Andre" medal to give to the three men who had captured British Major John Andre, who was later hanged as a spy. Andre had been plotting with Benedict Arnold for the overthrow of the American base of West Point. This was the first medal awarded to enlisted men in the American Army. What distinguished Washington's Badge of Military Merit from the Andre medal was the fact that the Badge of Military Merit could be earned by any soldier. The "Andre" medal was a special medal created by Congress to reward three specific men for a very specific act. It was not intended to be an ongoing award.

In the War of 1812 and the Mexican War special medals continued to be voted for generals, but not for enlisted men.

But in 1847, during the Mexican War, Congress created the Certificate of Merit. This certificate was originally for privates in the Army who distinguished themselves in action or by acts of heroism in peacetime. A soldier would receive the certificate and an extra $2.00 per month. In 1854, noncommissioned officers were made eligible. The drawback of a certificate, as opposed to a medal, lay in a person being deprived of having something to wear so that others could see and understand that he had performed a heroic deed. It was not until 1905 that a medal was given with the certificate. Different states and military commanders had their own medals created in order to reward soldiers, and this practice continued on into the Civil War, but there still was not a military-wide medal that could be earned by deserving soldiers and sailors.

Prior to the Civil War there was disagreement among the military leadership as to the necessity of having a medal of honor that soldiers could wear on their uniforms. One group of officers thought that the medals awarded to European military were a logical thing to copy, while others felt that since we were a democracy, we should not emulate things that were reminiscent of the old monarchies. In spite of these disagreements, a bill to "promote the efficiency of the Navy" was introduced in the Senate by Senator James W. Grimes of Iowa, chairman of the Senate Naval Committee. Navy Secretary Gideon Welles had been looking for a way to inspire reluctant sailors to improve their work. President Abraham Lincoln approved it on December 21, 1861, and this new act provided for the preparation of 200 Medals of Honor to be awarded "upon such petty officers, seamen, landsmen, and marines as shall most distinguish themselves by their gallantry in action and other seaman like qualities during the present war." Thus the Medal of Honor was created.

Secretary of the Navy Gideon Welles soon opened correspondence with the director of the Philadelphia Mint, James Pollock, in order to create a design for the new Medal. After numerous letters and proposed designs, the Navy Department approved a design and notified the Mint of their decision. The design was for a five-pointed-star-shaped emblem with a single point facing down. Each point of the star held a cluster of laurel leaves and a cluster of oak, the laurel representing victory while the oak stood for strength. In the center of the star were two figures. On the right was Minerva, Roman goddess of wisdom and war. On her helmet perched the owl of wisdom. Her left hand held a fasces, a bundle of rods with an ax blade projecting, which was a classical Roman symbol of authority. Her right hand held the shield of the Union, to dispel Discord, a small male figure on the left clutching snakes in both hands. Encircling both figures were 34 stars, one for each state in the Union at that time. The entire star-shaped emblem was suspended from a ribbon of red, white, and blue by an anchor tangled in rope. The reverse of the Medal was blank except for the inscription "Personal Valor," leaving room for engraving information about the man who had earned it. When one considers that the Medal was created during the Civil War, it is easy to see how the symbolism of the Goddess of Wisdom, using the shield of the Union to dispel Discord, would be favored.

Senator Henry Wilson of Massachusetts introduced a bill for an Army Medal of Honor on February 17, 1862, and on July 12, 1862, President Lincoln signed it into law. This provided for the president to present the medal "in the name of Congress to such noncommissioned officers and privates as shall most distinguish themselves by their gallantry in action, and other soldier-like qualities, during the present insurrection."

The Philadelphia firm of William Wilson & Sons, who had submitted the winning design for the Navy Medal through the Philadelphia Mint, approached Secretary of War Edwin M. Stanton and suggested that the design adopted by the Navy would serve just as well for the Army, and the upshot was that the Army adopted the same emblem for its Medal. The one visible difference between the two Medals was the suspension device between the star-shaped medal itself and the ribbon. Where the Navy had an anchor, the Army had an eagle perched on crossed cannon barrels, holding a saber in its talons. The wording on the reverse of the Army Medal was also different, reading "the Congress to." Underneath this inscription was room for engraving information about the Medal recipient. William Wilson & Sons were awarded contracts to assemble both the Army and Navy Medals using the star-shaped emblem that had been struck by the Philadelphia Mint.

Just four days after the approval of the Army Medal of Honor, the Navy further refined the legislation which had created its Medal. With the passage of the act on July 16, 1862, awards of the Navy Medal were extended beyond "the present war." The act also established a system for recommending sailors for the Medal and offered seamen who distinguished "themselves in battle or by extraordinary heroism in the line of their profession" a chance to be promoted, together with a gratuity of $100.00. By establishing a system for making recommendations for the Medal, the Navy avoided the problem that the Army would face many years later when soldiers began applying for the Medal on their own behalf.

At this time, the Navy and Army Medal legislation had two similarities of note. The first was that only enlisted men were eligible for the award and the second was that it was not a requirement that an act of heroism be performed in action against the enemy. On March 3, 1863, a law was passed for the Army that authorized the president to present Medals of Honor to "such officers, noncommissioned officers, and privates as have most distinguished, or who may thereafter most distinguish,

themselves in action." Army officers were now eligible to receive the Medal, and with the use of the word "thereafter," the Medal could be awarded later than the end of the "present insurrection." The act also allowed for awards for action prior to the Civil War. Many years later controversy would arise over whether or not this law negated the original Medal authorization of July 12, 1862. The July 12th act permitted the award of Medals for "soldier-like qualities," which meant that the act of heroism need not be performed in combat; however, the March 3rd law made no mention of "soldier-like qualities." At any rate, most Army awards of the Medal were made for gallantry in action, while the Navy awarded a great number of medals for "seaman-like qualities." Seamen confronted various hazards not commonly faced by soldiers, such as exploding boilers and the danger of drowning, which gave them occasion to distinguish themselves for bravery without having to be under enemy fire.

The Medal of Honor became a success from its very beginning. For Civil War action, 1,520 Medals of Honor were awarded. This number contrasts with the 238 Medals awarded for action in Vietnam, a war which lasted more than twice as long as the four-year Civil War. However, it is necessary to keep in mind that the Medal of Honor was the only military award for valor in the Civil War, and if a man did not receive this medal, there was no other which might be given in its place. Warfare was also very different then, and flags, which played a major part in battle, served as rallying points and as symbols of regimental pride. To have a regimental flag captured or fall to the ground in battle was considered a terrible disgrace. For this reason, 467 Medals of Honor were awarded for either the capture of an enemy flag or the protection of one's own. Capturing an enemy flag could almost guarantee the soldier a 30-day furlough and the Medal of Honor. There were no clear guidelines for earning and awarding the Medal of Honor until the 1890s. Veterans then began to apply for the Medals themselves, based on deeds that had taken place over 30 years before, and because the Army legislation had failed to include the recommendation of a commanding officer as a requirement, as the Navy's legislation had done, the Army continued to award the Medal when the application was initiated by the soldier himself.

The earliest action for which a Medal was awarded took place before the Civil War had even begun, February 13–14, 1861, in what is now Arizona. Bernard J. D. Irwin was an assistant surgeon in the Army who voluntarily led a command of troops to relieve a surrounded detachment of the 7th Infantry. Irwin's Medal was not awarded until January 24, 1894, over 30 years after his act of valor.

The first Medal of Honor in the Civil War was awarded to Francis Brownell of the 11th New York Infantry, on May 24, 1861, at the beginning of the conflict. Brownell's regiment was marching through Alexandria, Virginia when the regimental commander, Colonel Ellsworth, spotted a Confederate flag flying from the Marshall House Inn. Ellsworth went inside and upstairs, removed the flag, and started back down. The angry innkeeper met him on the stairs and shot him; Brownell returned the fire, shot the innkeeper, thereby earning himself the Medal of Honor. Although Francis Brownell performed the first act of the Civil War to be awarded the Medal of Honor, the Medal was not issued until 1877.

The first winner to be formally presented with a Medal of Honor was Private Jacob Parrott, and Secretary of War E. M. Stanton made the presentation. Parrott had been a member of Andrew's Raiders, a group of volunteers who set out to cut telegraph wires and to disrupt railroad lines between Atlanta, Georgia, and Chattanooga, Tennessee. The raiders had infiltrated into Confederate territory, where they stole a train and attempted to return north with it, stopping to cut telegraph wires and to burn bridges along the way. Although the mission was a failure and all of the men were captured, 19 members of the party were awarded the Medal of Honor. Parrott was one of six members of Andrew's Raiders who had been exchanged after their capture. On March 25, 1863, the six met with Stanton at the War Department, where he presented the Medal first to Parrott and then the other five. The group was then received at the White House where they enjoyed "a very interesting interview of half an hour's duration" with President Lincoln.

It was during the Civil War that one of the most amazing and controversial presentations of the Medal of Honor was made. In the summer of 1863 Robert E. Lee's Confederate Army was making its way into Pennsylvania. The War Department feared that the city of Washington would be in danger of attack when Lee turned south again and was looking for all available soldiers to defend the city. The 25th and 27th Maine regiments were two units that had been raised the previous October for a term of nine months and their enlistments were about to expire. They had spent their entire service in training or in garrison around Washington and were untried in combat. The 25th Maine refused to stay past their term to defend the city while the commander of the 27th Maine agreed to ask his men to stay. On June 30th, approximately 300 of the 864 men of the 27th Maine agreed to remain and the rest departed for home. The regimental commander then met with Secretary of War Stanton to offer the service of his volunteers. Surprisingly, Stanton then asked for the names of those who had agreed to stay so that they could each be awarded the Medal of Honor!

A few days later the battle of Gettysburg was resolved in favor of the North, and the volunteers from the 27th Maine left for home on the 4th of July. A record-keeping error eventually led to the submission of the entire roster of the 27th Maine, all 864, for the Medal of Honor authorized by Stanton. An accurate list of the approximately 300 who actually remained could not be produced and the Medals were eventually forwarded to the regimental commander who refused to give them all out, thinking that such an award was improper. All these men, however, were entered onto the list of Medal of Honor recipients, remaining there for over 50 years, until a board was convened to review all Medals of Honor awarded up to that time; as a result, all 864 men of the 27th Maine had their Medals taken away.

After the Civil War, the Indian Wars produced a steady stream of new heroes to earn the Medal. During this period abuses of the Medal began to appear. Because of the loose procedure for awarding the Medal, and poor record keeping, it became very difficult to tell who had actually earned it. In 1869, M. H. Beaumont, publisher of the magazine *The Soldier's Friend*, asked the War Department to give him a list of Medal of Honor recipients to publish. He wrote, "There are some who are using medals for the purpose of soliciting charity who obtained them surreptitiously." His request was granted, partly so that some of

the Medals could finally be delivered to those who might read their names on the list. In those days, the Medal of Honor presentation was not the prestigious ceremony that one might imagine. The Medal was often forwarded to the unit commander who might present it at a formation or in private, while for those who had left the service, the Medal was sent by registered mail. If the recipient had moved, the Medal would be returned to Washington, and hence the recipient might never know of the award to which he was entitled.

It was during the Indian Wars, after the disastrous battle at the Little Bighorn River in Montana, that some procedures began to be developed which would enhance the prestige of the Medal of Honor by closely examining the acts that would earn the Medal. While all of the men with General George Custer died at the Battle of the Little Bighorn on June 25, 1876, a detachment that he had sent to attack the Indian camp from the opposite direction managed to survive the fight. The surviving commanders recommended large numbers of their men for Medals of Honor, but Brigadier General Alfred A. Terry rejected them all saying "company commanders have recommended every man in the respective companies that behaved ordinarily well during the action. . . Medals of Honor are not intended for ordinarily good conduct, but for conspicuous acts of gallantry." In response, Colonel S. F. Sturgis assembled a board of officers to review the list of recommended men. One of the criteria the board used was "the conduct which deserves such recognition should not be the simple discharge of duty, but such acts beyond this that if omitted or refused to be done, should not justly subject the person to censure as a shortcoming or failure." As a result of the report of this review board, 24 men eventually received the Medal of Honor. Although the review process was not made standard after the battle of the Little Bighorn, it established a valuable precedent by which future recommendations for Medal awards could be evaluated.

In 1892, the War Department published a circular outlining the differences between the Medal of Honor and the Certificate of Merit. The circular stated that "Medals of Honor should be awarded to officers or enlisted men for distinguished bravery in action, while Certificates of Merit should . . . be awarded for distinguished service, whether in action or otherwise . . . by which the Government is saved losing men or material. Simple heroism in battle, on the contrary, is fitly rewarded by a Medal of Honor." Although the word "simple" does not fit very well when describing the Medal of Honor, this distinction between the Medal and the Certificate of Merit made the matter clear. The circular, however, did not preclude a man from receiving both the Medal and the certificate.

On April 23, 1890, in Washington, D.C., the Medal of Honor Legion was formed by Medal of Honor recipients to perpetuate the ideals and protect the integrity of the Medal of Honor. The Legion was to play a part in lobbying for changes.

Another problem was beginning to develop. Veterans' organizations were adopting medals that looked very similar to the Medal of Honor, and only close examination of these medals could distinguish them. In 1896, Adjutant General George D. Ruggles advised the secretary of war to change the pattern of the ribbon of the Medal of Honor to distinguish it from similar medals. On May 2, 1895, Congress had approved the creation of "a rosette or knot to be worn in lieu of the medal, and a ribbon to be worn with the medal . . . " The secretary of war was also authorized to issue replacement ribbons to those whose ribbons had worn out, and on November 10, 1896, the War Department issued a description of the new ribbon. Instead of having alternating red and white vertical stripes with a strip of blue across the top, it would feature a center stripe of white, flanked on either side by a stripe of blue, bordered by stripes of red. The secretary of war issued regulations for the distribution of the rosettes or knots on February 18, 1897. The regulations required that in order to be sold a rosette or bow, the man had to prove that he had earned the Medal of Honor by showing the Medal or proof of membership in the Medal of Honor Legion, or a statement of entitlement from the War Department. Tiffany & Company was given the contract for the ribbons, and with the proper proof, recipients were permitted to purchase the rosettes or knots directly. On May 4, 1898, a similar resolution passed, authorizing a rosette or knot for the Navy. In this way, the services had distinguished the real Medal from the imitations, and recipients were now also authorized to wear a rosette or knot.

The creation of the Medal of Honor Legion had sparked an increase in the number of applications made to the War Department for the Medal of Honor for deeds performed during the Civil War. This increase seems to have alarmed the members of the Legion for they began to push for legislation to make the Medal of Honor harder to receive and to prevent the Medal being awarded in cases like that of the 27th Maine during the Civil War. They even pushed to have the Medals taken away from those men. Legislation was not quick to come on this matter.

There were, however, stricter guidelines put in place for applying for the Medal, but because there were no regulations in place to deal with these new applications it became necessary to formulate a policy. President William McKinley directed that such a policy be incorporated into the Army Regulations. On June 26, 1897, paragraph 177 of the Regulations was amended to require that Medals only be awarded for service " . . . . performed in action of such a conspicuous character as to clearly distinguish the man for gallantry and intrepidity above his comrades . . . incontestable proof of performance of the service will be exacted." The new regulation also required that the claim for a Medal of Honor be made by someone other than the person in question whenever possible, and official records should also be used to support the claim. Failing this, " . . . testimony must embrace that of one or more eyewitnesses, who, under oath, describe specifically the act or acts they saw wherein the person recommended or applying clearly distinguished himself above his fellows for a most distinguished gallantry in action." Additionally, claims made for action which took place after January 1, 1890, could only be made by the commanding officer or a soldier " . . . having personal cognizance of the act for which the honor is claimed." For the first time, a time limit was set. All claims for a Medal of Honor for action that would take place after June 26, 1897, would have to be submitted within one year of the act.

The amended regulation defined the type of deed for which the Army would award the Medal, set up rules for applications, and set a time limit for award recommendations. All of these things can be found in present-day Medal of Honor regulations.

If one looks back to the review board of 1876, set up to screen the Little Bighorn recommendations, the origins of the June 26, 1897, regulation can be seen.

Elihu Root, when he became secretary of war, did much to push for legislation to tighten up procedures for awarding the Medal. Root wanted to clear up inconsistencies between Army regulations and legislation passed by Congress, and he was interested in setting a time limit in which Medal of Honor acts could be considered. He wrote, "Under existing law there is no limit to the time within which application for the award of Medals of Honor may be filed and considered . . . applications have been filed in recent years for the award of the Medals for gallantry alleged to have been performed more than 40 years ago . . . . It is needless to say that it is impossible at this late date to determine the facts in such cases with any degree of accuracy."

Because Congress was slow to implement his suggestions, on September 21, 1901, Root used his power as secretary of war to set up a review board, whose purpose was to examine claims for the Medal arising from the War with Spain and the Philippine Insurrection. The chairman of this review board was Major General Arthur MacArthur, himself a Civil War Medal of Honor recipient and the father of General Douglas MacArthur. The review board was in session for nine weeks and did such excellent work establishing procedures that it was recommended the board be continued, and this was done. On April 19, 1902, Root issued Special Order Number 95 to establish a board of officers to examine " . . . such applications and recommendations as may be referred to it."

Elihu Root also was in favor of changing the design of the Army Medal of Honor itself. There was a general consensus among military leaders including Medal of Honor winners General George L. Gillespie, chief of engineers, and Horace Porter, ambassador to France. Porter had the company of Messrs. Arthur, Bertrand, and Berenger of Paris draw up designs that he first showed to Root and then sent to the Medal of Honor Legion whose officers agreed to the new design. On April 23, 1904, Congress approved it and authorized the secretary of war to replace those Medals already issued.

The new Medal kept the star shape. The center of the star, however, now featured only the head of the goddess Minerva. A laurel wreath ringed the points of the star, while the oak leaves remained in the points of the star. The head of Minerva was encircled by the words "United States of America" instead of the old ring of 34 stars. The new emblem was suspended from a bar on which the word "valor" was inscribed and which had an eagle holding the olive branch of peace in one talon and the arrows of war in the other. The eagle's head was turned to the arrows of war because valor in time of war is what earns the Medal of Honor. This whole arrangement was suspended from a ribbon of light blue upon which were 13 white stars.

In order to receive the new Medal, Medal winners had to turn in their old decorations. This caused the recipients to complain because they had become attached to their original Medals. On February 27, 1907, Congress removed the requirement that the old Medals be turned in and directed the War Department to send back those Medals that had already been turned in. In order to protect the Medal from duplication, General George Gillespie took out a patent on it. The patent was issued on November 22, 1904, and on December 19, 1904, it was transferred to Secretary of War William Taft "and his successor or successors as Secretary of War of the United States of America." After the patent expired in 1918, Congress protected the Medal of Honor from duplication by passing a law on February 24, 1923, prohibiting the unauthorized manufacture of medals and badges awarded by the War Department.

The Navy changed its ribbon in 1913 to the same light blue with 13 stars that the Army had adopted. The anchor was now a clear one, not fouled by rope. In addition, regulations of 1917 stipulated that the Medal be worn around the neck, rather than pinned to the uniform.

In 1904, it was suggested that the presentation of the Medal be made a special and solemn occasion. As a result, on September 20, 1905, President Theodore Roosevelt issued an Executive Order which stated the presentation " . . . will always be made with formal and impressive . . . " ceremony. When possible, the ". . . presentation will be made by the President as Commander-in-Chief." This procedure has usually been followed, except in wartime, when the order authorized that "on campaign, the presentation will be made by the division or higher commander." This added greatly to the prestige of the Medal. A similar order was issued by the president for the Navy on October 19, 1906. The first person to be so presented the Medal of Honor by the president was Spanish-American War soldier James R. Church, to whom President Roosevelt presented the Medal on January 10, 1906, in a White House ceremony.

On March 3, 1915, Congress approved awarding the Medal of Honor to officers of the Navy. This legislation came exactly 42 years after the act permitting the Army to award the Medal to officers. The Navy bill authorized the president to award the Medal to " . . . any officer of the Navy, Marine Corps, or Coast Guard who shall have distinguished himself in battle or displayed extraordinary heroism in the line of his profession." Note that the act still allowed for the Medal to be awarded for heroism in the line of the naval profession.

The Medal of Honor Legion continued to press for legislation that would " . . . give the Medal of Honor the same position among the military orders of the world which similar medals occupy." Toward this end Representative Isaac R. Sherwood of Ohio introduced the bill to provide a pension for Medal recipients. The bill seemed innocent enough, but it stirred enormous controversy and it is still being argued about today. This bill, passed on April 27, 1916, authorized the establishment of the "Army and Navy Medal of Honor Roll." Those who were listed on the roll were to receive a special $10.00 per month pension for life. This roll was a list of " . . . holders of the Medal of Honor who had reached the age of 65 and who had been awarded the medal for action involving actual conflict with the enemy, distinguished by conspicuous gallantry or intrepidity, at the risk of life, above and beyond the call of duty." The wording of the bill excluded the members of the 27th Maine who had been awarded their Medals without ever seeing combat. In order to determine just who was eligible to be added to the roll, section 122 of the National Defense Act was added. Passed on June 3, 1916, it provided for a board of five retired Army generals who would review each case submitted to them. For those who did not meet the requirements, the bill stated: " . . . in any case in which said board shall find and report that said medal was issued for a cause other than that hereinbefore specified the name of

the recipient of the medal so issued shall be stricken permanently from the official Medal of Honor list."

This was a drastic step. The act of July 12, 1862, allowed for soldiers to receive the Medal of Honor for "soldier-like qualities." The March 3, 1865, act did not mention "soldier-like qualities," however, that act had not formally canceled the act of July 12, 1862. It could then be argued that the July 12th act was still in effect, and thus awards such as those made to the 27th Maine should be allowed to stand. The legislation required that the review board, presided over by Lieutenant General Nelson A. Miles, himself a Medal recipient, make a strict interpretation of the previous legislation in order to make its decisions. Nelson was also a past commander of the Medal of Honor Legion, an organization that had announced its disapproval of the awards made to the 27th Maine. As past commander, it is almost certain that he agreed with the Legion's stance. Miles also knew that a strict ruling would require the board to remove from the list some people who had displayed great courage in action, yet because they were not in the Army they could not legally receive the Medal. One of these men was a civilian scout named William F. Cody, better known as Buffalo Bill.

The board met from October 16, 1916, until January 17, 1917. All 2,625 Medals of Honor awarded by the Army up to that time were reviewed. In order to avoid bias, the case of each recipient was given a number so that the review board would not know the person's identity. The findings of the board were announced on February 5, 1917, and the names of 910 men and one woman had been removed from the list. Included in the total were Buffalo Bill and four other civilian scouts; Mary Walker, who had been awarded the Medal for service as a contract surgeon; 29 members of President Lincoln's funeral guard; and all 864 men of the 27th Maine. The board hoped that the Medals of the civilian scouts could be preserved through special legislation. They felt that these men had merited the Medal and they hoped that Congress did not intend to take the Medal away from deserving men on a technicality. The timing was not good, however. With America just about to enter the Great War in Europe, Congress did not have time to worry about such details. Of the 911 names removed from the list, only one, Mary Walker, was restored. This occurred in 1977 after her descendants lobbied for the restoration. Mary Walker remains the only woman to have been awarded the Medal of Honor.

Congress finally moved, in 1918, to establish a clear set of guidelines for awarding the Army Medal of Honor. On July 9 an act was passed that stated that " . . . the President is authorized to present, in the name of the Congress, a Medal of Honor only to each person who, while an officer or enlisted man of the Army, shall hereafter, in action involving actual conflict with an enemy, distinguish himself conspicuously by gallantry and intrepidity at risk of his life above and beyond the call of duty." The use of the word "hereafter" removed for good the problem of claims for Civil War action. The last three Medals for Civil War deeds had been awarded the previous year, in 1917. A time limit was also set. A recommendation had to be made within two years of the deed, and the Medal had to be awarded within three years. The July 9th act also abolished the Certificate of Merit, and the Distinguished Service Medal was created in its place. Two more awards, the Distinguished Service Cross and Silver Star were also created. With the award of any of these new medals or the Medal of Honor, a soldier was entitled to an extra $2.00 per month for the length of his service. The July 9th act also allowed the president to confer medals " . . . upon officers and enlisted men of the military forces of the countries concurrently engaged with the United States in the present war."

Up until this time, the only medal for valor in the military was the Medal of Honor. With the addition of the other medals came the beginning of a "Pyramid of Honor." It was then possible to recognize degrees of bravery and it was felt that this would help to protect the Medal of Honor at the top of the pyramid.

Only four Medals of Honor were awarded while World War I was still in progress. After the war ended, General John Pershing, commander of the American Expeditionary Force, made it a point to see that all worthy acts of bravery were properly reviewed to ensure that the appropriate medal was awarded. A total of 118 men received the Medal of Honor for valor in World War I. In addition, the Unknown Soldiers of Belgium, Great Britain, France, Italy, and Rumania were awarded the Medal of Honor. The Unknown Soldier of the United States was also awarded the Medal as would be the Unknown American Soldiers of World War II, Korea, and Vietnam. While the Army no longer allowed the award of the Medal of Honor for noncombat deeds, the Navy still did. On February 4, 1919, Congress allowed the awarding of two different Medals of Honor for the Navy. A new style of Medal would be designated for gallantry in action, while the old style would be awarded for bravery in the line of the naval profession. Tiffany & Company of New York came up with the new design, which is known by the nickname "Tiffany Cross." This cross featured an eagle in the center encircled by the words "United States Navy" and "1917–1918." In each of the four arms of the cross was an anchor, and on the back, the inscription "Awarded to." The Medal hung from a light blue ribbon with 13 stars, and was made to be either pinned to the uniform or worn with a neck ribbon.

Although it is not known how many "Tiffany Cross" Medals were awarded, it appears that there were at least 18 issued. The reason for the uncertainty is that there was no strict observation of the rules governing which Medal should be awarded in each case. Richard E. Byrd and Floyd Bennett were awarded the combat-style Medal for their flight over the North Pole. It is quite clear that these two should have received the old-style version for bravery in the line of the naval profession rather than the "Tiffany Cross."

The new-style Medal did not prove to be particularly popular, possibly because its shape resembled that of the German Iron Cross. On August 7, 1942, Congress restored the old-style Medal as the only Medal of Honor for the Navy. A sailor could still earn it for duty in the line of his profession, although this was not common during World War II. The last Medal of Honor to be awarded for noncombat bravery was to Owen Hammerberg who died while saving two fellow divers who had become trapped while clearing wreckage in Pearl Harbor on February 17, 1945.

While very few Medals of Honor were awarded posthumously for Civil War action, things began to change after the turn of the century. In World War II, posthumous awards outnumbered living awards and the same held true for Korea

and Vietnam. It has become very difficult to earn the Medal of Honor and survive the deed.

Following World War II, the Air Force became its own branch of the military. Prior to that time, and up to the Vietnam War, Army Air Corps or Air Force pilots who earned the Medal of Honor were awarded the Army-style Medal. In 1965 the Air Force adopted its own design. The Air Force Medal is almost twice as large as the Army and Navy Medals. While it retains the basic star shape, the center of the medal contains the head of the Statue of Liberty. A laurel wreath rings the Medal and the points of the star retain the oak leaves representing strength. The star is attached to the ribbon by a bar with the word "valor" on it; between the bar and star is the Air Force coat of arms with thunderbolts shooting out from all sides. The Medal is worn around the neck on a ribbon of blue. The Medal is attached to the ribbon by a pad of the same color as the ribbon, with 13 white stars upon it.

The neck ribbon for the Army Medal of Honor was first authorized on February 1, 1898, although it was usually worn pinned to the uniform until after World War II. The Navy adopted the neck ribbon in 1917 as did the Air Force when it created its own Medal in 1965. Today, the Medal of Honor is the only United States Military medal worn around the neck.

On July 25, 1963, Congress established the guidelines by which the Medal of Honor could be awarded:

1) while engaged in an action against an enemy of the United States;

2) while engaged in military operations involving conflict with an opposing foreign force; or,

3) while serving with friendly forces engaged in an armed conflict against an opposing armed force in which the United States is not a belligerent party.

For each of the three Medals of Honor, Army, Navy, and Air Force, the requirements are now the same. "The President may award, and present in the name of Congress, a Medal of Honor of appropriate design, with ribbons and appurtenances, to a person who, while a member of the Army (Navy, Air Force), distinguished himself conspicuously by gallantry and intrepidity at the risk of his life above and beyond the call of duty."

Currently, the regulations provide that an Army or Air Force Medal of Honor can only be awarded if the recommendation for the award is made within two years of the deed of valor and the award is made within three years. For the Navy, the requirements are that the recommendation be made within three years and the award made within five years of the deed of valor.

Gradually, the special pension awarded to Medal of Honor recipients was increased, and its current level now stands at $400.00 per month without any age requirement. Medal of Honor recipients are also permitted free travel on military aircraft on a space-available basis. A Medal of Honor recipient may be buried in Arlington Cemetery, and the children of Medal recipients may attend the military academies without a congressional appointment.

A reversal of the actions taken by the review board of February 15, 1917, by which 911 recipients had been removed from the Medal of Honor Roll, took place on June 12, 1989, and William F. Cody and the four other civilian scouts had their Medals restored. They were Amos Chapman, William Dixon, James B. Dosher (Dozier), and William H. Woodall. Their medals were presented to the next of kin at a ceremony held at the White House by President George Bush.

On April 24, 1991, President George Bush presented the family of Corporal Freddie Stowers his posthumous award. This soldier was killed in action in World War I.

President Bill Clinton presented Medals of Honor to the widows of two Army sergeants who were killed during "Operation Restore Hope" in Somalia. The two recipients were Master Sergeant Gary Ivan Gordon and Sergeant First Class Randall David Shughart. The presentation was made at the White House on May 23, 1994.

The Medal of Honor was first awarded during the Civil War (1861–1865) and has been awarded for all of the wars that we were engaged in since that date. However, we have also had members of the Armed Forces in many campaigns, actions, and operations over the years in which no Medals of Honor were awarded.

The history of the Medal of Honor is a long and interesting one, which adds to the prestige of the award that is our highest honor. The holders are true American heroes, whose sacrifices and accomplishments should be remembered and honored as an important part of our American heritage.

MEDAL OF HONOR
RECIPIENTS 1863–1994

Volume I
Civil War to 2nd Nicaraguan Campaign

CIVIL WAR

1 ◆ ADAMS, JAMES F.

Rank: Private (highest rank: Corporal)
Service: U.S. Army
Birthday: 26 August 1844
Place of Birth: Cabell County, West Virginia
Date of Death: 8 December 1922
Place of Death: Barboursville, West Virginia
Cemetery: Oaklawn Cemetery (MH)—Huntington, West Virginia
Entered Service at: Ceredo, Wayne County, West Virginia
Unit: Company D, 1st West Virginia Cavalry
Battle or Place of Action: Ninevah, Virginia
Date of Action: 12 November 1864
Date of Issue: 26 November 1864
Citation: Capture of state flag of 14th Virginia Cavalry (C.S.A.).
Notes: POW

2 ◆ ADAMS, JOHN GREGORY BISHOP

Rank: Second Lieutenant (highest rank: Captain)
Service: U.S. Army
Birthday: 6 October 1841
Place of Birth: Groveland, Essex County, Massachusetts
Date of Death: 19 October 1900
Place of Death: Lynn, Massachusetts
Cemetery: Pine Grove Cemetery (MH)—Lynn, Massachusetts
Entered Service at: West Newbury, Essex County, Massachusetts
Unit: Company I, 19th Massachusetts Infantry
Served as: Color Bearer
Battle or Place of Action: Fredericksburg, Virginia
Date of Action: 13 December 1862
Date of Issue: 16 December 1896
Citation: Seized the two colors from the hands of a corporal and a lieutenant as they fell mortally wounded, and with a color in each hand advanced across the field to a point where the regiment was reformed on those colors.

3 ◆ AHEAM, MICHAEL

Rank: Paymaster's Steward
Service: U.S. Navy
Entered Service at: France
Unit: U.S.S. *Kearsarge*
Battle or Place of Action: off Cherbourg, France
Date of Action: 19 June 1864

G.O. Number, Date: 45, 31 December 1864
Citation: Serving on board the U.S.S. *Kearsarge* when she destroyed the *Alabama* off Cherbourg, France, 19 June 1864. Carrying out his duties courageously, PmS. Aheam exhibited marked coolness and good conduct and was highly recommended by his divisional officer for gallantry under enemy fire.

4 ◆ ALBER, FREDERICK

Rank: Private
Service: U.S. Army
Birthday: 28 June 1838
Place of Birth: Germany
Date of Death: 12 September 1913
Place of Death: Elba, Michigan
Cemetery: Oregon Township Cemetery—Oregon Township, Michigan
Entered Service at: Manchester, Washtenaw County, Michigan
Unit: Company A, 17th Michigan Infantry
Battle or Place of Action: Spotsylvania, Virginia
Date of Action: 12 May 1864
Date of Issue: 30 July 1896
Citation: Bravely rescued Lt. Charles H. Todd of his regiment who had been captured by a party of Confederates by shooting down one, knocking over another with the butt of his musket, and taking them both prisoners.

5 ◆ ALBERT, CHRISTIAN

Rank: Private
Service: U.S. Army
Birthday: 1 May 1833
Place of Birth: Cincinnati, Hamilton County, Ohio
Date of Death: 6 March 1898
Cemetery: Reading Cemetery—Reading, Ohio
Entered Service at: Cincinnati, Hamilton County, Ohio
Unit: Company G, 47th Ohio Infantry
Battle or Place of Action: Vicksburg, Mississippi
Date of Action: 22 May 1863
Date of Issue: 10 August 1895
Citation: Gallantry in the charge of the "volunteer storming party."

6 ◆ ALLEN, ABNER PEELER

Rank: Corporal
Service: U.S. Army

Birthday: 9 October 1839
Place of Birth: Woodford County, Illinois
Date of Death: 22 August 1905
Cemetery: Centerburg Cemetery (MH)—Centerburg, Ohio
Entered Service at: Bloomington, McLean County, Illinois
Unit: Company K, 39th Illinois Infantry
Battle or Place of Action: Petersburg, Virginia
Date of Action: 2 April 1865
Date of Issue: 12 May 1865
Citation: Gallantry as color bearer in the assault on Fort Gregg.

7 ◆ ALLEN, JAMES

Rank: Private (highest rank: Corporal)
Service: U.S. Army
Birthday: 5 May 1843
Place of Birth: Ireland
Date of Death: 31 August 1913
Place of Death: St. Paul, Minnesota
Cemetery: Oakland Cemetery—St. Paul, Minnesota
Entered Service at: Potsdam, St. Lawrence County, New York
Unit: Company F, 16th New York Infantry
Battle or Place of Action: South Mountain, Maryland
Date of Action: 14 September 1862
Date of Issue: 11 September 1890
Citation: Singlehandedly and slightly wounded he accosted a squad of 14 Confederate soldiers bearing the colors of the 16th Georgia Infantry (C.S.A.). By an imaginary ruse he secured their surrender and kept them at bay when the regimental commander discovered him and rode away for assistance.

8 ◆ ALLEN, NATHANIEL M.

Rank: Corporal
Service: U.S. Army
Birthday: 29 April 1840
Place of Birth: Boston, Suffolk County, Massachusetts
Date of Death: 30 July 1900
Place of Death: South Acton, Massachusetts
Cemetery: Woodlawn Cemetery (MH)—Acton, Massachusetts
Entered Service at: Boston, Suffolk County, Massachusetts
Unit: Company B, 1st Massachusetts Infantry
Battle or Place of Action: Gettysburg, Pennsylvania
Date of Action: 2 July 1863
Date of Issue: 2 July 1899
Citation: When his regiment was falling back, this soldier, bearing the national color, returned in the face of the enemy's fire, pulled the regimental flag from under the body of its bearer, who had fallen, saved the flag from capture, and brought both colors off the field.

9 ◆ AMES, ADELBERT

Rank: First Lieutenant (highest rank: Brevet Major General)
Service: U.S. Army

Birthday: 31 October 1835
Place of Birth: Rockland, Knox County, Maine
Date of Death: 13 April 1933
Place of Death: Ormond, Florida
Cemetery: Hildreth Family Cemetery (MH)—Lowell, Massachusetts
Entered Service at: Rockland, Knox County, Maine
Unit: 5th U.S. Artillery
Battle or Place of Action: Bull Run, Virginia
Date of Action: 21 July 1861
Date of Issue: 22 June 1894
Citation: Remained upon the field in command of a section of Griffin's Battery, directing its fire after being severely wounded and refusing to leave the field until too weak to sit upon the caisson where he had been placed by men of his command.

10 ◆ AMMERMAN, ROBERT WESLEY

Rank: Private
Service: U.S. Army
Birthday: 1841
Place of Birth: Centre County, Pennsylvania
Date of Death: 30 September 1907
Place of Death: McAlisterville, Pennsylvania
Cemetery: Presbyterian Cemetery—McAlisterville, Pennsylvania
Entered Service at: Milesburg, Centre County, Pennsylvania
Unit: Company B, 148th Pennsylvania Infantry
Battle or Place of Action: Spotsylvania, Virginia
Date of Action: 12 May 1864
Date of Issue: 31 January 1865
Citation: Capture of battle flag of the 8th North Carolina (C.S.A.), being one of the foremost in the assault.

11 ◆ ANDERSON, BRUCE

Rank: Private
Service: U.S. Army
Birthday: 19 June 1845
Place of Birth: Mexico City, Mexico
Date of Death: 22 August 1922
Place of Death: Albany, New York
Cemetery: Green Hill Cemetery (MH)—Amsterdam, New York
Entered Service at: Albany, Albany County, New York
Unit: Company K, 142d New York Infantry
Battle or Place of Action: Fort Fisher, North Carolina
Date of Action: 15 January 1865
Date of Issue: 28 December 1914
Citation: Voluntarily advanced with the head of the column and cut down the palisading.

12 ◆ ANDERSON, CHARLES W.

Rank: Private
Service: U.S. Army
Birthday: 15 March 1844
Place of Birth: Baltimore, Baltimore County, Maryland

Date of Death: 25 February 1916
Place of Death: Stanton, Virginia
Cemetery: Thornrose Cemetery—Stanton, Virginia
Entered Service at: near Winchester, Frederick County, Virginia
Unit: 1st New York (Lincoln) Cavalry
Battle or Place of Action: Waynesboro, Virginia
Date of Action: 2 March 1865
Date of Issue: 26 March 1865
Citation: Capture of unknown Confederate flag.

13 ◆ ANDERSON, EVERETT W.

Rank: Sergeant (highest rank: Second Lieutenant)
Service: U.S. Army
Birthday: 12 July 1839
Place of Birth: near Phoenixville, Chester County, Pennsylvania
Date of Death: 4 February 1917
Cemetery: Morris Cemetery (MH)—Phoenixville, Pennsylvania
Entered Service at: Philadelphia, Philadelphia County, Pennsylvania
Unit: Company M, 15th Pennsylvania Cavalry
Battle or Place of Action: Crosby's Creek, Tennessee
Date of Action: 14 January 1864
Date of Issue: 3 December 1894
Citation: Captured, singlehandedly, Confederate Brig. Gen. Robert B. Vance during a charge upon the enemy.

14 ◆ ANDERSON, FREDERICK CHARLES

Rank: Private
Service: U.S. Army
Birthday: 24 March 1842
Place of Birth: Boston, Suffolk County, Massachusetts
Date of Death: 6 October 1882
Place of Death: Providence, Rhode Island
Cemetery: unknown cemetery (family plot)—Somerset, Massachusetts
Entered Service at: Dedham, Norfolk County, Massachusetts
Unit: Company A, 18th Massachusetts Infantry
Battle or Place of Action: Weldon Railroad, Virginia
Date of Action: 21 August 1864
Date of Issue: 3 December 1894
Citation: Capture of battle flag of 27th South Carolina (C.S.A.) and the color bearer.

15 ◆ ANDERSON, MARION T.

Rank: Captain
Service: U.S. Army
Birthday: 13 November 1839
Place of Birth: Decatur County, Indiana
Date of Death: 7 February 1904
Cemetery: Arlington National Cemetery (1-512)—Arlington, Virginia
Entered Service at: Kokomo, Howard County, Indiana

Unit: Company D, 51st Indiana Infantry
Battle or Place of Action: Nashville, Tennessee
Date of Action: 16 December 1864
Date of Issue: 1 September 1893
Citation: Lead his regiment over five lines of the enemy's works, where he fell, severely wounded.

16 ◆ ANDERSON, PETER T.

Rank: Private (highest rank: Brevet Captain)
Service: U.S. Army
Birthday: 4 September 1847
Place of Birth: Darlington, Lafayette County, Wisconsin
Date of Death: 26 July 1907
Place of Death: Storm Lake, Iowa
Cemetery: Newell Cemetery (MH)—Newell, Iowa
Entered Service at: Wiota, Wisconsin
Unit: Company B, 31st Wisconsin Infantry
Battle or Place of Action: Bentonville, North Carolina
Date of Action: 19 March 1865
Date of Issue: 16 June 1865
Citation: Entirely unassisted, brought from the field an abandoned piece of artillery and saved the gun from falling into the hands of the enemy.

17 ◆ ANDERSON, ROBERT N.

Rank: Quartermaster (highest rank: Acting Master's Mate)
Service: U.S. Navy
Birthday: 15 December 1843
Place of Birth: Ireland
Date of Death: 20 June 1900
Place of Death: Portsmouth, New Hampshire
Cemetery: Calvary Cemetery (MH)—Portsmouth, New Hampshire
Entered Service at: New Hampshire
Unit: U.S.S. *Crusader* and the U.S.S. *Keokuk*
Battle or Place of Action: Charleston, South Carolina
Date of Action: 10 July 1863
G.O. Number, Date: 17, 10 July 1863
Citation: Served on board the U.S.S. *Crusader* and the *Keokuk* during various actions of those vessels. Carrying out his duties skillfully while on board the U.S.S. *Crusader*, Q.M. Anderson, on all occasions, set forth the greatest intrepidity and devotion. During the attack on Charleston, while serving on board the U.S.S. *Keokuk*, Q.M. Anderson was stationed at the wheel when shot penetrated the house and, with the scattering of the iron, used his own body as a shield for his commanding officer.

18 ◆ ANDERSON, THOMAS

Rank: Corporal
Service: U.S. Army
Birthday: 12 July 1841
Place of Birth: Scenery Hill, Washington County, Pennsylvania
Date of Death: 8 September 1912
Place of Death: Washington County, Pennsylvania

Cemetery: Dunkard Cemetery—Washington, Pennsylvania
Entered Service at: Wheeling, Ohio County, West Virginia
Unit: Company I, 1st West Virginia Cavalry
Battle or Place of Action: Appomattox Station, Virginia
Date of Action: 8 April 1865
Date of Issue: 3 May 1865
Citation: Capture of Confederate flag.

19 ◆ ANGLING, JOHN

True Name: Anglin, John
Rank: Cabin Boy (highest rank: Cabin Boy First Class)
Service: U.S. Navy
Birthday: 6 October 1850
Place of Birth: Portland, Cumberland County, Maine
Date of Death: 6 September 1905
Cemetery: Calvary Cemetery (MH)—Portland, Maine
Entered Service at: Portland, Cumberland County, Maine
Unit: U.S.S. *Pontoosuc*
Battle or Place of Action: Fort Fisher & Wilmington, North Carolina
Date of Action: 24 December 1864—22 January 1865
G.O. Number, Date: 59, 22 June 1865
Citation: Served on board the U.S.S. *Pontoosuc* during the capture of Fort Fisher and Wilmington, 24 December 1864 to 22 January 1865. Carrying out his duties faithfully during this period, C.B. Angling was recommended for gallantry and skill and for his cool courage while under the fire of the enemy throughout these various actions.

20 ◆ APPLE, ANDREW O.

Rank: Corporal
Service: U.S. Army
Birthday: 1845
Place of Birth: Northampton, Northampton County, Pennsylvania
Date of Death: 7 June 1890
Cemetery: Bluff City Cemetery—Elgin, Illinois
Entered Service at: New Manchester, Hancock County, West Virginia
Unit: Company I, 12th West Virginia Infantry
Battle or Place of Action: Petersburg, Virginia
Date of Action: 2 April 1865
Date of Issue: 12 May 1865
Citation: Conspicuous gallantry as color bearer in the assault on Fort Gregg.

21 ◆ APPLETON, WILLIAM H.

Rank: First Lieutenant (highest rank: Brevet Major)
Service: U.S. Army
Birthday: 24 March 1843
Place of Birth: Chichester, New Hampshire
Date of Death: 9 September 1912
Cemetery: Evergreen Cemetery—Pembroke, New Hampshire
Entered Service at: Portsmouth, Rockingham County, New Hampshire

Unit: Company H, 4th U.S. Colored Infantry
Battle or Place of Action: Petersburg, Virginia
Date of Action: 15 June 1864
Date of Issue: 18 February 1891
Citation: The first man of the Eighteenth Corps to enter the enemy's works at Petersberg, Va., 15 June 1864. Valiant service in a desperate assault at New Market Heights, Va., inspiring the Union troops by his example of steady courage.

22 ◆ ARCHER, JAMES W.

Rank: First Lieutenant & Adjutant
Service: U.S. Army
Birthday: 6 September 1828
Place of Birth: Edgar County, Illinois
Date of Death: 28 January 1908
Cemetery: Riverside Cemetery—Spencer, Indiana
Entered Service at: Spencer, Owen County, Indiana
Unit: 59th Indiana Infantry
Battle or Place of Action: Corinth, Mississippi
Date of Action: 4 October 1862
Date of Issue: 2 August 1897
Citation: Voluntarily took command of another regiment, with the consent of one or more of his seniors, who were present, rallied the command and led it in the assault.

23 ◆ *ARCHER, LESTER

Rank: Sergeant
Service: U.S. Army
Birthday: 1838
Place of Birth: Fort Ann, Washington County, New York
Date of Death: 27 October 1864
Place of Death: Wilderness, Virginia (KIA)
Cemetery: NON-RECOVERABLE
Entered Service at: Plattsburgh, Clinton County, New York
Unit: Company E, 96th New York Infantry
Battle or Place of Action: Fort Harrison, Virginia
Date of Action: 29 September 1864
Date of Issue: 6 April 1865
Citation: Gallantry in placing the colors of his regiment on the fort.

24 ◆ ARCHINAL, WILLIAM J.

Rank: Corporal
Service: U.S. Army
Birthday: 3 June 1840
Place of Birth: Felsburg, Hesse, Germany
Date of Death: 10 May 1919
Cemetery: Riverview Cemetery—Trenton, New Jersey
Entered Service at: Canaldover, Ohio
Unit: Company I, 30th Ohio Infantry
Battle or Place of Action: Vicksburg, Mississippi
Date of Action: 22 May 1863
Date of Issue: 10 July 1894
Citation: Gallantry in the charge of the "volunteer storming party."
Notes: POW

25 ◆ ARMSTRONG, CLINTON LYCURGUS

Rank: Private
Service: U.S. Army
Birthday: 3 March 1844
Place of Birth: Franklin, Johnson County, Indiana
Date of Death: 5 January 1899
Place of Death: Cincinnati, Ohio
Cemetery: Mt. Fountain Park Cemetery—Winchester, Indiana
Entered Service at: Indianapolis, Marion County, Indiana
Unit: Company D, 83d Indiana Infantry
Battle or Place of Action: Vicksburg, Mississippi
Date of Action: 22 May 1863
Date of Issue: 15 August 1894
Citation: Gallantry in the charge of the "volunteer storming party."

26 ◆ ARNOLD, ABRAHAM KERNS

Rank: Captain (highest rank: Brigadier General)
Service: U.S. Army
Birthday: 24 March 1837
Place of Birth: Bedford, Bedford County, Pennsylvania
Date of Death: 23 November 1901
Place of Death: Cold Springs, New York
Cemetery: St. Philips-in-the-Highlands Cemetery—Garrison, New York
Entered Service at: Bedford, Bedford County, Pennsylvania
Unit: 5th U.S. Cavalry
Battle or Place of Action: Davenport Bridge, Virginia
Date of Action: 10 April 1864
Date of Issue: 1 September 1893
Citation: By a gallant charge against a superior force of the enemy, extricated his command from a perilous position in which it had been ordered.

27 ◆ ARTHER, MATTHEW

Rank: Signal Quartermaster
Service: U.S. Navy
Birthday: 1835
Place of Birth: Scotland
Entered Service at: Boston, Suffolk County, Massachusetts
Unit: U.S.S. *Carondelet*
Battle or Place of Action: Forts Henry & Donelson, Tennessee
Date of Action: 6, 14 February 1862
G.O. Number, Date: 17, 10 July 1863
Citation: Served on board the U.S.S. *Carondelet* at the reduction of Forts Henry and Donelson, 6 and 14 February 1862 and other actions. Carrying out his duties as signal quartermaster and captain of the rifled bow gun, S/Q.M. Arther was conspicuous for valor and devotion, serving most faithfully, effectively and valiantly.

28 ◆ ASTEN, CHARLES

True Name: Asten, Michael
Rank: Quarter Gunner
Service: U.S. Navy
Birthday: 1834
Place of Birth: Halifax, Nova Scotia, Canada
Date of Death: 14 September 1885
Place of Death: Providence, Rhode Island
Cemetery: St. Francis Cemetery—Pawtucket, Rhode Island
Entered Service at: Chicago, Cook County, Illinois
Unit: U.S.S. *Signal*
Battle or Place of Action: Red River, Louisiana
Date of Action: 5 May 1864
G.O. Number, Date: 45, 31 December 1864
Citation: Served on board the U.S.S. *Signal*, Red River, 5 May 1864. Proceeding up the Red River, the U.S.S. *Signal* engaged a large force of enemy field batteries and sharpshooters, returning their fire until the Federal ship was totally disabled, at which time the white flag was raised. Although on the sick list, Q.G. Asten courageously carried out his duties during the entire engagement.
Notes: POW

29 ◆ ATKINSON, THOMAS E.

Rank: Yeoman
Service: U.S. Navy
Birthday: 1824
Place of Birth: Salem, Essex County, Massachusetts
Entered Service at: Massachusetts
Unit: U.S.S. *Richmond*
Battle or Place of Action: Mobile Bay, Alabama
Date of Action: 5 August 1864
G.O. Number, Date: 45, 31 December 1864
Citation: On board the U.S.S. *Richmond*, Mobile Bay, 5 August 1864; commended for coolness and energy in supplying the rifle ammunition which was under his sole charge, in the action in Mobile Bay on the morning of 5 August 1864. He was a petty officer on board the U.S. Frigate *Congress* in 1842–46; was present and assisted in the capture the whole of the Buenos Ayrean fleet by that vessel off Montevideo; joined the *Richmond* in September 1860; was in the action with Fort McRea, the Head of the Passes of the Mississippi, Fort Jackson and St. Philip, the Chalmettes, the rebel ironclads and gunboats below New Orleans, Vicksburg, Port Hudson, and the surrender of New Orleans.

30 ◆ AVERY, JAMES

Rank: Seaman
Service: U.S. Navy
Birthday: 1825
Place of Birth: Scotland
Date of Death: 11 October 1898
Cemetery: U.S. Naval Hospital Cemetery (MH)—Norfolk, Virginia
Entered Service at: New York
Unit: U.S.S. *Metacomet*
Battle or Place of Action: Mobile Bay, Alabama
Date of Action: 5 August 1864
G.O. Number, Date: 71, 15 January 1866
Citation: Served on board the U.S.S. *Metacomet*. As a mem-

ber of the boat's crew which went to the rescue of the U.S. Monitor *Tecumseh* when that vessel was struck by a torpedo in passing the enemy forts in Mobile Bay, 5 August 1864, S/man Avery braved the enemy fire which was said by the admiral to be "one of the most galling" he had ever seen, and aided in rescuing from death 10 of the crew of the *Tecumseh*, eliciting the admiration of both friend and foe.

31 ◆ AVERY, WILLIAM B.

Rank: Second Lieutenant (highest rank: Captain)
Service: U.S. Army
Birthday: 10 September 1840
Place of Birth: Providence, Providence County, Rhode Island
Date of Death: 19 July 1894
Place of Death: Bayside, Kent County, Rhode Island
Cemetery: North Burial Grounds—Bayside, Rhode Island
Entered Service at: Providence, Providence County, Rhode Island
Unit: 1st New York Marine Artillery
Battle or Place of Action: Tranter's Creek, North Carolina
Date of Action: 5 June 1862
Date of Issue: 2 September 1893
Citation: Handled his battery with greatest coolness amidst the hottest fire.

32 ◆ AYERS, DAVID

True Name: Ayres, David
Rank: Sergeant (highest rank: Captain)
Service: U.S. Army
Birthday: 29 April 1841
Place of Birth: Kalida, Putnam County, Ohio
Date of Death: 11 December 1916
Place of Death: Chicago, Illinois
Cemetery: Oakwoods Cemetery—Chicago, Illinois
Entered Service at: Upper Sandusky, Wyandot County, Ohio
Unit: Company A, 57th Ohio Infantry
Battle or Place of Action: Vicksburg, Mississippi
Date of Action: 22 May 1863
Date of Issue: 13 April 1894
Citation: Gallantry in the charge of the "volunteer storming party."

33 ◆ AYERS, JOHN G. K.

Rank: Private
Service: U.S. Army
Birthday: 30 October 1837
Place of Birth: Washtenaw County, Michigan
Date of Death: 30 July 1913
Cemetery: Riverside Cemetery—Three Rivers, Michigan
Entered Service at: Pekin, Tazwell County, Illinois
Unit: Company H, 8th Missouri Infantry
Battle or Place of Action: Vicksburg, Mississippi
Date of Action: 22 May 1863

Date of Issue: 31 August 1895
Citation: Gallantry in the charge of the "volunteer storming party."

34 ◆ BABOCK, WILLIAM J.

Rank: Sergeant
Service: U.S. Army
Birthday: 8 April 1841
Place of Birth: Griswold, Connecticut
Date of Death: 29 October 1897
Cemetery: Riverside Cemetery (MH)—Wakefield, Rhode Island
Entered Service at: South Kingston, Washington County, Rhode Island
Unit: 2d Rhode Island Infantry
Battle or Place of Action: Petersburg, Virginia
Date of Action: 2 April 1865
Date of Issue: 2 March 1895
Citation: Planted the flag upon the parapet while the enemy still occupied the line; was the first of his regiment to enter the works.

35 ◆ *BACON, ELIJAH WILLIAM

Rank: Private
Service: U.S. Army
Birthday: 1836
Place of Birth: Burlington, Hartford County, Connecticut
Date of Death: 6 May 1864
Place of Death: Wilderness, Virginia
Cemetery: Maple Cemetery (MH)—Berlin, Connecticut
Entered Service at: New Britain, Hartford County, Connecticut
Unit: Company F, 14th Connecticut Infantry
Battle or Place of Action: Gettysburg, Pennsylvania
Date of Action: 3 July 1863
Date of Issue: 1 December 1864
Citation: Capture of flag of the 16th North Carolina regiment (C.S.A.).

36 ◆ BAIRD, ABSALOM

Rank: Brigadier General (highest rank: Brevet Major General)
Service: U.S. Army
Birthday: 20 August 1824
Place of Birth: Washington, Washington County, Pennsylvania
Date of Death: 14 June 1905
Place of Death: near Relay, Maryland
Cemetery: Arlington National Cemetery (1-55) (MH)—Arlington, Virginia
Entered Service at: Washington, Washington County, Pennsylvania
Unit: U.S. Volunteers
Battle or Place of Action: Jonesboro, Georgia
Date of Action: 1 September 1864
Date of Issue: 22 April 1896

Citation: Voluntarily led a detached brigade in an assault upon the enemy's works.

37 ◆ BAKER, CHARLES

Rank: Quarter Gunner
Service: U.S. Navy
Birthday: 1809
Place of Birth: Georgetown, D.C.
Date of Death: 3 August 1891
Place of Death: Philadelphia, Pennsylvania
Cemetery: Mount Moriah (VA plot 2-22-22) (MH)—Philadelphia, Pennsylvania
Entered Service at: New York, New York
Unit: U.S.S. *Metacomet*
Battle or Place of Action: Mobile Bay, Alabama
Date of Action: 5 August 1864
G.O. Number, Date: 71, 15 January 1866
Citation: Served on board the U.S.S. *Metacomet*. As a member of the boat's crew which went to the rescue of the U.S. Monitor *Tecumseh* when the vessel was struck by a torpedo in passing the enemy forts in Mobile Bay, 5 August 1864, Q.G. Baker braved the enemy fire which was said by the admiral to be "one of the most galling" he has ever seen, and aided in rescuing from death 10 of the crew of the *Tecumseh*, eliciting the admiration of both friend and foe.

38 ◆ BALDWIN, CHARLES H.

Rank: Coal Heaver (highest rank: Acting Master's Mate)
Service: U.S. Navy
Birthday: 30 June 1839
Place of Birth: Wilmington, New Castle County, Delaware
Date of Death: 22 November 1911
Cemetery: Christ Church Cemetery—Accokeek, Maryland
Entered Service at: Philadelphia, Philadelphia County, Pennsylvania
Unit: U.S.S. *Wyalusing*
Battle or Place of Action: Roanoke River, North Carolina
Date of Action: 25 May 1864
G.O. Number, Date: 45, 31 December 1864
Citation: Served on board the U.S.S. *Wyalusing* and participating in a plan to destroy the rebel ram *Albemarle* in Roanoke River, 25 May 1864. Volunteering for the hazardous mission, C.H. Baldwin participated in the transfer of two torpedoes across an island swamp. Weighted by a line which was used to transfer the torpedoes, he swam the river and, when challenged by a sentry, was forced to abandon the plan after erasing its detection and before it could be carried to completion. Escaping the fire of the muskets, C.H. Baldwin spent two days and nights of hazardous travel without food, and finally arrived, fatigued, at the mother ship.
Notes: POW

39 ◆ BALDWIN, FRANK DWIGHT✚

Rank: Captain (highest rank: Major General)
Service: U.S. Army

Birthday: 26 June 1842
Place of Birth: Manchester, Washtenaw County, Michigan
Date of Death: 22 April 1923
Cemetery: Arlington National Cemetery (3-1894)—Arlington Virginia,
Entered Service at: Constantine, St. Joseph County, Michigan
Unit: Company D, 19th Michigan Infantry
Battle or Place of Action: Peach Tree Creek, Georgia
Date of Action: 12 July 1864
Date of Issue: 3 December 1891
Citation: **First Award** Led his company in a countercharge at Peach Tree Creek, Ga., 12 July 1864, under a galling fire ahead of his own men, and singly entered the enemy's line, capturing and bringing back two commissioned officers, fully armed, besides a guidon of a Georgia regiment.
Notes: POW ✚Double Awardee: *see also* Indian Wars

40 ◆ BALLEN, FREDERICK A.

Rank: Private
Service: U.S. Army
Birthday: 11 August 1843
Place of Birth: Germany
Date of Death: 27 April 1916
Place of Death: Exeter Township, Michigan
Cemetery: Carleton Cemetery—Carleton, Michigan
Entered Service at: Adrian, Lenawee County, Michigan
Unit: Company B, 47th Ohio Infantry
Battle or Place of Action: Vicksburg, Mississippi
Date of Action: 3 May 1863
Date of Issue: 6 November 1908
Citation: Was one of a party that volunteered and attempted to run the enemy's batteries with a steam tug and two barges loaded with subsistence stores.

41 ◆ BANKS, GEORGE LOVELL

Rank: Sergeant
Service: U.S. Army
Birthday: 13 October 1839
Place of Birth: Lake County, Ohio
Date of Death: 20 August 1924
Place of Death: Independence, Kansas
Cemetery: Mount Hope Cemetery—Independence, Kansas
Entered Service at: Lafayette, Tippecanoe County, Indiana
Unit: Company C, 15th Indiana Infantry
Battle or Place of Action: Missionary Ridge, Tennessee
Date of Action: 25 November 1863
Date of Issue: 28 September 1897
Citation: As color bearer, led his regiment in the assault, and, though wounded, carried the flag forward to the enemy's works, where he was again wounded. In a brigade of eight regiments this flag was the first planted on the parapet.

42 ◆ BARBER, JAMES ALBERT

Rank: Corporal
Service: U.S. Army

Birthday: 11 July 1841
Place of Birth: Westerly, Washington County, Rhode Island
Date of Death: 26 June 1925
Cemetery: River Bend Cemetery (MH)—Westerly, Rhode Island
Entered Service at: Westerly, Washington County, Rhode Island
Unit: 1st Rhode Island Light Artillery
Battle or Place of Action: Petersburg, Virginia
Date of Action: 2 April 1865
Date of Issue: 20 June 1866
Citation: Was one of a detachment of 20 picked artillerymen who voluntarily accompanied an infantry assaulting party, and who turned upon the enemy the guns captured in the assault.

43 ◆ BARKER, NATHANIEL C.

Rank: Sergeant
Service: U.S. Army
Birthday: 28 September 1836
Place of Birth: Piermont, Grafton County, New Hampshire
Date of Death: 7 March 1904
Place of Death: Somerville, Massachusetts
Cemetery: Last Rest Cemetery (MH)—Merrimack, New Hampshire
Entered Service at: Manchester, Hillsborough County, New Hampshire
Unit: Company E, 11th New Hampshire Infantry
Battle or Place of Action: Spotsylvania, Virginia
Date of Action: 12 May 1864
Date of Presentation: 23 September 1897
Place of Presentation: at the Mass. Assoc. of N.H. Vets 27 Pemberton Square, Boston, Mass
Citation: Six color bearers of the regiment having been killed, he voluntarily took both flags of the regiment and carried them through the remainder of the battle.

44 ◆ BARNES, WILLIAM HENRY

Rank: Private (highest rank: Sergeant)
Service: U.S. Army
Birthday: 1845
Place of Birth: St. Marys County, Maryland
Date of Death: 24 December 1866
Place of Death: Indianola U.S. Army Hospital, Texas
Cemetery: San Antonio National Cemetery as an unknown (MH) ('In Memory' marker)—San Antonio, Texas
Entered Service at: Norfolk, Norfolk County, Virginia
Unit: Company C, 38th U.S. Colored Infantry
Battle or Place of Action: Chapin's Farm, Virginia
Date of Action: 29 September 1864
Date of Issue: 6 April 1865
Citation: Among the first to enter the enemy's works, although wounded.

45 ◆ BARNUM, HENRY ALANSON

Rank: Colonel (highest rank: Brevet Major General)
Service: U.S. Army

Birthday: 24 September 1833
Place of Birth: Jamesville, Onondaga County, New York
Date of Death: 29 January 1892
Place of Death: New York, New York
Cemetery: Oakwood Cemetery (MH)—Syracuse, New York
Entered Service at: Syracuse, Onondaga County, New York
Unit: 149th New York Infantry
Battle or Place of Action: Chattanooga, Tennessee
Date of Action: 23 November 1863
Date of Issue: 16 July 1889
Citation: Although suffering severely from wounds, he led his regiment, inciting his men to greater action by word and example until again severely wounded.
Notes: POW

46 ◆ BARNUM, JAMES

Rank: Boatswain's Mate
Service: U.S. Navy
Birthday: 1816
Place of Birth: Massachusetts
Entered Service at: Massachusetts
Unit: U.S.S. *New Ironsides*
Battle or Place of Action: Fort Fisher, North Carolina
Date of Action: 24-25 December 1864 & 13-15 January 1865
G.O. Number, Date: 59, 22 June 1865
Citation: Barnum served on board the U.S.S. *New Ironsides* during action in several attacks on Fort Fisher, 24 and 25 December 1864; and on 13, 14, and 15 January 1865. The ship steamed in and took the lead in the ironclad division close inshore and immediately opened its starboard battery in a barrage of well-directed fire to cause several fires and explosions and dismount several guns during the first two days of fighting. Taken under fire as she steamed into position on 13 January, the *New Ironsides* fought all day and took on ammunition at night despite severe weather conditions. When the enemy came out of his bombproofs to defend the fort against the storming party, the ship's battery disabled nearly every gun on the fort facing the shore before the cease-fire orders were given by the flagship. Barnum was commended for highly meritorious conduct during this period.

47 ◆ BARRELL, CHARLES L.

Rank: First Lieutenant (highest rank: Captain)
Service: U.S. Army
Birthday: 1 August 1842
Place of Birth: Conquest, New York
Date of Death: 18 April 1914
Place of Death: Ann Arbor, Michigan
Cemetery: Leighton Cemetery—Leighton, Michigan
Entered Service at: Leighton, Allegan County, Michigan
Unit: Company C, 102d U.S. Colored Infantry
Battle or Place of Action: near Camden, South Carolina
Date of Action: April 1865
Date of Issue: 14 May 1891
Citation: Hazardous service in marching through the enemy's country to bring relief to his command.

48 ◆ BARRICK, JESSE T.

Rank: Corporal (highest rank: Second Lieutenant)
Service: U.S. Army
Birthday: 18 January 1841
Place of Birth: Columbiana County, Ohio
Place of Death: Pasco, Washington
Date of Death: 3 November 1923
Cemetery: Pasco Cemetery—Pasco, Washington
Entered Service at: Fort Snelling, St. Paul County, Minnesota
Unit: Company H, 3d Minnesota Infantry
Battle or Place of Action: Duck River, Tennessee
Date of Action: 26 May-2 June 1863
Date of Issue: 3 March 1917
Citation: While on a scout singlehandedly captured two desperate Confederate guerrilla officers who were together and well-armed at the time.

49 ◆ BARRINGER, WILLIAM H.

Rank: Private
Service: U.S. Army
Birthday: 27 May 1841
Place of Birth: Long Bottom, Meigs County, Ohio
Date of Death: 7 April 1917
Place of Death: Oliver Township, Ohio
Cemetery: Mount Olive Cemetery—Racine, Ohio
Entered Service at: Mason City, Mason County, West Virginia
Unit: Company F, 4th West Virginia Infantry
Battle or Place of Action: Vicksburg, Mississippi
Date of Action: 22 May 1863
Date of Issue: 12 July 1894
Citation: Gallantry in the charge of the "volunteer storming party."

50 ◆ BARRY, AUGUSTUS

Rank: Sergeant Major
Service: U.S. Army
Birthday: 1840
Place of Birth: Ireland
Date of Death: 3 August 1871
Cemetery: Cold Harbor National Cemetery (MH) (A-309)—Mechanicsville, Virginia
Entered Service at: New York, New York
Unit: 16th U.S. Infantry
Battle or Place of Action: Tennessee & Georgia
Date of Action: 1863—1865
Date of Issue: 28 February 1870
Citation: Gallantry in various actions during the rebellion.

51 ◆ BARTER, GURDON H.

Rank: Landsman
Service: U.S. Navy
Birthday: 1843
Place of Birth: Williamsburg, Kings County, New York
Date of Death: 22 April 1900
Place of Death: Viola, Idaho
Cemetery: Viola Cemetery—Viola, Idaho
Entered Service at: New York, New York
Unit: U.S.S. *Minnesota*
Battle or Place of Action: Fort Fisher, North Carolina
Date of Action: 15 January 1865
G.O. Number, Date: 59, 22 June 1865
Citation: On board the U.S.S. *Minnesota* in action during the assault on Fort Fisher, 15 January 1865. Landing on the beach with the assaulting party from his ship, Landsman Barter advanced to the top of the sandhill and partly through the breach in the palisades despite enemy fire which killed and wounded many officers and men. When more than two-thirds of the men became seized with panic and retreated on the run, he remained with the party until dark, when it came safely away, bringing its wounded, its arms, and its colors.

52 ◆ BARTON, THOMAS

Rank: Seaman
Service: U.S. Navy
Birthday: 1831
Place of Birth: Cleveland, Cuyahoga County, Ohio
Entered Service at: Ohio
Unit: U.S.S. *Hunchback*
Battle or Place of Action: Franklin, Virginia
Date of Action: 3 October 1862
G.O. Number, Date: 11, 3 April 1863
Citation: On board the U.S.S. *Hunchback* in the attack on Franklin, Va., 3 October 1862. When an ignited shell, with cartridge attached, fell out of the howitzer upon the deck, S/man Barton promptly seized a pail of water and threw it upon the missle, thereby preventing it from exploding.

53 ◆ BASS, DAVID L.

Rank: Seaman
Service: U.S. Navy
Birthday: 3 February 1842
Place of Birth: Ireland
Date of Death: 14 October 1886
Place of Death: Little Falls, New York
Cemetery: Wilcox Cemetery (MH)—Little Falls, New York
Entered Service at: New York, New York
Unit: U.S.S. *Minnesota*
Battle or Place of Action: Fort Fisher, North Carolina
Date of Action: 15 January 1865
G.O. Number, Date: 59, 22 June 1865
Citation: On board the U.S.S. *Minnesota* in action during the assault on Fort Fisher, 15 January 1865. Landing on the beach with the assaulting party from his ship, S/man Bass advanced to the top of the sand hill and partly through the breach in the palisades despite enemy fire which killed and wounded many officers and men. When more than two-thirds of the men became seized with panic and retreated on the run, he remained with the party until dark, when it came safely away, bringing its wounded, its arms, and its colors.

54 ◆ BATCHELDER, RICHARD NAPOLEON

Rank: Lieutenant Colonel and Chief Quartermaster (highest rank: Brigadier General)
Service: U.S. Army
Birthday: 27 July 1832
Place of Birth: Lake Village (Now Lakeport), Belknap County, New Hampshire
Date of Death: 4 January 1901
Place of Death: Washington, D.C.
Cemetery: Arlington National Cemetery (2-998)—Arlington, Virginia
Entered Service at: Manchester, Hillsborough County, New Hampshire
Unit: 2d Corps
Battle or Place of Action: Catlett and Fairfax Stations, Virginia
Date of Action: 13-15 October 1863
Date of Issue: 20 May 1895
Citation: Being ordered to move his trains by a continuous day-and-night march, and without the usual military escort, armed his teamsters and personally commanded them, successfully fighting against heavy odds and bringing his trains through without the loss of a wagon.

55 ◆ BATES, DELAVAN

Rank: Colonel (highest rank: Brevet Brigadier General)
Service: U.S. Army
Birthday: 17 March 1840
Place of Birth: Schoharie County, New York
Date of Death: 19 December 1918
Cemetery: Aurora Cemetery (MH)—Aurora, Nebraska
Entered Service at: Mohawk, Herkimer County, New York
Unit: 30th U.S. Colored Troops
Battle or Place of Action: Cemetery Hill, Petersburg, Virginia
Date of Action: 30 July 1864
Date of Issue: 22 June 1891
Citation: Gallantry in action where he fell, shot through the face, at the head of his regiment.
Notes: POW

56 ◆ BATES, NORMAN FRANCIS

Rank: Sergeant
Service: U.S. Army
Birthday: 6 November 1839
Place of Birth: Derry, Vermont
Date of Death: 16 October 1915
Place of Death: Los Angeles, California
Cemetery: Forest Lawn Memorial Park—Glendale, California
Entered Service at: Grinnell, Poweshiek County, Iowa
Unit: 4th Iowa Cavalry
Battle or Place of Action: Columbus, Georgia
Date of Action: 16 April 1865
Date of Issue: 17 June 1865
Citation: Capture of flag and bearer.

57 ◆ BAYBUTT, PHILIP

Rank: Private
Service: U.S. Army
Birthday: 1844
Place of Birth: Manchester, Greater Manchester County, England
Date of Death: 17 April 1907
Place of Death: Manchester, England
Cemetery: unknown cemetery—Manchester, England
Entered Service at: Fall River, Bristol County, Massachusetts
Unit: Company A, 2d Massachusetts Cavalry
Battle or Place of Action: Luray, Virginia
Date of Action: 24 September 1864
Date of Issue: 14 October 1864
Citation: Capture of flag.

58 ◆ BAZAAR, PHILIP

Rank: Ordinary Seaman
Service: U.S. Navy
Place of Birth: Chile
Entered Service at: New Bedford, Bristol County, Massachusetts
Unit: U.S.S. *Santiago de Cuba*
Battle or Place of Action: Fort Fisher, North Carolina
Date of Action: 15 January 1865
G.O. Number, Date: 59, 22 June 1865
Citation: On board the U.S.S. *Santiago de Cuba* during the assault on Fort Fisher on 15 January 1865. As one of a boat crew detailed to one of the generals onshore, O.S. Bazaar bravely entered the fort in the assault and accompanied his party in carrying dispatches at the height of the battle. He was one of six men who entered the fort in the assault from the fleet.

59 ◆ BEATTY, ALEXANDER MITCHELL

True Name: Beattie, Alexander Mitchell
Rank: Captain
Service: U.S. Army
Birthday: 29 July 1828
Place of Birth: Ryegate, Caledonia County, Vermont
Date of Death: 7 March 1907
Cemetery: Summer Street Cemetery—Lancaster, New Hampshire
Entered Service at: Guildhall, Essex County, Vermont
Unit: Company F, 3d Vermont Infantry
Battle or Place of Action: Cold Harbor, Virginia
Date of Action: 5 June 1864
Date of Issue: 25 April 1894
Citation: Removed, under a hot fire, a wounded member of his command to a place of safety.

60 ◆ BEATY, POWHATAN

Rank: First Sergeant
Service: U.S. Army
Birthday: 8 October 1837

Place of Birth: Richmond, Richmond County, Virginia
Date of Death: 6 December 1916
Cemetery: Union Baptist Cemetery (MH)—Cincinnati, Ohio
Entered Service at: Cincinnati, Hamilton County, Ohio
Unit: Company G, 5th U.S. Colored Infantry
Battle or Place of Action: Chapin's Farm, Virginia
Date of Action: 29 September 1864
Date of Issue: 6 April 1865
Citation: Took command of his company, all the officers having been killed or wounded, and gallantly led it.

61 ◆ BEAUFORT, JEAN J.

True Name: Beaufort, John Joseph
Rank: Corporal
Service: U.S. Army
Birthday: 1832
Place of Birth: France
Date of Death: 15 September 1897
Cemetery: Arlington National Cemetery (13-13784) (MH)—Arlington, Virginia
Entered Service at: New Orleans, Orleans County, Louisiana
Unit: Company A, 2d Louisiana Infantry
Battle or Place of Action: Port Hudson, Louisiana
Date of Action: 20 May 1863
Date of Issue: 20 July 1897
Citation: Volunteered to go within the enemy's lines and at the head of a party of eight destroyed a signal station, thereby greatly aiding in the operations against Port Hudson that immediately followed.

62 ◆ BEAUMONT, EUGENE BEAUHARNAIS

Rank: Major and Assistant Adjutant General (highest rank: Colonel)
Service: U.S. Army
Birthday: 2 August 1837
Place of Birth: Wilks-Barre, Luzerne County, Pennsylvania
Date of Death: 17 August 1916
Place of Death: Harvey's Lake, Pennsylvania
Cemetery: Hollenbeck Cemetery—Wilkes-Barre, Pennsylvania
Entered Service at: Wilks-Barre, Luzerne County, Pennsylvania
Unit: Cavalry Corps, Army of the Mississippi
Battle or Place of Action: Harpeth River, Tennessee; Selma, Alabama
Date of Action: 17 December 1864 & 2 April 1865
Date of Issue: 30 March 1898
Citation: Obtained permission from the corps commander to advance upon enemy's position with the 4th U.S. Cavalry, of which he was a lieutenant; led an attack upon a battery, dispersed the enemy and captured the guns. At Selma, Ala., charged, at the head of his regiment, into the second and last line of the enemy's works.

63 ◆ BEBB, EDWARD JAMES

Rank: Private
Service: U.S. Army

Birthday: 28 April 1839
Place of Birth: Butler County, Ohio
Date of Death: 12 July 1916
Place of Death: Marshalltown, Iowa
Cemetery: New Salem Cemetery—Lynnville, Iowa
Entered Service at: Mount Pleasant, Henry County, Iowa
Unit: Company D, 4th Iowa Cavalry
Battle or Place of Action: Columbus, Georgia
Date of Action: 16 April 1865
Date of Issue: 17 June 1865
Citation: Capture of flag.

64 ◆ BECKWITH, WALLACE A.

Rank: Private
Service: U.S. Army
Birthday: 28 February 1843
Place of Birth: New London, New London County, Connecticut
Date of Death: 22 November 1929
Cemetery: Jordan Cemetery (MH)—Waterford, Connecticut
Entered Service at: New London, New London County, Connecticut
Unit: Company F, 21st Connecticut Infantry
Battle or Place of Action: Fredericksburg, Virginia
Date of Action: 13 December 1862
Date of Issue: 15 February 1897
Citation: Gallantly responded to a call for volunteers to man a battery, served with great heroism until the termination of the engagement.

65 ◆ BEDDOWS, RICHARD

Rank: Private
Service: U.S. Army
Birthday: 27 June 1843
Place of Birth: Liverpool, Merseyside County, England
Date of Death: 15 February 1922
Place of Death: Mt. Vernon, New York
Cemetery: Holy Sepulchre Cemetery—New Rochelle, New York
Entered Service at: Flushing, Queens County, New York
Unit: 34th New York Battery
Battle or Place of Action: Spotsylvania, Virginia
Date of Action: 18 May 1864
Date of Issue: 10 July 1896
Citation: Brought his guidon off in safety under a heavy fire of musketry after he had lost it by his horse becoming furious from the bursting of a shell.

66 ◆ BEEBE, WILLIAM SULLY

Rank: First lieutenant (highest rank: Major)
Service: U.S. Army
Birthday: 14 February 1841
Place of Birth: Ithaca, Tompkins County, New York
Date of Death: 12 October 1898
Cemetery: U.S. Military Academy Cemetery (N-15)—West Point, New York

Entered Service at: Philadelphia, Philadelphia County, Pennsylvania
Unit: Ordnance Department, U.S. Army
Battle or Place of Action: Cane River Crossing, Louisiana
Date of Action: 23 April 1864
Date of Issue: 30 June 1897
Citation: Voluntarily led a successful assault on a fortified position.

67 ◆ BEECH, JOHN P.

Rank: Sergeant
Service: U.S. Army
Birthday: 1 May 1844
Place of Birth: Stratfordshire County, England
Date of Death: 27 November 1926
Cemetery: Mercer Cemetery—Trenton, New Jersey
Entered Service at: Trenton, Mercer County, New Jersey
Unit: Company B, 4th New Jersey Infantry
Battle or Place of Action: Spotsylvania Courthouse, Virginia
Date of Action: 12 May 1864
Date of Issue: 1 June 1894
Citation: Voluntarily assisted in working the guns of a battery, all the members of which had been killed or wounded.

68 ◆ *BEGLEY, TERRENCE

Rank: Sergeant
Service: U.S. Army
Place of Birth: Ireland
Date of Death: 25 August 1864
Place of Death: Weldon RR, Reams Station
Entered Service at: Albany, Albany County, New York
Unit: Company D, 7th New York Heavy Artillery
Battle or Place of Action: Cold Harbor, Virginia
Date of Action: 3 June 1864
Date of Issue: 1 December 1864
Citation: Shot a Confederate color bearer, 26th Virginia Infantry, rushed forward and seized his colors, and although exposed to heavy fire, regained the lines in safety.

69 ◆ BELCHER, THOMAS

Rank: Private
Service: U.S. Army
Birthday: 1834
Place of Birth: Bangor, Penobscot County, Maine
Date of Death: 22 May 1898
Place of Death: Augusta, Maine
Cemetery: Togus, Maine (Per death certificate, no cemetery)
Entered Service at: Bangor, Penobscot County, Maine
Unit: Company I, 9th Maine Infantry
Battle or Place of Action: Chapin's Farm, Virginia
Date of Action: 29 September 1864
Date of Issue: 6 April 1865
Citation: Took a guidon from the hands of the bearer, mortally wounded, and advanced with it nearer to the battery than any other man.

70 ◆ BELL, GEORGE H.

Rank: Captain of the Afterguard
Service: U.S. Navy
Birthday: 12 March 1839
Place of Birth: Sunderland, England
Date of Death: 26 September 1917
Place of Death: Newcastle, England
Cemetery: Elswick Cemetery—Newcastle, England
Entered Service at: New York, New York
Unit: U.S.S. *Santee*
Battle or Place of Action: Galveston Bay, Texas
Date of Action: 7 November 1861
G.O. Number, Date: 17, 10 July 1863
Date of Presentation: 21 November 1864
Place of Presentation: Virginia, Hampton Roads, Virginia, on board the U.S.S. *Brooklyn*, presented by Capt. James Alden
Citation: Served as pilot of the U.S.S. *Santee* when that vessel was engaged in cutting out the rebel armed schooner *Royal Yacht* from Galveston Bay, 7 November 1861, and evinced more coolness, in passing the four forts and the rebel steamer *General Rusk*, than was ever before witnessed by his commanding officer. "Although severely wounded, in the encounter, he displayed extraordinary courage under the most painful and trying circumstances."

71 ◆ BELL, JAMES BENNETT

Rank: Sergeant
Service: U.S. Army
Birthday: 9 August 1835
Place of Birth: Branot, Ohio
Date of Death: 30 June 1910
Place of Death: Elkhart, Indiana
Cemetery: Gettysburg Cemetery (MH)—Gettysburg, Ohio
Entered Service at: Troy, Miami County, Ohio
Unit: Company H, 11th Ohio Infantry
Battle or Place of Action: Missionary Ridge, Tennessee
Date of Action: 25 November 1863
Date of Issue: 9 October 1907
Citation: Though severely wounded, was first of his regiment on the summit of the ridge, planted his colors inside the enemy's works, and did not leave the field until after he had been wounded five times.

72 ◆ BENEDICT, GEORGE GREENVILLE

Rank: Second Lieutenant
Service: U.S. Army
Birthday: 10 December 1826
Place of Birth: Burlington, Chittenden County, Vermont
Date of Death: 8 April 1907
Place of Death: Camden, North Carolina
Cemetery: Green Mount Cemetery—Burlington, Vermont
Entered Service at: Burlington, Chittenden County, Vermont
Unit: Company C (Howard Guards), 12th Vermont Infantry

Battle or Place of Action: Gettysburg, Pennsylvania
Date of Action: 3 July 1863
Date of Issue: 27 June 1892
Citation: Passed through a murderous fire of grape and canister in delivering order and re-formed the crowded lines.

73 ◆ BENJAMIN, JOHN FRANCIS

Rank: Corporal
Service: U.S. Army
Place of Birth: Orange County, New York
Entered Service at: Newburgh, Orange County, New York
Unit: Company M, 2d New York Cavalry
Battle or Place of Action: Deatonsville (Sailor's Creek), Virginia
Date of Action: 6 April 1865
Date of Issue: 3 May 1865
Citation: Capture of battle flag of 9th Virginia Infantry (C.S.A.)

74 ◆ BENJAMIN, SAMUEL NICHOLL

Rank: First Lieutenant (highest rank: Brevet Lieutenant Colonel)
Service: U.S. Army
Birthday: 3 January 1839
Place of Birth: New York, New York
Date of Death: 15 May 1886
Place of Death: Governor's Island, New York
Cemetery: St. Philips In The Highlands Church Cemetery—Garrison, New York
Entered Service at: New York, New York
Unit: 2d U.S. Artillery
Battle or Place of Action: Bull Run to Spotsylvania, Virginia
Date of Action: July 1861—May 1864
Date of Issue: 11 June 1877
Citation: Particularly distinguished services as an artillery officer.

75 ◆ BENNETT, ORRIN

Rank: Private
Service: U.S. Army
Place of Birth: Bradford County, Pennsylvania
Entered Service at: Towanda, Bradford County, Pennsylvania
Unit: Company D, 141st Pennsylvania Infantry
Battle or Place of Action: Deatonsville (Sailor's Creek), Virginia
Date of Action: 6 April 1865
Date of Issue: 10 May 1865
Citation: Capture of flag.

76 ◆ BENNETT, ORSON W.

Rank: First Lieutenant (highest rank: Major)
Service: U.S. Army
Birthday: 17 November 1841
Place of Birth: Union City, Branch County, Michigan

Date of Death: 8 January 1904
Cemetery: Westminster Cemetery—Philadelphia, Pennsylvania
Entered Service at: Dubuque, Dubuque County, Iowa
Unit: Company A, 102d U.S. Colored Infantry
Battle or Place of Action: Honey Hill, South Carolina
Date of Action: 30 November 1864
Date of Issue: 9 March 1887
Citation: After several unsuccessful efforts to recover three pieces of abandoned artillery, this officer gallantly led a small force fully 100 yards in advance of the Union lines and brought in the guns, preventing their capture.

77 ◆ BENSINGER, WILLIAM

Rank: Private (highest rank: Captain)
Service: U.S. Army
Birthday: 14 January 1840
Place of Birth: Waynesburg, Stark County, Ohio
Date of Death: 19 December 1918
Place of Death: McComb, Ohio
Cemetery: Union Cemetery—McComb, Ohio
Entered Service at: McComb, Hancock County, Ohio
Unit: Company G, 21st Ohio Infantry
Battle or Place of Action: Georgia
Date of Action: April 1862
Date of Presentation: 25 March 1863
Place of Presentation: Washington, D.C., presented by Sec. of War Edward M. Stanton
Citation: One of 19 of 24 men (including two civilians) who, by direction of Gen. Ormsby M. Mitchell, penetrated nearly 200 miles south into enemy territory and captured a railroad train at Big Shanty, Ga., in an attempt to destroy the bridges and track between Chattanaooga and Atlanta.

78 ◆ BENYAURD, WILLIAM HENRY HARRISON

Rank: First Lieutenant, Engineers (highest rank: Lieutenant Colonel)
Service: U.S. Army
Birthday: 17 May 1841
Place of Birth: Philadelphia, Philadelphia County, Pennsylvania
Date of Death: 7 February 1900
Cemetery: U.S. Military Academy Cemetery (T-1) (MH)— West Point, New York
Entered Service at: Philadelphia, Philadelphia County, Pennsylvania
Unit: Engineers
Battle or Place of Action: Five Forks, Virginia
Date of Action: 1 April 1865
Date of Issue: 7 September 1897
Citation: With one companion, voluntarily advanced in a reconnaissance beyond the skirmishers, where he was exposed to imminent peril; also, in the same battle, rode to the front with the commanding general to encourage wavering troops to resume the advance, which they did successfully.

79 ◆ BETHAM, ASA

Rank: Coxswain
Service: U.S. Navy
Birthday: 1838
Place of Birth: New York, New York
Entered Service at: New York, New York
Unit: U.S.S. *Pontoosuc*
Battle or Place of Action: Fort Fisher and Wilmington, North Carolina
Date of Action: 24 December 1864—22 June 1865
G.O. Number, Date: 59, 22 June 1865
Citation: Served on board the U.S.S. *Pontoosuc* during the capture of Fort Fisher and Wilmington, 24 December 1864, to 22 January 1865. Carrying out his duties faithfully during this period, Betham was recommended for gallantry and skill and for his cool courage while under the fire of the enemy throughout these various actions.

80 ◆ BETTS, CHARLES MALONE

Rank: Lieutenant Colonel
Service: U.S. Army
Birthday: 9 August 1838
Place of Birth: Bucks County, Pennsylvania
Date of Death: 10 November 1905
Place of Death: Germantown, Pennsylvania
Cemetery: West Laurel Hill Cemetery—Bala-Cynwyd, Pennsylvania
Entered Service at: Philadelphia, Philadelphia County, Pennsylvania
Unit: 15th Pennsylvania Cavalry
Battle or Place of Action: Greensboro, North Carolina
Date of Action: 19 April 1865
Date of Issue: 10 October 1892
Citation: With a force of but 75 men, while on a scouting expedition, by a judicious disposition of his men, surprised and captured an entire battalion of the enemy's cavalry.

81 ◆ BEYER, HILLARY

Rank: Second Lieutenant (highest rank: First Lieutenant)
Service: U.S. Army
Birthday: 28 September 1837
Place of Birth: Montgomery County, Pennsylvania
Date of Death: 24 September 1907
Cemetery: Presbyterian Church Yard Cemetery (MH)—Lower Providence, Pennsylvania
Entered Service at: Philadelphia, Philadelphia County, Pennsylvania
Unit: Company H, 90th Pennsylvania Infantry
Battle or Place of Action: Antietam, Maryland
Date of Action: 17 September 1862
Date of Issue: 30 October 1896
Citation: After his command had been forced to fall back, remained alone on the line of battle, caring for his wounded comrades and carrying one of them to a place of safety.

82 ◆ BIBBER, CHARLES JAMES

Rank: Gunner's Mate
Service: U.S. Navy
Birthday: 22 March 1837
Place of Birth: Portland, Cumberland County, Maine
Date of Death: 8 October 1883
Place of Death: Revere, Massachusetts
Cemetery: Woodlawn Cemetery (MH)—Everett, Massachusetts
Entered Service at: Portland, Cumberland County, Maine
Unit: U.S.S. *Agawam*
Battle or Place of Action: Fort Fisher, North Carolina
Date of Action: 23 December 1864
G.O. Number, Date: 45, 31 December 1864
Date of Presentation: 12 May 1865
Place of Presentation: On board the U.S.S. *Agawam* off New Bern, North Carolina
Citation: Bibber served on board the U.S.S. *Agawam*, as one of a volunteer crew of a powder boat which was exploded near Fort Fisher, 23 December 1864. The powder boat, towed in by the *Wilderness* to prevent detection by the enemy, cast off and slowly steamed to within 300 yards of the beach. After fuses and fires had been lit and a second anchor with short scope let go to assure the boat's tailing inshore, the crew again boarded the *Wilderness* and proceeded a distance of 12 miles from shore. Less than two hours later the explosion took place, and the following day fires were observed still burning at the forts.

83 ◆ BICKFORD, HENRY H.

Rank: Corporal (highest rank: Quartermaster Sergeant)
Service: U.S. Army
Birthday: 13 March 1838
Place of Birth: Ypsilanti, Washtenaw County, Michigan
Date of Death: 20 May 1917
Place of Death: Middleport, New York
Cemetery: Hartland Central Cemetery (MH)—Hartland, New York
Entered Service at: Middleport, Niagara County, New York
Unit: Company E, 8th New York Cavalry
Battle or Place of Action: Waynesboro, Virginia
Date of Action: 2 March 1865
Date of Issue: 26 March 1865
Citation: Recapture of flag.

84 ◆ BICKFORD, JOHN F.

Rank: Captain of the Top (highest rank: Master's Mate)
Service: U.S. Navy
Birthday: 12 March 1843
Place of Birth: Tremont, Maine
Date of Death: 28 April 1927
Place of Death: Glouchester, Massachusetts
Cemetery: Mount Pleasant Cemetery (MH)—East Glouchester, Massachusetts
Entered Service at: Boston, Suffolk County, Massachusetts
Unit: U.S.S. *Kearsarge*

Battle or Place of Action: off Cherbourg, France
Date of Action: 19 June 1864
G.O. Number, Date: 45, 31 December 1864
Citation: Served on board the U.S.S. *Kearsarge* when she destroyed the *Alabama* off Cherbourg, France, 19 June 1864. Acting as the first loader of the pivot gun during this bitter engagement, Bickford exhibited marked coolness and good conduct and was highly recommended for his gallantry under fire by his divisional officer.

85 ◆ BICKFORD, MATTHEW

Rank: Corporal
Service: U.S. Army
Birthday: 10 April 1839
Place of Birth: Peoria County, Illinois
Date of Death: 18 April 1918
Cemetery: Bayview Cemetery (MH)—Bellingham, Washington
Entered Service at: Trivolia, Peoria County, Illinois
Unit: Company G, 8th Missouri Infantry
Battle or Place of Action: Vicksburg, Mississippi
Date of Action: 22 May 1863
Date of Issue: 31 August 1894
Citation: Gallantry in the charge of the "volunteer storming party."

86 ◆ BIEGER, CHARLES

Rank: Private
Service: U.S. Army
Birthday: 25 March 1844
Place of Birth: Wiesbaden, Germany
Date of Death: 10 August 1930
Cemetery: Mount Hope Cemetery—St. Louis, Missouri
Entered Service at: St. Louis, St. Louis County, Missouri
Unit: Company D, 4th Missouri Cavalry
Battle or Place of Action: Ivy Farm, Mississippi
Date of Action: 22 February 1864
Date of Issue: 8 July 1897
Citation: Voluntarily risked his life by taking a horse, under heavy fire beyond the line of battle for the rescue of his captain, whose horse had been killed in a charge and who was surrounded by the enemy's skirmishers.

87 ◆ BINDER, RICHARD

True Name: Bigle, Richard
Rank: Sergeant
Service: U.S. Marine Corps
Birthday: 26 July 1839
Place of Birth: Germany
Date of Death: 26 February 1912
Place of Death: Philadelphia, Pennsylvania
Cemetery: West Laurel Hill Cemetery—Bala-Cynwyd, Pennsylvania
Entered Service at: Pennsylvania
Unit: U.S.S. *Ticonderoga*
Battle or Place of Action: Fort Fisher, North Carolina

Date of Action: 24-25 December 1864 & 13-15 January 1865
Citation: On board the U.S.S. *Ticonderoga* during the attacks on Fort Fisher, 24 and 25 December 1864 and 13 to 15 January 1865. Despite heavy return fire by the enemy and the explosion of the 100-pounder Parrott rifle which killed eight men and wounded 12 more, Sgt. Binder, as captain of a gun, performed his duties with skill and courage during the first two days of battle. As his ship again took position on the 13th, he remained steadfast on the *Ticonderoga*, maintained a well-placed fire upon the batteries onshore, and thereafter, as she materially lessened the power of guns on the mound which had been turned upon our assaulting columns. During this action the flag was planted on one of the strongest fortifications possessed by the rebels.

88 ◆ BINGHAM, HENRY HARRISON

Rank: Captain (highest rank: Brevet Brigadier General)
Service: U.S. Army
Birthday: 4 December 1841
Place of Birth: Philadelphia, Philadelphia County, Pennsylvania
Date of Death: 22 March 1912
Place of Death: Philadelphia, Pennsylvania
Cemetery: Laurel Hill Cemetery (MH)—Philadelphia, Pennsylvania
Entered Service at: Canonsburg, Washington County, Pensylvania
Unit: Company G, 140th Pennsylvania Infantry
Battle or Place of Action: Wilderness Campaign, Virginia
Date of Action: 6 May 1864
Date of Issue: 31 August 1893
Citation: Rallied and led into action a portion of the troops who had given way under the fierce assaults of the enemy.

89 ◆ BIRDSALL, HORATIO L.

Rank: Sergeant
Service: U.S. Army
Birthday: 1833
Place of Birth: Monroe County, New York
Date of Death: 29 November 1891
Cemetery: Arlington National Cemetery (13-6935) (MH)—Arlington, Virginia
Entered Service at: Keokuk, Lee County, Iowa
Unit: Company B, 3d Iowa Cavalry
Battle or Place of Action: Columbus, Georgia
Date of Action: 16 April 1865
Date of Issue: 17 June 1865
Citation: Capture of flag and bearer.

90 ◆ BISHOP, FRANCIS A.

Rank: Private (highest rank: Corporal)
Service: U.S. Army
Birthday: 3 December 1840
Place of Birth: Bradford County, Pennsylvania
Date of Death: 11 October 1937
Place of Death: State Veterans Home, Retsil, Washington

Cemetery: Blanchard Cemetery (MH)—Blanchard, Michigan
Entered Service at: Harrisburg, Dauphin County, Pennsylvania
Unit: Company C, 57th Pennsylvania Infantry
Battle or Place of Action: Spotsylvania, Virginia
Date of Action: 12 May 1864
Date of Issue: 1 December 1864
Citation: Capture of flag.

91 ◆ BLACK, JOHN CHARLES

Rank: Lieutenant Colonel (highest rank: Brevet Brigadier General)
Service: U.S. Army
Birthday: 27 January 1839
Place of Birth: Lexington, Holmes County, Mississippi
Date of Death: 17 August 1915
Place of Death: Chicago, Illinois
Cemetery: Spring Hill Cemetery—Danville, Illinois
Entered Service at: Danville, Vermillion County, Illinois
Unit: 37th Illinois Infantry
Battle or Place of Action: Prairie Grove, Arkansas
Date of Action: 7 December 1862
Date of Issue: 31 October 1893
Citation: Gallantly charged the position of the enemy at the head of his regiment, after two other regiments had been repulsed and driven down the hill, and captured a battery; was severely wounded.

92 ◆ BLACK, WILLIAM PERKINS

Rank: Captain
Service: U.S. Army
Birthday: 11 November 1842
Place of Birth: Woodford, Kentucky
Date of Death: 3 January 1916
Place of Death: Chicago, Illinois
Cemetery: Graceland Cemetery—Chicago, Illinois
Entered Service at: Danville, Vermillion County, Illinois
Unit: Company K, 37th Illinois Infantry
Battle or Place of Action: Pea Ridge, Arkansas
Date of Action: 7 March 1862
Date of Issue: 2 October 1893
Citation: Singlehandedly confronted the enemy, firing a rifle at them, and thus checked their advance within 100 yards of the lines.

93 ◆ BLACKMAR, WILMON WHILLDIN

Rank: Lieutenant (highest rank: Captain)
Service: U.S. Army
Birthday: 25 July 1841
Place of Birth: Bristol, Bucks County, Pennsylvania
Date of Death: 16 July 1905
Place of Death: Boise, Idaho
Cemetery: Cedar Grove Cemetery (MH)—Dorchester, Massachusetts

Entered Service at: Philadelphia, Philadelphia County, Pennsylvania
Unit: Company H, 1st West Virginia Cavalry
Battle or Place of Action: Five Forks, Virginia
Date of Action: 1 April 1865
Date of Issue: 23 October 1897
Citation: At a critical stage of the battle, without orders, led a successful advance upon the enemy.

94 ◆ BLACKWOOD, WILLIAM ROBERT DOUGLAS

Rank: Surgeon (highest rank: Brevet Lieutenant Colonel)
Service: U.S. Army
Birthday: 12 May 1838
Place of Birth: Hollywood, County Wicklow, Ireland
Date of Death: 26 April 1922
Place of Death: Philadelphia, Pennsylvania
Cemetery: Cheltin Hills Crematory (Cremated 29 April 1922. Disposition of remains unknown.)
Entered Service at: Philadelphia, Philadelphia County, Pennsylvania
Unit: 48th Pennsylvania Infantry
Served as: Surgeon
Battle or Place of Action: Petersburg, Virginia
Date of Action: 2 April 1865
Date of Issue: 21 July 1897
Citation: Removed severely wounded officers and soldiers from the field while under a heavy fire from the enemy, exposing himself beyond the call of duty, thus furnishing an example of most distinguished gallantry.

95 ◆ BLAGHEEN, WILLIAM

True Name: Blagden, William
Rank: Ship's Cook
Service: U.S. Navy
Birthday: 1832
Place of Birth: Devonshire County, England
Entered Service at: New York, New York
Unit: U.S.S. *Brooklyn*
Battle or Place of Action: Fort Morgan, Mobile Bay, Alabama
Date of Action: 5 August 1864
G.O. Number, Date: 45, 31 December 1864
Citation: On board the U.S.S. *Brooklyn* during successful attacks against Fort Morgan, rebel gunboats and the ram *Tennessee* in Mobile Bay, on 5 August 1864. Stationed in the immediate vicinity of the shell whips which were twice cleared of men by bursting shells, Blagheen remained steadfast at his post and performed his duties in the powder division throughout the furious action which resulted in the surrender of the prize rebel ram *Tennessee* and in the damaging and destruction of batteries at Fort Morgan.

96 ◆ BLAIR, ROBERT M.

Rank: Boatswain's Mate
Service: U.S. Navy

Birthday: 1836
Place of Birth: Peacham, Caledonia County, Vermont
Date of Death: 2 April 1899
Place of Death: Enid, Oklahoma
Cemetery: Enid Cemetery (MH)—Enid, Oklahoma
Entered Service at: Portland, Cumberland County, Maine
Unit: U.S.S. *Pontoosuc*
Battle or Place of Action: Fort Fisher and Wilmington, North Carolina
Date of Action: 23 December 1864—22 January 1865
G.O. Number, Date: 59, 22 June 1865
Citation: Served on board the U.S.S. *Pontoosuc* during the capture of Fort Fisher and Wilmington, 24 December 1864 to 22 January 1865. Carrying out his duties faithfully throughout this period, Blair was recommended for gallantry and skill and for his cool courage while under the fire of the enemy throughout these actions.

97 ◆ BLAKE, ROBERT

Rank: Contraband
Service: U.S. Navy
Place of Birth: Virginia
Entered Service at: Port Royal, Caroline County, Virginia
Unit: U.S. Steam Gunboat *Marblehead*
Battle or Place of Action: off Legareville, Stono River, John's Island, South Carolina
Date of Action: 25 December 1863
G.O. Number, Date: 32, 16 April 1864
Citation: On board the U.S. Steam Gunboat *Marblehead* off Legareville, Stono River, 25 December 1863, in an engagement with the enemy on John's Island. Serving the rifle gun, Blake, an escaped slave, carried out his duties bravely throughout the engagement, which resulted in the enemy's abandonment of positions, leaving a caisson and one gun behind.

98 ◆ BLASDEL, THOMAS A.

Rank: Private (highest rank: Corporal)
Service: U.S. Army
Birthday: 2 January 1843
Place of Birth: Dearborn County, Indiana
Date of Death: 12 October 1932
Place of Death: Sylvia, Kansas
Cemetery: Fairlawn Cemetery—Hutchinson, Kansas
Entered Service at: Guilford, Dearborn County, Indiana
Unit: Company H, 83d Indiana Infantry
Battle or Place of Action: Vicksburg, Mississippi
Date of Action: 22 May 1863
Date of Issue: 11 August 1894
Citation: Gallantry in the charge of the "volunteer storming party."

99 ◆ BLICKENSDERGER, MILTON

Rank: Corporal (highest rank: Sergeant)
Service: U.S. Army
Birthday: 20 May 1835
Place of Birth: Lancaster, Lancaster County, Pennsylvania

Date of Death: 17 March 1916
Cemetery: Shanesville Cemetery—Shanesville, Ohio
Entered Service at: Shanesville, Ohio
Unit: Company E, 126th Ohio Infantry
Battle or Place of Action: Petersburg, Virginia
Date of Action: 3 April 1865
Date of Issue: 10 May 1865
Citation: Capture of flag.

100 ◆ BLISS, GEORGE NEWMAN

Rank: Captain
Service: U.S. Army
Birthday: 22 July 1837
Place of Birth: Tiverton, Newport County, Rhode Island
Date of Death: 29 August 1928
Cemetery: Lakeside Cemetery (MH)—Rumford, Rhode Island
Entered Service at: Pawtucket, Providence County, Rhode Island
Unit: Company C, 1st Rhode Island Cavalry
Battle or Place of Action: Waynesboro, Virginia
Date of Action: 28 September 1864
Date of Issue: 3 August 1897
Citation: While in command of the provost guard in the village, he saw the Union lines returning before the attack of a greatly superior force of the enemy, mustered his guard, and, without orders, joined in the defense and charged the enemy without support. He received three saber wounds, his horse was shot, and he was taken prisoner.
Notes: POW

101 ◆ BLISS, ZENAS RANDALL

Rank: Colonel (highest rank: Major General)
Service: U.S. Army
Birthday: 17 April 1835
Place of Birth: Johnston, Providence County, Rhode Island
Date of Death: 2 January 1900
Place of Death: Washington, D.C.
Cemetery: Arlington National Cemetery (1-8-B)—Arlington, Virginia
Entered Service at: Johnston, Providence County, Rhode Island
Unit: 7th Rhode Island Infantry
Battle or Place of Action: Fredericksburg, Virginia
Date of Action: 13 December 1862
Date of Issue: 30 December 1898
Citation: This officer, to encourage his regiment which had never before been in action and which had been ordered to lie down to protect itself from the enemy's fire, rose to his feet, advanced in front of the line, and himself fired several shots at the enemy at short range, being fully exposed to their fire at the time.

102 ◆ BLODGETT, WELLS H.

Rank: First Lieutenant (highest rank: Colonel)
Service: U.S. Army

Birthday: 29 January 1839
Place of Birth: Downer's Grove, Du Page County, Illinois
Date of Death: 8 May 1929
Place of Death: St. Louis, Missouri
Cemetery: Bellefontaine Cemetery—St. Louis, Missouri
Entered Service at: Chicago, Cook County, Illinois
Unit: Company D, 37th Illinois Infantry
Battle or Place of Action: Newtonia, Missouri
Date of Action: 30 September 1862
Date of Issue: 15 February 1894
Citation: With a single orderly, captured an armed picket of eight men and marched them in as prisoners.

103 ◆ BLUCHER, CHARLES

Rank: Corporal (highest rank: Sergeant)
Service: U.S. Army
Place of Birth: Germany
Entered Service at: Philadelphia, Philadelphia County, Pennsylvania
Unit: Company H, 188th Pennsylvania Infantry
Battle or Place of Action: Fort Harrison, Virginia
Date of Action: 29 September 1864
Date of Issue: 6 April 1865
Citation: Planted first national colors on the fortifications.

104 ◆ BLUNT, JOHN W.

Rank: First Lieutenant (highest rank: Brevet Major)
Service: U.S. Army
Birthday: 18 May 1840
Place of Birth: Columbia County, New York
Date of Death: 21 January 1910
Cemetery: Chatham Rural Cemetery (MH)—Chatham, New York
Entered Service at: Four Corners, Chatham, Columbia County, New York
Unit: Company K, 6th New York Cavalry
Battle or Place of Action: Cedar Creek, Virginia
Date of Action: 19 October 1864
Date of Issue: 1 June 1908
Citation: Voluntarily led a charge across a narrow bridge over the creek, against the lines of the enemy.

105 ◆ BOEHM, PETER MARTIN

Rank: Second Lieutenant (highest rank: Major)
Service: U.S. Army
Birthday: 10 February 1845
Place of Birth: Albany, Albany County, New York
Date of Death: 14 June 1914
Place of Death: Chicago, Illinois
Cemetery: Arlington National Cemetery (2-3674)—Arlington, Virginia
Entered Service at: Brooklyn, Kings County, New York
Unit: Company K, 15th New York Cavalry
Battle or Place of Action: Dinwiddie Courthouse, Virginia
Date of Action: 31 March 1865
Date of Issue: 15 December 1898
Citation: While acting as aide to Gen. Custer, took a gun

from the hands of color bearer, rode in front of a line that was being driven back and, under a heavy fire, rallied the men, re-formed the line, and repulsed the charge.

106 ◆ BOIS, FRANK

Rank: Quartermaster
Service: U.S. Navy
Birthday: 13 September 1841
Place of Birth: Quebec, Canada
Date of Death: 25 January 1920
Place of Death: Seattle, Washington
Cemetery: Grand Army of the Republic Cemetery—Seattle, Washington
Entered Service at: Northampton, Hampshire County, Massachusetts
Unit: U.S.S. *Cincinnati*
Served as: Quartermaster
Battle or Place of Action: Vicksburg, Mississippi
Date of Action: 27 May 1863
G.O. Number, Date: 17, 10 July 1863
Citation: Served as quartermaster on board the U.S.S. *Cincinnati* during the attack on the Vicksburg batteries and at the time of her sinking, 27 May 1863. Engaging the enemy in a fierce battle, the *Cincinnati*, amidst an incessant fire of shot and shell, continued to fire her guns to the last, though so penetrated by enemy shellfire that her fate was sealed. Conspicuously cool in making signals throughout the battle, Bois, after all the *Cincinnati*'s staffs had been shot away, succeeded in nailing the flag to the stump of the forestaff to enable this proud ship to go down, "with her colors nailed to the mast."

107 ◆ BOND, WILLIAM S.

Rank: Boatswain's Mate (highest rank: Boatswain (WO))
Service: U.S. Navy
Birthday: 1839
Place of Birth: Boston, Suffolk County, Massachusetts
Date of Death: 17 March 1892
Cemetery: Sunrise Memorial Cemetery—Vallejo, California
Entered Service at: Boston, Suffolk County, Massachusetts
Unit: U.S.S. *Kearsarge*
Served as: Boatswain's Mate
Battle or Place of Action: off Cherbourg, France
Date of Action: 19 June 1864
G.O. Number, Date: 45, 31 December 1864
Citation: Served on board the U.S.S. *Kearsarge* when she destroyed the *Alabama* off Cherbourg, France, 19 June 1864. Carrying out his duties courageously, Bond exhibited marked coolness and good conduct and was highly recommended for his gallantry under fire by his divisional officer.

108 ◆ BONEBRAKE, HENRY G.

Rank: First Lieutenant
Service: U.S. Army
Birthday: 21 June 1838
Place of Birth: Waynesboro, Franklin County, Pennsylvania
Date of Death: 26 October 1912

Place of Death: Waynesboro, Pennsylvania
Cemetery: Green Hill Cemetery—Waynesboro, Pennsylvania
Entered Service at: Franklin County, Pennsylvania
Unit: Company G, 17th Pennsylvania Cavalry
Battle or Place of Action: Five Forks, Virginia
Date of Action: 1 April 1865
Date of Issue: 3 May 1865
Citation: As one of the first of Devin's Division to enter the works, he fought in a hand-to-hand struggle with a Confederate to capture his flag by superior physical strength.

109 ◆ BONNAFFON JR., SYLVESTER

Rank: First Lieutenant (highest rank: Brevet Lieutenant Colonel)
Service: U.S. Army
Birthday: 14 September 1844
Place of Birth: Philadelphia, Philadelphia County, Pennsylvania
Date of Death: 12 May 1922
Place of Death: Philadelphia, Pennsylvania
Cemetery: Woodlands Cemetery (MH)—Philadelphia, Pennsylvania
Entered Service at: Philadelphia, Philadelphia County, Pennsylvania
Unit: Company G, 99th Pennsylvania Infantry
Battle or Place of Action: Boydton Plank Road, Virginia
Date of Action: 27 October 1864
Date of Issue: 29 September 1893
Citation: Checked the rout and rallied the troops of his command in the face of a terrible fire of musketry; was severely wounded.

110 ◆ BOODY, ROBERT M.

Rank: Sergeant (highest rank: Second Lieutenant)
Service: U.S. Army
Birthday: 6 March 1836
Place of Birth: Lemington, Maine
Date of Death: 22 October 1913
Cemetery: Greenwood Cemetery (MH)—Haverhill, Massachusetts
Entered Service at: Amesbury, Essex County, Massachusetts
Unit: Company B, 40th New York Infantry
Battle or Place of Action: Williamsburg & Chancellorsville, Virginia
Date of Action: 5 May 1862 & 2 May 1863
Date of Issue: 8 July 1896
Citation: This soldier at Williamsburg, Va., then a corporal, at great personal risk, voluntarily saved the lives of and brought from the battlefield two wounded comrades. A year later, at Chancellorsville, voluntarily, and at great personal risk, brought from the field of battle and saved the life of Capt. George B. Carse, Company C, 40th New York Volunteer Infantry.

111 ◆ BOON, HUGH PATTERSON

Rank: Captain
Service: U.S. Army

Birthday: 24 July 1834
Place of Birth: Washington, Washington County, Pennsylvania
Date of Death: 14 January 1908
Cemetery: Washington Cemetery—Washington, Pennsylvania
Entered Service at: Washington, Washington County, Pennsylvania
Unit: Company B, 1st West Virginia Cavalry
Battle or Place of Action: Deatonsville (Sailor's Creek), Virginia
Date of Action: 6 April 1865
Date of Issue: 3 May 1865
Citation: Capture of flag.

112 ◆ BOSS, ORLANDO PHIDELIO

Rank: Corporal
Service: U.S. Army
Birthday: 30 July 1844
Place of Birth: Fitchburg, Worcester County, Massachusetts
Date of Death: 28 December 1931
Cemetery: Laurel Hill Cemetery—Fitchburg, Massachusetts
Entered Service at: Fitchburg, Worcester County, Massachusetts
Unit: Company F, 25th Massachusetts Infantry
Battle or Place of Action: Cold Harbor, Virginia
Date of Action: 3 June 1864
Date of Issue: 10 May 1888
Citation: Rescued his lieutenant, who was lying between the lines mortally wounded; this under a heavy fire from the enemy.

113 ◆ BOUQUET, NICHOLAS S.

Rank: Private (highest rank: Sergeant)
Service: U.S. Army
Birthday: 14 November 1842
Place of Birth: Landau, Bavaria, Germany
Date of Death: 27 December 1912
Place of Death: Burlington, Iowa
Cemetery: Aspen Grove Cemetery (MH)—Burlington, Iowa
Entered Service at: Burlington, Des Moines County, Iowa
Unit: Company D, 1st Iowa Infantry
Battle or Place of Action: Wilson's Creek, Missouri
Date of Action: 10 August 1861
Date of Issue: 16 February 1897
Citation: Voluntarily left the line of battle, and, exposing himself to imminent danger from a heavy fire from the enemy, Bouquet assisted in capturing a riderless horse at large between the lines and hitching him to a disabled gun, saved the gun from capture.

114 ◆ BOURKE, JOHN GREGORY

Rank: Private (highest rank: Brevet Major)
Service: U.S. Army
Birthday: 23 June 1846
Place of Birth: Philadelphia, Philadelphia County,

Pennsylvania
Date of Death: 8 June 1896
Cemetery: Arlington National Cemetery (1-32-A)—Arlington, Virginia
Entered Service at: Chicago, Cook County, Illinois
Unit: Company E, 15th Pennsylvania Cavalry
Battle or Place of Action: Stone River, Tennessee
Date of Action: 31 December 1862—1 January 1863
Date of Issue: 16 November 1887
Citation: Gallantry in action.

115 ◆ BOURNE, THOMAS

Rank: Seaman and Gun Captain (highest rank: Chief Quartermaster)
Service: U.S. Navy
Birthday: 1834
Place of Birth: England
Date of Death: 22 March 1888
Place of Death: Newburg, Michigan
Entered Service at: New York, New York
Unit: U.S.S. *Varuna*
Battle or Place of Action: Forts Jackson & St. Philip, Louisiana
Date of Action: 24 April 1862
G.O. Number, Date: 11, 3 April 1863
Citation: Served as a captain of a gun on board the U.S.S. *Varuna* during an attack on Forts Jackson and St. Philip and while under fire and ramming by the rebel ship *Morgan*, 24 April 1862. During this action at extremely close range, while his ship was under furious fire and was twice rammed by the rebel ship *Morgan*, Bourne remained steadfast at his gun and was instrumental in inflicting damage on the enemy until the *Varuna*, badly damaged and forced to beach, was finally sunk.

116 ◆ BOURY, RICHARD

True Name: Bowry, Richard
Rank: Sergeant
Service: U.S. Army
Birthday: 1836
Place of Birth: Monroe County, Ohio
Date of Death: 5 July 1914
Place of Death: Parkerburg, West Virginia
Cemetery: Odd Fellow Cemetery—Parkerburg, West Virginia
Entered Service at: Wirt Courthouse, West Virginia
Unit: Company G, 1st West Virginia Cavalry
Battle or Place of Action: Charlottesville, Virginia
Date of Action: 5 March 1865
Date of Issue: 25 March 1865
Citation: Capture of flag.

117 ◆ BOUTWELL, JOHN W.

Rank: Private
Service: U.S. Army
Birthday: 3 August 1845

Place of Birth: Hanover, Grafton County, New Hampshire
Date of Death: 11 December 1920
Cemetery: Arlington National Cemetery (33-2937) (MH)—Arlington, Virginia
Entered Service at: West Lebanon, Grafton County, New Hampshire
Unit: Company B, 18th New Hampshire Infantry
Battle or Place of Action: Petersburg, Virginia
Date of Action: 2 April 1865
Citation: Brought off from the picket line, under heavy fire, a comrade who had been shot through both legs.

118 ◆ BOWEN, CHESTER BENNETT

Rank: Corporal (highest rank: Sergeant)
Service: U.S. Army
Birthday: 1 April 1842
Place of Birth: Nunda, Livingston County, New York
Date of Death: 16 March 1905
Cemetery: City Greenwood Cemetery (MH)—Weatherford, Texas
Entered Service at: Nunda, Livingston County, New York
Unit: Company I, 19th New York Cavalry (1st New York Dragoons)
Battle or Place of Action: Winchester, Virginia
Date of Action: 19 September 1864
Date of Issue: 27 September 1864
Citation: Capture of flag.

119 ◆ BOWEN, EMMER

Rank: Private
Service: U.S. Army
Birthday: 25 October 1830
Place of Birth: Erie County, New York
Date of Death: 26 December 1912
Cemetery: Rosedale Cemetery—Los Angeles, California
Entered Service at: Hampshire, Kane County, Illinois
Unit: Company C, 127th Illinois Infantry
Battle or Place of Action: Vicksburg, Mississippi
Date of Action: 22 May 1863
Date of Issue: 21 July 1894
Citation: Gallantry in the charge of the "volunteer storming party."

120 ◆ BOWMAN, EDWARD R.

Rank: Quartermaster
Service: U.S. Navy
Birthday: 1826
Place of Birth: Eastport, Washington County, Maine
Date of Death: 20 October 1898
Cemetery: Hillside Cemetery (MH)—Eastport, Maine
Entered Service at: Maine
Unit: U.S.S. *Ticonderoga*
Battle or Place of Action: Fort Fisher, North Carolina
Date of Action: 13-15 January 1865
G.O. Number, Date: 59, 22 June 1865
Citation: On board the U.S.S. *Ticonderoga* during attacks

on Fort Fisher, 13 to 15 January 1865. Despite severe wounds sustained during the action, Bowman displayed outstanding courage in the performance of duty as his ship maintained its well-placed fire upon the batteries onshore, and thereafter, as she materially lessened the power of guns on the mound which had been turned upon our assaulting columns. During this battle the flag was planted on one of the strongest fortifications possessed by the rebels.

121 ◆ BOX, THOMAS J.

Rank: Captain
Service: U.S. Army
Birthday: 7 November 1833
Place of Birth: Indiana
Date of Death: 18 December 1914
Place of Death: Indianapolis, Marion County, Indiana
Cemetery: Greenhill Cemetery (MH)—Bedford, Indiana
Entered Service at: Bedford, Lawrence County, Indiana
Unit: Company D, 27th Indiana Infantry
Battle or Place of Action: Resaca, Georgia
Date of Action: 14 May 1864
Date of Issue: 7 April 1865
Citation: Capture of flag of the 38th Alabama Infantry (C.S.A.).

122 ◆ BOYNTON, HENRY VAN NESS

Rank: Lieutenant Colonel (highest rank: Brevet Brigadier General)
Service: U.S. Army
Birthday: 22 July 1835
Place of Birth: West Stockbridge, Berkshire County, Massachusetts
Date of Death: 3 June 1905
Place of Death: Atlantic City, New Jersey
Cemetery: Arlington National Cemetery (2-1096)—Arlington, Virginia
Entered Service at: Hamilton, Butler County, Ohio
Unit: 35th Ohio Infantry
Served as: Commanding Officer
Battle or Place of Action: Missionary Ridge, Tennessee
Date of Action: 25 November 1863
Date of Issue: 15 November 1893
Citation: Led his regiment in the face of a severe fire of the enemy; was severely wounded.

123 ◆ BRADLEY, AMOS

Rank: Landsman
Service: U.S. Navy
Birthday: 1837
Place of Birth: Dansville, Livingston County, New York
Entered Service at: New York
Unit: U.S.S. *Varuna*
Battle or Place of Action: Fort Jackson & St. Philip, Louisiana
Date of Action: 24 April 1862
G.O. Number, Date: 11, 3 April 1863

Citation: Served on board the U.S.S. *Varuna* in one of the most responsible positions, during the attacks on Forts Jackson and St. Philip, and while in action against the rebel ship *Morgan* 24 April 1862. Although guns were raking the decks from behind him, Bradley remained steadfast at the wheel throughout the thickest of the fight, continuing at his station and rendering service with the greatest courage until his ship, repeatedly holed and twice rammed by the rebel ship *Morgan*, was beached and sunk.

124 ◆ BRADLEY, CHARLES

Rank: Boatswain's Mate
Service: U.S. Navy
Birthday: 1838
Place of Birth: Ireland
Entered Service at: New York, New York
Unit: U.S.S. *Louisville*
Battle or Place of Action: Fort Hindman, Arkansas
Date of Action: 10-11 January 1863
G.O. Number, Date: 11, 3 April 1863
Citation: Served on board the U.S.S. *Louisville*. Carrying out his duties through the thick of the battle and acting as captain of a 9-inch gun, Bradley consistently showed "attention to duty, bravery, and coolness in action against the enemy."

125 ◆ BRADLEY, THOMAS WILSON

Rank: Sergeant (highest rank: Brevet Lieutenant Colonel)
Service: U.S. Army
Birthday: 6 April 1844
Place of Birth: Sheffield, Yorkshire County, England
Date of Death: 30 May 1920
Cemetery: Wallkill Valley Cemetery—Walden, New York
Entered Service at: Walden, Orange County, New York
Unit: Company H, 124th New York Infantry (American Guard)
Battle or Place of Action: Chancellorsville, Virginia
Date of Action: 3 May 1863
Date of Issue: 10 June 1896
Citation: Volunteered in response to a call and alone, in the face of a heavy fire of musketry and canister, went and procured ammunition for the use of his comrades.

126 ◆ BRADY, JAMES

Rank: Private
Service: U.S. Army
Birthday: 1842
Place of Birth: Boston, Suffolk County, Massachusetts
Date of Death: 7 October 1904
Cemetery: Old Pine Grove Cemetery (MH)—Raymond, New Hampshire
Entered Service at: Kingston, Rockingham County, New Hampshire
Unit: Company F, 10th New Hampshire Infantry (Irish Regiment)
Battle or Place of Action: Chapin's Farm, Virginia

Date of Action: 29 September 1864
Date of Issue: 6 April 1865
Citation: Capture of flag.

127 ◆ BRANDLE, JOSEPH E.

Rank: Private (highest rank: Color Sergeant)
Service: U.S. Army
Birthday: 8 October 1835
Place of Birth: Seneca County, Ohio
Date of Death: 13 May 1909
Place of Death: Coldwater, Michigan
Cemetery: Oak Grove Cemetery (MH)—Coldwater, Michigan
Entered Service at: Colon, St. Joseph County, Michigan
Unit: Company C, 17th Michigan Infantry
Battle or Place of Action: Lenoire, Tennessee
Date of Action: 16 November 1863
Date of Issue: 20 July 1897
Citation: While color bearer of his regiment, having been twice wounded and had the sight of one eye destroyed, Brandle still held to the colors until ordered to the rear by his regimental commander.

128 ◆ BRANNIGAN, FELIX

Rank: Private (highest rank: First Lieutenant)
Service: U.S. Army
Birthday: 1844
Place of Birth: Ireland
Date of Death: 10 June 1907
Cemetery: Arlington National Cemetery (3-1642)—Arlington, Virginia
Entered Service at: Pittsburgh, Allegheny County, Pennsylvania
Unit: Company A, 74th New York Infantry
Battle or Place of Action: Chancellorsville, Virginia
Date of Action: 2 May 1863
Date of Issue: 29 June 1866
Citation: Volunteered on a dangerous service and brought in valuable information.

129 ◆ BRANT JR., WILLIAM

Rank: Lieutenant (highest rank: Brevet Captain)
Service: U.S. Army
Birthday: 1840
Place of Birth: Elizabeth, Union County, New Jersey
Date of Death: 2 March 1898
Place of Death: Elizabeth, New Jersey
Cemetery: The Evergreen Cemetery (MH)—Hillside, New Jersey
Entered Service at: Trenton, Mercer County, New Jersey
Unit: Company B, 1st New Jersey Veteran Battalion
Battle or Place of Action: Petersburg, Virginia
Date of Action: 3 April 1865
Date of Issue: 10 May 1865
Citation: Capture of battle flag of 46th North Carolina (C.S.A.).

130 ◆ BRAS, EDGAR A.

Rank: Sergeant
Service: U.S. Army
Birthday: 6 October 1841
Place of Birth: Jefferson County, Iowa
Date of Death: 24 June 1923
Place of Death: Fort Lauderdale, Florida
Cemetery: Evergreen Cemetery—Fort Lauderdale, Florida
Entered Service at: Wapello, Louisa County, Iowa
Unit: Company K, 8th Iowa Infantry
Battle or Place of Action: Spanish Fort, Alabama
Date of Action: 8 April 1865
Date of Issue: 8 June 1865

131 ◆ BRAZELL, JOHN

Rank: Quartermaster (highest rank: Chief Quartermaster)
Service: U.S. Navy
Birthday: 1837
Place of Birth: Philadelphia, Philadelphia County, Pennsylvania
Date of Death: 12 August 1866
Place of Death: Philadelphia, Pennsylvania
Entered Service at: Pennsylvania
Unit: U.S.S. *Richmond*
Battle or Place of Action: Mobile Bay, Alabama
Date of Action: 5 August 1864
G.O. Number, Date: 45, 31 December 1864
Citation: Served on board the U.S.S. *Richmond* in the action at Mobile Bay, 5 August 1864, where he was recommended for coolness and good conduct as a gun captain during that engagement, which resulted in the capture of the rebel ram *Tennessee* and in the destruction of Fort Morgan. Brazell served gallantly throughout the actions with Forts Jackson and St. Philip, the Chalmettes, batteries below Vicksburg, and was present at the surrender of New Orleans while on board the U.S.S. *Brooklyn*.

132 ◆ BREEN, JOHN

Rank: Boatswain's Mate
Service: U.S. Navy
Birthday: 1827
Place of Birth: New York, New York
Date of Death: 13 December 1875
Place of Death: Milwaukee, Wisconsin
Cemetery: Calvary Cemetery—Milwaukee, Wisconsin
Entered Service at: New York, New York
Unit: U.S.S. *Commodore Perry*
Battle or Place of Action: Franklin, Virginia
Date of Action: 3 October 1862
G.O. Number, Date: 11, 3 April 1863
Citation: On board the U.S.S. *Commodore Perry* in the attack upon Franklin, Va., 3 October 1862. With enemy fire raking the deck of his ship and blockades thwarting her progress, Breen remained at his post and performed his duties with skill and courage as the *Commodore Perry* fought a gal-

lant battle to silence many rebel batteries as she steamed down the Blackwater River.

133 ◆ BRENNAN, CHRISTOPHER

Rank: Seaman
Service: U.S. Navy
Birthday: 1832
Place of Birth: Ireland
Entered Service at: Boston, Suffolk County, Massachusetts
Unit: U.S.S. *Mississippi* (temporarily assigned U.S.S. *Colorado*)
Battle or Place of Action: Forts Jackson & St. Philip and New Orleans, Louisiana
Date of Action: 24-25 April 1862
G.O. Number, Date: 17, 10 July 1863
Citation: On board the U.S.S. *Mississippi* during attacks on Forts Jackson and St. Philip and during the taking of New Orleans, 24–25 April 1862. Taking part in the actions which resulted in the damaging of the *Mississippi* and several casualties on it, Brennan showed skill and courage throughout the entire engagements which resulted in the taking of St. Philip and Jackson and in the surrender of New Orleans.

134 ◆ BREST, LEWIS FRANCIS

Rank: Private
Service: U.S. Army
Birthday: 15 May 1842
Place of Birth: Mercer, Mercer County, Pennsylvania
Date of Death: 2 December 1915
Place of Death: Mercer, Pennsylvania
Cemetery: Citizens Cemetery—Mercer, Pennsylvania
Entered Service at: Pittsburgh, Allegheny County, Pennsylvania
Unit: Company D, 57th Pennsylvania Infantry
Battle or Place of Action: Deatonsville (Sailor's Creek), Virginia
Date of Action: 6 April 1865
Date of Issue: 10 May 1865
Citation: Capture of flag.

135 ◆ BREWER, WILLIAM JOHN

Rank: Private (highest rank: Corporal)
Service: U.S. Army
Birthday: 1843
Place of Birth: Putnam County, New York
Date of Death: 19 June 1878
Place of Death: Cornwall, New York
Cemetery: Quaker Cemetery—Cornwall-on-the-Hudson, New York
Entered Service at: Newburgh, Orange County, New York
Unit: Company C, 2d New York Cavalry
Battle or Place of Action: Appomattox Campaign, Virginia
Date of Action: 4 April 1865
Date of Issue: 3 May 1865
Citation: Capture of engineer flag, Army of Northern Virginia.

136 ◆ BREYER, CHARLES

Rank: Sergeant
Service: U.S. Army
Birthday: 19 June 1844
Place of Birth: England
Date of Death: 9 September 1914
Place of Death: Pottstown, Pennsylvania
Cemetery: St. James Church Cemetery—Limerick, Pennsylvania
Entered Service at: Philadelphia, Philadelphia County, Pennsylvania
Unit: Company I, 90th Pennsylvania Infantry
Battle or Place of Action: Rappahannock Station, Virginia
Date of Action: 23 August 1862
Date of Issue: 8 July 1896
Citation: Voluntarily and at great personal risk, Breyer picked up an unexploded shell and threw it away, thus doubtless saving the life of a comrade whose arm had been taken off by the same shell.

137 ◆ BRIGGS, ELIJAH A.

Rank: Corporal (highest rank: Sergeant)
Service: U.S. Army
Birthday: 26 October 1843
Place of Birth: Salisbury, Litchfield County, Connecticut
Date of Death: 10 March 1922
Place of Death: Beacon, New York
Cemetery: Fishkill Rural Cemetery (MH)—Fishkill, New York
Entered Service at: Salisbury, Litchfield County, Connecticut
Unit: Company B, 2d Connecticut Heavy Artillery
Battle or Place of Action: Petersburg, Virginia
Date of Action: 3 April 1865
Date of Issue: 10 May 1865
Citation: Capture of battle flag.

138 ◆ BRINGLE, ANDREW

Rank: Corporal
Service: U.S. Army
Place of Birth: Buffalo, Erie County, New York
Entered Service at: Buffalo, Erie County, New York
Unit: Company F, 10th New York Cavalry (Porter Guard)
Battle or Place of Action: Deatonsville (Sailor's Creek), Virginia
Date of Action: 6 April 1865
Date of Issue: 3 July 1865
Citation: Charged the enemy and assisted Sgt. Llewllyn P. Norton in capturing a fieldpiece and two prisoners.

139 ◆ BRINN, ANDREW

Rank Seaman
Service: U.S. Navy
Birthday: 1829
Place of Birth: Scotland

Entered Service at: New York, New York
Unit: U.S.S. *Mississippi*
Battle or Place of Action: Port Hudson, Louisiana
Date of Action: 14 March 1864
G.O. Number, Date: 17, 10 July 1863
Citation: Served on board the U.S.S. *Mississippi* during her abandonment and firing in the engagement at Port Hudson, 14 March 1863. Remaining under enemy fire for 21/2 hours, Brinn remained on board the grounded vessel until all the abandoning crew had landed. After asking to be assigned some duty, he was finally ordered to save himself and to leave the *Mississippi*, which had been deliberately fired to prevent her falling into rebel hands.

140 ◆ BRONNER, AUGUST FREDERICK

Rank: Private
Service: U.S. Army
Birthday: 1835
Place of Birth: Germany
Date of Death: 31 October 1893
Place of Death: Newark, New Jersey
Cemetery: Fairmount Cemetery (MH)—Newark, New Jersey
Entered Service at: New York, New York
Unit: Company C, 1st New York Artillery
Battle or Place of Action: White Oak Swamp, Virginia
Date of Action: 30 June 1862
Date of Issue: 19 April 1892
Citation: Continued to fight after being severely wounded.

141 ◆ BRONSON, JAMES H.

Rank: First Sergeant
Service: U.S. Army
Birthday: 1838
Place of Birth: Indiana County, Pennsylvania
Date of Death: 16 March 1884
Cemetery: Chartiers Cemetery (MH)—Carnegie, Pennsylvania
Entered Service at: Trumbell County, Ohio
Unit: Company D, 5th U.S. Colored Infantry
Battle or Place of Action: Chapin's Farm, Virginia
Date of Action: 29 September 1864
Date of Issue: 6 April 1865
Citation: Took command of his company, all the officers having been killed or wounded, and gallantly led it.

142 ◆ BROSNAN, JOHN

Rank: Sergeant
Service: U.S. Army
Birthday: 1 July 1846
Place of Birth: Ireland
Date of Death: 7 August 1921
Place of Death: Brooklyn, New York
Cemetery: Holy Cross Cemetery—Brooklyn, New York
Entered Service at: New York, New York
Unit: Company E, 164th New York Infantry

Battle or Place of Action: Petersburg, Virginia
Date of Action: 17 June 1864
Date of Issue: 18 January 1894
Citation: Rescued a wounded comrade who lay exposed to the enemy's fire, receiving a severe wound in the effort.

143 ◆ BROUSE, CHARLES W.

Rank: Captain
Service: U.S. Army
Birthday: 30 November 1839
Date of Death: 26 October 1904
Cemetery: Crown Hill Cemetery (MH)—Indianapolis, Indiana
Entered Service at: Indianapolis, Marion County, Indiana
Unit: Company K, 100th Indiana Infantry
Battle or Place of Action: Missionary Ridge, Tennessee
Date of Action: 25 November 1863
Date of Issue: 16 May 1899
Citation: To encourage his men whom he had ordered to lie down while under severe fire and who were partially protected by slight earthworks, Brouse himself refused to lie down, but walked along the top of the works until he fell severely wounded.

144 ◆ BROWN, CHARLES E.

Rank: Sergeant (highest rank: Captain)
Service: U.S. Army
Birthday: 11 December 1841
Place of Birth: Schuylkill County, Pennsylvania
Date of Death: 20 February 1919
Place of Death: Schuylkill Haven, Pennsylvania
Cemetery: Union Cemetery (MH)—Schuylkill Haven, Pennsylvania
Entered Service at: Schuylkill Haven, Schuylkill County, Pennsylvania
Unit: Company C, 50th Pennsylvania Infantry
Battle or Place of Action: Weldon Railroad, Virginia
Date of Action: 19 August 1864
Date of Issue: 1 December 1864
Citation: Capture of flag of 47th Virginia Infantry (C.S.A.).

145 ◆ BROWN JR., EDWARD

True Name: Browne Jr., Edward
Rank: Corporal (highest rank: Sergeant)
Service: U.S. Army
Birthday: 6 July 1841
Place of Birth: Ireland
Date of Death: 5 November 1911
Place of Death: New York, New York
Cemetery: 1st Calvary Cemetery—Woodside, New York
Entered Service at: New York, New York
Unit: Company G, 62d New York Infantry
Battle or Place of Action: Fredericksburg & Salem Heights, Virginia
Date of Action: 3-4 May 1863
Date of Issue: 24 November 1880

Citation: Severely wounded while carrying the colors, he continued at his post, under fire, until ordered to the rear.

146 ◆ BROWN, HENRI LE FEVRE

Rank: Sergeant
Service: U.S. Army
Birthday: 30 May 1842
Place of Birth: Jamestown, Chautauqua County, New York
Date of Death: 29 April 1910
Place of Death: Jamestown, New York
Cemetery: Lakeview Cemetery—Jamestown, New York
Entered Service at: Ellicott, Erie County, New York
Unit: Company B, 72d New York Infantry
Battle or Place of Action: Wilderness Campaign, Virginia
Date of Action: 6 May 1864
Date of Issue: 23 June 1896
Citation: Voluntarily and under a heavy fire from the enemy, Brown three times crossed the field of battle with a load of ammunition in a blanket on his back, thus supplying the Federal forces, whose ammunition had nearly all been expended, and enabling them to hold their position until reinforcement arrived, when the enemy were driven from their position.

147 ◆ BROWN, JAMES

Rank: Quartermaster
Service: U.S. Navy
Birthday: 1826
Place of Birth: Rochester, Monroe County, New York
Entered Service at: New York
Unit: U.S.S. *Albatross*
Battle or Place of Action: Fort De Russy, Red River, Louisiana
Date of Action: 4 May 1863
G.O. Number, Date: 32, 16 April 1864
Citation: Served on board the U.S.S. *Albatross* during action against Fort De Russy in the Red River area on 4 May 1863. After the steering wheel and wheel ropes had been shot away by rebel fire, Brown stood on the gun platform of the quarterdeck, exposing himself to a close fire of musketry from the shore, and rendered invaluable assistance by his expert management of the relieving tackles in extricating the vessel from a perilous position, and thereby aided in the capture of Fort De Russy's heavyworks.

148 ◆ BROWN, JEREMIAH Z.

Rank: Captain (highest rank: Brevet Major)
Service: U.S. Army
Birthday: 7 November 1839
Place of Birth: near Rural Valley, Armstrong County, Pennsylvania
Date of Death: 19 February 1916
Place of Death: Porter Township, Pennsylvania
Cemetery: Squirriel Hill Cemetery—New Bethlehem, Pennsylvania
Entered Service at: Curllsville, Clarion County, Pennsylvania
Unit: Company K, 148th Pennsylvania Infantry

Battle or Place of Action: Petersburg, Virginia
Date of Action: 27 October 1864
Date of Issue: 22 June 1896
Citation: With 100 selected volunteers, Brown assaulted and captured the works of the enemy, together with a number of officers and men.

149 ◆ BROWN, JOHN

True Name: Hayes, Thomas
Rank: Captain of the Forecastle
Service: U.S. Navy
Birthday: 1826
Place of Birth: Glasgow, Scotland
Date of Death: 1 November 1883
Place of Death: Sonoma, California
Entered Service at: New York, New York
Unit: U.S.S. *Brooklyn*
Battle or Place of Action: Mobile Bay, Alabama
Date of Action: 5 August 1864
G.O. Number, Date: 45, 31 December 1864
Citation: On board the U.S.S. *Brooklyn* during action against rebel forts and gunboats and with the ram *Tennessee* in Mobile Bay, 5 August 1864. Despite severe damage to his ship and the loss of several men on board as enemy fire raked her decks from stem to stern, Brown fought his gun with skill and courage throughout the furious battle which resulted in the surrender of the prize rebel ram *Tennessee* and in the damaging and destruction of batteries at Fort Morgan.

150 ◆ BROWN, JOHN

Rank: First Sergeant (highest rank: Captain)
Service: U.S. Army
Birthday: 1842
Place of Birth: Boston, Suffolk County, Massachusetts
Date of Death: 7 August 1898
Cemetery: Spring Grove Cemetery—Cincinnati, Ohio
Entered Service at: Cincinnati, Hamilton County, Ohio
Unit: Company A, 47th Ohio Infantry
Battle or Place of Action: Vicksburg, Mississippi
Date of Action: 19 May 1863
Date of Issue: 24 August 1896
Citation: Voluntarily carried a verbal message from Col. A.C. Parry to Gen. Hugh Ewing through a terrific fire and in plain view of the enemy.

151 ◆ BROWN, JOHN HARTIES

Rank: Captain
Service: U.S. Army
Birthday: 1834
Place of Birth: New Brunswick, Canada
Date of Death: 30 January 1905
Place of Death: Washington, D.C.
Cemetery: Arlington National Cemetery (3-1486 1/2) (MH)—Arlington, Virginia
Entered Service at: Charlestown, Suffolk County, Massachusetts

Unit: Company D, 12th Kentucky Infantry
Battle or Place of Action: Franklin, Tennessee
Date of Action: 30 November 1864
Date of Issue: 13 February 1865
Citation: Capture of flag.

152 ◆ *BROWN JR., MORRIS

Rank: Captain
Service: U.S. Army
Birthday: August 1842
Place of Birth: Hammondsport, Steuben County, New York
Date of Death: 22 June 1864
Place of Death: Petersburg, Virginia
Cemetery: Lake View Cemetery—Penn Yan, New York
Entered Service at: Geneva, Ontario County, New York
Unit: Company A, 126th New York Infantry
Battle or Place of Action: Gettysburg, Pennsylvania
Date of Action: 3 July 1863
Date of Issue: 6 March 1869
Citation: Capture of flag.

153 ◆ BROWN, ROBERT

Rank: Captain of the Top
Service: U.S. Navy
Birthday: 1830
Place of Birth: Norway
Entered Service at: New York
Unit: U.S.S. *Richmond*
Battle or Place of Action: Fort Morgan, Mobile Bay, Alabama
Date of Action: 5 August 1864
G.O. Number, Date: 45, 31 December 1864
Citation: On board the U.S.S. *Richmond* in action at Mobile Bay, 5 August 1864. Cool and courageous at his station throughout the prolonged action, Brown rendered gallant service as his vessel trained her guns on Fort Morgan and on ships of the Confederacy despite extremely heavy return fire. He participated in the actions at Forts Jackson and St. Philip, with the Chalmette batteries, at the surrender of New Orleans and in the attacks on batteries below Vicksburg.

154 ◆ BROWN, ROBERT BURNS

Rank: Private
Service: U.S. Army
Birthday: 2 October 1844
Place of Birth: New Concord, Muskingum County, Ohio
Date of Death: 30 July 1916
Cemetery: Greenwood Cemetery (MH)—Zanesville, Ohio
Entered Service at: Zanesville, Muskingum County, Ohio
Unit: Company A, 15th Ohio Infantry
Battle or Place of Action: Missionary Ridge, Tennessee
Date of Action: 25 November 1863
Date of Issue: 27 March 1890
Citation: Upon reaching the ridge through concentrated fire, he approached the color bearer of the 9th Mississippi Infantry (C.S.A.), demanded his surrender with threatening gesture, and took him prisoner with his regimental flag.

155 ◆ BROWN, URIAH H.

Rank: Private (highest rank: Corporal)
Service: U.S. Army
Birthday: 4 July 1841
Place of Birth: Covington, Miami County, Ohio
Date of Death: 24 January 1927
Place of Death: Holiday Cove, West Virginia
Cemetery: Paris Cemetery—Paris, Pennsylvania
Entered Service at: Steubenville, Jefferson County, Ohio
Unit: Company G, 30th Ohio Infantry
Battle or Place of Action: Vicksburg, Mississippi
Date of Action: 22 May 1863
Date of Issue: 15 August 1894
Citation: Despite the death of his captain at his side during the assault, he continued carrying his log to the defense ditch. While he was laying his log in place he was shot down and thrown into the water. Unmindful of his own wound he, despite the intense fire, dragged five of his comrades from the ditch, wherein they lay wounded, to a place of safety.

156 ◆ BROWN, WILLIAM H.

Rank: Landsman
Service: U.S. Navy
Birthday: 1836
Place of Birth: Baltimore, Baltimore County, Maryland
Date of Death: 5 November 1896
Cemetery: Arlington National Cemetery (27-565-A) (MH)—Arlington, Virginia
Entered Service at: Maryland
Unit: U.S.S. *Brooklyn*
Battle or Place of Action: Fort Morgan, Mobile Bay, Alabama
Date of Action: 5 August 1864
G.O. Number, Date: 45, 31 December 1864
Citation: On board the U.S.S. *Brooklyn* during successful attacks against Fort Morgan rebel gunboats and the ram *Tennessee* in Mobile Bay, on 5 August 1864. Stationed in the immediate vicinity of the shell whips which were twice cleared of men by bursting shells, Brown remained steadfast at his post and performed his duties in the powder division throughout the furious action, which resulted in the surrender of the prize rebel ram *Tennessee* and in the damaging and destruction of batteries at Fort Morgan.

157 ◆ BROWN, WILSON

Rank: Landsman
Service: U.S. Navy
Birthday: 1841
Place of Birth: Natchez, Adams County, Mississippi
Date of Death: 24 January 1900
Cemetery: National Cemetery (G-3152) (MH)—Natchez, Mississippi
Entered Service at: Mississippi River, Mississippi
Unit: U.S.S. *Hartford*
Battle or Place of Action: Fort Morgan, Mobile Bay, Alabama

Date of Action: 5 August 1864
G.O. Number, Date: 45, 31 December 1864
Citation: On board the flagship U.S.S. *Hartford* during successful attacks against Fort Morgan, rebel gunboats, and the ram *Tennessee* in Mobile Bay, on 5 August 1864. Knocked unconscious into the hold of the ship when an enemy shell-burst fatally wounded a man on the ladder above him, Brown, upon regaining consciousness, promptly returned to the shell whip on the berth deck and zealously continued to perform his duties, although four of the six men at this station had been either killed or wounded by the enemy's terrific fire.

158 ◆ BROWN, WILSON W.

Rank: Private (highest rank: Second Lieutenant)
Service: U.S. Army
Birthday: 25 December 1837
Place of Birth: Logan County, Ohio
Date of Death: 25 February 1916
Place of Death: Toledo, Ohio
Cemetery: New Bellville Ridge Cemetery—Dowling, Ohio
Entered Service at: Findlay, Hancock County, Ohio
Unit: Company F, 21st Ohio Infantry
Battle or Place of Action: Georgia
Date of Action: April 1862
Date of Issue: September 1863
Citation: One of the 19 of 24 men (including two civilians) who, by direction of Gen. Ormsby M. Mitchell, penetrated nearly 200 miles south into enemy territory and captured a railroad train at Big Shanty, Ga., in an attempt to destroy the bridges and track between Chattanaooga and Atlanta.
Notes: POW 1862, 1863

159 ◆ BROWNELL, FRANCIS EDWIN

Rank: Private (highest rank: First Lieutenant)
Service: U.S. Army
Birthday: 1840
Place of Birth: Troy, Rensselaer County, New York
Date of Death: 15 March 1894
Place of Death: Washington, D.C.
Cemetery: Bellefontaine Cemetery—St. Louis, Missouri
Entered Service at: Troy, Rensselaer County, New York
Unit: Company A, 11th New York Infantry (Ellsworth's Zouaves)
Battle or Place of Action: Alexandria, Virginia
Date of Action: 24 May 1861
Date of Issue: 26 January 1877
Citation: Killed the murderer of Col. Ellsworth at the Marshall House, Alexandria, Va. First Civil War deed to merit Medal of Honor.

160 ◆ BROWNELL, WILLIAM P.

Rank: Coxswain (highest rank: Acting Master's Mate)
Service: U.S. Navy
Birthday: 12 July 1839
Place of Birth: New York
Date of Death: 26 April 1915

Place of Death: New York, New York
Cemetery: Oak Grove Cemetery (MH)—New Bedford, Massachusetts
Entered Service at: New York
Unit: U.S.S. *Benton*
Battle or Place of Action: Great Gulf Bay and Vicksburg, Mississippi
Date of Action: 2, 22 May 1863
G.O. Number, Date: 32, 16 April 1864
Citation: Served as coxswain on board the U.S.S. *Benton* during the attack on Great Gulf Bay, 2 May 1863, and Vicksburg, 22 May 1863. Carrying out his duties with coolness and courage, Brownell served gallantly against the enemy as captain of a 9-inch gun in the attacks on Great Gulf and Vicksburg and as a member of the Battery Benton before Vicksburg.

161 ◆ BRUNER, LOUIS J.

Rank: Private (highest rank: Quartermaster Sergeant)
Service: U.S. Army
Birthday: 6 October 1843
Place of Birth: Monroe County, Indiana
Date of Death: 28 January 1912
Cemetery: Green Park Cemetery—Portland, Indiana
Entered Service at: Clifty Brumer, Indiana
Unit: Company H, 5th Indiana Cavalry
Battle or Place of Action: Walker's Ford, Tennessee
Date of Action: 2 December 1863
Date of Issue: 9 March 1896
Citation: Voluntarily passed through the enemy's lines under fire and conveyed to a battalion, then in a perilous position and liable to capture, information which enabled it to reach a point of safety.

162 ◆ BRUSH, GEORGE WASHINGTON

Rank: Second Lieutenant (highest rank: Captain)
Service: U.S. Army
Birthday: 4 October 1842
Place of Birth: West Hills, Suffolk County, New York
Date of Death: 18 November 1927
Place of Death: Brooklyn, New York
Cemetery: Huntington Rural Cemetery—Huntington, New York
Entered Service at: Huntington, Suffolk County, New York
Unit: Company B, 34th U.S. Colored Infantry
Battle or Place of Action: Ashepoo River, South Carolina
Date of Action: 24 May 1864
Date of Issue: 21 January 1897
Citation: Voluntarily commanded a boat crew, which went to the rescue of a large number of Union soldiers on board the stranded steamer *Boston*, and with great gallantry succeeded in conveying them to shore, being exposed during the entire time to heavy fire from a Confederate battery.

163 ◆ BRUTON, CHRISTOPHER C.

True Name: Braton, Christopher
Rank: Captain (highest rank: Brevet Major)

Service: U.S. Army
Birthday: 1840
Place of Birth: Ireland
Entered Service at: Riga, Monroe County, New York
Unit: Company C, 22d New York Cavalry
Battle or Place of Action: Waynesboro, Virginia
Date of Action: 2 March 1865
Date of Issue: 26 March 1865
Citation: Capture of Gen. Early's headquarters flag. Confederate national standard.

164 ◆ BRUTSCHE, HENRY

Rank: Landsman
Service: U.S. Navy
Birthday: 1846
Place of Birth: Philadelphia, Philadelphia County, Pennsylvania
Entered Service at: Pennsylvania
Unit: U.S.S. *Tacony*
Battle or Place of Action: Plymouth, North Carolina
Date of Action: 23 May 1863
G.O. Number, Date: 45, 31 December 1864
Citation: Served on board the U.S.S. *Tacony* during the taking of Plymouth, N.C., 31 October 1864. Carrying out his duties faithfully during the capture of Plymouth, Brutsche distinguished himself by a display of coolness when he participated in landing and spiking a 9-inch gun while under a devastating fire from enemy musketry.

165 ◆ BRYANT, ANDREW SYMMES

Rank: Sergeant (highest rank: Sergeant Major)
Service: U.S. Army
Birthday: 3 March 1841
Place of Birth: Springfield, Hampden County, Massachusetts
Date of Death: 6 October 1931
Cemetery: Springfield Cemetery (MH)—Springfield, Massachusetts
Entered Service at: Springfield, Hampden County, Massachusetts
Unit: Company A, 46th Massachusetts Infantry
Battle or Place of Action: New Bern, North Carolina
Date of Action: 23 May 1863
Date of Issue: 13 August 1873
Citation: By his courage and judicious disposition of his guard of 16 men, stationed in a small earthwork at the head of the bridge, Bryant held in check and repulsed for a half hour a fierce attack of a strong force of the enemy, thus probably saving the city of New Bern from capture.

166 ◆ *BUCHANAN, GEORGE A.

Rank: Private
Service: U.S. Army
Birthday: 1842
Place of Birth: Victor, Ontario County, New York

Date of Death: 2 October 1864
Place of Death: Chapin's Farm, Virginia
Cemetery: Fort Harrison National Cemetery (A-224) (MH)—Richmond, Virginia
Entered Service at: Canaoaigua, Ontario County, New York
Unit: Company G, 148th New York Infantry
Battle or Place of Action: Chapin's Farm, Virginia
Date of Action: 29 September 1864
Date of Issue: 6 April 1865
Citation: Took position in advance of the skirmish line and drove the enemy's cannoneers from their guns; was mortally wounded.

167 ◆ BUCK, FREDERICK CLARENCE

Rank: Corporal (highest rank: First Lieutenant)
Service: U.S. Army
Birthday: 1843
Place of Birth: Hartford, Hartford County, Connecticut
Entered Service at: Windsor, Hartford County, Connecticut
Unit: Company A, 21st Connecticut Infantry
Battle or Place of Action: Chapin's Farm, Virginia
Date of Action: 29 September 1864
Date of Issue: 6 April 1865
Citation: Although wounded, refused to leave the field until the fight closed.

168 ◆ BUCK, JAMES

Rank: Quartermaster (highest rank: Acting Master's Mate)
Service: U.S. Navy
Birthday: 1808
Place of Birth: Baltimore, Baltimore County, Maryland
Unit: U.S.S. *Brooklyn*
Battle or Place of Action: Forts Jackson and St. Philip, Louisiana
Date of Action: 24-25 April 1862
G.O. Number, Date: 11, 3 April 1863
Citation: Served on board the U.S.S. *Brooklyn* in the attack upon Forts Jackson and St.Philip and at the taking of New Orleans, 24 and 25 April 1862. Although severely wounded by a heavy splinter, Buck continued to perform his duty until positively ordered below. Later stealing back to his post, he steered the ship for eight hours despite his critical condition. His bravery was typical of the type which resulted in the taking of the Forts Jackson and St. Philip and in the capture of New Orleans.

169 ◆ BUCKINGHAM, DAVID EASTBURN

Rank: First Lieutenant (highest rank: Captain)
Service: U.S. Army
Birthday: 3 February 1840
Place of Birth: Pleasant Hill (Stanton), Delaware
Date of Death: 23 November 1915
Cemetery: Arlington National Cemetery (2-3677)—Arlington, Virginia
Entered Service at: Wilmington, New Castle County, Delaware

Unit: Company E, 4th Delaware Infantry
Battle or Place of Action: Rowanty Creek, Virginia
Date of Action: 5 February 1865
Date of Issue: 13 February 1895
Citation: Swam the partly frozen creek under fire, in the attempt to capture a crossing.

170 ◆ BUCKLES, ABRAM J.

True Name: Buckles, Abraham Jay
Rank: Sergeant (highest rank: Second Lieutenant)
Service: U.S. Army
Birthday: 2 August 1846
Place of Birth: Delaware County, Indiana
Date of Death: 19 January 1915
Cemetery: Fairfield Cemetery—Fairfield, California
Entered Service at: Muncie, Delaware County, Indiana
Unit: Company E, 19th Indiana Infantry
Battle or Place of Action: Wilderness Campaign, Virginia
Date of Action: 5 May 1864
Date of Issue: 4 December 1893
Citation: Though suffering from an open wound, Buckles carried the regimental colors until again wounded.

171 ◆ *BUCKLEY, DENIS

True Name: Buckley, Dennis
Rank: Private
Service: U.S. Army
Birthday: 1844
Place of Birth: Canada
Date of Death: 20 July 1864
Place of Death: Peach Tree Creek, Georgia
Entered Service at: Avon, Livingston County, New York
Unit: Company G, 136th New York Infantry
Battle or Place of Action: Peach Tree Creek, Georgia
Date of Action: 20 July 1864
Date of Issue: 7 April 1865
Citation: Capture of flag of 31st Mississippi (C.S.A.).
Notes: POW

172 ◆ BUCKLEY, JOHN C.

Rank: Sergeant
Service: U.S. Army
Birthday: 1 April 1842
Place of Birth: Fayette County, West Virginia
Date of Death: 29 March 1913
Place of Death: Fitzgerald, Georgia
Cemetery: Evergreen Cemetery (MH)—Fitzgerald, Georgia
Entered Service at: Mount Pleasant, West Virginia
Unit: Company G, 4th West Virginia Infantry
Battle or Place of Action: Vicksburg, Mississippi
Date of Action: 22 May 1863
Date of Issue: 9 July 1894
Citation: Gallantry in the charge of the "volunteer storming party."

173 ◆ BUCKLYN, JOHN KNIGHT

Rank: First Lieutenant (highest rank: Brevet Captain)
Service: U.S. Army
Birthday: 15 March 1834
Place of Birth: Foster Creek, Providence County, Rhode Island
Date of Death: 15 May 1906
Cemetery: Lower Mystic Cemetery (MH)—Mystic, Connecticut
Entered Service at: Providence, Providence County, Rhode Island
Unit: Battery E, 1st Rhode Island Light Artillery
Battle or Place of Action: Chancellorsville, Virginia
Date of Action: 3 May 1863
Date of Issue: 13 July 1899
Citation: Though himself wounded, Bucklyn gallantly fought his section of the battery under a fierce fire from the enemy until his ammunition was all expended, many of the cannoneers and most of the horses killed or wounded, and the enemy within 25 yards of the gun, when, disabling one piece, he brought off the other in safety.

174 ◆ BUFFINGTON, JOHN C.

Rank: Sergeant (highest rank: First Lieutenant)
Service: U.S. Army
Birthday: 3 July 1841
Place of Birth: Carroll County, Maryland
Date of Death: 22 November 1924
Place of Death: Washington, D.C.
Cemetery: Trinity Lutheran Cemetery—Tanneytown, Maryland
Entered Service at: Westminster, Carroll County, Maryland
Unit: Company C, 6th Maryland Infantry
Battle or Place of Action: Petersburg, Virginia
Date of Action: 2 April 1865
Date of Issue: 6 March 1908
Citation: Was the first enlisted man of the 3d Division to mount the parapet of the enemy's line.

175 ◆ BUFFUM, ROBERT

Rank: Private (highest rank: Second Lieutenant)
Service: U.S. Army
Birthday: 1828
Place of Birth: Salem, Essex County, Massachusetts
Date of Death: 20 July 1871
Place of Death: Auburn, New York
Cemetery: Auburn Correctional Facility Cemetary ('In Memory' marker only)—Auburn, New York
Entered Service at: Gilead, Wood County, Ohio
Unit: Company H, 21st Ohio Infantry
Battle or Place of Action: Georgia
Date of Action: April 1862
Date of Presentation: 25 March 1863
Place of Presentation: Washington, D.C.; presented by Sec. of War Edward M. Stanton
Citation: One of the 19 of 24 men (including two civilians)

who, by direction of Gen. Mitchell (or Buell), penetrated nearly 200 miles south into enemy territory and captured a railroad train at Big Shanty, Ga., in an attempt to destroy the bridges and track between Chattanooga and Atlanta.

176 ◆ BUHRMAN, HENRY G.

Rank: Private –
Service: U.S. Army
Place of Birth: Cincinnati, Hamilton County, Ohio
Date of Death: 1 June 1906
Place of Death: Soldiers Home, Mountain Home, Tennessee
Entered Service at: Cincinnati, Hamilton County, Ohio
Unit: Company H, 54th Ohio Infantry
Battle or Place of Action: Vicksburg, Mississippi
Date of Action: 22 May 1863
Date of Issue: 12 July 1894
Citation: Gallantry in the charge of the "volunteer storming party."

177 ◆ BUMGARNER, WILLIAM

Rank: Sergeant
Service: U.S. Army
Birthday: 12 July 1837
Place of Birth: Mason County, West Virginia
Date of Death: 24 December 1911
Place of Death: Liberty Center, Indiana
Cemetery: Mossburg Cemetery—Wells County, Indiana
Entered Service at: Mason City, Mason County, West Virginia
Unit: Company A, 4th West Virginia Infantry
Battle or Place of Action: Petersburg, Virginia
Date of Action: 2 April 1862
Date of Issue: 10 July 1894
Citation: Gallantry in the charge of the "volunteer storming party."

178 ◆ BURBANK, JAMES H.

Rank: Sergeant
Service: U.S. Army
Birthday: 5 January 1838
Place of Birth: Stavorey, Holland
Date of Death: 15 February 1911
Cemetery: Miltonvale Cemetery (MH)—Miltonvale, Kansas
Entered Service at: Providence, Providence County, Rhode Island
Unit: Company K, 4th Rhode Island Infantry
Battle or Place of Action: Blackwater River, near Franklin, Virginia
Date of Action: 3 October 1862
Date of Issue: 27 July 1896
Citation: Gallantry in action while on detached service on board the gunboat *Barney*.

179 ◆ BURGER, JOSEPH

Rank: Private (highest rank: Captain)
Service: U.S. Army
Birthday: 16 April 1848
Place of Birth: Austria or Swiss Tyrol
Date of Death: 3 January 1921
Place of Death: St. Paul, Minnesota
Cemetery: Oakland Cemetery—St. Paul, Minnesota
Entered Service at: Crystal Lake, Hennepin County, Minnesota
Unit: Company H, 2d Minnesota Infantry
Battle or Place of Action: Nolensville, Tennessee
Date of Action: 15 February 1863
Date of Issue: 11 September 1897
Citation: Was one of a detachment of 16 men who heroically defended a wagon train against the attack of 125 cavalry, repulsed the attack, and saved the train.

180 ◆ BURK, E. MICHAEL

True Name: Burke, Michael
Rank: Private
Service: U.S. Army
Birthday: 1847
Place of Birth: Ireland
Date of Death: 3 February 1878
Cemetery: St. Mary's Cemetery (MH)—Troy, New York
Entered Service at: Troy, Rensselaer County, New York
Unit: Company D, 125th New York Infantry
Battle or Place of Action: Spotsylvania, Virginia
Date of Action: 12 May 1864
Date of Issue: 1 December 1864
Citation: Capture of flag, seizing it as his regiment advanced over the enemy's works. He received a bullet wound in the chest while capturing the flag.

181 ◆ BURK, THOMAS

Rank: Sergeant (highest rank: First Lieutenant)
Service: U.S. Army
Birthday: 7 August 1840
Place of Birth: Lewis County, New York
Date of Death: 15 February 1926
Place of Death: Lowville, New York
Cemetery: Lowville Rural Cemetery—Lowville, New York
Entered Service at: Harrisburgh, Lewis County, New York
Unit: Company H, 97th New York Infantry
Battle or Place of Action: Wilderness Campaign, Virginia
Date of Action: 6 May 1864
Date of Issue: 24 August 1896
Citation: At the risk of his own life, Burk went back while the rebels were still firing and, finding Col. Wheelock unable to move, alone and unaided, carried him off the field of battle.

182 ◆ BURKE, DANIEL WEBSTER

Rank: First Sergeant (highest rank: Brigadier General)
Service: U.S. Army
Birthday: 22 April 1841

Place of Birth: New Haven, New Haven County, Connecticut
Date of Death: 29 May 1911
Cemetery: Arlington National Cemetery (2-3739)—Arlington, Virginia
Entered Service at: New Haven, New Haven County, Connecticut
Unit: Company B, 2d U.S. Infantry
Battle or Place of Action: Shepherdstown Ford, West Virginia
Date of Action: 20 September 1862
Date of Issue: 21 April 1892
Citation: Voluntarily attempted to spike a gun in the face of the enemy.

183 ◆ BURKE, THOMAS

Rank: Private
Service: U.S. Army
Birthday: 1842
Place of Birth: Ireland
Date of Death: 15 March 1902
Cemetery: Calvary Cemetery—Woodside, New York
Entered Service at: New York, New York
Unit: Company A, 5th New York Cavalry
Battle or Place of Action: Hanover Courthouse, Virginia
Date of Action: 30 June 1863
Date of Issue: 11 February 1878
Citation: Capture of battle flag.

184 ◆ BURNS, JAMES MADISON

Rank: Sergeant (highest rank: Lieutenant Colonel)
Service: U.S. Army
Birthday: 9 August 1845
Place of Birth: Wells Township, Jefferson County, Ohio
Date of Death: 30 October 1910
Place of Death: Lebanon, Ohio
Cemetery: Lebanon Cemetery (MH)—Lebanon, Ohio
Entered Service at: Wellsburg, Brooke County, West Virginia
Unit: Company B, 1st West Virginia Infantry
Battle or Place of Action: New Market, Virginia
Date of Action: 15 May 1864
Date of Issue: 20 November 1896
Citation: Under a heavy fire of musketry, rallied a few men to the support of the colors, in danger of capture, and bore them to a place of safety. One of his comrades having been severely wounded in the effort, Sgt. Burns went back a hundred yards in the face of the enemy's fire and carried the wounded man from the field.

185 ◆ BURNS, JOHN M.

Rank: Seaman
Service: U.S. Navy
Birthday: 1835
Place of Birth: Hudson, Columbia County, New York
Entered Service at: New York

Unit: U.S.S. *Lackawanna*
Battle or Place of Action: Fort Morgan, Mobile Bay, Alabama
Date of Action: 5 August 1864
G.O. Number, Date: 45, 31 December 1864
Citation: On board the U.S.S. *Lackawanna* during the successful attacks against Fort Morgan, rebel gunboats and the ram *Tennessee* in Mobile Bay, on 5 August 1864. Although severely wounded and sent below under the surgeon's charge, Burns promptly returned to his station and assisted the powder division throughout the prolonged action which resulted in the capture of the rebel ram *Tennessee* and in the damaging and destruction of Fort Morgan.

186 ◆ BURRITT, WILLIAM WALLACE

Rank: Private
Service: U.S. Army
Birthday: 1831
Place of Birth: Campbell, Steuben County, New York
Date of Death: 18 October 1901
Place of Death: Wadsworth, Kansas
Cemetery: Leavenworth National Cemetery (16-5-7) (MH)—Leavenworth, Kansas
Entered Service at: Chicago, Cook County, Illinois
Unit: Company G, 113th Illinois Infantry
Battle or Place of Action: Vicksburg, Mississippi
Date of Action: 27 April 1863
Date of Issue: 8 July 1896
Citation: Voluntarily acted as a fireman on a steam tug which ran the blockade and passed the batteries under a heavy fire.

187 ◆ BURTON, ALBERT

Rank: Seaman
Service: U.S. Navy
Birthday: 1838
Place of Birth: England
Entered Service at: New York
Unit: U.S.S. *Wabash*
Battle or Place of Action: Fort Fisher, North Carolina
Date of Action: 15 January 1865
G.O. Number, Date: 59, 22 June 1865
Citation: Served on board the U.S.S. *Wabash* in the assault on Fort Fisher, 15 January 1865. Advancing gallantly through the severe enemy fire while armed only with a revolver and cutlass which made it impossible to return the fire at that range, Burton succeeded in reaching the angle of the fort and going on, to be one of the few who entered the fort. When the rest of the body of men to his rear were forced to retreat under a devastating fire, he was forced to withdraw through the lack of support, and to seek the shelter of one of the mounds near the stockade from which point he succeeded in regaining the safety of the ship.

188 ◆ BUTTERFIELD, DANIEL ADAMS

Rank: Brigadier General (highest rank: Major General)
Service: U.S. Army

Birthday: 31 October 1831
Place of Birth: Utica, Oneida County, New York
Date of Death: 17 July 1901
Place of Death: Cold Spring, New York
Cemetery: U.S. Military Academy Cemetery (R-15)—West Point, New York
Entered Service at: Washington, D.C.
Unit: U.S. Volunteers
Battle or Place of Action: Gaines' Mill, Virginia
Date of Action: 27 June 1862
Date of Issue: 26 September 1892
Citation: Seized the colors of the 83d Pennsylvania Volunteers at a critical moment and, under a galling fire of the enemy, encouraged the depleted ranks to renewed exertion.

189 ◆ BUTTERFIELD, FRANKLIN GEORGE

Rank: First Lieutenant (highest rank: Lieutenant Colonel)
Service: U.S. Army
Birthday: 11 March 1842
Place of Birth: Rockingham, Windham County, Vermont
Date of Death: 6 January 1916
Cemetery: Saxtons River Cemetery—Saxtons River, Vermont
Entered Service at: Rockingham, Windham County, Vermont
Unit: Company C, 6th Vermont Infantry
Battle or Place of Action: Salem Heights, Virginia
Date of Action: 4 May 1863
Date of Issue: 4 May 1891
Citation: Took command of the skirmish line and covered the movement of his regiment out of a precarious position.

190 ◆ BUTTS, GEORGE

Rank: Gunner's Mate
Service: U.S. Navy
Birthday: 1838
Place of Birth: Rome, Oneida County, New York
Date of Death: 17 February 1902
Cemetery: Ridgelawn Cemetery—Elyria, Ohio
Entered Service at: Cleveland, Cuyahoga County, Ohio
Unit: U.S.S. Signal
Battle or Place of Action: Red River, Louisiana
Date of Action: 5 May 1864
G.O. Number, Date: 45, 31 December 1864
Citation: Served on board the U.S.S. Signal, Red River, 5 May 1864. Proceeding up the Red River, the U.S.S. Signal engaged a large force of enemy field batteries and sharpshooters, returning their fire until the ship was totally disabled, at which time the white flag was raised. Although entered on the sick list, Butts courageously carried out his duties during the entire engagement.
Notes: POW

191 ◆ BYRNES, JAMES

Rank: Boatswain's Mate (highest rank: Master's Mate)
Service: U.S. Navy
Birthday: 1838

Place of Birth: Ireland
Entered Service at: New York
Unit: U.S.S. Louisville
Battle or Place of Action: Fort Hindman, Arkansas
Date of Action: 10-11 January 1863
G.O. Number, Date: 11, 3 April 1863
Citation: Served on board the U.S.S. Louisville. Carrying out his duties through the thick of battle and acting as captain of a 9-inch gun, Byrnes consistently showed "Attention to duty, bravery, and coolness in action against the enemy."

192 ◆ CADWALLADER, ABEL G.

Rank: Corporal (highest rank: Sergeant)
Service: U.S. Army
Birthday: 1841
Place of Birth: Baltimore, Baltimore County, Maryland
Date of Death: 6 July 1907
Place of Death: Baltimore, Maryland
Cemetery: Loudon Park Cemetery—Baltimore, Maryland
Entered Service at: Frederick, Frederick County, Maryland
Unit: Company H, 1st Maryland Infantry
Battle or Place of Action: Hatcher's Run & Dabney's Mills, Virginia
Date of Action: 6 February 1865
Date of Issue: 5 January 1897
Citation: Gallantly planted the colors on the enemy's works in advance of the arrival of his regiment.

193 ◆ CADWELL, LUMAN LEWIS

Rank: Sergeant (highest rank: First Lieutenant)
Service: U.S. Army
Birthday: 22 May 1836
Place of Birth: Nanticoke Springs, Broome County, New York
Date of Death: 9 July 1925
Place of Death: Decorah, Iowa
Cemetery: Phelps Cemetery—Decorah, Iowa
Entered Service at: Troy, Rensselaer County, New York
Unit: Company B, 2d New York Veteran Cavalry
Battle or Place of Action: Alabama Bayou, Louisiana
Date of Action: 20 September 1864
Date of Issue: 17 August 1894
Citation: Swam the bayou under fire of the enemy and captured and brought off a boat by means of which the command crossed and routed the enemy.

194 ◆ CALDWELL, DANIEL G.

Rank: Sergeant (highest rank: Captain)
Service: U.S. Army
Birthday: 1 June 1842
Place of Birth: Marble Hill, Montgomery County, Pennsylvania
Date of Death: 15 April 1917
Place of Death: Philadelphia, Pennsylvania
Cemetery: Mount Peace Cemetery—Rockledge, Pennsylvania

Entered Service at: Philadelphia, Philadelphia County, Pennsylvania
Unit: Company H, 13th Pennsylvania Cavalry (Volunteers 117th Regiment)
Battle or Place of Action: Hatcher's Run, Virginia
Date of Action: 6 February 1865
Date of Issue: 25 February 1865
Citation: In a mounted charge, Caldwell dashed into the center of the enemy's line and captured the colors of the 33d North Carolina Infantry.
Notes: POW

195 ◆ CALKIN, IVERS S.

Rank: First Sergeant
Service: U.S. Army
Birthday: 29 May 1836
Place of Birth: Elizabethtown, Essex County, New York
Date of Death: 16 February 1902
Place of Death: Montague, Michigan
Cemetery: Oak Grove Cemetery—Montague, Michigan
Entered Service at: Willsboro, Essex County, New York
Unit: Company M, 2d New York Cavalry
Battle or Place of Action: Deatonsville (Sailor's Creek), Virginia
Date of Action: 6 April 1865
Date of Issue: 3 May 1865
Citation: Capture of flag of 18th Virginia Infantry (C.S.A.).

196 ◆ CALLAHAN, JOHN H.

Rank: Private
Service: U.S. Army
Birthday: 25 January 1845
Place of Birth: Shelby County, Kentucky
Date of Death: 13 March 1914
Cemetery: Sunset Cemetery—Manhattan, Kansas
Entered Service at: Scottville, Macoupin County, Illinois
Unit: Company B, 122d Illinois Infantry
Battle or Place of Action: Fort Blakely, Alabama
Date of Action: 9 April 1865
Date of Issue: 8 June 1865
Citation: Capture of flag.

197 ◆ CAMP, CARLTON N.

Rank: Private
Service: U.S. Army
Birthday: 5 January 1845
Place of Birth: Hanover, Grafton County, New Hampshire
Date of Death: 1 September 1926
Cemetery: Etna Cemetery—Hanover, New Hampshire
Entered Service at: Hanover, Grafton County, New Hampshire
Unit: Company B, 18th New Hampshire Infantry
Battle or Place of Action: Petersburg, Virginia
Date of Action: 2 April 1865
Date of Issue: 21 December 1909

Citation: Brought off from the picket line, under heavy fire, a comrade who had been shot through both legs.

198 ◆ CAMPBELL, JAMES A.

Rank: Private
Service: U.S. Army
Birthday: 20 December 1844
Place of Birth: Brooklyn, Kings County, New York
Date of Death: 6 May 1904
Place of Death: Fort Snelling, Minnesota
Cemetery: Arlington National Cemetery (3-1468-55) (MH)—Arlington, Virginia
Entered Service at: New York, New York
Unit: Company A, 2d New York Cavalry
Battle or Place of Action: Woodstock & Amelia Courthouse, Virginia
Date of Action: 22 January & 5 April 1865
Date of Issue: 30 October 1897
Citation: While his command was retreating before superior numbers at Woodstock, Va., he voluntarily rushed back with one companion and rescued his commanding officer, who had been unhorsed and left behind. At Amelia Courthouse captured two battle flags.

199 ◆ CAMPBELL, WILLIAM

Rank: Private (highest rank: Corporal)
Service: U.S. Army
Birthday: 28 April 1840
Place of Birth: County Down, Ireland
Date of Death: 19 April 1919
Cemetery: Glendale Cemetery—Des Moines, Iowa
Entered Service at: New Philadelphia, Tuscarawas County, Ohio
Unit: Company I, 30th Ohio Infantry
Battle or Place of Action: Vicksburg, Mississippi
Date of Action: 22 May 1863
Date of Issue: 14 August 1894
Citation: Gallantry in the charge of the "volunteer storming party."

200 ◆ CAMPBELL, WILLIAM

Rank: Boatswain's Mate
Service: U.S. Navy
Birthday: 1838
Place of Birth: Indiana
Entered Service at: Indiana
Unit: U.S.S. *Ticonderoga*
Battle or Place of Action: Fort Fisher, North Carolina
Date of Action: 24-25 December 1864 & 13-15 January 1865
G.O. Number, Date: 59, 22 June 1865
Citation: On board the U.S.S. *Ticonderoga* during the attacks on Fort Fisher, 24 and 25 December 1864; and 13 to 15 January 1865. Despite heavy return fire by the enemy and the explosion of the 100-pounder Parrott rifle which killed eight men and wounded 12 more, Campbell, as captain of a

gun, performed his duties with skill and courage during the first two days of battle. As the ship again took position on the line of the 13th, he remained steadfast as the *Ticonderoga* maintained a well-placed fire upon the batteries onshore, and thereafter, as she materially lessened the power of guns on the mound which had been turned upon our assaulting columns. During this action the flag was planted on one of the strongest fortifications possessed by the rebels.

201 ◆ CAPEHART, CHARLES E.

Rank: Major (highest rank: Lieutenant Colonel)
Service: U.S. Army
Birthday: 1833
Place of Birth: Conemaugh Township, Pennsylvania
Date of Death: 11 July 1911
Place of Death: Washington, D.C.
Cemetery: Arlington National Cemetery (3-2033) (MH)—Arlington, Virginia
Entered Service at: Washington, D.C.
Unit: 1st West Virginia Cavalry
Battle or Place of Action: Monterey Mountain, Pennsylvania
Date of Action: 4 July 1863
Date of Issue: 7 April 1898
Citation: While commanding the regiment, Capehart charged down the mountain side at midnight, in a heavy rain, upon the enemy's fleeing wagon train. Many wagons were captured and destroyed and many prisoners taken.

202 ◆ CAPEHART, HENRY

Rank: Colonel (highest rank: Major General)
Service: U.S. Army
Birthday: 18 March 1825
Place of Birth: Johnstown, Cambria County, Pennsylvania
Date of Death: 15 April 1895
Place of Death: Fargo, North Dakota
Cemetery: Arlington National Cemetery (1-140-A&B) (MH)—Arlington, Virginia
Entered Service at: Bridgeport, Belmont County, Ohio
Unit: 1st West Virginia Cavalry
Battle or Place of Action: Greenbrier River, West Virginia
Date of Action: 22 May 1864
Date of Issue: 12 February 1895
Citation: Saved, under fire, the life of a drowning soldier.

203 ◆ *CAPRON JR., HORACE

Rank: Sergeant (highest rank: First Lieutenant)
Service: U.S. Army
Birthday: 1840
Place of Birth: Laurel, Prince George's County, Maryland
Date of Death: 6 February 1864
Place of Death: Blunt County, Tennessee
Cemetery: Springdale Cemetery—Peoria, Illinois
Entered Service at: Peoria, Peoria County, Illinois
Unit: Company G, 8th Illinois Cavalry
Battle or Place of Action: Chickahominy & Ashland, Virginia
Date of Action: June 1862

Date of Issue: 27 September 1865
Citation: Gallantry in action.

204 ◆ *CAREY, HUGH

Rank: Sergeant
Service: U.S. Army
Birthday: 1840
Place of Birth: Ireland
Date of Death: 26 March 1886
Place of Death: Brooklyn, New York
Cemetery: Holy Cross Cemetery—Brooklyn, New York
Entered Service at: New York, New York
Unit: Company E, 82d New York Infantry
Battle or Place of Action: Gettysburg, Pennsylvania
Date of Action: 2 July 1863
Date of Issue: 6 February 1888
Citation: Captured the flag of the 7th Virginia Infantry (C.S.A.), being twice wounded in the effort.

205 ◆ CAREY, JAMES LEMUEL

Rank: Sergeant
Service: U.S. Army
Birthday: 24 December 1839
Place of Birth: Jamesville, Onondaga County, New York
Date of Death: 15 May 1919
Place of Death: Grafton, Pennsylvania
Cemetery: Chartiers Cemetery, Soldier's Plot—Carnegie, Pennsylvania
Entered Service at: Syracuse, Onondaga County, New York
Unit: Company G, 10th New York Cavalry (Porter Guard)
Battle or Place of Action: Appomattox Courthouse, Virginia
Date of Action: 9 April 1865
Citation: Daring bravery and urging the men forward in a charge.

206 ◆ CARLISLE, CASPER R.

Rank: Private
Service: U.S. Army
Birthday: 1841
Place of Birth: Allegheny County, Pennsylvania
Date of Death: 29 April 1908
Cemetery: Mount Lebanon Cemetery (MH)—Pittsburgh, Pennsylvania
Entered Service at: Pittsburgh, Allegheny County, Pennsylvania
Unit: Company F, Independent Pennsylvania Light Artillery
Battle or Place of Action: Gettysburg, Pennsylvania
Date of Action: 2 July 1863
Date of Issue: 21 December 1892
Citation: Saved a gun of his battery under heavy musketry fire, most of the horses being killed and the drivers wounded.

207 ◆ CARMAN, WARREN

Rank: Private (highest rank: Corporal)
Service: U.S. Army

Birthday: 16 March 1845
Place of Birth: England
Date of Death: 17 October 1894
Place of Death: Rochester, New York
Cemetery: Mount Hope Cemetery (MH)—Rochester, New York
Entered Service at: Victor, Ontario County, New York
Unit: Company H, 1st New York (Lincoln) Cavalry
Battle or Place of Action: Waynesboro, Virginia
Date of Action: 2 March 1865
Date of Issue: 26 March 1865
Citation: Capture of flag and several prisoners.

208 ◆ CARMIN, ISAAC HARRISON

True Name: Carman, Isaac Harrison
Rank: Corporal
Service: U.S. Army
Birthday: 17 November 1841
Place of Birth: Monmouth County, New Jersey
Date of Death: 3 June 1919
Place of Death: Fayette County, Ohio
Cemetery: Washington Cemetery (MH)—Washington Courthouse, Ohio
Entered Service at: New Lexington, Perry County, Ohio
Unit: Company A, 48th Ohio Infantry
Battle or Place of Action: Vicksburg, Mississippi
Date of Action: 22 May 1863
Date of Issue: 25 February 1895
Citation: Saved his regimental flag; also seized and threw a shell, with burning fuse, from among his comrades.
Notes: POW

209 ◆ CARNEY, WILLIAM HARVEY

Rank: Sergeant
Service: U.S. Army
Birthday: 29 February 1840
Place of Birth: Norfolk, Norfolk County, Virginia
Date of Death: 9 December 1908
Place of Death: New Bedford, Massachusetts
Cemetery: Oak Grove Cemetery (MH)—New Bedford, Massachusetts
Entered Service at: New Bedford, Bristol County, Massachusetts
Unit: Company C, 54th Massachusetts Colored Infantry
Battle or Place of Action: Fort Wagner, South Carolina
Date of Action: 18 July 1863
Date of Issue: 23 May 1900
Citation: When the color sergeant was shot down, this soldier grasped the flag, led the way to the parapet, and planted the colors thereon. When the troops fell back he brought off the flag, under a fierce fire in which he was twice severely wounded.

210 ◆ CARR, EUGENE ASA

Rank: Colonel (highest rank: Brevet Major General)
Service: U.S. Army
Birthday: 20 March 1830

Place of Birth: Boston Corner, Erie County, New York
Date of Death: 2 December 1910
Cemetery: U.S. Military Academy Cemetery (K-14)—West Point, New York
Entered Service at: Hamburg, Erie County, New York
Unit: 3d Illinois Cavalry
Battle or Place of Action: Pea Ridge, Arkansas
Date of Action: 7 March 1862
Date of Issue: 16 January 1894
Citation: Directed the deployment of his command and held his ground, under a brisk fire of shot and shell in which he was several times wounded.

211 ◆ CARR, FRANKLIN

Rank: Corporal (highest rank: Sergeant)
Service: U.S. Army
Birthday: 1844
Place of Birth: Stark County, Ohio
Date of Death: 16 October 1904
Place of Death: McAlester, Oklahoma
Entered Service at: Toledo, Lucas County, Ohio
Unit: Company D, 124th Ohio Infantry
Battle or Place of Action: Nashville, Tennessee
Date of Action: 16 December 1864
Date of Issue: 24 February 1865
Citation: Recapture of U.S. guidon from a rebel battery.

212 ◆ CARR, WILLIAM M.

Rank: Master-at-Arms
Service: U.S. Navy
Birthday: 25 November 1829
Place of Birth: Baltimore, Baltimore County, Maryland
Date of Death: 2 May 1884
Place of Death: Newtown, Virginia
Cemetery: Norfolk City Cemetery (MH)—Norfolk, Virginia
Entered Service at: Baltimore, Baltimore County, Maryland
Unit: U.S.S. *Richmond*
Battle or Place of Action: Mobile Bay, Alabama
Date of Action: 5 August 1864
G.O. Number, Date: 45, 31 December 1864
Citation: On board the U.S.S. *Richmond* during action against rebel forts and gunboats and against the ram *Tennessee* in Mobile Bay, 5 August 1864. Despite damage to his ship and the loss of several men on board as enemy fire raked her decks, Carr performed his duties with skill and courage throughout the prolonged battle which resulted in the surrender of the rebel ram *Tennessee* and in the successful attacks carried out on Fort Morgan.

213 ◆ CARSON, WILLIAM J.

Rank: Musician
Service: U.S. Army
Birthday: 30 August 1840
Place of Birth: Washington County, Pennsylvania
Date of Death: 13 December 1913
Place of Death: Indianapolis, Indiana
Cemetery: Beech Grove Cemetery (MH)—Muncie, Indiana

Entered Service at: North Greenfield, Highland County, Ohio
Unit: Company E, 1st Battalion, 15th U.S. Infantry
Battle or Place of Action: Chickamauga, Georgia
Date of Action: 19 September 1863
Date of Issue: 27 January 1894
Citation: At a critical stage in the battle when the 14th Corps lines were wavering and in disorder, he on his own initiative bugled "to the colors" amid the 18th U.S. Infantry who formed by him, and held the enemy. Within a few minutes he repeated his action amid the wavering 2d Ohio Infantry. This bugling deceived the enemy who believed reinforcements had arrived. Thus, they delayed their attack.

214 ◆ CART, JACOB

Rank: Private (highest rank: Sergeant)
Service: U.S. Army
Birthday: 1843
Place of Birth: Carlisle, Cumberland County, Pennsylvania
Date of Death: 24 April 1882
Place of Death: Carlisle, Pennsylvania
Cemetery: Ashland Cemetery—Carlisle, Pennsylvania
Entered Service at: Carlisle, Cumberland County, Pennsylvania
Unit: Company A, 7th Pennsylvania Reserve Corps
Battle or Place of Action: Fredericksburg, Virginia
Date of Action: 13 December 1862
Date of Issue: 25 November 1864
Citation: Capture of flag of 19th Georgia Infantry (C.S.A.), wresting it from the hands of the color bearer.

215 ◆ CARTER, JOHN JOICE

Rank: Second Lieutenant (highest rank: Colonel)
Service: U.S. Army
Birthday: 16 June 1842
Place of Birth: Troy, Rensselaer County, New York
Date of Death: 3 January 1917
Cemetery: Woodlawn Cemetery (MH)—Titusville, Pennsylvania
Entered Service at: Nunda, Livingston County, New York
Unit: Company B, 33d New York Infantry
Served as: Commanding Officer
Battle or Place of Action: Antietam, Maryland
Date of Action: 17 September 1862
Date of Issue: 10 September 1897
Citation: While in command of a detached company, seeing his regiment thrown into confusion by a charge of the enemy, without orders made a countercharge upon the attacking column and checked the assault. Penetrated within the enemy's lines at night and obtained valuable information.

216 ◆ CARTER, JOSEPH FRANKLIN

Rank: Captain (highest rank: Major)
Service: U.S. Army
Birthday: 11 September 1842
Place of Birth: Baltimore, Baltimore County, Maryland
Date of Death: 10 April 1922

Cemetery: Arlington National Cemetery (3-1550)—Arlington, Virginia
Entered Service at: Baltimore, Baltimore County, Maryland
Unit: Company D, 3d Maryland Infantry
Battle or Place of Action: Fort Stedman, Virginia
Date of Action: 25 March 1865
Date of Issue: 9 July 1891
Citation: Captured the colors of the 51st Virginia Infantry (C.S.A.). During the battle he was captured and escaped, bringing a number of prisoners with him.

217 ◆ CARUANA, ORLANDO EMANUEL

Rank: Private (Highest rank Sergeant)
Service: U.S. Army
Birthday: 23 June 1844
Place of Birth: Ca Valletta, Malta
Date of Death: 14 September 1917
Cemetery: Mount Olivet Cemetery—Washington, D.C.
Entered Service at: New York, New York
Unit: Company K, 51st New York Infantry
Battle or Place of Action: New Bern, North Carolina & South Mountain, Maryland
Date of Action: 14 March & 14 September 1862
Date of Issue: 14 November 1890
Citation: At New Bern, N.C., brought off the wounded color sergeant and the colors under a heavy fire of the enemy. Was one of four soldiers who volunteered to determine the position of the enemy at South Mountain, Md. While so engaged was fired upon and his three companions killed, but he escaped and rejoined his command in safety.

218 ◆ CASEY, DAVID P.

Rank: Private (highest rank: Corporal)
Service: U.S. Army
Birthday: 1842
Place of Birth: Ireland
Date of Death: 4 January 1893
Cemetery: St. Patrick's Cemetery (MH)—Northbridge, Massachusetts
Entered Service at: Northbridge, Worcester County, Massachusetts
Unit: Company C, 25th Massachusetts Infantry
Battle or Place of Action: Cold Harbor, Virginia
Date of Action: 3 June 1864
Date of Issue: 14 September 1888
Citation: Two color bearers having been shot dead one after the other, the last one far in advance of his regiment and close to the enemy's lines, this soldier rushed forward, and, under a galling fire, after removing the dead body of the bearer therefrom, secured the flag and returned with it to the Union lines.
Notes: POW

219 ◆ CASEY, HENRY

Rank: Private (highest rank: Corporal)
Service: U.S. Army

Birthday: 28 October 1837
Place of Birth: New Geneva, Fayette County, Pennsylvania
Date of Death: 9 May 1919
Place of Death: Bloomingburg, Ohio
Cemetery: Bloomingburg Cemetery (MH)—Bloomingburg, Ohio
Entered Service at: Bloomingburg, Fayette County, Ohio
Unit: Company C, 20th Ohio Infantry
Battle or Place of Action: Vicksburg, Mississippi
Date of Action: 22 April 1863
Date of Issue: 17 September 1897
Citation: Voluntarily served as one of the crew of a transport that passed the forts under a heavy fire.

220 ◆ CASSIDY, MICHAEL

Rank: Landsman (highest rank: Ordinary Seaman)
Service: U.S. Navy
Birthday: 1837
Place of Birth: Ireland
Date of Death: 18 March 1908
Place of Death: Soldier's Home, Hampton, Virginia
Cemetery: Hampton National Cemetery (B-9503) (MH)—Hampton, Virginia
Entered Service at: New York, New York
Unit: U.S.S. *Lackawanna*
Battle or Place of Action: Mobile Bay, Alabama
Date of Action: 5 August 1864
G.O. Number, Date: 45, 31 December 1864
Citation: Served on board the U.S.S. *Lackawanna* during the successful attacks against Fort Morgan, rebel gunboats and the ram *Tennessee* in Mobile Bay, on 5 August 1864. Displaying great coolness and exemplary behavior as first sponger of a gun, Cassidy, by his coolness under fire, received the applause of his officers and the gun crew throughout the action which resulted in the capture of the prize ram *Tennessee* and in the destruction of batteries at Fort Morgan.

221 ◆ CATLIN, ISAAC SWARTWOOD

Rank: Colonel (highest rank: Brevet Major General)
Service: U.S. Army
Birthday: 8 July 1835
Place of Birth: Near Owego, Tioga County, New York
Date of Death: 19 January 1916
Place of Death: Brooklyn, New York
Cemetery: Arlington National Cemetery (2-3397) (MH)—Arlington, Virginia
Entered Service at: Owego, Tioga County, New York
Unit: 109th New York Infantry (Railway Brigade)
Battle or Place of Action: Petersburg, Virginia
Date of Action: 30 July 1864
Date of Issue: 13 January 1899
Citation: In a heroic effort to rally the disorganized troops was disabled by a severe wound. While being carried from the field he recovered somewhat and bravely started to return to his command, when he received a second wound, which necessitated amputation of his right leg.

222 ◆ CAYER, OVILA

Rank: Sergeant
Service: U.S. Army
Birthday: 9 February 1844
Place of Birth: St. Remi, Canada
Date of Death: 7 February 1909
Place of Death: Salinas, California
Cemetery: Garden of Memory Park Cemetery—Salinas, California
Entered Service at: Malone, Franklin County, New York
Unit: Company A, 14th U.S. Volunteer Infantry
Battle or Place of Action: Weldon Railroad, Virginia
Date of Action: 19 August 1864
Date of Issue: 15 February 1867
Citation: Commanded the regiment, all the officers being disabled.

223 ◆ CHAMBERLAIN, JOSHUA LAWRENCE

Rank: Colonel (highest rank: Brevet Major General)
Service: U.S. Army
Birthday: 8 September 1828
Place of Birth: Brewer, Penobscot County, Maine
Date of Death: 24 February 1914
Place of Death: Portland, Maine
Cemetery: Pine Grove Cemetery (MH)—Brunswick, Maine
Entered Service at: Brunswick, Cumberland County, Maine
Unit: 20th Maine Infantry
Battle or Place of Action: Gettysburg, Pennsylvania
Date of Action: 2 July 1863
Date of Issue: 11 August 1893
Citation: Daring heroism and great tenacity in holding his position on the Little Round Top against repeated assaults, and carrying the advance position on the Great Round Top.

224 ◆ CHAMBERLAIN, ORVILLE TYRON

Rank: Second Lieutenant (highest rank: Captain)
Service: U.S. Army
Birthday: 1 September 1841
Place of Birth: Leesburgh, Kosciusko County, Indiana
Date of Death: 27 May 1929
Place of Death: Prescott, Arizona
Cemetery: Gracelawn Cemetery—Elkhart, Indiana
Entered Service at: Elkhart, Elkhart County, Indiana
Unit: Company G, 74th Indiana Infantry
Battle or Place of Action: Chickamauga, Georgia
Date of Action: 20 September 1863
Date of Issue: 11 March 1896
Citation: While exposed to a galling fire, Chamberlain went in search of another regiment, found its location, procured ammunition from the men thereof, and returned with the ammunition to his own company.

225 ◆ CHAMBERS, JOSEPH B.

Rank: Private
Service: U.S. Army

Birthday: 4 May 1833
Place of Birth: Beaver County, Pennsylvania
Date of Death: 8 October 1909
Place of Death: East Brook, Pennsylvania
Cemetery: Oak Park Cemetery—New Castle, Pennsylvania
Entered Service at: East Brook, Pennsylvania
Unit: Company F, 100th Pennsylvania Infantry (Roundheads)
Battle or Place of Action: Petersburg, Virginia
Date of Action: 25 March 1865
Date of Issue: 27 July 1871
Citation: Capture of colors of 1st Virginia Infantry (C.S.A.).

226 ◆ CHANDLER, HENRY FLINT

Rank: Sergeant
Service: U.S. Army
Birthday: 26 September 1835
Place of Birth: Andover, Essex County, Massachusetts
Date of Death: 16 November 1906
Place of Death: Haver Hill, Massachusetts
Cemetery: West Parrish Cemetery (MH)—Andover, Massachusetts
Entered Service at: Andover, Essex County, Massachusetts
Unit: Company E, 59th Massachusetts Infantry
Battle or Place of Action: Petersburg, Virginia
Date of Action: 17 June 1864
Date of Issue: 30 March 1898
Citation: Though seriously wounded in a bayonet charge and directed to go to the rear, he declined to do so, but remained with his regiment and helped to carry the breastworks.

227 ◆ CHANDLER, JAMES B.

True Name: Chandler, John B.
Rank: Coxswain
Service: U.S. Navy
Birthday: 6 October 1837
Place of Birth: Plymouth, Plymouth County, Massachusetts
Date of Death: 12 July 1899
Place of Death: Taunton, Massachusetts
Cemetery: Vine Hill Cemetery (MH)—Plymouth, Massachusetts
Entered Service at: Boston, Suffolk County, Massachusetts
Unit: U.S.S. *Richmond*
Battle or Place of Action: Mobile Bay, Alabama
Date of Action: 5 August 1864
G.O. Number, Date: 45, 31 December 1864
Citation: On board the U.S.S. *Richmond* during action against rebel forts and gunboats and against the ram *Tennessee* in Mobile Bay, 5 August 1864. Cool and courageous although he had just come off the sick list, Chandler rendered gallant service throughout the prolonged action as his ship maintained accurate fire against Fort Morgan and ships of the Confederacy despite extremely heavy return fire. He participated in the actions at Forts Jackson and St. Philip, with the Chalmette batteries, at the surrender of New Orleans and in the attacks on batteries below Vicksburg.

228 ◆ CHANDLER, STEPHEN EDWIN

Rank: Quartermaster Sergeant
Service: U.S. Army
Birthday: 20 November 1841
Place of Birth: Convis, Michigan
Date of Death: 1 February 1919
Place of Death: Minneapolis, Minnesota
Cemetery: Lakewood Cemetery—Minneapolis, Minnesota
Entered Service at: Grandby, Oswego County, New York
Unit: Company A, 24th New York Cavalry
Battle or Place of Action: Amelia Springs, Virginia
Date of Action: 5 April 1865
Date of Issue: 4 April 1898
Citation: Under severe fire of the enemy and of the troops in retreat, Chandler went between the lines to the assistance of a wounded and helpless comrade, and rescued him from death or capture.

229 ◆ CHAPIN, ALARIC B.

Rank: Private
Service: U.S. Army
Birthday: 1847
Place of Birth: Ogdensburg, St. Lawrence County, New York
Date of Death: 27 November 1924
Place of Death: Portland, Oregon
Cemetery: Roselawn Cemetery—Portland, Oregon
Entered Service at: Pamelia, Jefferson County, New York
Unit: Company G, 142d New York Infantry
Battle or Place of Action: Fort Fisher, North Carolina
Date of Action: 15 January 1865
Date of Issue: 28 December 1914
Citation: Voluntarily advanced with the head of the column and cut down the palisading.

230 ◆ CHAPMAN, JOHN

True Name: Kaufman, Charles F.
Rank: Private
Service: U.S. Army
Birthday: 10 February 1844
Place of Birth: Strasburg, France
Date of Death: 30 September 1905
Place of Death: San Francisco, California
Cemetery: Holy Cross Cemetery—Colma, California
Entered Service at: Limerick, York County, Maine
Unit: Company B, 1st Maine Heavy Artillery
Battle or Place of Action: Deatonsville (Sailor's Creek), Virginia
Date of Action: 6 April 1865
Date of Issue: 10 May 1865
Citation: Capture of flag.

231 ◆ CHAPUT, LOUIS G.

Rank: Landsman
Service: U.S. Navy

Birthday: 1845
Place of Birth: Canada
Date of Death: 17 April 1916
Place of Death: Montreal, Canada
Entered Service at: New York, New York
Unit: U.S.S. *Lackawanna*
Battle or Place of Action: Mobile Bay, Alabama
Date of Action: 5 August 1864
G.O. Number, Date: 45, 31 December 1864
Citation: On board the U.S.S. *Lackawanna* during the successful attacks against Fort Morgan, rebel gunboats, and the ram *Tennessee* in Mobile Bay, on 5 August 1864. Severely wounded, Chaput remained at his gun until relieved, reported to the surgeon, and returned to his gun until the action was over. He was then carried below following the action, which resulted in the capture of the prize ram *Tennessee* and in the destruction of batteries at Fort Morgan.

232 ◆ CHASE, JOHN F.

Rank: Private (highest rank: Captain)
Service: U.S. Army
Birthday: 23 April 1843
Place of Birth: Chelsea, Maine
Date of Death: 28 November 1914
Place of Death: St. Petersburg, Florida
Cemetery: St. Bartholomew Cemetery (MH)—St. Petersburg, Florida
Entered Service at: Augusta, Kennebec County, Maine
Unit: 5th Battery, Maine Light Artillery
Battle or Place of Action: Chancellorsville, Virginia
Date of Action: 3 May 1863
Date of Issue: 7 February 1888
Citation: Nearly all the officers and men of the battery having been killed or wounded, this soldier with a comrade continued to fire his gun after the guns had ceased. The piece was then dragged off by the two, the horses having been shot, and its capture by the enemy was prevented.

233 ◆ CHILD, BENJAMIN HAM

Rank: Corporal (highest rank: Second Lieutenant)
Service: U.S. Army
Birthday: 8 May 1843
Place of Birth: Providence, Providence County, Rhode Island
Date of Death: 16 May 1902
Cemetery: Swan Point Cemetery (MH)—Providence, Rhode Island
Entered Service at: Providence, Providence County, Rhode Island
Unit: Battery A, 1st Rhode Island Light Artillery
Battle or Place of Action: Antietam, Maryland
Date of Action: 17 September 1862
Date of Issue: 20 July 1897
Citation: Was wounded and taken to the rear, insensible, but when partialy recovered, Child insisted on returning to the battery and resumed command of his piece, so remaining until the close of the battle.

234 ◆ CHISMAN, WILLIAM W.

Rank: Private (highest rank: Sergeant)
Service: U.S. Army
Birthday: 24 September 1843
Place of Birth: Dearborn County, Indiana
Date of Death: 25 April 1925
Cemetery: Elmwood Cemetery (MH)—Augusta, Kansas
Entered Service at: Wilmington, Indiana
Unit: Company I, 83d Indiana Infantry
Battle or Place of Action: Vicksburg, Mississippi
Date of Action: 22 May 1863
Date of Issue: 15 August 1894
Citation: Gallantry in the charge of the "volunteer storming party."

235 ◆ CHRISTIANCY, JAMES ISAAC

Rank: First Lieutenant
Service: U.S. Army
Birthday: 1844
Place of Birth: Monroe County, Michigan
Date of Death: 18 December 1899
Place of Death: Washington, D.C.
Cemetery: Arlington National Cemetery (1-580) (MH)—Arlington, Virginia
Entered Service at: Monroe County, Michigan
Unit: Company D, 9th Michigan Cavalry
Battle or Place of Action: Hawes Shops, Virginia
Date of Action: 28 May 1864
Date of Issue: 10 October 1892
Citation: While acting as aide, voluntarily led a part of the line into the fight, and was twice wounded.

236 ◆ CHURCHILL, SAMUEL JOSEPH

Rank: Corporal (highest rank: Quartermaster Sergeant)
Service: U.S. Army
Birthday: 1 November 1842
Place of Birth: Rutland, Rutland County, Vermont
Date of Death: 3 June 1932
Cemetery: Oak Hill Cemetery (MH)—Lawrence, Kansas
Entered Service at: DeKalb, DeKalb County, Illinois
Unit: Company G, 2d Illinois Light Artillery
Battle or Place of Action: Nashville, Tennessee
Date of Action: 15 December 1864
Date of Issue: 20 January 1897
Citation: When the fire of the enemy's batteries compelled the men of his detachment for a short time to seek shelter, he stood manfully at his post and for some minutes worked his gun alone.

237 ◆ CILLEY, CLINTON ALBERT

Rank: Captain (highest rank: Brevet Colonel)
Service: U.S. Army
Birthday: 16 February 1837
Place of Birth: Rockingham County, New Hampshire
Date of Death: 9 May 1900

Place of Death: Morgantown, North Carolina
Cemetery: Oakwood Cemetery (MH)—Hickory, North Carolina
Entered Service at: Sasioja, Minnesota
Unit: Company C, 2d Minnesota Infantry
Battle or Place of Action: Chickamauga, Georgia
Date of Action: 20 September 1863
Date of Issue: 12 June 1895
Citation: Seized the colors of a retreating regiment and led it into the thick of the attack.

238 ◆ CLANCY, JAMES T.

Rank: Sergeant (highest rank: Captain)
Service: U.S. Army
Birthday: 1833
Place of Birth: Albany, Albany County, New York
Entered Service at: Camden, Camden County, New Jersey
Unit: Company C, 1st New Jersey Cavalry
Battle or Place of Action: Vaughn Road, Virginia
Date of Action: 1 October 1864
Date of Issue: 3 July 1865
Citation: Shot the Confederate Brig. Gen. John Dunovant dead during a charge, thus confusing the enemy and greatly aiding in his repulse.

239 ◆ CLAPP, ALBERT ADAMS

Rank: First Sergeant (highest rank: Second Lieutenant)
Service: U.S. Army
Birthday: 1 May 1841
Place of Birth: Pompey, Onondaga County, New York
Date of Death: 8 May 1911
Place of Death: Alhambrah, California
Cemetery: Mountain View Cemetery—Altadena, California
Entered Service at: Painesville, Lake County, Ohio
Unit: Company G, 2d Ohio Cavalry
Battle or Place of Action: Deatonsville (Sailor's Creek), Virginia
Date of Action: 6 April 1865
Date of Issue: 24 April 1865
Citation: Capture of battle flag of the 8th Florida Infantry (C.S.A.).

240 ◆ CLARK, CHARLES AMORY

Rank: Lieutenant & Adjutant (highest rank: Brevet Lieutenant Colonel)
Service: U.S. Army
Birthday: 26 January 1841
Place of Birth: Sangerville, Piscataquis County, Maine
Date of Death: 22 December 1913
Cemetery: Oak Hill Cemetery (MH)—Cedar Rapids, Iowa
Entered Service at: Forcroft, Maine
Unit: 6th Maine Infantry
Battle or Place of Action: Brooks Ford, Virginia
Date of Action: 4 May 1863
Date of Issue: 13 May 1896
Citation: Having voluntarily taken command of his regi-

ment in the absence of its commander, at great personal risk and with remarkable presence of mind and fertility of resource, Clark led the command down an exceedingly precipitous embankment to the Rappahannock River and by his gallantry, coolness, and good judgment in the face of the enemy saved the command from capture or destruction.

241 ◆ CLARK, HARRISON

Rank: Corporal (highest rank: Second Lieutenant)
Service: U.S. Army
Birthday: 10 April 1842
Place of Birth: Chatham, Columbia County, New York
Date of Death: 18 April 1913
Cemetery: Albany Rural Cemetery (MH)—Albany, New York
Entered Service at: Chatham, Columbia County, New York
Unit: Company E, 125th New York Infantry
Battle or Place of Action: Gettysburg, Pennsylvania
Date of Action: 2 July 1863
Date of Issue: 11 June 1895
Citation: Seized the colors and advanced with them after the color bearer had been shot.

242 ◆ CLARK, JAMES G.

Rank: Private (highest rank: Drummer)
Service: U.S. Army
Birthday: 31 October 1843
Place of Birth: Germantown, Philadelphia County, Pennsylvania
Date of Death: 16 December 1911
Cemetery: Fernwood Cemetery (MH)—Fernwood, Pennsylvania
Entered Service at: Philadelphia, Philadelphia County, Pennsylvania
Unit: Company F, 88th Pennsylvania Infantry
Battle or Place of Action: Petersburg, Virginia
Date of Action: 18 June 1864
Date of Issue: 30 April 1892
Citation: Distinguished bravery in action; was severely wounded.

243 ◆ CLARK, JOHN WESLEY

Rank: First Lieutenant & Regimental Quartermaster (highest rank: Captain)
Service: U.S. Army
Birthday: 25 October 1830
Place of Birth: Montpelier, Washington County, Vermont
Date of Death: 4 August 1898
Place of Death: Montpelier, Vermont
Cemetery: Green Mount Cemetery—Montpelier, Vermont
Entered Service at: Vermont
Unit: 6th Vermont Infantry
Battle or Place of Action: near Warrenton, Virginia
Date of Action: 28 July 1863
Date of Issue: 17 August 1891
Citation: Defended the division train against a vastly superi-

or force of the enemy, he was severely wounded, but remained in the saddle for 20 hours afterward, until he had brought his train through in safety.

244 ◆ CLARK, WILLIAM A.

Rank: Corporal (highest rank: Sergeant)
Service: U.S. Army
Birthday: 24 July 1828
Place of Birth: Pennsylvania
Date of Death: 9 January 1916
Place of Death: Mankato, Minnesota
Cemetery: Hebron Cemetery (MH)—Nicollet County, Minnesota
Entered Service at: Shelbyville, Minnesota
Unit: Company H, 2d Minnesota Infantry
Battle or Place of Action: Nolensville, Tennessee
Date of Action: 15 February 1863
Date of Issue: 11 September 1897
Citation: Was one of a detachment of 16 men who heroically defended a wagon train against the attack of 125 cavalry, repulsed the attack and saved the train.

245 ◆ CLARKE, DAYTON P.

True Name: Clark, Dayton P.
Rank: Captain
Service: U.S. Army
Birthday: 15 December 1840
Place of Birth: DeKalb, St. Lawrence County, New York
Date of Death: 10 November 1915
Place of Death: Montpelier, Vermont
Cemetery: Green Mount Cemetery—Montpelier, Vermont
Entered Service at: Hermon, St. Lawrence County, New York
Unit: Company F, 2d Vermont Infantry
Battle or Place of Action: Spotsylvania, Virginia
Date of Action: 12 May 1864
Date of Issue: 30 June 1892
Citation: Distinguished conduct in a desperate hand-to-hand fight while commanding the regiment.

246 ◆ CLAUSEN, CHARLES H.

Rank: First Lieutenant
Service: U.S. Army
Birthday: 22 September 1842
Place of Birth: Philadelphia, Philadelphia County, Pennsylvania
Date of Death: 15 August 1922
Place of Death: Glenside, Pennsylvania
Cemetery: Mount Peace Cemetery—Philadelphia, Pennsylvania
Entered Service at: Philadelphia, Philadelphia County, Pennsylvania
Unit: Company H, 61st Pennsylvania Infantry
Battle or Place of Action: Spotsylvania, Virginia
Date of Action: 12 May 1864
Date of Issue: 25 June 1892

Citation: Although severely wounded, he led the regiment against the enemy, under a terrific fire, and saved a battery from capture.

247 ◆ CLAY, CECIL

Rank: Captain (highest rank: Brevet Brigadier General)
Service: U.S. Army
Birthday: 13 February 1842
Place of Birth: Philadelphia, Philadelphia County, Pennsylvania
Date of Death: 23 September 1907
Place of Death: Washington, D.C.
Cemetery: Arlington National Cemetery (2-1012)—Arlington, Virginia
Entered Service at: Philadelphia, Philadelphia County, Pennsylvania
Unit: Company K, 58th Pennsylvania Infantry
Battle or Place of Action: Fort Harrison, Virginia
Date of Action: 29 September 1864
Date of Issue: 19 April 1892
Citation: Led his regiment in the charge, carrying the colors of another regiment, and when severely wounded in the right arm, incurring loss of same, he shifted the colors to the left hand, which also became disabled by a gunshot wound.

248 ◆ CLEVELAND, CHARLES FRANKLIN

Rank: Private
Service: U.S. Army
Birthday: 14 August 1845
Place of Birth: Hartford, Washington County, New York
Date of Death: 29 September 1908
Cemetery: Forest Hill Cemetery—Utica, New York
Entered Service at: Elmira, Chemung County, New York
Unit: Company C, 26th New York Infantry
Battle or Place of Action: Antietam, Maryland
Date of Action: 17 September 1862
Date of Issue: 12 June 1895
Citation: Voluntarily took and carried the colors into action after the color bearer had been shot.

249 ◆ CLIFFORD, ROBERT TELEFORD

True Name: Kelley, Robert Teleford
Rank: Master-at-Arms (highest rank: Master's Mate)
Service: U.S. Navy
Birthday: 1835
Place of Birth: Pennsylvania
Date of Death: 24 July 1873
Place of Death: Philadelphia, Pennsylvania
Cemetery: Laurel Hill Cemetery (MH)—Philadelphia, Pennsylvania
Entered Service at: Pennsylvania
Unit: U.S.S. *Shokokon*
Battle or Place of Action: New Topsail Inlet, off Wilmington, North Carolina
Date of Action: 22 August 1863
G.O. Number, Date: 45, 31 December 1864

Citation: Served on board the U.S.S. *Shokokon* at New Topsail Inlet off Wilmington, N.C., 22 August 1863. Participating in a strategic plan to destroy an enemy schooner, Clifford aided in the portage of a dinghy across the narrow neck of land separating the sea from the sound. Launching the boat in the sound, the crew approached the enemy from the rear and Clifford gallantly crept into the rebel camp and counted the men who outnumbered his party three to one. Returning to his men, he ordered a charge in which the enemy was routed, leaving behind a schooner and a quantity of supplies.

250   ◆   CLOPP, JOHN E.

Rank: Private
Service: U.S. Army
Place of Birth: Philadelphia, Philadelphia County, Pennsylvania
Entered Service at: Philadelphia, Philadelphia County, Pennsylvania
Unit: Company F, 71st Pennsylvania Infantry
Battle or Place of Action: Gettysburg, Pennsylvania
Date of Action: 3 July 1863
Date of Issue: 2 February 1865
Citation: Capture of flag of 9th Virginia Infantry (C.S.A.), wresting it from the color bearer.

251   ◆   CLUTE, GEORGE WASHINGTON

Rank: Corporal
Service: U.S. Army
Birthday: 11 June 1842
Place of Birth: Marathon, Michigan
Date of Death: 13 February 1919
Place of Death: Flint, Michigan
Cemetery: Morris Cemetery (MH)—Mount Morris, Michigan
Entered Service at: Marathon, Michigan
Unit: Company I, 14th Michigan Infantry
Battle or Place of Action: Bentonville, North Carolina
Date of Action: 19 March 1865
Date of Issue: 26 August 1898
Citation: In a charge, captured the flag of the 40th North Carolina (C.S.A.), the flag being taken in a personal encounter with an officer who carried and defended it.

252   ◆   COATES, JEFFERSON

True Name: Coates, Francis Jefferson
Rank: Sergeant
Service: U.S. Army
Birthday: 24 August 1843
Place of Birth: Grant County, Wisconsin
Date of Death: 27 January 1880
Place of Death: Dorchester, Nebraska
Cemetery: Dorchester City Cemetery—Dorchester, Nebraska
Entered Service at: Boscobel, Grant County, Wisconsin

Unit: Company H, 7th Wisconsin Infantry
Battle or Place of Action: Gettysburg, Pennsylvania
Date of Action: 1 July 1863
Date of Issue: 29 June 1866
Citation: Unsurpassed courage in battle, where he had both eyes shot out.

253   ◆   COCKLEY, DAVID L.

Rank: First Lieutenant (highest rank: Captain)
Service: U.S. Army
Birthday: 8 June 1843
Place of Birth: Lexington, Richland County, Ohio
Date of Death: 26 December 1901
Cemetery: Oakland Cemetery (MH)—Shelby, Ohio
Entered Service at: Columbus, Franklin County, Ohio
Unit: Company L, 10th Ohio Cavalry
Battle or Place of Action: Waynesboro, Georgia
Date of Action: 4 December 1864
Date of Issue: 2 August 1897
Citation: While acting as aide-de-camp to a general officer, he three times asked permission to join his regiment in a proposed charge upon the enemy, and in response to the last request, having obtained such permission, joined his regiment and fought bravely at its head throughout the action.

254   ◆   COEY, JAMES

Rank: Major (highest rank: Brevet Colonel U.S. Volunteers)
Service: U.S. Army
Birthday: 12 February 1841
Place of Birth: New York, New York
Date of Death: 14 July 1918
Place of Death: Berkeley, California
Cemetery: San Francisco National Cemetery (OS-89-1) (MH)—San Francisco, California
Entered Service at: Oswego, Oswego County, New York
Unit: 147th New York Infantry
Battle or Place of Action: Hatcher's Run, Virginia
Date of Action: 6 February 1865
Date of Issue: 12 May 1892
Citation: Seized the regimental colors at a critical moment and by a prompt advance on the enemy caused the entire brigade to follow him; and, after himself being severely wounded, he caused himself to be lifted into the saddle and a second time rallied the line in an attempt to check the enemy.

255   ◆   COFFEY, ROBERT JOHN

Rank: Sergeant (highest rank: Major)
Service: U.S. Army
Birthday: 15 December 1842
Place of Birth: St. John, New Brunswick, Canada
Date of Death: 9 July 1901
Cemetery: Green Mount Cemetery—Montpelier, Vermont
Entered Service at: Montpelier, Washington County, Vermont
Unit: Company K, 4th Vermont Infantry

Battle or Place of Action: Bank's Ford, Virginia
Date of Action: 4 May 1863
Date of Issue: 13 May 1892
Citation: Singlehandedly captured two officers and five privates of the 8th Louisiana Regiment (C.S.A.).

256 ◆ COHN, ABRAHAM

Rank: Sergeant Major (highest rank: Captain)
Service: U.S. Army
Birthday: 1832
Place of Birth: Guttentag, Silesia, Prussia
Date of Death: 2 June 1897
Place of Death: New York, New York
Cemetery: Cypress Hills Cemetery (Private)—Brooklyn, New York
Entered Service at: Campton, Grafton County, New Hampshire
Unit: 6th New Hampshire Infantry
Battle or Place of Action: Wilderness Campaign & at the mine, Petersburg, Virginia
Date of Action: 6 May & 30 July 1864
Date of Issue: 24 August 1865
Citation: During Battle of the Wilderness rallied and formed, under heavy fire, disorganized and fleeing troops of different regiments. At Petersburg, Va., 30 July 1864, bravely and coolly carried orders to the advanced line under severe fire.

257 ◆ COLBERT, PATRICK

Rank: Coxswain
Service: U.S. Navy
Birthday: 1842
Place of Birth: Ireland
Date of Death: 19 January 1877
Place of Death: Detroit, Michigan
Cemetery: Mount Elliott Cemetery (MH)—Detroit, Michigan
Entered Service at: New York
Unit: U.S.S. *Commodore Hull*
Battle or Place of Action: Plymouth, North Carolina
Date of Action: 31 October 1864
G.O. Number, Date: 45, 31 December 1864
Citation: Served on board the U.S.S. *Commodore Hull* at the capture of Plymouth, 31 October 1864. Painfully wounded by a shell which killed the man at his side, Colbert, as captain of the forward pivot gun, remained at his post until the end of the action, braving the heavy enemy fire and appearing as cool as if mere target practice.

258 ◆ COLBY, CARLOS W.

Rank: Sergeant (highest rank: First Sergeant)
Service: U.S. Army
Birthday: 15 May 1837
Place of Birth: Merrimack, Hillsborough County, New Hampshire
Date of Death: 19 May 1922

Cemetery: Crest Hill Cemetery—Hillsboro, Illinois
Entered Service at: Madison County, Illinois
Unit: Company G, 97th Illinois Infantry
Battle or Place of Action: Vicksburg, Mississippi
Date of Action: 22 May 1863
Date of Issue: 31 January 1896
Citation: Gallantry in the charge of the "volunteer storming party."

259 ◆ COLE, GABRIEL

Rank: Corporal
Service: U.S. Army
Birthday: 22 March 1831
Place of Birth: Chenango County, New York
Date of Death: 7 January 1907
Cemetery: Sherman Township Cemetery (MH)—Tustin, Michigan
Entered Service at: New Salem, Washtenaw County, Michigan
Unit: Company I, 5th Michigan Cavalry
Battle or Place of Action: Winchester, Virginia
Date of Action: 19 September 1864
Date of Issue: 27 September 1864
Citation: Capture of flag, during which he was wounded in the leg.

260 ◆ COLLINS, HARRISON

Rank: Corporal
Service: U.S. Army
Birthday: 10 March 1836
Place of Birth: Hawkins County, Tennessee
Date of Death: 25 December 1890
Place of Death: Isabella, Missouri
Cemetery: Springfield National Cemetery (26-1357-B)—Springfield, Missouri
Entered Service at: Cumberland Gap, Claiborne County, Tennessee
Unit: Company A, 1st Tennessee Cavalry
Battle or Place of Action: Richland Creek, Tennessee
Date of Action: 24 December 1864
Date of Issue: 24 February 1865
Citation: Capture of flag of Chalmer's Division (C.S.A.).

261 ◆ COLLINS SR., THOMAS D.

Rank: Sergeant
Service: U.S. Army
Birthday: 14 August 1847
Place of Birth: Neversink Flats, Sullivan County, New York
Date of Death: 26 May 1935
Place of Death: Middletown, New York
Cemetery: Hillside Cemetery (MH)—Middletown, New York
Entered Service at: Liberty, Sullivan County, New York
Unit: Company H, 143d New York Infantry (Sullivan County Regiment)

Battle or Place of Action: Resaca, Georgia
Date of Action: 15 May 1864
Date of Issue: 14 August 1896
Citation: Captured a regimental flag of the enemy.

262 ◆ COLLIS, CHARLES HENRY TUCKY

Rank: Colonel (highest rank: Brevet Major General)
Service: U.S. Army
Birthday: 4 February 1838
Place of Birth: Cork, County Cork, Ireland
Date of Death: 11 May 1902
Place of Death: Bryn Mawr, Pennsylvania
Cemetery: Gettysburg National Cemetery (H-1 PA plot)—Gettysburg, Pennsylvania
Entered Service at: Philadelphia, Philadelphia County, Pennsylvania
Unit: 114th Pennsylvania Infantry (Collis' Regiment, Zouaves d'Afrique)
Battle or Place of Action: Fredericksburg, Virginia
Date of Action: 13 December 1862
Date of Issue: 10 March 1893
Citation: Gallantly led his regiment in battle at a critical moment.

263 ◆ COLWELL, OLIVER

Rank: First Lieutenant (highest rank: Captain)
Service: U.S. Army
Birthday: 1834
Place of Birth: Champaign County, Ohio
Date of Death: 12 October 1872
Place of Death: Rush Township, Ohio
Cemetery: Woodstock Cemetery—Rush Township, Ohio
Entered Service at: Columbus, Franklin County, Ohio
Unit: Company G, 95th Ohio Infantry
Battle or Place of Action: Nashville, Tennessee
Date of Action: 16 December 1864
Date of Issue: 24 February 1865
Citation: Capture of flag.
Notes: POW

264 ◆ COMPSON, HARTWELL B.

Rank: Major (highest rank: Brevet Lieutenant Colonel New York Volunteers)
Service: U.S. Army
Birthday: 1840
Place of Birth: Seneca Falls, Seneca County, New York
Date of Death: 31 August 1905
Cemetery: Grand Army of the Republic Cemetery—Portland, Oregon
Entered Service at: Seneca Falls, Seneca County, New York
Unit: 8th New York Cavalry
Battle or Place of Action: Waynesboro, Virginia
Date of Action: 2 March 1865
Date of Issue: 26 March 1865
Citation: Capture of flag belonging to Lt. Gen. Jubal Anderson Early's headquarters.

265 ◆ CONAWAY, JOHN WESLEY

Rank: Private (highest rank: Corporal)
Service: U.S. Army
Birthday: 19 September 1843
Place of Birth: Dearborn County, Indiana
Date of Death: 21 November 1913
Place of Death: Post Falls, Idaho
Cemetery: Evergreen Cemetery (MH)—Post Falls, Idaho
Entered Service at: Hartford, Blackford County, Indiana
Unit: Company C, 83d Indiana Infantry
Battle or Place of Action: Vicksburg, Mississippi
Date of Action: 22 May 1863
Date of Issue: 11 August 1894
Citation: Gallantry in the charge of the "volunteer storming party."

266 ◆ CONBOY, MARTIN

Rank: First Sergeant (highest rank: Second Lieutenant)
Service: U.S. Army
Birthday: 1833
Place of Birth: Roscommon, Ballagh County, Ireland
Date of Death: 21 December 1909
Place of Death: East Orange, New Jersey
Cemetery: Holy Sepulchre Cemetery—East Orange, New Jersey
Entered Service at: New York, New York
Unit: Company B, 37th New York Infantry
Battle or Place of Action: Williamsburg, Virginia
Date of Action: 5 May 1862
Date of Issue: 11 October 1892
Citation: Took command of the company in action, the captain having been wounded, the other commissioned officers being absent, and handled it with skill and bravery.

267 ◆ CONLAN, DENNIS

Rank: Seaman (highest rank: Gunner's Mate)
Service: U.S. Navy
Birthday: 1838
Place of Birth: New York, New York
Date of Death: 2 December 1870
Place of Death: New York, New York
Cemetery: Calvary Cemetery—Woodside, New York
Entered Service at: New York, New York
Unit: U.S.S. *Agawam*
Battle or Place of Action: Fort Fisher, North Carolina
Date of Action: 23 December 1864
G.O. Number, Date: 45, 31 December 1864
Date of Presentation: 12 May 1865
Place of Presentation: On board the U.S.S. *Agawam*, off New Bern, North Carolina
Citation: Conlan served on board the U.S.S. *Agawam*, as one of a volunteer crew of a powder boat which was exploded near Fort Fisher, 23 December 1864. The powder boat, towed in by the *Wilderness* to prevent detection by the enemy, cast off and slowly steamed to within 300 yards of the beach. After fuses and fires had been lit and a second anchor

with short scope let go to assure the boat's tailing inshore, the crew again boarded the *Wilderness* and proceeded a distance of 12 miles from shore. Less than two hours later the explosion took place, and the following day fires were observed still burning at the forts.

268 ◆ CONNELL, TRUSTRIM

Rank: Corporal
Service: U.S. Army
Birthday: 12 May 1844
Place of Birth: Lancaster, Lancaster County, Pennsylvania
Date of Death: 17 February 1937
Place of Death: Phoenix, Arizona
Cemetery: Rosedale Cemetery—Los Angeles, California
Entered Service at: Port Kennedy, Pennsylvania
Unit: Company I, 138th Pennsylvania Infantry
Battle or Place of Action: Deatonsville (Sailor's Creek), Virginia
Date of Action: 6 April 1865
Date of Issue: 10 May 1865
Citation: Capture of flag.

269 ◆ CONNER, RICHARD

Rank: Private (highest rank: Sergeant)
Service: U.S. Army
Birthday: 23 December 1840
Place of Birth: Philadelphia, Philadelphia County, Pennsylvania
Date of Death: 4 November 1923
Place of Death: Philadelphia, Pennsylvania
Cemetery: North Cedar Hills Cemetery—Philadelphia, Pennsylvania
Entered Service at: Burlington, Burlington County, New Jersey
Unit: Company F, 6th New Jersey Infantry
Battle or Place of Action: Bull Run, Virginia
Date of Action: 30 August 1862
Date of Issue: 17 September 1897
Citation: The flag of his regiment having been abandoned during retreat, he voluntarily returned with a single companion under a heavy fire and secured and brought off the flag, his companion being killed.

270 ◆ CONNOR, THOMAS

Rank: Ordinary Seaman
Service: U.S. Navy
Birthday: 1842
Place of Birth: Ireland
Entered Service at: Baltimore, Baltimore County, Maryland
Unit: U.S.S. *Minnesota*
Battle or Place of Action: Fort Fisher, North Carolina
Date of Action: 15 January 1865
G.O. Number, Date: 59, 22 June 1865
Citation: On board the U.S.S. *Minnesota*, in action during the assault on Fort Fisher, 15 January 1865. Landing on the beach with the assaulting party from his ship, Connor charged up to the palisades and, when more than two-thirds of the men became seized with panic and retreated on the run, risked

his life to remain with a wounded officer. With the enemy concentrating his fire on the group, he waited until after dark before assisting in carrying the wounded man from the field.

271 ◆ CONNOR, WILLIAM C.

Rank: Boatswain's Mate
Service: U.S. Navy
Birthday: 1832
Place of Birth: Cork, County Cork, Ireland
Entered Service at: Pennsylvania
Unit: U.S.S. *Howquah*
Battle or Place of Action: off Wilmington, Delaware
Date of Action: 25 September 1864
G.O. Number, Date: 45, 31 December 1864
Citation: Served on board the U.S.S. *Howquah* on the occasion of the destruction of the blockade runner *Lynx*, off Wilmington, 25 September 1864. Performing his duty faithfully under the most trying circumstances, Connor stood firmly at his post in the midst of a cross-fire from the rebel shore batteries and our own vessels.

272 ◆ CONNORS, JAMES

Rank: Private
Service: U.S. Army
Birthday: 1838
Place of Birth: Kildare, Ireland
Entered Service at: Canajoharie, Montgomery County, New York
Unit: Company E, 43rd New York Infantry
Battle or Place of Action: Fisher's Hill, Virginia
Date of Action: 22 September 1864
Date of Issue: 6 October 1864
Citation: Capture of flag.

273 ◆ COOK, JOHN

Rank: Bugler
Service: U.S. Army
Birthday: 16 August 1847
Place of Birth: Cincinnati, Hamilton County, Ohio
Date of Death: 3 August 1915
Cemetery: Arlington National Cemetery (17-18613)—Arlington, Virginia
Entered Service at: Cincinnati, Hamilton County, Ohio
Unit: Battery B, 4th U.S. Artillery
Battle or Place of Action: Antietam, Maryland
Date of Action: 17 September 1862
Date of Issue: 30 June 1894
Citation: Volunteered at the age of 15 years to act as a cannoneer, and as such volunteer served a gun under a terrific fire of the enemy.

274 ◆ COOK, JOHN HENRY

Rank: Sergeant
Service: U.S. Army
Birthday: 19 July 1840

Place of Birth: London, England
Date of Death: 22 July 1916
Place of Death: New York, New York
Cemetery: Woodlawn Cemetery—Bronx, New York
Entered Service at: Quincy, Adams County, Illinois
Unit: Company A, 119th Illinois Infantry
Battle or Place of Action: Pleasant Hill, Louisiana
Date of Action: 9 April 1864
Date of Issue: 19 September 1890
Citation: During an attack by the enemy, voluntarily left the brigade quartermaster, with whom he had been detailed as a clerk, rejoined his command, and, acting as first lieutenant, led the line farther toward the charging enemy.

275 ◆ COOKE, WALTER HOWARD

Rank: Captain (highest rank: Major)
Service: U.S. Army
Birthday: 21 July 1838
Place of Birth: Norristown, Montgomery County, Pennsylvania
Date of Death: 28 January 1909
Place of Death: Norristown, Pennsylvania
Cemetery: St. Thomas Church Cemetery (MH)—Whitemarsh, Pennsylvania
Entered Service at: Norristown, Montgomery County, Pennsylvania
Unit: Company K, 4th Pennsylvania Infantry Militia
Battle or Place of Action: Bull Run, Virginia
Date of Action: 21 July 1861
Date of Issue: 19 May 1887
Citation: Voluntarily served as an aide on the staff of Col. David Hunter and participated in the battle, his term of service having expired on the previous day.

276 ◆ COOPER, JOHN✝

True Name: Mather, John Laver
Rank: Coxswain
Service: U.S. Navy
Birthday: 24 July 1828
Place of Birth: Dublin, County Dublin, Ireland
Date of Death: 22 August 1891
Cemetery: Cypress Hills National Cemetery (2-5022) (MH)—Brooklyn, New York
Entered Service at: New York, New York
Unit: U.S.S. *Brooklyn*
Battle or Place of Action: Mobile Bay, Alabama
Date of Action: 5 August 1864
G.O. Number, Date: 45, 31 December 1864
Citation: On board the U.S.S. *Brooklyn* during action against rebel forts and gunboats and with the ram *Tennessee*, in Mobile Bay, on 5 August 1864. Despite severe damage to his ship and the loss of several men on board as enemy fire raked her decks from stem to stern, Cooper fought his gun with skill and courage throughout the furious battle which resulted in the surrender of the prize rebel ram *Tennessee* and in the damaging and destruction of batteries at Fort Morgan.
Notes: ✝Double Awardee: *see also* Interim 1865–1870

277 ◆ COPP, CHARLES DEARBORN

Rank: Second Lieutenant (highest rank: Captain)
Service: U.S. Army
Birthday: 11 April 1836
Place of Birth: Warren County, New Hampshire
Date of Death: 2 November 1912
Place of Death: Clinton, Massachusetts
Cemetery: Middle Yard Cemetery (MH)—Lancaster, Massachusetts
Entered Service at: Nashua, Hillsborough County, New Hampshire
Unit: Company C, 9th New Hampshire Infantry
Battle or Place of Action: Fredericksburg, Virginia
Date of Action: 13 December 1862
Date of Issue: 28 June 1890
Citation: Seized the regimental colors, the color bearer having been shot down, and, waving them, rallied the regiment under a heavy fire.

278 ◆ CORCORAN, JOHN

Rank: Private
Service: U.S. Army
Birthday: 24 June 1842
Place of Birth: Pawtucket, Providence County, Rhode Island
Date of Death: 19 June 1919
Cemetery: Oak Grove Cemetery (MH)—Pawtucket, Rhode Island
Entered Service at: Pawtucket, Providence County, Rhode Island
Unit: Company G, 1st Rhode Island Light Artillery
Battle or Place of Action: Petersburg, Virginia
Date of Action: 2 April 1865
Date of Issue: 2 November 1887
Citation: Was one of a detachment of 20 picked artillerymen who voluntarily accompanied an infantry assaulting party, and who turned upon the enemy the guns captured in the assault.

279 ◆ CORCORAN, THOMAS E.

Rank: Landsman
Service: U.S. Navy
Birthday: 1838
Place of Birth: Dublin, County Dublin, Ireland
Date of Death: 12 March 1904
Cemetery: 1st Calvary Cemetery—Woodside, New York
Entered Service at: New York, New York
Unit: U.S.S. *Cincinnati*
Battle or Place of Action: Vicksburg, Mississippi
Date of Action: 27 May 1863
G.O. Number, Date: 17, 10 July 1863
Citation: Served on board the U.S.S. *Cincinnati* during the attack on the Vicksburg batteries and at the time of her sinking, 27 May 1863. Engaging the enemy in a fierce battle, the *Cincinnati*, amidst an incessant fire of shot and shell, continued to fire her guns to the last, though so penetrated by shellfire that her fate was sealed. Serving bravely during this

action, Corcoran was conspicuously cool under the fire of the enemy, never ceasing to fight until this proud ship went down, "her colors nailed to the mast."

280 ◆ CORLISS, GEORGE W.

Rank: Captain (highest rank: Brevet Major)
Service: U.S. Army
Birthday: 1834
Place of Birth: Connecticut
Date of Death: 15 May 1903
Place of Death: New York, New York
Cemetery: Maple Grove Cemetery (MH)—Kew Gardens, New York
Entered Service at: Hartford, Hartford County, Connecticut
Unit: Company C, 5th Connecticut Infantry
Battle or Place of Action: Cedar Mountain, Virginia
Date of Action: 9 August 1862
Date of Issue: 10 September 1897
Citation: Seized a fallen flag of the regiment, the color bearer having been killed, carried it forward in the face of a severe fire, and though himself shot down and permanently disabled, planted the staff in the earth and kept the flag flying.

281 ◆ CORLISS, STEPHEN POTTER

Rank: First Lieutenant (highest rank: Brevet Colonel)
Service: U.S. Army
Birthday: 26 July 1842
Place of Birth: Albany, Albany County, New York
Date of Death: 9 May 1904
Place of Death: Pittsfield, Massachusetts
Cemetery: Albany Rural Cemetery (MH)—Albany, New York
Entered Service at: Albany, Albany County, New York
Unit: Company F, 4th New York Heavy Artillery
Battle or Place of Action: South Side Railroad, Virginia
Date of Action: 2 April 1865
Date of Issue: 17 January 1895
Citation: Raised the fallen colors and, rushing forward in advance of the troops, placed them on the enemy's works.

282 ◆ CORSON, JOSEPH KIRBY

Rank: Assistant Surgeon (highest rank: Major USA Ret.)
Service: U.S. Army
Birthday: 26 November 1836
Place of Birth: Plymouth Meeting, Montgomery County, Pennsylvania
Date of Death: 24 July 1913
Place of Death: Plymouth Meeting, Pennsylvania
Cemetery: West Laurel Hill Cemetery—Bala-Cynwyd, Pennsylvania
Entered Service at: Philadelphia, Philadelphia County, Pennsylvania
Unit: 6th Pennsylvania Reserves (35th Pennsylvania Volunteers)
Battle or Place of Action: near Bristoe Station, Virginia

Date of Action: 14 October 1863
Date of Issue: 13 May 1899
Citation: With one companion returned in the face of the enemy's heavy artillery fire and removed to a place of safety a severely wounded soldier who had been left behind as the regiment fell back.

283 ◆ COSGRIFF, RICHARD H.

Rank: Private
Service: U.S. Army
Birthday: 15 December 1844
Place of Birth: Dunkirk County, New York
Date of Death: 2 November 1910
Cemetery: Our Lady of Hope Cemetery—Chippewa Falls, Wisconsin
Entered Service at: Wapello, Louisa County, Iowa
Unit: Company L, 4th Iowa Cavalry
Battle or Place of Action: Columbus, Georgia
Date of Action: 16 April 1865
Date of Issue: 17 June 1865
Citation: Capture of flag in a personal encounter with its bearer.

284 ◆ COSGROVE, THOMAS

Rank: Private
Service: U.S. Army
Birthday: 12 June 1829
Place of Birth: County Galway, Ireland
Date of Death: 27 March 1912
Place of Death: East Lexington, Massachusetts
Cemetery: Munroe Cemetery (MH)—Lexington, Massachusetts
Entered Service at: East Stoughton, Norfolk County, Massachusetts
Unit: Company F, 40th Massachusetts Infantry
Battle or Place of Action: Drewry's Bluff, Virginia
Date of Action: 15 May 1864
Date of Issue: 7 November 1896
Citation: Individually demanded and received the surrender of seven armed Confederates concealed in a cellar, disarming and marching them in as prisoners of war.

285 ◆ COTTON, PETER

Rank: Ordinary Seaman (highest rank: Coxswain)
Service: U.S. Navy
Birthday: 1839
Place of Birth: New York, New York
Entered Service at: New York
Unit: U.S.S. *Baron De Kalb*
Battle or Place of Action: Yazoo River, Mississippi
Date of Action: 23-27 December 1862
G.O. Number, Date: 11, 3 April 1863
Citation: Cotton served on board the U.S.S. *Baron De Kalb* in the Yazoo River expedition, 23 to 27 December 1862. Proceeding under orders up the Yazoo River, the *Baron De Kalb*, with the object of capturing or destroying the enemy's

transports, came upon the steamers *John Walsh, R.J. Locklan, Golden Age,* and the *Scotland,* sunk on a bar where they were ordered to be burned. Continuing up the river, the *Baron De Kalb* was fired upon but, upon returning the fire, caused the enemy's retreat. Returning down the Yazoo, she destroyed and captured large quantities of enemy equipment and several prisoners. Serving bravely throughout this action, Cotton, as Coxswain, "distinguished himself in the various actions."

286 ◆ COUGHLIN, JOHN

Rank: Lieutenant Colonel (highest rank: Brevet Brigadier General)
Service: U.S. Army
Birthday: 1837
Place of Birth: Vermont
Date of Death: 27 May 1912
Cemetery: Arlington National Cemetery (2-936-WS) (MH)—Arlington, Virginia
Entered Service at: Manchester, Hillsborough County, New Hampshire
Unit: 10th New Hampshire Infantry (Irish Regiment)
Battle or Place of Action: Swift Creek, Virginia
Date of Action: 9 May 1864
Date of Issue: 31 August 1893
Citation: During a sudden night attack upon Burnham's Brigade, resulting in much confusion, this officer, without waiting for orders, led his regiment forward and interposed a line of battle between the advancing enemy and Hunt's Battery, repulsing the attack and saving the guns.

287 ◆ COX, ROBERT MITCHELL

Rank: Corporal
Service: U.S. Army
Birthday: 19 March 1845
Place of Birth: Guernsey County, Ohio
Date of Death: 26 October 1932
Place of Death: Prairie City, Illinois
Cemetery: Prairie City Cemetery (MH)—Prairie City, Illinois
Entered Service at: Prairie City, McDonough County, Illinois
Unit: Company K, 55th Illinois Infantry
Battle or Place of Action: Vicksburg, Mississippi
Date of Action: 22 May 1863
Date of Issue: 31 December 1892
Citation: Bravely defended the colors planted on the outward parapet of Fort Hill.

288 ◆ COYNE, JOHN NICHOLAS

Rank: Sergeant (highest rank: Lieutenant Colonel)
Service: U.S. Army
Birthday: 14 November 1839
Place of Birth: New York, New York
Date of Death: 4 March 1907
Place of Death: East Orange, New Jersey
Cemetery: The Green Wood Cemetery—Brooklyn, New York

Entered Service at: New York, New York
Unit: Company B, 70th New York Infantry
Battle or Place of Action: Williamsburg, Virginia
Date of Action: 5 May 1862
Date of Issue: 18 April 1888
Citation: Capture of a flag after a severe hand-to-hand contest; was mentioned in orders for his gallantry.

289 ◆ CRANSTON, WILLIAM WALLACE

Rank: Private (highest rank: Captain)
Service: U.S. Army
Birthday: 20 November 1838
Place of Birth: near Woodstock, Champaign County, Ohio
Date of Death: 7 December 1907
Place of Death: Parsons, Kansas
Cemetery: Oakwood Cemetery (MH)—Parsons, Kansas
Entered Service at: Urbana, Champaign County, Ohio
Unit: Company A, 66th Ohio Infantry
Battle or Place of Action: Chancellorsville, Virginia
Date of Action: 2 May 1863
Date of Issue: 15 December 1892
Citation: One of a party of four who voluntarily brought in a wounded Confederate officer from within the enemy's line in the face of a constant fire.

290 ◆ CRAWFORD, ALEXANDER

Rank: Fireman
Service: U.S. Navy
Birthday: 1842
Place of Birth: Philadelphia, Philadelphia County, Pennsylvania
Date of Death: 17 March 1886
Cemetery: Cedar Hill Cemetery—Philadelphia, Pennsylvania
Entered Service at: Philadelphia, Philadelphia County, Pennsylvania
Unit: U.S.S. *Wyalusing*
Battle or Place of Action: Roanoke River, North Carolina
Date of Action: 25 May 1864
G.O. Number, Date: 45, 31 December 1864
Citation: On board the U.S.S. *Wyalusing*, Crawford volunteered 25 May 1864, in a night attempt to destroy the rebel ram *Albemarle* in the Roanoke River. Taking part in a plan to explode the rebel ram *Albemarle*, Crawford executed his part in the plan with perfection, but upon being discovered, was forced to abandon the plan and retire, leaving no trace of the evidence. After spending two hazardous days and nights without food, he gained the safety of a friendly ship and was then transferred back to the *Wyalusing*. Though the plan failed, his skill and courage in preventing detection were an example of unfailing devotion to duty.

291 ◆ CREED, JOHN

Rank: Private (highest rank: Corporal)
Service: U.S. Army
Birthday: 1819
Place of Birth: Tipperary, County Tipperary, Ireland

Date of Death: 28 November 1872
Cemetery: Calvary Cemetery—Evanston, Illinois
Entered Service at: Chicago, Cook County, Illinois
Unit: Company D, 23d Illinois Infantry
Battle or Place of Action: Fisher's Hill, Virginia
Date of Action: 22 September 1864
Date of Issue: 6 October 1864
Citation: Capture of flag.

292 ◆ CRIPPS, THOMAS H.

Rank: Quartermaster
Service: U.S. Navy
Birthday: 29 November 1840
Place of Birth: Philadelphia, Philadelphia County, Pennsylvania
Date of Death: 8 December 1906
Place of Death: Philadelphia, Pennsylvania
Cemetery: Woodlands Cemetery (MH)—Philadelphia, Pennsylvania
Entered Service at: Pennsylvania
Unit: U.S.S. *Richmond*
Battle or Place of Action: Mobile Bay, Alabama
Date of Action: 5 August 1864
G.O. Number, Date: 45, 31 December 1864
Citation: As captain of a gun on board the U.S.S. *Richmond* during action against rebel forts and gunboats and with the ram *Tennessee* in Mobile Bay, 5 August 1864. Despite damage to his ship and the loss of several men on board as enemy fire raked her decks, Cripps fought his gun with skill and courage throughout a furious two-hour battle which resulted in the surrender of the rebel ram *Tennessee* and in the damaging and destruction of batteries at Fort Morgan.

293 ◆ CROCKER, HENRY H.

Rank: Captain
Service: U.S. Army
Birthday: 20 January 1839
Place of Birth: Colchester, New London County, Connecticut
Date of Death: 1913
Cemetery: Washington Cemetery (MH)—Washington, New Jersey
Entered Service at: San Francisco, San Francisco County, California
Unit: Company F, 2d Massachusetts Cavalry
Battle or Place of Action: Cedar Creek, Virginia
Date of Action: 19 October 1864
Date of Issue: 10 January 1896
Citation: Voluntarily led a charge, which resulted in the capture of 14 prisoners and in which he himself was wounded.

294 ◆ CROCKER, ULRIC LYONA

Rank: Private
Service: U.S. Army
Birthday: 5 September 1843
Place of Birth: Ohio

Date of Death: 2 February 1913
Place of Death: Manchester, Kansas
Cemetery: Medora Cemetery—Ruyle Township, Illinois
Entered Service at: Vergennes, Ohio
Unit: Company M, 6th Michigan Cavalry
Battle or Place of Action: Cedar Creek, Virginia
Date of Action: 19 October 1864
Date of Issue: 26 October 1864
Citation: Capture of flag of 18th Georgia (C.S.A.).

295 ◆ CROFT, JAMES E.

Rank: Private (highest rank: Second Lieutenant)
Service: U.S. Army
Birthday: 13 November 1833
Place of Birth: Yorkshire, England
Date of Death: 26 May 1914
Place of Death: Janesville, Wisconsin
Cemetery: Oak Hill Cemetery—Janesville, Wisconsin
Entered Service at: Janesville, Rock County, Wisconsin
Unit: 12th Battery, Wisconsin Light Artillery
Battle or Place of Action: Allatoona, Georgia
Date of Action: 5 October 1864
Date of Issue: 20 March 1897
Citation: Took the place of a gunner who had been shot down and inspired his comrades by his bravery and effective gunnery, which contributed largely to the defeat of the enemy.

296 ◆ CRONIN, CORNELIUS

Rank: Chief Quartermaster (highest rank: Chief Gunner)
Service: U.S. Navy
Birthday: 10 March 1838
Place of Birth: Ireland
Date of Death: 18 August 1912
Place of Death: Brooklyn, New York
Cemetery: 1st Calvary Cemetery—Woodside, New York
Entered Service at: Michigan
Unit: U.S.S. *Richmond*
Battle or Place of Action: Mobile Bay, Alabama; Forts Jackson & St. Philip; New Orleans, Louisiana; below Vicksburg, Mississippi
Date of Action: 5 August 1864
G.O. Number, Date: 45, 31 December 1864
Citation: On board the U.S.S. *Richmond* in action at Mobile Bay, 5 August 1864. Cool and vigilant at his station throughout the prolonged action, Cronin watched for signals and skillfully steered the ship as she trained her guns on Fort Morgan and on other ships of the Confederacy despite extremely heavy return fire. He participated in the actions at Forts Jackson and St. Philip, with the Chalmette batteries, at the surrender of New Orleans, and in the attacks on batteries below Vicksburg.

297 ◆ CROSIER, WILLIAM HENRY HARRISON

Rank: Sergeant (highest rank: Color Sergeant)
Service: U.S. Army

Birthday: 5 May 1844
Place of Birth: Skaneateles, Onondaga County, New York
Date of Death: 14 March 1903
Place of Death: Ogdensburg, New York
Cemetery: Oakwood Morningside Cemetery (MH)—Syracuse, New York
Entered Service at: Skaneateles, Onondaga County, New York
Unit: Company G, 149th New York Infantry
Battle or Place of Action: Peach Tree Creek, Georgia
Date of Action: 20 July 1864
Date of Issue: 12 January 1892
Citation: Severely wounded and ambushed by the enemy, he stripped the colors from the staff and brought them back into the line.

298 ◆ CROSS, JAMES EDWIN

Rank: Corporal (highest rank: Sergeant Major)
Service: U.S. Army
Birthday: 27 March 1840
Place of Birth: Darien, Genesee County, New York
Date of Death: 6 January 1917
Place of Death: Albany, New York
Cemetery: Albany Rural Cemetery (MH)—Albany, New York
Entered Service at: Batavia, Genesee County, New York
Unit: Company K, 12th New York Infantry (Independence Guard)
Battle or Place of Action: Blackburn's Ford, Virginia
Date of Action: 18 July 1861
Date of Issue: 5 April 1898
Citation: With a companion, refused to retreat when the part of the regiment to which he was attached was driven back in disorder, but remained upon the skirmish line for some time thereafter, firing upon the enemy.

299 ◆ CROWLEY, MICHAEL

Rank: Private
Service: U.S. Army
Birthday: 1829
Place of Birth: Rochester, Monroe County, New York
Date of Death: 12 May 1888
Place of Death: Worcester, Massachusetts
Cemetery: unknown cemetery—Boston, Massachusetts
Entered Service at: Rochester, Monroe County, New York
Unit: Company A, 22d New York Cavalry
Battle or Place of Action: Waynesboro, Virginia
Date of Action: 2 March 1865
Date of Issue: 26 March 1865
Citation: Capture of flag.

300 ◆ CULLEN, THOMAS

Rank: Corporal
Service: U.S. Army
Birthday: 26 February 1839
Place of Birth: Ireland
Date of Death: 17 August 1913

Cemetery: St. Mary's Cemetery (MH)—Kinny, Pennsylvania
Entered Service at: New York, New York
Unit: Company I, 82d New York Infantry
Battle or Place of Action: Bristoe Station, Virginia
Date of Action: 14 October 1863
Date of Issue: 1 December 1864
Citation: Capture of flag of 22d or 28th North Carolina (C.S.A.).

301 ◆ CUMMINGS, AMOS JAY

Rank: Sergeant Major
Service: U.S. Army
Birthday: 15 May 1838
Place of Birth: Conklin, Broome County, New York
Date of Death: 2 May 1902
Cemetery: Clinton Cemetery (MH)—Irvington, New Jersey
Entered Service at: Irvington, Essex County, New Jersey
Unit: 26th New Jersey Infantry
Battle or Place of Action: Salem Heights, Virginia
Date of Action: 4 May 1863
Date of Issue: 28 March 1894
Citation: Rendered great assistance in the heat of the action in rescuing a part of the field batteries from an extremely dangerous and exposed position.

302 ◆ CUMPSTON, JAMES M.

True Name: Compston, James M.
Rank: Private
Service: U.S. Army
Birthday: 1837
Place of Birth: Gallia County, Ohio
Date of Death: 24 May 1888
Place of Death: Coalton, Ohio
Cemetery: unknown cemetery—Coalton, Ohio
Entered Service at: Portsmouth, Scioto County, Ohio
Unit: Company D, 91st Ohio Infantry
Battle or Place of Action: Shenandoah Valley Campaign, Virginia
Date of Action: August-November 1864
Citation: Capture of flag.

303 ◆ CUNNINGHAM, FRANCIS MARION

Rank: First Sergeant (highest rank: First Lieutenant)
Service: U.S. Army
Birthday: 31 December 1837
Place of Birth: Somerset, Somerset County, Pennsylvania
Date of Death: 11 May 1919
Cemetery: Sugar Grove Cemetery—Ohiopyle, Pennsylvania
Entered Service at: Springfield, Delaware County, Pennsylvania
Unit: Company H, 1st West Virginia Cavalry
Battle or Place of Action: Deatonsville (Sailor's Creek), Virginia
Date of Action: 6 April 1865
Date of Issue: 3 May 1865

Citation: Capture of battle flag of 12th Virginia Infantry (C.S.A.) in hand-to-hand battle while wounded.

304 ◆ CUNNINGHAM, JAMES SMITH

Rank: Private
Service: U.S. Army
Birthday: 31 December 1840
Place of Birth: Washington County, Pennsylvania
Date of Death: 1 April 1921
Cemetery: Big Creek Cemetery—Burlington, Kansas
Entered Service at: Bloomington, McLean County, Illinois
Unit: Company D, 8th Missouri Infantry
Battle or Place of Action: Vicksburg, Mississippi
Date of Action: 22 May 1863
Date of Issue: 30 July 1894
Citation: Gallantry in the charge of the "volunteer storming party."

305 ◆ CURRAN, RICHARD J.

Rank: Assistant Surgeon (highest rank: Surgeon)
Service: U.S. Army
Birthday: 4 January 1834
Place of Birth: Ennis, County Clare, Ireland
Date of Death: 1 June 1915
Cemetery: Holy Sepulchre Cemetery (MH)—Rochester, New York
Entered Service at: Seneca Falls, Seneca County, New York
Unit: 33d New York Infantry
Battle or Place of Action: Antietam, Maryland
Date of Action: 17 September 1862
Date of Issue: 30 March 1898
Citation: Voluntarily exposed himself to great danger by going to the fighting line, there succoring the wounded and helpless, and conducting them to the field hospital.

306 ◆ CURTIS, JOHN CALVIN

Rank: Sergeant Major (highest rank: First Lieutenant)
Service: U.S. Army
Birthday: 19 April 1845
Place of Birth: Bridgeport, Fairfield County, Connecticut
Date of Death: 17 January 1917
Cemetery: Mountain Grove Cemetery (MH)—Bridgeport, Connecticut
Entered Service at: Bridgeport, Fairfield County, Connecticut
Unit: 9th Connecticut Infantry
Battle or Place of Action: Baton Rouge, Louisiana
Date of Action: 5 August 1862
Date of Issue: 16 December 1896
Citation: Voluntarily sought the line of battle and alone and unaided captured two prisoners, driving them before him to regimental headquarters at the point of the bayonet.

307 ◆ CURTIS, JOSIAH M.

Rank: Second Lieutenant (highest rank: First Lieutenant)
Service: U.S. Army

Birthday: 16 November 1844
Place of Birth: Ohio County, West Virginia
Date of Death: 17 June 1875
Place of Death: West Liberty, West Virginia
Cemetery: West Liberty Cemetery—West Liberty, West Virginia
Entered Service at: West Liberty, Ohio County, West Virginia
Unit: Company I, 12th West Virginia Infantry
Battle or Place of Action: Petersburg, Virginia
Date of Action: 2 April 1865
Date of Issue: 12 May 1865
Citation: Seized the colors of his regiment after two color bearers had fallen, bore them gallantly, and was among the first to gain a foothold, with his flag, inside the enemy's works.

308 ◆ CURTIS, NEWTON MARTIN

Rank: Brigadier General (highest rank: Major General)
Service: U.S. Army
Birthday: 21 May 1835
Place of Birth: De Peyster, St. Lawrence County, New York
Date of Death: 8 January 1910
Place of Death: New York, New York
Cemetery: Ogdensburg Cemetery—Ogdensburg, New York
Entered Service at: De Peyster, St. Lawrence County, New York
Unit: U.S. Volunteers
Battle or Place of Action: Fort Fisher, North Carolina
Date of Action: 15 January 1865
Date of Issue: 28 November 1891
Citation: The first man to pass through the stockade, he personally led each assault on the traverses and was four times wounded.

309 ◆ CUSTER, THOMAS WARD✚

Rank: Second Lieutenant (highest rank: Lieutenant Colonel)
Service: U.S. Army
Birthday: 15 March 1845
Place of Birth: New Rumley, Harrison County, Ohio
Date of Death: 25 June 1876
Place of Death: Little Big Horn, Montana
Cemetery: Fort Leavenworth Cemetery (H-1488)—Fort Leavenworth, Kansas
Entered Service at: Monroe, Monroe County, Michigan
Unit: Company B, 6th Michigan Cavalry
Battle or Place of Action: Willicomack (Namozine Church) & Deatonsville (Sailor's Creek), Virginia
Date of Action: 3 April 1865 & 6 April 1865
Date of Issue: 3 May 1865 & 26 May 1865
Citation: **First Award** Capture of flag on 3 April 1865.
Second Award Second Lt. Custer leaped his horse over the enemy's works and captured two stands of colors, having his horse shot from under him and receiving a severe wound.
Notes: ✚Double Awardee

310 ◆ CUTCHEON, BYRON M.

Rank: Major (highest rank: Brevet Brigadier General)
Service: U.S. Army
Birthday: 11 May 1836
Place of Birth: Pembroke, Suncook County, New Hampshire
Date of Death: 12 April 1908
Cemetery: Highland Cemetery—Ypsilanti, Michigan
Entered Service at: Ypsilanti, Washtenaw County, Michigan
Unit: 20th Michigan Infantry
Battle or Place of Action: Horseshoe Bend, Kentucky
Date of Action: 10 May 1863
Date of Issue: 29 June 1891
Citation: Distinguished gallantry in leading his regiment in a charge on a house occupied by the enemy.

311 ◆ CUTTS, JAMES MADISON

Rank: Captain (highest rank: Brevet Lieutenant Colonel)
Service: U.S. Army
Birthday: 1838
Place of Birth: Washington, D.C.
Date of Death: 24 February 1903
Cemetery: Arlington National Cemetery (3-1371-SS) (MH)—Arlington, Virginia
Entered Service at: Providence, Providence County, Rhode Island
Unit: 11th U.S. Infantry
Battle or Place of Action: Wilderness Campaign, Spotsylvania & Petersburg, Virginia
Date of Action: 1864
Date of Issue: 2 May 1891
Citation: Gallantry in actions.

312 ◆ DARROUGH, JOHN S.

Rank: Sergeant
Service: U.S. Army
Birthday: 6 April 1841
Place of Birth: Maysville, Mason County, Kentucky
Date of Death: 14 October 1920
Cemetery: Grand Army of the Republic Cemetery (MH)—Watseka, Illinois
Entered Service at: Concord, Morgan County, Illinois
Unit: Company F, 113th Illinois Infantry
Battle or Place of Action: Eastport, Mississippi
Date of Action: 10 October 1864
Date of Issue: 5 February 1895
Citation: Saved the life of a captain.

313 ◆ DAVIDSIZER, JOHN A.

Rank: Sergeant
Service: U.S. Army
Birthday: 26 April 1834
Place of Birth: Milford, Pike County, Pennsylvania
Date of Death: 19 October 1913
Place of Death: Lewistown, Pennsylvania
Cemetery: First Methodist Cemetery—Lewistown, Pennsylvania
Entered Service at: Lewistown, Mifflin County, Pennsylvania
Unit: Company A, 1st Pennsylvania Cavalry
Battle or Place of Action: Paine's Crossroads, Virginia
Date of Action: 5 April 1865
Date of Issue: 3 May 1865
Citation: Capture of flag.

314 ◆ DAVIDSON, ANDREW

Rank: Assistant Surgeon
Service: U.S. Army
Birthday: 1819
Place of Birth: Middlebury, Addison County, Vermont
Date of Death: 30 June 1901
Cemetery: Forest Rose Cemetery—Lancaster, Ohio
Entered Service at: Cincinnati, Hamilton County, Ohio
Unit: 47th Ohio Infantry
Battle or Place of Action: Vicksburg, Mississippi
Date of Action: 3 May 1863
Date of Issue: 17 October 1892
Citation: Voluntarily attempted to run the enemy's batteries.

315 ◆ DAVIDSON, ANDREW

Rank: First Lieutenant (highest rank: Colonel)
Service: U.S. Army
Birthday: 12 February 1840
Place of Birth: Morebattle, Roxburgshire, Scotland
Date of Death: 10 November 1902
Place of Death: Bath, New York
Cemetery: Lakewood Cemetery (MH)—Cooperstown, New York
Entered Service at: Middlefield, Otsego County, New York
Unit: Company H, 30th U.S. Colored Troops
Battle or Place of Action: Petersburg at the mine, Virginia
Date of Action: 30 July 1864
Date of Issue: 17 October 1892
Citation: One of the first to enter the enemy's works, where, after his colonel, major, and one-third of the company's officers had fallen, he gallantly assisted in rallying and saving the remnant of the command.

316 ◆ DAVIS, CHARLES C.

Rank: Major
Service: U.S. Army
Birthday: 15 August 1830
Place of Birth: Harrisburg, Dauphin County, Pennsylvania
Date of Death: 20 January 1909
Place of Death: Harrisburg, Pennsylvania
Cemetery: Harrisburg Cemetery—Harrisburg, Pennsylvania
Entered Service at: Harrisburg, Dauphin County, Pennsylvania
Unit: 7th Pennsylvania Cavalry
Battle or Place of Action: Shelbyville, Tennessee

Date of Action: 27 June 1863
Date of Issue: 14 June 1894
Citation: Led one of the most desperate and successful charges of the war.

317 ◆ DAVIS, FREEMAN

Rank: Sergeant (highest rank: Captain)
Service: U.S. Army
Birthday: 28 February 1842
Place of Birth: Newcomerstown, Tuscarawas County, Ohio
Date of Death: 23 February 1899
Place of Death: Butler, Missouri
Cemetery: Oak Hill Cemetery (MH)—Butler, Missouri
Entered Service at: Newcomerstown, Tuscarawas County, Ohio
Unit: Company B, 80th Ohio Infantry
Battle or Place of Action: Missionary Ridge, Tennessee
Date of Action: 25 November 1863
Date of Issue: 30 March 1898
Citation: This soldier, while his regiment was falling back, seeing the two color bearers shot down, under a severe fire and at imminent peril recovered both the flags and saved them from capture.

318 ◆ DAVIS, GEORGE EVANS

Rank: First Lieutenant (highest rank: Captain)
Service: U.S. Army
Birthday: 26 December 1839
Place of Birth: Dunstable, Middlesex County, Massachusetts
Date of Death: 28 June 1926
Place of Death: Soldier's Home, Burlington, Vermont
Cemetery: Lake View Cemetery (MH)—Burlington, Vermont
Entered Service at: Burlington, Chittenden County, Vermont
Unit: Company D, 10th Vermont Infantry
Battle or Place of Action: Monocacy, Maryland
Date of Action: 9 July 1864
Date of Issue: 27 May 1892
Citation: While in command of a small force, held the approaches to the two bridges against repeated assaults of superior numbers, thereby materially delaying Early's advance on Washington.

319 ◆ DAVIS, HARRY CLAY

Rank: Private (highest rank: Corporal)
Service: U.S. Army
Birthday: 5 February 1841
Place of Birth: Franklin County, Ohio
Date of Death: 9 July 1929
Place of Death: Pomona, California
Cemetery: Pomona Cemetery—Pomona, California
Entered Service at: Columbus, Franklin County, Ohio
Unit: Company G, 46th Ohio Infantry
Battle or Place of Action: Atlanta, Georgia
Date of Action: 28 July 1864

Date of Issue: 2 December 1864
Citation: Capture of flag of 30th Louisiana Infantry (C.S.A.).

320 ◆ DAVIS, JOHN

Rank: Quarter Gunner
Service: U.S. Navy
Place of Birth: Cedarville, Cumberland County, New Jersey
Entered Service at: New Jersey
Unit: U.S.S. *Valley City*
Battle or Place of Action: off Elizabeth City, North Carolina
Date of Action: 10 February 1862
G.O. Number, Date: 11, 3 April 1863
Citation: Served on board the U.S.S. *Valley City* during action against rebel fort batteries and ships off Elizabeth City, N.C., 10 February 1862. When a shell from the shore penetrated the side and passed through the magazine, exploding outside the screen on the berth deck, several powder divisions protecting bulkheads were torn to pieces and the forward part of the berth deck set on fire. Showing great presence of mind, Davis courageously covered a barrel of powder with his own body and prevented an explosion, while at the same time passing powder to provide the division on the upper deck while under fierce enemy fire.

321 ◆ DAVIS, JOHN

Rank: Private
Service: U.S. Army
Birthday: 1838
Place of Birth: Carroll, Kentucky
Date of Death: 30 December 1901
Place of Death: Cotopaxi, Colorado
Cemetery: unknown cemetery—Cotopaxi, Colorado (Now an abandoned town.)
Entered Service at: Indanapolis, Marion County, Indiana
Unit: Company F, 17th Indiana Mounted Infantry
Battle or Place of Action: Culloden, Georgia
Date of Action: April 1865
Date of Issue: 17 June 1865
Citation: Capture of flag of Worrill Grays (C.S.A.).
Notes: POW

322 ◆ DAVIS, JOSEPH

Rank: Corporal
Service: U.S. Army
Birthday: 22 May 1838
Place of Birth: Monmouth County, Wales
Entered Service at: East Palestine, Columbiana County, Ohio
Unit: Company C, 104th Ohio Infantry
Battle or Place of Action: Franklin, Tennessee
Date of Action: 30 October 1864
Date of Issue: 4 February 1865
Citation: Capture of flag.

323 ◆ DAVIS, MARTIN K.

Rank: Sergeant
Service: U.S. Army
Birthday: 12 March 1843
Place of Birth: Marion, Williamson County, Illinois
Date of Death: 14 December 1936
Cemetery: Demorest Cemetery (MH)—Demorest, Georgia
Entered Service at: Stonington, Christian County, Illinois
Unit: Company H, 116th Illinois Infantry
Battle or Place of Action: Vicksburg, Mississippi
Date of Action: 22 May 1863
Date of Issue: 26 July 1894
Citation: Gallantry in the charge of the "volunteer storming party."

324 ◆ DAVIS, SAMUEL W.

Rank: Ordinary Seaman
Service: U.S. Navy
Birthday: 1845
Place of Birth: Brewer, Penobscot County, Maine
Entered Service at: Maine
Unit: U.S.S. *Brooklyn*
Battle or Place of Action: Mobile Bay, Alabama
Date of Action: 5 August 1864
G.O. Number, Date: 45, 31 December 1864
Citation: On board the U.S.S. *Brooklyn* during successful attacks against Fort Morgan, rebel gunboats and the ram *Tennessee* in Mobile Bay, 5 August 1864. Despite severe damage to his ship and the loss of several men on board as enemy fire raked the decks from stem to stern, Davis exercised extreme courage and vigilance while acting as a lookout for torpedoes and other obstructions throughout the furious battle which resulted in the surrender of the prize rebel ram *Tennessee* and in the damaging and destruction of batteries at Fort Morgan.

325 ◆ DAVIS, THOMAS

Rank: Private
Service: U.S. Army
Birthday: 11 December 1837
Place of Birth: Haverford, West Wales
Date of Death: 24 March 1919
Place of Death: Brooklyn, New York
Cemetery: Mount Olivet Cemetery—Brooklyn, New York
Entered Service at: New York, New York
Unit: Company C, 2d New York Heavy Artillery
Battle or Place of Action: Deatonsville (Sailor's Creek), Virginia
Date of Action: 6 April 1865
Date of Issue: 3 May 1865
Citation: Capture of flag.

326 ◆ DAY, CHARLES

Rank: Private
Service: U.S. Army

Birthday: 28 May 1844
Place of Birth: West Laurens, Otsego County, New York
Date of Death: 29 July 1901
Place of Death: Lambs Creek, Pennsylvania
Cemetery: Prospect Cemetery (MH)—Mansfield, Pennsylvania
Entered Service at: Richmond, Philadelphia County, Pennsylvania
Unit: Company K, 210th Pennsylvania Infantry
Battle or Place of Action: Hatcher's Run, Virginia
Date of Action: 6 February 1865
Date of Issue: 20 July 1897
Citation: Seized the colors of another regiment of the brigade, the regiment having been thrown into confusion and the color bearer killed, and bore said colors throughout the remainder of the engagement.

327 ◆ DAY, DAVID FRAKES

Rank: Private
Service: U.S. Army
Birthday: 7 March 1847
Place of Birth: Dallasburg, Ohio
Date of Death: 22 June 1914
Place of Death: Durango, Colorado
Cemetery: Riverside Cemetery (MH)—Denver, Colorado
Entered Service at: Cincinnati, Hamilton County, Ohio
Unit: Company D, 57th Ohio Infantry
Battle or Place of Action: Vicksburg, Mississippi
Date of Action: 22 May 1863
Date of Issue: 2 January 1895
Citation: Gallantry in the charge of the "volunteer storming party."

328 ◆ DEAKIN, CHARLES

Rank: Boatswain's Mate
Service: U.S. Navy
Birthday: 1837
Place of Birth: New York, New York
Entered Service at: Philadelphia, Philadelphia County, Pennsylvania
Unit: U.S.S. *Richmond*
Battle or Place of Action: Mobile Bay, Alabama
Date of Action: 5 August 1864
G.O. Number, Date: 45, 31 December 1864
Citation: As captain of a gun on board the U.S.S. *Richmond* during action against rebel forts and gunboats and with the ram *Tennessee* in Mobile Bay, 5 August 1864. Despite damage to his ship and the loss of several men on board as enemy fire raked her decks, Deakin fought his gun with skill and courage throughout a furious two-hour battle which resulted in the surrender of the rebel ram *Tennessee* and in the damaging and destruction of batteries at Fort Morgan. He also participated in the actions at Forts Jackson and St. Philip.

329 ◆ DEANE, JOHN MILTON

Rank: Major
Service: U.S. Army

Birthday: 8 January 1840
Place of Birth: Assonet Village, Bristol County, Massachusetts
Date of Death: 2 September 1914
Cemetery: Assonet Burial Grounds (MH)—Freetown, Massachusetts
Entered Service at: Freetown, Bristol County, Massachusetts
Unit: 29th Massachusetts Infantry
Battle or Place of Action: Fort Stedman, Virginia
Date of Action: 25 March 1865
Date of Issue: 8 March 1895
Citation: This officer, observing an abandoned gun within Fort Haskell, called for volunteers, and under a heavy fire, worked the gun until the enemy's advancing line was routed.

330 ◆ DECASTRO, JOSEPH H.

Rank: Corporal (highest rank: Sergeant)
Service: U.S. Army
Birthday: 14 November 1844
Place of Birth: Boston, Suffolk County, Massachusetts
Date of Death: 8 May 1892
Place of Death: New York, New York
Cemetery: Fairmount Cemetery (MH)—Newark, New Jersey
Entered Service at: Boston, Suffolk County, Massachusetts
Unit: Company I, 19th Massachusetts Infantry
Battle or Place of Action: Gettysburg, Pennsylvania
Date of Action: 3 July 1863
Date of Issue: 1 December 1864
Citation: Capture of flag of 19th Virginia regiment (C.S.A.).

331 ◆ DELACEY, PATRICK

Rank: First Sergeant (highest rank: Second Lieutenant)
Service: U.S. Army
Birthday: 25 November 1835
Place of Birth: Carbondale, Lackawanna County, Pennsylvania
Date of Death: 27 April 1915
Place of Death: Scranton, Pennsylvania
Cemetery: St. Catherine's Cemetery (MH)—Moscow, Pennsylvania
Entered Service at: Scranton, Lackawanna County, Pennsylvania
Unit: Company A, 143d Pennsylvania Infantry
Battle or Place of Action: Wilderness Campaign, Virginia
Date of Action: 6 May 1864
Date of Issue: 24 April 1894
Citation: Running ahead of the line, under a concentrated fire, he shot the color bearer of a Confederate regiment on the works, thus contributing to the success of the attack.

332 ◆ DELAND, FREDERICK NELSON

Rank: Private
Service: U.S. Army
Birthday: 25 December 1843

Place of Birth: Sheffield, Berkshire County, Massachusetts
Date of Death: 23 August 1922
Place of Death: Pittsfield, Massachusetts
Cemetery: Mahaiwe Cemetery (MH)—Great Barrington, Massachusetts
Entered Service at: Great Barrington, Berkshire County, Massachusetts
Unit: Company B, 49th Massachusetts Infantry
Battle or Place of Action: Port Hudson, Louisiana
Date of Action: 27 May 1863
Date of Issue: 22 June 1896
Citation: Volunteered in response to a call and, under a heavy fire from the enemy, advanced and assisted in filling with fascines a ditch which presented a serious obstacle to the troops attempting to take the works of the enemy by assault.

333 ◆ DELANEY, JOHN CARROLL

Rank: Sergeant (highest rank: Brevet Captain)
Service: U.S. Army
Birthday: 22 April 1848
Place of Birth: Ireland
Date of Death: 4 April 1915
Cemetery: Arlington National Cemetery (3-2170-WS)—Arlington, Virginia
Entered Service at: Honesdale, Wayne County, Pennsylvania
Unit: Company I, 107th Pennsylvania Infantry
Battle or Place of Action: Danby's Mills, Virginia
Date of Action: 6 February 1865
Date of Issue: 29 August 1894
Citation: Sprang between the lines and brought out a wounded comrade about to be burned in the brush.

334 ◆ DELAVIE, HIRAM H.

True Name: Delavie, Hiram A.
Rank: Sergeant (highest rank: First Sergeant)
Service: U.S. Army
Place of Birth: Stark County, Ohio
Entered Service at: Allegheny County, Pennsylvania
Unit: Company I, 11th Pennsylvania Infantry (Washington Blues)
Battle or Place of Action: Five Forks, Virginia
Date of Action: 1 April 1865
Date of Issue: 10 May 1865
Citation: Capture of flag.

335 ◆ DEMPSTER, JOHN

Rank: Coxswain
Service: U.S. Navy
Birthday: 1839
Place of Birth: Scotland
Entered Service at: Philadelphia, Philadelphia County, Pennsylvania
Unit: U.S.S. *New Ironsides*
Battle or Place of Action: Fort Fisher, North Carolina
Date of Action: 24-25 December 1864 & 13-15 January 1865

G.O. Number, Date: 59, 22 June 1865
Citation: Dempster served on board the U.S.S. *New Ironsides* during action in several attacks on Fort Fisher, 24 and 25 December 1864; and 13, 14, and 15 January 1865. The ship steamed in and took the lead in the ironclad division close inshore and immediately opened its starboard battery in a barrage of well-directed fire to cause several fires and explosions and dismount several guns during the first two days of fighting. Taken under fire as she steamed into position on 13 January, the *New Ironsides* fought all day and took on ammunition at night despite severe weather conditions. When the enemy came out of his bomb-proofs to defend the fort against the storming party, the ship's battery disabled nearly every gun on the fort facing the shore before the cease-fire orders were given by the flagship.

336 ◆ DENIG, J. HENRY

Rank: Sergeant
Service: U.S. Marine Corps
Birthday: 1839
Place of Birth: York, York County, Pennsylvania
Entered Service at: Pennsylvania
Unit: U.S.S. *Brooklyn*
Battle or Place of Action: Mobile Bay, Alabama
Date of Action: 5 August 1864
G.O. Number, Date: 45, 31 December 1864
Citation: On board the U.S.S. *Brooklyn* during action against rebel forts and gunboats and with the ram *Tennessee*, in Mobile Bay, 5 August 1864. Despite severe damage to his ship and the loss of several men on board as enemy fire raked the decks, Sgt. Denig fought his gun with skill and courage throughout the furious two-hour battle which resulted in the surrender of the rebel ram *Tennessee* and in the damaging and destruction of batteries at Fort Morgan.

337 ◆ *DENNING, LORENZO

True Name: Deming, Lorenzo
Rank: Landsman
Service: U.S. Navy
Birthday: 6 September 1843
Place of Birth: Granby, Hartford County, Connecticut
Date of Death: 8 February 1865
Place of Death: Salisbury Prison, North Carolina
Cemetery: Salisbury National Cemetery—Salisbury, North Carolina (One of 11,700 unknowns buried in a long trench.)
Entered Service at: New Britain, Hartford County, Connecticut
Unit: U.S. Picket Boat No. 1
Battle or Place of Action: Plymouth, North Carolina
Date of Action: 27 October 1864
G.O. Number, Date: 45, 31 December 1864
Citation: Denning served on board the U.S. Picket Boat No. 1 in action, 27 October 1864, against the Confederate ram *Albemarle* which had resisted repeated attacks by our steamers and had kept a large force of vessels employed in watching her. The picket boat, equipped with a spar torpedo, succeeded in passing the enemy pickets within 20 yards without being discovered and then made for the *Albemarle* under a full head of steam. Immediately taken under fire by the ram, the small boat plunged on, jumped the log boom which encircled the target and exploded its torpedo under the port bow of the ram. The picket boat was destroyed by enemy fire and almost the entire crew was taken prisoner or lost.
Notes: POW

338 ◆ DENNIS, RICHARD

Rank: Boatswain's Mate
Service: U.S. Navy
Birthday: 1826
Place of Birth: Charlestown, Suffolk County, Massachusetts
Entered Service at: Boston, Suffolk County, Massachusetts
Unit: U.S.S. *Brooklyn*
Battle or Place of Action: Mobile Bay, Alabama
Date of Action: 5 August 1864
G.O. Number, Date: 45, 31 December 1864
Citation: On board the U.S.S. *Brooklyn* during successful attacks against Fort Morgan, rebel gunboats and the ram *Tennessee* in Mobile Bay, 5 August 1864. Despite severe damage to his ship and the loss of several men on board as enemy fire raked her decks from stem to stern, Dennis displayed outstanding skill and courage in operating the torpedo catcher and in assisting in working the bow chasers throughout the furious battle which resulted in the surrender of the prize rebel ram *Tennessee* and in the damaging and destruction of batteries at Fort Morgan.

339 ◆ DENSMORE, WILLIAM

Rank: Chief Boatswain's Mate
Service: U.S. Navy
Birthday: 1843
Place of Birth: New York
Date of Death: 17 June 1865
Place of Death: Philadelphia (Naval Hospital), Pennsylvania
Cemetery: unknown cemetery—Philadelphia, Pennsylvania
Entered Service at: New York
Unit: U.S.S. *Richmond*
Battle or Place of Action: Mobile Bay, Alabama
Date of Action: 5 August 1864
G.O. Number, Date: 45, 31 December 1864
Citation: As captain of a gun on board the U.S.S. *Richmond* during action against rebel forts and gunboats and with the ram *Tennessee* in Mobile Bay, 5 August 1864. Despite damage to his ship and the loss of several men on board as enemy fire raked her decks, Densmore fought his gun with skill and courage throughout a furious two-hour battle, which resulted in the surrender of the rebel ram *Tennessee* and in the damaging and destruction of batteries at Fort Morgan.

340 ◆ DEPUY, CHARLES H.

Rank: First Sergeant
Service: U.S. Army
Birthday: 8 September 1842
Place of Birth: Sherman, Michigan

Date of Death: 6 January 1935
Cemetery: Evergreen Cemetery—Kalkaska, Michigan
Entered Service at: St. Louis, St. Louis County, Missouri
Unit: Company H, 1st Michigan Sharpshooters
Battle or Place of Action: Petersburg, Virginia
Date of Action: 30 July 1864
Date of Issue: 30 July 1896
Citation: Being an old artillerist, De Puy aided Gen. Bartlett in working the guns of the dismantled fort.
Notes: POW

341 ◆ DEWITT, RICHARD WILLIS

Rank: Corporal (highest rank: Sergeant)
Service: U.S. Army
Birthday: 25 June 1838
Place of Birth: Butler County, Ohio
Date of Death: 16 September 1909
Place of Death: Terre Haute, Indiana
Cemetery: Oxford Cemetery—Oxford, Ohio
Entered Service at: Oxford, Butler County, Ohio
Unit: Company D, 47th Ohio Infantry
Battle or Place of Action: Vicksburg, Mississippi
Date of Action: 22 May 1863
Date of Issue: 10 August 1894
Citation: Gallantry in the charge of the "volunteer storming party."

342 ◆ DI CESNOLA, LOUIS PALMA

Rank: Colonel (highest rank: Brevet Brigadier General)
Service: U.S. Army
Birthday: 29 June 1832
Place of Birth: Rivarola, Piedmont, Italy
Date of Death: 20 November 1904
Cemetery: Kensico Cemetery—Valhalla, New York
Entered Service at: New York, New York
Unit: 4th New York Cavalry
Battle or Place of Action: Aldie, Virginia
Date of Action: 17 June 1863
Date of Issue: 6 December 1897
Citation: Was present, in arrest, when, seeing his regiment fall back, he rallied his men, accompanied them, without arms, in a second charge, and in recognition of his gallantry was released from arrest. He continued in the action at the head of his regiment until he was desperately wounded and taken prisoner.
Notes: POW

343 ◆ DICKEY, WILLIAM DONALDSON

Rank: Captain (highest rank: Colonel)
Service: U.S. Army
Birthday: 11 January 1845
Place of Birth: Newburgh, Orange County, New York
Date of Death: 14 May 1924
Place of Death: Brooklyn, New York
Cemetery: The Green Wood Cemetery—Brooklyn, New York

Entered Service at: Newburgh, Orange County, New York
Unit: Battery M, 15th New York Heavy Artillery
Battle or Place of Action: Petersburg, Virginia
Date of Action: 17 June 1864
Date of Issue: 10 June 1896
Citation: Refused to leave the field, remaining in command after being wounded by a piece of shell, and led his command in the assault on the enemy's works on the following day.

344 ◆ DICKIE, DAVID

Rank: Sergeant
Service: U.S. Army
Birthday: 13 July 1841
Place of Birth: Scotland
Date of Death: 26 August 1904
Cemetery: Gillespie Cemetery (MH)—Gillespie, Illinois
Entered Service at: Gillespie, Macoupin County, Illinois
Unit: Company A, 97th Illinois Infantry
Battle or Place of Action: Vicksburg, Mississippi
Date of Action: 22 May 1863
Date of Issue: 29 January 1896
Citation: Gallantry in the charge of the "volunteer storming party."

345 ◆ DIGGINS, BARTHOLOMEW

Rank: Ordinary Seaman
Service: U.S. Navy
Birthday: 9 October 1844
Place of Birth: Baltimore, Baltimore County, Maryland
Date of Death: 23 February 1917
Place of Death: Washington, D.C.
Cemetery: Arlington National Cemetery (13-5400-15)—Arlington, Virginia
Entered Service at: Maryland
Unit: U.S.S. *Hartford*
Battle or Place of Action: Mobile Bay, Alabama
Date of Action: 5 August 1864
G.O. Number, Date: 391, 12 November 1891
Citation: On board the flagship U.S.S. *Hartford*, during action against rebel forts and gunboats and with the ram *Tennessee* in Mobile Bay, 5 August 1864. Despite damage to his ship and the loss of several men on board as enemy fire raked her decks, Diggins as loader of a gun remained steadfast at his post throughout the furious two-hour battle which resulted in the surrender of the rebel ram *Tennessee* and in the damaging and destruction of batteries at Fort Morgan.

346 ◆ DILGER, HUBERT

Rank: Captain
Service: U.S. Army
Birthday: 5 March 1836
Place of Birth: Germany
Date of Death: 14 May 1911
Place of Death: near Front Royal, Virginia
Cemetery: Rock Creek Cemetery—Washington, D.C.

Entered Service at: New York, New York
Unit: Battery I, 1st Ohio Light Artillery
Battle or Place of Action: Chancellorsville, Virginia
Date of Action: 2 May 1863
Date of Issue: 17 August 1893
Citation: Fought his guns until the enemy were upon him, then with one gun hauled in the road by hand he formed the rear guard and kept the enemy at bay by the rapidity of his fire and was the last man in the retreat.

347 ◆ DILLON, MICHAEL A.

Rank: Private
Service: U.S. Army
Birthday: 29 September 1839
Place of Birth: Chelmsford, Middlesex County, Massachusetts
Date of Death: 6 October 1904
Cemetery: Arlington National Cemetery (13-14660)— Arlington, Virginia
Entered Service at: Wilton, Hillsborough County, New Hampshire
Unit: Company G, 2d New Hampshire Infantry
Battle or Place of Action: Williamsburg & Oak Grove, Virginia
Date of Action: 5 May & 25 June 1862
Date of Issue: 10 October 1889
Citation: Bravery in repulsing the enemy's charge on a battery, at Williamsburg, Va. At Oak Grove, Va., crawled outside the lines and brought in important information.

348 ◆ DITZENBACK, JOHN

Rank: Quartermaster
Service: U.S. Navy
Birthday: 1828
Place of Birth: New York, New York
Entered Service at: Indiana
Unit: U.S. Monitor *Neosho*
Battle or Place of Action: near Nashville, Tennessee
Date of Action: 6 December 1864
G.O. Number, Date: 59, 22 June 1865
Citation: Served on board the U.S. Monitor *Neosho* during the engagement with enemy batteries at Bells Mills, Cumberland River, near Nashville, Tenn., 6 December 1864. Carrying out his duties courageously during the engagement, Ditzenback gallantly left the pilot house after the flag and signal staffs of that vessel had been shot away and, taking the flag which was drooping over the wheelhouse, made it fast to the stump of the highest mast remaining, although the ship was still under a heavy fire from the enemy.

349 ◆ DOCKUM, WARREN C.

Rank: Private
Service: U.S. Army
Birthday: 1 January 1844
Place of Birth: Clintonville, Clinton County, New York

Date of Death: 2 October 1921
Place of Death: Colorado Springs, Colorado
Cemetery: Rosemont Cemetery (MH)—Pueblo, Colorado
Entered Service at: Plattsburgh, Clinton County, New York
Unit: Company H, 121st New York Infantry
Battle or Place of Action: Deatonsville (Sailor's Creek), Virginia
Date of Action: 6 April 1865
Date of Issue: 10 May 1865
Citation: Capture of flag of Savannah Guards (C.S.A.), after two other men had been killed in the effort.

350 ◆ DODD, ROBERT FULTON

Rank: Private (highest rank: Corporal)
Service: U.S. Army
Birthday: 1845
Place of Birth: Canada
Date of Death: 4 September 1903
Place of Death: Winnipeg, Canada
Entered Service at: Detroit, Wayne County, Michigan
Unit: Company E, 27th Michigan Infantry
Battle or Place of Action: Petersburg, Virginia
Date of Action: 30 July 1864
Date of Issue: 27 July 1896
Citation: While acting as orderly, voluntarily assisted to carry off the wounded from the ground in front of the crater while exposed to a heavy fire.

351 ◆ DODDS, EDWARD EDWIN

Rank: Sergeant
Service: U.S. Army
Birthday: 1845
Place of Birth: Canada
Date of Death: 12 January 1901
Place of Death: Port Hope, Canada
Cemetery: Canton Cemetery (MH)—Porthope, Ontario, Canada
Entered Service at: Rochester, Monroe County, New York
Unit: Company C, 21st New York Cavalry
Battle or Place of Action: Ashbys Gap, Virginia
Date of Action: 19 July 1864
Date of Issue: 11 June 1896
Citation: At great personal risk rescued his wounded captain and carried him from the field to a place of safety.

352 ◆ DOLLOFF, CHARLES W.

Rank: Corporal (highest rank: Sergeant)
Service: U.S. Army
Birthday: 10 May 1844
Place of Birth: Parishville, St. Lawrence County, New York
Date of Death: 2 August 1884
Place of Death: near Canton, Wisconsin
Cemetery: Forest Cemetery—Stevens Point, Wisconsin
Entered Service at: St. Johnsbury, Caledonia County, Vermont

Unit: Company K, 1st Vermont Heavy Artillery
Battle or Place of Action: Petersburg, Virginia
Date of Action: 2 April 1865
Date of Issue: 10 May 1865
Citation: Capture of flag.

353 ◆ DONALDSON, JOHN P.

Rank: Sergeant (highest rank: Commissary Sergeant)
Service: U.S. Army
Birthday: 14 August 1842
Place of Birth: Butler County, Pennsylvania
Date of Death: 7 January 1920
Place of Death: Dubuque, Iowa
Cemetery: Mars Hill Cemetery—Floris, Iowa
Entered Service at: Butler, Butler County, Pennsylvania
Unit: Company L, 4th Pennsylvania Cavalry
Battle or Place of Action: Appomattox Courthouse, Virginia
Date of Action: 9 April 1865
Date of Issue: 3 May 1865
Citation: Capture of flag of 14th Virginia Cavalry (C.S.A.).

354 ◆ DONNELLY, JOHN C.

Rank: Ordinary Seaman
Service: U.S. Navy
Birthday: 1839
Place of Birth: England
Date of Death: 1895
Entered Service at: New York, New York
Unit: U.S.S. *Metacomet*
Battle or Place of Action: Mobile Bay, Alabama
Date of Action: 5 August 1864
G.O. Number, Date: 71, 15 January 1866
Citation: Served on board the U.S.S. *Metacomet*. As a member of the boat's crew which went to the rescue of the U.S. Monitor *Tecumseh* when that vessel was struck by a torpedo in passing the enemy forts in Mobile Bay, 5 August 1864, Donnelly braved the enemy fire, which was said by the admiral to be "one of the most galling" he had ever seen, and aided in rescuing from death 10 of the crew of the *Tecumseh*, eliciting the admiration of both friend and foe.

355 ◆ DONOGHUE, TIMOTHY

True Name: Donahue, Timothy
Rank: Private
Service: U.S. Army
Birthday: 17 March 1825
Place of Birth: Ireland
Date of Death: 19 March 1908
Cemetery: Holy Cross Cemetery—Brooklyn, New York
Entered Service at: New York, New York
Unit: Company B, 69th New York Infantry
Battle or Place of Action: Fredericksburg, Virginia
Date of Action: 13 December 1862
Date of Issue: 17 January 1894
Citation: Voluntarily carried a wounded officer off the field from between the lines; while doing this he was himself wounded.

356 ◆ DOODY, PATRICK H.

Rank: Corporal (highest rank: First Lieutenant)
Service: U.S. Army
Birthday: 7 July 1840
Place of Birth: Ireland
Date of Death: 5 March 1924
Place of Death: Brooklyn, New York
Cemetery: 1st Calvary Cemetery—Woodside, New York
Entered Service at: New York, New York
Unit: Company E, 164th New York Infantry
Battle or Place of Action: Cold Harbor, Virginia
Date of Action: 7 June 1864
Date of Issue: 13 December 1893
Citation: After making a successful personal reconnaissance, he gallantly led the skirmishers in a night attack, charging the enemy, and thus enabling the pioneers to put up works.

357 ◆ DOOLEN, WILLIAM

Rank: Coal Heaver
Service: U.S. Navy
Birthday: 1841
Place of Birth: Ireland
Date of Death: 14 September 1895
Cemetery: unknown cemetery—Egbert, Wyoming
Entered Service at: Philadelphia, Philadelphia County, Pennsylvania
Unit: U.S.S. *Richmond*
Battle or Place of Action: Mobile Bay, Alabama
Date of Action: 5 August 1864
G.O. Number, Date: 45, 31 December 1864
Citation: On board the U.S.S. *Richmond* during action against rebel forts and gunboats and with the ram *Tennessee* in Mobile Bay, 5 August 1864. Although knocked down and seriously wounded in the head, Doolen refused to leave his station as shot and shell passed. Calm and courageous, he rendered gallant service throughout the prolonged battle, which resulted in the surrender of the rebel ram *Tennessee* and in the successful attacks carried out on Fort Morgan despite the enemy's heavy return fire.

358 ◆ DORE, GEORGE H.

Rank: Sergeant
Service: U.S. Army
Birthday: 24 June 1845
Place of Birth: England
Date of Death: 8 February 1927
Place of Death: Hornell, New York
Cemetery: Hope Cemetery—Hornell, New York
Entered Service at: West Bloomfield, Ontario County, New York
Unit: Company D, 126th New York Infantry
Battle or Place of Action: Gettysburg, Pennsylvania

Date of Action: 3 July 1863
Date of Issue: 1 Decembeer 1864
Citation: The colors being struck down by a shell as the enemy were charging, this soldier rushed out and seized it, exposing himself to the fire of both sides.

359 ◆ DORLEY, AUGUST

True Name: Doerle, August
Rank: Private
Service: U.S. Army
Birthday: 1842
Place of Birth: Germany
Date of Death: 17 October 1867
Cemetery: Natchez City Cemetery (MH)—Natchez, Mississippi
Entered Service at: Natchez, Adams County, Mississippi
Unit: Company B, 1st Louisiana Cavalry
Battle or Place of Action: Mount Pleasant, Alabama
Date of Action: 11 April 1865
Citation: Capture of flag.

360 ◆ DORMAN, JOHN HENRY

Rank: Seaman
Service: U.S. Navy
Birthday: 18 September 1843
Place of Birth: Cincinnati, Hamilton County, Ohio
Date of Death: 29 May 1921
Place of Death: Dayton, Ohio
Cemetery: Spring Grove Cemetery—Cincinnati, Ohio
Entered Service at: Cincinnati, Hamilton County, Ohio
Unit: U.S.S. *Carondelet*
Battle or Place of Action: Fort Henry, Tennessee & Vicksburg, Mississippi
Date of Action: 6 February 1862 & 22 May 1863
G.O. Number, Date: 32, 18 April 1864
Citation: Served on board the U.S.S. *Carondelet* in various actions of that vessel. Carrying out his duties courageously throughout the actions of the *Carondelet*, Dorman, although wounded several times, invariably returned to duty and constantly presented an example of devotion to the flag.

361 ◆ DORSEY, DANIEL ALLEN

Rank: Corporal (highest rank: First Lieutenant)
Service: U.S. Army
Birthday: 31 December 1838
Place of Birth: Lancaster, Fairfield County, Ohio
Date of Death: 10 May 1918
Place of Death: Leavenworth, Kansas
Cemetery: Leavenworth National Cemetery (11-19-8) (MH)—Leavenworth, Kansas
Entered Service at: Chillicothe, Ross County, Ohio
Unit: Company H, 33d Ohio Infantry
Battle or Place of Action: Georgia
Date of Action: April 1862
Date of Issue: 17 September 1863

Citation: One of 19 of 24 men (including two civilians) who, by direction of Gen. Ormsby M. Mitchell, penetrated nearly 200 miles south into enemy territory and captured a railroad train at Big Shanty, Ga., in an attempt to destroy the bridges and track between Chattanaooga and Atlanta.

362 ◆ DORSEY, DECATUR

Rank: Sergeant (highest rank: First Sergeant)
Service: U.S. Army
Birthday: 1836
Place of Birth: Howard County, Maryland
Date of Death: 11 July 1891
Place of Death: Hoboken, New Jersey
Cemetery: Flower Hill Cemetery (MH)—North Bergen, New Jersey
Entered Service at: Baltimore, Baltimore County, Maryland
Unit: Company B, 39th U.S. Colored Infantry
Battle or Place of Action: Petersburg, Virginia
Date of Action: 30 July 1864
Date of Issue: 8 November 1865
Citation: Planted his colors on the Confederate works in advance of his regiment, and when the regiment was driven back to the Union works he carried the colors there and bravely rallied the men.

363 ◆ DOUGALL, ALLAN HOUSTON

Rank: First Lieutenant & Adjutant
Service: U.S. Army
Birthday: 17 July 1836
Place of Birth: Scotland
Date of Death: 22 May 1912
Place of Death: Fort Wayne, Indiana
Cemetery: I.O.O.F. Cemetery—New Haven, Indiana
Entered Service at: New Haven, Allen County, Indiana
Unit: 88th Indiana Infantry
Battle or Place of Action: Bentonville, North Carolina
Date of Action: 19 March 1865
Date of Issue: 16 February 1897
Citation: In the face of a galling fire from the enemy he voluntarily returned to where the color bearer had fallen wounded and saved the flag of his regiment from capture.

364 ◆ DOUGHERTY, MICHAEL

Rank: Private
Service: U.S. Army
Birthday: 10 May 1844
Place of Birth: Falcarragh, County Donegal, Ireland
Date of Death: 19 February 1930
Place of Death: Bristol, Pennsylvania
Cemetery: St. Mark's Cemetery (MH)—Bristol, Pennsylvania
Entered Service at: Philadelphia, Philadelphia County, Pennsylvania
Unit: Company B, 13th Pennsylvania Cavalry (Volunteers 117th Regiment)
Battle or Place of Action: Jefferson, Virginia

Date of Action: 12 October 1863
Date of Issue: 23 January 1897
Citation: At the head of a detachment of his company, he dashed across an open field, exposed to a deadly fire from the enemy, and succeeded in dislodging them from an unoccupied house, which he and his comrades defended for several hours against repeated attacks, thus preventing the enemy from flanking the position of the Union forces.
Notes: POW

365 ◆ DOUGHERTY, PATRICK

Rank: Landsman
Service: U.S. Navy
Birthday: 1844
Place of Birth: Ireland
Entered Service at: New York, New York
Unit: U.S.S. *Lackawanna*
Battle or Place of Action: Fort Morgan, Mobile Bay, Alabama
Date of Action: 5 August 1864
G.O. Number, Date: 45, 31 December 1864
Citation: As a landsman on board the U.S.S. *Lackawanna*, Dougherty acted gallantly without orders when the powder boy at his gun was disabled under the heavy enemy fire, and maintained a supply of powder throughout the prolonged action. Dougherty also aided in the attacks on Fort Morgan and in the capture of the prize ram *Tennessee.*

366 ◆ DOW, GEORGE P.

Rank: Sergeant (highest rank: First Sergeant)
Service: U.S. Army
Birthday: 7 August 1840
Place of Birth: Atkinson, Rockingham County, New Hampshire
Date of Death: 28 September 1910
Cemetery: Old Cemetery—Atkinson, New Hampshire
Entered Service at: Manchester, Hillsborough County, New hampshire
Unit: Company C, 7th New Hampshire Infantry
Battle or Place of Action: near Richmond, Virginia
Date of Action: October 1864
Date of Issue: 10 May 1884
Citation: Gallantry while in command of his company during a reconnaissance toward Richmond.

367 ◆ DOW, HENRY

Rank: Boatswain's Mate
Service: U.S. Navy
Birthday: 1840
Place of Birth: Scotland
Entered Service at: Illinois
Unit: U.S.S. *Cincinnati*
Battle or Place of Action: Vicksburg, Mississippi
Date of Action: 27 May 1863
G.O. Number, Date: 17, 10 July 1863

Citation: Served on board the U.S.S. *Cincinnati* during the attack on the Vicksburg batteries and at the time of her sinking, 27 May 1863. Engaging the enemy in a fierce battle, the *Cincinnati*, amidst an incessant fire of shot and shell, continued to fire her guns to the last, though so penetrated by enemy shellfire that her fate was sealed. Serving courageously throughout this action, Dow carried out his duties to the end on this proud ship that went down with "her colors nailed to the mast."

368 ◆ DOWNEY, WILLIAM

Rank: Private
Service: U.S. Army
Birthday: 1832
Place of Birth: Ireland
Date of Death: 30 June 1909
Place of Death: New Bedford, Massachusetts
Cemetery: St. Mary's Cemetery (MH)—New Bedford, Massachusetts
Entered Service at: Fall River, Bristol County, Massachusetts
Unit: Company B, 4th Massachusetts Cavalry
Battle or Place of Action: Ashepoo River, South Carolina
Date of Action: 24 May 1864
Date of Issue: 21 January 1897
Citation: Volunteered as a member of a boatcrew which went to the rescue of a large number of Union soldiers on board the stranded steamer Boston, and with great gallantry assisted in conveying them to shore, being exposed the entire time to a heavy fire from a Confederate battery.

369 ◆ DOWNS, HENRY W.

Rank: Sergeant (highest rank: Second Lieutenant)
Service: U.S. Army
Birthday: 29 August 1844
Place of Birth: Jamaica, Windham County, Vermont
Date of Death: 2 July 1911
Place of Death: Dayton, Ohio
Cemetery: Dayton National Cemetery (0-7-24) (MH)—Dayton, Ohio
Entered Service at: Newfane, Windham County, Vermont
Unit: Company I, 8th Vermont Infantry
Battle or Place of Action: Winchester, Virginia
Date of Action: 19 September 1864
Date of Issue: 13 December 1893
Citation: With one comrade, voluntarily crossed an open field, exposed to a raking fire, and returned with a supply of ammunition, successfully repeating the attempt a short time thereafter.

370 ◆ DRAKE, JAMES MADISON

Rank: Second Lieutenant (highest rank: First Lieutenant)
Service: U.S. Army
Birthday: 25 March 1837
Place of Birth: Washington Valley, Somerset County, New Jersey

Date of Death: 28 November 1913
Place of Death: Elizabeth, New Jersey
Cemetery: Evergreen Cemetery (MH)—Hillside, New Jersey
Entered Service at: Elizabeth, Union County, New Jersey
Unit: Company D, 9th New Jersey Infantry
Battle or Place of Action: Bermuda Hundred, Virginia
Date of Action: 6 May 1864
Date of Presentation: 3 March 1873
Place of Presentation: The White House, presented by Pres. Ulysses S. Grant
Citation: Commanded the skirmish line in the advance and held his position all day and during the night.
Notes: POW

371 ◆ DRURY, JAMES

Rank: Sergeant
Service: U.S. Army
Birthday: 15 August 1837
Place of Birth: Limerick, County Limerick, Ireland
Date of Death: 25 December 1919
Place of Death: Lovilia, Iowa
Cemetery: St. Peter's Cemetery—Lovilia, Iowa
Entered Service at: Chester, Windsor County, Vermont
Unit: Company C, 4th Vermont Infantry
Battle or Place of Action: Weldon Railroad, Virginia
Date of Action: 23 June 1864
Date of Issue: 18 January 1893
Citation: Saved the colors of his regiment when it was surrounded by a much larger force of the enemy and after the greater part of the regiment had been killed or captured.

372 ◆ DUFFEY, JOHN

True Name: Duffy, John
Rank: Private (highest rank: Farrier)
Service: U.S. Army
Birthday: 17 March 1836
Place of Birth: New Bedford, Bristol County, Massachusetts
Date of Death: 21 August 1923
Cemetery: Oak Grove Cemetery (MH)—New Bedford, Massachusetts
Entered Service at: New Bedford, Bristol County, Massachusetts
Unit: Company B, 4th Massachusetts Cavalry
Battle or Place of Action: Ashepoo River, South Carolina
Date of Action: 24 May 1864
Date of Issue: 21 January 1897
Citation: Volunteered as a member of a boatcrew which went to the rescue of a large number of Union soldiers on board the stranded steamer Boston, and with great gallantry assisted in conveying them to shore, being exposed the entire time to a heavy fire from a Confederate battery.

373 ◆ DUNCAN, ADAM

Rank: Boatswain's Mate
Service: U.S. Navy

Birthday: 1833
Place of Birth: Maine
Entered Service at: Boston, Suffolk County, Massachusetts
Unit: U.S.S. *Richmond*
Battle or Place of Action: Mobile Bay, Alabama
Date of Action: 5 August 1864
G.O. Number, Date: 45, 31 December 1864
Citation: As captain of a gun on board the U.S.S. *Richmond* during action against rebel forts and gunboats and with the ram *Tennessee* in Mobile Bay, 5 August 1864. Despite damage to his ship and the loss of several men on board as enemy fire raked her decks, Duncan fought his gun with skill and courage throughout the prolonged battle, which resulted in the surrender of the rebel ram *Tennessee* and in the successful attacks carried out on Fort Morgan.

374 ◆ DUNCAN, JAMES K. L.

Rank: Ordinary Seaman
Service: U.S. Navy
Birthday: 6 July 1845
Place of Birth: Frankfort Mineral Springs, Washington County, Pennsylvania
Date of Death: 27 March 1913
Place of Death: Wood, Wisconsin
Cemetery: Wood National Cemetery (19-41) (MH)—Wood, Wisconsin
Entered Service at: Pennsylvania
Unit: U.S.S. *Fort Hindman*
Battle or Place of Action: near Harrisonburg, Louisiana
Date of Action: 2 March 1864
G.O. Number, Date: 32, 16 April 1864
Citation: Served on board the U.S.S. *Fort Hindman* during the engagement near Harrisonburg, La., 2 March 1864. Following a shellburst at one of the guns which started a fire at the cartridge tie, Duncan immediately seized the burning cartridge, took it from the gun, and threw it overboard, despite the immediate danger to himself. Carrying out his duties through the entire engagement, Duncan served courageously during this action in which the *Fort Hindman* was raked severely with shot and shell from the enemy guns.

375 ◆ DUNLAVY, JAMES

Rank: Private
Service: U.S. Army
Birthday: 4 February 1844
Place of Birth: Decatur County, Indiana
Date of Death: 6 March 1923
Place of Death: Enid, Oklahoma
Cemetery: Maramec Cemetery—Maramec, Oklahoma
Entered Service at: Bloomfield, Davis County, Iowa
Unit: Company D, 3d Iowa Cavalry
Battle or Place of Action: Osage, Kansas
Date of Action: 25 October 1864
Date of Issue: 4 April 1865
Citation: Gallantry in capturing Maj. Gen. John S. Marmaduke, C.S.A.

376 ◆ DUNN, WILLIAM

Rank: Quartermaster
Service: U.S. Navy
Birthday: 28 April 1834
Place of Birth: Lisbon, Androscoggin County, Maine
Date of Death: 18 March 1902
Place of Death: Lisbon, Maine
Cemetery: West Bowdoin Cemetery (MH)—West Bowdoin, Maine
Entered Service at: Maine
Unit: U.S.S. *Monadnock*
Battle or Place of Action: Fort Fisher, North Carolina
Date of Action: 24-25 December 1864 & 13-15 January 1865
G.O. Number, Date: 59, 22 June 1865
Citation: On board the U.S.S. *Monadnock* in action during several attacks on Fort Fisher, 24 and 25 December 1864; and 13, 14, and 15 January 1865. With his ship anchored well inshore to insure perfect range against the severe fire of rebel guns, Dunn continued his duties when the vessel was at anchor, as her propellers were kept in motion to make her turrets bear, and the shooting away of her chain might have caused her to ground. Disdainful of shelter despite severe weather conditions, he inspired his shipmates and contributed to the success of his vessel in reducing the enemy guns to silence.

377 ◆ DUNNE, JAMES

Rank: Corporal
Service: U.S. Army
Birthday: 26 December 1840
Place of Birth: Detroit, Wayne County, Michigan
Date of Death: 13 February 1915
Place of Death: Chicago, Illinois
Cemetery: Calvary Cemetery (MH)—Evanston, Illinois
Entered Service at: Chicago, Cook County, Illinois
Unit: Chicago Mercantile Battery, Illinois Light Artillery
Battle or Place of Action: Vicksburg, Mississippi
Date of Action: 22 May 1863
Date of Issue: 15 January 1895
Citation: Carried with others by hand a cannon up to and fired it through an embrasure of the enemy's works.

378 ◆ DUNPHY, RICHARD D.

Rank: Coal Heaver
Service: U.S. Navy
Birthday: 12 December 1841
Place of Birth: Ireland
Date of Death: 23 November 1904
Place of Death: San Francisco, California
Cemetery: St. Vincent's Cemetery—Vallejo, California
Entered Service at: New York, New York
Unit: U.S.S. *Hartford*
Battle or Place of Action: Mobile Bay, Alabama
Date of Action: 5 August 1864
G.O. Number, Date: 45, 31 December 1864

Citation: On board the flagship U.S.S. *Hartford*, during successful attacks against Fort Morgan, rebel gunboats, and the rebel ram *Tennessee* in Mobile Bay, 5 August 1864. With his ship under a terrific enemy shellfire, Dunphy performed his duties with skill and courage throughout this fierce engagement which resulted in the capture of the rebel ram *Tennessee*

379 ◆ DU PONT, HENRY ALGERNON

Rank: Captain (highest rank: Brevet Lieutenant Colonel)
Service: U.S. Army
Birthday: 30 July 1838
Place of Birth: Eleutherean Mills, New Castle County, Delaware
Date of Death: 31 December 1926
Place of Death: Winterthur, Delaware
Cemetery: Du Pont Family Cemetery—Christians Hundred, Delaware
Entered Service at: Wilmington, New Castle County, Delaware
Unit: 5th U.S. Artillery
Battle or Place of Action: Cedar Creek, Virginia
Date of Action: 19 October 1864
Date of Issue: 2 April 1898
Citation: By his distinguished gallantry and voluntary exposure to the enemy's fire at a critical moment, when the Union line had been broken, encouraged his men to stand to their guns, checked the advance of the enemy and brought off most of his pieces.

380 ◆ DURHAM, JAMES R.

Rank: Second Lieutenant
Service: U.S. Army
Birthday: 7 February 1833
Place of Birth: Richmond, Richmond County, Virginia
Date of Death: 6 August 1904
Cemetery: Arlington National Cemetery (3-1435)—Arlington, Virginia
Entered Service at: Clarksburg, Harrison County, West Virginia
Unit: Company E, 12th West Virginia Infantry
Battle or Place of Action: Winchester, Virginia
Date of Action: 14 June 1863
Date of Issue: 6 March 1890
Citation: Led his command over the stone wall, where he was wounded.

381 ◆ DURHAM, JOHN S.

Rank: Sergeant
Service: U.S. Army
Birthday: 8 June 1843
Place of Birth: New York, New York
Date of Death: 2 January 1918
Place of Death: Leavenworth, Kansas
Cemetery: Leavenworth National Cemetery (33-10-18) (MH)—Leavenworth, Kansas

Entered Service at: Malone, Fond Du Lac County, Wisconsin
Unit: Company F, 1st Wisconsin Infantry
Battle or Place of Action: Perryville, Kentucky
Date of Action: 8 October 1862
Date of Issue: 20 November 1896
Citation: Seized the flag of his regiment when the color sergeant was shot and advanced with the flag midway between the lines, amid a shower of shot, shell, and bullets, until stopped by his commanding officer.

382 ◆ ECKES, JOHN N.

Rank: Private
Service: U.S. Army
Place of Birth: Lewis County, West Virginia
Date of Death: 20 April 1912
Place of Death: Cushing, Oklahoma
Entered Service at: Weston, Lewis County, West Virginia
Unit: Company E, 47th Ohio Infantry
Battle or Place of Action: Vicksburg, Mississippi
Date of Action: 22 May 1863
Citation: Gallantry in the charge of the "volunteer storming party."

383 ◆ EDDY, SAMUEL E.

Rank: Private
Service: U.S. Army
Birthday: 2 June 1822
Place of Birth: Whitingham, Windham County, Vermont
Date of Death: 7 March 1909
Cemetery: Mount Cemetery (MH)—West Chesterfield, Massachusetts
Entered Service at: Chesterfield, Hampshire County, Massachusetts
Unit: Company D, 37th Massachusetts Infantry
Battle or Place of Action: Deatonville—Sailor's Creek, Virginia
Date of Action: 6 April 1885
Citation: Saved the life of the adjutant of his regiment by voluntarily going beyond the line and there killing one of the enemy then in the act of firing upon the wounded officer. Was assailed by several of the enemy, run through the body with a bayonet, and pinned to the ground, but while so situated he shot and killed his assailant.

384 ◆ EDGERTON, NATHAN HUNTLEY

Rank: First Lieutenant & Adjutant (highest rank: Captain)
Service: U.s. Army
Birthday: 25 August 1838
Place of Birth: Barnesville, Belmont County, Ohio
Date of Death: 27 October 1932
Place of Death: Agnes, Oregon
Cemetery: At his mountain homestead—Agnes, Oregon
Entered Service at: Philadelphia, Philadelphia County, Pennsylvania
Unit: 6th U.S. Colored Infantry

Battle or Place of Action: Chapin's Farm, Virginia
Date of Action: 29 September 1884
Citation: Took up the flag after three color bearers had been shot down and bore it forward, though himself wounded

385 ◆ EDWARDS, DAVID

Rank: Private (highest rank: Corporal)
Service: U.S. Army
Birthday: 1841
Place of Birth: Wales
Date of Death: 14 April 1897
Cemetery: Waterville Cemetery (MH)—Waterville, New York
Entered Service at: Sangerfield, Oneida County, New York
Unit: Company H, 146th New York Infantry
Battle or Place of Action: Five Forks, Virginia
Date of Action: 1 April 1865
Date of Issue: 10 May 1865
Citation: Capture of flag.

386 ◆ EDWARDS, JOHN

Rank: Captain of the Top
Service: U.S. Navy
Birthday: 1831
Place of Birth: Providence, Providence County, Rhode Island
Date of Death: 27 December 1902
Cemetery: Pocasset Cemetery (MH)—Cranston, Rhode Island
Entered Service at: Rhode Island
Unit: U.S.S. *Lackawanna*
Battle or Place of Action: Mobile Bay, Alabama
Date of Action: 5 August 1864
G.O. Number, Date: 45, 31 December 1864
Citation: As second captain of a gun on board the U.S.S. *Lackawanna* during successful attacks against Fort Morgan, rebel gunboats and the ram *Tennessee* in Mobile Bay, 5 August 1864. Wounded when an enemy shell struck, Edwards refused to go below for aid and, as heavy return fire continued to strike his vessel, took the place of the first captain and carried out his duties during the prolonged action which resulted in the capture of the prize ram *Tennessee* and in the damaging and destruction of batteries at Fort Morgan.

387 ◆ ELLIOTT, ALEXANDER

Rank: Sergeant
Service: U.S. Army
Birthday: 1831
Place of Birth: Beaver County, Pennsylvania
Date of Death: 9 February 1905
Place of Death: Emsworth, Pennsylvania
Cemetery: Highwood Cemetery (MH)—Pittsburgh, Pennsylvania
Entered Service at: North Sewickley, Allegheny County, Pennsylvania
Unit: Company A, 1st Pennsylvania Cavalry

Battle or Place of Action: Paine's Crossroads, Virginia
Date of Action: 5 April 1865
Date of Issue: 3 May 1865
Citation: Capture of flag.

388 ◆ ELLIOTT, RUSSELL C.

Rank: Sergeant (highest rank: Second Lieutenant)
Service: U.S. Army
Birthday: 1842
Place of Birth: Concord, Merrimack County, New Hampshire
Date of Death: 23 October 1898
Place of Death: East Somerville, Massachusetts
Cemetery: Woodlawn Cemetery (MH)—Everett, Massachusetts
Entered Service at: Boston, Suffolk County, Massachusetts
Unit: Company B, 3d Massachusetts Cavalry
Battle or Place of Action: Natchitoches, Louisiana
Date of Action: 19 April 1864
Date of Issue: 20 November 1896
Citation: Seeing a Confederate officer in advance of his command, charged on him alone and unaided and captured him.

389 ◆ ELLIS, HORACE

Rank: Private
Service: U.S. Army
Birthday: 23 May 1843
Place of Birth: Mercer County, Pennsylvania
Date of Death: 27 June 1867
Cemetery: O'Neil Creek Cemetery—Eagle Point, Wisconsin
Entered Service at: Chippewa Falls, Chippewa County, Wisconsin
Unit: Company A, 7th Wisconsin Infantry
Battle or Place of Action: Weldon Railroad, Virginia
Date of Action: 21 August 1864
Date of Issue: 1 December 1864
Citation: Capture of flag of 16th Mississippi (C.S.A.).

390 ◆ ELLIS, WILLIAM

Rank: First Sergeant (highest rank: Second Lieutenant)
Service: U.S. Army
Birthday: 1834
Place of Birth: England
Date of Death: 1 February 1875
Place of Death: Cahon Pap, California
Cemetery: County PAP Cemetery—San Bernardino, California
Entered Service at: Watertown, Jefferson County, Wisconsin
Unit: Company K, 3d Wisconsin Cavalry
Battle or Place of Action: Dardanelles, Arkansas
Date of Action: 14 January 1865
Citation: Remained at his post after receiving three wounds, and only retired, by his commanding officer's orders, after being wounded a fourth time.

391 ◆ ELLSWORTH, THOMAS FOULDS

Rank: Captain
Service: U.S. Army
Birthday: 12 November 1840
Place of Birth: Ipswich, Essex County, Massachusetts
Date of Death: 29 August 1911
Place of Death: Pasadena, California
Cemetery: Mountain View Cemetery—Pasadena, California
Entered Service at: Boston, Suffolk County, Massachusetts
Unit: Company B, 55th Massachusetts Colored Infantry
Battle or Place of Action: Honey Hill, South Carolina
Date of Action: 30 November 1864
Date of Issue: 18 November 1895
Citation: Under a heavy fire carried his wounded commanding officer from the field.

392 ◆ ELSON, JAMES M.

Rank: Sergeant (highest rank: First Lieutenant)
Service: U.S. Army
Birthday: 6 November 1838
Place of Birth: Coshocton, Coshocton County, Ohio
Date of Death: 26 March 1894
Place of Death: Vinton, Iowa
Cemetery: Oakwood Cemetery (MH)—Shellsburg, Iowa
Entered Service at: Shellsburg, Benton County, Iowa
Unit: Company C, 9th Iowa Infantry
Battle or Place of Action: Vicksburg, Mississippi
Date of Action: 22 May 1863
Date of Issue: 12 September 1891
Citation: Carried the colors in advance of his regiment and was shot down while attempting to plant them on the enemy's works.

393 ◆ EMBLER, ANDREW HENRY

Rank: Captain (highest rank: Brevet Colonel U.S. Vols.)
Service: U.S. Army
Birthday: 29 June 1834
Place of Birth: New York, New York
Cemetery: Evergreen Cemetery (MH)—New Haven, Connecticut
Entered Service at: New York
Unit: Company D, 59th New York Infantry
Battle or Place of Action: Boydton Plank Road, Virginia
Date of Action: 27 October 1864
Date of Issue: 19 October 1893
Citation: Charged at the head of two regiments, which drove the enemy's main body, gained the crest of the hill near the Burgess house, and forced a barricade on the Boydton road.

394 ◆ ENDERLIN, RICHARD

Rank: Musician (highest rank: Sergeant)
Service: U.S. Army
Birthday: 11 January 1843
Place of Birth: Germany

Date of Death: 11 February 1930
Place of Death: Chillicothe, Ohio
Cemetery: Grandview Cemetery—Chillicothe, Ohio
Entered Service at: Chillicothe, Ross County, Ohio
Unit: Company B, 73d Ohio Infantry
Battle or Place of Action: Gettysburg, Pennsylvania
Date of Action: 1-3 July 1863
Date of Issue: 11 September 1897
Citation: Voluntarily took a rifle and served as a soldier in the ranks during the first and second days of the battle. Voluntarily and at his own imminent peril went into the enemy's lines at night and, under a sharp fire, rescued a wounded comrade.

395 ◆ ENGLE, JAMES EDGAR

Rank: Sergeant (highest rank: Brevet Captain)
Service: U.S. Army
Birthday: 1844
Place of Birth: Chester, Delaware County, Pennsylvania
Date of Death: 19 November 1897
Cemetery: Arlington National Cemetery (1-569)—Arlington, Virginia
Entered Service at: Chester, Delaware County, Pennsylvania
Unit: Company I, 97th Pennsylvania Infantry
Battle or Place of Action: Bermuda Hundred, Virginia
Date of Action: 18 May 1864
Date of Issue: 17 December 1896
Citation: Responded to a call for volunteers to carry ammunition to the regiment on the picket line and under a heavy fire from the enemy, assisted in carrying a box of ammunition to the front, and remained to distribute the same.

396 ◆ ENGLISH, EDMUND

Rank: First Sergeant (highest rank: Captain)
Service: U.S. Army
Birthday: 16 November 1844
Place of Birth: New York, New York
Date of Death: 27 May 1912
Place of Death: Philadelphia, Pennsylvania
Cemetery: Old Cathedral Cemetery—Philadelphia, Pennsylvania
Entered Service at: Newark, Essex County, New Jersey
Unit: Company C, 2d New Jersey Infantry
Battle or Place of Action: Wilderness Campaign, Virginia
Date of Action: 6 May 1864
Date of Issue: 13 February 1891
Citation: During a rout and while under orders to retreat, seized the colors, rallied the men, and drove the enemy back.
Notes: POW

397 ◆ ENGLISH, THOMAS

Rank: Signal Quartermaster
Service: U.S. Navy
Birthday: 1819
Place of Birth: New York, New York
Entered Service at: New York, New York

Unit: U.S.S. *New Ironsides*
Battle or Place of Action: Fort Fisher, North Carolina
Date of Action: 24-25 December 1864—13-15 January 1865
G.O. Number, Date: 59, 22 June 1865
Date of Issue: 22 June 1865
Citation: English served on board the U.S.S. *New Ironsides* during action in several attacks on Fort Fisher, 24 and 25 December 1864; and 13, 14 and 15 January 1865. The ship steamed in and took the lead in the ironclad division close inshore and immediately opened its starboard battery in a barrage of well-directed fire to cause several fires and explosions and dismount several guns during the first two days of fighting. Taken under fire as she steamed into position on 13 January, the *New Ironsides* fought and took on ammunition at night despite severe weather conditions. When the enemy came out of his bombproofs to defend the fort against the storming party, the ship's battery disabled nearly every gun on the fort facing the shore before the cease-fire orders were given by the flagship.

398 ◆ ENNIS, CHARLES D.

Rank: Private
Service: U.S. Army
Birthday: 8 August 1843
Place of Birth: Stonington, New London County, Connecticut
Date of Death: 29 December 1930
Place of Death: Potter Hill, Rhode Island
Cemetery: White Brook Cemetery (MH)—Richmond, Rhode Island
Entered Service at: Charleston, Washington County, Rhode Island
Unit: Company G, 1st Rhode Island Light Artillery
Battle or Place of Action: Petersburg, Virginia
Date of Action: 2 April 1865
Date of Issue: 28 June 1892
Citation: Was one of a detachment of 20 picked artillerymen who voluntarily accompanied an infantry assaulting party and who turned upon the enemy the guns captured in the assault.

399 ◆ ERICKSON, JOHN P.

Rank: Captain of the Forecastle
Service: U.S. Navy
Birthday: 1826
Place of Birth: London, England
Date of Death: 2 August 1907
Place of Death: Brooklyn, New York
Cemetery: The Green Wood Cemetery—Brooklyn, New York
Entered Service at: Brooklyn, Kings County, New York
Unit: U.S.S. *Pontoosuc*
Battle or Place of Action: Forts Fisher & Wilmington, North Carolina
Date of Action: 24 December 1864—22 February 1865
G.O. Number, Date: 59, 22 June 1865

Citation: Served on board the U.S.S. *Pontoosuc* during the capture of Fort Fisher and Wilmington, 24 December 1864 to 22 February 1865. Carrying out his duties faithfully throughout this period, Erickson was so severely wounded in the assault upon Fort Fisher that he was sent to the hospital at Portsmouth, Va. Erickson was recommended for his gallantry, skill, and coolness in action while under the fire of the enemy.

400 ◆ ESTES, LEWELLYN GARRISH

Rank: Captain & Assistant Adjutant General (highest rank: Brevet Brigadier General)
Service: U.S. Army
Birthday: 27 December 1843
Place of Birth: Oldtown, Penobscot County, Maine
Date of Death: 21 February 1905
Place of Death: Washington, D.C.
Cemetery: Arlington National Cemetery (3-1437)—Arlington, Virginia
Entered Service at: Oldtown, Penobscot County, Maine
Unit: U.S. Volunteers
Battle or Place of Action: Flint River, Georgia
Date of Action: 30 August 1864
Date of Issue: 29 August 1894
Citation: Voluntarily led troops in a charge over a burning bridge.

401 ◆ EVANS, CORON D.

Rank: Private
Service: U.S. Army
Birthday: 1844
Place of Birth: Jefferson County, Indiana
Entered Service at: Madison, Jefferson County, Indiana
Unit: Company A, 3d Indiana Cavalry
Battle or Place of Action: Deatonsville (Sailor's Creek), Virginia
Date of Action: 6 April 1865
Date of Issue: 3 May 1865
Citation: Capture of flag of 26th Virginia Infantry (C.S.A.).

402 ◆ EVANS, IRA HOBART

Rank: Captain (highest rank: Brevet Major)
Service: U.S. Army
Birthday: 11 April 1844
Place of Birth: Piermont, Grafton County, New Hampshire
Date of Death: 19 April 1922
Place of Death: San Diego, California
Cemetery: Corners Cemetery—Berlin, Vermont
Entered Service at: Barre, Washington County, Vermont
Unit: Company B, 116th U.S. Colored Infantry
Battle or Place of Action: Hatcher's Run, Virginia
Date of Action: 2 April 1865
Date of Issue: 24 March 1892
Citation: Voluntarily passed between the lines, under a heavy fire from the enemy, and obtained important information.

403 ◆ EVANS, JAMES ROBERT

Rank: Private (highest rank: Captain)
Service: U.S. Army
Birthday: 12 September 1843
Place of Birth: New York, New York
Date of Death: 27 December 1918
Place of Death: Caldwell, New Jersey
Cemetery: First Reformed Church Cemetery—Pompton Plains, New Jersey
Entered Service at: New York, New York
Unit: Company H, 62d New York Infantry
Battle or Place of Action: Wilderness Campaign, Virginia
Date of Action: 5 May 1864
Date of Issue: 25 February 1895
Citation: Went out in front of the line under a fierce fire and, in the face of the rapidly advancing enemy, rescued the regimental flag with which the color bearer had fallen.

404 ◆ EVANS, THOMAS

Rank: Private
Service: U.S. Army
Birthday: 1824
Place of Birth: Wales
Entered Service at: Johnstown, Cambria County, Pennsylvania
Unit: Company D, 54th Pennsylvania Infantry
Battle or Place of Action: Piedmont, Virginia
Date of Action: 5 June 1864
Date of Issue: 26 November 1864
Citation: Capture of flag of 45th Virginia (C.S.A.).

405 ◆ EVERSON, ADELBERT

Rank: Private
Service: U.S. Army
Birthday: 12 April 1841
Place of Birth: Cicero, Onondaga County, New York
Date of Death: 23 July 1913
Place of Death: Brewerton, New York
Cemetery: Riverside Cemetery—Brewerton, New York
Entered Service at: Salina, Onondaga County, New York
Unit: Company D, 185th New York Infantry
Battle or Place of Action: Five Forks, Virginia
Date of Action: 1 April 1865
Date of Issue: 10 May 1865
Citation: Capture of flag.

406 ◆ EWING, JOHN C.

Rank: Private
Service: U.S. Army
Birthday: 4 March 1843
Place of Birth: Ligonier Valley, Westmoreland County, Pennsylvania
Date of Death: 23 May 1918
Place of Death: Johnstown, Pennsylvania
Cemetery: Ligonier Valley Cemetery—Ligonier, Pennsylvania

Entered Service at: Greensburg, Westmoreland County, Pennsylvania
Unit: Company E, 211th Pennsylvania Infantry
Battle or Place of Action: Petersburg, Virginia
Date of Action: 2 April 1865
Date of Issue: 20 May 1865
Citation: Capture of flag.

407 ◆ FALCONER, JOHN A.

Rank: Corporal
Service: U.S. Army
Birthday: 1844
Place of Birth: Washtenaw, Michigan
Date of Death: 1 April 1900
Cemetery: Sunset Hill Cemetery—Warrensburg, Missouri
Entered Service at: Manchester, Washtenaw County, Michigan
Unit: Company A, 17th Michigan Infantry
Battle or Place of Action: Fort Sanders, Knoxville, Tennessee
Date of Action: 20 November 1863
Date of Issue: 27 July 1896
Citation: Conducted the "burning party" of his regiment at the time a charge was made on the enemy's picket line, and burned the house which had sheltered the enemy's sharpshooters, thus insuring success to a hazardous enterprise.

408 ◆ FALL, CHARLES S.

Rank: Sergeant
Service: U.S. Army
Birthday: 1842
Place of Birth: Noble County, Indiana
Date of Death: 4 June 1918
Place of Death: Pasadena, California
Cemetery: I.O.O.F. Cemetery—Alhambra, California
Entered Service at: Hamburg, Livingston County, Michigan
Unit: Company E, 26th Michigan Infantry
Battle or Place of Action: Spotsylvania Courthouse, Virginia
Date of Action: 12 May 1864
Date of Issue: 13 May 1899
Citation: Was one of the first to mount the Confederate works, where he bayoneted two of the enemy and captured a Confederate flag, but threw it away to continue the pursuit of the enemy.

409 ◆ FALLON, THOMAS TIMOTHY

Rank: Private (highest rank: Sergeant)
Service: U.S. Army
Birthday: 12 August 1837
Place of Birth: County Galway, Ireland
Date of Death: 26 August 1916
Cemetery: St. Rose of Lima Cemetery (MH)—Freehold, New Jersey
Entered Service at: Freehold, Monmouth County, New Jersey
Unit: Company K, 37th New York Infantry

Battle or Place of Action: Williamsburg & Fair Oaks, Virginia & Big Shanty, Georgia
Date of Action: 5,30-31 May 1862 & 14-15 June 1864
Date of Issue: 13 February 1891
Citation: At Williamsburg, Va., assisted in driving rebel skirmishers to their main line. Participated in action, at Fair Oaks, Va., though excused from duty because of disability. In a charge with his company at Big Shanty, Ga., was the first man on the enemy's works.

410 ◆ *FALLS, BENJAMIN FRANK

Rank: Color Sergeant
Service: U.S. Army
Place of Birth: Portsmouth, Rockingham County, New Hampshire
Date of Death: 12 May 1864
Place of Death: Wilderness, Virginia
Cemetery: Pine Grove Cemetery (MH)—Lynn, Massachusetts
Entered Service at: Lynn, Essex County, Massachusetts
Unit: Company A, 19th Massachusetts Infantry
Battle or Place of Action: Gettysburg, Pennsylvania
Date of Action: 3 July 1863
Date of Issue: 1 December 1864
Citation: Capture of flag.

411 ◆ FANNING, NICHOLAS

Rank: Private
Service: U.S. Army
Place of Birth: Carroll County, Indiana
Entered Service at: Independence, Buchanan County, Iowa
Unit: Company B, 4th Iowa Cavalry
Battle or Place of Action: Selma, Alabama
Date of Action: 2 April 1865
Date of Issue: 17 June 1865
Citation: Capture of silk Confederate States flag and two staff officers.

412 ◆ FARLEY, WILLIAM

Rank: Boatswain's Mate
Service: U.S. Navy
Birthday: 1835
Place of Birth: Whitefield, Lincoln County, Maine
Entered Service at: Maine
Unit: U.S.S. *Marblehead*
Battle or Place of Action: off Legareville, John's Island, Stono River, South Carolina
Date of Action: 25 December 1863
G.O. Number, Date: 32, 16 April 1864
Citation: Served on board the U.S.S. *Marblehead* off Legareville, Stono River, 25 December 1863, during an engagement with the enemy on John's Island. Behaving in a gallant manner, Farley animated his men and kept up a rapid and effective fire on the enemy throughout the engagement, which resulted in the enemy's abandonment of his positions, leaving a caisson and one gun behind.

413 ◆ FARNSWORTH, HERBERT E.

Rank: Sergeant Major (highest rank: Captain)
Service: U.S. Army
Birthday: 23 August 1834
Place of Birth: Perrysburg, Cattaraugus County, New York
Date of Death: 4 July 1908
Place of Death: Clarkston, Washington
Cemetery: Pomeroy City Cemetery—Pomeroy, Washington
Entered Service at: Gowanda, Cattaraugus County, New York
Unit: 10th New York Cavalry (Porter Guard)
Battle or Place of Action: Trevilian Station, Virginia
Date of Action: 11 June 1864
Date of Issue: 1 April 1898
Citation: Voluntarily carried a message which stopped the firing of a Union battery into his regiment, in which service he crossed a ridge in plain view and swept by the fire of both armies.

414 ◆ FARQUHAR, JOHN MCGREATH

Rank: Sergeant Major
Service: U.S. Army
Birthday: 17 April 1832
Place of Birth: near Ayr, Scotland
Date of Death: 24 April 1918
Place of Death: Buffalo, New York
Cemetery: Forest Lawn Cemetery (MH)—Buffalo, New York
Entered Service at: Chicago, Cook County, Illinois
Unit: 89th Illinois Infantry
Battle or Place of Action: Stone River, Tennessee
Date of Action: 31 December 1862
Date of Issue: 6 August 1902
Citation: When a break occurred on the extreme right wing of the Army of the Cumberland, this soldier rallied fugitives from other commands, and deployed his own regiment, thereby checking the Confederate advance until a new line was established.

415 ◆ FARRELL, EDWARD

Rank: Quartermaster
Service: U.S. Navy
Birthday: 1833
Place of Birth: Saratoga, Saratoga County, New York
Entered Service at: New York, New York
Unit: U.S.S. *Owasco*
Battle or Place of Action: Forts Jackson and St. Philip, Louisiana
Date of Action: 24 April 1862
G.O. Number, Date: 11, 3 April 1863
Citation: Served on board the U.S.S. *Owasco* during the attack upon Forts Jackson and St. Philip, 24 April 1862. Stationed at the masthead during these operations, Farrell observed and reported the effect of the fire of our guns in such a manner as to make his intelligence, coolness, and capacity conspicuous.

416 ◆ FASNACHT, CHARLES H.

Rank: Sergeant (highest rank: First Lieutenant)
Service: U.S. Army
Birthday: 27 March 1842
Place of Birth: Lancaster County, Pennsylvania
Date of Death: 21 July 1902
Cemetery: Greenwood Cemetery (MH)—Lancaster, Pennsylvania
Entered Service at: Philadelphia, Philadelphia County, Pennsylvania
Unit: Company A, 99th Pennsylvania Infantry
Battle or Place of Action: Spotsylvania, Virginia
Date of Action: 12 May 1864
Date of Issue: 2 April 1878
Citation: Capture of flag of 2d Louisiana Tigers (C.S.A.), in a hand-to-hand contest.
Notes: POW

417 ◆ FASSETT, JOHN BARCLAY

Rank: Captain (highest rank: Major)
Service: U.S. Army
Birthday: 1843
Place of Birth: Philadelphia, Philadelphia County, Pennsylvania
Date of Death: 18 January 1905
Place of Death: Pasadena, California
Cemetery: Woodlawn Cemetery—Bronx, New York
Entered Service at: Philadelphia, Philadelphia County, Pennsylvania
Unit: Company F, 23d Pennsylvania Infantry
Battle or Place of Action: Gettysburg, Pennsylvania
Date of Action: 2 July 1863
Date of Issue: 29 December 1894
Citation: While acting as an aide, voluntarily led a regiment to the relief of a battery and recaptured its gun from the enemy.

418 ◆ FERNALD, ALBERT E.

Rank: First Lieutenant
Service: U.S. Army
Birthday: 13 May 1838
Place of Birth: Winterport, Waldo County, Maine
Date of Death: 3 December 1908
Cemetery: Oak Hill Cemetery (MH)—Winterport, Maine
Entered Service at: Winterport, Waldo County, Maine
Unit: Company F, 20th Maine Infantry
Battle or Place of Action: Five Forks, Virginia
Date of Action: 1 April 1865
Date of Issue: 10 May 1865
Citation: During a rush at the enemy, Lt. Fernald seized, during a scuffle, the flag of the 9th Virginia Infantry (C.S.A.).

419 ◆ FERRELL, JOHN H.

Rank: Pilot (Civilian)
Service: U.S. Navy

Birthday: 15 April 1829
Place of Birth: Bedford County, Tennessee
Place of Death: Elizabethtown, Illinois
Cemetery: Price Cemetery—Elizabethtown, Illinois
Entered Service at: Illinois
Unit: U.S. Monitor *Neosho*
Battle or Place of Action: Bells Mills, Cumberland River, near Nashville, Tennessee
Date of Action: 6 December 1864
G.O. Number, Date: 59, 22 June 1865
Citation: Served on board the U.S. Monitor *Neosho* during the engagement with enemy batteries at Bells Mills, Cumberland River, near Nashville, Tenn., 6 December 1864. Carrying out his duties courageously during the engagement, Ferrell gallantly left the pilothouse after the flag and signal staffs of that vessel had been shot away and, taking the flag which was drooping over the wheelhouse, made it fast to the stump of the highest mast remaining, although the ship was still under a heavy fire from the enemy.

420 ◆ FERRIER, DANIEL TWEED

Rank: Sergeant (highest rank: Quartermaster Sergeant)
Service: U.S. Army
Birthday: 26 November 1841
Place of Birth: Indiana
Date of Death: 18 March 1914
Cemetery: Nebo Cemetery (MH)—Camden, Indiana
Entered Service at: Delphi, Carroll County, Indiana
Unit: Company K, 2d Indiana Cavalry
Battle or Place of Action: Varnells Station, Georgia
Date of Action: 9 May 1864
Date of Issue: 30 March 1898
Citation: While his regiment was retreating, voluntarily gave up his horse to his brigade commander who had been unhorsed and was in danger of capture, thereby enabling him to rejoin and rally the disorganized troops. Sgt. Ferrier himself was captured and confined in Confederate prisons, from which he escaped and, after great hardship, rejoined the Union lines.
Notes: POW

421 ◆ FERRIS, EUGENE W.

Rank: First Lieutenant & Adjutant (highest rank: Captain)
Service: U.S. Army
Birthday: 18 November 1841
Place of Birth: Springfield, Windsor County, Vermont
Date of Death: 26 February 1907
Place of Death: Rockville, Indiana
Cemetery: Rockville Cemetery—Rockville, Indiana
Entered Service at: Lowell, Middlesex County, Massachusetts
Unit: 30th Massachusetts Infantry
Battle or Place of Action: Berryville, Virginia
Date of Action: 1 April 1865
Date of Issue: 16 October 1897
Citation: Accompanied only by an orderly, outside the lines of the Army, he gallantly resisted an attack of five of Mosby's cavalry, mortally wounded the leader of the party, seized his

horse and pistols, wounded three more, and, though wounded himself, escaped.

422 ◆ FESQ, FRANK E.

Rank: Private
Service: U.S. Army
Birthday: 4 April 1840
Place of Birth: Germany
Date of Death: 6 May 1920
Cemetery: Rosedale Cemetery (MH)—Orange, New Jersey
Entered Service at: Newark, Essex County, New Jersey
Unit: Company A, 40th New Jersey Infantry
Battle or Place of Action: Petersburg, Virginia
Date of Action: 2 April 1865
Date of Issue: 10 May 1865
Citation: Capture of flag of 18th North Carolina (C.S.A.), within the enemy's works.

423 ◆ FINKENBINER, HENRY S.

Rank: Private (highest rank: Corporal)
Service: U.S. Army
Birthday: 29 July 1842
Place of Birth: North Industry, Stark County, Ohio
Date of Death: 3 June 1922
Place of Death: Danville, Illinois
Cemetery: Hopewell Cemetery (MH)—Largo, Indiana
Entered Service at: Pike Township, Ohio
Unit: Company D, 107th Ohio Infantry
Battle or Place of Action: Dingles Mill, South Carolina
Date of Action: 9 April 1865
Date of Issue: 30 March 1898
Citation: While on the advance skirmish line and within direct and close fire of the enemy's artillery, crossed the mill race on a burning bridge and ascertained the enemy's position.

424 ◆ FISHER, JOHN H.

Rank: First Lieutenant
Service: U.S. Army
Birthday: 1837
Place of Birth: Monmouth, Pennsylvania
Date of Death: 16 September 1895
Place of Death: Spencer, Iowa
Cemetery: Mountain View Cemetery (MH)—Longmount, Colorado
Entered Service at: Chicago, Cook County, Illinois
Unit: Company B, 55th Illinois Infantry
Battle or Place of Action: Vicksburg, Mississippi
Date of Action: 22 May 1863
Date of Issue: 2 September 1893
Citation: Gallantry in the charge of the "volunteer storming party."

425 ◆ FISHER, JOSEPH

Rank: Corporal
Service: U.S. Army

Birthday: 24 August 1843
Place of Birth: Philadelphia, Philadelphia County, Pennsylvania
Date of Death: 8 October 1903
Cemetery: Fernwood Cemetery (MH)—Fernwood, Pennsylvania
Entered Service at: Philadelphia, Philadelphia County, Pennsylvania
Unit: Company C, 61st Pennsylvania Infantry
Battle or Place of Action: Petersburg, Virginia
Date of Action: 2 April 1865
Date of Issue: 16 January 1894
Citation: Carried the colors 50 yards in advance of his regiment, and after being painfully wounded attempted to crawl into the enemy's works in an endeavor to plant his flag thereon.

426 ◆ FITZPATRICK, THOMAS

Rank: Coxswain
Service: U.S. Navy
Birthday: 1837
Place of Birth: Canada
Entered Service at: Taunton, Bristol County, Massachusetts
Unit: U.S.S. *Hartford*
Battle or Place of Action: Mobile Bay, Alabama
Date of Action: 5 August 1864
G.O. Number, Date: 45, 31 December 1864
Citation: As captain of the No. 1 gun on board the flagship U.S.S. *Hartford*, during action against rebel gunboats, the ram *Tennessee* and Fort Morgan in Mobile Bay, 5 August 1864. Although struck several times in the face by splinters, and with his gun disabled when a shell burst between the two forward 9-inch guns, killing and wounding 15 men, Fitzpatrick, within a few minutes, had the gun in working order again with new track, breeching, and side tackle, had sent the wounded below, cleared the area of other casualties, and was fighting his gun as before. He served as an inspiration to the members of his crew and contributed to the success of the action in which the *Tennessee* was captured.

427 ◆ FLANAGAN, AUGUSTIN D.

Rank: Sergeant
Service: U.S. Army
Birthday: 10 August 1844
Place of Birth: Loretto, Cambria County, Pennsylvania
Date of Death: 22 January 1924
Place of Death: Tecumseh, Nebraska
Cemetery: Tecumseh Cemetery (MH)—Tecumseh, Nebraska
Entered Service at: Chester Springs, Chester County, Pennsylvania
Unit: Company A, 55th Pennsylvania Infantry
Battle or Place of Action: Chapin's Farm, Virginia
Date of Action: 29 September 1864
Date of Issue: 6 April 1865
Citation: Gallantry in the charge on the enemy's works; rushing forward with the colors and calling upon the men to follow him; was severely wounded.

428 ◆ FLANNIGAN, JAMES

Rank: Private (highest rank: Sergeant)
Service: U.S. Army
Birthday: 1833
Place of Birth: Canada
Date of Death: 4 October 1905
Place of Death: Louisville, New York
Cemetery: St. Lawrence Cemetery (MH)—Louisville, New York
Entered Service at: Fort Snelling, St. Paul County, Minnesota
Unit: Company H, 2d Minnesota Infantry
Battle or Place of Action: Nolensville, Tennessee
Date of Action: 15 February 1863
Date of Issue: 11 September 1897
Citation: Was one of a detachment of 16 men who heroically defended a wagon train against the attack of 125 cavalry, repulsed the attack, and saved the train.

429 ◆ FLEETWOOD, CHRISTIAN A.

Rank: Sergeant Major
Service: U.S. Army
Birthday: 21 July 1840
Place of Birth: Baltimore, Baltimore County, Maryland
Date of Death: 28 September 1914
Place of Death: Washington, D.C.
Cemetery: Harmony Memorial Park (MH)—Landover, Maryland
Entered Service at: Baltimore, Baltimore County, Maryland
Unit: 4th U.S. Colored Infantry
Battle or Place of Action: Chapin's Farm, Virginia
Date of Action: 29 September 1864
Date of Issue: 6 April 1865
Citation: Seized the colors, after two color bearers had been shot down, and bore them nobly through the fight.

430 ◆ FLOOD, THOMAS S.

Rank: Boy
Service: U.S. Navy
Birthday: 1840
Place of Birth: Ireland
Entered Service at: New York
Unit: U.S.S. *Pensacola*
Battle or Place of Action: Forts Jackson and St. Philip, Louisiana
Date of Action: 24-25 April 1862
G.O. Number, Date: 11, 3 April 1863
Citation: Served on board the U.S.S. *Pensacola* in the attack on Forts Jackson and St. Philip and the taking of New Orleans, 24 and 25 April 1862. Swept from the bridge by a shell which wounded the signal quartermaster, Flood returned to the bridge after assisting the wounded man below and taking over his duties, "Performed them with coolness, exactitude and the fidelity of a veteran seaman. His intelligence and character cannot be spoken of too warmly."

431 ◆ FLYNN, CHRISTOPHER

Rank: Corporal (highest rank: Sergeant)
Service: U.S. Army
Birthday: December 1828
Place of Birth: Ireland
Date of Death: 15 October 1889
Place of Death: Sprague, Connecticut
Cemetery: St. Mary's Cemetery (MH)—Sprague, Connecticut
Entered Service at: Hartford, Hartford County, Connecticut
Unit: Company K, 14th Connecticut Infantry
Battle or Place of Action: Gettysburg, Pennsylvania
Date of Action: 3 July 1863
Date of Issue: 1 December 1864
Citation: Capture of flag of 52d North Carolina Infantry (C.S.A.).

432 ◆ FLYNN, JAMES EDWARD

Rank: Sergeant
Service: U.S. Army
Birthday: 17 July 1843
Place of Birth: Pittsfield, Pike County, Illinois
Date of Death: 1 January 1913
Cemetery: Calvary Cemetery—St. Louis, Missouri
Entered Service at: St. Louis, St. Louis County, Missouri
Unit: Company G, 6th Missouri Infantry
Battle or Place of Action: Vicksburg, Mississippi
Date of Action: 22 May 1863
Date of Issue: 19 June 1894
Citation: Gallantry in the charge of the "volunteer storming party."

433 ◆ FOLLETT, JOSEPH LEONARD

Rank: Sergeant (highest rank: Second Lieutenant)
Service: U.S. Army
Birthday: 16 February 1843
Place of Birth: Newark, Essex County, New Jersey
Date of Death: 1 April 1907
Place of Death: New York, New York
Cemetery: Albany Rural Cemetery (MH)—Albany, New York
Entered Service at: St. Louis, St. Louis County, Missouri
Unit: Company G, 1st Missouri Light Artillery
Battle or Place of Action: New Madrid, Missouri & Stone River, Tennessee
Date of Action: 3 March & 31 December 1862
Date of Issue: 19 September 1890
Citation: At New Madrid, Mo., remained on duty though severely wounded. While procuring ammunition from the supply train at Stone River, Tenn., Follett was captured, but made his escape, secured the ammunition, and in less than an hour from the time of his capture had the batteries supplied.

434 ◆ FORCE, MANNING FERGUSON

Rank: Brigadier General (highest rank: Brevet Major General)
Service: U.S. Army
Birthday: 17 December 1824
Place of Birth: Washington, D.C.
Date of Death: 8 May 1899
Cemetery: Spring Grove Cemetery—Cincinnati, Ohio
Entered Service at: Cincinnati, Hamilton County, Ohio
Unit: U.S. Volunteers
Battle or Place of Action: Atlanta, Georgia
Date of Action: 22 July 1864
Date of Issue: 31 March 1892
Citation: Charged upon the enemy's works, and after their capture defended his position against assaults of the enemy until he was severely wounded.

435 ◆ FORD, GEORGE W.

Rank: First Lieutenant (highest rank: Captain)
Service: U.S. Army
Birthday: 1844
Place of Birth: Ireland
Date of Death: 29 November 1883
Cemetery: 1st Calvary Cemetery—Woodside, New York
Entered Service at: New York, New York
Unit: Company E, 88th New York Infantry
Battle or Place of Action: Deatonsville (Sailor's Creek), Virginia
Date of Action: 6 April 1865
Date of Issue: 10 May 1865
Citation: Capture of flag.

436 ◆ FORMAN, ALEXANDER A.

Rank: Corporal
Service: U.S. Army
Birthday: 14 January 1843
Place of Birth: Scipio Township, Hillsdale County, Michigan
Date of Death: 3 March 1922
Cemetery: Cypress Hills Cemetery (Private)—Brooklyn, New York
Entered Service at: Jonesville, Hillsdale County, Michigan
Unit: Company C, 7th Michigan Infantry
Battle or Place of Action: Fair Oaks, Virginia
Date of Action: 31 May 1862
Date of Issue: 17 August 1895
Citation: Although wounded, he continued fighting until, fainting from loss of blood, he was carried off the field.

437 ◆ FOUT, FREDERICK W.

Rank: Second Lieutenant
Service: U.S. Army
Place of Birth: Germany
Date of Death: 6 June 1905
Place of Death: St. Louis, Missouri
Cemetery: Bellefontaine Cemetery—St. Louis, Missouri
Entered Service at: Indanapolis, Marion County, Indiana
Unit: 15th Battery, Indiana Light Artillery
Battle or Place of Action: near Harpers Ferry, West Virginia

Date of Action: 15 September 1862
Date of Issue: 2 November 1896
Citation: Voluntarily gathered the men of the battery together, remanned the guns, which had been ordered abandoned by an officer, opened fire, and kept up the same on the enemy until after the surrender.

438 ◆ FOX, HENRY

Rank: Sergeant (highest rank: Captain)
Service: U.S. Army
Birthday: 3 October 1833
Place of Birth: Reuthingen, Wurtemberg, Germany
Date of Death: 3 September 1906
Cemetery: Oaklawn Cemetery—Dwight, Illinois
Entered Service at: Lincoln, Logan County, Illinois
Unit: Company H, 106th Illinois Infantry
Battle or Place of Action: near Jackson, Tennessee
Date of Action: 23 December 1862
Date of Issue: 16 May 1899
Citation: When his command was surrounded by a greatly superior force, voluntarily left the shelter of the breastworks, crossed an open railway trestle under a concentrated fire from the enemy, made his way out, and secured reinforcements for the relief of his command.

439 ◆ FOX, HENRY M.

Rank: Sergeant (highest rank: Second Lieutenant)
Service: U.S. Army
Birthday: 15 November 1844
Place of Birth: Trumbull, Ohio
Date of Death: 2 March 1923
Place of Death: Middlebury, Indiana
Cemetery: Mottville Cemetery (MH)—Mottville, Michigan
Entered Service at: Coldwater, Branch County, Michigan
Unit: Company M, 5th Michigan Cavalry
Battle or Place of Action: Winchester, Virginia
Date of Action: 19 September 1864
Date of Issue: 27 September 1864
Citation: Capture of flag.

440 ◆ FOX, NICHOLAS

Rank: Private
Service: U.S. Army
Birthday: 1844
Date of Death: 2 October 1929
Place of Death: Port Chester, New York
Cemetery: St. Mary's Cemetery (MH)—Rye Brook, New York
Entered Service at: Greenwich, Fairfield County, Connecticut
Unit: Company H, 28th Connecticut Infantry
Battle or Place of Action: Port Hudson, Louisiana
Date of Action: 14 June 1863
Date of Issue: 1 April 1898
Citation: Made two trips across an open space, in the face of the enemy's concentrated fire, and secured water for the sick and wounded.

441 ◆ FOX, WILLIAM R.

Rank: Private (highest rank: Corporal)
Service: U.S. Army
Birthday: 1837
Place of Birth: Philadelphia, Philadelphia County, Pennsylvania
Entered Service at: Philadelphia, Philadelphia County, Pennsylvania
Unit: Company A, 95th Pennsylvania Infantry
Battle or Place of Action: Petersburg, Virginia
Date of Action: 2 April 1865
Date of Issue: 28 March 1879
Citation: Bravely assisted in the capture of one of the enemy's guns; with the first troops to enter the city, captured the flag of the Confederate customhouse.

442 ◆ FOY, CHARLES H.

Rank: Signal Quartermaster
Service: U.S. Navy
Birthday: 1809
Place of Birth: Portsmouth, Rockingham County, New Hampshire
Entered Service at: Springfield, Hampden County, Massachusetts
Unit: U.S.S. *Rhode Island*
Battle or Place of Action: Fort Fisher and the Federal Point batteries, North Carolina
Date of Action: 13-15 January 1865
G.O. Number, Date: 59, 22 June 1865
Citation: Served on board the U.S.S. *Rhode Island* during the actions with Fort Fisher and the Federal Point batteries, 13 to 15 January 1865. Carrying out his duties courageously during the battle, Foy continued to be outstanding by his good conduct and faithful services throughout the engagement, which resulted in a heavy casualty list when an attempt was made to storm Fort Fisher.

443 ◆ FRANKS, WILLIAM J.

Rank: Seaman (highest rank: Acting Master's Mate)
Service: U.S. Navy
Birthday: 1830
Place of Birth: Chatham County, North Carolina
Entered Service at: De Valls Bluff, Prairie County, Arkansas
Unit: U.S.S. *Marmora*
Battle or Place of Action: off Yazoo City, Mississippi
Date of Action: 5 March 1864
G.O. Number, Date: 32, 16 April 1864
Citation: Served on board the U.S.S. *Marmora* off Yazoo City, Miss., 5 March 1864. Embarking from the *Marmora* with a 12-pound howitzer mounted on a field carriage. Franks landed with the gun and crew in the midst of heated battle and, bravely standing by his gun despite enemy rifle fire

which cut the gun carriage and rammer, contributed to the turning back of the enemy during the fierce engagement.

444 ◆ FRANTZ, JOSEPH

Rank: Private
Service: U.S. Army
Birthday: 9 March 1837
Place of Birth: Eurapae, France
Date of Death: 14 October 1913
Cemetery: Calvary Catholic Cemetery—Northfield, Minnesota
Entered Service at: Osgood, Ripley County, Indiana
Unit: Company E, 83d Indiana Infantry
Battle or Place of Action: Vicksburg, Mississippi
Date of Action: 22 May 1863
Date of Issue: 13 August 1894
Citation: Gallantry in the charge of the "volunteer storming party."

445 ◆ FRASER, WILLIAM W.

Rank: Private (highest rank: Corporal)
Service: U.S. Army
Birthday: 7 March 1844
Place of Birth: Burn Brac, Scotland
Date of Death: 9 February 1915
Place of Death: Los Angeles, California
Cemetery: Odd Fellow Cemetery—Los Angeles, California
Entered Service at: Alton, Madison County, Illinois
Unit: Company I, 97th Illinois Infantry
Battle or Place of Action: Vicksburg, Mississippi
Date of Action: 22 May 1863
Date of Issue: 24 October 1895
Citation: Gallantry in the charge of the "volunteer storming party."

446 ◆ FREEMAN, ARCHIBALD

Rank: Private (highest rank: Sergeant)
Service: U.S. Army
Birthday: 13 August 1847
Place of Birth: Newburgh, Orange County, New York
Date of Death: 26 January 1918
Cemetery: Bethel Cemetery (MH)—Groesbeck, Texas
Entered Service at: Newburgh, Orange County, New York
Unit: Company E, 124th New York Infantry
Battle or Place of Action: Spotsylvania, Virginia
Date of Action: 12 May 1864
Date of Issue: 1 December 1864
Citation: Capture of flag.

447 ◆ FREEMAN, HENRY BLANCHARD

Rank: First Lieutenant (highest rank: Brigadier General)
Service: U.S. Army
Birthday: 17 January 1837
Place of Birth: Mount Vernon, Knox County, Ohio
Date of Death: 16 October 1915

Cemetery: Arlington National Cemetery (2-937)—Arlington, Virginia
Entered Service at: Mount Vernon, Knox County, Ohio
Unit: 18th U.S. Infantry
Battle or Place of Action: Stone River, Tennessee
Date of Action: 31 December 1862
Date of Issue: 17 February 1894
Citation: Voluntarily went to the front and picked up and carried to a place of safety, under a heavy fire from the enemy, an acting field officer who had been wounded, and was about to fall into enemy hands.
Notes: POW

448 ◆ FREEMAN, MARTIN

Rank: 1st Class Pilot (Civilian) (highest rank: Acting Volunteer Lieutenant)
Service: U.S. Navy
Birthday: 18 May 1814
Place of Birth: Germany
Date of Death: 11 September 1894
Place of Death: Pascagoula, Mississippi
Cemetery: Greenwood Cemetery—Pascagoula, Mississippi
Entered Service at: Ship's Island, Jackson County, Mississippi
Unit: U.S.S. *Hartford*
Battle or Place of Action: Mobile Bay, Alabama
Date of Action: 5 August 1864
G.O. Number, Date: 45, 31 December 1864
Citation: As pilot of the flagship U.S.S. *Hartford*, during action against Fort Morgan, rebel gunboats, the ram *Tennessee* in Mobile Bay, 5 August 1864. With his ship under a terrific enemy shellfire, Freeman calmly remained at his station in the maintop and skillfully piloted the ships into the bay. He rendered gallant service throughout the prolonged battle in which the rebel gunboats were captured or driven off, the prize ram *Tennessee* forced to surrender, and the fort successfully attacked.

449 ◆ FREEMAN, WILLIAM HENRY

Rank: Private
Service: U.S. Army
Birthday: 10 May 1844
Place of Birth: Troy, Rensselaer County, New York
Date of Death: 26 August 1911
Place of Death: Troy, New York
Cemetery: Oakwood Cemetery (MH)—Troy, New York
Entered Service at: Troy, Rensselaer County, New York
Unit: Company B, 169th New York Infantry
Battle or Place of Action: Fort Fisher, North Carolina
Date of Action: 15 January 1865
Date of Issue: 27 May 1905
Citation: Volunteered to carry the brigade flag after the bearer was wounded.

450 ◆ FRENCH, SAMUEL S.

Rank: Private
Service: U.S. Army
Birthday: 23 April 1841

Place of Birth: Erie County, New York
Date of Death: 17 February 1913
Place of Death: Gilford, Michigan
Cemetery: Gilford Township Cemetery—Gilford, Michigan
Entered Service at: Gifford, Tuscola County, Michigan
Unit: Company E, 7th Michigan Infantry
Battle or Place of Action: Fair Oaks, Virginia
Date of Action: 31 May 1862
Date of Issue: 24 October 1895
Citation: Continued fighting, although wounded, until he fainted from loss of blood.

451 ◆ FREY, FRANZ

Rank: Corporal
Service: U.S. Army
Birthday: 8 December 1837
Place of Birth: Switzerland
Date of Death: 13 March 1900
Cemetery: Lakeview Cemetery—Cleveland, Ohio
Entered Service at: Cleveland, Cuyahoga County, Ohio
Unit: Company H, 37th Ohio Infantry
Battle or Place of Action: Vicksburg, Mississippi
Date of Action: 22 May 1863
Date of Issue: 14 August 1894
Citation: Gallantry in the charge of the "volunteer storming party."

452 ◆ FRICK, JACOB G.

Rank: Colonel
Service: U.S. Army
Birthday: 23 January 1825
Place of Birth: Northumberland, Northumberland County, Pennsylvania
Date of Death: 5 March 1902
Cemetery: Presbyterian Church Cemetery (MH)—Pottsville, Pennsylvania
Entered Service at: Pottsville, Schuylkill County, Pennsylvania
Unit: 129th Pennsylvania Infantry
Battle or Place of Action: Fredericksburg & Chancellorsville, Virginia
Date of Action: 13 December 1862 & 3 May 1863
Date of Issue: 7 June 1892
Citation: At Fredericksburg seized the colors and led the command through a terrible fire of cannon and musketry. In a hand-to-hand fight at Chancellorsville, recaptured the colors of his regiment.

453 ◆ FRISBEE, JOHN B.

Rank: Gunner's Mate
Service: U.S. Navy
Birthday: 7 January 1825
Place of Birth: Phippsburg, Sagadahoc County, Maine
Date of Death: 9 September 1903
Place of Death: Bath, Maine
Cemetery: Fairview Cemetery (MH)—Winnegance, Maine
Entered Service at: Brookline, Norfolk County, Massachusetts

Unit: U.S. Steam Gunboat *Pinola*
Battle or Place of Action: Forts Jackson & St. Philip and New Orleans, Louisiana
Date of Action: 24 April 1862
G.O. Number, Date: 11, 3 April 1863
Citation: Served on board the U.S. steam gunboat *Pinola* during action against Forts Jackson and St. Philip, and during the taking of New Orleans, 24 April 1862. While engaged in the bombardment of Fort St. Philip, Frisbee, acting courageously and without personal regard, closed the powder magazine which had been set afire by enemy shelling and shut off his avenue of escape, thereby setting a high example of bravery. He served courageously throughout these engagements which resulted in the taking of the Forts Jackson and St Philip and in the surrender of New Orleans.

454 ◆ FRIZZELL, HENRY F.

Rank: Private (highest rank: Corporal)
Service: U.S. Army
Place of Birth: Madison County, Missouri
Date of Death: 25 May 1904
Place of Death: St. Louis, Missouri
Cemetery: Mount Lebanon Cemetery (MH)—St. Louis, Missouri
Entered Service at: Pilot Knob, Iron County, Missouri
Unit: Company B, 6th Missouri Infantry
Battle or Place of Action: Vicksburg, Mississippi
Date of Action: 22 May 1863
Date of Issue: 30 July 1894
Citation: Gallantry in the charge of the "volunteer storming party."

455 ◆ FRY, ISAAC N.

Rank: Orderly Sergeant
Service: U.S. Marine Corps
Place of Birth: Lancaster, Lancaster County, Pennsylvania
Entered Service at: Philadelphia, Philadelphia County, Pennsylvania
Unit: U.S.S. *Ticonderoga*
Battle or Place of Action: Fort Fisher, North Carolina
Date of Action: 13-15 January 1865
G.O. Number, Date: 59, 22 June 1865
Citation: On board the U.S.S. *Ticonderoga* during attacks on Fort Fisher, 13 to 15 January 1865. As orderly sergeant of marine guard and captain of a gun, Orderly Sgt. Fry performed his duties with skill and courage as the *Ticonderoga* maintained a well-placed fire upon the batteries to the left of the palisades during the initial phases of the three-day battle, and thereafter, as she considerably lessened the firing power of guns on the mount which had been turned upon our assaulting columns. During this action the flag was planted on one of the strongest fortifications possessed by the rebels.

456 ◆ FUGER, FREDERICK W.

Rank: Sergeant (highest rank: Lieutenant Colonel USA Ret.)
Service: U.S. Army

Birthday: 18 June 1836
Place of Birth: Wurttemberg, Germany
Date of Death: 13 October 1913
Place of Death: Washington, D.C.
Cemetery: Arlington National Cemetery (1-511)—Arlington, Virginia
Entered Service at: New York, New York
Unit: Battery A, 4th U.S. Artillery
Battle or Place of Action: Gettysburg, Pennsylvania
Date of Action: 3 July 1863
Date of Issue: 24 August 1897
Citation: All the officers of his battery having been killed or wounded and five of its guns disabled in Pickett's assault, he succeeded to the command and fought the remaining gun with most distinguished gallantry until the battery was ordered withdrawn.

457 ◆ FUNK, WEST

Rank: Major
Service: U.S. Army
Place of Birth: Boston, Suffolk County, Massachusetts
Date of Death: 30 July 1897
Place of Death: Philadelphia, Pennsylvania
Entered Service at: Philadelphia, Philadelphia County, Pennsylvania
Unit: 121st Pennsylvania Infantry
Battle or Place of Action: Appomattox Courthouse, Virginia
Date of Action: 9 April 1865
Date of Issue: 15 October 1872
Citation: Capture of flag of 46th Virginia Infantry (C.S.A.).

458 ◆ FURMAN, CHESTER S.

Rank: Corporal
Service: U.S. Army
Birthday: 14 February 1842
Place of Birth: Columbia, Lancaster County, Pennsylvania
Date of Death: 22 July 1910
Cemetery: Old Rosemont Cemetery—Bloomsburg, Pennsylvania
Entered Service at: Bloomsburg, Columbia County, Pennsylvania
Unit: Company A, 6th Pennsylvania Reserves
Battle or Place of Action: Gettysburg, Pennsylvania
Date of Action: 2 July 1863
Date of Issue: 3 August 1897
Citation: Was one of six volunteers who charged upon a log house near Devil's Den, where a squad of the enemy's sharpshooters were sheltered, and compelled their surrender.

459 ◆ FURNESS, FRANK

Rank: Captain
Service: U.S. Army
Birthday: 12 November 1839
Place of Birth: Philadelphia, Philadelphia County, Pennsylvania

Date of Death: 27 June 1912
Place of Death: Media, Pennsylvania
Cemetery: Laurel Hill Cemetery (MH)—Philadelphia, Pennsylvania
Entered Service at: Philadelphia, Philadelphia County, Pennsylvania
Unit: Company F, 6th Pennsylvania Cavalry
Battle or Place of Action: Trevilian Station, Virginia
Date of Action: 12 June 1864
Date of Issue: 20 October 1899
Citation: Voluntarily carried a box of ammunition across an open space swept by the enemy's fire to the relief of an outpost whose ammunition had become almost exhausted, but which was thus enabled to hold its important position.

460 ◆ GAGE, RICHARD J.

Rank: Private
Service: U.S. Army
Birthday: 1842
Place of Birth: Grafton County, New Hampshire
Date of Death: 28 April 1903
Cemetery: Maxton Cemetery (MH)—Seneca, Illinois
Entered Service at: Ottawa, La Salle County, Illinois
Unit: Company D, 104th Illinois Infantry
Battle or Place of Action: Elk River, Tennessee
Date of Action: 2 July 1863
Date of Issue: 30 October 1897
Citation: Voluntarily joined a small party that, under a heavy fire, captured a stockade and saved the bridge.

461 ◆ GALLOWAY, GEORGE NORTON

Rank: Private
Service: U.S. Army
Birthday: 1841/42
Place of Birth: Philadelphia, Philadelphia County, Pennsylvania
Date of Death: 9 February 1904
Place of Death: Philadelphia, Pennsylvania
Cemetery: Mount Moriah Cemetery—Philadelphia, Pennsylvania
Entered Service at: Philadelphia, Philadelphia County, Pennsylvania
Unit: Company G, 95th Pennsylvania Infantry
Battle or Place of Action: Alsops Farm, Virginia
Date of Action: 8 May 1864
Date of Issue: 24 October 1895
Citation: Voluntarily held an important position under heavy fire.

462 ◆ GALLOWAY, JOHN

Rank: Commissary Sergeant (highest rank: First Lieutenant)
Service: U.S. Army
Place of Birth: Philadelphia, Philadelphia County, Pennsylvania
Date of Death: 23 May 1904
Place of Death: Philadelphia, Pennsylvania

Cemetery: Mount Moriah Cemetery—Philadelphia, Pennsylvania
Entered Service at: Philadelphia, Philadelphia County, Pennsylvania
Unit: 8th Pennsylvania Cavalry
Battle or Place of Action: Farmville, Virginia
Date of Action: 7 April 1865
Date of Issue: 30 October 1897
Citation: His regiment being surprised and nearly overwhelmed, he dashed forward under a heavy fire, reached the right of the regiment, where the danger was greatest, rallied the men, and prevented a disaster that was imminent.

463 ◆ GARDINER, JAMES

True Name: Gardner, James Daniel
Rank: Private
Service: U.S. Army
Birthday: 16 September 1839
Place of Birth: Gloucester, Gloucester County, Virginia
Date of Death: 29 September 1905
Place of Death: Clark's Summit, Pennsylvania
Cemetery: Calvary Crest Cemetery (MH)—Ottumwa, Iowa
Entered Service at: Yorktown, York County, Virginia
Unit: Company I, 36th U.S. Colored Infantry
Battle or Place of Action: Chapin's Farm, Virginia
Date of Action: 29 September 1864
Date of Issue: 6 April 1865
Citation: Rushed in advance of his brigade, shot a rebel officer who was on the parapet rallying his men, and then ran him through with his bayonet.

464 ◆ GARDNER, CHARLES N.

Rank: Private (highest rank: Second Lieutenant)
Service: U.S. Army
Birthday: 29 March 1845
Place of Birth: South Scituate, Plymouth County, Massachusetts
Date of Death: 22 February 1919
Place of Death: Accord, Massachusetts
Cemetery: Washington Street Cemetery (MH)—Norwell, Massachusetts
Entered Service at: Scituate, Plymouth County, Massachusetts
Unit: Company E, 32d Massachusetts Infantry
Battle or Place of Action: Five Forks, Virginia
Date of Action: 1 April 1865
Date of Issue: 10 May 1865
Citation: Capture of flag.

465 ◆ GARDNER, ROBERT J.

Rank: Sergeant (highest rank: First Sergeant)
Service: U.S. Army
Birthday: 28 September 1837
Place of Birth: Livingston, Columbia County, New York
Date of Death: 23 September 1902
Place of Death: Iosco, Michigan

Cemetery: Munsell Cemetery—Iosco Township, Michigan
Entered Service at: Egremont, Berkshire County, Massachusetts
Unit: Company K, 34th Massachusetts Infantry
Battle or Place of Action: Petersburg, Virginia
Date of Action: 2 April 1865
Date of Issue: 12 May 1865
Citation: Was among the first to enter Fort Gregg, clearing his way by using his musket on the heads of the enemy.

466 ◆ GARDNER, WILLIAM

Rank: Seaman (highest rank: Ship's Cook)
Service: U.S. Navy
Birthday: 1832
Place of Birth: Ireland
Entered Service at: New York, New York
Unit: U.S.S. *Galena*
Battle or Place of Action: Mobile Bay, Alabama
Date of Action: 5 August 1864
G.O. Number, Date: 45, 31 December 1864
Citation: As seaman on board the U.S.S. *Galena* in the engagement at Mobile Bay, 5 August 1864. Serving gallantly during this fierce battle which resulted in the capture of the rebel ram *Tennessee* and the damaging of Fort Morgan, Gardner behaved with conspicuous coolness under the fire of the enemy.

467 ◆ GARRETT, WILLIAM

Rank: Sergeant
Service: U.S. Army
Birthday: 6 February 1842
Place of Birth: Isle of Man, England
Date of Death: 30 December 1916
Place of Death: Leavenworth, Kansas
Cemetery: Leavenworth National Cemetery (32-3-26) (MH)—Leavenworth, Kansas
Entered Service at: Chardon, Geauga County, Ohio
Unit: Company G, 41st Ohio Infantry
Battle or Place of Action: Nashville, Tennessee
Date of Action: 16 December 1864
Date of Issue: 24 February 1865
Citation: With several companions dashed forward, the first to enter the enemy's works, taking possession of four pieces of artillery and captured the flag of the 13th Mississippi Infantry (C.S.A.).

468 ◆ GARRISON, JAMES R.

Rank: Coal Heaver
Service: U.S. Navy
Birthday: 22 June 1838
Place of Birth: Poughkeepsie, Dutchess County, New York
Date of Death: 19 April 1908
Place of Death: Hampton, Virginia
Cemetery: Hampton National Cemetery (B-9523) (MH)—Hampton, Virginia
Entered Service at: New York, New York

Unit: U.S.S. *Hartford*
Battle or Place of Action: Mobile Bay, Alabama
Date of Action: 5 August 1864
G.O. Number, Date: 45, 31 December 1864
Citation: On board the flagship, U.S.S. *Hartford*, during successful engagements against Fort Morgan, rebel gunboats, the ram *Tennessee* in Mobile Bay, 5 August 1864. When a shell struck his foot and severed one of his toes, Garrison remained at his station at the shell whip and, after crudely bandaging the wound, continued to perform his duties until severely wounded by another shell burst.

469 ◆ GARVIN, WILLIAM

Rank: Captain of the Forecastle (highest rank: Boatswain's Mate)
Service: U.S. Navy
Birthday: 1835
Place of Birth: west Canada
Entered Service at: Plymouth, Litchfield County, Connecticut
Unit: U.S.S. *Agawam*
Battle or Place of Action: Fort Fisher, North Carolina
Date of Action: 23 December 1864
G.O. Number, Date: 45, 31 December 1864
Citation: Garvin served on board the U.S.S. *Agawam*, as one of a volunteer crew of a powder boat which was exploded near Fort Fisher, 23 December 1864. The powder boat, towed in by the *Wilderness* to prevent detection by the enemy, cast off and slowly steamed to within 300 yards of the beach. After fuses and fires had been lit and a second anchor with short scope let go to assure the boat's tailing inshore, the crew again boarded the *Wilderness* and proceeded a distance of 12 miles from shore. Less than two hours later the explosion took place, and the following day fires were observed still burning at the fort.

470 ◆ *GASSON, RICHARD

Rank: Sergeant
Service: U.S. Army
Birthday: 1842
Place of Birth: Ireland
Date of Death: 29 September 1864
Place of Death: Chapins Farm, Virginia
Entered Service at: New York, New York
Unit: Company K, 47th New York Infantry
Battle or Place of Action: Chapin's Farm, Virginia
Date of Action: 29 September 1864
Date of Issue: 6 April 1865
Citation: Fell dead while planting the colors of his regiment on the enemy's works.

471 ◆ GAUNT, JOHN C.

Rank: Private
Service: U.S. Army
Place of Birth: Columbiana County, Ohio
Date of Death: 13 January 1886

Cemetery: unknown cemetery—Garfield, Ohio
Entered Service at: Damascoville, Ohio
Unit: Company G, 104th Ohio Infantry
Battle or Place of Action: Franklin, Tennessee
Date of Action: 30 November 1864
Date of Issue: 13 February 1865
Citation: Capture of flag.

472 ◆ GAUSE, ISAAC

Rank: Corporal (highest rank: Sergeant)
Service: U.S. Army
Birthday: 9 December 1843
Place of Birth: Trumbull County, Ohio
Date of Death: 23 April 1920
Place of Death: Johnson City, Tennessee
Cemetery: Arlington National Cemetery (17-19595) (MH)—Arlington, Virginia
Entered Service at: Canfield, Mahoning County, Ohio
Unit: Company E, 2d Ohio Cavalry
Battle or Place of Action: near Berryville, Virginia
Date of Action: 13 September 1864
Date of Issue: 19 September 1864
Citation: Capture of the colors of the 8th South Carolina Infantry while engaged in a reconnaissance along the Berryville and Winchester Pike.

473 ◆ GAYLORD, LEVI B.

Rank: Sergeant
Service: U.S. Army
Birthday: 23 September 1840
Place of Birth: Boston, Suffolk County, Massachusetts
Date of Death: 6 December 1900
Place of Death: Dorchester, Massachusetts
Cemetery: Cohasset Central Cemetery (MH)—Cohasset, Massachusetts
Entered Service at: Boston, Suffolk County, Massachusetts
Unit: Company A, 29th Massachusetts Infantry
Battle or Place of Action: Fort Stedman, Virginia
Date of Action: 25 March 1865
Date of Issue: 22 June 1896
Citation: Voluntarily assisted in working an abandoned gun, while exposed to heavy fire, until the enemy's advancing line was routed by a charge on its left flank.

474 ◆ GEORGE, DANIEL GRIFFIN

Rank: Ordinary Seaman
Service: U.S. Navy
Birthday: 7 July 1840
Place of Birth: Plaistow, Rockingham County, New Hampshire
Date of Death: 26 February 1916
Place of Death: Amesbury, Massachusetts
Cemetery: Locust Grove Cemetery (MH)—Merrimac, Massachusetts
Entered Service at: New Hampshire
Unit: U.S. Picket Boat No. 1

Battle or Place of Action: Plymouth, North Carolina
Date of Action: 27 October 1864
G.O. Number, Date: 45, 31 December 1864
Citation: George served on board the U.S. Picket Boat No. 1 in action, 27 October 1864, against the Confederate ram *Albemarle*, which had resisted repeated attacks by our steamers and had kept a large force of vessels employed in watching her. The picket boat, equipped with a spar torpedo, succeeded in passing the enemy pickets within 20 yards without being discovered and then made for the *Albemarle* under a full head of steam. Immediately taken under fire by the ram, the small boat plunged on, jumped the log boom which encircled the target, and exploded its torpedo under the port bow of the ram. The picket boat was destroyed by enemy fire and almost the entire crew was taken prisoner or lost.
Notes: POW

475 ◆ GERE, THOMAS PARKE

Rank: First Lieutenant & Adjutant
Service: U.S. Army
Birthday: 10 December 1842
Place of Birth: Wellsburg, Chemung County, New York
Date of Death: 8 January 1912
Cemetery: Arlington National Cemetery (1-361) (MH)—Arlington, Virginia
Entered Service at: Fort Snelling, St. Paul County, Minnesota
Unit: 5th Minnesota Infantry
Battle or Place of Action: Nashville, Tennessee
Date of Action: 16 December 1864
Date of Issue: 24 February 1865
Citation: Capture of flag of 4th Mississippi (C.S.A.).

476 ◆ GESCHWIND, NICHOLAS

Rank: Captain
Service: U.S. Army
Place of Birth: France
Date of Death: 2 January 1897
Cemetery: Springdale Cemetery—Peoria, Illinois
Entered Service at: Pleasant Hill, Pike County, Illinois
Unit: Company F, 116th Illinois Infantry
Battle or Place of Action: Vicksburg, Mississippi
Date of Action: 22 May 1863
Date of Issue: 24 August 1894
Citation: Gallantry in the charge of the "volunteer storming party."

477 ◆ GIBBS, WESLEY

Rank: Sergeant
Service: U.S. Army
Birthday: 24 July 1842
Place of Birth: Sharon, Litchfield County, Connecticut
Date of Death: 29 May 1917
Cemetery: Forest View Cemetery (MH)—Winchester, Connecticut

Entered Service at: Salisbury, Litchfield County, Connecticut
Unit: Company B, 2d Connecticut Heavy Artillery
Battle or Place of Action: Petersburg, Virginia
Date of Action: 2 April 1865
Date of Issue: 10 May 1865
Citation: Capture of flag.

478 ◆ GIFFORD, BENJAMIN

Rank: Private
Service: U.S. Army
Birthday: 13 September 1833
Place of Birth: German Flats, Herkimer County, New York
Date of Death: 14 July 1901
Cemetery: Hinsdale Cemetery (MH)—Hinsdale, New York
Entered Service at: German Flats, Herkimer County, New York
Unit: Company H, 121st New York Infantry
Battle or Place of Action: Deatonsville (Sailor's Creek), Virginia
Date of Action: 6 April 1865
Date of Issue: 10 May 1865
Citation: Capture of flag.

479 ◆ GIFFORD, DAVID L.

Rank: Private
Service: U.S. Army
Birthday: 18 September 1844
Place of Birth: Dartmouth, Bristol County, Massachusetts
Date of Death: 13 January 1904
Place of Death: Dartmouth, Massachusetts
Cemetery: South Dartmouth Cemetery—South Dartmouth, Massachusetts
Entered Service at: New Bedford, Bristol County, Massachusetts
Unit: Company B, 4th Massachusetts Cavalry
Battle or Place of Action: Ashepoo River, South Carolina
Date of Action: 24 May 1864
Date of Issue: 21 January 1897
Citation: Volunteered as a member of a boat crew which went to the rescue of a large number of Union soldiers on board the stranded steamer Boston and with great gallantry assisted in conveying them to shore, being exposed during the entire time to a heavy fire from a Confederate battery.

480 ◆ GILE, FRANK S.

Rank: Landsman
Service: U.S. Navy
Birthday: 15 September 1847
Place of Birth: Massachusetts
Date of Death: 19 March 1898
Place of Death: South Andover, Massachusetts
Cemetery: Ridgewood Cemetery (MH)—North Andover, Massachusetts
Entered Service at: Massachusetts
Unit: U.S.S. *Lehigh*

Battle or Place of Action: Charleston Harbor, South Carolina
Date of Action: 16 November 1863
G.O. Number, Date: 32, 16 April 1864
Citation: On board the U.S.S. *Lehigh*, Charleston Harbor, 16 November 1863, during the hazardous task of freeing the *Lehigh*, which had been grounded and was under heavy enemy fire from Fort Moultrie. After several previous attempts had been made, Gile succeeded in passing in a small boat from the *Lehigh* to the *Nahant* with a line bent on a hawser. This courageous action while under severe enemy fire enabled the *Lehigh* to be freed from her helpless position.

481 ◆ GILLESPIE JR., GEORGE LEWIS

Rank: First Lieutenant (highest rank: Major General)
Service: U.S. Army
Birthday: 7 October 1841
Place of Birth: Kingston, Roane County, Tennessee
Date of Death: 27 September 1913
Place of Death: Saratoga, New York
Cemetery: U.S. Military Academy Cemetery (S-37)—West Point, New York
Entered Service at: Chattanooga, Hamilton County, Tennessee
Unit: Corps of Engineers
Battle or Place of Action: near Bethesda Church, Virginia
Date of Action: 31 May 1864
Date of Issue: 27 October 1897
Citation: Exposed himself to great danger by voluntarily making his way through the enemy's lines to communicate with Gen. Sheridan. While rendering this service he was captured, but escaped; again came in contact with the enemy, was again ordered to surrender, but escaped by dashing away under fire.

482 ◆ GILLIGAN, EDWARD LYONS

Rank: First Sergeant (highest rank: Captain)
Service: U.S. Army
Birthday: 18 April 1843
Place of Birth: Philadelphia, Philadelphia County, Pennsylvania
Date of Death: 2 April 1922
Place of Death: Oxford, Pennsylvania
Cemetery: Oxford Cemetery (MH)—Oxford, Pennsylvania
Entered Service at: Philadelphia, Philadelphia County, Pennsylvania
Unit: Company E, 88th Pennsylvania Infantry
Battle or Place of Action: Gettysburg, Pennsylvania
Date of Action: 1 July 1863
Date of Issue: 30 April 1892
Citation: Assisted in the capture of a Confederate flag by knocking down the color sergeant.

483 ◆ GILMORE, JOHN CURTIS

Rank: Major (highest rank: Brigadier General USA)
Service: U.S. Army

Birthday: 18 April 1837
Place of Birth: Canada
Date of Death: 22 December 1922
Cemetery: Arlington National Cemetery (1-270)—Arlington, Virginia
Entered Service at: Potsdam, St. Lawrence County, New York
Unit: 16th New York Infantry
Battle or Place of Action: Salem Heights, Virginia
Date of Action: 3 May 1863
Date of Issue: 10 October 1892
Citation: Seized the colors of his regiment and gallantly rallied his men under a very severe fire.

484 ◆ GINLEY, PATRICK

Rank: Private
Service: U.S. Army
Birthday: 11 December 1822
Place of Birth: Ireland
Date of Death: 5 April 1917
Place of Death: New York, New York
Cemetery: 1st Calvary Cemetery—Woodside, New York
Entered Service at: New York, New York
Unit: Company G, 1st New York Light Artillery
Battle or Place of Action: Reams' Station, Virginia
Date of Action: 25 August 1864
Date of Issue: 31 October 1890
Citation: The command having been driven from the works, he, having been left alone between the opposing lines, crept back into the works, put three charges of canister in one of the guns and fired the piece directly into a body of the enemy about to seize the works; he then rejoined his command, took the colors, and ran toward the enemy, followed by the command, which recaptured the works and guns.

485 ◆ GION, JOSEPH

Rank: Private
Service: U.S. Army
Birthday: 1826
Place of Birth: Alsace-Lorraine area, Germany
Date of Death: 16 January 1889
Place of Death: Chartiers Township, Pennsylvania
Cemetery: St. Martin's Cemetery (MH)—Pittsburgh, Pennsylvania
Entered Service at: Allegheny County, Pennsylvania
Unit: Company A, 74th New York Infantry
Battle or Place of Action: Chancellorsville, Virginia
Date of Action: 2 May 1863
Date of Issue: 26 November 1884
Citation: Voluntarily and under heavy fire advanced toward the enemy's lines and secured valuable information.

486 ◆ GODLEY, LEONIDAS MAHLON

Rank: First Sergeant
Service: U.S. Army
Birthday: 13 June 1836

Place of Birth: Mason County, West Virginia
Date of Death: 23 May 1904
Place of Death: Ottumwa, Iowa
Cemetery: Ottumwa Cemetery—Ottumwa, Iowa
Entered Service at: Ashland, Iowa
Unit: Company E, 22d Iowa Infantry
Battle or Place of Action: Vicksburg, Mississippi
Date of Action: 22 May 1863
Date of Issue: 3 August 1897
Citation: Led his company in the assault on the enemy's works and gained the parapet, there receiving three very severe wounds. He lay all day in the sun, was taken prisoner, and had his leg amputated without anesthetics.
Notes: POW

487 ◆ GOETTEL, PHILIP

Rank: Private (highest rank: Corporal)
Service: U.S. Army
Birthday: 2 September 1840
Place of Birth: Salina, Onondaga County, New York
Date of Death: 30 January 1920
Place of Death: Syracuse, New York
Cemetery: Woodlawn Cemetery (MH)—Syracuse, New York
Entered Service at: Syracuse, Onondaga County, New York
Unit: Company B, 149th New York Infantry
Battle or Place of Action: Ringgold, Georgia
Date of Action: 27 November 1863
Date of Issue: 28 June 1865
Citation: Capture of flag and a battery guidon.

488 ◆ GOHEEN, CHARLES ARTHUR

Rank: First Sergeant (highest rank: First Lieutenant)
Service: U.S. Army
Birthday: 5 August 1843
Place of Birth: Groveland, Livingston County, New York
Date of Death: 8 May 1889
Place of Death: Mendon, New York
Cemetery: Honeoye Falls Cemetery (MH)—Honeoye Falls, New York
Entered Service at: Rochester, Monroe County, New York
Unit: Company G, 8th New York Cavalry
Battle or Place of Action: Waynesboro, Virginia
Date of Action: 2 March 1865
Date of Issue: 26 March 1865
Citation: Capture of flag.

489 ◆ GOLDSBERY, ANDREW E.

True Name: Goldsberry, Andrew E.
Rank: Private
Service: U.S. Army
Birthday: 25 September 1840
Place of Birth: St. Charles, Kane County, Illinois
Date of Death: 27 October 1910
Place of Death: Fairbank, Iowa
Cemetery: Long Grove Cemetery—Maynard, Iowa

Entered Service at: St. Charles, Kane County, Illinois
Unit: Company E, 127th Illinois Infantry
Battle or Place of Action: Vicksburg, Mississippi
Date of Action: 22 May 1863
Date of Issue: 9 August 1894
Citation: Gallantry in the charge of the "volunteer storming party."

490 ◆ GOODALL, FRANCIS HENRY

Rank: First Sergeant
Service: U.S. Army
Birthday: 10 January 1838
Place of Birth: Bath, Grafton County, New Hampshire
Date of Death: 12 April 1925
Place of Death: Takoma Park, Maryland
Cemetery: Rock Creek Cemetery—Washington, D.C.
Entered Service at: Bath, Grafton County, New Hampshire
Unit: Company G, 11th New Hampshire Infantry
Battle or Place of Action: Fredericksburg, Virginia
Date of Action: 13 December 1862
Date of Issue: 14 December 1894
Citation: With the assistance of another soldier brought a wounded comrade into the lines, under heavy fire.

491 ◆ GOODMAN, WILLAIM ERNEST

Rank: First Lieutenant (highest rank: Major)
Service: U.S. Army
Birthday: 10 December 1838
Place of Birth: Philadelphia, Philadelphia County, Pennsylvania
Date of Death: 22 March 1912
Place of Death: Philadelphia, Pennsylvania
Cemetery: St. Thomas Church Cemetery (MH)—Whitemarsh, Pennsylvania
Entered Service at: Philadelphia, Philadelphia County, Pennsylvania
Unit: Company D, 147th Pennsylvania Infantry
Battle or Place of Action: Chancellorsville, Virginia
Date of Action: 3 May 1863
Date of Issue: 11 January 1894
Citation: Rescued the colors of the 107th Ohio Volunteers from the enemy.

492 ◆ GOODRICH, EDWIN

Rank: First Lieutenant (highest rank: Major)
Service: U.S. Army
Birthday: 22 March 1843
Place of Birth: New York, New York
Date of Death: 26 November 1910
Cemetery: Graceland Cemetery—Chicago, Illinois
Entered Service at: Westfield, Chautauqua County, New York
Unit: Company D, 9th New York Cavalry
Battle or Place of Action: near Cedar Creek, Virginia
Date of Action: November 1864
Date of Issue: 14 May 1894

Citation: While the command was falling back, he returned and in the face of the enemy rescued a sergeant from under his fallen horse.

493 ◆ GOULD, CHARLES GILBERT

Rank: Captain (highest rank: Brevet Major)
Service: U.S. Army
Birthday: 5 May 1845
Place of Birth: Windham County, Vermont
Date of Death: 5 December 1916
Cemetery: Windham Central Cemetery—Windham, Vermont
Entered Service at: Windham County, Vermont
Unit: Company H, 5th Vermont Infantry
Battle or Place of Action: Petersburg, Virginia
Date of Action: 2 April 1865
Date of Issue: 30 July 1890
Citation: Among the first to mount the enemy's works in the assault, he received a serious bayonet wound in the face, was struck several times with clubbed muskets, but bravely stood his ground, and with his sword killed the man who had bayoneted him.

494 ◆ GOULD, NEWTON THOMAS

Rank: Private (highest rank: Sergeant)
Service: U.S. Army
Birthday: 14 May 1843
Place of Birth: Elk Grove, Cook County, Illinois
Date of Death: 2 April 1925
Cemetery: Sacramento City Cemetery (MH)—Sacramento, California
Entered Service at: Elk Grove, Cook County, Illinois
Unit: Company G, 113th Illinois Infantry
Battle or Place of Action: Vicksburg, Mississippi
Date of Action: 22 May 1863
Date of Issue: 6 September 1894
Citation: Gallantry in the charge of the "volunteer storming party."
Notes: POW

495 ◆ GOURAUD, GEORGE EDWARD

Rank: Captain & Aide-de-Camp (highest rank: Brevet Lieutenant Colonel U.S. Vols.)
Service: U.S. Army
Birthday: 1840
Place of Birth: New York, New York
Date of Death: 17 February 1912
Place of Death: England
Entered Service at: New York, New York
Unit: U.S. Volunteers
Battle or Place of Action: Honey Hill, South Carolina
Date of Action: 30 November 1864
Date of Issue: 21 August 1893
Citation: While under severe fire of the enemy, which drove back the command, rendered valuable assistance in rallying the men.

496 ◆ GRACE, PETER

Rank: Sergeant (highest rank: Captain)
Service: U.S. Army
Birthday: 18 March 1845
Place of Birth: Berkshire, Berkshire County, Massachusetts
Date of Death: 27 March 1914
Cemetery: Arlington National Cemetery (3-2556)—Arlington, Virginia
Entered Service at: Berkshire, Berkshire County, Massachusetts
Unit: Company G, 83d Pennsylvania Infantry
Battle or Place of Action: Wilderness Campaign, Virginia
Date of Action: 5 May 1864
Date of Issue: 27 December 1894
Citation: Singlehandedly rescued a comrade from two Confederate guards, knocking down one and compelling the surrender of the other.

497 ◆ GRAHAM, ROBERT

True Name: Hall, Frederick, reenlisted U.S. Marine Corps 1881
Rank: Landsman
Service: U.S. Navy
Birthday: 1841
Place of Birth: England
Entered Service at: New York
Unit: U.S.S. *Tacony*
Battle or Place of Action: Plymouth, North Carolina
Date of Action: 31 October 1864
G.O. Number, Date: 45, 31 December 1864
Citation: Served on board the U.S.S. *Tacony* during the taking of Plymouth, N.C., 31 October 1864. Carrying out his duties faithfully during the capture of Plymouth, Graham distinguished himself by a display of coolness when he participated in landing and spiking a 9-inch gun while under a devastating fire from enemy musketry.

498 ◆ GRAHAM, THOMAS N.

Rank: Second Lieutenant
Service: U.S. Army
Birthday: 16 September 1837
Date of Death: 4 February 1911
Cemetery: Oak Hill Cemetery (MH)—Lawrence, Kansas
Entered Service at: Westville, La Porte County, Indiana
Unit: Company G, 15th Indiana Infantry
Battle or Place of Action: Missionary Ridge, Tennessee
Date of Action: 25 November 1863
Date of Issue: 15 February 1897
Citation: Seized the colors from the color bearer, who had been wounded, and, exposed to a terrible fire, carried them forward, planting them on the enemy's breastworks.

499 ◆ GRANT, GABRIEL

Rank: Surgeon (highest rank: Major)
Service: U.S. Army

Place of Birth: Newark, Essex County, New Jersey
Date of Death: 8 November 1909
Cemetery: Sleepy Hollow Cemetery (MH)—Tarrytown, New York
Entered Service at: Trenton, Mercer County, New Jersey
Unit: U.S. Volunteers
Battle or Place of Action: Fair Oaks, Virginia
Date of Action: 1 June 1862
Date of Issue: 21 July 1897
Citation: Removed severely wounded officers and soldiers from the field while under a heavy fire from the enemy, exposing himself beyond the call of duty, thus furnishing an example of most distinguished gallantry.

500 ◆ GRANT, LEWIS ADDISON

Rank: Colonel (highest rank: Brevet Major General U.S. Vols.)
Service: U.S. Army
Birthday: 17 January 1829
Place of Birth: Winhall, Vermont
Date of Death: 20 March 1918
Cemetery: Lakewood Cemetery—Minneapolis, Minnesota
Entered Service at: Bellows Falls, Windham County, Vermont
Unit: 5th Vermont Infantry
Battle or Place of Action: Salem Heights, Virginia
Date of Action: 3 May 1864
Date of Issue: 11 May 1893
Citation: Personal gallantry and intrepidity displayed in the management of his brigade and in leading it in the assault in which he was wounded.

501 ◆ GRAUL, WILLIAM L.

Rank: Corporal
Service: U.S. Army
Birthday: 27 July 1846
Place of Birth: Reading, Berks County, Pennsylvania
Date of Death: 2 September 1909
Place of Death: Reading, Berks County, Pennsylvania
Cemetery: Charles Evans Cemetery (MH)—Reading, Pennsylvania
Entered Service at: Reading, Berks County, Pennsylvania
Unit: Company I, 188th Pennsylvania Infantry
Battle or Place of Action: Fort Harrison, Virginia
Date of Action: 29 September 1864
Date of Issue: 6 April 1865
Citation: First to plant the colors of his State on the fortifications.

502 ◆ GRAY, JOHN

Rank: Private (highest rank: Musician)
Service: U.S. Army
Birthday: 1836
Place of Birth: Dundee, Scotland
Date of Death: 1 June 1887
Place of Death: Leavenworth, Kansas

Cemetery: Leavenworth National Cemetery (9-1-23) (MH)—Leavenworth, Kansas
Entered Service at: Cincinnati, Hamilton County, Ohio
Unit: Company B, 5th Ohio Infantry
Battle or Place of Action: Port Republic, Virginia
Date of Action: 9 June 1862
Date of Issue: 14 March 1864
Citation: Mounted an artillery horse of the enemy and captured a brass six-pound piece in the face of the enemy's fire and brought it to the rear.

503 ◆ GRAY, ROBERT A.

Rank: Sergeant
Service: U.S. Army
Birthday: 21 September 1834
Place of Birth: Philadelphia, Philadelphia County, Pennsylvania
Date of Death: 22 November 1906
Place of Death: Groton, Connecticut
Cemetery: Colonel Ledyard Cemetery (MH)—Groton, Connecticut
Entered Service at: Groton, New London County, Connecticut
Unit: Company C, 21st Connecticut Infantry
Battle or Place of Action: Drewry's Bluff, Virginia
Date of Action: 16 May 1864
Date of Issue: 13 July 1897
Citation: While retreating with his regiment, which had been repulsed, he voluntarily returned, in the face of the enemy's fire, to a former position and rescued a wounded officer of his company who was unable to walk.

504 ◆ GREBE, M. R. WILLIAM

Rank: Captain (highest rank: Major)
Service: U.S. Army
Birthday: 4 August 1838
Place of Birth: Hildesheim, Germany
Date of Death: 24 December 1916
Place of Death: Bonner Springs, Kansas
Cemetery: Mount St. Mary's Cemetery—Kansas City, Missouri
Entered Service at: St. Louis, St. Louis County, Missouri
Unit: Company F, 4th Missouri Cavalry
Battle or Place of Action: Jonesboro, Georgia
Date of Action: 31 August 1864
Date of Issue: 24 February 1899
Citation: While acting as aide and carrying orders across a most dangerous part of the battlefield, being hindered by a Confederate advance, seized a rifle, took a place in the ranks and was conspicuous in repulsing the enemy.

505 ◆ GREEN, GEORGE

Rank: Corporal
Service: U.S. Army
Birthday: 16 July 1840
Place of Birth: Elsham, Lincolnshire County, England

Date of Death: 10 February 1898
Cemetery: Riverside Cemetery—Troy, Ohio
Entered Service at: Columbus, Franklin County, Ohio
Unit: Company H, 11th Ohio Infantry
Battle or Place of Action: Missionary Ridge, Tennessee
Date of Action: 25 November 1863
Date of Issue: 12 January 1892
Citation: Scaled the enemy's works and in a hand-to-hand fight helped capture the flag of the 18th Alabama Infantry (C.S.A.).

506 ◆ GREENAWALT, ABRAHAM

Rank: Private
Service: U.S. Army
Birthday: 1834
Place of Birth: Montgomery County, Pennsylvania
Date of Death: 27 October 1922
Cemetery: City Cemetery—Alliance, Ohio
Entered Service at: Salem, Columbiana County, Ohio
Unit: Company G, 104th Ohio Infantry
Battle or Place of Action: Franklin, Tennessee
Date of Action: 30 November 1864
Date of Issue: 13 February 1865
Citation: Capture of corps headquarters flag (C.S.A.).

507 ◆ GREENE, JOHN

Rank: Captain of the Forecastle
Service: U.S. Navy
Entered Service at: New York
Unit: U.S.S. *Varuna*
Battle or Place of Action: Forts Jackson and St. Philip, Louisiana
Date of Action: 24 April 1862
G.O. Number, Date: 11, 3 April 1863
Citation: Captain of a gun on board the U.S.S. *Varuna* during the attacks on Forts Jackson and St. Philip, and while under fire and ramming by the rebel ship *Morgan*, 24 April 1862. During this action at extremely close-range while his ship was under furious fire and twice rammed by the rebel ship *Morgan*, Greene remained steadfast at his gun throughout the thickest of the fight and was instrumental in inflicting damage on the enemy until the *Varuna*, badly damaged and forced to beach, was finally sunk.

508 ◆ GREENE, OLIVER DUFF

Rank: Major & Assistant Adjutant General (highest rank: Brevet Brigadier General)
Service: U.S. Army
Birthday: 25 January 1833
Place of Birth: Scott, Cortland County, New York
Date of Death: 19 March 1904
Cemetery: San Francisco National Cemetery OS-49-8—San Francisco, California
Entered Service at: Scott, Cortland County, New York
Unit: U.S. Army

Battle or Place of Action: Antietam, Maryland
Date of Action: 17 September 1862
Date of Issue: 13 December 1893
Citation: Formed the columns under heavy fire and put them into position.

509 ◆ GREGG, JOSEPH OLDS

Rank: Private (highest rank: Captain)
Service: U.S. Army
Birthday: 5 January 1841
Place of Birth: Lithopolis, Fairfield County, Ohio
Date of Death: 25 February 1930
Place of Death: Columbus, Ohio
Cemetery: Lithopolis Cemetery—Lithopolis, Ohio
Entered Service at: Columbus, Franklin County, Ohio
Unit: Company F, 133d Ohio National Guard Infantry
Battle or Place of Action: near the Richmond & Petersburg Railway, Virginia
Date of Action: 16 June 1864
Date of Issue: 13 May 1899
Citation: Voluntarily returned to the breastworks, which his regiment had been forced to abandon, to notify three missing companies that the regiment was falling back; found the enemy already in the works, refused a demand to surrender, returning to his command under a concentrated fire, several bullets passing through his hat and clothing.

510 ◆ GREIG, THEODORE W.

Rank: Second Lieutenant (highest rank: Major)
Service: U.S. Army
Birthday: 13 March 1843
Place of Birth: New York
Date of Death: 17 November 1893
Place of Death: New York, New York
Cemetery: Woodlawn Cemetery—Bronx, New York
Entered Service at: Staten Island, Richmond County, New York
Unit: Company C, 61st New York Infantry
Battle or Place of Action: Antietam, Maryland
Date of Action: 17 September 1862
Date of Issue: 10 February 1887
Citation: A Confederate regiment, the 4th Alabama Infantry (C.S.A.), having planted its battle flag slightly in advance of the regiment, this officer rushed forward and seized it, and, although shot through the neck, retained the flag and brought it within the Union lines.

511 ◆ GRESSER, IGNATZ

Rank: Corporal
Service: U.S. Army
Birthday: 15 August 1835
Place of Birth: Malach, Germany
Date of Death: 1 August 1929
Place of Death: Allentown, Pennsylvania
Cemetery: West Cemetery—Allentown, Pennsylvania

Entered Service at: Allentown, Lehigh County, Pennsylvania
Unit: Company D, 128th Pennsylvania Infantry
Battle or Place of Action: Antietam, Maryland
Date of Action: 17 September 1862
Date of Issue: 12 December 1895
Citation: While exposed to the fire of the enemy, carried from the field a wounded comrade.

512 ◆ GRIBBEN, JAMES H.

Rank: First Lieutenant
Service: U.S. Army
Birthday: April 1839
Place of Birth: Ireland
Date of Death: 6 August 1878
Place of Death: New York, New York
Cemetery: The Green Wood Cemetery—Brooklyn, New York
Entered Service at: New York, New York
Unit: Company C., 2d New York Cavalry
Battle or Place of Action: Deatonsville (Sailor's Creek), Virginia
Date of Action: 6 April 1865
Date of Issue: 3 May 1865
Citation: Capture of flag of 12th Virginia Infantry (C.S.A.).

513 ◆ GRIFFITHS, JOHN

Rank: Captain of the Forecastle
Service: U.S. Navy
Birthday: 1835
Place of Birth: Wales
Entered Service at: Massachusetts
Unit: U.S.S. *Santiago de Cuba*
Battle or Place of Action: Fort Fisher, North Carolina
Date of Action: 15 January 1865
G.O. Number, Date: 59, 22 June 1865
Citation: On board the U.S.S. *Santiago de Cuba* during the assault on Fort Fisher, 15 January 1865. As one of a boatcrew detailed to one of the generals onshore, Griffiths bravely entered the fort in the assault and accompanied his party in carrying dispatches at the height of the battle. He was one of the six men who entered the fort in the assault from the fleet.

514 ◆ GRIMSHAW, SAMUEL

Rank: Private (highest rank: Corporal)
Service: U.S. Army
Birthday: 2 March 1840
Place of Birth: Jefferson County, Ohio
Date of Death: 9 November 1918
Place of Death: Holton, Kansas
Cemetery: Holton Cemetery—Holton, Kansas
Entered Service at: Smithfield, Jefferson County, Ohio
Unit: Company B, 52d Ohio Infantry
Battle or Place of Action: Atlanta, Georgia
Date of Action: 6 August 1864
Date of Issue: 5 April 1894

Citation: Saved the lives of some of his comrades, and greatly imperiled his own by picking up and throwing away a lighted shell which had fallen in the midst of the company.

515 ◆ GRINDLAY, JAMES G.

Rank: Colonel (highest rank: Brevet Brigadier General)
Service: U.S. Army
Birthday: 14 February 1840
Place of Birth: Odinburgh, Scotland
Date of Death: 19 October 1907
Place of Death: Troy, New York
Cemetery: Forest Hill Cemetery—Utica, New York
Entered Service at: Utica, Oneida County, New York
Unit: 146th New York Infantry
Battle or Place of Action: Five Forks, Virginia
Date of Action: 1 April 1865
Date of Issue: 14 August 1891
Citation: The first to enter the enemy's works, where he captured two flags.

516 ◆ GRISWOLD, LUKE M.

Rank: Ordinary Seaman
Service: U.S. Navy
Birthday: 1837
Place of Birth: Massachusetts
Entered Service at: Springfield, Hampden County, Massachusetts
Unit: U.S.S. *Rhode Island*
Battle or Place of Action: off Cape Hatteras, North Carolina
Date of Action: 30 December 1862
G.O. Number, Date: 59, 22 June 1865
Citation: Served on board the U.S.S. *Rhode Island* which was engaged in saving the lives of the officers and crew of the *Monitor*, 30 December 1862. Participating in the hazardous rescue of the officers and crew of the sinking *Monitor*, Griswold, after rescuing several of the men, became separated in a heavy gale with other members of the cutter that had set out from the *Rhode Island*, and spent many hours in the small boat at the mercy of the weather and high seas until finally picked up by a schooner 50 miles east of Cape Hatteras

517 ◆ GRUEB, GEORGE M.

Rank: Private (highest rank: Corporal)
Service: U.S. Army
Birthday: 1835
Place of Birth: Wurttemberg, Germany
Date of Death: 26 September 1893
Cemetery: Bath National Cemetery (A-2-3) (MH)—Bath, New York
Entered Service at: Brooklyn, Kings County, New York
Unit: Company E, 158th New York Infantry
Battle or Place of Action: Chapin's Farm, Virginia
Date of Action: 29 September 1864
Date of Issue: 6 April 1865

Citation: Gallantry in advancing to the ditch of the enemy's works.

518 ◆ GUERIN, FITZ W.

Rank: Private
Service: U.S. Army
Birthday: 17 March 1846
Place of Birth: New York, New York
Date of Death: 11 July 1903
Place of Death: San Francisco, California
Cemetery: Bellefontaine Cemetery—St. Louis, Missouri
Entered Service at: St. Louis, St. Louis County, Missouri
Unit: Battery A, 1st Missouri Light Artillery
Battle or Place of Action: Grand Gulf, Mississippi
Date of Action: 28-29 April 1863
Date of Issue: 10 March 1896
Citation: With two comrades voluntarily took position on board the steamer *Cheeseman*, in charge of all the guns and ammunition of the battery, and remained in charge of the same for a considerable time while the steamer was unmanageable and subjected to a heavy fire from the enemy.

519 ◆ GUINN, THOMAS

Rank: Private
Service: U.S. Army
Birthday: 5 March 1836
Place of Birth: Clinton County, Ohio
Date of Death: 12 September 1908
Place of Death: New Westville, Ohio
Cemetery: Springlawn Cemetery (MH)—New Paris, Ohio
Entered Service at: Oxford, Butler County, Ohio
Unit: Company D, 47th Ohio Infantry
Battle or Place of Action: Vicksburg, Mississippi
Date of Action: 22 May 1863
Date of Issue: 21 August 1894
Citation: Gallantry in the charge of the "volunteer storming party."

520 ◆ GWYNNE, NATHANIEL MCCLEAN

Rank: Private (highest rank: Second Lieutenant)
Service: U.S. Army
Birthday: 5 July 1849
Place of Birth: Urbana, Champaign County, Ohio
Date of Death: 6 January 1883
Place of Death: Kansas City, Missouri
Cemetery: Union Cemetery (MH)—Kansas City, Missouri
Entered Service at: Fairmount, Missouri
Unit: Company H, 13th Ohio Cavalry
Battle or Place of Action: Petersburg, Virginia
Date of Action: 30 July 1864
Date of Issue: 27 January 1865
Citation: When about entering upon the charge, this soldier, then but 15 years old, was cautioned not to go in, as he had not been mustered. He indignantly protested and participated in the charge, his left arm being crushed by a shell and amputated soon afterward.

521 ◆ HACK, JOHN

Rank: Private
Service: U.S. Army
Birthday: 26 November 1842
Place of Birth: Germany
Date of Death: 29 March 1933
Cemetery: Maple Grove Cemetery (MH)—Trenton, Missouri
Entered Service at: Adrian, Lenawee County, Michigan
Unit: Company B, 47th Ohio Infantry
Battle or Place of Action: Vicksburg, Mississippi
Date of Action: 3 May 1863
Date of Issue: 3 January 1907
Citation: Was one of a party which volunteered and attempted to run the enemy's batteries with a steam tug and two barges loaded with subsistence stores.

522 ◆ HACK, LESTER GOODEL

Rank: Sergeant
Service: U.S. Army
Birthday: 18 January 1844
Place of Birth: Cadwell, Warren County, New York
Date of Death: 24 April 1928
Place of Death: Copenhagen, New York
Cemetery: Mount Hope Cemetery (MH)—Ticonderoga, New York
Entered Service at: Salisbury, Addison County, Vermont
Unit: Company F, 5th Vermont Infantry
Battle or Place of Action: Petersburg, Virginia
Date of Action: 2 April 1865
Date of Issue: 10 May 1865
Citation: Capture of flag of 23d Tennessee Infantry (C.S.A.) and several of the enemy.

523 ◆ HADLEY, CORNELIUS MINOR

Rank: Sergeant (highest rank: First Lieutenant)
Service: U.S. Army
Birthday: 27 April 1838
Place of Birth: Sandy Creek, Oswego County, New York
Date of Death: 22 March 1902
Cemetery: Mount Hope Cemetery—Litchfield, Michigan
Entered Service at: Adrian, Lenawee County, Michigan
Unit: Company F, 9th Michigan Cavalry
Battle or Place of Action: Knoxville, Tennessee
Date of Action: 20 November 1863
Date of Issue: 5 April 1898
Citation: With one companion, voluntarily carried through the enemy's lines important dispatches from Gen. Grant to Gen. Burnside, then besieged within Knoxville, and brought back replies, his comrade's horse being killed and the man taken prisoner.

524 ◆ HADLEY, OSGOOD TOWNS

Rank: Corporal (highest rank: Sergeant)
Service: U.S. Army

Birthday: 19 January 1838
Place of Birth: Nashua, Hillsborough County, New Hampshire
Date of Death: 5 October 1914
Place of Death: Southboro, Massachusetts
Cemetery: Rural Cemetery (MH)—Southboro, Massachusetts
Entered Service at: Peterborough, Hillsborough County, New Hampshire
Unit: Company E, 6th New Hampshire Veteran Infantry
Battle or Place of Action: near Pegram House, Virginia
Date of Action: 30 September 1864
Date of Issue: 27 July 1896
Citation: As color bearer of his regiment he defended his colors with great personal gallantry and brought them safely out of the action.

525 ◆ HAFFEE, EDMUND

Rank: Quarter Gunner
Service: U.S. Navy
Birthday: 1832
Place of Birth: Philadelphia, Philadelphia County, Pennsylvania
Entered Service at: Philadelphia, Philadelphia County, Pennsylvania
Unit: U.S.S. *New Ironsides*
Battle or Place of Action: Fort Fisher, North Carolina
Date of Action: 24-25 December 1864 & 13-15 January 1865
G.O. Number, Date: 59, 22 June 1865
Citation: Haffee served on board the U.S.S. *New Ironsides* during action in several attacks on Fort Fisher, 24 and 25 December 1864; and 13, 14, and 15 January 1865. The ship steamed in and took the lead in the ironclad division close inshore, and immediately opened its starboard battery in a barrage of well-directed fire to cause several fires and explosions and dismount several guns during the first two days of fighting. Taken under fire, as she steamed into position on 13 January, the *New Ironsides* fought all day and took on ammunition at night despite severe weather conditions. When the enemy came out of his bombproof to defend the fort against the storming party, the ship's battery disabled nearly every gun on the fort facing the shore before the cease-fire orders were given by the flagship.

526 ◆ HAGERTY, ASEL

True Name: Hagert, Asa
Rank: Private
Service: U.S. Army
Birthday: 30 June 1837
Place of Birth: Canada
Date of Death: 30 March 1919
Cemetery: Riverside Cemetery—Defiance, Ohio
Entered Service at: New York, New York
Unit: Company A, 61st New York Infantry
Battle or Place of Action: Deatonsville (Sailor's Creek), Virginia

Date of Action: 6 April 1865
Date of Issue: 10 May 1865
Citation: Capture of flag.

527 ◆ HAIGHT, JOHN H.

Rank: Sergeant
Service: U.S. Army
Birthday: 1 July 1841
Place of Birth: Westfield, Chautauqua County, New York
Date of Death: 8 April 1917
Place of Death: Westfield, New York
Cemetery: East Ripley Cemetery (MH)—Ripley, New York
Entered Service at: Westfield, Chautauqua County, New York
Unit: Company G, 72d New York Infantry
Battle or Place of Action: Williamsburg & Bristol Station & Manassas, Virginia
Date of Action: 5 May & 27,29,30 August 1862
Date of Issue: 8 June 1888
Citation: At Williamsburg, Va., voluntarily carried a severely wounded comrade off the field in the face of a large force of the enemy; in doing so was himself severely wounded and taken prisoner. Went into the fight at Bristol Station, Va., although severely disabled. At Manassas, volunteered to search the woods for the wounded.
Notes: POW

528 ◆ HAIGHT, SIDNEY

Rank: Corporal
Service: U.S. Army
Birthday: 21 August 1847
Place of Birth: Reading, Hillsdale County, Michigan
Date of Death: 17 September 1918
Cemetery: West Reading Cemetery—Hillsdale, Michigan
Entered Service at: Goodland, Michigan
Unit: Company E, 1st Michigan Sharpshooters
Battle or Place of Action: Petersburg, Virginia
Date of Action: 30 July 1864
Date of Issue: 31 July 1896
Citation: Instead of retreating, remained in the captured works, regardless of his personal safety and exposed to the firing, which he boldly and deliberately returned until the enemy was close upon him.
Notes: POW

529 ◆ HALEY, JAMES

Rank: Captain of the Forecastle
Service: U.S. Navy
Birthday: 1824
Place of Birth: Ireland
Entered Service at: Ohio
Unit: U.S.S. *Kearsarge*
Battle or Place of Action: off Cherbourg, France
Date of Action: 19 June 1864
G.O. Number, Date: 45, 31 December 1864
Citation: Served as captain of the forecastle on board the U.S.S. *Kearsarge* when she destroyed the *Alabama* off

Cherbourg, France, 19 June 1864. Acting as captain of a gun during the bitter engagement, Haley exhibited marked coolness and good conduct and was highly commended by his division officer for his gallantry and meritorious achievement under enemy fire.

530 ◆ HALL, FRANCIS BLOODGOOD

Rank: Chaplain
Service: U.S. Army
Birthday: 16 November 1827
Place of Birth: New York, New York
Date of Death: 4 October 1903
Cemetery: Riverside Cemetery—Plattsburgh, New York
Entered Service at: Plattsburgh, Clinton County, New York
Unit: 16th New York Infantry
Served as: Chaplain
Battle or Place of Action: Salem Heights, Virginia
Date of Action: 3 May 1863
Date of Issue: 16 February 1897
Citation: Voluntarily exposed himself to a heavy fire during the thickest of the fight and carried wounded men to the rear for treatment and attendance.

531 ◆ HALL, HENRY SEYMOUR

True Name: Hall, Hiram Seymour
Rank: Second Lieutenant & Captain (highest rank: Brevet Brigadier General U.S. Vols.)
Service: U.S. Army
Birthday: 26 September 1835
Place of Birth: Barkersville, Saratoga County, New York
Date of Death: 1 July 1908
Place of Death: Kansas City, Kansas
Cemetery: Oak Hill Cemetery (MH)—Lawrence, Kansas
Entered Service at: Elmira, Chemung County, New York
Unit: Company G, 27th New York Infantry; Company F, 121st New York Infantry
Battle or Place of Action: Gaines' Mill & Rappahannock Station, Virginia
Date of Action: 27 June 1862 & 7 November 1863
Date of Issue: 17 August 1891
Citation: Although wounded at Gaines' Mill, Va., he remained on duty and participated in the battle with his company. At Rappahannock Station, Va., while acting as aide, rendered gallant and prompt assistance in reforming the regiments inside the enemy's works.

532 ◆ HALL, NEWTON H.

Rank: Corporal
Service: U.S. Army
Birthday: 4 August 1842
Place of Birth: Brimfield, Portage County, Ohio
Date of Death: 19 October 1911
Cemetery: Standing Rock Cemetery—Kent, Ohio
Entered Service at: Brimfield, Portage County, Ohio
Unit: Company I, 104th Ohio Infantry
Battle or Place of Action: Franklin, Tennessee

Date of Action: 30 November 1864
Date of Issue: 13 February 1865
Citation: Capture of flag, believed to have belonged to Stewart's Corps (C.S.A.).

533 ◆ HALLOCK, NATHAN MULLOCK

Rank: Private (highest rank: Corporal)
Service: U.S. Army
Birthday: 23 August 1844
Place of Birth: Mount Hope, Orange County, New York
Date of Death: 21 March 1903
Place of Death: Los Angeles, California
Cemetery: Hillside Cemetery (MH)—Middletown, New York
Entered Service at: Middletown, Orange County, New York
Unit: Company K, 124th New York Infantry
Battle or Place of Action: Bristoe Station, Virginia
Date of Action: 15 June 1863
Date of Issue: 10 September 1897
Citation: At imminent peril saved from death or capture a disabled officer of his company by carrying him under a hot musketry fire to a place of safety.

534 ◆ HALSTEAD, WILLIAM W.

Rank: Coxswain
Service: U.S. Navy
Birthday: 9 January 1837
Place of Birth: Alplaus, Schenectady County, New York
Date of Death: 23 July 1916
Place of Death: Wyandotte, Michigan
Cemetery: Forest Cemetery—Toledo, Ohio
Entered Service at: New York
Unit: U.S.S. *Brooklyn*
Battle or Place of Action: Mobile Bay, Alabama
Date of Action: 5 August 1864
G.O. Number, Date: 45, 31 December 1864
Citation: On board the U.S.S. *Brooklyn* during action against rebel forts and gunboats and with the ram *Tennessee*, in Mobile Bay, 5 August 1864. Despite severe damage to his ship and the loss of several men on board as enemy fire raked her decks from stem to stern, Halstead fought his gun with skill and courage throughout the furious battle which resulted in the surrender of the prize rebel ram *Tennessee* and in the damaging and destruction of batteries at Fort Morgan.

535 ◆ HAM, MARK G.

Rank: Carpenter's Mate
Service: U.S. Navy
Birthday: 1820
Place of Birth: Portsmouth, Rockingham County, New Hampshire
Date of Death: 11 March 1869
Place of Death: Portsmouth, New Hampshire
Cemetery: Harmony Grove Cemetery (MH)—Portsmouth, New Hampshire
Entered Service at: Portsmouth, Rockingham County, New Hampshire

Unit: U.S.S. *Kearsarge*
Battle or Place of Action: off Cherbourg, France
Date of Action: 19 June 1864
G.O. Number, Date: 45, 31 December 1864
Citation: Served on board the U.S.S. *Kearsarge* when she destroyed the *Alabama* off Cherbourg, France, 19 June 1864. Performing his duties intelligently and faithfully, Ham distinguished himself in the face of the bitter enemy fire and was highly commended by his divisional officer.

536 ◆ HAMILTON, HUGH

Rank: Coxswain
Service: U.S. Navy
Birthday: 1830
Place of Birth: New York, New York
Entered Service at: New York, New York
Unit: U.S.S. *Richmond*
Battle or Place of Action: Mobile Bay, Alabama
Date of Action: 5 August 1864
G.O. Number, Date: 45, 31 December 1864
Citation: On board the U.S.S. *Richmond* during the action against rebel forts and gunboats and with the ram *Tennessee* in Mobile Bay, 5 August 1864. Despite damage to his ship and the loss of several men on board as enemy fire raked her decks, Hamilton performed his duties with skill and courage throughout the prolonged battle, which resulted in the surrender of the rebel ram *Tennessee* and in the successful attacks carried out on Fort Morgan.

537 ◆ HAMILTON, RICHARD

Rank: Coal Heaver
Service: U.S. Navy
Birthday: 1836
Place of Birth: Philadelphia, Philadelphia County, Pennsylvania
Date of Death: 6 July 1881
Place of Death: Camden, New Jersey
Cemetery: Evergreen Cemetery—Camden, New Jersey
Entered Service at: Pennsylvania
Unit: U.S. Picket Boat No. 1
Battle or Place of Action: Plymouth, North Carolina
Date of Action: 27 October 1864
G.O. Number, Date: 45, 31 December 1864
Citation: Hamilton served on board the U.S. Picket Boat No. 1, in action, 27 October 1864, against the Confederate ram, *Albemarle*, which had resisted repeated attacks by our steamers and had kept a large force of vessels employed in watching her. The picket boat, equipped with a spar torpedo, succeeded in passing the enemy pickets within 20 yards without being discovered and then made for the *Albemarle* under a full head of steam. Immediately taken under fire by the ram, the small boat plunged on, jumped the log boom which encircled the target and exploded its torpedo under the port bow of the ram. The picket boat was destroyed by enemy fire and almost the entire crew was taken prisoner or lost.
Notes: POW

538 ◆ HAMILTON, THOMAS W.

Rank: Quartermaster
Service: U.S. Navy
Birthday: 1833
Place of Birth: Scotland
Entered Service at: Weymouth, Norfolk County, Massachusetts
Unit: U.S.S. *Cincinnati*
Battle or Place of Action: Vicksburg, Mississippi
Date of Action: 27 May 1863
G.O. Number, Date: 17, 10 July 1863
Citation: Served as quartermaster on board the U.S.S. *Cincinnati* during the attack on the Vicksburg batteries and at the time of her sinking, 27 May 1863. Engaging the enemy in a fierce battle, the *Cincinnati*, amidst an incessant fire of shot and shell, continued to fire her guns to the last although so penetrated by enemy shell fire that her fate was sealed. Conspicuously gallant during this action, Hamilton, severely wounded at the wheel, returned to his post and had to be sent down below, to hear the incessant roar of guns as the gallant ship went down, "her colors nailed to the mast."

539 ◆ HAMMEL, HENRY A.

Rank: Sergeant (highest rank: First Sergeant)
Service: U.S. Army
Birthday: 20 September 1840
Place of Birth: Germany
Date of Death: 29 November 1902
Cemetery: Bellefontaine Cemetery (MH)—St. Louis, Missouri
Entered Service at: St. Louis, St. Louis County, Missouri
Unit: Battery A, 1st Missouri Light Artillery
Battle or Place of Action: Grand Gulf, Mississippi
Date of Action: 28-29 April 1863
Date of Issue: 10 March 1896
Citation: With two comrades, voluntarily took position on board the steamer *Cheeseman*, in charge of all the guns and ammunition of the battery, and remained in charge of the same for considerable time while the steamer was unmanageable and subjected to a heavy fire from the enemy.

540 ◆ HAND, ALEXANDER

Rank: Quartermaster
Service: U.S. Navy
Birthday: 1836
Place of Birth: Delaware
Entered Service at: Delaware
Unit: U.S.S. *Ceres*
Battle or Place of Action: near Hamilton, Roanoke River, North Carolina
Date of Action: 9 July 1862
G.O. Number, Date: 11, 3 April 1863
Citation: Served on board the U.S.S. *Ceres* in the fight near Hamilton, Roanoke River, 9 July 1862. Fired on by the enemy with small arms, Hand courageously returned the raking enemy fire and was spoken of for "good conduct and cool bravery under enemy fire" by the commanding officer.

541 ◆ HANEY, MILTON LORENZI

Rank: Regimental Chaplain
Service: U.S. Army
Birthday: 23 January 1825
Place of Birth: Savannah, Ashland County, Ohio
Date of Death: 20 January 1922
Place of Death: Pasadena, California
Cemetery: Mountain View Cemetery—Altadena, California
Entered Service at: Bushnell, McDonough County, Illinois
Unit: 55th Illinois Infantry
Battle or Place of Action: Atlanta, Georgia
Date of Action: 22 July 1864
Date of Issue: 3 November 1896
Citation: Voluntarily carried a musket in the ranks of his regiment and rendered heroic service in retaking the Federal works which had been captured by the enemy.

542 ◆ HANFORD, EDWARD R.

Rank: Private
Service: U.S. Army
Birthday: 1841
Place of Birth: Allegany County, New York
Date of Death: 30 January 1890
Place of Death: Chili Gulch, California
Cemetery: Mokelumne Hill Protestant Cemetery (MH)—Mokelumne Hill, California
Entered Service at: Cortland, Cortland County, New York
Unit: Company H, 2d U.S. Cavalry
Battle or Place of Action: Woodstock, Virginia
Date of Action: 9 October 1864
Date of Issue: 14 October 1864
Citation: Capture of flag of 32d Battalion Virginia Cavalry (C.S.A.).

543 ◆ HANKS, JOSEPH

Rank: Private
Service: U.S. Army
Birthday: 22 March 1843
Place of Birth: Chillicothe, Ross County, Ohio
Date of Death: 28 December 1922
Place of Death: North Bend, Nebraska
Cemetery: Woodland Cemetery (MH)—North Bend, Nebraska
Entered Service at: Chillicothe, Ross County, Ohio
Unit: Company E, 37th Ohio Infantry
Battle or Place of Action: Vicksburg, Mississippi
Date of Action: 22 May 1863
Date of Issue: 19 November 1897
Citation: Voluntarily and under fire went to the rescue of a wounded comrade lying between the lines, gave him water, and brought him off the field.

544 ◆ HANNA, MARCUS A.

Rank: Sergeant
Service: U.S. Army
Birthday: 3 November 1842
Place of Birth: Bristol, Lincoln County, Maine
Date of Death: 12 December 1921
Place of Death: South Portland, Maine
Cemetery: Mount Pleasant Cemetery (MH)—Portland, Maine
Entered Service at: Rockport, Essex County, Massachusetts
Unit: Company B, 50th Massachusetts Infantry
Battle or Place of Action: Port Hudson, Louisiana
Date of Action: 4 July 1863
Date of Issue: 2 November 1895
Citation: Voluntarily exposed himself to a heavy fire to get water for comrades in rifle pits.

545 ◆ HANNA, MILTON

Rank: Corporal (highest rank: Sergeant)
Service: U.S. Army
Birthday: 12 January 1842
Place of Birth: Licking County, Ohio
Date of Death: 21 January 1913
Place of Death: Minnetiaha, Minnesota
Cemetery: Glenwood Cemetery—Mankato, Minnesota
Entered Service at: Henderson, Sibley County, Minnesota
Unit: Company H, 2d Minnesota Infantry
Battle or Place of Action: Nolensville, Tennessee
Date of Action: 15 February 1863
Date of Issue: 11 September 1897
Citation: Was one of a detachment of 16 men who heroically defended a wagon train against the attack of 125 cavalry, repulsed the attack, and saved the train.

546 ◆ HANSCOM, MOSES C.

Rank: Corporal
Service: U.S. Army
Birthday: 1842
Place of Birth: Danville, Androscoggin County, Maine
Date of Death: 26 July 1873
Place of Death: Auburn, Maine
Cemetery: Oak Hill Cemetery (MH)—Auburn, Maine
Entered Service at: Bowdoinham, Sagadahoc County, Maine
Unit: Company F, 19th Maine Infantry
Battle or Place of Action: Bristoe Station, Virginia
Date of Action: 14 October 1863
Date of Issue: 1 December 1864
Citation: Capture of the flag of 26th North Carolina (C.S.A.).

547 ◆ HAPEMAN, DOUGLAS

Rank: Lieutenant Colonel (highest rank: Colonel)
Service: U.S. Army
Birthday: 15 January 1839
Place of Birth: Ephrata, Fulton County, New York
Date of Death: 3 June 1905
Cemetery: Ottawa Avenue Cemetery—Ottawa, Illinois
Entered Service at: Ottawa, La Salle County, Illinois

Unit: 104th Illinois Infantry
Battle or Place of Action: Peach Tree Creek, Georgia
Date of Action: 20 July 1864
Date of Issue: 5 April 1898
Citation: With conspicuous coolness and bravery rallied his men under a severe attack, reformed the broken ranks, and repulsed the attack.
Notes: POW

548 ◆ HARBOURNE, JOHN H.

Rank: Private
Service: U.S. Army
Birthday: 9 September 1840
Place of Birth: England
Date of Death: 29 November 1928
Place of Death: Philadelphia, Pennsylvania
Cemetery: Fernwood Cemetery (no marker at all)—Fernwood, Pennsylvania
Entered Service at: Readville, Suffolk County, Massachusetts
Unit: Company K, 29th Massachusetts Infantry
Battle or Place of Action: Petersburg, Virginia
Date of Action: 17 June 1864
Date of Issue: 24 February 1897
Citation: Capture of flag along with three enemy men.

549 ◆ HARCOURT, THOMAS

Rank: Ordinary Seaman
Service: U.S. Navy
Birthday: 1841
Place of Birth: Boston, Suffolk County, Massachusetts
Entered Service at: Massachusetts
Unit: U.S.S. *Minnesota*
Battle or Place of Action: Fort Fisher, North Carolina
Date of Action: 15 January 1865
G.O. Number, Date: 59, 22 June 1865
Citation: On board the U.S.S. *Minnesota* in action during the assault on Fort Fisher, 15 January 1865. Landing on the beach with the assaulting party from his ship, Harcourt advanced to the top of the sandhill and partly through the breach in the palisades despite enemy fire, which killed and wounded many officers and men. When more than two-thirds of the men became seized with panic and retreated on the run, he remained with the party until dark when it came safely away, bringing its wounded, its arms, and its colors.

550 ◆ *HARDENBERGH, HENRY M.

Rank: Private
Service: U.S. Army
Place of Birth: Noble County, Indiana
Date of Death: 28 August 1864
Place of Death: Petersburg, Virginia
Cemetery: Poplar Grove National Cemetery (D-1283) (MH)—Petersburg, Virginia
Entered Service at: Bremen, Illinois
Unit: Company G, 39th Illinois Infantry

Battle or Place of Action: Deep Run, Virginia
Date of Action: 16 August 1864
Date of Issue: 6 April 1865
Citation: Capture of flag. He was wounded in the shoulder during this action. He was killed in action at Petersburg on 28 August 1864.

551 ◆ HARDING, THOMAS

Rank: Captain of the Forecastle (highest rank: Acting Master's Mate)
Service: U.S. Navy
Birthday: 1837
Place of Birth: Middletown, Middlesex County, Connecticut
Entered Service at: Connecticut
Unit: U.S.S. *Dacotah*
Battle or Place of Action: Beaufort, North Carolina
Date of Action: 9 June 1864
G.O. Number, Date: 45, 31 December 1864
Date of Issue: 31 December 1864
Citation: Served as captain of the forecastle on board the U.S.S. *Dacotah* on the occasion of the destruction of the blockade runner *Pevensey*, near Beaufort, N.C., 9 June 1864. "Learning that one of the officers in the boat, which was in danger of being, and subsequently was, swamped, could not swim, Harding remarked to him: 'If we are swamped, sir, I shall carry you to the beach or I will never go there myself.' He did not succeed in carrying out his promise, but made desperate efforts to do so, while others thought only of themselves. Such conduct is worthy of appreciation and admiration—a sailor risking his own life to save that of an officer."

552 ◆ HARING, ABRAM PYE

Rank: First Lieutenant
Service: U.S. Army
Birthday: 15 November 1840
Place of Birth: New York, New York
Date of Death: 22 February 1915
Place of Death: Montclair, New Jersey
Cemetery: Canterbury Presbyterian Cemetery—Cornwall-on-the-Hudson, New York
Entered Service at: New York, New York
Unit: Company G, 132d New York Infantry
Battle or Place of Action: Bachelor's Creek, North Carolina
Date of Action: 1 February 1864
Date of Issue: 28 June 1890
Citation: With a command of 11 men, on picket, resisted the attack of an overwhelming force of the enemy.

553 ◆ HARLEY, BERNARD

Rank: Ordinary Seaman
Service: U.S. Navy
Birthday: 1842
Place of Birth: Brooklyn, Kings County, New York
Date of Death: 15 January 1886
Cemetery: Holy Cross Cemetery—Brooklyn, New York

Entered Service at: New York, New York
Unit: U.S. Picket Boat No. 1
Battle or Place of Action: Plymouth, North Carolina
Date of Action: 27 October 1864
G.O. Number, Date: 45, 31 December 1864
Citation: Harley served on board the U.S. Picket Boat No. 1, in action, 27 October 1864, against the Confederate ram *Albemarle*, which had resisted repeated attacks by our steamers and had kept a large force of vessels employed in watching her. The picket boat, equipped with a spar torpedo, succeeded in passing the enemy pickets within 20 yards without being discovered and then made for the *Albemarle* under a full head of steam. Immediately taken under fire by the ram, the small boat plunged on, jumped the log boom which encircled the target and exploded its torpedo under the port bow of the ram. The picket boat was destroyed by enemy fire and almost the entire crew taken prisoner or lost.
Notes: POW

554 ◆ HARMON, AMZI DAVIS

True Name: Harman, Amzi Davis
Rank: Corporal
Service: U.S. Army
Birthday: 18 April 1845
Place of Birth: Wilkinsburg, Allegheny County, Pennsylvania
Date of Death: 9 October 1927
Place of Death: St. Cloud, Florida
Cemetery: Mount Peace Cemetery (MH)—St. Cloud, Florida
Entered Service at: Greensburg, Westmoreland County, Pennsylvania
Unit: Company K, 211th Pennsylvania Infantry
Battle or Place of Action: Petersburg, Virginia
Date of Action: 2 April 1865
Date of Issue: 20 May 1865
Citation: Capture of flag.

555 ◆ HARRINGTON, DANIEL C.

Rank: Landsman (highest rank: Acting Masters Mate)
Service: U.S. Navy
Birthday: 1849
Place of Birth: Ireland
Entered Service at: Massachusetts
Unit: U.S.S. *Pocahontas*
Battle or Place of Action: near Brunswick, Georgia
Date of Action: 11 March 1862
G.O. Number, Date: 11, 3 April 1863
Date of Presentation: 1 June 1863
Place of Presentation: Off Wilmington, North Carolina, aboard the U.S.S. Steamer *Sacramento*, presented by Capt. Charles S. Boggs.
Citation: Harrington, a landsman from the U.S.S. *Pocahontas*, participated in a shore mission to procure meat for the ship's crew. While returning to the beach, the party was fired on from ambush and several men killed or wounded. Cool and courageous throughout this action, Harrington

rendered gallant service against the enemy and in administering to the casualties.

556 ◆ HARRINGTON, EPHRAIM W.

Rank: Sergeant (highest rank: Major)
Service: U.S. Army
Birthday: 16 January 1833
Place of Birth: Waterford, Oxford County, Maine
Date of Death: 19 October 1914
Place of Death: St. Johnsbury, Vermont
Cemetery: Grove Cemetery (MH)—St. Johnsbury, Vermont
Entered Service at: Kirby, Vermont
Unit: Company G, 2d Vermont Infantry
Battle or Place of Action: Fredericksburg, Virginia
Date of Action: 3 May 1863
Date of Issue: 13 December 1893
Citation: Carried the colors to the top of the heights and almost to the muzzle of the enemy's guns.

557 ◆ HARRIS, GEORGE W.

Rank: Private
Service: U.S. Army
Birthday: 6 March 1835
Place of Birth: Schuylkill, Philadelphia County, Pennsylvania
Date of Death: 30 January 1921
Place of Death: Bellefonte, Pennsylvania
Cemetery: Union Cemetery (MH)—Bellefonte, Pennsylvania
Entered Service at: Bellefonte, Centre County, Pennsylvania
Unit: Company B, 148th Pennsylvania Infantry
Battle or Place of Action: Spotsylvania, Virginia
Date of Action: 12 May 1864
Date of Issue: 1 December 1864
Citation: Capture of flag, wresting it from the color bearer and shooting an officer who attempted to regain it.

558 ◆ HARRIS, JAMES H.

Rank: Sergeant
Service: U.S. Army
Birthday: 1828
Place of Birth: St. Mary's County, Maryland
Date of Death: 28 January 1898
Cemetery: Arlington National Cemetery (27-985-H) (MH)—Arlington, Virginia
Entered Service at: Great Mills, St. Mary's County, Maryland
Unit: Company B, 38th U.S. Colored Infantry
Battle or Place of Action: New Market Heights, Virginia
Date of Action: 29 September 1864
Date of Issue: 18 February 1874
Citation: Gallantry in the assault.

559 ◆ HARRIS, JOHN

Rank: Captain of the Forecastle
Service: U.S. Navy

Birthday: 1839
Place of Birth: Norway
Entered Service at: New York, New York
Unit: U.S.S. *Metacomet*
Battle or Place of Action: Mobile Bay, Alabama
Date of Action: 5 August 1864
G.O. Number, Date: 17, 15 January 1866
Citation: As captain of the forecastle on board the U.S.S. *Metacomet*, Harris was a member of the boat's crew which went to the rescue of the officers and crew of the U.S. Monitor *Tecumseh*, when the vessel was struck by a torpedo in passing the enemy forts in Mobile Bay, 5 August 1864. Harris braved the enemy fire which was said by the admiral to be "one of the most galling" he had ever seen, and aided in rescuing from death 10 of the crew of the *Tecumseh*, thereby eliciting the admiration of both friend and foe.

560 ◆ HARRIS, MOSES

Rank: First Lieutenant (highest rank: Major)
Service: U.S. Army
Birthday: 1839
Place of Birth: Andover, Merrimack County, New Hampshire
Date of Death: 27 June 1927
Cemetery: U.S. Military Academy Cemetery (4-C-60)—West Point, New York
Entered Service at: Boston, Suffolk County, Massachusetts
Unit: 1st U.S. Cavalry
Battle or Place of Action: Smithfield, Virginia
Date of Action: 28 August 1864
Date of Issue: 23 November 1896
Citation: In an attack upon a largely superior force, his personal gallantry was so conspicuous as to inspire the men to extraordinary efforts, resulting in complete rout of the enemy.

561 ◆ HARRIS, SAMPSON

Rank: Private
Service: U.S. Army
Place of Birth: Noble County, Ohio
Date of Death: 29 October 1905
Cemetery: Olive Cemetery—Caldwell, Ohio
Entered Service at: Olive, Ohio
Unit: Company K, 30th Ohio Infantry
Battle or Place of Action: Vicksburg, Mississippi
Date of Action: 22 May 1863
Date of Issue: 10 July 1894
Citation: Gallantry in the charge of the "volunteer storming party."

562 ◆ HARRISON, GEORGE H.

Rank: Seaman
Service: U.S. Navy
Birthday: 9 April 1841
Place of Birth: Middleton, Essex County, Massachusetts
Date of Death: 18 January 1919
Place of Death: Chelsea, Massachusetts

Cemetery: Fort Dale Cemetery (MH)—Malden, Massachusetts
Entered Service at: Somerset, Bristol County, Massachusetts
Unit: U.S.S. *Kearsarge*
Battle or Place of Action: off Cherbourg, France
Date of Action: 19 June 1864
G.O. Number, Date: 45, 31 December 1864
Citation: Served on board the U.S.S. *Kearsarge* when she destroyed the *Alabama* off Cherbourg, France, 19 June 1864. Acting as sponger and loader of the 11-inch pivot gun during the bitter engagement, Harrison exhibited marked coolness and good conduct and was highly recommended for his gallantry under fire by the divisional officer.

563 ◆ HART, JOHN WILLIAM

Rank: Sergeant
Service: U.S. Army
Birthday: 30 July 1833
Place of Birth: Germany
Date of Death: 2 June 1908
Place of Death: Cumberland, Maryland
Cemetery: German Lutheran Cemetery—Cumberland, Maryland
Entered Service at: Cumberland, Allegany County, Maryland
Unit: Company D, 6th Pennsylvania Reserves
Battle or Place of Action: Gettysburg, Pennsylvania
Date of Action: 2 July 1863
Date of Issue: 3 August 1897
Citation: Was one of six volunteers who charged upon a log house near the Devil's Den, where a squad of the enemy's sharpshooters were sheltered, and compelled their surrender.

564 ◆ HART, WILLIAM E.

Rank: Private (highest rank: Corporal)
Service: U.S. Army
Birthday: 1843
Place of Birth: Rushville, Yates County, New York
Date of Death: 21 October 1874
Place of Death: Champlain Canal, New York
Cemetery: unknown cemetery—Halfmoon, New York
Entered Service at: Rushville, Yates County, New York
Unit: Company B, 8th New York Cavalry
Battle or Place of Action: Shenandoah Valley, Virginia
Date of Action: 1864 & 1865
Date of Issue: 3 July 1872
Citation: Gallant conduct and services as scout in connection with capture of the guerrilla Harry Gilmore, and other daring acts.

565 ◆ HARTRANFT, JOHN FREDERIC

Rank: Colonel (highest rank: Brevet Major General)
Service: U.S. Army
Birthday: 16 December 1830
Place of Birth: New Hanover Township, Montgomery County, Pennsylvania

Date of Death: 17 October 1889
Cemetery: Montgomery Cemetery (MH)—Norristown, Pennsylvania
Entered Service at: Norristown, Montgomery County, Pennsylvania
Unit: 4th Pennsylvania Militia
Battle or Place of Action: Bull Run, Virginia
Date of Action: 21 July 1861
Date of Issue: 26 August 1886
Citation: Voluntarily served as an aide and participated in the battle after expiration of his term of service, distinguishing himself in rallying several regiments which had been thrown into confusion.

566 ◆ HARVEY, HARRY

True Name: Huckman, Harry
Rank: Corporal
Service: U.S. Army
Birthday: 14 December 1846
Place of Birth: England
Date of Death: 2 April 1896
Place of Death: Elmwood, New York
Cemetery: Myrtle Hill Cemetery (MH)—Syracuse, New York
Entered Service at: Rochester, Monroe County, New York
Unit: Company A, 22d New York Cavalry
Battle or Place of Action: Waynesboro, Virginia
Date of Action: 2 March 1865
Date of Issue: 26 March 1865
Citation: Capture of flag and bearer, with two other prisoners.

567 ◆ HASKELL, FRANK W.

Rank: Sergeant Major
Service: U.S. Army
Birthday: 1843
Place of Birth: Benton, Maine
Date of Death: 9 October 1903
Cemetery: Pine Grove Cemetery—Waterville, Maine
Entered Service at: Waterville, Kennebec County, Maine
Unit: 3d Maine Infantry
Battle or Place of Action: Fair Oaks, Virginia
Date of Action: 1 June 1862
Date of Issue: 8 December 1898
Citation: Assumed command of a portion of the left wing of his regiment, all the company officers present having been killed or disabled, led it gallantly across a stream and contributed most effectively to the success of the action.

568 ◆ HASKELL, MARCUS M.

Rank: Sergeant
Service: U.S. Army
Birthday: 12 February 1843
Place of Birth: Chelsea, Suffolk County, Massachusetts
Date of Death: 29 October 1925
Place of Death: Centerville, Massachusetts
Cemetery: Beechwood Cemetery (MH)—Centerville,

Massachusetts
Entered Service at: Chelsea, Suffolk County, Massachusetts
Unit: Company C, 35th Massachusetts Infantry
Battle or Place of Action: Antietam, Maryland
Date of Action: 17 September 1862
Date of Issue: 18 November 1896
Citation: Although wounded and exposed to a heavy fire from the enemy, at the risk of his own life he rescued a badly wounded comrade and succeeded in conveying him to a place of safety.

569 ◆ HASTINGS, SMITH H.

Rank: Captain (highest rank: Colonel)
Service: U.S. Army
Birthday: 27 December 1843
Place of Birth: Quincy, Branch County, Michigan
Date of Death: 13 October 1905
Place of Death: Denver, Colorado
Cemetery: Riverside Cemetery (MH)—Denver, Colorado
Entered Service at: Coldwater, Branch County, Michigan
Unit: Troop M, 5th Michigan Cavalry
Battle or Place of Action: Newbys Crossroads, Virginia
Date of Action: 24 July 1863
Date of Issue: 2 August 1897
Citation: While in command of a squadron in rear guard of a cavalry division, then retiring before the advance of a corps of infantry, was attacked by the enemy and, orders having been given to abandon the guns of a section of field artillery with the rear guard that were in imminent danger of capture, he disregarded the orders received and aided in repelling the attack and saving the guns.

570 ◆ HATCH, JOHN PORTER

Rank: Brigadier General (highest rank: Brevet Major General)
Service: U.S. Army
Birthday: 9 January 1822
Place of Birth: Oswego, Oswego County, New York
Date of Death: 12 April 1901
Place of Death: New York, New York
Cemetery: Arlington National Cemetery (1-333-C)—Arlington, Virginia
Entered Service at: Oswego, Oswego County, New York
Unit: 1st Division, U.S. Volunteers
Battle or Place of Action: South Mountain, Maryland
Date of Action: 14 September 1862
Date of Issue: 28 October 1893
Citation: Was severely wounded while leading one of his brigades in the attack under a heavy fire from the enemy.

571 ◆ HATHAWAY, EDWARD W.

Rank: Seaman
Service: U.S. Navy
Birthday: 9 July 1839
Place of Birth: Plymouth, Plymouth County, Massachusetts
Date of Death: 6 April 1916
Place of Death: Salem, Massachusetts

Cemetery: Woodlawn Cemetery (MH)—Everett, Massachusetts
Entered Service at: Plymouth, Plymouth County, Massachusetts
Unit: U.S.S. *Sciota*
Battle or Place of Action: near Vicksburg, Mississippi
Date of Action: 28 June 1862
G.O. Number, Date: 84, 3 October 1867
Citation: On board the U.S.S. *Sciota* prior to the battle of Vicksburg, 28 June 1862. Struck by a bullet which severed his left arm above the elbow, Hathaway displayed exceptional courage as his ship sustained numerous damaging hits from stem to stern while proceeding down the river to fight the battle of Vicksburg.

572 ◆ HAVRON, JOHN H.

Rank: Sergeant
Service: U.S. Army
Birthday: 23 December 1843
Place of Birth: Ireland
Date of Death: 28 October 1910
Place of Death: New Orleans, Louisiana
Entered Service at: Providence, Providence County, Rhode Island
Unit: Company G, 1st Rhode Island Light Artillery
Battle or Place of Action: Petersburg, Virginia
Date of Action: 2 April 1865
Date of Issue: 16 June 1866
Citation: Was one of a detachment of 20 picked artillerymen who voluntarily accompanied an infantry assaulting party and who turned upon the enemy the guns captured in the assault.

573 ◆ HAWKINS, CHARLES

Rank: Seaman (highest rank: Boatswain's Mate)
Service: U.S. Navy
Birthday: 1834
Place of Birth: Scotland
Date of Death: 29 February 1908
Place of Death: Cranston, Rhode Island
Cemetery: St. Mary's Cemetery—Cranston, Rhode Island
Entered Service at: Portsmouth, Rockingham County, New Hampshire
Unit: U.S.S. *Agawam*
Battle or Place of Action: Fort Fisher, North Carolina
Date of Action: 23 December 1864
G.O. Number, Date: 45, 31 December 1864
Date of Presentation: 12 May 1865
Place of Presentation: On board the U.S.S. *Agawam* off New Bern, North Carolina
Citation: Hawkins served on board the U.S.S. *Agawam* as one of a volunteer crew of a powder boat which was exploded near Fort Fisher, 23 December 1864. The powder boat, towed in by the *Wilderness*, to prevent detection by the enemy, cast off and slowly steamed to within 300 yards of the beach. After fuses and fires had been lit and a second anchor with short scope let go to assure the boat's tailing inshore, the crew again boarded the *Wilderness* and and proceeded a distance of 12 miles from shore. Less than two hours later the explosion took place, and the following day fires were observed still burning at the forts.

574 ◆ HAWKINS, GARDNER C.

Rank: First Lieutenant (highest rank: Colonel)
Service: U.S. Army
Birthday: 11 February 1846
Place of Birth: Pomfret, Vermont
Date of Death: 15 December 1913
Place of Death: Winthrop, Massachusetts
Cemetery: Lindenwood Cemetery—Stoneham, Massachusetts
Entered Service at: Woodstock, Windsor County, Vermont
Unit: Company E, 3d Vermont Infantry
Battle or Place of Action: Petersburg, Virginia
Date of Action: 2 April 1865
Date of Issue: 30 September 1893
Citation: When the lines were wavering from the well-directed fire of the enemy, this officer, acting adjutant of the regiment, sprang forward, and with encouraging words cheered the soldiers on and, although dangerously wounded, refused to leave the field until the enemy's works were taken.

575 ◆ HAWKINS, MARTIN JONES

Rank: Corporal (highest rank: First Lieutenant)
Service: U.S. Army
Place of Birth: Mercer County, Pennsylvania
Date of Death: 7 February 1886
Cemetery: Woodlawn Cemetery (MH)—Quincy, Illinois
Entered Service at: Portsmouth, Scioto County, Ohio
Unit: Company A, 33d Ohio Infantry
Battle or Place of Action: Georgia
Date of Action: April 1862
Date of Issue: September 1863
Citation: One of 19 of 24 men (including two civilians) who, by direction of Gen. Ormsby M. Mitchell, penetrated nearly 200 miles south into enemy territory and captured a railroad train at Big Shanty, Ga., in an attempt to destroy the bridges and track between Chattanooga and Atlanta.
Notes: POW

576 ◆ HAWKINS, THOMAS R.

Rank: Sergeant Major
Service: U.S. Army
Birthday: 1840
Place of Birth: Cincinnati, Hamilton County, Ohio
Date of Death: 28 February 1870
Place of Death: Washington, D.C.
Cemetery: Harmony Cemetery—Landover, Maryland
Entered Service at: Philadelphia, Philadelphia County, Pennsylvania
Unit: 6th U.S. Colored Infantry
Battle or Place of Action: Chapin's Farm, Virginia
Date of Action: 29 September 1864
Date of Issue: 8 February 1870
Citation: Rescue of regimental colors.

577 ◆ HAWTHORNE, HARRIS SMITH

Rank: Corporal (highest rank: Sergeant)
Service: U.S. Army
Birthday: 29 February 1832
Place of Birth: Salem, Washington County, New York
Date of Death: 23 March 1911
Place of Death: Hoosick Falls, New York
Cemetery: Maple Grove Cemetery—Hoosick Falls, New York
Entered Service at: Otsego County, New York
Unit: Company F, 121st New York Infantry
Battle or Place of Action: Deatonsville (Sailor's Creek), Virginia
Date of Action: 6 April 1865
Date of Issue: 29 December 1894
Citation: Capture of Confederate Maj. Gen. George Washington Custis Lee.

578 ◆ HAYDEN, JOSEPH B.

Rank: Quartermaster
Service: U.S. Navy
Birthday: 1834
Place of Birth: St. Mary's City, St. Mary's County, Maryland
Entered Service at: Maryland
Unit: U.S.S. *Ticonderoga*
Battle or Place of Action: Fort Fisher, North Carolina
Date of Action: 13-15 January 1865
G.O. Number, Date: 59, 22 June 1865
Citation: On board the U.S.S. *Ticonderoga*, as quartermaster in charge of steering the ship into action, during attacks on Fort Fisher, 13 to 15 January 1865. Hayden steered the ship into position in the line of battle where she maintained a well-directed fire upon the batteries to the left of the palisades during the initial phases of the engagement. Although several of the enemy's shots fell over and around the vessel, the *Ticonderoga* fought her guns gallantly throughout three consecutive days of battle until the flag was planted on one of the strongest fortifications possessed by the rebels.

579 ◆ HAYES, JOHN

Rank: Coxswain
Service: U.S. Navy
Birthday: 20 July 1832
Place of Birth: Brogus, Newfoundland, Canada
Date of Death: 28 January 1911
Place of Death: Blairstown, Iowa
Cemetery: Pleasant Hill Cemetery (MH)—Blairstown, Iowa
Entered Service at: New Bedford, Bristol County, Massachusetts
Unit: U.S.S. *Kearsarge*
Battle or Place of Action: off Cherbourg, France
Date of Action: 19 June 1864
G.O. Number, Date: 45, 31 December 1864
Citation: Served on board the U.S.S. *Kearsarge* when she destroyed the *Alabama* off Cherbourg, France, 19 June 1864. Acting as second captain of the No. 2 gun during the bitter engagement, Hayes exhibited marked coolness and good conduct and was highly recommended for his gallantry under fire by the divisional officer.

580 ◆ HAYES, THOMAS

Rank: Coxswain
Service: U.S. Navy
Birthday: 1840
Place of Birth: Rhode Island
Date of Death: 24 May 1914
Entered Service at: Rhode Island
Unit: U.S.S. *Richmond*
Battle or Place of Action: Mobile Bay, Alabama
Date of Action: 5 August 1864
G.O. Number, Date: 45, 31 December 1864
Citation: As captain of No. 1 gun on board the U.S.S. *Richmond* during action against rebel forts and gunboats and with the ram *Tennessee* in Mobile Bay, 5 August 1864. Cool and courageous at his station throughout the prolonged action, Hayes maintained fire from his gun on Fort Morgan and on ships of the Confederacy despite extremely heavy return fire.

581 ◆ HAYNES, ASBURY F.

Rank: Corporal (highest rank: First Sergeant)
Service: U.S. Army
Birthday: 4 September 1842
Place of Birth: Edinburgh, Maine
Date of Death: 8 July 1931
Place of Death: Retsil, Washington
Cemetery: Lakeview Cemetery—Seattle, Washington
Entered Service at: Passadumkeag, Penobscot County, Maine
Unit: Company F, 17th Maine Infantry
Battle or Place of Action: Deatonsville (Sailor's Creek), Virginia
Date of Action: 6 April 1865
Date of Issue: 10 May 1865
Citation: Capture of flag.

582 ◆ HAYS, JOHN H.

Rank: Private
Service: U.S. Army
Birthday: 4 August 1844
Place of Birth: Jefferson County, Ohio
Date of Death: 27 January 1904
Cemetery: Moscow Cemetery—Moscow, Idaho
Entered Service at: Oskaloosa, Mahaska County, Iowa
Unit: Company F, 4th Iowa Cavalry
Battle or Place of Action: Columbus, Georgia
Date of Action: 16 April 1865
Date of Issue: 17 June 1865
Citation: Capture of flag and bearer, Austin's Battery (C.S.A.).

4-20-05

W. B. Lipes, 84; Performed Surgery on Sub

By RICHARD GOLDSTEIN

Lt. Cmdr. Wheeler B. Lipes, who performed a storied appendectomy while a pharmacist's mate aboard a submarine in the Pacific during World War II, died on Sunday in New Bern, N.C. He was 84.

The cause was pancreatic cancer, said his daughter-in-law, Berniece Lipes.

On Sept. 11, 1942, Pharmacist's Mate Lipes become a surgeon aboard the submarine Seadragon, on patrol at a depth of 120 feet in the South China Sea.

A 19-year-old seaman from Kansas, Darrell Dean Rector, had suffered appendicitis. With the Seadragon about a week's journey from the nearest Allied port, in Australia, the skipper, Lt. Cmdr. William Ferrall, obtained Seaman Rector's permission for surgery by a team of sailors, not one of them a doctor.

Pharmacist's Mate Lipes had observed several appendectomies as a laboratory technician at a naval hospital in Philadelphia, so he was designated to lead the surgical team, amid much trepidation.

In a 1999 interview with the Naval Historical Center, he recalled the moment when the commanding officer approached him after the diagnosis of appendicitis was made.

"The C.O. and I had a long talk and he asked me what I was going to do. 'Nothing,' I replied. He lectured me about the fact that we were there to do the best we could. 'I fire torpedoes every day and some of them miss,' he reminded me. I told him that I could not fire this torpedo and miss. He asked me if I could do the surgery, and I said yes. He then ordered me to do it."

Seaman Rector was placed on a mess table. A tea strainer covered with gauze became an ether mask, and the anesthesia was monitored by the communications officer, Lt. Franz P. Hoskins.

Metal spoons bent at right angles became muscle retractors, holding the wound open after Pharmacist's Mate Lipes made a three-inch incision with a scalpel. Sulfa pills were ground into powder to use as an antiseptic. Boiled water and alcohol milked from the torpedo mechanism sterilized the instruments and operating "gowns," actually the crew's pajamas.

Pharmacist's Mate Lipes removed the appendix in about two and a half hours in the first appendectomy ever

Gary Thompson/Las Vegas Review-Journal
Wheeler B. Lipes, center, with former shipmates in Las Vegas in 1997.

performed on board a submerged submarine. His patient was soon back on duty.

When the Seadragon returned to Australia, its report told of the Japanese ships it had sunk and it related another eventful moment, headlined "One Merchant Ship, One Oil Tanker and One Successful Appendectomy."

George Weller, a correspondent for The Chicago Daily News, received a Pulitzer Prize for his article in December 1942 about the surgery. The operation was recounted in the 1950's television series "The Silent Service," and dramatized in the Hollywood movies "Destination Tokyo" and "Run Silent, Run Deep."

But Seaman Rector did not survive the war. He was among 78 crewmen lost aboard the submarine Tang when it sank off Formosa in October 1944, having been struck by a torpedo that veered back at the submarine after being fired.

Wheeler Bryson Lipes, a native of New Castle, Va., joined the Navy in 1936 and served on several submarines during the war.

Upon returning to the United States in 1943, he spoke at war-bond rallies, representing the Navy, although he did not receive a commendation for his surgical feat.

He retired from the Navy medical corps in 1962 as a lieutenant commander and later served as a hospital executive. He is survived by his second wife, Audrey, of New Bern; his son, Bruce, of Corpus Christi, Tex.; four grandchildren; and four great-grandchildren. His first wife, Myrtle, died in 1997.

In his interview with Navy historians, Commander Lipes said that many doctors in the Navy's wartime Bureau of Medicine and Surgery were unhappy with his achievement.

"I guess they were afraid that because I had performed an appendectomy everyone in the fleet would be running around looking for the first opportunity to do one," he said.

Two appendectomies were performed by corpsmen aboard submarines later in World War II, the Navy said.

In February, Commander Lipes was presented with the Navy Commendation Medal, as a result of a belated study of the surgery by the Navy Medical Department.

"I just didn't think it was that big a deal," he said of the surgery in an interview with The Roanoke Times, in Virginia, after receiving the medal. "I was just proud to save a guy's life."

Earnings at Merrill Decline 3%

By The Associated Press

Merrill Lynch & Company said yesterday that its first-quarter earnings fell 3 percent from a year earlier. The results exceeded analysts' estimates, and Merrill shares rose as it also announced a 25 percent increase in its quarterly dividend and a $4 billion stock buyback program.

For the three months ended April 1, Merrill Lynch's net income dropped to $1.21 billion, or $1.21 a share, from $1.25 billion, or $1.21 a share, a year ago. Net revenue grew 3 percent, to $6.22 billion, from $6.06 billion a year ago — the highest the company has generated since the first quarter of 2001.

Analysts surveyed by Thomson Financial were forecasting earnings of $1.18 a share on sales of $6.15 billion in the latest quarter.

With uncertainty about the economy, inflation and stocks continuing to pervade Wall Street, the chief administrative officer, Ahmass Fakahany, was cautious in his assessment of Merrill's earnings potential for the second quarter and 2005. He did not give estimates on earnings per share or revenue for future quarters.

"So far, we have seen the sentiment that brought the markets lower

in the first quarter accelerate into April," Mr. Fakahany said. "We strongly believe that the best is yet to come out of this franchise. But we need to be cautious about our outlook."

Mr. Fakahany said Wall Street's woes had the potential to erode revenues in both retail brokerage, with customers less likely to trade in a down market, and Merrill's own institutional trading, where the company's stockholdings may decrease in value.

The bond markets are another matter, however. Like other Wall Street firms that have already reported their first-quarter earnings, Merrill Lynch benefited from strong gains in its bond transactions as the stock market lost traction. Of the $2.6 billion in revenue generated from its global markets unit, $1.6 billion of that came from debt markets, with only $990 million in revenue generated from the equity markets.

Likewise, Merrill's investment banking division, which had revenue of $682 million, benefited from companies issuing corporate bonds, while new equity offerings were flat compared with a year ago.

Shares of Merrill Lynch rose 80 cents, to $54.04.

FASTEST PALM OS® DEVICE EVER: THE TREO™ 650

do-it-all device does-it-faster

---

ail costs drove up the most in four months, the Labor Department said yesterday. But a smaller-than-expected increase in prices excluding energy and food helped ease concern that inflation was accelerating.

The Commerce Department issued a report yesterday that said that home construction plunged last month by the most since January 1991. Housing starts dropped a greater-than-expected 18 percent in March. Work began on 1.837 million homes at an annual rate, the fewest since November, after a 21-year high of 2.229 million in February.

The drop in home building, combined with lower core inflation, added to evidence that the economy slowed in the first quarter.

The measure of prices paid to factories, farmers and other producers rose 0.7 percent, the Labor Department said.

...ale prices in March by ings fell 3 percent from a year earlier.

583 ◆ HEALEY, GEORGE WASHINGTON

Rank: Private (highest rank: Corporal)
Service: U.S. Army
Birthday: 22 February 1842
Place of Birth: Dubuque, Dubuque County, Iowa
Date of Death: 9 May 1913
Cemetery: Lindwood Cemetery (MH)—Dubuque, Iowa
Entered Service at: Dubuque, Dubuque County, Iowa
Unit: Company E, 5th Iowa Cavalry
Battle or Place of Action: Newman, Georgia
Date of Action: 29 July 1864
Date of Issue: 13 January 1899
Citation: When nearly surrounded by the enemy, captured a Confederate soldier, and with the aid of a comrade who joined him later, captured four other Confederate soldiers, disarmed the five prisoners, and brought them all into the Union lines.
Notes: POW

584 ◆ HEDGES, JOSEPH S.

Rank: First Lieutenant (highest rank: Captain)
Service: U.S. Army
Birthday: 12 June 1836
Place of Birth: Mansfield, Richland County, Ohio
Date of Death: 12 August 1910
Cemetery: Mansfield Memorial Park—Mansfield, Ohio
Entered Service at: Mansfield, Richland County, Ohio
Unit: 4th U.S. Cavalry
Battle or Place of Action: near Harpeth River, Tennessee
Date of Action: 17 December 1864
Date of Issue: 5 April 1898
Citation: At the head of his regiment charged a field battery with strong infantry supports, broke the enemy's line, and, with other mounted troops, captured three guns and many prisoners.

585 ◆ HEERMANCE, WILLIAM LAING

Rank: Captain
Service: U.S. Army
Birthday: 28 February 1837
Place of Birth: Kinderhook, Columbia County, New York
Date of Death: 25 February 1903
Place of Death: Yonkers, New York
Cemetery: Oakland Cemetery (MH)—Yonkers, New York
Entered Service at: Kinderhook, Columbia County, New York
Unit: Company C, 6th New York Cavalry
Battle or Place of Action: Chancellorsville, Virginia
Date of Action: 30 April 1863
Date of Issue: 30 March 1898
Citation: Took command of the regiment as its senior officer when surrounded by Stuart's Cavalry. The regiment cut its way through the enemy's line and escaped, but Capt. Heermance was desperately wounded, left for dead on the field and was taken prisoner.
Notes: POW

586 ◆ HELLER, HENRY

Rank: Sergeant
Service: U.S. Army
Birthday: 1841
Date of Death: 14 December 1895
Cemetery: Kings Creek Baptist Church Cemetery—Kings Creek, Ohio
Entered Service at: Urbana, Champaign County, Ohio
Unit: Company A, 66th Ohio Infantry
Battle or Place of Action: Chancellorsville, Virginia
Date of Action: 2 May 1863
Date of Issue: 29 July 1892
Citation: One of a party of four who, under heavy fire, voluntarily brought into the Union lines a wounded Confederate officer from whom was obtained valuable information concerning the positions of the enemy.

587 ◆ HELMS, DAVID H.

Rank: Private (highest rank: First Sergeant)
Service: U.S. Army
Birthday: 21 September 1838
Place of Birth: Dearborn County, Indiana
Date of Death: 7 July 1921
Cemetery: Silverlake Cemetery (MH)—Silverlake, Kansas
Entered Service at: Farmers Retreat, Indiana
Unit: Company B, 83d Indiana Infantry
Battle or Place of Action: Vicksburg, Mississippi
Date of Action: 22 May 1863
Date of Issue: 26 July 1894
Citation: Gallantry in the charge of the "volunteer storming party."

588 ◆ HENRY, GUY VERNOR

Rank: Colonel (highest rank: Major General)
Service: U.S. Army
Birthday: 9 March 1839
Place of Birth: Fort Smith, Indian Territory
Date of Death: 27 October 1899
Cemetery: Arlington National Cemetery (2-990)—Arlington, Virginia
Entered Service at: Reading, Berks County, Pennsylvania
Unit: 40th Massachusetts Infantry
Battle or Place of Action: Cold Harbor, Virginia
Date of Action: 1 June 1864
Date of Issue: 5 December 1893
Citation: Led the assaults of his brigade upon the enemy's works, where he had two horses shot under him.

589 ◆ HENRY, JAMES

Rank: Sergeant (highest rank: First Sergeant)
Service: U.S. Army
Birthday: 7 April 1833
Place of Birth: Sunfish, Ohio
Date of Death: 7 June 1911
Place of Death: Geneva, Illinois

Cemetery: Oak Hill Cemetery (MH)—Geneva, Illinois
Entered Service at: Kankakee, Kankakee County, Illinois
Unit: Company B, 113th Illinois Infantry
Battle or Place of Action: Vicksburg, Mississippi
Date of Action: 22 May 1863
Date of Issue: 9 July 1894
Citation: Gallantry in the charge of the "volunteer storming party."

590 ◆ HENRY, WILLIAM WIRT

Rank: Colonel (highest rank: Brevet Brigadier General)
Service: U.S. Army
Birthday: 21 November 1831
Place of Birth: Waterbury, Washington County, Vermont
Date of Death: 31 August 1915
Cemetery: Lake View Cemetery—Burlington, Vermont
Entered Service at: Waterbury, Washington County, Vermont
Unit: 10th Vermont Infantry
Battle or Place of Action: Cedar Creek, Virginia
Date of Action: 19 October 1864
Date of Issue: 21 December 1892
Citation: Though suffering from severe wounds, rejoined his regiment and led it in a brilliant charge, recapturing the guns of an abandoned battery.

591 ◆ HERINGTON, PITT B.

Rank: Private
Service: U.S. Army
Birthday: 5 February 1841
Place of Birth: Michigan
Date of Death: 15 January 1919
Place of Death: Wapalla, Illinois
Cemetery: Park Cemetery—Clinton, Illinois
Entered Service at: Tipton, Cedar County, Iowa
Unit: Company E, 11th Iowa Infantry
Battle or Place of Action: near Kenesaw Mountain, Georgia
Date of Action: 15 June 1864
Date of Issue: 27 November 1899
Citation: With one companion and under a fierce fire of the enemy at close-range, went to the rescue of a wounded comrade who had fallen between the lines and carried him to a place of safety.

592 ◆ HERRON, FRANCIS JAY

Rank: Lieutenant Colonel (highest rank: Major General)
Service: U.S. Army
Birthday: 17 February 1837
Place of Birth: Pittsburgh, Allegheny County, Pennsylvania
Date of Death: 8 January 1902
Cemetery: First Calvary Cemetery—Woodside, New York
Entered Service at: Pittsburgh, Allegheny County, Pennsylvania
Unit: 9th Iowa Infantry
Battle or Place of Action: Pea Ridge, Arkansas
Date of Action: 7 March 1862
Date of Issue: 26 September 1893

Citation: Was foremost in leading his men, rallying them to repeated acts of daring, until himself disabled and taken prisoner.
Notes: POW

593 ◆ HESSELTINE, FRANCIS SNOW

Rank: Lieutenant Colonel
Service: U.S. Army
Birthday: 10 December 1833
Place of Birth: Bangor, Penobscot County, Maine
Date of Death: 17 February 1916
Place of Death: Texas
Cemetery: Wyoming Cemetery (MH)—Melrose, Massachusetts
Entered Service at: Waterville, Kennebec County, Maine
Unit: 13th Maine Infantry
Battle or Place of Action: Matagorda Bay, Texas
Date of Action: 30 December 1863
Date of Issue: 2 March 1895
Citation: In command of a detachment of 100 men, conducted a reconnaissance for two days, baffling and beating back an attacking force of more than 1000 Confederate cavalry, and regained his transport without loss.

594 ◆ HIBSON, JOSEPH C.

Rank: Private (highest rank: Bugler)
Service: U.S. Army
Birthday: 3 August 1843
Place of Birth: London, England
Date of Death: 14 April 1911
Place of Death: Flushing, New York
Cemetery: Cypress Hills Cemetery (Private)—Brooklyn, New York
Entered Service at: New York, New York
Unit: Company C, 48th New York Infantry
Battle or Place of Action: near Fort Wagner, South Carolina
Date of Action: 13-14, 18 July 1863
Date of Issue: 23 October 1897
Citation: While voluntarily performing picket duty under fire, 13 July 1863, was attacked and his surrender demanded, but he killed his assailant. The day following Hibson responded to a call for a volunteer to reconnoiter the enemy's position, and went within the enemy's lines under fire and was exposed to great danger. On 18 July voluntarily exposed himself with great gallantry during an assault, and received three wounds that permanently disabled him for active service.

595 ◆ HICKEY, DENNIS WILLIAM

Rank: Sergeant
Service: U.S. Army
Birthday: 20 September 1844
Place of Birth: Troy, Rensselaer County, New York
Date of Death: 26 October 1908
Place of Death: Newburgh, New York
Cemetery: St. George's Cemetery—Newburgh, New York
Entered Service at: Plattsburgh, Clinton County, New York
Unit: Company E, 2d New York Cavalry

Battle or Place of Action: Stony Creek Bridge, Virginia
Date of Action: 29 June 1864
Date of Issue: 18 April 1891
Citation: With a detachment of three men, tore up the bridge at Stony Creek, being the last man on the bridge and covering the retreat until he was shot down.

596 ◆ HICKMAN, JOHN S.

Rank: Second Class Fireman
Service: U.S. Navy
Birthday: 2 March 1837
Place of Birth: Blair County, Pennsylvania
Date of Death: 24 December 1904
Cemetery: Calvary Cemetery (MH)—Altoona, Pennsylvania
Entered Service at: Pennsylvania
Unit: U.S.S. *Richmond*
Battle or Place of Action: Port Hudson, Louisiana
Date of Action: 14 March 1863
G.O. Number, Date: 17, 10 July 1863
Citation: Served on board the U.S.S. *Richmond* in the attack on Port Hudson, 14 March 1863. Damaged by a 6-inch solid rifle shot which shattered the starboard safety-valve chamber and also damaged the port safety valve, the fireroom of the U.S.S. *Richmond* immediately became filled with steam to place it in an extremely critical condition. Acting courageously in this crisis, Hickman persisted in penetrating the steam-filled room in order to haul the hot fires of the furnaces and continued this action until the gravity of the situation had been lessened.

597 ◆ HICKOK, NATHAN E.

Rank: Corporal
Service: U.S. Army
Birthday: 1839
Place of Birth: Danbury, Fairfield County, Connecticut
Cemetery: Wooster Cemetery—Danbury, Connecticut (Name inscribed on monument honoring local men in unknown graves.)
Entered Service at: Danbury, Fairfield County, Connecticut
Unit: Company A, 8th Connecticut Infantry
Battle or Place of Action: Chapin's Farm, Virginia
Date of Action: 29 September 1864
Date of Issue: 6 April 1865
Citation: Capture of flag.

598 ◆ HIGBY, CHARLES

Rank: Private
Service: U.S. Army
Birthday: 1841
Place of Birth: Pittsburgh, Allegheny County, Pennsylvania
Date of Death: 19 February 1903
Place of Death: McLoud, Oklahoma
Cemetery: unknown cemetery—McLoud, Oklahoma
Entered Service at: New Brighton, Beaver County, Pennsylvania
Unit: Company F, 1st Pennsylvania Cavalry
Battle or Place of Action: Appomattox Campaign, Virginia

Date of Action: 29 March-9 April 1865
Date of Issue: 3 May 1865
Citation: Capture of flag.

599 ◆ HIGGINS, THOMAS J.

Rank: Sergeant
Service: U.S. Army
Birthday: 8 June 1831
Place of Birth: Riverlequerre, Quebec, Canada
Date of Death: 15 August 1917
Place of Death: Hannibal, Missouri
Cemetery: Holy Family Cemetery—Hannibal, Missouri
Entered Service at: Barry, Pike County, Illinois
Unit: Company D, 99th Illinois Infantry
Battle or Place of Action: Vicksburg, Mississippi
Date of Action: 22 May 1863
Date of Issue: 1 April 1898
Citation: When his regiment fell back in the assault, repulsed, this soldier continued to advance and planted the flag on the parapet, where he was captured by the enemy.
Notes: POW

600 ◆ HIGHLAND, PATRICK

Rank: Corporal (highest rank: Sergeant)
Service: U.S. Army
Place of Birth: Tipperary, Ireland
Entered Service at: Chicago, Cook County, Illinois
Unit: Company D, 23rd Illinois Infantry
Battle or Place of Action: Petersburg, Virginia
Date of Action: 2 April 1865
Date of Issue: 12 May 1865
Citation: Conspicuous gallantry as color bearer in the assault on Fort Gregg.

601 ◆ HILL, EDWARD

Rank: Captain (highest rank: Lieutenant Colonel)
Service: U.S. Army
Birthday: 13 April 1835
Place of Birth: Liberty, Sullivan County, New York
Date of Death: 23 October 1900
Place of Death: Green Bay, Wisconsin
Cemetery: Fredericksburg National Military Park Cemetery (OS-2) (MH)—Fredericksburg, Virginia
Entered Service at: Detroit, Wayne County, Michigan
Unit: Company K, 16th Michigan Infantry
Battle or Place of Action: Cold Harbor, Virginia
Date of Action: 1 June 1864
Date of Issue: 4 December 1893
Citation: Led the brigade skirmish line in a desperate charge on the enemy's masked batteries to the muzzles of the guns, where he was severely wounded.

602 ◆ HILL, HENRY

Rank: Corporal (highest rank: Sergeant)
Service: U.S. Army
Birthday: 1843

Place of Birth: Schuylkill County, Pennsylvania
Date of Death: 2 August 1909
Place of Death: Schuylkill Haven, Pennsylvania
Cemetery: Union Cemetery (MH)—Schuylkill Haven, Pennsylvania
Entered Service at: Harrisburg, Dauphin County, Pennsylvania
Unit: Company C, 50th Pennsylvania Infantry
Battle or Place of Action: Wilderness Campaign, Virginia
Date of Action: 6 May 1864
Date of Issue: 23 September 1897
Citation: This soldier, with one companion, would not retire when his regiment fell back in confusion after an unsuccessful charge, but instead advanced and continued firing upon the enemy until the regiment re-formed and regained its position.

603 ◆ HILL, JAMES

Rank: First Lieutenant
Service: U.S. Army
Birthday: 6 December 1822
Place of Birth: Bristol, Avon County, England
Date of Death: 22 September 1899
Cemetery: Cascade Community Cemetery (MH)—Cascade, Iowa
Entered Service at: Cascade, Dubuque County, Iowa
Unit: Company I, 21st Iowa Infantry
Battle or Place of Action: Champion Hill, Mississippi
Date of Action: 16 May 1863
Date of Issue: 15 March 1893
Citation: By skillful and brave management captured three of the enemy's pickets.

604 ◆ HILL, JAMES SAMUEL

Rank: Sergeant
Service: U.S. Army
Birthday: 1845
Place of Birth: Lyons, Wayne County, New York
Date of Death: 10 April 1865
Place of Death: Danville, Virginia
Entered Service at: Lyons, Wayne County, New York
Unit: Company C, 14th New York Heavy Artillery
Battle or Place of Action: Petersburg, Virginia
Date of Action: 30 July 1864
Date of Issue: 1 December 1864
Citation: Capture of flag, shooting a Confederate officer who was rallying his men with the colors in his hand.
Notes: POW

605 ◆ HILLIKER, BENJAMIN F.

Rank: Musician
Service: U.S. Army
Birthday: 23 May 1843
Place of Birth: Golden, Erie County, New York
Date of Death: 18 October 1916
Place of Death: Los Angeles, California

Cemetery: Hollywood Cemetery—Hollywood, California
Entered Service at: Waupaca Township, Waupaca County, Wisconsin
Unit: Company A, 8th Wisconsin Infantry
Battle or Place of Action: Mechanicsburg, Mississippi
Date of Action: 4 June 1863
Date of Issue: 17 December 1897
Citation: When men were needed to oppose a superior Confederate force he laid down his drum for a rifle and proceeded to the front of the skirmish line which was about 120 feet from the enemy. While on this volunteer mission and firing at the enemy he was hit in the head with a minie ball which passed through him. An order was given to "lay him in the shade; he won't last long." He recovered from this wound being left with an ugly scar.

606 ◆ HILLS, WILLIAM GILES

Rank: Private
Service: U.S. Army
Birthday: 26 June 1841
Place of Birth: Conewango, Cattaraugus County, New York
Date of Death: 18 April 1912
Place of Death: St. Louis, Missouri
Cemetery: unknown cemetery—St. Louis, Missouri
Entered Service at: East Randolph, Cattaraugus County, New York
Unit: Company E, 9th New York Cavalry
Battle or Place of Action: North Fork, Virginia
Date of Action: 26 September 1864
Date of Issue: 26 September 1893
Citation: Voluntarily carried a severely wounded comrade out of a heavy fire from the enemy.

607 ◆ *HILTON, ALFRED B.

Rank: Sergeant
Service: U.S. Army
Birthday: 1842
Place of Birth: Harford County, Maryland
Date of Death: 21 October 1864
Place of Death: Fortress Monroe, Virginia
Cemetery: Hampton National Cemetery (E-1231) (MH)—Hampton, Virginia
Entered Service at: Baltimore, Baltimore County, Maryland
Unit: Company H, 4th U.S. Colored Infantry
Battle or Place of Action: Chapin's Farm, Virginia
Date of Action: 29 September 1864
Date of Issue: 6 April 1865
Citation: When the regimental color bearer fell, this soldier seized the colors and carried it forward, together with the national standard, until disabled at the enemy's inner line.

608 ◆ HINCKS, WILLIAM B.

Rank: Sergeant Major (highest rank: Major)
Service: U.S. Army
Birthday: 1841
Place of Birth: Bucksport, Hancock County, Maine

Date of Death: 7 November 1903
Cemetery: Mountain Grove Cemetery (MH)—Bridgeport, Connecticut
Entered Service at: Bridgeport, Fairfield County, Connecticut
Unit: 14th Connecticut Infantry
Battle or Place of Action: Gettysburg, Pennsylvania
Date of Action: 3 July 1863
Date of Issue: 1 December 1864
Citation: During the highwater mark of Pickett's charge on 3 July 1863 the colors of the 14th Tennessee Infantry C.S.A. were planted 50 yards in front of the center of Sgt. Maj. Hincks' regiment. There were no Confederates standing near it but several were lying down around it. Upon a call for volunteers by Maj. Ellis, commanding, to capture this flag, this soldier and two others leaped the wall. One companion was instantly shot. Sgt. Maj. Hincks outran his remaining companion, running straight and swift for the colors amid a storm of shot. Swinging his saber over the prostrate Confederates and uttering a terrific yell, he seized the flag and hastily returned to his lines. The 14th Tenn. carried 12 battle honors on its flag. The devotion to duty shown by Sgt. Maj. Hincks gave encouragement to many of his comrades at a crucial moment of the battle.

609 ◆ HINNEGAN, WILLIAM

Rank: Second Class Fireman
Service: U.S. Navy
Birthday: 1841
Place of Birth: Ireland
Entered Service at: New York
Unit: U.S.S. *Agawam*
Battle or Place of Action: Fort Fisher, North Carolina
Date of Action: 23 December 1864
G.O. Number, Date: 45, 31 December 1864
Date of Presentation: 12 May 1865
Citation: Hinnegan served on board the U.S.S. *Agawam*, as one of a volunteer crew of powder boat which was exploded near Fort Fisher, 23 December 1864. The powder boat, towed in by the *Wilderness* to prevent detection by the enemy, cast off and slowly steamed to within 300 yards of the beach. After fuses and fires had been lit and a second anchor with short scope let go to assure the boat's tailing inshore, the crew again boarded the *Wilderness* and proceeded a distance of 12 miles from shore. Less than two hours later the explosion took place, and the following day fires were observed still burning at the forts.

610 ◆ HODGES, ADDISON J.

Rank: Private (highest rank: Corporal)
Service: U.S. Army
Birthday: 24 October 1841
Place of Birth: Hillsdale, Hillsdale County, Michigan
Date of Death: 28 July 1923
Place of Death: Adrian, Michigan
Cemetery: Zion Cemetery (MH)—Ogden Township, Michigan

Entered Service at: Adrian, Lenawee County, Michigan
Unit: Company B, 47th Ohio Infantry
Battle or Place of Action: Vicksburg, Mississippi
Date of Action: 3 May 1863
Date of Issue: 31 December 1907
Citation: Was one of a party that volunteered and attempted to run the enemy's batteries with a steam tug and two barges loaded with subsistence stores.
Notes: POW

611 ◆ HOFFMAN, HENRY

Rank: Corporal
Service: U.S. Army
Birthday: 23 December 1836
Place of Birth: Wurttemberg, Germany
Date of Death: 8 January 1894
Cemetery: Old Joseph's Cemetery—Cincinnati, Ohio
Entered Service at: Cincinnati, Hamilton County, Ohio
Unit: Company M, 2d Ohio Cavalry
Battle or Place of Action: Deatonsville (Sailor's Creek), Virginia
Date of Action: 6 April 1865
Date of Issue: 3 May 1865
Citation: Capture of flag.

612 ◆ HOFFMAN, THOMAS W.

Rank: Captain (highest rank: Brevet Lieutenant Colonel)
Service: U.S. Army
Birthday: 21 July 1839
Place of Birth: Perrysburg, Allegheny County, Pennsylvania
Date of Death: 18 April 1905
Place of Death: Scranton, Pennsylvania
Cemetery: Pomfret Manor Cemetery—Sunbury, Pennsylvania
Entered Service at: Harrisburg, Dauphin County, Pennsylvania
Unit: Company A, 208th Pennsylvania Infantry
Battle or Place of Action: Petersburg, Virginia
Date of Action: 2 April 1865
Date of Issue: 19 July 1895
Citation: Prevented a retreat of his regiment during the battle.

613 ◆ HOGAN, FRANKLIN

Rank: Corporal
Service: U.S. Army
Birthday: 7 January 1843
Place of Birth: Centre County, Pennsylvania
Date of Death: 5 April 1932
Place of Death: Hutchinson, Kansas
Cemetery: Eastside Cemetery—Hutchinson, Kansas
Entered Service at: Howard, Centre County, Pennsylvania
Unit: Company A, 45th Pennsylvania Infantry
Battle or Place of Action: Petersburg, Virginia
Date of Action: 30 July 1864
Date of Issue: 1 October 1864
Citation: Capture of flag of 6th Virginia Infantry (C.S.A.).

614 ◆ HOGARTY, WILLIAM P.

Rank: Private (highest rank: Lieutenant U.S.A.—Captain U.S. Vols.)
Service: U.S. Army
Birthday: 16 February 1840
Place of Birth: New York, New York
Date of Death: 23 October 1914
Place of Death: Stillwater, Oklahoma
Cemetery: Mount Hope Cemetery—Kansas City, Kansas
Entered Service at: Elmira, Chemung County, New York
Unit: Company D, 23d New York Infantry
Battle or Place of Action: Antietam, Maryland & Fredericksburg, Virginia
Date of Action: 17 September, 13 December 1862
Date of Issue: 22 June 1891
Citation: Distinguished gallantry in actions while attached to Battery B, 4th U.S. Artillery; lost his left arm at Fredericksburg.

615 ◆ HOLCOMB, DANIEL IRVING

Rank: Private (highest rank: Corporal)
Service: U.S. Army
Birthday: 13 November 1845
Place of Birth: Hartford, Trumbull County, Ohio
Date of Death: 14 December 1900
Place of Death: Sedalia, Missouri
Cemetery: Crown Hill Cemetery—Sedalia, Missouri
Entered Service at: Hartford, Trumbull County, Ohio
Unit: Company A, 41st Ohio Infantry
Battle or Place of Action: Brentwood Hills, Tennessee
Date of Action: 16 December 1864
Date of Issue: 22 February 1865
Citation: Capture of Confederate guidon.

616 ◆ HOLEHOUSE, JAMES

Rank: Private
Service: U.S. Army
Birthday: 25 December 1839
Place of Birth: Stockport, Greater Manchester County, England
Date of Death: 20 May 1915
Place of Death: Chelsea, Massachusetts
Cemetery: Oak Grove Cemetery (MH)—Fall River, Massachusetts
Entered Service at: Fall River, Bristol County, Massachusetts
Unit: Company B, 7th Massachusetts Infantry
Battle or Place of Action: Marye's Heights, Virginia
Date of Action: 3 May 1863
Date of Issue: 10 September 1897
Citation: With one companion voluntarily and with conspicuous daring advanced beyond his regiment, which had been broken in the assault, and halted beneath the crest. Following the example of these two men, the colors were brought to the summit, the regiment was advanced, and the position held.

617 ◆ HOLLAND, LEMUEL F.

Rank: Corporal (highest rank: Sergeant)
Service: U.S. Army
Birthday: 28 July 1840
Place of Birth: Burlington, Ohio
Date of Death: 13 January 1914
Cemetery: Greenwood Cemetery—Decatur, Illinois
Entered Service at: Tiskilwa, Bureau County, Illinois
Unit: Company D, 104th Illinois Infantry
Battle or Place of Action: Elk River, Tennessee
Date of Action: 2 July 1863
Date of Issue: 30 October 1897
Citation: Voluntarily joined a small party that, under a heavy fire, captured a stockade and saved the bridge.

618 ◆ HOLLAND, MILTON MURRAY

Rank: Sergeant Major
Service: U.S. Army
Birthday: 1 August 1844
Place of Birth: Austin, Travis County, Texas
Date of Death: 15 May 1910
Place of Death: Silver Springs, Maryland
Cemetery: Arlington National Cemetery (23-21713)—Arlington, Virginia
Entered Service at: Albany, Athens County, Ohio
Unit: 5th U.S. Colored Infantry
Battle or Place of Action: Chapin's Farm, Virginia
Date of Action: 29 September 1864
Date of Issue: 6 April 1865
Citation: Took command of Company C, after all the officers had been killed or wounded, and gallantly led it.

619 ◆ HOLLAT, GEORGE

Rank: Third Class Boy
Service: U.S. Navy
Birthday: 1846
Entered Service at: New York
Unit: U.S.S. *Varuna*
Battle or Place of Action: Forts Jackson and St. Philip, Louisiana
Date of Action: 24 April 1862
G.O. Number, Date: 11, 3 April 1863
Citation: Hollat served as third class boy on board the U.S.S. *Varuna* during an attack on Forts Jackson and St. Philip, 24 April 1862. He rendered gallant service through the perilous action and remained steadfast and courageous at his battle station despite extremely heavy fire and the ramming of the *Varuna* by the rebel ship *Morgan*, continuing his efforts until his ship, repeatedly holed and fatally damaged, was beached and sunk.

620 ◆ HOLMES, LOVILO N.

Rank: First Sergeant (highest rank: Captain)
Service: U.S. Army
Birthday: 10 October 1830

Place of Birth: Farmersville, Cattaraugus County, New York
Date of Death: 7 May 1914
Place of Death: Mankato, Minnesota
Cemetery: Glenwood Cemetery—Mankato, Minnesota
Entered Service at: Mankato, Blue Earth County, Minnesota
Unit: Company H, 2d Minnesota Infantry
Battle or Place of Action: Nolensville, Tennessee
Date of Action: 15 February 1863
Date of Issue: 11 September 1897
Citation: Was one of a detachment of 16 men who heroically defended a wagon train against the attack of 125 cavalry, repulsed the attack, and saved the train.

621 ◆ HOLMES, WILLIAM T.

Rank: Private
Service: U.S. Army
Birthday: 7 June 1846
Place of Birth: Vermilion County, Illinois
Date of Death: 31 August 1916
Place of Death: Osage Township, Missouri
Cemetery: Bean Cemetery—St. Clair County, Missouri
Entered Service at: Indanapolis, Marion County, Indiana
Unit: Company A, 3d Indiana Cavalry
Battle or Place of Action: Deatonsville (Sailor's Creek), Virginia
Date of Action: 6 April 1865
Date of Issue: 3 May 1865
Citation: Capture of flag of 27th Virginia Infantry (C.S.A.).

622 ◆ HOLTON, CHARLES MAYNARD

Rank: First Sergeant (highest rank: Second Lieutenant)
Service: U.S. Army
Birthday: 25 May 1838
Place of Birth: Potter, Yates County, New York
Date of Death: 25 August 1899
Place of Death: Yakima, Washington
Cemetery: Oak Hill Cemetery (MH)—Battle Creek, Michigan
Entered Service at: Battle Creek, Calhoun County, Michigan
Unit: Company A, 7th Michigan Cavalry
Battle or Place of Action: Falling Waters, Virginia
Date of Action: 14 July 1863
Date of Issue: 21 March 1889
Citation: Capture of flag of 55th Virginia Infantry (C.S.A.). In the midst of the battle with foot soldiers he dismounted to capture the flag.

623 ◆ HOLTON, EDWARD A.

Rank: First Sergeant (highest rank: Captain)
Service: U.S. Army
Birthday: 28 August 1835
Place of Birth: Westminster, Windham County, Vermont
Date of Death: 29 January 1906
Place of Death: Bernardston, Massachusetts
Cemetery: Westminster Old Cemetery—Westminster, Vermont

Entered Service at: Williston, Chittenden County, Vermont
Unit: Company I, 6th Vermont Infantry
Battle or Place of Action: Lee's Mills, Virginia
Date of Action: 16 April 1862
Date of Issue: 9 July 1892
Citation: Rescued the colors of his regiment under heavy fire, the color bearer having been shot down while the troops were in retreat.

624 ◆ HOMAN, CONRAD

Rank: Color Sergeant (highest rank: First Lieutenant)
Service: U.S. Army
Birthday: 27 February 1840
Place of Birth: Roxbury, Suffolk County, Massachusetts
Date of Death: 30 January 1922
Cemetery: Edwards Cemetery (MH)—Framingham, Massachusetts
Entered Service at: Boston, Suffolk County, Massachusetts
Unit: Company A, 29th Massachusetts Infantry
Battle or Place of Action: near Petersburg, Virginia
Date of Action: 30 July 1864
Date of Issue: 3 June 1869
Citation: Fought his way through the enemy's lines with the regimental colors, the rest of the color guard being killed or captured.

625 ◆ HOOKER, GEORGE WHITE

Rank: First Lieutenant (highest rank: Brevet Lieutenant Colonel U.S. Vols.)
Service: U.S. Army
Birthday: 6 February 1838
Place of Birth: Salem, Washington County, New York
Date of Death: 6 August 1902
Place of Death: Brattleboro, Vermont
Cemetery: Prospect Hill Cemetery—Brattleboro, Vermont
Entered Service at: Boston, Suffolk County, Massachusetts
Unit: Company E, 4th Vermont Infantry
Battle or Place of Action: South Mountain, Maryland
Date of Action: 14 September 1862
Date of Issue: 17 September 1891
Citation: Rode alone, in advance of his regiment, into the enemy's lines, and before his own men came up, received the surrender of the major of a Confederate regiment, together with the colors and 116 men.

626 ◆ HOOPER, WILLIAM B.

Rank: Corporal (highest rank: Quartermaster Sergeant)
Service: U.S. Army
Birthday: 1841
Place of Birth: Willimantic, Windham County, Connecticut
Date of Death: 16 January 1870
Place of Death: Caldera, Chile
Cemetery: Old Willimatic Cemetery (MH)—Windham, Connecticut
Entered Service at: Jersey City, Hudson County, New Jersey

Unit: Company L, 1st New Jersey Cavalry
Battle or Place of Action: Chamberlains Creek, Virginia
Date of Action: 31 March 1865
Date of Issue: 3 July 1865
Citation: With the assistance of a comrade, headed off the advance of the enemy, shooting two of his color bearers; also posted himself between the enemy and the lead horses of his own command, thus saving the herd from capture.

627 ◆ HOPKINS, CHARLES F.

Rank: Corporal
Service: U.S. Army
Birthday: 16 May 1842
Place of Birth: Hope, Warren County, New Jersey
Date of Death: 14 February 1934
Place of Death: Boonton, New Jersey
Cemetery: Greenwood Cemetery—Boonton, New Jersey
Entered Service at: Trenton, Mercer County, New Jersey
Unit: Company I, 1st New Jersey Infantry
Battle or Place of Action: Gaines' Mill, Virginia
Date of Action: 27 June 1862
Date of Issue: 9 July 1892
Citation: Voluntarily carried a wounded comrade, under heavy fire, to a place of safety; though twice wounded in the act, he continued in action until again severely wounded.
Notes: POW

628 ◆ HORAN, THOMAS

Rank: Sergeant
Service: U.S. Army
Birthday: 1839
Date of Death: 1902
Place of Death: Madison, Illinois
Cemetery: St. Mary's Cemetery—Dunkirk, New York
Entered Service at: Dunkirk, Chautauqua County, New York
Unit: Company E, 72d New York Infantry
Battle or Place of Action: Gettysburg, Pennsylvania
Date of Action: 2 July 1863
Date of Issue: 5 April 1898
Citation: In a charge of his regiment this soldier captured the regimental flag of the 8th Florida Infantry (C.S.A.).

629 ◆ HORNE, SAMUEL BELTON

Rank: Captain
Service: U.S. Army
Birthday: 3 March 1843
Place of Birth: Belleek, County Fermanagh, Ireland
Date of Death: 18 September 1928
Place of Death: Winchester, Connecticut
Cemetery: Forest View Cemetery (MH)—Winsted, Connecticut
Entered Service at: Winsted, Litchfield County, Connecticut
Unit: Company H, 11th Connecticut Infantry
Battle or Place of Action: Fort Harrison, Virginia
Date of Action: 29 September 1864

Date of Issue: 19 November 1897
Citation: While acting as an aide and carrying an important message, Horne was severely wounded and his horse killed, but delivered the order and rejoined his general.

630 ◆ HORSFALL, WILLIAM H.

Rank: Drummer
Service: U.S. Army
Birthday: 3 March 1847
Place of Birth: Campbell County, Kentucky
Date of Death: 22 October 1922
Place of Death: Newport, Kentucky
Cemetery: Evergreen Cemetery (MH)—Southgate, Kentucky
Entered Service at: Fort Cox, Charleston, West Virginia
Unit: Company G, 1st Kentucky Infantry
Battle or Place of Action: Corinth, Mississippi
Date of Action: 21 May 1862
Date of Issue: 17 August 1895
Citation: Saved the life of a wounded officer lying between the lines.

631 ◆ HORTON, JAMES

True Name: Horton, Joseph
Rank: Gunner's Mate (highest rank: Paymaster's Steward)
Service: U.S. Navy
Birthday: 1 July 1840
Place of Birth: England
Date of Death: 15 April 1894
Cemetery: Cypress Hills (Private Sec. 5 Lot 175 East Half—Brooklyn, New York
Entered Service at: Massachusetts
Unit: U.S.S. *Montauk*
Battle or Place of Action: off Port Royal, South Carolina
G.O. Number, Date: 59, 22 June 1865
Citation: Served as gunner's mate on board the U.S.S. *Montauk*, 21 September 1864. During the night of 21 September 1864, when fire was discovered in the magazine lightroom of the vessel, causing a panic and demoralizing the crew, Horton rushed into the cabin, obtained the magazine keys, sprang into the lightroom and began passing out combustibles, including the box of signals in which the fire originated.

632 ◆ HORTON, LEWIS AUGUSTINE

Rank: Seaman
Service: U.S. Navy
Birthday: 26 May 1842
Place of Birth: Bristol County, Massachusetts
Date of Death: 8 June 1916
Place of Death: Boston, Massachusetts
Cemetery: Forest Hill Cemetery—Boston, Massachusetts
Entered Service at: Taunton, Bristol County, Massachusetts
Unit: U.S.S. *Rhode Island*
Battle or Place of Action: off Cape Hatteras, North Carolina
Date of Action: 30 December 1862
G.O. Number, Date: 59, 22 June 1865

Citation: Served on board the U.S.S. *Rhode Island* which was engaged in saving the lives of the officers and crew of the *Monitor*, 30 December 1862. Participating in the hazardous rescue of the officers and crew of the sinking *Monitor*, Horton, after rescuing several of the men, became separated in a heavy gale with other members of the cutter that had set out from the *Rhode Island*, and spent many hours in the small boat at the mercy of the weather and the high seas until finally picked up by a schooner 50 miles east of Cape Hatteras.

633 ◆ HOTTENSTINE, SOLOMON J.

True Name: Hottenstein, Solomon J.
Rank: Private (highest rank: Sergeant)
Service: U.S. Army
Birthday: 5 May 1844
Place of Birth: Lehigh County, Pennsylvania
Date of Death: 24 May 1896
Place of Death: Manassas, Virginia
Cemetery: Manassas Cemetery (MH)—Manassas, Virginia
Entered Service at: Philadelphia, Philadelphia County, Pennsylvania
Unit: Company C, 107th Pennsylvania Infantry
Battle or Place of Action: Petersburg & Norfolk Railroad, Virginia
Date of Action: 19 August 1864
Date of Issue: 2 February 1865
Citation: Captured flag belonging to a North Carolina regiment, and through a ruse led them into the arms of Federal troops.

634 ◆ HOUGH, IRA

Rank: Private
Service: U.S. Army
Birthday: 2 July 1843
Place of Birth: Henry County, Indiana
Date of Death: 18 October 1916
Place of Death: Chipley, Florida
Cemetery: Slocum Church Cemetery—Jackson County, Florida
Entered Service at: Middletown, Henry County, Indiana
Unit: Company E, 8th Indiana Infantry
Battle or Place of Action: Cedar Creek, Virginia
Date of Action: 19 October 1864
Date of Issue: 26 October 1864
Citation: Capture of flag.

635 ◆ HOUGHTON, CHARLES H.

Rank: Captain (highest rank: Colonel)
Service: U.S. Army
Birthday: 30 April 1842
Place of Birth: Macomb, St. Lawrence County, New York
Date of Death: 6 April 1914
Cemetery: Arlington National Cemetery (3-2411-WS)—Arlington, Virginia
Entered Service at: Ogdensburg, St. Lawrence County, New York

Unit: Company L, 14th New York Artillery
Battle or Place of Action: Petersburg, Virginia
Date of Action: 30 July 1864 & 25 March 1865
Date of Issue: 5 April 1898
Citation: In the Union assault at the Crater (30 July 1864), and in the Confederate assault repelled at Fort Haskell, Houghton displayed most conspicuous gallantry and repeatedly exposed himself voluntarily to great danger, was three times wounded, and the suffered loss of a leg.

636 ◆ HOUGHTON, EDWARD J.

Rank: Ordinary Seaman
Service: U.S. Navy
Birthday: 1843
Place of Birth: Mobile, Mobile County, Alabama
Date of Death: 16 July 1865
Place of Death: Norfolk, Virginia
Cemetery: Hollywood Cemetery (MH)—Brookline, Massachusetts
Entered Service at: Alabama
Unit: U.S. Picket Boat No. 1
Battle or Place of Action: Plymouth, North Carolina
Date of Action: 27 October 1864
G.O. Number, Date: 45, 31 December 1864
Citation: Houghton served on board the U.S. Picket Boat No. 1, in action, 27 October 1864, against the Confederate ram, *Albemarle*, which had resisted repeated attacks by our steamers and had kept a large force of vessels employed in watching her. The picket boat, equipped with a spar torpedo, succeeded in passing the enemy pickets within 20 yards without being discovered and then made for the *Albemarle* under a full head of steam. Immediately taken under fire by the ram, the small boat plunged on, jumped the log boom which encircled the target, and exploded its torpedo under the port bow of the ram. The picket boat was destroyed by enemy fire and almost the entire crew taken prisoner or lost.

637 ◆ HOUGHTON, GEORGE L.

Rank: Private
Service: U.S. Army
Birthday: 28 August 1841
Place of Birth: Yarmouth, West Canada
Date of Death: 25 February 1917
Cemetery: Soldier's Home Cemetery—Orting, Washington
Entered Service at: Brookfield, Cook County, Illinois
Unit: Company D, 104th Illinois Infantry
Battle or Place of Action: Elk River, Tennessee
Date of Action: 2 July 1863
Date of Issue: 27 March 1900
Citation: Voluntarily joined a small party that, under a heavy fire, captured a stockade and saved the bridge.

638 ◆ HOULTON, WILLIAM M.

Rank: Commissary Sergeant
Service: U.S. Army
Birthday: 1 September 1835

Place of Birth: Clymer, Chautauqua County, New York
Date of Death: 13 February 1918
Place of Death: Abilene, Kansas
Cemetery: Abilene Cemetery—Abilene, Kansas
Entered Service at: Athens, Athens County, Ohio
Unit: 1st West Virginia Cavalry
Battle or Place of Action: Deatonsville (Sailor's Creek), Virginia
Date of Action: 6 April 1865
Date of Issue: 3 May 1865
Citation: Capture of flag.

639 ◆ HOWARD, HENDERSON CALVIN

Rank: Corporal (highest rank: First Sergeant)
Service: U.S. Army
Birthday: 16 September 1839
Place of Birth: Indiana County, Pennsylvania
Date of Death: 13 December 1919
Place of Death: Fort Collins, Colorado
Cemetery: Grand View Cemetery (MH)—Fort Collins, Colorado
Entered Service at: Indiana, Indiana County, Pennsylvania
Unit: Company B, 11th Pennsylvania Reserves
Battle or Place of Action: Glendale, Virginia
Date of Action: 30 June 1862
Date of Issue: 30 March 1898
Citation: While pursuing one of the enemy's sharpshooters, encountered two others, whom he bayoneted in hand-to-hand encounters; was three times wounded in action.

640 ◆ HOWARD, HIRAM REESE

Rank: Private
Service: U.S. Army
Birthday: 17 February 1843
Place of Birth: Urbana, Champaign County, Ohio
Date of Death: 9 May 1912
Place of Death: Point Pleasant, West Virginia
Cemetery: Lone Oak Cemetery (MH)—Point Pleasant, West Virginia
Entered Service at: Cincinnati, Hamilton County, Ohio
Unit: Company H, 11th Ohio Infantry
Battle or Place of Action: Missionary Ridge, Tennessee
Date of Action: 25 November 1863
Date of Issue: 29 July 1892
Citation: Scaled the enemy's works and in a hand-to-hand fight helped capture the flag of the 18th Alabama Infantry (C.S.A.).

641 ◆ HOWARD, JAMES

True Name: Brown, James
Rank: Sergeant
Service: U.S. Army
Place of Birth: Newton, Sussex County, New Jersey
Place of Death: Brooklyn, New York
Entered Service at: Brooklyn, Kings County, New York

Unit: Company K, 158th New York Infantry
Battle or Place of Action: near Petersburg (Battery Gregg), Virginia
Date of Action: 2 April 1865
Date of Issue: 12 May 1865
Citation: Carried the colors in advance of the line of battle, the flagstaff being shot off while he was planting it on the parapet of the fort.

642 ◆ HOWARD, MARTIN

True Name: Horgan, Michael C.
Rank: Landsman
Service: U.S. Navy
Birthday: 1843
Place of Birth: Ireland
Date of Death: 27 November 1910
Place of Death: Boston, Massachusetts
Cemetery: Holy Cross Cemetery (MH)—Malden, Massachusetts
Entered Service at: New York, New York
Unit: U.S.S. *Tacony*
Battle or Place of Action: Plymouth, North Carolina
Date of Action: 31 October 1864
G.O. Number, Date: 45, 31 December 1864
Citation: Served on board the U.S.S. *Tacony* during the taking of Plymouth, N.C., 31 October 1864. Carrying out his duties faithfully during the capture of Plymouth, Howard distinguished himself by a display of coolness when he participated in landing and spiking a 9-inch gun while under a devastating fire from enemy musketry.

643 ◆ HOWARD, OLIVER OTIS

Rank: Brigadier General (highest rank: Major General)
Service: U.S. Army
Birthday: 8 November 1830
Place of Birth: Leeds, Androscoggin County, Maine
Date of Death: 26 October 1909
Place of Death: Burlington, Vermont
Cemetery: Lake View Cemetery—Burlington, Vermont
Entered Service at: Leeds, Androscoggin County, Maine
Unit: U.S. Volunteers
Battle or Place of Action: Fair Oaks, Virginia
Date of Action: 1 June 1862
Date of Issue: 29 March 1893
Citation: Led the 61st New York Infantry in a charge in which he was twice severely wounded in the right arm, necessitating amputation.

644 ◆ HOWARD, PETER

Rank: Boatswain's Mate (highest rank: Acting Ensign)
Service: U.S. Navy
Birthday: 1829
Place of Birth: France
Date of Death: 25 March 1875
Place of Death: Brooklyn, New York

Entered Service at: Boston, Suffolk County, Massachusetts
Unit: U.S.S. *Mississippi*
Battle or Place of Action: Port Hudson, Louisiana
Date of Action: 14 March 1863
G.O. Number, Date: 17, 10 July 1863
Citation: Served on board the U.S.S. *Mississippi* during the action against Port Hudson, 14 March 1863. Running aground during the darkness and in the midst of battle while exposed to a devastating fire from enemy shore batteries, the *Mississippi* was ordered abandoned after a long and desperate attempt to free her. Serving courageously throughout this period in which a steady fire was kept up against the enemy until the ship was enveloped in flames and abandoned, Howard acted gallantly in his duties as boatswain's mate. Soon after the firing of the *Mississippi* and its abandonment, it was seen to slide off the shoal, drift downstream, and explode, leaving no possibility of its falling into enemy hands.

645 ◆ HOWARD, SQUIRE EDWARD

Rank: First Sergeant (highest rank: Captain)
Service: U.S. Army
Birthday: 15 May 1840
Place of Birth: Jamaica, Windham County, Vermont
Date of Death: 26 November 1912
Place of Death: West Newton, Massachusetts
Cemetery: Newton Cemetery—Newton Center, Massachusetts
Entered Service at: Townshend, Windham County, Vermont
Unit: Company H, 8th Vermont Infantry
Battle or Place of Action: Bayou Teche, Louisiana
Date of Action: 14 January 1863
Date of Issue: 29 January 1894
Citation: Voluntarily carried an important message through the heavy fire of the enemy to bring aid and save the gunboat *Calhoun*.

646 ◆ HOWE, ORION P.

Rank: Musician (highest rank: Corporal)
Service: U.S. Army
Birthday: 29 December 1849
Place of Birth: Hiram, Portage County, Ohio
Date of Death: 27 January 1930
Place of Death: Springfield, Missouri
Cemetery: Springfield National Cemetery (4-207A) (MH)—Springfield, Missouri
Entered Service at: Waukegan, Lake County, Illinois
Unit: Company C, 55th Illinois Infantry
Battle or Place of Action: Vicksburg, Mississippi
Date of Action: 19 May 1863
Date of Issue: 23 April 1896
Citation: A drummer boy, 14 years of age, and severely wounded and exposed to a heavy fire from the enemy, he persistently remained upon the field of battle until he had reported to Gen. W.T. Sherman the necessity of supplying cartridges for the use of troops under command of Col. Malmborg.

647 ◆ HOWE, WILLIAM H.

Rank: Sergeant (highest rank: First Lieutenant)
Service: U.S. Army
Birthday: 11 April 1837
Place of Birth: Haverhill, Essex County, Massachusetts
Date of Death: 23 April 1907
Place of Death: Everett, Massachusetts
Cemetery: Woodlawn Cemetery (MH)—Everett, Massachusetts
Entered Service at: Boston, Suffolk County, Massachusetts
Unit: Company K, 29th Massachusetts Infantry
Battle or Place of Action: Fort Stedman, Virginia
Date of Action: 25 March 1865
Date of Issue: 8 March 1895
Citation: Saved an abandoned gun under heavy fire.

648 ◆ HUBBELL, WILLIAM STONE

Rank: Captain (highest rank: Brevet Major)
Service: U.S. Army
Birthday: 19 April 1837
Place of Birth: Wolcottville, New Haven County, Connecticut
Date of Death: 28 August 1930
Place of Death: Plymouth, Massachusetts
Cemetery: Indian Hill Cemetery (MH)—Middletown, Connecticut
Entered Service at: North Stonington, New London County, Connecticut
Unit: Company A, 21st Connecticut Infantry
Battle or Place of Action: Fort Harrison, Virginia
Date of Action: 30 September 1864
Date of Issue: 13 June 1894
Citation: Led out a small flanking party and by a clash and at great risk captured a large number of prisoners.

649 ◆ HUDSON, AARON R.

Rank: Private
Service: U.S. Army
Place of Birth: Madison County, Kentucky
Date of Death: 7 May 1907
Cemetery: Regan Cemetery (MH)—Neosho, Missouri
Entered Service at: Indanapolis, Marion County, Indiana
Unit: Company C, 17th Indiana Mounted Infantry
Battle or Place of Action: Culloden, Georgia
Date of Action: April 1865
Date of Issue: 17 June 1865
Citation: Capture of flag of Worrill Grays (C.S.A.).

650 ◆ HUDSON, MICHAEL

Rank: Sergeant
Service: U.S. Marine Corps

Birthday: 1834
Place of Birth: County Sligo, Ireland
Date of Death: 28 December 1891
Cemetery: Maple Hill Cemetery (MH)—Charlotte, Michigan
Entered Service at: New York
Unit: U.S.S. *Brooklyn*
Battle or Place of Action: Mobile Bay, Alabama
Date of Action: 5 August 1864
G.O. Number, Date: 45, 31 December 1864
Citation: On board the U.S.S. *Brooklyn* during action against rebel forts and gunboats and with the ram *Tennessee*, in Mobile Bay, 5 August 1864. Despite severe damage to his ship and the loss of several men on board as enemy fire raked the decks, Sgt. Hudson fought his gun with skill and courage throughout the furious two-hour battle, which resulted in the surrender of the rebel ram *Tennessee*.

651 ◆ HUGHES, OLIVER

Rank: Corporal
Service: U.S. Army
Birthday: 21 January 1844
Place of Birth: Fentress County, Tennessee
Date of Death: 5 January 1911
Place of Death: Macon, Missouri
Cemetery: Old Callao Cemetery—Callao, Missouri
Entered Service at: Albany, Clinton County, Kentucky
Unit: Company C, 12th Kentucky Infantry
Battle or Place of Action: Town Creek, North Carolina
Date of Action: 20 February 1865
Date of Issue: 1 August 1865
Citation: Capture of flag of 11th South Carolina (C.S.A.).

652 ◆ HUGHEY, JOHN P.

Rank: Corporal
Service: U.S. Army
Birthday: 1836
Place of Birth: Louisville, Jefferson County, Kentucky
Date of Death: 29 January 1900
Place of Death: Near Hickman, Kentucky
Cemetery: unknown cemetery—Fulton County, Kentucky
Entered Service at: Anna, Union County, Illinois
Unit: Company L, 2d Ohio Cavalry
Battle or Place of Action: Deatonsville (Sailor's Creek), Virginia
Date of Action: 6 April 1865
Date of Issue: 3 May 1865
Citation: Capture of flag of 38th Virginia Infantry (C.S.A.).

653 ◆ HUIDEKOPER, HENRY SHIPPEN

Rank: Lieutenant Colonel (highest rank: Major General) PA National Guard
Service: U.S. Army
Birthday: 7 July 1839
Place of Birth: Meadville, Crawford County, Pennsylvania
Date of Death: 9 November 1918
Place of Death: Philadelphia, Pennsylvania
Cemetery: Greendale Cemetery (MH)—Meadville, Pennsylvania
Entered Service at: Philadelphia, Philadelphia County, Pennsylvania
Unit: 150th Pennsylvania Infantry
Battle or Place of Action: Gettysburg, Pennsylvania
Date of Action: 1 July 1863
Date of Issue: 27 May 1905
Citation: While engaged in repelling an attack of the enemy, received a severe wound of the right arm, but instead of retiring remained at the front in command of his regiment.

654 ◆ HUNT, LOUIS T.

Rank: Private
Service: U.S. Army
Place of Birth: Montgomery County, Indiana
Date of Death: 14 March 1901
Cemetery: Evangelical Lutheran Cemetery—St. Louis, Missouri
Entered Service at: Jefferson County, Missouri
Unit: Company H, 6th Missouri Infantry
Battle or Place of Action: Vicksburg, Mississippi
Date of Action: 22 May 1863
Date of Issue: 12 July 1894
Citation: Gallantry in the charge of the "volunteer storming party."

655 ◆ HUNTER, CHARLES ADAMS

Rank: Sergeant
Service: U.S. Army
Birthday: 26 August 1843
Place of Birth: Spencer, Worcester County, Massachusetts
Date of Death: 31 December 1912
Place of Death: Ashland, Massachusetts
Cemetery: Pine Grove Cemetery (MH)—Spencer, Massachusetts
Entered Service at: Spencer, Worcester County, Massachusetts
Unit: Company E, 34th Massachusetts Infantry
Battle or Place of Action: Petersburg, Virginia
Date of Action: 2 April 1865
Date of Issue: 12 May 1865
Citation: In the assault on Fort Gregg, bore the regimental flag bravely and was among the foremost to enter the work.

656 ◆ HUNTERSON, JOHN C.

Rank: Private
Service: U.S. Army
Birthday: 4 August 1841
Place of Birth: Philadelphia, Philadelphia County, Pennsylvania
Date of Death: 6 November 1927
Place of Death: New Haven, Connecticut
Cemetery: Old Swedes Burial Grounds (MH)—Philadelphia, Pennsylvania

Entered Service at: Philadelphia, Philadelphia County, Pennsylvania
Unit: Company B, 3d Pennsylvania Cavalry
Battle or Place of Action: On the Peninsula, Virginia
Date of Action: 5 June 1862
Date of Issue: 2 August 1897
Citation: While under fire, between the lines of the two armies, voluntarily gave up his own horse to an engineer officer whom he was accompanying on a reconnaissance and whose horse had been killed, thus enabling the officer to escape with valuable papers in his possession.

657 ◆ HUSKEY, MICHAEL

Rank: Fireman (highest rank: Fireman First Class)
Service: U.S. Navy
Birthday: 1841
Place of Birth: Niagara County, New York
Entered Service at: New York
Unit: U.S.S. *Carondelet*
Battle or Place of Action: Deer Creek Expedition, Mississippi
Date of Action: March 1863
G.O. Number, Date: 32, 16 April 1864
Citation: Fireman on board the U.S.S. *Carondelet*, Deer Creek Expedition, March 1863. Carrying out his duties gallantly, Huskey volunteered to aid in the rescue of the tug *Ivy* under the fire of the enemy, and set forth general meritorious conduct during this hazardous mission.

658 ◆ HYATT, THEODORE

Rank: First Sergeant
Service: U.S. Army
Birthday: 3 July 1830
Place of Birth: Pennsylvania
Date of Death: 7 May 1900
Place of Death: Woliet, Illinois
Cemetery: Lockport Cemetery (MH)—Lockport, Illinois
Entered Service at: Gardner, Grundy County, Illinois
Unit: Company D, 127th Illinois Infantry
Battle or Place of Action: Vicksburg, Mississippi
Date of Action: 22 May 1863
Date of Issue: 9 July 1894
Citation: Gallantry in the charge of the "volunteer storming party."

659 ◆ HYDE, THOMAS WORCESTER

Rank: Major (highest rank: Brevet Brigadier General)
Service: U.S. Army
Birthday: 16 January 1841
Place of Birth: Florence, Italy
Date of Death: 14 November 1899
Place of Death: Fortress Monroe, Virginia
Cemetery: Oak Grove Cemetery (Hyde Mausoleum) (MH)—Bath, Maine
Entered Service at: Bath, Sagadahoc County, Maine
Unit: 7th Maine Infantry

Battle or Place of Action: Antietam, Maryland
Date of Action: 17 September 1862
Date of Issue: 8 April 1891
Citation: Led his regiment in an assault on a strong body of the enemy's infantry and kept up the fight until the greater part of his men had been killed or wounded, bringing the remainder safely out of the fight.

660 ◆ HYLAND, JOHN

Rank: Seaman (highest rank: Assistant Gunner)
Service: U.S. Navy
Birthday: 1819
Place of Birth: Ireland
Date of Death: 10 August 1867
Place of Death: Manistee, Michigan
Entered Service at: Illinois
Unit: U.S.S. *Signal*
Battle or Place of Action: Red River, Louisiana
Date of Action: 5 May 1864
G.O. Number, Date: 45, 31 December 1864
Citation: Served as seaman on board the U.S.S. *Signal* which was attacked by field batteries and sharpshooters and destroyed in Red River, 5 May 1864. Proceeding up the Red River, the U.S.S. *Signal* engaged a large force of enemy field batteries and sharpshooters, returning their fire until the ship was totally disabled, at which time the white flag was raised. Although wounded, Hyland courageously went in full view of several hundred sharpshooters and let go the anchor, and again to slip the cable, when he was again wounded by the raking enemy fire.

661 ◆ HYMER, SAMUEL

Rank: Captain
Service: U.S. Army
Birthday: 17 May 1829
Place of Birth: Harrison County, Indiana
Date of Death: 9 May 1906
Cemetery: Rushville Cemetery—Rushville, Illinois
Entered Service at: Rushville, Schuyler County, Illinois
Unit: Company D, 115th Illinois Infantry
Battle or Place of Action: Buzzard's Roost Gap, Georgia
Date of Action: 13 October 1864
Date of Issue: 28 March 1896
Citation: With only 41 men under his command, defended and held a blockhouse against the attack of Hood's Division for nearly 10 hours, thus checking the advance of the enemy and insuring the safety of the balance of the regiment, as well as that of the 8th Kentucky Infantry, then stationed at Ringgold, Ga.

662 ◆ ILGENFRITZ, CHARLES HENRY

Rank: Sergeant (highest rank: First Sergeant)
Service: U.S. Army
Birthday: 4 March 1837
Place of Birth: York County, Pennsylvania
Date of Death: 31 March 1920

Place of Death: York, Pennsylvania
Cemetery: Prospect Hill Cemetery—York, Pennsylvania
Entered Service at: Harrisburg, Dauphin County, Pennsylvania
Unit: Company E, 207th Pennsylvania Infantry
Battle or Place of Action: Fort Sedgwick, Virginia
Date of Action: 2 April 1865
Date of Issue: 20 March 1917
Citation: The color bearer falling, pierced by seven balls, he immediately sprang forward and grasped the colors, planting them upon the enemy's forts amid a murderous fire of grape, canister, and musketry from the enemy.

663 ◆ IMMELL, LORENZO DOW

Rank: Corporal (highest rank: First Lieutenant)
Service: U.S. Army
Birthday: 18 June 1837
Place of Birth: Ross, Butler County, Ohio
Date of Death: 31 October 1912
Cemetery: Jefferson Barracks National Cemetery (4-12342) (MH)—St. Louis, Missouri
Entered Service at: Fort Leavenworth, Leavenworth County, Kansas
Unit: Company F, 2d U.S. Artillery
Battle or Place of Action: Wilson's Creek, Missouri
Date of Action: 10 August 1861
Date of Issue: 19 July 1890
Citation: Bravery in action.

664 ◆ INGALLS, LEWIS J.

Rank: Private
Service: U.S. Army
Birthday: 11 October 1837
Place of Birth: Boston, Suffolk County, Massachusetts
Date of Death: 31 December 1913
Place of Death: Irasburg, Vermont
Cemetery: Irasburg Cemetery—Irasburg, Vermont
Entered Service at: Belvidere, Lamoille County, Vermont
Unit: Company K, 8th Vermont Infantry
Battle or Place of Action: Boutte Station, Louisiana
Date of Action: 4 September 1862
Date of Issue: 20 October 1899
Citation: A railroad train guarded by about 60 men on flat cars having been sidetracked by a misplaced switch into an ambuscade of guerrillas who were rapidly shooting down the unprotected guards, this soldier, under a severe fire in which he was wounded, ran to another switch and, opening it, enabled the train and the surviving guards to escape.

665 ◆ INSCHO, LEONIDAS H.

Rank: Corporal (highest rank: First Lieutenant)
Service: U.S. Army
Birthday: 20 February 1840
Place of Birth: Chatham, Licking County, Ohio
Date of Death: 12 November 1907
Cemetery: Cedar Hill Cemetery (MH)—Newark, Ohio

Entered Service at: Newark, Licking County, Ohio
Unit: Company E, 12th Ohio Infantry
Battle or Place of Action: South Mountain, Maryland
Date of Action: 14 September 1862
Date of Issue: 31 January 1894
Citation: Alone and unaided and with his left hand disabled, captured a Confederate captain and four men.

666 ◆ IRLAM, JOSEPH

Rank: Seaman
Service: U.S. Navy
Birthday: 1840
Place of Birth: Liverpool, Merseyside County, England
Entered Service at: New York, New York
Unit: U.S.S. *Brooklyn*
Battle or Place of Action: Mobile Bay, Alabama
Date of Action: 5 August 1864
G.O. Number, Date: 45, 31 December 1864
Citation: Stationed at the wheel on board the U.S.S. *Brooklyn* during action against rebel forts and gunboats and with the ram *Tennessee* in Mobile Bay, 5 August 1864. When heavy enemy fire struck down several men at their guns and replacements were not available, Irlam voluntarily released two men who were stationed with him and carried on at the wheel with the assistance of only one of the crew throughout the furious battle.

667 ◆ IRSCH, FRANCIS

Rank: Captain
Service: U.S. Army
Birthday: 4 December 1840
Place of Birth: Saarburg, Germany
Date of Death: 19 August 1906
Place of Death: Tampa, Florida
Cemetery: Woodlawn Cemetery (MH)—Tampa, Florida
Entered Service at: New York, New York
Unit: Company D, 45th New York Infantry
Battle or Place of Action: Gettysburg, Pennsylvania
Date of Action: 1 July 1863
Date of Issue: 27 May 1892
Citation: Gallantry in flanking the enemy and capturing a number of prisoners and in holding a part of the town against heavy odds while the Army was rallying on Cemetery Hill.

668 ◆ IRVING, JOHN

Rank: Coxswain
Service: U.S. Navy
Birthday: 1839
Place of Birth: East Brooklyn, Kings County, New York
Entered Service at: New York, New York
Unit: U.S.S. *Brooklyn*
Battle or Place of Action: Mobile Bay, Alabama
Date of Action: 5 August 1864
G.O. Number, Date: 45, 31 December 1864
Citation: On board the U.S.S. *Brooklyn* during action against rebel forts and gunboats and with the ram *Tennessee*,

in Mobile Bay, 5 August 1864. Despite severe damage to his ship and loss of several men on board as enemy fire raked her decks from stem to stern, Irving fought his gun with skill and courage throughout the furious battle which resulted in the surrender of the prize rebel ram *Tennessee* and in the damaging and destruction of batteries at Fort Morgan.

669 ◆ IRVING, THOMAS

Rank: Coxswain (highest rank: Acting Master's Mate)
Service: U.S. Navy
Birthday: 1842
Place of Birth: England
Entered Service at: New York, New York
Unit: U.S.S. *Lehigh*
Battle or Place of Action: Charleston Harbor, South Carolina
Date of Action: 16 November 1863
G.O. Number, Date: 32, 16 April 1864
Citation: Served on board the U.S.S. *Lehigh*, Charleston Harbor, 16 November 1863, during the hazardous task of freeing the *Lehigh*, which had grounded, and was under heavy enemy fire from Fort Moultrie. Rowing the small boat which was used in the hazardous task of transferring hawsers from the *Lehigh* to the *Nahant*, Irving twice succeeded in making the trip, while under severe fire from the enemy, only to find that each had been in vain when the hawsers were cut by hostile fire and chaffing.

670 ◆ IRWIN, NICHOLAS

Rank: Seaman
Service: U.S. Navy
Birthday: 1833
Place of Birth: Denmark
Date of Death: 19 April 1896
Place of Death: Marion, Indiana
Cemetery: Marion National Cemetery (I-382) (MH)—Marion, Indiana
Entered Service at: New York, New York
Unit: U.S.S. *Brooklyn*
Battle or Place of Action: Mobile Bay, Alabama
Date of Action: 5 August 1864
G.O. Number, Date: 45, 31 December 1864
Citation: On board the U.S.S. *Brooklyn* during action against rebel forts and gunboats and with the ram *Tennessee*, in Mobile Bay, 5 August 1864. Despite severe damage to his ship and loss of several men on board as enemy fire raked her decks from stem to stern, Irwin fought his gun with skill and courage throughout the furious battle which resulted in the surrender of the prize rebel ram *Tennessee* and in the damaging and destruction of batteries at Fort Morgan.

671 ◆ IRWIN, PATRICK

Rank: First Sergeant (highest rank: First Lieutenant)
Service: U.S. Army
Birthday: 1839
Place of Birth: Ireland

Date of Death: 6 February 1910
Cemetery: St. Thomas' Cemetery—Ann Arbor, Michigan
Entered Service at: Ann Arbor, Washtenaw County, Michigan
Unit: Company H, 14th Michigan Infantry
Battle or Place of Action: Jonesboro, Georgia
Date of Action: 1 September 1864
Date of Issue: 28 April 1896
Citation: In a charge by the 14th Michigan Infantry against the entrenched enemy, Irwin was the first man over the line of works of the enemy, and demanded and received the surrender of Confederate Gen. Daviel Govan and his command.

672 ◆ JACKSON, FREDERICK RANDOLPH

Rank: First Sergeant (highest rank: Sergeant Major)
Service: U.S. Army
Birthday: 18 February 1844
Place of Birth: New Haven, New Haven County, Connecticut
Date of Death: 14 February 1925
Place of Death: Smithville, New York
Cemetery: Smithfield Cemetery (MH)—Smithville, New York
Entered Service at: New Haven, New Haven County, Connecticut
Unit: Company F, 7th Connecticut Infantry
Battle or Place of Action: James Island, South Carolina
Date of Action: 16 June 1862
Date of Issue: 1863
Citation: Having his left arm shot away in a charge on the enemy, he continued on duty, taking part in a second and a third charge until he fell exhausted from the loss of blood.

673 ◆ JACOBSON, EUGENE PHILIP

Rank: Sergeant Major (highest rank: Brevet Captain U.S. Vols.)
Service: U.S. Army
Birthday: 3 May 1841
Place of Birth: Prussia
Date of Death: 12 April 1881
Place of Death: Denver, Colorado
Cemetery: Green Mount Cemetery—Baltimore, Maryland
Entered Service at: New York, New York
Unit: 74th New York Infantry
Battle or Place of Action: Chancellorsville, Virginia
Date of Action: 2 May 1863
Date of Issue: 29 March 1865
Citation: Bravery in conducting a scouting party in front of the enemy.

674 ◆ JAMES, ISAAC

Rank: Private
Service: U.S. Army
Birthday: 8 March 1838
Place of Birth: Jefferson Township, Ashtabula County, Ohio

Date of Death: 26 September 1914
Place of Death: Union City, Indiana
Entered Service at: Mississinawa Township, Ohio
Unit: Company H, 110th Ohio Infantry
Battle or Place of Action: Petersburg, Virginia
Date of Action: 2 April 1865
Date of Issue: 10 May 1865
Citation: Capture of flag.

675 ◆ JAMES, JOHN H.

Rank: Captain of the Top
Service: U.S. Navy
Birthday: 1835
Place of Birth: Boston, Suffolk County, Massachusetts
Date of Death: 3 August 1914
Cemetery: Dayton National Cemetery (I-19-58) (MH)—Dayton, Ohio
Entered Service at: Massachusetts
Unit: U.S.S. *Richmond*
Battle or Place of Action: Mobile Bay, Alabama
Date of Action: 5 August 1864
G.O. Number, Date: 45, 31 December 1864
Citation: As captain of a gun on board the U.S.S. *Richmond* during action against rebel forts and gunboats and with the ram *Tennessee* in Mobile Bay, 5 August 1864. Despite damage to his ship and the loss of several men on board as enemy fire raked her decks, James fought his gun with skill and courage throughout the furious two-hour battle which resulted in the surrender of the rebel ram *Tennessee* and in the damaging and destruction of batteries at Fort Morgan.

676 ◆ JAMES, MILES

Rank: Corporal (highest rank: First Sergeant)
Service: U.S. Army
Birthday: 1829
Place of Birth: Princess Anne County, Virginia
Date of Death: 28 August 1871
Place of Death: Norfolk, Virginia
Cemetery: unknown cemetery—Norfolk, Virginia
Entered Service at: Portsmouth, Portsmouth County, Virginia
Unit: Company B, 36th U.S. Colored Infantry
Battle or Place of Action: Chapin's Farm, Virginia
Date of Action: 30 September 1864
Date of Issue: 6 April 1865
Citation: Having had his arm mutilated, making immediate amputation necessary, he loaded and discharged his piece with one hand and urged his men forward; this within 30 yards of the enemy's works.

677 ◆ JAMIESON, WALTER

Rank: First Sergeant (highest rank: Captain)
Service: U.S. Army
Birthday: 1842
Place of Birth: Boulogne, France
Date of Death: 6 December 1904

Place of Death: Brooklyn, New York
Cemetery: Cypress Hills Cemetery (Private)—Brooklyn, New York
Entered Service at: New York, New York
Unit: Company B, 139th New York Infantry
Battle or Place of Action: Petersburg & Fort Harrison, Virginia
Date of Action: 30 July, 29 September 1864
Date of Issue: 5 April 1898
Citation: Voluntarily went between the lines under a heavy fire at Petersburg, Va., to the assistance of a wounded and helpless officer, whom he carried within the Union lines. At Fort Harrison, Va., seized the regimental color, the color bearer and guard having been shot down, and, rushing forward, planted it upon the fort in full view of the entire brigade.

678 ◆ JARDINE, JAMES

Rank: Sergeant (highest rank: First Lieutenant)
Service: U.S. Army
Birthday: 16 April 1837
Place of Birth: Helensburgh, Dunbartonshire, Scotland
Date of Death: 9 December 1922
Cemetery: Ohio Veterans' Home Cemetery (MH)—Sandusky, Ohio
Entered Service at: Hamilton County, Ohio
Unit: Company F, 54th Ohio Infantry
Battle or Place of Action: Vicksburg, Mississippi
Date of Action: 22 May 1863
Date of Issue: 5 April 1894
Citation: Gallantry in the charge of the "volunteer storming party."

679 ◆ JELLISON, BENJAMIN H.

Rank: Sergeant (highest rank: Captain)
Service: U.S. Army
Birthday: 29 December 1845
Place of Birth: Newburyport, Essex County, Massachusetts
Date of Death: 5 April 1924
Place of Death: Reading, Massachusetts
Cemetery: Elmwood Cemetery (MH)—Haverhill, Massachusetts
Entered Service at: Newburyport, Essex County, Massachusetts
Unit: Company C, 19th Massachusetts Infantry
Battle or Place of Action: Gettysburg, Pennsylvania
Date of Action: 3 July 1863
Date of Issue: 1 December 1864
Citation: Capture of flag of 57th Virginia Infantry (C.S.A.). He also assisted in taking prisoners.

680 ◆ JENKINS, THOMAS

Rank: Seaman
Service: U.S. Navy
Unit: U.S.S. *Cincinnati*
Battle or Place of Action: Vicksburg, Mississippi

Date of Action: 27 May 1863
G.O. Number, Date: 17, 10 July 1863
Citation: Served on board the U.S.S. *Cincinnati* during the attack on the Vicksburg batteries and at the time of her sinking, 27 May 1863. Engaging the enemy in a fierce battle, the *Cincinnati*, amidst an incessant fire of shot and shell, continued to fire her guns to the last, though so penetrated by shell fire that her fate was sealed. Serving bravely during this action, Jenkins was conspicuously cool under the fire of the enemy, never ceasing to fight until this proud ship went down, "her colors nailed to the mast."

681 ◆ JENNINGS, JAMES T.

Rank: Private (highest rank: Corporal)
Service: U.S. Army
Birthday: April 1818
Place of Birth: Devonshire, England
Date of Death: 22 March 1865
Place of Death: Baltimore, Maryland
Cemetery: Louden Park National Cemetery (A-1410) (MH)—Baltimore, Maryland
Entered Service at: Luzerne, Luzerne County, Pennsylvania
Unit: Company K, 56th Pennsylvania Infantry
Battle or Place of Action: Weldon Railroad, Virginia
Date of Action: 20 August 1864
Date of Issue: 1 December 1864
Citation: Capture of flag of 55th North Carolina Infantry (C.S.A.).

682 ◆ JEWETT, ERASTUS W.

Rank: First Lieutenant
Service: U.S. Army
Birthday: 1 April 1839
Place of Birth: St. Albans, Franklin County, Vermont
Date of Death: 20 February 1906
Cemetery: Church Street Cemetery—Swanton, Vermont
Entered Service at: St. Albans, Franklin County, Vermont
Unit: Company A, 9th Vermont Infantry
Battle or Place of Action: Newport Barracks, North Carolina
Date of Action: 2 February 1864
Date of Issue: 8 September 1891
Citation: By long and persistent resistance and burning the bridges, Jewett kept a superior force of the enemy at a distance and thus covered the retreat of the garrison.
Notes: POW

683 ◆ JOHN, WILLIAM F.

Rank: Private
Service: U.S. Army
Birthday: 23 October 1844
Place of Birth: Germany
Date of Death: 29 August 1927
Place of Death: Hutchings, Kansas
Cemetery: Prattsburg Cemetery (MH)—Macksville, Kansas
Entered Service at: Chillicothe, Ross County, Ohio

Unit: Company E, 37th Ohio Infantry
Battle or Place of Action: Vicksburg, Mississippi
Date of Action: 22 May 1863
Date of Issue: 14 July 1894
Citation: Gallantry in the charge of the "volunteer storming party."

684 ◆ JOHNDRO, FRANKLIN

Rank: Private
Service: U.S. Army
Birthday: 1835
Place of Birth: Highgate Falls, Franklin County, Vermont
Date of Death: 5 April 1901
Place of Death: North Bay City, Michigan
Cemetery: Glens Falls Cemetery—Glens Falls, New York
Entered Service at: Queensbury, Warren County, New York
Unit: Company A, 118th New York Infantry
Battle or Place of Action: Chapin's Farm, Virginia
Date of Action: 30 September 1864
Date of Issue: 6 April 1865
Citation: Capture of 40 prisoners.

685 ◆ JOHNS, ELISHA

Rank: Corporal (highest rank: Sergeant)
Service: U.S. Army
Birthday: 25 August 1837
Place of Birth: Clinton, Summit County, Ohio
Date of Death: 14 June 1920
Place of Death: Elkhart, Indiana
Cemetery: Plum Grove Cemetery—Union, Michigan
Entered Service at: Martinton, Iroquois County, Illinois
Unit: Company B, 113th Illinois Infantry
Battle or Place of Action: Vicksburg, Mississippi
Date of Action: 22 May 1863
Date of Issue: 9 August 1894
Citation: Gallantry in the charge of the "volunteer storming party."

686 ◆ JOHNS, HENRY T.

Rank: Private (highest rank: First Lieutenant)
Service: U.S. Army
Birthday: 8 April 1828
Place of Birth: Philadelphia, Philadelphia County, Pennsylvania
Date of Death: 13 May 1906
Place of Death: Glendale, California
Cemetery: Mountain View Cemetery—Oakland, California
Entered Service at: Hinsdale, Berkshire County, Massachusetts
Unit: Company C, 49th Massachusetts Infantry
Battle or Place of Action: Port Hudson, Louisiana
Date of Action: 27 May 1863
Date of Issue: 25 November 1893
Citation: Volunteered in response to a call and took part in the movement that was made upon the enemy's works under a heavy fire therefrom in advance of the general assault.

687 ◆ JOHNSON, ANDREW

Rank: Private
Service: U.S. Army
Birthday: 1833
Place of Birth: Delaware County, Ohio
Date of Death: 7 February 1912
Place of Death: Tower Hill Township, Illinois
Cemetery: Tower Hill Cemetery (MH)—Tower Hill Township, Illinois
Entered Service at: Assumption, Christian County, Illinois
Unit: Company G, 116th Illinois Infantry
Battle or Place of Action: Vicksburg, Mississippi
Date of Action: 22 May 1863
Date of Issue: 9 August 1894
Citation: Gallantry in the charge of the "volunteer storming party."

688 ◆ JOHNSON, FOLLETT

Rank: Corporal
Service: U.S. Army
Birthday: 20 April 1843
Place of Birth: Brasher, St. Lawrence County, New York
Date of Death: 9 March 1909
Place of Death: Massena, New York
Cemetery: Pine Grove Cemetery No.1 (MH)—Massena, New York
Entered Service at: Ogdensburg, St. Lawrence County, New York
Unit: Company H, 60th New York Infantry
Battle or Place of Action: New Hope Church, Georgia
Date of Action: 27 May 1864
Date of Issue: 6 April 1892
Citation: Voluntarily exposed himself to the fire of a Confederate sharpshooter, thus drawing fire upon himself and enabling his comrade to shoot the sharpshooter.
Notes: POW

689 ◆ JOHNSON, HENRY

Rank: Seaman
Service: U.S. Navy
Birthday: 1824
Place of Birth: Norway
Entered Service at: New York, New York
Unit: U.S.S. *Metacomet*
Battle or Place of Action: Mobile Bay, Alabama
Date of Action: 5 August 1864
G.O. Number, Date: 82, 23 February 1867
Citation: As seaman on board the U.S.S. *Metacomet*, Johnson served as a member of the boat's crew which went to the rescue of the U.S. Monitor *Tecumseh* when that vessel was struck by a torpedo in passing the enemy forts in Mobile Bay, 5 August 1864. He braved the enemy fire, which was said by the admiral to be "one of the most galling" he had ever seen, and aided in rescuing from death 10 of the crew of the *Tecumseh*, thereby eliciting the admiration of both friend and foe.

690 ◆ JOHNSON, JOHN

Rank: Private
Service: U.S. Army
Birthday: 25 March 1842
Place of Birth: Toten Christiana (now Olso), Norway
Date of Death: 3 April 1907
Place of Death: Detroit, Michigan
Cemetery: Rock Creek Cemetery—Washington, D.C.
Entered Service at: Janesville, Rock County, Wisconsin
Unit: Company D, 2d Wisconsin Infantry
Battle or Place of Action: Fredericksburg, Virginia
Date of Action: 13 December 1862
Date of Issue: 28 August 1893
Citation: Conspicuous gallantry in battle in which he was severely wounded. While serving as cannoneer he manned the positions of fallen gunners.

691 ◆ JOHNSON, JOSEPH ESREY

Rank: First Lieutenant (highest rank: Brevet Major)
Service: U.S. Army
Birthday: 5 February 1843
Place of Birth: Lower Merion, Montgomery County, Pennsylvania
Date of Death: 30 April 1911
Cemetery: Arlington National Cemetery (3-2278)—Arlington, Virginia
Entered Service at: Philadelphia, Philadelphia County, Pennsylvania
Unit: Company A, 58th Pennsylvania Infantry
Battle or Place of Action: Fort Harrison, Virginia
Date of Action: 29 September 1864
Date of Issue: 1 April 1898
Citation: Though twice severely wounded while advancing in the assault, he disregarded his injuries and was among the first to enter the fort, where he was wounded for the third time.

692 ◆ JOHNSON, RUEL M.

Rank: Major (highest rank: Colonel)
Service: U.S. Army
Birthday: 5 June 1843
Place of Birth: Harbor Creek Township, Erie County, Pennsylvania
Date of Death: 12 November 1901
Place of Death: Goshen, Indiana
Cemetery: Oak Ridge Cemetery (MH)—Goshen, Indiana
Entered Service at: Goshen, Elkhart County, Indiana
Unit: 100th Indiana Infantry
Battle or Place of Action: Chattanooga, Tennessee
Date of Action: 25 November 1863
Date of Issue: 24 August 1896
Citation: While in command of the regiment bravely exposed himself to the fire of the enemy, encouraging and cheering his men.

693 ◆ JOHNSON, SAMUEL

Rank: Private (highest rank: Second Lieutenant)
Service: U.S. Army
Birthday: 28 January 1845
Place of Birth: Springfield Township, Delaware County, Pennsylvania
Date of Death: 24 November 1915
Place of Death: West Fork, Arkansas
Entered Service at: Connellsville, Fayette County, Pennsylvania
Unit: Company G, 9th Pennsylvania Reserves
Battle or Place of Action: Antietam, Maryland
Date of Action: 17 September 1862
G.O. Number, Date: 160, 30 May 1863
Citation: Individual bravery and daring in capturing from the enemy two colors of the 1st Texas Rangers (C.S.A.), receiving in the act a severe wound.

694 ◆ JOHNSON, WALLACE W.

Rank: Sergeant
Service: U.S. Army
Birthday: 30 December 1842
Place of Birth: Newfield, Thompkins County, New York
Date of Death: 30 December 1911
Place of Death: Walter's Park, Pennsylvania
Cemetery: West Laurel Hill Cemetery—Bala Cynwyd, Pennsylvania
Entered Service at: Waverly, Tioga County, New York
Unit: Company G, 6th Pennsylvania Reserves
Battle or Place of Action: Gettysburg, Pennsylvania
Date of Action: 2 July 1863
Date of Issue: 8 August 1900
Citation: With five other volunteers gallantly charged on a number of the enemy's sharpshooters concealed in a log house, captured them, and brought them into the Union lines.

695 ◆ JOHNSTON, DAVID H.

Rank: Private
Service: U.S. Army
Birthday: 19 August 1838
Place of Birth: Indiana County, Pennsylvania
Date of Death: 1931
Place of Death: Stanfield, Missouri
Cemetery: Pierce Chapel Cemetery (MH)—Clark, Nebraska
Entered Service at: Warsaw, Hancock County, Illinois
Unit: Company K, 8th Missouri Infantry
Battle or Place of Action: Vicksburg, Mississippi
Date of Action: 22 May 1863
Date of Issue: 16 August 1884
Citation: Gallantry in the charge of the "volunteer storming party."

696 ◆ JOHNSTON, WILLIAM P.

Rank: Landsman
Service: U.S. Navy
Birthday: 1849
Place of Birth: Chicago, Cook County, Illinois
Entered Service at: Chicago, Cook County, Illinois
Unit: U.S.S. *Fort Hindman*
Battle or Place of Action: Harrisonburg, Louisiana
Date of Action: 2 March 1864
G.O. Number, Date: 32, 16 April 1864
Citation: Served on board the U.S.S. *Fort Hindman* during the engagement near Harrisonburg, La., 2 March 1864. Badly wounded in the hand during the action, Johnston, despite his wound, took the place of another man to sponge and lead one of the guns throughout the entire action in which the Fort Hindman was raked severely with shot and shell from the enemy guns.

697 ◆ JOHNSTON, WILLIAM (WILLIE)

Rank: Musician
Service: U.S. Army
Birthday: July 1850
Place of Birth: Morristown, Morristown County, New York
Entered Service at: St. Johnsbury, Caledonia County, Vermont
Unit: Company D, 3d Vermont Infantry
Served as: Drummer
Battle or Place of Action: Seven Day Battle & on the Peninsula Campaign, Virginia
Date of Action: 26 June-1 July 1862
Date of Issue: 16 September 1863
Citation: Gallantry in Seven Day Battle and Peninsula campaign.

698 ◆ JONES, ANDREW

Rank: Chief Boatswain's Mate
Service: U.S. Navy
Birthday: 1835
Place of Birth: Limerick, County Limerick, Ireland
Entered Service at: New York, New York
Unit: U.S. Ironclad *Chickasaw*
Battle or Place of Action: Mobile Bay, Alabama
Date of Action: 4 August 1864
G.O. Number, Date: 45, 31 December 1864
Citation: Served as chief boatswain's mate on board the U.S. Ironclad *Chickasaw*, Mobile Bay, 5 August 1864. Although his enlistment was up, Jones volunteered for the battle of Mobile Bay, going on board the *Chickasaw* from the *Vincennes* where he then carried out his duties gallantly throughout the engagement with the enemy, which resulted in the capture of the rebel ram *Tennessee*.

699 ◆ JONES, DAVID

Rank: Private (highest rank: First Lieutenant)
Service: U.S. Army
Birthday: 13 April 1841
Place of Birth: Fayette County, Ohio
Date of Death: 18 June 1911

Cemetery: Good Hope Cemetery—Good Hope, Ohio
Entered Service at: Washington Courthouse, Fayette County, Ohio
Unit: Company I, 54th Ohio Infantry
Battle or Place of Action: Vicksburg, Mississippi
Date of Action: 22 May 1863
Date of Issue: 13 June 1894
Citation: Gallantry in the charge of the "volunteer storming party."

700 ◆ JONES, JOHN

Rank: Landsman
Service: U.S. Navy
Birthday: 25 August 1841
Place of Birth: Bridgeport, Fairfield County, Connecticut
Date of Death: 15 August 1907
Place of Death: Portsmouth, New Hampshire
Cemetery: St. Mary's Cemetery—Portsmouth, New Hampshire
Entered Service at: Acton, Middlesex County, Massachusetts
Unit: U.S.S. *Rhode Island*
Battle or Place of Action: off Cape Hatteras, North Carolina
Date of Action: 30 December 1862
G.O. Number, Date: 59, 22 June 1865
Citation: Served on board the U.S.S. *Rhode Island* which was engaged in saving the lives of the officers and crew of the *Monitor*, 30 December 1862. Participating in the hazardous rescue of the officers and crew of the sinking *Monitor*, Jones, after rescuing several of the men, became separated in a heavy gale with other members of the cutter that had set out from the *Rhode Island*, and spent many hours in the small boat at the mercy of the weather and the high seas until finally picked up by a schooner 50 miles east of Cape Hatteras.

701 ◆ JONES, JOHN E.

Rank: Quartermaster
Service: U.S. Navy
Place of Birth: New York, New York
Entered Service at: New York
Unit: U.S.S. *Oneida*
Battle or Place of Action: Mobile Bay, Alabama
Date of Action: 5 August 1864
G.O. Number, Date: 45, 31 December 1864
Citation: Served as quartermaster on board the U.S.S. *Oneida* in the engagement at Mobile Bay, 5 August 1864. Stationed at the wheel during the fierce action, Jones, though wounded, carried out his duties gallantly by going to the poop to assist at the signals after the wheel ropes were shot away and remained there until ordered to reeve new wheel ropes.

702 ◆ JONES, THOMAS

Rank: Coxswain
Service: U.S. Navy
Birthday: 1820

Place of Birth: Baltimore, Baltimore County, Maryland
Place of Death: Annapolis, Maryland
Entered Service at: Baltimore, Baltimore County, Maryland
Unit: U.S.S. *Ticonderoga*
Battle or Place of Action: Fort Fisher, North Carolina
Date of Action: 24-25 December 1864 & 13-15 January 1865
G.O. Number, Date: 59, 22 June 1865
Citation: On board the U.S.S. *Ticonderoga* during attacks on Fort Fisher, 24 and 25 December 1864; and 13 to 15 January 1865. Despite heavy return fire by the enemy and the explosion of the 100-pounder Parrott rifle which killed eight men and wounded 12 more, Jones, as captain of a gun, performed his duties with skill and courage during the first two days of battle. As his ship again took position on the line on the 13th, he remained steadfast as the *Ticonderoga* maintained a well-placed fire upon the batteries onshore, and thereafter, as she materially lessened the power of the guns on the mound which had been turned upon our assaulting columns. During this action the flag was planted on one side of the strongest fortifications possessed by the rebels.

703 ◆ JONES, WILLIAM

Rank: Captain of the Top
Service: U.S. Navy
Birthday: 1831
Place of Birth: Philadelphia, Philadelphia County, Pennsylvania
Entered Service at: Pennsylvania
Unit: U.S.S. *Richmond*
Battle or Place of Action: Mobile Bay, Alabama
Date of Action: 5 August 1864
G.O. Number, Date: 45, 31 December 1864
Citation: As captain of a gun on board the U.S.S. *Richmond* during action against rebel forts and gunboats and with the ram *Tennessee* in Mobile Bay, 5 August 1864. Despite damage to his ship and the loss of several men on board as enemy fire raked her decks, Jones fought his gun with skill and courage throughout the prolonged battle, which resulted in the surrender of the rebel ram *Tennessee* and in the damaging and destruction of batteries at Fort Morgan.

704 ◆ *JONES, WILLIAM

Rank: First Sergeant
Service: U.S. Army
Birthday: 1836
Place of Birth: Wicklow, County Wicklow, Ireland
Date of Death: 12 May 1864
Place of Death: Spotsylvania, Virginia
Cemetery: Fredericksburg National Military Park (2448) (MH)—Fredericksburg, Virginia
Entered Service at: New York, New York
Unit: Company A, 73d New York Infantry
Battle or Place of Action: Spotsylvania, Virginia
Date of Action: 12 May 1864
Date of Issue: 1 December 1864
Citation: Capture of flag of 65th Virginia Infantry (C.S.A.).

705 ◆ JORDAN, ABSALOM

Rank: Corporal
Service: U.S. Army
Place of Birth: Brown County, Ohio
Date of Death: 3 May 1888
Cemetery: Centerville Cemetery—Lovett, Indiana
Entered Service at: North Madison, Jefferson County, Indiana
Unit: Company A, 3d Indiana Cavalry
Battle or Place of Action: Deatonsville (Sailor's Creek), Virginia
Date of Action: 6 April 1865
Date of Issue: 3 May 1865
Citation: Capture of flag.

706 ◆ JORDAN, ROBERT

Rank: Coxswain
Service: U.S. Navy
Birthday: 1826
Place of Birth: New York, New York
Entered Service at: New York
Unit: U.S.S. *Minnesota* (temporarily on U.S.S. *Mount Washington*)
Battle or Place of Action: Nansemond River, Virginia
Date of Action: 14 April 1863
G.O. Number, Date: 17, 10 July 1863
Date of Issue: 10 July 1863
Citation: Attached to the U.S.S. *Minnesota* and temporarily serving on the U.S.S. *Mount Washington*, during action against the enemy in the Nansemond River, 14 April 1863. When the *Mount Washington* drifted against the bank following several successive hits which struck her boilers and stopped her engines, Jordan boarded the stricken vessel and, for six hours as fierce artillery and musketry continued to rake her decks, calmly assisted in manning a 12-pound howitzer which had been mounted on the open hurricane deck.

707 ◆ JORDAN, THOMAS H.

Rank: Quartermaster
Service: U.S. Navy
Birthday: 12 April 1840
Place of Birth: Portsmouth, Portsmouth County, Virginia
Date of Death: 17 July 1930
Place of Death: Baltimore, Maryland
Cemetery: Mount Olivet Cemetery—Chicago, Illinois
Entered Service at: Baltimore, Baltimore County, Maryland
Unit: U.S.S. *Galena*
Battle or Place of Action: Mobile Bay, Alabama
Date of Action: 5 August 1864
G.O. Number, Date: 59, 22 June 1865
Citation: On board the U.S.S. *Galena* during the attack on enemy forts at Mobile Bay, 5 August 1864. Securely lashed to the side of the *Oneida*, which had suffered the loss of her steering apparatus and an explosion of her boiler from enemy fire, the *Galena* aided the stricken vessel past the enemy forts to safety. Despite heavy damage to his ship from raking

enemy fire, Jordan performed his duties with skill and courage throughout the action.

708 ◆ JOSSELYN, SIMEON T.

Rank: First Lieutenant
Service: U.S. Army
Birthday: 14 January 1842
Place of Birth: Buffalo, Erie County, New York
Date of Death: 4 April 1905
Place of Death: Skagway, Alaska
Cemetery: Forest Lawn Cemetery—Omaha, Nebraska
Entered Service at: Amboy, Lee County, Illinois
Unit: Company C, 13th Illinois Infantry
Battle or Place of Action: Missionary Ridge, Tennessee
Date of Action: 25 November 1863
Date of Issue: 4 April 1898
Citation: While commanding his company, deployed as skirmishers, Josselyn came upon a large body of the enemy, taking a number of them prisoner. Lt. Josselyn himself shot their color bearer, seized the colors, and brought them back to his regiment.

709 ◆ JUDGE, FRANCIS W.

Rank: First Sergeant (highest rank: Brevet Major U.S. Vols.)
Service: U.S. Army
Birthday: 10 February 1838
Place of Birth: England
Date of Death: 3 December 1904
Place of Death: New York, New York
Cemetery: Greenwood Cemetery—Brooklyn, New York
Entered Service at: New York, New York
Unit: Company K, 79th New York Infantry
Battle or Place of Action: Fort Sanders, Knoxville, Tennessee
Date of Action: 29 November 1863
Date of Issue: 2 November 1870
Citation: The color bearer of the 51st Georgia Infantry (C.S.A.), having planted his flag upon the side of the work, Sgt. Judge leaped from his position of safety, sprang upon the parapet, and in the face of a concentrated fire seized the flag and returned with it in safety to the fort.

710 ◆ KAISER, JOHN

Rank: First Sergeant (highest rank: Ordnance Sergeant)
Service: U.S. Army
Birthday: 1825
Place of Birth: Nerzogenaurach, Germany
Date of Death: 9 January 1894
Place of Death: Buffalo, New York
Cemetery: Forest Lawn Cemetery (MH)—Buffalo, New York
Entered Service at: New York, New York
Unit: Company E, 2d U.S. Artillery
Battle or Place of Action: Richmond, Virginia
Date of Action: 27 June 1862
Date of Issue: 2 April 1878

Citation: Gallant and meritorious service during the Seven Days' Battles before Richmond, Va.

711 ◆ KALTENBACH, LUTHER

Rank: Corporal (highest rank: Sergeant)
Service: U.S. Army
Birthday: 16 August 1843
Place of Birth: Germany
Date of Death: 1 September 1922
Place of Death: Los Angeles, California
Cemetery: Los Angeles National Cemetery (43-A-15)(MH)—Los Angeles, California
Entered Service at: Honey Creek, Pottawattamie County, Iowa
Unit: Company F, 12th Iowa Infantry
Battle or Place of Action: Nashville, Tennessee
Date of Action: 16 December 1864
Date of Issue: 24 February 1865
Citation: Capture of flag of 44th Mississippi Infantry (C.S.A.).

712 ◆ KANE, JOHN

Rank: Corporal (highest rank: Sergeant)
Service: U.S. Army
Place of Birth: Ireland
Entered Service at: Marilla, Erie County, New York
Unit: Company K, 100th New York Infantry
Served as: Color Bearer
Battle or Place of Action: Petersburg, Virginia
Date of Action: 2 April 1865
Date of Issue: 12 May 1865
Citation: Gallantry as color bearer in the assault on Fort Gregg.

713 ◆ KANE, THOMAS

Rank: Captain of the Hold
Service: U.S. Navy
Birthday: 1841
Place of Birth: Jersey City, Hudson County, New Jersey
Entered Service at: New Jersey
Unit: U.S.S. *Nereus*
Served as: Captain of the Hold
Battle or Place of Action: Fort Fisher, North Carolina
Date of Action: 15 January 1865
G.O. Number, Date: 84, 3 October 1867
Citation: On board the U.S.S. *Nereus* during the attack on Fort Fisher, 15 January 1865. Kane, as captain of the hold, displayed outstanding skill and courage as his ship maintained its well-directed fire against fortifications onshore despite the enemy's return fire. When a rebel steamer was discovered in the river back of the fort, the *Nereus*, with forward rifle guns trained, drove the ship off at the third fire. The gallant ship's participation contributed to the planting of the flag on one of the strongest fortifications possessed by the rebels.

714 ◆ KAPPESSER, PETER

Rank: Private
Service: U.S. Army

Birthday: 8 January 1839
Place of Birth: Germany
Date of Death: 31 May 1930
Place of Death: Syracuse, New York
Cemetery: Woodlawn Cemetery (Soldiers' Plot)(MH)—Syracuse, New York
Entered Service at: Syracuse, Onondaga County, New York
Unit: Company B, 149th New York Infantry
Battle or Place of Action: Lookout Mountain, Tennessee
Date of Action: 24 November 1863
Date of Issue: 28 June 1865
Citation: Capture of Confederate flag (Bragg's army).

715 ◆ KARPELES, LEOPOLD

Rank: Sergeant (highest rank: Color Sergeant)
Service: U.S. Army
Birthday: 9 September 1838
Place of Birth: Prague, Austria-Hungary
Date of Death: 2 February 1909
Place of Death: Washington, D.C.
Cemetery: Hebrew Congregation Cemetery—Washington, D.C.
Entered Service at: Springfield, Hampden County, Massachusetts
Unit: Company E, 57th Massachusetts Infantry
Battle or Place of Action: Wilderness Campaign, Virginia
Date of Action: 6 May 1864
Date of Issue: 30 April 1870
Citation: While color bearer, rallied the retreating troops and induced them to check the enemy's advance.

716 ◆ KAUSS, AUGUST

Rank: Corporal
Service: U.S. Army
Birthday: 6 November 1843
Place of Birth: Germany
Date of Death: 27 April 1913
Place of Death: Hurley, New York
Cemetery: Hurley Cemetery (MH)—Hurley, New York
Entered Service at: New York, New York
Unit: Company H, 15th New York Heavy Artillery
Battle or Place of Action: Five Forks, Virginia
Date of Action: 1 April 1865
Date of Issue: 10 May 1865
Citation: Capture of battle flag.

717 ◆ KEELE, JOSEPH

Rank: Sergeant Major (highest rank: Captain)
Service: U.S. Army
Birthday: 1 August 1840
Place of Birth: Ireland
Date of Death: 16 October 1906
Place of Death: Jersey City, New Jersey
Cemetery: Bayview Cemetery (MH)—Jersey City, New Jersey
Entered Service at: Staten Island, Richmond County, New York

Unit: 182d New York Infantry
Battle or Place of Action: North Anna River, Virginia
Date of Action: 23 May 1864
Date of Issue: 25 October 1867
Citation: Voluntarily and at the risk of his life carried orders to the brigade commander, which resulted in saving the works his regiment was defending.

718 ◆ KEEN, JOSEPH S.

Rank: Sergeant
Service: U.S. Army
Birthday: 24 July 1843
Place of Birth: Vale, Guernsey, England
Date of Death: 3 December 1926
Place of Death: Detroit, Michigan
Cemetery: Elmwood Cemetery (MH)—Detroit, Michigan
Entered Service at: Detroit, Wayne County, Michigan
Unit: Company D, 13th Michigan Infantry
Battle or Place of Action: near the Chattahoochee River, Georgia
Date of Action: 1 October 1864
Date of Issue: 4 August 1899
Citation: While an escaped prisoner of war within the enemy's lines, Keen witnessed an important movement of the enemy, and at great personal risk made his way through the enemy's lines and brought news of the movement to Sherman's army.
Notes: POW

719 ◆ KEENE, JOSEPH

Rank: Private (highest rank: Corporal)
Service: U.S. Army
Birthday: 3 April 1839
Place of Birth: England
Date of Death: 1 December 1921
Place of Death: Willowvale, New York
Cemetery: Grand View Cemetery—Whitesboro, New York
Entered Service at: Utica, Oneida County, New York
Unit: Company B, 26th New York Infantry
Battle or Place of Action: Fredericksburg, Virginia
Date of Action: 13 December 1862
Date of Issue: 2 December 1892
Citation: Voluntarily seized the colors after several color bearers had been shot down and led the regiment in the charge.

720 ◆ KELLEY, ANDREW JOHN

Rank: Private (highest rank: Sergeant)
Service: U.S. Army
Birthday: 2 September 1845
Place of Birth: La Grange County, Indiana
Date of Death: 4 June 1918
Place of Death: Crookston, Minnesota
Cemetery: Oakdale Cemetery (MH)—Crookston, Minnesota
Entered Service at: Ypsilanti, Washtenaw County, Michigan
Unit: Company E, 17th Michigan Infantry

Battle or Place of Action: Knoxville, Tennessee
Date of Action: 20 November 1863
Date of Issue: 17 April 1900
Citation: Having voluntarily accompanied a small party to destroy buildings within the enemy's lines whence sharp-shooters had been firing, Kelley disregarded an order to retire, remained, and completed the firing of the buildings, thus insuring their total destruction; this at the imminent risk of his life from the fire of the advancing enemy.

721 ◆ KELLEY, GEORGE V.

Rank: Captain
Service: U.S. Army
Birthday: 23 March 1843
Place of Birth: Massillon, Stark County, Ohio
Date of Death: 4 November 1905
Cemetery: Riverside Cemetery (MH)—Denver, Colorado
Entered Service at: Massillon, Stark County, Ohio
Unit: Company A, 104th Ohio Infantry
Battle or Place of Action: Franklin, Tennessee
Date of Action: 30 November 1864
Date of Issue: 13 February 1865
Citation: Capture of flag supposed to be of Cheatham's Corps (C.S.A.).

722 ◆ KELLEY, JOHN

Rank: Second Class Fireman
Service: U.S. Navy
Place of Birth: Ireland
Unit: U.S.S. *Ceres*
Battle or Place of Action: Roanoke River, near Hamilton, North Carolina
Date of Action: 9 July 1862
G.O. Number, Date: 11, 3 April 1863
Citation: Served as second-class fireman on board the U.S.S. *Ceres* in the fight near Hamilton, Roanoke River, 9 July 1862. When his ship was fired upon by the enemy with small arms, Kelley returned the raking fire, courageously carrying out his duties throughout the engagement, and was spoken of for "good conduct and cool bravery under enemy fire" by the commanding officer.

723 ◆ KELLEY, LEVERETT MANSFIELD

Rank: Sergeant (highest rank: Captain)
Service: U.S. Army
Birthday: 28 September 1841
Place of Birth: Schenectady, Schenectady County, New York
Date of Death: 9 April 1924
Place of Death: Washington, D.C.
Cemetery: Arlington National Cemetery (2-3756)—Arlington, Virginia
Entered Service at: Rutland, La Salle County, Illinois
Unit: Company A, 36th Illinois Infantry
Battle or Place of Action: Missionary Ridge, Tennessee
Date of Action: 25 November 1863
Date of Issue: 4 April 1900

Citation: Sprang over the works just captured from the enemy and calling upon his comrades to follow, rushed forward in the face of a deadly fire and was among the first over the works on the summit, where he compelled the surrender of a Confederate officer and received his sword.

724 ◆ KELLY, ALEXANDER

Rank: First Sergeant
Service: U.S. Army
Birthday: 7 April 1840
Place of Birth: Saltsburg, Indiana County, Pennsylvania
Date of Death: 19 June 1907
Cemetery: St. Peter's Cemetery (MH)—Pittsburgh, Pennsylvania
Entered Service at: Allegheny, Allegheny County, Pennsylvania
Unit: Company F, 6th U.S. Colored Infantry
Battle or Place of Action: Chapin's Farm, Virginia
Date of Action: 29 September 1864
Date of Issue: 6 April 1865
Citation: Gallantly seized the colors, which had fallen near the enemy's lines of abatis, raised them, and rallied the men at a time of confusion and in a place of the greatest danger.

725 ◆ KELLY, DANIEL ARMER

Rank: Sergeant (highest rank: Quartermaster Sergeant)
Service: U.S. Army
Birthday: 19 March 1841
Place of Birth: Groveland, Livingston County, New York
Date of Death: 18 January 1912
Cemetery: Maple Wood Cemetery (MH)—Reading, Michigan
Entered Service at: Groveland, Livingston County, New York
Unit: Company G, 8th New York Cavalry
Battle or Place of Action: Waynesboro, Virginia
Date of Action: 26 March 1865
Date of Issue: 26 March 1865
Citation: Capture of flag.

726 ◆ KELLY, THOMAS

Rank: Private
Service: U.S. Army
Place of Birth: Ireland
Entered Service at: New York, New York
Unit: Company A, 6th New York Cavalry
Battle or Place of Action: Front Royal, Virginia
Date of Action: 16 August 1864
Date of Issue: 26 August 1864
Citation: Capture of flag.

727 ◆ KEMP, JOSEPH BELL

Rank: First Sergeant (highest rank: Captain)
Service: U.S. Army
Birthday: 1 July 1844

Place of Birth: Lima, Allen County, Ohio
Date of Death: 13 July 1917
Place of Death: Ann Arbor, Michigan
Cemetery: Forest Hill Cemetery—Ann Arbor, Michigan
Entered Service at: Sault Ste. Marie, Chippewa County, Michigan
Unit: Company D, 5th Michigan Infantry
Battle or Place of Action: Wilderness Campaign, Virginia
Date of Action: 6 May 1864
Date of Issue: 1 December 1864
Citation: Capture of flag of 31st North Carolina (C.S.A.) in a personal encounter.

728 ◆ KENDALL, WILLIAM WESLEY

Rank: First Sergeant (highest rank: First Lieutenant)
Service: U.S. Army
Birthday: 31 August 1839
Place of Birth: Hall Township, Dubois County, Indiana
Date of Death: 14 August 1920
Place of Death: West Baden, Indiana
Cemetery: Ames Chapel Cemetery—Abydel, Indiana
Entered Service at: Jeffersonville, Clark County, Indiana
Unit: Company A, 49th Indiana Infantry
Battle or Place of Action: Black River Bridge, Mississippi
Date of Action: 17 May 1863
Date of Issue: 12 February 1894
Citation: Voluntarily led the company in a charge and was the first to enter the enemy's works, taking a number of prisoners.

729 ◆ KENDRICK, THOMAS

Rank: Coxswain
Service: U.S. Navy
Birthday: 1839
Place of Birth: Bath, Sagadahoc County, Maine
Entered Service at: Maine
Unit: U.S.S. *Oneida*
Battle or Place of Action: Mobile Bay, Alabama
Date of Action: 5 August 1864
G.O. Number, Date: 45, 31 December 1864
Citation: Served as coxswain on board the U.S.S. *Oneida* in the engagement at Mobile Bay, 5 August 1864. Volunteering for the Mobile Bay action from Bienville, Kendrick displayed courageous devotion to duty, and his excellent conduct throughout the battle which resulted in the capture of the rebel ram *Tennessee* and in the damaging of Fort Morgan, attracted the attention of the commanding officer and those serving around him.

730 ◆ KENNA, BARNETT

Rank: Quartermaster
Service: U.S. Navy
Birthday: 1827
Place of Birth: Canterbury, Kent County, England
Date of Death: 28 May 1890
Place of Death: Glouchester, Massachusetts

Cemetery: Cherry Hill Cemetery (MH)—Gloucester, Massachusetts
Entered Service at: Newburyport, Essex County, Massachusetts
Unit: U.S.S. *Brooklyn*
Battle or Place of Action: Mobile Bay, Alabama
Date of Action: 5 August 1864
G.O. Number, Date: 45, 31 December 1864
Citation: On board the U.S.S. *Brooklyn* during action against rebel forts and gunboats and with the ram *Tennessee*, in Mobile Bay, 5 August 1864. Despite severe damage to his ship and the loss of several men on board as enemy fire raked her decks from stem to stern, Kenna fought his gun with skill and courage throughout the furious action which resulted in the surrender of the rebel ram *Tennessee* and in the damaging and destruction of batteries at Fort Morgan.

731 ◆ KENNEDY, JOHN

Rank: Private (highest rank: Ordance Sergeant Ret.)
Service: U.S. Army
Birthday: 14 May 1834
Place of Birth: Cavan, County Cavan, Ireland
Date of Death: 28 September 1910
Cemetery: Oakland Cemetery (MH)—Little Rock, Arkansas
Entered Service at: New York, New York
Unit: Company M, 2d U.S. Artillery
Battle or Place of Action: Trevilian Station, Virginia
Date of Action: 11 June 1864
Date of Issue: 19 August 1892
Citation: Remained at his gun, resisting with its implements the advancing cavalry, and thus secured the retreat of his detachment.

732 ◆ KENYON, CHARLES W.

Rank: Fireman (highest rank: Acting Third Assistant Engineer)
Service: U.S. Navy
Birthday: 1840
Place of Birth: Oneida, Madison County, New York
Entered Service at: New York, New York
Unit: U.S.S. *Galena*
Battle or Place of Action: Drewry's Bluff, James River, Virginia
Date of Action: 15 May 1862
G.O. Number, Date: 11, 3 April 1863
Citation: On board the U.S.S. *Galena* in the attack upon Drewry's Bluff, 15 May 1862. Severely burned while extricating a priming wire which had become bent and fixed in the bow gun while the ship underwent terrific shelling from the enemy, Kenyon hastily dressed his hands with cotton waste and oil and courageously returned to his gun while enemy sharpshooters in rifle pits along the banks continued to direct their fire at the men at the guns.

733 ◆ KENYON, JOHN SNYDERS

Rank: Sergeant
Service: U.S. Army

Birthday: 5 May 1843
Place of Birth: Grosvenors Corners, Schoharie County, New York
Date of Death: 16 February 1902
Cemetery: Oakwood Cemetery (MH)—Syracuse, New York
Entered Service at: Schenevus, Otsego County, New York
Unit: Company D, 3d New York Cavalry
Battle or Place of Action: Trenton, North Carolina
Date of Action: 15 May 1862
Date of Issue: 28 September 1897
Citation: Voluntarily left a retiring column, returned in the face of the enemy's fire, helped a wounded man upon a horse, and so enabled him to escape capture or death.

734 ◆ KENYON, SAMUEL P.

Rank: Private (highest rank: Quartermaster Sergeant)
Service: U.S. Army
Birthday: 1846
Place of Birth: Ira, Cayuga County, New York
Date of Death: 14 June 1884
Place of Death: Cullen, New York
Entered Service at: Augusta, New York
Unit: Company B, 24th New York Cavalry
Battle or Place of Action: Deatonsville (Sailor's Creek), Virginia
Date of Action: 6 April 1865
Date of Issue: 3 May 1865
Citation: Capture of battle flag.

735 ◆ KEOUGH, JOHN

Rank: Corporal
Service: U.S. Army
Birthday: 1835
Place of Birth: County Tipperary, Ireland
Entered Service at: Annapolis, Anne Arundel County, Maryland
Unit: Company E, 67th Pennsylvania Infantry
Battle or Place of Action: Deatonsville (Sailor's Creek), Virginia
Date of Action: 6 April 1865
Date of Issue: 10 May 1865
Citation: Capture of battle flag of 50th Georgia Infantry (C.S.A.).
Notes: POW

736 ◆ KEPHART, JAMES

Rank: Private
Service: U.S. Army
Birthday: 22 April 1842
Place of Birth: Venango County, Pennsylvania
Date of Death: 17 April 1932
Place of Death: Gooding, Idaho
Cemetery: Elmwood Cemetery (MH)—Gooding, Idaho
Entered Service at: Dubuque, Dubuque County, Iowa
Unit: Company C, 13th U.S. Infantry
Battle or Place of Action: Vicksburg, Mississippi

Date of Action: 19 May 1863
Date of Issue: 13 May 1899
Citation: Voluntarily and at the risk of his life, under a severe fire of the enemy, aided and assisted to the rear an officer who had been severely wounded and left on the field.

737 ◆ KERR, THOMAS R.

Rank: Captain
Service: U.S. Army
Birthday: 24 April 1843
Place of Birth: near Colleraine, County Derry, Ireland
Date of Death: 14 November 1926
Place of Death: Pittsburgh, Pennsylvania
Cemetery: Arlington National Cemetery (3-1623)—Arlington, Virginia
Entered Service at: Pittsburgh, Allegheny County, Pennsylvania
Unit: Company C, 14th Pennsylvania Cavalry
Battle or Place of Action: Moorfield, West Virginia
Date of Action: 7 August 1864
Date of Issue: 13 June 1894
Citation: After being most desperately wounded, he captured the colors of the 8th Virginia Cavalry (C.S.A.).

738 ◆ KIGGINS, JOHN

Rank: Sergeant
Service: U.S. Army
Birthday: 2 February 1837
Place of Birth: Syracuse, Onondaga County, New York
Date of Death: 29 September 1914
Place of Death: Bath, New York
Cemetery: Bath National Cemetery (H-32-9) (MH)—Bath, New York
Entered Service at: Syracuse, Onondaga County, New York
Unit: Company D, 149th New York Infantry
Battle or Place of Action: Lookout Mountain, Tennessee
Date of Action: 24 November 1863
Date of Issue: 12 January 1892
Citation: Waved the colors to save the lives of the men who were being fired upon by their own batteries, and thereby drew upon himself a concentrated fire from the enemy.

739 ◆ KIMBALL, JOSEPH

Rank: Private (highest rank: Corporal)
Service: U.S. Army
Birthday: 2 February 1836
Place of Birth: Littleton, Grafton County, New Hampshire
Date of Death: 20 July 1909
Place of Death: Alma, West Virginia
Cemetery: Beechwood Cemetery (MH)—Middle Bourne, West Virginia
Entered Service at: Ironton, Lawrence County, Ohio
Unit: Company B, 2d West Virginia Cavalry
Battle or Place of Action: Deatonsville (Sailor's Creek), Virginia
Date of Action: 6 April 1865

Date of Issue: 3 May 1865
Citation: Capture of flag of 6th North Carolina Infantry (C.S.A.).

740 ◆ KINDIG, JOHN M.

Rank: Corporal (highest rank: Sergeant)
Service: U.S. Army
Place of Birth: East Liberty, Allegheny County, Pennsylvania
Entered Service at: Wilkins, Allegheny County, Pennsylvania
Unit: Company A, 63d Pennsylvania Infantry
Battle or Place of Action: Spotsylvania, Virginia
Date of Action: 12 May 1864
Date of Issue: 1 December 1864
Citation: Capture of flag of 28th North Carolina Infantry (C.S.A.).
Notes: POW

741 ◆ KING, HORATIO COLLINS

Rank: Major & Quartermaster (highest rank: Brevet Colonel)
Service: U.S. Army
Birthday: 22 December 1837
Place of Birth: Portland, Cumberland County, Maine
Date of Death: 15 November 1918
Place of Death: Brooklyn, New York
Cemetery: The Green Wood Cemetery—Brooklyn, New York
Entered Service at: Brooklyn, Kings County, New York
Unit: U.S. Volunteers
Battle or Place of Action: near Dinwiddie Courthouse, Virginia
Date of Action: 31 March 1865
Date of Issue: 23 September 1897
Citation: While serving as a volunteer aide, carried orders to the reserve brigade and participated with it in the charge which repulsed the enemy.

742 ◆ KING, ROBERT HENRY

Rank: Landsman
Service: U.S. Navy
Birthday: 1845
Place of Birth: New York
Date of Death: 10 April 1865
Cemetery: Albany Rural Cemetery (MH)—Albany, New York
Entered Service at: New York
Unit: U.S. Picket Boat No. 1
Battle or Place of Action: Plymouth, North Carolina
Date of Action: 27 October 1864
G.O. Number, Date: 45, 31 December 1864
Citation: King served on board the U.S. Picket Boat No. 1, in action, 27 October 1864, against the Confederate ram, *Albemarle*, which had resisted repeated attacks by our steamers and had kept a large force of vessels employed in watching

her. The picket boat, equipped with a spar torpedo, succeeded in passing the enemy pickets within 20 yards without being discovered and then made for the *Albemarle* under a full head of steam. Immediately taken under fire by the ram, the small boat plunged on, jumped the log boom which encircled the target, and exploded its torpedo under the port bow of the ram. The picket boat was destroyed by enemy fire and almost the entire crew taken prisoner or lost.
Notes: POW

743 ◆ KING JR., RUFUS

Rank: First Lieutenant (highest rank: Brevet Major)
Service: U.S. Army
Birthday: 21 March 1838
Place of Birth: New York
Date of Death: 18 March 1900
Place of Death: New York, New York
Cemetery: Evergreen Cemetery (MH)—Hillside, New Jersey
Entered Service at: New York
Unit: 4th U.S. Artillery
Battle or Place of Action: White Oak Swamp Bridge, Virginia
Date of Action: 30 June 1862
Date of Issue: 2 April 1898
Citation: This officer, when his captain was wounded, succeeded to the command of two batteries while engaged against a superior force of the enemy and fought his guns most gallantly until compelled to retire.

744 ◆ KINNAIRD, SAMUEL W.

Rank: Landsman (highest rank: Ordinary Seaman)
Service: U.S. Navy
Birthday: 2 May 1840
Place of Birth: New York, New York
Date of Death: 20 April 1923
Place of Death: South Berne, New York
Cemetery: 1st Calvary Cemetery—Woodside, New York
Entered Service at: New York, New York
Unit: U.S.S. *Lackawanna*
Battle or Place of Action: Mobile Bay, Alabama
Date of Action: 5 August 1864
G.O. Number, Date: 45, 31 December 1864
Citation: Served as a landsman on board the U.S.S. *Lackawanna* during successful attacks against Fort Morgan, rebel gunboats, and the ram *Tennessee* in Mobile Bay, 5 August 1864. Showing a presence of mind and cheerfulness that had much to do with maintaining the crew's morale, Kinnaird served gallantly through the action which resulted in the capture of the prize rebel ram *Tennessee* and in the destruction of batteries at Fort Morgan.

745 ◆ KINSEY, JOHN

Rank: Corporal
Service: U.S. Army
Birthday: 1844

Place of Birth: Lancaster County, Pennsylvania
Date of Death: 19 December 1904
Cemetery: Crown Hill Cemetery—Indianapolis, Indiana
Entered Service at: Maytown, Lancaster County, Pennsylvania
Unit: Company B, 45th Pennsylvania Infantry
Battle or Place of Action: Spotsylvania, Virginia
Date of Action: 18 May 1864
Date of Issue: 2 March 1897
Citation: Seized the colors, the color bearer having been shot, and with great gallantry succeeded in saving them from capture.

746 ◆ KIRBY, DENNIS THOMAS

Rank: Major (highest rank: Brevet Brigadier General)
Service: U.S. Army
Birthday: 15 September 1835
Place of Birth: Niagara Falls, Niagara County, New York
Date of Death: 18 April 1922
Place of Death: Washington, D.C.
Cemetery: Arlington National Cemetery (1-334)—Arlington, Virginia
Entered Service at: St. Louis, St. Louis County, Missouri
Unit: 8th Missouri Infantry
Battle or Place of Action: Vicksburg, Mississippi
Date of Action: 22 May 1863
Date of Issue: 31 January 1894
Citation: Seized the colors when the color bearer was killed and bore them himself in the assault.

747 ◆ KIRK, JONATHAN C.

Rank: Captain
Service: U.S. Army
Place of Birth: Clinton County, Ohio
Date of Death: 30 July 1907
Cemetery: Maple Grove Cemetery (MH)—Wichita, Kansas
Entered Service at: Wilmington, Clinton County, Ohio
Unit: Company F, 20th Indiana Infantry
Battle or Place of Action: North Anna River, Virginia
Date of Action: 23 May 1864
Date of Issue: 13 June 1894
Citation: Volunteered for dangerous service and singlehandedly captured 13 armed Confederate soldiers and marched them to the rear.

748 ◆ KLINE, HARRY

True Name: Klien, Henry
Rank: Private (highest rank: Corporal)
Service: U.S. Army
Birthday: 4 October 1841
Place of Birth: Germany
Date of Death: 5 December 1901
Place of Death: Syracuse, New York
Cemetery: Woodlawn Cemetery (MH)—Syracuse, New York

Entered Service at: Syracuse, Onondaga County, New York
Unit: Company E, 40th New York Infantry
Battle or Place of Action: Deatonsville (Sailor's Creek), Virginia
Date of Action: 6 April 1865
Date of Issue: 10 May 1865
Citation: Capture of battle flag.

749 ◆ KLOTH, CHARLES H.

Rank: Private
Service: U.S. Army
Place of Birth: Europe
Entered Service at: Chicago, Cook County, Illinois
Unit: Chicago Mercantile Battery, Illinois Light Artillery
Battle or Place of Action: Vicksburg, Mississippi
Date of Action: 22 May 1863
Date of Issue: 15 January 1895
Citation: Carried with others by hand a cannon up to and fired it through an embrasure of the enemy's works.

750 ◆ KNIGHT, CHARLES H.

Rank: Corporal
Service: U.S. Army
Birthday: 1839
Place of Birth: Keene, Cheshire County, New Hampshire
Date of Death: 9 August 1904
Place of Death: West Springfield, Massachusetts
Cemetery: Oak Grove Cemetery (MH)—Springfield, Massachusetts
Entered Service at: Keene, Cheshire County, New Hampshire
Unit: Company I, 9th New Hampshire Infantry
Battle or Place of Action: Petersburg, Virginia
Date of Action: 30 July 1864
Date of Issue: 27 July 1896
Citation: In company with a sergeant, was the first to enter the exploded mine; was wounded but took several prisoners to the Federal lines.

751 ◆ KNIGHT, WILLIAM J.

Rank: Private
Service: U.S. Army
Birthday: 24 January 1837
Place of Birth: Apple Creek, Wayne County, Ohio
Date of Death: 26 September 1916
Cemetery: Oakwood Cemetery—Stryker, Ohio
Entered Service at: Farmers Center, Defiance County, Ohio
Unit: Company E, 21st Ohio Infantry
Battle or Place of Action: Georgia
Date of Action: April 1862
Date of Issue: September 1863
Citation: One of 19 of 24 men (including two civilians) who, by direction of Gen. Ormsby M. Mitchell, penetrated nearly 200 miles south into enemy territory and captured a railroad train at Big Shanty, Ga., in an attempt to destroy the bridges and track between Chattanooga and Atlanta.

752 ◆ KNOWLES, ABIATHER J.

Rank: Private (highest rank: Captain)
Service: U.S. Army
Birthday: 15 March 1830
Place of Birth: La Grange, Penobscot County, Maine
Date of Death: 11 February 1905
Place of Death: North Bradfort, Maine
Cemetery: Hill Crest Cemetery (MH)—La Grange, Maine
Entered Service at: Willets Point, Queens County, New York
Unit: Company D, 2d Maine Infantry
Battle or Place of Action: Bull Run, Virginia
Date of Action: 21 July 1861
Date of Issue: 27 December 1894
Citation: Removed the dead and wounded under heavy fire.

753 ◆ KNOX, EDWARD M.

Rank: Second Lieutenant
Service: U.S. Army
Birthday: 12 February 1842
Place of Birth: New York, New York
Date of Death: 28 March 1916
Place of Death: New York, New York
Cemetery: Woodlawn Cemetery—Bronx, New York
Entered Service at: New York, New York
Unit: 15th New York Battery Light Artillery
Battle or Place of Action: Gettysburg, Pennsylvania
Date of Action: 2 July 1863
Date of Issue: 18 October 1892
Citation: Held his ground with the battery after the other batteries had fallen back until compelled to draw his piece off by hand; he was severely wounded.

754 ◆ KOOGLE, JACOB

Rank: First Lieutenant
Service: U.S. Army
Birthday: 5 December 1841
Place of Birth: Frederick, Frederick County, Maryland
Date of Death: 16 March 1915
Place of Death: Hagerstown, Maryland
Cemetery: St. Paul's Lutheran Cemetery (MH)—Myersville, Maryland
Entered Service at: Middletown, Frederick County, Maryland
Unit: Company G, 7th Maryland Infantry
Battle or Place of Action: Five Forks, Virginia
Date of Action: 1 April 1865
Date of Issue: 10 May 1865
Citation: Capture of battle flag.

755 ◆ KOUNTZ, JOHN S.

Rank: Musician
Service: U.S. Army
Birthday: 25 March 1845
Place of Birth: Maumee, Lucas County, Ohio

Date of Death: 14 June 1909
Cemetery: Calvary Cemetery—Toledo, Ohio
Entered Service at: Maumee, Lucas County, Ohio
Unit: Company G, 37th Ohio Infantry
Battle or Place of Action: Missionary Ridge, Tennessee
Date of Action: 25 November 1863
Date of Issue: 13 August 1895
Citation: Seized a musket and joined in the charge in which he was severely wounded.

756 ◆ KRAMER, THEODORE L.

Rank: Private
Service: U.S. Army
Birthday: 1847
Place of Birth: Luzerne County, Pennsylvania
Date of Death: 2 March 1910
Place of Death: Chicago, Illinois
Cemetery: Arlington Cemetery (MH)—Elmhurst, Illinois
Entered Service at: Danville, Montour County, Pennsylvania
Unit: Company G, 188th Pennsylvania Infantry
Battle or Place of Action: Chapin's Farm, Virginia
Date of Action: 29 September 1864
Date of Issue: 6 April 1865
Citation: Took one of the first prisoners, a captain.

757 ◆ KRETSINGER, GEORGE

Rank: Private
Service: U.S. Army
Birthday: 20 June 1844
Place of Birth: Fairfield, Herkimer County, New York
Date of Death: 20 April 1906
Place of Death: Chicago, Illinois
Cemetery: Rose Hill Cemetery—Chicago, Illinois
Entered Service at: Chicago, Cook County, Illinois
Unit: Chicago Mercantile Battery, Illinois Light Artillery
Battle or Place of Action: Vicksburg, Mississippi
Date of Action: 22 May 1863
Date of Issue: 20 July 1897
Citation: Carried with others by hand a cannon up to and fired it through an embrasure of the enemy's works.

758 ◆ KUDER, ANDREW

Rank: Second Lieutenant (highest rank: Captain)
Service: U.S. Army
Birthday: 1838
Place of Birth: Groveland, Livingston County, New York
Date of Death: 30 April 1899
Place of Death: South Livonia, New York
Cemetery: Arnold Cemetery (MH)—Conesus, New York
Entered Service at: Rochester, Monroe County, New York
Unit: Company G, 8th New York Cavalry
Battle or Place of Action: Waynesboro, Virginia
Date of Action: 2 March 1865
Date of Issue: 26 March 1865
Citation: Capture of flag.

759 ◆ KUDER, JEREMIAH

Rank: Lieutenant (highest rank: Captain)
Service: U.S. Army
Birthday: 12 July 1835
Place of Birth: Tiffin, Seneca County, Ohio
Date of Death: 25 May 1916
Place of Death: Marion, Indiana
Cemetery: Marion National Cemetery (4-2464) (MH)—Marion, Indiana
Entered Service at: Warsaw, Kosciusko County, Indiana
Unit: Company A, 74th Indiana Infantry
Battle or Place of Action: Jonesboro, Georgia
Date of Action: 1 September 1864
Date of Issue: 7 April 1865
Citation: Capture of flag of 8th and 19th Arkansas (C.S.A.).

760 ◆ LABILL, JOSEPH S.

True Name: Labille, Joseph S.
Rank: Private
Service: U.S. Army
Birthday: 1837
Place of Birth: Belgium
Date of Death: 1911
Cemetery: South Hill Cemetery (MH)—Vandalia, Illinois
Entered Service at: Vandalia, Fayette County, Illinois
Unit: Company C, 6th Missouri Infantry
Battle or Place of Action: Vicksburg, Mississippi
Date of Action: 22 May 1863
Date of Issue: 14 August 1894
Citation: Gallantry in the charge of the "volunteer storming party."

761 ◆ LADD, GEORGE

Rank: Private
Service: U.S. Army
Place of Birth: Camillus, Onondaga County, New York
Date of Death: 13 August 1869
Place of Death: Bath, New York
Cemetery: Bath National Cemetery (C6-6) (MH)—Bath, New York
Entered Service at: Camillus, Onondaga County, New York
Unit: Company H, 22d New York Cavalry
Battle or Place of Action: Waynesboro, Virginia
Date of Action: 2 March 1865
Date of Issue: 26 March 1865
Citation: Captured a standard bearer, his flag, horse, and equipment.

762 ◆ LAFFERTY, JOHN✝

True Name: Laverty, John
Rank: Fireman
Service: U.S. Navy
Birthday: 1842
Place of Birth: New York, New York
Date of Death: 13 November 1903

Place of Death: Philadelphia, Pennsylvania
Cemetery: Mount Moriah (VA plot 3-3-17) (MH)—Philadelphia, Pennsylvania
Entered Service at: Pennsylvania
Unit: U.S.S. *Wyalusing*
Battle or Place of Action: Roanoke River, North Carolina
Date of Action: 25 May 1864
G.O. Number, Date: 45, 31 December 1864
Date of Issue: 14 March 1865
Citation: **First Award** Served on board the U.S.S. *Wyalusing* and participated in a plan to destroy the rebel ram *Abemarle* in Roanoke River, 25 May 1864. Volunteering for the hazardous mission, Lafferty participated in the transfer of two torpedoes across an island swamp and then served as sentry to keep guard of clothes and arms left by other members of the party. After being rejoined by others of the party who had been discovered before the plan could be completed, Lafferty succeeded in returning to the mother ship after spending 24 hours of discomfort in the rain and swamp.
Notes: ✛Double Awardee: *see also* Interim 1871-1898 during which he served under the name John Laverty

763 ◆ LAFFEY, BARTLETT

Rank: Seaman (highest rank: Acting Master's Mate)
Service: U.S. Navy
Birthday: 1841
Place of Birth: Galway, County Galway, Ireland
Date of Death: 22 March 1901
Place of Death: Chelsea, Massachusetts
Cemetery: Old Calvary Cemetery (MH)—Roslindale, Massachusetts
Entered Service at: Boston, Suffolk County, Massachusetts
Unit: U.S.S. *Marmora*
Battle or Place of Action: off Yazoo City, Mississippi
Date of Action: 5 March 1864
G.O. Number, Date: 32, 16 April 1864
Citation: Off Yazoo City, Miss., 5 March 1864, embarking from the *Marmora* with a 12-pound howitzer mounted on a field carriage, Laffey landed with the gun and crew in the midst of heated battle and, bravely standing by his gun despite enemy rifle fire which cut the gun carriage and rammer, contributed to the turning back of the enemy during the fierce engagement.

764 ◆ *LAING, WILLIAM

Rank: Sergeant
Service: U.S. Army
Birthday: 1831
Place of Birth: Hempstead, Nassau County, New York
Date of Death: 29 September 1864
Place of Death: Chapin's Bluff, Virginia
Entered Service at: Brooklyn, Kings County, New York
Unit: Company F, 158th New York Infantry
Battle or Place of Action: Chapin's Farm, Virginia
Date of Action: 29 September 1864
Date of Issue: 6 April 1865
Citation: Was among the first to scale the parapet.

765 ◆ LAKIN, DANIEL

Rank: Seaman
Service: U.S. Navy
Birthday: 1834
Place of Birth: Baltimore, Baltimore County, Maryland
Entered Service at: Maryland
Unit: U.S.S. *Commodore Perry*
Battle or Place of Action: Franklin, Virginia
Date of Action: 3 October 1862
G.O. Number, Date: 11, 3 April 1863
Citation: On board the U.S.S. *Commodore Perry* in the attack upon Franklin, Va., 3 October 1862. With enemy fire raking the deck of his ship and blockades thwarting her progress, Lakin remained at his post and performed his duties with skill and courage as the *Commodore Perry* fought a gallant battle to silence many rebel batteries as she steamed down the Blackwater River.

766 ◆ LANDIS, JAMES PARKER

Rank: Chief Bugler
Service: U.S. Army
Birthday: 20 July 1843
Place of Birth: Mifflin County, Pennsylvania
Date of Death: 1 December 1924
Place of Death: Yeagertown, Pennsylvania
Cemetery: Holy Communion Lutheran Cemetery—Yeagertown, Pennsylvania
Entered Service at: Reedsville, Mifflin County, Pennsylvania
Unit: 1st Pennsylvania Cavalry
Battle or Place of Action: Paines Crossroads, Virginia
Date of Action: 5 April 1865
Date of Issue: 3 May 1865
Citation: Capture of flag.

767 ◆ LANE, MORGAN D.

Rank: Private
Service: U.S. Army
Birthday: 1844
Place of Birth: Monroe, Orange County, New York
Date of Death: 19 July 1892
Cemetery: Mount Vernon Cemetery (MH)—Atchison, Kansas
Entered Service at: Allegan, Allegan County, Michigan
Unit: Signal Corps
Battle or Place of Action: Jetersville, Virginia
Date of Action: 6 April 1865
Date of Issue: 16 March 1866
Citation: Capture of flag of gunboat *Nansemond*.

768 ◆ LANFARE, AARON STEVEN

Rank: First Lieutenant (highest rank: Captain)
Service: U.S. Army
Birthday: 9 September 1824
Place of Birth: Branford, New Haven County, Connecticut
Date of Death: 19 September 1875
Place of Death: At Sea & buried at Sea

Cemetery: Branford Center Cemetery (MH) (Marker Only)—Branford, Connecticut
Entered Service at: Branford, New Haven County, Connecticut
Unit: Company B, 1st Connecticut Cavalry
Battle or Place of Action: Deatonsville (Sailor's Creek), Virginia
Date of Action: 6 April 1865
Date of Issue: 3 May 1865
Citation: Capture of flag of 11th Florida Infantry (C.S.A.).

769 ◆ LANGBEIN, JOHANN CHRISTOPH JULIUS

Rank: Musician (highest rank: Drummer)
Service: U.S. Army
Birthday: 22 September 1845
Place of Birth: Germany
Date of Death: 28 January 1910
Place of Death: New York, New York
Cemetery: Woodlawn Cemetery (Mausoleum) (125-92)—Bronx, New York
Entered Service at: New York, New York
Unit: Company B, 9th New York Infantry
Battle or Place of Action: Camden, North Carolina
Date of Action: 19 April 1862
Date of Issue: 7 January 1895
Citation: A drummer boy, 15 years of age, he voluntarily and under a heavy fire went to the aid of a wounded officer, procured medical assistance for him, and aided in carrying him to a place of safety.

770 ◆ LANN, JOHN S.

True Name: Lanning, John S.
Rank: Landsman
Service: U.S. Navy
Birthday: 29 August 1843
Place of Birth: Rochester, Monroe County, New York
Date of Death: 13 April 1907
Cemetery: Yankton Municipal Cemetery (MH)—Yankton, South Dakota
Entered Service at: New York, New York
Unit: U.S.S. *Magnolia*
Battle or Place of Action: St. Marks, Florida
Date of Action: 5-6 March 1865
G.O. Number, Date: 59, 22 June 1865
Citation: As landsman on board the U.S.S. *Magnolia*, St. Marks, Fla., 5 and 6 March, Lann served with the Army in charge of the Navy howitzers during the attack on St. Marks and throughout this fierce engagement made remarkable efforts in assisting transport of the gun. His coolness and determination in standing by his gun while under fire of the enemy were a credit to the service to which he belonged.

771 ◆ LARIMER, SMITH

Rank: Corporal
Service: U.S. Army
Birthday: 17 March 1829

Place of Birth: Richland County, Ohio
Date of Death: 20 February 1881
Cemetery: Marlow Cemetery—Ontario, Ohio
Entered Service at: Columbus, Franklin County, Ohio
Unit: Company G, 2d Ohio Cavalry
Battle or Place of Action: Deatonsville (Sailor's Creek), Virginia
Date of Action: 6 April 1865
Date of Issue: 3 May 1865
Citation: Capture of flag of Maj. Gen. Joseph Brezard Kershaw's headquarters.

772 ◆ LARRABEE, JAMES W.

Rank: Corporal (highest rank: First Sergeant)
Service: U.S. Army
Birthday: 1839
Place of Birth: Rensselaer County, New York
Date of Death: 30 December 1907
Place of Death: Lee County, Illinois
Cemetery: Four Mile Grove Cemetery—Meriden, Illinois
Entered Service at: Mendota, La Salle County, Illinois
Unit: Company I, 55th Illinois Infantry
Battle or Place of Action: Vicksburg, Mississippi
Date of Action: 22 May 1863
Date of Issue: 2 September 1893
Citation: Gallantry in the charge of the "volunteer storming party."

773 ◆ LAWSON, GAINES

Rank: First Sergeant (highest rank: Brevet Lieutenant Colonel)
Service: U.S. Army
Birthday: 4 September 1840
Place of Birth: Hawkins County, Tennessee
Date of Death: 12 September 1906
Cemetery: Arlington National Cemetery (1-37-A)—Arlington, Virginia
Entered Service at: Rogersville, Hawkins County, Tennessee
Unit: Company D, 4th East Tennessee Infantry
Battle or Place of Action: Minville, Tennessee
Date of Action: 3 October 1863
Date of Issue: 11 June 1895
Citation: Went to the aid of a wounded comrade between the lines and carried him to a place of safety.

774 ◆ LAWSON, JOHN

Rank: Landsman
Service: U.S. Navy
Birthday: 16 June 1837
Place of Birth: Philadelphia, Philadelphia County, Pennsylvania
Date of Death: 3 May 1919
Place of Death: Philadelphia, Pennsylvania
Cemetery: Mount Peace Cemetery—Camden, New Jersey
Entered Service at: Pennsylvania
Unit: U.S.S. *Hartford*

Battle or Place of Action: Mobile Bay, Alabama
Date of Action: 5 August 1864
G.O. Number, Date: 45, 31 December 1864
Citation: On board the flagship U.S.S. *Hartford* during successful attacks against Fort Morgan, rebel gunboats, and the ram *Tennessee* in Mobile Bay on 5 August 1864. Wounded in the leg and thrown violently against the side of the ship when an enemy shell killed or wounded the six-man crew as the shell whipped on the berth deck, Lawson, upon regaining his composure, promptly returned to his station and, although urged to go below for treatment, steadfastly continued his duties throughout the remainder of the action.

775 ◆ LAWTON, HENRY WARE

Rank: Captain (highest rank: Major General)
Service: U.S. Army
Birthday: 17 March 1843
Place of Birth: Manhattan, Lucas County, Ohio
Date of Death: 19 December 1899
Place of Death: Philippine Islands
Cemetery: Arlington National Cemetery (2-841-842)—Arlington, Virginia
Entered Service at: Fort Wayne, Allen County, Indiana
Unit: Company A, 30th Indiana Infantry
Battle or Place of Action: Atlanta, Georgia
Date of Action: 3 August 1864
Date of Issue: 22 May 1893
Citation: Led a charge of skirmishers against the enemy rifle pits and stubbornly and successfully resisted two determined attacks of the enemy to retake the works.

776 ◆ LEAR, NICHOLAS

Rank: Quartermaster
Service: U.S. Navy
Birthday: 1826
Place of Birth: Rhode Island
Date of Death: 4 July 1902
Place of Death: Philadelphia, Pennsylvania
Cemetery: Mount Moriah Cemetery (VA plot 3-3-3) (MH)—Philadelphia, Pennsylvania
Entered Service at: Philadelphia, Philadelphia County, Pennsylvania
Unit: U.S.S. *New Ironsides*
Battle or Place of Action: Fort Fisher, North Carolina
Date of Action: 24-25 December 1864 & 13-15 January 1865
G.O. Number, Date: 59, 22 June 1865
Citation: Lear served on board the U.S.S. *New Ironsides* during action in several attacks on Fort Fisher, 24 and 25 December 1864; and 13, 14 and 15 January 1865. The ship steamed in and took the lead in the ironclad division close inshore and immediately opened its starboard battery in a barrage of well-directed fire to cause several fires and explosions and dismount several guns during the first two days of fighting. Taken under fire as she steamed into position on 13 January, the *New Ironsides* fought all day and took on ammunition at night, despite severe weather conditions. When the

enemy came out of their bombproofs to defend the fort against the storming party, the ship's battery disabled nearly every gun on the fort facing the shore before the cease-fire order was given by the flagship.

777 ◆ LEE, JAMES H.

Rank: Seaman (highest rank: Captain of the Top)
Service: U.S. Navy
Birthday: 1840
Place of Birth: New York
Date of Death: 9 August 1877
Place of Death: Oswego, New York
Cemetery: The Rural Cemetery—Oswego, New York
Entered Service at: New York, New York
Unit: U.S.S. *Kearsarge*
Battle or Place of Action: off Cherbourg, France
Date of Action: 19 June 1864
G.O. Number, Date: 45, 31 December 1864
Citation: Served as seaman on board the U.S.S. *Kearsarge* when she destroyed the *Alabama* off Cherbourg, France, 19 June 1864. Acting as sponger of the No. 1 gun, during this bitter engagement, Lee exhibited marked coolness and good conduct and was highly recommended for his gallantry under fire by the divisional officer.

778 ◆ LELAND, GEORGE W.

Rank: Gunner's Mate (highest rank: Acting Master's Mate)
Service: U.S. Navy
Birthday: 1834
Place of Birth: Savannah, Chatham County, Georgia
Date of Death: 18 March 1880
Cemetery: Riverside Cemetery (MH)—Lewiston, Maine
Entered Service at: Georgia
Unit: U.S.S. *Lehigh*
Battle or Place of Action: Charleston Harbor, South Carolina
Date of Action: 16 November 1863
G.O. Number, Date: 32, 16 April 1864
Citation: Served on board the U.S.S. *Lehigh*, Charleston Harbor, 16 November 1863, during the hazardous task of freeing the *Lehigh*, which had grounded and was under heavy enemy fire from Fort Moultrie. Rowing the small boat which was used in the hazardous task of transferring hawsers from the *Lehigh* to the *Nahant*, Leland twice succeeded in making the trip, only to find that each had been in vain when the hawsers were cut by enemy fire and chaffing.

779 ◆ LEON, PIERRE

Rank: Captain of the Forecastle
Service: U.S. Navy
Birthday: 23 August 1838
Place of Birth: France
Date of Death: 7 December 1915
Place of Death: Riverside, New Jersey
Cemetery: St. Peter's Cemetery (MH)—Riverside, New Jersey

Entered Service at: Philadelphia, Philadelphia County, Pennsylvania
Unit: U.S.S. *Baron De Kalb*
Battle or Place of Action: Yazoo River, Mississippi
Date of Action: 23-27 December 1862
G.O. Number, Date: 11, 3 April 1863
Citation: Served on board the U.S.S. *Baron De Kalb*, Yazoo River Expedition, 23 to 27 December 1862. Proceeding under orders up the Yazoo River, the U.S.S. *Baron De Kalb*, with the object of capturing or destroying the enemy's transports, came upon the steamers *John Walsh*, *R.J. Locklan*, *Golden Age*, and the *Scotland* sunk on a bar where they were ordered fired. Continuing up the river, she was fired on, but upon returning the fire, caused the enemy's retreat. Returning down the Yazoo, she destroyed and captured larger quantities of enemy equipment and several prisoners. Serving bravely throughout this action, Leon, as captain of the forecastle, "distinguished himself in the various actions."

780 ◆ LEONARD, EDWIN

Rank: Sergeant
Service: U.S. Army
Birthday: 17 November 1823
Place of Birth: Agawam, Hampden County, Massachusetts
Date of Death: 5 April 1900
Cemetery: The White Church Cemetery (MH)—West Springfield, Massachusetts
red Service at: Agawam, Hampden County, Massachusetts
Unit: Company I, 37th Massachusetts Infantry
Battle or Place of Action: near Petersburg, Virginia
Date of Action: 18 June 1864
Date of Issue: 16 August 1894
Citation: Voluntarily exposed himself to the fire of a Union brigade to stop their firing on the Union skirmish line.

781 ◆ LEONARD, WILLIAM EDMAN

Rank: Private (highest rank: Second Lieutenant)
Service: U.S. Army
Birthday: 1836
Place of Birth: Greene County, Pennsylvania
Date of Death: 8 February 1891
Place of Death: Harvey's, Pennsylvania
Cemetery: unknown cemetery—Greene County, Pennsylvania
Entered Service at: Jacksonville, Pennsylvania
Unit: Company F, 85th Pennsylvania Infantry
Battle or Place of Action: Deep Bottom, Virginia
Date of Action: 16 August 1864
Date of Issue: 6 April 1865
Citation: Capture of battle flag.

782 ◆ LESLIE, FRANK

Rank: Private (highest rank: Corporal)
Service: U.S. Army
Birthday: 1841
Place of Birth: London, England

Date of Death: 1 August 1882
Place of Death: Minneapolis, Kansas
Entered Service at: New York, New York
Unit: Company B, 4th New York Cavalry
Battle or Place of Action: Front Royal, Virginia
Date of Action: 15 August 1864
Date of Issue: 26 August 1864
Citation: Capture of colors of 3d Virginia Infantry (C.S.A.).
Notes: POW

783 ◆ LEVY, BENJAMIN BENNETT

Rank: Private (highest rank: Color Sergeant)
Service: U.S. Army
Birthday: 22 February 1845
Place of Birth: New York, New York
Date of Death: 20 July 1921
Place of Death: New York, New York
Cemetery: Cypress Hills Cemetery (Private) (Sec.9 Lot 538, Grave 170)—Brooklyn, New York
Entered Service at: Newport News, Newport News County, Virginia
Unit: Company G, 1st New York Infantry
Served as: Orderly
Battle or Place of Action: Glendale, Virginia
Date of Action: 30 June 1862
Date of Issue: 1 March 1865
Citation: This soldier, a drummer boy, took the gun of a sick comrade, went into the fight, and when the color bearers were shot down, carried the colors and saved them from capture.

784 ◆ LEWIS, DEWITT CLINTON

Rank: Captain (highest rank: Brevet Lieutenant Colonel)
Service: U.S. Army
Birthday: 30 July 1822
Place of Birth: West Chester, Chester County, Pennsylvania
Date of Death: 28 June 1899
Place of Death: Morton, Pennsylvania
Cemetery: Oakland Cemetery—West Chester, Pennsylvania
Entered Service at: West Chester, Chester County, Pennsylvania
Unit: Company F, 97th Pennsylvania Infantry
Battle or Place of Action: Secessionville, South Carolina
Date of Action: 16 June 1862
Date of Issue: 23 April 1896
Citation: While retiring with his men before a heavy fire of canister shot at short-range, returned in the face of the enemy's fire and rescued an exhausted private of his company who but for this timely action would have lost his life by drowning in the morass through which the troops were retiring.

785 ◆ LEWIS, HENRY

Rank: Corporal (highest rank: First Sergeant)
Service: U.S. Army
Birthday: 14 December 1844
Place of Birth: Belleville, Wayne County, Michigan

Date of Death: 29 March 1930
Place of Death: Belleville, Michigan
Cemetery: Shoop Cemetery—Belleville, Van Buren Township, Michigan
Entered Service at: Adrian, Lenawee County, Michigan
Unit: Company B, 47th Ohio Infantry
Battle or Place of Action: Vicksburg, Mississippi
Date of Action: 3 May 1863
Date of Issue: 17 April 1917
Citation: Was one of a party that volunteered and attempted to run the enemy's batteries with a steam tug and two barges loaded with subsistence stores.
Notes: POW

786 ◆ LEWIS, SAMUEL E.

Rank: Corporal
Service: U.S. Army
Place of Birth: Coventry, Kent County, Rhode Island
Date of Death: 22 March 1907
Cemetery: North Burial Grounds Cemetery (MH)—Providence, Rhode Island
Entered Service at: Coventry, Kent County, Rhode Island
Unit: Company G, 1st Rhode Island Light Artillery
Battle or Place of Action: Petersburg, Virginia
Date of Action: 2 April 1865
Date of Issue: 16 June 1866
Citation: Was one of a detachment of 20 picked artillerymen who voluntarily accompanied an infantry assaulting party and who turned upon the enemy the guns captured in the assault.

787 ◆ LIBAIRE, ADOLPH

True Name: Libaire, Adolphe
Rank: Captain
Service: U.S. Army
Birthday: 2 May 1840
Place of Birth: Baccarat, France
Date of Death: 5 September 1920
Place of Death: Deal, New Jersey
Cemetery: The Green Wood Cemetery—Brooklyn, New York
Entered Service at: New York, New York
Unit: Company E, 9th New York Infantry
Battle or Place of Action: Antietam, Maryland
Date of Action: 17 September 1862
Date of Issue: 2 April 1898
Citation: In the advance on the enemy and after his color bearer and the entire color guard of eight men had been shot down, this officer seized the regimental flag and with conspicuous gallantry carried it to the extreme front, urging the line forward.

788 ◆ LILLEY, JOHN

Rank: Private
Service: U.S. Army
Birthday: February 1826
Place of Birth: Mifflin County, Pennsylvania
Date of Death: 12 May 1902

Place of Death: Lewistown, Pennsylvania
Cemetery: First Methodist Cemetery—Lewistown, Pennsylvania
Entered Service at: Lewistown, Mifflin County, Pennsylvania
Unit: Company F, 205th Pennsylvania Infantry
Battle or Place of Action: Petersburg, Virginia
Date of Action: 2 April 1865
Date of Issue: 20 May 1865
Citation: After his regiment had began to waiver, he rushed on alone to capture the enemy flag. He reached the works and the Confederate color bearer who, at bayonet point, he caused to surrender with several enemy soldiers. He kept his prisoners in tow when they realized he was alone as his regiment in the meantime withdrawn further to the rear.

789 ◆ LITTLE, HENRY F. W.

Rank: Sergeant (highest rank: First Lieutenant)
Service: U.S. Army
Birthday: 27 June 1842
Place of Birth: Manchester, Hillsborough County, New Hampshire
Date of Death: 7 February 1907
Cemetery: Valley Cemetery (MH)—Manchester, New Hampshire
Entered Service at: Manchester, Hillsborough County, New Hampshire
Unit: Company D, 7th New Hampshire Infantry
Battle or Place of Action: near Richmond, Virginia
Date of Action: September 1864
Date of Issue: 14 January 1870
Citation: Gallantry on the skirmish line.

790 ◆ LITTLEFIELD, GEORGE H.

Rank: Corporal
Service: U.S. Army
Birthday: 2 May 1842
Place of Birth: Skowhegan, Somerset County, Maine
Date of Death: 25 December 1919
Place of Death: Richmond, Maine
Cemetery: The Cotton Cemetery (MH)—Richmond, Maine
Entered Service at: Skowhegan, Somerset County, Maine
Unit: Company G, 1st Maine Veteran Infantry
Battle or Place of Action: Fort Fisher, North Carolina
Date of Action: 25 March 1865
Date of Issue: 22 June 1885
Citation: The color sergeant having been wounded, this soldier picked up the flag and bore it to the front, to the great encouragement of the charging column.

791 ◆ LIVINGSTON, JOSIAH O.

Rank: First Lieutenant & Adjutant (highest rank: Captain)
Service: U.S. Army
Birthday: 3 February 1837
Place of Birth: Walden, Vermont
Date of Death: 23 July 1917
Cemetery: Robinson Cemetery—Calais, Vermont

Entered Service at: Marshfield, Washington County, Vermont
Unit: 9th Vermont Infantry
Battle or Place of Action: Newport Barracks, North Carolina
Date of Action: 2 February 1864
Date of Issue: 8 September 1891
Citation: When, after desperate resistance, the small garrison had been driven back to the river by a vastly superior force, this officer, while a small force held back the enemy, personally fired the railroad bridge, and, although wounded himself, assisted a wounded officer over the burning structure.

792 ◆ LLOYD, BENJAMIN

Rank: Coal Heaver (highest rank: Fireman Second Class)
Service: U.S. Navy
Birthday: 1839
Place of Birth: Liverpool, Merseyside County, England
Entered Service at: Philadelphia, Philadelphia County, Pennsylvania
Unit: U.S.S. *Wyalusing*
Battle or Place of Action: Roanoke River, North Carolina
Date of Action: 25 May 1864
G.O. Number, Date: 45, 31 December 1864
Citation: Serving on board the U.S.S. *Wyalusing* and paticipating in a plan to destroy the rebel ram *Albemarle* in Roanoke River, 25 May 1864. Volunteering for the hazardous mission, Lloyd participated in the transfer of two torpedoes across an island swamp. Serving as boatkeeper, he aided in rescuing others of the party who had been detected before the plan could be completed, but who escaped, leaving detection of the plan impossible. By his skill and courage, Lloyd succeeded in returning to the mother ship after spending 24 hours of discomfort in the rain and swamp.

793 ◆ LLOYD, JOHN W.

Rank: Coxswain
Service: U.S. Navy
Birthday: 1831
Place of Birth: New York, New York
Entered Service at: New York
Unit: U.S.S. *Wyalusing*
Battle or Place of Action: Roanoke River, North Carolina
Date of Action: 25 May 1864
G.O. Number, Date: 45, 31 December 1864
Citation: Serving on board the U.S.S. *Wyalusing* during an attempt to destroy the rebel ram *Albemarle* in Roanoke River, 25 May 1864. Lloyd participated in this daring plan by swimming the Roanoke River heavily weighted with a line which was used for hauling torpedoes across. Thwarted by discovery just before the completion of the plan, Lloyd cut the torpedo guiding line to prevent detection of the plan by the enemy and again swam the river, narrowly escaping enemy musket fire and regaining the ship in safety.

794 ◆ LOCKE, LEWIS

Rank: Private
Service: U.S. Army

Place of Birth: Clintonville, Essex County, New York
Date of Death: 1892
Place of Death: Ashuelot, New Hampshire
Entered Service at: Jersey City, Hudson County, New Jersey
Unit: Company A, 1st New Jersey Cavalry
Battle or Place of Action: Paines Crossroads, Virginia
Date of Action: 5 April 1865
Date of Issue: 3 May 1865
Citation: Capture of a Confederate flag.

795 ◆ LOGAN, HUGH

Rank: Captain of the Afterguard
Service: U.S. Navy
Birthday: 1834
Place of Birth: Ireland
Date of Death: 22 November 1903
Place of Death: Glasgow, Scotland
Entered Service at: Boston, Suffolk County, Massachusetts
Unit: U.S.S. *Rhode Island*
Battle or Place of Action: off Cape Hatteras, North Carolina
Date of Action: 30 December 1862
G.O. Number, Date: 59, 22 June 1865
Citation: On board the U.S.S. *Rhode Island* which was engaged in saving the lives of the officers and crew of the *Monitor*, 30 December 1862. Participating in the hazardous rescue of the officers and crew of the sinking *Monitor*, Logan, after rescuing several of the men, became separated in a heavy gale with other members of the cutter that had set out from the *Rhode Island*, and spent many hours in the small boat at the mercy of the weather and high seas until finally picked up by a schooner 50 miles east of Cape Hatteras.

796 ◆ LONERGAN, JOHN

Rank: Captain
Service: U.S. Army
Birthday: 7 April 1839
Place of Birth: Carrick, County Donegal, Ireland
Date of Death: 6 August 1902
Place of Death: Montreal, Canada
Cemetery: St. Joseph's Cemetery—Burlington, Vermont
Entered Service at: Burlington, Chittenden County, Vermont
Unit: Company A, 13th Vermont Infantry
Battle or Place of Action: Gettysburg, Pennsylvania
Date of Action: 2 July 1863
Date of Issue: 28 October 1893
Citation: Gallantry in the recapture of four guns and the capture of two additional guns from the enemy; also the capture of a number of prisoners.

797 ◆ LONGSHORE, WILLIAM HENRY

Rank: Private
Service: U.S. Army
Birthday: 18 February 1841
Place of Birth: Zanesville, Muskingum County, Ohio

Date of Death: 20 December 1909
Place of Death: Fort Scott, Kansas
Cemetery: Evergreen Cemetery (MH)—Fort Scott, Kansas
Entered Service at: Columbus, Franklin County, Ohio
Unit: Company D, 30th Ohio Infantry
Battle or Place of Action: Vicksburg, Mississippi
Date of Action: 22 May 1863
Date of Issue: 10 August 1894
Citation: Gallantry in the charge of the "volunteer storming party."

798 ◆ LONSWAY, JOSEPH

Rank: Private
Service: U.S. Army
Birthday: 17 March 1844
Place of Birth: Clayton, Jefferson County, New York
Date of Death: 22 January 1925
Place of Death: Clayton, New York
Cemetery: St. Mary's Cemetery (MH)—Clayton, New York
Entered Service at: Sackets Harbor, Jefferson County, New York
Unit: Company D, 20th New York Cavalry
Battle or Place of Action: Murfrees Station, Virginia
Date of Action: 16 October 1864
Date of Issue: 7 March 1917
Citation: Volunteered to swim Blackwater River to get a large flat used as a ferry on the other side; succeeded in getting the boat safely across, making it possible for a detachment to cross the river and take possession of the enemy's breastworks.

799 ◆ LORD, WILLIAM

Rank: Musician
Service: U.S. Army
Birthday: 13 February 1841
Place of Birth: Bradford, England
Date of Death: 4 August 1915
Place of Death: New York, New York
Cemetery: The Lutheran Cemetery—Middle Village, New York
Entered Service at: Lawrence, Essex County, Massachusetts
Unit: Company C, 40th Massachusetts Infantry
Battle or Place of Action: Drewry's Bluff, Virginia
Date of Action: 16 May 1864
Date of Issue: 4 April 1898
Citation: Went to the assistance of a wounded officer lying helpless between the lines, and under fire from both sides removed him to a place of safety.

800 ◆ LORISH, ANDREW J.

Rank: Commissary Sergeant (highest rank: Brevet First Lieutenant)
Service: U.S. Army
Birthday: 8 November 1832
Place of Birth: Dansville, Livingston County, New York
Date of Death: 11 August 1897

Place of Death: Warsaw, New York
Cemetery: Forest Hill Cemetery (MH)—Attica, New York
Entered Service at: Attica, Wyoming County, New York
Unit: 19th New York Cavalry (1st New York Dragoons)
Battle or Place of Action: Winchester, Virginia
Date of Action: 19 September 1864
Date of Issue: 27 September 1864
Citation: Amid the enemy he grabbed the flag from a color bearer who then called for help. When the bearer's comrades were readying their rifles, he dashed directly at them securing their disarming. As he rode away, the Confederates picked up their guns firing at the captor of their flag.

801 ◆ LOVE, GEORGE MALTBY

Rank: Colonel (highest rank: Brevet Brigadier General U.S. Volunteers)
Service: U.S. Army
Birthday: 1 January 1831
Place of Birth: Buffalo, Erie County, New York
Date of Death: 15 March 1887
Place of Death: Buffalo, New York
Cemetery: Forest Lawn Cemetery (MH)—Buffalo, New York
Entered Service at: Elmira, Chemung County, New York
Unit: 116th New York Infantry
Battle or Place of Action: Cedar Creek, Virginia
Date of Action: 19 October 1864
Date of Issue: 6 March 1865
Citation: Capture of battle flag of 2d South Carolina (C.S.A.).

802 ◆ LOVERING, GEORGE MASON

Rank: First Sergeant (highest rank: First Lieutenant)
Service: U.S. Army
Birthday: 10 January 1832
Place of Birth: Springfield, New Hampshire
Date of Death: 2 April 1919
Cemetery: Union Cemetery (MH)—Holbrook, Massachusetts
Entered Service at: East Randolph, Norfolk County, Massachusetts
Unit: Company I, 4th Massachusetts Infantry
Battle or Place of Action: Port Hudson, Louisiana
Date of Action: 14 June 1863
Date of Issue: 19 November 1891
Citation: During a momentary confusion in the ranks caused by other troops rushing upon the regiment, this soldier, with coolness and determination, rendered efficient aid in preventing a panic among the troops.

803 ◆ LOWER, CYRUS B.

Rank: Private
Service: U.S. Army
Birthday: 28 February 1843
Place of Birth: Lawrence, Pennsylvania
Date of Death: 21 May 1924

Place of Death: Washington, D.C.
Cemetery: Arlington National Cemetery (17-19971) (MH)—Arlington, Virginia
Entered Service at: New Castle, Lawrence County, Pennsylvania
Unit: Company K, 13th Pennsylvania Reserves
Battle or Place of Action: Wilderness Campaign, Virginia
Date of Action: 7 May 1864
Date of Issue: 20 July 1887
Citation: Gallant services and soldierly qualities in voluntarily rejoining his command after having been wounded.

804 ◆ LOWER, ROBERT A.

Rank: Private
Service: U.S. Army
Birthday: 1844
Place of Birth: Illinois
Cemetery: Yates City Cemetery—Yates City, Illinois
Entered Service at: Elmwood, Peoria County, Illinois
Unit: Company K, 55th Illinois Infantry
Battle or Place of Action: Vicksburg, Mississippi
Date of Action: 22 May 1863
Date of Issue: 2 September 1893
Citation: Gallantry in the charge of the "volunteer storming party."

805 ◆ LOYD, GEORGE A.

Rank: Private
Service: U.S. Army
Birthday: 9 May 1844
Place of Birth: Muskingum County, Ohio
Date of Death: 13 May 1917
Cemetery: Spring Grove Cemetery—Cincinnati, Ohio
Entered Service at: Zanesville, Muskingum County, Ohio
Unit: Company A, 122d Ohio Infantry
Battle or Place of Action: Petersburg, Virginia
Date of Action: 2 April 1865
Date of Issue: 16 April 1891
Citation: Capture of division flag of Maj. Gen. Henry Heth, (C.S.A.).

806 ◆ LUCAS, GEORGE WASHINGTON

Rank: Private
Service: U.S. Army
Birthday: 1845
Place of Birth: Adams County, Illinois
Date of Death: 17 May 1921
Place of Death: Quincy, Illinois
Cemetery: Mounds Cemetery (MH)—Timewell, Illinois
Entered Service at: Mount Sterling, Brown County, Illinois
Unit: Company C, 3d Missouri Cavalry
Battle or Place of Action: Benton, Arkansas
Date of Action: 25 July 1864
Date of Issue: December 1864
Citation: Pursued and killed Confederate Brig. Gen. George M. Holt, Arkansas Militia, capturing his arms and horse.

807 ◆ LUCE, MOSES AUGUSTINE

Rank: Sergeant
Service: U.S. Army
Birthday: 14 May 1842
Place of Birth: Payson, Adams County, Illinois
Date of Death: 13 April 1933
Place of Death: San Diego, California
Cemetery: Greenwood Memorial Park—San Diego, California
Entered Service at: Adrian, Lenawee County, Michigan
Unit: Company E, 4th Michigan Infantry
Battle or Place of Action: Laurel Hill, Virginia
Date of Action: 10 May 1864
Date of Issue: 7 February 1895
Citation: Voluntarily returned in the face of the advancing enemy to the assistance of a wounded and helpless comrade, and carried him, at imminent peril, to a place of safety.

808 ◆ LUDGATE, WILLIAM

Rank: Captain (highest rank: Brevet Major)
Service: U.S. Army
Birthday: 11 March 1836
Place of Birth: London, England
Date of Death: 14 June 1912
Cemetery: Arlington National Cemetery (3-1488)—Arlington, Virginia
Entered Service at: New York, New York
Unit: Company G, 59th New York Veteran Infantry
Battle or Place of Action: Farmville, Virginia
Date of Action: 7 April 1865
Date of Issue: 10 August 1889
Citation: Gallantry and promptness in rallying his men and advancing with a small detachment to save a bridge about to be fired by the enemy.

809 ◆ LUDWIG, CARL

Rank: Private (highest rank: Corporal)
Service: U.S. Army
Birthday: 10 May 1841
Place of Birth: France
Date of Death: 16 May 1913
Place of Death: College Point, New York
Cemetery: Flushing Cemetery—Flushing, New York
Entered Service at: Flushing, Queens County, New York
Unit: 34th New York Battery
Battle or Place of Action: Petersburg, Virginia
Date of Action: 18 June 1864
Date of Issue: 30 July 1896
Citation: As gunner of his piece, inflicted singly a great loss upon the enemy and distinguished himself in the removal of the piece while under a heavy fire.

810 ◆ LUNT, ALPHONSO M.

Rank: Sergeant
Service: U.S. Army

Birthday: 6 September 1837
Place of Birth: Berwick, York County, Maine
Date of Death: 18 December 1917
Place of Death: Mountain Home, Tennessee
Cemetery: Cambridge Cemetery (MH)—Cambridge, Massachusetts
Entered Service at: Cambridge, Middlesex County, Massachusetts
Unit: Company F, 38th Massachusetts Infantry
Battle or Place of Action: Opequan Creek, Virginia
Date of Action: 19 September 1864
Date of Issue: 10 May 1894
Citation: Carried his flag to the most advanced position where, left almost alone close to the enemy's lines, he refused their demand to surrender, withdrew at great personal peril, and saved his flag.

811 ◆ LUTES, FRANKLIN W.

Rank: Corporal
Service: U.S. Army
Birthday: 1840
Place of Birth: Dundee, Yates County, New York
Date of Death: 6 April 1915
Cemetery: Glenside Cemetery—Wolcott, New York
Entered Service at: Geddes, New York
Unit: Company D, 111th New York Infantry
Battle or Place of Action: Petersburg, Virginia
Date of Action: 31 March 1865
Date of Issue: 3 April 1865
Citation: Capture of flag of 41st Alabama Infantry (C.S.A.), together with the color bearer and one of the color guard.
Notes: POW

812 ◆ LUTHER, JAMES HEZIKIAH

Rank: Private (highest rank: Corporal)
Service: U.S. Army
Birthday: 24 January 1841
Place of Birth: Dighton, Bristol County, Massachusetts
Date of Death: 3 March 1916
Place of Death: North Dighton, Massachusetts
Cemetery: Westville Cemetery (MH)—Taunton, Massachusetts
Entered Service at: Taunton, Bristol County, Massachusetts
Unit: Company D, 7th Massachusetts Infantry
Battle or Place of Action: Fredericksburg, Virginia
Date of Action: 3 May 1863
Date of Issue: 28 June 1890
Citation: Among the first to jump into the enemy's rifle pits, he himself captured and brought out three prisoners.

813 ◆ LUTY, GOTLIEB

Rank: Corporal
Service: U.S. Army
Birthday: 1842
Place of Birth: Allegheny County, Pennsylvania

Date of Death: 12 July 1904
Place of Death: Allegheny, Pennsylvania
Cemetery: Uniondale Cemetery (MH)—Pittsburgh, Pennsylvania
Entered Service at: West Manchester, York County, Pennsylvania
Unit: Company A, 74th New York Infantry
Battle or Place of Action: Chancellorsville, Virginia
Date of Action: 3 May 1863
Date of Issue: 5 October 1876
Citation: Bravely advanced to the enemy's line under heavy fire and brought back valuable information.

814 ◆ LYMAN, JOEL H.

Rank: Quartermaster Sergeant (highest rank: First Lieutenant)
Service: U.S. Army
Birthday: 11 May 1845
Place of Birth: East Randolph, Cattaraugus County, New York
Date of Death: 4 May 1922
Place of Death: Randolph, New York
Cemetery: Randolph Cemetery—Randolph, New York
Entered Service at: East Randolph, Cattaraugus County, New York
Unit: Company B, 9th New York Cavalry
Battle or Place of Action: Winchester, Virginia
Date of Action: 19 September 1864
Date of Issue: 20 August 1894
Citation: In an attempt to capture a Confederate flag, he captured one of the enemy's officers and brought him within the lines.

815 ◆ LYON, FREDERICK A.

Rank: Corporal (highest rank: Sergeant)
Service: U.S. Army
Birthday: 25 June 1843
Place of Birth: Williamsburg, Hampshire County, Massachusetts
Date of Death: 23 September 1911
Place of Death: Jackson, Michigan
Cemetery: Mount Evergreen Cemetery—Jackson, Michigan
Entered Service at: Burlington, Chittenden County, Vermont
Unit: Company A, 1st Vermont Cavalry
Battle or Place of Action: Cedar Creek, Virginia
Date of Action: 19 October 1864
Date of Issue: 26 November 1864
Citation: With one companion, captured the flag of a Confederate regiment, three officers, and an ambulance with its mules and driver.

816 ◆ LYONS, THOMAS G.

Rank: Seaman
Service: U.S. Navy
Birthday: 1838

Place of Birth: Salem, Essex County, Massachusetts
Date of Death: 29 August 1904
Place of Death: Philadelphia, Pennsylvania
Cemetery: Mount Moriah Cemetery (VA plot 3-4-3) (MH)—Philadelphia, Pennsylvania
Entered Service at: Massachusetts
Unit: U.S.S. *Pensacola*
Battle or Place of Action: Forts Jackson & St. Philip, Louisiana
Date of Action: 24 April 1862
G.O. Number, Date: 169, 8 February 1872
Citation: Served as seaman on board the U.S.S. *Pensacola* in the attack on Forts Jackson and St. Philip, 24 April 1862. Carrying out his duties throughout the din and roar of the battle, Lyons never once erred in his brave performance. Lashed outside of that vessel, on the port-sheet chain, with the lead in hand to lead the ship past the forts, Lyons never flinched, although under a heavy fire from the forts and rebel gunboats.

817 ◆ MacARTHUR JR., ARTHUR

Rank: First Lieutenant & Adjutant (highest rank: Lieutenant General)
Service: U.S. Army
Birthday: 2 June 1845
Place of Birth: Springfield, Hampden County, Massachusetts
Date of Death: 5 September 1912
Cemetery: Arlington National Cemetery (2-845-A)—Arlington, Virginia
Entered Service at: Milwaukee, Milwaukee County, Wisconsin
Unit: 24th Wisconsin Infantry
Battle or Place of Action: Missionary Ridge, Tennessee
Date of Action: 25 November 1863
Date of Issue: 30 June 1890
Citation: Seized the colors of his regiment at a critical moment and planted them on the captured works on the crest of Missionary Ridge.

818 ◆ MACHON, JAMES

Rank: Boy (highest rank: Boy First Class)
Service: U.S. Navy
Birthday: 1848
Place of Birth: Derby, Derbyshire, England
Entered Service at: New York, New York
Unit: U.S.S. *Brooklyn*
Battle or Place of Action: Mobile Bay, Alabama
Date of Action: 5 August 1864
G.O. Number, Date: 45, 31 December 1864
Citation: On board the U.S.S. *Brooklyn* during successful attacks against Fort Morgan, rebel gunboats, and the ram *Tennessee* in Mobile Bay, on 5 August 1864. Stationed in the immediate vicinity of the shell whips which were twice cleared of men by bursting shells, Machon remained steadfast at his post and performed his duties in the powder division throughout the furious action which resulted in the surrender

of the prize rebel ram *Tennessee* and in the damaging and destruction of batteries at Fort Morgan.

819 ◆ MACK, ALEXANDER

Rank: Captain of the Top (highest rank: Chief Boatswain's Mate Ret.)
Service: U.S. Navy
Birthday: 17 May 1834
Place of Birth: Rotterdam, Holland
Date of Death: 25 September 1907
Place of Death: New London, Connecticut
Cemetery: Oak Grove Cemetery (MH)—Fall River, Massachusetts
Entered Service at: New York, New York
Unit: U.S.S. *Brooklyn*
Battle or Place of Action: Mobile Bay, Alabama
Date of Action: 5 August 1864
G.O. Number, Date: 45, 31 December 1864
Citation: On board the U.S.S. *Brooklyn* during successful attacks against Fort Morgan, rebel gunboats, and the ram *Tennessee* in Mobile Bay, on 5 August 1864. Although wounded and sent below for treatment, Mack immediately returned to his post, took charge of his gun, and, as heavy enemy return fire continued to fall, performed his duties with skill and courage until he was again wounded and totally disabled.

820 ◆ MACK, JOHN

True Name: Connely, Michael
Rank: Seaman
Service: U.S. Navy
Birthday: 1843
Place of Birth: Brooksville, Hancock County, Maine
Date of Death: 10 November 1881
Place of Death: Lynn, Massachusetts
Cemetery: St. Mary's Cemetery (MH)—Lynn, Massachusetts
Entered Service at: Maine
Unit: U.S.S. *Hendrick Hudson*
Battle or Place of Action: St. Marks, Florida
Date of Action: 5-6 March 1865
G.O. Number, Date: 59, 22 June 1865
Citation: As seaman on board the U.S.S. *Hendrick Hudson*, St. Marks, Fla., 5 and 6 March 1865, Mack served with the Army in charge of Navy howitzers during the attack on St. Marks and, throughout this fierce engagement, made remarkable efforts in assisting transport of the gun. His coolness and determination in courageously standing by his gun while under the fire of the enemy were a credit to the service to which he belonged.

821 ◆ MACKIE, JOHN FREEMAN

Rank: Corporal (highest rank: Orderly Sergeant)
Service: U.S. Marine Corps
Birthday: 1 October 1835
Place of Birth: New York, New York

Date of Death: 18 June 1910
Cemetery: Arlington Cemetery—Drexel Hill, Pennsylvania
Entered Service at: New York, New York
Unit: U.S.S. *Galena*
Battle or Place of Action: Fort Darling at Drewry's Bluff, Virginia
Date of Action: 15 May 1862
G.O. Number, Date: 17, 10 July 1863
Place of Presentation: Texas, off Sabine pass, on board the U.S.S. *Seminole*
Citation: On board the U.S.S. *Galena* in the attack on Fort Darling, at Drewry's Bluff, James River, on 15 May 1862. As enemy shellfire raked the deck of his ship, Cpl. Mackie fearlessly maintained his musket fire against the rifle pits along the shore and, when ordered to fill vacancies at guns caused by men wounded and killed in action, manned the weapon with skill and courage.

822 ◆ MADDEN, MICHAEL

Rank: Private
Service: U.S. Army
Birthday: 28 September 1841
Place of Birth: County Limerick, Ireland
Date of Death: 7 August 1920
Place of Death: Harrisburg, Pennsylvania
Cemetery: Mount Calvary Cemetery—Harrisburg, Pennsylvania
Entered Service at: New York, New York
Unit: Company K, 42d New York Infantry
Battle or Place of Action: Mason's Island, Maryland
Date of Action: 3 September 1861
Date of Issue: 22 March 1898
Citation: Assisted a wounded comrade to the riverbank and, under heavy fire of the enemy, swam with him across a branch of the Potomac to the Union lines.

823 ◆ MADDEN, WILLIAM

Rank: Coal Heaver
Service: U.S. Navy
Birthday: 1843
Place of Birth: Devonshire, England
Entered Service at: New York, New York
Unit: U.S.S. *Brooklyn*
Battle or Place of Action: Mobile Bay, Alabama
Date of Action: 5 August 1864
G.O. Number, Date: 45, 31 December 1864
Citation: On board the U.S.S. *Brooklyn* during the successful attacks against Fort Morgan, rebel gunboats, and the ram *Tennessee* in Mobile Bay, 5 August 1864. Stationed in the immediate vicinity of the shell whips, which were twice cleared of men by bursting shells, Madden remained steadfast at his post and performed his duties in the powder division throughout the furious action, which resulted in the surrender of the prize rebel ram *Tennessee* and in the damaging and destruction of batteries at Fort Morgan.

824 ◆ MADISON, JAMES

True Name: Congdon, James
Rank: Sergeant
Service: U.S. Army
Birthday: 1842
Place of Birth: Niagara, Niagara County, New York
Date of Death: 7 August 1926
Cemetery: San Francisco National Cemetery OS-A-7-(MH)—San Francisco, California
Entered Service at: Fairport, Monroe County, New York
Unit: Company E, 8th New York Cavalry
Battle or Place of Action: Waynesboro, Virginia
Date of Action: 2 March 1865
Date of Issue: 26 March 1865
Citation: Recapture of Gen. Crook's headquarters flag.

825 ◆ MAGEE, WILLIAM

Rank: Drummer
Service: U.S. Army
Place of Birth: Newark, Essex County, New Jersey
Entered Service at: Newark, Essex County, New Jersey
Unit: Company C, 33d New Jersey Infantry
Battle or Place of Action: Murfreesboro, Tennessee
Date of Action: 5 December 1864
Date of Issue: 7 February 1866
Citation: In a charge, Magee was among the first to reach a battery of the enemy and, with one or two others, mounted the artillery horses and took two guns into the Union lines.

826 ◆ MAHONEY, JEREMIAH

Rank: First Sergeant
Service: U.S. Army
Birthday: 1840
Date of Death: 24 November 1902
Place of Death: Boston, Massachusetts
Cemetery: Holy Cross Cemetery (MH)—Malden, Massachusetts
Entered Service at: Fall River, Bristol County, Massachusetts
Unit: Company A, 29th Massachusetts Infantry
Battle or Place of Action: Fort Sanders, Knoxville, Tennessee
Date of Action: 29 November 1863
Date of Issue: 1 December 1864
Citation: Capture of flag of 17th Mississippi Infantry (C.S.A.).

827 ◆ MANDY, HARRY J.

Rank: First Sergeant (highest rank: First Lieutenant)
Service: U.S. Army
Birthday: 2 June 1840
Place of Birth: England
Date of Death: 14 August 1904
Place of Death: Hampton, Virginia

Cemetery: Hampton National Cemetery (B-8709) (MH)—Hampton, Virginia
Entered Service at: New York, New York
Unit: Company B, 4th New York Cavalry
Battle or Place of Action: Front Royal, Virginia
Date of Action: 15 August 1864
Date of Issue: 26 August 1864
Citation: Capture of flag of 3d Virginia Infantry (C.S.A.).

828   ◆   MANGAM, RICHARD CHRISTOPHER

Rank: Private
Service: U.S. Army
Place of Birth: Ireland
Date of Death: 17 November 1893
Place of Death: Decatur, New York
Entered Service at: Auburn, Cayuga County, New York
Unit: Company H, 148th New York Infantry
Battle or Place of Action: Hatcher's Run, Virginia
Date of Action: 2 April 1865
Date of Issue: 21 September 1888
Citation: Capture of flag of 8th Mississippi Infantry (C.S.A.).

829   ◆   MANNING, JOSEPH S.

Rank: Private
Service: U.S. Army
Birthday: 13 April 1845
Place of Birth: Ipswich, Essex County, Massachusetts
Date of Death: 27 December 1905
Place of Death: Somerville, Massachusetts
Cemetery: Old North Cemetery (MH)—Ipswich, Massachusetts
Entered Service at: Boston, Suffolk County, Massachusetts
Unit: Company K, 29th Massachusetts Infantry
Battle or Place of Action: Fort Sanders, Knoxville, Tennessee
Date of Action: 29 November 1863
Date of Issue: 1 December 1864
Citation: Capture of flag of 16th Georgia Infantry (C.S.A.).

830   ◆   MARLAND, WILLIAM

Rank: First Lieutenant (highest rank: Brevet Major)
Service: U.S. Army
Birthday: 11 March 1839
Place of Birth: Andover, Essex County, Massachusetts
Date of Death: 17 April 1905
Place of Death: Griffin, Georgia
Cemetery: Oak Hill Cemetery (MH)—Griffin, Georgia
Entered Service at: Andover, Essex County, Massachusetts
Unit: 2d Independent Battery, Massachusetts Light Artillery
Battle or Place of Action: Grand Coteau, Louisiana
Date of Action: 3 November 1863
Date of Issue: 16 February 1897
Citation: After having been surrounded by the enemy's cavalry, his support having surrendered, he ordered a charge and saved the section of the battery that was under his command.

831   ◆   MARQUETTE, CHARLES D.

Rank: Sergeant
Service: U.S. Army
Birthday: 9 February 1845
Place of Birth: Lebanon County, Pennsylvania
Date of Death: 25 November 1907
Place of Death: Carlisle, Pennsylvania
Cemetery: Fairview Cemetery—Wrightsville, Pennsylvania
Entered Service at: Campbelltown, Lebanon County, Pennsylvania
Unit: Company F, 93d Pennsylvania Infantry
Battle or Place of Action: Petersburg, Virginia
Date of Action: 2 April 1865
Date of Issue: 10 May 1865
Citation: Sgt. Marquette, although wounded, was one of the first to plant colors on the enemy's breastworks.

832   ◆   MARSH, ALBERT

Rank: Sergeant
Service: U.S. Army
Birthday: 15 February 1831
Place of Birth: Randolph, Cattaraugus County, New York
Date of Death: 17 February 1895
Place of Death: Randolph, New York
Cemetery: Randolph Cemetery—Randolph, New York
Entered Service at: Randolph, Cattaraugus County, New York
Unit: Company B, 64th New York Infantry
Battle or Place of Action: Spotsylvania, Virginia
Date of Action: 12 May 1864
Date of Issue: 1 December 1864
Citation: Capture of flag.

833   ◆   MARSH, CHARLES H.

Rank: Private
Service: U.S. Army
Birthday: 1840
Place of Birth: Milford, New Haven County, Connecticut
Date of Death: 25 January 1867
Cemetery: Quaker Burying Groungs (MH)—New Milford, Connecticut
Entered Service at: New Milford, Litchfield County, Connecticut
Unit: Company D, 1st Connecticut Cavalry
Battle or Place of Action: Back Creek Valley, near North Mountain, West Virginia
Date of Action: 31 July 1864
Date of Issue: 23 January 1865
Citation: For gallantry in capturing a Black Flag and its bearer from Lt. Gen. Jubal A. Early's (C.S.A.) command, at Back Creek Valley, near North Mountain, W. Va., 31 July 1864.

834 ◆ MARSH, GEORGE

Rank: Sergeant
Service: U.S. Army
Place of Birth: Brookfield, Cook County, Illinois
Date of Death: 18 June 1915
Cemetery: Ottawa Avenue Cemetery—Ottawa, Illinois
Entered Service at: Brookfield, Cook County, Illinois
Unit: Company D, 104th Illinois Infantry
Battle or Place of Action: Elk River, Tennessee
Date of Action: 2 July 1863
Date of Issue: 17 September 1897
Citation: Voluntarily led a small party and, under a heavy fire, captured a stockade and saved the bridge.

835 ◆ MARTIN, EDWARD S.

Rank: Quartermaster
Service: U.S. Navy
Birthday: 1840
Place of Birth: Ireland
Date of Death: 23 December 1901
Place of Death: Brooklyn, New York
Cemetery: Cypress Hills National Cemetery (5766) (MH)—Brooklyn, New York
Entered Service at: Philadelphia, Philadelphia County, Pennsylvania
Unit: U.S.S. *Galena*
Battle or Place of Action: Mobile Bay, Alabama
Date of Action: 5 August 1864
G.O. Number, Date: 59, 22 June 1865
Citation: On board the U.S.S. *Galena* during the attack on enemy forts at Mobile Bay, 5 August 1864. Securely lashed to the side of the *Oneida*, which had suffered the loss of her steering apparatus and an explosion of her boiler from enemy fire, the *Galena* aided the stricken vessel past the enemy forts to safety. Despite heavy damage to his ship from raking enemy fire, Martin performed his duties with skill and courage throughout the action.

836 ◆ MARTIN, JAMES

Rank: Sergeant
Service: U.S. Marine Corps
Birthday: 1826
Place of Birth: Derry, Ireland
Date of Death: 29 October 1895
Cemetery: Mount Moriah Cemetery (VA plot 2-24-5) (MH)—Philadelphia, Pennsylvania
Entered Service at: Pennsylvania
Unit: U.S.S. *Richmond*
Battle or Place of Action: Mobile Bay, Alabama
Date of Action: 5 August 1864
G.O. Number, Date: 45, 31 December 1864
Citation: As captain of a gun on board the U.S.S. *Richmond* during action against rebel forts and gunboats and with the ram *Tennessee* in Mobile Bay, 5 August 1864. Despite damage to his ship and the loss of several men on board as enemy fire raked her decks, Sgt. Martin fought his gun with skill and

courage throughout a furious two-hour battle which resulted in the surrender of the rebel ram *Tennessee* and in the damaging and destruction of batteries at Fort Morgan.

837 ◆ MARTIN, SYLVESTER HOPKINS

Rank: Lieutenant (highest rank: Captain)
Service: U.S. Army
Birthday: 9 August 1841
Place of Birth: Chester County, Pennsylvania
Date of Death: 25 September 1927
Place of Death: Erie, Pennsylvania
Cemetery: unknown cemetery—Philadelphia, Pennsylvania
Entered Service at: Philadelphia, Philadelphia County, Pennsylvania
Unit: Company K, 88th Pennsylvania Infantry
Battle or Place of Action: Weldon Railroad, Virginia
Date of Action: 19 August 1864
Date of Issue: 5 April 1894
Citation: Gallantly made a most dangerous reconnaissance, discovering the position of the enemy and enabling the division to repulse an attack made in strong force.

838 ◆ MARTIN, WILLIAM

Rank: Seaman
Service: U.S. Navy
Birthday: 1839
Place of Birth: Ireland
Entered Service at: New York
Unit: U.S.S. *Varuna*
Battle or Place of Action: Forts Jackson and St. Philip, Louisiana
Date of Action: 24 April 1862
G.O. Number, Date: 11, 3 April 1863
Citation: Captain of a gun on board the U.S.S. *Varuna* during an attack on Forts Jackson and St. Philip, 24 April 1862. His ship was taken under furious fire by the rebel *Morgan* and severely damaged by ramming. Steadfast at his station through the thickest of the fight, Martin inflicted damage on the enemy, remaining cool and courageous although the *Varuna*, so badly damaged that she was forced to beach, was finally sunk.

839 ◆ MARTIN, WILLIAM

Rank: Boatswain's Mate (highest rank: Master's Mate)
Service: U.S. Navy
Birthday: 22 September 1835
Place of Birth: New York, New York
Date of Death: 3 April 1914
Place of Death: Alto Pass, Illinois
Cemetery: Alto Pass Cemetery, Block 14, Lot 3—Alto Pass, Illinois
Entered Service at: Cairo, Alexander County, Illinois
Unit: U.S.S. *Benton*
Battle or Place of Action: Haines Bluff, Yazoo River, Mississippi
Date of Action: 27 December 1862

G.O. Number, Date: 11, 3 April 1863
Citation: Served as boatswain's mate on board U.S.S. *Benton* during the attack on Haines Bluff, Yazoo River, 27 December 1862. Taking part in the hour-and-a-half engagement with the enemy, who had the dead-range of the vessel and was punishing her with heavy fire, Martin served courageously throughout the battle until the *Benton* was ordered to withdraw.

840 ◆ MASON, ELIHU H.

Rank: Sergeant (highest rank: Second Lieutenant)
Service: U.S. Army
Birthday: 23 March 1831
Place of Birth: Wayne County, Indiana
Date of Death: 24 September 1896
Cemetery: Pemberville Cemetery—Pemberville, Ohio
Entered Service at: Pemberville, Wood County, Ohio
Unit: Company K, 21st Ohio Infantry
Battle or Place of Action: Georgia
Date of Action: April 1862
Date of Presentation: 25 March 1863
Place of Presentation: Washington, D.C., presented by Sec. of War Edward M. Stanton
Citation: One of 19 of 24 men (including two civilians) who, by direction of Gen. Ormsby M. Mitchell, penetrated nearly 200 miles south into enemy territory and captured a railroad train at Big Shanty, Ga., in an attempt to destroy the bridges and track between Chattanooga and Atlanta.

841 ◆ MATHEWS, WILLIAM HENRY

Rank: First Sergeant (highest rank: Captain)
Service: U.S. Army
Birthday: 3 March 1844
Place of Birth: Devizes, Wiltshire, England
Date of Death: 7 February 1928
Place of Death: Brooklyn, New York
Cemetery: The Green Wood Cemetery—Brooklyn, New York
Entered Service at: Baltimore, Baltimore County, Maryland
Unit: Company E, 2d Maryland Veteran Infantry
Battle or Place of Action: Petersburg, Virginia
Date of Action: 30 July 1864
Date of Issue: 10 July 1892
Citation: Finding himself among a squad of Confederates, he fired into them, killing one, and was himself wounded, but succeeded in bringing in a sergeant and two men of the 17th South Carolina Regiment (C.S.A.) as prisoners.

842 ◆ MATTHEWS, JOHN C.

Rank: Corporal (highest rank: Sergeant)
Service: U.S. Army
Birthday: 1843
Place of Birth: Westmoreland County, Pennsylvania
Date of Death: 20 February 1924
Place of Death: Dayton, Ohio
Cemetery: Dayton National Cemetery (3-7-50) (MH)—Dayton, Ohio

Entered Service at: Greensburg, Westmoreland County, Pennsylvania
Unit: Company A, 61st Pennsylvania Infantry
Battle or Place of Action: Petersburg, Virginia
Date of Action: 2 April 1865
Date of Issue: 13 February 1891
Citation: Voluntarily took the colors, whose bearer had been disabled, and, although himself severely wounded, carried the same until the enemy's works were taken.

843 ◆ MATTHEWS, MILTON

Rank: Private
Service: U.S. Army
Place of Birth: Pittsburgh, Allegheny County, Pennsylvania
Date of Death: 11 April 1896
Place of Death: Milwaukee, Wisconsin
Cemetery: Wood National Cemetery (11-61) (MH)—Wood, Wisconsin
Entered Service at: Pittsburgh, Allegheny County, Pennsylvania
Unit: Company C, 61st Pennsylvania Infantry
Battle or Place of Action: Petersburg, Virginia
Date of Action: 2 April 1865
Date of Issue: 10 May 1865
Citation: Capture of flag of 7th Tennessee Infantry (C.S.A.).

844 ◆ MATTINGLY, HENRY B.

Rank: Private
Service: U.S. Army
Place of Birth: Marion County, Kentucky
Date of Death: 30 November 1893
Place of Death: Shepherdsville, Kentucky
Cemetery: Lebanon Junction Cemetery—Lebanon, Kentucky
Entered Service at: Lebanon, Marion County, Kentucky
Unit: Company C, 10th Kentucky Infantry
Battle or Place of Action: Jonesboro, Georgia
Date of Action: 1 September 1864
Date of Issue: 7 April 1865
Citation: Capture of flags of 6th and 7th Arkansas Infantry (C.S.A.).

845 ◆ MATTOCKS, CHARLES PORTER

Rank: Major
Service: U.S. Army
Birthday: 11 October 1840
Place of Birth: Danville, Caledonia County, Vermont
Date of Death: 16 May 1910
Cemetery: Evergreen Cemetery—Portland, Maine
Entered Service at: Portland, Cumberland County, Maine
Unit: 17th Maine Infantry
Battle or Place of Action: Deatonsville (Sailor's Creek), Virginia
Date of Action: 6 April 1865
Date of Issue: 29 March 1899

Citation: Displayed extraordinary gallantry in leading a charge of his regiment which resulted in the capture of a large number of prisoners and a stand of colors.

846 ◆ MAXHAM, LOWELL MASON

Rank: Corporal
Service: U.S. Army
Birthday: 6 December 1841
Place of Birth: Carver, Plymouth County, Massachusetts
Date of Death: 13 February 1931
Cemetery: Mayflower Hill Cemetery (MH)—Taunton, Massachusetts
Entered Service at: Taunton, Bristol County, Massachusetts
Unit: Company F, 7th Massachusetts Infantry
Battle or Place of Action: Fredericksburg, Virginia
Date of Action: 3 May 1863
Date of Issue: 24 August 1896
Citation: Though severely wounded and in the face of a deadly fire from the enemy at short-range, he rushed bravely forward and was among the first to enter the enemy's works on the crest of Marye's Heights and helped to plant his regimental colors there.

847 ◆ MAY, WILLIAM C.

Rank: Private
Service: U.S. Army
Birthday: 16 January 1826
Place of Birth: Pennsylvania
Date of Death: 21 October 1894
Place of Death: Howard Lake, Minnesota
Cemetery: Winsted Public Cemetery (MH)—Winsted, Minnesota
Entered Service at: Maysville, Franklin County, Iowa
Unit: Company H, 32d Iowa Infantry
Battle or Place of Action: Nashville, Tennessee
Date of Action: 16 December 1864
Date of Issue: 24 February 1865
Citation: Ran ahead of his regiment over the enemy's works and captured from its bearer the flag of Bonanchad's Confederate battery (C.S.A.).

848 ◆ MAYBERRY, JOHN B.

True Name: Maberry, John B.
Rank: Private (highest rank: Sergeant)
Service: U.S. Army
Birthday: 17 December 1841
Place of Birth: Smyrna, Kent County, Delaware
Date of Death: 17 December 1922
Cemetery: Glenwood Cemetery (MH)—Smyrna, Delaware
Entered Service at: Dover, Kent County, Delaware
Unit: Company F, 1st Delaware Infantry
Battle or Place of Action: Gettysburg, Pennsylvania
Date of Action: 3 July 1863
Date of Issue: 1 December 1864
Citation: Capture of flag.

849 ◆ MAYES, WILLIAM B.

Rank: Private
Service: U.S. Army
Birthday: 1838
Place of Birth: Marion County, Ohio
Date of Death: 16 August 1900
Place of Death: Los Angeles, California
Cemetery: Rosedale Cemetery—Los Angeles, California
Entered Service at: DeWitt, Clinton County, Iowa
Unit: Company K, 11th Iowa Infantry
Battle or Place of Action: near Kenesaw Mountain, Georgia
Date of Action: 15 June 1864
Date of Issue: 27 November 1899
Citation: With one companion and under a fierce fire from the enemy at short-range went to the rescue of a wounded comrade who had fallen between the lines and carried him to a place of safety.

850 ◆ MAYNARD, GEORGE HENRY

Rank: Private (highest rank: Brevet Major)
Service: U.S. Army
Birthday: 2 February 1836
Place of Birth: Waltham, Middlesex County, Massachusetts
Date of Death: 26 December 1927
Cemetery: Mount Feake Cemetery—Walthan, Massachusetts
Entered Service at: Boston, Suffolk County, Massachusetts
Unit: Company D, 13th Massachusetts Infantry
Battle or Place of Action: Fredericksburg, Virginia
Date of Action: 13 December 1862
Date of Issue: 1898
Citation: A wounded and helpless comrade, having been left on the skirmish line, this soldier voluntarily returned to the front under a severe fire and carried the wounded man to a place of safety.

851 ◆ McADAMS, PETER

Rank: Corporal (highest rank: Second Lieutenant)
Service: U.S. Army
Birthday: 21 April 1834
Place of Birth: Armagh, County Armagh, Ireland
Date of Death: 29 September 1926
Place of Death: Roxborough, Pennsylvania
Cemetery: St. John the Baptist Cemetery—Philadelphia, Pennsylvania
Entered Service at: Philadelphia, Philadelphia County, Pennsylvania
Unit: Company A, 98th Pennsylvania Infantry
Battle or Place of Action: Salem Heights, Virginia
Date of Action: 3 May 1863
Date of Issue: 1 April 1898
Citation: Went 250 yards in front of his regiment toward the position of the enemy and, under fire, brought within the lines a wounded and unconscious comrade.

852 ◆ McALWEE, BENJAMIN FRANKLIN

Rank: Sergeant (highest rank: Sergeant Major)
Service: U.S. Army
Birthday: 7 January 1838
Place of Birth: Washington, D.C.
Date of Death: 28 June 1918
Place of Death: Washington, D.C.
Cemetery: Congressional Cemetery—Washington, D.C.
Entered Service at: Baltimore, Baltimore County, Maryland
Unit: Company D, 3d Maryland Infantry
Battle or Place of Action: Petersburg, Virginia
Date of Action: 30 July 1864
Date of Issue: 4 April 1898
Citation: Picked up a shell with burning fuse and threw it over the parapet into the ditch, where it exploded; by this act he probably saved the lives of comrades at the great peril of his own.

853 ◆ McANALLY, CHARLES

Rank: Second Lieutenant (highest rank: Captain)
Service: U.S. Army
Birthday: 12 May 1836
Place of Birth: Ireland
Date of Death: 1905
Place of Death: Austin, Texas
Entered Service at: Philadelphia, Philadelphia County, Pennsylvania
Unit: Company D, 69th Pennsylvania Infantry
Battle or Place of Action: Spotsylvania, Virginia
Date of Action: 12 May 1864
Date of Issue: 2 August 1897
Citation: In a hand-to-hand encounter with the enemy captured flag, was wounded in the act, but continued on duty until he received a second wound.

854 ◆ McCAMMON, WILLIAM WALLACE

Rank: First Lieutenant (highest rank: Major Ret.)
Service: U.S. Army
Birthday: 28 May 1838
Place of Birth: Shippensburg, Cumberland County, Pennsylvania
Date of Death: 27 March 1903
Cemetery: Vancouver Barracks Post Cemetery (4-W-412) (MH)—Vancouver, Washington
Entered Service at: Montgomery City, Montgomery County, Missouri
Unit: Company E, 24th Missouri Infantry
Battle or Place of Action: Corinth, Mississippi
Date of Action: 3 October 1862
Date of Issue: 9 July 1896
Citation: While on duty as provost marshal, voluntarily assumed command of his company, then under fire, and so continued in command until the repulse and retreat of the enemy on the following day, the loss to his company during the battle being very great.

855 ◆ McCARREN, BERNARD

Rank: Private (highest rank: Corporal)
Service: U.S. Army
Birthday: 1830
Place of Birth: Ireland
Date of Death: 20 June 1870
Place of Death: Wilmington, Delaware
Cemetery: Old Cathedral Cemetery—Wilmington, Delaware
Entered Service at: Wilmimgton, New Castle County, Delaware
Unit: Company C, 1st Delaware Infantry
Battle or Place of Action: Gettysburg, Pennsylvania
Date of Action: 3 July 1863
Date of Issue: 1 December 1864
Citation: Capture of flag.

856 ◆ McCAUSLIN, JOSEPH

Rank: Private
Service: U.S. Army
Birthday: 1840
Place of Birth: Ohio County, West Virginia
Date of Death: 6 July 1906
Place of Death: West Liberty, West Virginia
Cemetery: West Alexander Cemetery—West Alexander, Pennsylvania
Entered Service at: West Liberty, Ohio County, West Virginia
Unit: Company D, 12th West Virginia Infantry
Battle or Place of Action: Petersburg, Virginia
Date of Action: 2 April 1865
Date of Issue: 12 May 1865
Citation: Conspicuous gallantry as color bearer in the assault on Fort Gregg.

857 ◆ McCLEARY, CHARLES H.

Rank: First Lieutenant (highest rank: Captain)
Service: U.S. Army
Birthday: 1842
Place of Birth: Sandusky County, Ohio
Date of Death: 23 June 1906
Cemetery: McPherson Cemetery (MH)—Clyde, Ohio
Entered Service at: Clyde, Sandusky County, Ohio
Unit: Company C, 72d Ohio Infantry
Battle or Place of Action: Nashville, Tennessee
Date of Action: 16 December 1864
Date of Issue: 24 February 1865
Citation: Capture of flag of 4th Florida Infantry (C.S.A.), while in advance of his lines.

858 ◆ McCLELLAND, JAMES M.

Rank: Private
Service: U.S. Army
Birthday: 12 August 1830

Place of Birth: Harrison County, Ohio
Date of Death: 10 April 1915
Cemetery: Riverside Cemetery (MH)—Cleveland, Ohio
Entered Service at: Ohio
Unit: Company B, 30th Ohio Infantry
Battle or Place of Action: Vicksburg, Mississippi
Date of Action: 22 May 1863
Date of Issue: 13 August 1894
Citation: Gallantry in the charge of the "volunteer storming party."

859 ◆ McCLELLAND, MATTHEW

Rank: First Class Fireman
Service: U.S. Navy
Birthday: 1833
Place of Birth: Brooklyn, Kings County, New York
Date of Death: 30 January 1883
Entered Service at: Brooklyn, Kings County, New York
Unit: U.S.S. *Richmond*
Battle or Place of Action: Port Hudson, Louisiana
Date of Action: 14 March 1863
G.O. Number, Date: 17, 10 July 1863
Citation: Served on board the U.S.S. *Richmond* in the attack on Port Hudson, 14 March 1863. Damaged by a 6-inch solid rifle shot which shattered the starboard safety-valve chamber and also damaged the port safety valve, the fireroom of the *Richmond* immediately became filled with steam to place it in an extremely critical condition. Acting courageously in this crisis, McClelland persisted in penetrating the steam-filled room in order to haul the hot fires of the furnaces and continued this gallant action until the gravity of the situation had lessened.

860 ◆ McCONNELL, SAMUEL

Rank: Captain
Service: U.S. Army
Birthday: 1 June 1830
Place of Birth: Belmont County, Ohio
Date of Death: 26 March 1915
Place of Death: Havelock, Nebraska
Cemetery: Arborville Rural Cemetery (MH)—Bradshaw, Nebraska
Entered Service at: Bushnell, McDonough County, Illinois
Unit: Company H, 119th Illinois Infantry
Battle or Place of Action: Fort Blakely, Alabama
Date of Action: 9 April 1865
Date of Issue: 8 June 1865
Citation: While leading his company in an assault, Capt. McConnell braved an intense fire that mowed down his unit. Upon reaching the breastworks, he found that he had only one member of his company with him, Pvt. Wagner. He was so close to an enemy gun that the blast knocked him down a ditch. Getting up, he entered the gun pit, the gun crew fleeing before him. About 30 paces away he saw a Confederate flag bearer and guard which he captured with the last shot in his pistol.

861 ◆ McCORMICK, MICHAEL

Rank: Boatswain's Mate
Service: U.S. Navy
Birthday: 1833
Place of Birth: Ireland
Date of Death: 19 May 1865
Place of Death: Milwaukee, Wisconsin
Entered Service at: Chicago, Cook County, Illinois
Unit: U.S.S. *Signal*
Battle or Place of Action: Red River, Louisiana
Date of Action: 5 May 1864
G.O. Number, Date: 45, 31 December 1864
Citation: Served as boatswain's mate on board the U.S.S. *Signal*, Red River, 5 May 1864. Proceeding up the Red River, the U.S.S. *Signal* engaged a large force of enemy field batteries and sharpshooters, returning the fire until the ship was totally disabled, at which time the white flag was raised. Serving as gun captain and wounded early in the battle, McCormick bravely stood by his gun in the face of the enemy fire until ordered to withdraw.

862 ◆ McCORNACK, ANDREW

Rank: Private
Service: U.S. Army
Birthday: 2 April 1844
Place of Birth: Kane, Greene County, Illinois
Date of Death: 4 May 1920
Cemetery: Hillside Cemetery (MH)—Monticello, Minnesota
Entered Service at: Rutland, La Salle County, Illinois
Unit: Company I, 127th Illinois Infantry
Battle or Place of Action: Vicksburg, Mississippi
Date of Action: 22 May 1863
Date of Issue: 10 January 1895
Citation: Gallantry in the charge of the "volunteer storming party."

863 ◆ McCULLOCK, ADAM

Rank: Seaman
Service: U.S. Navy
Birthday: 1834
Place of Birth: Maine
Entered Service at: Augusta, Kennebec County, Maine
Unit: U.S.S. *Lackawanna*
Battle or Place of Action: Mobile Bay, Alabama
Date of Action: 5 August 1864
G.O. Number, Date: 45, 31 December 1864
Citation: On board the U.S.S. *Lackawanna* during successful attacks against Fort Morgan, rebel gunboats, and the ram *Tennessee* in Mobile Bay, on 5 August 1864. Wounded when an enemy shell struck and ordered to go below, McCullock refused to leave his station and continued to perform his duties throughout the prolonged action which resulted in the capture of the prize ram *Tennessee* and in the damaging and destruction of Fort Morgan.

864 ◆ McDONALD, GEORGE E.

Rank: Private
Service: U.S. Army
Place of Birth: Warwick, Kent County, Rhode Island
Date of Death: 8 September 1897
Cemetery: Oak Grove Cemetery (MH)—Pawtucket, Rhode Island
Entered Service at: Warwick, Kent County, Rhode Island
Unit: Company L, 1st Connecticut Heavy Artillery
Battle or Place of Action: Fort Stedman, Virginia
Date of Action: 25 March 1865
Date of Issue: 21 July 1865
Citation: Capture of flag of the 26th North Carolina Infantry (C.S.A.).

865 ◆ McDONALD, JOHN

Rank: Boatswain's Mate
Service: U.S. Navy
Birthday: 1817
Place of Birth: Perth, Scotland
Entered Service at: Boston, Suffolk County, Massachusetts
Unit: U.S.S. *Baron De Kalb*
Battle or Place of Action: Yazoo River Expedition, Mississippi
Date of Action: 23-27 December 1862
G.O. Number, Date: 11, 3 April 1863
Citation: Served on board the U.S.S. *Baron De Kalb*, Yazoo River Expedition, 23 to 27 December 1862. Proceeding under orders up the Yazoo River, the U.S.S. *Baron de Kalb*, with the object of capturing or destroying the enemy's transports, came upon the steamers *John Walsh, R.J. Locklan, Golden Age*, and the *Scotland*, sunk on a bar where they were ordered burned. Continuing up the river, she was fired on but, upon returning the fire, caused the enemy's retreat. Returning down the Yazoo, she destroyed and captured large quantities of enemy equipment and several prisoners. Serving bravely throughout this action, McDonald, as boatswain's mate, "distinguished himself in the various actions."

866 ◆ McDONALD, JOHN WADE

Rank: Private
Service: U.S. Army
Birthday: 10 September 1843
Place of Birth: Lancaster, Fairfield County, Ohio
Date of Death: 27 July 1910
Place of Death: San Diego, California
Cemetery: Greenwood Memorial Park—San Diego, California
Entered Service at: Waynesville, DeWitt County, Illinois
Unit: Company E, 20th Illinois Infantry
Battle or Place of Action: Pittsburg Landing, Tennessee
Date of Action: 6 April 1862
Date of Issue: 27 August 1900
Citation: Was severely wounded while endeavoring, at the risk of his life, to carry to a place of safety a wounded and helpless comrade.

867 ◆ McELHINNY, SAMUEL O.

Rank: Private
Service: U.S. Army
Birthday: 1845
Place of Birth: Meigs County, Ohio
Date of Death: 15 May 1923
Cemetery: Pine Street Cemetery (MH)—Gallipolis, Ohio
Entered Service at: Point Pleasant, Mason County, West Virginia
Unit: Company A, 2d West Virginia Cavalry
Battle or Place of Action: Deatonsville (Sailor's Creek), Virginia
Date of Action: 6 April 1865
Date of Issue: 3 May 1865
Citation: Capture of flag.

868 ◆ McENROE, PATRICK H.

Rank: Sergeant
Service: U.S. Army
Place of Birth: Ireland
Entered Service at: Schodack, Rensselaer County, New York
Unit: Company D, 6th New York Cavalry
Battle or Place of Action: Winchester, Virginia
Date of Action: 19 September 1864
Date of Issue: 19 September 1864
Citation: Capture of colors of 36th Virginia Infantry (C.S.A.).

869 ◆ McFALL, DANIEL ROBERT

Rank: Sergeant
Service: U.S. Army
Birthday: 1836
Place of Birth: Niagara County, New York
Date of Death: 5 November 1919
Place of Death: Milan, Missouri
Cemetery: Rice Cemetery—Dundee, Illinois
Entered Service at: Ypsilanti, Washtenaw County, Michigan
Unit: Company E, 17th Michigan Infantry
Battle or Place of Action: Spotsylvania, Virginia
Date of Action: 12 May 1864
Date of Issue: 27 July 1896
Citation: Captured Col. Barker, commanding the Confederate brigade that charged the Union batteries; on the same day rescued Lt. George W. Harmon of his regiment from the enemy.

870 ◆ McFARLAND, JOHN C.

Rank: Captain of the Forecastle
Service: U.S. Navy
Birthday: 1840
Place of Birth: Boston, Suffolk County, Massachusetts
Date of Death: 3 October 1881

Place of Death: Lowell, Massachusetts
Cemetery: St. Patrick's Cemetery (MH)—Lowell, Massachusetts
Entered Service at: Boston, Suffolk County, Massachusetts
Unit: U.S.S. *Hartford*
Battle or Place of Action: Mobile Bay, Alabama
Date of Action: 5 August 1864
G.O. Number, Date: 45, 31 December 1864
Citation: Stationed at the wheel on board the flagship U.S.S. *Hartford* during successful actions against Fort Morgan, rebel gunboats, and the ram *Tennessee* in Mobile Bay, 5 August 1864. With his ship under terrific enemy shellfire, McFarland performed his duties with skill and courage and, when the *Lackawanna* ran into his ship and every man at the wheel was in danger of being crushed, remained steadfast at his station and continued to steer his ship.

871 ◆ McGINN, EDWARD

Rank: Private (highest rank: First Lieutenant)
Service: U.S. Army
Birthday: 20 November 1843
Place of Birth: New York, New York
Date of Death: 28 September 1908
Place of Death: Milwaukee, Wisconsin
Cemetery: Calvary Cemetery (MH)—Milwaukee, Wisconsin
Entered Service at: Cincinnati, Hamilton County, Ohio
Unit: Company F, 54th Ohio Infantry
Battle or Place of Action: Vicksburg, Mississippi
Date of Action: 22 May 1863
Date of Issue: 28 June 1894
Citation: Gallantry in the charge of the "volunteer storming party."

872 ◆ McGONAGLE, WILSON

Rank: Private
Service: U.S. Army
Birthday: 9 August 1838
Place of Birth: Jefferson County, Ohio
Date of Death: 15 September 1912
Place of Death: Dayton (Soldier's Home), Ohio
Cemetery: unknown cemetery—Saxonburg, Pennsylvania
Entered Service at: Cadiz, Harrison County, Ohio
Unit: Company B, 30th Ohio Infantry
Battle or Place of Action: Vicksburg, Mississippi
Date of Action: 22 May 1863
Date of Issue: 15 August 1894
Citation: Gallantry in the charge of the "volunteer storming party."

873 ◆ McGONNIGLE, ANDREW JACKSON

Rank: Captain & Assistant Quartermaster (highest rank: Colonel)
Service: U.S. Army
Birthday: 4 March 1829
Place of Birth: New York, New York
Date of Death: 25 January 1901

Place of Death: Ashville, North Carolina
Cemetery: Riverside Cemetery (MH)—Ashville, North Carolina
Entered Service at: Cumberland, Allegany County, Maryland
Unit: U.S. Volunteers
Battle or Place of Action: Cedar Creek, Virginia
Date of Action: 19 October 1864
Date of Issue: 21 July 1897
Citation: While acting as chief quartermaster of Gen. Sheridan's forces operating in the Shenandoah Valley, McGonnigle was severely wounded while voluntarily leading a brigade of infantry and was commended for the greatest gallantry by Gen. Sheridan.

874 ◆ McGOUGH, OWEN

Rank: Corporal
Service: U.S. Army
Birthday: 29 June 1829
Place of Birth: Monaghan, Ireland
Date of Death: 5 January 1908
Place of Death: Troy, New York
Cemetery: St. Peter's Cemetery—Troy, New York
Entered Service at: Cornwall, Orange County, New York
Unit: Battery D, 5th U.S. Artillery
Battle or Place of Action: Bull Run, Virginia
Date of Action: 21 July 1861
Date of Issue: 28 August 1897
Citation: Through his personal exertions under a heavy fire, one of the guns of his battery was brought off the field; all the other guns were lost.

875 ◆ McGOWAN, JOHN

Rank: Quartermaster
Service: U.S. Navy
Birthday: 1831
Place of Birth: Ireland
Entered Service at: New York, New York
Unit: U.S.S. *Varuna*
Battle or Place of Action: Forts Jackson and St. Philip, Louisiana
Date of Action: 24 April 1864
G.O. Number, Date: 11, 3 April 1863
Citation: McGowan occupied one of the most responsible positions in the U.S.S. *Varuna*, during the attacks on Forts Jackson and St. Philip and in action against the rebel ship *Morgan*, 24 April 1862. Although guns were raking the decks from behind him, McGowan remained steadfast at the wheel throughout the thickest of the fight, continuing at his station and rendering service with the greatest courage and skill until his ship, repeatedly holed and twice rammed by the enemy, was beached and sunk.

876 ◆ McGRAW, THOMAS

Rank: Sergeant
Service: U.S. Army

Birthday: 1834
Place of Birth: Ireland
Date of Death: 1899
Cemetery: LaCrosse City Cemetery (MH)—LaCrosse, Kansas
Entered Service at: Chicago, Cook County, Illinois
Unit: Company B, 23d Illinois Infantry
Battle or Place of Action: Petersburg, Virginia
Date of Action: 2 April 1865
Date of Issue: 12 May 1865
Citation: One of the three soldiers most conspicuous for gallantry in the final assault.

877 ◆ McGUIRE, PATRICK

Rank: Private
Service: U.S. Army
Birthday: 1840
Place of Birth: Ireland
Date of Death: 8 September 1898
Place of Death: Chicago, Illinois
Cemetery: Calvary Cemetery—Evanston, Illinois
Entered Service at: Chicago, Cook County, Illinois
Unit: Chicago Mercantile Battery, Illinois Light Artillery
Battle or Place of Action: Vicksburg, Mississippi
Date of Action: 22 May 1863
Date of Issue: 15 January 1895
Citation: Carried with others by hand a cannon up to and fired it through the embrasure of the enemy's works.

878 ◆ McHALE, ALEXANDER U.

Rank: Corporal (highest rank: Sergeant)
Service: U.S. Army
Birthday: 16 March 1837
Place of Birth: Ireland
Date of Death: 13 March 1911
Cemetery: Lake View Cemetery—Seattle, Washington
Entered Service at: Muskegon, Muskegon County, Michigan
Unit: Company H, 26th Michigan Infantry
Battle or Place of Action: Spotsylvania Courthouse, Virginia
Date of Action: 12 May 1864
Date of Issue: 11 January 1900
Citation: Captured a Confederate color in a charge, threw the flag over in front of the works, and continued in the charge upon the enemy.

879 ◆ McHUGH, MARTIN

Rank: Seaman
Service: U.S. Navy
Birthday: 1837
Place of Birth: Cincinnati, Hamilton County, Ohio
Entered Service at: Ohio
Unit: U.S.S. *Cincinnati*
Battle or Place of Action: Vicksburg, Mississippi
Date of Action: 27 May 1863
G.O. Number, Date: 17, 10 July 1863
Citation: Served on board the U.S.S. *Cincinnati* during the attack on the Vicksburg batteries and at the time of her sinking, 27 May 1863. Engaging the enemy in a fierce battle, the *Cincinnati*, amidst an incessant fire of shot and shell, continued to fire her guns to the last, though so penetrated by shellfire that her fate was sealed. Serving bravely during this action, McHugh was conspicuously cool under the fire of the enemy, never ceasing to fire until this proud ship went down, "her colors nailed to the mast."

880 ◆ McINTOSH, JAMES

Rank: Captain of the Top
Service: U.S. Navy
Birthday: 17 November 1829
Place of Birth: Canada
Date of Death: 28 May 1908
Place of Death: Kearney, New Jersey
Cemetery: Arlington Cemetery—Kearney, New Jersey
Entered Service at: New York, New York
Unit: U.S.S. *Richmond*
Battle or Place of Action: Mobile Bay, Alabama
Date of Action: 5 August 1864
G.O. Number, Date: 45, 31 December 1864
Citation: On board the U.S.S. *Richmond* during action against rebel forts and gunboats and with the ram *Tennessee* in Mobile Bay, 5 August 1864. Despite damage to his ship and the loss of several men on board as enemy fire raked her decks, McIntosh performed his duties with skill and courage throughout the prolonged battle, which resulted in the surrender of the rebel ram *Tennessee* and in the successful attacks carried out on Fort Morgan.

881 ◆ McKAY, CHARLES W.

Rank: Sergeant (highest rank: Captain)
Service: U.S. Army
Birthday: 25 January 1847
Place of Birth: Mansfield, Cattaraugus County, New York
Date of Death: 25 August 1912
Place of Death: Staples, Minnesota
Cemetery: Oak Grove Cemetery—Fergus Falls, Minnesota
Entered Service at: Allegany, Cattaraugus County, New York
Unit: Company C, 154th New York Infantry
Battle or Place of Action: Dug Gap, Georgia
Date of Action: 8 May 1864
Date of Issue: 13 April 1894
Citation: Voluntarily risked his life in rescuing under the fire of the enemy a wounded comrade who was lying between the lines.

882 ◆ McKEE, GEORGE

Rank: Color Sergeant
Service: U.S. Army
Birthday: 1845
Place of Birth: County Tyrone, Ireland
Date of Death: 8 July 1892

Place of Death: Sawtella, California
Cemetery: Los Angeles National Cemetery (1-6-2) (MH)—Los Angeles, California
Entered Service at: Rochester, Monroe County, New York
Unit: Company D, 89th New York Infantry
Battle or Place of Action: Petersburg, Virginia
Date of Action: 2 April 1865
Date of Issue: 12 May 1865
Citation: Gallantry as color bearer in the assault on Fort Gregg.
Notes: POW

883 ◆ McKEEN, NINEVEH S.

Rank: First Lieutenant (highest rank: Brevet Major)
Service: U.S. Army
Place of Birth: Marshall, Clark County, Illinois
Date of Death: 22 December 1890
Place of Death: Collinsville, Illinois
Cemetery: Greenwood Cemetery (MH)—Collinsville, Illinois
Entered Service at: Marshall, Clark County, Illinois
Unit: Company H, 21st Illinois Infantry
Battle or Place of Action: Stone River & Liberty Gap, Tennessee
Date of Action: 30 December 1862 & 25 June 1863
Date of Issue: 23 June 1890
Citation: Conspicuous in the charge at Stone River, Tenn., where he was three times wounded. At Liberty Gap, Tenn., captured colors of 8th Arkansas Infantry (C.S.A.).

884 ◆ McKEEVER, MICHAEL

Rank: Private (highest rank: First Sergeant)
Service: U.S. Army
Birthday: 25 March 1842
Place of Birth: Ireland
Date of Death: 24 December 1916
Place of Death: Philadelphia, Pennsylvania
Cemetery: Holy Sepulchre Cemetery—Philadelphia, Pennsylvania
Entered Service at: Philadelphia, Philadelphia County, Pennsylvania
Unit: Company K, 5th Pennsylvania Cavalry
Battle or Place of Action: Burnt Ordinary, Virginia
Date of Action: 19 January 1863
Date of Issue: 2 August 1897
Citation: Was one of a small scouting party that charged and routed a mounted force of the enemy six times their number. He led the charge in a most gallant and distinguished manner, going far beyond the call of duty.

885 ◆ McKNIGHT, WILLIAM

Rank: Coxswain (highest rank: Master's Mate)
Service: U.S. Navy
Birthday: 3 May 1842
Place of Birth: Ulster County, New York
Date of Death: 4 November 1914

Place of Death: Woodhaven, New York
Cemetery: The Green Wood Cemetery—Brooklyn, New York
Entered Service at: New York, New York
Unit: U.S.S. *Varuna*
Battle or Place of Action: Forts Jackson & St. Philip, Louisiana
Date of Action: 24 April 1862
G.O. Number, Date: 11, 3 April 1863
Citation: Captain of a gun on board the U.S.S. *Varuna* during the attacks on Forts Jackson and St. Philip and in action against the rebel ship *Morgan*, 24 April 1862. During this action at extremely close-range, while the ship was under furious fire and was twice rammed by the rebel ship *Morgan*, McKnight remained steadfast at his gun throughout the thickest of the fight and was instrumental in inflicting damage on the enemy until the *Varuna*, so badly damaged that she was forced to beach, was finally sunk.

886 ◆ McKOWN, NATHANIEL A.

Rank: Sergeant (highest rank: First Lieutenant)
Service: U.S. Army
Birthday: 11 March 1838
Place of Birth: Susquehanna County, Pennsylvania
Date of Death: 11 August 1902
Cemetery: Sunnyside Cemetery—Tunkhannock, Pennsylvania
Entered Service at: Philadelphia, Philadelphia County, Pennsylvania
Unit: Company B, 58th Pennsylvania Infantry
Battle or Place of Action: Chapin's Farm, Virginia
Date of Action: 29 September 1864
Date of Issue: 6 April 1865
Citation: Capture of flag.

887 ◆ McLEOD, JAMES

Rank: Captain of the Foretop
Service: U.S. Navy
Place of Birth: Scotland
Entered Service at: Maine
Unit: U.S.S. *Pensacola*
Battle or Place of Action: Forts Jackson & St. Philip and New Orleans, Louisiana
Date of Action: 24-25 April 1862
G.O. Number, Date: 11, 3 April 1863
Citation: Captain of the foretop, and a volunteer from the *Colorado*, McLeod served on board the U.S.S. *Pensacola* during the attack on Forts Jackson and St. Philip and the taking of New Orleans, 24 and 25 April 1862. Acting as gun captain of the rifled howitzer aft, which was much exposed, he served this piece with great ability and activity, although no officer superintended it.

888 ◆ McMAHON, MARTIN THOMAS

Rank: Captain & Aide-de-Camp (highest rank: Brevet Major General)

Service: U.S. Army
Birthday: 21 March 1838
Place of Birth: LaPrairie, Quebec, Canada
Date of Death: 21 April 1906
Place of Death: New York, New York
Cemetery: Arlington National Cemetery (2-1101)—Arlington, Virginia
Entered Service at: California
Unit: U.S. Volunteers
Battle or Place of Action: White Oak Swamp, Virginia
Date of Action: 30 June 1862
Date of Issue: 10 March 1891
Citation: Under fire of the enemy, successfully destroyed a valuable train that had been abandoned and prevented it from falling into the hands of the enemy.

889 ◆ McMILLEN, FRANCIS M.

Rank: Sergeant (highest rank: Sergeant Major)
Service: U.S. Army
Birthday: 25 March 1832
Place of Birth: Bracken County, Kentucky
Date of Death: 8 March 1913
Place of Death: Dayton, Ohio
Cemetery: Washington Cemetery (MH)—Washington Courthouse, Ohio
Entered Service at: Piqua, Miami County, Ohio
Unit: Company C, 110th Ohio Infantry
Battle or Place of Action: Petersburg, Virginia
Date of Action: 2 April 1865
Date of Issue: 10 May 1865
Citation: Capture of flag.

890 ◆ *McVEANE, JOHN P.

True Name: McVean, John P.
Rank: Corporal
Service: U.S. Army
Birthday: 1842
Place of Birth: Toronto, Canada
Date of Death: 10 May 1864
Place of Death: Wilderness, Virginia
Cemetery: Forest Lawn Cemetery (MH)—Buffalo, New York
Entered Service at: Buffalo, Erie County, New York
Unit: Company D, 49th New York Infantry
Battle or Place of Action: Fredericksburg Heights, Virginia
Date of Action: 4 May 1863
Date of Issue: 21 September 1870
Citation: Shot a Confederate color bearer and seized the flag; also approached, alone, a barn between the lines and demanded and received the surrender of a number of the enemy therein.

891 ◆ McWHORTER, WALTER F.

Rank: Commissary Sergeant
Service: U.S. Army
Birthday: 14 July 1836
Place of Birth: Lewis County, West Virginia

Date of Death: 17 May 1877
Place of Death: New Milton, West Virginia
Cemetery: Greenbrier (S.B.O.) Cemetery—Nina, West Virginia
Entered Service at: Clarksburg, Harrison County, West Virginia
Unit: Company E, 3d West Virginia Cavalry
Battle or Place of Action: Deatonsville (Sailor's Creek), Virginia
Date of Action: 6 April 1865
Date of Issue: 3 May 1865
Citation: Capture of flag of 6th Tennessee Infantry (C.S.A.).

892 ◆ McWILLIAMS, GEORGE WASHINGTON

Rank: Landsman
Service: U.S. Navy
Birthday: 1844
Place of Birth: Waterford, Erie County, Pennsylvania
Date of Death: 11 August 1900
Place of Death: Ida Grove, Iowa
Cemetery: Ida Grove Cemetery—Ida Grove, Iowa
Entered Service at: Pennsylvania
Unit: U.S.S. *Pontoosuc*
Battle or Place of Action: Fort Fisher & Wilmington, North Carolina
Date of Action: 24 December 1864—22 February 1865
G.O. Number, Date: 59, 22 June 1865
Citation: Served on board the U.S.S. *Pontoosuc* during the capture of Fort Fisher and Wilmington, 24 December 1864 to 22 February 1865. Carrying out his duties faithfully throughout this period, McWilliams was so severely wounded in the assault upon Fort Fisher that he was sent to the hospital at Portsmouth, Va. McWilliams was recommended for his gallantry, skill, and coolness in action while under the fire of the enemy.

893 ◆ MEACH, GEORGE E.

Rank: Farrier (highest rank: Sergeant)
Service: U.S. Army
Birthday: 1844
Place of Birth: New York
Date of Death: 21 March 1873
Cemetery: Pine Grove Cemetery (MH)—Fillmore, New York
Entered Service at: New York, New York
Unit: Company I, 6th New York Cavalry
Battle or Place of Action: Winchester, Virginia
Date of Action: 19 September 1864
Date of Issue: 27 September 1864
Citation: Capture of flag.

894 ◆ MEAGHER, THOMAS

True Name: Marr, Thomas W.
Rank: First Sergeant (highest rank: Brevet First Lieutenant NY Volunteers)

Service: U.S. Army
Birthday: 1842
Place of Birth: Scotland
Date of Death: 16 January 1890
Place of Death: Brooklyn, New York
Cemetery: Holy Cross Cemetery—Brooklyn, New York
Entered Service at: Brooklyn, Kings County, New York
Unit: Company G, 158th New York Infantry
Battle or Place of Action: Chapin's Farm, Virginia
Date of Action: 29 September 1864
Date of Issue: 6 April 1865
Citation: Led a section of his men on the enemy's works, receiving a wound while scaling a parapet.

895 ◆ MEARS, GEORGE W.

Rank: Sergeant
Service: U.S. Army
Birthday: 3 January 1843
Place of Birth: Bloomsburg, Columbia County, Pennsylvania
Date of Death: 24 November 1921
Place of Death: Bloomsburg, Pennsylvania
Cemetery: Old Rosemont Cemetery—Bloomsburg, Pennsylvania
Entered Service at: Bloomsburg, Columbia County, Pennsylvania
Unit: Company A, 6th Pennsylvania Reserves
Battle or Place of Action: Gettysburg, Pennsylvania
Date of Action: 2 July 1863
Date of Issue: 16 February 1897
Citation: With five volunteers he gallantly charged on a number of the enemy's sharpshooters concealed in a log house, captured them, and brought them into the Union lines.

896 ◆ MELVILLE, CHARLES

True Name: Ramsbottom, James
Rank: Ordinary Seaman
Service: U.S. Navy
Birthday: 1828
Place of Birth: Dover, Strafford County, New Hampshire
Date of Death: 5 January 1867
Cemetery: Family Cemetery, Old Dover Road (SR-16B) (MH)—Rochester, New Hampshire
Entered Service at: New Hampshire
Unit: U.S.S. *Hartford*
Battle or Place of Action: Mobile Bay, Alabama
Date of Action: 5 August 1864
G.O. Number, Date: 45, 31 December 1864
Citation: On board the flagship U.S.S. *Hartford* during action against rebel gunboats, the ram *Tennessee*, and Fort Morgan in Mobile Bay, 5 August 1864. Wounded and taken below to the surgeon when a shell burst between the two forward 9-inch guns, killing and wounding 15 men, Melville promptly returned to his gun on the deck and, although scarcely able to stand, refused to go below and continued to man his post throughout the remainder of the action resulting in the capture of the rebel ram *Tennessee*.

897 ◆ MENTER, JOHN WILLIAM

Rank: Sergeant
Service: U.S. Army
Birthday: 7 September 1840
Place of Birth: Palmer, New York
Date of Death: 18 April 1925
Place of Death: Ovid, Michigan
Entered Service at: Detroit, Wayne County, Michigan
Unit: Company D, 5th Michigan Infantry
Battle or Place of Action: Deatonsville (Sailor's Creek), Virginia
Date of Action: 6 April 1865
Date of Issue: 10 May 1865
Citation: Capture of flag.

898 ◆ MERRIAM, HENRY CLAY

Rank: Lieutenant Colonel (highest rank: Major General)
Service: U.S. Army
Birthday: 13 November 1837
Place of Birth: Houlton, Aroostook County, Maine
Date of Death: 18 November 1912
Cemetery: Arlington National Cemetery (1-114-13) (MH)—Arlington, Virginia
Entered Service at: Houlton, Aroostook County, Maine
Unit: 73d U.S. Colored Infantry
Battle or Place of Action: Fort Blakely, Alabama
Date of Action: 9 April 1865
Date of Issue: 28 June 1894
Citation: Volunteered to attack the enemy's works in advance of orders and, upon permission being given, made a most gallant assault.

899 ◆ MERRIFIELD, JAMES K.

Rank: Corporal
Service: U.S. Army
Birthday: 20 August 1844
Place of Birth: Hyde Park, Westmoreland County, Pennsylvania
Date of Death: 7 September 1918
Place of Death: St. Louis, Missouri
Cemetery: Valhalla Cemetery—St. Louis, Missouri
Entered Service at: Manlius, Bureau County, Illinois
Unit: Company C, 88th Illinois Infantry
Battle or Place of Action: Franklin, Tennessee
Date of Action: 30 November 1864
Date of Issue: 28 March 1896
Citation: Captured two battle flags from the enemy and returned with them to his own lines.

900 ◆ MERRILL, AUGUSTUS

Rank: Captain
Service: U.S. Army
Birthday: 4 October 1843
Place of Birth: Byron, Maine
Date of Death: 14 November 1895

Place of Death: Eagle Rock, California
Cemetery: Graceland Cemetery—Chicago, Illinois
Entered Service at: Lyndon, Maine
Unit: Company B, 1st Maine Veteran Infantry
Battle or Place of Action: Petersburg, Virginia
Date of Action: 2 April 1865
Date of Issue: 23 October 1891
Citation: With six men, captured 69 Confederate prisoners and recaptured several soldiers who had fallen into the enemy's hands.

901 ◆ MERRILL, GEORGE

Rank: Private
Service: U.S. Army
Birthday: 11 February 1847
Place of Birth: Queensberry, Warren County, New York
Date of Death: 29 August 1925
Place of Death: Glens Falls, New York
Cemetery: Glens Falls Cemetery—Glens Falls, New York
Entered Service at: Moreau, New York
Unit: Company I, 142d New York Infantry
Battle or Place of Action: Fort Fisher, North Carolina
Date of Action: 15 January 1865
Date of Issue: 28 December 1914
Citation: Voluntarily advanced with the head of the column and cut down the palisading.

902 ◆ MERRITT, JOHN G.

Rank: Sergeant
Service: U.S. Army
Birthday: 31 October 1837
Place of Birth: New York, New York
Date of Death: 17 December 1892
Place of Death: Washington, D.C.
Cemetery: Congressional Cemetery—Washington, D.C.
Entered Service at: Fort Snelling, St. Paul County, Minnesota
Unit: Company K, 1st Minnesota Infantry
Battle or Place of Action: Bull Run, Virginia
Date of Action: 21 July 1861
Date of Issue: 1 April 1880
Citation: Gallantry in action; was wounded while capturing flag in advance of his regiment.

903 ◆ MEYER, HENRY CODDINGTON

Rank: Captain (highest rank: Brevet Major NY Volunteers)
Service: U.S. Army
Birthday: 14 April 1844
Place of Birth: Hamburg, Erie County, New York
Date of Death: 27 March 1935
Place of Death: Montclair, New Jersey
Cemetery: Rosedale Cemetery (MH)—Orange, New Jersey
Entered Service at: Dobbs Ferry, Westchester County, New York
Unit: Company D, 24th New York Cavalry
Battle or Place of Action: Petersburg, Virginia

Date of Action: 17 June 1864
Date of Issue: 29 March 1899
Citation: During an assault and in the face of a heavy fire rendered heroic assistance to a wounded and helpless officer, thereby saving his life and in the performance of this gallant act sustained a severe wound.

904 ◆ MIFFLIN, JAMES

Rank: Engineer's Cook
Service: U.S. Navy
Birthday: 1839
Place of Birth: Richmond, Richmond County, Virginia
Entered Service at: Virginia
Unit: U.S.S. *Brooklyn*
Battle or Place of Action: Mobile Bay, Alabama
Date of Action: 5 August 1864
G.O. Number, Date: 45, 31 December 1864
Citation: On board the U.S.S. *Brooklyn* during successful attacks against Fort Morgan, rebel gunboats, and the ram *Tennessee* in Mobile Bay, 5 August 1864. Stationed in the immediate vicinity of the shell whips, which were twice cleared of men by bursting shells, Mifflin remained steadfast at his post and performed his duties in the powder division throughout the furious action which resulted in the surrender of the prize ram *Tennessee* and in the damaging and destruction of batteries at Fort Morgan.

905 ◆ MILES, NELSON APPLETON

Rank: Colonel (highest rank: Lieutenant General Ret.)
Service: U.S. Army
Birthday: 8 August 1839
Place of Birth: Westminster, Worcester County, Massachusetts
Date of Death: 15 May 1925
Place of Death: Washington, D.C.
Cemetery: Arlington National Cemetery (3-1873) (MH)—Arlington, Virginia
Entered Service at: Roxbury, Suffolk County, Massachusetts
Unit: 61st New York Infantry
Battle or Place of Action: Chancellorsville, Virginia
Date of Action: 2-3 May 1863
Date of Issue: 23 July 1892
Citation: Distinguished gallantry while holding with his command an advanced position against repeated assaults by a strong force of the enemy; was severely wounded.

906 ◆ MILLER, ANDREW

Rank: Sergeant
Service: U.S. Marine Corps
Birthday: 1836
Place of Birth: Germany
Entered Service at: Washington, D.C.
Unit: U.S.S. *Richmond*
Battle or Place of Action: Mobile Bay, Alabama
Date of Action: 5 August 1864
G.O. Number, Date: 45, 31 December 1864

Citation: As a captain of a gun on board the U.S.S. *Richmond* during action against rebel forts and gunboats and with the ram *Tennessee* in Mobile Bay, 5 August 1864. Despite damage to his ship and the loss of several men on board as enemy fire raked her desks, Sgt. Miller fought his gun with skill and courage throughout the furious two-hour battle which resulted in the surrender of the rebel ram *Tennessee* and in the damaging and destruction of batteries at Fort Morgan.

907 ◆ MILLER, FRANK

Rank: Private
Service: U.S. Army
Birthday: 1848
Place of Birth: New York
Date of Death: 12 September 1903
Place of Death: San Francisco, California
Cemetery: unknown cemetery—San Francisco, California
Entered Service at: Jamaica, Queens County, New York
Unit: Company M, 2d New York Cavalry
Battle or Place of Action: Deatonsville (Sailor's Creek), Virginia
Date of Action: 6 April 1865
Date of Issue: 24 April 1865
Citation: Capture of flag of 25th Battalion Virginia Infantry (C.S.A.); was taken prisoner, but successfully retained his trophy until recaptured.

908 ◆ MILLER, HENRY AUGUST

Rank: Captain
Service: U.S. Army
Birthday: 22 March 1839
Place of Birth: Germany
te of Death: 12 June 1919
Place of Death: Urbana, Illinois
Cemetery: Mount Hope Cemetery—Champaign, Illinois
Entered Service at: Decatur, Macon County, Illinois
Unit: Company B, 8th Illinois Infantry
Battle or Place of Action: Fort Blakely, Alabama
Date of Action: 9 April 1865
Date of Issue: 8 June 1865
Citation: Capture of flag.

909 ◆ MILLER, JACOB C.

Rank: Private (highest rank: Sergeant)
Service: U.S. Army
Birthday: 4 August 1840
Place of Birth: Bellevue, Huron County, Ohio
Date of Death: 13 January 1917
Place of Death: Omaha, Nebraska
Cemetery: Cedar Dale Cemetery (MH)—Papillon, Nebraska
Entered Service at: Elgin, Kane County, Illinois
Unit: Company G, 113th Illinois Infantry
Battle or Place of Action: Vicksburg, Mississippi
Date of Action: 22 May 1863

Date of Issue: 20 August 1894
Citation: Gallantry in the charge of the "volunteer storming party."

910 ◆ MILLER, JAMES

Rank: Quartermaster (highest rank: Acting Master's Mate)
Service: U.S. Navy
Birthday: 21 September 1836
Place of Birth: Denmark
Date of Death: 4 March 1914
Place of Death: Philadelphia, Pennsylvania
Cemetery: unknown cemetery—Philadelphia, Pennsylvania
Entered Service at: Boston, Suffolk County, Massachusetts
Unit: U.S. Steam Gunboat *Marblehead*
Battle or Place of Action: off Legareville, John's Island, Stono River, South Carolina
Date of Action: 25 December 1863
G.O. Number, Date: 32, 16 April 1864
Date of Presentation: July 1864
Place of Presentation: Presented by Rear Adm. John A. Dahlgren on his flagship
Citation: Served as quartermaster on board the U.S. steam gunboat *Marblehead* off Legareville, Stono River, 25 December 1863, during an engagement with the enemy on John's Island. Acting courageously under the fierce hostile fire, Miller behaved gallantly throughout the engagement, which resulted in the enemy's withdrawal and abandonment of his arms.

911 ◆ MILLER, JAMES P.

Rank: Private
Service: U.S. Army
Birthday: 29 April 1834
Place of Birth: Franklin, Warren County, Ohio
Date of Death: 2 July 1918
Cemetery: Greenwood Cemetery (MH)—York, Nebraska
Entered Service at: Henry County, Iowa
Unit: Company D, 4th Iowa Cavalry
Battle or Place of Action: Selma, Alabama
Date of Action: 2 April 1865
Date of Issue: 17 June 1865
Citation: Capture of standard of 12th Mississippi Cavalry (C.S.A.).

912 ◆ MILLER, JOHN

True Name: Fey, Henry
Rank: Private
Service: U.S. Army
Birthday: 1839
Place of Birth: Kurhessen, Germany
Date of Death: 8 March 1882
Place of Death: Philadelphia, Pennsylvania
Cemetery: Glenwood Memorial Gardens Cemetery—Broomall, Pennsylvania
Entered Service at: Rochester, Monroe County, New York
Unit: Company H, 8th New York Cavalry

Battle or Place of Action: Waynesboro, Virginia
Date of Action: 2 March 1865
Date of Issue: 26 March 1865
Citation: Capture of flag.

913 ◆ MILLER, JOHN G.

Rank: Corporal (highest rank: Sergeant)
Service: U.S. Army
Birthday: 1841
Place of Birth: Germany
Date of Death: 11 June 1909
Place of Death: Freemont, Ohio
Cemetery: St. Mary's Cemetery—Champaign, Illinois
Entered Service at: Camp Dennison, Hamilton County, Ohio
Unit: Company G, 8th Ohio Infantry
Battle or Place of Action: Gettysburg, Pennsylvania
Date of Action: 3 July 1863
Date of Issue: 1 December 1864
Citation: Capture of two flags.

914 ◆ MILLER, WILLIAM EDWARD

Rank: Captain
Service: U.S. Army
Birthday: 5 February 1836
Place of Birth: West Hill, Cumberland County, Pennsylvania
Date of Death: 10 December 1919
Cemetery: Gettysburg National Military Park (OFF-8) (MH) —Gettysburg, Pennsylvania
Entered Service at: Newville, Cumberland County, Pennsylvania
Unit: Company H, 3d Pennsylvania Cavalry
Battle or Place of Action: Gettysburg, Pennsylvania
Date of Action: 3 July 1863
Date of Issue: 21 July 1897
Citation: Without orders, led a charge of his squadron upon the flank of the enemy, checked his attack, and cut off and dispersed the rear of his column.

915 ◆ MILLIKEN, DANIEL

Rank: Quarter Gunner
Service: U.S. Navy
Birthday: 1838
Place of Birth: Saco, York County, Maine
Entered Service at: New York, New York
Unit: U.S.S. *New Ironsides*
Battle or Place of Action: Fort Fisher, North Carolina
Date of Action: 24-25 December 1864 & 13-15 January 1865
G.O. Number, Date: 59, 22 June 1865
Citation: Milliken served on board the U.S.S. *New Ironsides* during the action in several attacks on Fort Fisher, 24 and 25 December 1864; and 13, 14 and 15 January 1865. The ship steamed in and took the lead in the ironclad division close inshore and immediately opened its starboard battery in a bar-

rage of well-directed fire to cause several fires and explosions and dismount several guns during the first two days of fighting. Taken under fire as she steamed into position on 13 January, the *New Ironsides* fought all day and took on ammunition at night despite severe weather conditions. When the enemy came out of his bombproofs to defend the fort against the storming party, the ship's battery disabled nearly every gun on the fort facing the shore before the cease-fire orders were given by the flagship.

916 ◆ MILLS, CHARLES

Rank: Seaman
Service: U.S. Navy
Birthday: September 1840
Place of Birth: Ulster, Ulster County, New York
Entered Service at: Brooklyn, Kings County, New York
Unit: U.S.S. *Minnesota*
Battle or Place of Action: Fort Fisher, North Carolina
Date of Action: 15 January 1865
G.O. Number, Date: 59, 22 June 1865
Citation: On board the U.S.S. *Minnesota*, in action during the assault on Fort Fisher, 15 January 1865. Landing on the beach with the assaulting party from his ship, Mills charged up the palisades and, when more than two-thirds of the men became seized with panic and retreated on the run, risked his life to remain with a wounded officer. With the enemy concentrating his fire on the group, he waited until after dark before assisting the wounded officer from the field.

917 ◆ MILLS, FRANK W.

Rank: Sergeant (highest rank: First Sergeant)
Service: U.S. Army
Birthday: 5 August 1845
Place of Birth: Middletown, Orange County, New York
Date of Death: 25 November 1923
Place of Death: Pittsburgh, Pennsylvania
Cemetery: St. John's Reformed Church Cemetery (MH)—Chicore, Pennsylvania
Entered Service at: Middletown, Orange County, New York
Unit: Company C, 1st New York Mounted Rifles
Battle or Place of Action: Sandy Cross Roads, North Carolina
Date of Action: 4 September 1862
Date of Issue: 2 April 1898
Citation: While scouting, this soldier, in command of an advance of but three or four men, came upon the enemy, and charged them without orders, the rest of the troops following, the whole force of the enemy, 120 men, being captured.

918 ◆ MINDIL, GEORGE WASHINGTON

Rank: Captain (highest rank: Brevet Major General)
Service: U.S. Army
Birthday: 9 August 1843
Place of Birth: near Frankfort, Germany
Date of Death: 20 July 1907

Cemetery: Arlington National Cemetery (3-1568)—Arlington, Virginia
Entered Service at: Philadelphia, Philadelphia County, Pennsylvania
Unit: Company I, 61st Pennsylvania Infantry
Battle or Place of Action: Williamsburg, Virginia
Date of Action: 5 May 1862
Date of Issue: 25 October 1893
Citation: As aide-de-camp led the charge with a part of a regiment, pierced the enemy's center, silenced some of his artillery, and, getting in his rear, caused him to abandon his position.

919 ◆ MITCHELL, ALEXANDER H.

Rank: First Lieutenant (highest rank: Captain)
Service: U.S. Army
Birthday: 13 November 1840
Place of Birth: Perrysville, Allegheny County, Pennsylvania
Date of Death: 17 March 1913
Cemetery: Arlington National Cemetery (3-2515)—Arlington, Virginia
Entered Service at: Hamilton, Jefferson County, Pennsylvania
Unit: Company A, 105th Pennsylvania Infantry
Battle or Place of Action: Spotsylvania, Virginia
Date of Action: 12 May 1864
Date of Issue: 27 March 1890
Citation: Capture of flag of 18th North Carolina Infantry (C.S.A.), in a personal encounter with the color bearer.

920 ◆ MITCHELL, THEODORE

Rank: Private
Service: U.S. Army
Birthday: 5 May 1835
Place of Birth: Tarentum, Allegheny County, Pennsylvania
Date of Death: 2 March 1910
Place of Death: Cleveland, Ohio
Cemetery: Woodland Cemetery (MH)—Cleveland, Ohio
Entered Service at: Pittsburgh, Allegheny County, Pennsylvania
Unit: Company C, 61st Pennsylvania Infantry
Battle or Place of Action: Petersburg, Virginia
Date of Action: 2 April 1865
Date of Issue: 10 May 1865
Citation: Capture of flag of the Tennessee Brigade (C.S.A.).

921 ◆ MOFFITT, JOHN HENRY

Rank: Corporal (highest rank: Sergeant)
Service: U.S. Army
Birthday: 8 January 1843
Place of Birth: Chazy, Clinton County, New York
Date of Death: 14 August 1926
Place of Death: Plattsburg, New York
Cemetery: Mount Carmel Cemetery—Plattsburg, New York
Entered Service at: Plattsburgh, Clinton County, New York

Unit: Company C, 16th New York Infantry
Battle or Place of Action: Gaines' Mill, Virginia
Date of Action: 27 June 1862
Date of Issue: 3 March 1891
Citation: Voluntarily took up the regimental colors after several color bearers had been shot down and carried them until himself wounded.

922 ◆ MOLBONE, ARCHIBALD

True Name: Malbourne, Archibald
Rank: Sergeant
Service: U.S. Army
Birthday: 3 May 1840
Place of Birth: West Greenwich, Rhode Island
Date of Death: 28 February 1912
Cemetery: Bennett Gardner Cemetery (MH)—Scituate, Massachusetts
Entered Service at: Johnston, Providence County, Rhode Island
Unit: Company G, 1st Rhode Island Light Artillery
Battle or Place of Action: Petersburg, Virginia
Date of Action: 2 April 1865
Date of Issue: 20 June 1866
Citation: Was one of a detachment of 20 picked artillerymen who voluntarily accompanied an infantry assaulting party and who turned upon the enemy the guns captured in the assault.

923 ◆ MOLLOY, HUGH

Rank: Ordinary Seaman
Service: U.S. Navy
Birthday: 25 September 1841
Place of Birth: County Wexford, Ireland
Date of Death: 8 March 1922
Place of Death: Chicago, Illinois
Cemetery: Calvary Cemetery—Evanston, Illinois
Entered Service at: Joliet, Will County, Illinois
Unit: U.S.S. *Fort Hindman*
Battle or Place of Action: near Harrisonburg, Louisiana
Date of Action: 2 March 1864
G.O. Number, Date: 32, 16 April 1864
Citation: Served on board the U.S.S. *Fort Hindman* during the engagement near Harrisonburg, La., 2 March 1864. Following a shellburst which mortally wounded the first sponger, who dropped the sponge out of the forecastle port, Molloy jumped out of the port to the forecastle, recovered the sponge and sponged and loaded the gun for the remainder of the action from his exposed position, despite the extreme danger to his person from the raking fire of enemy musketry.

924 ◆ MONAGHAN, PATRICK H.

Rank: Corporal (highest rank: Lieutenant Colonel)
Service: U.S. Army
Birthday: 19 November 1843
Place of Birth: Ireland
Date of Death: 22 October 1916

Cemetery: St. Joseph's Cemetery—Girardville, Pennsylvania
Entered Service at: Minersville, Schuylkill County, Pennsylvania
Unit: Company F, 48th Pennsylvania Infantry
Battle or Place of Action: Petersburg, Virginia
Date of Action: 17 June 1864
Date of Issue: 1 December 1864
Citation: Recapture of colors of 7th New York Heavy Artillery.

925 ◆ MONTGOMERY, ROBERT WILLIAM

Rank: Captain of the Afterguard
Service: U.S. Navy
Birthday: 1838
Place of Birth: Ireland
Date of Death: 1898
Place of Death: Liverpool, England
Entered Service at: Norwich, New London County, Connecticut
Unit: U.S.S. *Agawam*
Battle or Place of Action: Fort Fisher, North Carolina
Date of Action: 23 December 1864
G.O. Number, Date: 45, 31 December 1864
Date of Presentation: 12 May 1865
Place of Presentation: off New Bern, NC, on board the U.S.S. *Agawam*
Citation: Montgomery on board the U.S.S. *Agawam* as one of a volunteer crew of a powder boat which was exploded near Fort Fisher, 23 December 1864. The powder boat, towed in by the *Wilderness* to prevent detection by the enemy, cast off and slowly steamed to within 300 yards of the beach. After fuses and fires had been lit and a second anchor with short scope let go to assure the boat's tailing inshore, the crew boarded the *Wilderness* and proceeded a distance of 12 miles from shore. Less than two hours later the explosion took place, and the following day fires were observed still burning at the forts.

926 ◆ MOORE, CHARLES

Rank: Seaman
Service: U.S. Navy
Birthday: 1835
Place of Birth: Holland
Date of Death: 30 March 1891
Place of Death: Long Island City, New York
Cemetery: St. Michael's Cemetery—East Elmhurst, New York
Entered Service at: Gibraltar
Unit: U.S.S. *Kearsarge*
Battle or Place of Action: off Cherbourg, France
Date of Action: 19 June 1864
G.O. Number, Date: 45, 31 December 1864
Citation: Served as seaman on board the U.S.S. *Kearsarge* when she destroyed the *Alabama* off Cherbourg, France, 19 June 1864. Acting as sponger and loader on the 11-inch pivot gun of the second division during this bitter engage-

ment, Moore exhibited marked coolness and good conduct and was highly recommended for gallantry under fire by the divisional officer.

927 ◆ MOORE, CHARLES

Rank: Landsman
Service: U.S. Navy
Birthday: 1839
Place of Birth: Ireland
Entered Service at: New York, New York
Unit: U.S. Steam Gunboat *Marblehead*
Battle or Place of Action: off Legareville, John's Island, Stono River, South Carolina
Date of Action: 25 December 1863
G.O. Number, Date: 32, 16 April 1864
Citation: Served on board the U.S. steam gunboat *Marblehead* off Legareville, Stono River, 25 December 1863, during an engagement with the enemy on John's Island. Wounded in the fierce battle, Moore returned to his quarters until so exhausted by loss of blood that he had to be taken below. This engagement resulted in the enemy's abandonment of his positions, leaving a caisson and one gun behind.

928 ◆ MOORE, DANIEL B.

Rank: Corporal (highest rank: Brevet Captain)
Service: U.S. Army
Birthday: 12 June 1838
Place of Birth: Mifflin, Iowa County, Wisconsin
Date of Death: 2 July 1914
Place of Death: Mifflin, Wisconsin
Cemetery: Graceland Cemetery—Mineral Point, Wisconsin
Entered Service at: Mifflin, Iowa County, Wisconsin
Unit: Company E, 11th Wisconsin Infantry
Battle or Place of Action: Fort Blakely, Alabama
Date of Action: 9 April 1865
Date of Issue: 8 August 1900
Citation: At the risk of his own life saved the life of an officer who had been shot down and overpowered by superior umbers.

929 ◆ MOORE, GEORGE

Rank: Seaman
Service: U.S. Navy
Birthday: 1838
Place of Birth: Philadelphia, Philadelphia County, Pennsylvania
Entered Service at: Boston, Suffolk County, Massachusetts
Unit: U.S.S. *Rhode Island*
Battle or Place of Action: off Cape Hatteras, North Carolina
Date of Action: 30 December 1862
G.O. Number, Date: 59, 22 June 1865
Citation: Served on board the U.S.S. *Rhode Island* which was engaged in saving lives of the officers and crew of the *Monitor*, 30 December 1862. Participating in the hazardous task of rescuing the officers and crew of the sinking *Monitor*,

Moore, after rescuing several of the men, became separated in a heavy gale with other members of the cutter that had set out from the *Rhode Island*, and spent many hours in the small boat at the mercy of the weather and high seas until finally picked up by a schooner 50 miles east of Cape Hatteras.

930 ◆ MOORE, GEORGE G.

Rank: Private
Service: U.S. Army
Birthday: 2 July 1844
Place of Birth: Tyler County, West Virginia
Date of Death: 26 November 1925
Place of Death: Greeley, Colorado
Cemetery: Eaton Cemetery (MH)—Eaton, Colorado
Entered Service at: Parkersburg, Wood County, West Virginia
Unit: Company D, 11th West Virginia Infantry
Battle or Place of Action: Fisher's Hill, Virginia
Date of Action: 22 September 1864
Date of Issue: 6 October 1864
Citation: Capture of flag.

931 ◆ MOORE, WILBUR F.

Rank: Private
Service: U.S. Army
Birthday: 1840
Place of Birth: Lebanon, St. Clair County, Illinois
Date of Death: 9 December 1924
Cemetery: Forest Hills Cemetery (MH)—Kansas City, Missouri
Entered Service at: Lebanon, St. Clair County, Illinois
Unit: Company C, 117th Illinois Infantry
Battle or Place of Action: Nashville, Tennessee
Date of Action: 16 December 1864
Date of Issue: 22 February 1865
Citation: Captured the flag of a Confederate battery while far in advance of the Union lines.

932 ◆ MOORE, WILLIAM

Rank: Boatswain's Mate
Service: U.S. Navy
Birthday: 18 May 1837
Place of Birth: Boston, Suffolk County, Massachusetts
Date of Death: 16 February 1918
Place of Death: Austin, Texas
Cemetery: Oakwood Cemetery (MH)—Austin, Texas
Entered Service at: Massachusetts
Unit: U.S.S. *Benton*
Battle or Place of Action: Haines Bluff, Yazoo River, Mississippi
Date of Action: 27 December 1862
G.O. Number, Date: 32, 16 April 1864
Citation: Served as boatswain's mate on board the U.S.S. *Benton* during the attack on Haines Bluff, Yazoo River, 27 December 1862. Wounded during the hour-and-a-half engagement in which the enemy had the dead-range of the

vessel and was punishing her with heavy fire, Moore served courageously in carrying lines to the shore until the Benton was ordered to withdraw.

933 ◆ MOREY, DELANO

Rank: Private
Service: U.S. Army
Birthday: 14 July 1845
Place of Birth: Licking County, Ohio
Date of Death: 24 April 1911
Cemetery: Grove Cemetery (MH)—Canton, Ohio
Entered Service at: Kenton, Hardin County, Ohio
Unit: Company B, 82d Ohio Infantry
Battle or Place of Action: McDowell, Virginia
Date of Action: 8 May 1862
Date of Issue: 14 August 1893
Citation: After the charge of the command had been repulsed, he rushed forward alone with an empty gun and captured two of the enemy's sharpshooters.
Notes: POW

934 ◆ MORFORD, JEROME

Rank: Private
Service: U.S. Army
Birthday: 13 June 1841
Place of Birth: Mercer County, Pennsylvania
Date of Death: 11 June 1910
Place of Death: Seattle, Washington
Cemetery: Riverton Crest Cemetery—Seattle, Washington
Entered Service at: Bridgers County, Illinois
Unit: Company K, 55th Illinois Infantry
Battle or Place of Action: Vicksburg, Mississippi
Date of Action: 22 May 1863
Date of Issue: 2 September 1893
Citation: Gallantry in the charge of the "volunteer storming party."

935 ◆ MORGAN, JAMES H.

True Name: Creevey, James H.
Rank: Captain of the Top
Service: U.S. Navy
Birthday: 1840
Place of Birth: New York
Date of Death: 6 April 1877
Cemetery: 1st Calvary Cemetery—Woodside, New York
Entered Service at: New York, New York
Unit: U.S.S. *Richmond*
Battle or Place of Action: Mobile Bay, Alabama
Date of Action: 5 August 1864
G.O. Number, Date: 45, 31 December 1864
Citation: As a captain of a gun on board the U.S.S. *Richmond* during action against rebel forts and gunboats and with the ram *Tennessee* in Mobile Bay, 5 August 1864. Despite damage to his ship and the loss of several men on board as enemy fire raked her decks, Morgan fought his gun with skill and courage throughout the furious two-hour battle

Alain Le Ray, 96, Top Figure In French Resistance and Army

PARIS, June 7 (AP) — Gen. Alain Le Ray, whose famous escape from a notorious Nazi prison laid the basis for leadership in the French Resistance in World War II and then in the postwar army, died Monday at the age of 96.

His family announced the death but did not give the place or cause.

General Le Ray, a career army officer who later fought in colonial wars in Indochina and Algeria, was captured by the Germans in June 1940 and less than a year later became the first to escape from the infamous Colditz prison in Germany. The Nazis had boasted that the prison was escape-proof, and his exploits were recounted in the 1976 book "Première à Colditz" — "First in Colditz."

Back in France, General Le Ray entered the Resistance, and as an expert mountain climber, he helped in an operation in the Alpine region of Vercors, becoming the first military chief of the Vercors network in May 1943.

General Le Ray rose within the Resistance to become commander of the French Forces of the Interior in Isère, another Alpine region. In 1945, his forces moved to Mont-Cenis, where they forced the Germans from their last French mountain strongholds. He organized the liberation of the Isère area with Allied forces.

He later was named a lieutenant colonel, taking part in the 1953-54 Indochina campaign.

From 1956 to 1958, General Le Ray served as chief of staff of the paratrooper division in Algeria when it

PBS

Alain Le Ray in 1940.

was waging war for independence from France. He then was named military attaché in Bonn. He was promoted to brigadier general in 1961, and a year later was made commander of the 27th Alpine Division in Kabylia, in Algeria.

He was promoted to general of army corps in 1968, two years before retiring.

Survivors include his wife, Luce, the daughter of the famed French writer François Mauriac.

The New York Times Magazine illuminates the news.

tropolitan Almanac

entral Park, for the 16 hours ended at 4 p.m. yesterday.

perature

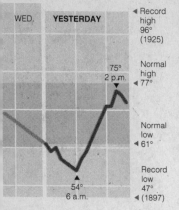

WED. | **YESTERDAY**

◄ Record high 96° (1925)

75° 2 p.m. ▲

Normal high ◄ 77°

Normal low ◄ 61°

Record low 47° ◄ (1897)

54° 6 a.m. ▲

| 4 | 12 | 6 | 12 | 4 |
| o.m. | a.m. | a.m. | p.m. | p.m. |

daily departure normal
nonth ....+2.6°

Avg. daily departure from normal
this year ....+0.1°

ervoir levels (New York City water supply)

erday 97%
nated normal...99%

Precipitation (in inches)

Yesterday 0.00
Record 1.95 (1918)

For the last 30 days
Actual 5.37
Normal 4.41

For the last 365 days
Actual 64.86
Normal 49.69

LAST 30 DAYS

Air pressure

High ...... 30.14, 10 a.m.
Low ..... 30.05, midnight

Humidity

High .... 72%, 6 a.m.
Low .... 42%, noon

Cooling degree days

An index of power use that tracks how far the day's mean temperature rose above 65°.

Yesterday 10
So far this month 42
So far this season (since Jan. 1) 158
Normal to date for the season 105

Trends

	Temperature		Precipitation	
	Average		Average	
	Below	Above	Below	Above
Last 10 days		●		●
30 days		●		●
90 days		●		●
365 days		●		●

Chart shows how recent temperature and precipitation trends compare with those of the last 30 years.

creational Forecast

, Moon and Planets

quarter	New	First quarter	Full
une 8	June 14	June 22	June 30
	11:13 p.m.		9:49 a.m.

	RISE	5:25 a.m.	**Moon**	R	1:13 a.m.
	SET	8:26 p.m.		S	1:02 p.m.
	NEXT R	5:25 a.m.		**NEXT R**	1:36 a.m.
ter	S	5:23 a.m.	**Mars**	R	2:35 a.m.
	R	7:57 p.m.		S	3:19 p.m.
rn	S	12:20 a.m.	**Venus**	R	8:48 a.m.
	R	10:19 a.m.		S	11:36 p.m.

ating

n *Montauk Point to Sandy Hook, N.J., out to 20 ical miles, including Long Island Sound and York Harbor.*

ds from the south at 10 to 15 knots, with higher s in the afternoon. Visibility of 5 miles or more, ess in morning fog patches. Wave heights will

Beaches and Ocean Temperatures

Today's forecast

Kennebunkport
69/52 Mostly to partly cloudy, cool

Cape Cod
65/55 Patchy clouds, cool breezes

L.I. North Shore
84/57 Partly sunny, warm

L.I. South Shore
79/59 Some sunshine, warm

N.J. Shore
89/63 Mainly sunny, warm

Eastern Shore
92/68 Sunny, hot

Ocean City, Md.

which resulted in the surrender of the rebel ram *Tennessee* and in the damaging and destruction of batteries at Fort Morgan.

936 ◆ *MORGAN, LEWIS

Rank: Private (highest rank: Sergeant)
Service: U.S. Army
Birthday: 1836
Place of Birth: Delaware County, Ohio
Date of Death: 27 October 1864
Place of Death: Hatchers Run, Virginia
Entered Service at: Delaware County, Ohio
Unit: Company I, 4th Ohio Infantry
Battle or Place of Action: Spotsylvania, Virginia
Date of Action: 12 May 1864
Date of Issue: 1 December 1864
Citation: Capture of flag from the enemy's works.

937 ◆ MORGAN, RICHARD H.

Rank: Corporal
Service: U.S. Army
Birthday: 2 April 1840
Place of Birth: Dubois County, Indiana
Date of Death: 17 December 1916
Cemetery: Memory Cemetery (MH)—New Market, Iowa
Entered Service at: Taylor, Freemont County, Iowa
Unit: Company A, 4th Iowa Cavalry
Battle or Place of Action: Columbus, Georgia
Date of Action: 16 April 1865
Date of Issue: 17 June 1865
Citation: Capture of flag inside the enemy's works, contesting for its possession with its bearer.

938 ◆ MORRILL, WALTER GOODALE

Rank: Captain (highest rank: Colonel)
Service: U.S. Army
Birthday: 30 November 1840
Place of Birth: Williamsburg, Maine
Date of Death: 3 March 1935
Cemetery: Village Cemetery (MH)—Pittsfield, Maine
Entered Service at: Brownville, Piscataquis County, Maine
Unit: Company B, 20th Maine Infantry
Battle or Place of Action: Rappahannock Station, Virginia
Date of Action: 7 November 1863
Date of Issue: 5 April 1898
Citation: Learning that an assault was to be made upon the enemy's works by other troops, this officer voluntarily joined the storming party with about 50 men of his regiment, and by his dash and gallantry rendered effective service in the assault.

939 ◆ MORRIS, WILLIAM POWERS

Rank: Sergeant
Service: U.S. Army
Birthday: 18 December 1844
Place of Birth: Philadelphia, Philadelphia County, Pennsylvania

Date of Death: 8 December 1916
Place of Death: Banning, California
Cemetery: Banning Cabazon Cemetery—Banning, California
Entered Service at: Philadelphia, Philadelphia County, Pennsylvania
Unit: Company C, 1st New York (Lincoln) Cavalry
Battle or Place of Action: Deatonsville (Sailor's Creek), Virginia
Date of Action: 6 April 1865
Date of Issue: 3 May 1865
Citation: Capture of flag of 40th Virginia Infantry (C.S.A.).

940 ◆ MORRISON, FRANCIS

Rank: Private
Service: U.S. Army
Birthday: 15 January 1845
Place of Birth: Ohiopyle, Fayette County, Pennsylvania
Date of Death: 30 April 1913
Place of Death: Hopwood, Pennsylvania
Cemetery: Sugar Grove Cemetery (MH)—Ohiopyle, Pennsylvania
Entered Service at: Drakestown, Pennsylvania
Unit: Company H, 85th Pennsylvania infantry
Battle or Place of Action: Bermuda Hundred, Virginia
Date of Action: 17 June 1864
Date of Issue: 2 August 1897
Citation: Voluntarily exposed himself to a heavy fire to bring off a wounded comrade.

941 ◆ MORRISON, JOHN G.

Rank: Coxswain
Service: U.S. Navy
Birthday: 3 November 1842
Place of Birth: Ireland
Date of Death: 9 June 1897
Cemetery: Cypress Hills Cemetery (Private) (MH)—Brooklyn, New York
Entered Service at: Lansingburg, Tompkins County, New York
Unit: U.S.S. *Carondelet*
Battle or Place of Action: Yazoo River, Mississippi
Date of Action: 15 July 1862
G.O. Number, Date: 59, 22 June 1865
Citation: Served as coxswain on board the U.S.S. *Carondelet*, Morrison was commended for meritorious conduct in general and especially for his heroic conduct and his inspiring example to the crew in the engagement with the rebel ram *Arkansas*, Yazoo River, 15 July 1862. When the *Carondelet* was badly cut up, several of her crew killed, many wounded, and others almost suffocated from the effects of escaped steam, Morrison was the leader when boarders were called on deck and the first to return to the guns and give the ram a broadside as she passed. His presence of mind in time of battle or trial is reported as always conspicuous and encouraging.

942 ◆ MORSE, BENJAMIN

Rank: Private (highest rank: Corporal)
Service: U.S. Army
Birthday: 20 September 1844
Place of Birth: Livingston, Columbia County, New York
Date of Death: 24 November 1908
Cemetery: Oakwood Cemetery—Lowell, Michigan
Entered Service at: Grand Rapids, Kent County, Michigan
Unit: Company C, 3d Michigan Infantry
Battle or Place of Action: Spotsylvania, Virginia
Date of Action: 12 May 1864
Date of Issue: 24 February 1891
Citation: Capture of colors of 4th Georgia Battery (C.S.A.).
Notes: POW

943 ◆ MORSE, CHARLES E.

Rank: Sergeant
Service: U.S. Army
Birthday: 5 May 1841
Place of Birth: France
Date of Death: 31 August 1920
Place of Death: Bath, New York
Cemetery: Bath National Cemetery (J-4-24) (MH)—Bath, New York
Entered Service at: New York
Unit: Company I, 62d New York Infantry
Battle or Place of Action: Wilderness Campaign, Virginia
Date of Action: 5 May 1864
Date of Issue: 14 January 1890
Citation: Voluntarily rushed back into the enemy's lines, took the colors from the color sergeant, who was mortally wounded, and, although himself wounded, carried them through the fight.

944 ◆ MORTON, CHARLES W.

Rank: Boatswain's Mate
Service: U.S. Navy
Birthday: 1836
Place of Birth: Ireland
Date of Death: 4 August 1899
Place of Death: Portsmouth, Virginia
Cemetery: U.S. Naval Hospital Cemetery (MH)—Portsmouth, Virginia
Entered Service at: Maryland
Unit: U.S.S. *Benton*
Battle or Place of Action: Yazoo River Expedition, Mississippi
Date of Action: 23-27 December 1863
G.O. Number, Date: 11, 3 April 1863
Citation: Served as boatswain's mate on board the U.S.S. *Benton* during the Yazoo River Expedition, 23 to 27 December 1863. Taking part in the hour-and-a-half engagement with the enemy at Drumgould's Bluff, 27 December, Morton served courageously throughout the battle against the hostile forces, who had the dead-range of the vessel and were punishing her with heavy fire, until the *Benton* was ordered to withdraw.

945 ◆ MOSTOLLER, JOHN WILLIAM

Rank: Private
Service: U.S. Army
Birthday: 14 January 1843
Place of Birth: Stoystown, Somerset County, Pennsylvania
Date of Death: 5 December 1925
Place of Death: Somerset County, Pennsylvania
Cemetery: I.O.O.F. Cemetery—Stoystown, Pennsylvania
Entered Service at: Stoystown, Somerset County, Pennsylvania
Unit: Company B, 54th Pennsylvania Infantry
Battle or Place of Action: Lynchburg, Virginia
Date of Action: 18 June 1864
Date of Issue: 27 December 1894
Citation: Voluntarily led a charge on a Confederate battery (the officers of the company being disabled) and compelled its hasty removal.

946 ◆ MULHOLLAND, ST. CLAIR AGUSTIN

Rank: Major (highest rank: Brevet Major General)
Service: U.S. Army
Birthday: 1 April 1839
Place of Birth: Lisburn, County Antrim, Ireland
Date of Death: 17 February 1910
Place of Death: Philadelphia, Pennsylvania
Cemetery: Old Cathedral Cemetery—Philadelphia, Pennsylvania
Entered Service at: Philadelphia, Philadelphia County, Pennsylvania
Unit: 116th Pennsylvania Infantry
Battle or Place of Action: Chancellorsville, Virginia
Date of Action: 4-5 May 1863
Date of Presentation: 26 March 1895
Place of Presentation: Presented by Ass. Sec. of War Doe
Citation: In command of the picket line, held the enemy in check all night to cover the retreat of the Army.

947 ◆ MULLEN, PATRICK✦

Rank: Boatswain's Mate
Service: U.S. Navy
Birthday: 6 May 1844
Place of Birth: Ireland
Date of Death: 14 February 1897
Cemetery: New Cathedral Cemetery—Baltimore, Maryland
Entered Service at: Baltimore, Baltimore County, Maryland
Unit: U.S.S. *Wyandank*
Battle or Place of Action: Mattox Creek, Virginia
Date of Action: 17 March 1865
G.O. Number, Date: 59, 22 June 1865
Citation: **First Award** Served as boatswain's mate on board the U.S.S. *Wyandank* during a boat expedition up Mattox Creek, 17 March 1865. Rendering gallant assistance to his commanding officer, Mullen, lying on his back, loaded the

howitzer and then fired so carefully as to kill and wound many rebels, causing their retreat.
Notes: ✠Double Awardee: *see also* Interim 1865-1870

948 ◆ MUNDELL, WALTER L.

Rank: Corporal
Service: U.S. Army
Birthday: 4 August 1838
Place of Birth: Michigan
Date of Death: 20 April 1900
Place of Death: Fowler, Michigan
Cemetery: Oak Ridge Cemetery—Bengal Township, Michigan
Entered Service at: Dallas, Michigan
Unit: Company E, 5th Michigan Infantry
Battle or Place of Action: Deatonsville (Sailor's Creek), Virginia
Date of Action: 6 April 1865
Date of Issue: 10 May 1865
Citation: Capture of flag.

949 ◆ MUNSELL, HARVEY MAY

Rank: Sergeant (highest rank: Captain)
Service: U.S. Army
Birthday: 5 January 1843
Place of Birth: Painted Post, Steuben County, New York
Date of Death: 9 February 1913
Place of Death: Mount Vernon, New York
Cemetery: Mount Auburn Cemetery (MH)—Cambridge, Massachusetts
Entered Service at: Philadelphia, Philadelphia County, Pennsylvania
Unit: Company A, 99th Pennsylvania Infantry
Battle or Place of Action: Gettysburg, Pennsylvania
Date of Action: 1-3 July 1863
Date of Issue: 5 February 1866
Citation: Gallant and courageous conduct as color bearer. (This noncommissioned officer carried the colors of his regiment through 13 engagements.)
Notes: POW

950 ◆ MURPHY, CHARLES JOSEPH

Rank: First Lieutenant & Quartermaster (highest rank: Colonel)
Service: U.S. Army
Birthday: 3 June 1832
Place of Birth: Stockport, Greater Manchester County, England
Date of Death: 29 May 1921
Place of Death: New York, New York
Cemetery: Calvary Cemetery—Woodside, New York
Entered Service at: New York, New York
Unit: 38th New York Infantry
Battle or Place of Action: Bull Run, Virginia
Date of Action: 21 July 1861
Date of Issue: 5 April 1898

Citation: Took a rifle and voluntarily fought with his regiment in the ranks; when the regiment was forced back, voluntarily remained on the field caring for the wounded and was there taken prisoner.
Notes: POW

951 ◆ MURPHY, DANIEL J.

Rank: Sergeant (highest rank: Second Lieutenant)
Service: U.S. Army
Birthday: 1843
Place of Birth: Philadelphia, Philadelphia County, Pennsylvania
Date of Death: 19 September 1870
Cemetery: Oakwood Cemetery (MH)—Jefferson, Texas
Entered Service at: Lowell, Middlesex County, Massachusetts
Unit: Company F, 19th Massachusetts Infantry
Battle or Place of Action: Hatcher's Run, Virginia
Date of Action: 27 October 1864
Date of Issue: 1 December 1864
Citation: Capture of flag of 47th North Carolina Infantry (C.S.A.).

952 ◆ MURPHY, DENNIS J. F.

Rank: Sergeant
Service: U.S. Army
Birthday: 28 July 1830
Place of Birth: County Cork, Ireland
Date of Death: 19 June 1901
Place of Death: Green Bay, Wisconsin
Cemetery: Allouez Catholic Cemetery (MH)—Green Bay, Wisconsin
Entered Service at: Lowell, Middlesex County, Massachusetts
Unit: Company F, 14th Wisconsin Infantry
Battle or Place of Action: Corinth, Mississippi
Date of Action: 3 October 1862
Date of Issue: 22 January 1892
Citation: Although wounded three times, carried the colors throughout the conflict.

953 ◆ MURPHY, JAMES T.

Rank: Private (highest rank: Sergeant)
Service: U.S. Army
Birthday: 1839
Place of Birth: Canada
Date of Death: 11 January 1904
Place of Death: New Haven, Connecticut
Cemetery: St. Bernard's Cemetery (MH)—New Haven, Connecticut
Entered Service at: New Haven, New Haven County, Connecticut
Unit: Company L, 1st Connecticut Artillery
Battle or Place of Action: Petersburg, Virginia
Date of Action: 25 March 1865
Date of Issue: 29 October 1886

Citation: A piece of artillery having been silenced by the enemy, this soldier voluntarily assisted in working the piece, conducting himself throughout the engagement in a gallant and fearless manner.

954 ◆ MURPHY, JOHN P.

Rank: Private (highest rank: First Sergeant)
Service: U.S. Army
Birthday: 24 June 1844
Place of Birth: Killarney, County Kerry, Ireland
Date of Death: 1 January 1911
Place of Death: Cincinnati, Ohio
Cemetery: Spring Grove Cemetery—Cincinnati, Ohio
Entered Service at: Cincinnati, Hamilton County, Ohio
Unit: Company K, 5th Ohio Infantry
Battle or Place of Action: Antietam, Maryland
Date of Action: 17 September 1862
Date of Issue: 11 September 1866
Citation: Capture of flag of 13th Alabama Infantry (C.S.A.).

955 ◆ MURPHY, MICHAEL C.

Rank: Lieutenant Colonel (highest rank: Colonel)
Service: U.S. Army
Birthday: 1836
Place of Birth: Limerick, County Limerick, Ireland
Date of Death: 4 March 1903
Cemetery: Kensico Cemetery—Valhalla, New York
Entered Service at: New York, New York
Unit: 170th New York Infantry
Battle or Place of Action: North Anna River, Virginia
Date of Action: 24 May 1864
Date of Issue: 15 January 1897
Citation: This officer, commanding the regiment, kept it on the field exposed to the fire of the enemy for three hours without being able to fire one shot in return because of the ammunition being exhausted.

956 ◆ MURPHY, PATRICK

Rank: Boatswain's Mate (highest rank: Chief Boatswain's Mate)
Service: U.S. Navy
Birthday: 1823
Place of Birth: Ireland
Date of Death: 1 December 1896
Entered Service at: New York, New York
Unit: U.S.S. *Metacomet*
Battle or Place of Action: Mobile Bay, Alabama
Date of Action: 5 August 1864
G.O. Number, Date: 84, 3 October 1867
Citation: Served as boatswain's mate on board the U.S.S. *Metacomet* during action against rebel forts and gunboats and with the ram *Tennessee* in Mobile Bay, 5 August 1864. Despite damage to his ship and the loss of several men on board as enemy fire raked her decks, Murphy performed his duties with skill and courage throughout a furious two-hour battle, which resulted in the surrender of the rebel ram *Tennessee* and in the damaging and destruction of batteries at Fort Morgan.

957 ◆ MURPHY, ROBINSON BARR

Rank: Musician
Service: U.S. Army
Birthday: 11 May 1849
Place of Birth: Oswego, Kendall County, Illinois
Date of Death: 2 October 1934
Place of Death: Washington, D.C.
Cemetery: Arlington National Cemetery (6-9749)—Arlington, Virginia
Entered Service at: Oswego, Kendall County, Illinois
Unit: Company A, 127th Illinois Infantry
Battle or Place of Action: Atlanta, Georgia
Date of Action: 28 July 1864
Date of Issue: 22 July 1890
Citation: Being orderly to the brigade commander, he voluntarily led two regiments as reinforcements into line of battle, where he had his horse shot under him.

958 ◆ MURPHY, THOMAS

Rank: Corporal
Service: U.S. Army
Place of Birth: New York, New York
Entered Service at: Brooklyn, Kings County, New York
Unit: Company K, 158th New York Infantry
Battle or Place of Action: Chapin's Farm, Virginia
Date of Action: 30 September 1864
Date of Issue: 15 October 1864
Citation: Capture of flag.

959 ◆ MURPHY, THOMAS C.

Rank: Corporal
Service: U.S. Army
Birthday: 1842
Place of Birth: Ireland
Date of Death: 31 December 1920
Cemetery: Glendale Cemetery—Washington, Illinois
Entered Service at: Pekin, Tazewell County, Illinois
Unit: Company I, 31st Illinois Infantry
Battle or Place of Action: Vicksburg, Mississippi
Date of Action: 22 May 1863
Date of Issue: 14 August 1893
Citation: Voluntarily crossed the line of heavy fire of Union and Confederate forces, carrying a message to stop the firing of one Union regiment on another.

960 ◆ MURPHY, THOMAS J.

Rank: First Sergeant
Service: U.S. Army
Birthday: 1833
Place of Birth: Ireland
Date of Death: 2 December 1901
Place of Death: High Ridge, Connecticut

Cemetery: Pound Ridge Cemetery (MH)—Pound Ridge, New York
Entered Service at: New York, New York
Unit: Company F, 146th New York Infantry
Battle or Place of Action: Five Forks, Virginia
Date of Action: 1 April 1865
Date of Issue: 10 May 1865
Citation: Capture of flag.

961 ◆ MYERS, GEORGE S.

Rank: Private
Service: U.S. Army
Birthday: 26 January 1843
Place of Birth: Fairfield, Butler County, Ohio
Date of Death: 21 August 1917
Place of Death: Hermosa Beach, California
Cemetery: Inglewood Park Cemetery—Inglewood, California
Entered Service at: Tiffin, Seneca County, Ohio
Unit: Company F, 101st Ohio Infantry
Battle or Place of Action: Chickamauga, Georgia
Date of Action: 19 September 1863
Date of Issue: 9 April 1894
Citation: Saved the regimental colors by greatest personal devotion and bravery.

962 ◆ MYERS, WILLIAM H.

True Name: Meyers, William H.
Rank: Private
Service: U.S. Army
Place of Birth: Philadelphia, Philadelphia County, Pennsylvania
Entered Service at: Baltimore, Baltimore County, Maryland
Unit: Company A, 1st Maryland Cavalry
Battle or Place of Action: Appomattox Courthouse, Virginia
Date of Action: 9 April 1865
Date of Issue: 14 June 1871
Citation: Gallantry in action; was five times wounded.

963 ◆ NASH, HENRY H.

Rank: Corporal
Service: U.S. Army
Birthday: 4 March 1842
Place of Birth: Lenawee County, Michigan
Date of Death: 30 March 1917
Place of Death: Palmyra, Michigan
Cemetery: Palmyra Cemetery (MH)—Palmyra, Michigan
Entered Service at: Adrian, Lenawee County, Michigan
Unit: Company B, 47th Ohio Infantry
Battle or Place of Action: Vicksburg, Mississippi
Date of Action: 3 May 1863
Date of Issue: 15 February 1909
Citation: Was one of a party that volunteered and attempted to run the enemy's batteries with a steam tug and two barges loaded with subsistence stores.
Notes: POW

964 ◆ NAYLOR, DAVID JOHNSON

Rank: Landsman
Service: U.S. Navy
Birthday: 14 November 1843
Place of Birth: Thompsonville, Sullivan County, New York
Date of Death: 7 February 1926
Place of Death: Potter Hill, Rhode Island
Cemetery: River Bend Cemetery (MH)—Westerly, Rhode Island
Entered Service at: New York, New York
Unit: U.S.S. *Oneida*
Battle or Place of Action: Mobile Bay, Alabama
Date of Action: 5 August 1864
G.O. Number, Date: 45, 31 December 1864
Citation: Served on board the U.S.S. *Oneida* in the engagement at Mobile Bay, 5 August 1864. Acting as powder boy at the 30-pounder Parrott rifle, Naylor had his passing box shot from his hands and knocked overboard where it fell into one of the *Galena*'s boats which was under the bow. Jumping overboard, Naylor recovered his box, returned to his station, and continued to carry out his courageous actions throughout the engagement, which resulted in the capture of the rebel ram *Tennessee* and the damaging of Fort Morgan.

965 ◆ NEAHR, ZACHARIAH C.

Rank: Private
Service: U.S. Army
Birthday: 9 December 1830
Place of Birth: Palatine, Montgomery County, New York
Date of Death: 21 July 1903
Place of Death: Canajoharie, New York
Cemetery: Canajoharie Falls Cemetery (MH)—Canajoharie, New York
Entered Service at: Canajoharie, Montgomery County, New York
Unit: Company K, 142d New York Infantry
Battle or Place of Action: Fort Fisher, North Carolina
Date of Action: 16 January 1865
Date of Issue: 11 September 1890
Citation: Voluntarily advanced with the head of the column and cut down the palisading.

966 ◆ NEIL, JOHN

Rank: Quarter Gunner (highest rank: Master-at-Arms)
Service: U.S. Navy
Birthday: 1840
Place of Birth: Newfoundland, Canada
Entered Service at: Norwich, New London County, Connecticut
Unit: U.S.S. *Agawam*
Battle or Place of Action: Fort Fisher, North Carolina
Date of Action: 23 December 1864
G.O. Number, Date: 45, 31 December 1864
Date of Presentation: 12 May 1865
Place of Presentation: off New Bern, NC, on board the U.S.S. *Agawam*

Citation: Neil served on board the U.S.S. *Agawam*, as one of a volunteer crew of a powder boat which was exploded near Fort Fisher, 23 December 1864. The powder boat, towed in by the *Wilderness* to prevent detection by the enemy, cast off and slowly steamed to within 300 yards of the beach. After fuses and fires had been lit and a second anchor with short scope let go to assure the boat's tailing inshore, the crew again boarded the *Wilderness* and proceeded a distance of 12 miles from shore. Less then two hours later the explosion took place, and the following day fires were observed still burning at the forts.

967 ◆ NEVILLE, EDWIN MICHAEL

Rank: Captain
Service: U.S. Army
Birthday: 27 January 1843
Place of Birth: Waterbury, New Haven County, Connecticut
Date of Death: 4 October 1886
Cemetery: Old St. Joseph's Cemetery (MH)—Waterbury, Connecticut
Entered Service at: Waterbury, New Haven County, Connecticut
Unit: Company C, 1st Connecticut Cavalry
Battle or Place of Action: Deatonsville (Sailor's Creek), Virginia
Date of Action: 6 April 1865
Date of Issue: 3 May 1865
Citation: Capture of flag.

968 ◆ NEWLAND, WILLIAM D.

Rank: Ordinary Seaman
Service: U.S. Navy
Birthday: 5 January 1841
Place of Birth: Medway, Norfolk County, Massachusetts
Date of Death: 1914
Cemetery: Prospect Hill Cemetery (MH)—Millis, Massachusetts
Entered Service at: Massachusetts
Unit: U.S.S. *Oneida*
Battle or Place of Action: Mobile Bay, Alabama
Date of Action: 5 August 1864
G.O. Number, Date: 45, 31 December 1864
Citation: Served on board the U.S.S. *Oneida* in the engagement at Mobile Bay, 5 August 1864. Carrying out his duties as loader of the after 11-inch gun, Newland distinguished himself on board for his good conduct and faithful discharge of his station, behaving spendidly under the fire of the enemy and throughout the battle, which resulted in the capture of the rebel ram *Tennessee* and the damaging of Fort Morgan.

969 ◆ NEWMAN, MARCELLUS J.

Rank: Private
Service: U.S. Army
Birthday: 1836
Place of Birth: Richview, Washington County, Illinois

Date of Death: 15 November 1905
Place of Death: Meeker, Oklahoma
Cemetery: Elmwood Cemetery—Centralia, Illinois
Entered Service at: Richview, Washington County, Illinois
Unit: Company B, 111th Illinois Infantry
Battle or Place of Action: Resaca, Georgia
Date of Action: 14 May 1864
Date of Issue: 13 May 1899
Citation: Voluntarily returned, in the face of a severe fire from the enemy, and rescued a wounded comrade who had been left behind as the regiment fell back.

970 ◆ NEWMAN, WILLIAM HENRY

Rank: Lieutenant (highest rank: Captain)
Service: U.S. Army
Birthday: 12 December 1838
Place of Birth: Highland Mills, Orange County, New York
Date of Death: 7 April 1917
Place of Death: Freemont Center, New York
Cemetery: Heavenly Rest Cemetery (MH)—North Branch, New York
Entered Service at: Port Jervis, Orange County, New York
Unit: Company B, 86th New York Infantry
Battle or Place of Action: Amelia Springs, Virginia
Date of Action: 6 April 1865
Date of Issue: 10 May 1865
Citation: Capture of flag.

971 ◆ NIBBE, JOHN H.

Rank: Quartermaster
Service: U.S. Navy
Birthday: 25 November 1847
Place of Birth: Germany
Date of Death: 15 June 1902
Cemetery: Ivy Green Cemetery (MH)—Bremerton, Washington
Entered Service at: New York
Unit: U.S.S. *Petrel*
Battle or Place of Action: Yazoo River, Mississippi
Date of Action: 22 April 1864
G.O. Number, Date: 59, 22 June 1865
Citation: Served as quartermaster on board the U.S.S. *Petrel* during its capture in Yazoo River, 22 April 1864. Standing his ground when a shot came through the stern, raking the gundeck and entering and exploding the boilers, when all the others had deserted the flag, Nibbe assisted in getting the wounded off the guard and proceeded to get ready to fire the ship despite the escaping steam from the boilers, at which time he was surrounded on all sides by the rebels and forced to surrender.
Notes: POW

972 ◆ NICHOLS, HENRY CLAY

Rank: Captain
Service: U.S. Army
Birthday: 30 March 1832

Place of Birth: Brandon, Rutland County, Vermont
Date of Death: 10 February 1904
Place of Death: Coventry, Vermont
Cemetery: Coventry Cemetery—Coventry, Vermont
Entered Service at: St. Albans, Franklin County, Vermont
Unit: Company E, 73d U.S. Colored Infantry
Battle or Place of Action: Fort Blakely, Alabama
Date of Action: 9 April 1865
Date of Issue: 3 August 1897
Citation: Voluntarily made a reconnaissance in advance of the line held by his regiment and, under a heavy fire, obtained information of great value.

973 ◆ NICHOLS, WILLIAM

Rank: Quartermaster
Service: U.S. Navy
Birthday: 1837
Place of Birth: New York, New York
Entered Service at: New York
Unit: U.S.S. *Brooklyn*
Battle or Place of Action: Mobile Bay, Alabama
Date of Action: 5 August 1864
G.O. Number, Date: 45, 31 December 1864
Citation: On board the U.S.S. *Brooklyn* during the successful attacks against Fort Morgan, rebel gunboats, and the ram *Tennessee*, in Mobile Bay, 5 August 1864. Despite severe damage to his ship and the loss of several men on board as enemy fire raked her decks from stem to stern, Nichols fought his gun with skill and courage throughout the furious battle which resulted in the surrender of the prize rebel ram *Tennessee* and in the damaging and destruction of batteries at Fort Morgan.

974 ◆ NIVEN, ROBERT

Rank: Second Lieutenant (highest rank: Captain)
Service: U.S. Army
Birthday: 18 December 1833
Place of Birth: Harlem, New York
Date of Death: 21 December 1921
Place of Death: Providence, Rhode Island
Cemetery: Highland Cemetery—Lakewood, Rhode Island
Entered Service at: Rochester, Monroe County, New York
Unit: Company H, 8th New York Cavalry
Battle or Place of Action: Waynesboro, Virginia
Date of Action: 2 March 1865
Date of Issue: 26 March 1865
Citation: Capture of two flags.

975 ◆ NOBLE, DANIEL

Rank: Landsman
Service: U.S. Navy
Birthday: 1840
Place of Birth: Bath County, Kentucky
Entered Service at: Chicago, Cook County, Illinois
Unit: U.S.S. *Metacomet*
Battle or Place of Action: Mobile Bay, Alabama

Date of Action: 5 August 1864
G.O. Number, Date: 71, 15 January 1866
Citation: As landsman on board the U.S.S. *Metacomet*, Noble served among the boat's crew which went to the rescue of the U.S. Monitor *Tecumseh* when that vessel was struck by a torpedo in passing enemy forts in Mobile Bay, 5 August 1864. Noble braved the enemy fire, which was said by the admiral to be "one of the most galling" he had ever seen, and aided in rescuing from death 10 of the crew of the *Tecumseh*, thereby eliciting the admiration of both friend and foe.

976 ◆ NOLAN, JOHN J.

Rank: Sergeant (highest rank: Second Lieutenant)
Service: U.S. Army
Birthday: 24 June 1842
Place of Birth: Thurles, County Tipperary, Ireland
Date of Death: 13 June 1912
Place of Death: Bronx, New York
Cemetery: St. Raymond's Cemetery—Bronx, New York
Entered Service at: Nashua, Hillsborough County, New Hampshire
Unit: Company K, 8th New Hampshire Infantry
Served as: Color Bearer
Battle or Place of Action: Georgia Landing, Louisiana
Date of Action: 27 October 1862
Date of Issue: 3 August 1897
Citation: Although prostrated by a cannon shot, refused to give up the flag which he was carrying as color bearer of his regiment and continued to carry it at the head of the regiment throughout the engagement.

977 ◆ NOLL, CONRAD

Rank: Sergeant
Service: U.S. Army
Birthday: 20 February 1836
Place of Birth: Germany
Date of Death: 26 May 1925
Place of Death: Ann Arbor, Michigan
Cemetery: Forest Hill Cemetery—Ann Arbor, Michigan
Entered Service at: Ann Arbor, Washtenaw County, Michigan
Unit: Company D, 20th Michigan Infantry
Battle or Place of Action: Spotsylvania, Virginia
Date of Action: 12 May 1864
Date of Issue: 28 July 1896
Citation: Seized the colors, the color bearer having been shot down, and gallantly fought his way out with them, though the enemy were on the left flank and rear.

978 ◆ NORTH, JASPER N.

Rank: Private
Service: U.S. Army
Birthday: 15 September 1842
Place of Birth: Ohio
Date of Death: 10 February 1918
Place of Death: Federal, Ohio

Cemetery: Rightstown Cemetery—Amesville, Ohio
Entered Service at: Amesville, Athens County, Ohio
Unit: Company D, 4th West Virginia Infantry
Battle or Place of Action: Vicksburg, Mississippi
Date of Action: 22 May 1863
Date of Issue: 27 July 1894
Citation: Gallantry in the charge of the "volunteer storming party."

979 ◆ NORTON, ELLIOTT MALLOY

Rank: Second Lieutenant (highest rank: First Lieutenant)
Service: U.S. Army
Birthday: 15 June 1834
Place of Birth: Connecticut
Date of Death: 5 January 1899
Place of Death: Carson City, Michigan
Cemetery: Liberty Street Cemetery—Alamo Township, Michigan
Entered Service at: Cooper, Michigan
Unit: Company H, 6th Michigan Cavalry
Battle or Place of Action: Deatonsville (Sailor's Creek), Virginia
Date of Action: 6 April 1865
Date of Issue: 3 May 1865
Citation: Rushed ahead of his column and captured the flag of the 44th Tennessee Infantry (C.S.A.).

980 ◆ NORTON, JOHN R.

Rank: Second Lieutenant
Service: U.S. Army
Birthday: 20 June 1830
Place of Birth: St. John's Parish, Roscommon, County Ballaugh, Ireland
Date of Death: 19 December 1905
Cemetery: St. Parick's Cemetery—Ada, Michigan
Entered Service at: Grand Rapids, Kent County, Michigan
Unit: Company M, 1st New York (Lincoln) Cavalry
Battle or Place of Action: Deatonsville (Sailor's Creek), Virginia
Date of Action: 6 April 1865
Date of Issue: 3 May 1865
Citation: Capture of flag.

981 ◆ NORTON, LLEWELLYN POWELL

Rank: Sergeant (highest rank: Sergeant Major)
Service: U.S. Army
Birthday: 11 May 1837
Place of Birth: Scott, Cortland County, New York
Date of Death: 16 February 1914
Place of Death: Homer, New York
Cemetery: Elmwood Cemetery—Preble, New York
Entered Service at: Scott, Cortland County, New York
Unit: Company L, 10th New York Cavalry
Battle or Place of Action: Deatonsville (Sailor's Creek), Virginia
Date of Action: 6 April 1865

Date of Issue: 3 July 1865
Citation: Charged the enemy and, with the assistance of Cpl. Andrew Bringle, captured a fieldpiece with two prisoners.

982 ◆ NOYES, WILLIAM W.

Rank: Private
Service: U.S. Army
Birthday: 23 April 1846
Place of Birth: Montpelier, Washington County, Vermont
Date of Death: 1 July 1910
Cemetery: Cutler Cemetery—East Montpelier, Vermont
Entered Service at: Montpelier, Washington County, Vermont
Unit: Company F, 2d Vermont Infantry
Battle or Place of Action: Spotsylvania, Virginia
Date of Action: 12 May 1864
Date of Issue: 22 March 1892
Citation: Standing upon the top of the breastworks, deliberately took aim and fired no less than 15 shots into the enemy's lines, but a few yards away.

983 ◆ NUGENT, CHRISTOPHER

Rank: Orderly Sergeant
Service: U.S. Marine Corps
Birthday: 1838
Place of Birth: County Cavan, Ireland
Date of Death: 6 May 1898
Cemetery: St. Raymond's Cemetery (MH)—Bronx, New York
Entered Service at: Massachusetts
Unit: U.S.S. *Fort Henry*
Battle or Place of Action: Crystal River, Florida
Date of Action: 15 June 1863
G.O. Number, Date: 32, 16 April 1864
Citation: Served on board the U.S.S. *Fort Henry*, Crystal River, Fla., 15 June 1863. Reconnoitering on the Crystal River on this date and in charge of a boat from the *Fort Henry*, Orderly Sgt. Nugent ordered an assault upon a rebel breastwork fortification. In this assault, the orderly sergeant and his comrades drove a guard of 11 rebels into the swamp, capturing their arms and destroying their camp equipage while gallantly withholding fire to prevent harm to a woman among the fugitives. On 30 July 1863, he further proved his courage by capturing a boat off Depot Key, Fla., containing two men and a woman with their baggage.

984 ◆ NUTTING, LEE

Rank: Captain
Service: U.S. Army
Birthday: 14 October 1837
Place of Birth: New York, New York
Date of Death: 11 July 1908
Cemetery: Brookside Cemetery (MH)—Brightwater, Nova Scotia, Canada
Entered Service at: New York, New York
Unit: Company C, 61st New York Infantry

Battle or Place of Action: Todds Tavern, Virginia
Date of Action: 8 May 1864
Date of Issue: 21 August 1893
Citation: Led the regiment in charge at a critical moment under a murderous fire until he fell desperately wounded.

985 ◆ O'BEIRNE, JAMES ROWAN

Rank: Captain (highest rank: Brigadier General)
Service: U.S. Army
Birthday: 25 September 1844
Place of Birth: Roscommon, County Ballagh, Ireland
Date of Death: 17 February 1917
Cemetery: Calvary Cemetery—Woodside, New York
Entered Service at: New York, New York
Unit: Company C, 37th New York Infantry
Battle or Place of Action: Fair Oaks, Virginia
Date of Action: 31 May & 1 June 1862
Date of Issue: 20 January 1891
Citation: Gallantly maintained the line of battle until ordered to fall back.

986 ◆ O'BRIEN, HENRY D.

Rank: Corporal (highest rank: Major)
Service: U.S. Army
Birthday: 21 January 1842
Place of Birth: Colois, Maine
Date of Death: 2 November 1902
Place of Death: St. Louis, Missouri
Cemetery: Bellefontaine Cemetery—St. Louis, Missouri
Entered Service at: St. Anthony Falls, Minnesota
Unit: Company E, 1st Minnesota Infantry
Battle or Place of Action: Gettysburg, Pennsylvania
Date of Action: 3 July 1863
Date of Issue: 9 April 1890
Citation: Taking up the colors where they had fallen, he rushed ahead of his regiment, close to the muzzles of the enemy's guns, and engaged in the desperate struggle in which the enemy was defeated, and though severely wounded, he held the colors until wounded a second time.

987 ◆ O'BRIEN, OLIVER ALBERT

Rank: Coxswain (highest rank: Acting Master's Mate)
Service: U.S. Navy
Birthday: 1839
Place of Birth: Boston, Suffolk County, Massachusetts
Date of Death: 1 October 1894
Place of Death: Glouchester, Massachusetts
Cemetery: St. Ann's Oak Hill Cemetery (MH)—Glouchester, Massachusetts
Entered Service at: Boston, Suffolk County, Massachusetts
Unit: U.S. Sloop *John Adams*
Battle or Place of Action: Sullivan's Island Channel, South Carolina
Date of Action: 28 November 1864
G.O. Number, Date: 45, 31 December 1864
Citation: Served as coxswain on board the U.S. sloop *John Adams*, Sullivan's Island Channel, 28 November 1864. Taking part in the boarding of the blockade runner *Beatrice* while under heavy enemy fire from Fort Moultrie, O'Brien, who was in charge of one of the boarding launches, carried out his duties with prompt and energetic conduct. This action resulted in the firing of the *Beatrice* and the capture of a quantity of supplies from her.

988 ◆ O'BRIEN, PETER

Rank: Private (highest rank: Corporal)
Service: U.S. Army
Birthday: 1842
Place of Birth: Dublin, County Dublin, Ireland
Date of Death: 30 September 1898
Place of Death: Chicago, Illinois
Cemetery: Rose Hill Cemetery—Chicago, Illinois
Entered Service at: New York, New York
Unit: Company A, 1st New York (Lincoln) Cavalry
Battle or Place of Action: Waynesboro, Virginia
Date of Action: 2 March 1865
Date of Issue: 26 March 1865
Citation: Capture of flag and of a Confederate officer with his horse and equipment.

989 ◆ O'CONNELL, THOMAS

Rank: Coal Heaver
Service: U.S. Navy
Birthday: 1842
Place of Birth: Ireland
Date of Death: 1899
Place of Death: New York, New York
Entered Service at: New York, New York
Unit: U.S.S. *Hartford*
Battle or Place of Action: Mobile Bay, Alabama
Date of Action: 5 August 1864
G.O. Number, Date: 45, 31 December 1864
Citation: On board the flagship U.S.S. *Hartford*, during successful attacks against Fort Morgan, rebel gunboats, and the ram *Tennessee* in Mobile Bay, 5 August 1864. Although a patient in the sick bay, O'Connell voluntarily reported at his station at the shell whip and continued to perform his duties with zeal and courage until his right hand was severed by an enemy shellburst.

990 ◆ O'CONNOR, ALBERT

Rank: Sergeant (highest rank: First Sergeant)
Service: U.S. Army
Birthday: 15 July 1843
Place of Birth: Herford, Canada
Date of Death: 3 April 1928
Cemetery: Soldier's Home Cemetery (MH)—Orting, Washington
Entered Service at: Lodi, Columbia County, Wisconsin
Unit: Company A, 7th Wisconsin Infantry
Battle or Place of Action: Gravelly Run, Virginia
Date of Action: 31 March & 1 April 1865

Date of Issue: 27 February 1917
Citation: On 31 March 1865, with a comrade, recaptured a Union officer from a detachment of nine Confederates, capturing three of the detachment and dispersing the remainder, and on 1 April 1865, seized a stand of Confederate colors, killing a Confederate officer in a hand-to-hand contest over the colors and retaining the colors until surrounded by Confederates and compelled to relinquish them.
Notes: POW

991 ◆ O'CONNOR, TIMOTHY

Rank: Private (highest rank: Sergeant)
Service: U.S. Army
Place of Birth: Ireland
Entered Service at: New Creek, Virginia
Unit: Company E, 1st U.S. Cavalry
Battle or Place of Action: near Malvern, Virginia
Date of Action: 28 July 1864
Date of Issue: 5 January 1865
Citation: Capture of flag of the 18th North Carolina Infantry (C.S.A.).

992 ◆ O'DEA, JOHN

Rank: Private
Service: U.S. Army
Birthday: 1839
Place of Birth: Limerick, County Limerick, Ireland
Place of Death: Quincy, Illinois
Cemetery: Sunset Cemetery, Illinois Veterans Home (MH)—Quincy, Illinois
Entered Service at: Bloomington, McLean County, Illinois
Unit: Company D, 8th Missouri Infantry
Battle or Place of Action: Vicksburg, Mississippi
Date of Action: 22 May 1863
Date of Issue: 12 July 1894
Citation: Gallantry in the charge of the "volunteer storming party."

993 ◆ O'DONNELL, MENOMEN

Rank: First Lieutenant (highest rank: Captain)
Service: U.S. Army
Birthday: 20 April 1830
Place of Birth: Drumbarty, Ireland
Date of Death: 3 September 1911
Cemetery: Mount Calvary Cemetery (MH)—Vincennes, Indiana
Entered Service at: Sumner, Lawrence County, Illinois
Unit: Company A, 11th Missouri Infantry
Battle or Place of Action: Vicksburg, Mississippi & Fort DeRussey, Louisiana
Date of Action: 22 May 1863 & 14 March 1864
Date of Issue: 11 September 1897
Citation: Voluntarily joined the color guard in the assault on the enemy's works when he saw indications of wavering and caused the colors of his regiment to be planted on the parapet. Voluntarily placed himself in the ranks of an assault-ing column (being then on staff duty) and rode with it into the enemy's works, being the only mounted officer present; was twice wounded in battle.

994 ◆ O'DONOGHUE, TIMOTHY

Rank: Seaman
Service: U.S. Navy
Birthday: 1841
Place of Birth: Rochester, Monroe County, New York
Entered Service at: New York
Unit: U.S.S. *Signal*
Battle or Place of Action: Red River, Louisiana
Date of Action: 5 May 1864
G.O. Number, Date: 45, 31 December 1864
Citation: Served as boatswain's mate on board the U.S.S. *Signal*, Red River, 5 May 1864. Proceeding up the Red River, the U.S.S. *Signal* engaged a large force of enemy field batteries and sharpshooters, returning the fire until the ship was totally disabled, at which time the white flag was raised. Serving as gun captain, wounded early in the battle, O'Donoghue bravely stood by his gun in the face of enemy fire until ordered to withdraw.
Notes: POW

995 ◆ OLIVER, CHARLES

Rank: Sergeant (highest rank: Brevet Captain)
Service: U.S. Army
Birthday: 1840
Place of Birth: Allegheny County, Pennsylvania
Date of Death: 30 August 1920
Cemetery: Richland Cemetery (MH)—Dravosburg, Pennsylvania
Entered Service at: Webster, Westmoreland County, Pennsylvania
Unit: Company M, 100th Pennsylvania Infantry
Battle or Place of Action: Petersburg, Virginia
Date of Action: 25 March 1865
Date of Issue: 3 July 1865
Citation: Capture of flag of 31st Georgia Infantry (C.S.A.).

996 ◆ OLIVER, PAUL AMBROSE

Rank: Captain (highest rank: Brevet Brigadier General)
Service: U.S. Army
Birthday: 18 July 1831
Place of Birth: At sea in the English Channel aboard American flagship Louisiana.
Date of Death: 18 May 1928
Place of Death: Laurel Run, Pennsylvania
Cemetery: The Green Wood Cemetery—Brooklyn, New York
Entered Service at: New York, New York
Unit: Company D, 12th New York Infantry
Battle or Place of Action: Resaca, Georgia
Date of Action: 15 May 1864
Date of Issue: 12 October 1892
Citation: While acting as aide assisted in preventing a disaster caused by Union troops firing into each other.

997 ◆ O'NEILL, STEPHEN

Rank: Corporal (highest rank: Ordance Sergeant Ret.)
Service: U.S. Army
Birthday: 23 December 1837
Place of Birth: St. Johns, New Brunswick, Canada
Date of Death: 20 October 1909
Place of Death: Sault Ste. Marie, Michigan
Cemetery: Riverside Cemetery—Sault Ste. Marie, Michigan
Entered Service at: New York, New York
Unit: Company E, 7th U.S. Infantry
Battle or Place of Action: Chancellorsville, Virginia
Date of Action: 1 May 1863
Date of Issue: 28 September 1891
Citation: Took up the colors from the hands of the color bearer who had been shot down and bore them through the remainder of the battle.

998 ◆ OPEL, JOHN N.

Rank: Private
Service: U.S. Army
Birthday: 30 July 1843
Place of Birth: Hoflas, Bavaria, Germany
Date of Death: 21 February 1925
Place of Death: Cora, Missouri
Cemetery: Mount Zion Cemetery—Pleasant Hill Township, Missouri
Entered Service at: Rossburg, Decatur County, Indiana
Unit: Company G, 7th Indiana Infantry
Battle or Place of Action: Wilderness Campaign, Virginia
Date of Action: 5 May 1864
Date of Issue: 1 December 1864
Citation: Capture of flag of 50th Virginia Infantry (C.S.A.).

999 ◆ ORBANSKY, DAVID

Rank: Private (highest rank: Corporal)
Service: U.S. Army
Birthday: 1843
Place of Birth: Lautenburg, Prussia
Date of Death: 22 January 1897
Cemetery: Cedar Hill Cemetery—Piqua, Ohio
Entered Service at: Columbus, Franklin County, Ohio
Unit: Company B, 58th Ohio Infantry
Battle or Place of Action: Shiloh, Tennessee & Vicksburg, Mississippi, etc.
Date of Action: 1862 & 1863
Date of Issue: 2 August 1879
Citation: Gallantry in actions.

1000 ◆ ORR, CHARLES ALVIN

Rank: Private
Service: U.S. Army
Birthday: 28 June 1848
Place of Birth: Holland, Erie County, New York
Date of Death: 28 October 1923
Place of Death: Buffalo, New York

Cemetery: Forest Lawn Cemetery—Buffalo, New York
Entered Service at: Bennington, Wyoming County, New York
Unit: Company G, 187th New York Infantry
Battle or Place of Action: Hatcher's Run, Virginia
Date of Action: 27 October 1864
Date of Issue: 1 April 1898
Citation: This soldier and two others, voluntarily and under fire, rescued several wounded and helpless soldiers.

1001 ◆ ORR, ROBERT LEVAN

Rank: Major (highest rank: Colonel)
Service: U.S. Army
Birthday: 28 March 1836
Place of Birth: Philadelphia, Philadelphia County, Pennsylvania
Date of Death: 14 November 1894
Cemetery: Lawnview Cemetery—Philadelphia, Pennsylvania
Entered Service at: Philadelphia, Philadelphia County, Pennsylvania
Unit: 61st Pennsylvania Infantry
Battle or Place of Action: Petersburg, Virginia
Date of Action: 2 April 1865
Date of Issue: 28 November 1892
Citation: Carried the colors at the head of the column in the assault after two color bearers had been shot down.

1002 ◆ ORTEGA, JOHN

Rank: Seaman (highest rank: Acting Master's Mate)
Service: U.S. Navy
Birthday: 1840
Place of Birth: Spain
Entered Service at: Pennsylvania
Unit: U.S.S. *Saratoga*
Battle or Place of Action: off the Coast, Georgia
Date of Action: Unknown
G.O. Number, Date: 45, 31 December 1864
Citation: Served as seaman on board the U.S.S. *Saratoga* during actions of that vessel on two occasions. Carrying out his duties courageously during these actions, Ortega conducted himself gallantly through both periods. Promoted to acting master's mate.

1003 ◆ ORTH, JACOB GEORGE

Rank: Corporal (highest rank: Sergeant)
Service: U.S. Army
Birthday: 25 November 1837
Place of Birth: Philadelphia, Philadelphia County, Pennsylvania
Date of Death: 11 September 1907
Place of Death: Philadelphia, Pennsylvania
Cemetery: West Laurel Cemetery (MH)—Bala-Cynwyd, Pennsylvania
Entered Service at: Philadelphia, Philadelphia County, Pennsylvania
Unit: Company D, 28th Pennsylvania Infantry

Battle or Place of Action: Antietam, Maryland
Date of Action: 17 September 1862
Date of Issue: 15 January 1867
Citation: Capture of flag of 7th South Carolina Infantry (C.S.A.), in hand-to-hand encounter, although he was wounded in the shoulder.

1004 ◆ OSBORNE, WILLIAM HENRY

Rank: Private
Service: U.S. Army
Birthday: 16 September 1839
Place of Birth: Scituate, Plymouth County, Massachusetts
Date of Death: 5 June 1910
Cemetery: Village Cemetery of Elmwood (MH)—East Bridgewater, Massachusetts
Entered Service at: East Bridgewater, Plymouth County, Massachusetts
Unit: Company C, 29th Massachusetts Infantry
Battle or Place of Action: Malvern Hill, Virginia
Date of Action: 1 July 1862
Date of Issue: 1 April 1898
Citation: Although wounded and carried to the rear, he secured a rifle and voluntarily returned to the front, where, failing to find his own regiment, he joined another and fought with it until again severely wounded and taken prisoner.
Notes: POW

1005 ◆ OSS, ALBERT

Rank: Private
Service: U.S. Army
Birthday: 1818
Place of Birth: Belgium
Date of Death: 18 December 1898
Place of Death: Kearney, New Jersey
Cemetery: The Holy Sepulchre Cemetery—East Orange, New Jersey
Entered Service at: Newark, Essex County, New Jersey
Unit: Company B, 11th New Jersey Infantry
Battle or Place of Action: Chancellorsville, Virginia
Date of Action: 3 May 1863
Date of Issue: 6 May 1892
Citation: Remained in the rifle pits after the others had retreated, firing constantly, and contesting the ground step by step.

1006 ◆ OVERTURF, JACOB H.

Rank: Private (highest rank: Sergeant)
Service: U.S. Army
Birthday: 7 January 1842
Place of Birth: Jefferson County, Indiana
Date of Death: 10 September 1900
Cemetery: Holton Cemetery (MH)—Holton, Indiana
Entered Service at: Holton, Ripley County, Indiana
Unit: Company K, 83d Indiana Infantry
Battle or Place of Action: Vicksburg, Mississippi

Date of Action: 22 May 1863
Date of Issue: 13 August 1894
Citation: Gallantry in the charge of the "volunteer storming party."

1007 ◆ OVIATT, MILES M.

Rank: Corporal
Service: U.S. Marine Corps
Birthday: 1 December 1840
Place of Birth: Cattaraugus County, New York
Date of Death: 1 November 1880
Cemetery: Pleasant Valley Cemetery (MH)—Olean, New York
Entered Service at: New York
Unit: U.S.S. *Brooklyn*
Battle or Place of Action: Mobile Bay, Alabama
Date of Action: 5 August 1864
G.O. Number, Date: 45, 31 December 1864
Citation: On board the U.S.S. *Brooklyn* during action against rebel forts and gunboat and with the ram *Tennessee* in Mobile Bay, 5 August 1864. Despite severe damage to his ship and the loss of several men on board as enemy fire raked the deck, Cpl. Oviatt fought his gun with skill and courage throughout the furious two-hour battle which resulted in the surrender of the rebel ram *Tennessee*.

1008 ◆ PACKARD, LORON F.

Rank: Private
Service: U.S. Army
Place of Birth: Cattaraugus County, New York
Date of Death: 16 July 1903
Cemetery: Cuba Cemetery (MH)—Cuba, New York
Entered Service at: Cuba, Allegany County, New York
Unit: Company E, 5th New York Cavalry
Battle or Place of Action: Raccoon Ford, Virginia
Date of Action: 27 November 1863
Date of Issue: 20 August 1894
Citation: After his command had retreated, this soldier, voluntarily and alone, returned to the assistance of a comrade and rescued him from the hands of three armed Confederates,

1009 ◆ PALMER, GEORGE HENRY

Rank: Musician (highest rank: Major)
Service: U.S. Army
Birthday: 1842
Place of Birth: New York
Date of Death: 7 April 1901
Cemetery: Arlington National Cemetery (3-2104)—Arlington, Virginia
Entered Service at: Monmouth, Warren County, Illinois
Unit: 1st Illinois Cavalry
Battle or Place of Action: Lexington, Missouri
Date of Action: 20 September 1861
Date of Issue: 10 March 1896
Citation: Volunteered to fight in the trenches and also led a charge which resulted in the recapture of a Union hospital,

together with Confederate sharpshooters then occupying the same.

1010 ◆ PALMER, JOHN GIDEON

Rank: Corporal
Service: U.S. Army
Birthday: 14 October 1845
Place of Birth: Montville, New London County, Connecticut
Date of Death: 17 November 1901
Place of Death: New Haven, Connecticut
Cemetery: Indian Hill Cemetery (MH)—Middletown, Connecticut
Entered Service at: Montville, New London County, Connecticut
Unit: Company F, 21st Connecticut Infantry
Battle or Place of Action: Fredericksburg, Virginia
Date of Action: 13 December 1862
Date of Issue: 30 October 1896
Citation: First of six men who volunteered to assist gunner of a battery upon which the enemy was concentrating its fire, and fought with the battery until the close of the engagement. His commanding officer felt he would never see this man alive again.

1011 ◆ PALMER, WILLIAM JACKSON

Rank: Colonel (highest rank: Brevet Brigadier General)
Service: U.S. Army
Birthday: 17 September 1836
Place of Birth: Leipsic, Kent County, Delaware
Date of Death: 13 March 1909
Place of Death: Colorado Springs, Colorado
Cemetery: Evergreen Cemetery (MH)—Colorado Springs, Colorado
Entered Service at: Philadelphia, Philadelphia County, Pennsylvania
Unit: 15th Pennsylvania Cavalry
Battle or Place of Action: Red Hill, Alabama
Date of Action: 14 January 1865
Date of Issue: 24 February 1894
Citation: With less than 200 men attacked and defeated a superior force of the enemy, capturing their fieldpiece and about 100 prisoners without losing a man.

1012 ◆ PARKER, THOMAS

Rank: Corporal
Service: U.S. Army
Birthday: 1822
Place of Birth: England
Date of Death: 27 April 1872
Cemetery: Mechanics Cemetery—Philadelphia, Pennsylvania
Entered Service at: Providence, Providence County, Rhode Island
Unit: Company B, 2d Rhode Island Infantry
Battle or Place of Action: Petersburg & Deatonsville (Sailors Creek) Virginia

Date of Action: 2 April & 6 April 1865
Date of Issue: 29 May 1867
Citation: Planted the first color on the enemy's works. Carried the regimental colors over the creek after the regiment had broken and been repulsed.

1013 ◆ PARKER, WILLIAM

Rank: Captain of the Afterguard
Service: U.S. Navy
Place of Birth: Boston, Suffolk County, Massachusetts
Entered Service at: Massachusetts
Unit: U.S.S. *Cayuga*
Battle or Place of Action: Forts Jackson & St. Philip and New Orleans, Louisiana
Date of Action: 24-25 April 1862
G.O. Number, Date: 11, 3 April 1863
Citation: At the wheel on board the U.S.S. *Cayuga* during the capture of Forts St. Philip and Jackson, and of New Orleans, 24 and 25 April 1862. As his ship led the advance column toward the barrier and both forts opened fire simultaneously, striking the vessel from stem to stern, Parker conscientiously performed his duties throughout the action in which attempts by three rebel steamers to butt and board were thwarted, and the ships driven off. Eleven gunboats were successfully engaged and the enemy garrisons forced to surrender during this battle in which the *Cayuga* sustained 46 hits.

1014 ◆ PARKS, GEORGE

Rank: Captain of the Forecastle
Service: U.S. Navy
Birthday: 1823
Place of Birth: Schenectady, Schenectady County, New York
Entered Service at: New York, New York
Unit: U.S.S. *Richmond*
Battle or Place of Action: Fort Morgan, Mobile Bay, Alabama
Date of Action: 5 August 1864
G.O. Number, Date: 45, 31 December 1864
Citation: On board the U.S.S. *Richmond* during action against rebel forts and gunboats and with the ram *Tennessee* in Mobile Bay, 5 August 1864. Despite damage to his ship the and loss of several men on board as enemy fire raked her decks, Parks performed his duties with skill and courage throughout a furious two-hour battle which resulted in the surrender of the rebel ram *Tennessee* and in the damaging and destruction of batteries at Fort Morgan.

1015 ◆ PARKS, HENRY JEREMIAH

Rank: Private (highest rank: Captain)
Service: U.S. Army
Birthday: 24 February 1848
Place of Birth: Orangeville, Wyoming County, New York
Date of Death: 19 October 1927
Place of Death: San Diego, California

Cemetery: Arlington National Cemetery (2-1200-SS)—Arlington, Virginia
Entered Service at: Orangeville, Wyoming County, New York
Unit: Company A, 9th New York Cavalry
Battle or Place of Action: Cedar Creek, Virginia
Date of Action: 19 October 1864
Date of Presentation: 26 October 1864
Place of Presentation: Presented by Pres. Abraham Lincoln
Citation: While alone and in advance of his unit and attempting to cut off the retreat of a supply wagon, he fought and sent to flight a Confederate color bearer. After capturing the color bearer and leaving him in the rear, he returned to the front and captured three more wagons and drivers.

1016 ◆ PARKS, JAMES W.

Rank: Corporal
Service: U.S. Army
Birthday: 1840
Place of Birth: Lawrence County, Ohio
Date of Death: 14 January 1906
Place of Death: Massac County, Illinois
Entered Service at: Xenia, Clay County, Illinois
Unit: Company F, 11th Missouri Infantry
Battle or Place of Action: Nashville, Tennessee
Date of Action: 16 December 1864
Date of Issue: 24 February 1865
Citation: Capture of flag.

1017 ◆ PARROTT, JACOB

Rank: Private (highest rank: First Lieutenant)
Service: U.S. Army
Birthday: 17 July 1843
Place of Birth: Fairfield County, Ohio
Date of Death: 22 December 1908
Cemetery: Grove Cemetery (MH)—Kenton, Ohio
Entered Service at: Kenton, Hardin County, Ohio
Unit: Company K, 33d Ohio Infantry
Battle or Place of Action: Georgia
Date of Action: April 1862
Date of Presentation: 25 March 1863
Place of Presentation: Washington, D.C., presented by Sec. of War Edward M. Stanton
Citation: One of 19 of 24 men (including two civilians) who, by direction of Gen. Ormsby M. Mitchell, penetrated nearly 200 miles south into enemy territory and captured a railroad train at Big Shanty, Ga., in an attempt to destroy the bridges and track between Chattanooga and Atlanta.
Notes: POW

1018 ◆ PARSONS, JOEL

Rank: Private
Service: U.S. Army
Birthday: 23 August 1840
Place of Birth: Jackson County, West Virginia
Date of Death: 10 November 1919

Place of Death: Columbus, Ohio
Cemetery: Union Cemetery—Columbus, Ohio
Entered Service at: Mason City, Mason County, West Virginia
Unit: Company B, 4th West Virginia Infantry
Battle or Place of Action: Vicksburg, Mississippi
Date of Action: 22 May 1863
Date of Issue: 16 August 1894
Citation: Gallantry in the charge of the "volunteer storming party."

1019 ◆ PATTERSON, JOHN HENRY

Rank: First Lieutenant (highest rank: Brigadier General Ret.)
Service: U.S. Army
Birthday: 10 February 1843
Place of Birth: New York
Date of Death: 5 October 1920
Place of Death: Selkirk, New York
Cemetery: Albany Rural Cemetery (MH)—Albany, New York
Entered Service at: New York
Unit: 11th U.S. Infantry
Battle or Place of Action: Wilderness Campaign, Virginia
Date of Action: 5 May 1864
Date of Issue: 23 July 1897
Citation: Under the heavy fire of the advancing enemy, picked up and carried several hundred yards to a place of safety a wounded officer of his regiment who was helpless and would otherwise have been burned in the forest.

1020 ◆ PATTERSON, JOHN T.

Rank: Principal Musician
Service: U.S. Army
Birthday: 3 February 1838
Place of Birth: Morgan County, Ohio
Date of Death: 3 March 1922
Place of Death: Mauston, Wisconsin
Cemetery: Oakwood Cemetery—Mauston, Wisconsin
Entered Service at: McConnelsville, Morgan County, Ohio
Unit: 122d Ohio Infantry
Battle or Place of Action: Winchester, Virginia
Date of Action: 14 June 1863
Date of Issue: 13 May 1899
Citation: With one companion, voluntarily went in front of the Union lines, under a heavy fire from the enemy, and carried back a helpless, wounded comrade, thus saving him from death or capture.

1021 ◆ PAUL, WILLIAM H.

Rank: Private (highest rank: First Sergeant)
Service: U.S. Army
Birthday: 3 October 1844
Place of Birth: Philadelphia, Philadelphia County, Pennsylvania
Date of Death: 23 February 1911

Cemetery: Wesleyan Chapel Cemetery—Havre De Grace, Maryland
Entered Service at: Philadelphia, Philadelphia County, Pennsylvania
Unit: Company E, 90th Pennsylvania Infantry
Battle or Place of Action: Antietam, Maryland
Date of Action: 17 September 1862
Date of Issue: 3 November 1896
Citation: Under a most withering and concentrated fire, voluntarily picked up the colors of his regiment, when the bearer and two of the color guard had been killed, and bore them aloft throughout the entire battle.

1022 ◆ PAY, BYRON E.

Rank: Private
Service: U.S. Army
Birthday: 21 October 1844
Place of Birth: LeRoy Township, Jefferson County, New York
Date of Death: 19 February 1906
Place of Death: Volga, South Dakota
Entered Service at: Mankato, Blue Earth County, Minnesota
Unit: Company H, 2d Minnesota Infantry
Battle or Place of Action: Nolensville, Tennessee
Date of Action: 15 February 1863
Date of Issue: 11 September 1897
Citation: Was one of a detachment of 16 men who heroically defended a wagon train against the attack of 125 cavalry, repulsed the attack, and saved the train.

1023 ◆ PAYNE, IRVIN C.

Rank: Corporal (highest rank: Sergeant)
Service: U.S. Army
Birthday: 1830
Place of Birth: Wayne County, Pennsylvania
Date of Death: 3 April 1887
Place of Death: Dunmore, Pennsylvania
Cemetery: Dunmore Cemetery—Dunmore, Pennsylvania
Entered Service at: New York, New York
Unit: Company M, 2d New York Cavalry
Battle or Place of Action: Deatonsville (Sailor's Creek), Virginia
Date of Action: 6 April 1865
Date of Issue: 3 May 1865
Citation: Capture of Virginia state colors.

1024 ◆ PAYNE, THOMAS H. L.

Rank: First Lieutenant (highest rank: Captain)
Service: U.S. Army
Birthday: 5 October 1840
Place of Birth: Boston Suffolk County, Massachusetts
Date of Death: 13 September 1909
Place of Death: Philadelphia, Pennsylvania
Cemetery: Fernwood Cemetery—Fernwood, Pennsylvania
Entered Service at: Mendota, La Salle County, Illinois

Unit: Company E, 37th Illinois Infantry
Battle or Place of Action: Fort Blakely, Alabama
Date of Action: 9 April 1865
Date of Issue: 1 April 1898
Citation: While acting regimental quartermaster, learning of an expected assault, Payne requested assignment to a company that had no commissioned officers present; was so assigned, and was one of the first to lead his men into the enemy's works.

1025 ◆ PEARSALL, PLATT

Rank: Corporal
Service: U.S. Army
Birthday: 27 December 1841
Place of Birth: Meigs County, Ohio
Date of Death: 18 June 1931
Place of Death: Farmington, Missouri
Cemetery: Pendleton Cemetery (MH)—Farmington, Missouri
Entered Service at: Downington, Ohio
Unit: Company C, 30th Ohio Infantry
Battle or Place of Action: Vicksburg, Mississippi
Date of Action: 22 May 1863
Date of Issue: 14 August 1894
Citation: Gallantry in the charge of the "volunteer storming party."

1026 ◆ PEARSON, ALFRED L.

Rank: Colonel (highest rank: Brevet Major General)
Service: U.S. Army
Birthday: 28 December 1838
Place of Birth: Pittsburgh, Allegheny County, Pennsylvania
Date of Death: 6 January 1903
Place of Death: Sewickley, Pennsylvania
Cemetery: Allegheny Cemetery (MH)—Pittsburgh, Pennsylvania
Entered Service at: Pittsburgh, Allegheny County, Pennsylvania
Unit: 155th Pennsylvania Infantry
Battle or Place of Action: Lewis' Farm, Virginia
Date of Action: 29 March 1865
Date of Issue: 17 September 1897
Citation: Seeing a brigade forced back by the enemy, he seized his regimental color, called on his men to follow him, and advanced upon the enemy under a severe fire. The whole brigade took up the advance, the lost ground was regained, and the enemy was repulsed.

1027 ◆ PEASE, JOACHIM

Rank: Seaman
Service: U.S. Navy
Birthday: 1842
Place of Birth: Long Island, New York
Entered Service at: New York, New York
Unit: U.S.S. *Kearsarge*
Battle or Place of Action: off Cherbourg, France

Date of Action: 19 June 1864
G.O. Number, Date: 45, 31 December 1864
Citation: Served as seaman on board the U.S.S. *Kearsarge* when she destroyed the *Alabama* off Cherbourg, France, 19 June 1864. Acting as loader on the No. 2 gun during this bitter engagement, Pease exhibited marked coolness and good conduct and was highly recommended by the divisional officer for gallantry under fire.

1028 ◆ PECK, CASSIUS

Rank: Private (highest rank: Sergeant)
Service: U.S. Army
Birthday: 3 March 1842
Place of Birth: Brookfield, Orange County, Vermont
Date of Death: 12 July 1913
Place of Death: Burlington, Vermont
Cemetery: Brookfield New Cemetery—Brookfield, Vermont
Entered Service at: West Randolph, Orange County, Vermont
Unit: Company F, 1st U.S. Sharpshooters
Battle or Place of Action: near Blackburn's Ford, West Virginia
Date of Action: 19 September 1862
Date of Issue: 12 October 1892
Citation: Took command of such soldiers as he could get and attacked and captured a Confederate battery of four guns. Also, while on a reconnaissance, overtook and captured a Confederate soldier.

1029 ◆ PECK, OSCAR E.

Rank: Second Class Boy
Service: U.S. Navy
Birthday: 1848
Place of Birth: Bridgeport, Fairfield County, Connecticut
Date of Death: 23 October 1906
Place of Death: Norton Heights, Connecticut
Cemetery: Fitch's Home Cemetery (MH)—Darien, Connecticut
Entered Service at: Connecticut
Unit: U.S.S. *Varuna*
Battle or Place of Action: Forts Jackson & St. Philip, Louisiana
Date of Action: 24 April 1862
G.O. Number, Date: 11, 3 April 1863
Citation: Peck served as second class boy on board the *Varuna* during attacks on Forts Jackson and St. Philip, 24 April 1862. Acting as powder boy of the after rifle, Peck served gallantly while the *Varuna* was repeatedly attacked and rammed and finally sunk. This was an extremely close-range action and, although badly damaged, the *Varuna* delivered shells abaft the *Morgan*'s armor.

1030 ◆ PECK, THEODORE SAFFORD

Rank: First Lieutenant (highest rank: Major General)
Service: U.S. Army
Birthday: 22 March 1843

Place of Birth: Burlington, Chittenden County, Vermont
Date of Death: 15 March 1918
Cemetery: Lake View Cemetery—Burlington, Vermont
Entered Service at: Burlington, Chittenden County, Vermont
Unit: Company H, 9th Vermont Infantry
Battle or Place of Action: Newport Barracks, North Carolina
Date of Action: 2 February 1864
Date of Issue: 8 September 1891
Citation: By long and persistent resistance and burning the bridges, kept a superior force of the enemy at bay and covered the retreat of the garrison.

1031 ◆ PEIRSOL, JAMES KASTOR

Rank: Sergeant (highest rank: First Lieutenant)
Service: U.S. Army
Birthday: 21 September 1843
Place of Birth: Beaver County, Pennsylvania
Date of Death: 1 March 1927
Place of Death: Claremont, California
Cemetery: Grove Cemetery—New Brighton, Pennsylvania
Entered Service at: Waynesboro, Ohio
Unit: Company F, 13th Ohio Cavalry
Battle or Place of Action: Paines Crossroads, Virginia
Date of Action: 5 April 1865
Date of Issue: 3 May 1865
Citation: Capture of flag.

1032 ◆ PELHAM, WILLIAM

Rank: Landsman
Service: U.S. Navy
Birthday: 8 December 1847
Place of Birth: Halifax, Nova Scotia, Canada
Date of Death: 30 March 1933
Place of Death: Brooklyn, New York
Cemetery: Holy Cross Cemetery—Brooklyn, New York
Entered Service at: New York, New York
Unit: U.S.S. *Hartford*
Battle or Place of Action: Mobile Bay, Alabama
Date of Action: 5 August 1864
G.O. Number, Date: 45, 31 December 1864
Citation: On board the flagship U.S.S. *Hartford*, during successful actions against Fort Morgan, rebel gunboats and the ram *Tennessee* in Mobile Bay, 5 August 1864. When other members of his crewgun were killed or wounded under the enemy's terrific shellfire, Pelham calmly assisted the casualties below and voluntarily returned and took his place at an adjoining gun where another man had been struck down. He continued to fight his gun throughout the remainder of the battle which resulted in the capture of the *Tennessee*.

1033 ◆ PENNYPACKER, GALUSHA

Rank: Colonel (highest rank: Major General U.S.A.)
Service: U.S. Army
Birthday: 1 June 1844

Place of Birth: Near Valley Forge, Chester County, Pennsylvania
Date of Death: 1 October 1916
Place of Death: Philadelphia, Pennsylvania
Cemetery: Philadelphia National Cemetery (0-175)—Philadelphia, Pennsylvania
Entered Service at: West Chester, Chester County, Pennsylvania
Unit: 97th Pennsylvania Infantry
Battle or Place of Action: Fort Fisher, North Carolina
Date of Action: 15 January 1865
Date of Issue: 17 August 1891
Citation: Gallantly led the charge over a traverse and planted the colors of one of his regiments thereon; was severely wounded.

1034 ◆ PENTZER, PATRICK HENRY

Rank: Captain
Service: U.S. Army
Birthday: 1839
Place of Birth: Marion County, Missouri
Date of Death: 16 October 1901
Place of Death: Nevada, Missouri
Cemetery: Springfield National Cemetery (24-1696) (MH)—Springfield, Missouri
Entered Service at: Gillespie, Macoupin County, Illinois
Unit: Company C, 97th Illinois Infantry
Battle or Place of Action: Fort Blakely, Alabama
Date of Action: 9 April 1865
Date of Issue: 9 October 1879
Citation: Among the first to enter the enemy's entrenchments, he received the surrender of a Confederate general officer and his headquarters flag.

1035 ◆ PERRY, THOMAS

Rank: Boatswain's Mate
Service: U.S. Navy
Birthday: 1836
Place of Birth: New York
Entered Service at: New York
Unit: U.S.S. *Kearsarge*
Battle or Place of Action: off Cherbourg, France
Date of Action: 19 June 1864
G.O. Number, Date: 45, 31 December 1864
Citation: Served as boatswain's mate on board the U.S.S. *Kearsarge* when she destroyed the *Alabama* off Cherbourg, France, 19 June 1864. Acting as captain of the No. 2 gun during this bitter engagement, Perry exhibited marked coolness and good conduct under the enemy fire and was recommended for gallantry by his divisional officer.

1036 ◆ PESCH, JOSEPH M.

Rank: Private
Service: U.S. Army
Birthday: 18 July 1835
Place of Birth: Grossleiton, Prussia

Date of Death: 11 October 1903
Cemetery: Bellefontaine Cemetery—St. Louis, Missouri
Entered Service at: St. Louis, St. Louis County, Missouri
Unit: Battery A, 1st Missouri Light Artillery
Battle or Place of Action: Grand Gulf, Mississippi
Date of Action: 28-29 April 1863
Date of Issue: 10 March 1896
Citation: With two comrades voluntarily took position on board the steamer *Cheeseman*, in charge of all the guns and ammunition of the battery, and remained in charge of the same, although the steamer became unmanageable and was exposed for some time to a heavy fire from the enemy.

1037 ◆ PETERS, HENRY CARLTON

Rank: Private (highest rank: Sergeant)
Service: U.S. Army
Birthday: 29 February 1840
Place of Birth: Monroe County, Michigan
Date of Death: 19 March 1923
Place of Death: Manning, Iowa
Cemetery: Riverside Cemetery (MH)—South Rockwood, Michigan
Entered Service at: Adrian, Lenawee County, Michigan
Unit: Company B, 47th Ohio Infantry
Battle or Place of Action: Vicksburg, Mississippi
Date of Action: 3 May 1863
Date of Issue: 17 April 1917
Citation: Was one of a party that volunteered and attempted to run the enemy's batteries with a steam tug and two barges loaded with subsistence stores.
Notes: POW

1038 ◆ PETERSON, ALFRED

Rank: Seaman
Service: U.S. Navy
Birthday: 1838
Place of Birth: Sweden
Entered Service at: New York, New York
Unit: U.S.S. *Commodore Perry*
Battle or Place of Action: Franklin, Virginia
Date of Action: 3 October 1862
G.O. Number, Date: 11, 3 April 1863
Citation: On board the U.S.S. *Commodore Perry* in the attack upon Franklin, Va., 3 October 1862. With enemy fire raking the deck of his ship and blockades thwarting her progress, Peterson remained at his post and performed his duties with skill and courage as the *Commodore Perry* fought a gallant battle to silence many rebel batteries as she steamed down the Blackwater River.

1039 ◆ PETTY, PHILIP

Rank: Sergeant (highest rank: Color Sergeant)
Service: U.S. Army
Birthday: 17 May 1840
Place of Birth: Tingswich, Buckinghamshire, England
Date of Death: 22 December 1917

Place of Death: Daggett, Pennsylvania
Cemetery: Daggett Cemetery (MH)—Daggett, Pennsylvania
Entered Service at: Troy, Bradford County, Pennsylvania
Unit: Company A, 136th Pennsylvania Infantry
Battle or Place of Action: Fredericksburg, Virginia
Date of Action: 13 December 1862
Date of Issue: 21 August 1893
Citation: Took up the colors as they fell out of the hands of the wounded color bearer and carried them forward in the charge.

1040 ◆ PHELPS, CHARLES EDWARDS

Rank: Colonel (highest rank: Brevet Brigadier General)
Service: U.S. Army
Birthday: 1 May 1833
Place of Birth: Guilford, Vermont
Date of Death: 27 December 1908
Cemetery: Woodlawn Cemetery—Baltimore, Maryland
Entered Service at: Baltimore, Baltimore County, Maryland
Unit: 7th Maryland Infantry
Battle or Place of Action: Laurel Hill, Virginia
Date of Action: 8 May 1864
Date of Issue: 30 March 1898
Citation: Rode to the head of the assaulting column, then much broken by severe losses and faltering under the close fire of artillery, placed himself conspicuously in front of the troops, and gallantly rallied and led them to within a few feet of the enemy's works, where he was severely wounded and captured.

1041 ◆ PHILLIPS, JOSIAH

Rank: Private
Service: U.S. Army
Birthday: 1830
Place of Birth: Wyoming County, New York
Date of Death: 11 December 1894
Place of Death: Lawrence, Wisconsin
Cemetery: Lawrence Cemetery—Lawrence, Wisconsin
Entered Service at: Ulysses, Potter County, Pennsylvania
Unit: Company E, 148th Pennsylvania Infantry
Battle or Place of Action: Sutherland Station, Virginia
Date of Action: 2 April 1865
Date of Issue: 10 May 1865
Citation: Capture of flag.

1042 ◆ PHINNEY, WILLIAM

Rank: Boatswain's Mate
Service: U.S. Navy
Birthday: 1824
Place of Birth: Norway
Entered Service at: New York, New York
Unit: U.S.S. *Lackawanna*
Battle or Place of Action: Fort Morgan, Mobile Bay, Alabama

Date of Action: 5 August 1864
G.O. Number, Date: 45, 31 December 1864
Citation: On board the U.S.S. *Lackawanna* during successful attacks against Fort Morgan, rebel gunboats, and the rebel ram *Tennessee* in Mobile Bay, 5 August 1864. Serving as gun captain, Phinney showed much presence of mind in managing the gun and gave much needed encouragement to the crew during the engagement, which resulted in the capture of the prize rebel ram *Tennessee* and in the damaging and destruction of Fort Morgan.

1043 ◆ PHISTERER, FREDERICK

Rank: First Lieutenant (highest rank: Brevet Major General)
Service: U.S. Army
Birthday: 11 October 1836
Place of Birth: Germany
Date of Death: 13 July 1909
Cemetery: Greenlawn Cemetery—Columbus, Ohio
Entered Service at: Medina County, Ohio
Unit: 18th U.S. Infantry
Battle or Place of Action: Stone River, Tennessee
Date of Action: 31 December 1862
Date of Issue: 12 December 1894
Citation: Voluntarily conveyed, under a heavy fire, information to the commander of a battalion of regular troops by which the battalion was saved from capture or annihilation.

1044 ◆ PICKLE, ALONZO H.

Rank: Sergeant
Service: U.S. Army
Birthday: 2 July 1843
Place of Birth: Canada
Date of Death: 24 May 1925
Cemetery: Home Cemetery (MH)—Sleepy Eye, Minnesota
Entered Service at: Dover, Olmsted County, Minnesota
Unit: Company B, 1st Battalion, Minnesota Infantry
Battle or Place of Action: Deep Bottom, Virginia
Date of Action: 14 August 1864
Date of Issue: 12 June 1895
Citation: At the risk of his life, voluntarily went to the assistance of a wounded officer lying close to the enemy's lines and, under fire, carried him to a place of safety.

1045 ◆ PIKE, EDWARD M.

Rank: First Sergeant
Service: U.S. Army
Birthday: 1 July 1838
Place of Birth: Casco, Cumberland County, Maine
Date of Death: 10 August 1924
Cemetery: Payne Cemetery—Chenoa, Illinois
Entered Service at: Bloomington, McLean County, Illinois
Unit: Company A, 33d Illinois Infantry
Battle or Place of Action: Cache River, Arkansas
Date of Action: 7 July 1862
Date of Issue: 29 March 1899

Citation: While the troops were falling back before a superior force, this soldier, assisted by one companion, and while under severe fire at close-range, saved a cannon from capture by the enemy.

1046 ◆ PINGREE, SAMUEL E.

Rank: Captain (highest rank: Colonel)
Service: U.S. Army
Birthday: 2 August 1832
Place of Birth: Salisbury, Merrimack County, New Hampshire
Date of Death: 1 June 1922
Cemetery: Hartford Cemetery—White River Junction, Vermont
Entered Service at: Hartford, Windsor County, Vermont
Unit: Company F, 3d Vermont Infantry
Battle or Place of Action: Lee's Mills, Virginia
Date of Action: 16 April 1862
Date of Issue: 17 August 1891
Citation: Gallantly led his company across a wide, deep creek, drove the enemy from the rifle pits, which were within two yards of the farther bank, and remained at the head of his men until a second time severely wounded.

1047 ◆ PINKHAM, CHARLES H.

Rank: Sergeant Major (highest rank: Brevet Captain)
Service: U.S. Army
Birthday: 18 August 1844
Place of Birth: Grafton, Worcester County, Massachusetts
Date of Death: 6 November 1920
Cemetery: Hope Cemetery (MH)—Worcester, Massachusetts
Entered Service at: Worcester, Worcester County, Massachusetts
Unit: 57th Massachusetts Infantry
Battle or Place of Action: Fort Stedman, Virginia
Date of Action: 25 March 1865
Date of Issue: 15 April 1895
Citation: Captured the flag of the 57th North Carolina Infantry (C.S.A.), and saved his own colors by tearing them from the staff while the enemy was in the camp.

1048 ◆ PINN, ROBERT A.

Rank: First Sergeant
Service: U.S. Army
Birthday: 1 March 1843
Place of Birth: Stark County, Ohio
Date of Death: 1 January 1911
Cemetery: City Cemetery (MH)—Massillon, Ohio
Entered Service at: Massillon, Stark County, Ohio
Unit: Company I, 5th U.S. Colored Infantry
Battle or Place of Action: Chapin's Farm, Virginia
Date of Action: 29 September 1864
Date of Issue: 6 April 1865
Citation: Took command of his company after all the officers had been killed or wounded and gallantly led it in battle.

1049 ◆ PIPES, JAMES MILTON

Rank: Captain
Service: U.S. Army
Birthday: 10 November 1840
Place of Birth: Morrisville, Bucks County, Pennsylvania
Date of Death: 1 December 1928
Place of Death: Washington, D.C.
Cemetery: Arlington National Cemetery (3-1332-A)—Arlington, Virginia
Entered Service at: Waynesburg, Greene County, Pennsylvania
Unit: Company A, 140th Pennsylvania Infantry
Battle or Place of Action: Gettysburg, Pennsylvania & Reams Station, Virginia
Date of Action: 2 July 1863 & 25 August 1864
Date of Issue: 5 April 1898
Citation: While a sergeant and retiring with his company before the rapid advance of the enemy at Gettysburg, he and a companion stopped and carried to a place of safety a wounded and helpless comrade; in this act both he and his companion were severely wounded. A year later, at Reams Station, Va., while commanding a skirmish line, voluntarily assisted in checking a flank movement of the enemy, and while so doing was severely wounded, suffering the loss of an arm.

1050 ◆ PITMAN, GEORGE J.

Rank: Sergeant
Service: U.S. Army
Birthday: 1839
Place of Birth: Recklestown, New Jersey
Date of Death: 30 April 1884
Place of Death: Philadelphia, Pennsylvania
Cemetery: South Section Laruel Hill Cemetery (MH)—Philadelphia, Pennsylvania
Entered Service at: Philadelphia, Philadelphia County, Pennsylvania
Unit: Company C, 1st New York (Lincoln) Cavalry
Battle or Place of Action: Deatonsville (Sailor's Creek), Virginia
Date of Action: 6 April 1865
Date of Issue: 3 May 1865
Citation: Capture of flag of the Sumter Heavy Artillery (C.S.A.).

1051 ◆ PITTINGER, WILLIAM

True Name: Pittenger, William
Rank: Sergeant
Service: U.S. Army
Birthday: 31 January 1840
Place of Birth: Knoxville, Jefferson County, Ohio
Date of Death: 24 April 1904
Place of Death: Fallbrook, California
Cemetery: Odd Fellow Cemetery (MH)—Fallbrook, California

Entered Service at: Steubenville, Jefferson County, Ohio
Unit: Company G, 2d Ohio Infantry
Battle or Place of Action: Georgia
Date of Action: April 1862
Date of Presentation: 25 March 1863
Place of Presentation: Washington, D.C., presented by Sec. of War Edward M. Stanton
Citation: One of 19 of 24 men (including two civilians) who, by direction of Gen. Ormsby M. Mitchell, penetrated nearly 200 miles south into enemy territory and captured a railroad train at Big Shanty, Ga., in an attempt to destroy the bridges and track between Chattanooga and Atlanta.

1052 ◆ PLANT, HENRY E.

Rank: Corporal (highest rank: Color Sergeant)
Service: U.S. Army
Birthday: 11 October 1841
Place of Birth: Oswego County, New York
Date of Death: 16 April 1925
Cemetery: Nunica Cemetery (MH)—Nunica, Michigan
Entered Service at: Cockery, Michigan
Unit: Company F, 14th Michigan Infantry
Battle or Place of Action: Bentonville, North Carolina
Date of Action: 19 March 1865
Date of Issue: 27 April 1896
Citation: Rushed into the midst of the enemy and rescued the colors, the color bearer having fallen mortally wounded.

1053 ◆ PLATT, GEORGE CRAWFORD

Rank: Private (highest rank: Sergeant)
Service: U.S. Army
Birthday: 17 February 1842
Place of Birth: Ireland
Date of Death: 20 June 1912
Cemetery: Holy Cross Cemetery (MH)—Yeadon, Pennsylvania
Entered Service at: Philadelphia, Philadelphia County, Pennsylvania
Unit: Troop H, 6th U.S. Cavalry
Battle or Place of Action: Fairfield, Pennsylvania
Date of Action: 3 July 1863
Date of Issue: 12 July 1895
Citation: Seized the regimental flag upon the death of the standard bearer in a hand-to-hand fight and prevented it from falling into the hands of the enemy.

1054 ◆ PLIMLEY, WILLIAM

Rank: First Lieutenant (highest rank: Major)
Service: U.S. Army
Birthday: 12 August 1839
Place of Birth: Catskill, Greene County, New York
Date of Death: 2 October 1913
Place of Death: New York, New York
Cemetery: Catskill Rural Cemetery (MH)—Catskill, New York

Entered Service at: Catskill, Greene County, New York
Unit: Company F, 120th New York Infantry
Battle or Place of Action: Hatcher's Run, Virginia
Date of Action: 2 April 1865
Date of Issue: 4 April 1898
Citation: While acting as aide to a general officer, voluntarily accompanied a regiment in an assault on the enemy's works and acted as leader of the movement which resulted in the rout of the enemy and the capture of large numbers of prisoners.

1055 ◆ PLOWMAN, GEORGE H.

Rank: Sergeant Major (highest rank: Captain)
Service: U.S. Army
Birthday: 10 March 1840
Place of Birth: Oxford, Oxfordshire, England
Date of Death: 27 February 1921
Place of Death: Woodward, Oklahoma
Cemetery: Arlington National Cemetery (3-4417-EH) (MH)—Arlington, Virginia
Entered Service at: Washington, D.C.
Unit: 3d Maryland Infantry
Battle or Place of Action: Petersburg, Virginia
Date of Action: 17 June 1864
Date of Issue: 1 December 1864
Citation: Recaptured the colors of the 2d Pennsylvania Provisional Artillery.

1056 ◆ PLUNKETT, THOMAS

Rank: Sergeant
Service: U.S. Army
Birthday: 1841
Place of Birth: Ireland
Date of Death: 10 March 1885
Cemetery: Hope Cemetery—Worcester, Massachusetts
Entered Service at: West Boylston, Worcester County, Massachusetts
Unit: Company E, 21st Massachusetts Infantry
Battle or Place of Action: Fredericksburg, Virginia
Date of Action: 11 December 1862
Date of Issue: 30 March 1866
Citation: Seized the colors of his regiment, the color bearer having been shot down, and bore them to the front where both his arms were carried off by a shell.

1057 ◆ POND, GEORGE F.

Rank: Private
Service: U.S. Army
Birthday: 5 October 1844
Place of Birth: Libertyville, Lake County, Illinois
Date of Death: 21 June 1911
Place of Death: Fort Scott, Kansas
Cemetery: Evergreen Cemetery (MH)—Fort Scott, Kansas
Entered Service at: Fairwater, Fond du Lac County, Wisconsin

Unit: Company C, 3d Wisconsin Cavalry
Battle or Place of Action: Drywood, Kansas
Date of Action: 15 May 1864
Date of Issue: 16 May 1899
Citation: With two companions, attacked a greatly superior force of guerrillas, routed them, and rescued several prisoners.

1058 ◆ POND, JAMES BURTON

Rank: First Lieutenant (highest rank: Major)
Service: U.S. Army
Birthday: 11 June 1838
Place of Birth: Allegany, Cattaraugus County, New York
Date of Death: 21 June 1903
Place of Death: Jersey City, New Jersey
Cemetery: Woodlawn Cemetery—Bronx, New York
Entered Service at: Janesville, Rock County, Wisconsin
Unit: Company C, 3d Wisconsin Cavalry
Battle or Place of Action: Baxter Springs, Kansas
Date of Action: 6 October 1863
Date of Issue: 30 March 1898
Citation: While in command of two companies of cavalry, was surprised and attacked by several times his own number of guerrillas, but gallantly rallied his men, and after a severe struggle drove the enemy outside the fortifications. First Lt. Pond then went outside the works and, alone and unaided, fired a howitzer three times, throwing the enemy into confusion and causing him to retire.

1059 ◆ POOLE, WILLIAM B.

Rank: Quartermaster
Service: U.S. Navy
Birthday: 1833
Place of Birth: Cape Elizabeth Cumberland County, Maine
Date of Death: 15 August 1904
Place of Death: Lynn, Massachusetts
Cemetery: Pine Grove Cemetery (MH)—Lynn, Massachusetts
Entered Service at: Maine
Unit: U.S.S. *Kearsarge*
Battle or Place of Action: off Cherbourg, France
Date of Action: 19 June 1864
G.O. Number, Date: 45, 31 December 1864
Citation: Served as quartermaster on board the U.S.S. *Kearsarge* when she destroyed the *Alabama* off Cherbourg, France, 19 June 1864. Stationed at the helm, Poole steered the ship during the engagement in a cool and most creditable manner and was highly commended by his divisional officer for his gallantry under fire.

1060 ◆ PORTER, AMBROSE

Rank: Commissary Sergeant (highest rank: First Lieutenant)
Service: U.S. Army
Birthday: 2 February 1839
Place of Birth: Allegany County, Maryland
Date of Death: 21 January 1916

Place of Death: Phelps City, Missouri
Cemetery: Elmwood Cemetery (MH)—Rockport, Missouri
Entered Service at: Rockport, Atchison County, Missouri
Unit: Company D, 12th Missouri Cavalry
Battle or Place of Action: Tallahatchie River, Mississippi
Date of Action: 7 August 1864
Date of Issue: 24 August 1905
Citation: Was one of four volunteers who swam the river under a brisk fire of the enemy's sharpshooters and brought over a ferry boat, by means of which the troops crossed and dislodged the enemy from a strong position.

1061 ◆ PORTER, HORACE

Rank: Captain (highest rank: Brevet Brigadier General)
Service: U.S. Army
Birthday: 15 April 1837
Place of Birth: Huntingdon, Huntingdon County, Pennsylvania
Date of Death: 29 May 1921
Place of Death: New York, New York
Cemetery: Old First United Methodist Church—West Long Branch, New Jersey
Entered Service at: Harrisburg, Dauphin County, Pennsylvania
Unit: Ordnance Department
Battle or Place of Action: Chickamauga, Georgia
Date of Action: 20 September 1863
Date of Issue: 8 July 1902
Citation: While acting as a volunteer aide, at a critical moment when the lines were broken, rallied enough fugitives to hold the ground under heavy fire long enough to effect the escape of wagon trains and batteries.

1062 ◆ PORTER, JOHN REED

Rank: Private (highest rank: First Lieutenant)
Service: U.S. Army
Birthday: 14 November 1838
Place of Birth: Delaware County, Ohio
Date of Death: 17 October 1923
Cemetery: Union Cemetery—Macomb, Ohio
Entered Service at: McComb, Hancock County, Ohio
Unit: Company G, 21st Ohio Infantry
Battle or Place of Action: Georgia
Date of Action: April 1862
Date of Issue: September 1863
Citation: One of 19 of 24 men (including two civilians) who, by direction of Gen. Ormsby M. Mitchell, penetrated nearly 200 miles south into enemy territory and captured a railroad train at Big Shanty, Ga., in an attempt to destroy the bridges and track between Chattanooga and Atlanta.
Notes: POW

1063 ◆ PORTER, WILLIAM

Rank: Sergeant
Service: U.S. Army

Place of Birth: New York, New York
Entered Service at: Trenton, Mercer County, New Jersey
Unit: Company H, 1st New Jersey Cavalry
Battle or Place of Action: Deatonsville (Sailor's Creek), Virginia
Date of Action: 6 April 1865
Date of Issue: 3 July 1865
Citation: Among the first to check the enemy's countercharge.

1064 ◆ POST, PHILIP SIDNEY

Rank: Colonel (highest rank: Brevet Brigadier General)
Service: U.S. Army
Birthday: 19 March 1833
Place of Birth: Florida, Orange County, New York
Date of Death: 5 January 1895
Cemetery: Hope Cemetery—Galesburg, Illinois
Entered Service at: Galesburg, Knox County, Illinois
Unit: 59th Illinois Infantry
Battle or Place of Action: Nashville, Tennessee
Date of Action: 15-16 December 1864
Date of Issue: 18 March 1893
Citation: Led his brigade in an attack upon a strong position under a terrific fire of grape, canister, and musketry; was struck down by a grapeshot after he had reached the enemy's works.

1065 ◆ POSTLES, JAMES PARKE

Rank: Captain
Service: U.S. Army
Birthday: 28 September 1840
Place of Birth: Camden, Kent County, Delaware
Date of Death: 27 May 1908
Cemetery: Wilmington Cemetery—Wilmington, Delaware
Entered Service at: Wilmimgton, New Castle County, Delaware
Unit: Company A, 1st Delaware Infantry
Battle or Place of Action: Gettysburg, Pennsylvania
Date of Action: 2 July 1863
Date of Issue: 22 July 1892
Citation: Voluntarily delivered an order in the face of heavy fire from the enemy.

1066 ◆ POTTER, GEORGE W.

Rank: Private
Service: U.S. Army
Birthday: 11 December 1843
Place of Birth: Coventry, Kent County, Rhode Island
Date of Death: 30 November 1918
Cemetery: Swan Point Cemetery (MH)—Providence, Rhode Island
Entered Service at: Coventry, Kent County, Rhode Island
Unit: Company G, 1st Rhode Island Light Artillery
Battle or Place of Action: Petersburg, Virginia
Date of Action: 2 April 1865
Date of Issue: 4 March 1886
Citation: Was one of a detachment of 20 picked artillerymen

who voluntarily accompanied an infantry assaulting party, and who turned upon the enemy the guns captured in the assault.

1067 ◆ POTTER, NORMAN F.

Rank: First Sergeant
Service: U.S. Army
Birthday: 10 June 1826
Place of Birth: Pompey, Onondaga County, New York
Date of Death: 25 April 1900
Cemetery: Delphi Falls Baptist Church Cemetery (MH)—Delphi Falls, New York
Entered Service at: Pompey, Onondaga County, New York
Unit: Company E, 149th New York Infantry
Battle or Place of Action: Lookout Mountain, Tennessee
Date of Action: 24 November 1863
Date of Issue: 24 June 1865
Citation: Capture of flag (Bragg's army).

1068 ◆ POWELL, WILLIAM HENRY

Rank: Major (highest rank: Brevet Major General)
Service: U.S. Army
Birthday: 25 May 1825
Place of Birth: Pontypool, Monmouthshire, South Wales
Date of Death: 26 December 1904
Place of Death: Sacket Harbor, New York
Cemetery: Graceland Cemetery—Chicago, Illinois
Entered Service at: Ironton, Lawrence County, Ohio
Unit: 2d West Virginia Cavalry
Battle or Place of Action: Sinking Creek, Virginia
Date of Action: 26 November 1862
Date of Issue: 22 July 1890
Citation: Distinguished services in raid, where with 20 men, he charged and captured the enemy's camp, 500 strong, without the loss of a man or gun.

1069 ◆ POWER, ALBERT

Rank: Private (highest rank: First Sergeant)
Service: U.S. Army
Birthday: 18 June 1842
Place of Birth: Liberty, Guernsey County, Ohio
Date of Death: 26 April 1923
Cemetery: I.O.O.F. Cemetery—Bloomfield, Iowa
Entered Service at: Bloomfield, Davis County, Iowa
Unit: Company A, 3d Iowa Cavalry
Battle or Place of Action: Pea Ridge, Arkansas
Date of Action: 7 March 1862
Date of Issue: 6 March 1899
Citation: Under a heavy fire and at great personal risk went to the aid of a dismounted comrade who was surrounded by the enemy, took him up on his own horse, and carried him to a place of safety.

1070 ◆ POWERS, WESLEY JAMES

Rank: Corporal
Service: U.S. Army
Birthday: 26 October 1845

Place of Birth: Orono, Ontario, Canada
Date of Death: 14 December 1902
Place of Death: St. Charles, Illinois
Cemetery: North Cemetery—St. Charles, Illinois
Entered Service at: Virgil, Kane County, Illinois
Unit: Company F, 147th Illinois Infantry
Battle or Place of Action: Oostanaula River, Georgia
Date of Action: 3 April 1865
Date of Issue: 24 October 1895
Citation: Voluntarily swam the river under heavy fire and secured a ferryboat, by means of which the command crossed.

1071 ◆ PRANCE, GEORGE

Rank: Captain of the Main Top
Service: U.S. Navy
Birthday: 1827
Place of Birth: France
Entered Service at: Boston, Suffolk County, Massachusetts
Unit: U.S.S. *Ticonderoga*
Battle or Place of Action: Fort Fisher, North Carolina
Date of Action: December 1864 & January 1865
G.O. Number, Date: 59, 22 June 1865
Citation: On board the U.S.S. *Ticonderoga* during attacks on Fort Fisher, 24 and 25 December 1864; and 13 to 15 January 1865. Despite heavy return fire by the enemy and the explosion of the 100-pounder Parrott rifle which killed eight men and wounded 12 more, Prance, as captain of a gun, performed his duties with skill and courage during the first two days of battle. As his ship again took position on the line on the 13th, he remained steadfast as the *Ticonderoga* maintained a well-placed fire upon the batteries onshore, and thereafter as she materially lessened the power of guns on the mound which had been turned upon our assaulting columns. During this action the flag was planted on one of the strongest fortifications possessed by the rebels.

1072 ◆ PRENTICE, JOSEPH ROLLIN

Rank: Private
Service: U.S. Army
Birthday: 6 December 1838
Place of Birth: Lancaster, Fairfield County, Ohio
Date of Death: 7 August 1908
Place of Death: Colorado Springs, Colorado
Cemetery: Sacred Heart Cemetery—Hebron, Nebraska
Entered Service at: Fort Wayne, Allen County, Indiana
Unit: Company E, 19th U.S. Infantry
Battle or Place of Action: Stone River, Tennessee
Date of Action: 31 December 1862
Date of Issue: 3 February 1894
Citation: Voluntarily rescued the body of his commanding officer, who had fallen mortally wounded. He brought off the field his mortally wounded leader under direct and constant rifle fire.

1073 ◆ PRESTON, JOHN

Rank: Landsman
Service: U.S. Navy

Birthday: 1841
Place of Birth: Ireland
Entered Service at: Boston, Suffolk County, Massachusetts
Unit: U.S.S. *Oneida*
Battle or Place of Action: Fort Morgan, Mobile Bay, Alabama
Date of Action: 5 August 1864
G.O. Number, Date: 45, 31 December 1864
Citation: Served on board the U.S.S. *Oneida* in the engagement at Mobile Bay, 5 August 1864. Severely wounded, Preston remained at his gun throughout the engagement which resulted in the capture of the rebel ram *Tennessee* and the damaging of Fort Morgan, carrying on until obliged to go to the surgeon to whom he reported himself as "only slightly injured." He then assisted in taking care of the wounded below and wanted to be allowed to return to his battle station on deck. Upon close examination it was found that he was wounded quite severely in both eyes.

1074 ◆ PRESTON, NOBLE DELANCE

Rank: First Lieutenant & Commissary (highest rank: Lieutenant Colonel)
Service: U.S. Army
Birthday: 2 February 1842
Place of Birth: Madison, Madison County, New York
Date of Death: 27 December 1919
Place of Death: Philadelphia, Pennsylvania
Entered Service at: Fulton, Oswego County, New York
Unit: 10th New York Cavalry
Battle or Place of Action: Trevilian Station, Virginia
Date of Action: 11 June 1864
Date of Issue: 22 November 1889
Citation: Voluntarily led a charge in which he was severely wounded.

1075 ◆ PRICE, EDWARD

Rank: Coxswain
Service: U.S. Navy
Birthday: 1840
Place of Birth: New York, New York
Entered Service at: New York, New York
Unit: U.S.S. *Brooklyn*
Battle or Place of Action: Fort Morgan, Mobile Bay, Alabama
Date of Action: 5 August 1864
G.O. Number, Date: 45, 31 December 1864
Citation: On board the U.S.S. *Brooklyn* during successful attacks against Fort Morgan, rebel gunboats and the ram *Tennessee* in Mobile Bay, 5 August 1864. When the sponge broke, leaving the head in the gun and completely disabling the weapon, Price immediately cleared it by pouring powder into the vent and blowing the sponge head out, thereafter continuing to man the weapon until the close of the furious action which resulted in the capture of the prize rebel ram *Tennessee* and in the infliction of damage and destruction of Fort Morgan.

1076 ◆ PROVINCE, GEORGE

Rank: Ordinary Seaman
Service: U.S. Navy
Birthday: 1842
Place of Birth: Newport, Newport County, Rhode Island
Entered Service at: Boston, Suffolk County, Massachusetts
Unit: U.S.S. *Santiago de Cuba*
Battle or Place of Action: Fort Fisher, North Carolina
Date of Action: 15 January 1865
G.O. Number, Date: 59, 22 June 1865
Citation: On board the U.S.S. *Santiago de Cuba* during the assault on Fort Fisher, 15 January 1865. As one of a boat crew detailed to one of the generals onshore, Province bravely entered the fort in the assault and accompanied his party in carrying dispatches at the height of the battle. He was one of six men who entered the fort in the assault from the fleet.

1077 ◆ PURCELL, HIRAM W.

Rank: Sergeant
Service: U.S. Army
Birthday: 1 August 1837
Place of Birth: Upper Black Eddy, Bucks County, Pennsylvania
Date of Death: 13 May 1918
Place of Death: White Haven, Pennsylvania
Cemetery: Laurel Hill Cemetery—White Haven, Pennsylvania
Entered Service at: Doylestown, Bucks County, Pennsylvania
Unit: Company G, 104th Pennsylvania Infantry
Battle or Place of Action: Fair Oaks, Virginia
Date of Action: 31 May 1862
Date of Issue: 12 May 1894
Citation: While carrying the regimental colors on the retreat he returned to face the advancing enemy, flag in hand, and saved the other color, which would otherwise have been captured.

1078 ◆ PURMAN, JAMES JACKSON

Rank: Lieutenant (highest rank: First Lieutenant)
Service: U.S. Army
Birthday: 1841
Place of Birth: Greene County, Pennsylvania
Date of Death: 10 May 1915
Place of Death: Washington, D.C.
Cemetery: Arlington National Cemetery (1-615)—Arlington, Virginia
Entered Service at: Waynesburg, Greene County, Pennsylvania
Unit: Company A, 140th Pennsylvania Infantry
Battle or Place of Action: Gettysburg, Pennsylvania
Date of Action: 2 July 1863
Date of Issue: 30 October 1896
Citation: Voluntarily assisted a wounded comrade to a place of apparent safety while the enemy were in close proximity; he received the fire of the enemy and a wound which resulted in the amputation of his left leg.

1079 ◆ PUTNAM, EDGAR PIERPONT

Rank: Sergeant (highest rank: Brevet Major New York Volunteers)
Service: U.S. Army
Birthday: 4 May 1844
Place of Birth: Stockton, Chautauqua County, New York
Date of Death: 20 May 1921
Cemetery: Lake View Cemetery—Jamestown, New York
Entered Service at: Stockton, Chautauqua County, New York
Unit: Company D, 9th New York Cavalry
Battle or Place of Action: Crumps Creek, Virginia
Date of Action: 27 May 1864
Date of Issue: 13 May 1892
Citation: With a small force on a reconnaissance, drove off a strong body of the enemy, charged into another force of the enemy's cavalry and stampeded them, taking 27 prisoners.

1080 ◆ PUTNAM, WINTHROP D.

Rank: Corporal
Service: U.S. Army
Birthday: 18 September 1837
Place of Birth: Southbridge, Worcester County, Massachusetts
Date of Death: 15 January 1907
Place of Death: Wood, Wisconsin
Cemetery: Wood National Cemetery (16-09) (MH)—Wood, Wisconsin
Entered Service at: Peoria, Peoria County, Illinois
Unit: Company A, 77th Illinois Infantry
Battle or Place of Action: Vicksburg, Mississippi
Date of Action: 22 May 1863
Date of Issue: 4 April 1898
Citation: Carried, with others, by hand, a cannon up to and fired it through an embrasure of the enemy's works.

1081 ◆ PYNE, GEORGE

Rank: Seaman
Service: U.S. Navy
Birthday: 1841
Place of Birth: England
Entered Service at: New York, New York
Unit: U.S.S. *Magnolia*
Battle or Place of Action: St. Marks, Florida
Date of Action: 5, 6 March 1865
G.O. Number, Date: 59, 22 June 1865
Citation: As seaman on board the U.S.S. *Magnolia*, St. Marks, Fla., 5 and 6 March 1865. Serving with the Army in charge of Navy howitzers during the attack on St. Marks and throughout this fierce engagement, Pyne, although wounded, made remarkable efforts in assisting transport of the gun, and his coolness and determination in courageously standing by

his gun while under the fire of the enemy were a credit to the service to which he belonged.

1082 ◆ QUAY, MATTHEW STANLEY

Rank: Colonel
Service: U.S. Army
Birthday: 30 September 1833
Place of Birth: Dillsburg, York County, Pennsylvania
Date of Death: 28 May 1904
Cemetery: Beaver Cemetery—Beaver, Pennsylvania
Entered Service at: Harrisburg, Dauphin County, Pennsylvania
Unit: 134th Pennsylvania Infantry
Battle or Place of Action: Fredericksburg, Virginia
Date of Action: 13 December 1862
Date of Issue: 9 July 1888
Citation: Although out of service, he voluntarily resumed duty on the eve of the battle and took a conspicuous part in the charge on the heights.

1083 ◆ QUINLAN, JAMES

Rank: Major (highest rank: Lieutenant Colonel)
Service: U.S. Army
Birthday: 13 September 1833
Place of Birth: Clomwell, County Tipperary, Ireland
Date of Death: 29 August 1906
Place of Death: New York, New York
Cemetery: Calvary Cemetery—Woodside, New York
Entered Service at: New York, New York
Unit: 88th New York Infantry
Battle or Place of Action: Savage Station, Virginia
Date of Action: 29 June 1862
Date of Issue: 18 February 1891
Citation: Led his regiment on the enemy's battery, silenced the guns, held the position against overwhelming numbers, and covered the retreat of the 2d Army Corps.

1084 ◆ RAFFERTY, PETER F.

Rank: Private (highest rank: Captain)
Service: U.S. Army
Birthday: 12 June 1845
Place of Birth: County Tyrone, Ireland
Date of Death: 30 April 1910
Cemetery: Calvary Cemetery (First)—Woodside, New York
Entered Service at: New York, New York
Unit: Company B, 69th New York Infantry
Battle or Place of Action: Malvern Hill, Virginia
Date of Action: 1 July 1862
Date of Issue: 2 August 1897
Citation: Having been wounded and directed to the rear, declined to go, but continued in action, receiving several additional wounds, which resulted in his capture by the enemy and his total disability for military service.
Notes: POW

1085 ◆ RAND, CHARLES FRANKLIN

Rank: Private (highest rank: Captain)
Service: U.S. Army
Birthday: 1839
Place of Birth: Batavia, Genesee County, New York
Date of Death: 13 October 1908
Cemetery: Arlington National Cemetery (1-125-B)—Arlington, Virginia
Entered Service at: Batavia, Genesee County, New York
Unit: Company K, 12th New York Infantry
Battle or Place of Action: Blackburn's Ford, Virginia
Date of Action: 18 July 1861
Date of Issue: 23 October 1897
Citation: Remained in action when a part of his regiment broke in disorder, joined another company, and fought with it through the remainder of the engagement.

1086 ◆ RANNAHAN, JOHN

Rank: Corporal
Service: U.S. Marine Corps
Birthday: 1836
Place of Birth: County Monaghan, Ireland
Entered Service at: Pennsylvania
Unit: U.S.S. *Minnesota*
Battle or Place of Action: Fort Fisher, North Carolina
Date of Action: 15 January 1865
G.O. Number, Date: 59, 22 June 1865
Citation: On board the U.S.S. *Minnesota*, in the assault on Fort Fisher, 15 January 1865. Landing on the beach with the assaulting party from his ship, Cpl. Rannahan advanced to the top of the sandhill and partly through the breach in the palisades, despite enemy fire which killed or wounded many officers and men. When more than two-thirds of the men became seized with panic and retreated on the run, he remained with the party until dark when it came safely away, bringing its wounded, its arms, and its colors.

1087 ◆ RANNEY, GEORGE E.

Rank: Assistant Surgeon (highest rank: Surgeon)
Service: U.S. Army
Birthday: 13 June 1839
Place of Birth: Batavia, Genesee County, New York
Date of Death: 10 November 1915
Place of Death: Lansing, Michigan
Cemetery: Mount Hope Cemetery—Lansing, Michigan
Entered Service at: Grand Rapids, Kent County, Michigan
Unit: 2d Michigan Cavalry
Battle or Place of Action: Resaca, Georgia
Date of Action: 14 May 1864
Date of Issue: 24 April 1901
Citation: At great personal risk, went to the aid of a wounded soldier, Pvt. Charles W. Baker, lying under heavy fire between the lines and with the aid of an orderly, carried him to a place of safety.
Notes: POW

1088 ◆ RANNEY, MYRON H.

Rank: Private (highest rank: Corporal)
Service: U.S. Army
Birthday: 1846
Place of Birth: Franklinville, Cattaraugus County, New York
Date of Death: 26 September 1910
Cemetery: I.O.O.F. Cemetery—Olympia, Washington
Entered Service at: Dansville, Livingston County, New York
Unit: Company G, 13th New York Infantry
Battle or Place of Action: Bull Run, Virginia
Date of Action: 30 August 1862
Date of Issue: 23 March 1895
Citation: Picked up the colors and carried them off the field after the color bearer had been shot down; was himself wounded.

1089 ◆ RANSBOTTOM, ALFRED

Rank: First Sergeant
Service: U.S. Army
Birthday: 1831
Place of Birth: South Zanesville, Delaware County, Ohio
Date of Death: 14 April 1893
Place of Death: Springfield Township, Ohio
Cemetery: Roseville Cemetery (MH)—Roseville, Ohio
Entered Service at: Nashport, Muskingum County, Ohio
Unit: Company K, 97th Ohio Infantry
Battle or Place of Action: Franklin, Tennessee
Date of Action: 30 November 1864
Date of Issue: 24 February 1865
Citation: Captured the flag of the 2d Mississippi Infantry (C.S.A.), in a hand-to-hand fight with the color bearer.

1090 ◆ RATCLIFF, EDWARD

Rank: First Sergeant (highest rank: Sergeant Major)
Service: U.S. Army
Birthday: 8 February 1835
Place of Birth: James County, Virginia
Date of Death: 10 March 1915
Place of Death: Nelson, Virginia
Cemetery: Chescake Cemetery Naval Station—Lackey, Virginia
Entered Service at: Yorktown, York County, Virginia
Unit: Company C, 38th U.S. Colored Troops
Battle or Place of Action: Chapin's Farm, Virginia
Date of Action: 29 September 1864
Date of Issue: 6 April 1865
Citation: Commanded and gallantly led his company after the commanding officer had been killed; was the first enlisted man to enter the enemy's works.

1091 ◆ RAUB, JACOB F.

Rank: Assistant Surgeon
Service: U.S. Army
Birthday: 13 May 1840

Place of Birth: Raubsville, Northampton County, Pennsylvania
Date of Death: 21 May 1906
Cemetery: Arlington National Cemetery (3-1469)—Arlington, Virginia
Entered Service at: Weaversville, Pennsylvania
Unit: 210th Pennsylvania Infantry
Battle or Place of Action: Hatcher's Run, Virginia
Date of Action: 5 February 1865
Date of Issue: 20 April 1896
Citation: Discovering a flank movement by the enemy, appraised the commanding general at great peril, and though a noncombatant voluntarily participated with the troops in repelling this attack.

1092 ◆ RAYMOND, WILLIAM H.

Rank: Corporal (highest rank: Second Lieutenant)
Service: U.S. Army
Birthday: 30 May 1844
Place of Birth: Penfield, Monroe County, New York
Date of Death: 7 December 1916
Place of Death: Washington, D.C.
Cemetery: Arlington National Cemetery (2-4853) (MH)—Arlington, Virginia
Entered Service at: Penfield, Monroe County, New York
Unit: Company A, 108th New York Infantry
Battle or Place of Action: Gettysburg, Pennsylvania
Date of Action: 3 July 1863
Date of Issue: 10 March 1896
Citation: Voluntarily and under a severe fire brought a box of ammunition to his comrades on the skirmish line.

1093 ◆ READ, CHARLES

Rank: Ordinary Seaman (highest rank: Ship's Cook)
Service: U.S. Navy
Birthday: 1840
Place of Birth: Cambridge, Washington County, New York
Entered Service at: New York, New York
Unit: U.S.S. *Magnolia*
Battle or Place of Action: St. Marks, Florida
Date of Action: 5, 6 March 1865
G.O. Number, Date: 59, 22 June 1865
Citation: As seaman on board the U.S.S. *Magnolia*, St. Marks, Fla., 5 and 6 March 1865. Serving with the Army in charge of Navy howitzers during the attack on St. Marks and throughout this fierce engagement, Read made remarkable efforts in assisting transport of the gun, and his coolness and determination in courageously standing by his gun while under the fire of the enemy were a credit to the service to which he belonged.

1094 ◆ READ, CHARLES A.

Rank: Coxswain
Service: U.S. Navy
Birthday: 1837
Place of Birth: Sweden

Entered Service at: Ohio
Unit: U.S.S. *Kearsarge*
Battle or Place of Action: off Cherbourg, France
Date of Action: 19 June 1864
G.O. Number, Date: 45, 31 December 1864
Citation: Served as coxswain on board the U.S.S. *Kearsarge* when she destroyed the *Alabama* off Cherbourg, France, 19 June 1864. Acting as the first sponger of the pivot gun during this bitter engagement, Read exhibited marked coolness and good conduct and was highly recommended for his gallantry under fire by his divisional officer.

1095 ◆ READ, GEORGE E.

Rank: Seaman
Service: U.S. Navy
Birthday: 1838
Place of Birth: Rhode Island
Date of Death: 1910
Cemetery: Little Neck Cemetery (MH)—Riverside, Rhode Island
Entered Service at: Rhode Island
Unit: U.S.S. *Kearsarge*
Battle or Place of Action: off Cherbourg, France
Date of Action: 19 June 1864
G.O. Number, Date: 45, 31 December 1864
Citation: Served as seaman on board the U.S.S. *Kearsarge* when she destroyed the *Alabama* off Cherbourg, France, 19 June 1864. Acting as the first loader of the No. 2 gun during this bitter engagement, Read exhibited marked coolness and good conduct and was highly recommended for his gallantry under fire by his divisional officer.

1096 ◆ READ, MORTON A.

Rank: First Lieutenant
Service: U.S. Army
Birthday: 1843
Place of Birth: Brockport, Monroe County, New York
Date of Death: 10 July 1921
Place of Death: Danville, Illinois
Cemetery: Danville National Cemetery (10-3033-R-8) (MH)—Danville, Illinois
Entered Service at: Brockport, Monroe County, New York
Unit: Company D, 8th New York Cavalry
Battle or Place of Action: Appomattox Station, Virginia
Date of Action: 8 April 1865
Date of Issue: 3 May 1865
Citation: Capture of flag of 1st Texas Infantry (C.S.A.).

1097 ◆ REBMANN, GEORGE F.

Rank: Sergeant
Service: U.S. Army
Birthday: 10 April 1840
Place of Birth: Schuyler County, Illinois
Date of Death: 20 August 1918
Cemetery: Messerer Cemetery—Rushville, Illinois
Entered Service at: Rushville, Schuyler County, Illinois

Unit: Company B, 119th Illinois Infantry
Battle or Place of Action: Fort Blakely, Alabama
Date of Action: 9 April 1865
Date of Issue: 8 June 1865
Citation: Capture of flag.

1098 ◆ REDDICK, WILLIAM HENRY HARRISON

Rank: Corporal (highest rank: Second Lieutenant)
Service: U.S. Army
Birthday: 18 September 1840
Place of Birth: Locust Grove, Adams County, Ohio
Date of Death: 8 November 1903
Cemetery: Letts Cemetery (MH)—Letts, Iowa
Entered Service at: Portsmouth, Scioto County, Ohio
Unit: Company B, 33d Ohio Infantry
Battle or Place of Action: Georgia
Date of Action: April 1862
Date of Presentation: 25 March 1863
Place of Presentation: Washington, D.C., presented by Sec. of War Stanton
Citation: One of 19 of 24 men (including two civilians) who, by direction of Gen. Ormsby M. Mitchell, penetrated nearly 200 miles south into enemy territory and captured a railroad train at Big Shanty, Ga., in an attempt to destroy the bridges and track between Chattanooga and Atlanta.

1099 ◆ REED, AXEL HAYFORD

Rank: Sergeant (highest rank: Captain)
Service: U.S. Army
Birthday: 13 March 1835
Place of Birth: Hartford, Oxford County, Maine
Date of Death: 21 January 1917
Place of Death: Glencoe, Minnesota
Cemetery: Mount Auburn Cemetery (MH)—Glencoe, Minnesota
Entered Service at: Glencoe, McLeod County, Minnesota
Unit: Company K, 2d Minnesota Infantry
Battle or Place of Action: Chickamauga, Georgia and Missionary Ridge, Tennessee
Date of Action: 19 September 1863 & 15 November 1863
Date of Issue: 2 April 1898
Citation: While in arrest at Chickamagua, Ga., left his place in the rear and voluntarily went to the line of battle, secured a rifle, and fought gallantly during the two-day battle; was released from arrest in recognition of his bravery. At Missionary Ridge Reed commanded his company and gallantly led it, being among the first to enter the enemy's works; was severely wounded, losing an arm, but declined a discharge and remained in active service to the end of the war.

1100 ◆ REED, CHARLES WELLINGTON

Rank: Bugler (highest rank: Chief Bugler)
Service: U.S. Army
Birthday: 1 April 1842
Place of Birth: Charlestown, Suffolk County, Massachusetts

Date of Death: 29 April 1926
Place of Death: Norwell, Massachusetts
Cemetery: Mount Auburn Cemetery (MH)—Cambridge, Massachusetts
Entered Service at: Malden, Middlesex County, Massachusetts
Unit: 9th Independent Battery, Massachusetts Light Artillery
Served as: Bugler
Battle or Place of Action: Gettysburg, Pennsylvania
Date of Action: 2 July 1863
Date of Issue: 16 August 1895
Citation: Rescued his wounded captain from between the lines.

1101 ◆ REED, GEORGE W.

Rank: Private
Service: U.S. Army
Birthday: 1831
Place of Birth: Cambria County, Pennsylvania
Date of Death: 21 December 1906
Place of Death: Chicago, Illinois
Cemetery: Grand View Cemetery—Johnstown, Pennsylvania
Entered Service at: Johnstown, Cambria County, Pennsylvania
Unit: Company E, 11th Pennsylvania Infantry
Battle or Place of Action: Weldon Railroad, Virginia
Date of Action: 21 August 1864
Date of Issue: 6 September 1864
Citation: Capture of flag of 24th North Carolina Volunteers (C.S.A.).

1102 ◆ REED, WILLIAM

Rank: Private
Service: U.S. Army
Birthday: 21 February 1839
Place of Birth: Union County, Pennsylvania
Date of Death: 30 May 1918
Cemetery: Riverview Cemetery (MH)—Huntingdon, Pennsylvania
Entered Service at: Pekin, Tazewell County, Illinois
Unit: Company H, 8th Missouri Infantry
Battle or Place of Action: Vicksburg, Mississippi
Date of Action: 22 May 1863
Date of Issue: 12 December 1895
Citation: Gallantry in the charge of the "volunteer storming party."

1103 ◆ REEDER, CHARLES A.

Rank: Private (highest rank: Corporal)
Service: U.S. Army
Birthday: 20 November 1843
Place of Birth: Harrison, Clay County, West Virginia
Date of Death: 28 September 1902
Place of Death: Morgantown, West Virginia
Cemetery: Masonic Cemetery—Shinnston, West Virginia

Entered Service at: Shinnston, Harrison County, West Virginia
Unit: Company G, 12th West Virginia Infantry
Battle or Place of Action: Battery Gregg, near Petersburg, Virginia
Date of Action: 2 April 1865
Date of Issue: 3 April 1867
Citation: Capture of flag.

1104 ◆ REGAN, JEREMIAH

Rank: Quartermaster
Service: U.S. Navy
Birthday: 1832
Place of Birth: Boston, Suffolk County, Massachusetts
Entered Service at: Boston, Suffolk County, Massachusetts
Unit: U.S.S. *Galena*
Battle or Place of Action: Drewry's Bluff, Virginia
Date of Action: 15 May 1862
G.O. Number, Date: 11, 3 April 1863
Citation: As captain of No. 2 gun on board the U.S.S. *Galena* in the attack upon Drewry's Bluff, 15 May 1862. With his ship severely damaged by the enemy's shellfire and several men killed and wounded, Regan continued to man his gun throughout the engagement despite the concentration of fire directed against men at their guns by enemy sharpshooters in rifle pits along the banks.

1105 ◆ REID, ROBERT ALEXANDER

Rank: Private (highest rank: Ordnance Sergeant)
Service: U.S. Army
Birthday: 22 January 1842
Place of Birth: Raploch, Scotland
Date of Death: 25 April 1929
Place of Death: Pottsville, Pennsylvania
Cemetery: I.O.O.F. Cemetery (MH)—Pottsville, Pennsylvania
Entered Service at: Pottsville, Schuylkill County, Pennsylvania
Unit: Company G, 48th Pennsylvania Infantry
Battle or Place of Action: Petersburg, Virginia
Date of Action: 17 June 1864
Date of Issue: 1 December 1864
Citation: Capture of flag of 44th Tennessee Infantry (C.S.A.).

1106 ◆ REIGLE, DANIEL P.

Rank: Corporal (highest rank: Sergeant)
Service: U.S. Army
Birthday: 19 February 1841
Place of Birth: Adams County, Pennsylvania
Date of Death: 19 March 1917
Place of Death: Gettysburg, Pennsylvania
Cemetery: Mount Carmel Cemetery—Littlestown, Pennsylvania
Entered Service at: Gettysburg, Adams County, Pennsylvania
Unit: Company F, 87th Pennsylvania Infantry
Battle or Place of Action: Cedar Creek, Virginia

Date of Action: 19 October 1864
Date of Issue: 26 October 1864
Citation: For gallantry while rushing forward to capture a Confederate flag at the stone fence where the enemy's last stand was made.

1107 ◆ REISINGER, JAMES MONROE

Rank: Corporal (highest rank: First Lieutenant)
Service: U.S. Army
Birthday: 28 October 1842
Place of Birth: Beaver County, Pennsylvania
Date of Death: 25 May 1925
Place of Death: Franklin, Pennsylvania
Cemetery: Greenville Cemetery (MH)—Meadville, Pennsylvania
Entered Service at: Meadville, Crawford County, Pennsylvania
Unit: Company H, 150th Pennsylvania Infantry
Battle or Place of Action: Gettysburg, Pennsylvania
Date of Action: 1 July 1863
Citation: Specially brave and meritorious conduct in the face of the enemy. Awarded under Act of Congress, January 25, 1907.

1108 ◆ RENNINGER, LOUIS

Rank: Corporal
Service: U.S. Army
Birthday: 25 August 1841
Place of Birth: Liverpool, Ohio
Date of Death: 17 November 1908
Place of Death: Eugene, Oregon
Cemetery: Eugene Pioneer Cemetery—Eugene, Oregon
Entered Service at: Liverpool, Ohio
Unit: Company H, 37th Ohio Infantry
Battle or Place of Action: Vicksburg, Mississippi
Date of Action: 22 May 1863
Date of Issue: 15 August 1894
Citation: Gallantry in the charge of the "volunteer storming party."

1109 ◆ REYNOLDS, GEORGE

Rank: Private
Service: U.S. Army
Place of Birth: Ireland
Entered Service at: New York, New York
Unit: Company M, 9th New York Cavalry
Battle or Place of Action: Winchester, Virginia
Date of Action: 19 September 1864
Date of Issue: 27 September 1864
Citation: Capture of Virginia state flag.

1110 ◆ RHODES, JULIUS DEXTER

Rank: Private (highest rank: Sergeant Major)
Service: U.S. Army
Birthday: 1 October 1841
Place of Birth: Monroe County, Michigan

Date of Death: 19 February 1906
Place of Death: Washington, D.C.
Entered Service at: Springville, Erie County, New York
Unit: Company F, 5th New York Cavalry
Battle or Place of Action: Thoroughfare Gap & Bull Run, Virginia
Date of Action: 28,30 August 1862
Date of Issue: 9 March 1887
Citation: After having had his horse shot under him in the fight at Thoroughfare Gap, Va., he voluntarily joined the 105th New York Volunteers and was conspicuous in the advance on the enemy's lines. Displayed gallantry in the advance on the skirmish line at Bull Run, Va., where he was wounded.

1111 ◆ RHODES, SYLVESTER D.

Rank: Sergeant (highest rank: Captain)
Service: U.S. Army
Birthday: December 1842
Place of Birth: Plains, Pennsylvania
Date of Death: 29 August 1904
Place of Death: Parsons, Pennsylvania
Cemetery: Hollenbeck Cemetery—Wilkes-Barre, Pennsylvania
Entered Service at: Wilkes-Barre, Luzerne County, Pennsylvania
Unit: Company D, 61st Pennsylvania Infantry
Battle or Place of Action: Fisher's Hill, Virginia
Date of Action: 22 September 1864
Date of Issue: 16 February 1897
Citation: Was on the skirmish line which drove the enemy from the first entrenchment and was the first man to enter the breastworks, capturing one of the guns and turning it upon the enemy.

1112 ◆ RICE, CHARLES

Rank: Coal Heaver (highest rank: Fireman Second Class)
Service: U.S. Navy
Birthday: 1840
Place of Birth: Russia
Entered Service at: Portland, Cumberland County, Maine
Unit: U.S.S. *Agawam*
Battle or Place of Action: Fort Fisher, North Carolina
Date of Action: 23 December 1864
G.O. Number, Date: 45, 31 December 1864
Date of Presentation: 12 May 1865
Place of Presentation: On board the U.S.S. *Agawam* off New Bern, North Carolina
Citation: On board the U.S.S. *Agawam* as one of a volunteer crew of a powder boat which was exploded near Fort Fisher, 23 December 1864. The powder boat, towed in by the *Wilderness* to prevent detection by the enemy, cast off and slowly steamed to within 300 yards of the beach. After fuses and fires had been lit and a second anchor with short scope let go to assure the boat's tailing inshore, the crew boarded the *Wilderness* and proceeded a distance of 12 miles from shore. Less than two hours later the explosion took place, and the following day, fires were observed still burning at the fort.

1113 ◆ RICE, EDMUND

Rank: Major (highest rank: Brigadier General)
Service: U.S. Army
Birthday: 2 December 1842
Place of Birth: Brighton, Suffolk County, Massachusetts
Date of Death: 20 July 1906
Place of Death: Boston, Massachusetts
Cemetery: Arlington National Cemetery (3-1875)—Arlington, Virginia
Entered Service at: Cambridge, Middlesex Ccounty, Massachusetts
Unit: 19th Massachusetts Infantry
Battle or Place of Action: Gettysburg, Pennsylvania
Date of Action: 3 July 1863
Date of Issue: 6 October 1891
Citation: Conspicuous bravery on the third day of the battle on the countercharge against Pickett's division where he fell severely wounded within the enemy's lines.

1114 ◆ RICH, CARLOS H.

Rank: First Sergeant
Service: U.S. Army
Birthday: 11 February 1841
Place of Birth: Canada
Date of Death: 29 May 1918
Place of Death: Bennington, Vermont
Cemetery: Roxbury Cemetery—Roxbury, Vermont
Entered Service at: Northfield, Franklin County, Massachusetts
Unit: Company K, 4th Vermont Infantry
Battle or Place of Action: Wilderness Campaign, Virginia
Date of Action: 5 May 1864
Date of Issue: 4 January 1895
Citation: Saved the life of an officer.

1115 ◆ RICHARDS, LOUIS

Rank: Quartermaster (highest rank: Acting Master's Mate)
Service: U.S. Navy
Birthday: 1835
Place of Birth: New York, New York
Date of Death: 7 January 1894
Place of Death: Brooklyn, New York
Cemetery: Evergreen Cemetery—Brooklyn, New York
Entered Service at: New York, New York
Unit: U.S.S. *Pensacola*
Battle or Place of Action: Forts Jackson & St. Philip and New Orleans, Louisiana
Date of Action: 24-25 April 1862
G.O. Number, Date: 11, 3 April 1863
Citation: Richards served as quartermaster on board the U.S.S. *Pensacola* in the attacks upon Forts Jackson and St. Philip, and at the taking of New Orleans, 24 and 25 April 1862. Through all the din and roar of battle, he steered the ship through the narrow opening of the barricade, and his attention to orders contributed to the successful passage of the ship without once fouling the shore or the obstacles of the barricade.

1116 ◆ RICHARDSON, WILLIAM R.

Rank: Private
Service: U.S. Army
Birthday: 1842
Place of Birth: Cleveland, Cuyahoga County, Ohio
Date of Death: 24 October 1873
Cemetery: City Cemetery—Massillon, Ohio
Entered Service at: Washington, Ohio
Unit: Company A, 2d Ohio Cavalry
Battle or Place of Action: Deatonsville (Sailor's Creek), Virginia
Date of Action: 6 April 1865
Date of Issue: 7 April 1866
Citation: Having been captured and taken to the rear, Richardson made his escape, rejoined the Union lines, and furnished information of great importance as to the enemy's position and the approaches thereto.

1117 ◆ RICHEY, WILLIAM E.

Rank: Corporal (highest rank: Sergeant)
Service: U.S. Army
Birthday: 1841
Place of Birth: Athens County, Ohio
Date of Death: 21 June 1909
Cemetery: Harveyville Cemetery—Harveyville, Kansas
Entered Service at: New Concord, Muskingum County, Ohio
Unit: Company A, 15th Ohio Infantry
Battle or Place of Action: Chickamauga, Georgia
Date of Action: 19 September 1863
Date of Issue: 9 November 1893
Citation: While on the extreme front, between the lines of the combatants single-handedly he captured a Confederate major who was armed and mounted.

1118 ◆ *RICHMOND, JAMES

Rank: Private
Service: U.S. Army
Birthday: 1843
Place of Birth: Maine
Date of Death: 3 June 1864
Place of Death: Washington, D.C.
Cemetery: Arlington National Cemetery (27-886) (MH)—Arlington, Virginia
Entered Service at: Fremont, Sandusky County, Ohio
Unit: Company F, 8th Ohio Infantry
Battle or Place of Action: Gettysburg, Pennsylvania
Date of Action: 3 July 1863
Date of Issue: 1 December 1864
Citation: Capture of flag.

1119 ◆ RICKSECKER, JOHN HENRY

Rank: Private
Service: U.S. Army
Birthday: 14 November 1843

Place of Birth: Mansfield, Richland County, Ohio
Date of Death: 2 August 1929
Place of Death: Kansas City, Missouri
Cemetery: Forest Hills Cemetery (MH)—Kansas City, Missouri
Entered Service at: Aurora, Portage County, Ohio
Unit: Company D, 104th Ohio Infantry
Battle or Place of Action: Franklin, Tennessee
Date of Action: 30 November 1864
Date of Issue: 3 February 1865
Citation: Capture of flag of 16th Alabama Artillery (C.S.A.).

1120 ◆ RIDDELL, RUDOLPH R.

Rank: Lieutenant (highest rank: Brevet Lieutenant Colonel)
Service: U.S. Army
Birthday: 11 February 1847
Place of Birth: Hamilton, Madison County, New York
Date of Death: 8 September 1913
Place of Death: Albany, New York
Cemetery: Madison Street Cemetery (MH)—Hamilton, New York
Entered Service at: Hamilton, Madison County, New York
Unit: Company I, 61st New York Infantry
Battle or Place of Action: Deatonsville (Sailor's Creek), Virginia
Date of Action: 6 April 1865
Date of Issue: 10 May 1865
Citation: Captured the flag of the 6th Alabama Cavalry (C.S.A.).

1121 ◆ RILEY, THOMAS

Rank: Private (highest rank: Corporal)
Service: U.S. Army
Place of Birth: Ireland
Entered Service at: New Orleans, Orleans County, Louisiana
Unit: Company D, 1st Louisiana Cavalry
Battle or Place of Action: Fort Blakely, Alabama
Date of Action: 4 April 1865
Date of Issue: 8 June 1865
Citation: Captured the flag of the 6th Alabama Cavalry (C.S.A.).

1122 ◆ RINGOLD, EDWARD

Rank: Coxswain
Service: U.S. Navy
Birthday: 1827
Place of Birth: Baltimore, Baltimore County, Maryland
Entered Service at: Maryland
Unit: U.S.S. *Wabash*
Battle or Place of Action: Pocataligo, South Carolina
Date of Action: 22 October 1862
G.O. Number, Date: 17, 10 July 1863
Citation: Served as coxswain on board the U.S.S. *Wabash* in the engagement at Pocataligo, 22 October 1862. Soliciting permission to accompany the howitzer corps and performing his

duty with such gallantry and presence of mind as to attract the attention of all around him, Ringold, knowing there was a scarcity of ammunition, went through the whole line of fire with his shirt slung over his shoulder filled with fixed ammunition which he had brought from two miles to the rear of the lines.

1123 ◆ RIPLEY, WILLIAM YOUNG WARREN

Rank: Lieutenant Colonel (highest rank: Major General)
Service: U.S. Army
Birthday: 31 December 1832
Place of Birth: Middlebury, Addison County, Vermont
Date of Death: 16 December 1905
Cemetery: Evergreen Cemetery (MH)—Rutland, Vermont
Entered Service at: Rutland, Rutland County, Vermont
Unit: 1st U.S. Sharpshooters
Battle or Place of Action: Malvern Hill, Virginia
Date of Action: 1 July 1862
Date of Issue: 11 March 1893
Citation: At a critical moment brought up two regiments, which he led against the enemy himself, being severely wounded.

1124 ◆ ROANTREE, JAMES S.

Rank: Sergeant (highest rank: First Sergeant)
Service: U.S. Marine Corps
Birthday: 1835
Place of Birth: Dublin, County Dublin, Ireland
Date of Death: 24 February 1873
Place of Death: Boston, Massachusetts
Cemetery: Calvary Cemetery—Roslindale, Massachusetts
Entered Service at: New York
Unit: U.S.S. *Oneida*
Battle or Place of Action: Mobile Bay, Alabama
Date of Action: 5 August 1864
G.O. Number, Date: 45, 31 December 1864
Citation: On board the U.S.S. *Oneida* during action against rebel forts and gunboats and with the ram *Tennessee* in Mobile Bay, 5 August 1864. Despite damage to his ship and the loss of several men onboard as the enemy fire raked her decks and penetrated her boilers, Sgt. Roantree performed his duties with skill and courage throughout the furious battle which resulted in the surrender of the rebel ram *Tennessee* and in the damaging and destruction of batteries at Fort Morgan.

1125 ◆ ROBBINS, AUGUSTUS J.

Rank: Second Lieutenant
Service: U.S. Army
Birthday: 17 November 1839
Place of Birth: Grafton, Windham County, Vermont
Date of Death: 6 September 1909
Place of Death: Lakewood, New Jersey
Cemetery: Woodlawn Cemetery (MH)—Lakewood, New Jersey
Entered Service at: Grafton, Windham County, Vermont
Unit: Company B, 2d Vermont Infantry
Battle or Place of Action: Spotsylvania, Virginia

Date of Action: 12 May 1864
Date of Issue: 24 March 1892
Citation: While voluntarily serving as a staff officer, successfully withdrew a regiment across and around a severely exposed position to the rest of the command; was severely wounded.

1126 ◆ ROBERTS, JAMES

Rank: Seaman
Service: U.S. Navy
Birthday: 14 February 1837
Place of Birth: England
Date of Death: 19 October 1908
Place of Death: Bath, New York
Cemetery: Bath National Cemetery (1-26-2) (MH)—Bath, New York
Entered Service at: Hartford, Hartford County, Connecticut
Unit: U.S.S. *Agawan*
Battle or Place of Action: Fort Fisher, North Carolina
Date of Action: 23 December 1864
G.O. Number, Date: 45, 31 December 1864
Date of Presentation: 12 May 1865
Place of Presentation: off New Bern, NC, on board the U.S.S. *Agawam*
Citation: Roberts served on board the U.S.S. *Agawam*, as one of a volunteer crew of a powder boat which was exploded near Fort Fisher, 23 December 1864. The powder boat, towed in by the *Wilderness* to prevent detection by the enemy, cast off and slowly steamed to within 300 yards of the beach. After fuses and fires had been lit and a second anchor with short scope let go to insure the boat's tailing inshore, the crew again boarded the *Wilderness* and proceeded a distance of 12 miles from shore. Less than two hours later the explosion took place, and the following day fires were observed still burning at the fort.

1127 ◆ ROBERTS, OTIS O.

Rank: Sergeant
Service: U.S. Army
Birthday: 20 March 1842
Place of Birth: Sangerville, Piscataquis County, Maine
Date of Death: 8 February 1930
Place of Death: Dexter, Maine
Cemetery: Mount Pleasant Cemetery (MH)—Dexter, Maine
Entered Service at: Dexter, Penobscot County, Maine
Unit: Company H, 6th Maine Infantry
Battle or Place of Action: Rappahannock Station, Virginia
Date of Action: 7 November 1863
Date of Issue: 28 December 1863
Citation: Capture of flag of 8th Louisiana (C.S.A.) in a hand-to-hand struggle with the color bearer.

1128 ◆ ROBERTSON, ROBERT STODDART

Rank: First Lieutenant (highest rank: Brevet Colonel NY Volunteers)
Service: U.S. Army
Birthday: 16 April 1839

Place of Birth: Argyle, Washington County, New York
Date of Death: 25 August 1906
Cemetery: Lindenwood Cemetery—Fort Wayne, Indiana
Entered Service at: Argyle, Washington County, New York
Unit: Company K, 93d New York Infantry
Battle or Place of Action: Corbins Bridge, Virginia
Date of Action: 8 May 1864
Date of Issue: 2 August 1897
Citation: While acting as aide-de-camp to a general officer, seeing a regiment break to the rear, he seized its colors, rode with them to the front in the face of the advancing enemy, and rallied the retreating regiment.

1129 ◆ *ROBERTSON, SAMUEL

Rank: Private
Service: U.S. Army
Birthday: 1843
Place of Birth: Muskingum County, Ohio
Date of Death: 18 June 1862
Cemetery: Chattanooga National Cemetery (H-11177) (MH)—Chattanooga, Tennessee
Entered Service at: Boarneville, Ross County, Ohio
Unit: Company G, 33d Ohio Infantry
Battle or Place of Action: Georgia
Date of Action: April 1862
Date of Issue: September 1863
Citation: One of 19 of 24 men (including two civilians) who, by direction of Gen. Ormsby M. Mitchell, penetrated nearly 200 miles south into enemy territory and captured a railroad train at Big Shanty, Ga., in an attempt to destroy the bridges and track between Chattanooga and Atlanta.

1130 ◆ ROBIE, GEORGE FRANK

Rank: Sergeant (highest rank: First Lieutenant)
Service: U.S. Army
Birthday: 17 June 1844
Place of Birth: Candia, Rockingham County, New Hampshire
Date of Death: 10 June 1891
Place of Death: Galveston, Texas
Entered Service at: Manchester, Hillsborough County, New Hampshire
Unit: Company D, 7th New Hampshire Infantry
Battle or Place of Action: before Richmond, Virginia
Date of Action: September 1864
Date of Issue: 12 June 1883
Citation: Gallantry on the skirmish line.

1131 ◆ ROBINSON, ALEXANDER

Rank: Boatswain's Mate
Service: U.S. Navy
Birthday: 1831
Place of Birth: England
Entered Service at: New York, New York
Unit: U.S.S. *Howquah*
Battle or Place of Action: off Wilmington, North Carolina
Date of Action: 25 September 1864

G.O. Number, Date: 45, 31 December 1864
Date of Issue: 25 August 1868
Citation: Served as boatswain's mate on board the U.S.S. *Howquah* on the occasion of the destruction of the blockade runner, *Lynx*, off Wilmington, 25 September 1864. Performing his duty faithfully under the most trying circumstances, Robinson stood firmly at his post in the midst of a crossfire from the rebel shore batteries and our own vessels.

1132 ◆ ROBINSON, CHARLES

Rank: Boatswain's Mate
Service: U.S. Navy
Birthday: 1840
Place of Birth: Dundee, Scotland
Date of Death: 21 April 1896
Place of Death: Halifax, Nova Scotia, Canada
Cemetery: Holy Cross Cemetery (MH)—Halifax, Nova Scotia, Canada
Entered Service at: New York, New York
Unit: U.S.S. *Baron de Kalb*
Battle or Place of Action: Yazoo River, Mississippi
Date of Action: 23-27 December 1862
G.O. Number, Date: 11, 3 April 1863
Citation: Served on board the U.S.S. *Baron de Kalb* Yazoo River Expedition, 23 to 27 December 1862. Proceeding under orders up the Yazoo River, the U.S.S. *Baron de Kalb*, with the object of capturing or destroying the enemy's transports, came upon the steamers *John Walsh*, *R.J. Locklan*, *Golden Age*, and the *Scotland* sunk on a bar where they were ordered fired. Continuing up the river, she was fired on by the enemy, but upon returning the fire, caused the rebels to retreat. Returning down the Yazoo, she destroyed and captured large quantities of enemy equipment and several prisoners. Serving bravely throughout this action, Robinson, as boatswain's mate, "distinguished himself in the various actions."

1133 ◆ ROBINSON, ELBRIDGE

Rank: Private
Service: U.S. Army
Birthday: 7 January 1844
Place of Birth: Morgan County, Ohio
Date of Death: 19 January 1918
Place of Death: Vernon, Illinois
Cemetery: Patoka Cemetery—Patoka, Illinois
Entered Service at: McConnelsville, Morgan County, Ohio
Unit: Company C, 122d Ohio Infantry
Battle or Place of Action: Winchester, Virginia
Date of Action: 14 June 1863
Date of Issue: 5 April 1898
Citation: With one companion voluntarily went in front of the Union line, under a heavy fire from the enemy, and carried back a helpless wounded comrade, thus saving him from death or capture.

1134 ◆ *ROBINSON, JAMES H.

Rank: Private
Service: U.S. Army

Place of Birth: Oakland County, Michigan
Place of Death: Memphis, Tennessee
Cemetery: Memphis National Cemetery (H-4131) (MH)—Memphis, Tennessee
Entered Service at: Victor, Michigan
Unit: Company B, 3d Michigan Cavalry
Battle or Place of Action: Brownsville Station, Arkansas
Date of Action: 27 January 1865
Date of Issue: 4 April 1865
Citation: Successfully defended himself, singlehandedly, against seven guerrillas, killing the leader (Capt. W.C. Stephenson) and driving off the remainder of the party.

1135 ◆ ROBINSON, JOHN CLEVELAND

Rank: Brigadier General (highest rank: Major General)
Service: U.S. Army
Birthday: 10 April 1817
Place of Birth: Binghamton, Broome County, New York
Date of Death: 18 February 1897
Cemetery: Spring Forest Cemetery (MH)—Binghamton, New York
Entered Service at: Binghamton, Broome County, New York
Unit: U.S. Volunteers
Battle or Place of Action: Laurel Hill, Virginia
Date of Action: 8 May 1864
Date of Issue: 28 March 1894
Citation: Placed himself at the head of the leading brigade in a charge upon the enemy's breastworks; was severely wounded.

1136 ◆ ROBINSON, JOHN H.

Rank: Private
Service: U.S. Army
Birthday: 1846
Place of Birth: Ireland
Date of Death: 30 November 1883
Place of Death: Boston, Massachusetts
Cemetery: St. Benedict Cemetery (MH)—West Roxbury, Massachusetts
Entered Service at: Roxbury, Suffolk County, Massachusetts
Unit: Company I, 19th Massachusetts Infantry
Battle or Place of Action: Gettysburg, Pennsylvania
Date of Action: 3 July 1863
Date of Issue: 1 December 1864
Citation: Capture of flag of 57th Virginia Infantry (C.S.A.).
Notes: POW

1137 ◆ ROBINSON, THOMAS

Rank: Private
Service: U.S. Army
Place of Birth: Ireland
Entered Service at: Tamaqua, Schuylkill County, Pennsylvania
Unit: Company H, 81st Pennsylvania Infantry
Battle or Place of Action: Spotsylvania, Virginia
Date of Action: 12 May 1864

Date of Issue: 1 December 1864
Citation: Capture of flag in a hand-to-hand conflict.

1138 ◆ ROCK, FREDERICK

Rank: Private
Service: U.S. Army
Birthday: 1840
Place of Birth: Darmstadt, Germany
Date of Death: 7 November 1924
Cemetery: Woodlawn Cemetery (MH)—Tampa, Florida
Entered Service at: Cleveland, Cuyahoga County, Ohio
Unit: Company A, 37th Ohio Infantry
Battle or Place of Action: Vicksburg, Mississippi
Date of Action: 22 May 1863
Date of Issue: 10 August 1894
Citation: Gallantry in the charge of the "volunteer storming party."

1139 ◆ ROCKEFELLER, CHARLES MORTIMER

Rank: Lieutenant (highest rank: Major)
Service: U.S. Army
Birthday: 18 September 1844
Place of Birth: Gallatin Columbia County, New York
Date of Death: 28 April 1899
Place of Death: M.I.A. Declared dead near Manila
Entered Service at: New York, New York
Unit: Company A, 178th New York Infantry
Battle or Place of Action: Fort Blakely, Alabama
Date of Action: 9 April 1865
Date of Issue: 2 August 1897
Citation: Voluntarily and alone, under a heavy fire, obtained valuable information which a reconnoitering party of 25 men had previously attempted and failed to obtain, suffering severe loss in the attempt. The information obtained by him was made the basis of the orders for the assault that followed. He also advanced with a few followers, under the fire of both sides, and captured 300 of the enemy who would otherwise have escaped.
Notes: POW

1140 ◆ RODENBOUGH, THEOPHILUS FRANCIS

Rank: Captain (highest rank: Brigadier General)
Service: U.S. Army
Birthday: 5 November 1838
Place of Birth: Easton, Northampton County, Pennsylvania
Date of Death: 19 December 1912
Place of Death: New York, New York
Cemetery: Easton Heights Cemetery (MH)—Easton, Pennsylvania
Entered Service at: Pennsylvania
Unit: 2d U.S. Cavalry
Battle or Place of Action: Trevilian Station, Virginia
Date of Action: 11 June 1864
Date of Issue: 21 September 1893

Citation: Handled the regiment with great skill and valor; was severely wounded.

1141 ◆ ROHM, FERDINAND FREDERICK

Rank: Chief Bugler
Service: U.S. Army
Birthday: 30 August 1843
Place of Birth: Patterson, Juniata County, Pennsylvania
Date of Death: 24 November 1917
Place of Death: Harrisburg, Pennsylvania
Cemetery: Westminster Presbyterian Cemetery—Mifflintown, Pennsylvania
Entered Service at: Juniata County, Pennsylvania
Unit: 16th Pennsylvania Cavalry
Battle or Place of Action: Reams' Station, Virginia
Date of Action: 25 August 1864
Date of Issue: 16 October 1897
Citation: While his regiment was retiring under fire, voluntarily remained behind to succor a wounded officer who was in great danger, secured assistance, and removed the officer to a place of safety.

1142 ◆ ROOD, OLIVER P.

Rank: Private
Service: U.S. Army
Birthday: 1844
Place of Birth: Frankfort County, Kentucky
Date of Death: 11 June 1885
Place of Death: Nashville, Tennessee
Cemetery: Mount Olivet Cemetery (MH)—Nashville, Tennessee
Entered Service at: Terre Haute, Vigo County, Indiana
Unit: Company B, 20th Indiana Infantry
Battle or Place of Action: Gettysburg, Pennsylvania
Date of Action: 3 July 1863
Date of Issue: 1 December 1864
Citation: Capture of flag of 21st North Carolina Infantry (C.S.A.).

1143 ◆ ROOSEVELT, GEORGE WASHINGTON

Rank: First Sergeant (highest rank: Brevet Captain)
Service: U.S. Army
Birthday: 14 February 1844
Place of Birth: Chester County, Pennsylvania
Date of Death: 15 April 1907
Place of Death: Brussels, Belgium
Cemetery: Oak Hill Cemetery—Washington, D.C.
Entered Service at: Chester County, Pennsylvania
Unit: Company K, 26th Pennsylvania Infantry
Battle or Place of Action: Bull Run, Virginia & Gettysburg, Pennsylvania
Date of Action: 30 August 1862 & 2 July 1863
Date of Issue: 2 July 1887
Citation: At Bull Run, Va., recaptured the colors, which had been seized by the enemy. At Gettysburg captured a

Confederate color bearer and colors, in which effort he was severely wounded.

1144 ◆ *ROSS, MARION A.

Rank: Sergeant Major
Service: U.S. Army
Birthday: 1833
Place of Birth: Christianburg, Champaign County, Ohio
Date of Death: 18 June 1862
Cemetery: Chattanooga National Cemetery (H-11179) (MH)—Chattanooga, Tennessee
Entered Service at: Christianburg, Champaign County, Ohio
Unit: 2d Ohio Infantry
Battle or Place of Action: Georgia
Date of Action: April 1862
Date of Issue: September 1863
Citation: One of 19 of 24 men (including two civilians) who, by direction of Gen. Ormsby M. Mitchell, penetrated nearly 200 miles south into enemy territory and captured a railroad train at Big Shanty, Ga., in an attempt to destroy the bridges and track between Chattanooga and Atlanta.

1145 ◆ ROSSBACH, VALENTINE

Rank: Sergeant
Service: U.S. Army
Birthday: 1842
Place of Birth: Germany
Date of Death: 20 February 1897
Cemetery: Cypress Hills National Cemetery (2-5427) (MH)—Brooklyn, New York
Entered Service at: Flushing, Queens County, New York
Unit: 34th New York Battery
Battle or Place of Action: Spotsylvania, Virginia
Date of Action: 12 May 1864
Date of Issue: 10 July 1896
Citation: Encouraged his cannoneers to hold a very dangerous position, and when all depended on several good shots it was from his piece that the most effective were delivered, causing the enemy's fire to cease and thereby relieving the critical position of the Federal troops.

1146 ◆ ROUGHT, STEPHEN

Rank: Sergeant
Service: U.S. Army
Birthday: 3 April 1840
Place of Birth: Bradford County, Pennsylvania
Date of Death: 16 March 1919
Place of Death: Wyalusing, Pennsylvania
Cemetery: Lacy Street Cemetery—Lacyville, Pennsylvania
Entered Service at: Crampton, Pennsylvania
Unit: Company A, 141st Pennsylvania Infantry
Battle or Place of Action: Wilderness Campaign, Virginia
Date of Action: 6 May 1864
Date of Issue: 1 December 1864
Citation: Capture of flag of the 13th North Carolina Infantry (C.S.A.).

1147 ◆ ROUNDS, LEWIS A.

Rank: Private (highest rank: Brevet Major)
Service: U.S. Army
Birthday: 7 June 1843
Place of Birth: Cattaraugus County, New York
Date of Death: 1 May 1916
Place of Death: Wood Soldier's Home, Wisconsin
Cemetery: Wood National Cemetery (MH)—Wood, Wisconsin
Entered Service at: Norwalk, Huron County, Ohio
Unit: Company D, 8th Ohio Infantry
Battle or Place of Action: Spotsylvania, Virginia
Date of Action: 12 May 1864
Date of Issue: 1 December 1864
Citation: Capture of flag.

1148 ◆ ROUNTRY, JOHN

Rank: First Class Fireman
Service: U.S. Navy
Birthday: 1843
Place of Birth: Massachusetts
Date of Death: 3 October 1901
Place of Death: New York, New York
Cemetery: Holy Cross Cemetery—Brooklyn, New York
Entered Service at: Boston, Suffolk County, Massachusetts
Unit: U.S.S. *Montauk*
Battle or Place of Action: off Port Royal, South Carolina
Date of Action: 21 September 1864
G.O. Number, Date: 59, 22 June 1865
Citation: Served as first class fireman on board the U.S.S. *Montauk*, 21 September 1864. During the night of 21 September, when fire was discovered in the magazine lightroom of that vessel, causing a panic and demoralizing the crew, Rountry, notwithstanding the cry of "fire in the magazine," forced his way with hose in hand, through the frightened crowd to the lightroom, and put out the flames.

1149 ◆ ROUSH, JAMES LEVI

Rank: Corporal
Service: U.S. Army
Birthday: 11 February 1838
Place of Birth: Bedford County, Pennsylvania
Date of Death: 12 February 1906
Place of Death: McKee's Gap, Pennsylvania
Cemetery: St. Patrick's Cemetery (MH)—Newry, Pennsylvania
Entered Service at: Chambersburg, Franklin County, Pennsylvania
Unit: Company D, 6th Pennsylvania Reserves
Battle or Place of Action: Gettysburg, Pennsylvania
Date of Action: 2 July 1863
Date of Issue: 3 August 1897
Citation: Was one of six volunteers who charged upon a log house near the Devil's Den, where a squad of the enemy's sharpshooters were sheltered, and compelled their surrender.

1150 ◆ ROWAND JR., ARCHIBALD HAMILTON

Rank: Private
Service: U.S. Army
Birthday: 6 March 1845
Place of Birth: Philadelphia, Philadelphia County, Pennsylvania
Date of Death: 14 December 1913
Cemetery: Allegheny Cemetery (MH)—Pittsburgh, Pennsylvania
Entered Service at: Pittsburgh, Allegheny County, Pennsylvania
Unit: Company K, 1st West Virginia Cavalry
Served as: Scout
Battle or Place of Action: from Columbia Virginia to City Point on the James River, west of Richmond
Date of Action: winter 1864-65
Date of Issue: 3 March 1873
Citation: Was one of two men who succeeded in getting through the enemy's lines with dispatches to Gen. Grant.

1151 ◆ ROWE, HENRY WALKER

Rank: Private
Service: U.S. Army
Birthday: 1 April 1840
Place of Birth: Candia, Rockingham County, New Hampshire
Date of Death: 9 October 1913
Place of Death: Roxbury, Massachusetts
Cemetery: Hill Cemetery—Candia, New Hampshire
Entered Service at: Candia, Rockingham County, New Hampshire
Unit: Company I, 11th New Hampshire Infantry
Battle or Place of Action: Petersburg, Virginia
Date of Action: 17 June 1864
Date of Issue: 1 December 1864
Citation: With two companions, he rushed and disarmed 27 enemy pickets, capturing a stand of flags.

1152 ◆ RUNDLE, CHARLES WESLEY

Rank: Private
Service: U.S. Army
Birthday: 14 December 1842
Place of Birth: Covington, Campbell County, Kentucky
Date of Death: 11 July 1924
Place of Death: Los Angeles, California
Cemetery: Los Angeles National Cemetery (34-I-11) (MH)—Los Angeles, California
Entered Service at: Oakley, Macon County, Illinois
Unit: Company A, 116th Illinois Infantry
Battle or Place of Action: Vicksburg, Mississippi
Date of Action: 22 May 1863
Date of Issue: 26 July 1894
Citation: Gallantry in the charge of the "volunteer storming party."

1153 ◆ RUSH, JOHN

True Name: Little, Israel W.
Rank: First Class Fireman
Service: U.S. Navy
Birthday: 21 February 1837
Place of Birth: Washington, D.C.
Date of Death: 29 April 1916
Place of Death: Washington, D.C.
Cemetery: Arlington National Cemetery (17-18768)—Arlington, Virginia
Entered Service at: Washington, D.C.
Unit: U.S.S. *Richmond*
Battle or Place of Action: Port Hudson, Louisiana
Date of Action: 14 March 1863
G.O. Number, Date: 17, 10 July 1863
Citation: Served on board the U.S.S. *Richmond* in the attack on Port Hudson, 14 March 1863. Damaged by a 6-inch solid rifle shot which shattered the starboard safety-valve chamber and also damaged the port safety valve, the fireroom of the Richmond immediately became filled with steam to place it in an extremely critical condition. Acting courageously in this crisis, Rush persisted in penetrating the steam-filled room in order to haul the hot fires of the furnaces, and continued this action until the gravity of the situation had been lessened.

1154 ◆ RUSSELL, CHARLES L.

Rank: Corporal (highest rank: Second Lieutenant)
Service: U.S. Army
Place of Birth: Malone, Franklin County, New York
Date of Death: 7 June 1910
Cemetery: Hot Springs National Cemetery (3-12-R1)—Hot Springs, South Dakota
Entered Service at: Malone, Franklin County, New York
Unit: Company H, 93d New York Infantry
Battle or Place of Action: Spotsylvania, Virginia
Date of Action: 12 May 1864
Date of Issue: 1 December 1864
Citation: Capture of flag of 42d Virginia Infantry (C.S.A.).

1155 ◆ RUSSELL, MILTON F.

Rank: Captain
Service: U.S. Army
Birthday: 25 September 1836
Place of Birth: Hendricks County, Indiana
Date of Death: 2 July 1908
Place of Death: Oakland, California
Cemetery: Odd Fellow Columbarium Cemetery—San Francisco, California
Entered Service at: North Salem, Hendricks County, Indiana
Unit: Company A, 51st Indiana Infantry
Battle or Place of Action: Stone River, Tennessee
Date of Action: 29 December 1862
Date of Issue: 28 September 1897

Citation: Was the first man to cross Stone River and, in the face of a galling fire from the concealed skirmishers of the enemy, led his men up the hillside, driving the opposing skirmishers before them.

1156 ◆ RUTHERFORD, JOHN T.

Rank: First Lieutenant (highest rank: Brevet Major)
Service: U.S. Army
Birthday: 23 August 1823
Place of Birth: Russell, St. Lawrence County, New York
Date of Death: 27 August 1898
Place of Death: Chicago, Illinois
Cemetery: Brookside Cemetery—Waddington, New York
Entered Service at: Canton, St. Lawrence County, New York
Unit: Company L, 9th New York Cavalry
Battle or Place of Action: Yellow Tavern & Hanovertown, Virginia
Date of Action: 11, 27 May 1864
Date of Issue: 22 March 1892
Citation: Made a successful charge at Yellow Tavern, Va., 11 May 1864, by which 90 prisoners were captured. On 27 May 1864, in a gallant dash on a superior force of the enemy and a personal encounter, captured his opponent.

1157 ◆ RUTTER, JAMES MAY

Rank: Sergeant
Service: U.S. Army
Birthday: 13 May 1841
Place of Birth: Wilkes-Barre, Luzerne County, Pennsylvania
Date of Death: 23 November 1907
Place of Death: Wilkes-Barre, Pennsylvania
Cemetery: Hollenbeck Cemetery—Wilkes-Barre, Pennsylvania
Entered Service at: Wilkes-Barre, Luzerne County, Pennsylvania
Unit: Company C, 143d Pennsylvania Infantry
Battle or Place of Action: Gettysburg, Pennsylvania
Date of Action: 1 July 1863
Date of Issue: 30 October 1896
Citation: At great risk of his life went to the assistance of a wounded comrade and while under fire removed him to a place of safety.

1158 ◆ RYAN, PETER J.

Rank: Private
Service: U.S. Army
Birthday: 1841
Place of Birth: Tipperary, County Tipperary, Ireland
Date of Death: 8 January 1908
Cemetery: Calvary Cemetery—Terre Haute, Indiana
Entered Service at: Terre Haute, Vigo County, Indiana
Unit: Company D, 11th Indiana Infantry
Battle or Place of Action: Winchester, Virginia
Date of Action: 19 September 1864

Date of Issue: 4 April 1865
Citation: With one companion, captured 14 Confederates in the severest part of the battle.

1159 ◆ SACRISTE, LOUIS JEANOTTELLE

Rank: First Lieutenant (highest rank: Brevet Major)
Service: U.S. Army
Birthday: 15 June 1843
Place of Birth: New Castle County, Delaware
Date of Death: 18 August 1904
Place of Death: La Grange, Illinois
Cemetery: Mount Carmel Cemetery—Hillside, Illinois
Entered Service at: Philadelphia, Philadelphia County, Pennsylvania
Unit: Company D, 116th Pennsylvania Infantry
Battle or Place of Action: Chancellorsville & Auburn, Virginia
Date of Action: 3 May & 14 October 1863
Date of Issue: 31 January 1889
Citation: Saved from capture a gun of the 5th Maine Battery. Voluntarily carried orders which resulted in saving from destruction or capture the picket line of the 1st Division, 2d Army Corps.

1160 ◆ SAGELHURST, JOHN CHRISTOPHER

True Name: Segelhurst
Rank: Sergeant (highest rank: First Sergeant)
Service: U.S. Army
Birthday: 1 June 1841
Place of Birth: Buffalo, Erie County, New York
Date of Death: 10 May 1907
Place of Death: Buffalo, New York
Cemetery: Forest Lawn Cemetery (MH)—Buffalo, New York
Entered Service at: Jersey City, Hudson County, New Jersey
Unit: Company B, 1st New Jersey Cavalry
Battle or Place of Action: Hatcher's Run, Virginia
Date of Action: 6 February 1865
Date of Issue: 3 January 1906
Citation: Under a heavy fire from the enemy carried off the field a commissioned officer who was severely wounded and also led a charge on the enemy's rifle pits.

1161 ◆ SANCRAINTE, CHARLES FRANCIS

True Name: Sanscrainte
Rank: Private
Service: U.S. Army
Birthday: 28 February 1838
Place of Birth: Monroe, Monroe County, Michigan
Date of Death: 5 May 1910
Place of Death: Buffalo, New York
Cemetery: Pine Hill Roman Catholic Cemetery (MH)—Buffalo, New York
Entered Service at: Monroe, Monroe County, Michigan

Unit: Company B, 15th Michigan Infantry
Battle or Place of Action: Atlanta, Georgia
Date of Action: 22 July 1864
Date of Issue: 25 July 1892
Citation: Voluntarily scaled the enemy's breastworks and signaled to his commanding officer in charge; also in single combat captured the colors of the 5th Texas Regiment (C.S.A.).

1162 ◆ SANDERSON, AARON

True Name: Anderson
Rank: Landsman
Service: U.S. Navy
Birthday: 1811
Place of Birth: North Carolina
Entered Service at: Philadelphia, Philadelphia County, Pennsylvania
Unit: U.S.S. *Wyandank*
Battle or Place of Action: Mattox Creek, Virginia
Date of Action: 17 March 1865
G.O. Number, Date: 59, 22 June 1865
Citation: Served on board the U.S.S. *Wyandank* during a boat expedition up Mattox Creek, 17 March 1865. Participating with a boat crew in the clearing of Mattox Creek, Landsman Sanderson carried out his duties courageously in the face of a devastating fire which cut away half the oars, pierced the launch in many places, and cut the barrel off a musket being fired at the enemy.

1163 ◆ SANDS, WILLIAM

Rank: First Sergeant
Service: U.S. Army
Birthday: 14 October 1835
Place of Birth: Reading, Berks County, Pennsylvania
Date of Death: 31 October 1918
Place of Death: Norristown, Pennsylvania
Cemetery: Charles Evans Cemetery (MH)—Reading, Pennsylvania
Entered Service at: Reading, Berks County, Pennsylvania
Unit: Company G, 88th Pennsylvania Infantry
Battle or Place of Action: Dabney's Mills, Virginia
Date of Action: 6-7 February 1865
Date of Issue: 9 November 1893
Citation: Grasped the enemy's colors in the face of a deadly fire and brought them inside the lines.

1164 ◆ SANFORD, JACOB

Rank: Private (highest rank: Commissary Sergeant)
Service: U.S. Army
Birthday: 1840
Place of Birth: Fulton County, Illinois
Date of Death: 3 September 1901
Cemetery: Prairie City Cemetery (MH)—Prairie City, Illinois
Entered Service at: Prairie City, McDonough County, Illinois

Unit: 55th Illinois Infantry
Battle or Place of Action: Vicksburg, Mississippi
Date of Action: 22 May 1863
Date of Issue: 2 September 1893
Citation: Gallantry in the charge of the "volunteer storming party."

1165 ◆ SARGENT, JACKSON G.

Rank: Sergeant
Service: U.S. Army
Birthday: 29 December 1841
Place of Birth: Stowe, Lamoille County, Vermont
Date of Death: 2 October 1921
Cemetery: River View Cemetery (MH)—Stowe, Vermont
Entered Service at: Stowe, Lamoille County, Vermont
Unit: Company D, 5th Vermont Infantry
Battle or Place of Action: Petersburg, Virginia
Date of Action: 2 April 1865
Date of Issue: 28 October 1891
Citation: First to scale the enemy's works and plant the colors thereon.

1166 ◆ SARTWELL, HENRY

Rank: Sergeant
Service: U.S. Army
Birthday: 7 March 1837
Place of Birth: Ticonderoga, Essex County, New York
Date of Death: 26 February 1910
Place of Death: Fort Ann, New York
Cemetery: Fish Hill Cemetery (MH)—Fort Ann, New York
Entered Service at: Fort Ann, Washington County, New York
Unit: Company D, 123d New York Infantry
Battle or Place of Action: Chancellorsville, Virginia
Date of Action: 3 May 1863
Date of Issue: 17 November 1896
Citation: Was severely wounded by a gunshot to his left arm, went half a mile to the rear but insisted on returning to his company and continued to fight bravely until he became exhausted from the loss of blood and was compelled to retire from the field.

1167 ◆ SAUNDERS, JAMES

Rank: Quartermaster (highest rank: Chief Quartermaster)
Service: U.S. Navy
Birthday: 1809
Place of Birth: Massachusetts
Entered Service at: Boston, Suffolk County, Massachusetts
Unit: U.S.S. *Kearsarge*
Battle or Place of Action: off Cherbourg, France
Date of Action: 19 June 1864
G.O. Number, Date: 59, 22 June 1865
Citation: Served as quartermaster on board the U.S.S. *Kearsarge* when she destroyed the *Alabama* off Cherbourg, France, 19 June 1864. Carrying out his duties courageously throughout the bitter engagement, Saunders was prompt in

reporting damages done to both ships, and it is testified to by Commodore Winslow that he is deserving of all commendation, both for gallantry and for encouragement of others in his division.

1168 ◆ SAVACOOL, EDWIN F.

Rank: Captain
Service: U.S. Army
Birthday: 1842
Place of Birth: Jackson, Jackson County, Michigan
Date of Death: 5 June 1865
Place of Death: Washington, D.C.
Cemetery: Elmwood Cemetery (MH)—Detroit, Michigan
Entered Service at: Marshall, Calhoun County, Michigan
Unit: Company K, 1st New York (Lincoln) Cavalry
Battle or Place of Action: Deatonsville (Sailor's Creek), Virginia
Date of Action: 6 April 1865
Date of Issue: 24 April 1865
Citation: Capture of flag, during which he was wounded and died several days later in Washington, D.C.

1169 ◆ SAVAGE, AUZELLA

Rank: Ordinary Seaman
Service: U.S. Navy
Birthday: 1846
Place of Birth: Anson, Somerset County, Maine
Date of Death: February 1882
Place of Death: Lost at sea, Atlantic Ocean
Entered Service at: Boston, Suffolk County, Massachusetts
Unit: U.S.S. *Santiago de Cuba*
Battle or Place of Action: Fort Fisher, North Carolina
Date of Action: 15 January 1865
G.O. Number, Date: 59, 22 May 1865
Citation: On board the U.S.S. *Santiago de Cuba* during the assault on Fort Fisher, 15 January 1865. When the landing party to which he was attached charged on the fort with a cheer and the determination to plant the colors on the ramparts, Savage remained steadfast when more than two-thirds of the marines and sailors fell back in panic during the fight. When enemy fire shot away the flagstaff above his hand, he bravery seized the remainder of the staff and brought his colors safely off.

1170 ◆ SAXTON JR., RUFUS

Rank: Brigadier General (highest rank: Brevet Major General)
Service: U.S. Army
Birthday: 19 October 1824
Place of Birth: Greenfield, Franklin County, Massachusetts
Date of Death: 23 February 1908
Place of Death: Washington, D.C.
Cemetery: Arlington National Cemetery (1-20-A) (MH)—Arlington, Virginia
Entered Service at: Deerfield, Franklin County, Massachusetts
Unit: U.S. Volunteers
Battle or Place of Action: Harpers Ferry, West Virginia

Date of Action: 26-30 May 1862
Date of Issue: 25 April 1893
Citation: Distinguished gallantry and good conduct in the defense.

1171 ◆ SCANLAN, PATRICK

True Name: Scanlon, Patrick
Rank: Private (highest rank: Sergeant)
Service: U.S. Army
Birthday: 1838
Place of Birth: Ireland
Date of Death: 5 September 1903
Place of Death: Farmington, Connecticut
Cemetery: St. Mary's Cemetery (MH)—Farmington, Connecticut
Entered Service at: Spencer, Worcester County, Massachusetts
Unit: Company A, 4th Massachusetts Cavalry
Battle or Place of Action: Ashepoo River, South Carolina
Date of Action: 24 May 1864
Date of Issue: 21 January 1897
Citation: Volunteered as a member of a boat crew which went to the rescue of a large number of Union soldiers on board the stranded steamer *Boston*, and with great gallantry assisted in conveying them to shore, being exposed the entire time to a heavy fire from a Confederate battery.

1172 ◆ SCHEIBNER, MARTIN E.

Rank: Private (highest rank: Corporal)
Service: U.S. Army
Birthday: 13 October 1842
Place of Birth: Valdai, Russia
Date of Death: 29 November 1908
Place of Death: Camden, New Jersey
Cemetery: Charles Evans Cemetery (MH)—Reading, Pennsylvania
Entered Service at: Philadelphia, Philadelphia County, Pennsylvania
Unit: Company G, 90th Pennsylvania Infantry
Battle or Place of Action: Mine Run, Virginia
Date of Action: 27 November 1863
Date of Issue: 23 June 1896
Citation: Voluntarily extinguished the burning fuse of a shell which had been thrown into the lines of the regiment by the enemy.

1173 ◆ SCHENCK, BENJAMIN W.

Rank: Private (highest rank: Corporal)
Service: U.S. Army
Birthday: 12 August 1837
Place of Birth: Butler County, Ohio
Date of Death: 28 February 1916
Place of Death: Danville, Illinois
Cemetery: Greenwood Cemetery—Decatur, Illinois
Entered Service at: Maroa, Macon County, Illinois
Unit: Company D, 116th Illinois Infantry

Battle or Place of Action: Vicksburg, Mississippi
Date of Action: 22 May 1863
Date of Issue: 14 August 1894
Citation: Gallantry in the charge of the "volunteer storming party."

1174 ◆ SCHILLER, JOHN

True Name: Schilling, John
Rank: Private
Service: U.S. Army
Birthday: 16 August 1847
Place of Birth: Hessen, Germany
Date of Death: 3 June 1926
Cemetery: Cypress Hills National Cemetery (5-3)—Brooklyn, New York
Entered Service at: New York, New York
Unit: Company E, 158th New York Infantry
Battle or Place of Action: Chapin's Farm, Virginia
Date of Action: 29 September 1864
Date of Issue: 6 April 1865
Citation: Advanced to the ditch of the enemy's works.

1175 ◆ SCHLACHTER, PHILIPP

Rank: Private
Service: U.S. Army
Birthday: 17 June 1841
Place of Birth: Germany
Date of Death: 9 September 1923
Place of Death: Sturgis, Michigan
Cemetery: Oakland Cemetery—Sturgis, Michigan
Entered Service at: New York, New York
Unit: Company F, 73d New York Infantry
Battle or Place of Action: Spotsylvania, Virginia
Date of Action: 12 May 1864
Date of Issue: 1 December 1864
Citation: Capture of flag of 15th Louisiana Infantry (C.S.A.).

1176 ◆ SCHMAL, GEORGE WILLIAM

Rank: Blacksmith
Service: U.S. Army
Birthday: 1849
Place of Birth: Germany
Date of Death: 4 August 1923
Cemetery: Forest Lawn Cemetery (MH)—Buffalo, New York
Entered Service at: Buffalo, Erie County, New York
Unit: Company M, 24th New York Cavalry
Battle or Place of Action: Paines Crossroads, Virginia
Date of Action: 5 April 1865
Date of Issue: 3 May 1865
Citation: Capture of flag.

1177 ◆ SCHMAUCH, ANDREW

Rank: Private (highest rank: First Sergeant)
Service: U.S. Army
Birthday: 1841

Place of Birth: Germany
Entered Service at: Portsmouth, Scioto County, Ohio
Unit: Company A, 30th Ohio Infantry
Battle or Place of Action: Vicksburg, Mississippi
Date of Action: 22 May 1863
Date of Issue: 9 July 1894
Citation: Gallantry in the charge of the "volunteer storming party."

1178 ◆ SCHMIDT, CONRAD

Rank: First Sergeant (highest rank: Quartermaster Sergeant)
Service: U.S. Army
Birthday: 27 February 1830
Place of Birth: Wurttemberg, Germany
Date of Death: 26 December 1908
Cemetery: Catholic Cemetery—Ogden, Kansas
Entered Service at: Fort Leavenworth, Leavenworth County, Kansas
Unit: Company K, 2d U.S. Cavalry
Battle or Place of Action: Winchester, Virginia
Date of Action: 19 September 1864
Date of Issue: 16 March 1896
Citation: Went to the assistance of his regimental commander, whose horse had been killed under him in a charge, mounted the officer behind him, under a heavy fire from the enemy, and returned him to his command.

1179 ◆ SCHMIDT, WILLIAM

Rank: Private
Service: U.S. Army
Birthday: 10 July 1846
Place of Birth: Tiffin, Seneca County, Ohio
Date of Death: 12 January 1888
Cemetery: St. Mary's Cemetery—Cincinnati, Ohio
Entered Service at: Maumee, Lucas County, Ohio
Unit: Company G, 37th Ohio Infantry
Battle or Place of Action: Missionary Ridge, Tennessee
Date of Action: 25 November 1863
Date of Issue: 9 November 1895
Citation: Rescued a wounded comrade under terrific fire.

1180 ◆ SCHNEIDER, GEORGE

Rank: Sergeant
Service: U.S. Army
Birthday: 8 November 1844
Place of Birth: Baltimore, Baltimore County, Maryland
Date of Death: 2 January 1929
Place of Death: Baltimore, Maryland
Cemetery: The Baltimore Cemetery—Baltimore, Maryland
Entered Service at: Baltimore, Baltimore County, Maryland
Unit: Company A, 3d Maryland Veteran Infantry
Battle or Place of Action: Petersburg, Virginia
Date of Action: 30 July 1864
Date of Issue: 27 July 1896
Citation: After the color sergeant had been shot down, seized the colors and planted them on the enemy's works during the charge.

1181 ◆ SCHNELL, CHRISTIAN

Rank: Corporal
Service: U.S. Army
Birthday: 19 February 1838
Place of Birth: Virginia
Date of Death: 14 December 1908
Cemetery: Greenlawn Cemetery—Wapakoneta, Ohio
Entered Service at: Wapakoneta, Auglaize County, Ohio
Unit: Company C, 37th Ohio Infantry
Battle or Place of Action: Vicksburg, Mississippi
Date of Action: 22 May 1863
Date of Issue: 10 July 1894
Citation: Gallantry in the charge of the "volunteer storming party."

1182 ◆ SCHOFIELD, JOHN MCALLISTER

Rank: Major (highest rank: Lieutenant General)
Service: U.S. Army
Birthday: 29 September 1831
Place of Birth: Gerry, Chautauga County, New York
Date of Death: 4 March 1906
Place of Death: St. Augustine, Florida
Cemetery: Arlington National Cemetery (2-1108)—Arlington, Virginia
Entered Service at: Freeport, Stephenson County, Illinois
Unit: 1st Missouri Infantry
Battle or Place of Action: Wilson's Creek, Missouri
Date of Action: 10 August 1861
Date of Issue: 2 July 1892
Citation: Was conspicuously gallant in leading a regiment in a successful charge against the enemy.

1183 ◆ SCHOONMAKER, JAMES MARTINUS

Rank: Colonel
Service: U.S. Army
Birthday: 30 June 1842
Place of Birth: Pittsburgh, Allegheny County, Pennsylvania
Date of Death: 11 October 1927
Place of Death: Pittsburgh, Pennsylvania
Cemetery: Mary S. Brown Memorial Cemetery—Pittsburgh, Pennsylvania
Entered Service at: Pittsburgh, Allegheny County, Pennsylvania
Unit: 14th Pennsylvania Cavalry
Battle or Place of Action: Winchester, Virginia
Date of Action: 19 September 1864
Date of Issue: 19 May 1899
Citation: At a critical period, gallantly led a cavalry charge against the left of the enemy's line of battle, drove the enemy out of his works, and captured many prisoners.

1184 ◆ SCHORN, CHARLES

Rank: Chief Bugler
Service: U.S. Army
Birthday: 1 May 1842
Place of Birth: Germany

Date of Death: 25 March 1915
Place of Death: Pomeroy, Ohio
Cemetery: Catholic Cemetery—Pomeroy, Ohio
Entered Service at: Mason City, Mason County, West Virginia
Unit: Company M, 1st West Virginia Cavalry
Battle or Place of Action: Appomattox, Virginia
Date of Action: 8 April 1865
Date of Issue: 3 May 1865
Citation: Capture of flag of the Sumter Flying Artillery (C.S.A.).

1185 ◆ SCHUBERT, MARTIN

Rank: Private (highest rank: First Lieutenant)
Service: U.S. Army
Birthday: 29 June 1838
Place of Birth: Germany
Date of Death: 25 April 1912
Place of Death: St. Louis, Missouri
Cemetery: Jefferson Barracks National Cemetery 4-12310 (MH)—St. Louis, Missouri
Entered Service at: Elmira, Chemung County, New York
Unit: Company E, 26th New York Infantry
Battle or Place of Action: Fredericksburg, Virginia
Date of Action: 13 December 1862
Date of Issue: 1 September 1893
Citation: Relinquished a furlough granted for wounds, entered the battle, where he picked up the colors after several bearers had been killed or wounded, and carried them until himself again wounded.

1186 ◆ SCHUTT, GEORGE

Rank: Coxswain
Service: U.S. Navy
Birthday: 1833
Place of Birth: Ireland
Entered Service at: New York, New York
Unit: U.S.S. *Hendrick Hudson*
Battle or Place of Action: St. Marks, Florida
Date of Action: 5-6 March 1865
G.O. Number, Date: 59, 22 June 1865
Citation: As coxswain on board the U.S.S. *Hendrick Hudson*, St. Marks, Fla., 5 and 6 March 1865. Serving with the Army in charge of Navy howitzers during the attack on St. Marks and throughout this fierce engagement, Schutt made remarkable efforts in assisting transport of the gun, and his coolness and determination in courageously remaining by his gun while under the heavy fire of the enemy were a credit to the service to which he belonged.

1187 ◆ SCHWAN, THEODORE

Rank: First Lieutenant (highest rank: Major General)
Service: U.S. Army
Birthday: 9 July 1841
Place of Birth: Hanover, Germany
Date of Death: 27 May 1926
Place of Death: Washington, D.C.
Cemetery: Arlington National Cemetery (2-860-)—Arlington, Virginia

Entered Service at: New York
Unit: 10th U.S. Infantry
Battle or Place of Action: Peebles Farm, Virginia
Date of Action: 1 October 1864
Date of Issue: 12 December 1898
Citation: At the imminent risk of his own life, while his regiment was falling back before a superior force of the enemy, he dragged a wounded and helpless officer to the rear, thus saving him from death or capture.

1188 ◆ SCHWENK, MARTIN

Rank: Sergeant
Service: U.S. Army
Birthday: 28 April 1839
Place of Birth: Baden, Germany
Date of Death: 20 June 1924
Cemetery: Arlington National Cemetery (17-20472) (MH)—Arlington, Virginia
Entered Service at: Boston, Suffolk County, Massachusetts
Unit: Company B, 6th U.S. Cavalry
Battle or Place of Action: Millerstown, Pennsylvania
Date of Action: July 1863
Date of Issue: 23 April 1889
Citation: Bravery in an attempt to carry a communication through the enemy's lines; also rescued an officer from the hands of the enemy.

1189 ◆ SCOFIELD, DAVID H.

Rank: Quartermaster Sergeant (highest rank: Regimental Quartermaster Sergeant)
Service: U.S. Army
Birthday: 10 December 1840
Place of Birth: Mamaroneck, Westchester County, New York
Date of Death: 30 September 1905
Place of Death: Bath, New York
Cemetery: Slasson Cemetery (MH)—Darien, Connecticut
Entered Service at: Stamford, Fairfield County, Connecticut
Unit: Company K, 5th New York Cavalry
Battle or Place of Action: Cedar Creek, Virginia
Date of Action: 19 October 1864
Date of Issue: 26 October 1864
Citation: Capture of flag of 13th Virginia Infantry (C.S.A.).

1190 ◆ SCOTT, ALEXANDER

Rank: Corporal
Service: U.S. Army
Birthday: 19 August 1844
Place of Birth: Montreal, Canada
Date of Death: 26 May 1923
Place of Death: Washington, D.C.
Cemetery: Arlington National Cemetery (17-18563) (MH)—Arlington, Virginia
Entered Service at: Winooski, Chittenden County, Vermont
Unit: Company D, 10th Vermont Infantry
Battle or Place of Action: Monocacy, Maryland
Date of Action: 9 July 1864

Date of Issue: 28 September 1897
Citation: Under a very heavy fire from the enemy saved the national flag of his regiment from capture.

1191 ◆ *SCOTT, JOHN MOREHEAD

Rank: Sergeant
Service: U.S. Army
Birthday: 1839
Place of Birth: Stark County, Ohio
Date of Death: 18 June 1862
Cemetery: Chattanooga National Cemetery (H-11182)—Chattanooga, Tennessee
Entered Service at: Findley, Hancock County, Ohio
Unit: Company F, 21st Ohio Infantry
Battle or Place of Action: Georgia
Date of Action: April 1862
Date of Issue: 4 August 1866
Citation: One of 19 of 24 men (including two civilians) who, by direction of Gen. Ormsby M. Mitchell, penetrated nearly 200 miles south into enemy territory and captured a railroad train at Big Shanty, Ga., in an attempt to destroy the bridges and track between Chattanooga and Atlanta.
Notes: POW

1192 ◆ SCOTT, JOHN WALLACE

Rank: Captain (highest rank: Brevet Major)
Service: U.S. Army
Birthday: 31 August 1832
Place of Birth: Chester County, Pennsylvania
Date of Death: 12 May 1903
Place of Death: Philadelphia, Pennsylvania
Cemetery: Presbyterian Church Cemetery—Parkesburg, Pennsylvania
Entered Service at: Philadelphia, Philadelphia County, Pennsylvania
Unit: Company D, 157th Pennsylvania Infantry
Battle or Place of Action: Five Forks, Virginia
Date of Action: 1 April 1865
Date of Issue: 27 April 1865
Citation: Capture of the flag of the 16th South Carolina Infantry, in hand-to-hand combat.

1193 ◆ SCOTT, JULIAN A.

Rank: Drummer
Service: U.S. Army
Birthday: 15 February 1846
Place of Birth: Johnson, Lamoille County, Vermont
Date of Death: 4 July 1901
Cemetery: Hillside Cemetery (MH)—Plainfield, New Jersey
Entered Service at: Johnson, Lamoille County, Vermont
Unit: Company E, 3d Vermont Infantry
Battle or Place of Action: Lee's Mill, Virginia
Date of Action: 16 April 1862
Date of Issue: February 1865
Citation: Crossed the creek under a terrific fire of musketry several times to assist in bringing off the wounded.

1194 ◆ SEAMAN, ELISHA B.

Rank: Private
Service: U.S. Army
Birthday: 1838
Place of Birth: Logan County, Ohio
Date of Death: 12 June 1919
Cemetery: Mount Tabor Cemetery—Salem Township, Ohio
Entered Service at: Logan County, Ohio
Unit: Company A, 66th Ohio Infantry
Battle or Place of Action: Chancellorsville, Virginia
Date of Action: 2 May 1863
Date of Issue: 24 June 1892
Citation: Was one of a party of four who voluntarily brought into the Union lines, under fire, a wounded Confederate officer from whom was obtained valuable information concerning the enemy.

1195 ◆ SEANOR, JAMES

Rank: Master-at-Arms
Service: U.S. Navy
Birthday: 1833
Place of Birth: Boston, Suffolk County, Massachusetts
Entered Service at: New York, New York
Unit: U.S. Ironclad *Chickasaw*
Battle or Place of Action: Fort Morgan, Mobile Bay, Alabama
Date of Action: 5 August 1864
G.O. Number, Date: 45, 31 December 1864
Citation: Served as master-at-arms on board the U.S. Ironclad *Chickasaw*, Mobile Bay, 5 August 1864. Although his enlistment was up, Seanor volunteered for the battle of Mobile Bay, going on board the *Chickasaw* from the *Vincennes* where he carried out his duties gallantly throughout the engagement which resulted in the capture of the rebel ram *Tennessee*.

1196 ◆ SEARS, CYRUS

Rank: First Lieutenant (highest rank: Colonel)
Service: U.S. Army
Birthday: 10 March 1832
Place of Birth: Meredith Township, Delaware County, New York
Date of Death: 30 November 1909
Cemetery: Oak Hill Cemetery (MH)—Upper Sandusky, Ohio
Entered Service at: Bucyrus, Crawford County, Ohio
Unit: Ohio Light Artillery, 11th Battery
Battle or Place of Action: Iuka, Mississippi
Date of Action: 19 September 1862
Date of Issue: 31 December 1892
Citation: Although severely wounded, fought his battery until the cannoneers and horses were nearly all killed or wounded.

1197 ◆ SEAVER, THOMAS ORVILLE

Rank: Colonel
Service: U.S. Army
Birthday: 23 December 1833
Place of Birth: Cavendish, Windsor County, Vermont
Date of Death: 11 July 1912
Place of Death: Woodstock, Vermont
Cemetery: River Street Cemetery—Woodstock, Vermont
Entered Service at: Pomfret, Vermont
Unit: 3d Vermont Infantry
Battle or Place of Action: Spotsylvania Courthouse, Virginia
Date of Action: 10 May 1864
Date of Issue: 8 April 1892
Citation: At the head of three regiments and under a most galling fire, attacked and occupied the enemy's works.

1198 ◆ SEITZINGER, JAMES M.

Rank: Private (highest rank: Sergeant)
Service: U.S. Army
Birthday: 24 November 1846
Place of Birth: Germany
Date of Death: 14 January 1924
Place of Death: Gordon, Pennsylvania
Cemetery: Christ Church Cemetery—Fountain Springs, Pennsylvania
Entered Service at: Worcester, Montgomery County, Pennsylvania
Unit: Company G, 116th Pennsylvania Infantry
Battle or Place of Action: Cold Harbor, Virginia
Date of Action: 3 June 1864
Date of Issue: 1 March 1906
Citation: When the color bearer was shot down, this soldier seized the colors and bore them gallantly in a charge against the enemy.

1199 ◆ SELLERS, ALFRED JACOB

Rank: Major (highest rank: Brevet Colonel)
Service: U.S. Army
Birthday: 2 March 1836
Place of Birth: Plumsteadville, Bucks County, Pennsylvania
Date of Death: 20 September 1908
Place of Death: Philadelphia, Pennsylvania
Cemetery: Mount Vernon Cemetery (MH)—Philadelphia, Pennsylvania
Entered Service at: Philadelphia, Philadelphia County, Pennsylvania
Unit: 90th Pennsylvania Infantry
Battle or Place of Action: Gettysburg, Pennsylvania
Date of Action: 1 July 1863
Date of Issue: 21 July 1894
Citation: Voluntarily led the regiment under a withering fire to a position from which the enemy was repulsed.

1200 ◆ *SESTON, CHARLES H.

Rank: Sergeant
Service: U.S. Army
Birthday: 1840
Place of Birth: New Albany, Floyd County, Indiana
Date of Death: 19 September 1864
Place of Death: Winchester, Virginia

Cemetery: New Albany Cemetery—Floyd County, Indiana
Entered Service at: New Albany, Floyd County, Indiana
Unit: Company I, 11th Indiana Infantry
Battle or Place of Action: Winchester, Virginia
Date of Action: 19 September 1864
Date of Issue: 6 April 1865
Citation: Gallant and meritorious service in carrying the regimental colors.

1201 ◆ SEWARD, RICHARD HENRY

True Name: Seaward, Richard Henry
Rank: Paymaster's Steward (highest rank: Master's Mate)
Service: U.S. Navy
Birthday: 10 October 1840
Place of Birth: Kittery, York County, Maine
Date of Death: 30 May 1899
Cemetery: First Christian Church Cemetery (MH)—Kittery Point, Maine
Entered Service at: Kittery, York County, Maine
Unit: U.S.S. *Commodore*
Battle or Place of Action: Ship Island Sound, Louisiana
Date of Action: 23 November 1863
G.O. Number, Date: 32, 16 April 1864
Citation: Served as paymaster's steward on board the U.S.S. *Commodore*, November 1863. Carrying out his duties courageously, Seward "volunteered to go on the field amidst a heavy fire to recover the bodies of two soldiers which he brought off with the aid of others; a second instance of personal valor within a fortnight." Promoted to acting master's mate.

1202 ◆ SEWELL, WILLIAM JOYCE

Rank: Colonel (highest rank: Brevet Major General)
Service: U.S. Army
Birthday: 6 December 1835
Place of Birth: Castlebar, County Mayo, Ireland
Date of Death: 27 December 1901
Place of Death: Camden, New Jersey
Cemetery: Harleigh Cemetery—Camden, New Jersey
Entered Service at: Camden, Camden County, New Jersey
Unit: 5th New Jersey Infantry
Battle or Place of Action: Chancellorsville, Virginia
Date of Action: 3 May 1863
Date of Issue: 25 March 1896
Citation: Assuming command of a brigade, he rallied around his colors a mass of men from other regiments and fought these troops with great brilliancy through several hours of desperate conflict, remaining in command though wounded and inspired them by his presence and the gallantry of his personal example.

1203 ◆ SHAFTER, WILLIAM RUFUS

Rank: First Lieutenant (highest rank: Major General U.S. Army)
Service: U.S. Army
Birthday: 16 October 1835
Place of Birth: Kalamazoo, Kalamazoo County, Michigan

Date of Death: 12 November 1906
Place of Death: Bakersfield, California
Cemetery: San Francisco National Cemetery OS-30-46 (MH)—San Francisco, California
Entered Service at: Galesburg, Kalamazoo County, Michigan
Unit: Company I, 7th Michigan Infantry
Battle or Place of Action: Fair Oaks, Virginia
Date of Action: 31 May 1862
Date of Issue: 12 June 1895
Citation: Lt. Shafter was engaged in bridge construction and not being needed there returned with his men to engage the enemy participating in a charge across an open field that resulted in casualties to 18 of the 22 men. At the close of the battle his horse was shot from under him and he was severely flesh wounded. He remained on the field that day and stayed to fight the next day only by concealing his wounds. In order not to be sent home with the wounded he kept his wounds concealed for another three days until other wounded had left the area.

1204 ◆ SHAHAN, EMISIRE

Rank: Corporal (highest rank: Sergeant)
Service: U.S. Army
Birthday: 14 August 1843
Place of Birth: Preston County, West Virginia
Date of Death: 17 November 1919
Cemetery: Masonic Cemetery (MH)—Elma, Washington
Entered Service at: Clarksburg, Harrison County, West Virginia
Unit: Company A, 1st West Virginia Cavalry
Battle or Place of Action: Deatonsville (Sailor's Creek), Virginia
Date of Action: 6 April 1865
Date of Issue: 3 May 1865
Citation: Capture of flag of 76th Georgia Infantry (C.S.A.).

1205 ◆ SHALER, ALEXANDER

Rank: Colonel (highest rank: Brevet Major General)
Service: U.S. Army
Birthday: 19 March 1827
Place of Birth: Haddam, Middlesex County, Connecticut
Date of Death: 28 December 1911
Place of Death: New York, New York
Cemetery: English Neighborhood Reform Church Cemetery—Ridgefield, New Jersey
Entered Service at: New York, New York
Unit: 65th New York Infantry
Battle or Place of Action: Marye's Heights, Virginia
Date of Action: 3 May 1863
Date of Issue: 25 November 1893
Citation: At a most critical moment, the head of the charging column being about to be crushed by the severe fire of the enemy's artillery and infantry, he pushed forward with a supporting column, pierced the enemy's works, and turned their flank.
Notes: POW

1206 ◆ SHAMBAUGH, CHARLES

Rank: Corporal
Service: U.S. Army
Birthday: 25 August 1839
Place of Birth: Prussia, Germany
Date of Death: 12 October 1913
Place of Death: Hyattsville, Maryland
Cemetery: Prospect Hill Cemetery—Washington, D.C.
Entered Service at: Indian Town, Lebanon County, Pennsylvania
Unit: Company B, 11th Pennsylvania Reserves
Battle or Place of Action: Charles City Crossroads, Virginia
Date of Action: 30 June 1862
Date of Issue: 17 July 1866
Citation: Capture of flag.
Notes: POW

1207 ◆ SHANES, JOHN

Rank: Private
Service: U.S. Army
Birthday: 23 July 1844
Place of Birth: Monongalia County, West Virginia
Date of Death: 26 January 1904
Place of Death: Brave, Pennsylvania
Cemetery: Lantz Cemetery—Brave, Pennsylvania
Entered Service at: Warren, West Virginia
Unit: Company K, 14th West Virginia Infantry
Battle or Place of Action: Carter's Farm, Virginia
Date of Action: 20 July 1864
Date of Issue: 31 January 1896
Citation: Charged upon a Confederate fieldpiece in advance of his comrades and by his individual exertions silenced the piece.

1208 ◆ SHAPLAND, JOHN

Rank: Private
Service: U.S. Army
Birthday: 4 March 1832
Place of Birth: Barnstable, Devonshire, England
Date of Death: 5 February 1923
Cemetery: Greenwood Cemetery (MH)—York, Nebraska
Entered Service at: Ottawa, La Salle County, Illinois
Unit: Company D, 104th Illinois Infantry
Battle or Place of Action: Elk River, Tennessee
Date of Action: 2 July 1863
Date of Issue: 30 October 1897
Citation: Voluntarily joined a small party that, under heavy fire, captured a stockade and saved the bridge.

1209 ◆ SHARP, HENDRICK

Rank: Seaman
Service: U.S. Navy
Birthday: 1815
Place of Birth: Spain
Entered Service at: New York, New York

Unit: U.S.S. *Richmond*
Battle or Place of Action: Fort Mogan, Mobile Bay, Alabama
Date of Action: 5 August 1864
G.O. Number, Date: 45, 31 December 1864
Citation: As captain of a 100-pounder rifle gun on topgallant forecastle on board the U.S.S. *Richmond* during action against rebel forts and gunboats and against the ram *Tennessee* in Mobile Bay, 5 August 1864. Despite damage to his ship and the loss of several men on board as enemy fire raked her decks, Sharp fought his gun with skill and courage throughout a furious two-hour battle which resulted in the surrender of the rebel ram *Tennessee* and in the damaging and destruction of batteries at Fort Morgan.

1210 ◆ SHEA, JOSEPH HENRY

Rank: Private
Service: U.S. Army
Place of Birth: Baltimore, Baltimore County, Maryland
Entered Service at: New Bern, Craven County, North Carolina
Unit: Company K, 92d New York Infantry
Battle or Place of Action: Chapin's Farm, Virginia
Date of Action: 29 September 1864
Date of Issue: March 1866
Citation: Gallantry in bringing wounded from the field under heavy fire.

1211 ◆ SHELLENBERGER, JOHN

Rank: Corporal
Service: U.S. Army
Birthday: 30 August 1839
Place of Birth: Fayette County, Pennsylvania
Date of Death: 16 January 1911
Cemetery: Welsh Hill Cemetery (MH)—Grandville Township, Ohio
Entered Service at: Perryopolis, Fayette County, Pennsylvania
Unit: Company B, 85th Pennsylvania Infantry
Battle or Place of Action: Deep Run, Virginia
Date of Action: 16 August 1864
Date of Issue: 6 April 1865
Citation: Capture of flag.

1212 ◆ SHEPARD, IRWIN

Rank: Corporal (highest rank: First Sergeant)
Service: U.S. Army
Birthday: 5 July 1843
Place of Birth: Skaneateles, Onondaga County, New York
Date of Death: 17 April 1916
Cemetery: Woodlawn Cemetery—Winona, Minnesota
Entered Service at: Chelsea, Washtenaw County, Michigan
Unit: Company E, 17th Michigan Infantry
Battle or Place of Action: Knoxville, Tennessee
Date of Action: 20 November 1863
Date of Issue: 3 August 1897

Citation: Having voluntarily accompanied a small party to destroy buildings within the enemy's lines, whence sharpshooters had been firing, disregarded an order to retire, remained, and completed the firing of the buildings, thus insuring their total destruction; this at the imminent risk of his life from the fire of the advancing enemy.

1213 ◆ SHEPARD, LOUIS CAPET

Rank: Ordinary Seaman
Service: U.S. Navy
Birthday: 2 September 1841
Place of Birth: Ashtabula, Ashtabula County, Ohio
Date of Death: 27 April 1919
Place of Death: Danbury, Ohio
Cemetery: Lakeview Cemetery—Port Clinton, Ohio
Entered Service at: Ohio
Unit: U.S.S. *Wabash*
Battle or Place of Action: Fort Fisher, North Carolina
Date of Action: 15 January 1865
G.O. Number, Date: 59, 22 June 1865
Citation: Served as seaman on board the U.S.S. *Wabash* in the assault on Fort Fisher, 15 January 1865. Advancing gallantly through severe enemy fire while armed only with a revolver and cutlass which made it impossible to return the fire at that range, Shepard succeeded in reaching the angle of the fort and in going on to be one of the few who entered the fort. When the rest of the body of men to his rear were forced to retreat under a devastating fire, he was forced to withdraw through lack of support and to seek the shelter of one of the mounds near the stockade from which point he succeeded in regaining the safety of his ship.

1214 ◆ SHEPHERD, WILLIAM

Rank: Private (highest rank: Sergeant)
Service: U.S. Army
Birthday: 1837
Place of Birth: Dillsboro, Ohio County, Indiana
Date of Death: 19 March 1899
Cemetery: Conaway Family Cemetery (MH)—Dillsboro, Indiana
Entered Service at: Washington, D.C.
Unit: Company A, 3d Indiana Cavalry
Battle or Place of Action: Deatonsville (Sailor's Creek), Virginia
Date of Action: 6 April 1865
Date of Issue: 3 May 1865
Citation: Capture of flag.
Notes: POW

1215 ◆ SHERIDAN, JAMES

Rank: Quartermaster
Service: U.S. Navy
Birthday: 1831
Place of Birth: Newark, Essex County, New Jersey
Entered Service at: New York, New York
Unit: U.S.S. *Oneida*

Battle or Place of Action: Mobile Bay, Alabama
Date of Action: 5 August 1864
G.O. Number, Date: 45, 31 December 1864
Citation: Served as quartermaster on board the U.S.S. *Oneida* in the engagement at Mobile Bay, 5 August 1864. Acting as captain of the after 11-inch gun, and wounded in several places, Sheridan remained at his gun until the firing had ceased and then took the place of the signal quartermaster who had been injured by a fall. Recommended for his gallantry and intelligence, Sheridan served courageously throughout this battle which resulted in the capture of the rebel ram *Tennessee* and the damaging of Fort Morgan.

1216 ◆ SHERMAN, MARSHALL

Rank: Private
Service: U.S. Army
Birthday: 1823
Place of Birth: Burlington, Chittenden County, Vermont
Date of Death: 19 April 1896
Cemetery: Oakland Cemetery (MH)—St. Paul, Minnesota
Entered Service at: St. Paul, Ramsey County, Minnesota
Unit: Company C, 1st Minnesota Infantry
Battle or Place of Action: Gettysburg, Pennsylvania
Date of Action: 3 July 1863
Date of Issue: 1 December 1864
Citation: Capture of flag of 28th Virginia Infantry (C.S.A.).

1217 ◆ SHIELDS, BERNARD

Rank: Private
Service: U.S. Army
Birthday: 1833
Place of Birth: Ireland
Date of Death: 20 April 1887
Cemetery: Mount Calvary Cemetery—Columbus, Ohio
Entered Service at: Ironton, Lawrence County, Ohio
Unit: Company E, 2d West Virginia Cavalry
Battle or Place of Action: Appomattox, Virginia
Date of Action: 8 April 1865
Date of Issue: 3 May 1865
Citation: Capture of flag of the Washington Artillery (C.S.A.).

1218 ◆ SHIEL, JOHN

True Name: Shields, John
Rank: Corporal (highest rank: Sergeant)
Service: U.S. Army
Birthday: May 1828
Place of Birth: Scotland
Date of Death: 11 June 1908
Place of Death: Philadelphia, Pennsylvania
Cemetery: Greenmount Cemetery—Philadelphia, Pennsylvania
Entered Service at: Philadelphia, Philadelphia County, Pennsylvania
Unit: Company E, 90th Pennsylvania Infantry

Battle or Place of Action: Fredericksburg, Virginia
Date of Action: 13 December 1862
Date of Issue: 21 January 1897
Citation: Carried a dangerously wounded comrade into the Union lines, thereby preventing his capture by the enemy.

1219 ◆ SHILLING, JOHN

Rank: First Sergeant
Service: U.S. Army
Birthday: 15 February 1832
Place of Birth: England
Date of Death: 22 July 1884
Cemetery: Riverside Cemetery—Wilmington, Delaware
Entered Service at: Felton, Kent County, Delaware
Unit: Company H, 3d Delaware Infantry
Battle or Place of Action: Weldon Railroad, Virginia
Date of Action: 21 August 1864
Date of Issue: 6 September 1864
Citation: Capture of flag.

1220 ◆ SHIPLEY, ROBERT F.

Rank: First Sergeant
Service: U.S. Army
Birthday: 8 May 1838
Place of Birth: Wayne, Schuyler County, New York
Date of Death: 29 April 1903
Cemetery: Restland Cemetery—Mendota, Illinois
Entered Service at: Penn Yan, Yates County, New York
Unit: Company A, 140th New York Infantry
Battle or Place of Action: Five Forks, Virginia
Date of Action: 1 April 1865
Date of Issue: 10 May 1865
Citation: Captured the flag of the 9th Virginia Infantry (C.S.A.) in hand-to-hand combat.

1221 ◆ SHIPMAN, WILLIAM

Rank: Coxswain
Service: U.S. Navy
Birthday: 1831
Place of Birth: New York, New York
Date of Death: 17 April 1894
Cemetery: Holy Cross Cemetery—Philadelphia, Pennsylvania
Entered Service at: New York, New York
Unit: U.S.S. *Ticonderoga*
Battle or Place of Action: Fort Fisher, North Carolina
Date of Action: 15 January 1865
G.O. Number, Date: 59, 22 June 1865
Citation: On board the U.S.S. *Ticonderoga* in the attack upon Fort Fisher, 15 January 1865. As captain of No. 2 gun, stationed near the 100-pound Parrott rifle when it burst into fragments, killing eight men and wounding 12 more, Shipman promptly recognized the effect produced by the explosion and, despite the carnage surrounding them and the enemy's fire, encouraged the men at their guns by exclaiming, "Go ahead, boys! This is only the fortunes of war!"

1222 ◆ SHIVERS, JOHN

Rank: Private
Service: U.S. Marine Corps
Birthday: 1830
Place of Birth: Canada
Entered Service at: New Jersey
Battle or Place of Action: Fort Fisher, North Carolina
Date of Action: 15 January 1865
G.O. Number, Date: 59, 22 June 1865
Citation: On board the U.S.S. *Minnesota*, in the assault on Fort Fisher, 15 January 1865. Landing on the beach with the assaulting party from his ship, Pvt. Shivers advanced to the top of the sandhill and partly through the breach in the palisades despite enemy fire which killed or wounded many officers and men. When more than two-thirds of the men became seized with panic and retreated on the run, he remained with the party until dark when it came safely away, bringing its wounded, its arms, and its colors.

1223 ◆ SHOEMAKER, LEVI

Rank: Sergeant
Service: U.S. Army
Birthday: 25 June 1840
Place of Birth: Monongalia County, West Virginia
Date of Death: 3 April 1917
Place of Death: Morgantown, West Virginia
Cemetery: East Oak Grove Cemetery (MH)—Morgantown, West Virginia
Entered Service at: Clarksburg, Harrison County, West Virginia
Unit: Company A, 1st West Virginia Cavalry
Battle or Place of Action: Nineveh, Virginia
Date of Action: 12 November 1864
Date of Issue: 26 November 1864
Citation: Capture of flag of 22d Virginia Cavalry (C.S.A.).

1224 ◆ SHOPP, GEORGE J.

Rank: Private
Service: U.S. Army
Birthday: 8 September 1834
Place of Birth: Equinunk, Wayne County, Pennsylvania
Date of Death: 24 March 1924
Place of Death: Denver, Colorado
Cemetery: Yuma Cemetery (MH)—Yuma, Colorado
Entered Service at: Reading, Berks County, Pennsylvania
Unit: Company E, 191st Pennsylvania Infantry
Battle or Place of Action: Five Forks, Virginia
Date of Action: 1 April 1865
Date of Issue: 27 April 1865
Citation: Capture of flag.

1225 ◆ SHUBERT, FRANK

Rank: Sergeant (highest rank: Second Lieutenant)
Service: U.S. Army
Birthday: 12 January 1841

Place of Birth: Hesse, Germany
Date of Death: 24 December 1920
Cemetery: Prospect Hill Cemetery (MH)—Canojaharie, New York
Entered Service at: Canojaharie, Montgomery County, New York
Unit: Company E, 43d New York Infantry
Battle or Place of Action: Petersburg, Virginia
Date of Action: 2 April 1865
Date of Issue: 10 May 1865
Citation: Capture of two markers.

1226 ◆ SHUTES, HENRY

Rank: Captain of the Forecastle
Service: U.S. Navy
Birthday: 1804
Place of Birth: Baltimore Baltimore County, Maryland
Date of Death: 10 September 1889
Place of Death: Philadelphia, Pennsylvania
Cemetery: Mount Moriah Cemetery VA plot 2-22-01 (MH)—Philadelphia, Pennsylvania
Entered Service at: Maryland
Unit: U.S.S. *Wissahickon*
Battle or Place of Action: New Orleans, Louisiana & Fort McAllister, Georgia
Date of Action: 24-25 April 1862 & 27 February 1863
G.O. Number, Date: 71, 15 January 1866
Citation: Served as captain of the forecastle on board the U.S.S. *Wissahickon* during the battle of New Orleans, 24 and 25 April 1862; and in the engagement at Fort McAllister, 27 February 1863. Going on board the U.S.S. *Wissahickon* from the U.S.S. *Don*, where his seamanlike qualities as gunner's mate were outstanding, Shutes performed his duties with skill and courage. Showing a presence of mind and prompt action when a shot from Fort McAllister penetrated the *Wissahickon* below the water line and entered the powder magazine, Shutes contributed materially to the preservation of the powder and safety of the ship.

1227 ◆ SICKLES, DANIEL EDGAR

Rank: Major General
Service: U.S. Army
Birthday: 20 October 1819
Place of Birth: New York, New York
Date of Death: 3 May 1914
Place of Death: New York, New York
Cemetery: Arlington National Cemetery (3-1906) (MH)—Arlington, Virginia
Entered Service at: New York, New York
Unit: U.S. Volunteers
Battle or Place of Action: Gettysburg, Pennsylvania
Date of Action: 2 July 1863
Date of Issue: 30 October 1897
Citation: Displayed most conspicuous gallantry on the field vigorously contesting the advance of the enemy and continuing to encourage his troops after being himself severely wounded.

1228 ◆ SICKLES, WILLIAM H.

Rank: Sergeant
Service: U.S. Army
Birthday: 27 October 1844
Place of Birth: Danube, Herkimer County, New York
Date of Death: 26 September 1938
Place of Death: Orting, Washington
Cemetery: Soldier's Home Cemetery (MH)—Orting, Washington
Entered Service at: Fall River, Columbia County, Wisconsin
Unit: Company B, 7th Wisconsin Infantry
Battle or Place of Action: Gravelly Run, Virginia
Date of Action: 31 March 1865
Date of Issue: 28 February 1917
Citation: With a comrade, attempted capture of a stand of Confederate colors and detachment of nine Confederates, actually taking prisoner three members of the detachment, dispersing the remainder, and recapturing a Union officer who was a prisoner in hands of the detachment.

1229 ◆ SIDMAN, GEORGE DALLAS

Rank: Private (highest rank: Corporal)
Service: U.S. Army
Birthday: 25 November 1844
Place of Birth: Rochester, Monroe County, New York
Date of Death: 3 February 1920
Place of Death: Lakeland, Florida
Cemetery: Arlington National Cemetery (3-2492) (MH)—Arlington, Virginia
Entered Service at: Owosso, Shiawassee County, Michigan
Unit: Company C, 16th Michigan Infantry
Battle or Place of Action: Gaines' Mill, Virginia
Date of Action: 27 June 1862
Date of Issue: 6 April 1892
Citation: Distinguished bravery in battle. Rallied his comrades to charge vastly superior force until wounded in the hip. He was a 16-year old drummer.
Notes: POW

1230 ◆ SIMKINS, LEBBEUS

True Name: Simpkins, Lebbeus
Rank: Coxswain
Service: U.S. Navy
Birthday: 1836
Place of Birth: Utica, Oneida County, New York
Date of Death: 10 September 1884
Place of Death: Sacramento, California
Cemetery: I.O.O.F. Tier, City Cemetery (MH)—Sacramento, California
Entered Service at: New York
Unit: U.S.S. *Richmond*
Battle or Place of Action: Mobile Bay, Alabama
Date of Action: 5 August 1864
G.O. Number, Date: 45, 31 December 1864
Citation: On board the U.S.S. *Richmond* during action against rebel forts and gunboats and against the ram *Tennessee*

in Mobile Bay, 5 August 1864. Despite damage to his ship and the loss of several men on board as enemy fire raked her decks, Simkins performed his duties with skill and courage throughout the furious two-hour battle, which resulted in the surrender of the rebel ram *Tennessee* and in the damaging and destruction of batteries at Fort Morgan.

1231 ◆ SIMMONS, JOHN

Rank: Private
Service: U.S. Army
Place of Birth: Bethel, Sullivan County, New York
Date of Death: 9 January 1891
Cemetery: Andes Cemetery (MH)—Andes, New York
Entered Service at: Liberty, Sullivan County, New York
Unit: Company D, 2d New York Heavy Artillery
Battle or Place of Action: Deatonsville (Sailor's Creek), Virginia
Date of Action: 6 April 1865
Date of Issue: 24 April 1865
Citation: Capture of flag.

1232 ◆ SIMMONS, WILLIAM THOMAS

Rank: First Lieutenant
Service: U.S. Army
Birthday: 29 January 1843
Place of Birth: Greene County, Illinois
Date of Death: 27 December 1908
Place of Death: Caliatoga, California
Cemetery: St. Helena Public Cemetery (MH)—St. Helena, California
Entered Service at: Springfield, Sangamon County, Illinois
Unit: Company C, 11th Missouri Infantry
Battle or Place of Action: Nashville, Tennessee
Date of Action: 16 December 1864
Date of Issue: 25 February 1865
Citation: Capture of flag of 34th Alabama Infantry (C.S.A.). Being the first to enter the works, he shot and wounded the enemy color bearer.

1233 ◆ SIMONDS, WILLIAM EDGAR

Rank: Sergeant Major (highest rank: Second Lieutenant)
Service: U.S. Army
Birthday: 24 November 1842
Place of Birth: Collinsville, Hartford County, Connecticut
Date of Death: 14 March 1903
Place of Death: Hartford, Connecticut
Cemetery: Collinsville Cemetery (MH)—Collinsville, Connecticut
Entered Service at: Canton, Hartford County, Connecticut
Unit: 25th Connecticut Infantry
Battle or Place of Action: Irish Bend, Louisiana
Date of Action: 14 April 1863
Date of Issue: 25 February 1899
Citation: Displayed great gallantry, under a heavy fire from the enemy, in calling in the skirmishers and assisting in forming the line of battle.

1234 ◆ SIMONS, CHARLES JENKS

Rank: Sergeant (highest rank: First Lieutenant)
Service: U.S. Army
Birthday: 29 March 1843
Place of Birth: Bombay, India
Date of Death: 18 June 1914
Place of Death: Chicago, Illinois
Cemetery: Oakwood Cemetery—Chicago, Illinois
Entered Service at: Exeter, Rockingham County, New Hampshire
Unit: Company A, 9th New Hampshire Infantry
Battle or Place of Action: Petersburg, Virginia
Date of Action: 30 July 1864
Date of Issue: 27 July 1896
Citation: Was one of the first in the exploded mine, captured a number of prisoners, and was himself captured, but escaped.

1235 ◆ SKELLIE, EBENEZER

Rank: Corporal (highest rank: Brevet Second Lieutenant NY Volunteers)
Service: U.S. Army
Birthday: August 1844
Place of Birth: Mina, Chautauqua County, New York
Date of Death: 2 July 1898
Place of Death: Findley Lake, New York
Cemetery: Mina Cemetery (MH)—Mina, New York
Entered Service at: Mina, Chautauqua County, New York
Unit: Company D, 112th New York Infantry
Battle or Place of Action: Chapin's Farm, Virginia
Date of Action: 29 September 1864
Date of Issue: 6 April 1865
Citation: Took the colors of his regiment, the color bearer having fallen, and carried them through the first charge; also, in the second charge, after all the color guards had been killed or wounded he carried the colors up to the enemy's works, where he fell wounded.

1236 ◆ SLADEN, JOSEPH ALTON

Rank: Private (highest rank: Major U.S.A. Retired)
Service: U.S. Army
Birthday: 9 April 1841
Place of Birth: Rockdale, England
Date of Death: 25 January 1911
Place of Death: Portland, Oregon
Cemetery: U.S. Military Academy Cemetery (4-22)—West Point, New York
Entered Service at: Lowell, Middlesex County, Massachusetts
Unit: Company A, 33d Massachusetts Infantry
Battle or Place of Action: Resaca, Georgia
Date of Action: 14 May 1864
Date of Issue: 19 July 1895
Citation: While detailed as clerk at headquarters, voluntarily engaged in action at a critical moment and personal example inspired the troops to repel the enemy.

1237 ◆ SLAGLE, OSCAR

Rank: Private
Service: U.S. Army
Birthday: 2 April 1844
Place of Birth: Fulton County, Ohio
Date of Death: 12 April 1913
Place of Death: Cullom, Illinois
Cemetery: Broughton Township Cemetery—Kempton, Illinois
Entered Service at: Manlius, Bureau County, Illinois
Unit: Company D, 104th Illinois Infantry
Battle or Place of Action: Elk River, Tennessee
Date of Action: 2 July 1863
Date of Issue: 30 October 1897
Citation: Voluntarily joined a small party that, under a heavy fire, captured a stockade and saved the bridge.

1238 ◆ *SLAVENS, SAMUEL

Rank: Private
Service: U.S. Army
Birthday: 1830
Place of Birth: Pike County, Ohio
Date of Death: 18 June 1862
Place of Death: Atlanta, Georgia
Cemetery: Chattanooga National Cemetery (H-11176) (MH)—Chattanooga, Tennessee
Entered Service at: Wakefield, Pike County, Ohio
Unit: Company E, 33d Ohio Infantry
Battle or Place of Action: Georgia
Date of Action: April 1862
Date of Issue: 28 July 1883
Citation: One of 19 of 24 men (including two civilians) who, by direction of Gen. Ormsby M. Mitchell, penetrated nearly 200 miles south into enemy territory and captured a railroad train at Big Shanty, Ga., in an attempt to destroy the bridges and track between Chattanooga and Atlanta.

1239 ◆ SLOAN, ANDREW JACKSON

Rank: Private
Service: U.S. Army
Birthday: 1835
Place of Birth: Bedford County, Pennsylvania
Date of Death: 1875
Cemetery: Platt Cemetery (MH)—Colesburg, Iowa
Entered Service at: Colesburg, Delaware County, Iowa
Unit: Company H, 12th Iowa Infantry
Battle or Place of Action: Nashville, Tennessee
Date of Action: 16 December 1864
Date of Issue: 24 February 1865
Citation: Captured flag of 1st Louisiana Battery (C.S.A.).

1240 ◆ SLUSHER, HENRY C.

Rank: Private
Service: U.S. Army
Birthday: 10 May 1846

Place of Birth: Washington County, Pennsylvania
Date of Death: 12 March 1923
Place of Death: Washington, Pennsylvania
Cemetery: Lone Pine Cemetery—Amwell Township, Pennsylvania
Entered Service at: Washington, Washington County, Pennsylvania
Unit: Troop F, 22d Pennsylvania Volunteer Cavalry
Battle or Place of Action: near Moorefield, West Virginia
Date of Action: 11 September 1863
Date of Issue: 4 April 1898
Citation: Voluntarily crossed a branch of the Potomac River under fire to rescue a wounded comrade held prisoner by the enemy. Was wounded and taken prisoner in the attempt.
Notes: POW

1241 ◆ SMALLEY, REUBEN

Rank: Private
Service: U.S. Army
Birthday: 29 April 1839
Place of Birth: Reading, Schuyler County, New York
Date of Death: 9 July 1926
Place of Death: Greensburg, Indiana
Cemetery: South Park Cemetery (MH)—Greensburg, Indiana
Entered Service at: Holton, Ripley County, Indiana
Unit: Company F, 83d Indiana Infantry
Battle or Place of Action: Vicksburg, Mississippi
Date of Action: 22 May 1863
Date of Issue: 9 July 1894
Citation: Gallantry in the charge of the "volunteer storming party."

1242 ◆ SMALLEY, REUBEN S.

Rank: Private
Service: U.S. Army
Birthday: 8 April 1837
Place of Birth: Washington County, Pennsylvania
Date of Death: 17 February 1916
Place of Death: Quincy, Illinois
Cemetery: Allen Cemetery—Allen, Illinois
Entered Service at: Brookfield, Cook County, Illinois
Unit: Company D, 104th Illinois Infantry
Battle or Place of Action: Elk River, Tennessee
Date of Action: 2 July 1863
Date of Issue: 30 October 1897
Citation: Voluntarily joined a small party that, under a heavy fire, captured a stockade and saved the bridge.

1243 ◆ SMITH, ALONZO

Rank: Sergeant (highest rank: First Lieutenant)
Service: U.S. Army
Birthday: 9 August 1842
Place of Birth: Niagara County, New York
Date of Death: 17 January 1927
Place of Death: Buffalo, New York

Cemetery: St. Stephen's RC Cemetery (MH)—Middleport, New York
Entered Service at: Jonesville, Hillsdale County, Michigan
Unit: Company C, 7th Michigan Infantry
Battle or Place of Action: Hatcher's Run, Virginia
Date of Action: 27 October 1864
Date of Issue: 1 December 1864
Citation: Capture of flag of 26th North Carolina Infantry (C.S.A.), while outside his lines far from his comrades.

1244 ◆ SMITH, CHARLES H.

Rank: Coxswain (highest rank: Master's Mate)
Service: U.S. Navy
Birthday: 1826
Place of Birth: Standish, Cumberland County, Maine
Date of Death: 4 February 1898
Place of Death: West Concord, Vermont
Entered Service at: Maine
Unit: U.S.S. *Rhode Island*
Battle or Place of Action: off Cape Hatteras, North Carolina
Date of Action: 30 December 1862
G.O. Number, Date: 59, 22 June 1865
Citation: Served on board the U.S.S. *Rhode Island* which was engaged in saving the lives of the officers and crew of the *Monitor*, 30 December 1862. Participating in the hazardous rescue of the officers and crew of the sinking *Monitor*, Smith, after rescuing several of the men, became separated in a heavy gale with other members of the cutter that had set out from the *Rhode Island*, and spent many hours in the small boat at the mercy of the weather and high seas until finally picked up by a schooner 50 miles east of Cape Hatteras.

1245 ◆ SMITH, CHARLES HENRY

Rank: Colonel (highest rank: Brevet Major General)
Service: U.S. Army
Birthday: 1 November 1827
Place of Birth: Hollis, York County, Maine
Date of Death: 17 July 1902
Cemetery: Arlington National Cemetery (1-128-A)—Arlington, Virginia
Entered Service at: Eastport, Washington County, Maine
Unit: 1st Maine Cavalry
Battle or Place of Action: St. Mary's Church, Virginia
Date of Action: 24 June 1864
Date of Issue: 11 April 1895
Citation: Remained in the fight to the close, although severely wounded.

1246 ◆ SMITH, DAVID LAFAYETTE

Rank: Sergeant (highest rank: First Lieutenant)
Service: U.S. Army
Birthday: 1 May 1835
Place of Birth: Cameron, Steuben County, New York
Date of Death: 8 June 1916
Place of Death: Orlean, New York

Cemetery: Pleasant Valley Cemetery—Orlean, New York
Entered Service at: Bath, Steuben County, New York
Unit: Battery E, 1st New York Light Artillery
Battle or Place of Action: Warwick Courthouse, Virginia
Date of Action: 6 April 1862
Date of Issue: 6 August 1906
Citation: This soldier, when a shell struck an ammunition chest, exploding a number of cartridges and setting fire to the packing tow, procured water and extinguished the fire, thus preventing the explosion of the remaining ammunition.

1247 ◆ SMITH, EDWIN

Rank: Ordinary Seaman
Service: U.S. Navy
Place of Birth: New York, New York
Entered Service at: New York
Unit: U.S.S. *Whitehead*
Battle or Place of Action: Franklin, Virginia
Date of Action: 3 October 1862
Citation: On board the U.S.S. *Whitehead* in the attack upon Franklin, Va., 3 October 1862. When his ship became grounded in a narrow passage as she rounded a bend in the Blackwater River, Smith, realizing the hazards of lowering a boat, voluntarily swam to shore with a line under the enemy's heavy fire. His fearless action enabled his ship to maintain steady fire and keep the enemy in check during the battle.

1248 ◆ SMITH, FRANCIS M.

Rank: First Lieutenant & Adjutant (highest rank: Captain)
Service: U.S. Army
Birthday: 29 November 1842
Place of Birth: Baltimore, Baltimore County, Maryland
Date of Death: 22 September 1917
Place of Death: Baltimore, Maryland
Cemetery: Loudon Park Cemetery (Private)—Baltimore, Maryland
Entered Service at: Frederick, Frederick County, Maryland
Unit: 1st Maryland Infantry
Battle or Place of Action: Dabney's Mills, Virginia
Date of Action: 6 February 1865
Date of Issue: 13 August 1895
Citation: Voluntarily remained with the body of his regimental commander under a heavy fire after the brigade had retired, and brought the body off the field.

1249 ◆ SMITH, HENRY I.

Rank: First Lieutenant (highest rank: Major)
Service: U.S. Army
Birthday: 4 May 1840
Place of Birth: Nottingham, Nottinghamshire, England
Date of Death: 15 November 1910
Place of Death: Mason City, Iowa
Cemetery: Elmwood Cemetery (MH)—Mason City, Iowa
Entered Service at: Shell Rock Fall, Butler County, Iowa
Unit: Company B, 7th Iowa Infantry
Battle or Place of Action: Black River, North Carolina

Date of Action: 15 March 1865
Date of Issue: 7 September 1894
Citation: Voluntarily and under fire rescued a comrade from death by drowning.

1250 ◆ SMITH, JAMES

Rank: Captain of the Forecastle
Service: U.S. Navy
Birthday: 1826
Place of Birth: Belfast, County Antrim, Ireland
Date of Death: 31 October 1881
Place of Death: New York, New York
Cemetery: Arlington National Cemetery (45-1485) (MH)—Arlington, Virginia
Entered Service at: New York, New York
Unit: U.S.S. *Richmond*
Battle or Place of Action: Mobile Bay, Alabama
Date of Action: 5 August 1864
G.O. Number, Date: 45, 31 December 1864
Citation: As captain of a gun on board the U.S.S. *Richmond* during action against rebel forts and gunboats and against the ram *Tennessee* in Mobile Bay, 5 August 1864. Despite damage to his ship and the loss of several men on board as enemy fire raked her decks, Smith fought his gun with skill and courage throughout the prolonged battle which resulted in the surrender of the rebel ram *Tennessee* and in the successful attacks carried out on Fort Morgan.

1251 ◆ SMITH, JAMES (OVID)

True Name: Smith, Ovid Wellford
Rank: Private (highest rank: Corporal)
Service: U.S. Army
Birthday: 9 November 1844
Place of Birth: Fredericksburg, Fredericksburg County, Virginia
Date of Death: 28 January 1868
Cemetery: Greenlawn Cemetery (MH)—Columbus, Ohio
Entered Service at: Circleville, Pickaway County, Ohio
Unit: Company I, 2d Ohio Infantry
Battle or Place of Action: Georgia
Date of Action: April 1862
Date of Issue: 6 July 1864
Citation: One of the 24 men (including two civilians) who, by direction of Gen. Ormsby M. Mitchell, penetrated nearly 200 miles south into enemy territory. Smith was captured near Huntsville, Ala., and did not participate in the remainder of the raid.

1252 ◆ SMITH, JOHN

Rank: Captain of the Forecastle
Service: U.S. Navy
Birthday: 1831
Place of Birth: Boston, Suffolk County, Massachusetts
Entered Service at: Massachusetts
Unit: U.S.S. *Lackawanna*

Battle or Place of Action: Fort Morgan, Mobile Bay, Alabama
Date of Action: 5 August 1864
G.O. Number, Date: 45, 31 December 1864
Citation: On board the U.S.S. *Lackawanna* during successful attacks against Fort Morgan, rebel gunboats, and the rebel ram *Tennessee* in Mobile Bay, 5 August 1864. Serving as gun captain and finding he could not depress his gun when alongside the rebel ironclad *Tennessee*, Smith threw a hand holystone into one of the ports at a rebel using abusive language against the crew of the ship. He continued his daring action throughout the engagement which resulted in the capture of the prize ram *Tennessee* and in the damaging and destruction of Fort Morgan.

1253 ◆ SMITH, JOHN

Rank: Second Captain of the Top
Service: U.S. Navy
Birthday: 1826
Place of Birth: Albany, Albany County, New York
Entered Service at: New York, New York
Unit: U.S.S. *Richmond*
Battle or Place of Action: Fort Morgan, Mobile Bay, Alabama
Date of Action: 5 August 1864
G.O. Number, Date: 45, 31 December 1864
Citation: As captain of a gun on board the U.S.S. *Richmond* during action against rebel forts and gunboats and against the ram *Tennessee* in Mobile Bay, 5 August 1864. Despite damage to his ship and the loss of several men on board as enemy fire raked her decks, Smith fought his gun with skill and courage throughout a furious two-hour battle, which resulted in the surrender of the rebel ram *Tennessee* and in the damaging and destruction of batteries at Fort Morgan.

1254 ◆ SMITH, JOSEPH SEWALL

Rank: Lieutenant Colonel (highest rank: Brevet Brigadier General)
Service: U.S. Army
Birthday: 27 November 1836
Place of Birth: Wiscasset, Lincoln County, Maine
Date of Death: 25 January 1919
Place of Death: Fort Monroe, Virginia
Cemetery: Arlington National Cemetery (2-996)—Arlington, Virginia
Entered Service at: Wiscasset, Lincoln County, Maine
Unit: 2d Army Corps
Battle or Place of Action: Hatcher's Run, Virginia
Date of Action: 27 October 1864
Date of Issue: 25 May 1892
Citation: Led a part of a brigade, saved two pieces of artillery, captured a flag, and secured a number of prisoners.

1255 ◆ SMITH, OLOFF

Rank: Coxswain
Service: U.S. Navy

Birthday: 1833
Place of Birth: Sweden
Entered Service at: New York, New York
Unit: U.S.S. *Richmond*
Battle or Place of Action: Fort Morgan, Mobile Bay, Alabama
Date of Action: 5 August 1864
G.O. Number, Date: 45, 31 December 1864
Citation: On board the U.S.S. *Richmond* during action against rebel forts and gunboats and against the ram *Tennessee* in Mobile Bay, 5 August 1864. Despite damage to his ship and the loss of several men on board as enemy fire raked her decks, Smith performed his duties with skill and courage throughout the furious two-hour battle, which resulted in the surrender of the rebel ram *Tennessee* and in the damaging and destruction of batteries at Fort Morgan.

1256 ◆ SMITH, OTIS W.

Rank: Private (highest rank: Corporal)
Service: U.S. Army
Birthday: 4 October 1844
Place of Birth: Logan County, Ohio
Date of Death: 10 March 1923
Place of Death: Yountville, California
Cemetery: Arroyo Grande Cemetery—Arroyo Grande, California
Entered Service at: Champaign, Ohio
Unit: Company G, 95th Ohio Infantry
Battle or Place of Action: Nashville, Tennessee
Date of Action: 16 December 1864
Date of Issue: 24 February 1865
Citation: Capture of flag of 6th Florida Infantry (C.S.A.).

1257 ◆ SMITH, RICHARD

Rank: Private
Service: U.S. Army
Birthday: 9 January 1840
Place of Birth: Haverstraw, Rockland County, New York
Date of Death: 13 June 1918
Cemetery: Mount Repose Cemetery—Hayerstraw, New York
Entered Service at: Haverstraw, Rockland County, New York
Unit: Company B, 95th New York Infantry
Battle or Place of Action: Weldon Railroad, Virginia
Date of Action: 21 August 1864
Date of Issue: 13 March 1865
Citation: Captured two officers and 20 men of Hagood's brigade while they were endeavoring to make their way back through the woods.

1258 ◆ SMITH, SAMUEL RODMOND

Rank: Captain (highest rank: Brevet Major)
Service: U.S. Army
Birthday: 20 April 1841
Place of Birth: Wilmington, New Castle County, Delaware

Date of Death: 30 September 1912
Place of Death: Miami, Florida
Cemetery: Wilmington Cemetery—Wilmington, Delaware
Entered Service at: Wilmington, New Castle County, Delaware
Unit: Company C, 4th Delaware Infantry
Battle or Place of Action: Rowanty Creek, Virginia
Date of Action: 5 February 1865
Date of Issue: 8 April 1895
Citation: Swam the partly frozen creek under fire to establish a crossing.

1259 ◆ SMITH, THADDEUS S.

Rank: Corporal
Service: U.S. Army
Birthday: 13 May 1847
Place of Birth: Cumberland, Franklin County, Pennsylvania
Date of Death: 14 March 1933
Place of Death: Port Townsend, Washington
Cemetery: Laurel Grove Cemetery (GAR plot) (MH)—Port Townsend, Washington
Entered Service at: Harrisburg, Dauphin County, Pennsylvania
Unit: Company E, 6th Pennsylvania Reserve Infantry
Battle or Place of Action: Gettysburg, Pennsylvania
Date of Action: 2 July 1863
Date of Issue: 5 May 1900
Citation: Was one of six volunteers who charged upon a log house near the Devil's Den, where a squad of the enemy's sharpshooters were sheltered, and compelled their surrender.

1260 ◆ SMITH, THOMAS

Rank: Seaman
Service: U.S. Navy
Birthday: 1838
Place of Birth: England
Entered Service at: New York, New York
Unit: U.S.S. *Magnolia*
Battle or Place of Action: St. Marks, Florida
Date of Action: 5-6 March 1865
G.O. Number, Date: 59, 22 June 1865
Citation: As seaman on board the U.S.S. *Magnolia*, St. Marks, Fla., 5 and 6 March 1865. Serving with the Army in charge of Navy howitzers during the attack on St. Marks and throughout this fierce engagement, Smith made remarkable efforts in assisting transport of the gun, and his coolness and determination in courageously standing by his gun while under the fire of the enemy were a credit to the service to which he belonged.

1261 ◆ SMITH, WALTER B.

Rank: Ordinary Seaman
Service: U.S. Navy
Birthday: 1827
Place of Birth: New York
Entered Service at: New York, New York

Unit: U.S.S. *Richmond*
Battle or Place of Action: Fort Morgan, Mobile Bay, Alabama
Date of Action: 5 August 1864
G.O. Number, Date: 45, 31 December 1864
Citation: On board the U.S.S. *Richmond* during action against rebel forts and gunboats and with the ram *Tennessee* in Mobile Bay, 5 August 1864. Cool and courageous at his station throughout the prolonged action, Smith rendered outstanding service at the 100-pounder rifle on the topgallant forecastle and while firing his musket into the gun ports of the rebel *Tennessee*.

1262 ◆ SMITH, WILLARD M.

Rank: Corporal
Service: U.S. Marine Corps
Birthday: 1840
Place of Birth: Allegany, Cattaraugus County, New York
Date of Death: 26 March 1918
Place of Death: Brooklyn, New York
Cemetery: Elm Lawn Cemetery—Buffalo, New York
Entered Service at: New York
Unit: U.S.S. *Brooklyn*
Battle or Place of Action: Mobile Bay, Alabama
Date of Action: 5 August 1864
G.O. Number, Date: 45, 31 December 1864
Citation: On board the U.S.S. *Brooklyn* during action against rebel forts and gunboats, and with the ram *Tennessee* in Mobile Bay, on 5 August 1864. Despite severe damage to his ship and the loss of several men on board as enemy fire continued to fall, Cpl. Smith fought his gun with skill and courage throughout the furious two-hour battle which resulted in the surrender of the rebel ram *Tennessee*.

1263 ◆ SMITH, WILLIAM

Rank: Quartermaster (highest rank: Master's Mate)
Service: U.S. Navy
Birthday: 1838
Place of Birth: Ireland
Date of Death: 12 January 1902
Place of Death: Concord, New Hampshire
Cemetery: Blossom Hill Cemetery—Concord, New Hampshire
Entered Service at: Concord, Merrimack County, New Hampshire
Unit: U.S.S. *Kearsarge*
Battle or Place of Action: off Cherbourg, France
Date of Action: 19 June 1864
G.O. Number, Date: 45, 31 December 1864
Citation: Served as second quartermaster on board the U.S.S. *Kearsarge* when she destroyed the *Alabama* off Cherbourg, France, 19 June 1864. Acting as captain of the 11-inch pivot gun of the second division, Smith carried out his duties courageously and deserved special notice for the deliberate and cool manner in which he acted throughout the bitter engagement. It is stated by rebel officers that this gun

was more destructive and did more damage than any other gun of the *Kearsarge*

1264 ◆ SMITH, WILSON

Rank: Corporal (highest rank: Sergeant)
Service: U.S. Army
Birthday: 6 September 1841
Place of Birth: Madison, Madison County, New York
Date of Death: 22 February 1901
Place of Death: Rome, New York
Cemetery: Rome Cemetery (MH)—Rome, New York
Entered Service at: Madison, Madison County, New York
Unit: Battery H, 3d New York Light Artillery
Battle or Place of Action: Washington, North Carolina
Date of Action: 6 September 1862
Date of Issue: 24 April 1896
Citation: Took command of a gun (the lieutenant in charge having disappeared) and fired the same so rapidly and effectively that the enemy was repulsed, although for a time a hand-to-hand conflict was had over the gun.

1265 ◆ SNEDDEN, JAMES

Rank: Musician (highest rank: Bugler)
Service: U.S. Army
Birthday: 19 September 1849
Place of Birth: Edinburgh, Scotland
Date of Death: 14 June 1919
Cemetery: Odd Fellow Cemetery—Lexington, Mississippi
Entered Service at: Johnstown, Cambria County, Pennsylvania
Unit: Company E, 54th Pennsylvania Infantry
Battle or Place of Action: Piedmont, Virginia
Date of Action: 5 June 1864
Date of Issue: 11 September 1897
Citation: Left his place in the rear, took the rifle of a disabled soldier, and fought through the remainder of the action.

1266 ◆ SOUTHARD, DAVID

Rank: Sergeant
Service: U.S. Army
Birthday: 1845
Place of Birth: Ocean County, New Jersey
Date of Death: 6 May 1894
Cemetery: Zion Methodist Cemetery (MH)—Zion, New Jersey
Entered Service at: Florence, Burlington County, New Jersey
Unit: Company C, 1st New Jersey Cavalry
Battle or Place of Action: Deatonsville (Sailor's Creek), Virginia
Date of Action: 6 April 1865
Date of Issue: 3 July 1865
Citation: Capture of flag; and was the first man over the works in the charge.

1267 ◆ SOVA, JOSEPH E.

Rank: Saddler
Service: U.S. Army
Birthday: 1840
Place of Birth: Chili, Monroe County, New York
Date of Death: 23 October 1866
Place of Death: Walworth, New York
Entered Service at: Rochester, Monroe County, New York
Unit: Company H, 8th New York Cavalry
Battle or Place of Action: Appomattox Campaign, Virginia
Date of Action: 29 March-9 April 1865
Date of Issue: 3 May 1865
Citation: Capture of flag.

1268 ◆ SOWERS, MICHAEL

Rank: Private
Service: U.S. Army
Birthday: 14 September 1844
Place of Birth: Pittsburgh, Allegheny County, Pennsylvania
Date of Death: 7 January 1920
Place of Death: Findley, Pennsylvania
Cemetery: Catholic Cemetery—Findley, Pennsylvania
Entered Service at: Pittsburgh, Allegheny County, Pennsylvania
Unit: Company L, 4th Pennsylvania Cavalry
Battle or Place of Action: Stony Creek Station, Virginia
Date of Action: 1 December 1864
Date of Issue: 16 February 1897
Citation: His horse having been shot from under him, he voluntarily and on foot participated in the cavalry charge made upon one of the forts, conducting himself throughout with great personal bravery.

1269 ◆ SPALDING, EDWARD BURSON

Rank: Sergeant (highest rank: First Lieutenant)
Service: U.S. Army
Birthday: 2 February 1840
Place of Birth: Byron, Ogle County, Illinois
Date of Death: 4 March 1920
Cemetery: Floyd Cemetery (MH)—Sioux City, Iowa
Entered Service at: Rockford, Winnebago County, Illinois
Unit: Company E, 52d Illinois Infantry
Battle or Place of Action: Pittsburg Landing, Tennessee
Date of Action: 6 April 1862
Date of Issue: 15 January 1894
Citation: Although twice wounded, and thereby crippled for life, he remained fighting in open ground to the close of the battle.

1270 ◆ SPERRY, WILLIAM JOSEPH

Rank: Major (highest rank: Lieutenant Colonel)
Service: U.S. Army
Birthday: 28 December 1840
Place of Birth: Cavendish, Windsor County, Vermont

Date of Death: 3 March 1914
Cemetery: Mount Union Cemetery—Cavendish Village, Vermont
Entered Service at: Cavendish, Windsor County, Vermont
Unit: 6th Vermont Infantry
Battle or Place of Action: Petersburg, Virginia
Date of Action: 2 April 1865
Date of Issue: 12 August 1892
Citation: With the assistance of a few men, captured two pieces of artillery and turned them upon the enemy.

1271 ◆ SPILLANE, TIMOTHY

Rank: Private (highest rank: Ordnance Sergeant) (highest rank: U.S.A. Ret.)
Service: U.S. Army
Birthday: 1842
Place of Birth: County Kerry, Ireland
Date of Death: 3 December 1901
Place of Death: Knoxville, Tennessee
Cemetery: Knoxville National Cemetery (A-3319) (MH)—Knoxville, Tennessee
Entered Service at: Waterford, Saratoga County, New York
Unit: Company C, 16th Pennsylvania Cavalry
Battle or Place of Action: Hatcher's Run, Virginia
Date of Action: 5-7 February 1865
Date of Issue: 16 September 1880
Citation: Gallantry and good conduct in action; bravery in a charge and reluctance to leave the field after being twice wounded.

1272 ◆ SPRAGUE, BENONA

Rank: Corporal (highest rank: Sergeant)
Service: U.S. Army
Birthday: 15 February 1833
Place of Birth: Satina Onondaga County, New York
Date of Death: 19 June 1908
Place of Death: Cheney Grove, Illinois
Cemetery: Riverside Cemetery—Saybrook, Illinois
Entered Service at: Cheney Grove, Illinois
Unit: Company F, 116th Illinois Infantry
Battle or Place of Action: Vicksburg, Mississippi
Date of Action: 22 May 1863
Date of Issue: 10 July 1894
Citation: Gallantry in the charge of the "volunteer storming party."

1273 ◆ *SPRAGUE, JOHN WILSON

Rank: Colonel (highest rank: Brevet Major General)
Service: U.S. Army
Birthday: 4 April 1817
Place of Birth: White Creek, Washington County, New York
Date of Death: 24 December 1893
Cemetery: Old Tacoma Cemetery—Tacoma, Washington
Entered Service at: Sandusky, Erie County, Ohio

Unit: 63d Ohio Infantry
Battle or Place of Action: Decatur, Georgia
Date of Action: 22 July 1862
Date of Issue: 18 January 1894
Citation: With a small command defeated an overwhelming force of the enemy and saved the trains of the corps.

1274 ◆ SPROWLE, DAVID

True Name: Sprowls, David
Rank: Orderly Sergeant
Service: U.S. Marine Corps
Birthday: 1811
Place of Birth: Lisbon, St. Lawrence County, New York
Cemetery: Red Mills Cemetery—Lisbon, New York
Entered Service at: New York
Unit: U.S.S. *Richmond*
Battle or Place of Action: Mobile Bay, Alabama
Date of Action: 5 August 1864
G.O. Number, Date: 45, 31 December 1864
Citation: On board the U.S.S. *Richmond* during action against rebel forts and gunboats and with the ram *Tennessee* in Moblie Bay, 5 August 1864. Despite damage to his ship and the loss of several men on board as enemy fire raked her decks, Orderly Sgt. Sprowle inspired the men of the marine guard and directed a division of great guns throughout the furious battle which resulted in the surrender of the rebel ram *Tennessee* and in the damaging and destruction of batteries at Fort Morgan.

1275 ◆ SPURLING, ANDREW BARCLAY

Rank: Lieutenant Colonel (highest rank: Brevet Brigadier General)
Service: U.S. Army
Birthday: 20 March 1833
Place of Birth: Cranberry Isles, Hancock County, Maine
Date of Death: 13 August 1906
Place of Death: Chicago, Illinois
Cemetery: Rose Hill Cemetery—Chicago, Illinois
Entered Service at: Augusta, Kennebec County, Maine
Unit: 2d Maine Cavalry
Battle or Place of Action: Evergreen, Alabama
Date of Action: 23 March 1865
Date of Issue: 10 September 1897
Citation: Advanced alone in the darkness beyond the picket line, came upon three of the enemy, fired upon them (his fire being returned), wounded two, and captured the whole party.

1276 ◆ STACEY, CHARLES

Rank: Private
Service: U.S. Army
Birthday: 22 January 1842
Place of Birth: England
Date of Death: 17 October 1924
Cemetery: Woodlawn Cemetery (Mausoleum) (MH)—

Norwalk, Ohio
Entered Service at: Norwalk, Huron County, Ohio
Unit: Company D, 55th Ohio Infantry
Battle or Place of Action: Gettysburg, Pennsylvania
Date of Action: 2 July 1863
Date of Issue: 23 June 1896
Citation: Voluntarily took an advanced position on the skirmish line for the purpose of ascertaining the location of Confederate sharpshooters and under heavy fire held the position thus taken until the company of which he was a member went back to the main line.
Notes: POW from 2 July 1863—19 May 1864

1277 ◆ STAHEL, JULIUS H.

Rank: Major General
Service: U.S. Army
Birthday: 5 November 1825
Place of Birth: Szegedin, Hungary
Date of Death: 4 December 1912
Place of Death: New York, New York
Cemetery: Arlington National Cemetery (2-998)—Arlington, Virginia
Entered Service at: New York, New York
Unit: U.S. Volunteers
Battle or Place of Action: Piedmont, Virginia
Date of Action: 5 June 1864
Date of Issue: 4 November 1893
Citation: Led his division into action until he was severely wounded.

1278 ◆ STANLEY, DAVID SLOANE

Rank: Major General
Service: U.S. Army
Birthday: 1 June 1828
Place of Birth: Cedar Valley, Ohio
Date of Death: 13 March 1902
Place of Death: Washington, D.C.
Cemetery: Soldier's Home National Cemetery (O-20)—Washington, D.C.
Entered Service at: Congress, Wayne County, Ohio
Unit: U.S. Volunteers
Battle or Place of Action: Franklin, Tennessee
Date of Action: 30 November 1864
Date of Issue: 29 March 1893
Citation: At a critical moment rode to the front of one of his brigades, reestablished its lines, and gallantly led it in a successful assault.

1279 ◆ STANLEY, WILLIAM A.

Rank: Shell Man
Service: U.S. Navy
Birthday: 1831
Place of Birth: Massachusetts
Entered Service at: Massachusetts
Unit: U.S.S. *Hartford*

Battle or Place of Action: Fort Morgan, Mobile Bay, Alabama
Date of Action: 5 August 1864
G.O. Number, Date: 45, 31 December 1864
Citation: Shell man on No. 8 on board the U.S.S. *Hartford* during successful actions against Fort Morgan, rebel gunboats, and the ram *Tennessee* in Mobile Bay, 5 August 1864. Although severely wounded when his ship sustained numerous hits under the enemy's terrific shellfire, Stanley continued to pass shell until forced by the loss of blood to go below.

1280 ◆ STARKINS, JOHN H.

Rank: Sergeant (highest rank: First Sergeant)
Service: U.S. Army
Birthday: 1841
Place of Birth: Great Neck, Nassau County, New York
Date of Death: 4 April 1897
Place of Death: Flushing, New York
Cemetery: Zion Church Cemetery—Little Neck, New York
Entered Service at: Flushing, Queens County, New York
Unit: 34th New York Battery
Battle or Place of Action: Campbell Station, Tennessee
Date of Action: 16 November 1863
Date of Issue: 30 July 1896
Citation: Brought off his piece without losing a man.

1281 ◆ STEELE, JOHN WHEDON

Rank: Major & Aide-de-Camp (highest rank: Lieutenant Colonel)
Service: U.S. Army
Birthday: 21 December 1835
Place of Birth: Middleburg, Logan County, Ohio
Date of Death: 26 April 1905
Place of Death: Oberlin, Ohio
Cemetery: Westwood Cemetery—Oberlin, Ohio
Entered Service at: Oberlin, Lorain County, Ohio
Unit: U.S. Volunteers
Battle or Place of Action: Spring Hill, Tennessee
Date of Action: 29 November 1864
Date of Issue: 28 September 1897
Citation: During a night attack of the enemy upon the wagon and ammunition train of this officer's corps, he gathered up a force of stragglers and others, assumed command of it, though himself a staff officer, and attacked and dispersed the enemy's forces, thus saving the train.

1282 ◆ STEINMETZ, WILLIAM

Rank: Private (highest rank: Corporal)
Service: U.S. Army
Birthday: 2 September 1847
Place of Birth: Newport, Campbell County, Kentucky
Date of Death: 10 June 1903
Cemetery: Wesleyan Cemetery—Cincinnati, Ohio
Entered Service at: Sunman, Ripley County, Indiana
Unit: Company G, 83d Indiana Infantry

Battle or Place of Action: Vicksburg, Mississippi
Date of Action: 22 May 1863
Date of Issue: 12 July 1894
Citation: Gallantry in the charge of the "volunteer storming party."

1283 ◆ STEPHENS, WILLIAM G.

Rank: Private
Service: U.S. Army
Birthday: 26 December 1843
Place of Birth: New York, New York
Date of Death: 21 March 1904
Place of Death: Chicago, Illinois
Cemetery: Rose Hill Cemetery—Chicago, Illinois
Entered Service at: Chicago, Cook County, Illinois
Unit: Chicago Mercantile Battery, Illinois Light Artillery
Battle or Place of Action: Vicksburg, Mississippi
Date of Action: 22 May 1863
Date of Issue: 21 December 1894
Citation: Carried with others by hand a cannon up to and fired it through an embrasure of the enemy's works.

1284 ◆ STERLING, JAMES E.

Rank: Coal Heaver
Service: U.S. Navy
Birthday: 1838
Place of Birth: Baltimore, Baltimore County, Maryland
Entered Service at: Maryland
Unit: U.S.S. *Brooklyn*
Battle or Place of Action: Fort Morgan, Mobile Bay, Alabama
Date of Action: 5 August 1864
G.O. Number, Date: 45, 31 December 1864
Citation: On board the U.S.S. *Brooklyn* during successful attacks against Fort Morgan, rebel gunboats and the ram *Tennessee* in Mobile Bay, 5 August 1864. Although wounded when heavy enemy return-fire raked the decks of his ship, Sterling courageously remained at his post and continued passing shell until struck down a second time and completely disabled.

1285 ◆ STERLING, JOHN T.

Rank: Private (highest rank: Corporal)
Service: U.S. Army
Birthday: 1841
Place of Birth: Edgar County, Illinois
Date of Death: 2 February 1920
Cemetery: Bethesda Cemetery—West Terre Haute, Indiana
Entered Service at: Indianapolis, Marion County, Indiana
Unit: Company D, 11th Indiana Infantry
Battle or Place of Action: Winchester, Virginia
Date of Action: 19 September 1864
Date of Issue: 4 April 1865
Citation: With one companion captured 14 of the enemy in the severest part of the battle.

1286 ◆ STEVENS, DANIEL DICKERSON

True Name: Stephens, Daniel Dickerson
Rank: Quartermaster (highest rank: Chief Quartermaster)
Service: U.S. Navy
Birthday: 19 December 1839
Place of Birth: La Grange, Fayette County, Tennessee
Date of Death: 7 November 1916
Place of Death: Peabody, Massachusetts
Cemetery: Walnut Grove Cemetery (MH)—Danvers, Massachusetts
Entered Service at: Massachusetts
Unit: U.S.S. *Canonicus*
Battle or Place of Action: Fort Fisher, North Carolina
Date of Action: 13 January 1865
Citation: On board the U.S.S. *Canonicus* during attacks on Fort Fisher, 13 January 1865. As the *Canonicus* moved into position at 700 yards from shore, the enemy troops soon obtained her range and opened with heavy artillery fire, subjecting her to several hits and near misses until late in the afternoon when the heavy ships coming into line drove them into their bombproofs. Twice during the battle, in which his ship sustained 36 hits, the flag was shot away and gallantly replaced by Stevens.

1287 ◆ STEVENS, HAZARD

Rank: Captain & Assistant Adjutant General (highest rank: Brevet Brigadier General)
Service: U.S. Army
Birthday: 9 June 1842
Place of Birth: Newport, Newport County, Rhode Island
Date of Death: 11 October 1918
Place of Death: Olympia, Washington
Cemetery: Island Cemetery—Newport, Rhode Island
Entered Service at: Olympia, Thurston County, Washington Territory
Unit: U.S. Volunteers
Battle or Place of Action: Fort Huger, Virginia
Date of Action: 19 April 1863
Date of Issue: 13 June 1894
Citation: Gallantly led a party that assaulted and captured the fort.

1288 ◆ STEWART, GEORGE W.

Rank: First Sergeant
Service: U.S. Army
Birthday: 25 March 1839
Place of Birth: Salem, Salem County, New Jersey
Date of Death: 17 November 1911
Cemetery: New Camden Cemetery (MH)—New Camden, New Jersey
Entered Service at: Salem, Salem County, New Jersey
Unit: Company E, 1st New Jersey Cavalry
Battle or Place of Action: Paines Crossroads, Virginia
Date of Action: 5 April 1865
Date of Issue: 3 May 1865
Citation: Capture of flag.

1289 ◆ STEWART, JOSEPH

Rank: Private
Service: U.S. Army
Place of Birth: Ireland
Entered Service at: Baltimore, Baltimore County, Maryland
Unit: Company G, 1st Maryland Infantry
Battle or Place of Action: Five Forks, Virginia
Date of Action: 1 April 1865
Date of Issue: 27 April 1865
Citation: Capture of flag.

1290 ◆ STICKELS, JOSEPH

True Name: Stickles, Joseph
Rank: Sergeant
Service: U.S. Army
Birthday: 1843
Place of Birth: Butler County, Ohio
Date of Death: 6 December 1876
Place of Death: Quincy, Illinois
Cemetery: Monroe Cemetery—Monroe, Iowa
Entered Service at: Bethany, Ohio
Unit: Company A, 83d Ohio Infantry
Battle or Place of Action: Fort Blakely, Alabama
Date of Action: 9 April 1865
Date of Issue: 8 June 1865
Citation: Capture of flag.
Notes: POW

1291 ◆ STOCKMAN, GEORGE HENRY

Rank: First Lieutenant
Service: U.S. Army
Birthday: 3 July 1833
Place of Birth: Muenden, Germany
Date of Death: 30 June 1912
Cemetery: West Laurel Hill Cemetery (MH)—Bala-Cynwyd, Pennsylvania
Entered Service at: Chicago, Cook County, Illinois
Unit: Company C, 6th Missouri Infantry
Battle or Place of Action: Vicksburg, Mississippi
Date of Action: 22 May 1863
Date of Issue: 9 July 1894
Citation: Gallantry in the charge of the "volunteer storming party."

1292 ◆ STODDARD, JAMES

Rank: Seaman (highest rank: Acting Master's Mate)
Service: U.S. Navy
Birthday: 1838
Place of Birth: Port Robinson, Canada (West)
Entered Service at: Detroit, Wayne County, Michigan
Unit: U.S.S. *Marmora*
Battle or Place of Action: off Yazoo City, Mississippi
Date of Action: 5 March 1864
G.O. Number, Date: 32, 16 April 1864
Citation: Off Yazoo City, Miss., 5 March 1864. Embarking

from the *Marmora* with a 12-pound howitzer mounted on a field carriage, Stoddard landed with the gun and crew in the midst of heated battle and, bravely standing by his gun despite enemy rifle fire which cut the gun carriage and rammer, contributed to the turning back of the enemy during the fierce engagement.

1293 ◆ STOKES, GEORGE

Rank: Private (highest rank: Corporal)
Service: U.S. Army
Birthday: 24 December 1838
Place of Birth: England
Date of Death: 25 March 1919
Cemetery: Oakland Cemetery—Dolton, Illinois
Entered Service at: Jerseyville, Jersey County, Illinois
Unit: Company C, 122d Illinois Infantry
Battle or Place of Action: Nashville, Tennessee
Date of Action: 16 December 1864
Date of Issue: 24 February 1865
on: Capture of flag.

1294 ◆ STOLZ, FRANK

Rank: Private
Service: U.S. Army
Birthday: 20 July 1844
Place of Birth: Dearborn County, Indiana
Date of Death: 19 November 1926
Place of Death: Indianapolis, Indiana
Cemetery: St. Joseph's Cemetery—Indianapolis, Indiana
Entered Service at: Sunman, Ripley County, Indiana
Unit: Company G, 83d Indiana Infantry
Battle or Place of Action: Vicksburg, Mississippi
Date of Action: 22 May 1863
Date of Issue: 9 July 1894
Citation: Gallantry in the charge of the "volunteer storming party."

1295 ◆ STOREY, JOHN HAMILTON REID

Rank: Sergeant
Service: U.S. Army
Birthday: 14 April 1836
Place of Birth: Philadelphia, Philadelphia County, Pennsylvania
Date of Death: 10 April 1916
Place of Death: Philadelphia, Pennsylvania
Cemetery: Laurel Hill Cemetery (MH)—Philadelphia, Pennsylvania
Entered Service at: Philadelphia, Philadelphia County, Pennsylvania
Unit: Company F, 109th Pennsylvania Infantry
Battle or Place of Action: Dallas, Georgia
Date of Action: 28 May 1864
Date of Issue: 29 August 1896
Citation: While bringing in a wounded comrade, under a destructive fire, he was himself wounded in the right leg, which was amputated on the same day.

1296 ◆ STOUT, RICHARD

Rank: Landsman
Service: U.S. Navy
Birthday: 1836
Place of Birth: Owego, Tioga County, New York
Date of Death: 6 August 1896
Place of Death: Owego, New York
Cemetery: Evergreen Cemetery—Owego, New York
Entered Service at: New York
Unit: U.S.S. *Isaac Smith*
Battle or Place of Action: Stono River, South Carolina
Date of Action: 30 January 1863
G.O. Number, Date: 32, 16 April 1864
Citation: Serving on board the U.S.S. *Isaac Smith*, Stono River, 30 January 1863. While reconnoitering on the Stono River on this date, the U.S.S. *Isaac Smith* became trapped in a rebel ambush. Fired on from two sides, she fought her guns until disabled. Suffering heavy casualties and at the mercy of the enemy who was delivering a raking fire from every side, she struck her colors out of regard for the wounded aboard, and all aboard were taken prisoners. Carrying out his duties bravely through this action, Stout was severely wounded and lost his right arm while returning the rebel fire.
Notes: POW

1297 ◆ STRAHAN, ROBERT

Rank: Captain of the Top
Service: U.S. Navy
Birthday: 1836
Place of Birth: New Jersey
Entered Service at: New Jersey
Unit: U.S.S. *Kearsarge*
Battle or Place of Action: off Cherbourg, France
Date of Action: 19 June 1864
G.O. Number, Date: 45, 31 December 1864
Citation: Served as captain of the top on board the U.S.S. *Kearsarge* when she destroyed the *Alabama* off Cherbourg, France, 19 June 1864. Acting as captain of the No. 1 gun, Strahan carried out his duties in the face of heavy enemy fire and exhibited marked coolness and good conduct throughout the engagement. Strahan was highly recommended by his division officer for his gallantry and meritorious achievements.

1298 ◆ *STRAUSBURGH, BERNARD A.

Rank: First Sergeant
Service: U.S. Army
Birthday: 1831
Place of Birth: Adams County, Pennsylvania
Date of Death: 5 November 1864
Place of Death: Beverly, New Jersey
Cemetery: General Hospital Cemetery Grave 133—Beverly, New Jersey
Entered Service at: Warfordsburg, Fulton County, Pennsylvania
Unit: Company A, 3d Maryland Infantry
Battle or Place of Action: Petersburg, Virginia

Date of Action: 17 June 1864
Date of Issue: 1 December 1864
Citation: Recaptured the colors of 2nd Pennsylvania Provisional Artillery.

1299 ◆ STREILE, CHRISTIAN

Rank: Private
Service: U.S. Army
Birthday: 1839
Place of Birth: Germany
Date of Death: 4 December 1886
Place of Death: New York, New York
Cemetery: The Lutheran Cemetery—Middle Village, New York
Entered Service at: Jersey City, Hudson County, New Jersey
Unit: Company I, 1st New Jersey Cavalry
Battle or Place of Action: Paines Crossroads, Virginia
Date of Action: 5 April 1865
Date of Issue: 3 May 1865
Citation: Capture of flag.

1300 ◆ STRONG, JAMES N.

Rank: Sergeant (highest rank: Second Lieutenant)
Service: U.S. Army
Birthday: 28 February 1818
Place of Birth: Pittsfield, Berkshire County, Massachusetts
Date of Death: 17 December 1900
Place of Death: Fairfield, Iowa
Cemetery: City Cemetery (MH)—Fairfield, Iowa
Entered Service at: Pittsfield, Berkshire County, Massachusetts
Unit: Company C, 49th Massachusetts Infantry
Battle or Place of Action: Port Hudson, Louisiana
Date of Action: 27 May 1863
Date of Issue: 25 November 1893
Citation: Volunteered in response to a call and took part in the movement that was made upon the enemy's works under a heavy fire therefrom in advance of the general assault.

1301 ◆ STURGEON, JAMES K.

Rank: Private
Service: U.S. Army
Birthday: 5 November 1846
Place of Birth: Perry County, Ohio
Date of Death: 19 August 1898
Place of Death: Los Angeles, California
Cemetery: Evergreen Cemetery—Los Angeles, California
Entered Service at: Lancaster, Fairfield County, Ohio
Unit: Company F, 46th Ohio Infantry
Battle or Place of Action: Kenesaw Mountain, Georgia
Date of Action: 15 June 1864
Date of Issue: 2 January 1895
Citation: Advanced beyond the lines and in an encounter with three Confederates shot two and took the other prisoner.

1302 ◆ SULLIVAN, JAMES

Rank: Ordinary Seaman
Service: U.S. Navy
Birthday: 1833
Place of Birth: New York, New York
Entered Service at: Danbury, Fairfield County, Connecticut
Unit: U.S.S. *Agawam*
Battle or Place of Action: Fort Fisher, North Carolina
Date of Action: 2 December 1864
G.O. Number, Date: 45, 31 December 1864
Date of Presentation: 12 May 1865
Place of Presentation: off New Bern, NC, on board the U.S.S. *Agawam*
Citation: On board the U.S.S. *Agawam* as one of a volunteer crew of a powder boat which was exploded near Fort Fisher, 2 December 1864. The powder boat, towed in by the *Wilderness* to prevent detection by the enemy, cast off and slowly steamed to within 300 yards of the beach. After fuses and fires had been lit and a second anchor with short scope let go to assure the boat's tailing inshore, the crew boarded the *Wilderness* and proceeded a distance of 12 miles from shore. Less than two hours later the explosion took place, and the following day fires were observed still burning at the forts.

1303 ◆ SULLIVAN, JOHN

Rank: Seaman
Service: U.S. Navy
Birthday: 17 March 1840
Place of Birth: New York, New York
Date of Death: 23 June 1913
Cemetery: Harmony Grove Cemetery—Portsmouth, New Hampshire
Entered Service at: New York
Unit: U.S.S. *Monticello*
Battle or Place of Action: Wilmington, North Carolina
Date of Action: 23-25 June 1864
G.O. Number, Date: 45, 31 December 1864
Citation: Served as seaman on board the U.S.S. *Monticello* during the reconnaissance of the harbor and water defenses of Wilmington, N.C., 23 to 25 June 1864. Taking part in a reconnaissance of the enemy defenses which covered a period of 2 days and nights, Sullivan courageously carried out his duties during this action, which resulted in the capture of a mail carrier and mail, the cutting of a telegraph wire, and the capture of a large group of prisoners. Although in immediate danger from the enemy at all times, Sullivan showed gallantry and coolness throughout this action, which resulted in the gaining of much vital information of the rebel defenses.

1304 ◆ SULLIVAN, TIMOTHY

Rank: Coxswain
Service: U.S. Navy
Birthday: 1835
Place of Birth: Ireland
Date of Death: 6 October 1910

Place of Death: Sawtella, California
Cemetery: Los Angeles National Cemetery (18-H-2)—Los Angeles, California
Entered Service at: New York, New York
Unit: U.S.S. *Louisville*
Battle or Place of Action: Arkansas, Tennessee & Mississippi
Date of Action: Unknown
G.O. Number, Date: 11, 3 April 1863
Citation: Served on board the U.S.S. *Louisville* during various actions of that vessel. During the engagements of the *Louisville*, Sullivan served as first captain of a 9-inch gun and throughout this period of service was "especially commended for his attention to duty, bravery, and coolness in action."

1305 ◆ SUMMERS, JAMES CALVIN

Rank: Private
Service: U.S. Army
Birthday: 14 February 1838
Place of Birth: on Elk River six miles above Charleston, Kanawha County, West Virginia
Date of Death: 9 May 1927
Place of Death: Frame, West Virginia
Cemetery: Reynolds Cemetery—Elkview, West Virginia
Entered Service at: Point Pleasant, Mason County, West Virginia
Unit: Company H, 4th West Virginia Infantry
Battle or Place of Action: Vicksburg, Mississippi
Date of Action: 22 May 1863
Date of Issue: 25 February 1895
Citation: Gallantry in charge of the "volunteer storming party."

1306 ◆ SUMMERS, ROBERT

True Name: Sommers, Robert
Rank: Chief Quartermaster (highest rank: Chief Gunner)
Service: U.S. Navy
Birthday: 17 December 1837
Place of Birth: Prussia
Date of Death: 1 December 1919
Cemetery: U.S. Naval Academy Cemetery (Lot 235) (MH)—Annapolis, Maryland
Entered Service at: New York, New York
Unit: U.S.S. *Ticonderoga*
Battle or Place of Action: Fort Fisher, North Carolina
Date of Action: 13-15 January 1865
G.O. Number, Date: 59, 22 June 1865
Citation: Summers served on board the U.S.S. *Ticonderoga* in the attacks on Fort Fisher, 13 to 15 January 1865. The ship took position in the line of battle and maintained a well-directed fire upon the batteries to the left of the palisades during the initial phase of the engagement. Although several of the enemy's shots fell over and around the vessel, the *Ticonderoga* fought her guns gallantly throughout three consecutive days of battle until the flag was planted on one of the strongest fortifications possessed by the rebels.

1307 ◆ SURLES, WILLIAM H.

Rank: Private
Service: U.S. Army
Birthday: 24 February 1845
Place of Birth: Steubenville, Jefferson County, Ohio
Date of Death: 19 March 1919
Cemetery: Riverview Cemetery (MH)—East Liverpool, Ohio
Entered Service at: Steubenville, Jefferson County, Ohio
Unit: Company G, 2d Ohio Infantry
Battle or Place of Action: Perryville, Kentucky
Date of Action: 8 October 1862
Date of Issue: 19 August 1891
Citation: In the hottest part of the fire he stepped in front on his colonel to shield him from the enemy's fire.

1308 ◆ SWAN, CHARLES ALEXANDER

Rank: Private
Service: U.S. Army
Birthday: 29 May 1838
Place of Birth: Greene County, Pennsylvania
Date of Death: 8 January 1914
Place of Death: Mount Pleasant, Iowa
Cemetery: Forest Home Cemetery—Mount Pleasant, Iowa
Entered Service at: Mount Pleasant, Henry County, Iowa
Unit: Company K, 4th Iowa Cavalry
Battle or Place of Action: Selma, Alabama
Date of Action: 2 April 1865
Date of Issue: 17 June 1865
Citation: Capture of flag (supposed to be 11th Mississippi, C.S.A.) and bearer.

1309 ◆ SWANSON, JOHN

Rank: Seaman
Service: U.S. Navy
Birthday: 1842
Place of Birth: Gothenburg, Sweden
Entered Service at: Massachusetts
Unit: U.S.S. *Santiago de Cuba*
Battle or Place of Action: Fort Fisher, North Carolina
Date of Action: 15 January 1865
G.O. Number, Date: 59, 22 June 1865
Citation: On board the U.S.S. *Santiago de Cuba* during the assault on Fort Fisher, 15 January 1865. As one of a boat crew detailed to one of the generals onshore, Swanson bravely entered the fort in the assault and accompanied his party in carrying dispatches at the height of the battle. He was one of six men who entered the fort in the assault from the fleet.

1310 ◆ SWAP, JACOB E.

Rank: Private
Service: U.S. Army
Birthday: 12 August 1846
Place of Birth: Coeymans, Albany County, New York

Date of Death: 22 January 1925
Place of Death: Lakeport, California
Cemetery: Oakland Cemetery—Lakeport, California
Entered Service at: Springs, Somerset County, Pennsylvania
Unit: Company H, 83d Pennsylvania Infantry
Battle or Place of Action: Wilderness Campaign, Virginia
Date of Action: 5 May 1864
Date of Issue: 19 November 1897
Citation: Although assigned to other duty, he voluntarily joined his regiment in a charge and fought with it until severely wounded.

1311 ◆ SWATTON, EDWARD

Rank: Seaman
Service: U.S. Navy
Birthday: 1836
Place of Birth: New York, New York
Entered Service at: Boston, Suffolk County, Massachusetts
Unit: U.S.S. *Santiago de Cuba*
Battle or Place of Action: Fort Fisher, North Carolina
Date of Action: 15 January 1865
G.O. Number, Date: 59, 22 June 1865
Citation: On board the U.S.S. *Santiago de Cuba* during the assault on Fort Fisher on 15 January 1865. As one of a boat crew detailed to one of the generals onshore, Swatton bravely entered the fort in the assault and accompanied his party in carrying dispatches at the height of the battle. He was one of six men who entered the fort in the assault from the fleet.

1312 ◆ SWAYNE, WAGER

Rank: Lieutenant Colonel (highest rank: Major General)
Service: U.S. Army
Birthday: 10 November 1834
Place of Birth: Columbus, Franklin County, Ohio
Date of Death: 18 December 1902
Place of Death: New York, New York
Cemetery: Arlington National Cemetery (3-1406)—Arlington, Virginia
Entered Service at: Columbus, Franklin County, Ohio
Unit: 43d Ohio Infantry
Battle or Place of Action: Corinth, Mississippi
Date of Action: 4 October 1862
Date of Issue: 19 August 1893
Citation: Conspicuous gallantry in restoring order at a critical moment and leading his regiment in a charge.

1313 ◆ SWEARER, BENJAMIN

Rank: Seaman (highest rank: Captain of the Foretop)
Service: U.S. Navy
Birthday: 18 May 1825
Place of Birth: Baltimore, Baltimore County, Maryland
Entered Service at: Maryland
Unit: U.S.S. *Pawnee*
Battle or Place of Action: Fort Clark, off Baltimore Inlet, Maryland
Date of Action: 29 August 1861

G.O. Number, Date: 11, 3 April 1863
Date of Issue: 14 April 1864
Citation: Embarked in a surfboat from the U.S.S. *Pawnee* during action against Fort Clark, off Baltimore Inlet, 29 August 1861. Taking part in a mission to land troops and to remain inshore and provide protection, Swearer rendered gallant service throughout the action and had the honor of being the first man to raise the flag on the captured fort.

1314 ◆ SWEATT, JOSEPH SEWELL GERRISH

Rank: Private
Service: U.S. Army
Birthday: 23 October 1843
Place of Birth: Boscawen, Merrimack County, New Hampshire
Date of Death: 14 February 1914
Place of Death: East Billerica, Massachusetts
Cemetery: Oak Grove Cemetery (MH)—Medford, Massachusetts
Entered Service at: Lowell, Middlesex County, Massachusetts
Unit: Company C, 6th Massachusetts Infantry
Battle or Place of Action: Carrsville, Virginia
Date of Action: 15 May 1863
Date of Issue: 22 March 1892
Citation: When ordered to retreat, this soldier turned and rushed back to the front, in the face of heavy fire from the enemy, in an endeavor to rescue his wounded comrades, remaining by them until overpowered and taken prisoner.
Notes: POW

1315 ◆ SWEENEY, JAMES

Rank: Private (highest rank: Corporal)
Service: U.S. Army
Birthday: 24 September 1845
Place of Birth: Manchester, Greater Manchester County, England
Date of Death: 26 June 1931
Place of Death: Sawtella, California
Cemetery: Los Angeles National Cemetery (MH)—Los Angeles, California
Entered Service at: Essex, Chittenden County, Vermont
Unit: Company A, 1st Vermont Cavalry
Battle or Place of Action: Cedar Creek, Virginia
Date of Action: 19 October 1864
Date of Issue: 26 October 1864
Citation: With one companion captured the state flag of a North Carolina regiment, together with three officers and an ambulance with its mules and driver.

1316 ◆ SWEGHEIMER, JACOB

True Name: Swegheimer, John
Rank: Private
Service: U.S. Army
Birthday: 25 February 1843
Place of Birth: Oldtown, Baden, Germany
Date of Death: 15 March 1917

Place of Death: Delaware, Ohio
Cemetery: Oak Grove Cemetery—Delaware, Ohio
Entered Service at: Paducah, McCracken County, Kentucky
Unit: Company I, 54th Ohio Infantry
Battle or Place of Action: Vicksburg, Mississippi
Date of Action: 22 May 1863
Date of Issue: 14 July 1894
Citation: Gallantry in the charge of the "volunteer storming party."

1317 ◆ SWIFT, FREDERIC WILLIAM

Rank: Lieutenant Colonel (highest rank: Brevet Brigadier General)
Service: U.S. Army
Birthday: 30 January 1831
Place of Birth: Mansfield Center, Tolland County, Connecticut
Date of Death: 30 January 1916
Place of Death: Detroit, Michigan
Cemetery: Elmwood Cemetery (MH)—Detroit, Michigan
Entered Service at: Detroit, Wayne County, Michigan
Unit: 17th Michigan Infantry
Battle or Place of Action: Lenoire Station, Tennessee
Date of Action: 16 November 1863
Date of Issue: 15 February 1897
Citation: Gallantly seized the colors and rallied the regiment after three color bearers had been shot and the regiment, having become demoralized, was in imminent danger of capture.

1318 ◆ SWIFT, HARLAN J.

Rank: Second Lieutenant (highest rank: Captain)
Service: U.S. Army
Birthday: 2 October 1843
Place of Birth: New Hudson, Columbia County, New York
Date of Death: 6 October 1910
Cemetery: Cuba Cemetery (MH)—Cuba, New York
Entered Service at: Buffalo, Erie County, New York
Unit: Company H, 2d New York Mounted Rifles
Battle or Place of Action: Petersburg, Virginia
Date of Action: 30 July 1864
Date of Issue: 20 July 1897
Citation: Having advanced with his regiment and captured the enemy's line, saw four of the enemy retiring toward their second line of works. He advanced upon them alone, compelled their surrender and regained his regiment with the four prisoners.

1319 ◆ SYPE, PETER

Rank: Private
Service: U.S. Army
Birthday: 11 October 1841
Place of Birth: Monroe County, Michigan
Date of Death: 20 April 1923
Place of Death: Newport, Michigan
Cemetery: Trinity Lutheran Cemetery (MH)—Monroe, Michigan

Entered Service at: Adrian, Lenawee County, Michigan
Unit: Company B, 47th Ohio Infantry
Battle or Place of Action: Vicksburg, Mississippi
Date of Action: 3 May 1863
Date of Issue: 12 September 1911
Citation: Was one of a party that volunteered and attempted to run the enemy's batteries with a steam tug and two barges loaded with subsistence stores.

1320 ◆ TABOR, WILLIAM L. S.

Rank: Private
Service: U.S. Army
Birthday: 2 June 1843
Place of Birth: Metheun, Essex County, Massachusetts
Date of Death: 15 December 1921
Place of Death: Derry, New Hampshire
Cemetery: Forest Hill Cemetery (MH)—East Derry, New Hampshire
Entered Service at: Concord, Merrimack County, New Hampshire
Unit: Company K, 15th New Hampshire Infantry
Battle or Place of Action: Port Hudson, Louisiana
Date of Action: July 1863
Date of Issue: 10 March 1896
Citation: Voluntarily exposed himself to the enemy only a few feet away to render valuable services for the protection of his comrades.

1321 ◆ TAGGART, CHARLES A.

Rank: Private
Service: U.S. Army
Birthday: 17 January 1843
Place of Birth: Blandford, Hampden County, Massachusetts
Date of Death: 10 April 1938
Place of Death: Dayton, Ohio
Cemetery: Dayton National Cemetery (R-9-14) (MH)—Dayton, Ohio
Entered Service at: Otis, Berkshire County, Massachusetts
Unit: Company B, 37th Massachusetts Infantry
Battle or Place of Action: Deatonsville (Sailor's Creek), Virginia
Date of Action: 6 April 1865
Date of Issue: 10 May 1865
Citation: Capture of flag.

1322 ◆ TALBOTT, WILLIAM

True Name: Talbot, William
Rank: Captain of the Forecastle
Service: U.S. Navy
Birthday: 1812
Place of Birth: England
Date of Death: 5 September 1899
Place of Death: Bath, Maine
Cemetery: Maple Grove Cemetery—Bath, Maine
Entered Service at: Boston, Suffolk County, Massachusetts
Unit: U.S.S. *Louisville*

Battle or Place of Action: Arkansas post (Fort Hindman), Arkansas
Date of Action: 10-11 January 1863
G.O. Number, Date: 32, 16 April 1865
Citation: Served as captain of the forecastle on board the U.S.S. *Louisville* at the capture of the Arkansas post, 10 and 11 January 1863. Carrying out his duties as captain of a 9-inch gun, Talbott was conspicuous for ability and bravery throughout this engagement with the enemy.

1323 ◆ *TALLENTINE, JAMES

Rank: Quarter Gunner
Service: U.S. Navy
Birthday: 1840
Place of Birth: England
Date of Death: 15 January 1865
Place of Death: Fort Fisher, North Carolina
Entered Service at: Baltimore, Baltimore County, Maryland
Unit: U.S.S. *Tacony*
Battle or Place of Action: Plymouth, North Carolina
Date of Action: 31 October 1864
G.O. Number, Date: 45, 31 December 1864
Citation: Served as quarter gunner on board the U.S.S. *Tacony* during the taking of Plymouth, N.C., 31 October 1864. Carrying out his duties faithfully during the capture of Plymouth, Tallentine distinguished himself by a display of coolness when he participated in landing and spiking a 9-inch gun while under devastating fire from enemy musketry. Tallentine later gave his life while courageously engaged in storming Fort Fisher, 15 January 1865.

1324 ◆ TANNER, CHARLES B.

Rank: Second Lieutenant (highest rank: First Lieutenant)
Service: U.S. Army
Birthday: 25 November 1842
Place of Birth: Philadelphia, Philadelphia County, Pennsylvania
Date of Death: 16 December 1911
Place of Death: Floral Park, New York
Cemetery: Greenfield Cemetery—Hempstead, New York
Entered Service at: Wilmimgton, New Castle County, Delaware
Unit: Company H, 1st Delaware Infantry
Battle or Place of Action: Antietam, Maryland
Date of Action: 17 September 1862
Date of Issue: 13 December 1889
Citation: Carried off the regimental colors, which had fallen within 20 yards of the enemy's lines, the color guard of nine men having all been wounded or killed; was himself three times wounded.

1325 ◆ TAYLOR, ANTHONY

Rank: First Lieutenant
Service: U.S. Army
Birthday: 11 October 1837

Place of Birth: Burlington, Burlington County, New Jersey
Date of Death: 21 May 1894
Place of Death: Philadelphia, Pennsylvania
Cemetery: St. James The Less Cemetery—Philadelphia, Pennsylvania
Entered Service at: Philadelphia, Philadelphia County, Pennsylvania
Unit: Company A, 15th Pennsylvania Cavalry
Battle or Place of Action: Chickamauga, Georgia
Date of Action: 20 September 1863
Date of Issue: 4 December 1893
Citation: Held out to the last with a small force against the advance of superior numbers of the enemy.

1326 ◆ TAYLOR, FORRESTER L.

Rank: Captain (highest rank: Brevet Major)
Service: U.S. Army
Birthday: 30 October 1833
Place of Birth: Philadelphia, Philadelphia County, Pennsylvania
Date of Death: 21 April 1907
Place of Death: Lawers, Virginia
Cemetery: Family Cemetery, Wards Road, U.S. 29 South—Lynchburg, Virginia
Entered Service at: Beverly, Burlington County, New Jersey
Unit: Company H, 23d New Jersey Infantry
Battle or Place of Action: Chancellorsville, Virginia
Date of Action: 3 May 1863
Date of Issue: 2 November 1896
Citation: At great risk voluntarily saved the lives of and brought from the battlefield two wounded comrades.

1327 ◆ TAYLOR, GEORGE

True Name: Johnson, George Taylor F.
Rank: Armorer
Service: U.S. Navy
Birthday: 15 November 1830
Place of Birth: Reddich, Hereford & Worcester County, England
Date of Death: 7 October 1893
Place of Death: Paragould, Arkansas
Cemetery: Linwood Cemetery—Paragould, Arkansas
Entered Service at: New York, New York
Unit: U.S.S. *Lackawanna*
Battle or Place of Action: Mobile Bay, Alabama
Date of Action: 5 August 1864
G.O. Number, Date: 45, 31 December 1864
Citation: On board the U.S.S. *Lackawanna* during successful attacks against Fort Morgan, rebel gunboats, and the ram *Tennessee* in Mobile Bay, 5 August 1864. When an enemy shell exploded in the shellroom, Taylor, although wounded, went into the room and, with his hand, extinguished the fire from the explosion. He then carried out his duties during the remainder of the prolonged action which resulted in the capture of the prize rebel ram *Tennessee* and the damaging and destruction of Fort Morgan.

1328 ◆ TAYLOR, HENRY H.

Rank: Sergeant
Service: U.S. Army
Birthday: 4 July 1841
Place of Birth: Near Galena, Jo Daviess County, Illinois
Date of Death: 3 May 1909
Place of Death: Leavenworth, Kansas
Cemetery: Greenwood Cemetery (MH)—Clay Center, Kansas
Entered Service at: Galena, Jo Daviess County, Illinois
Unit: Company C, 45th Illinois Infantry
Served as: Color Sergeant
Battle or Place of Action: Vicksburg, Mississippi
Date of Action: 25 June 1863
Date of Issue: 1 September 1863
Citation: Was the first to plant the Union colors upon the enemy's works.

1329 ◆ TAYLOR, JOSEPH

Rank: Private
Service: U.S. Army
Place of Birth: England
Date of Death: 16 February 1912
Cemetery: Greenwood Cemetery (MH)—Coventry, Rhode Island
Entered Service at: Burrillville, Rhode Island
Unit: Company E, 7th Rhode Island Infantry
Battle or Place of Action: Weldon Railroad, Virginia
Date of Action: 18 August 1864
Date of Issue: 20 July 1897
Citation: While acting as an orderly to a general officer on the field and alone, encountered a picket of three of the enemy and compelled their surrender.

1330 ◆ TAYLOR, RICHARD

Rank: Private
Service: U.S. Army
Birthday: 1834
Place of Birth: Madison County, Alabama
Date of Death: 23 February 1890
Cemetery: St. John's Cemetery (MH)—Washington, Indiana
Entered Service at: Indianapolis, Marion County, Indiana
Unit: Company E, 18th Indiana Infantry
Battle or Place of Action: Cedar Creek, Virginia
Date of Action: 19 October 1864
Date of Issue: 21 November 1864
Citation: Capture of Flag.

1331 ◆ TAYLOR, THOMAS

Rank: Coxswain
Service: U.S. Navy
Birthday: 1834
Place of Birth: Bangor, Penobscot County, Maine

Entered Service at: Maine
Unit: U.S.S. *Metacomet*
Battle or Place of Action: Mobile Bay, Alabama
Date of Action: 5 August 1864
G.O. Number, Date: 59, 22 June 1865
Citation: Served on board the U.S.S. *Metacomet* during the action against rebel forts and gunboats and with the rebel ram *Tennessee* in Mobile Bay, 5 August 1864. Despite damage to his ship and the loss of several men on board as enemy fire raked her decks, Taylor encouraged the men of the forward pivot gun when the officer in command displayed cowardice, doing honor to the occasion.

1332 ◆ TAYLOR, WILLIAM

Rank: Sergeant & Second Lieutenant (highest rank: Captain)
Service: U.S. Army
Birthday: 1836
Place of Birth: Washington, D.C.
Date of Death: 6 April 1902
Place of Death: Baltimore, Maryland
Cemetery: Louden Park National Cemetery (Off-16)—Baltimore, Maryland
Entered Service at: Frederick, Frederick County, Maryland
Unit: Company H & Company M, 1st Maryland Infantry
Battle or Place of Action: Front Royal & Weldon Railroad, Virginia
Date of Action: 23 May 1862 & 19 August 1864
Date of Issue: 2 August 1897
Citation: When a sergeant at Front Royal, Va., he was painfully wounded while obeying an order to burn a bridge, but, persevering in the attempt, he burned the bridge and prevented its use by the enemy. Later, at Weldon Railroad, Va., then a lieutenant, he voluntarily took the place of a disabled officer and undertook a hazardous reconnaissance beyond the lines of the army; was taken prisoner in the attempt.
Notes: POW

1333 ◆ TAYLOR, WILLIAM G.

Rank: Captain of the Forecastle
Service: U.S. Navy
Birthday: 9 August 1829
Place of Birth: Philadelphia, Philadelphia County, Pennsylvania
Date of Death: 28 March 1910
Cemetery: Sunset Cemetery—Quincy, Illinois
Entered Service at: Philadelphia, Philadelphia County, Pennsylvania
Unit: U.S.S. *Ticonderoga*
Battle or Place of Action: Fort Fisher, North Carolina
Date of Action: 24-25 December 1864
G.O. Number, Date: 59, 22 June 1865
Citation: On board the U.S.S. *Ticonderoga* during attacks on Fort Fisher, 24 and 25 December 1864. As captain of a gun, Taylor performed his duties with coolness and skill as his

ship took position in the line of battle and delivered its fire on the batteries onshore. Despite the depressing effect caused when an explosion of the 100-pounder Parrott rifle killed eight men and wounded 12 more, and the enemy's heavy return fire, he calmly remained at his station during the two days' operations.

1334 ◆ TERRY, JOHN DARLING

Rank: Sergeant (highest rank: Major)
Service: U.S. Army
Birthday: 3 September 1845
Place of Birth: Montville, Maine
Date of Death: 4 March 1919
Cemetery: Woodlawn Cemetery—Bronx, New York
Entered Service at: Boston, Suffolk County, Massachusetts
Unit: Company E, 23d Massachusetts Infantry
Battle or Place of Action: New Bern, North Carolina
Date of Action: 14 March 1862
Date of Issue: 12 October 1867
Citation: In the thickest of the fight, where he lost his leg by a shot, still encouraged the men until carried off the field.

1335 ◆ THACKRAH, BENJAMIN

Rank: Private
Service: U.S. Army
Birthday: 13 August 1845
Place of Birth: Scotland
Date of Death: 20 May 1912
Place of Death: Amsterdam, New York
Cemetery: St. Mary's Cemetery (MH)—Fort Johnston, New York
Entered Service at: Johnsonville, Rensselaer County, New York
Unit: Company H, 115th New York Infantry
Battle or Place of Action: near Fort Gates, Florida
Date of Action: 1 April 1864
Date of Issue: 2 May 1890
Citation: Was a volunteer in the surprise and capture of the enemy's picket.

1336 ◆ THATCHER, CHARLES M.

Rank: Private
Service: U.S. Army
Birthday: 1844
Place of Birth: Coldwater, Branch County, Michigan
Date of Death: 13 December 1900
Cemetery: Evergreen Cemetery—Kalkaska, Michigan
Entered Service at: Grand Haven, Ottawa County, Michigan
Unit: Company B, 1st Michigan Sharpshooters
Battle or Place of Action: Petersburg, Virginia
Date of Action: 30 July 1864
Date of Issue: 31 July 1896
Citation: Instead of retreating or surrendering when the works were captured, regardless of his personal safety, contin-

ued to return the enemy's fire until he was captured.
Notes: POW

1337 ◆ THAXTER, SIDNEY WARREN

Rank: Major
Service: U.S. Army
Birthday: 8 September 1839
Place of Birth: Bangor, Penobscot County, Maine
Date of Death: 10 November 1908
Place of Death: Portland, Maine
Cemetery: Evergreen Cemetery (MH)—Portland, Maine
Entered Service at: Bangor, Penobscot County, Maine
Unit: 1st Maine Cavalry
Battle or Place of Action: Hatcher's Run, Virginia
Date of Action: 27 October 1864
Date of Issue: 10 September 1897
Citation: Voluntarily remained and participated in the battle with conspicuous gallantry, although his term of service had expired and he had been ordered home to be mustered out.

1338 ◆ THIELBERG, HENRY

Rank: Seaman
Service: U.S. Navy
Birthday: 1833
Place of Birth: Germany
Entered Service at: Dudley, Webster County, Massachusetts
Unit: U.S.S. *Mount Washington* (temporarily assigned) U.S.S. *Minnesota*
Battle or Place of Action: Nansemond River, Virginia
Date of Action: 14 April 1863
G.O. Number, Date: 17, 10 July 1863
Citation: Served temporarily on board the U.S.S. *Mount Washington* during the Nansemond River action, 14 April 1863. After assisting in hauling up and raising the flagstaff, Thielberg volunteered to go up on the pilothouse and observe the movements of the enemy and although three shells struck within a few inches of his head, remained at his post until ordered to descend.

1339 ◆ THOMAS, HAMPTON SIDNEY

Rank: Major (highest rank: Brevet Colonel)
Service: U.S. Army
Birthday: 3 November 1837
Place of Birth: Quakertown, Bucks County, Pennsylvania
Date of Death: 21 May 1899
Place of Death: Philadelphia, Pennsylvania
Cemetery: Lawnview Cemetery—Philadelphia, Pennsylvania
Entered Service at: Harrisburg, Dauphin County, Pennsylvania
Unit: 1st Pennsylvania Veteran Cavalry
Battle or Place of Action: Amelia Springs, Virginia
Date of Action: 5 April 1865
Date of Issue: 15 January 1894
Citation: Conspicuous gallantry in the capture of a field battery and a number of battle flags and in the destruction of the enemy's wagon train. Maj. Thomas lost a leg in this action.

1340 ◆ THOMAS, STEPHEN

Rank: Colonel (highest rank: Brigadier General)
Service: U.S. Army
Birthday: 6 December 1809
Place of Birth: Bethel, Windsor County, Vermont
Date of Death: 18 December 1903
Place of Death: Montpelier, Vermont
Cemetery: Green Mount Cemetery—Montpelier, Vermont
Entered Service at: West Fairlee, Orange County, Vermont
Unit: 8th Vermont Infantry
Battle or Place of Action: Cedar Creek, Virginia
Date of Action: 19 October 1864
Date of Issue: 25 July 1892
Citation: Distinguished conduct in a desperate hand-to-hand encounter, in which the advance of the enemy was checked.

1341 ◆ THOMPKINS, GEORGE W.

True Name: Tompkins, George W.
Rank: Corporal
Service: U.S. Army
Birthday: 9 April 1841
Place of Birth: Orange County, New York
Date of Death: 22 February 1934
Place of Death: Schenectady, New York
Cemetery: Vale Cemetery—Schenectady, New York
Entered Service at: Port Jervis, Orange County, New York
Unit: Company F, 124th New York Infantry
Battle or Place of Action: Petersburg, Virginia
Date of Action: 25 March 1865
Date of Issue: 6 April 1865
Citation: Capture of flag of 49th Alabama Infantry (C.S.A.) from an officer who, with colors in hand, was rallying his men.

1342 ◆ THOMPSON, ALLEN

Rank: Private
Service: U.S. Army
Birthday: 1 October 1847
Place of Birth: New York, New York
Date of Death: 27 February 1906
Cemetery: Lake View Cemetery (MH)—Cheyenne, Wyoming
Entered Service at: Sandy Creek, Oswego County, New York
Unit: Company K, 4th New York Heavy Artillery
Battle or Place of Action: White Oak Road, Virginia
Date of Action: 1 April 1865
Date of Issue: 22 April 1896
Citation: Made a hazardous reconnaissance through timber and slashings, preceding the Union line of battle, signaling the troops, and leading them through the obstructions.

1343 ◆ THOMPSON, CHARLES AUGUSTUS

Rank: Sergeant (highest rank: Second Lieutenant)
Service: U.S. Army
Birthday: 16 February 1843
Place of Birth: Perrysburg, Wood County, Ohio
Date of Death: 24 August 1900
Place of Death: Rutland, Vermont
Cemetery: Evergreen Cemetery—Rutland, Vermont
Entered Service at: Kalamazoo, Kalamazoo County, Michigan
Unit: Company D, 17th Michigan Infantry
Battle or Place of Action: Spotsylvania, Virginia
Date of Action: 12 May 1864
Date of Issue: 27 July 1896
Citation: After the regiment was surrounded and all resistance seemed useless, fought singlehanded for the colors and refused to give them up until he had appealed to his superior officers.

1344 ◆ THOMPSON, FREEMAN C.

Rank: Corporal
Service: U.S. Army
Birthday: 25 February 1845
Place of Birth: Monroe County, Ohio
Date of Death: 10 August 1887
Cemetery: Olive Cemetery—Caldwell, Ohio
Entered Service at: Marietta, Washington County, Ohio
Unit: Company F, 116th Ohio Infantry
Battle or Place of Action: Petersburg, Virginia
Date of Action: 2 April 1865
Date of Issue: 12 May 1865
Citation: Was twice knocked from the parapet of Fort Gregg by blows from the enemy's muskets, but at the third attempt fought his way into the works.

1345 ◆ THOMPSON, HENRY A.

True Name: Connelly, Roderick P.
Rank: Private
Service: U.S. Marine Corps
Birthday: 1841
Place of Birth: England
Date of Death: 16 February 1889
Cemetery: Calvary Cemetery—Woodside, New York
Entered Service at: Pennsylvania
Unit: U.S.S. *Minnesota*
Battle or Place of Action: Fort Fisher, North Carolina
Date of Action: 15 January 1865
G.O. Number, Date: 59, 22 June 1865
Date of Issue: On board the U.S.S. *Minnesota* in the assault on Ft. Fisher, 15 January 1865
Citation: On board the U.S.S. *Minnesota* in the assault on Ft. Fisher, 15 January 1865. Landing on the beach with the assaulting party from his ship, Pvt. Thompson advanced partly through a breach in the palisades and nearer to the fort than any man from his ship despite enemy fire which killed or wounded many officers and men. When more than two-thirds of the men became seized with panic and retreated on the run, he remained with the party until dark, when it came safely away, bringing its wounded, its arms and its colors.

1346 ◆ THOMPSON, JAMES B.

Rank: Sergeant (highest rank: First Sergeant)
Service: U.S. Army
Birthday: 1843
Place of Birth: Juniata County, Pennsylvania
Date of Death: 31 August 1875
Place of Death: Port Royal, Pennsylvania
Cemetery: Old Churchill Cemetery—Port Royal, Pennsylvania
Entered Service at: Perrysville, Allegheny County, Pennsylvania
Unit: Company G, 1st Pennsylvania Rifles
Battle or Place of Action: Gettysburg, Pennsylvania
Date of Action: 3 July 1863
Date of Issue: 1 December 1864
Citation: Capture of flag of 15th Georgia Infantry (C.S.A.).
Notes: POW

1347 ◆ THOMPSON, JAMES GRANVILLE

Rank: Private
Service: U.S. Army
Birthday: 25 December 1849
Place of Birth: Sandy Creek, Oswego County, New York
Date of Death: 23 May 1921
Cemetery: Mount Hope Cemetery (MH)—San Diego, California
Entered Service at: Sandy Creek, Oswego County, New York
Unit: Company K, 4th New York Heavy Artillery
Battle or Place of Action: White Oak Road, Virginia
Date of Action: 1 April 1865
Date of Issue: 22 April 1896
Citation: Made a hazardous reconnaissance through timber and slashings, preceding the Union line of battle, signaling the troops, and leading them through the obstructions.

1348 ◆ THOMPSON, JAMES HARRY

Rank: Surgeon (highest rank: Major)
Service: U.S. Army
Birthday: 1824
Place of Birth: England
Date of Death: 4 November 1896
Place of Death: Great Yarmouth, England
Entered Service at: New York, New York
Unit: U.S. Volunteers
Battle or Place of Action: New Bern, North Carolina
Date of Action: 14 March 1862
Date of Issue: 11 November 1870
Citation: Voluntarily reconnoitered the enemy's position and carried orders under the hottest fire.

1349 ◆ THOMPSON, JOHN J.

Rank: Corporal
Service: U.S. Army
Birthday: 14 August 1838

Place of Birth: Holstein, Germany
Date of Death: 2 July 1915
Place of Death: Baltimore, Maryland
Cemetery: Immanuel Cemetery—Baltimore, Maryland
Entered Service at: Baltimore, Baltimore County, Maryland
Unit: Company C, 1st Maryland Infantry
Battle or Place of Action: Hatcher's Run, Virginia
Date of Action: 6 February 1865
Date of Issue: 10 September 1897
Citation: As color bearer with most conspicuous gallantry preceded his regiment in the assault and planted his flag upon the enemy's works.

1350 ◆ THOMPSON, THOMAS W.

Rank: Sergeant
Service: U.S. Army
Birthday: 27 May 1839
Place of Birth: Champaign County, Ohio
Date of Death: 25 March 1927
Place of Death: Mechanicsburg, Ohio
Cemetery: Maple Grove Cemetery—Mechanicsburg, Ohio
Entered Service at: Urbana, Champaign County, Ohio
Unit: Company A, 66th Ohio Infantry
Battle or Place of Action: Chancellorsville, Virginia
Date of Action: 2 May 1863
Date of Issue: 16 July 1892
Citation: One of a party of four who voluntarily brought into the Union lines, under fire, a wounded Confederate officer from whom was obtained valuable information concerning the enemy.

1351 ◆ THOMPSON, WILLIAM

Rank: Signal Quartermaster
Service: U.S. Navy
Birthday: 1812
Place of Birth: Cape May County, New Jersey
Date of Death: 12 September 1872
Place of Death: Philadelphia, Pennsylvania
Cemetery: Mount Moriah Cemetery VA plot 14-12—Philadelphia, Pennsylvania
Entered Service at: Boston, Suffolk County, Massachusetts
Unit: U.S.S. *Mohican*
Battle or Place of Action: Hilton Head, South Carolina
Date of Action: 7 November 1861
G.O. Number, Date: 17, 10 July 1863
Citation: During action of the main squadron of ships against heavily defended Forts Beauregard and Walker on Hilton Head, 7 November 1861. Serving as a signal quartermaster on board the U.S.S. *Mohican*, Thompson steadfastly steered the ship with a steady and bold heart under the batteries; was wounded by a piece of shell but remained at his station until he fell from loss of blood. Leg since amputated.

1352 ◆ *THOMPSON, WILLIAM P.

Rank: Sergeant (highest rank: First Lieutenant)
Service: U.S. Army

Birthday: 11 January 1844
Place of Birth: Brooklyn, Kings County, New York
Date of Death: 7 October 1864
Place of Death: Wilderness, Virginia
Cemetery: Greenbush Cemetery (MH)—Lafayette, Indiana
Entered Service at: Lafayette, Tippecanoe County, Indiana
Unit: Company G, 20th Indiana Infantry
Battle or Place of Action: Wilderness Campaign, Virginia
Date of Action: 6 May 1864
Date of Issue: 1 December 1864
Citation: Capture of flag of 55th Virginia Infantry (C.S.A.).

1353 ◆ THOMSON, CLIFFORD

Rank: First Lieutenant (highest rank: Brevet Major)
Service: U.S. Army
Birthday: 15 April 1834
Place of Birth: Fulton, Oswego County, New York
Date of Death: 29 September 1912
Cemetery: Holy Sepulchre Cemetery—East Orange, New Jersey
Entered Service at: New York, New York
Unit: Company A, 1st New York Cavalry
Battle or Place of Action: Chancellorsville, Virginia
Date of Action: 2 May 1863
Date of Issue: 27 November 1896
Citation: Volunteered to ascertain the character of approaching troops; rode up so close as to distinguish the features of the enemy, and as he wheeled to return they opened fire with musketry, the Union troops returning same. Under a terrific fire from both sides, Lt. Thompson rode back unhurt to the Federal lines, averting a disaster to the Army by his heroic act.

1354 ◆ THORN, WALTER

Rank: Second Lieutenant (highest rank: Brevet Captain)
Service: U.S. Army
Birthday: 18 November 1844
Place of Birth: Brooklyn, Kings County, New York
Date of Death: 29 July 1920
Place of Death: Hampton, Virginia
Cemetery: Arlington National Cemetery (2-3689-WH) (MH)—Arlington, Virginia
Entered Service at: Camp Nelson, Kentucky
Unit: Company G, 116th U.S. Colored Infantry
Battle or Place of Action: Dutch Gap Canal, Virginia
Date of Action: 1 January 1865
Date of Issue: 8 December 1898
Citation: After the fuse to the mined bulkhead had been lit, this officer, learning that the picket guard had not been withdrawn, mounted the bulkhead and at great personal peril warned the guard of its danger.

1355 ◆ TIBBETS, ANDREW W.

Rank: Private
Service: U.S. Army
Birthday: 1830

Place of Birth: Clark County, Indiana
Date of Death: 18 May 1898
Cemetery: Alberton Cemetery (MH)—Alberton, Iowa
Entered Service at: Centerville, Appanoose County, Iowa
Unit: Company I, 3d Iowa Cavalry
Battle or Place of Action: Columbus, Georgia
Date of Action: 16 April 1865
Date of Issue: 17 June 1865
Citation: Capture of flag and bearer, Austin's Battery (C.S.A.).

1356 ◆ TILTON, WILLIAM

Rank: Sergeant
Service: U.S. Army
Birthday: 27 October 1834
Place of Birth: St. Albans, Franklin County, Vermont
Date of Death: 8 March 1910
Place of Death: Enfield, New Hampshire
Cemetery: Oak Grove Cemetery—Enfield, New Hampshire
Entered Service at: Hanover, Grafton County, New Hampshire
Unit: Company C, 7th New Hampshire Infantry
Battle or Place of Action: Richmond Campaign, Virginia
Date of Action: 1864
Date of Issue: 20 February 1884
Citation: Gallant conduct in the field.

1357 ◆ TINKHAM, EUGENE M.

Rank: Corporal (highest rank: Sergeant)
Service: U.S. Army
Birthday: 19 April 1842
Place of Birth: Sprague, Connecticut
Date of Death: 21 October 1909
Place of Death: Springfield, Massachusetts
Cemetery: New Hanover Cemetery (MH)—Hanover, Connecticut
Entered Service at: Waterloo, Seneca County, New York
Unit: Company H, 148th New York Infantry
Battle or Place of Action: Cold Harbor, Virginia
Date of Action: 3 June 1864
Date of Issue: 5 April 1898
Citation: Though himself wounded, voluntarily left the rifle pits, crept out between the lines and, exposed to the severe fire of the enemy's guns at close-range, brought within the lines two wounded and helpless comrades.

1358 ◆ TITUS, CHARLES

Rank: Sergeant (highest rank: Quartermaster Sergeant)
Service: U.S. Army
Birthday: 1 January 1838
Place of Birth: Millstone, New Jersey
Date of Death: 26 March 1921
Place of Death: Belmar, New Jersey
Cemetery: Gledola Cemetery—Wall Township, New Jersey
Entered Service at: New Brunswick, Middlesex County, New Jersey

Unit: Company H, 1st New Jersey Cavalry
Battle or Place of Action: Deatonsville (Sailor's Creek), Virginia
Date of Action: 6 April 1865
Date of Issue: 3 July 1865
Citation: Was among the first to check the enemy's counter-charge.

1359 ◆ TOBAN, JAMES W.

True Name: Toban, Jacobus W.
Rank: Sergeant
Service: U.S. Army
Birthday: 23 November 1845
Place of Birth: Northfield, Michigan
Date of Death: 2 November 1903
Place of Death: Lansing, Michigan
Cemetery: Catholic Cemetery—Northfield, Michigan
Entered Service at: Northfield, Michigan
Unit: Company C, 9th Michigan Cavalry
Battle or Place of Action: Aiken, South Carolina
Date of Action: 11 February 1865
Date of Issue: 9 July 1896
Citation: Voluntarily and at great personal risk returned, in the face of the advance of the enemy, and rescued from impending death or capture, Maj. William C. Stevens, 9th Michigan Cavalry, who had been thrown from his horse.

1360 ◆ TOBIE JR., EDWARD PARSONS

Rank: Sergeant Major (highest rank: Second Lieutenant)
Service: U.S. Army
Birthday: 19 March 1838
Place of Birth: Lewiston, Androscoggin County, Maine
Date of Death: 21 January 1900
Cemetery: Swain Point Cemetery (MH)—Providence, Rhode Island
Entered Service at: Lewiston, Androscoggin County, Maine
Unit: 1st Maine Cavalry
Battle or Place of Action: Appomattox Campaign, Virginia
Date of Action: 29 March-9 April 1865
Date of Issue: 1 April 1898
Citation: Though severely wounded at Sailors Creek, 6 April, and at Farmville, 7 April, refused to go to the hospital, but remained with his regiment, performed the full duties of adjutant upon the wounding of that officer, and was present for duty at Appomattox.
Notes: POW

1361 ◆ TOBIN, JOHN MICHAEL

Rank: First Lieutenant & Adjutant (highest rank: Captain)
Service: U.S. Army
Place of Birth: Waterford, Ireland
Date of Death: 27 December 1898
Cemetery: Mount Auburn Cemetery (MH)—Cambridge, Massachusetts
Entered Service at: Boston, Suffolk County, Massachusetts

Unit: Company I, 9th Massachusetts Infantry
Battle or Place of Action: Malvern Hill, Virginia
Date of Action: 1 July 1862
Date of Issue: 11 March 1896
Citation: Voluntarily took command of the 9th Massachusetts while adjutant, bravely fighting from 3:00 P.M. until dusk, rallying and reforming the regiment under fire; twice picked up the regimental flag, the color bearer having been shot down, and placed it in worthy hands.

1362 ◆ TODD, SAMUEL

Rank: Quartermaster
Service: U.S. Navy
Birthday: 1815
Place of Birth: Portsmouth, Rockingham County, New Hampshire
Entered Service at: New Hampshire
Unit: U.S.S. *Brooklyn*
Battle or Place of Action: Fort Morgan, Mobile Bay, Alabama
Date of Action: 5 August 1864
G.O. Number, Date: 45, 31 December 1864
Citation: Stationed at the conn on board the U.S.S. *Brooklyn* during action against rebel forts and gunboats and with the ram *Tennessee* in Mobile Bay, 5 August 1864. Despite severe damage to his ship and the loss of several men on board as enemy fire raked her decks from stem to stern, Todd performed his duties with outstanding skill and courage throughout the furious battle which resulted in the surrender of the prize rebel ram *Tennessee* and in the damaging and destruction of batteries at Fort Morgan.

1363 ◆ TOFFEY, JOHN JAMES

Rank: First Lieutenant
Service: U.S. Army
Birthday: 1 June 1844
Place of Birth: Quaker Hill, Dutchess County, New York
Date of Death: 13 March 1911
Cemetery: Fishkill Cemetery—Pauling, New York
Entered Service at: Hudson, Hudson County, New Jersey
Unit: Company G, 33d New Jersey Infantry
Battle or Place of Action: Chattanooga, Tennessee
Date of Action: 23 November 1863
Date of Issue: 10 September 1897
Citation: Although excused from duty on account of sickness, went to the front in command of a storming party and with conspicuous gallantry participated in the assault of Missionary Ridge; was here wounded and permanently disabled.

1364 ◆ TOMLIN, ANDREW J.

Rank: Corporal (highest rank: Sergeant)
Service: U.S. Marine Corps
Birthday: 15 March 1845
Place of Birth: Goshen, Cape May County, New Jersey
Date of Death: 1 November 1905

Cemetery: Goshen Methodist Cemetery (MH)—Goshen, New Jersey
Entered Service at: New Jersey
Unit: U.S.S. *Wabash*
Battle or Place of Action: Fort Fisher, North Carolina
Date of Action: 15 January 1865
G.O. Number, Date: 59, 22 June 1865
Citation: As corporal of the guard on board the U.S.S. *Wabash* during the assault on Fort Fisher, 15 January 1865. As one of 200 marines assembled to hold a line of entrenchments in the rear of the fort which the enemy threatened to attack in force following a retreat in panic by more than two-thirds of the assaulting ground forces, Cpl. Tomlin took position in line and remained until morning when relief troops arrived from the fort. When one of his comrades was struck down by enemy fire, he unhesitatingly advanced under a withering fire of musketry into an open plain close to the fort and assisted the wounded man to a place of safety.

1365 ◆ TOMPKINS, AARON B.

Rank: Sergeant (highest rank: First Sergeant)
Service: U.S. Army
Birthday: 15 February 1844
Place of Birth: Orange, Essex County, New Jersey
Date of Death: 25 November 1931
Cemetery: Rosedale Cemetery (MH)—Orange, New Jersey
Entered Service at: Jersey City, Hudson County, New Jersey
Unit: Company G, 1st New Jersey Cavalry
Battle or Place of Action: Deatonsville (Sailor's Creek), Virginia
Date of Action: 5 April 1865
Date of Issue: 3 July 1865
Citation: Charged into the enemy's ranks and captured a battle flag, having a horse shot under him and his cheeks and shoulders cut with a saber.

1366 ◆ TOMPKINS, CHARLES HENRY

Rank: First Lieutenant (highest rank: Brevet Brigadier General)
Service: U.S. Army
Birthday: 12 September 1830
Place of Birth: Fort Monroe, Hampton County, Virginia
Date of Death: 18 January 1915
Place of Death: Washington, D.C.
Cemetery: Oak Hill Cemetery—Washington D.C.
Entered Service at: Brooklyn, Kings County, New York
Unit: 2d U.S. Cavalry
Battle or Place of Action: Fairfax, Virginia
Date of Action: 1 June 1861
Date of Issue: 13 November 1893
Citation: Twice charged through the enemy's lines and, taking a carbine from an enlisted man, shot the enemy's captain.

1367 ◆ TOOHEY, THOMAS

Rank: Sergeant (highest rank: First Sergeant)
Service: U.S. Army

Birthday: 1 January 1835
Place of Birth: New York, New York
Date of Death: 19 November 1918
Cemetery: Mount Washington Cemetery (MH)—Independence, Missouri
Entered Service at: Milwaukee, Milwaukee County, Wisconsin
Unit: Company F, 24th Wisconsin Infantry
Battle or Place of Action: Franklin, Tennessee
Date of Action: 30 November 1864
Date of Issue: 12 March 1917
Citation: Gallantry in action; voluntarily assisting in working guns of battery near right of regiment after nearly every man had left them, the fire of the enemy being hotter at this than at any other point on the line.

1368 ◆ TOOMER, WILLIAM

Rank: Sergeant
Service: U.S. Army
Birthday: 12 January 1830
Place of Birth: Dublin, Ireland
Date of Death: 27 December 1901
Cemetery: Graceland Cemetery—Chicago, Illinois
Entered Service at: Chicago, Cook County, Illinois
Unit: Company G, 127th Illinois Infantry
Battle or Place of Action: Vicksburg, Mississippi
Date of Action: 22 May 1863
Date of Issue: 9 July 1894
Citation: Gallantry in the charge of the "volunteer storming party."

1369 ◆ TORGLER, ERNEST R.

Rank: Sergeant
Service: U.S. Army
Birthday: 29 March 1840
Place of Birth: Mecklenburg, Germany
Date of Death: 3 August 1923
Cemetery: Woodlawn Cemetery (MH)—Toledo, Ohio
Entered Service at: Toledo, Lucas County, Ohio
Unit: Company G, 37th Ohio Infantry
Battle or Place of Action: Ezra Chapel, Georgia
Date of Action: 28 July 1864
Date of Issue: 10 May 1894
Citation: At great hazard of his life he saved his commanding officer, then badly wounded, from capture.

1370 ◆ TOZIER, ANDREW JACKSON

Rank: Sergeant (highest rank: First Sergeant)
Service: U.S. Army
Birthday: 11 February 1838
Place of Birth: Monmouth, Kennebec County, Maine
Date of Death: 28 March 1910
Cemetery: Litchfield Plains Cemetery (MH)—Litchfield, Maine
Entered Service at: Bangor, Penobscot County, Maine
Unit: Company I, 20th Maine Infantry

Battle or Place of Action: Gettysburg, Pennsylvania
Date of Action: 2 July 1863
Date of Issue: 13 August 1898
Citation: At the crisis of the engagement this soldier, a color bearer, stood alone in an advanced position, the regiment having been borne back, and defended his colors with musket and ammunition picked up at his feet.

1371 ◆ TRACY, AMASA SAWYER

Rank: Lieutenant Colonel (highest rank: Brevet Colonel)
Service: U.S. Army
Birthday: 16 March 1829
Place of Birth: Dover, Piscataquis County, Maine
Date of Death: 26 February 1908
Place of Death: Orleans, Vermont
Cemetery: West Cemetery—Middlebury, Vermont
Entered Service at: Middlebury, Addison County, Vermont
Unit: 2d Vermont Infantry
Battle or Place of Action: Cedar Creek, Virginia
Date of Action: 19 October 1864
Date of Issue: 24 June 1892
Citation: Took command and led the brigade in the assault on the enemy's works.

1372 ◆ TRACY, BENJAMIN FRANKLIN

Rank: Colonel (highest rank: Brevet Brigadier General)
Service: U.S. Army
Birthday: 26 April 1830
Place of Birth: Owego, Tioga County, New York
Date of Death: 6 August 1915
Place of Death: New York, New York
Cemetery: The Green Wood Cemetery—Brooklyn, New York
Entered Service at: Owego, Tioga County, New York
Unit: 109th New York Infantry
Served as: Commanding Officer
Battle or Place of Action: Wilderness Campaign, Virginia
Date of Action: 6 May 1864
Date of Issue: 21 June 1895
Citation: Seized the colors and led the regiment when other regiments had retired and then reformed his line and held it.

1373 ◆ TRACY, CHARLES H.

Rank: Sergeant
Service: U.S. Army
Birthday: 1833
Place of Birth: Jewett City, New London County, Connecticut
Date of Death: 13 September 1911
Cemetery: Fairview Cemetery (MH)—Chicopee, Massachusetts
Entered Service at: Springfield, Hampden County, Massachusetts
Unit: Company A, 37th Massachusetts Infantry
Battle or Place of Action: Spotsylvania & Petersburg, Virginia

Date of Action: 12 May 1864 & 2 April 1865
Date of Issue: 19 November 1897
Citation: At the risk of his own life, at Spotsylvania, 12 May 1864, assisted in carrying to a place of safety a wounded and helpless officer. On 2 April 1865, advanced with the pioneers, and, under heavy fire, assisted in removing two lines of chevaux-de-frise; was twice wounded but advanced to the third line, where he was again severely wounded, losing a leg.

1374 ◆ TRACY, WILLIAM GARDNER

Rank: Second Lieutenant (highest rank: Major)
Service: U.S. Army
Birthday: 7 April 1842
Place of Birth: Syracuse, Onondaga County, New York
Date of Death: 8 December 1924
Cemetery: Oakwood Morningside Cemetery (MH)—Syracuse, New York
Entered Service at: Albany, Albany County, New York
Unit: Company I, 122d New York Infantry
Battle or Place of Action: Chancellorsville, Virginia
Date of Action: 2 May 1863
Date of Issue: 2 May 1895
Citation: Having been sent outside the lines to obtain certain information of great importance and having succeeded in his mission, was surprised upon his return by a large force of the enemy, regaining the Union lines only after greatly imperiling his life.

1375 ◆ TRAYNOR, ANDREW

Rank: Corporal
Service: U.S. Army
Birthday: 9 February 1843
Place of Birth: Newark, Essex County, New Jersey
Date of Death: 6 July 1920
Place of Death: Omaha, Nebraska
Cemetery: Forest Lawn Cemetery—Omaha, Nebraska
Entered Service at: Rome, Oneida County, New York
Unit: Company D, 1st Michigan Cavalry
Battle or Place of Action: Mason's Hill, Virginia
Date of Action: 16 March 1864
Date of Issue: 28 September 1897
Citation: Having been surprised and captured by a detachment of guerrillas, this soldier, with other prisoners, seized the arms of the guard over them, killed two of the guerrillas, and enabled all the prisoners to escape.

1376 ◆ TREAT, HOWELL B.

Rank: Sergeant
Service: U.S. Army
Birthday: 31 March 1833
Place of Birth: Painesville, Lake County, Ohio
Date of Death: 21 July 1912
Cemetery: Evergreen Cemetery—Painesville, Ohio
Entered Service at: Painesville, Lake County, Ohio
Unit: Company I, 52d Ohio Infantry
Battle or Place of Action: Buzzard's Roost, Georgia

Date of Action: 11 May 1864
Date of Issue: 14 August 1894
Citation: Risked his life in saving a wounded comrade.

1377 ◆ TREMAIN, HENRY EDWIN

Rank: Major & Aide-de-Camp (highest rank: Brevet Brigadier General)
Service: U.S. Army
Birthday: 14 November 1840
Place of Birth: New York, New York
Date of Death: 9 December 1910
Place of Death: New York, New York
Cemetery: Woodlawn Cemetery—Bronx, New York
Entered Service at: New York, New York
Unit: U.S. Volunteers
Battle or Place of Action: Resaca, Georgia
Date of Action: 15 May 1864
Date of Issue: 30 June 1892
Citation: Voluntarily rode between the lines while two brigades of Union troops were firing into each other and stopped the firing.

1378 ◆ TRIBE, JOHN

Rank: Private (highest rank: Quartermaster Sergeant)
Service: U.S. Army
Birthday: 4 December 1841
Place of Birth: Tioga County, New York
Date of Death: 4 December 1917
Place of Death: Barton, New York
Cemetery: Halsey Valley Cemetery (MH)—Halsey Valley, New York
Entered Service at: Oswego, Oswego County, New York
Unit: Company G, 5th New York Cavalry
Battle or Place of Action: Waterloo Bridge, Virginia
Date of Action: 25 August 1862
Date of Issue: 11 June 1895
Citation: Voluntarily assisted in the burning and destruction of the bridge under heavy fire from the enemy.

1379 ◆ TRIPP, OTHNIEL

Rank: Chief Boatswain's Mate
Service: U.S. Navy
Birthday: 1826
Place of Birth: Maine
Entered Service at: Maine
Unit: U.S.S. *Seneca*
Battle or Place of Action: Fort Fisher, North Carolina
Date of Action: 15 January 1865
G.O. Number, Date: 59, 22 June 1865
Citation: On board the U.S.S. *Seneca* in the assault on Fort Fisher, 15 January 1865. Despite severe enemy fire which halted an attempt by his assaulting party to enter the stockade, Tripp boldly charged through the gap in the stockade although the center of the line, being totally unprotected, fell back along the open beach and left too few in the ranks to attempt an offensive operation.

1380 ◆ TROGDEN, HOWELL G.

Rank: Private
Service: U.S. Army
Birthday: 24 October 1840
Place of Birth: Cedar Falls, Randolph County, North Carolina
Date of Death: 2 December 1910
Cemetery: Calvary Cemetery (MH)—Los Angeles, California
Entered Service at: St. Louis, St. Louis County, Missouri
Unit: Company B, 8th Missouri Infantry
Battle or Place of Action: Vicksburg, Mississippi
Date of Action: 22 May 1863
Date of Issue: 3 August 1894
Citation: Gallantry in the charge of the "volunteer storming party." He carried his regiment's flag and tried to borrow a gun to defend it.

1381 ◆ TRUELL, EDWIN M.

Rank: Private (highest rank: First Lieutenant)
Service: U.S. Army
Birthday: 19 August 1841
Place of Birth: Lowell, Middlesex County, Massachusetts
Date of Death: 12 October 1907
Place of Death: Washington, D.C.
Cemetery: Arlington National Cemetery (13-5274-C)—Arlington, Virginia
Entered Service at: Mantson, Wisconsin
Unit: Company E, 12th Wisconsin Infantry
Battle or Place of Action: near Atlanta, Georgia
Date of Action: 21 July 1864
Date of Issue: 11 March 1870
Citation: Although severely wounded in a charge, he remained with the regiment until again severely wounded, losing his leg.

1382 ◆ TRUETT, ALEXANDER H.

Rank: Coxswain
Service: U.S. Navy
Birthday: 4 July 1833
Place of Birth: Baltimore, Baltimore County, Maryland
Entered Service at: Maryland
Unit: U.S.S. *Richmond*
Battle or Place of Action: Fort Morgan, Mobile Bay, Alabama
Date of Action: 5 August 1864
G.O. Number, Date: 45, 31 December 1864
Date of Issue: 24 October 1865
Citation: On board the U.S.S. *Richmond* during action against rebel forts and gunboats and with the ram *Tennessee* in Mobile Bay, 5 August 1864. Despite damage to his ship the loss of several men on board as enemy fire raked her decks, Truett performed his duties with skill and courage throughout a furious two-hour battle which resulted in the surrender of the rebel ram *Tennessee* and in the damaging and destruction of batteries at Fort Morgan.

1383 ◆ TUCKER, ALLEN

Rank: Sergeant
Service: U.S. Army
Birthday: 1838
Place of Birth: Lyme, Connecticut
Date of Death: 22 February 1903
Place of Death: New Haven, Connecticut
Cemetery: Evergreen Cemetery (MH)—New Haven, Connecticut
Entered Service at: Sprague, Connecticut
Unit: Company F, 10th Connecticut Infantry
Battle or Place of Action: Petersburg, Virginia
Date of Action: 2 April 1865
Date of Issue: 12 May 1865
Citation: Gallantry as color bearer in the assault on Fort Gregg.

1384 ◆ TUCKER, JACOB R.

Rank: Corporal
Service: U.S. Army
Birthday: 1 April 1845
Place of Birth: Chester County, Pennsylvania
Date of Death: 16 February 1926
Cemetery: The Baltimore Cemetery—Baltimore, Maryland
Entered Service at: Baltimore, Baltimore County, Maryland
Unit: Company G, 4th Maryland Infantry
Battle or Place of Action: Petersburg, Virginia
Date of Action: 1 April 1865
Date of Issue: 22 April 1871
Citation: Was one of three soldiers most conspicuous in the final assault.

1385 ◆ TWEEDALE, JOHN

Rank: Private (highest rank: Colonel)
Service: U.S. Army
Birthday: 10 June 1841
Place of Birth: Frankford, Philadelphia County, Pennsylvania
Date of Death: 21 December 1920
Cemetery: Arlington National Cemetery (1-470-WS)—Arlington, Virginia
Entered Service at: Philadelphia, Philadelphia County, Pennsylvania
Unit: Company B, 15th Pennsylvania Cavalry
Battle or Place of Action: Stone River, Tennessee
Date of Action: 31 December 1862—1 January 1863
Date of Issue: 18 November 1887
Citation: Gallantry in action.

1386 ◆ TWOMBLY, VOLTARE PAINE

Rank: Corporal (highest rank: Captain)
Service: U.S. Army
Birthday: 21 February 1842
Place of Birth: Farmington, Van Buren County, Iowa
Date of Death: 24 February 1918
Place of Death: Des Moines, Iowa
Cemetery: Pitsburg Rural Cemetery (MH)—Keosauqua, Iowa
Entered Service at: Keosauqua, Van Buren County, Iowa
Unit: Company F, 2d Iowa Infantry
Battle or Place of Action: Fort Donelson, Tennessee
Date of Action: 15 February 1862
Date of Issue: 12 March 1897
Citation: Took the colors after three of the color guard had fallen, and although most instantly knocked down by a spent ball, immediately arose and bore the colors to the end of the engagement.

1387 ◆ TYRRELL, GEORGE WILLIAM

Rank: Corporal (highest rank: First Sergeant)
Service: U.S. Army
Place of Birth: Ireland
Entered Service at: Cincinnati, Hamilton County, Ohio
Unit: Company H, 5th Ohio Infantry
Battle or Place of Action: Resaca, Georgia
Date of Action: 14 May 1864
Date of Issue: 7 April 1865
Citation: Capture of flag.

1388 ◆ UHRL, GEORGE

True Name: Uhri, George
Rank: Sergeant
Service: U.S. Army
Birthday: 21 October 1838
Place of Birth: Baden, Germany
Date of Death: 28 September 1911
Place of Death: New York, New York
Cemetery: The Lutheran Cemetery—Middle Village, New York
Entered Service at: New York, New York
Unit: Light Battery F, 5th U.S. Artillery
Battle or Place of Action: White Oak Swamp Bridge, Virginia
Date of Action: 30 June 1862
Date of Issue: 4 April 1898
Citation: Was one of a party of three who, under heavy fire of advancing enemy, voluntarily secured and saved from capture a field gun belonging to another battery and which had been deserted by its officers and men.

1389 ◆ URELL, MICHAEL EMMET

Rank: Private (highest rank: Brevet Major)
Service: U.S. Army
Birthday: 8 November 1844
Place of Birth: County Cork, Ireland
Date of Death: 6 September 1910
Place of Death: County Cork, Ireland
Cemetery: Arlington National Cemetery (1-51-D-WS)—Arlington, Virginia
Entered Service at: New York, New York
Unit: Company E, 82d New York Infantry

Served as: Color Bearer
Battle or Place of Action: Bristoe Station, Virginia
Date of Action: 14 October 1863
Date of Issue: 6 June 1870
Citation: Gallantry in action while detailed as color bearer; was severely wounded.
Notes: POW

1390 ◆ VALE, JOHN

Rank: Private (highest rank: Sergeant)
Service: U.S. Army
Birthday: 9 August 1836
Place of Birth: London, England
Date of Death: 4 February 1909
Place of Death: Davenport, Iowa
Cemetery: Oakdale Cemetery—Davenport, Iowa
Entered Service at: Rochester, Olmsted County, Minnesota
Unit: Company H, 2d Minnesota Infantry
Battle or Place of Action: Nolensville, Tennessee
Date of Action: 15 February 1863
Date of Issue: 11 September 1897
Citation: Was one of a detachment of 16 men who heroically defended a wagon train against the attack of 125 cavalry, repulsed the attack and saved the train.

1391 ◆ VANCE, WILSON J.

Rank: Private (highest rank: Brevet Captain)
Service: U.S. Army
Birthday: 20 December 1845
Place of Birth: Findlay, Hancock County, Ohio
Date of Death: 10 November 1911
Place of Death: Chattanooga, Tennessee
Cemetery: Arlington National Cemetery (3-2360-WS) (MH)—Arlington, Virginia
Entered Service at: Findlay, Hancock County, Ohio
Unit: Company B, 21st Ohio Infantry
Battle or Place of Action: Stone River, Tennessee
Date of Action: 31 December 1862
Date of Issue: 17 September 1897
Citation: Voluntarily and under a heavy fire, while his command was falling back, rescued a wounded and helpless comrade from death or capture.

1392 ◆ VANDERSLICE, JOHN MITCHELL

Rank: Private
Service: U.S. Army
Birthday: 31 August 1846
Place of Birth: near Valley Forge, Chester County, Pennsylvania
Date of Death: 12 March 1915
Place of Death: Collegeville, Pennsylvania
Cemetery: St. James Perkiomen Cemetery (MH)—Evansburg, Pennsylvania
Entered Service at: Philadelphia, Philadelphia County, Pennsylvania
Unit: Company D, 8th Pennsylvania Cavalry

Battle or Place of Action: Hatcher's Run, Virginia
Date of Action: 6 February 1865
Date of Issue: 1 September 1893
Citation: Was the first man to reach the enemy's rifle pits, which were taken in the charge.
Notes: POW

1393 ◆ VAN MATRE, JOSEPH

Rank: Private
Service: U.S. Army
Birthday: 9 October 1828
Place of Birth: Mason County, West Virginia
Date of Death: 14 January 1892
Cemetery: Hill Cemetery—Middleport, Ohio
Entered Service at: Middleport, Meigs County, Ohio
Unit: Company G, 116th Ohio Infantry
Battle or Place of Action: Petersburg, Virginia
Date of Action: 2 April 1865
Date of Issue: 12 May 1865
Citation: In the assault on Fort Gregg, this soldier climbed upon the parapet and fired down into the fort as fast as the loaded guns could be passed up to him by comrades.

1394 ◆ VANTINE, JOSEPH E.

Rank: First Class Fireman
Service: U.S. Navy
Birthday: March 1835
Place of Birth: Philadelphia, Philadelphia County, Pennsylvania
Date of Death: 5 May 1904
Cemetery: Globe Cemetery—New Castle, Delaware
Entered Service at: Pennslyvania
Unit: U.S.S. *Richmond*
Battle or Place of Action: Port Hudson, Louisiana
Date of Action: 14 March 1863
G.O. Number, Date: 17, 10 July 1863
Citation: Served on board the U.S.S. *Richmond* in the attack on Port Hudson, 14 March 1863. Damaged by a 6-inch solid rifle shot which shattered the starboard safety-valve chamber and also damaged the port safety valve, the fireroom of the *Richmond* immediately filled with steam, to place it in an extremely critical condition. Acting courageously in this crisis, Vantine persisted in penetrating the steam-filled room in order to haul the hot fires of the furnaces and continued this action until the gravity of the situation had been lessened.

1395 ◆ VAN WINKLE, EDWARD (EDWIN)

Rank: Corporal (highest rank: Sergeant)
Service: U.S. Army
Birthday: 1839
Place of Birth: Phelps, Ontario County, New York
Date of Death: 30 July 1891
Cemetery: Oak Hill Cemetery (MH)—Battle Creek, Michigan
Entered Service at: Phelps, Ontario County, New York
Unit: Company C, 148th New York Infantry

Battle or Place of Action: Chapin's Farm, Virginia
Date of Action: 29 September 1864
Date of Issue: 6 April 1865
Citation: Took position in advance of the skirmish line and drove the enemy's cannoneers from their guns.

1396 ◆ VAUGHN, PINKERTON ROSS

Rank: Sergeant
Service: U.S. Marine Corps
Birthday: 1839
Place of Birth: Downingtown, Chester County, Pennsylvania
Date of Death: 22 August 1866
Cemetery: Laurel Hill Cemetery (MH)—Philadelphia, Pennsylvania
Entered Service at: Pennsylvania
Unit: U.S.S. *Mississippi*
Battle or Place of Action: Port Hudson, Louisiana
Date of Action: 14 March 1863
G.O. Number, Date: 17, 10 July 1863
Citation: Serving on board the U.S.S. *Mississippi* during her abandonment and firing in the action with the Port Hudson batteries, 14 March 1863. During the abandonment of the *Mississippi* which had to be grounded, Sgt. Vaughn rendered invaluable assistance to his commanding officer, remaining with the ship until all of the crew had landed and the ship had been fired to prevent its falling into enemy hands. Persistent until the last, and conspicuously cool under the heavy shellfire, Sgt. Vaughn was finally ordered to save himself as he saw fit.

1397 ◆ VEAL, CHARLES

True Name: Veale, Charles
Rank: Private
Service: U.S. Army
Birthday: 1838
Place of Birth: Portsmouth, Portsmouth County, Virginia
Date of Death: 27 July 1872
Place of Death: Hampton, Virginia
Cemetery: Hampton National Cemetery (F-5097) (MH)—Hampton, Virginia
Entered Service at: Baltimore, Baltimore County, Maryland
Unit: Company D, 4th U.S. Colored Infantry
Battle or Place of Action: Chapin's Farm, Virginia
Date of Action: 29 September 1864
Date of Issue: 6 April 1865
Citation: Seized the national colors, after two color bearers had been shot down close to the enemy's works, and bore them through the remainder of the battle.

1398 ◆ VEALE, MOSES

Rank: Captain (highest rank: Major)
Service: U.S. Army
Birthday: 9 November 1832
Place of Birth: Bridgeton, Cumberland County, New Jersey
Date of Death: 27 July 1917

Place of Death: Philadelphia, Pennsylvania
Cemetery: West Laurel Hill Cemetery—Bala-Cynwyd, Pennsylvania
Entered Service at: Philadelphia, Philadelphia County, Pennsylvania
Unit: Company F, 109th Pennsylvania Infantry
Battle or Place of Action: Wauhatchie, Tennessee
Date of Action: 28 October 1863
Date of Issue: 17 January 1894
Citation: Gallantry in action; manifesting throughout the engagement coolness, zeal, judgment, and courage. His horse was shot from under him and he was hit by four enemy bullets.

1399 ◆ VEAZEY, WHEELOCK GRAVES

Rank: Colonel
Service: U.S. Army
Birthday: 5 December 1835
Place of Birth: Brentwood, Coos County, New Hampshire
Date of Death: 22 March 1898
Cemetery: Arlington National Cemetery (2-1026))—Arlington, Virginia
Entered Service at: Springfield, Windsor County, Vermont
Unit: 16th Vermont Infantry
Battle or Place of Action: Gettysburg, Pennsylvania
Date of Action: 3 July 1863
Date of Issue: 8 September 1891
Citation: Rapidly assembled his regiment and charged the enemy's flank; charged front under heavy fire, and charged and destroyed a Confederate brigade, all this with new troops in their first battle.

1400 ◆ VERNAY, JAMES DAVID

Rank: Second Lieutenant (highest rank: Brevet Major)
Service: U.S. Army
Birthday: 24 December 1834
Place of Birth: Lacon, Marshall County, Illinois
Date of Death: 19 July 1918
Place of Death: Washington, D.C.
Cemetery: Arlington National Cemetery (3-4052) (MH)—Arlington, Virginia
Entered Service at: Lacon, Marshall County, Illinois
Unit: Company B, 11th Illinois Infantry
Battle or Place of Action: Vicksburg, Mississippi
Date of Action: 22 April 1863
Date of Issue: 1 April 1898
Citation: Served gallantly as a volunteer with the crew of the steamer *Horizon* that, under a heavy fire, passed the Confederate batteries.

1401 ◆ VERNEY, JAMES W.

Rank: Chief Quartermaster
Service: U.S. Navy
Birthday: 17 January 1834
Place of Birth: Bath, Sagadahoc County, Maine
Date of Death: 29 November 1902
Place of Death: Boston, Massachusetts

Cemetery: Cedar Grove Cemetery (MH)—Dorchester, Massachusetts
Entered Service at: Portland, Cumberland County, Maine
Unit: U.S.S. *Pontoosuc*
Battle or Place of Action: Fort Fisher & Wilmington, North Carolina
Date of Action: 24 December 1864—22 February 1865
G.O. Number, Date: 59, 22 June 1865
Citation: Seved as chief quartermaster on board the U.S.S. *Pontoosuc* during the capture of Fort Fisher and Wilmington, 24 December 1864 to 22 February 1865. Carrying out his duties faithfully throughout this period, Verney was recommended for gallantry and skill and for his cool courage while under fire of the enemy throughout these various actions.

1402 ◆ VIFQUAIN, VICTOR

Rank: Lieutenant Colonel (highest rank: Brevet Brigadier General)
Service: U.S. Army
Birthday: 20 May 1836
Place of Birth: Brussels, Belgium
Date of Death: 7 January 1904
Place of Death: Lincoln, Nebraska
Cemetery: Calvary Cemetery (MH)—Lincoln, Nebraska
Entered Service at: Salene County, Nebraska
Unit: 97th Illinois Infantry
Battle or Place of Action: Fort Blakely, Alabama
Date of Action: 9 April 1865
Date of Issue: 8 June 1865
Citation: Capture of flag.

1403 ◆ VON VEGESACK, ERNEST

Rank: Major & Aide-de-Camp (highest rank: Brevet Brigadier General)
Service: U.S. Army
Birthday: 18 June 1820
Place of Birth: Gotland, Sweden
Date of Death: 12 January 1903
Place of Death: Stockholm, Sweden
Cemetery: Churchyard Cemetery—Stockholm, Sweden
Entered Service at: New York, New York
Unit: U.S. Volunteers
Battle or Place of Action: Gaines' Mill, Virginia
Date of Action: 27 June 1862
Date of Issue: 23 August 1893
Citation: While voluntarily serving as aide-de-camp, successfully and advantageously charged the position of troops under fire.

1404 ◆ WAGEMAN, JOHN H.

Rank: Private (highest rank: Corporal)
Service: U.S. Army
Birthday: 22 March 1841
Place of Birth: Amelia, Clermont County, Ohio
Date of Death: 9 January 1916
Place of Death: Williamsburg, Ohio

Cemetery: Clover Cemetery—Clover, Ohio
Entered Service at: Amelia, Clermont County, Ohio
Unit: Company I, 60th Ohio Infantry
Battle or Place of Action: Petersburg, Virginia
Date of Action: 17 June 1864
Date of Issue: 27 July 1896
Citation: Remained with the command after being severely wounded until he had fired all the cartridges in his possession, when he had to be carried from the field.

1405 ◆ WAGG, MAURICE

Rank: Coxswain (highest rank: Master's Mate)
Service: U.S. Navy
Birthday: 23 July 1840
Place of Birth: Hampshire, England
Date of Death: 22 June 1926
Place of Death: London, England
Entered Service at: New York, New York
Unit: U.S.S. *Rhode Island*
Battle or Place of Action: off Cape Hatteras, North Carolina
Date of Action: 31 December 1862
G.O. Number, Date: 45, 31 December 1864
Citation: Served on board the U.S.S. *Rhode Island*, which was engaged in saving the lives of the officers and crew of the *Monitor* off Hatteras, 31 December 1862. Participating in the hazardous task of rescuing the officers and crew of the sinking *Monitor*, Wagg distinguished himself by meritorious conduct during this operation.

1406 ◆ WAGNER, JOHN W.

Rank: Corporal
Service: U.S. Army
Birthday: 1837
Place of Birth: Clear Spring, Washington County, Maryland
Date of Death: 24 August 1896
Place of Death: Boston, Massachusetts
Cemetery: Forest Hills Cemetery (PM)—Jamaica Plain, Massachusetts
Entered Service at: St. Louis, St. Louis County, Missouri
Unit: Company F, 8th Missouri Infantry
Battle or Place of Action: Vicksburg, Mississippi
Date of Action: 22 May 1863
Date of Issue: 14 December 1894
Citation: Gallantry in the charge of the "volunteer storming party."

1407 ◆ WAINWRIGHT, JOHN

Rank: First Lieutenant (highest rank: Colonel)
Service: U.S. Army
Birthday: 13 July 1839
Place of Birth: Syracuse, Onondaga County, New York
Date of Death: 15 April 1915
Place of Death: Wilmington, Delaware
Cemetery: Arlington National Cemetery (2-1061)—Arlington, Virginia

Entered Service at: West Chester, Chester County, Pennsylvania
Unit: Company F, 97th Pennsylvania Infantry
Battle or Place of Action: Fort Fisher, North Carolina
Date of Action: 15 January 1865
Date of Issue: 24 June 1890
Citation: Gallant and meritorious conduct, where, as first lieutenant, he commanded the regiment.

1408 ◆ WALKER, JAMES C.

Rank: Private (highest rank: Color Sergeant)
Service: U.S. Army
Birthday: 30 November 1843
Place of Birth: Harmony, Clark County, Ohio
Date of Death: 8 April 1923
Cemetery: Ferncliff Cemetery (MH)—Springfield, Ohio
Entered Service at: Springfield, Clark County, Ohio
Unit: Company K, 31st Ohio Infantry
Battle or Place of Action: Missionary Ridge, Tennessee
Date of Action: 25 November 1863
Date of Issue: 25 November 1895
Citation: After two color bearers had fallen, seized the flag and carried it forward, assisting in the capture of the battery. Shortly thereafter he captured the flag of the 41st Alabama and the color bearer.

1409 ◆ WALKER, MARY EDWARDS

Service: U.S. Army
Birthday: 26 November 1832
Place of Birth: Oswego County, New York
Date of Death: 21 February 1919
Cemetery: The Rural Cemetery (MH)—Oswego, New York
Entered Service at: Louisville, Jefferson County, Kentucky
Served as: Contract Acting Assistant Surgeon (Civilian)
Battle or Place of Action: Battle of Bull Run; Patent Office Hospital, Washington, D.C.; Chattanooga, Tenn.; following Battle of Chickamauga; Battle of Atlanta
Date of Action: 21 July 1861; October 1861; September 1863; September 1864
Date of Issue: 11 November 1865
Citation: *Whereas* it appears from official reports that Dr. Mary E. Walker, a graduate of medicine, "has rendered valuable service to the Government, and her efforts have been earnest and untiring in a variety of ways," and that she was assigned to duty and served as an assistant surgeon in charge of female prisoners at Louisville, Ky., upon the recommendation of Maj. Gens. Sherman and Thomas, and faithfully served as contract surgeon in the service of the United States, and has devoted herself with much patriotic zeal to the sick and wounded soldiers, both in the field and hospitals, to the detriment of her own health, and has also endured hardships as a prisoner of war four months in a Southern prison while acting as contract surgeon; and *Whereas,* by reason of her not being a commissioned officer in the military service, a brevet or honorary rank cannot, under existing laws, be conferred upon her; and *Whereas,* in the opinion of the President an honorable recognition of her services and sufferings should be made; *It is ordered,* That a testimonial thereof shall be hereby made and given to the said Dr. Mary E. Walker, and that the usual medal of honor for meritorious services be given her. Given under my hand in the city of Washington, D.C., this 11th day of November, A.D. 1865. Andrew Johnson
Notes: POW from 10 April 1864—12 August 1864, Richmond, Virginia

1410 ◆ WALL, JERRY C.

Rank: Private
Service: U.S. Army
Birthday: 1 July 1841
Place of Birth: Geneva Ontario County, New York
Date of Death: 8 April 1923
Place of Death: Dansville, New York
Cemetery: Greenmount Cemetery (MH)—Dansville, New York
Entered Service at: Milo, New York
Unit: Company B, 126th New York Infantry
Battle or Place of Action: Gettysburg, Pennsylvania
Date of Action: 3 July 1863
Date of Issue: 1 December 1864
Citation: Capture of flag.

1411 ◆ WALLER, FRANCIS A.

Rank: Corporal (highest rank: First Lieutenant)
Service: U.S. Army
Birthday: 15 August 1840
Place of Birth: Gurney, Ohio
Date of Death: 30 April 1911
Place of Death: Bentford, South Dakota
Cemetery: Walnut Mound Cemetery—DeSoto, Wisconsin
Entered Service at: DeSoto, Vernon County, Wisconsin
Unit: Company I, 6th Wisconsin Infantry
Battle or Place of Action: Gettysburg, Pennsylvania
Date of Action: 1 July 1863
Date of Issue: 1 December 1864
Citation: Capture of flag of 2d Mississippi Infantry (C.S.A.).

1412 ◆ WALLING, WILLIAM HENRY

Rank: Captain (highest rank: Brevet Lieutenant Colonel)
Service: U.S. Army
Birthday: 3 September 1830
Place of Birth: Hartford, Washington County, New York
Date of Death: 16 June 1912
Place of Death: Potsdam, New York
Cemetery: Bayside Cemetery—Potsdam, New York
Entered Service at: Folly Island, Charleston County, South Carolina
Unit: Company C, 142d New York Infantry
Battle or Place of Action: Fort Fisher, North Carolina
Date of Action: 25 December 1864
Date of Issue: 28 March 1892
Citation: During the bombardment of the fort by the fleet, captured and brought the flag of the fort, the flagstaff having been shot down.

1413 ◆ WALSH, JOHN

Rank: Corporal
Service: U.S. Army
Birthday: 4 December 1841
Place of Birth: Tipperary, Ireland
Date of Death: 25 May 1924
Place of Death: Springfield, Massachusetts
Cemetery: St. Benedict's Cemetery—Springfield, Massachusetts
Entered Service at: Springfield, Hampden County, Massachusetts
Unit: Company D, 5th New York Cavalry
Battle or Place of Action: Cedar Creek, Virginia
Date of Action: 19 October 1864
Date of Issue: 26 October 1864
Citation: Recapture of the flag of the 15th New Jersey Infantry.
Notes: POW

1414 ◆ WALTON, GEORGE WASHINGTON

Rank: Private (highest rank: Sergeant)
Service: U.S. Army
Birthday: 27 March 1844
Place of Birth: Upper Oxford Township, Chester County, Pennsylvania
Date of Death: 8 February 1920
Place of Death: Oxford, Pennsylvania
Cemetery: Oxford Cemetery (MH)—Oxford, Pennsylvania
Entered Service at: Upper Oxford Township, Chester County, Pennsylvania
Unit: Company C, 97th Pennsylvania Infantry
Battle or Place of Action: Fort Hell, Petersberg, Virginia
Date of Action: 29 August 1864
Date of Issue: 6 August 1902
Citation: Went outside the trenches, under heavy fire at short-range, and rescued a comrade who had been wounded and thrown out of the trench by an exploding shell.

1415 ◆ WAMBSGAN, MARTIN

Rank: Private (highest rank: Sergeant)
Service: U.S. Army
Birthday: 19 August 1839
Place of Birth: Nusdorof, Bavaria, Germany
Date of Death: 3 May 1911
Place of Death: Baldwinsville, New York
Cemetery: Woodlawn Cemetery (MH)—Syracuse, New York
Entered Service at: Clyde, Wayne County, New York
Unit: Company D, 90th New York Infantry
Battle or Place of Action: Cedar Creek, Virginia
Date of Action: 19 October 1864
Date of Issue: 3 November 1896
Citation: While the enemy were in close proximity, this soldier sprang forward and bore off in safety the regimental colors, the color bearer having fallen on the field of battle.

1416 ◆ WARD, JAMES

Rank: Quarter Gunner (highest rank: Captain of the Forecastle)
Service: U.S. Navy
Birthday: 1833
Place of Birth: New York, New York
Entered Service at: New York, New York
Unit: U.S.S. *Lackawanna*
Battle or Place of Action: Fort Morgan, Mobile Bay, Alabama
Date of Action: 5 August 1864
G.O. Number, Date: 45, 31 December 1864
Citation: Served as gunner on board the U.S.S. *Lackawanna* during successful attacks against Fort Morgan, rebel gunboats, and the rebel ram *Tennessee* in Mobile Bay, 5 August 1864. Although wounded and ordered below, Ward refused to go, but rendered aid at one of the guns when the crew was disabled. He subsequently remained in the chains, heaving the lead, until nearly caught in the collision with the ram *Tennessee*. He continued to serve bravely throughout the action which resulted in the capture of the prize ram *Tennessee* and in the damaging and destruction of Fort Morgan.

1417 ◆ WARD, NELSON W.

Rank: Private (highest rank: Quartermaster Sergeant)
Service: U.S. Army
Birthday: 20 November 1837
Place of Birth: Madison Township, Columbiana County, Ohio
Date of Death: 5 February 1929
Place of Death: Long Beach, California
Cemetery: Sunnyside Cemetery—Long Beach, California
Entered Service at: Rutland, Meigs County, Ohio
Unit: Company M, 11th Pennsylvania Cavalry
Battle or Place of Action: Staunton River Bridge, Virginia
Date of Action: 25 June 1864
Date of Issue: 10 September 1897
Citation: Voluntarily took part in the charge; went alone in the front of his regiment under a heavy fire to secure the body of his captain, who had been killed in the action.

1418 ◆ WARD, THOMAS J.

Rank: Private (highest rank: Sergeant Major)
Service: U.S. Army
Birthday: 18 August 1837
Place of Birth: Romney, Hampshire County, West Virginia
Date of Death: 30 March 1924
Place of Death: Anaconda, Montana
Cemetery: Upper Hill Cemetery (MH)—Anaconda, Montana
Entered Service at: Decatur, Macon County, Illinois
Unit: Company C, 116th Illinois Infantry
Battle or Place of Action: Vicksburg, Mississippi
Date of Action: 22 May 1863
Date of Issue: 27 July 1894

Citation: Gallantry in the charge of the "volunteer storming party."

1419 ◆ WARD, WILLIAM HENRY

Rank: Captain
Service: U.S. Army
Birthday: 9 December 1840
Place of Birth: Adrian, Lenawee County, Michigan
Date of Death: 11 April 1927
Place of Death: Kansas City, Kansas
Cemetery: Highland Park Cemetery (MH)—Kansas City, Kansas
Entered Service at: Adrian, Lenawee County, Michigan
Unit: Company B, 47th Ohio Infantry
Battle or Place of Action: Vicksburg, Mississippi
Date of Action: 3 May 1863
Date of Issue: 2 January 1895
Citation: Voluntarily commanded the expedition which, under cover of darkness, attempted to run the enemy's batteries.

1420 ◆ WARDEN, JOHN

Rank: Corporal (highest rank: First Lieutenant)
Service: U.S. Army
Birthday: 11 June 1841
Place of Birth: Cook County, Illinois
Date of Death: 2 July 1906
Place of Death: Sumner, Washington
Cemetery: Orting Cemetery—Orting, Washington
Entered Service at: Lemont, Du Page County, Illinois
Unit: Company E, 55th Illinois Infantry
tle or Place of Action: Vicksburg, Mississippi
Date of Action: 22 May 1863
Date of Issue: 2 September 1893
Citation: Gallantry in the charge of the "volunteer storming party."

1421 ◆ WARFEL, HENRY CLAY

Rank: Private
Service: U.S. Army
Birthday: 14 September 1844
Place of Birth: Mill Creek, Huntingdon County, Pennsylvania
Date of Death: 17 June 1923
Place of Death: Philipsburg, Pennsylvania
Cemetery: Philipsburg Cemetery (MH)—Philipsburg, Pennsylvania
Entered Service at: Monocacy Junction, Maryland
Unit: Company A, 1st Pennsylvania Cavalry
Battle or Place of Action: Paine's Crossroads, Virginia
Date of Action: 5 April 1865
Date of Issue: 3 May 1865
Citation: Capture of Virginia state colors.

1422 ◆ WARREN, DAVID

Rank: Coxswain
Service: U.S. Navy

Birthday: 1836
Place of Birth: Glasgow, Scotland
Date of Death: 2 August 1900
Place of Death: Hampton, Virginia
Cemetery: Hampton National Cemetery (C-7972) (MH)—Hampton, Virginia
Entered Service at: New York, New York
Unit: U.S.S. *Monticello*
Battle or Place of Action: Wilmington, North Carolina
Date of Action: 23-25 June 1864
G.O. Number, Date: 45, 31 December 1864
Citation: Served as coxswain on board the U.S.S. *Monticello* during the reconnaissance of the harbor and water defenses of Wilmington, N.C., 23 to 25 June 1864. Taking part in a reconnaissance of the enemy defenses which lasted two days and nights, Warren courageously carried out his duties during this action which resulted in the capture of a mail carrier and mail, the cutting of the telegraph wire, and the capture of a large group of prisoners. Although in immediate danger from the enemy, Warren showed gallantry and coolness throughout this action which resulted in the gaining of much vital information of the rebel defenses.

1423 ◆ WARREN, FRANCIS EMROY

Rank: Corporal
Service: U.S. Army
Birthday: 20 June 1844
Place of Birth: Hinsdale, Berkshire County, Massachusetts
Date of Death: 24 November 1929
Place of Death: Washington, D.C.
Cemetery: Lake View Cemetery (MH)—Cheyenne, Wyoming
Entered Service at: Hinsdale, Berkshire County, Massachusetts
Unit: Company C, 49th Massachusetts Infantry
Battle or Place of Action: Port Hudson, Louisiana
Date of Action: 27 May 1863
Date of Issue: 30 September 1893
Citation: Volunteered in response to a call, and took part in the movement that was made upon the enemy's works under a heavy fire therefrom in advance of the general assault.

1424 ◆ WEBB, ALEXANDER STEWART

Rank: Brigadier General (highest rank: Major General U.S.A.)
Service: U.S. Army
Birthday: 15 February 1835
Place of Birth: New York, New York
Date of Death: 12 February 1911
Place of Death: Riverdale, New York
Cemetery: U.S. Military Academy Cemetery (M-18)—West Point, New York
Entered Service at: New York, New York
Unit: U.S. Volunteers
Battle or Place of Action: Gettysburg, Pennsylvania
Date of Action: 3 July 1863
Date of Issue: 28 September 1891

Citation: Distinguished personal gallantry in leading his men forward at a critical period in the contest.

1425 ◆ WEBB, JAMES W.

Rank: Private (highest rank: Brevet Captain)
Service: U.S. Army
Birthday: 2 September 1841
Place of Birth: Brooklyn, Kings County, New York
Date of Death: 7 June 1915
Place of Death: Brooklyn, New York
Cemetery: Cypress Hills Cemetery (2-7410) (MH)—Brooklyn, New York
Entered Service at: New York, New York
Unit: Company F, 5th New York Infantry
Battle or Place of Action: Bull Run, Virginia
Date of Action: 30 August 1862
Date of Issue: 17 September 1897
Citation: Under heavy fire voluntarily carried information to a battery commander that enabled him to save his guns from capture. Was severely wounded, but refused to go to the hospital and participated in the remainder of the campaign.

1426 ◆ WEBBER, ALASON P.

True Name: Webber, Alanson P.
Rank: Musician (highest rank: Principal Musician)
Service: U.S. Army
Birthday: 16 March 1828
Place of Birth: Greene County, New York
Date of Death: 27 July 1902
Cemetery: Saratoga Cemetery—Henry, Illinois
Entered Service at: Chillicothe, Ross County, Ohio
Unit: 86th Illinois Infantry
Battle or Place of Action: Kenesaw Mountain, Georgia
Date of Action: 27 June 1864
Date of Issue: 22 June 1896
Citation: Voluntarily joined in a charge against the enemy, which was repulsed, and by his rapid firing in the face of the enemy enabled many of the wounded to return to the Federal lines; with others, held the advance of the enemy while temporary works were being constructed.

1427 ◆ WEBSTER, HENRY S.

Rank: Landsman
Service: U.S. Navy
Birthday: 7 January 1845
Place of Birth: Stockholm, New York
Date of Death: 2 July 1910
Place of Death: Brattleboro, Vermont
Cemetery: Cedar Grove Cemetery—Fairhaven, Vermont
Entered Service at: Brooklyn, Kings County, New York
Unit: U.S.S. *Susquehanna*
Battle or Place of Action: Fort Fisher, North Carolina
Date of Action: 15 January 1865
G.O. Number, Date: 59, 22 June 1865
Citation: On board the U.S.S. *Susquehanna* during the assault on Fort Fisher, 15 January 1865. When enemy fire halted the attempt by his landing party to enter the fort and

more than two-thirds of the men fell back along the open beach, Webster voluntarily remained with one of his wounded officers, under fire, until aid could be obtained to bring him to the rear.

1428 ◆ WEEKS, CHARLES H.

Rank: Captain of the Foretop
Service: U.S. Navy
Birthday: 1837
Place of Birth: New Jersey
Entered Service at: New Jersey
Unit: U.S.S. *Montauk*
Battle or Place of Action: off Port Royal, South Carolina
Date of Action: 21 September 1864
G.O. Number, Date: 84, 3 October 1867
Citation: Served as captain of the foretop on board the U.S.S. *Montauk*, 21 September 1864. During the night of 21 September, when fire was discovered in the magazine light-room of that vessel, causing a panic and demoralizing the crew, Weeks, notwithstanding the cry of "fire in the magazine," displayed great presence of mind and rendered valuable service in extinguishing the flames which were imperiling the ship and the men on board.

1429 ◆ WEEKS, JOHN HENRY

Rank: Private
Service: U.S. Army
Birthday: 15 March 1845
Place of Birth: Hampton, Windham County, Connecticut
Date of Death: 10 March 1911
Cemetery: Hartwick Seminary Cemetery (MH)—Hartwick Seminary, New York
Entered Service at: Hartwick Seminary, Oswego County, New York
Unit: Company H, 152d New York Infantry
Battle or Place of Action: Spotsylvania, Virginia
Date of Action: 12 May 1864
Date of Issue: 1 December 1864
Citation: Capture of flag and color bearer using an empty cocked rifle while outnumbered by five or six.

1430 ◆ WEIR, HENRY CARY

Rank: Captain & Assistant Adjutant General (highest rank: Brevet Lieutenant Colonel)
Service: U.S. Army
Birthday: 22 August 1840
Place of Birth: West Point, Orange County, New York
Date of Death: 22 April 1927
Place of Death: Warwick, New York
Cemetery: The Green Wood Cemetery—Brooklyn, New York
Entered Service at: Bolivar, West Virginia
Unit: U.S. Volunteers
Battle or Place of Action: St. Mary's Church, Virginia
Date of Action: 24 June 1864
Date of Issue: 18 May 1899
Citation: The division being hard-pressed and falling back,

this officer dismounted, gave his horse to a wounded officer, and thus enabled him to escape. Afterwards, on foot, Capt. Weir rallied and took command of some stragglers and helped to repel the last charge of the enemy.

1431 ◆ WELCH, GEORGE W.

Rank: Private
Service: U.S. Army
Place of Birth: Brown County, Iowa
Entered Service at: Keokuk, Lee County, Iowa
Unit: Company A, 11th Missouri Infantry
Battle or Place of Action: Nashville, Tennessee
Date of Action: 16 December 1864
Date of Issue: 24 February 1865
Citation: Captured the flag of the 13th Alabama Infantry (C.S.A.).

1432 ◆ WELCH, RICHARD

Rank: Corporal (highest rank: Sergeant)
Service: U.S. Army
Birthday: 1828
Place of Birth: Ireland
Date of Death: 13 March 1894
Place of Death: Williamstown, Massachusetts
Cemetery: Eastlawn Cemetery (MH)—Williamstown, Massachusetts
Entered Service at: Williamstown, Berkshire County, Massachusetts
Unit: Company E, 37th Massachusetts Infantry
Battle or Place of Action: Petersburg, Virginia
Date of Action: 2 April 1865
Date of Issue: 10 May 1865
Citation: Capture of flag.

1433 ◆ WELCH, STEPHEN

Rank: Sergeant (highest rank: Captain)
Service: U.S. Army
Birthday: 14 June 1824
Place of Birth: Groton, Tompkins County, New York
Date of Death: 30 March 1906
Cemetery: Allegany Cemetery—Allegany, New York
Entered Service at: Allegany, Cattaraugus County, New York
Unit: Company C, 154th New York Infantry
Battle or Place of Action: Dug Gap, Georgia
Date of Action: 8 May 1864
Date of Issue: 13 April 1894
Citation: Risked his life in rescuing a wounded comrade under fire of the enemy.

1434 ◆ *WELLS, HENRY S.

Rank: Private
Service: U.S. Army
Birthday: 1842
Date of Death: 27 October 1864
Place of Death: Fair Oaks, Virginia

Entered Service at: Phelps, Ontario County, New York
Unit: Company C, 148th New York Infantry
Battle or Place of Action: Chapin's Farm, Virginia
Date of Action: 29 September 1864
Date of Issue: 6 April 1865
Citation: With two comrades, took position in advance of the skirmish line, within short distance of the enemy's gunners, and drove them from their guns.
Notes: POW

1435 ◆ WELLS, THOMAS MCCOY

Rank: Chief Bugler (highest rank: First Lieutenant)
Service: U.S. Army
Birthday: 1841
Place of Birth: Ather, Ireland
Date of Death: 5 February 1901
Place of Death: Canton, New York
Cemetery: East Dekalb Cemetery—Dekalb, New York
Entered Service at: DeKalb, St. Lawrence County, New York
Unit: 6th New York Cavalry
Battle or Place of Action: Cedar Creek, Virginia
Date of Action: 19 October 1864
Date of Issue: 26 October 1864
Citation: Capture of colors of 44th Georgia Infantry (C.S.A.).

1436 ◆ WELLS, WILLIAM

Rank: Quartermaster
Service: U.S. Navy
Birthday: 1832
Place of Birth: Germany
Entered Service at: New York, New York
Unit: U.S.S. *Richmond*
Battle or Place of Action: Fort Morgan, Mobile Bay, Alabama
Date of Action: 5 August 1864
G.O. Number, Date: 45, 31 December 1864
Place of Presentation: Lisbon, on board the U.S.S. *Colorado*
Citation: As landsman and lookout on board the U.S.S. *Richmond* during action against rebel forts and gunboats and with the ram *Tennessee* in Mobile Bay, 5 August 1864. Despite damage to his ship and the loss of several men on board as enemy fire raked her decks, Wells performed his duties with skill and courage throughout a furious two-hour battle which resulted in the surrender of the rebel ram *Tennessee* and in the damaging and destruction of batteries at Fort Morgan.

1437 ◆ WELLS, WILLIAM

Rank: Major (highest rank: Brevet Major General)
Service: U.S. Army
Birthday: 14 December 1837
Place of Birth: Waterbury, Washington County, Vermont
Date of Death: 29 April 1892

Place of Death: New York, New York
Cemetery: Lakeview Cemetery—Burlington, Vermont
Entered Service at: Waterbury, Washington County, Vermont
Unit: 2d Battalion, 1st Vermont Cavalry
Battle or Place of Action: Gettysburg, Pennsylvania
Date of Action: 3 July 1863
Date of Issue: 8 September 1891
Citation: Led the second battalion of his regiment in a daring charge.
Notes: POW

1438 ◆ WELSH, EDWARD

Rank: Private (highest rank: Sergeant)
Service: U.S. Army
Birthday: 3 January 1843
Place of Birth: Ireland
Date of Death: 1 February 1929
Place of Death: Soldier's Home, Washington, D.C.
Cemetery: Mount Olivet Cemetery—Washington, D.C.
Entered Service at: Cincinnati, Hamilton County, Ohio
Unit: Company D, 54th Ohio Infantry
Battle or Place of Action: Vicksburg, Mississippi
Date of Action: 22 May 1863
Date of Issue: 11 May 1894
Citation: Gallantry in the charge of the "volunteer storming party."

1439 ◆ WELSH, JAMES

Rank: Private
Service: U.S. Army
Birthday: 11 May 1846
Place of Birth: Ireland
Date of Death: 17 December 1916
Place of Death: Elizabeth City, Virginia
Entered Service at: Slatersville, Providence County, Rhode Island
Unit: Company E, 4th Rhode Island Infantry
Battle or Place of Action: Petersburg, Virginia
Date of Action: 30 July 1864
Date of Issue: 3 June 1905
Citation: Bore off the regimental colors after the color sergeant had been wounded and the color corporal bearing the colors killed, thereby saving the colors from capture.

1440 ◆ WESTERHOLD, WILLIAM

Rank: Sergeant (highest rank: First Lieutenant)
Service: U.S. Army
Birthday: 21 January 1836
Place of Birth: Binde, Prussia
Date of Death: 12 May 1910
Place of Death: New York, New York
Entered Service at: New York, New York
Unit: Company G, 52d New York Infantry
Battle or Place of Action: Spotsylvania, Virginia
Date of Action: 12 May 1864
Date of Issue: 1 December 1864

Citation: Capture of flag of 23d Virginia Infantry (C.S.A.) and its bearer.

1441 ◆ WESTON, JOHN FRANCIS

Rank: Major (highest rank: Major General)
Service: U.S. Army
Birthday: 13 November 1845
Place of Birth: Louisville, Jefferson County, Kentucky
Date of Death: 3 August 1917
Place of Death: Briarcliff Manor, New York
Cemetery: Arlington National Cemetery (2-856)—Arlington, Virginia
Entered Service at: Camp Anderson, Kentucky
Unit: 4th Kentucky Cavalry
Battle or Place of Action: Wetumpka, Alabama
Date of Action: 13 April 1865
Date of Issue: 9 April 1898
Citation: This officer, with a small detachment, while en route to destroy steamboats loaded with supplies for the enemy, was stopped by an unfordable river, but with five of his men swam the river, captured two leaky canoes, and ferried his men across. He then encountered and defeated the enemy, and on reaching Wetumpka found the steamers anchored in midstream. By a ruse obtained possession of a boat, with which he reached the steamers and demanded and received their surrender.

1442 ◆ WHEATON, LOYD

Rank: Lieutenant Colonel (highest rank: Major General)
Service: U.S. Army
Birthday: 15 July 1838
Place of Birth: Penfield, Michigan
Date of Death: 17 September 1918
Cemetery: Greenwood Cemetery—Rockford, Illinois
Entered Service at: Peoria, Peoria County, Illinois
Unit: 8th Illinois Infantry
Battle or Place of Action: Fort Blakely, Alabama
Date of Action: 9 April 1865
Date of Issue: 16 January 1894
Citation: Led the right wing of his regiment, and, springing through an embrasure, was the first to enter the enemy's works, against a strong fire of artillery and infantry.

1443 ◆ WHEELER, DANIEL DAVIS

Rank: First Lieutenant (highest rank: Brigadier General Ret.)
Service: U.S. Army
Birthday: 12 July 1841
Place of Birth: Cavendish, Windsor County, Vermont
Date of Death: 27 July 1916
Place of Death: Fredericksburg, Virginia
Cemetery: Fredericksburg City Cemetery—Fredericksburg, Virginia
Entered Service at: Cavendish, Windsor County, Vermont
Unit: Company G, 4th Vermont Infantry
Battle or Place of Action: Salem Heights, Virginia

Date of Action: 3 May 1863
Date of Issue: 28 March 1892
Citation: Distinguished bravery in action where he was wounded and had a horse shot from under him.

1444 ◆ WHEELER, HENRY W.

Rank: Private (highest rank: Brevet Captain, U.S. Volunteers)
Service: U.S. Army
Birthday: 23 September 1841
Place of Birth: Fort Smith, Sebastian County, Arkansas
Date of Death: 18 April 1904
Cemetery: Arlington National Cemetery (3-1496)—Arlington, Virginia
Entered Service at: Bangor, Penobscot County, Maine
Unit: Company A, 2d Maine Infantry
Battle or Place of Action: Bull Run, Virginia
Date of Action: 21 July 1861
Date of Issue: 5 April 1898
Citation: Voluntarily accompanied his commanding officer and assisted in removing the dead and wounded from the field under a heavy fire of artillery and musketry.

1445 ◆ WHERRY, WILLIAM MACKY

Rank: First Lieutenant (highest rank: Brigadier General USA)
Service: U.S. Army
Birthday: 13 September 1836
Place of Birth: St. Louis, St. Louis County, Missouri
Date of Death: 3 November 1918
Place of Death: Cincinnati, Ohio
Cemetery: Bellefontaine Cemetery—St. Louis, Missouri
Entered Service at: St. Louis, St. Louis County, Missouri
Unit: Company D, 3d U.S. Reserve Missouri Infantry
Battle or Place of Action: Wilson's Creek, Missouri
Date of Action: 10 August 1861
Date of Issue: 30 October 1895
Citation: Displayed conspicuous coolness and heroism in rallying troops that were recoiling under heavy fire.

1446 ◆ WHITAKER, EDWARD WASHBURN

Rank: Captain (highest rank: Brigadier General, U.S. Volunteers)
Service: U.S. Army
Birthday: 15 June 1841
Place of Birth: Killingly, Connecticut
Date of Death: 30 July 1922
Place of Death: Washington, D.C.
Cemetery: Arlington National Cemetery (3-1324)—Arlington, Virginia
Entered Service at: Hartford, Hartford County, Connecticut
Unit: Company E, 1st Connecticut Cavalry
Battle or Place of Action: Reams' Station, Virginia
Date of Action: 29 June 1864
Date of Issue: 2 April 1898
Citation: While acting as an aide, voluntarily carried dispatches from the commanding general to Gen. Meade, forcing his way with a single troop of cavalry, through an infantry division of the enemy in the most distinguished manner, though he lost half his escort.

1447 ◆ WHITE, ADAM

Rank: Corporal
Service: U.S. Army
Birthday: 21 December 1823
Place of Birth: Switzerland
Date of Death: 19 May 1895
Place of Death: Tyner, West Virginia
Cemetery: Wadesville Cemetery—Wadesville, West Virginia
Entered Service at: Parkersburg, Wood County, West Virginia
Unit: Company G, 11th West Virginia Infantry
Battle or Place of Action: Hatcher's Run, Virginia
Date of Action: 2 April 1865
Date of Issue: 13 June 1865
Citation: Capture of flag.

1448 ◆ WHITE, JOHN HENRY

Rank: Private
Service: U.S. Army
Birthday: 1 March 1835
Place of Birth: Philadelphia, Philadelphia County, Pennsylvania
Date of Death: 27 April 1912
Place of Death: Darby, Pennsylvania
Entered Service at: Philadelphia, Philadelphia County, Pennsylvania
Unit: Company A, 90th Pennsylvania Infantry
Battle or Place of Action: Rappahannock Station, Virginia
Date of Action: 23 August 1862
Date of Issue: 5 May 1900
Citation: At the imminent risk of his life, crawled to a nearby spring within the enemy's range and, exposed to constant fire, filled a large number of canteens, and returned in safety to the relief of his comrades who were suffering from want of water.
Notes: POW

1449 ◆ WHITE, JOSEPH

Rank: Coxswain
Service: U.S. Navy
Birthday: 1840
Place of Birth: Washington, D.C.
Entered Service at: Philadelphia, Philadelphia County, Pennsylvania
Unit: U.S.S. *New Ironsides*
Battle or Place of Action: Fort Fisher, North Carolina
Date of Action: December 1864 & January 1865
G.O. Number, Date: 59, 22 June 1865
Citation: White served on board the U.S.S. *New Ironsides* during action in several attacks on Fort Fisher, 24 and 25 December 1864; and 13, 14 and 15 January 1865. The ship steamed in and took the lead in the ironclad division close inshore and immediately opened its starboard battery in a barrage of well-directed fire to cause several fires and explosions and dismount several guns during the first two days of fight-

ing. Taken under fire as she steamed into position on 13 January, the *New Ironsides* fought all day and took on ammunition at night, despite severe weather conditions. When the enemy came out of their bombproofs to defend the fort against the storming party, the ship's battery disabled nearly every gun on the fort facing the shore before the cease-fire order was given by the flagship.

1450 ◆ WHITE, PATRICK H.

Rank: Captain
Service: U.S. Army
Birthday: 1 June 1832
Place of Birth: County Sligo, Ireland
Date of Death: 25 November 1915
Place of Death: Albany, New York
Cemetery: St. Agnes Cemetery—Menands, New York
Entered Service at: Chicago, Cook County, Illinois
Unit: Chicago Mercantile Battery, Illinois Light Artillery
Battle or Place of Action: Vicksburg, Mississippi
Date of Action: 22 May 1863
Date of Issue: 15 January 1895
Citation: Carried with others by hand a cannon up to and fired it through an embrasure of the enemy's works.
Notes: POW

1451 ◆ WHITEHEAD, JOHN MILTON

Rank: Chaplain
Service: U.S. Army
Birthday: 6 March 1823
Place of Birth: Wayne County, Indiana
Date of Death: 8 March 1909
Place of Death: Topeka, Kansas
Cemetery: Topeka Cemetery (MH)—Topeka, Kansas
Entered Service at: Westville, La Porte County, Indiana
Unit: 15th Indiana Infantry
Battle or Place of Action: Stone River, Tennessee
Date of Action: 31 December 1862
Date of Issue: 4 April 1898
Citation: Went to the front during a desperate contest and unaided carried to the rear several wounded and helpless soldiers.

1452 ◆ WHITFIELD, DANIEL

Rank: Quartermaster
Service: U.S. Navy
Birthday: 1821
Place of Birth: Newark, Essex County, New Jersey
Entered Service at: New Jersey
Unit: U.S.S. *Lackawanna*
Battle or Place of Action: Fort Morgan, Mobile Bay, Alabama
Date of Action: 5 August 1864
G.O. Number, Date: 45, 31 December 1864
Citation: Serving as quartermaster on board the U.S.S. *Lackawanna* during successful attacks against Fort Morgan, rebel gunboats, and the rebel ram *Tennessee* in Mobile Bay, 5 August 1864. Acting as captain of a gun, Whitfield coolly stood by his gun, holding on to the lock string, and waited alongside the rebel ram *Tennessee* until able to fire the shot

that entered her port. Whitfield courageously carried out his duties during the prolonged action which resulted in the capture of the prize ram *Tennessee* and in the damaging and destruction of Fort Morgan.

1453 ◆ WHITMAN, FRANK M.

Rank: Private (highest rank: Sergeant)
Service: U.S. Army
Birthday: 30 September 1838
Place of Birth: Woodstock, Maine
Date of Death: 9 July 1918
Place of Death: Boston, Massachusetts
Cemetery: Riverview Cemetery—Groveland, Massachusetts
Entered Service at: Ayersville, Massachusetts
Unit: Company G, 35th Massachusetts Infantry
Battle or Place of Action: Antietam, Maryland
Date of Action: 17 September 1862
Date of Issue: 21 February 1874
Citation: Was among the last to leave the field at Antietam and was instrumental in saving the lives of several of his comrades at the imminent risk of his own. At Spotsylvania was foremost in line in the assault, where he lost a leg.

1454 ◆ WHITMORE, JOHN W.

Rank: Private
Service: U.S. Army
Birthday: 3 July 1844
Place of Birth: Brown County, Illinois
Date of Death: 26 February 1913
Place of Death: New London, Iowa
Cemetery: Shiner Cemetery—New London, Iowa
Entered Service at: Camden, Schuyler County, Illinois
Unit: Company F, 119th Illinois Infantry
Battle or Place of Action: Fort Blakely, Alabama
Date of Action: 9 April 1865
Date of Issue: 8 June 1865
Citation: Capture of flag.

1455 ◆ WHITNEY, WILLIAM G.

Rank: Sergeant (highest rank: Captain)
Service: U.S. Army
Birthday: 13 December 1840
Place of Birth: Allen, Hillsdale County, Michigan
Date of Death: 7 May 1915
Place of Death: Allen, Michigan
Cemetery: Allen Cemetery—Allen, Michigan
Entered Service at: Quincy, Branch County, Michigan
Unit: Company B, 11th Michigan Infantry
Battle or Place of Action: Chickamauga, Georgia
Date of Action: 20 September 1863
Date of Issue: 21 October 1895
Citation: As the enemy were about to charge, this officer went outside the temporary Union works among the dead and wounded enemy and at great exposure to himself cut off and removed their cartridge boxes, bringing the same within the Union lines, the ammunition being used with good effect in again repulsing the attack.

1456 ◆ WHITTIER, EDWARD NEWTON

Rank: First Lieutenant (highest rank: Captain)
Service: U.S. Army
Birthday: 1 July 1840
Place of Birth: Portland, Cumberland County, Maine
Date of Death: 14 June 1902
Place of Death: Boston, Massachusetts
Cemetery: Pierce Family Grave Yard (MH)—Baldwin, Maine
Entered Service at: Gorham, Cumberland County, Maine
Unit: 5th Battery, Maine Light Artillery
Battle or Place of Action: Fisher's Hill, Virginia
Date of Action: 22 September 1864
Date of Issue: 13 January 1892
Citation: While acting as assistant adjutant general, Artillery Brigade, 6th Army Corps, went over the enemy's works, mounted, with the assaulting column, to gain quicker possession of the guns and to turn them upon the enemy.

1457 ◆ WIDICK, ANDREW J.

Rank: Private
Service: U.S. Army
Birthday: 27 March 1842
Place of Birth: Macon County, Illinois
Date of Death: 24 January 1929
Place of Death: Bertrand, Nebraska
Cemetery: Bertrand Cemetery (MH)—Bertrand, Nebraska
Entered Service at: Decatur, Macon County, Illinois
Unit: Company B, 116th Illinois Infantry
Battle or Place of Action: Vicksburg, Mississippi
Date of Action: 22 May 1863
Date of Issue: 11 August 1894
Citation: Gallantry in the charge of the "volunteer storming party."

1458 ◆ WILCOX, FRANKLIN L.

Rank: Ordinary Seaman
Service: U.S. Navy
Birthday: November 1830
Place of Birth: Paris, Oneida County, New York
Date of Death: 16 November 1898
Place of Death: Grand Rapids (Soldier's Home), Michigan
Cemetery: Michigan Veterans Cemetery—Grand Rapids, Michigan
Entered Service at: New York
Unit: U.S.S. *Minnesota*
Battle or Place of Action: Fort Fisher, North Carolina
Date of Action: 15 January 1865
G.O. Number, Date: 59, 22 June 1865
Citation: On board the U.S.S. *Minnesota* in action during the assault on Fort Fisher, 15 January 1865. Landing on the beach with the assaulting party from his ship, Wilcox advanced to the top of the sandhill and partly through the breach in the palisades, despite enemy fire which killed and wounded many officers and men. When more than two-thirds of the men became seized with panic and retreated on the run, he remained with the party until dark when it came safely away, bringing its wounded, its arms and its colors.

1459 ◆ WILCOX, WILLIAM H.

Rank: Sergeant
Service: U.S. Army
Birthday: 12 November 1840
Place of Birth: Lempster, Sullivan County, New Hampshire
Date of Death: 27 October 1913
Place of Death: Kalamazoo, Michigan
Cemetery: Lake View Cemetery—South Haven, Michigan
Entered Service at: Lempster, Sullivan County, New Hampshire
Unit: Company G, 9th New Hampshire Infantry
Battle or Place of Action: Spotsylvania, Virginia
Date of Action: 12 May 1864
Date of Issue: 28 July 1896
Citation: Took command of his company, deployed as skirmishers, after the officers in the command of the skirmish line had both been wounded, conducting himself gallantly; afterwards, becoming separated from command, he asked and obtained permission to fight in another company.

1460 ◆ *WILEY, JAMES

Rank: Sergeant
Service: U.S. Army
Birthday: 1835
Place of Birth: Ohio
Date of Death: 7 February 1865
Place of Death: Andersonville, Georgia
Cemetery: Andersonville National Historical Site (H-10607) (MH)—Andersonville, Georgia
Entered Service at: Bellville, Richland County, Ohio
Unit: Company B, 59th New York Infantry
Battle or Place of Action: Gettysburg, Pennsylvania
Date of Action: 3 July 1863
Date of Issue: 1 December 1864
Citation: Capture of flag of a Georgia regiment.

1461 ◆ WILHELM, GEORGE

Rank: Captain (highest rank: Lieutenant Colonel)
Service: U.S. Army
Birthday: 2 April 1829
Place of Birth: Scioto County, Ohio
Date of Death: 20 August 1920
Place of Death: Dayton, Ohio
Cemetery: Greenville Cemetery—Greenville, Mississippi
Entered Service at: Lancaster, Fairfield County, Ohio
Unit: Company F, 56th Ohio Infantry
Battle or Place of Action: Champion Hill or Baker's Creek, Mississippi
Date of Action: 16 May 1863
Date of Issue: 17 November 1887
Citation: Having been badly wounded in the breast and captured, he made a prisoner of his captor and brought him into camp.

1462 ◆ WILKES, HENRY

Rank: Landsman
Service: U.S. Navy

Birthday: 1845
Place of Birth: New York, New York
Date of Death: 3 March 1888
Place of Death: Rensselaer, New York
Cemetery: Beverwyck Cemetery (MH)—Rensselaer, New York
Entered Service at: New York, New York
Unit: U.S. Picket Boat No. 1
Battle or Place of Action: Plymouth, North Carolina
Date of Action: 27 October 1864
G.O. Number, Date: 45, 31 December 1864
Citation: Wilkes served on board the U.S. Picket Boat No. 1 in action, 27 October 1864, against the Confederate ram, *Albemarle*, which had resisted repeated attacks by our steamers and had kept a large force of vessels employed in watching her. The picket boat, equipped with a spar torpedo, succeeded in passing the enemy pickets within 20 yards without being discovered and then made for the *Albemarle* under a full head of steam. Immediately taken under fire by the ram, the small boat plunged on, jumped the log boom which encircled the target and exploded its torpedo under the port bow of the ram. The picket boat was destroyed by enemy fire and almost the entire crew taken prisoner or lost.
Notes: POW

1463 ◆ WILKES, PERRY

Rank: Pilot
Service: U.S. Navy
Birthday: 6 June 1830
Place of Birth: Indiana
Date of Death: 19 March 1889
Place of Death: Louisville, Kentucky
Cemetery: Cave Hill Cemetery South One-Half-866 Section P, (MH)—Louisville, Kentucky
Entered Service at: Jeffersonville, Clark County, Indiana
Unit: U.S.S. *Signal*
Battle or Place of Action: Red River, Louisiana
Date of Action: 5 May 1864
G.O. Number, Date: 45, 31 December 1864
Citation: Served as pilot on board the U.S.S. *Signal*, Red River, 5 May 1864. Proceeding up the Red River, the U.S.S. *Signal* engaged a large force of enemy field batteries and sharpshooters, returning their fire until the ship was totally disabled, at which time the white flag was ordered raised. Acting as pilot throughout the battle, Wilkes stood by his wheel until it was disabled in his hands by a bursting enemy shell.

1464 ◆ WILKINS, LEANDER A.

Rank: Sergeant
Service: U.S. Army
Place of Birth: Lancaster, Coos County, New Hampshire
Entered Service at: Northumberland, New Hampshire
Unit: Company H, 9th New Hampshire Infantry
Battle or Place of Action: Petersburg, Virginia
Date of Action: 30 July 1864
Date of Issue: 1 December 1864
Citation: Recaptured the colors of 21st Massachusetts Infantry in a hand-to-hand encounter.

1465 ◆ WILLCOX, ORLANDO BOLIVAR

Rank: Colonel (highest rank: Major General)
Service: U.S. Army
Birthday: 16 April 1823
Place of Birth: Detroit, Wayne County, Michigan
Date of Death: 10 May 1907
Place of Death: Ontario, Canada
Cemetery: Arlington National Cemetery (1-18)—Arlington, Virginia
Entered Service at: Detroit, Wayne County, Michigan
Unit: 1st Michigan Infantry
Battle or Place of Action: Bull Run, Virginia
Date of Action: 21 July 1861
Date of Issue: 2 March 1895
Citation: Led repeated charges until wounded and taken prisoner.
Notes: POW

1466 ◆ WILLIAMS, ANTHONY

Rank: Sailmaker's Mate
Service: U.S. Navy
Birthday: 1822
Place of Birth: Plymouth, Plymouth County, Massachusetts
Entered Service at: Portsmouth, Maine
Unit: U.S.S. *Pontoosuc*
Battle or Place of Action: Fort Fisher and Wilmington, North Carolina
Date of Action: 24 December 1864
G.O. Number, Date: 59, 22 June 1865
Citation: Served as sailmaker's mate on board the U.S.S. *Pontoosuc* during the capture of Fort Fisher and Wilmington, 24 December 1864 to 22 February 1865. Carrying out his duties faithfully throughout this period, Williams was recommended for gallantry and skill and for his cool courage while under the fire of the enemy throughout these various actions.

1467 ◆ WILLIAMS, AUGUSTUS

Rank: Seaman
Service: U.S. Navy
Birthday: 1842
Place of Birth: Kristiansand, Norway
Entered Service at: Massachusetts
Unit: U.S.S. *Santiago de Cuba*
Battle or Place of Action: Fort Fisher, North Carolina
Date of Action: 15 January 1865
G.O. Number, Date: 59, 22 June 1865
Citation: On board the U.S.S. *Santiago de Cuba* during the assault by the fleet on Fort Fisher, 15 January 1865. When the landing party to which he was attached charged on the fort with a cheer, and with determination to plant their colors on the ramparts, Williams remained steadfast when they reached the foot of the fort and more than two-thirds of the marines and sailors fell back in panic. Taking cover when the enemy concentrated his fire on the remainder of the group, he alone remained with his executive officer, subsequently withdrawing from the field after dark.

1468 ◆ WILLIAMS, ELWOOD N.

Rank: Private
Service: U.S. Army
Birthday: 11 November 1842
Place of Birth: Philadelphia, Philadelphia County, Pennsylvania
Date of Death: 8 March 1921
Place of Death: Philadelphia, Pennsylvania
Entered Service at: Havana, Mason County, Illinois
Unit: Company A, 28th Illinois Infantry
Battle or Place of Action: Shiloh, Tennessee
Date of Action: 6 April 1862
Date of Issue: 28 September 1897
Citation: A box of ammunition having been abandoned between the lines, this soldier voluntarily went forward with one companion, under a heavy fire from both armies, secured the box, and delivered it within the lines of his regiment, his companion being mortally wounded.

1469 ◆ WILLIAMS, GEORGE C.

Rank: Quartermaster Sergeant
Service: U.S. Army
Birthday: 9 December 1839
Place of Birth: England
Date of Death: 14 November 1926
Place of Death: New London, Connecticut
Cemetery: Cedar Grove Cemetery (MH)—New London, Connecticut
Entered Service at: New London, New London County, Connecticut
Unit: 14th U.S. Infantry, 1st Battalion
Battle or Place of Action: Gaines' Mill, Virginia
Date of Action: 27 June 1862
Date of Issue: 28 August 1897
Citation: While on duty with the wagon train as quartermaster sergeant he voluntarily left his place of safety in the rear, joined a company, and fought with distinguished gallantry through the action.

1470 ◆ WILLIAMS, JOHN

Rank: Captain of the Maintop (highest rank: Master's Mate)
Service: U.S. Navy
Birthday: 1828
Place of Birth: New Orleans, Orleans County, Louisiana
Entered Service at: Louisiana
Unit: U.S.S. *Pawnee*
Battle or Place of Action: Matthias Point, Virginia
Date of Action: 26 June 1861
G.O. Number, Date: 11, 3 April 1863
Citation: Served as captain of the maintop of the U.S.S. *Pawnee* in the attack upon Mathias Point, 26 June 1861, Williams told his men, while lying off in the boat, that every man must die on his thwart sooner than leave a man behind. Although wounded by a musket ball in the thigh he retained the charge of his boat; and when the staff was shot away, held the stump in his hand, with the flag, until alongside the *Freeborn*.

1471 ◆ WILLIAMS, JOHN

Rank: Seaman
Service: U.S. Navy
Birthday: 1832
Place of Birth: Blair County, Pennsylvania
Entered Service at: Pennsylvania
Unit: U.S.S. *Commodore Perry*
Battle or Place of Action: Franklin, Virginia
Date of Action: 3 October 1862
G.O. Number, Date: 11, 3 April 1863
Citation: On board the U.S.S. *Commodore Perry* in the attack upon Franklin, Va., 3 October 1862. With enemy fire raking the deck of his ship and blockades thwarting her progress, Williams remained at his post and performed his duties with skill and courage as the *Commodore Perry* fought a gallant battle to silence many rebel batteries as she steamed down the Blackwater River.

1472 ◆ WILLIAMS II, JOHN

Rank: Boatswain's Mate
Service: U.S. Navy
Place of Birth: Elizabethtown, New Jersey
Entered Service at: New York
Unit: U.S.S. *Mohican*
Battle or Place of Action: Hilton Head, South Carolina
Date of Action: 7 November 1861
G.O. Number, Date: 17, 10 July 1863
Citation: Captain of an 11-inch gun aboard the U.S.S. *Mohican* during action of the main squadron of ships against the heavily defended Forts Beauregard and Walker on Hilton Head, and against ships of the Confederate fleet, 7 November 1861. Cool and courageous at his battle station, Williams maintained steady fire against the enemy while under the fort batteries during a four-hour engagement which resulted in silencing the batteries of the forts and in the rout of the rebel steamers.

1473 ◆ WILLIAMS, LEROY

Rank: Sergeant (highest rank: First Lieutenant)
Service: U.S. Army
Birthday: 18 August 1845
Place of Birth: Oswego, Oswego County, New York
Date of Death: 14 February 1930
Place of Death: Cleveland, Ohio
Cemetery: Oakwood Cemetery (MH)—Niagara Falls, New York
Entered Service at: Batavia, Genesee County, New York
Unit: Company G, 8th New York Heavy Artillery
Battle or Place of Action: Cold Harbor, Virginia
Date of Action: 3 June 1864
Date of Issue: 1 April 1898
Citation: Voluntarily exposed himself to the fire of the enemy's sharpshooters and located the body of his colonel who had been killed close to the enemy's lines. Under cover of darkness, with four companions, he recovered the body and brought it within the Union lines, having approached within a few feet of the Confederate pickets while so engaged.

1474 ◆ WILLIAMS, PETER

Rank: Seaman (highest rank: Quartermaster)
Service: U.S. Navy
Birthday: 1831
Place of Birth: Norway
Entered Service at: Pennsylvania
Unit: U.S. Ironclad Steamer *Monitor*
Battle or Place of Action: Hampton Roads, Virginia
Date of Action: 9 March 1862
G.O. Number, Date: 11, 3 April 1863
Citation: Served on board the U.S. Ironclad Steamer *Monitor*, at Hampton Roads, 9 March 1862. During the engagement between the U.S.S. *Monitor* and the C.S.S. *Merrimack*, Williams gallantly served throughout the engagement as quartermaster, piloting the *Monitor* throughout the battle in which the *Merrimack*, after being damaged, retired from the scene of the battle.

1475 ◆ WILLIAMS, ROBERT

Rank: Signal Quartermaster
Service: U.S. Navy
Birthday: 1837
Place of Birth: New York, New York
Entered Service at: New York
Unit: U.S.S. *Benton*
Battle or Place of Action: Drumgould's Bluff, Mississippi
Date of Action: 27 December 1862
G.O. Number, Date: 11, 3 April 1863
Date of Presentation: 15 May 1863
Place of Presentation: Brooklyn Navy Yard, New York, on board the U.S.S. *North Carolina*, presented by Capt. Richard Meade
Citation: Served as quartermaster on board the U.S.S. *Benton* during the Yazoo River Expedition, 23 to 27 December 1862. Taking part in the hour-and-a-half engagement with the enemy at Drumgould's Bluff, 27 December, Williams served courageously throughout that battle against hostile forces in which the enemy had the dead-range of the vessel and were punishing her with heavy fire and various other action in which he took part during the Yazoo River Expedition.

1476 ◆ WILLIAMS, WILLIAM

Rank: Landsman
Service: U.S. Navy
Birthday: 1840
Place of Birth: Ireland
Entered Service at: Pennsylvania
Unit: U.S.S. *Lehigh*
Battle or Place of Action: Charleston Harbor, South Carolina
Date of Action: 16 November 1863
G.O. Number, Date: 32, 16 April 1864
Citation: On board the U.S.S. *Lehigh*, Charleston Harbor, 16 November 1863, during the hazardous task of freeing the *Lehigh*, which had been grounded, and was under heavy enemy fire from Fort Moultrie. After several previous attempts had been made, Williams succeeded in passing in a small boat from the *Lehigh* to the *Nahant* with a line bent on a hawser. This courageous action while under severe enemy fire enabled the *Lehigh* to be freed from her helpless position.

1477 ◆ WILLIAMS, WILLIAM HALIDAY

Rank: Private
Service: U.S. Army
Birthday: 13 December 1845
Place of Birth: Williamstown, Hancock County, Ohio
Date of Death: 1 September 1916
Place of Death: Schuyler, Nebraska
Cemetery: Schuyler Cemetery (MH)—Schuyler, Nebraska
Entered Service at: Lima, Allen County, Ohio
Unit: Company C, 82d Ohio Infantry
Battle or Place of Action: Peach Tree Creek, Georgia
Date of Action: 20 July 1864
Date of Issue: 19 June 1894
Citation: Voluntarily went beyond the lines to observe the enemy; also aided a wounded comrade.

1478 ◆ WILLIAMSON, JAMES ALEXANDER

Rank: Colonel (highest rank: Brevet Major General U.S. Volunteers)
Service: U.S. Army
Birthday: 8 February 1829
Place of Birth: Columbia, Adair County, Kentucky
Date of Death: 7 September 1902
Place of Death: Jamestown, Rhode Island
Cemetery: Rock Creek Cemetery—Washington, D.C.
Entered Service at: Des Moines, Polk County, Iowa
Unit: 4th Iowa Infantry
Battle or Place of Action: Chickasaw Bayou, Mississippi
Date of Action: 29 December 1862
Date of Issue: 17 January 1895
Citation: Led his regiment against a superior force, strongly entrenched, and held his ground when all support had been withdrawn.

1479 ◆ WILLIS, RICHARD

Rank: Coxswain (highest rank: Quartermaster)
Service: U.S. Navy
Birthday: 1826
Place of Birth: England
Entered Service at: Philadelphia, Philadelphia County, Pennsylvania
Unit: U.S.S. *New Ironsides*
Battle or Place of Action: Fort Fisher, North Carolina
Date of Action: 24-25 December 1864 & 13-15 January 1865
G.O. Number, Date: 59, 22 June 1865
Citation: Willis served on board the U.S.S. *New Ironsides* during action in several attacks on Fort Fisher, 24 and 25 December 1864; and 13, 14 and 15 January 1865. The ship steamed in and took the lead in the ironclad division close inshore and immediately opened its starboard battery in a barrage of well-directed fire to cause several fires and explosions and dismount several guns during the first two days of fighting. Taken under fire as she steamed into position on 13

January, the *New Ironsides* fought all day and took on ammunition at night, despite severe weather conditions. When the enemy troops came out of their bombproofs to defend the fort against the storming party, the ship's battery disabled nearly every gun on the fort facing the shore before the cease-fire order was given by the flagship.

1480 ◆ WILLISTON, EDWARD BANCROFT

Rank: First Lieutenant (highest rank: Brigadier General)
Service: U.S. Army
Birthday: 15 July 1836
Place of Birth: Norwich, Windsor County, Vermont
Date of Death: 24 April 1920
Cemetery: Arlington National Cemetery (1-422) (MH)—Arlington, Virginia
Entered Service at: San Francisco, San Francisco County, California
Unit: Horse Battery D, 2d U.S. Artillery
Served as: Commanding Officer
Battle or Place of Action: Trevilian Station, Virginia
Date of Action: 12 June 1864
Date of Issue: 6 April 1892
Citation: Distinguished gallantry.

1481 ◆ WILSON, CHARLES E.

Rank: Sergeant (highest rank: First Lieutenant)
Service: U.S. Army
Birthday: 1840
Place of Birth: Bucks County, Pennsylvania
Date of Death: 15 August 1915
Place of Death: Trenton, New Jersey
Cemetery: Highland Cemetery (MH)—Hopewell Township, New Jersey
Entered Service at: Hatborough, Montgomery County, New Jersey
Unit: Company A, 1st New Jersey Cavalry
Battle or Place of Action: Deatonsville (Sailor's Creek), Virginia
Date of Action: 6 April 1865
Date of Issue: 3 July 1865
Citation: Charged the enemy's works, colors in hand, and had two horses shot from under him.

1482 ◆ WILSON, CHRISTOPHER W.

Rank: Private
Service: U.S. Army
Birthday: 1846
Place of Birth: Ireland
Date of Death: 12 September 1916
Place of Death: Seacliff, New York
Cemetery: The Evergreen Cemetery (MH)—Brooklyn, New York
Entered Service at: West Meriden, New Haven County, Connecticut
Unit: Company E, 73d New York Infantry
Battle or Place of Action: Spotsylvania, Virginia

Date of Action: 12 May 1864
Date of Issue: 30 December 1898
Citation: Took the flag from the wounded color bearer and carried it in the charge over the Confederate works, in which charge he also captured the colors of the 56th Virginia (C.S.A.) bringing off both flags in safety.

1483 ◆ WILSON, FRANCIS A.

Rank: Corporal
Service: U.S. Army
Birthday: 1840
Place of Birth: Philadelphia, Philadelphia County, Pennsylvania
Date of Death: 11 July 1888
Cemetery: Mount Moriah Cemetery (No marker.)—Philadelphia, Pennsylvania
Entered Service at: Philadelphia, Philadelphia County, Pennsylvania
Unit: Company B, 95th Pennsylvania Infantry
Battle or Place of Action: Petersburg, Virginia
Date of Action: 2 April 1865
Date of Issue: 25 June 1880
Citation: Was among the first to penetrate the enemy's lines and himself captured a gun of the two batteries captured.

1484 ◆ WILSON, JOHN

Rank: Sergeant
Service: U.S. Army
Place of Birth: England
Entered Service at: Jersey City, Hudson County, New Jersey
Unit: Company L, 1st New Jersey Cavalry
Battle or Place of Action: Chamberlains Creek, Virginia
Date of Action: 31 March 1865
Date of Issue: 3 July 1865
Citation: With the assistance of one comrade, headed off the advance of the enemy, shooting two of his color bearers; also posted himself between the enemy and the lead horses of his own command, thus saving the herd from capture.

1485 ◆ WILSON, JOHN ALFRED

Rank: Private (highest rank: Corporal)
Service: U.S. Army
Birthday: 25 July 1833
Place of Birth: Columbus, Franklin County, Ohio
Date of Death: 28 March 1904
Cemetery: Union Hill Cemetery (MH)—Bowling Green, Ohio
Entered Service at: Perrysburg, Wood County, Ohio
Unit: Company C, 21st Ohio Infantry
Battle or Place of Action: Georgia
Date of Action: April 1862
Date of Issue: September 1863
Citation: One of 19 of 24 men (including two civilians) who, by direction of Gen. Ormsby M. Mitchell, penetrated

nearly 200 miles south into enemy territory and captured a railroad train at Big Shanty, Ga., in an attempt to destroy the bridges and track between Chattanooga and Atlanta.
Notes: POW

1486 ◆ WILSON, JOHN MOULDER

Rank: First Lieutenant (highest rank: Brigadier General)
Service: U.S. Army
Birthday: 8 October 1837
Place of Birth: Washington, D.C.
Date of Death: 1 February 1919
Place of Death: Washington, D.C.
Cemetery: U.S. Military Academy Cemetery (K-9)—West Point, New York
Entered Service at: Olympia, Thurston County, Washington Territory
Unit: U.S. Engineers
Battle or Place of Action: Malvern Hill, Virginia
Date of Action: 6 August 1862
Date of Issue: 3 July 1897
Citation: Remained on duty, while suffering from an acute illness and very weak, and participated in the action of that date. A few days previous he had been transferred to a staff corps, but preferred to remain until the close of the campaign, taking part in several actions.

1487 ◆ WINEGAR, WILLIAM W.

Rank: First Lieutenant (highest rank: Brevet Captain)
Service: U.S. Army
Birthday: 20 October 1844
Place of Birth: Springport, New York
Date of Death: 3 September 1916
Place of Death: Bath, New York
Cemetery: Nondago Cemetery (MH)—Bath, New York
Entered Service at: Mount Morris, Livingston County, New York
Unit: Company B, 19th New York Cavalry (1st New York Dragoons)
Battle or Place of Action: Five Forks, Virginia
Date of Action: 1 April 1865
Date of Issue: 3 May 1865
Citation: While advancing in front of his company and alone, he found himself surrounded by the enemy. He accosted a nearby enemy flag-bearer demanding the surrender of the group. His effective firing of one shot so demoralized the unit that it surrendered with flag.

1488 ◆ WISNER, LEWIS S.

Rank: First Lieutenant (highest rank: Captain)
Service: U.S. Army
Birthday: 11 August 1841
Place of Birth: Wallkill, Ulster County, New York
Date of Death: 6 October 1906
Place of Death: Middletown, New York
Cemetery: Hillside Cemetery (MH)—Middletown, New York

Entered Service at: Wallkill, Ulster County, New York
Unit: Company K, 124th New York Infantry
Served as: Engineer Officer
Battle or Place of Action: Spotsylvania, Virginia
Date of Action: 12 May 1864
Date of Issue: 2 January 1895
Citation: While serving as an engineer officer voluntarily exposed himself to the enemy's fire.

1489 ◆ WITHINGTON, WILLIAM HERBERT

Rank: Captain (highest rank: Brevet Brigadier General)
Service: U.S. Army
Birthday: 1 February 1835
Place of Birth: Dorchester, Suffolk County, Massachusetts
Date of Death: 27 June 1903
Place of Death: Jackson, Michigan
Cemetery: Mount Evergreen Cemetery (MH)—Jackson, Michigan
Entered Service at: Jackson, Jackson County, Michigan
Unit: Company B, 1st Michigan Infantry
Battle or Place of Action: Bull Run, Virginia
Date of Action: 21 July 1861
Date of Issue: 7 January 1895
Citation: Remained on the field under heavy fire to succor his superior officer.

1490 ◆ WOLLAM, JOHN

Rank: Private
Service: U.S. Army
Birthday: 1838
Place of Birth: Hamilton, Butler County, Ohio
Date of Death: 26 September 1890
Cemetery: Fairmount Cemetery—Jackson, Ohio
Entered Service at: Jackson, Jackson County, Ohio
Unit: Company C, 33d Ohio Infantry
Battle or Place of Action: Georgia
Date of Action: April 1862
Date of Issue: 20 July 1864
Citation: One of 19 of 24 men (including two civilians) who, by direction of Gen. Ormsby M. Mitchell, penetrated nearly 200 miles south into enemy territory and captured a railroad train at Big Shanty, Ga., in an attempt to destroy the bridges and track between Chattanooga and Atlanta.
Notes: POW

1491 ◆ WOOD, HENRY CLAY

Rank: First Lieutenant (highest rank: Brigadier General)
Service: U.S. Army
Birthday: 26 May 1832
Place of Birth: Winthrop, Kennebec County, Maine
Date of Death: 29 August 1918
Cemetery: Arlington National Cemetery (1-80-A) (MH)—Arlington, Virginia
Entered Service at: Winthrop, Kennebec County, Maine
Unit: 11th U.S. Infantry
Battle or Place of Action: Wilson's Creek, Missouri

Date of Action: 10 August 1861
Date of Issue: 28 October 1893
Citation: Distinguished gallantry.

1492 ◆ WOOD, MARK

Rank: Private
Service: U.S. Army
Birthday: 1839
Place of Birth: England
Date of Death: 11 July 1866
Cemetery: Forest Cemetery—Toledo, Ohio
Entered Service at: Portage, Wood County, Ohio
Unit: Company C, 21st Ohio Infantry
Battle or Place of Action: Georgia
Date of Action: April 1862
Date of Issue: September 1863
Citation: One 19 of 24 men (including two civilians) who, by direction of Gen. Ormsby M. Mitchell, penetrated nearly 200 miles south into enemy territory and captured a railroad train at Big Shanty, Ga., in an attempt to destroy the bridges and track between Chattanooga and Atlanta.
Notes: POW

1493 ◆ WOOD, RICHARD H.

Rank: Captain
Service: U.S. Army
Birthday: 15 November 1833
Place of Birth: Canton, New Jersey
Date of Death: 8 March 1903
Cemetery: Woodburn Cemetery (MH)—Bunker Hill, Illinois
Entered Service at: Woodburn, Macoupin County, Illinois
Unit: Company A, 97th Illinois Infantry
Battle or Place of Action: Vicksburg, Mississippi
Date of Action: 22 May 1863
Date of Issue: 12 December 1895
Citation: Led the "volunteer storming party," which made a most gallant assault upon the enemy's works.

1494 ◆ WOOD, ROBERT B.

True Name: Woods, Robert B.
Rank: Coxswain
Service: U.S. Navy
Place of Birth: New Garden, Ohio
Date of Death: 1 July 1878
Place of Death: Columbus, Ohio
Entered Service at: Ohio
Unit: attached to the U.S.S. *Minnesota* & temporarily serving on the U.S.S. *Mount Washington*
Battle or Place of Action: Nansemond River, Virginia
Date of Action: 14 April 1863
G.O. Number, Date: 17, 10 July 1863
Citation: Attached to the U.S.S. *Minnesota* and temporarily served on the U.S.S. *Mount Washington* during action against the enemy in the Nansemond River, 14 April 1863. When the U.S.S. *Mount Washington* drifted against the bank and all men were driven from the decks by escaping steam following several successive hits which struck her boilers and stopped her engines, Wood boarded the stricken vessel and, despite a strike on the head by a spent ball, continued at his gun for six hours as fierce artillery and musketry continued to rake her decks.

1495 ◆ WOODALL, WILLIAM H.

Rank: Scout
Service: U.S. Army
Place of Birth: Lynchburg, Lynchburg County, Virginia
Entered Service at: Winchester, Frederic County, Virginia
Battle or Place of Action: Deatonsville (Sailor's Creek), Virginia
Date of Action: 29 March-9 April 1865
Date of Issue: 3 May 1865
Citation: Capture of flag.

1496 ◆ WOODBURY, ERI DAVIDSON

Rank: Sergeant (highest rank: Brevet Captain)
Service: U.S. Army
Birthday: 30 May 1837
Place of Birth: Francistown, Hillsborough County, New Hampshire
Date of Death: 14 April 1928
Place of Death: Cheshire, Connecticut
Cemetery: St. Peter's Episcopal Cemetery (MH)—Cheshire, Connecticut
Entered Service at: St. Johnsbury, Caledonia County, Vermont
Unit: Company E, 1st Vermont Cavalry
Battle or Place of Action: Cedar Creek, Virginia
Date of Action: 19 October 1864
Date of Issue: 26 October 1864
Citation: During the regiment's charge when the enemy was in retreat, Sgt. Woodbury encountered four Confederate infantrymen retreating. He drew his saber and ordered them to surrender, overcoming by his determined actions their willingness to further resist. They surrendered to him together with their rifles and 12th North Carolina (C.S.A.) regimental flag.

1497 ◆ WOODRUFF, ALONZO

Rank: Sergeant
Service: U.S. Army
Birthday: 31 March 1839
Place of Birth: Ionia, Ionia County, Michigan
Date of Death: 10 February 1917
Cemetery: Valley Cemetery—Luther, Michigan
Entered Service at: Ionia, Ionia County, Michigan
Unit: Company I, 1st U.S. Sharpshooters
Battle or Place of Action: Hatcher's Run, Virginia
Date of Action: 27 October 1864
Date of Issue: 29 January 1896
Citation: Went to the assistance of a wounded and overpowered comrade, and in a hand-to-hand encounter effected his rescue.

1498 ◆ WOODRUFF, CARLE AUGUSTUS

Rank: First Lieutenant (highest rank: Brigadier General)
Service: U.S. Army

Birthday: 8 August 1841
Place of Birth: Buffalo, Erie County, New York
Date of Death: 20 July 1913
Place of Death: Raleigh, North Carolina
Cemetery: Oakwood Cemetery (MH)—Raleigh, North Carolina
Entered Service at: Washington, D.C.
Unit: Horse Battery M, 2d U.S. Artillery
Battle or Place of Action: Newbys Crossroads, Virginia
Date of Action: 24 July 1863
Date of Issue: 1 September 1893
Citation: While in command of a section of a battery constituting a portion of the rear guard of a division then retiring before the advance of a corps of Infantry, Woodruff was attacked by the enemy and ordered to abandon his guns. Lt. Woodruff disregarded the orders received and aided in repelling the attack and saving the guns.

1499 ◆ WOODS, DANIEL A. (WOOD)

True Name: Wood, Daniel A.
Rank: Private
Service: U.S. Army
Birthday: 1843
Place of Birth: Ohio County, West Virginia
Date of Death: 10 August 1894
Place of Death: Wheeling, West Virginia
Cemetery: Greenwood Cemetery (MH)—Wheeling, West Virginia
Entered Service at: Wheeling, Ohio County, West Virginia
Unit: Company K, 1st West Virginia Cavalry
Battle or Place of Action: Deatonsville (Sailor's Creek), Virginia
Date of Action: 6 April 1865
Date of Issue: 3 May 1865
Citation: Capture of flag, 18th Florida Infantry (C.S.A.).

1500 ◆ WOODS, SAMUEL

Rank: Seaman (highest rank: Boatswain's Mate)
Service: U.S. Navy
Birthday: 1838
Place of Birth: San Francisco, San Francisco County, California
Date of Death: 23 May 1885
Place of Death: Portsmouth, Virginia
Cemetery: Oak Grove Cemetery (MH)—Portsmouth, Virginia
Entered Service at: California
Unit: U.S.S. *Mount Washington*
Battle or Place of Action: Nansemond River, Virginia
Date of Action: 14 April 1863
G.O. Number, Date: 17, 10 July 1863
Citation: As captain of the gun, served temporarily on board the U.S.S. *Mount Washington* during the Nansemond River action, 14 April 1863. When one of his comrades was struck by a bullet and knocked overboard, Woods fearlessly jumped into the water and swam after him. Before he reached him, the man sank beneath the surface and Woods promptly swam back to the vessel, went to his gun, and fought it to the close of the action. At the close of the battle, he tirelessly cared for the wounded.

1501 ◆ WOODWARD, EVAN M.

Rank: First Lieutenant & Adjutant (highest rank: Brevet Major)
Service: U.S. Army
Birthday: 11 March 1838
Place of Birth: Philadelphia Philadelphia County, Pennsylvania
Date of Death: 15 August 1904
Place of Death: Trenton, New Jersey
Cemetery: Riverview Cemetery—Trenton, New Jersey
Entered Service at: Sandy Hook, Maryland
Unit: 2d Pennsylvania Reserve Infantry
Battle or Place of Action: Fredericksburg, Virginia
Date of Action: 13 December 1862
Date of Issue: 14 December 1894
Citation: Advanced between the lines, demanded and received the surrender of the 19th Georgia Infantry (C.S.A.) and captured their battle flag.

1502 ◆ WOON, JOHN

Rank: Boatswain's Mate
Service: U.S. Navy
Birthday: 1823
Place of Birth: England
Entered Service at: New York, New York
Unit: U.S.S. *Pittsburgh*
Battle or Place of Action: Grand Gulf, Mississippi River, Mississippi
Date of Action: 29 April 1863
G.O. Number, Date: 17, 10 July 1863
Citation: Serving on board the U.S.S. *Pittsburgh*, Mississippi River, 29 April 1863. Engaging the enemy batteries at Grand Gulf, the U.S.S. *Pittsburgh*, although severely damaged and suffering many personnel casualties, continued to fire her batteries until ordered to withdraw. Taking part in a similar action after nightfall, the U.S.S. *Pittsburgh* received further damage, but received no personnel casualties in the latter action. Woon showed courage and devotion to duty throughout these bitter engagements.

1503 ◆ WORAM, CHARLES B.

Rank: Seaman (highest rank: Landsman)
Service: U.S. Navy
Birthday: 29 March 1845
Place of Birth: New York, New York
Date of Death: 1 November 1897
Place of Death: New York, New York
Cemetery: Woodlawn Cemetery—Bronx, New York
Entered Service at: New York, New York
Unit: U.S.S. *Oneida*
Battle or Place of Action: Mobile Bay, Alabama
Date of Action: 5 August 1864
G.O. Number, Date: 45, 31 December 1864

Citation: Served on board the U.S.S. *Oneida* in the engagement at Moblie Bay, 5 August 1864. Acting as an aid to the executive officer, Woram carried orders intelligently and correctly, distinguishing himself by his cool courage throughout the battle which resulted in the capture of the rebel ram *Tennessee* and the damaging of Fort Morgan.

1504 ◆ WORTICK, JOSEPH

True Name: Wertick, Joseph
Rank: Private
Service: U.S. Army
Birthday: 1838
Place of Birth: Fayette County, Pennsylvania
Place of Death: Leon, Kansas
Cemetery: Leon Cemetery (MH)—Leon, Kansas
Entered Service at: Hannibal, Marion County, Missouri
Unit: Company A, 6th Missouri Infantry
Battle or Place of Action: Vicksburg, Mississippi
Date of Action: 22 May 1863
Date of Issue: 14 July 1894
Citation: Gallantry in the charge of the "volunteer storming party."

1505 ◆ WRAY, WILLIAM J.

Rank: Sergeant
Service: U.S. Army
Birthday: 16 May 1845
Place of Birth: Philadelphia, Philadelphia County, Pennsylvania
Date of Death: 2 June 1919
Place of Death: Philadelphia, Pennsylvania
Cemetery: Philadelphia Memorial Park—Frazier, Pennsylvania
Entered Service at: Philadelphia, Philadelphia County, Pennsylvania
Unit: Company K, 1st Veterans Reserve Corps
Battle or Place of Action: Fort Steven's, Washington, D.C.
Date of Action: 12 July 1864
Date of Issue: 15 December 1892
Citation: Rallied the company at a critical moment during a change of position under fire.

1506 ◆ WRIGHT, ALBERT D.

Rank: Captain
Service: U.S. Army
Birthday: 10 December 1842
Place of Birth: Elkland, Tioga County, Pennsylvania
Date of Death: 15 February 1926
Place of Death: Tampa, Florida
Cemetery: Greenwood Cemetery (MH)—Eustis, Florida
Entered Service at: Wellsboro, Tioga County, Pennsylvania
Unit: Company G, 43d U.S. Colored Troops
Battle or Place of Action: Petersburg, Virginia
Date of Action: 30 July 1864
Date of Issue: 1 May 1893
Citation: Advanced beyond the enemy's lines, capturing a stand of colors and its color guard; was severely wounded.

1507 ◆ WRIGHT, EDWARD

Rank: Quartermaster
Service: U.S. Navy
Birthday: 1829
Place of Birth: New York, New York
Date of Death: 17 February 1901
Place of Death: New York, New York
Cemetery: Maple Grove Cemetery—Kew Gardens, New York
Entered Service at: New York, New York
Unit: U.S.S. *Cayuga*
Battle or Place of Action: Fts. St. Philip & Jackson and New Orleans, Louisiana
Date of Action: 24-25 April 1862
G.O. Number, Date: 11, 3 April 1863
Citation: On board the U.S.S. *Cayuga* during the capture of Forts St. Philip and Jackson and the taking of New Orleans, 24 and 25 April 1862. As his ship led the advance column toward the barrier and both forts opened fire simultaneously, striking the vessel from stem to stern, Wright conscientiously performed his duties throughout the action in which the attempts of three rebel steamers to butt and board were repelled, and the ships driven off or forced to surrender. Eleven gunboats were successfully engaged and garrisons captured during this battle in which the *Cayuga* sustained 46 hits.

1508 ◆ WRIGHT, ROBERT

Rank: Private
Service: U.S. Army
Birthday: 1828
Place of Birth: Ireland
Date of Death: 22 October 1885
Cemetery: Cedar Lawn Cemetery (MH)—Patterson, New Jersey
Entered Service at: Woodstock, Windham County, Connecticut
Unit: Company G, 14th U.S. Infantry
Battle or Place of Action: Chapel House Farm, Virginia
Date of Action: 1 October 1864
Date of Issue: 25 November 1869
Citation: Gallantry in action.

1509 ◆ WRIGHT, SAMUEL

Rank: Corporal
Service: U.S. Army
Birthday: 20 January 1828
Place of Birth: Indiana
Date of Death: 7 July 1918
Place of Death: Tribune, Kansas
Cemetery: Maple Grove Cemetery (MH)—Wichita, Kansas
Entered Service at: Mankato, Blue Earth County, Minnesota
Unit: Company H, 2d Minnesota Infantry
Battle or Place of Action: Nolensville, Tennessee
Date of Action: 15 February 1863

Date of Issue: 11 September 1897
Citation: Was one of a detachment of 16 men who heroically defended a wagon train against the attack of 125 cavalry, repulsed the attack, and saved the train.

1510 ◆ WRIGHT, SAMUEL COLE

Rank: Private (highest rank: Sergeant)
Service: U.S. Army
Birthday: 7 September 1842
Place of Birth: Plympton, Plymouth County, Massachusetts
Date of Death: 6 July 1906
Place of Death: Plympton, Massachusetts
Cemetery: Oak Grove Cemetery (MH)—Plymouth, Massachusetts
Entered Service at: Plympton, Plymouth County, Massachusetts
Unit: Company E, 29th Massachusetts Infantry
Battle or Place of Action: Antietam, Maryland
Date of Action: 17 September 1862
Date of Issue: 29 January 1896
Citation: Voluntarily advanced under a destructive fire and removed a fence which would have impeded a contemplated charge.

1511 ◆ WRIGHT, WILLIAM

Rank: Yeoman
Service: U.S. Navy
Birthday: 1835
Place of Birth: London, England
Entered Service at: Baltimore, Baltimore County, Maryland
Unit: U.S.S. *Monticello*
Battle or Place of Action: Wilmington, North Carolina
Date of Action: 23-25 June 1864
G.O. Number, Date: 45, 31 December 1864
Citation: Served as yeoman on board the U.S.S. *Monticello* during the reconnaissance of the harbor and water defenses of Wilmington, N.C., 23 to 25 June 1864. Taking part in a reconnaissance of enemy defenses which covered a period of two days and nights, Wright courageously carried out his cutting of a telegraph wire and the capture of a large group of prisoners. Although in immediate danger from the enemy at all times, Wright showed gallantry and coolness throughout this action which resulted in the gaining of much vital information on the rebel defenses.

1512 ◆ YEAGER, JACOB F.

Rank: Private
Service: U.S. Army
Birthday: 27 January 1841
Place of Birth: New Texas, Lehigh County, Pennsylvania
Date of Death: 13 November 1909
Cemetery: Greenlawn Cemetery (MH)—Tiffin, Ohio
Entered Service at: Tiffin, Seneca County, Ohio
Unit: Company H, 101st Ohio Infantry
Battle or Place of Action: Buzzard's Roost, Georgia
Date of Action: 11 May 1864

Date of Issue: 3 August 1897
Citation: Seized a shell with fuse burning that had fallen in the ranks of his company and threw it into a stream, thereby probably saving his comrades from injury.
Notes: POW

1513 ◆ YOUNG, ANDREW J.

Rank: Sergeant
Service: U.S. Army
Birthday: 28 December 1837
Place of Birth: Greene County, Pennsylvania
Date of Death: 27 January 1910
Place of Death: Jefferson, Pennsylvania
Cemetery: Jefferson Cemetery—Jefferson, Pennsylvania
Entered Service at: Carmichaels, Greene County, Pennsylvania
Unit: Company F, 1st Pennsylvania Cavalry
Battle or Place of Action: Paines Crossroads, Virginia
Date of Action: 5 April 1865
Date of Issue: 3 May 1865
Citation: Capture of flag.

1514 ◆ YOUNG, BENJAMIN F.

Rank: Corporal
Service: U.S. Army
Birthday: 1841
Place of Birth: Canada
Date of Death: 27 January 1927
Place of Death: Los Angeles, California
Cemetery: Odd Fellow Cemetery—Los Angeles, California
Entered Service at: Detroit, Wayne County, Michigan
Unit: 1st Michigan Sharpshooters
Battle or Place of Action: Petersburg, Virginia
Date of Action: 17 June 1864
Date of Issue: 1 December 1864
Citation: Capture of flag of 35th North Carolina Infantry (C.S.A.).
Notes: POW

1515 ◆ YOUNG, CALVARY MORRIS

Rank: Sergeant
Service: U.S. Army
Birthday: 12 March 1840
Place of Birth: Washington County, Ohio
Date of Death: 11 July 1909
Place of Death: Ludlow, Kentucky
Cemetery: Highland Cemetery (MH)—Fort Mitchell, Kentucky
Entered Service at: Hopeville, Clark County, Iowa
Unit: Company L, 3d Iowa Cavalry
Battle or Place of Action: Osage, Kansas
Date of Action: 25 October 1864
Date of Issue: 4 April 1865
Citation: Gallantry in capturing Brig. Gen. William Lewis Cabell, (C.S.A.).

1516 ◆ YOUNG, EDWARD B.

Rank: Coxswain (highest rank: Wardroom Steward)
Service: U.S. Navy
Birthday: 1835
Place of Birth: Bergen, Hudson County, New Jersey
Date of Death: 24 February 1867
Place of Death: Philadelphia, Pennsylvania
Cemetery: Lafayette Cemetery—Philadelphia, Pennsylvania
Entered Service at: New Jersey
Unit: U.S.S. *Galena*
Battle or Place of Action: Mobile Bay, Alabama
Date of Action: 5 August 1864
G.O. Number, Date: 59, 22 June 1865
Citation: On board the U.S.S. *Galena* during the attack on enemy forts at Mobile Bay, 5 August 1864. Securely lashed to the side of the *Oneida*, which had suffered the loss of her steering apparatus and an explosion of her boiler from enemy fire, the *Galena* aided the stricken vessel past the enemy forts to safety. Despite heavy damage to his ship from raking enemy fire, Young performed his duties with skill and courage throughout the action.

1517 ◆ YOUNG, HORATIO NELSON

Rank: Seaman
Service: U.S. Navy
Birthday: 19 July 1845
Place of Birth: Calais, Washington County, Maine
Date of Death: 3 July 1913
Place of Death: Calais (Red Beach), Maine
Cemetery: The Rural Cemetery (MH)—St. Stephen, New Brunswick, Canada
Entered Service at: Boston, Suffolk County, Massachusetts
Unit: U.S.S. *Lehigh*
Battle or Place of Action: Charleston Harbor, South Carolina
Date of Action: 16 November 1863
G.O. Number, Date: 32, 16 April 1864
Citation: On board the U.S.S. *Lehigh*, Charleston Harbor, 16 November 1863, during the hazardous task of freeing the *Lehigh*, which had grounded and was under heavy enemy fire from Fort Moultrie. After several previous attempts had been made, Young succeeded in passing in a small boat from the *Lehigh* to the *Nahant* with a line bent on a hawser. This courageous action while under severe enemy fire enabled the *Lehigh* to be freed from her helpless position.

1518 ◆ YOUNG, JAMES MARVIN

Rank: Private
Service: U.S. Army
Birthday: 2 December 1843
Place of Birth: Ellicott, Erie County, New York
Date of Death: 30 November 1913
Place of Death: Jamestown, New York
Cemetery: Lake View Cemetery—Jamestown, New York
Entered Service at: Chautauqua County, New York
Unit: Company B, 72d New York Infantry
Battle or Place of Action: Wilderness Campaign, Virginia
Date of Action: 6 May 1864
Date of Issue: 2 April 1898
Citation: With two companions, voluntarily went forward in the forest to reconnoiter the enemy's position; was fired upon and one of his companions disabled. Pvt. Young took the wounded man upon his back and, under fire, carried him to within the Union lines.

1519 ◆ YOUNG, WILLIAM

Rank: Boatswain's Mate
Service: U.S. Navy
Birthday: 1835
Place of Birth: New York
Entered Service at: New York, New York
Unit: U.S.S. *Cayuga*
Battle or Place of Action: Fts. St. Philip & Jackson and New Orleans, Louisiana
Date of Action: 24-25 April 1862
G.O. Number, Date: 11, 3 April 1863
Citation: On board the U.S.S. *Cayuga* during the capture of Forts St. Philip and Jackson and the taking of New Orleans, 24 and 25 April 1862. As his ship led the advance column toward the barrier and both forts opened fire simultaneously, striking the vessel from stem to stern, Young calmly manned a Parrot gun throughout the action in which attempts by three rebel steamers to butt and board were thwarted and the ships driven off or captured, 11 gunboats were successfully engaged, and garrisons forced to surrender. During the battle, the *Cayuga* sustained 46 hits.

1520 ◆ YOUNKER, JOHN L.

Rank: Private
Service: U.S. Army
Birthday: 16 November 1836
Place of Birth: Wurttemberg, Germany
Date of Death: 18 May 1911
Place of Death: Logan, Ohio
Cemetery: Oak Grove Cemetery—Logan, Ohio
Entered Service at: Lancaster, Fairfield County, Ohio
Unit: Company A, 12th U.S. Infantry
Battle or Place of Action: Cedar Mountain, Virginia
Date of Action: 9 August 1862
Date of Issue: 1 November 1893

INTERIM 1865–1870

1521 ◆ BATES, RICHARD

Rank: Seaman
Service: U.S. Navy
Birthday: 1829
Place of Birth: Wales
Entered Service at: New York
Unit: U.S.S. *Winooski*
Battle or Place of Action: off Eastport, Maine
Date of Action: 10 May 1866
G.O. Number, Date: 77, 1 August 1866
Citation: For heroic conduct in rescuing from drowning James Rose and John Russell, seamen of the U.S.S. *Winooski*, off Eastport, Maine, 10 May 1866.

1522 ◆ BROWN, JOHN

Rank: Captain of the Afterguard
Service: U.S. Navy
Birthday: 1838
Place of Birth: Denmark
Entered Service at: Maryland
Unit: U.S.S. *Winooski*
Battle or Place of Action: off Eastport, Maine
Date of Action: 10 May 1866
G.O. Number, Date: 77, 1 August 1866
Citation: For heroic conduct with two comrades, in rescuing from drowning James Rose and John Russell, seamen of the U.S.S. *Winooski*, off Eastport, Maine, 10 May 1866.

1523 ◆ BURKE, THOMAS

Rank: Seaman
Service: U.S. Navy
Birthday: 1833
Place of Birth: Ireland
Entered Service at: New York
Unit: U.S.S. *Winooski*
Battle or Place of Action: off Eastport, Maine
Date of Action: 10 May 1866
G.O. Number, Date: 77, 1 August 1866
Citation: For heroic conduct with two comrades, in rescuing from drowning James Rose and John Russell, seamen of the U.S.S. *Winooski*, off Eastport, Maine, 10 May 1866.

1524 ◆ CAREY, JAMES

Rank: Seaman
Service: U.S. Navy
Birthday: 1844
Place of Birth: Ireland
Entered Service at: New York
Unit: U.S.S. *Huron*
Citation: Seaman on board the U.S.S. *Huron*, for saving three shipmates from drowning.

1525 ◆ COOPER, JOHN✠

True Name: Mather, John Laver
Rank: Quartermaster
Service: U.S. Navy
Birthday: 24 July 1828
Place of Birth: Dublin, Ireland
Date of Death: 22 August 1891
Cemetery: Cypress Hills National Cemetery (2-5022) (MH)—Brooklyn, New York
Entered Service at: New York, New York
Unit: on Acting Rear Adm. Thatcher's staff
Battle or Place of Action: Mobile, Alabama
Date of Action: 26 April 1865
G.O. Number, Date: 62, 29 June 1865
Citation: **Second Award** Served as quartermaster on Acting Rear Adm. Thatcher's staff. During the terrific fire at Mobile, on 26 April 1865, at the risk of being blown to pieces by exploding shells, Cooper advanced through the burning locality, rescued a wounded man from certain death, and bore him on his back to a place of safety.
Notes: ✠Double Awardee: *see also* Civil War

1526 ◆ DU MOULIN, FRANK

Rank: Apprentice
Service: U.S. Navy
Birthday: 1850
Place of Birth: Philadelphia, Philadelphia County, Pennsylvania
Entered Service at: Pennsylvania
Unit: U.S.S. *Sabine*
Battle or Place of Action: in New London Harbor, Connecticut
Date of Action: 5 September 1867
G.O. Number, Date: 84, 3 October 1867
Citation: On 5 September 1867, Du Moulin jumped overboard and saved from drowning Apprentice D'Orsay, who had fallen from the mizzen topmast rigging of the *Sabine*, in New London Harbor and was rendered helpless by striking the mizzen rigging and boat davit in the fall.

1527 ◆ GERBER, FREDERICK WILLIAM

Rank: Sergeant Major
Service: U.S. Army
Birthday: 1813
Place of Birth: Dresden, Germany
Date of Death: 10 November 1875
Cemetery: Cypress Hills National Cemetery (2-6101) (MH)—Brooklyn, New York
Entered Service at: Brooklyn, Kings County, New York
Unit: U.S. Engineers
Date of Action: 1839—1871
Date of Issue: 8 November 1871
Citation: Distinguished gallantry in many actions and in recognition of long, faithful, and meritorious services covering a period of 32 years.

1528 ◆ HALFORD, WILLIAM

Rank: Coxswain (highest rank: Lieutenant)
Service: U.S. Navy
Birthday: 18 August 1841
Place of Birth: Gloucester, Gloucestershire, England
Date of Death: 17 February 1919
Place of Death: Vallejo, California
Cemetery: Mare Island Shipyard Cemetery (MH)—Vallejo, California
Entered Service at: San Francisco, San Francisco County, California
Unit: U.S.S. *Saginaw*
Battle or Place of Action: Sandwich Islands
Date of Action: October 1870
G.O. Number, Date: 169, 8 February 1872
Citation: Halford was sole survivor of the boat's crew sent to the Sandwich Islands for assistance after the wreck of the *Saginaw*, October 1870. Promoted to acting gunner.

1529 ◆ MULLEN, PATRICK✛

Rank: Boatswain's Mate
Service: U.S. Navy
Birthday: 6 May 1844
Place of Birth: Ireland
Date of Death: 14 February 1897
Cemetery: New Cathedral Cemetery—Baltimore, Maryland
Entered Service at: Baltimore, Baltimore County, Maryland
Unit: U.S.S. *Don*
Battle or Place of Action: off the coast of Virginia
Date of Action: 1 May 1865
G.O. Number, Date: 62, 29 June 1865
Citation: **Second Award** Served as boatswain's mate on board the U.S.S. *Don*, 1 May 1865. Engaged in picking up the crew of Picket Launch No. 6, which had swamped. Mullen, seeing an officer who at that time was no longer able to keep up and was below the surface of the water, jumped overboard and brought the officer to the boat, thereby rescuing him from drowning, which brave action entitled him to wear a bar on the medal he had already received at Mattox Creek, 17 March 1865.
Notes: ✛Double Awardee: *see also* Civil War

1530 ◆ ROBINSON, JOHN

Rank: Captain of the Hold
Service: U.S. Navy
Birthday: 1840
Place of Birth: Cuba
Entered Service at: Maine
Unit: U.S.S. *Yucca*
Battle or Place of Action: in Pensacola Bay, Florida
Date of Action: 19 January 1867
G.O. Number, Date: 82, 23 February 1867
Citation: With Acting Ens. James H. Bunting, during the heavy gale which occurred in Pensacola Bay on the night of 19 January 1867, Robinson swam ashore with a line for the purpose of sending off a blowcock, which would facilitate getting upsteam and prevent the vessel from stranding, thus voluntarily periling his life to save the vessel and the lives of others.

1531 ◆ ROBINSON, THOMAS

Rank: Captain of the Afterguard
Service: U.S. Navy
Birthday: 17 May 1837
Place of Birth: Norway
Date of Death: 12 May 1915
Cemetery: Lakewood Cemetery (no marker on grave)—Minneapolis, Minnesota
Entered Service at: New York
Unit: U.S.S. *Tallapoosa*
Battle or Place of Action: off New Orleans, Louisiana
Date of Action: 15 July 1866
G.O. Number, Date: 77, 1 August 1866
Citation: For heroic efforts to save from drowning Wellington Brocar, landsman, of the *Tallapoosa*, off New Orleans, 15 July 1866.

1532 ◆ STACY, WILLIAM BRADFORD

Rank: Seaman
Service: U.S. Navy
Birthday: 4 March 1838
Place of Birth: Fall River, Bristol County, Massachusetts
Date of Death: 3 May 1921
Place of Death: Haswell, Colorado
Cemetery: Highland Cemetery—Iola, Kansas
Entered Service at: New Bedford, Bristol County, Massachusetts
Unit: U.S.S. *Rhode Island*
Battle or Place of Action: in the harbor, Cape Haiten, Haiti
G.O. Number, Date: 71, 15 January 1866
Citation: While coaling ship in the harbor of Cape Haiten, one of the crew of the U.S.S. *Rhode Island* fell overboard,

and, after catching a rope, had been forced by exhaustion to relinquish his hold. Although the sea was running high at the time, Stacy, at the peril of his life, jumped overboard, secured the rope around his shipmate, and thus saved him from drowning.

1533 ◆ TAYLOR, JOHN

Rank: Seaman
Service: U.S. Navy

Battle or Place of Action: New York Navy Yard
Date of Action: 9 September 1865
G.O. Number, Date: 71, 15 January 1866
Citation: Seaman in charge of the picket boat attached to the Navy Yard, New York, 9 September 1865. Acting with promptness, coolness, and good judgment, Taylor rescued from drowning Comdr. S.D. Trenchard of the U.S. Navy, who fell overboard in attempting to get on a ferryboat which had collided with an English steamer and who needed immediate assistance.

INDIAN CAMPAIGNS

1534 ◆ ALBEE, GEORGE EMERSON

Rank: First Lieutenant (highest rank: Captain)
Service: U.S. Army
Birthday: 27 January 1845
Place of Birth: Lisbon, Grafton County, New Hampshire
Date of Death: 24 March 1918
Place of Death: Laurel, Maryland
Cemetery: Arlington National Cemetery (2-850)—Arlington, Virginia
Entered Service at: Owatonna, Steele County, Minnesota
Unit: Company L, 41st U.S. Infantry
Battle or Place of Action: Brazos River, Texas
Date of Action: 28 October 1869
Date of Issue: 18 January 1894
Citation: Attacked with two men a force of 11 Indians, drove them from the hills, and reconnoitered the country beyond.

1535 ◆ ALCHESAY, WILLIAM

Rank: Sergeant
Service: U.S. Army
Birthday: 17 May 1853
Place of Birth: Arizona
Date of Death: 6 August 1928
Cemetery: Fort Apache Indian Reservation near Little Round Top Peak—White River, Arizona
Entered Service at: Camp Verde, Yavapai County, Arizona Territory
Unit: Indian Scouts
Battle or Place of Action: Apache Campaigns
Date of Action: winter 1872-73
Date of Presentation: 12 April 1875
Place of Presentation: Fort Apache, Arizona, presented by Gen. Crook
Citation: Gallant conduct during campaigns and engagements with Apaches.

1536 ◆ ALLEN, WILLIAM

Rank: First Sergeant (highest rank: First Lieutenant)
Service: U.S. Army
Birthday: 1846
Place of Birth: Philadelphia, Philadelphia County, Pennsylvania
Date of Death: 8 January 1892
Cemetery: San Francisco National Cemetery (OS-48-2)—San Francisco, California
Entered Service at: Philadelphia, Philadelphia County, Pennsylvania

Unit: Company I, 23d U.S. Infantry
Battle or Place of Action: Turret Mountain, Arizona Territory
Date of Action: 27 March 1873
Date of Issue: 12 April 1875
Citation: Gallantry in action.

1537 ◆ ANDERSON, JAMES

True Name: Smyth, James
Rank: Private (highest rank: Sergeant)
Service: U.S. Army
Birthday: 28 May 1849
Place of Birth: Canada East
Date of Death: 31 May 1918
Cemetery: St. Peter & Paul Cemetery—St. Louis, Missouri
Entered Service at: St. Louis, St. Louis County, Missouri
Unit: Company M, 6th U.S. Cavalry
Battle or Place of Action: Wichita River, Texas
Date of Action: 5 October 1870
Date of Issue: 19 November 1870
Citation: Gallantry during the pursuit and fight with Indians.

1538 ◆ ASTON, EDGAR R.

Rank: Private
Service: U.S. Army
Birthday: 1846
Place of Birth: Clermont County, Ohio
Date of Death: 14 April 1932
Cemetery: Tate Township Cemetery—Bethel, Ohio
Entered Service at: Cincinnati, Hamilton County, Ohio
Unit: Company L, 8th U.S. Cavalry
Battle or Place of Action: San Carlos, Arizona
Date of Action: 30 May 1868
Date of Issue: 28 July 1868
Citation: With two other men he volunteered to search for a wagon passage out of a 4,000-foot valley wherein an infantry column was immobile. This small group passed six miles through hostile Apache terrain, finding the sought passage. On their return trip down the canyon they were attacked by Apaches, who were successfully held at bay.

1539 ◆ AUSTIN, WILLIAM GRAFTON

Rank: Sergeant
Service: U.S. Army
Birthday: 6 January 1868

Place of Birth: Galveston, Galveston County, Texas
Date of Death: 15 July 1929
Place of Death: Los Altos, California
Cemetery: Cypress Lawn Cemetery—Colma, California
Entered Service at: New York, New York
Unit: Company E, 7th U.S. Cavalry
Battle or Place of Action: Wounded Knee Creek, South Dakota
Date of Action: 29 December 1890
Date of Issue: 27 June 1891
Citation: While the Indians were concealed in a ravine, assisted men on the skirmish line, directing their fire, etc., and using every effort to dislodge the enemy.

1540 ◆ AYERS, JAMES F.

Rank: Private
Service: U.S. Army
Birthday: 1847
Place of Birth: Collinstown, Henry County, Virginia
Date of Death: 18 January 1895
Place of Death: Fort Reily, Kansas
Cemetery: Post Cemetery (F-27) (MH)—Fort Riley, Kansas
Entered Service at: Richmond, Richmond County, Virginia
Unit: Company H, 6th U.S. Cavalry
Battle or Place of Action: Sappa Creek, Kansas
Date of Action: 23 April 1875
Date of Issue: 16 November 1876
Citation: Rapid pursuit, gallantry, energy, and enterprise in an engagement with Indians.

1541 ◆ BABCOCK, JOHN BRECKINRIDGE

True Name: Breckenridge, John
Rank: First Lieutenant (highest rank: Brigadier General U.S. Vols.)
Service: U.S. Army
Birthday: 7 February 1847
Place of Birth: New Orleans, Orleans County, Louisiana
Date of Death: 26 April 1909
Cemetery: Evergreen Cemetery (MH)—Stonington, Connecticut
Entered Service at: Stonington, New London County, Connecticut
Unit: 5th U.S. Cavalry
Battle or Place of Action: Spring Creek, Nebraska
Date of Action: 16 May 1869
Date of Issue: 18 September 1897
Citation: While serving with a scouting column, this officer's troop was attacked by a vastly superior force of Indians. Advancing to high ground, he dismounted his men, remaining mounted himself to encourage them, and there fought the Indians until relieved, his horse being wounded.

1542 ◆ BAILEY, JAMES E.

Rank: Sergeant
Service: U.S. Army
Place of Birth: Dexter, Penobscot County, Maine

Entered Service at: Boston, Suffolk County, Massachusetts
Unit: Company E, 5th U.S. Cavalry
Battle or Place of Action: Apache campaigns
Date of Action: 1872—1873
Date of Issue: 12 April 1875
Citation: Gallant conduct during campaigns and engagements with Apaches.

1543 ◆ BAIRD, GEORGE WILLIAM

Rank: First Lieutenant, Adjutant (highest rank: Major General)
Service: U.S. Army
Birthday: 13 December 1839
Place of Birth: Milford, New Haven County, Connecticut
Date of Death: 28 November 1906
Place of Death: Ashville, North Carolina
Cemetery: Old Milford Cemetery (MH)—Milford, Connecticut
Entered Service at: Milford, New Haven County, Connecticut
Unit: 5th U.S. Infantry
Battle or Place of Action: Bear Paw Mountain, Montana
Date of Action: 30 September 1877
Date of Issue: 27 November 1894
Citation: Most distinguished gallantry in action with the Nez Perce Indians.

1544 ◆ BAKER, JOHN

Rank: Musician
Service: U.S. Army
Birthday: 1853
Place of Birth: Hessen, Germany
Entered Service at: Brooklyn, Kings County, New York
Unit: Company D, 5th U.S. Infantry
Battle or Place of Action: Cedar Creek, etc., Montana
Date of Action: October 1876—January 1877
Date of Issue: 27 April 1877
Citation: Gallantry in engagements.

1545 ◆ BALDWIN, FRANK DWIGHT✚

Rank: First Lieutenant (highest rank: Major General)
Service: U.S. Army
Birthday: 26 June 1842
Place of Birth: Manchester, Washtenaw County, Michigan
Date of Death: 22 April 1923
Cemetery: Arlington National Cemetery (3-1894)—Arlington, Virginia
Entered Service at: Constantine, St. Joseph County, Michigan
Unit: 5th U.S. Infantry
Battle or Place of Action: McClellans Creek, Texas
Date of Action: 8 November 1874
Date of Issue: 3 December 1891
Citation: **Second Award** Rescued, with two companies, two white girls by a voluntary attack upon Indians whose superior numbers and strong position would have warranted delay for

reinforcements, but which delay would have permitted the Indians to escape and kill their captives.
Notes: ✚Double Awardee: *see also* Civil War

1546 ◆ BANCROFT, NEIL

Rank: Private
Service: U.S. Army
Birthday: 1846
Place of Birth: Oswego, Oswego County, New York
Entered Service at: Chicago, Cook County, Illinois
Unit: Company A, 7th U.S. Cavalry
Battle or Place of Action: Little Big Horn, Montana
Date of Action: 25 June 1876
Date of Issue: 5 October 1878
Citation: Brought water for the wounded under a most galling fire.

1547 ◆ BARNES, WILL CROFT

Rank: Private First Class
Service: U.S. Army
Birthday: 21 June 1858
Place of Birth: San Francisco, San Francisco County, California
Date of Death: 17 December 1936
Place of Death: Phoenix, Arizona
Cemetery: Arlington National Cemetery (6-9754)—Arlington, Virginia
Entered Service at: Washington, D.C.
Unit: U.S. Army, Signal Corps
Battle or Place of Action: Arizona
Date of Action: 1 September 1881
Date of Issue: 8 November 1882
Citation: Bravery in action.

1548 ◆ BARRETT, RICHARD

Rank: First Sergeant
Service: U.S. Army
Birthday: 1838
Date of Birth: County Mayo, Ireland
Date of Death: 20 March 1898
Cemetery: Soldiers Home National Cemetery (K-6765) (MH)—Washington, D.C.,
Entered Service at: Buffalo, Erie County, New York
Unit: Company A, 1st U.S. Cavalry
Battle or Place of Action: Sycamore Canyon, Arizona
Date of Action: 23 May 1872
Date of Issue: 12 April 1875
Citation: Conspicuous gallantry in a charge upon the Tonto Apaches.

1549 ◆ BEAUFORD, CLAY

True Name: Bridwell, Welford Chapman
Rank: First Sergeant
Service: U.S. Army

Birthday: 1847
Place of Birth: Washington County, Maryland
Date of Death: 1 February 1905
Cemetery: Rosedale Cemetery—Los Angeles, California
Entered Service at: Nashville, Davidson County, Tennessee
Unit: Company B, 5th U.S. Cavalry
Battle or Place of Action: Apache campaigns
Date of Action: 1872-73
Date of Issue: 12 April 1875
Citation: Gallant conduct during campaigns and engagements with Apaches.

1550 ◆ BELL, JAMES

Rank: Private (highest rank: Sergeant)
Service: U.S. Army
Birthday: 1845
Place of Birth: County Antrim, Ireland
Date of Death: 1 July 1901
Place of Death: Chicago, Illinois
Cemetery: Mount Olivet Cemetery—Chicago, Illinois
Entered Service at: Troy, Rensselaer County, New York
Unit: Company E, 7th U.S. Infantry
Battle or Place of Action: Big Horn, Montana
Date of Action: 9 July 1876
Date of Issue: 2 December 1876
Citation: Carried dispatches to Gen. Crook at the imminent risk of his life.

1551 ◆ BERGENDAHL, FREDERICK

Rank: Private (highest rank: Sergeant)
Service: U.S. Army
Birthday: 26 February 1858
Place of Birth: Gothenburg, Sweden
Date of Death: 15 December 1889
Place of Death: Gothenburg, Sweden
Cemetery: The Cast Cemetery, Ostra Kyrkcogardco—Gothenburg, Sweden
Entered Service at: Boston, Suffolk County, Massachusetts
Unit: Band, 4th U.S. Cavalry
Battle or Place of Action: Staked Plains, Texas
Date of Action: 8 December 1874
Date of Issue: 13 October 1875
Citation: Gallantry in a long chase after Indians.

1552 ◆ BERTRAM, HEINRICH

Rank: Corporal
Service: U.S. Army
Birthday: 1842
Place of Birth: Brunswick, Germany
Entered Service at: Cincinnati, Hamilton County, Ohio
Unit: Company B, 8th U.S. Cavalry
Battle or Place of Action: Arizona
Date of Action: 1868
Date of Issue: 24 July 1869
Citation: Bravery in scouts and actions against Indians.

1553 ◆ BESSEY, CHARLES ALBERT

Rank: Corporal (highest rank: Chief Musician-Ret.)
Service: U.S. Army
Birthday: 6 November 1848
Place of Birth: Reading, Middlesex County, Massachusetts
Date of Death: 4 June 1909
Place of Death: Biloxi, Mississippi
Cemetery: Old Biloxi Cemetery—Biloxi, Mississippi
Entered Service at: Boston, Suffolk County, Massachusetts
Unit: Company A, 3d U.S. Cavalry
Battle or Place of Action: Elkhorn Creek, Wyoming
Date of Action: 13 January 1877
Date of Issue: 15 May 1890
Citation: While scouting with four men and being attacked in ambush by 14 hostile Indians, held his ground, two of his men being wounded, and kept up the fight until himself wounded in the side, and then went to the assistance of his wounded comrades.

1554 ◆ BISHOP, DANIEL

Rank: Sergeant
Service: U.S. Army
Birthday: 1846
Place of Birth: Monroe County, Ohio
Date of Death: 23 May 1891
Place of Death: Bellaire, Ohio
Cemetery: Greenwood Cemetery—Bellaire, Ohio
Entered Service at: Wheeling, Ohio County, West Virginia
Unit: Company A, 5th U.S. Cavalry
Battle or Place of Action: Turret Mountain, Arizona Territory
Date of Action: 25 March 1873
Date of Issue: 12 April 1875
Citation: Gallantry in engagements.

1555 ◆ BLAIR, JAMES

Rank: First Sergeant
Service: U.S. Army
Birthday: 1841
Place of Birth: Schuyler County, Pennsylvania
Entered Service at: Camp Winfield Scott, Humbolt County, Nevada
Unit: Company I, 1st U.S. Cavalry
Battle or Place of Action: Apache campaigns
Date of Action: 1872-73
Date of Issue: 12 April 1875
Citation: Gallant conduct during campaigns and engagements with Apaches.

1556 ◆ BLANQUET

Rank: Indian Scout
Service: U.S. Army
Place of Birth: Arizona
Unit: Indian Scouts
Battle or Place of Action: Apache campaigns

Date of Action: 1872-73
Date of Issue: 12 April 1875
Citation: Gallant conduct during campaigns and engagements with Apaches.

1557 ◆ BOWDEN, SAMUEL

Rank: Corporal
Service: U.S. Army
Birthday: 1846
Place of Birth: Salem, Essex County, Massachusetts
Entered Service at: Boston, Suffolk County, Massachusetts
Unit: Company M, 6th U.S. Cavalry
Battle or Place of Action: Wichita River, Texas
Date of Action: 5 October 1870
Date of Issue: 19 November 1870
Citation: Gallantry in pursuit of and fight with Indians.

1558 ◆ BOWMAN, ALONZO

Rank: Sergeant
Service: U.S. Army
Birthday: 15 June 1848
Place of Birth: Washington Township, Knox County, Maine
Date of Death: 4 October 1885
Place of Death: Fort Bayard, New Mexico
Cemetery: Fort Bayard National Cemetery (A-I-31)—Fort Bayard, New Mexico
Entered Service at: Boston, Suffolk County, Massachusetts
Unit: Company D, 6th U.S. Cavalry
Battle or Place of Action: Cibicu Creek, Arizona
Date of Action: 30 August 1881
Date of Issue: 4 November 1882
Citation: Conspicuous and extraordinary bravery in attacking mutinous scouts.

1559 ◆ BOYNE, THOMAS

Rank: Sergeant
Service: U.S. Army
Birthday: 1849
Place of Birth: Prince Georges County, Maryland
Date of Death: 21 April 1896
Place of Death: Washington, D.C.
Cemetery: Soldiers Home National Cemetery (J-5859) (MH)—Washington, D.C.,
Entered Service at: Norfolk, Norfolk County, Virginia
Unit: Company C, 9th U.S. Cavalry
Battle or Place of Action: Cuchillo Negro River & Mimbres Mountains, New Mexico
Date of Action: 29 May & 27 September 1879
Date of Issue: 6 January 1882
Citation: Bravery in action.

1560 ◆ BRADBURY, SANFORD

Rank: First Sergeant
Service: U.S. Army

Birthday: 1840
Place of Birth: Newton, Sussex County, New Jersey
Date of Death: 7 December 1911
Cemetery: Arlington National Cemetery (3-2162WS)—Arlington, Virginia
Entered Service at: Washington, D.C.
Unit: Company L, 8th U.S. Cavalry
Battle or Place of Action: Hell Canyon, Arizona
Date of Action: 3 July 1869
Date of Issue: 3 March 1870
Citation: Conspicuous gallantry in action.

1561 ◆ BRANAGAN, EDWARD

Rank: Private
Service: U.S. Army
Birthday: 1846
Place of Birth: County Louth, Ireland
Cemetery: Fort Concho National Historic Landmark (MH) (Marker Only)—San Angelo, Texas
Entered Service at: New York, New York
Unit: Company F, 4th U.S. Cavalry
Battle or Place of Action: Red River, Texas
Date of Action: 29 September 1872
Date of Issue: 19 November 1872
Citation: Gallantry in action.

1562 ◆ *BRANT, ABRAM B.

Rank: Private
Service: U.S. Army
Birthday: 1849
Place of Birth: New York, New York
Date of Death: 4 October 1878
Place of Death: near Camp Ruhlen, Dakota Territory
Cemetery: Fort Meade National Cemetery—Fort Meade, South Dakota (as unknown)
Entered Service at: St. Louis, St. Louis County, Missouri
Unit: Company D, 7th U.S. Cavalry
Battle or Place of Action: Little Big Horn, Montana
Date of Action: 25 June 1876
Date of Issue: 5 October 1878
Citation: Brought water for the wounded under a most galling fire.

1563 ◆ *BRATLING, FRANK

Rank: Corporal
Service: U.S. Army
Birthday: 1845
Place of Birth: Bavaria, Germany
Date of Death: 13 July 1873
Place of Death: near Canada Alamos, New Mexico
Cemetery: Post Cemetery—Fort McRae, New Mexico; Fort Bliss National Cemetery (MH)(marker only)—Fort Bliss, Texas
Entered Service at: Louisville, Jefferson County, Kentucky
Unit: Company C, 8th U.S. Cavalry
Battle or Place of Action: Fort Selden, New Mexico

Date of Action: 8-11 July 1873
Date of Issue: 12 August 1875
Citation: Services against hostile Indians.

1564 ◆ BRETT, LLOYD MILTON

Rank: Second Lieutenant (highest rank: Brigadier General-Ret.)
Service: U.S. Army
Birthday: 22 February 1856
Place of Birth: Dead River, Maine
Date of Death: 23 September 1927
Place of Death: Washington, D.C.
Cemetery: Arlington National Cemetery {6-8367)—Arlington, Virginia
Entered Service at: Malden, Middlesex County, Massachusetts
Unit: 2d U.S. Cavalry
Battle or Place of Action: O'Fallons Creek, Montana
Date of Action: 1 April 1880
Date of Issue: 7 February 1895
Citation: Fearless exposure and dashing bravery in cutting off the Indians' pony herd, thereby greatly crippling the hostiles.

1565 ◆ BROGAN, JAMES

True Name: Brogan, Edward James
Rank: Sergeant
Service: U.S. Army
Birthday: 1834
Place of Birth: County Donegal, Ireland
Date of Death: 30 October 1908
Place of Death: Summit Hill, Pennsylvania
Cemetery: Saint Joseph's Cemetery (MH)—Summit Hill, Pennsylvania
Entered Service at: Harrisburg, Dauphin County, Pennsylvania
Unit: Company G, 6th U.S. Cavalry
Battle or Place of Action: Simon Valley, Arizona
Date of Action: 14 December 1877
Date of Issue: 9 January 1880
Citation: Engaged singlehandedly two renegade Indians until his horse was shot under him and then pursued them so long as he was able.

1566 ◆ BROPHY, JAMES

Rank: Private
Service: U.S. Army
Birthday: 20 May 1846
Place of Birth: Kilkenny, Ireland
Date of Death: 7 August 1929
Cemetery: Soldiers Home National Cemetery (L-9086) (MH)—Washington, D.C.
Entered Service at: Stockton, San Joaquin County, California
Unit: Company B, 8th U.S. Cavalry
Battle or Place of Action: Arizona

Date of Action: 1868
Date of Issue: 24 July 1869
Citation: Bravery in scouts and actions against Indians.

1567 ◆ BROWN, BENJAMIN

Rank: Sergeant
Service: U.S. Army
Birthday: 1859
Place of Birth: Spotsylvania County, Virginia
Date of Death: 5 September 1910
Place of Death: Washington, D.C.
Cemetery: Soldier's Home National Cemetery (K-7519) (MH)—Washington, D.C.
Entered Service at: Harrisburg, Dauphin County, Pennsylvania
Unit: Company C, 24th U.S. Infantry
Battle or Place of Action: Arizona
Date of Action: 11 May 1889
Date of Issue: 19 February 1890
Citation: Although shot in the abdomen, in a fight between a paymaster's escort and robbers, did not leave the field until again wounded through both arms.

1568 ◆ BROWN, JAMES

Rank: Sergeant
Service: U.S. Army
Birthday: 1847
Place of Birth: Wexford, Ireland
Entered Service at: New York, New York
Unit: Company F, 5th U.S. Cavalry
Battle or Place of Action: Davidson Canyon, Arizona
Date of Action: 27 August 1872
Date of Issue: 4 December 1874
Citation: In command of a detachment of four men, defeated a superior force.

1569 ◆ BROWN, LORENZO DOW

Rank: Private
Service: U.S. Army
Birthday: December 1851
Place of Birth: Davidson County, North Carolina
Date of Death: 17 April 1906
Place of Death: near Jonesboro, Arkansas
Entered Service at: Indianapolis, Marion County, Indiana
Unit: Company A, 7th U.S. Infantry
Battle or Place of Action: Big Hole, Montana
Date of Action: 9 August 1877
Date of Issue: 8 May 1878
Citation: After having been severely wounded in right shoulder, continued to do duty in a most courageous manner.

1570 ◆ BRYAN, WILLIAM C.

Rank: Hospital Steward
Service: U.S. Army
Birthday: 9 September 1852

Place of Birth: Zanesville, Muskingum County, Ohio
Date of Death: 27 March 1933
Place of Death: Santa Monica, California
Cemetery: Forest Lawn Cemetery (MH)—Los Angeles, California
Entered Service at: St. Louis, St. Louis County, Missouri
Unit: U.S. Army
Battle or Place of Action: Powder River, Wyoming
Date of Action: 17 March 1876
Date of Issue: 15 June 1899
Citation: Accompanied a detachment of cavalry in a charge on a village of hostile Indians and fought through the engagements, having his horse killed under him. He continued to fight on foot, and under severe fire and without assistance conveyed two wounded comrades to places of safety, saving them from capture.

1571 ◆ BURKARD, OSCAR R.

Rank: Private (highest rank: Major, Medical Corps)
Service: U.S. Army
Birthday: 21 December 1877
Place of Birth: Baden Achern, Germany
Date of Death: 18 February 1950
Place of Death: Rome, New York
Cemetery: Rome Cemetery (MH)—Rome, New York
Entered Service at: Fort Snelling, St. Paul County, Minnesota
Unit: U.S. Army, Hospital Corps
Served as: Medic
Battle or Place of Action: Leech Lake, Minnesota
Date of Action: 5 October 1898
Date of Issue: 21 August 1899
Citation: For distinguished bravery in action against hostile Indians.
Notes: This, the last Medal of Honor won in an Indian campaign, was awarded for an action during the uprising of Chippewa Indians, on Lake Leech, northern Minn., 5 October 1898.

1572 ◆ BURKE, PATRICK J.

Rank: Farrier
Service: U.S. Army
Birthday: 1835
Place of Birth: Kilkenny, Ireland
Entered Service at: Vallejo, Solano County, California
Unit: Company B, 8th U.S. Cavalry
Battle or Place of Action: Arizona
Date of Action: 1868
Date of Issue: 24 July 1869
Citation: Bravery in scouts and actions against Indians.

1573 ◆ BURKE, RICHARD

Rank: Private
Service: U.S. Army
Birthday: 1847
Place of Birth: Tipperary, Ireland

Entered Service at: New York, New York
Unit: Company G., 5th U.S. Infantry
Battle or Place of Action: Cedar Creek, etc., Montana
Date of Action: October 1876—January 1877
Date of Issue: 27 April 1877
Citation: Gallantry in engagements.

1574 ◆ BURNETT, GEORGE RITTER

Rank: Second Lieutenant (highest rank: First Lieutenant)
Service: U.S. Army
Birthday: 21 April 1858
Place of Birth: Lower Providence Township, Pennsylvania
Date of Death: 1 November 1908
Place of Death: Lincoln, Nebraska
Cemetery: Arlington National Cemetery (3-2193WS)—Arlington, Virginia
Entered Service at: Spring Mills, Centre County, Pennsylvania
Unit: 9th U.S. Cavalry
Battle or Place of Action: Cuchillo Negro Mountains, New Mexico
Date of Action: 16 August 1881
Date of Issue: 23 July 1897
Citation: Saved the life of a dismounted soldier, who was in imminent danger of being cut off, by alone galloping quickly to his assistance under heavy fire and escorting him to a place of safety, his horse being twice shot in this action.

1575 ◆ BUTLER, EDMOND THOMAS

Rank: Captain (highest rank: Lieutenant Colonel)
Service: U.S. Army
Birthday: 19 March 1827
Place of Birth: Clonmel, County Tipperary, Ireland
Date of Death: 21 August 1895
Place of Death: Paris, France
Cemetery: Holy Sepulchre Cemetery (MH)—Omaha, Nebraska
Entered Service at: Brooklyn, Kings County, New York
Unit: 5th U.S. Infantry
Battle or Place of Action: Wolf Mountain, Montana
Date of Action: 8 January 1877
Date of Issue: 27 April 1877
Citation: Most distinguished gallantry in action with hostile Indians.

1576 ◆ BYRNE, DENIS

Rank: Sergeant
Service: U.S. Army
Birthday: 1833
Place of Birth: Wexford, Ireland
Date of Death: 31 December 1905
Place of Death: Birds Island, Minnesota
Entered Service at: New York, New York
Unit: Company G, 5th U.S. Infantry
Battle or Place of Action: Cedar Creek, etc., Montana

Date of Action: October 1876—January 1877
Date of Issue: 27 April 1877
Citation: Gallantry in engagements.

1577 ◆ CABLE, JOSEPH A.

Rank: Private (highest rank: Corporal)
Service: U.S. Army
Birthday: 1848
Place of Birth: Cape Girardeau, Cape Girardeau County, Missouri
Date of Death: 15 October 1877
Place of Death: Bear Paw Mountain, Montana
Cemetery: Custer Battlefield National Cemetery—Crow Agency, Montana
Entered Service at: Madison, Dane County, Wisconsin
Unit: Company I, 5th U.S. Infantry
Battle or Place of Action: Cedar Creek, etc., Montana
Date of Action: October 1876—January 1877
Date of Issue: 27 April 1877
Citation: Gallantry in action.

1578 ◆ CALLEN, THOMAS JOSEPH

True Name: Callan, Thomas Joseph
Rank: Private
Service: U.S. Army
Birthday: 13 July 1853
Place of Birth: County Louth, Ireland
Date of Death: 5 March 1908
Cemetery: Holy Sepulchre Cemetery (MH)—East Orange, New Jersey
Entered Service at: Boston, Suffolk County, Massachusetts
Unit: Company B, 7th U.S. Cavalry
Battle or Place of Action: Little Big Horn, Montana
Date of Action: 25-26 June 1876
Date of Issue: 24 October 1896
Citation: Volunteered and succeeded in obtaining water for the wounded of the command; also displayed conspicuously good conduct in assisting to drive away the Indians.

1579 ◆ CALVERT, JAMES SPENCER

Rank: Private (highest rank: Regimental Quartermaster Sergeant)
Service: U.S. Army
Birthday: 27 June 1852
Place of Birth: Athens County, Ohio
Date of Death: 26 February 1929
Place of Death: Washington, D.C.
Cemetery: Arlington National Cemetery (3-2490)—Arlington, Virginia
Entered Service at: Springfield, Sangamon County, Illinois
Unit: Company C, 5th U.S. Infantry
Battle or Place of Action: Cedar Creek, etc., Montana
Date of Action: October 1876—January 1877
Date of Issue: 27 April 1877
Citation: Gallantry in action.

1580 ◆ CANFIELD, HETH

Rank: Private
Service: U.S. Army
Birthday: 1849
Place of Birth: New Milford, Litchfield County, Connecticut
Date of Death: 16 December 1913
Place of Death: St. Augustine, Florida
Cemetery: Evergreen Cemetery (MH)—St. Augustine, Florida
Entered Service at: Carlisle, Cumberland County, Pennsylvania
Unit: Company C, 2d U.S. Cavalry
Battle or Place of Action: Little Blue, Nebraska
Date of Action: 15 May 1870
Date of Issue: 22 June 1870
Citation: Gallantry in action.

1581 ◆ CARPENTER, LOUIS HENRY

Rank: Captain (highest rank: Brigadier General Ret.)
Service: U.S. Army
Birthday: 11 February 1839
Place of Birth: Glassboro, Gloucester County, New Jersey
Date of Death: 21 January 1916
Place of Death: Philadelphia, Pennsylvania
Cemetery: Trinity Church Cemetery—Swedesboro, New Jersey
Entered Service at: Philadelphia, Philadelphia County, Pennsylvania
Unit: Company H, 10th U.S. Cavalry
Battle or Place of Action: Indian Campaigns, Kansas and Colorado
Date of Action: September, October 1868
Date of Issue: 8 April 1898
Citation: Was gallant and meritorious throughout the campaigns, especially in the combat of October 15 and in the forced march on September 23, 24 and 25 to the relief of Forsyth's Scouts, who were known to be in danger of annihilation by largely superior forces of Indians.

1582 ◆ CARR, JOHN

Rank: Private (highest rank: Corporal)
Service: U.S. Army
Birthday: 1847
Place of Birth: Columbus, Franklin County, Ohio
Date of Death: 15 July 1891
Place of Death: Columbian Arsenel, Tennessee
Cemetery: Nashville National Cemetery (A-16550) (MH)—Nashville, Tennessee
Entered Service at: San Jose, Santa Clara County, California
Unit: Company G, U.S. Cavalry
Battle or Place of Action: Chiricahua Mountains, Arizona Territory
Date of Action: 29 October 1869

Date of Issue: 14 February 1870
Citation: Gallantry in action.

1583 ◆ CARROLL, THOMAS

Rank: Private
Service: U.S. Army
Birthday: 1842
Place of Birth: Kilkenny, Ireland
Entered Service at: Chicago, Cook County, Illinois
Unit: Company L, 8th U.S. Cavalry
Battle or Place of Action: Arizona
Date of Action: August-October 1868
Date of Issue: 24 July 1869
Citation: Bravery in scouts and actions against Indians.

1584 ◆ CARTER, GEORGE

Rank: Private
Service: U.S. Army
Birthday: 1839
Place of Birth: Dublin, Ireland
Entered Service at: Vallejo, Solano County, California
Unit: Company B, 8th U.S. Cavalry
Battle or Place of Action: Arizona
Date of Action: August-October 1868
Date of Issue: 24 July 1869
Citation: Bravery in scouts and actions against Indians.

1585 ◆ CARTER, MASON

Rank: First Lieutenant (highest rank: Brevet Major)
Service: U.S. Army
Birthday: 26 January 1834
Place of Birth: Augusta, Richmond County, Georgia
Date of Death: 11 December 1909
Cemetery: Fort Rosecrans National Cemetery (PS-4-102)—San Diego, California
Entered Service at: Augusta, Richmond County, Georgia
Unit: 5th U.S. Infantry
Battle or Place of Action: Bear Paw Mountain, Montana
Date of Action: 30 October 1877
Date of Issue: 27 November 1894
Citation: Led a charge under a galling fire, in which he inflicted great loss upon the enemy.

1586 ◆ CARTER, ROBERT GOLDTHWAITE

Rank: Second Lieutenant (highest rank: Brevet Captain)
Service: U.S. Army
Birthday: 18 April 1847
Place of Birth: Bridgton, Cumberland County, Maine
Date of Death: 4 January 1936
Place of Death: Walter Reed Hospital, Washington, D.C.
Cemetery: Arlington National Cemetery (1-106A)—Arlington, Virginia
Entered Service at: Bradford, Essex County, Massachusetts
Unit: 4th U.S. Cavalry

Battle or Place of Action: Brazos River, Texas
Date of Action: 10 October 1871
Date of Issue: 27 February 1900
Citation: Held the left of the line with a few men during the charge of a large body of Indians, after the right of the line had retreated, and by delivering a rapid fire, succeeded in checking the enemy until other troops came to the rescue.

1587 ◆ CARTER, WILLIAM HARDING

Rank: First Lieutenant (highest rank: Major General)
Service: U.S. Army
Birthday: 19 November 1851
Place of Birth: Nashville, Davidson County, Tennessee
Date of Death: 24 May 1925
Place of Death: Washington, D.C.
Cemetery: Arlington National Cemetery (1-443-WS)— Arlington, Virginia
Entered Service at: New York, New York
Unit: 6th U.S. Cavalry
Battle or Place of Action: Cibicu, Arizona
Date of Action: 30 August 1881
Date of Issue: 17 October 1891
Citation: Rescued, with the voluntary assistance of two soldiers, the wounded from under a heavy fire.

1588 ◆ CASEY, JAMES SEAMAN

Rank: Captain (highest rank: Colonel-USA-Ret.)
Service: U.S. Army
Birthday: 28 January 1833
Place of Birth: Philadelphia, Philadelphia County, Pennsylvania
Date of Death: 24 December 1899
Place of Death: New York, New York
Cemetery: Vale Cemetery—Schenectady, New York
Entered Service at: New York, New York
Unit: 5th U.S. Infantry
Battle or Place of Action: Wolf Mountain, Montana
Date of Action: 8 January 1877
Date of Issue: 27 November 1894
Citation: Led his command in a successful charge against superior numbers of the enemy strongly posted.

1589 ◆ CHAPMAN, AMOS

Rank: Scout (Civilian)
Service: U.S. Army
Birthday: 15 March 1839
Place of Birth: Kalamazoo, Kalamazoo County, Michigan
Date of Death: 18 July 1925
Cemetery: Bromfield Cemetery—Seiling, Oklahoma
Entered Service at: Fort Supply, Indian Territory (Oklahoma)
Unit: 6th U.S. Cavalry (Assigned)
Battle or Place of Action: Washita River, Texas
Date of Action: 12 September 1874
Date of Issue: 7 November 1874
Citation: Gallantry in action.

1590 ◆ CHEEVER JR., BENJAMIN HARRISON

Rank: First Lieutenant (highest rank: Colonel)
Service: U.S. Army
Birthday: 7 June 1850
Place of Birth: Washington, D.C.
Date of Death: 21 October 1930
Place of Death: Atlantic City, New Jersey
Cemetery: Arlington National Cemetery (1-421) (MH)— Arlington, Virginia
Entered Service at: Washington, D.C.
Unit: 6th U.S. Cavalry
Battle or Place of Action: White River, South Dakota
Date of Action: 1 January 1891
Date of Issue: 25 April 1891
Citation: Headed the advance across White River, partly frozen, in a spirited movement to the effective assistance of Troop K, 6th U.S. Cavalry.

1591 ◆ CHIQUITO

Rank: Scout
Service: U.S. Army
Place of Birth: Arizona
Entered Service at: San Carlos, Gila County, Arizona
Unit: Indian Scouts
Battle or Place of Action: Arizona
Date of Action: winter 1872-73
Date of Issue: 12 April 1875
Citation: Gallant conduct during campaigns and engagements with Apaches.

1592 ◆ CLANCY, JOHN E.

Rank: Musician (highest rank: First Sergeant Ret.)
Service: U.S. Army
Birthday: 25 October 1869
Place of Birth: New York, New York
Date of Death: 11 July 1932
Cemetery: Fort Riley Post Cemetery (I-5) (MH)—Fort Riley, Kansas
Entered Service at: Vancouver Barracks, Clark County, Washington
Unit: Company E, 1st U.S. Artillery
Battle or Place of Action: Wounded Knee Creek, South Dakota
Date of Action: 29 December 1890
Date of Issue: 23 January 1892
Citation: Twice voluntarily rescued wounded comrades under fire of the enemy.

1593 ◆ CLARK, WILFRED

Rank: Private
Service: U.S. Army
Birthday: 1841
Place of Birth: Philadelphia, Philadelphia County, Pennsylvania
Entered Service at: Philadelphia, Philadelphia County, Pennsylvania

Unit: Company L, 2d U.S. Cavalry
Battle or Place of Action: Big Hole, Montana-Camas Meadows, Idaho
Date of Action: 9-20 August 1877
Date of Issue: 28 February 1878
Citation: Conspicuous gallantry; especial skill as sharpshooter.

1594 ◆ CLARKE, POWHATAN HENRY

Rank: Second Lieutenant
Service: U.S. Army
Birthday: 9 October 1862
Place of Birth: Alexandria, Rapides County, Louisiana
Date of Death: 21 July 1893
Place of Death: Little Big Horn River, Montana
Cemetery: Calvary Cemetery—St.Louis, Missouri
Entered Service at: Baltimore, Baltimore County, Maryland
Unit: 10th U.S. Cavalry
Battle or Place of Action: Pinito Mountains, Sonora, Mexico
Date of Action: 3 May 1886
Date of Issue: 12 March 1891
Citation: Rushed forward to the rescue of a soldier who was severely wounded and lay, disabled, exposed to the enemy's fire, and carried him to a place of safety.

1595 ◆ CODY, WILLIAM FREDERICK "BUFFALO BILL"

Rank: Guide (Civilian)
Service: U.S. Army
Birthday: 16 February 1846
Place of Birth: Scott County, Iowa
Date of Death: 10 January 1917
Place of Death: Denver, Colorado
Cemetery: Lookout Mountain (MH)—Golden, Colorado
Entered Service at: Fort McPherson, Nebraska
Unit: Indian Scouts attached to 3d U.S. Cavalry
Battle or Place of Action: Loupe Fork of the Platte River, Nebraska
Date of Action: 26 April 1872
Date of Issue: 22 May 1872
Citation: Gallantry in action.

1596 ◆ COMFORT, JOHN W.

Rank: Corporal
Service: U.S. Army
Birthday: 1844
Place of Birth: Philadelphia, Philadelphia County, Pennsylvania
Date of Death: 29 November 1893
Place of Death: Philadelphia, Pennsylvania
Cemetery: Mount Peace Cemetery—Rockledge, Pennsylvania
Entered Service at: Philadelphia, Philadelphia County, Pennsylvania
Unit: Company A, 4th U.S. Cavalry

Battle or Place of Action: Staked Plains, Texas
Date of Action: 5 November 1874
Date of Issue: 13 October 1875
Citation: Ran down and killed an Indian.

1597 ◆ CONNOR, JOHN

Rank: Corporal (highest rank: Sergeant Ret.)
Service: U.S. Army
Birthday: 1845
Place of Birth: Galway, Ireland
Date of Death: 5 February 1907
Place of Death: Washington, D.C.
Cemetery: Soldier's Home National Cemetery (K-7258) (MH)—Washington, D.C.
Entered Service at: Jefferson, Marion County, Texas
Unit: Company H, 6th U.S. Cavalry
Battle or Place of Action: Wichita River, Texas
Date of Action: 12 July 1870
Date of Issue: 25 August 1870
Citation: Gallantry in action.

1598 ◆ COONROD, AQUILLA

Rank: Sergeant (highest rank: First Sergeant)
Service: U.S. Army
Birthday: 1831
Place of Birth: Williams County, Ohio
Date of Death: 14 May 1884
Cemetery: Custer Battlefield National Monument (A-372)—Crow Agency, Montana
Entered Service at: Bryan, Williams County, Ohio
Unit: Company C, 5th U.S. Infantry
Battle or Place of Action: Cedar Creek, etc., Montana
Date of Action: October 1876—January 1877
Date of Issue: 27 April 1877
Citation: Gallantry in action.

1599 ◆ CORCORAN, MICHAEL

Rank: Corporal
Service: U.S. Army
Birthday: 1847
Place of Birth: Philadelphia, Philadelphia County, Pennsylvania
Date of Death: 3 October 1919
Cemetery: Calvary Cemetery—Cleveland, Ohio
Entered Service at: Wheeling, Ohio County, West Virginia
Unit: Company E, 8th U.S. Cavalry
Battle or Place of Action: Agua Fria River, Arizona
Date of Action: 25 August 1869
Date of Issue: 3 March 1870
Citation: Gallantry in action.

1600 ◆ CO-RUX-TE-CHOD-ISH (MAD BEAR)

Rank: Sergeant
Service: U.S. Army
Place of Birth: Nebraska

Entered Service at: Columbus, Platte County, Nebraska
Unit: U.S. Army
Battle or Place of Action: Republican River, Kansas
Date of Action: 8 July 1869
Date of Issue: 24 August 1869
Citation: Ran out from the command in pursuit of a dismounted Indian; was shot down and badly wounded by a bullet from his own command.

1601 ◆ CRAIG, SAMUEL HENRY

Rank: Sergeant (highest rank: First Sergeant)
Service: U.S. Army
Birthday: 31 October 1863
Place of Birth: New Market, Rockingham County, New Hampshire
Date of Death: 1 June 1929
Place of Death: Kittery, Maine
Cemetery: Laurel Hill Cemetery (MH)—Saco, Maine
Entered Service at: Chicago, Cook County, Illinois
Unit: Company D, 4th U.S. Cavalry
Battle or Place of Action: Santa Cruz Mountains, Mexico
Date of Action: 15 May 1886
Date of Issue: 27 April 1887
Citation: Conspicuous gallantry during an attack on a hostile Apache Indian camp; seriously wounded.

1602 ◆ CRANDALL, CHARLES

Rank: Private
Service: U.S. Army
Birthday: 1847
Place of Birth: Worcester, Worcester County, Massachusetts
Entered Service at: Philadelphia, Philadelphia County, Pennsylvania
Unit: Company B, 8th U.S. Cavalry
Battle or Place of Action: Arizona
Date of Action: August-October 1868
Date of Issue: 24 July 1869
Citation: Bravery in scouts and actions against Indians.

1603 ◆ CRIST, JOHN

Rank: Sergeant
Service: U.S. Army
Birthday: 1845
Place of Birth: Baltimore, Baltimore County, Maryland
Entered Service at: Baltimore, Baltimore County, Maryland
Unit: Company L, 8th U.S. Cavalry
Battle or Place of Action: Arizona
Date of Action: 26 November 1869
Date of Issue: 3 March 1870
Citation: Gallantry in action.

1604 ◆ CRISWELL, BENJAMIN C.

Rank: Sergeant (highest rank: First Sergeant)
Service: U.S. Army

Birthday: 9 February 1849
Place of Birth: Moundsville, Marshall County, West Virginia
Date of Death: 17 October 1921
Place of Death: Eldorado, Oklahoma
Entered Service at: Cincinnati, Hamilton County, Ohio
Unit: Company B, 7th U.S. Cavalry
Battle or Place of Action: Little Big Horn River, Montana
Date of Action: 25 June 1876
Date of Issue: 5 October 1878
Citation: Rescued the body of Lt. Hodgson from within the enemy's lines; brought up ammunition and encouraged the men in the most exposed positions under heavy fire.

1605 ◆ CRUSE, THOMAS

Rank: Second Lieutenant (highest rank: Brigadier General)
Service: U.S. Army
Birthday: 29 December 1857
Place of Birth: Owensboro, Daviess County, Kentucky
Date of Death: 8 June 1943
Cemetery: Arlington National Cemetery (3-1763)—Arlington, Virginia
Entered Service at: Owensboro, Daviess County, Kentucky
Unit: 6th U.S. Cavalry
Battle or Place of Action: Big Dry Fork (Chevelon's Fork), Arizona
Date of Action: 17 July 1882
Date of Issue: 12 July 1892
Citation: Gallantly charged hostile Indians and with his carbine compelled a party of them to keep under cover of their breastworks, thus being enabled to recover a severely wounded soldier.

1606 ◆ CUBBERLY, WILLIAM G.

Rank: Private
Service: U.S. Army
Birthday: 26 November 1847
Place of Birth: Butler County, Ohio
Date of Death: 27 July 1919
Cemetery: Union Cemetery—Lyonsville, Indiana
Entered Service at: Cincinnati, Hamilton County, Ohio
Unit: Company L, 8th U.S. Cavalry
Battle or Place of Action: San Carlos, Arizona
Date of Action: 30 May 1868
Date of Issue: 28 July 1868
Citation: With two other men he volunteered to search for a wagon passage out of a 4,000-foot valley wherein an infantry column was immobile. This small group passed six miles among hostile Apache terrain finding the sought passage. On their return trip down the canyon they were attacked by Apache, who were successfully held at bay.

1607 ◆ CUNNINGHAM, CHARLES

Rank: Corporal
Service: U.S. Army
Birthday: 1845
Place of Birth: Hudson, Columbia County, New York

Entered Service at: New York, New York
Unit: Company B, 7th U.S. Cavalry
Battle or Place of Action: Little Big Horn River, Montana
Date of Action: 25 June 1876
Date of Issue: 5 October 1878
Citation: Declined to leave the line when wounded in the neck during heavy fire and fought bravely all next day.

1608 ◆ DAILY, CHARLES

Rank: Private
Service: U.S. Army
Birthday: 1841
Place of Birth: Mallow, County Cork, Ireland
Entered Service at: Philadelphia, Philadelphia County, Pennsylvania
Unit: Company B, 8th U.S. Cavalry
Battle or Place of Action: Arizona
Date of Action: August-October 1868
Date of Issue: 24 July 1869
Citation: Bravery in scouts and actions against Indians.

1609 ◆ DANIELS, JAMES THOMAS

Rank: Sergeant
Service: U.S. Army
Birthday: 1860
Place of Birth: Richland County, Illinois
Date of Death: 2 January 1933
Place of Death: Richmond, Virginia
Cemetery: Riverview Cemetery—Richmond, Virginia
Entered Service at: Fort Leavenworth, Leavenworth County, Kansas
Unit: Company L, 4th U.S. Cavalry
Battle or Place of Action: Arizona
Date of Action: 7 March 1890
Date of Issue: 15 May 1890
Citation: Untiring energy and cool gallantry under fire in an engagement with Apache Indians.

1610 ◆ DAWSON, MICHAEL

Rank: Trumpeter (highest rank: Musician)
Service: U.S. Army
Birthday: 1845
Place of Birth: Boston, Suffolk County, Massachusetts
Entered Service at: New York, New York
Unit: Company H, 6th U.S. Cavalry
Battle or Place of Action: Sappa Creek, Kansas
Date of Action: 23 April 1875
Date of Issue: 16 November 1876
Citation: Gallantry in action.

1611 ◆ DAY, MATTHIAS WALTER

Rank: Second Lieutenant (highest rank: Colonel Ret.)
Service: U.S. Army
Birthday: 8 August 1853

Place of Birth: Mansfield, Richland County, Ohio
Date of Death: 12 September 1927
Place of Death: Los Angeles, California
Cemetery: San Francisco National Cemetery OS-2-11—San Francisco, California
Entered Service at: Oberlin, Lorain County, Ohio
Unit: 9th U.S. Cavalry
Battle or Place of Action: Las Animas Canyon, New Mexico
Date of Action: 18 September 1879
Date of Issue: 7 May 1890
Citation: Advanced alone into the enemy's lines and carried off a wounded soldier of his command under a hot fire and after he had been ordered to retreat.

1612 ◆ DAY, WILLIAM L.

Rank: First Sergeant
Service: U.S. Army
Birthday: 1837
Place of Birth: Barron County, Kentucky
Entered Service at: Louisville, Jefferson County, Kentucky
Unit: Company E, 5th U.S. Cavalry
Battle or Place of Action: Apache campaigns
Date of Action: 1872-73
Date of Issue: 12 April 1875
Citation: Gallant conduct during campaigns and engagements with Apaches.

1613 ◆ *DE ARMOND, WILLIAM

Rank: Sergeant
Service: U.S. Army
Birthday: 1838
Place of Birth: Butler County, Ohio
Date of Death: 9 September 1874
Cemetery: San Antonio National Cemetery (MH)—San Antonio, Texas
Entered Service at: New York, New York
Unit: Company I, 5th U.S. Infantry
Battle or Place of Action: Upper Washita, Texas
Date of Action: 9-11 September 1874
Date of Issue: 23 April 1875
Citation: Gallantry in action.

1614 ◆ DEARY, GEORGE

Rank: Sergeant
Service: U.S. Army
Birthday: 1845
Place of Birth: Philadelphia, Philadelphia County, Pennsylvania
Date of Death: 26 September 1901
Place of Death: Philadelphia, Pennsylvania
Cemetery: Mount Moriah Cemetery—Philadelphia, Pennsylvania
Entered Service at: Philadelphia, Philadelphia County, Pennsylvania
Unit: Company L, 5th U.S. Cavalry

Battle or Place of Action: Apache Creek, Arizona
Date of Action: 2 April 1874
Date of Issue: 12 April 1875
Citation: Gallantry in action.

1615 ◆ DEETLINE, FREDERICK

Rank: Private (highest rank: Quartermaster Sergeant)
Service: U.S. Army
Birthday: 1846
Place of Birth: Offenheim, Germany
Date of Death: 13 December 1910
Cemetery: San Antonio National Cemetery (F-921) (MH)—San Antonio, Texas
Entered Service at: Baltimore, Baltimore County, Maryland
Unit: Company D, 7th U.S. Cavalry
Battle or Place of Action: Little Big Horn, Montana
Date of Action: 25 June 1876
Date of Issue: 15 October 1878
Citation: Voluntarily brought water to wounded under fire.

1616 ◆ DENNY, JOHN

Rank: Sergeant
Service: U.S. Army
Birthday: 1846
Place of Birth: Big Flats, Chemung County, New York
Date of Death: 28 November 1901
Place of Death: Washington, D.C.
Cemetery: Soldier's Home Cemetery (K-7020) (MH)—Washington, D.C.
Entered Service at: Elmira, Chemung County, New York
Unit: Company C, 9th U.S. Cavalry
Battle or Place of Action: Las Animas Canyon, New Mexico
Date of Action: 18 September 1879
Date of Issue: 27 November 1894
Citation: Removed a wounded comrade, under a heavy fire, to a place of safety.

1617 ◆ DICKENS, CHARLES H.

Rank: Corporal
Service: U.S. Army
Place of Birth: Dublin, Ireland
Date of Death: 1 March 1880
Cemetery: St. John's Cemetery—Worcester, Massachusetts
Entered Service at: San Francisco, San Francisco County, California
Unit: Company G, 8th U.S. Cavalry
Battle or Place of Action: Chiricahua Mountains, Arizona Territory
Date of Action: 20 October 1869
Date of Issue: 14 February 1870
Citation: Gallantry in action.

1618 ◆ DIXON, WILLIAM "BILLY"

Rank: Scout (Civilian)
Service: U.S. Army

Birthday: 25 September 1850
Place of Birth: Ohio County, West Virginia
Date of Death: 9 March 1913
Place of Death: Cimmarron County, Oklahoma
Cemetery: Adobe Walls Battlefield Site (MH)—Adobe Walls, Texas
Entered Service at: Indian Territory
Unit: Indian Scouts
Battle or Place of Action: Washita River, Texas
Date of Action: 12 September 1874
Date of Issue: 7 November 1874
Citation: Gallantry in action.

1619 ◆ DODGE, FRANCIS SAFFORD

Rank: Captain (highest rank: Brigadier General)
Service: U.S. Army
Birthday: 9 November 1842
Place of Birth: Danvers, Essex County, Massachusetts
Date of Death: 19 February 1908
Cemetery: Arlington National Cemetery (3-1874)—Arlington, Virginia
Entered Service at: Danvers, Essex County, Massachusetts
Unit: Troop D, 9th U.S. Cavalry
Battle or Place of Action: White River Agency, Colorado
Date of Action: 29 September 1879
Date of Issue: 2 April 1898
Citation: With a force of 40 men rode all night to the relief of a command that had been defeated and was besieged by an overwhelming force of Indians, reached the field at daylight, joined in the action, and fought for three days.

1620 ◆ DONAHUE, JOHN L.

True Name: Donohue, John L.
Rank: Private
Service: U.S. Army
Birthday: 1847
Place of Birth: Baltimore County, Maryland
Date of Death: 16 March 1900
Cemetery: Arlington National Cemetery (13-14045)—Arlington, Virginia
Entered Service at: Baltimore, Baltimore County, Maryland
Unit: Company G, 8th U.S. Cavalry
Battle or Place of Action: Chiricahua Mountains, Arizona Territory
Date of Action: 20 October 1869
Date of Issue: 14 February 1870
Citation: Gallantry in action.

1621 ◆ DONAVAN, CORNELIUS

True Name: Donovan, Cornelius
Rank: Sergeant
Service: U.S. Army
Birthday: 1839
Place of Birth: County Cork, Ireland
Entered Service at: New York, New York
Unit: Company E, 8th U.S. Cavalry

Battle or Place of Action: Agua Fria River, Arizona
Date of Action: 25 August 1869
Date of Issue: 3 March 1870
Citation: Gallantry in action.

1622 ◆ DONELLY, JOHN S.

True Name: Donnelly, John S.
Rank: Private
Service: U.S. Army
Birthday: 1850
Place of Birth: County Kerry, Ireland
Entered Service at: Jersey City, Hudson County, New Jersey
Unit: Company G, 5th U.S. Infantry
Battle or Place of Action: Cedar Creek, etc., Montana
Date of Action: October 1876—January 1877
Date of Issue: 27 April 1877
Citation: Gallantry in action.

1623 ◆ DOUGHERTY, WILLIAM

Rank: Blacksmith
Service: U.S. Army
Birthday: 1841
Place of Birth: Detroit, Wayne County, Michigan
Entered Service at: Philadelphia, Philadelphia County, Pennsylvania
Unit: Company B, 8th U.S. Cavalry
Battle or Place of Action: Arizona
Date of Action: August-October 1868
Date of Issue: 24 July 1869
Citation: Bravery in scouts and actions against Indians.

1624 ◆ DOWLING, JAMES

Rank: Corporal (highest rank: Sergeant)
Service: U.S. Army
Birthday: August 1846
Place of Birth: County Meath, Ireland
Date of Death: 26 December 1891
Place of Death: Washington, D.C.
Cemetery: Soldier's Home National Cemetery (J-6352) (MH)—Washington, D.C.
Entered Service at: Cleveland, Cuyahoga County, Ohio
Unit: Company B, 8th U.S. Cavalry
Battle or Place of Action: Arizona
Date of Action: August-October 1868
Date of Issue: 24 July 1869
Citation: Bravery in scouts and actions against Indians.

1625 ◆ DOZIER, JAMES B.

True Name: Dosher, James B.
Rank: Civilian Guide
Service: U.S. Army
Birthday: 2 May 1820
Place of Birth: Warren County, Tennessee
Date of Death: Early 1900's

Place of Death: Jacksboro, Texas
Cemetery: Bottom Cemetery (MH)—Jack County, Texas
Entered Service at: Fort Richardson, Texas
Unit: Indian Scouts
Battle or Place of Action: Wichita River, Texas
Date of Action: 5 October 1870
Date of Issue: 19 November 1870
Citation: Gallantry in action and on the march.

1626 ◆ EDWARDS, WILLIAM D.

Rank: First Sergeant
Service: U.S. Army
Birthday: 1849
Place of Birth: Brooklyn, Kings County, New York
Date of Death: 24 January 1903
Place of Death: Washington, D.C.
Cemetery: Soldier's Home National Cemetery (K-7023) (MH)—Washington, D.C.
Entered Service at: Brooklyn, Kings County, New York
Unit: Company F, 7th U.S. Infantry
Battle or Place of Action: Big Hole, Montana
Date of Action: 9 August 1877
Date of Issue: 2 December 1878
Citation: Bravery in action.

1627 ◆ ELDRIDGE, GEORGE H.

Rank: Sergeant
Service: U.S. Army
Birthday: 12 May 1846
Place of Birth: Sackets Harbor, Jefferson County, New York
Date of Death: 20 November 1918
Place of Death: Los Angeles, California
Cemetery: Los Angeles National Cemetery (37-B-1) (MH)—Los Angeles, California
Entered Service at: Detroit, Wayne County, Michigan
Unit: Company C, 6th U.S. Cavalry
Battle or Place of Action: Wichita River, Texas
Date of Action: 12 July 1870
Date of Issue: 25 August 1870
Citation: Gallantry in action.

1628 ◆ ELSATSOOSH

Rank: Corporal
Service: U.S. Army
Place of Birth: Arizona Territory
Unit: Indian Scouts
Battle or Place of Action: Apache campaigns
Date of Action: winter 1872-73
Date of Issue: 12 April 1875
Citation: Gallant conduct during campaigns and engagements with Apaches.

1629 ◆ ELWOOD, EDWIN L.

Rank: Private
Service: U.S. Army

Birthday: 1847
Place of Birth: St. Louis, St Louis County, Missouri
Date of Death: 13 September 1907
Cemetery: Santa Fe National Cemetery (H-705) (MH)—Santa Fe, New Mexico
Entered Service at: San Jose, Santa Clara County, California
Unit: Company G, 8th U.S. Cavalry
Battle or Place of Action: Chiricahua Mountains, Arizona Territory
Date of Action: 20 October 1869
Date of Issue: 14 February 1870
Citation: Gallantry in action.

1630 ◆ EMMET, ROBERT TEMPLE

Rank: Second Lieutenant (highest rank: Colonel)
Service: U.S. Army
Birthday: 13 December 1854
Place of Birth: New York, New York
Date of Death: 25 October 1936
Place of Death: Ashfield, Massachusetts
Cemetery: Beechwoods Cemetery—New Rochelle, New York
Entered Service at: New York, New York
Unit: 9th U.S. Cavalry
Battle or Place of Action: Las Animas Canyon, New Mexico
Date of Action: 18 September 1879
Date of Issue: 24 August 1899
Citation: Lt. Emmet was in G Troop, which was sent to relieve a detachment of soldiers under attack by hostile Apaches. During a flank attack on the Indian camp, made to divert the hostiles, Lt. Emmet and five of his men became surrounded when the Indians returned to defend their camp. Finding that the Indians were making for a position from which they could direct their fire on the retreating troop, the lieutenant held his point with his party until the soldiers reached the safety of a canyon. Lt. Emmet then continued to hold his position while his party recovered their horses. The enemy force consisted of approximately 200.

1631 ◆ EVANS, WILLIAM

Rank: Private
Service: U.S. Army
Birthday: 1851
Place of Birth: Annagh, Ireland
Date of Death: 27 August 1881
Place of Death: St. Louis, Missouri
Cemetery: Bellefontaine Cemetery (MH)—St. Louis, Missouri
Entered Service at: St. Louis, St. Louis County, Missouri
Unit: Company E, 7th U.S. Infantry
Battle or Place of Action: Big Horn, Montana
Date of Action: 9 July 1876
Date of Issue: 9 July 1876
Citation: Carried dispatches to Brig. Gen. Crook through a country occupied by Sioux.

1632 ◆ FACTOR, POMPEY

Rank: Private
Service: U.S. Army
Birthday: 1849
Place of Birth: Arkansas
Date of Death: 29 March 1928
Cemetery: Seminole Indian Scout Cemetery (MH)—Brackettsville, Texas
Entered Service at: Fort Duncan, Texas
Unit: Indian Scouts
Battle or Place of Action: Pecos River, Texas
Date of Action: 25 April 1875
Date of Issue: 28 May 1875
Citation: With three other men, he participated in a charge against 25 hostiles while on a scouting patrol.

1633 ◆ FALCOTT, HENRY

Rank: Sergeant (highest rank: First Sergeant)
Service: U.S. Army
Birthday: 1835
Place of Birth: Champagne, France
Date of Death: 2 December 1910
Place of Death: San Antonio, Texas
Cemetery: San Antonio National Cemetery (F-918) (MH)—San Antonio, Texas
Entered Service at: San Francisco, San Francisco County, California
Unit: Company L, 8th U.S. Cavalry
Battle or Place of Action: Arizona
Date of Action: August-October 1868
Date of Issue: 24 July 1869
Citation: Bravery in scouts and actions against Indians.

1634 ◆ FARREN, DANIEL

Rank: Private
Service: U.S. Army
Birthday: 1848
Place of Birth: County Derry, Ireland
Entered Service at: Philadelphia, Philadelphia County, Pennsylvania
Unit: Company B, 8th U.S. Cavalry
Battle or Place of Action: Arizona
Date of Action: August-October 1868
Date of Issue: 24 July 1869
Citation: Bravery in scouts and actions against Indians.

1635 ◆ FEASTER, MOSHEIM

Rank: Private
Service: U.S. Army
Birthday: 27 May 1867
Place of Birth: Schellsburg, Bedford County, Pennsylvania
Date of Death: 18 March 1950
Cemetery: Golden Gate National Cemetery (0-319)—San Bruno, California

Entered Service at: Cleveland, Cuyahoga County, Ohio
Unit: Company E, 7th U.S. Cavalry
Battle or Place of Action: Wounded Knee Creek, South Dakota
Date of Action: 29 December 1890
Date of Issue: 23 June 1891
Citation: Extraordinary gallantry.

1636 ◆ FEGAN, JAMES

Rank: Sergeant
Service: U.S. Army
Birthday: 1827
Place of Birth: Athlone, County Westmeath, Ireland
Date of Death: 25 June 1886
Cemetery: Custer Battlefield National Monument (A-749)—Crow Agency, Montana
Entered Service at: New York, New York
Unit: Company H, 3d U.S. Infantry
Battle or Place of Action: Plum Creek, Kansas
Date of Action: March 1868
Date of Issue: 19 October 1878
Citation: While in charge of a powder train en route from Fort Harker to Fort Dodge, Kan., was attacked by a party of desperadoes, who attempted to rescue a deserter in his charge and to fire the train. Sgt. Fegan, singlehandedly, repelled the attacking party, wounding two of them, and brought his train through in safety.

1637 ◆ FERRARI, GEORGE

Rank: Corporal
Service: U.S. Army
Birthday: 1845
Place of Birth: New York, New York
Entered Service at: Cleveland, Cuyahoga County, Ohio
Unit: Company D, 8th U.S. Cavalry
Battle or Place of Action: Red Creek, Arizona
Date of Action: 23 September 1869
Date of Issue: 23 November 1869
Citation: Gallantry in action.

1638 ◆ FICHTER, HERMANN EMIL

Rank: Private (highest rank: Corporal)
Service: U.S. Army
Birthday: 30 March 1845
Place of Birth: Baden, Germany
Date of Death: 5 August 1912
Place of Death: Quincy, Illinois
Cemetery: St. Boniface Cemetery (MH)—Quincy, Illinois
Entered Service at: New York, New York
Unit: Company F, 3d U.S. Cavalry
Battle or Place of Action: Whetstone Mountains, Arizona Territory
Date of Action: 5 May 1871
Date of Issue: 13 November 1871
Citation: Gallantry in action.

1639 ◆ FOLEY, JOHN H.

Rank: Sergeant
Service: U.S. Army
Birthday: 1839
Place of Birth: Cork, Ireland
Date of Death: 18 November 1874
Place of Death: Benicia Barracks, California
Cemetery: Post Cemetery as Unknown—Benicia Barracks, California
Entered Service at: Boston, Suffolk County, Massachusetts
Unit: Company B, 3d U.S. Cavalry
Battle or Place of Action: Loupe Fork of the Platte River, Nebraska
Date of Action: 26 April 1872
Date of Issue: 22 May 1872
Citation: Gallantry in action.

1640 ◆ FOLLY, WILLIAM H.

Rank: Private
Service: U.S. Army
Birthday: 1845
Place of Birth: Bergen County, New Jersey
Entered Service at: New York, New York
Unit: Company B, 8th U.S. Cavalry
Battle or Place of Action: Arizona
Date of Action: August-October 1868
Citation: Bravery in scouts and actions against Indians.

1641 ◆ FORAN, NICHOLAS

Rank: Private (highest rank: Sergeant)
Service: U.S. Army
Birthday: 3 June 1844
Place of Birth: County Waterford, Ireland
Date of Death: 29 September 1927
Place of Death: Prescott, Arizona
Cemetery: Prescott National Cemetery (1-2-54) (MH)—Prescott, Arizona
Entered Service at: St. Louis, St. Louis County, Missouri
Unit: Company L, 8th U.S. Cavalry
Battle or Place of Action: Arizona
Date of Action: August-October 1868
Date of Issue: 24 July 1869
Citation: Bravery in scouts and actions against Indians.

1642 ◆ FORSYTH, THOMAS HALL

Rank: First Sergeant (highest rank: Commissary Sergeant Ret.)
Service: U.S. Army
Birthday: 17 December 1842
Place of Birth: Hartford, Hartford County, Connecticut
Date of Death: 22 March 1908
Place of Death: San Diego, California
Cemetery: Mount Hope Cemetery (MH)—San Diego, California

Entered Service at: St. Louis, St. Louis County, Missouri
Unit: Company M, 4th U.S. Cavalry
Battle or Place of Action: Powder River, Wyoming
Date of Action: 25 November 1876
Date of Issue: 14 July 1891
Citation: Though dangerously wounded, he maintained his ground with a small party against a largely superior force after his commanding officer had been shot down during a sudden attack and rescued that officer and a comrade from the enemy.

1643 ◆ FOSTER, WILLIAM

Rank: Sergeant
Service: U.S. Army
Birthday: 1832
Place of Birth: Somerset County, England
Date of Death: 16 July 1880
Place of Death: Presido of San Francisco, California
Cemetery: San Francisco National Cemetery (WS-187) (MH)—San Francisco, California
Entered Service at: Bakersville, Maryland
Unit: Company F, 4th U.S. Cavalry
Battle or Place of Action: Red River, Texas
Date of Action: 29 September 1872
Date of Issue: 19 November 1872
Citation: Gallantry in action.

1644 ◆ FREEMEYER, CHRISTOPHER

Rank: Private
Service: U.S. Army
Birthday: 1838
Place of Birth: Bavaria, Germany
Date of Death: 14 October 1894
Cemetery: Cypress Hills National Cemetery (2-5259) (MH)—Brooklyn, New York
Entered Service at: New York, New York
Unit: Company D, 5th U.S. Infantry
Battle or Place of Action: Cedar Creek, etc., Montana
Date of Action: 21 October 1876—8 January 1877
Date of Issue: 27 April 1877
Citation: Gallantry in action.

1645 ◆ GARDINER, PETER W.

Rank: Private
Service: U.S. Army
Birthday: 1841
Place of Birth: Carlisle, Schoharie County, New York
Date of Death: 1883
Place of Death: Fort Lowell, Arizona
Entered Service at: New York, New York
Unit: Company H, 6th U.S. Cavalry
Battle or Place of Action: Sappa Creek, Kansas
Date of Action: 23 April 1875
Date of Issue: 16 November 1876
Citation: With five other men he waded in mud and water up the creek to a position directly behind an entrenched Cheyenne position, who were using natural bank pits to good

advantage against the main column. This surprise attack from the enemy rear broke their resistance.

1646 ◆ GARDNER, CHARLES

True Name: Suhler, Simon
Rank: Private
Service: U.S. Army
Birthday: 1844
Place of Birth: Bavaria, Germany
Date of Death: 16 May 1895
Cemetery: San Antonio National Cemetery (I-1610) (MH)—San Antonio, Texas
Entered Service at: San Francisco, San Francisco County, California
Unit: Company B, 8th U.S. Cavalry
Battle or Place of Action: Arizona
Date of Action: August-October 1868
Date of Issue: 24 July 1869
Citation: Bravery in scouts and actions against Indians.
Notes: POW—Civil War

1647 ◆ GARLAND, HARRY

Rank: Corporal (highest rank: Hospital Steward)
Service: U.S. Army
Birthday: 1844
Place of Birth: Boston, Suffolk County, Massachusetts
Date of Death: 7 May 1883
Cemetery: unknown gravesite, Fort Ellis, Wyoming
Entered Service at: Indianapolis, Marion County, Indiana
Unit: Company L, 2d U.S. Cavalry
Battle or Place of Action: Little Muddy Creek, Montana & Camas Meadows, Idaho
Date of Action: 7 May & 29 August 1877
Date of Issue: 28 February 1878
Citation: Gallantry in action with hostile Sioux at Little Muddy Creek, Mont.; having been wounded in the hip so as to be unable to stand, at Camas Meadows, Idaho, he still continued to direct the men under his charge until the enemy withdrew.

1648 ◆ GARLINGTON, ERNEST ALBERT

Rank: First Lieutenant (highest rank: Brigadier General)
Service: U.S. Army
Birthday: 20 February 1853
Place of Birth: Newberry Hill, Newberry County, South Carolina
Date of Death: 16 October 1934
Place of Death: California
Cemetery: Arlington National Cemetery (3-1735-B)—Arlington, Virginia
Entered Service at: Athens, Clarke County, Georgia
Unit: 7th U.S. Cavalry
Battle or Place of Action: Wounded Knee Creek, South Dakota
Date of Action: 29 December 1890
Date of Issue: 26 September 1893
Citation: Distinguished gallantry.

1649 ◆ GATES, GEORGE

Rank: Bugler (highest rank: Blacksmith)
Service: U.S. Army
Birthday: 30 July 1844
Place of Birth: Delaware County, Ohio
Date of Death: 18 March 1915
Place of Death: Quincy, Illinois
Cemetery: Illinois Veteran Home Sunset Cemetery (MH)—Quincy, Illinois
Entered Service at: Dubuque, Dubuque County, Iowa
Unit: 8th U.S. Cavalry
Battle or Place of Action: Picacho Mountain, Arizona Territory
Date of Action: 4 June 1869
Date of Issue: 3 March 1870
Citation: Killed an Indian warrior and captured his arms.

1650 ◆ GAY, THOMAS H.

Rank: Private (highest rank: Sergeant)
Service: U.S. Army
Birthday: 8 June 1848
Place of Birth: Prince Edward Island, Canada
Date of Death: 28 February 1895
Place of Death: Attleboro, Massachusetts
Cemetery: Woodlawn Cemetery (MH)—Attleboro, Massachusetts
Entered Service at: Boston, Suffolk County, Massachusetts
Unit: Company B, 8th U.S. Cavalry
Battle or Place of Action: Arizona
Date of Action: August-October 1868
Date of Issue: 24 July 1869
Citation: Bravery in scouts and actions against Indians.

1651 ◆ GEIGER, GEORGE

Rank: Sergeant
Service: U.S. Army
Birthday: 1843
Place of Birth: Cincinnati, Hamilton County, Ohio
Date of Death: 23 January 1904
Place of Death: Dayton, Ohio
Cemetery: Dayton National Cemetery (N-20-47) (MH)—Dayton, Ohio
Entered Service at: St. Louis, St. Louis County, Missouri
Unit: Company H, 7th U.S. Cavalry
Battle or Place of Action: Little Big Horn River, Montana
Date of Action: 25 June 1876
Date of Issue: 5 October 1878
Citation: With three comrades during the entire engagement courageously held a position that secured water for the command.

1652 ◆ GEORGIAN, JOHN

Rank: Private
Service: U.S. Army
Birthday: 1842

Place of Birth: Germany
Entered Service at: Buffalo, Erie County, New York
Unit: Company G, 8th U.S. Cavalry
Battle or Place of Action: Chiricahua Mountains, Arizona Territory
Date of Action: 20 October 1869
Date of Issue: 14 February 1870
Citation: Bravery in action.

1653 ◆ *GIVEN, JOHN J.

Rank: Corporal
Service: U.S. Army
Birthday: 1840
Place of Birth: Daviess County, Kentucky
Date of Death: 12 July 1870
Cemetery: San Antonio National Cemetery (MH)—San Antonio, Texas
Entered Service at: Cincinnati, Hamilton County, Ohio
Unit: Company K, 6th U.S. Cavalry
Battle or Place of Action: Wichita River, Texas
Date of Action: 12 July 1870
Date of Issue: 25 August 1870
Citation: Bravery in action.

1654 ◆ GLAVINSKI, ALBERT

True Name: Glawinski, Albert
Rank: Blacksmith
Service: U.S. Army
Birthday: 1852
Place of Birth: Germany (Prussia)
Entered Service at: Pittsburgh, Allegheny County, Pennsylvania
Unit: Company M, 3d U.S. Cavalry
Battle or Place of Action: Powder River, Montana
Date of Action: 17 March 1876
Date of Issue: 16 October 1877
Citation: During a retreat he selected exposed positions; he was part of the rear guard.

1655 ◆ GLOVER, THADDEUS BROWN

Rank: Sergeant (highest rank: Major, Quartermaster Corps)
Service: U.S. Army
Birthday: 2 January 1852
Place of Birth: New York, New York
Date of Death: 18 December 1932
Place of Death: Buffalo, New York
Cemetery: Willow Mill Cemetery—Southold, New York
Entered Service at: New York, New York
Unit: Troop B, 2d U.S. Cavalry
Battle or Place of Action: Mizpah & Pumpkin Creek, Montana
Date of Action: 10 April 1879 & 10 February 1880
Date of Issue: 20 November 1897
Citation: While in charge of small scouting parties, fought, charged, surrounded, and captured war parties of Sioux Indians.

1656 ◆ GLYNN, MICHAEL

Rank: Private
Service: U.S. Army
Birthday: 1845
Place of Birth: Galway, Ireland
Entered Service at: New York, New York
Unit: Company F, 5th U.S. Cavalry
Battle or Place of Action: Whetstone Mountains, Arizona Territory
Date of Action: 13 July 1872
Date of Issue: 4 December 1874
Citation: Drove off, singlehandedly, eight hostile Indians, killing and wounding five.

1657 ◆ GODFREY, EDWARD SETTLE

Rank: Captain (highest rank: Brigadier General)
Service: U.S. Army
Birthday: 9 October 1843
Place of Birth: Kalida, Putnam County, Ohio
Date of Death: 1 April 1932
Place of Death: Mount Holly, New Jersey
Cemetery: Arlington National Cemetery (3-4175-E)—Arlington, Virginia
Entered Service at: Ottawa, Putnam County, Ohio
Unit: 7th U.S. Cavalry
Battle or Place of Action: Bear Paw Mountain, Montana
Date of Action: 30 September 1877
Date of Issue: 27 November 1894
Citation: Led his command into action when he was severely wounded.

1658 ◆ GOLDEN, PATRICK

Rank: Sergeant
Service: U.S. Army
Birthday: 1836
Place of Birth: County Sligo, Ireland
Date of Death: 25 May 1872
Place of Death: Fort Columbus, New York
Cemetery: Cypress Hills National Cemetery (2-4316) (MH)—Brooklyn, New York
Entered Service at: San Francisco, San Francisco County, California
Unit: Company B, 8th U.S. Cavalry
Battle or Place of Action: Arizona
Date of Action: August-October 1868
Date of Issue: 24 July 1869
Citation: Bravery in scouts and actions against Indians.

1659 ◆ GOLDIN, THEODORE W. B.

Rank: Private
Service: U.S. Army
Birthday: 25 July 1858
Place of Birth: Avon, Rock County, Wisconsin
Date of Death: 15 February 1935

Place of Death: Waupaca, Wisconsin
Cemetery: King Veterans Memorial Cemetery (MH)—Waupaca, Wisconsin
Entered Service at: Chicago, Cook County, Illinois
Unit: Troop G, 7th U.S. Cavalry
Battle or Place of Action: Little Big Horn, Montana
Date of Action: 26 June 1876
Date of Issue: 21 December 1895
Citation: One of a party of volunteers who, under a heavy fire from the Indians, went for and brought water to the wounded.

1660 ◆ GOODMAN, DAVID

Rank: Private
Service: U.S. Army
Birthday: 1846
Place of Birth: Paxton, Worcester County, Massachusetts
Entered Service at: Boston, Suffolk County, Massachusetts
Unit: Company L, 8th U.S. Cavalry
Battle or Place of Action: Lyry Creek, Arizona Territory
Date of Action: 14 October 1869
Date of Issue: 3 March 1870
Citation: Bravery in action.

1661 ◆ GRANT, GEORGE

Rank: Sergeant
Service: U.S. Army
Birthday: 1834
Place of Birth: Raleigh, Shelby County, Tennessee
Date of Death: 1 September 1876
Cemetery: Arbor Cemetery—Stockville, Nebraska
Entered Service at: Indianapolis, Marion County, Indiana
Unit: Company E, 18th U.S. Infantry
Battle or Place of Action: Ft. Phil Kearny to Ft. C. F. Smith, Dakota Territory
Date of Action: February 1867
Date of Issue: 6 May 1871
Citation: Bravery, energy and perseverance, involving much suffering and privation through attacks by hostile Indians, deep snows, etc., while voluntarily carrying dispatches .

1662 ◆ GREAVES, CLINTON

Rank: Corporal
Service: U.S. Army
Birthday: 12 August 1855
Place of Birth: Madison County, Virginia
Date of Death: 18 August 1906
Cemetery: Greenlawn Cemetery—Columbus, Ohio
Entered Service at: Baltimore, Baltimore County, Maryland
Unit: Company C, 9th U.S. Cavalry
Battle or Place of Action: Florida Mountains, New Mexico
Date of Action: 24 January 1877
Date of Issue: 26 June 1879
Citation: While part of a small detachment to persuade a band of renegade Apache Indians to surrender, his group was

surrounded. Cpl. Greaves in the center of the savage hand-to-hand fighting, managed to shoot and bash a gap through the swarming Apaches, permitting his companions to break free.

1663 ◆ GREEN, FRANCIS C.

Rank: Sergeant
Service: U.S. Army
Birthday: 4 September 1835
Place of Birth: Mount Vernon, Posey County, Indiana
Date of Death: 13 March 1905
Cemetery: Nicolas Graveyard—Erin, Tennessee
Entered Service at: Sacramento, Sacramento County, California
Unit: Company K, 8th U.S. Cavalry
Battle or Place of Action: Arizona
Date of Action: 1868 & 1869
Date of Issue: 6 September 1869
Citation: Bravery in action.

1664 ◆ GREEN, JOHN

Rank: Major (highest rank: Brevet Brigadier General)
Service: U.S. Army
Birthday: 20 November 1825
Place of Birth: Wurttemberg, Germany
Date of Death: 22 November 1908
Cemetery: Morris Hill Cemetery (MH)—Boise, Idaho
Entered Service at: Columbus, Franklin County, Ohio
Unit: 1st U.S. Cavalry
Battle or Place of Action: Lava Beds, California
Date of Action: 17 January 1873
Date of Issue: 18 November 1897
Citation: In order to reassure his command, this officer, in the most fearless manner and exposed to very great danger, walked in front of the line; the command, thus encouraged, advanced over the lava upon the Indians who were concealed among the rocks.

1665 ◆ GRESHAM, JOHN CHOWNING

Rank: First Lieutenant (highest rank: Colonel)
Service: U.S. Army
Birthday: 25 September 1851
Place of Birth: Virginia
Date of Death: 2 September 1926
Place of Death: San Diego, California
Cemetery: San Francisco National Cemetery (OS-4P5)—San Francisco, California
Entered Service at: Lancaster Courthouse, Lancaster County, Virginia
Unit: 7th U.S. Cavalry
Battle or Place of Action: Wounded Knee Creek, South Dakota
Date of Action: 29 December 1890
Date of Issue: 26 March 1895
Citation: Voluntarily led a party into a ravine to dislodge Sioux Indians concealed therein. He was wounded during this action.

1666 ◆ GRIMES, EDWARD P.

Rank: Sergeant (highest rank: First Sergeant)
Service: U.S. Army
Birthday: 18 May 1848
Place of Birth: Dover, Strafford County, New Hampshire
Date of Death: 17 June 1913
Cemetery: Cypress Hills National Cemetery (2-7210) (MH)—Brooklyn, New York
Entered Service at: Boston, Suffolk County, Massachusetts
Unit: Company F, 5th U.S. Cavalry
Battle or Place of Action: Milk River, Colorado
Date of Action: 29 September-5 October 1879
Date of Issue: 27 January 1880
Citation: The command being almost out of ammunition and surrounded on three sides by the enemy, he voluntarily brought up a supply under heavy fire at almost point-blank range.

1667 ◆ GUNTHER, JACOB

True Name: Guenther, Jacob
Rank: Corporal
Service: U.S. Army
Birthday: 13 November 1844
Place of Birth: Schuylkill County, Pennsylvania
Date of Death: 29 March 1871
Place of Death: Fort Wingate (near Gallup), New Mexico
Cemetery: Santa Fe National Cemetery (A3-1055) (MH)—Santa Fe, New Mexico
Entered Service at: Philadelphia, Philadelphia County, Pennsylvania
Unit: Company E, 8th U.S. Cavalry
Battle or Place of Action: Arizona
Date of Action: 1868-1869
Date of Issue: 6 September 1869
Citation: Bravery in scouts and actions against Indians.

1668 ◆ *HADDOO, JOHN

True Name: Haddo Jr., John
Rank: Corporal
Service: U.S. Army
Birthday: 13 August 1851
Place of Birth: Hooksett, Merrimack County, New Hampshire
Date of Death: 30 September 1877
Place of Death: Bear Paw Mountain, Montana
Cemetery: Custer Battlefield National Cemetery—Crow Agency, Montana
Entered Service at: Columbus, Cherokee County, Kansas
Unit: Company B, 5th U.S. Infantry
Battle or Place of Action: Cedar Creek, etc., Montana
Date of Action: October 1876—8 January 1877
Date of Issue: 18 July 1877
Citation: Gallantry in action.

1669 ◆ HALL, JOHN

Rank: Private
Service: U.S. Army
Birthday: 1834
Place of Birth: Logan County, Illinois
Entered Service at: Sacramento, Sacramento County, California
Unit: Company B, 8th U.S. Cavalry
Battle or Place of Action: Arizona
Date of Action: August-October 1868
Date of Issue: 24 July 1869
Citation: Bravery in scouts and actions against Indians.

1670 ◆ HALL, WILLIAM PREBLE

Rank: First Lieutenant (highest rank: Brigadier General)
Service: U.S. Army
Birthday: 11 June 1848
Place of Birth: Randolph County, Missouri
Date of Death: 14 December 1927
Place of Death: Washington, D.C.
Cemetery: Arlington National Cemetery (1-653)—Arlington, Virginia
Entered Service at: Huntsville, Randolph County, Missouri
Unit: 5th U.S. Cavalry
Battle or Place of Action: near Camp, White River, Colorado
Date of Action: 20 October 1879
Date of Issue: 18 September 1897
Citation: With a reconnoitering party of three men, was attacked by 35 Indians and several times exposed himself to draw the fire of the enemy, giving his small party opportunity to reply with much effect.

1671 ◆ HAMILTON, FRANK

Rank: Private
Service: U.S. Army
Birthday: 1840
Place of Birth: County Tyrone, Ireland
Entered Service at: Sacramento, Sacramento County, California
Unit: Company E, 8th U.S. Cavalry
Battle or Place of Action: Agua Fria River, Arizona
Date of Action: 25 August 1869
Date of Issue: 3 March 1870
Citation: Gallantry in action.

1672 ◆ HAMILTON, MATHEW H.

Rank: Private
Service: U.S. Army
Birthday: 1865
Place of Birth: Hobart, Australia
Entered Service at: New York, New York
Unit: Company G, 7th U.S. Cavalry
Battle or Place of Action: Wounded Knee Creek, South Dakota
Date of Action: 29 December 1890

Date of Issue: 25 May 1891
Citation: Bravery in action.

1673 ◆ HANLEY, RICHARD P.

Rank: Sergeant
Service: U.S. Army
Birthday: 1843
Place of Birth: Boston, Suffolk County, Massachusetts
Entered Service at: Cincinnati, Hamilton County, Ohio
Unit: Company C, 7th U.S. Cavalry
Battle or Place of Action: Little Big Horn River, Montana
Date of Action: 25 June 1876
Date of Issue: 5 October 1878
Citation: Recaptured, singlehandedly, and without orders, within the enemy's lines and under a galling fire lasting some 20 minutes, a stampeded pack mule loaded with ammunition.

1674 ◆ HARDING, MOSHER A.

Rank: Blacksmith
Service: U.S. Army
Birthday: 2 May 1847
Place of Birth: Canada West
Date of Death: 10 May 1931
Place of Death: Denison, Iowa
Cemetery: Oakland Cemetery—Denison, Iowa
Entered Service at: St. Louis, St. Louis County, Missouri
Unit: Company G, 8th U.S. Cavalry
Battle or Place of Action: Chiricahua Mountains, Arizona Territory
Date of Action: 20 October 1869
Date of Issue: 14 February 1870
Citation: Gallantry in action.

1675 ◆ HARRINGTON, JOHN

Rank: Private (highest rank: Sergeant)
Service: U.S. Army
Birthday: 1848
Place of Birth: Detroit, Wayne County, Michigan
Date of Death: 3 January 1905
Cemetery: San Antonio National Cemetery (F-1012) (MH)—San Antonio, Texas
Entered Service at: Cleveland, Cuyahoga County, Ohio
Unit: Company H, 6th U.S. Cavalry
Battle or Place of Action: Washita River, Texas
Date of Action: 12 September 1874
Date of Issue: 4 November 1874
Citation: While carrying dispatches was attacked by 125 hostile Indians, whom he and his comrades fought throughout the day. He was severely wounded in the hip and unable to move. He continued to fight, defending an exposed dying man.

1676 ◆ HARRIS, CHARLES D.

Rank: Sergeant
Service: U.S. Army
Birthday: 1845

Place of Birth: Albion, Orleans County, New York
Entered Service at: Rochester, Monroe County, New York
Unit: Company D, 8th U.S. Cavalry
Battle or Place of Action: Red Creek, Arizona
Date of Action: 23 September 1869
Date of Issue: 23 November 1869
Citation: Gallantry in action.

1677 ◆ HARRIS, DAVID W.

Rank: Private
Service: U.S. Army
Birthday: 1851
Place of Birth: Indianapolis, Marion County, Indiana
Entered Service at: Cincinnati, Hamilton County, Ohio
Unit: Company A, 7th U.S. Cavalry
Battle or Place of Action: Little Big Horn River, Montana
Date of Action: 25 June 1876
Date of Issue: 5 October 1878
Citation: Brought water to the wounded, at great danger to his life, under a most galling fire from the enemy.

1678 ◆ HARRIS, WILLIAM M.

Rank: Private
Service: U.S. Army
Birthday: 1850
Place of Birth: Madison County, Kentucky
Entered Service at: Mount Vernon, Rockcastle County, Kentucky
Unit: Company D, 7th U.S. Cavalry
Battle or Place of Action: Little Big Horn River, Montana
Date of Action: 25 June 1876
Date of Issue: 5 October 1878
Citation: Voluntarily brought water to the wounded under fire of the enemy.

1679 ◆ HARTZOG, JOSHUA B.

Rank: Private (highest rank: Sergeant)
Service: U.S. Army
Birthday: 3 February 1866
Place of Birth: Paulding County, Ohio
Date of Death: 27 May 1939
Place of Death: Beebe, Arkansas
Cemetery: Gum Springs Cemetery (MH)—Searcy, Arkansas
Entered Service at: Detroit, Wayne County, Michigan
Unit: Company E, 1st U.S. Artillery
Battle or Place of Action: Wounded Knee Creek, South Dakota
Date of Action: 29 December 1890
Date of Issue: 24 March 1891
Citation: Went to the rescue of the commanding officer who had fallen severely wounded, picked him up, and carried him out of range of the hostile guns.

1680 ◆ HAUPT, PAUL

Rank: Corporal
Service: U.S. Army

Birthday: 1842
Place of Birth: Germany (Prussia)
Entered Service at: Baltimore, Baltimore County, Maryland
Unit: Company L, 8th U.S. Cavalry
Battle or Place of Action: Hell Canyon, Arizona
Date of Action: 3 July 1869
Date of Issue: 3 March 1870
Citation: Gallantry in action.

1681 ◆ HAWTHORNE, HARRY LEROY

Rank: Second Lieutenant (highest rank: Colonel)
Service: U.S. Army
Birthday: 27 November 1859
Place of Birth: Minnesota
Date of Death: 9 April 1948
Place of Death: Pasadena, California
Cemetery: Arlington National Cemetery (3-1952) (MH)—Arlington, Virginia
Entered Service at: Kentucky
Unit: 2d U.S. Artillery
Battle or Place of Action: Wounded Knee Creek, South Dakota
Date of Action: 29 December 1890
Date of Issue: 11 October 1892
Citation: Distinguished conduct in battle with hostile Indians.

1682 ◆ HAY, FRED STEWART

True Name: Schwabe, Frederick H.
Rank: Sergeant (highest rank: Drum Major U.S.A. ret.)
Service: U.S. Army
Birthday: 1850
Place of Birth: Stirlingshire, Scotland
Date of Death: 14 January 1914
Place of Death: Highlands, New Jersey
Cemetery: Bayview Cemetery—Leonardo, New Jersey
Entered Service at: Fort Leavenworth, Leavenworth County, Kansas
Unit: Company I, 5th U.S. Infantry
Battle or Place of Action: Upper Wichita River, Texas
Date of Action: 9 September 1874
Date of Issue: 23 April 1875
Citation: Gallantry in action.

1683 ◆ HEARTERY, RICHARD

Rank: Private
Service: U.S. Army
Birthday: 1847
Place of Birth: Ireland
Date of Death: 7 June 1912
Place of Death: Chicago, Illinois
Cemetery: Mount Carmel Cemetery—Hillside, Illinois
Entered Service at: San Francisco, San Francisco County, California
Unit: Company D, 6th U.S. Cavalry
Battle or Place of Action: Cibicu, Arizona
Date of Action: 30 August 1881

Date of Issue: 20 July 1888
Citation: Bravery in action.

1684 ◆ HEISE, CLAMOR

Rank: Private (highest rank: Quartermaster Sergeant)
Service: U.S. Army
Birthday: 12 December 1844
Place of Birth: Germany
Date of Death: October 1921
Cemetery: Heise Hot Springs Cemetery (MH)—Heise, Idaho
Entered Service at: New York, New York
Unit: Company B, 8th U.S. Cavalry
Battle or Place of Action: Arizona
Date of Action: August-October 1868
Date of Issue: 24 July 1869
Citation: Bravery in scouts and actions against Indians.

1685 ◆ HERRON, LEANDER

Rank: Corporal
Service: U.S. Army
Birthday: 29 December 1846
Place of Birth: Bucks County, Pennsylvania
Date of Death: 5 April 1937
Place of Death: St. Paul, Nebraska
Cemetery: Elmwood Cemetery (MH)—St. Paul, Nebraska
Entered Service at: Pittsburgh, Allegheny County, Pennsylvania
Unit: Company A, 3d U.S. Infantry
Battle or Place of Action: Fort Dodge, Kansas
Date of Action: 2 September 1868
Citation: While detailed as mail courier from the fort, voluntarily went to the assistance of a party of four enlisted men, who were attacked by about 50 Indians at some distance from the fort and remained with them until the party was relieved.

1686 ◆ HEYL, CHARLES PETTIT HEATH

Rank: Second Lieutenant (highest rank: Colonel)
Service: U.S. Army
Birthday: 22 July 1849
Place of Birth: Philadelphia, Philadelphia County, Pennsylvania
Date of Death: 12 October 1926
Cemetery: Arlington National Cemetery (1-135-B-WH) (MH)—Arlington, Virginia
Entered Service at: Camden, Camden County, New Jersey
Unit: 23d U.S. Infantry
Battle or Place of Action: Fort Hartsuff, Nebraska
Date of Action: 28 April 1876
Date of Issue: 26 October 1897
Citation: Voluntarily, and with most conspicuous gallantry, charged with three men upon six Indians who were entrenched upon a hillside.

1687 ◆ HIGGINS, THOMAS P.

Rank: Private
Service: U.S. Army

Birthday: 1839
Place of Birth: Longford, Ireland
Entered Service at: Napa, Napa County, California
Unit: Company B, 8th U.S. Cavalry
Battle or Place of Action: Arizona
Date of Action: August-October 1868
Date of Issue: 24 July 1869
Citation: Bravery in scouts and actions against Indians.

1688 ◆ HILL, FRANK E.

Rank: Sergeant (highest rank: First Sergeant)
Service: U.S. Army
Birthday: 1849
Place of Birth: Mayfield, Wisconsin
Date of Death: 20 March 1906
Place of Death: Manhattan, Nevada
Cemetery: San Francisco Columbarium—San Francisco, California
Entered Service at: St. Louis, St. Louis County, Missouri
Unit: Company E, 5th U.S. Cavalry
Battle or Place of Action: Date Creek, Arizona
Date of Action: 8 September 1872
Date of Issue: 12 August 1875
Citation: Secured the person of a hostile Apache chief, although while holding the chief he was severely wounded in the back by another Indian.

1689 ◆ HILL, JAMES MADISON

Rank: First Sergeant (highest rank: Commissary Sergeant)
Service: U.S. Army
Birthday: 25 April 1845
Place of Birth: Washington County, Pennsylvania
Date of Death: 17 September 1919
Place of Death: Vancouver, Washington
Cemetery: Vancouver Barracks Post Cemetery (4-W-650) (MH)—Vancouver, Washington
Entered Service at: Cincinnati, Hamilton County, Ohio
Unit: Company A, 5th U.S. Cavalry
Battle or Place of Action: Turret Mountain, Arizona Territory
Date of Action: 25 March 1873
Date of Issue: 12 August 1875
Citation: Gallantry in action.

1690 ◆ HILLOCK, MARVIN C.

Rank: Private
Service: U.S. Army
Birthday: 1868
Place of Birth: Port Huron, St. Clair County, Michigan
Entered Service at: Detroit, Wayne County, Michigan
Unit: Company B, 7th U.S. Cavalry
Battle or Place of Action: Wounded Knee Creek, South Dakota
Date of Action: 29 December 1890
Date of Issue: 16 April 1891
Citation: Distinguished bravery.

1691 ◆ HIMMELSBACK, MICHAEL

Rank: Private
Service: U.S. Army
Birthday: 1849
Place of Birth: Allegheny County, Pennsylvania
Date of Death: 5 January 1881
Place of Death: Fort Ellis, Montana
Entered Service at: Harrisburg, Dauphin County, Pennsylvania
Unit: Company C, 2d U.S. Cavalry
Battle or Place of Action: Little Blue, Nebraska
Date of Action: 15 May 1870
Date of Issue: 22 June 1870
Citation: Gallantry in action.

1692 ◆ HINEMANN, LEHMANN

Rank: Sergeant
Service: U.S. Army
Birthday: 1844
Place of Birth: Lanback, Germany
Date of Death: 11 November 1920
Place of Death: Newport, Kentucky
Cemetery: St. Stephen's Cemetery—Fort Thomas, Kentucky
Entered Service at: Baltimore, Baltimore County, Maryland
Unit: Company L, 1st U.S. Cavalry
Battle or Place of Action: Arizona
Date of Action: winter 1872-73
Date of Issue: 12 August 1875
Citation: Gallant conduct during campaigns and engagements with Apaches.

1693 ◆ HOBDAY, GEORGE

Rank: Private
Service: U.S. Army
Birthday: 1842
Place of Birth: Pulaski County, Illinois
Date of Death: 22 November 1891
Cemetery: Jefferson Barracks National Cemetery—St. Louis, Missouri
Entered Service at: Memphis, Shelby County, Tennessee
Unit: Company A, 7th U.S. Cavalry
Battle or Place of Action: Wounded Knee Creek, South Dakota
Date of Action: 29 December 1890
Date of Issue: 23 June 1891
Citation: Conspicuous and gallant conduct in battle.

1694 ◆ HOGAN, HENRY✠

Rank: Private (highest rank: Corporal)
Service: U.S. Army
Birthday: 8 March 1840
Place of Birth: County Clare, Ireland
Date of Death: 20 April 1916
Cemetery: Custer County Cemetery (MH)—Miles City, Montana
Entered Service at: New York, New York

Unit: Company G, 5th U.S. Infantry
Battle or Place of Action: Cedar Creek, etc., Montana; at Bear Paw Mountain, Montana
Date of Action: 21 October 1876—8 January 1877; 30 September 1877
Date of Issue: 26 June 1894
Citation: **First Award** Gallantry in actions. **Second Award** Carried Lt. Romeyn, who was severely wounded, off the field of battle under heavy fire.
Notes: ✠Double Awardee

1695 ◆ HOLDEN, HENRY

Rank: Private (highest rank: Corporal)
Service: U.S. Army
Birthday: 1836
Place of Birth: Brighton, Sussex County, England
Date of Death: 14 December 1905
Place of Death: Brighton, England
Cemetery: Brighton & Preston Cemetery (MH)—Brighton, England
Entered Service at: Boston, Suffolk County, Massachusetts
Unit: Company D, 7th U.S. Cavalry
Battle or Place of Action: Little Big Horn River, Montana
Date of Action: 25 June 1876
Date of Issue: 5 October 1878
Citation: Brought up ammunition under a galling fire from the enemy.

1696 ◆ HOLLAND, DAVID

Rank: Corporal (highest rank: Sergeant)
Service: U.S. Army
Birthday: 1839
Place of Birth: Dearborn, Wayne County, Michigan
Entered Service at: Fort Leavenworth, Leavenworth County, Kansas
Unit: Company A, 5th U.S. Infantry
Battle or Place of Action: Cedar Creek, etc., Montana
Date of Action: 21 October 1876—8 January 1877
Date of Issue: 27 April 1877
Citation: Gallantry in actions.

1697 ◆ *HOOKER, GEORGE

Rank: Private
Service: U.S. Army
Birthday: 1847
Place of Birth: Frederick, Frederick County, Maryland
Date of Death: 22 January 1873
Place of Death: Tonto Creek, Arizona
Cemetery: Fort Bliss National Cemetery (MH)—Fort Bliss, Texas
Entered Service at: Washington, D.C.
Unit: Company K, 5th U.S. Cavalry
Battle or Place of Action: Tonto Creek, Arizona
Date of Action: 22 January 1873
Date of Issue: 12 August 1875
Citation: Gallantry in action in which he was killed.

1698 ◆ HOOVER, SAMUEL

Rank: Bugler
Service: U.S. Army
Birthday: 1851
Place of Birth: Dauphin County, Pennsylvania
Entered Service at: Harrisburg, Dauphin County, Pennsylvania
Unit: Company A, 1st U.S. Cavalry
Battle or Place of Action: Santa Maria Mountains, Arizona
Date of Action: 6 May 1873
Date of Issue: 12 August 1875
Citation: Gallantry in action; also services as trailer in May 1872.

1699 ◆ HORNADAY, ELISHA SIMPSON

Rank: Private (highest rank: First Sergeant)
Service: U.S. Army
Birthday: 24 March 1851
Place of Birth: Hendricks County, Indiana
Date of Death: 9 July 1923
Place of Death: San Diego, California
Cemetery: Greenwood Cemetery—San Diego, California
Entered Service at: Des Moines, Polk County, Iowa
Unit: Company H, 6th U.S. Cavalry
Battle or Place of Action: Sappa Creek, Kansas
Date of Action: 23 April 1875
Date of Issue: 16 November 1876
Citation: With five other men he waded in mud and water up the creek to a position directly behind an entrenched Cheyenne position, who were using natural bank pits to good advantage against the main column. This surprise attack from the enemy rear broke their resistance.

1700 ◆ HOWZE, ROBERT LEE

Rank: Second Lieutenant (highest rank: Major General)
Service: U.S. Army
Birthday: 22 August 1864
Place of Birth: Overton, Rusk County, Texas
Date of Death: 19 September 1926
Place of Death: Columbus, Ohio
Cemetery: U.S. Military Academy Cemetery (I-14)—West Point, New York
Entered Service at: Overton, Rusk County, Texas
Unit: Company K, 6th U.S. Cavalry
Battle or Place of Action: White River, South Dakota
Date of Action: 1 January 1891
Date of Issue: 25 July 1891
Citation: Bravery in action.

1701 ◆ HUBBARD, THOMAS H.

Rank: Private
Service: U.S. Army
Birthday: 1848
Place of Birth: Philadelphia, Philadelphia County, Pennsylvania
Date of Death: 19 September 1889
Place of Death: Philadelphia, Pennsylvania
Entered Service at: Philadelphia, Philadelphia County, Pennsylvania
Unit: Company C, 2d U.S. Cavalry
Battle or Place of Action: Little Blue, Nebraska
Date of Action: 15 May 1870
Date of Issue: 22 June 1870
Citation: Gallantry in action.

1702 ◆ HUFF, JAMES W.

Rank: Private (highest rank: Sergeant)
Service: U.S. Army
Birthday: 7 February 1840
Place of Birth: Washington, Washington County, Pennsylvania
Date of Death: 30 November 1927
Place of Death: Port Richey, Florida
Cemetery: Pine Hill Cemetery—New Port Richey, Florida
Entered Service at: Vanburan, Pennsylvania
Unit: Company L, 1st U.S. Cavalry
Battle or Place of Action: Arizona
Date of Action: winter 1872-73
Date of Issue: 12 April 1875
Citation: Gallant conduct during campaigns and engagements with Apaches.

1703 ◆ HUGGINS, ELI LUNDY

Rank: Captain (highest rank: Brigadier General)
Service: U.S. Army
Birthday: 1 August 1842
Place of Birth: Schuyler County, Illinois
Date of Death: 22 October 1929
Cemetery: Mountview View Cemetery—Oakland, California
Entered Service at: Minnesota
Unit: 2d U.S. Cavalry
Battle or Place of Action: O'Fallons Creek, Montana
Date of Action: 1 April 1880
Date of Issue: 27 November 1894
Citation: Surprised the Indians in their strong position and fought them until dark with great boldness.

1704 ◆ HUMPHREY, CHARLES FREDERIC

Rank: First Lieutenant (highest rank: Major General)
Service: U.S. Army
Birthday: 2 September 1844
Place of Birth: Cortland, Cortland County, New York
Date of Death: 4 June 1926
Place of Death: Washington, D.C.
Cemetery: Arlington National Cemetery (4-3115)—Arlington, Virginia
Entered Service at: Buffalo, Erie County, New York
Unit: 4th U.S. Artillery
Battle or Place of Action: Clearwater, Idaho
Date of Action: 11 July 1877
Date of Issue: 2 March 1897
Citation: Voluntarily and successfully conducted, in the face of a withering fire, a party which recovered possession of an abandoned howitzer and two Gatling guns lying between the lines a few yards from the Indians.

1705 ◆ HUNT, FREDERICK O.

Rank: Private (highest rank: Corporal)
Service: U.S. Army
Birthday: 31 January 1848
Place of Birth: London, England
Date of Death: 21 July 1918
Place of Death: Columbia Falls, Montana
Cemetery: Soldier's Home Cemetery (MH)—Columbia Falls, Montana
Entered Service at: Fort Leavenworth, Leavenworth County, Kansas
Unit: 5th U.S. Infantry
Battle or Place of Action: Cedar Creek, etc., Montana
Date of Action: 21 October 1876—8 January 1877
Date of Issue: 27 April 1877
Citation: Gallantry in action.

1706 ◆ HUTCHINSON, RUFUS D.

Rank: Sergeant
Service: U.S. Army
Birthday: 1850
Place of Birth: Butlerville, Ohio
Entered Service at: Cincinnati, Hamilton County, Ohio
Unit: Company B, 7th U.S. Cavalry
Battle or Place of Action: Little Big Horn River, Montana
Date of Action: 25 June 1876
Date of Issue: 5 October 1878
Citation: Guarded and carried the wounded, brought water for the same, and posted and directed the men in his charge under galling fire from the enemy.

1707 ◆ HYDE, HENRY J.

Rank: Sergeant
Service: U.S. Army
Birthday: 11 February 1846
Place of Birth: Bangor, Penobscot County, Maine
Date of Death: 25 July 1893
Place of Death: Marion, Indiana
Cemetery: Marion National Cemetery (I-97) (MH)—Marion, Indiana
Entered Service at: New York, New York
Unit: Company M, 1st U.S. Cavalry
Battle or Place of Action: Arizona
Date of Action: winter 1872-73
Date of Issue: 12 August 1875
Citation: Gallant conduct during campaigns and engagements with Apaches.

1708 ◆ IRWIN, BERNARD JOHN DOWLING

Rank: Assistant Surgeon (highest rank: Brigadier General)
Service: U.S. Army
Birthday: 24 June 1830
Place of Birth: Ireland
Date of Death: 15 December 1927
Place of Death: Cobourg, Ontario, Canada
Cemetery: U.S. Military Academy Cemetery (D-17)

(MH)—West Point, New York
Entered Service at: New York, New York
Unit: 7th U.S. Infantry
Battle or Place of Action: Apache Pass, Arizona
Date of Action: 13 February 1861
Date of Issue: 24 January 1894
Citation: Voluntarily took command of troops and attacked and defeated hostile Indians he met on the way. Surg. Irwin volunteered to go to the rescue of 2d Lt. George N. Bascom, 7th Infantry, who with 60 men was trapped by Chiricahua Apaches under Cochise. Irwin and 14 men, not having horses, began the 100-mile march riding mules. After fighting and capturing Indians, recovering stolen horses and cattle, he reached Bascom's column and helped break his siege.

1709 ◆ JACKSON, JAMES

Rank: Captain (highest rank: Brigadier General)
Service: U.S. Army
Birthday: 21 November 1833
Place of Birth: New Jersey
Date of Death: 21 October 1916
Place of Death: Portland, Oregon
Cemetery: Riverside Cemetery—Portland, Oregon
Entered Service at: New Jersey
Unit: 1st U.S. Cavalry
Battle or Place of Action: Camas Meadows, Idaho
Date of Action: 20 August 1877
Date of Issue: 17 April 1896
Citation: Dismounted from his horse in the face of a heavy fire from pursuing Indians and, with the assistance of one or two of the men of his command, secured to a place of safety the body of his trumpeter, who had been shot and killed.

1710 ◆ JAMES, JOHN

Rank: Corporal
Service: U.S. Army
Birthday: 1838
Place of Birth: Manchester, Greater Manchester County, England
Date of Death: 23 May 1902
Place of Death: Washington, D.C.
Cemetery: Soldier's Home National Cemetery (K-6991) (MH)—Washington, D.C.
Entered Service at: Albany, Albany County, New York
Unit: Company I, 5th U.S. Infantry
Battle or Place of Action: Upper Washita River, Texas
Date of Action: 9-11 September 1874
Date of Issue: 23 May 1875
Citation: Gallantry in action.

1711 ◆ JARVIS, FREDERICK

Rank: Sergeant
Service: U.S. Army
Birthday: 1841
Place of Birth: Essex County, New York
Date of Death: 8 April 1894
Place of Death: Salt Lake City, Utah

Cemetery: City Cemetery (MH)—Salt Lake City, Utah
Entered Service at: Hudson, Lenawee County, Michigan
Unit: Company G, 1st U.S. Cavalry
Battle or Place of Action: Chiricahua Mountains, Arizona Territory
Date of Action: 20 October 1869
Date of Issue: 14 February 1870
Citation: Gallantry in action.

1712 ◆ JETTER, BERNHARD

Rank: Sergeant (highest rank: First Sergeant)
Service: U.S. Army
Birthday: 1862
Place of Birth: Wurttemberg, Germany
Date of Death: 23 August 1927
Cemetery: Cypress Hills National Cemetery (5-1) (MH)—Brooklyn, New York
Entered Service at: New York, New York
Unit: Company K, 7th U.S. Cavalry
Battle or Place of Action: Sioux Campaign, South Dakota
Date of Action: 29 December 1890
Date of Issue: 24 April 1891
Citation: Distinguished bravery.

1713 ◆ JIM

Rank: Sergeant
Service: U.S. Army
Birthday: 1850
Place of Birth: Arizona Territory
Date of Death: 1889
Place of Death: Ash Flats, Arizona
Entered Service at: Camp Verde, Yavapia County, Arizona Territory
Unit: Indian Scouts
Battle or Place of Action: Arizona
Date of Action: winter 1872-73
Date of Issue: 12 April 1875
Citation: Gallant conduct during campaigns and engagements with Apaches.

1714 ◆ JOHNSON, HENRY

Rank: Sergeant
Service: U.S. Army
Birthday: 11 June 1850
Place of Birth: Boydton, Mecklenburg County, Virginia
Date of Death: 31 January 1904
Place of Death: Washington, D.C.
Cemetery: Arlington National Cemetery (23-16547) (MH)—Arlington, Virginia
Entered Service at: Detroit, Wayne County, Michigan
Unit: Company D, 9th U.S. Cavalry
Battle or Place of Action: Milk River, Colorado
Date of Action: 2-5 October 1879
Date of Issue: 22 September 1890
Citation: Voluntarily left fortified shelter and under heavy fire at close-range made the rounds of the pits to instruct the guards; fought his way to the creek and back to bring water to the wounded.

1715 ◆ JOHNSTON, EDWARD

Rank: Corporal (highest rank: Sergeant)
Service: U.S. Army
Birthday: 8 February 1844
Place of Birth: Pen Yan, Yates County, New York
Date of Death: 20 January 1920
Cemetery: Lakeview Cemetery (MH)—Penn Yan, New York
Entered Service at: Chicago, Cook County, Illinois
Unit: 5th U.S. Infantry
Battle or Place of Action: Cedar Creek, etc., Montana
Date of Action: 21 October 1876—8 January 1877
Date of Issue: 27 April 1877
Citation: Gallantry in action.

1716 ◆ JONES, WILLIAM H.

Rank: Farrier (highest rank: Blacksmith)
Service: U.S. Army
Birthday: 1842
Place of Birth: Davidson County, North Carolina
Date of Death: 23 December 1911
Cemetery: Efland Methodist Church Cemetery (MH)—Efland, North Carolina
Entered Service at: Louisville, Jefferson County, Kentucky
Unit: Company L, 2d U.S. Cavalry
Battle or Place of Action: Little Muddy Creek, Montana
Date of Action: 7 May 1877
Date of Issue: 28 February 1878
Citation: Gallantry in the attack against hostile Sioux Indians 7 May 1877 at Muddy Creek, Mont., and in the engagement with Nez Perce Indians at Camas Meadows, Idaho, 20 August 1877, in which he sustained a painful knee wound.

1717 ◆ JORDAN, GEORGE

Rank: Sergeant
Service: U.S. Army
Birthday: 1847
Place of Birth: Williamson County, Tennessee
Date of Death: 24 October 1904
Cemetery: Fort McPherson National Cemetery (F-1131) (MH)—Maxwell, Nebraska
Entered Service at: Nashville, Davidson County, Tennessee
Unit: Company K, 9th U.S. Cavalry
Battle or Place of Action: Fort Tularosa & Carrizo Canyon, New Mexico
Date of Action: 14 May 1880 & 12 August 1881
Date of Issue: 7 May 1890
Citation: While commanding a detachment of 25 men at Fort Tularosa, N. Mex., repulsed a force of more than 100 Indians. At Carrizo Canyon, N. Mex., while commanding the right of a detachment of 19 men, 12 August 1881, he stubbornly held his ground in an extremely exposed position and gallantly forced back a much superior number of the enemy, preventing them from surrounding the command.

1718 ◆ KAY, JOHN

Rank: Private
Service: U.S. Army
Birthday: 1846
Place of Birth: Lancashire, England
Entered Service at: Philadelphia, Philadelphia County, Pennsylvania
Unit: Company L, 8th U.S. Cavalry
Battle or Place of Action: Arizona
Date of Action: 21 October 1868
Date of Issue: 3 March 1870
Citation: Brought a comrade, severely wounded, from under the fire of a large party of the enemy.

1719 ◆ KEATING, DANIEL

Rank: Corporal (highest rank: Sergeant)
Service: U.S. Army
Birthday: 1846
Place of Birth: County Cork, Ireland
Date of Death: 20 June 1912
Place of Death: East Boston, Massachusetts
Cemetery: Holy Cross Cemetery (MH)—Malden, Massachusetts
Entered Service at: Boston, Suffolk County, Massachusetts
Unit: Company M, 6th U.S. Cavalry
Battle or Place of Action: Wichita River, Texas
Date of Action: 5 October 1870
Date of Issue: 5 October 1870
Citation: Gallantry in action and in pursuit of Indians.

1720 ◆ KEENAN, BARTHOLOMEW T.

Rank: Trumpeter
Service: U.S. Army
Birthday: 1843
Place of Birth: Brooklyn, Kings County, New York
Entered Service at: Cincinnati, Hamilton County, Ohio
Unit: Company G, 1st U.S. Cavalry
Battle or Place of Action: Chiricahua Mountains, Arizona Territory
Date of Action: 20 October 1869
Date of Issue: 14 February 1870
Citation: Gallantry in action.

1721 ◆ KEENAN, JOHN

Rank: Private
Service: U.S. Army
Birthday: 1843
Place of Birth: Tubbercurry, County Sligo, Ireland
Date of Death: 18 March 1906
Place of Death: McIntyre, Iowa
Entered Service at: San Francisco, San Francisco County, California
Unit: 8th U.S. Cavalry
Battle or Place of Action: Arizona
Date of Action: August-October 1868

Date of Issue: 24 July 1869
Citation: Bravery in scouts and actions against Indians.

1722 ◆ KELLEY, CHARLES

Rank: Private
Service: U.S. Army
Birthday: 1840
Place of Birth: County Clare, Ireland
Entered Service at: New York, New York
Unit: U.S. Cavalry
Battle or Place of Action: Chiricahua Mountains, Arizona Territory
Date of Action: 20 October 1869
Date of Issue: 14 February 1870
Citation: Gallantry in action.

1723 ◆ KELLY, JOHN J. H.

Rank: Corporal (highest rank: Ordnance Sergeant)
Service: U.S. Army
Birthday: 1851
Place of Birth: Schuyler County, Illinois
Date of Death: 4 February 1907
Cemetery: Oak Ridge Cemetery—Springfield, Illinois
Entered Service at: Springfield, Sangamon County, Illinois
Unit: Company I, 5th U.S. Infantry
Battle or Place of Action: Upper Wichita River, Texas
Date of Action: 9 September 1874
Date of Issue: 23 April 1875
Citation: Gallantry in action.

1724 ◆ KELLY, THOMAS

Rank: Private
Service: U.S. Army
Birthday: June 1837
Place of Birth: County Mayo, Ireland
Date of Death: 25 March 1919
Place of Death: Leavenworth, Kansas
Cemetery: Mount Calvary Cemetery (MH)—Leavenworth, Kansas
Entered Service at: New York, New York
Unit: Company I, 5th U.S. Infantry
Battle or Place of Action: Upper Wichita River, Texas
Date of Action: 9 September 1874
Date of Issue: 23 April 1875
Citation: Gallantry in action.

1725 ◆ KELSAY

Rank: Scout
Service: U.S. Army
Place of Birth: Arizona Territory
Entered Service at: Arizona Territory
Unit: Indian Scouts
Battle or Place of Action: Arizona Territory
Date of Action: winter 1872-73
Date of Issue: 23 April 1875

Citation: Gallant conduct during campaigns and engagements with Apaches.

1726 ◆ *KENNEDY, PHILIP

Rank: Private
Service: U.S. Army
Birthday: 1841
Place of Birth: County Galway, Ireland
Date of Death: 3 November 1883
Place of Death: Cincinnati, Ohio
Entered Service at: Evansville, Randolph County, Illinois
Unit: Company C, 5th U.S. Infantry
Battle or Place of Action: Cedar Creek, etc., Montana
Date of Action: 21 October 1876—8 January 1877
Date of Issue: 27 April 1887
Citation: Gallantry in action.

1727 ◆ KERR, JOHN BROWN

Rank: Captain (highest rank: Brigadier General)
Service: U.S. Army
Birthday: 12 March 1847
Place of Birth: Lexington, Fayette County, Kentucky
Date of Death: 27 February 1928
Place of Death: Washington, D.C.
Cemetery: Arlington National Cemetery (3-1950-SH)—Arlington, Virginia
Entered Service at: Hutchison Station, Bourbon County, Kentucky
Unit: 6th U.S. Cavalry
Battle or Place of Action: White River, South Dakota
Date of Action: 1 January 1891
Date of Issue: 25 April 1891
Citation: For distinguished bravery while in command of his troop in action against hostile Sioux Indians on the north bank of the White River, near the mouth of Little Grass Creek, S. Dak., where he defeated a force of 300 Brule Sioux warriors, and turned the Sioux tribe, which was endeavoring to enter the Bad Lands, back into the Pine Ridge Agency.

1728 ◆ KERRIGAN, THOMAS

Rank: Sergeant
Service: U.S. Army
Birthday: 1845
Place of Birth: County Tipperary, Ireland
Entered Service at: New York, New York
Unit: Company H, 6th U.S. Cavalry
Battle or Place of Action: Wichita River, Texas
Date of Action: 12 July 1870
Date of Issue: 25 August 1870
Citation: Gallantry in action.

1729 ◆ KILMARTIN, JOHN

True Name: Gilmartin, John
Rank: Private
Service: U.S. Army

Birthday: 20 February 1850
Place of Birth: Montreal, Canada
Date of Death: 23 March 1890
Place of Death: Toledo, Ohio
Cemetery: Calvary Cemetery—Toledo, Ohio
Entered Service at: Philadelphia, Philadelphia County, Pennsylvania
Unit: Company F, 3d U.S. Cavalry
Battle or Place of Action: Whetstone Mountains, Arizona Territory
Date of Action: 5 May 1871
Date of Issue: 13 November 1871
Citation: Gallantry in action.

1730 ◆ KIRK, JOHN

Rank: First Sergeant (highest rank: Sergeant Major)
Service: U.S. Army
Birthday: 20 November 1846
Place of Birth: York, York County, Pennsylvania
Date of Death: 2 March 1920
Place of Death: New Cumberland, Pennsylvania
Cemetery: Mount Olivet Cemetery—New Cumberland, Pennsylvania
Entered Service at: Harrisburg, Dauphin County, Pennsylvania
Unit: Company L, 6th U.S. Cavalry
Battle or Place of Action: Wichita River, Texas
Date of Action: 12 July 1870
Date of Issue: 25 August 1870
Citation: Gallantry in action.

1731 ◆ KIRKWOOD, JOHN A.

Rank: Sergeant
Service: U.S. Army
Birthday: 29 October 1851
Place of Birth: Allegheny City, Allegheny County, Pennsylvania
Date of Death: 10 May 1930
Place of Death: Washington, D.C.
Cemetery: Soldier's Home National Cemetery (L-9102) (MH)—Washington, D.C.
Entered Service at: North Platte Barracks, Lincoln County, Nebraska
Unit: Company M, 3d U.S. Cavalry
Battle or Place of Action: Slim Butts, Dakota Territory
Date of Action: 9 September 1876
Date of Issue: 16 October 1877
Citation: Bravely endeavored to dislodge some Sioux Indians secreted in a ravine.

1732 ◆ KITCHEN, GEORGE KRAUSE

Rank: Sergeant (highest rank: First Sergeant)
Service: U.S. Army
Birthday: 5 October 1844
Place of Birth: Lebanon County, Pennsylvania
Date of Death: 22 November 1922

Place of Death: San Antonio, Texas
Cemetery: St. Mary's Cemetery (MH)—San Antonio, Texas
Entered Service at: Harrisburg, Dauphin County, Pennsylvania
Unit: Company H, 6th U.S. Cavalry
Battle or Place of Action: Upper Wichita River, Texas
Date of Action: 9 September 1874
Date of Issue: 23 April 1875
Citation: Gallantry in action.

1733 ◆ KNAAK, ALBERT

Rank: Private (highest rank: Ordnance Sergeant)
Service: U.S. Army
Birthday: 1840
Place of Birth: Luxenburg, Switzerland
Date of Death: 7 April 1897
Cemetery: Fort Meade National Cemetery (2-101) (MH)—Sturgis, South Dakota
Entered Service at: Cincinnati, Hamilton County, Ohio
Unit: Company B, 8th U.S. Cavalry
Battle or Place of Action: Arizona
Date of Action: August-October 1868
Date of Issue: 24 July 1869
Citation: Bravery in scouts and actions against Indians.

1734 ◆ KNIGHT, JOSEPH F.

Rank: Sergeant
Service: U.S. Army
Birthday: 23 November 1863
Place of Birth: Danville, Vermilion County, Illinois
Date of Death: 24 May 1940
Cemetery: City of Lubbock Cemetery (MH)—Lubbock, Texas
Entered Service at: Denver, Denver County, Colorado
Unit: Troop F, 6th U.S. Cavalry
Battle or Place of Action: White River, South Dakota
Date of Action: 1 January 1891
Date of Issue: 1 May 1891
Citation: Led the advance in a spirited movement to the assistance of Troop K, 6th U.S. Cavalry.

1735 ◆ KNOX, JOHN W.

Rank: Sergeant
Service: U.S. Army
Birthday: 1851
Place of Birth: Burlington, Des Moines County, Iowa
Date of Death: 1895
Place of Death: Philadelphia, Pennsylvania
Entered Service at: Fort Leavenworth, Leavenworth County, Kansas
Unit: Company I, 5th U.S. Infantry
Battle or Place of Action: Upper Wichita River, Texas
Date of Action: 9 September 1874
Date of Issue: 23 April 1875
Citation: Gallantry in action.

1736 ◆ KOELPIN, WILLIAM

Rank: Sergeant
Service: U.S. Army
Birthday: 5 October 1845
Place of Birth: Stetten, Prussia
Date of Death: 2 January 1912
Place of Death: Brooklyn, New York
Cemetery: Lutheran Cemetery—Middle Village, New York
Entered Service at: Brooklyn, Kings County, New York
Unit: Company I, 5th U.S. Infantry
Battle or Place of Action: Upper Wichita River, Texas
Date of Action: 9 September 1874
Date of Issue: 23 April 1875
Citation: Gallantry in action.

1737 ◆ KOSOHA

Rank: Scout
Service: U.S. Army
Place of Birth: Arizona Territory
Unit: Indian Scouts
Battle or Place of Action: Arizona Territory
Date of Action: winter 1872-73
Date of Issue: 12 April 1875
Citation: Gallant conduct during campaigns and engagements with Apaches.

1738 ◆ *KREHER, WENDELIN

Rank: First Sergeant
Service: U.S. Army
Birthday: 1846
Place of Birth: Stetten, Prussia
Date of Death: 17 March 1877
Place of Death: Tongue River, Montana
Cemetery: Custer Battlefield National Monument (A-466)—Crow Agency, Montana
Entered Service at: Philadelphia, Philadelphia County, Pennsylvania
Unit: Company C, 5th U.S. Infantry
Battle or Place of Action: Cedar Creek, etc., Montana
Date of Action: 21 October 1876
Date of Issue: 27 April 1877
Citation: Gallantry in action.

1739 ◆ KYLE, JOHN

Rank: Corporal
Service: U.S. Army
Birthday: 1846
Place of Birth: Cincinnati, Hamilton County, Ohio
Date of Death: 18 July 1870
Place of Death: Fort Hays, Kansas
Cemetery: Fort Leavenworth National Cemetery (H-3341)—Fort Leavenworth, Kansas
Entered Service at: Nashville, Davidson County, Tennessee
Unit: Company M, 5th U.S. Cavalry
Battle or Place of Action: Republican River, Kansas

Date of Action: 8 July 1869
Date of Issue: 24 August 1869
Citation: This soldier and two others were attacked by eight Indians, but beat them off and badly wounded two of them.

1740 ◆ LARKIN, DAVID

Rank: Farrier
Service: U.S. Army
Birthday: 1845
Place of Birth: Cork, Ireland
Date of Death: 8 May 1905
Cemetery: St. Paul's Cemetery (MH)—Arlington, Massachusetts
Entered Service at: Boston, Suffolk County, Massachusetts
Unit: Company F, 4th U.S. Cavalry
Battle or Place of Action: Red River, Texas
Date of Action: 29 September 1872
Date of Issue: 19 November 1872
Citation: Gallantry in action.

1741 ◆ LAWRENCE, JAMES

Rank: Private
Service: U.S. Army
Birthday: 1832
Place of Birth: Aberdeen, Scotland
Entered Service at: Sacramento, Sacramento County, California
Unit: Company B, 8th U.S. Cavalry
Battle or Place of Action: Arizona
Date of Action: August-October 1868
Date of Issue: 24 July 1869
Citation: Bravery in scouts and actions against Indians.

1742 ◆ LAWTON, JOHN STERLING

Rank: Sergeant
Service: U.S. Army
Birthday: 13 May 1858
Place of Birth: Bristol, Bristol County, Rhode Island
Date of Death: 12 June 1909
Place of Death: Presido of San Francisco, California
Cemetery: San Francisco National Cemetery (WS-1392)—San Francisco, California
Entered Service at: Boston, Suffolk County, Massachusetts
Unit: Company D, 5th U.S. Cavalry
Battle or Place of Action: Milk River, Colorado
Date of Action: 29 October 1879
Date of Issue: 7 June 1880
Citation: Coolness and steadiness under fire; volunteered to accompany a small detachment on a very dangerous mission.

1743 ◆ LENIHAN, JAMES

Rank: Private
Service: U.S. Army
Birthday: 1846

Place of Birth: County Kerry, Ireland
Entered Service at: Washington, D.C.
Unit: Company K, 5th U.S. Cavalry
Battle or Place of Action: Clear Creek, Arizona
Date of Action: 2 January 1873
Date of Issue: 12 April 1875
Citation: Gallantry in action.

1744 ◆ LEONARD, PATRICK JAMES

Rank: Sergeant (highest rank: First Sergeant)
Service: U.S. Army
Birthday: 19 May 1847
Place of Birth: County Meath, Ireland
Date of Death: 24 January 1899
Place of Death: Kansas City, Missouri
Cemetery: St. Joseph's Cemetery (MH)—New Almelo, Kansas
Entered Service at: Cincinnati, Hamilton County, Ohio
Unit: Company C, 2d U.S. Cavalry
Battle or Place of Action: Little Blue, Nebraska
Date of Action: 15 May 1870
Date of Issue: 22 June 1870
Citation: Gallantry in action.

1745 ◆ LEONARD, PATRICK THOMAS

Rank: Corporal (highest rank: Sergeant)
Service: U.S. Army
Birthday: 1828
Place of Birth: County Clare, Ireland
Date of Death: 1 March 1905
Place of Death: Leavenworth, Kansas
Cemetery: Mount Calvary Cemetery (MH)—Leavenworth, Kansas
Entered Service at: New York, New York
Unit: Company A, 23d U.S. Infantry
Battle or Place of Action: Fort Hartsuff (Grace Creek), Nebraska
Date of Action: 28 April 1876
Date of Issue: 26 August 1876
Citation: Gallantry in charge on hostile Sioux.

1746 ◆ LEONARD, WILLIAM

Rank: Private
Service: U.S. Army
Birthday: 14 July 1855
Place of Birth: Ypsilanti, Washtenaw County, Michigan
Date of Death: 15 September 1923
Place of Death: White Sulphur Springs, Montana
Cemetery: Main Cemetery (MH)—White Sulphur Springs, Montana
Entered Service at: Detroit, Wayne County, Michigan
Unit: Company L, 2d U.S. Cavalry
Battle or Place of Action: Muddy Creek, Montana
Date of Action: 7 May 1877
Date of Issue: 8 August 1877
Citation: Bravery in action.

1747 ◆ LEWIS, WILLIAM B.

Rank: Sergeant
Service: U.S. Army
Birthday: 1847
Place of Birth: Boston, Suffolk County, Massachusetts
Date of Death: 1 November 1900
Place of Death: Mamaroneck, New York
Cemetery: Beechwoods Cemetery—New Rochelle, New York
Entered Service at: Boston, Suffolk County, Massachusetts
Unit: Company B, 3d U.S. Cavalry
Battle or Place of Action: Bluff Station, Wyoming
Date of Action: 20-22 January 1879
Date of Issue: 28 March 1879
Citation: Bravery in skirmish.

1748 ◆ LITTLE, THOMAS

Rank: Bugler
Service: U.S. Army
Birthday: 1830
Place of Birth: Barbados, West Indians
Date of Death: 11 February 1880
Place of Death: Washington, D.C.
Cemetery: Soldier's Home National Cemetery (I-5627) (MH)—Washington, D.C.
Entered Service at: New York, New York
Unit: Company B, 8th U.S. Cavalry
Battle or Place of Action: Arizona
Date of Action: August-October 1868
Date of Issue: 24 July 1869
Citation: Bravery in scouts and actions against Indians.

1749 ◆ LLOYD, GEORGE

True Name: Loyd, George
Rank: Sergeant (highest rank: First Sergeant)
Service: U.S. Army
Birthday: 1843
Place of Birth: County Tyrone, Ireland
Date of Death: 17 December 1892
Place of Death: Fort Riley, Kansas
Cemetery: Post Cemetery (MH)—Fort Riley, Kansas
Entered Service at: Canton, Van Zandt County, Texas
Unit: Company I, 7th U.S. Cavalry
Battle or Place of Action: Wounded Knee Creek, South Dakota
Date of Action: 29 December 1890
Date of Issue: 16 April 1891
Citation: Bravery, especially after having been severely wounded through the lung.

1750 ◆ LOHNES, FRANK W.

True Name: Lohnas, Frank W.
Rank: Private
Service: U.S. Army
Birthday: 1840

Place of Birth: Oneida County, New York
Date of Death: 18 September 1889
Place of Death: Near Shubert, Nebraska
Cemetery: Maple Grove Cemetery (MH)—Shubert, Nebraska
Entered Service at: Omaha, Douglas County, Nebraska
Unit: Company H, 1st Nebraska Veteran Cavalry
Battle or Place of Action: Gilmans Ranch, Nebraska
Date of Action: 12 May 1865
Date of Issue: 24 July 1865
Citation: Gallantry in defending Government property against Indians.

1751 ◆ LONG, OSCAR FITZALAN

Rank: Second Lieutenant (highest rank: Brigadier General Ret.)
Service: U.S. Army
Birthday: 16 June 1852
Place of Birth: Utica, Oneida County, New York
Date of Death: 23 December 1928
Place of Death: Piedmont, California
Cemetery: Mountain View Cemetery—Oakland, California
Entered Service at: Utica, Oneida County, New York
Unit: 5th U.S. Infantry
Battle or Place of Action: Bear Paw Mountain, Montana
Date of Action: 30 September 1877
Date of Issue: 22 March 1895
Citation: Having been directed to order a troop of cavalry to advance, and finding both its officers killed, he voluntarily assumed command, and under a heavy fire from the Indians advanced the troop to its proper position.

1752 ◆ LOWTHERS, JAMES

Rank: Private
Service: U.S. Army
Birthday: 1852
Place of Birth: Boston, Suffolk County, Massachusetts
Entered Service at: Boston, Suffolk County, Massachusetts
Unit: Company H, 6th U.S. Cavalry
Battle or Place of Action: Sappa Creek, Kansas
Date of Action: 23 April 1875
Date of Issue: 16 November 1876
Citation: With five other men he waded in mud and water up the creek to a position directly behind an entrenched Cheyenne position, who were using natural bank pits to good advantage against the main column. This surprise attack from the enemy rear broke their resistance.

1753 ◆ LYTLE, LEONIDAS S.

Rank: Sergeant (highest rank: First Sergeant)
Service: U.S. Army
Birthday: 4 September 1846
Place of Birth: Warren County, Pennsylvania
Date of Death: 23 January 1924
Place of Death: Silver City, New Mexico
Cemetery: Memory Lane Cemetery (MH)—Silver City, New Mexico

Entered Service at: Cleveland, Cuyahoga County, Ohio
Unit: Company C, 8th U.S. Cavalry
Battle or Place of Action: Fort Selden, New Mexico
Date of Action: 8-11 July 1873
Date of Issue: 12 April 1875
Citation: Services against hostile Indians.

1754 ◆ LYTTON, JEPTHA L.

Rank: Corporal (highest rank: Sergeant)
Service: U.S. Army
Birthday: 18 November 1849
Place of Birth: Lawrence County, Indiana
Date of Death: 27 December 1932
Place of Death: Washington, D.C.
Cemetery: Soldier's Home National Cemetery (M-9370) (MH)—Washington, D.C.
Entered Service at: San Francisco, San Francisco County, California
Unit: Company A, 23d U.S. Infantry
Battle or Place of Action: Fort Hartsuff, Nebraska
Date of Action: 28 April 1876
Date of Issue: 26 August 1876
Citation: Gallantry in charge on hostile Sioux.

1755 ◆ MACHOL

Rank: Private
Service: U.S. Army
Place of Birth: Arizona Territory
Unit: Indian Scouts
Battle or Place of Action: Arizona Territory
Date of Action: 1872-73
Date of Issue: 12 April 1875
Citation: Gallant conduct during campaign and engagements with Apaches.

1756 ◆ MAHERS, HERBERT

Rank: Private
Service: U.S. Army
Birthday: 1846
Place of Birth: Canada
Entered Service at: Wilmington, Los Angeles County, California
Unit: Company F, 8th U.S. Cavalry
Battle or Place of Action: Seneca Mountain, Arizona
Date of Action: 25 August 1869
Date of Issue: 3 March 1870
Citation: Gallantry in action.

1757 ◆ MAHONEY, GREGORY

Rank: Private
Service: U.S. Army
Birthday: 1850
Place of Birth: Pettypool, South Wales
Cemetery: Fort Concho National Historic Landmark (MH) (Marker Only)—San Angelo, Texas

Entered Service at: Boston, Suffolk County, Massachusetts
Unit: Company E, 4th U.S. Cavalry
Battle or Place of Action: Red River, Texas
Date of Action: 26-28 September 1874
Date of Issue: 13 October 1875
Citation: Gallantry in attack on a large party of Cheyennes.

1758 ◆ MARTIN, PATRICK

Rank: Sergeant
Service: U.S. Army
Birthday: 1846
Place of Birth: County Offaly, Ireland
Date of Death: 12 December 1895
Entered Service at: New York, New York
Unit: Company G, 5th U.S. Cavalry
Battle or Place of Action: Castle Dome and Santa Maria Mountains, Arizona
Date of Action: June-July 1873
Date of Issue: 12 April 1875
Citation: Gallant services in operations of Capt. James Burns, 5th U.S. Cavalry.

1759 ◆ MATTHEWS, DAVID A.

Rank: Corporal (highest rank: First Sergeant)
Service: U.S. Army
Birthday: 7 March 1847
Place of Birth: Boston, Suffolk County, Massachusetts
Date of Death: 12 September 1923
Cemetery: St. John's Cemetery—Worcester, Massachusetts
Entered Service at: Boston, Suffolk County, Massachusetts
Unit: Company E, 8th U.S. Cavalry
Battle or Place of Action: Arizona Territory
Date of Action: 1868 & 1869
Date of Issue: 6 September 1869
Citation: Bravery in scouts and actions against Indians.

1760 ◆ MAUS, MARION PERRY

Rank: First Lieutenant (highest rank: Brigadier General-USA-Ret.)
Service: U.S. Army
Birthday: 25 August 1850
Place of Birth: Burnt Mills, Montgomery County, Maryland
Date of Death: 9 February 1930
Place of Death: New Windsor, Maryland
Cemetery: Arlington National Cemetery (3-3886-B)—Arlington, Virginia
Entered Service at: Tennallytown, Montgomery County, Maryland
Unit: 1st U.S. Infantry
Battle or Place of Action: Rio Aros, Sierra Madre Mountains, Mexico
Date of Action: 11 January 1886
Date of Issue: 27 November 1894
Citation: Most distinguished gallantry in action with hostile Apaches led by Geronimo and Natchez.

1761 ◆ MAY, JOHN

Rank: Sergeant
Service: U.S. Army
Birthday: 1839
Place of Birth: Wurttemberg, Germany
Date of Death: 19 March 1886
Place of Death: La Junta, Colorado
Cemetery: Fairview Cemetery (MH)—La Junta, Colorado
Entered Service at: Philadelphia, Philadelphia County, Pennsylvania
Unit: Company L, 6th U.S. Cavalry
Battle or Place of Action: Wichita River, Texas
Date of Action: 12 July 1870
Date of Issue: 25 August 1870
Citation: Gallantry in action.

1762 ◆ MAYS, ISAIAH

Rank: Corporal
Service: U.S. Army
Birthday: 16 February 1858
Place of Birth: Carters Bridge, Virginia
Date of Death: 2 May 1925
Place of Death: Phoenix, Arizona
Cemetery: Arizona State Hospital Cemetery (MH)—Phoenix, Arizona
Entered Service at: Columbus Barracks, Franklin County, Ohio
Unit: Company B, 24th U.S. Infantry
Battle or Place of Action: Cedar Springs, Arizona Territory
Date of Action: 11 May 1889
Date of Issue: 19 February 1890
Citation: Gallantry in the fight between Paymaster Wham's escort and robbers. Mays walked and crawled two miles to a ranch for help.

1763 ◆ McBRIDE, BERNARD

Rank: Private
Service: U.S. Army
Birthday: 1845
Place of Birth: Brooklyn, Kings County, New York
Entered Service at: Washington, D.C.
Unit: Company B, 8th U.S. Cavalry
Battle or Place of Action: Arizona Territory
Date of Action: August-October 1868
Date of Issue: 24 July 1869
Citation: Bravery in scouts and actions against Indians.

1764 ◆ McBRYAR, WILLIAM

Rank: Sergeant (highest rank: First Lieutenant)
Service: U.S. Army
Birthday: 14 February 1861
Place of Birth: Elizabethtown, Bladen County, North Carolina
Date of Death: 8 March 1941
Place of Death: Philadelphia, Pennsylvania
Cemetery: Arlington National Cemetery (4-2738-B) (MH)—Arlington, Virginia
Entered Service at: New York, New York
Unit: 10th U.S. Cavalry
Battle or Place of Action: Arizona Territory
Date of Action: 7 March 1890
Date of Issue: 15 May 1890
Citation: Distinguished himself for coolness, bravery, and marksmanship while his troop was in pursuit of hostile Apache Indians.

1765 ◆ McCABE, WILLIAM

Rank: Private
Service: U.S. Army
Birthday: 1848
Place of Birth: Belfast, County Antrim, Ireland
Cemetery: Fort Concho National Historic Landmark (MH) (Marker Only)—San Angelo, Texas
Entered Service at: Fort Duncan, Texas
Unit: Company E, 4th U.S. Cavalry
Battle or Place of Action: Red River, Texas
Date of Action: 26-28 September 1874
Date of Issue: 13 October 1875
Citation: Gallantry in attack on a large party of Cheyennes.

1766 ◆ *McCANN, BERNARD

Rank: Private
Service: U.S. Army
Birthday: 1850
Place of Birth: County Roscommon, Ireland
Date of Death: 12 January 1877
Cemetery: Custer Battlefield National Monument (A-859)—Crow Agency, Montana
Entered Service at: New York, New York
Unit: Company F, 22d U.S. Infantry
Battle or Place of Action: Cedar Creek, etc., Montana
Date of Action: 21 October 1876—8 January 1877
Date of Issue: 27 April 1877
Citation: Gallantry in action.

1767 ◆ McCARTHY, MICHAEL

Rank: First Sergeant (highest rank: Colonel–WAANG)
Service: U.S. Army
Birthday: 19 April 1845
Place of Birth: St. John's, Newfoundland, Canada
Date of Death: 15 January 1914
Cemetery: Mountain View Cemetery (IOOF Section)—Walla Walla, Washington
Entered Service at: New York, New York
Unit: Troop H, 1st U.S. Cavalry
Battle or Place of Action: White Bird Canyon, Idaho
Date of Action: June 1876—January 1877
Date of Issue: 20 November 1897
Citation: Was detailed with six men to hold a commanding position and held it with great gallantry until the troops fell back. He then fought his way through the Indians, rejoined a

portion of his command, and continued the fight in retreat. He had two horses shot from under him and was captured, but escaped and reported for duty after three days' hiding and wandering in the mountains.

1768 ◆ McCLERNAND, EDWARD JOHN

Rank: Second Lieutenant (highest rank: Brigadier General)
Service: U.S. Army
Birthday: 29 December 1848
Place of Birth: Jacksonville, Morgan County, Illinois
Date of Death: 9 February 1926
Place of Death: Washington, D.C.
Cemetery: Arlington National Cemetery (3-1931-SW)—Arlington, Virginia
Entered Service at: Springfield, Sangamon County, Illinois
Unit: 2d U.S. Cavalry
Battle or Place of Action: Bear Paw Mountain, Montana
Date of Action: 30 September 1877
Date of Issue: 27 November 1894
Citation: Gallantly attacked a band of hostiles and conducted the combat with excellent skill and boldness.

1769 ◆ McCORMICK, MICHAEL P.

Rank: Private (highest rank: First Sergeant Ret.)
Service: U.S. Army
Birthday: 23 January 1848
Place of Birth: Rutland, Rutland County, Vermont
Date of Death: 27 March 1909
Place of Death: Rutland, Vermont
Cemetery: Calvary Cemetery—Rutland, Vermont
Entered Service at: Harrisburg, Dauphin County, Pennsylvania
Unit: Company G, 5th U.S. Infantry
Battle or Place of Action: Cedar Creek, etc., Montana
Date of Action: 21 October 1876—8 January 1877
Date of Issue: 27 April 1877
Citation: Gallantry in action.

1770 ◆ McDONALD, FRANKLIN M.

Rank: Private
Service: U.S. Army
Birthday: 1850
Place of Birth: Bowling Green, Warren County, Kentucky
Entered Service at: Fort Griffin, Texas
Unit: Company G, 11th U.S. Infantry
Battle or Place of Action: Fort Griffin, Texas
Date of Action: 5 August 1872
Date of Issue: 31 August 1872
Citation: Gallantry in defeating Indians who attacked the mail.

1771 ◆ McDONALD, JAMES

Rank: Corporal (highest rank: Sergeant)
Service: U.S. Army
Birthday: 1834

Place of Birth: Edinburgh, Scotland
Entered Service at: Chicago, Cook County, Illinois
Unit: Company B, 8th U.S. Cavalry
Battle or Place of Action: Arizona Territory
Date of Action: August-October 1868
Date of Issue: 24 July 1869
Citation: Bravery in scouts and actions against Indians.

1772 ◆ McDONALD, ROBERT

Rank: First Lieutenant (highest rank: Captain)
Service: U.S. Army
Birthday: 12 May 1822
Place of Birth: Erie County, New York
Date of Death: 21 May 1901
Place of Death: San Francisco, California
Cemetery: Lone Tree Cemetery—Hayward, California
Entered Service at: Newport, Campbell County, Kentucky
Unit: 5th U.S. Infantry
Battle or Place of Action: Wolf Mountain, Montana
Date of Action: 8 January 1877
Date of Issue: 27 November 1894
Citation: Led his command in a successful charge against superior numbers of hostile Indians, strongly posted.

1773 ◆ McGANN, MICHAEL A.

Rank: First Sergeant (highest rank: Sergeant Major, Ordnance Corps)
Service: U.S. Army
Birthday: 1846
Place of Birth: County Roscommon, Ireland
Date of Death: 27 September 1918
Place of Death: Los Angeles, California
Cemetery: Calvary Cemetery—Los Angeles, California
Entered Service at: St. Louis, St. Louis County, Missouri
Unit: Company F, 3d U.S. Cavalry
Battle or Place of Action: Rosebud River, Montana
Date of Action: 17 June 1876
Date of Issue: 9 September 1880
Citation: Gallantry in action.

1774 ◆ McGAR, OWEN

Rank: Private
Service: U.S. Army
Birthday: 1851
Place of Birth: North Attleboro, Bristol County, Massachusetts
Date of Death: 5 November 1899
Cemetery: St. Francis Cemetery (MH)—Pawtucket, Rhode Island
Entered Service at: Providence, Providence County, Rhode Island
Unit: Company C, 5th U.S. Infantry
Battle or Place of Action: Cedar Creek, etc., Montana
Date of Action: 21 October 1876—8 January 1877
Date of Issue: 27 April 1877
Citation: Gallantry in action.

1775 ◆ McHUGH, JOHN

Rank: Private
Service: U.S. Army
Birthday: 1844
Place of Birth: Syracuse, Onondaga County, New York
Entered Service at: New York, New York
Unit: Company A, 5th U.S. Infantry
Battle or Place of Action: Cedar Creek, etc., Montana
Date of Action: 21 October 1876—8 January 1877
Date of Issue: 27 April 1877
Citation: Gallantry in action.

1776 ◆ McKINLEY, DANIEL

Rank: Private
Service: U.S. Army
Birthday: 1845
Place of Birth: Boston, Suffolk County, Massachusetts
Entered Service at: San Francisco, San Francisco County, California
Unit: Company B, 8th U.S. Cavalry
Battle or Place of Action: Arizona Territory
Date of Action: August-October 1868
Date of Issue: 24 July 1869
Citation: Bravery in scouts and actions against Indians.

1777 ◆ McLENNON, JOHN

Rank: Musician (highest rank: Sergeant)
Service: U.S. Army
Birthday: 1855
Place of Birth: Fort Belknap, Texas
Date of Death: 14 May 1888
Cemetery: St. Joseph's Catholic Cemetary (MH)—Rock Springs, Wyoming
Entered Service at: Fort Ellis, Montana
Unit: Company A, 7th U.S. Infantry
Battle or Place of Action: Big Hole, Montana
Date of Action: 9 August 1877
Date of Issue: 2 December 1878
Citation: Gallantry in action.

1778 ◆ McLOUGHLIN, MICHAEL

Rank: Sergeant
Service: U.S. Army
Birthday: 4 January 1840
Place of Birth: County Sligo, Ireland
Date of Death: 8 June 1921
Place of Death: Orting, Washington
Cemetery: Calvary Cemetery—Tacoma, Washington
Entered Service at: Louisville, Jefferson County, Kentucky
Unit: Company A, 5th U.S. Infantry
Battle or Place of Action: Cedar Creek, etc., Montana
Date of Action: 21 October 1876—8 January 1877
Date of Issue: 27 April 1877
Citation: Gallantry in action.

1779 ◆ *McMASTERS, HENRY A.

Rank: Corporal
Service: U.S. Army
Birthday: 1845
Place of Birth: Augusta, Kennebec County, Maine
Date of Death: 11 November 1872
Place of Death: Fort Griffin, Texas
Cemetery: San Antonio National Cemetery (D-729) (MH)—San Antonio, Texas
Entered Service at: Augusta, Kennebec County, Maine
Unit: Company A, 4th U.S. Cavalry
Battle or Place of Action: Red River, Texas
Date of Action: 29 September 1872
Date of Issue: 19 November 1872
Citation: Gallantry in action.

1780 ◆ McMILLIAN, ALBERT WALTER

Rank: Sergeant
Service: U.S. Army
Birthday: 13 October 1862
Place of Birth: Stillwater, Washington County, Minnesota
Date of Death: 2 October 1948
Place of Death: St. Paul, Minnesota
Cemetery: Oakland Cemetery—St. Paul, Minnesota
Entered Service at: Jefferson Barracks, Missouri
Unit: Company E, 7th U.S. Cavalry
Battle or Place of Action: Wounded Knee Creek, South Dakota
Date of Action: 29 December 1890
Date of Issue: 23 June 1891
Citation: While engaged with Indians concealed in a ravine, he assisted the men on the skirmish line, directed their fire, encouraged them by example, and used every effort to dislodge the enemy.

1781 ◆ McNALLY, JAMES

Rank: First Sergeant
Service: U.S. Army
Birthday: 1839
Place of Birth: County Monaghan, Ireland
Date of Death: 26 November 1904
Place of Death: Kingston, New Mexico
Entered Service at: Albany, Albany County, New York
Unit: Company E, 8th U.S. Cavalry
Battle or Place of Action: Arizona Territory
Date of Action: 1868 & 1869
Date of Issue: 6 September 1869
Citation: Bravery in scouts and actions against Indians.

1782 ◆ McNAMARA, WILLIAM

Rank: First Sergeant
Service: U.S. Army
Birthday: 1835
Place of Birth: County Cork, Ireland
Date of Death: 6 March 1912

Cemetery: Calvary Cemetery—Woodside, New York
Entered Service at: Baltimore, Baltimore County, Maryland
Unit: Company F, 4th U.S. Cavalry
Battle or Place of Action: Red River, Texas
Date of Action: 29 September 1872
Date of Issue: 19 November 1872
Citation: Gallantry in action.

1783 ◆ McPHELAN, ROBERT

Rank: Sergeant
Service: U.S. Army
Birthday: 1837
Place of Birth: County Laois, Ireland
Date of Death: 1 February 1884
Cemetery: Mount Calvary Cemetery (MH)—Leavenworth, Kansas
Entered Service at: New York, New York
Unit: Company E, 5th U.S. Infantry
Battle or Place of Action: Cedar Creek, etc., Montana
Date of Action: 21 October 1876—8 January 1877
Date of Issue: 27 April 1877
Citation: Gallantry in action.

1784 ◆ McVEAGH, CHARLES H.

Rank: Private
Service: U.S. Army
Birthday: 1833
Place of Birth: New York, New York
Entered Service at: San Francisco, San Francisco County, California
Unit: Company B, 8th U.S. Cavalry
Battle or Place of Action: Arizona
Date of Action: August-October 1868
Date of Issue: 24 July 1869
Citation: Bravery in scouts and actions against Indians.

1785 ◆ MEAHER, NICHOLAS

Rank: Corporal (highest rank: Sergeant)
Service: U.S. Army
Birthday: 1845
Place of Birth: Perry County, Ohio
Entered Service at: Cincinnati, Hamilton County, Ohio
Unit: Company G, 1st U.S. Cavalry
Battle or Place of Action: Chiricahua Mountains, Arizona Territory
Date of Action: 20 October 1869
Date of Issue: 14 February 1870
Citation: Gallantry in action.

1786 ◆ MECHLIN, HENRY W.B.

True Name: Mechling, Henry W.B.
Rank: Blacksmith
Service: U.S. Army

Birthday: 14 October 1851
Place of Birth: Mount Pleasant, Westmoreland County, Pennsylvania
Date of Death: 10 April 1926
Place of Death: Washington, D.C.
Cemetery: Soldier's Home National Cemetery (L-8861) (MH)—Washington, D.C.
Entered Service at: Pittsburgh, Allegheny County, Pennsylvania
Unit: Company H, 7th U.S. Cavalry
Battle or Place of Action: Little Big Horn, Montana
Date of Action: 25 June 1876
Date of Issue: 29 August 1878
Citation: With three comrades during the entire engagement courageously held a position that secured water for the command.

1787 ◆ MERRILL, JOHN MITCHELL

Rank: Sergeant
Service: U.S. Army
Birthday: 1846
Place of Birth: New York, New York
Date of Death: 10 June 1883
Place of Death: Fort D.A. Russell, Wyoming
Cemetery: Olivet Catholic Cemetery—Cheyenne, Wyoming
Entered Service at: New York, New York
Unit: Company F, 5th U.S. Cavalry
Battle or Place of Action: Milk River, Colorado
Date of Action: 29 September 1879
Date of Issue: 7 June 1880
Citation: Though painfully wounded, he remained on duty and rendered gallant and valuable service.

1788 ◆ MILLER, DANIEL H.

Rank: Private
Service: U.S. Army
Birthday: 1841
Place of Birth: Fairfield County, Ohio
Date of Death: 6 October 1874
Cemetery: Fort McPherson National Cemetery (A-380) (MH)—Maxwell, Nebraska
Entered Service at: Columbus, Franklin County, Ohio
Unit: Company F, 3d U.S. Cavalry
Battle or Place of Action: Whetstone Mountains, Arizona Territory
Date of Action: 5 May 1871
Date of Issue: 13 November 1871
Citation: Gallantry in action.

1789 ◆ MILLER, GEORGE

Rank: Corporal
Service: U.S. Army
Birthday: 1851
Place of Birth: Brooklyn, Kings County, New York
Date of Death: 10 June 1888

Place of Death: Sheridan, Kansas
Cemetery: Red Top Cemetery (MH)—Baker Township, Kansas
Entered Service at: Boston, Suffolk County, Massachusetts
Unit: Company H, 5th U.S. Infantry
Battle or Place of Action: Cedar Creek, etc., Montana
Date of Action: 21 October 1876—8 January 1877
Date of Issue: 27 April 1877
Citation: Gallantry in action.

1790 ◆ MILLER, GEORGE W.

Rank: Private
Service: U.S. Army
Birthday: 1839
Place of Birth: Philadelphia, Philadelphia County, Pennsylvania
Date of Death: 29 September 1869
Place of Death: Wickensburg, Arizona
Entered Service at: Philadelphia, Philadelphia County, Pennsylvania
Unit: Company B, 8th U.S. Cavalry
Battle or Place of Action: Arizona
Date of Action: August-October 1868
Date of Issue: 24 July 1869
Citation: Bravery in scouts and actions against Indians.

1791 ◆ MITCHELL, JOHN

Rank: First Sergeant (highest rank: Ordnance Sergeant)
Service: U.S. Army
Birthday: 1846
Place of Birth: Dublin, Ireland
Date of Death: 1 May 1904
Cemetery: San Francisco National Cemetery (NAWS-411-Row 51) (MH)—San Francisco, California
Entered Service at: Peoria, Peoria County, Illinois
Unit: Company I, 5th U.S. Infantry
Battle or Place of Action: Upper Washita, Texas
Date of Action: 9-11 September 1874
Date of Issue: 23 April 1875
Citation: Gallantry in engagement with Indians.

1792 ◆ MITCHELL, JOHN JAMES

Rank: Corporal
Service: U.S. Army
Birthday: 1846
Place of Birth: County Tyrone, Ireland
Date of Death: 15 May 1898
Place of Death: Tucson, Arizona
Entered Service at: Philadelphia, Philadelphia County, Pennsylvania
Unit: Company L, 8th U.S. Cavalry
Battle or Place of Action: Hell Canyon, Arizona
Date of Action: 3 July 1869
Date of Issue: 3 March 1870
Citation: Gallantry in action.

1793 ◆ MONTROSE, CHARLES H.

True Name: Munson, Alexander D.
Rank: Private
Service: U.S. Army
Birthday: 1853
Place of Birth: St. Paul, Ramsey County, Minnesota
Entered Service at: New York, New York
Unit: Company I, 5th U.S. Infantry
Battle or Place of Action: Cedar Creek, etc., Montana
Date of Action: 21 October 1876—8 January 1877
Date of Issue: 27 April 1877
Citation: Gallantry in action.

1794 ◆ MOQUIN, GEORGE

Rank: Corporal
Service: U.S. Army
Birthday: 1855
Place of Birth: New York, New York
Entered Service at: Brooklyn, Kings County, New York
Unit: Company F, 5th U.S. Cavalry
Battle or Place of Action: Milk River, Colorado
Date of Action: 29 September-5 October 1879
Date of Issue: 27 January 1880
Citation: Gallantry in action.

1795 ◆ MORAN, JOHN

Rank: Private
Service: U.S. Army
Birthday: 1842
Place of Birth: Lyon, France
Entered Service at: Marysville, Yuba County, California
Unit: Company F, 8th U.S. Cavalry
Battle or Place of Action: Seneca Mountain, Arizona
Date of Action: 25 August 1869
Date of Issue: 3 March 1870
Citation: Gallantry in action.

1796 ◆ MORGAN, GEORGE HORACE

Rank: Second Lieutenant (highest rank: Colonel)
Service: U.S. Army
Birthday: 1 January 1855
Place of Birth: St. Catherines, Canada
Date of Death: 14 February 1948
Place of Death: Washington, D.C.
Cemetery: Arlington National Cemetery (3-2053)—Arlington, Virginia
Entered Service at: Minneapolis, Hennepin County, Minnesota
Unit: 3d U.S. Cavalry
Battle or Place of Action: Big Dry Fork, Arizona
Date of Action: 17 July 1882
Date of Issue: 15 July 1892
Citation: Gallantly held his ground at a critical moment and

fired upon the advancing enemy (hostile Indians) until he was disabled by a shot.

1797 ◆ MORIARITY, JOHN

Rank: Sergeant
Service: U.S. Army
Birthday: 10 March 1846
Place of Birth: Huddersfield, Yorkshire, England
Date of Death: 12 October 1913
Place of Death: Yountville, California
Cemetery: Veterans Home of California Cemetery (MH)—Yountville, California
Entered Service at: Boston, Suffolk County, Massachusetts
Unit: Company E, 8th U.S. Cavalry
Battle or Place of Action: Arizona Territory
Date of Action: 1868 & 1869
Date of Issue: 6 September 1869
Citation: Bravery in scouts and actions against Indians.

1798 ◆ MORRIS, JAMES L.

Rank: First Sergeant
Service: U.S. Army
Birthday: 1844
Place of Birth: County Kerry, Ireland
Date of Death: 9 February 1903
Cemetery: Fairview Memorial Park (MH)—Albuquerque, New Mexico
Entered Service at: Philadelphia, Philadelphia County, Pennsylvania
Unit: Company C, 8th U.S. Cavalry
Battle or Place of Action: Fort Selden, New Mexico
Date of Action: 8-11 July 1873
Date of Issue: 12 August 1875
Citation: Services against hostile Indians.

1799 ◆ MORRIS, WILLIAM W.

Rank: Corporal
Service: U.S. Army
Birthday: 1843
Place of Birth: Stewart County, Tennessee
Entered Service at: Louisville, Jefferson County, Kentucky
Unit: Company H, 6th U.S. Cavalry
Battle or Place of Action: Upper Washita, Texas
Date of Action: 9-11 September 1874
Date of Issue: 23 April 1875
Citation: Gallantry in engagement with Indians.

1800 ◆ MOTT, JOHN

True Name: McMahan, John Mott
Rank: Sergeant (highest rank: Quartermaster Sergeant)
Service: U.S. Army
Birthday: 25 August 1842
Place of Birth: Fifeshire, Scotland
Date of Death: 30 August 1917
Place of Death: Omaha, Nebraska

Cemetery: Forest Lawn Cemetery—Omaha, Nebraska
Entered Service at: Baltimore, Baltimore County, Maryland
Unit: Company F, 3d U.S. Cavalry
Battle or Place of Action: Whetstone Mountains, Arizona Territory
Date of Action: 5 May 1871
Date of Issue: 13 November 1871
Citation: Gallantry in action.

1801 ◆ MOYLAN, MYLES

Rank: Captain (highest rank: Major)
Service: U.S. Army
Birthday: 17 December 1838
Place of Birth: Amesbury, Essex County, Massachusetts
Date of Death: 11 December 1909
Place of Death: San Diego, California
Cemetery: Greenwood Cemetery—San Diego, California
Entered Service at: Essex, Essex County, Massachusetts
Unit: 7th U.S. Cavalry
Battle or Place of Action: Bear Paw Mountain, Montana
Date of Action: 30 September 1877
Date of Issue: 27 November 1894
Citation: Gallantly led his command in action against Nez Perce Indians until he was severely wounded.

1802 ◆ MURPHY, EDWARD

Rank: Private (highest rank: Sergeant)
Service: U.S. Army
Birthday: 1845
Place of Birth: County Cork, Ireland
Date of Death: 27 January 1924
Place of Death: Los Angeles, California
Cemetery: Los Angeles National Cemetery (44-I-22) (MH)—Los Angeles, California
Entered Service at: New York, New York
Unit: Company G, 1st U.S. Cavalry
Battle or Place of Action: Chiricahua Mountains, Arizona Territory
Date of Action: 20 October 1869
Citation: Gallantry in action.

1803 ◆ MURPHY, EDWARD F.

Rank: Corporal
Service: U.S. Army
Birthday: 16 July 1850
Place of Birth: Wayne County, Pennsylvania
Date of Death: 20 April 1908
Place of Death: Philadelphia, Pennsylvania
Cemetery: Old Cathedral Cemetery—Philadelphia, Pennsylvania
Entered Service at: Philadelphia, Philadelphia County, Pennsylvania
Unit: Company D, 5th U.S. Cavalry
Battle or Place of Action: Milk River, Colorado
Date of Action: 29 September 1879

Date of Issue: 23 April 1880
Citation: Gallantry in action.

1804 ◆ MURPHY, JEREMIAH J.

Rank: Private
Service: U.S. Army
Birthday: 2 February 1858
Place of Birth: County Cork, Ireland
Date of Death: 12 May 1932
Place of Death: Detroit, Michigan
Cemetery: Mount Olivet Cemetery—Washington, D.C.
Entered Service at: Boston, Suffolk County, Massachusetts
Unit: Company M, 3d U.S. Cavalry
Battle or Place of Action: Powder River, Montana
Date of Action: 17 March 1876
Date of Issue: 16 October 1877
Citation: Being the only member of his picket not disabled, he attempted to save a wounded comrade.

1805 ◆ MURPHY, PHILIP

Rank: Corporal
Service: U.S. Army
Birthday: 1 November 1844
Place of Birth: County Killkenny, Ireland
Date of Death: 12 February 1923
Place of Death: Freewater, Oregon
Cemetery: Mountain View Cemetery—Walla Walla, Washington
Entered Service at: Chicago, Cook County, Illinois
Unit: Company F, 8th U.S. Cavalry
Battle or Place of Action: Seneca Mountain, Arizona
Date of Action: 25 August 1869
Date of Issue: 3 March 1870
Citation: Gallantry in action.

1806 ◆ MURPHY, THOMAS

Rank: Corporal
Service: U.S. Army
Birthday: 1836
Place of Birth: County Kerry, Ireland
Entered Service at: San Francisco, San Francisco County, California
Unit: Company F, 8th U.S. Cavalry
Battle or Place of Action: Seneca Mountain, Arizona
Date of Action: 25 August 1869
Date of Issue: 3 March 1870
Citation: Gallantry in action.

1807 ◆ MURRAY, THOMAS

Rank: Sergeant
Service: U.S. Army
Birthday: 1836
Place of Birth: County Monaghan, Ireland
Date of Death: 4 August 1888
Cemetery: Soldier's Home National Cemetery (K-6502) (MH)—Washington, D.C.

Entered Service at: New York, New York
Unit: Company B, 7th U.S. Cavalry
Battle or Place of Action: Little Big Horn, Montana
Date of Action: 25 June 1876
Date of Issue: 5 October 1878
Citation: Brought up the pack train, and on the second day the rations, under a heavy fire from the enemy.

1808 ◆ MYERS, FRED

Rank: Sergeant
Service: U.S. Army
Birthday: 1848
Place of Birth: Brunswick, Germany
Date of Death: 5 May 1900
Cemetery: Arlington National Cemetery (13-14034) (MH)—Arlington, Virginia
Entered Service at: St. Louis, St. Louis County, Missouri
Unit: Company K, 6th U.S. Cavalry
Battle or Place of Action: White River, South Dakota
Date of Action: 1 January 1891
Date of Issue: 4 February 1891
Citation: With five men repelled a superior force of the enemy and held his position against their repeated efforts to recapture it.

1809 ◆ NANNASADDIE

Rank: Scout
Service: U.S. Army
Place of Birth: Arizona Territory
Unit: Indian Scouts
Battle or Place of Action: Arizona Territory
Date of Action: 1872-73
Date of Issue: 12 April 1875
Citation: Gallant conduct during campaigns and engagements with Apaches.

1810 ◆ NANTAJE (NANTAHE)

Rank: Scout
Service: U.S. Army
Place of Birth: Arizona Territory
Unit: Indian Scouts
Battle or Place of Action: Arizona Territory
Date of Action: 1872-73
Date of Issue: 12 April 1875
Citation: Gallant conduct during campaigns and engagements with Apaches.

1811 ◆ NEAL, SOLON D.

Rank: Private (highest rank: Sergeant)
Service: U.S. Army
Birthday: 1846
Place of Birth: Hanover, Grafton County, New Hampshire
Date of Death: 1 November 1920
Cemetery: San Antonio National Cemetery (G-1323) (MH)—San Antonio, Texas

Entered Service at: Boston, Suffolk County, Massachusetts
Unit: Company L, 6th U.S. Cavalry
Battle or Place of Action: Wichita River, Texas
Date of Action: 12 July 1870
Date of Issue: 25 August 1870
Citation: Gallantry in action.

1812 ◆ NEDER, ADAM

Rank: Corporal
Service: U.S. Army
Birthday: 1865
Place of Birth: Bavaria, Germany
Date of Death: 17 September 1910
Place of Death: Manila, Philippine Islands
Cemetery: San Francisco National Cemetery (NAWS-1805) (MH)—San Francisco, California
Entered Service at: St. Louis, St. Louis County, Missouri
Unit: Company A, 7th U.S. Cavalry
Battle or Place of Action: Sioux Campaign
Date of Action: December 1890
Date of Issue: 25 April 1891
Citation: Distinguished bravery.

1813 ◆ NEILON, FREDERICK S.

Rank: Sergeant
Service: U.S. Army
Birthday: 22 June 1846
Place of Birth: Boston, Suffolk County, Massachusetts
Date of Death: 13 September 1916
Place of Death: Somerville, Massachusetts
Cemetery: St. Paul's Cemetery (MH)—Arlington, Massachusetts
Entered Service at: Watertown, Middlesex County, Massachusetts
Unit: Company A, 6th U.S. Cavalry
Battle or Place of Action: Upper Washita, Texas
Date of Action: 9-11 September 1874
Date of Issue: 23 April 1875
Citation: Gallantry in action.

1814 ◆ NEWMAN, HENRY

Rank: First Sergeant
Service: U.S. Army
Birthday: 1845
Place of Birth: Hanover, Germany
Date of Death: 13 July 1915
Cemetery: Loudon Park National Cemetery (PS-739)—Baltimore, Maryland
Entered Service at: Cincinnati, Hamilton County, Ohio
Unit: Company F, 5th U.S. Cavalry
Battle or Place of Action: Whetstone Mountains, Arizona Territory
Date of Action: 13 July 1872
Date of Issue: 4 December 1874
Citation: He and two companions covered the withdrawal of wounded comrades from the fire of an Apache band well concealed among rocks.

1815 ◆ NIHILL, JOHN

Rank: Private (highest rank: Sergeant)
Service: U.S. Army
Birthday: 25 May 1850
Place of Birth: Nenagh, County Tipperary, Ireland
Date of Death: 29 May 1908
Cemetery: Cypress Hills National Cemetery (2-6640) (MH)—Brooklyn, New York
Entered Service at: Brooklyn, Kings County, New York
Unit: Company F, 5th U.S. Cavalry
Battle or Place of Action: Whetstone Mountains, Arizona Territory
Date of Action: 13 July 1872
Date of Issue: 4 December 1874
Citation: Fought and defeated four hostile Apaches located between him and his comrades.

1816 ◆ NOLAN, RICHARD J.

Rank: Farrier
Service: U.S. Army
Birthday: 1848
Place of Birth: Ireland
Date of Death: 26 August 1905
Place of Death: Washington, D.C.
Cemetery: Soldier's Home National Cemetery (K-7179) (MH)—Washington, D.C.
Entered Service at: Milwaukee, Milwaukee County, Wisconsin
Unit: Company I, 7th U.S. Cavalry
Battle or Place of Action: White Clay Creek, South Dakota
Date of Action: 30 December 1890
Date of Issue: 1 April 1891
Citation: Bravery.

1817 ◆ O'CALLAGHAN, JOHN

Rank: Sergeant
Service: U.S. Army
Birthday: 1838
Place of Birth: New York, New York
Entered Service at: San Francisco, San Francisco County, California
Unit: Company B, 8th U.S. Cavalry
Battle or Place of Action: Arizona
Date of Action: August-October 1868
Date of Issue: 24 July 1869
Citation: Bravery in scouts and actions against Indians.

1818 ◆ OLIVER, FRANCIS

Rank: First Sergeant
Service: U.S. Army

Birthday: 1832
Place of Birth: Baltimore, Baltimore County, Maryland
Date of Death: 28 July 1880
Place of Death: Lewiston, Idaho
Cemetery: Normal Hill Cemetery (MH)—Lewiston, Idaho
Entered Service at: Fort Filmore, New Mexico
Unit: Company G, 1st U.S. Cavalry
Battle or Place of Action: Chiricahua Mountains, Arizona Territory
Date of Action: 20 October 1869
Date of Issue: 14 February 1870
Citation: Bravery in action.

1819 ◆ O'NEILL, WILLIAM

Rank: Corporal
Service: U.S. Army
Birthday: 1848
Place of Birth: Tariffville, Hartford County, Connecticut
Cemetery: Fort Concho National Historic Landmark (MH) (Marker Only)—San Angelo, Texas
Entered Service at: New York, New York
Unit: Company I, 4th U.S. Cavalry
Battle or Place of Action: Red River, Texas
Date of Action: 29 September 1872
Date of Issue: 19 November 1872
Citation: Bravery in action.

1820 ◆ O'REGAN, MICHAEL

Rank: Private
Service: U.S. Army
Birthday: 1846
Place of Birth: Fall River, Bristol County, Massachusetts
Entered Service at: Boston, Suffolk County, Massachusetts
Unit: Company B, 8th U.S. Cavalry
Battle or Place of Action: Arizona
Date of Action: August-October 1868
Date of Issue: 24 July 1869
Citation: Bravery in scouts and actions against Indians.

1821 ◆ ORR, MOSES

Rank: Private
Service: U.S. Army
Birthday: 1840
Place of Birth: County Tyrone, Ireland
Date of Death: 1897
Place of Death: Philadelphia, Pennsylvania
Entered Service at: Philadelphia, Philadelphia County, Pennsylvania
Unit: Company A, 1st U.S. Cavalry
Battle or Place of Action: Apache campaigns
Date of Action: winter 1872-73
Date of Issue: 12 April 1875
Citation: Gallant conduct during campaigns and engagements with Apaches.

1822 ◆ OSBORNE, WILLIAM

True Name: Osborn, William
Rank: Sergeant
Service: U.S. Army
Birthday: 1837
Place of Birth: Boston, Suffolk County, Massachusetts
Date of Death: 17 May 1876
Place of Death: Washington, D.C.
Cemetery: Soldier's Home National Cemetery (K-6512)—Washington, D.C.
Entered Service at: Boston, Suffolk County, Massachusetts
Unit: Company M, 1st U.S. Cavalry
Battle or Place of Action: Apache campaigns
Date of Action: winter 1872-73
Date of Issue: 12 April 1875
Citation: Gallant conduct during campaigns and engagements with Apaches.

1823 ◆ O'SULLIVAN, JOHN FRANCIS

Rank: Private
Service: U.S. Army
Birthday: 1850
Place of Birth: County Kerry, Ireland
Date of Death: 19 May 1907
Place of Death: New York, New York
Cemetery: Calvary Cemetery—Woodside, New York
Entered Service at: New York, New York
Unit: Company I, 4th U.S. Cavalry
Battle or Place of Action: Staked Plains, Texas
Date of Action: 8 December 1874
Date of Issue: 13 October 1875
Citation: Gallantry in a long chase after Indians.

1824 ◆ PAINE, ADAM

True Name: Payne, Adan
Rank: Private
Service: U.S. Army
Birthday: 1843
Place of Birth: Florida
Date of Death: 1 January 1877
Cemetery: Seminole Indian Scout Cemetery (MH)—Brackettville, Texas
Entered Service at: Fort Duncan, Texas
Unit: Indian Scouts
Battle or Place of Action: Canyon Blanco tributary of the Red River, Texas
Date of Action: 26-27 September 1874
Date of Issue: 13 October 1875
Citation: Rendered invaluable service to Col. R.S. Mackenzie, 4th U.S. Cavalry, during this engagement.

1825 ◆ PARNELL, WILLIAM RUSSELL

Rank: First Lieutenant (highest rank: Colonel)
Service: U.S. Army

Birthday: 13 August 1836
Place of Birth: Dublin, Ireland
Date of Death: 20 August 1910
Cemetery: San Francisco National Cemetery (OS-68 Row 54)—San Francisco, California
Entered Service at: Brooklyn, Kings County, New York
Unit: 1st U.S. Cavalry
Battle or Place of Action: White Bird Canyon, Idaho
Date of Action: 17 June 1877
Date of Issue: 16 September 1897
Citation: With a few men, in the face of a heavy fire from pursuing Indians and in imminent peril, returned and rescued a soldier whose horse had been killed and who had been left behind in the retreat.

1826 ◆ PAYNE, ISAAC

Rank: Trumpeter
Service: U.S. Army
Birthday: 1854
Place of Birth: Mexico
Date of Death: 12 January 1904
Cemetery: Seminole Indian Scout Cemetery (MH)—Brackettville, Texas
Entered Service at: Fort Duncan, Texas
Unit: Indian Scouts
Battle or Place of Action: Pecos River, Texas
Date of Action: 25 April 1875
Date of Issue: 28 May 1875
Citation: With three other men, he participated in a charge against 25 hostiles while on a scouting patrol.

1827 ◆ PENGALLY, EDWARD

Rank: Private
Service: U.S. Army
Birthday: 1824
Place of Birth: Devonshire, England
Date of Death: 25 November 1874
Place of Death: Fort Supply, Oklahoma
Cemetery: Fort Leavenworth National Cemetery (G-3032 (MH)—Leavenworth, Kansas
Entered Service at: Albany, Albany County, New York
Unit: Company B, 8th U.S. Cavalry
Battle or Place of Action: Chiricahua Mountains, Arizona Territory
Date of Action: 20 October 1869
Date of Issue: 14 February 1870
Citation: Gallantry in action.

1828 ◆ PENNSYL, JOSIAH

Rank: Sergeant
Service: U.S. Army
Birthday: 15 September 1850
Place of Birth: Frederick County, Maryland
Date of Death: 22 January 1920
Place of Death: Pima, Arizona
Cemetery: Pima Cemetery (MH)—Pima, Arizona

Entered Service at: Carlisle, Cumberland County, Pennsylvania
Unit: Company M, 6th U.S. Cavalry
Battle or Place of Action: Upper Washita, Texas
Date of Action: 11 September 1874
Date of Issue: 23 April 1875
Citation: Gallantry in action.

1829 ◆ PHIFE, LEWIS

True Name: Pheiff, Louis
Rank: Sergeant
Service: U.S. Army
Birthday: 31 October 1841
Place of Birth: Des Moines County, Iowa
Date of Death: 31 January 1913
Place of Death: Wever, Iowa
Cemetery: Tierney Cemetery—Wever, Iowa
Entered Service at: Marion, Marion County, Oregon
Unit: Company B, 8th U.S. Cavalry
Battle or Place of Action: Arizona Territory
Date of Action: August-October 1868
Date of Issue: 24 July 1869
Citation: Bravery in scouts and actions against Indians.

1830 ◆ PHILIPSEN, WILHELM O.

Rank: Blacksmith
Service: U.S. Army
Birthday: 1852
Place of Birth: Schleswig, Germany
Entered Service at: Baltimore, Baltimore County, Maryland
Unit: Troop D, 5th U.S. Cavalry
Battle or Place of Action: Milk Creek, Colorado
Date of Action: 29 September 1879
Date of Issue: 12 December 1894
Citation: With nine others voluntarily attacked and captured a strong position held by Indians.

1831 ◆ PHILLIPS, SAMUEL D.

Rank: Private
Service: U.S. Army
Birthday: 28 January 1845
Place of Birth: Butler County, Ohio
Date of Death: 12 November 1915
Cemetery: Oakland Cemetery—St. Paul, Minnesota
Entered Service at: St. Louis, St. Louis County, Missouri
Unit: Company H, 2d U.S. Cavalry
Battle or Place of Action: Muddy Creek, Montana
Date of Action: 7 May 1877
Date of Issue: 8 August 1877
Citation: Gallantry in action.

1832 ◆ PHOENIX, EDWIN

Rank: Corporal
Service: U.S. Army
Birthday: 1846
Place of Birth: St. Louis, St. Louis County, Missouri

Date of Death: 26 September 1932
Place of Death: Los Angeles, California
Cemetery: Los Angeles National Cemetery (67-H-22) (MH)—Los Angeles, California
Entered Service at: St. Louis, St. Louis County, Missouri
Unit: Company E, 4th U.S. Cavalry
Battle or Place of Action: Red River, Texas
Date of Action: 26-28 September 1874
Date of Issue: 13 October 1875
Citation: Gallantry in action.

1833 ◆ PLATTEN, FREDERICK

Rank: Sergeant (highest rank: First Sergeant)
Service: U.S. Army
Birthday: 1849
Place of Birth: Torbeck, Ireland
Date of Death: 2 March 1939
Cemetery: Williams Cemetery—Williams, Arizona
Entered Service at: New York, New York
Unit: Company H, 6th U.S. Cavalry
Battle or Place of Action: Sappa Creek, Kansas
Date of Action: 23 April 1875
Date of Issue: 16 November 1876
Citation: With five other men he waded in mud and water up the creek to a position directly behind an entrenched Cheyenne position, who were using natural bank pits to good advantage against the main column. This surprise attack from the enemy rear broke their resistance.

1834 ◆ POPPE, JOHN A.

Rank: Sergeant
Service: U.S. Army
Birthday: 1854
Place of Birth: Cincinnati, Hamilton County, Ohio
Entered Service at: Fort Dodge, Ford County, Kansas
Unit: Company F, 5th U.S. Cavalry
Battle or Place of Action: Milk River, Colorado
Date of Action: 29 September-5 October 1879
Date of Issue: 27 January 1880
Citation: Gallantry in action.

1835 ◆ PORTER, SAMUEL

Rank: Farrier
Service: U.S. Army
Birthday: 5 December 1843
Place of Birth: Montgomery County, Maryland
Date of Death: 17 April 1920
Place of Death: Los Angeles, California
Cemetery: Los Angeles National Cemetery (40-E-6) (MH)—Los Angeles, California
Entered Service at: Washington, D.C.
Unit: Company L, 6th U.S. Cavalry
Battle or Place of Action: Wichita River, Texas
Date of Action: 12 July 1870
Date of Issue: 25 August 1870
Citation: Gallantry in action.

1836 ◆ POWERS, THOMAS

Rank: Corporal
Service: U.S. Army
Birthday: 1841
Place of Birth: New York, New York
Date of Death: 8 December 1884
Place of Death: Vience, Michigan
Entered Service at: Detroit, Wayne County, Michigan
Unit: Company G, 1st U.S. Cavalry
Battle or Place of Action: Chiricahua Mountains, Arizona Territory
Date of Action: 20 October 1869
Date of Issue: 14 February 1870
Citation: Gallantry in action.

1837 ◆ PRATT, JAMES N.

Rank: Blacksmith
Service: U.S. Army
Birthday: 12 September 1852
Place of Birth: Bellefontaine, Logan County, Ohio
Date of Death: 13 October 1903
Place of Death: Bellefontaine, Ohio
Cemetery: Bellefontaine Cemetery (MH)—Bellefontaine, Ohio
Entered Service at: Bellefontaine, Logan County, Ohio
Unit: Company I, 4th U.S. Cavalry
Battle or Place of Action: Red River, Texas
Date of Action: 29 September 1872
Date of Issue: 19 November 1872
Citation: Gallantry in action.

1838 ◆ PYM, JAMES

Rank: Private
Service: U.S. Army
Birthday: 1852
Place of Birth: Oxfordshire, England
Date of Death: 6 December 1893
Cemetery: Custer County Cemetery (MH)—Miles City, Missouri
Entered Service at: Boston, Suffolk County, Massachusetts
Unit: Company B, 7th U.S. Cavalry
Battle or Place of Action: Little Big Horn River, Montana
Date of Action: 25 June 1876
Date of Issue: 5 October 1878
Citation: Voluntarily went for water and secured the same under heavy fire.

1839 ◆ RAERICK, JOHN

Rank: Private
Service: U.S. Army
Birthday: 1844
Place of Birth: Baden, Germany
Entered Service at: Cincinnati, Hamilton County, Ohio
Unit: Company L, 8th U.S. Cavalry
Battle or Place of Action: Lyry Creek, Arizona Territory

Date of Action: 14 October 1869
Date of Issue: 3 March 1870
Citation: Gallantry in action with Indians.

1840 ◆ RAGNAR, THEODORE

True Name: Ling-Vannerus, Ragnar Theodor
Rank: First Sergeant
Service: U.S. Army
Birthday: 1 June 1856
Place of Birth: Linkoping, Sweden
Date of Death: 2 November 1943
Place of Death: Gothenburg, Sweden
Cemetery: St. Elius Cemetery—Skorde, Sweden
Entered Service at: New York, New York
Unit: Company K, 7th U.S. Cavalry
Battle or Place of Action: White Clay Creek, South Dakota
Date of Action: 30 December 1890
Date of Issue: 13 April 1891
Citation: Bravery.

1841 ◆ RANKIN, WILLIAM

Rank: Private (highest rank: Farrier-USA-Ret.)
Service: U.S. Army
Birthday: 1836
Place of Birth: Lewistown, Mifflin County, Pennsylvania
Date of Death: 2 February 1916
Place of Death: Lewiston, Pennsylvania
Cemetery: St. Mark's Episcopal Cemetery—Lewiston, Pennsylvania
Entered Service at: Harrisburg, Dauphin County, Pennsylvania
Unit: Company F, 4th U.S. Cavalry
Battle or Place of Action: Red River, Texas
Date of Action: 29 September 1872
Date of Issue: 19 November 1872
Citation: Gallantry in action with Indians.

1842 ◆ REED, JAMES C.

Rank: Private
Service: U.S. Army
Birthday: 1833
Place of Birth: Kilkenny, Ireland
Entered Service at: San Francisco, San Francisco County, California
Unit: Company A, 8th U.S. Cavalry
Battle or Place of Action: Arizona Territory
Date of Action: 29 April 1868
Date of Issue: 24 July 1869
Citation: Defended his position (with three others) against a party of 17 hostile Indians under heavy fire at close quarters, the entire party except himself being severely wounded.

1843 ◆ RICHMAN, SAMUEL

Rank: Private
Service: U.S. Army

Birthday: 1845
Place of Birth: Cleveland, Cuyahoga County, Ohio
Entered Service at: Cleveland, Cuyahoga County, Ohio
Unit: Company E, 8th U.S. Cavalry
Battle or Place of Action: Arizona Territory
Date of Action: 1868 & 1869
Date of Issue: 6 September 1869
Citation: Bravery in actions with Indians.

1844 ◆ ROACH, HAMPTON MITCHELL

Rank: Corporal (highest rank: Second Lieutenant)
Service: U.S. Army
Birthday: 1854
Place of Birth: Concord, Louisiana
Date of Death: 24 January 1923
Cemetery: Arlington National Cemetery (3-2393-WS) (MH)—Arlington, Virginia
Entered Service at: Fort Dodge, Ford County, Kansas
Unit: Company F, 5th U.S. Cavalry
Battle or Place of Action: Milk River, Colorado
Date of Action: 29 September-5 October 1879
Date of Issue: 27 January 1880
Citation: Erected breastworks under fire; also kept the command supplied with water three consecutive nights while exposed to fire from ambushed Indians at close-range.

1845 ◆ ROBBINS, MARCUS M.

Rank: Private (highest rank: Sergeant)
Service: U.S. Army
Birthday: 25 July 1851
Place of Birth: Elba, Dodge County, Wisconsin
Date of Death: 21 June 1924
Cemetery: Pittsfield Cemetery (MH)—Pittsfield, Massachusetts
Entered Service at: Boston, Suffolk County, Massachusetts
Unit: Company H, 6th U.S. Cavalry
Battle or Place of Action: Sappa Creek, Kansas
Date of Action: 23 April 1875
Date of Issue: 16 November 1876
Citation: With five other men he waded in mud and water up the creek to a position directly behind an entrenched Cheyenne position, who were using natural bank pits to good advantage against the main column. This suprise attack from the enemy rear broke their resistance.

1846 ◆ ROBINSON, JOSEPH

Rank: First Sergeant
Service: U.S. Army
Birthday: 12 October 1845
Place of Birth: Montreal, Canada
Date of Death: 18 December 1917
Cemetery: Fort Leavenworth National Cemetery (D-1269-D) (MH)—Fort Leavenworth, Kansas
Entered Service at: Boston, Suffolk County, Massachusetts
Unit: Company D, 3d U.S. Cavalry

Battle or Place of Action: Rosebud River, Montana
Date of Action: 17 June 1876
Date of Issue: 23 January 1880
Citation: Discharged his duties while in charge of the skirmish line under fire with judgment and great coolness and brought up the lead horses at a critical moment.

1847 ◆ ROCHE, DAVID

Rank: First Sergeant
Service: U.S. Army
Birthday: 1 May 1838
Place of Birth: County Kerry, Ireland
Date of Death: 19 November 1914
Place of Death: Worcester, Massachusetts
Cemetery: Hope Cemetery (MH)—Worcester, Massachusetts
Entered Service at: New York, New York
Unit: Company A, 5th U.S. Infantry
Battle or Place of Action: Cedar Creek, etc., Montana
Date of Action: 21 October 1876—8 January 1877
Date of Issue: 27 April 1877
Citation: Gallantry in action.

1848 ◆ RODENBURG, HENRY

Rank: Private (highest rank: Corporal)
Service: U.S. Army
Birthday: 1851
Date of Death: 13 December 1899
Place of Death: Fort Columbus, New York
Cemetery: Cypress Hills National Cemetery (2-5825) (MH)—Brooklyn, New York
Entered Service at: Fort Leavenworth, Leavenworth County, Kansas
Unit: Company A, 5th U.S. Infantry
Battle or Place of Action: Cedar Creek, etc., Montana
Date of Action: 21 October 1876—8 January 1877
Date of Issue: 27 April 1877
Citation: Gallantry in action.

1849 ◆ ROGAN, PATRICK

Rank: Sergeant (highest rank: First Sergeant)
Service: U.S. Army
Birthday: 1847
Place of Birth: County Leitrim, Ireland
Date of Death: 27 December 1912
Place of Death: Rock Springs, Wyoming
Cemetery: St. Joseph's Catholic Cemetary (MH)—Rock Springs, Wyoming
Entered Service at: Reading, Berks County, Pennsylvania
Unit: Company A, 7th U.S. Infantry
Battle or Place of Action: Big Hole, Montana
Date of Action: 9 August 1877
Date of Issue: 2 December 1878
Citation: Verified and reported the company while subjected to a galling fire from the enemy.

1850 ◆ ROMEYN, HENRY

Rank: First Lieutenant (highest rank: Major)
Service: U.S. Army
Birthday: 1 June 1833
Place of Birth: Galen, Wayne County, New York
Date of Death: 21 February 1913
Cemetery: Arlington National Cemetery (3-1750)—Arlington, Virginia
Entered Service at: Michigan
Unit: 5th U.S. Infantry
Battle or Place of Action: Bear Paw Mountain, Montana
Date of Action: 30 September 1877
Date of Issue: 27 November 1894
Citation: Led his command into close-range of the enemy, there maintained his position, and vigorously prosecuted the fight until he was severely wounded.

1851 ◆ ROONEY, EDWARD

Rank: Private (highest rank: First Sergeant)
Service: U.S. Army
Birthday: 1847
Place of Birth: Poughkeepsie, Dutchess County, New York
Entered Service at: Poughkeepsie, Dutchess County, New York
Unit: Company D, 5th U.S. Infantry
Battle or Place of Action: Cedar Creek, etc., Montana
Date of Action: 21 October 1876—8 January 1877
Date of Issue: 27 April 1877
Citation: Gallantry in action.

1852 ◆ ROTH, PETER PAUL

Rank: Private
Service: U.S. Army
Birthday: 1849
Place of Birth: Wurttemberg, Germany
Date of Death: 18 January 1907
Cemetery: Rottenmunster Cemetery—Rottenmunster, Germany
Entered Service at: Brooklyn, Kings County, New York
Unit: Company A, 6th U.S. Cavalry
Battle or Place of Action: Washita River, Texas
Date of Action: 12 September 1874
Date of Issue: 4 November 1874
Citation: While carrying dispatches was attacked by 125 hostile Indians, whom he and his comrades fought throughout the day.

1853 ◆ ROWALT, JOHN F.

Rank: Private
Service: U.S. Army
Birthday: 1847
Place of Birth: Belleville, Richland County, Ohio
Entered Service at: Cincinnati, Hamilton County, Ohio
Unit: Company L, 8th U.S. Cavalry

Battle or Place of Action: Lyry Creek, Arizona Territory
Date of Action: 14 October 1869
Date of Issue: 3 March 1870
Citation: Gallantry in action with Indians.

1854 ◆ ROWDY

Rank: Sergeant
Service: U.S. Army
Place of Birth: Arizona Territory
f Death: 29 March 1893
Cemetery: Santa Fe National Cemetery (A-894) (MH)—Santa Fe, New Mexico
Entered Service at: San Carlos, Gila County, Arizona
Unit: Company A, Indian Scouts
Battle or Place of Action: Arizona Territory
Date of Action: 7 March 1890
Date of Issue: 15 May 1890
Citation: Bravery in action with Apache Indians.

1855 ◆ ROY, STANISLAUS

True Name: Roy, Stanilas
Rank: Sergeant (highest rank: Color Sergeant)
Service: U.S. Army
Birthday: 12 November 1846
Place of Birth: France
Date of Death: 10 February 1913
Cemetery: Columbus Barracks, Green Lawn Cemetery–Post Cemetery (51-A-1A3) (MH)—Columbus, Ohio
Entered Service at: Cincinnati, Hamilton County, Ohio
Unit: Company A, 7th U.S. Cavalry
Battle or Place of Action: Little Big Horn, Montana
Date of Action: 25 June 1876
Date of Issue: 5 October 1878
Citation: Brought water to the wounded at great danger to life and under a most galling fire of the enemy.

1856 ◆ RUSSELL, JAMES

Rank: Private
Service: U.S. Army
Birthday: 1846
Place of Birth: New York, New York
Entered Service at: New York, New York
Unit: Company G, 1st U.S. Cavalry
Battle or Place of Action: Chiricahua Mountains, Arizona Territory
Date of Action: 20 October 1869
Date of Issue: 14 February 1870
Citation: Gallantry in action with Indians.

1857 ◆ RYAN, DAVID

Rank: Private (highest rank: Sergeant)
Service: U.S. Army
Birthday: 1836
Place of Birth: County Kilkenny, Ireland

Date of Death: 8 September 1896
Place of Death: St. Louis, Missouri
Cemetery: Jefferson Barracks National Cemetery (59-11715) (MH)—St. Louis, Missouri
Entered Service at: Philadelphia, Philadelphia County, Pennsylvania
Unit: Company G, 5th U.S. Infantry
Battle or Place of Action: Cedar Creek, etc., Montana
Date of Action: 21 October 1876—8 January 1877
Date of Issue: 27 April 1877
Citation: Gallantry in action.

1858 ◆ RYAN, DENIS

Rank: First Sergeant
Service: U.S. Army
Birthday: 1848
Place of Birth: Cork, Ireland
Entered Service at: New York, New York
Unit: Company I, 6th U.S. Cavalry
Battle or Place of Action: Gageby Creek, Indian Territory
Date of Action: 2 December 1874
Date of Issue: 23 April 1875
Citation: Courage while in command of a detachment.

1859 ◆ SALE, ALBERT

Rank: Private (highest rank: Corporal)
Service: U.S. Army
Birthday: 1850
Place of Birth: Broome County, New York
Date of Death: 29 November 1874
Place of Death: Fort Union, New Mexico
Entered Service at: Dubuque, Dubuque County, Iowa
Unit: Company F, 8th U.S. Cavalry
Battle or Place of Action: Santa Maria River, Arizona
Date of Action: 29 June 1869
Date of Issue: 3 March 1870
Citation: Gallantry in killing an Indian warrior and capturing pony and effects.

1860 ◆ SCHNITZER, JOHN

Rank: Wagoner
Service: U.S. Army
Birthday: 1854
Place of Birth: Kempten, Bavaria, Germany
Date of Death: 26 October 1904
Cemetery: Fort Bayard Post Cemetery (A-O-43) (MH)—Fort Bayard, New Mexico
Entered Service at: New York, New York
Unit: Troop G, 4th U.S. Cavalry
Battle or Place of Action: Horseshoe Canyon, New Mexico
Date of Action: 23 April 1882
Date of Issue: 17 August 1896
Citation: Assisted, under a heavy fire, in rescuing a wounded comrade.

1861 ◆ SCHOU, JULIUS ALEXIS

Rank: Corporal (highest rank: Sergeant)
Service: U.S. Army
Birthday: 17 July 1849
Place of Birth: Copenhagen, Denmark
Date of Death: 19 November 1929
Place of Death: Washington, D.C.
Cemetery: Arlington National Cemetery (17-21482) (MH)—Arlington, Virginia
Entered Service at: Brooklyn, Kings County, New York
Unit: Company I, 22d U.S. Infantry
Battle or Place of Action: Sioux Campaign
Date of Action: 1870
Date of Issue: 19 November 1884
Citation: Carried dispatches to Fort Buford.

1862 ◆ SCHROETER, CHARLES

Rank: Private (highest rank: Sergeant)
Service: U.S. Army
Birthday: 1839
Place of Birth: Lindberg, Hanover, Germany
Entered Service at: St. Louis, St. Louis County, Missouri
Unit: Company G, 8th U.S. Cavalry
Battle or Place of Action: Chiricahua Mountains, Arizona Territory
Date of Action: 20 October 1869
Date of Issue: 14 February 1870
Citation: Gallantry in action.

1863 ◆ SCOTT, GEORGE D.

Rank: Private
Service: U.S. Army
Birthday: 1850
Place of Birth: Lancaster, Garrard County, Kentucky
Entered Service at: Mount Vernon, Rockcastle County, Kentucky
Unit: Company D, 7th U.S. Cavalry
Battle or Place of Action: Little Big Horn, Montana
Date of Action: 25-26 June 1876
Date of Issue: 5 October 1878
Citation: Voluntarily brought water to the wounded under fire.

1864 ◆ SCOTT, ROBERT B.

Rank: Private
Service: U.S. Army
Birthday: 1845
Place of Birth: Washington County, New York
Date of Death: 3 March 1908
Place of Death: Argyle, New York
Cemetery: Prospect Hill Cemetery—Argyle, New York
Entered Service at: St. Louis, St. Louis County, Missouri
Unit: Company G, 8th U.S. Cavalry
Battle or Place of Action: Chiricahua Mountains, Arizona Territory

Date of Action: 20 October 1869
Date of Issue: 14 February 1870
Citation: Gallantry in action.

1865 ◆ SEWARD, GRIFFIN

Rank: Wagoner
Service: U.S. Army
Birthday: 8 October 1842
Place of Birth: Dover, Kent County, Delaware
Date of Death: 10 September 1908
Place of Death: Los Angeles, California
Cemetery: Los Angeles National Cemetery (15-D-10) (MH)—Los Angeles, California
Entered Service at: Philadelphia, Philadelphia County, Pennsylvania
Unit: Company G, 8th U.S. Cavalry
Battle or Place of Action: Chiricahua Mountains, Arizona Territory
Date of Action: 20 October 1869
Date of Issue: 14 February 1870
Citation: Gallantry in action.

1866 ◆ SHAFFER, WILLIAM

True Name: Schaffer, William
Rank: Private
Service: U.S. Army
Birthday: 1841
Place of Birth: Bavaria, Germany
Date of Death: 2 January 1910
Place of Death: Los Angeles, California
Cemetery: I.O.O.F. Cemetery—Los Angeles, California
Entered Service at: Cincinnati, Hamilton County, Ohio
Unit: Company B, 8th U.S. Cavalry
Battle or Place of Action: Arizona Territory
Date of Action: August-October 1868
Date of Issue: 24 July 1869
Citation: Bravery in scouts and actions against Indians.

1867 ◆ SHARPLESS, EDWARD CLAY

Rank: Corporal
Service: U.S. Army
Birthday: 10 August 1853
Place of Birth: Marion County, Ohio
Date of Death: 12 January 1934
Place of Death: Mountainair, New Mexico
Cemetery: Mountainair Cemetery (MH)—Mountainair, New Mexico
Entered Service at: Columbus, Franklin County, Ohio
Unit: Company H, 6th U.S. Cavalry
Battle or Place of Action: Upper Washita River, Texas
Date of Action: 9-11 September 1874
Date of Issue: 23 April 1875
Citation: While carrying dispatches was attacked by 125 hostile Indians, whom he (and a comrade) fought throughout the day.

1868 ◆ SHAW, THOMAS

Rank: Sergeant (highest rank: First Sergeant)
Service: U.S. Army
Birthday: 1846
Place of Birth: Covington, Kenton County, Kentucky
Date of Death: 23 June 1895
Place of Death: Washington, D.C.
Cemetery: Arlington National Cemetery (27-952-B) (MH)—Arlington, Virginia
Entered Service at: Baton Rouge, Baton Rouge County, Louisiana
Unit: Company K, 9th U.S. Cavalry
Battle or Place of Action: Carrizo Canyon, New Mexico
Date of Action: 12 August 1881
Date of Issue: 7 December 1890
Citation: Forced the enemy back after stubbornly holding his ground in an extremely exposed position and prevented the enemy's superior numbers from surrounding his command.

1869 ◆ SHEERIN, JOHN

Rank: Blacksmith
Service: U.S. Army
Birthday: 1841
Place of Birth: Camden County, New Jersey
Entered Service at: Baltimore, Baltimore County, Maryland
Unit: Company C, 8th U.S. Cavalry
Battle or Place of Action: Fort Selden, New Mexico
Date of Action: 8-11 July 1873
Date of Issue: 12 August 1875
Citation: Services against hostile Indians.

1870 ◆ SHEPPARD, CHARLES

Rank: Private
Service: U.S. Army
Birthday: 27 November 1850
Place of Birth: Rocky Hill, Hartford County, Connecticut
Entered Service at: St. Louis, St. Louis County, Missouri
Unit: Company A, 5th U.S. Infantry
Battle or Place of Action: Cedar Creek, etc, Montana
Date of Action: 21 October 1876—8 January 1877
Date of Issue: 27 April 1877
Citation: Bravery in action with Sioux.

1871 ◆ SHINGLE, JOHN HENRY

Rank: First Sergeant
Service: U.S. Army
Birthday: 25 November 1842
Place of Birth: Philadelphia, Philadelphia County, Pennsylvania
Date of Death: 29 July 1907
Place of Death: Leavenworth, Kansas
Cemetery: Leavenworth National Cemetery (22-4-2) (MH)—Leavenworth, Kansas
Entered Service at: St. Louis, St. Louis County, Missouri
Unit: Troop I, 3d U.S. Cavalry

Battle or Place of Action: Rosebud River, Montana
Date of Action: 17 June 1876
Date of Issue: 1 June 1880
Citation: Gallantry in action.

1872 ◆ SKINNER, JOHN OSCAR

Rank: Contract Surgeon (highest rank: Lieutenant Colonel)
Service: U.S. Army
Birthday: 4 May 1845
Place of Birth: Baltimore, Baltimore County, Maryland
Date of Death: 12 September 1932
Cemetery: Arlington National Cemetery (3-1662)—Arlington, Virginia
Entered Service at: Maryland
Unit: U.S. Army
Battle or Place of Action: Lava Beds, California
Date of Action: 17 January 1873
Date of Issue: 6 April 1915
Citation: Rescued a wounded soldier who lay under a close and heavy fire during the assault on the Modoc stronghold after two soldiers had unsuccessfully attempted to make the rescue and both had been wounded in doing so.

1873 ◆ SMITH, ANDREW J.

Rank: Sergeant
Service: U.S. Army
Birthday: 1848
Place of Birth: Baltimore, Baltimore County, Maryland
Entered Service at: Baltimore, Baltimore County, Maryland
Unit: Company G, 8th U.S. Cavalry
Battle or Place of Action: Chiricahua Mountains, Arizona Territory
Date of Action: 20 October 1869
Date of Issue: 14 February 1870
Citation: Gallantry in action.

1874 ◆ SMITH, CHARLES E.

Rank: Corporal
Service: U.S. Army
Birthday: 1844
Place of Birth: Auburn, Cayuga County, New York
Entered Service at: St. Louis, St. Louis County, Missouri
Unit: Company H, 6th U.S. Cavalry
Battle or Place of Action: Wichita River, Texas
Date of Action: 12 July 1870
Date of Issue: 25 August 1870
Citation: Gallantry in action.

1875 ◆ SMITH, CORNELIUS COLE

Rank: First Sergeant (highest rank: Colonel U.S. Army Ret.)
Service: U.S. Army
Birthday: 7 April 1869
Place of Birth: Tucson, Pima County, Arizona
Date of Death: 10 January 1936

Cemetery: Evergreen Memorial Park (MH)—Riverside, California
Entered Service at: Helena, Lewis & Clark County, Montana
Unit: Company K, 6th U.S. Cavalry
Battle or Place of Action: White River, South Dakota
Date of Action: 1 January 1891
Date of Issue: 4 February 1891
Citation: With four men of his troop drove off a superior force of the enemy and held his position against their repeated efforts to recapture it, and subsequently pursued them a great distance.

1876 ◆ *SMITH, GEORGE W.

Rank: Private
Service: U.S. Army
Birthday: 1848
Place of Birth: Greenfield, Saratoga County, New York
Date of Death: 13 September 1874
Place of Death: Buffalo Wallow Battlegrounds remains not recovered, Texas
Cemetery: San Antonio National Cemetery (marker only) (MH)—San Antonio, Texas
Entered Service at: New York, New York
Unit: Company M, 6th U.S. Cavalry
Battle or Place of Action: Washita River, Texas
Date of Action: 12 September 1874
Date of Issue: 4 November 1874
Citation: While carrying dispatches was attacked by 125 hostile Indians, whom he and his comrades fought throughout the day. Pvt. Smith was mortally wounded during the engagement and died early the next day.

1877 ◆ SMITH, OTTO

Rank: Private
Service: U.S. Army
Birthday: 1840
Place of Birth: Baltimore, Baltimore County, Maryland
Entered Service at: Sacramento, Sacramento County, California
Unit: Company K, 8th U.S. Cavalry
Battle or Place of Action: Arizona Territory
Date of Action: 1868 & 1869
Date of Issue: 6 September 1869
Citation: Bravery in scouts and actions against Indians.

1878 ◆ SMITH, ROBERT

Rank: Private
Service: U.S. Army
Birthday: 1851
Place of Birth: Philadelphia, Philadelphia County, Pennsylvania
Entered Service at: Philadelphia, Philadelphia County, Pennsylvania
Unit: Company M, 3d U.S. Cavalry
Battle or Place of Action: Slim Buttes, Montana
Date of Action: 9 September 1876

Date of Issue: 16 October 1877
Citation: Special bravery in endeavoring to dislodge Indians secreted in a ravine.

1879 ◆ SMITH, THEODORE F.

Rank: Private (highest rank: Corporal)
Service: U.S. Army
Birthday: 6 September 1852
Place of Birth: Rahway, Union County, New Jersey
Date of Death: 6 June 1925
Place of Death: Washington, D.C.
Cemetery: Arlington Cemetery—Drexel Hill, Pennsylvania
Entered Service at: Harrisburg, Dauphin County, Pennsylvania
Unit: Company G, 1st U.S. Cavalry
Battle or Place of Action: Chiricahua Mountains, Arizona Territory
Date of Action: 20 October 1869
Date of Issue: 14 February 1879
Citation: Gallantry in action.

1880 ◆ SMITH, THOMAS

Rank: Private
Service: U.S. Army
Birthday: 4 July 1847
Place of Birth: Boston, Suffolk County, Massachusetts
Date of Death: 1 September 1909
Place of Death: Washington, D.C.
Cemetery: Soldier's Home National Cemetery (K-7492) (MH)—Washington, D.C.
Entered Service at: Fort Adams, Rhode Island
Unit: Company G, 1st U.S. Cavalry
Battle or Place of Action: Chiricahua Mountains, Arizona Territory
Date of Action: 20 October 1869
Date of Issue: 14 February 1870
Citation: Gallantry in action.

1881 ◆ SMITH, THOMAS J.

True Name: Smith, Thomas J.
Rank: Private
Service: U.S. Army
Birthday: 1833
Place of Birth: Liverpool, Merseyside County, England
Entered Service at: New York, New York
Unit: Company G, 1st U.S. Cavalry
Battle or Place of Action: Chiricahua Mountains, Arizona Territory
Date of Action: 20 October 1869
Date of Issue: 14 February 1870
Citation: Gallantry in action.

1882 ◆ SMITH, WILLIAM

Rank: Private
Service: U.S. Army

Birthday: 1848
Place of Birth: Bath, Sagadahoc County, Maine
Entered Service at: San Francisco, San Francisco County, California
Unit: Company G, 8th U.S. Cavalry
Battle or Place of Action: Chiricahua Mountains, Arizona Territory
Date of Action: 20 October 1869
Date of Issue: 14 February 1870
Citation: Gallantry in action.

1883 ◆ SMITH, WILLIAM H.

Rank: Private
Service: U.S. Army
Birthday: 1847
Place of Birth: Lapeer, Lapeer County, Michigan
Entered Service at: Cincinnati, Hamilton County, Ohio
Unit: Company G, 1st U.S. Cavalry
Battle or Place of Action: Chiricahua Mountains, Arizona Territory
Date of Action: 20 October 1869
Date of Issue: 14 February 1870
Citation: Gallantry in action.

1884 ◆ SNOW, ELMER A.

Rank: Trumpeter
Service: U.S. Army
Birthday: 1851
Place of Birth: Hardwick, Worcester County, Massachusetts
Date of Death: 21 January 1892
Cemetery: Highland Cemetery (MH)—Athol, Massachusetts
Entered Service at: Chicago, Cook County, Illinois
Unit: Company M, 3d U.S. Cavalry
Battle or Place of Action: Rosebud Creek, Montana
Date of Action: 17 June 1876
Date of Issue: 16 October 1877
Citation: Bravery in action; was wounded in both arms.

1885 ◆ SPENCE, ORIZOBA

True Name: Spence, Orisoba
Rank: Private
Service: U.S. Army
Birthday: 1847
Place of Birth: Forest County, Pennsylvania
Date of Death: 7 April 1876
Cemetery: Post Cemetery (Sec. E-16 Grave #58)—Fort Bowie, Arizona
Entered Service at: Cincinnati, Hamilton County, Ohio
Unit: Company G, 8th U.S. Cavalry
Battle or Place of Action: Chiricahua Mountains, Arizona Territory
Date of Action: 20 October 1869
Date of Issue: 14 February 1870
Citation: Gallantry in action.

1886 ◆ SPRINGER, GEORGE

Rank: Private
Service: U.S. Army
Birthday: 7 May 1848
Place of Birth: York County, Pennsylvania
Date of Death: 11 June 1931
Cemetery: Mount Olivet Cemetery—New Cumberland, Pennsylvania
Entered Service at: Harrisburg, Dauphin County, Pennsylvania
Unit: Company G, 1st U.S. Cavalry
Battle or Place of Action: Chiricahua Mountains, Arizona Territory
Date of Action: 20 October 1869
Date of Issue: 14 February 1870
Citation: Gallantry in action.

1887 ◆ STANCE, EMANUEL

Rank: Sergeant (highest rank: First Sergeant)
Service: U.S. Army
Birthday: 1843
Place of Birth: Carroll Parish, Louisiana
Date of Death: 25 December 1887
Place of Death: Fort Robinson, Nebraska
Cemetery: Fort McPherson National Cemetery (F-1040) (MH)—Maxwell, Nebraska
Entered Service at: East Carroll Parish, Louisiana
Unit: Company F, 9th U.S. Cavalry
Battle or Place of Action: Kickapoo Springs, Texas
Date of Action: 20 May 1870
Date of Issue: 28 June 1870
Citation: Gallantry on scout after Indians.

1888 ◆ STANLEY, EBEN

Rank: Private
Service: U.S. Army
Birthday: 1844
Place of Birth: Decatur County, Iowa
Date of Death: 19 November 1904
Place of Death: Hillsboro, New Mexico
Cemetery: Hillsboro Cemetery—Hillsboro, New Mexico
Entered Service at: Santa Fe, Santa Fe County, New Mexico
Unit: Company A, 5th U.S. Cavalry
Battle or Place of Action: Turret Mountain, Arizona Territory
Date of Action: 25, 27 March 1873
Date of Issue: 12 April 1875
Citation: Gallantry in action.

1889 ◆ STANLEY, EDWARD

Rank: Corporal
Service: U.S. Army
Birthday: 1846
Place of Birth: New York, New York
Entered Service at: San Francisco, San Francisco County, California

Unit: Company F, 8th U.S. Cavalry
Battle or Place of Action: Seneca Mountain, Arizona
Date of Action: 26 August 1869
Date of Issue: 3 March 1870
Citation: Gallantry in action.

1890 ◆ STAUFFER, RUDOLPH

Rank: First Sergeant
Service: U.S. Army
Birthday: 27 November 1836
Place of Birth: Berne, Switzerland
Date of Death: 9 June 1918
Place of Death: Washington, D.C.
Cemetery: Soldier's Home National Cemetery (K-8132) (MH)—Washington, D.C.
Entered Service at: Cincinnati, Hamilton County, Ohio
Unit: Company K, 5th U.S. Cavalry
Battle or Place of Action: Camp Hualpai, Arizona Territory
Date of Action: 1872
Date of Issue: 30 July 1875
Citation: Gallantry on scouts after Indians.

1891 ◆ STEINER, CHRISTIAN

Rank: Saddler
Service: U.S. Army
Birthday: 1833
Place of Birth: Wurttemberg, Germany
Date of Death: 5 August 1880
Place of Death: Hot Springs, Arkansas
Entered Service at: St. Louis, St. Louis County, Missouri
Unit: Company G, 8th U.S. Cavalry
Battle or Place of Action: Chiricahua Mountains, Arizona Territory
Date of Action: 20 October 1869
Date of Issue: 14 February 1870
Citation: Gallantry in action.

1892 ◆ STEVERS, THOMAS W.

True Name: Stivers, Thomas W.
Rank: Private
Service: U.S. Army
Birthday: 1850
Place of Birth: Madison County, Kentucky
Entered Service at: Mount Vernon, Rockcastle County, Kentucky
Unit: Company D, 7th U.S. Cavalry
Battle or Place of Action: Little Big Horn, Montana
Date of Action: 25-26 June 1876
Date of Issue: 5 October 1878
Citation: Voluntarily brought water to the wounded under fire.

1893 ◆ STEWART, BENJAMIN F.

Rank: Private
Service: U.S. Army

Birthday: 1851
Place of Birth: Norfolk, Norfolk County, Virginia
Entered Service at: Boston, Suffolk County, Massachusetts
Unit: Company E, 7th U.S. Infantry
Battle or Place of Action: Big Horn River, Montana
Date of Action: 9 July 1876
Date of Issue: 2 December 1876
Citation: Carried dispatches to Gen. Crook at imminent risk of his life.

1894 ◆ STICKOFFER, JULIUS HENRY

Rank: Saddler (highest rank: First Sergeant)
Service: U.S. Army
Birthday: 1845
Place of Birth: Switzerland
Date of Death: 3 September 1925
Place of Death: Yountville, California
Cemetery: Veterans Home of California Cemetery (MH)—Yountville, California
Entered Service at: Cincinnati, Hamilton County, Ohio
Unit: Company L, 8th U.S. Cavalry
Battle or Place of Action: Cienaga Springs, Utah
Date of Action: 11 November 1868
Date of Issue: 3 March 1870
Citation: Gallantry in action.

1895 ◆ STOKES, ALONZO

Rank: First Sergeant
Service: U.S. Army
Birthday: 1837
Place of Birth: Logan County, Ohio
Date of Death: 4 July 1876
Place of Death: St. Louis, Missouri
Cemetery: Jefferson Barracks National Cemetery (63-114-50) (MH)—St. Louis, Missouri
Entered Service at: Cincinnati, Hamilton County, Ohio
Unit: Company H, 6th U.S. Cavalry
Battle or Place of Action: Wichita River, Texas
Date of Action: 12 July 1870
Date of Issue: 25 August 1870
Citation: Gallantry in action.

1896 ◆ STRAYER, WILLIAM H.

Rank: Private (highest rank: Sergeant)
Service: U.S. Army
Birthday: 1847
Place of Birth: Maytown, Lancaster County, Pennsylvania
Entered Service at: Carlisle, Cumberland County, Pennsylvania
Unit: Company B, 3d U.S. Cavalry
Battle or Place of Action: Loupe Fork of the Platte River, Nebraska
Date of Action: 26 April 1872
Date of Issue: 22 May 1872
Citation: Gallantry in action.

1897 ◆ STRIVSON, BENONI

True Name: Stinson, Benoni
Rank: Private
Service: U.S. Army
Birthday: 1831
Place of Birth: Overton, Tennessee
Entered Service at: Sacramento, Sacramento County, California
Unit: Company B, 8th U.S. Cavalry
Battle or Place of Action: Arizona
Date of Action: August-October 1868
Date of Issue: 24 July 1869
Citation: Bravery in scouts and actions against Indians.

1898 ◆ SULLIVAN, THOMAS

Rank: Private (highest rank: First Sergeant)
Service: U.S. Army
Birthday: 20 April 1859
Place of Birth: County Meath, Ireland
Date of Death: 10 January 1940
Cemetery: Holy Sepulchre Cemetery—East Orange, New Jersey
Entered Service at: Newark, Essex County, New Jersey
Unit: Company E, 7th U.S. Cavalry
Battle or Place of Action: Wounded Knee Creek, South Dakota
Date of Action: 29 December 1890
Date of Issue: 17 December 1891
Citation: Conspicuous bravery in action against Indians concealed in a ravine.

1899 ◆ SULLIVAN, THOMAS

Rank: Private
Service: U.S. Army
Birthday: 1847
Place of Birth: Covington, Kenton County, Kentucky
Entered Service at: Cincinnati, Hamilton County, Ohio
Unit: Company G, 1st U.S. Cavalry
Battle or Place of Action: Chiricahua Mountains, Arizona Territory
Date of Action: 20 October 1869
Date of Issue: 14 February 1870
Citation: Gallantry in action against Indians concealed in a ravine.

1900 ◆ SUMNER, JAMES

Rank: Private
Service: U.S. Army
Birthday: 1840
Place of Birth: London, England
Date of Death: 5 July 1912
Place of Death: Ventura, California
Cemetery: Ventura Cemetery (MH)—Ventura, California
Entered Service at: Chicago, Cook County, Illinois
Unit: Company G, 1st U.S. Cavalry

Battle or Place of Action: Chiricahua Mountains, Arizona Territory
Date of Action: 20 October 1869
Date of Issue: 14 February 1870
Citation: Gallantry in action.

1901 ◆ SUTHERLAND, JOHN ALEXANDER

Rank: Corporal
Service: U.S. Army
Birthday: 19 February 1849
Place of Birth: Harrodsburg, Monroe County, Indiana
Date of Death: 2 December 1891
Cemetery: El Reno Cemetery (PM)—El Reno, Oklahoma
Entered Service at: Indianapolis, Marion County, Indiana
Unit: Company L, 8th U.S. Cavalry
Battle or Place of Action: Arizona Territory
Date of Action: August-October 1868
Date of Issue: 24 July 1869
Citation: Bravery in scouts and actions against Indians.

1902 ◆ *TAYLOR, BERNARD

Rank: Sergeant
Service: U.S. Army
Birthday: 1844
Place of Birth: St. Louis, St. Louis County, Missouri
Date of Death: 14 April 1875
Cemetery: San Francisco National Cemetery (WS-1090)—San Francisco, California
Entered Service at: Washington, D.C.
Unit: Company A, 5th U.S. Cavalry
Battle or Place of Action: Sunset Pass, Arizona Territory
Date of Action: 1 November 1874
Date of Issue: 12 April 1875
Citation: Bravery in rescuing Lt. Charles King, 5th U.S. Cavalry, from Indians.

1903 ◆ TAYLOR, CHARLES

Rank: First Sergeant
Service: U.S. Army
Birthday: 1840
Place of Birth: Baltimore, Baltimore County, Maryland
Date of Death: 3 August 1899
Place of Death: Washington, D.C.
Cemetery: Soldier's Home National Cemetery (K-0851) (MH)—Washington, D.C.
Entered Service at: St. Louis, St. Louis County, Missouri
Unit: Company D, 3d U.S. Cavalry
Battle or Place of Action: Big Dry Wash, Arizona Territory
Date of Action: 17 July 1882
Date of Issue: 16 December 1882
Citation: Gallantry in action.

1904 ◆ TAYLOR, WILBUR NELSON

Rank: Corporal (highest rank: Sergeant)
Service: U.S. Army

Birthday: 2 December 1846
Place of Birth: Hampden, Penobscot County, Maine
Date of Death: 20 November 1903
Place of Death: Minneapolis, Minnesota
Cemetery: Lakewood Cemetery—Minneapolis, Minnesota
Entered Service at: Boston, Suffolk County, Massachusetts
Unit: Company K, 8th U.S. Cavalry
Battle or Place of Action: Arizona Territory
Date of Action: 1868 & 1869
Date of Issue: 6 September 1869
Citation: Bravery in actions with Indians.

1905 ◆ TEA, RICHARD LONGSTREET

Rank: Sergeant
Service: U.S. Army
Birthday: February 1842
Place of Birth: Philadelphia, Philadelphia County, Pennsylvania
Date of Death: 14 September 1911
Place of Death: Fort Whipple, Arizona
Cemetery: Mountain View Cemetery (MH)—Prescott, Arizona
Entered Service at: Philadelphia, Philadelphia County, Pennsylvania
Unit: Company H, 6th U.S. Cavalry
Battle or Place of Action: Sappa Creek, Kansas
Date of Action: 23 April 1875
Date of Issue: 16 November 1876
Citation: With five other men he waded in mud and water up the creek to a position directly behind an entrenched Cheyenne position, who were using natural bank pits to good advantage against the main column. This surprise attack from the enemy rear broke their resistance.

1906 ◆ *THOMAS, CHARLES L.

Rank: Sergeant
Service: U.S. Army
Birthday: 12 February 1843
Place of Birth: Philadelphia, Philadelphia County, Pennsylvania
Date of Death: 24 February 1893
Place of Death: Dwight, Kansas
Cemetery: Dwight-Morris Cemetery (MH)—Dwight, Kansas
Entered Service at: Cincinnati, Hamilton County, Ohio
Unit: Company E, 11th Ohio Cavalry
Battle or Place of Action: Powder River Expedition, Dakota Territory
Date of Action: 17 September 1865
Date of Issue: 24 August 1894
Citation: Carried a message through a country infested with hostile Indians and saved the life of a comrade en route.

1907 ◆ THOMPSON, GEORGE WASHINGTON

Rank: Private
Service: U.S. Army

Birthday: 1847
Place of Birth: Victory, Cayuga County, New York
Entered Service at: Syracuse, Onondaga County, New York
Unit: Company C, 2d U.S. Cavalry
Battle or Place of Action: Little Blue, Nebraska
Date of Action: 15 May 1870
Date of Issue: 22 June 1870
Citation: Gallantry in action.

1908 ◆ THOMPSON, JOHN

Rank: Sergeant
Service: U.S. Army
Birthday: 1842
Place of Birth: Glasgow, Scotland
Entered Service at: Chicago, Cook County, Illinois
Unit: Company G, 1st U.S. Cavalry
Battle or Place of Action: Chiricahua Mountains, Arizona Territory
Date of Action: 20 October 1869
Date of Presentation: 24 February 1870
Place of Presentation: Fort Camp Bowie, Arizona
Citation: Bravery in action with Indians.

1909 ◆ THOMPSON, PETER

Rank: Private
Service: U.S. Army
Birthday: 28 December 1854
Place of Birth: Scotland
Date of Death: 4 December 1928
Place of Death: Hot Springs, South Dakota
Cemetery: West Lead Cemetery (MH)—Hot Springs, South Dakota
Entered Service at: Pittsburgh, Allegheny County, Pennsylvania
Unit: Company C, 7th U.S. Cavalry
Battle or Place of Action: Little Big Horn, Montana
Date of Action: 25 June 1876
Date of Issue: 5 October 1878
Citation: After having voluntarily brought water to the wounded, during which effort he was shot through the head, he made two successful trips for the same purpose, notwithstanding remonstrances of his sergeant.

1910 ◆ TILTON, HENRY REMSEN

Rank: Major and Surgeon (highest rank: Colonel)
Service: U.S. Army
Birthday: 1 February 1836
Place of Birth: Barnegat, Ocean County, New Jersey
Date of Death: 25 June 1906
Cemetery: Arlington National Cemetery (1-392)—Arlington, Virginia
Entered Service at: Jersey City, Hudson County, New Jersey
Unit: U.S. Army
Battle or Place of Action: Bear Paw Mountain, Montana
Date of Action: 30 September 1877

Date of Issue: 22 March 1895
Citation: Fearlessly risked his life and displayed great gallantry in rescuing and protection the wounded men.

1911 ◆ TOLAN, FRANK

Rank: Private
Service: U.S. Army
Birthday: 1854
Place of Birth: Malone, Franklin County, New York
Entered Service at: Boston, Suffolk County, Massachusetts
Unit: Company D, 7th U.S. Cavalry
Battle or Place of Action: Little Big Horn, Montana
Date of Action: 25 June 1876
Date of Issue: 5 October 1878
Citation: Voluntarily brought water to the wounded under fire.

1912 ◆ TOY, FREDERICK ERNEST

Rank: First Sergeant (highest rank: Captain)
Service: U.S. Army
Birthday: 1866
Place of Birth: Buffalo, Erie County, New York
Date of Death: 5 August 1933
Place of Death: Youngstown, New York
Cemetery: Riverdale Cemetery—Lewiston, New York
Entered Service at: Chicago, Cook County, Illinois
Unit: Company G, 7th U.S. Cavalry
Battle or Place of Action: Wounded Knee Creek, South Dakota
Date of Action: 29 December 1890
Date of Issue: 26 May 1891
Citation: Bravery.

1913 ◆ TRACY, JOHN

True Name: Nabers, Henry G.
Rank: Private
Service: U.S. Army
Birthday: 28 December 1848
Place of Birth: Dublin, Ireland
Date of Death: 29 May 1918
Place of Death: St. Louis, Missouri
Cemetery: Calvary Cemetery—St. Louis, Missouri
Entered Service at: Chicago, Cook County, Illinois
Unit: Company G, 8th U.S. Cavalry
Battle or Place of Action: Chiricahua Mountains, Arizona Territory
Date of Action: 20 October 1869
Date of Issue: 14 February 1870
Citation: Bravery in action with Indians.

1914 ◆ TRAUTMAN, JACOB

Rank: First Sergeant
Service: U.S. Army
Birthday: 1840
Place of Birth: Hamburg, Germany

Date of Death: 7 November 1898
Cemetery: Southside Cemetery (MH)—Pittsburgh, Pennsylvania
Entered Service at: Pittsburgh, Allegheny County, Pennsylvania
Unit: Company I, 7th U.S. Cavalry
Battle or Place of Action: Wounded Knee Creek, South Dakota
Date of Action: 29 December 1890
Date of Issue: 27 March 1891
Citation: Killed a hostile Indian at close quarters, and, although entitled to retirement from service, remained to the close of the campaign.

1915 ◆ TURPIN, JAMES H.

Rank: First Sergeant
Service: U.S. Army
Birthday: 1846
Place of Birth: Easton, Bristol County, Massachusetts
Date of Death: 30 May 1893
Place of Death: Denver, Colorado
Cemetery: Fairmount Cemetery (MH)—Denver, Colorado
Entered Service at: Boston, Suffolk County, Massachusetts
Unit: Company L, 5th U.S. Cavalry
Battle or Place of Action: Arizona Territory
Date of Action: 1872-74
Date of Issue: 12 April 1875
Citation: Gallantry in actions with Apaches.

1916 ◆ VARNUM, CHARLES ALBERT

Rank: Captain (highest rank: Colonel)
Service: U.S. Army
Birthday: 21 June 1849
Place of Birth: Troy, Rensselaer County, New York
Date of Death: 26 February 1936
Cemetery: San Francisco National Cemetery (OS-3-3A) (MH)—San Francisco, California
Entered Service at: Pensacola, Escambia County, Florida
Unit: Company B, 7th U.S. Cavalry
Battle or Place of Action: White Clay Creek, South Dakota
Date of Action: 30 December 1890
Date of Issue: 22 September 1897
Citation: While executing an order to withdraw, seeing that a continuance of the movement would expose another troop of his regiment to being cut off and surrounded, he disregarded orders to retire, placed himself in front of his men, led a charge upon the advancing Indians, regained a commanding position that had just been vacated, and thus insured a safe withdrawal of both detachments without further loss.

1917 ◆ VEUVE, ERNEST

Rank: Farrier (highest rank: Sergeant)
Service: U.S. Army
Birthday: 19 March 1843

Place of Birth: New Castle, Switzerland
Date of Death: 17 June 1916
Place of Death: Missoula, Montana
Cemetery: Missoula Cemetery—Missoula, Montana
Entered Service at: Jackson Barracks, Louisanna
Unit: Company A, 4th U.S. Cavalry
Battle or Place of Action: Staked Plains, Texas
Date of Action: 3 November 1874
Date of Issue: 13 October 1875
Citation: Gallant manner in which he faced a desperate Indian.

1918 ◆ VOIT, OTTO EMIL

Rank: Saddler
Service: U.S. Army
Birthday: 5 February 1845
Place of Birth: Baden, Germany
Date of Death: 1 June 1906
Place of Death: Louisville, Kentucky
Cemetery: St. Stephen's Cemetery—Louisville, Kentucky
Entered Service at: Louisville, Jefferson County, Kentucky
Unit: Company H, 7th U.S. Cavalry
Battle or Place of Action: Little Big Horn, Montana
Date of Action: 25 June 1876
Date of Issue: 5 October 1878
Citation: Volunteered with George Geiger, Charles Windolph, and Henry Mechlin to hold an exposed position standing erect on the brow of the hill facing the Little Big Horn River. They fired constantly in this manner for more than 20 minutes diverting fire and attention from another group filling canteens of water that were desperately needed.

1919 ◆ VOKES, LEROY H.

Rank: First Sergeant
Service: U.S. Army
Birthday: 12 November 1849
Place of Birth: Lake County, Illinois
Entered Service at: St. Louis, St. Louis County, Missouri
Unit: Company B, 3d U.S. Cavalry
Battle or Place of Action: Loupe Fork of the Platte River, Nebraska
Date of Action: 26 April 1872
Date of Issue: 22 May 1872
Citation: Gallantry in action.

1920 ◆ VON MEDEM, RUDOLPH

Rank: Sergeant
Service: U.S. Army
Birthday: 1846
Place of Birth: Germany (Prussia)
Entered Service at: New York, New York
Unit: Company A, 5th U.S. Cavalry
Battle or Place of Action: Apache campaigns
Date of Action: 1872-73
Date of Issue: 12 April 1875
Citation: Gallantry in actions and campaigns.

1921 ◆ WALKER, ALLEN

Rank: Private (highest rank: Captain)
Service: U.S. Army
Birthday: 19 January 1866
Place of Birth: Patriot, Switzerland County, Indiana
Date of Death: 11 September 1953
Cemetery: Catholic Cemetery (MH)—Laredo, Texas
Entered Service at: Cincinnati, Hamilton County, Ohio
Unit: Company C, 3d U.S. Cavalry
Battle or Place of Action: Texas
Date of Action: 30 December 1891
Date of Issue: 25 April 1892
Citation: While carrying dispatches, he attacked a party of three armed men and secured papers valuable to the United States.

1922 ◆ WALKER, JOHN

Rank: Private
Service: U.S. Army
Birthday: 1845
Place of Birth: Leon, France
Entered Service at: Detroit, Wayne County, Michigan
Unit: Company D, 8th U.S. Cavalry
Battle or Place of Action: Red Creek, Arizona Territory
Date of Action: 23 September 1869
Date of Issue: 23 November 1869
Citation: Gallantry in action with Indians.

1923 ◆ WALLACE, WILLIAM

True Name: Wallace, John A.
Rank: Sergeant
Service: U.S. Army
Birthday: 31 October 1847
Place of Birth: County Donegal, Ireland
Date of Death: 9 January 1928
Place of Death: Walnut, Kansas
Cemetery: Walnut Cemetery—Walnut, Kansas
Entered Service at: New York, New York
Unit: Company C, 5th U.S. Infantry
Battle or Place of Action: Cedar Creek, etc., Montana
Date of Action: 21 October 1876—8 January 1877
Date of Issue: 27 April 1877
Citation: Gallantry in action.

1924 ◆ WALLEY, AUGUSTUS

Rank: Private (highest rank: First Sergeant)
Service: U.S. Army
Birthday: 10 March 1856
Place of Birth: Reistertown, Baltimore County, Maryland
Date of Death: 9 April 1938
Place of Death: Baltimore, Maryland
Cemetery: St. Luke's Cemetery (MH)—Reistertown, Maryland
Entered Service at: Baltimore, Baltimore County, Maryland
Unit: Company I, 9th U.S. Cavalry
Battle or Place of Action: Cuchillo Negro Mountains, New Mexico

Date of Action: 16 August 1881
Date of Issue: 1 October 1890
Citation: Bravery in action with hostile Apaches.

1925 ◆ WARD, CHARLES H.

Rank: Private
Service: U.S. Army
Birthday: 1845
Place of Birth: Bradford, England
Entered Service at: Philadelphia, Philadelphia County, Pennsylvania
Unit: Company G, 1st U.S. Cavalry
Battle or Place of Action: Chiricahua Mountains, Arizona Territory
Date of Action: 20 October 1869
Date of Issue: 14 February 1870
Citation: Gallantry in action with Indians.

1926 ◆ WARD, JAMES

Rank: Sergeant
Service: U.S. Army
Birthday: 6 December 1858
Place of Birth: Quincy, Norfolk County, Massachusetts
Date of Death: 11 March 1901
Place of Death: Boston, Massachusetts
Cemetery: New Calvary Cemetery (MH)—Boston, Massachusetts
Entered Service at: Boston, Suffolk County, Massachusetts
Unit: Company B, 7th U.S. Cavalry
Battle or Place of Action: Wounded Knee Creek, South Dakota
Date of Action: 29 December 1890
Date of Issue: 16 April 1891
Citation: Continued to fight after being severely wounded.

1927 ◆ WARD, JOHN

True Name: Warrior, John
Rank: Sergeant
Service: U.S. Army
Birthday: 1847
Place of Birth: Arkansas
Date of Death: 24 May 1911
Cemetery: Seminole Indian Scout Cemetery (MH)—Brackettville, Texas
Entered Service at: Fort Duncan, Texas
Unit: 24th U.S. Infantry, Indian Scouts
Battle or Place of Action: Pecos River, Texas
Date of Action: 25 April 1875
Date of Issue: 28 May 1875
Citation: With three other men, he participated in a charge against 25 hostiles while on a scouting patrol.

1928 ◆ WARRINGTON, LEWIS

Rank: First Lieutenant
Service: U.S. Army

Place of Birth: Washington, D.C.
Date of Death: 5 January 1879
Place of Death: San Antonio, Texas
Cemetery: San Antonio National Cemetery (A-60) (MH)—San Antonio, Texas
Entered Service at: Washington, D.C.
Unit: 4th U.S. Cavalry
Battle or Place of Action: Muchague Valley, Texas
Date of Action: 8 December 1874
Date of Issue: 12 April 1875
Citation: Gallantry in combat with five Indians.

1929 ◆ WATSON, JAMES C.

Rank: Corporal (highest rank: Sergeant)
Service: U.S. Army
Birthday: 1842
Place of Birth: Cochecton, Sullivan County, New York
Date of Death: 7 January 1890
Place of Death: Chicago, Illinois
Cemetery: Rose Hill Cemetery—Chicago, Illinois
Entered Service at: Philadelphia, Philadelphia County, Pennsylvania
Unit: Company L, 6th U.S. Cavalry
Battle or Place of Action: Wichita River, Texas
Date of Action: 12 July 1870
Date of Issue: 25 August 1870
Citation: Gallantry in action.

1930 ◆ WATSON, JOSEPH

Rank: Private
Service: U.S. Army
Birthday: 1846
Place of Birth: Union City, Branch County, Michigan
Entered Service at: Chicago, Cook County, Illinois
Unit: Company F, 8th U.S. Cavalry
Battle or Place of Action: Picacho Mountain, Arizona Territory
Date of Action: 4 June 1869
Date of Issue: 3 March 1870
Citation: Killed an Indian warrior and captured his arms.

1931 ◆ WEAHER, ANDREW J.

True Name: Weaber, Andrew J.
Rank: Private
Service: U.S. Army
Birthday: 22 May 1842
Place of Birth: Philadelphia, Philadelphia County, Pennsylvania
Date of Death: 27 August 1920
Place of Death: Phoenix, Arizona
Cemetery: Greenwood Memorial Park—Phoenix, Arizona
Entered Service at: Philadelphia, Philadelphia County, Pennsylvania
Unit: Company B, 8th U.S. Cavalry
Battle or Place of Action: Arizona Territory
Date of Action: August-October 1868

Date of Issue: 24 July 1869
Citation: Bravery in scouts and against Indians.

1932 ◆ WEINERT, PAUL H.

Rank: Corporal (highest rank: Sergeant)
Service: U.S. Army
Birthday: 15 July 1869
Place of Birth: Frankfort, Germany
Date of Death: 19 January 1919
Place of Death: Mattapan, Massachusetts
Cemetery: Milton Cemetery (MH)—Milton, Massachusetts
Entered Service at: Baltimore, Baltimore County, Maryland
Unit: Battery E, 1st U.S. Artillery
Battle or Place of Action: Wounded Knee Creek, South Dakota
Date of Action: 29 December 1890
Date of Issue: 24 March 1891
Citation: Taking the place of his commanding officer, who had fallen severely wounded, he gallantly served his piece, after each fire advancing it to a better position.

1933 ◆ WEISS, ENOCH R.

Rank: Private
Service: U.S. Army
Birthday: 13 February 1848
Place of Birth: Kosciusko County, Indiana
Date of Death: 29 December 1917
Cemetery: South Bend Cemetery—South Bend, Indiana
Entered Service at: St. Louis, St. Louis County, Missouri
Unit: Company G, 1st U.S. Cavalry
Battle or Place of Action: Chiricahua Mountains, Arizona Territory
Date of Action: 20 October 1869
Date of Issue: 14 February 1870
Citation: Gallantry in action with Indians.

1934 ◆ WELCH, CHARLES H.

Rank: Sergeant
Service: U.S. Army
Birthday: 16 March 1845
Place of Birth: New York, New York
Date of Death: 22 June 1915
Place of Death: LaSalle, Colorado
Cemetery: Evans Cemetery (MH)—Evans, Colorado
Entered Service at: Fort Snelling, St. Paul County, Minnesota
Unit: Company D, 7th U.S. Cavalry
Battle or Place of Action: Little Big Horn, Montana
Date of Action: 25-26 June 1876
Date of Issue: 5 October 1878
Citation: Voluntarily brought water to the wounded, under fire.

1935 ◆ WELCH, MICHAEL

Rank: Sergeant
Service: U.S. Army
Birthday: 1843

Place of Birth: Poughkeepsie, Dutchess County, New York
Entered Service at: New York, New York
Unit: Company M, 6th U.S. Cavalry
Battle or Place of Action: Wichita River, Texas
Date of Action: 5 October 1870
Date of Issue: 19 November 1870
Citation: Gallantry in action.

1936 ◆ WEST, FRANK

Rank: First Lieutenant (highest rank: Colonel)
Service: U.S. Army
Birthday: 26 September 1850
Place of Birth: Mohawk, Herkimer County, New York
Date of Death: 26 August 1923
Place of Death: Mohawk, New York
Cemetery: Arlington National Cemetery (1-549)—Arlington, Virginia
Entered Service at: Mohawk, Herkimer County, New York
Unit: 6th U.S. Cavalry
Battle or Place of Action: Big Dry Wash, Arizona
Date of Action: 17 July 1882
Date of Issue: 12 July 1892
Citation: Rallied his command and led it in the advance against the enemy's fortified position.

1937 ◆ WHITEHEAD, PATTON G.

True Name: Whited, Patton G.
Rank: Private (highest rank: Corporal)
Service: U.S. Army
Birthday: 25 September 1840
Place of Birth: Russell County, Virginia
Date of Death: 8 December 1900
Place of Death: Los Angeles, California
Cemetery: New Calvary Cemetery—Los Angeles, California
Entered Service at: Louisville, Jefferson County, Kentucky
Unit: Company C, 5th U.S. Infantry
Battle or Place of Action: Cedar Creek, etc., Montana
Date of Action: 21 October 1876—8 January 1877
Date of Issue: 27 April 1877
Citation: Gallantry in action.

1938 ◆ WIDMER, JACOB

Rank: First Sergeant
Service: U.S. Army
Birthday: 1845
Place of Birth: Wurttemberg, Germany
Date of Death: 5 July 1880
Place of Death: Fort Niobrara, Nebraska
Cemetery: Fort Leavenworth National Cemetery (G-3529) (MH)—Fort Leavenworth, Kansas
Entered Service at: Philadelphia, Philadelphia County, Pennsylvania
Unit: Company D, 5th U.S. Cavalry
Battle or Place of Action: Milk River, Colorado
Date of Action: 29 September 1879
Date of Issue: 4 May 1880

Citation: Volunteered to accompany a small detachment on a very dangerous mission.

1939 ◆ WILDER, WILBER ELLIOTT

Rank: First Lieutenant (highest rank: Brigadier General)
Service: U.S. Army
Birthday: 16 August 1857
Place of Birth: Atlas, Genesee County, Michigan
Date of Death: 30 January 1952
Place of Death: Governors Island, New York
Cemetery: Fairlawn Cemetery—Ridgefield, Connecticut
Entered Service at: Detroit, Wayne County, Michigan
Unit: 4th U.S. Cavalry
Battle or Place of Action: Horseshoe Canyon, New Mexico
Date of Action: 23 April 1882
Date of Issue: 17 August 1896
Citation: Assisted, under a heavy fire, in rescuing a wounded comrade.

1940 ◆ WILKENS, HENRY

Rank: First Sergeant (highest rank: Ordnance Sergeant)
Service: U.S. Army
Birthday: 1855
Place of Birth: Germany
Date of Death: 2 August 1895
Cemetery: Cypress Hills National Cemetery (2-5325)—Brooklyn, New York
Entered Service at: Pittsburgh, Allegheny County, Pennsylvania
Unit: Company L, 2d U.S. Cavalry
Battle or Place of Action: Little Muddy Creek, Montana; Camas Meadows, Idaho
Date of Action: 7 May & 20 August 1877
Date of Issue: 28 February 1878
Citation: Bravery in actions with Indians.

1941 ◆ WILLIAMS, MOSES

Rank: First Sergeant (highest rank: Ordnance Sergeant)
Service: U.S. Army
Birthday: 1845
Place of Birth: Carrollton, Orleans Parish, Louisiana
Date of Death: 23 August 1899
Cemetery: Vancouver Barracks National Cemetery (8-W-393) (MH)—Vancouver, Washington
Entered Service at: East Carroll Parish, Louisiana
Unit: Company I, 9th U.S. Cavalry
Battle or Place of Action: foothills of the Cuchillo Negro Mountains, New Mexico
Date of Action: 16 August 1881
Date of Issue: 12 November 1896
Citation: Rallied a detachment, skillfully conducted a running fight of three or four hours, and by his coolness, bravery, and unflinching devotion to duty in standing by his commanding officer in an exposed position under a heavy fire

from a large party of Indians saved the lives of at least three of his comrades.

1942 ◆ WILLS, HENRY

Rank: Private (highest rank: Sergeant)
Service: U.S. Army
Birthday: 1842
Place of Birth: Gracon, Virginia
Entered Service at: St. Louis, St. Louis County, Missouri
Unit: Company C, 8th U.S. Cavalry
Battle or Place of Action: Fort Selden, New Mexico
Date of Action: 8-11 July 1873
Date of Issue: 12 August 1875
Citation: Services against hostile Indians.

1943 ◆ WILSON, BENJAMIN

Rank: Private
Service: U.S. Army
Birthday: 1843
Place of Birth: Pittsburgh, Allegheny County, Pennsylvania
Entered Service at: Cincinnati, Hamilton County, Ohio
Unit: Company M, 6th U.S. Cavalry
Battle or Place of Action: Wichita River, Texas
Date of Action: 5 October 1870
Date of Issue: 19 November 1870
Citation: Gallantry in action.

1944 ◆ WILSON, CHARLES

Rank: Corporal (highest rank: Sergeant)
Service: U.S. Army
Birthday: 1852
Place of Birth: Petersburg, Menard County, Illinois
Date of Death: 16 February 1943
Place of Death: Los Angeles, California
Cemetery: Inglewood Park Cemetery—Inglewood, California
Entered Service at: Springfield, Sangamon County, Illinois
Unit: Company H, 5th U.S. Infantry
Battle or Place of Action: Cedar Creek, etc., Montana
Date of Action: 21 October 1876—8 January 1877
Date of Issue: 27 April 1877
Citation: Gallantry in action.

1945 ◆ WILSON, MILDEN H.

Rank: Sergeant (highest rank: Ordnance Sergeant)
Service: U.S. Army
Birthday: 25 July 1847
Place of Birth: Huron County, Ohio
Date of Death: 6 February 1924
Entered Service at: Newark, Licking County, Ohio
Unit: Company I, 7th U.S. Infantry
Battle or Place of Action: Big Hole, Montana
Date of Action: 9 August 1877

Date of Issue: 2 December 1878
Citation: Gallantry in forming company from line of skirmishers and deploying again under a galling fire, and in carrying dispatches at the imminent risk of his life.

1946 ◆ WILSON, WILLIAM✠

Rank: Sergeant
Service: U.S. Army
Birthday: 1847
Place of Birth: Philadelphia, Philadelphia County, Pennsylvania
Date of Death: 22 December 1895
Cemetery: San Francisco National Cemetery (WS-527-Row 28) (MH)—San Francisco, California
Entered Service at: Philadelphia, Philadelphia County, Pennsylvania
Unit: Company I, 4th U.S. Cavalry
Battle or Place of Action: Colorado Valley and Red River, Texas
Date of Action: 28 March 1872; 29 September 1872
Date of Issue: 27 April 1872
Citation: **First Award** In pursuit of a band of cattle thieves from New Mexico. **Second Award** Distinguished conduct in action with Indians.
Notes: ✠Double Awardee

1947 ◆ WILSON, WILLIAM O.

Rank: Corporal
Service: U.S. Army
Birthday: 1867
Place of Birth: Hagerstown, Washington County, Maryland
Date of Death: 18 January 1928
Place of Death: Washington County, Maryland
Cemetery: Jewish Cemetery—Halfway, Maryland
Entered Service at: St. Paul, Ramsey County, Minnesota
Unit: Company I, 9th U.S. Cavalry
Battle or Place of Action: Sioux Campaign
Date of Action: 1890
Date of Issue: 17 September 1891
Citation: Bravery.

1948 ◆ WINDOLPH, CHARLES

Rank: Private (highest rank: First Sergeant)
Service: U.S. Army
Birthday: 9 December 1851
Place of Birth: Bergen, Germany
Date of Death: 11 March 1950
Place of Death: Lead, South Dakota
Cemetery: Black Hills National Cemetery (A-239) (MH)—Sturgis, South Dakota
Entered Service at: Brooklyn, Kings County, New York
Unit: Company H, 7th U.S. Cavalry
Battle or Place of Action: Little Big Horn, Montana
Date of Action: 25-26 June 1876
Date of Issue: 5 October 1878

Citation: With three comrades, during the entire engagement, courageously held a position that secured water for the command.

1949 ◆ WINDUS, CLARON

Rank: Bugler (highest rank: Captain)
Service: U.S. Army
Birthday: 10 January 1850
Place of Birth: Janesville, Rock County, Wisconsin
Date of Death: 18 October 1927
Place of Death: Fort Sam Houston, Texas
Cemetery: Masonic Cemetery (MH)—Brackettville, Texas
Entered Service at: Indianapolis, Marion County, Indiana
Unit: Company L, 6th U.S. Cavalry
Battle or Place of Action: Wichita River, Texas
Date of Action: 12 July 1870
Date of Issue: 25 August 1870
Citation: Gallantry in action.

1950 ◆ WINTERBOTTOM, WILLIAM

Rank: Sergeant
Service: U.S. Army
Birthday: 1847
Place of Birth: Manchester, Greater Manchester County, England
Date of Death: 4 April 1932
Cemetery: Bayview Cemetery (MH)—Jersey City, New Jersey
Entered Service at: Boston, Suffolk County, Massachusetts
Unit: Company A, 6th U.S. Cavalry
Battle or Place of Action: Wichita River, Texas
Date of Action: 12 July 1870
Date of Issue: 25 August 1870
Citation: Gallantry in action.

1951 ◆ WITCOME, JOSEPH

Rank: Private
Service: U.S. Army
Birthday: 1846
Place of Birth: Mechanicsburg, Cumberland County, Pennsylvania
Date of Death: 7 October 1869
Place of Death: Ash Creek, Arizona
Entered Service at: Carlisle, Cumberland County, Pennsylvania
Unit: Company B, 8th U.S. Cavalry
Battle or Place of Action: Arizona Territory
Date of Action: August-October 1868
Date of Issue: 24 July 1869
Citation: Bravery in scouts and actions against Indians.

1952 ◆ WOOD, LEONARD

Rank: Assistant Surgeon (highest rank: Major General)
Service: U.S. Army

Birthday: 9 October 1860
Place of Birth: Winchester, Cheshire County, New Hampshire
Date of Death: 7 August 1927
Place of Death: Boston, Massachusetts
Cemetery: Arlington National Cemetery (21-S-10)—Arlington, Virginia
Entered Service at: Boston, Suffolk County, Massachusetts
Unit: U.S. Army
Served as: Assistant Surgeon
Battle or Place of Action: Apache Campaign, Arizona Territory
Date of Action: summer 1886
Date of Issue: 8 April 1898
Citation: Voluntarily carried dispatches through a region infested with hostile Indians, making a journey of 70 miles in one night and walking 30 miles the next day. Also for several weeks, while in close pursuit of Geronimo's band and constantly expecting an encounter, commanded a detachment of infantry, which was then without an officer and to the command of which he was assigned upon his own request.

1953 ◆ WOODALL, ZACHARIAH

True Name: Woodall, Zachery T.
Rank: Sergeant (highest rank: Ordnance Sergeant)
Service: U.S. Army
Birthday: 1850
Place of Birth: Alexandria, Alexandria County, Virginia
Date of Death: 12 September 1899
Place of Death: Havana, Cuba
Cemetery: Arlington National Cemetery (22-15788) (MH)—Arlington, Virginia
Entered Service at: Carlisle, Cumberland County, Pennsylvania
Unit: Company I, 6th U.S. Cavalry
Battle or Place of Action: Washita River, Texas
Date of Action: 12 September 1874
Date of Issue: 7 November 1874
Citation: While in command of five men and carrying dispatches, was attacked by 125 Indians, whom he with his command fought throughout the day, he being severely wounded.

1954 ◆ WOODS, BRENT

Rank: Sergeant
Service: U.S. Army
Birthday: 1850
Place of Birth: Pulaski County, Kentucky
Date of Death: 31 March 1906
Cemetery: Mill Springs National Cemetery (A-930) (MH)—Nancy, Kentucky
Entered Service at: Louisville, Jefferson County, Kentucky
Unit: Company B, 9th U.S. Cavalry

Battle or Place of Action: New Mexico
Date of Action: 19 August 1881
Date of Issue: 12 July 1894
Citation: Saved the lives of his comrades and citizens of the detachment.

1955 ◆ WORTMAN, GEORGE G.

Rank: Sergeant (highest rank: Quartermaster Sergeant)
Service: U.S. Army
Birthday: 15 August 1841
Place of Birth: Monckton, New Brunswick, Canada
Date of Death: 19 May 1913
Cemetery: Crown Hill Cemetery (MH)—Denver, Colorado
Entered Service at: Boston, Suffolk County, Massachusetts
Unit: Company B, 8th U.S. Cavalry
Battle or Place of Action: Arizona Territory
Date of Action: August-October 1868
Date of Issue: 24 July 1869
Citation: Bravery in scouts and actions against Indians.

1956 ◆ YOUNT, JOHN P.

Rank: Private
Service: U.S. Army
Birthday: 1849
Place of Birth: Putnam County, Indiana
Date of Death: 11 December 1872
Place of Death: Fort McPherson, Nebraska
Entered Service at: Sacramento, Sacramento County, California
Unit: Company F, 3d U.S. Cavalry
Battle or Place of Action: Whetstone Mountains, Arizona Territory
Date of Action: 5 May 1871
Date of Issue: 13 November 1871
Citation: Gallantry in action with Indians.

1957 ◆ ZIEGNER, HERMAN

Rank: Private
Service: U.S. Army
Birthday: 1864
Place of Birth: Aploda, Germany
Date of Death: 9 September 1898
Cemetery: Calvary Cemetery—Woodside, New York
Entered Service at: Baltimore, Baltimore County, Maryland
Unit: Company E, 7th U.S. Cavalry
Battle or Place of Action: South Dakota Wounded Knee Creek and White Clay Creek
Date of Action: 29-30 December 1890
Date of Issue: 23 June 1891
Citation: Conspicuous bravery.

KOREAN CAMPAIGN 1871

1958 ◆ ANDREWS, JOHN

Rank: Ordinary Seaman
Service: U.S. Navy
Birthday: 1821
Place of Birth: York County, Pennsylvania
Entered Service at: Maryland
Unit: U.S.S. *Benicia*
Battle or Place of Action: Korean Forts
Date of Action: 9-10 June 1871
G.O. Number, Date: 176, 9 July 1872
Citation: On board the U.S.S. *Benicia* in action against Korean forts on 9 and 10 June 1871. Stationed at the lead in passing the forts, Andrews stood on the gunwale on the *Benicia*'s launch, lashed to the ridgerope. He remained unflinchingly in this dangerous position and gave his soundings with coolness and accuracy under a heavy fire.

1959 ◆ BROWN, CHARLES

Rank: Corporal
Service: U.S. Marine Corps
Place of Birth: New York, New York
Enlisted at: Hong Kong
Unit: U.S.S. *Colorado*
Battle or Place of Action: Korean Forts
Date of Action: 11 June 1871
G.O. Number, Date: 169, 8 February 1872
Citation: On board the U.S.S. *Colorado* in action against a Korean fort, 11 June 1871. Assisted in capturing the Korean standard in the center of the citadel of the fort.

1960 ◆ COLEMAN, JOHN

Rank: Private
Service: U.S. Marine Corps
Birthday: 9 October 1847
Place of Birth: County Cork, Ireland
Entered Service at: California
Unit: U.S.S. *Colorado*
Battle or Place of Action: Korean Forts
Date of Action: 11 June 1871
G.O. Number, Date: 169, 8 February 1872
Citation: On board the U.S.S. *Colorado* in action at Korea, 11 June 1871. Fighting hand-to-hand with the enemy, Coleman succeeded in saving the life of Alexander McKenzie.

1961 ◆ DOUGHERTY, JAMES

Rank: Private
Service: U.S. Marine Corps
Birthday: 16 November 1839
Place of Birth: Langhash, Ireland
Date of Death: 25 November 1897
Cemetery: Cypress Hills National Cemetery (6-12374) (MH)—Brooklyn, New York
Entered Service at: Pennsylvania
Unit: U.S.S. *Benicia*
Battle or Place of Action: Korean Forts
Date of Action: 11 June 1871
G.O. Number, Date: 169, 8 February 1872
Citation: On board the U.S.S. *Carondelet* in various actions of that vessel. Wounded several times, Dougherty invariably returned to duty, presenting an example of constancy and devotion to the flag.

1962 ◆ FRANKLIN, FREDERICK H.

Rank: Quartermaster
Service: U.S. Navy
Birthday: 1840
Place of Birth: Portsmouth, Rockingham County, New Hampshire
Date of Death: 10 May 1873
Cemetery: Proprietors Cemetery (MH)—Portsmouth, New Hampshire
Entered Service at: New Hampshire
Unit: Ship's Company D, U.S.S. *Colorado*
Battle or Place of Action: Korean Forts
Date of Action: 11 June 1871
G.O. Number, Date: 169, 8 February 1872
Citation: On board the U.S.S. *Colorado* during the attack and capture of the Korean forts, 11 June 1871. Assuming command of Company D, after Lt. McKee was wounded, Franklin handled the company with great credit until relieved.

1963 ◆ GRACE, PATRICK HENRY

True Name: Grace, Henry Patrick
Rank: Chief Quartermaster
Service: U.S. Navy
Birthday: 1832
Place of Birth: Ireland
Date of Death: 24 February 1896
Place of Death: Dorchester, Massachusetts

Entered Service at: Pennsylvania
Unit: U.S.S. *Benicia*
Battle or Place of Action: Korean Forts
Date of Action: 10-11 June 1871
G.O. Number, Date: 177, 4 December 1915
Citation: On board the U.S.S. *Benicia* during the attack on Korean forts, 10 and 11 June 1871. Carrying out his duties with coolness, Grace set forth gallant and meritorious conduct throughout this action.

1964 ◆ HAYDEN, CYRUS

Rank: Carpenter
Service: U.S. Navy
Birthday: 1843
Place of Birth: York, York County, Maine
Entered Service at: Maine
Unit: U.S.S. *Colorado*
Served as: Color Bearer
Battle or Place of Action: Korean Forts
Date of Action: 11 June 1871
G.O. Number, Date: 169, 8 February 1872
Citation: On board the U.S.S. *Colorado* during the attack and capture of the Korean forts, 11 June 1871. Serving as color bearer of the battalion, Hayden planted his flag on the ramparts of the citadel and protected it under a heavy fire from the enemy.

1965 ◆ LUKES, WILLIAM F.

Rank: Landsman (highest rank: Seaman)
Service: U.S. Navy
Birthday: 19 February 1847
Place of Birth: Niderbergdorf, Bohemia
Date of Death: 17 December 1923
Place of Death: Los Angeles, California
Cemetery: Los Angeles National Cemetery (7-F-19) (MH)—Los Angeles, California
Entered Service at: Enlisted in Tientsin, China
Unit: Company D, U.S.S. *Colorado*
Battle or Place of Action: Korean Forts
Date of Action: 9-10 June 1871
G.O. Number, Date: 180, 10 October 1872
Citation: Served with Company D during the capture of the Korean forts, 9 and 10 June 1871. Fighting the enemy inside the fort, Lukes received a severe cut over the head.

1966 ◆ McKENZIE, ALEXANDER

Rank: Boatswain's Mate
Service: U.S. Navy
Birthday: 1837
Place of Birth: Glasgow, Scotland
Entered Service at: New York
Unit: U.S.S. *Colorado*
Battle or Place of Action: Korean Forts
Date of Action: 11 June 1871
G.O. Number, Date: 169, 8 February 1872
Citation: On board the U.S.S. *Colorado* during the capture

of the Korean forts, 11 June 1871. Fighting at the side of Lt. McKee during this action, McKenzie was struck by a sword and received a severe cut in the head from the blow.

1967 ◆ McNAMARA, MICHAEL

Rank: Private
Service: U.S. Marine Corps
Birthday: 1841
Place of Birth: Clure, Ireland
Entered Service at: New York
Unit: U.S.S. *Benicia*
Battle or Place of Action: Korean Forts
Date of Action: 11 June 1871
G.O. Number, Date: 169, 8 February 1872
Citation: On board the U.S.S. *Benicia* during the capture of the Korean forts, 11 June 1871. Advancing to the parapet, McNamara wrenched the matchlock from the hands of an enemy and killed him.

1968 ◆ MERTON, JAMES F.

Rank: Landsman (highest rank: Carpenter)
Service: U.S. Navy
Birthday: 1845
Place of Birth: Cheshire, England
Entered Service at: Portsmouth, Rockingham County, New Hampshire
Unit: Ship's Company D, U.S.S. *Colorado*
Battle or Place of Action: Korean Forts
Date of Action: 9-10 June 1871
G.O. Number, Date: 180, 10 October 1872
Citation: Landsman and member of Company D during the capture of the Korean forts, 9 and 10 June 1871. Merton was severely wounded in the arm while trying to force his way into the fort.

1969 ◆ OWENS, MICHAEL

Rank: Private
Service: U.S. Marine Corps
Birthday: 6 February 1837
Place of Birth: New York, New York
Date of Death: 8 December 1890
Entered Service at: New York
Unit: U.S.S. *Colorado*
Battle or Place of Action: Korean Forts
Date of Action: 11 June 1871
G.O. Number, Date: 169, 8 February 1872
Citation: On board the U.S.S. *Colorado* during the capture of Korean forts, 11 June 1871. Fighting courageously in hand-to-hand combat, Owens was badly wounded by the enemy during this action.

1970 ◆ PURVIS, HUGH

Rank: Private
Service: U.S. Marine Corps
Birthday: 5 March 1846

Place of Birth: Philadelphia, Philadelphia County, Pennsylvania
Date of Death: 12 February 1922
Place of Death: Annapolis, Maryland
Cemetery: Cedar Bluff Cemetery (MH)—Annapolis, Maryland
Entered Service at: Pennsylvania
Unit: U.S.S. *Alaska*
Battle or Place of Action: Korean Forts
Date of Action: 11 June 1871
G.O. Number, Date: 169, 8 February 1872
Citation: On board the U.S.S. *Alaska* during the attack on and capture of the Korean forts, 11 June 1871. Braving the enemy fire, Purvis was the first to scale the walls of the fort and capture the flag of the Korean forces.

1971 ◆ ROGERS, SAMUEL F.

Rank: Quartermaster
Service: U.S. Navy
Birthday: 1845
Place of Birth: Buffalo, Erie County, New York
Date of Death: 1 November 1905
Cemetery: Forest Homes Cemetery—Forest Park, Illinois
Entered Service at: New York
Unit: U.S.S. *Colorado*

Battle or Place of Action: Korean Forts
Date of Action: 11 June 1871
G.O. Number, Date: 169, 8 February 1872
Citation: On board the U.S.S. *Colorado* during the attack and capture of the Korean forts, 11 June 1871. Fighting courageously at the side of Lt. McKee during this action, Rogers was wounded by the enemy.

1972 ◆ TROY, WILLIAM

Rank: Ordinary Seaman
Service: U.S. Navy
Birthday: 1848
Place of Birth: Boston, Suffolk County, Massachusetts
Date of Death: 8 March 1907
Cemetery: Stockton State Hospital Cemetery—Stockton, California
Entered Service at: Massachusetts
Unit: U.S.S. *Colorado*
Battle or Place of Action: Korean Forts
Date of Action: 11 June 1871
G.O. Number, Date: 169, 8 February 1872
Citation: On board the U.S.S. *Colorado* during the capture of the Korean forts, 11 June 1871. Fighting at the side of Lt. McKee, by whom he was especially commended, Troy was badly wounded by the enemy.

INTERIM 1871–1898

1973 ◆ AHERN, WILLIAM

Rank: Watertender
Service: U.S. Navy
Birthday: 1861
Place of Birth: Ireland
Entered Service at: New York
Unit: U.S.S. *Puritan*
Battle or Place of Action: U.S.S. *Puritan*
Date of Action: 1 July 1897
G.O. Number, Date: 482, 1 November 1897
Citation: On board the U.S.S. *Puritan* at the time of the collapse of one of the crown sheets of boiler E of that vessel, 1 July 1897. Wrapped in wet cloths to protect his face and arms, Ahern entered the fireroom, crawled over the tops of the boilers and closed the auxiliary stop valve, disconnecting boiler E and removing the danger of disabling the other boilers.

1974 ◆ ANDERSON, WILLIAM

Rank: Coxswain
Service: U.S. Navy
Birthday: 1852
Place of Birth: Sweden
Entered Service at: New York
Unit: U.S.S. *Powhatan*
Battle or Place of Action: U.S.S. *Powhatan*
Date of Action: 28 June 1878
Citation: On board the U.S.S. *Powhatan*, 28 June 1878. Acting courageously, Anderson rescued from drowning W.H. Moffatt, first class boy.

1975 ◆ ATKINS, DANIEL

Rank: Ship's Cook First Class (highest rank: Chief Commissary Steward)
Service: U.S. Navy
Birthday: 18 November 1866
Place of Birth: Brunswick, Virginia
Date of Death: 11 May 1923
Place of Death: Portsmouth, Virginia
Cemetery: U.S. Navy Hospital Cemetery (MH)—Portsmouth, Virginia
Entered Service at: Virginia
Unit: U.S.S. *Cushing*
Battle or Place of Action: U.S.S. *Cushing*
Date of Action: 11 February 1898
G.O. Number, Date: 489, 20 May 1898
Citation: On board the U.S.S. *Cushing*, 11 February 1898.

Showing gallant conduct, Atkins attempted to save the life of the late Ens. Joseph C. Breckenridge, U.S. Navy, who fell overboard at sea from that vessel on this date.

1976 ◆ AUER, JOHN F.

Rank: Ordinary Seaman Apprentice
Service: U.S. Navy
Birthday: 1866
Place of Birth: New York
Entered Service at: New York
Unit: U.S.S. *Lancaster*
Battle or Place of Action: Marseille, France
Date of Action: 20 November 1883
Citation: On board the U.S.S. *Lancaster*, Marseille, France, 20 November 1883. Jumping overboard, Auer rescued from drowning a French lad who had fallen into the sea from a stone pier astern of the ship.

1977 ◆ BARRETT, EDWARD

Rank: Second Class Fireman
Service: U.S. Navy
Birthday: 1855
Place of Birth: Philadelphia, Philadelphia County, Pennsylvania
Entered Service at: Pennsylvania
Unit: U.S.S. *Alaska*
Battle or Place of Action: Callao Bay, Peru
Date of Action: 14 September 1881
G.O. Number, Date: 326, 18 October 1884
Citation: On board the U.S.S. *Alaska* at Callao Bay, Peru, 14 September 1881. Following the rupture of the stop-valve chamber, Barrett courageously hauled the fires from under the boiler of that vessel.

1978 ◆ BELPITT, WILLIAM HENRY

Rank: Captain of the Afterguard
Service: U.S. Navy
Birthday: 3 May 1860
Place of Birth: Ryde, Australia
Unit: U.S.S. *Monocacy*
Battle or Place of Action: Foochow, China
Date of Action: 7 October 1884
G.O. Number, Date: Letter No. 126 LCDR Iverson, U.S. Navy; 27 October 1884
Citation: On board the U.S.S. *Monocacy*, Foochow, China, 7 October 1884. Jumping overboard from that vessel on the morning of this date, Belpitt sustained, until picked up, a

Chinaman who had been thrown into the water by the capsizing of a canoe.

1979 ◆ BENSON, JAMES

Rank: Seaman
Service: U.S. Navy
Birthday: 1842
Place of Birth: Denmark
Date of Death: 4 August 1890
Place of Death: Boston Harbor, Massachusetts
Enlisted at: Yokohama, Japan
Unit: U.S.S. *Ossipee*
Battle or Place of Action: at sea
Date of Action: 20 June 1872
G.O. Number, Date: 180, 10 October 1872
Date of Issue: 1872
Citation: On board the U.S.S. *Ossipee*, 20 June 1872. Risking his life, Benson leaped into the sea while the ship was going at a speed of four knots and endeavored to save John K. Smith, landsman, of the same vessel, from drowning.

1980 ◆ BRADLEY, ALEXANDER

Rank: Landsman
Service: U.S. Navy
Birthday: 19 September 1851
Place of Birth: Boston, Suffolk County, Massachusetts
Date of Death: 6 March 1925
Place of Death: Akron, Ohio
Cemetery: Holy Cross Cemetery—Akron, Ohio
Entered Service at: Massachusetts
Unit: U.S.S. *Wachusett*
Battle or Place of Action: off Cowes, Isle of Wight, England
Date of Action: 7 August 1872
G.O. Number, Date: 180, 10 October 1872
Citation: On board the U.S.S. *Wachusett* off Cowes, 7 August 1872. Jumping overboard into a strong tideway, Bradley attempted to save Philip Cassidy, landsman, of the U.S.S. *Wabash*, from drowning.

1981 ◆ BUCHANAN, DAVID M.

Rank: Apprentice
Service: U.S. Navy
Birthday: 1862
Place of Birth: Philadelphia, Philadelphia County, Pennsylvania
Entered Service at: Pennsylvania
Unit: U.S.S. *Saratoga*
Battle or Place of Action: off The Battery, New York Harbor, New York
Date of Action: 15 July 1879
G.O. Number, Date: 246, 22 July 1879
Citation: On board the U.S.S. *Saratoga* off Battery, New York Harbor, 15 July 1879. On the morning of this date, Robert Lee Robey, apprentice, fell overboard from the after part of the ship into the tide which was running strong ebb at

the time and, not being an expert swimmer, was in danger of drowning. Instantly springing over the rail after him, Buchanan never hesitated for an instant to remove even a portion of his clothing. Both men were picked up by the ship's boat following this act of heroism.

1982 ◆ CAVANAUGH, THOMAS

Rank: Fireman First Class
Service: U.S. Navy
Birthday: 10 May 1869
Place of Birth: Ireland
Entered Service at: New York
Unit: U.S.S. *Potomac*
Served as: Fireman
Battle or Place of Action: at sea between Cat Island and Nassau
Date of Action: 14 November 1898
G.O. Number, Date: 503, 12 December 1898
Citation: On board the U.S.S. *Potomac* during the passage of that vessel from Cat Island to Nassau, 14 November 1898. Volunteering to enter the fireroom, which was filled with steam, Cavanaugh, after repeated attempts, succeeded in reaching the auxiliary valve and opening it, thereby relieving the vessel from further danger.

1983 ◆ CHANDRON, AUGUST

Rank: Seaman Apprentice Second Class
Service: U.S. Navy
Birthday: 1866
Place of Birth: France
Entered Service at: New York
Unit: U.S.S. *Quinnebaug*
Battle or Place of Action: Alexandria, Egypt
Date of Action: 21 November 1885
G.O. Number, Date: Letter, Capt. N. Judlow, U.S. Navy, No. 8326B; 21 November 1885
Citation: On board the U.S.S. *Quinnebaug*, Alexandria, Egypt, on the morning of 21 November 1885. Jumping overboard from that vessel, Chandron, with the aid of Hugh Miller, boatswain's mate, rescued William Evans, ordinary seaman, from drowning.

1984 ◆ CONNOLLY, MICHAEL

Rank: Ordinary Seaman
Service: U.S. Navy
Birthday: 1855
Place of Birth: Boston, Suffolk County, Massachusetts
Entered Service at: Massachusetts
Unit: U.S.S. *Plymouth*
Battle or Place of Action: Halifax Harbor, Nova Scotia, Canada
Date of Action: 7 August 1876
G.O. Number, Date: 218, 24 August 1876
Citation: On board the U.S.S. *Plymouth*, Halifax Harbor, Nova Scotia, 7 August 1876. Acting gallantly, Connolly succeeded in rescuing a citizen from drowning on this date.

1985 ◆ COREY, WILLIAM

Rank: Landsman
Service: U.S. Navy
Birthday: 1853
Place of Birth: New York, New York
Entered Service at: New York
Unit: U.S.S. *Plymouth*
Battle or Place of Action: Navy Yard, New York
Date of Action: 26 July 1876
G.O. Number, Date: 215, 9 August 1876
Citation: On board the U.S.S. *Plymouth*, Navy Yard, New York, 26 July 1876. Showing heroic conduct, Corey endeavored to save the life of one of the crew of that ship who had fallen overboard from aloft.

1986 ◆ COSTELLO, JOHN

Rank: Ordinary Seaman
Service: U.S. Navy
Birthday: 1850
Place of Birth: Rouses Point, Clinton County, New York
Entered Service at: New York
Unit: U.S.S. *Hartford*
Battle or Place of Action: Philadelphia, Pennsylvania
Date of Action: 16 July 1876
G.O. Number, Date: 214, 27 July 1876
Citation: On board the U.S.S. *Hartford*, Philadelphia, Pa., 16 July 1876. Showing gallantry, Costello rescued from drowning a landsman of that vessel.

1987 ◆ COURTNEY, HENRY C.

Rank: Seaman
Service: U.S. Navy
Birthday: 1856
Place of Birth: Springfield, Sangamon County, Illinois
Entered Service at: Illinois
Unit: U.S. Training Ship *Portsmouth*
Battle or Place of Action: Navy Yard, Washington, D.C.
Date of Action: 7 February 1882
G.O. Number, Date: 326, 18 October 1884
Citation: On board the U.S. training ship *Portsmouth*, Washington Navy Yard, 7 February 1882. Jumping overboard from that vessel, Courtney assisted in rescuing Charles Taliaferro, jack-of-the-dust, from drowning.

1988 ◆ CRAMEN, THOMAS

Rank: Boatswain's Mate
Service: U.S. Navy
Birthday: 1848
Place of Birth: Ireland
Entered Service at: Massachusetts
Unit: U.S.S. *Portsmouth*
Battle or Place of Action: Navy Yard, Washington, D.C.
Date of Action: 7 February 1882
G.O. Number, Date: 326, 18 October 1884
Citation: On board the U.S.S. *Portsmouth*, Washington Navy Yard, 7 February 1882. Jumping overboard from that vessel, Cramen rescued Charles Taliaferro, jack-of-the-dust, from drowning.

1989 ◆ CREELMAN, WILLIAM JAMES

Rank: Landsman (highest rank: Chief Gunner)
Service: U.S. Navy
Birthday: 3 August 1874
Place of Birth: Brooklyn, Kings County, New York
Date of Death: 24 March 1928
Place of Death: Brooklyn, New York
Cemetery: 1st Calvary Cemetery—Woodside, New York
Entered Service at: New York
Unit: U.S.S. *Maine*
Battle or Place of Action: at Sea
Date of Action: 7 February 1897
Citation: Attached to the U.S.S. *Maine*, 6 February 1897. Distinguishing himself, Creelman showed extraordinary heroism in the line of his profession during an attempt to save life at sea.

1990 ◆ CUTTER, GEORGE W.

Rank: Landsman
Service: U.S. Navy
Birthday: 1849
Place of Birth: Philadelphia, Philadelphia County, Pennsylvania
Entered Service at: Pennsylvania
Unit: U.S.S. *Powhatan*
Battle or Place of Action: Norfolk, Virginia
Date of Action: 27 May 1872
G.O. Number, Date: 176, 9 July 1872
Citation: On board the U.S.S. *Powhatan*, Norfolk, Va., 27 May 1872. Jumping overboard on this date, Cutter aided in saving one of the crew of that vessel from drowning.

1991 ◆ DAVIS, JOHN

Rank: Ordinary Seaman
Service: U.S. Navy
Birthday: 1854
Place of Birth: Kingston, Jamaica
Date of Death: 19 August 1903
Place of Death: Hampton, Virginia
Cemetery: Hampton National Cemetery (C-8534) (MH)—Hampton, Virginia
Unit: U.S.S. *Trenton*
Battle or Place of Action: Toulon, France
Date of Action: February 1881
G.O. Number, Date: 326, 18 October 1884
Citation: On board the U.S.S. *Trenton*, Toulon, France, February 1881. Jumping overboard, Davis rescued Augustus Ohlensen, coxswain, from drowning.

1992 ◆ DAVIS, JOSEPH H.

Rank: Landsman
Service: U.S. Navy

Birthday: 22 July 1860
Place of Birth: Philadelphia, Philadelphia County, Pennsylvania
Entered Service at: Philadelphia, Philadelphia County, Pennsylvania
Unit: U.S. Receiving Ship *Dale*
Battle or Place of Action: off the wharf, Norfolk, Virginia
Date of Action: 22 January 1886
G.O. Number, Date: Letter Mate J.W. Baxter, U.S Navy, No. 8985; 25 January 1886
Citation: On board the U.S. receiving ship *Dale* off the Wharf at Norfolk, Va., 22 January 1886. Jumping overboard from the ferryboat, Davis rescued from drowning John Norman, ordinary seaman.

1993 ◆ DEMPSEY, JOHN

Rank: Seaman
Service: U.S. Navy
Birthday: 1848
Place of Birth: Ireland
Entered Service at: Boston, Suffolk County, Massachusetts
Unit: U.S.S. *Kearsarge*
Battle or Place of Action: Shanghai, China
Date of Action: 23 January 1875
Citation: On board the U.S.S. *Kearsarge* at Shanghai, China, 23 January 1875. Displaying gallant conduct, Dempsey jumped overboard from the *Kearsarge* and rescued from drowning one of the crew of that vessel.

1994 ◆ DENEEF, MICHAEL

Rank: Captain of the Top
Service: U.S. Navy
Birthday: 1851
Place of Birth: Massachusetts
Entered Service at: Massachusetts
Unit: U.S.S. *Swatara*
Battle or Place of Action: Para, Brazil
Date of Action: 1 December 1875
G.O. Number, Date: 201, 18 January 1876
Citation: On board the U.S.S. *Swatara* at Para, Brazil, 1 December 1875. Displaying gallant conduct, Deneef jumped overboard and rescued one of the crew of that vessel from drowning.

1995 ◆ DENHAM, AUSTIN

Rank: Seaman
Service: U.S. Navy
Birthday: 29 September 1850
Place of Birth: England
Date of Death: 2 June 1948
Place of Death: Los Angeles, California
Cemetery: Calvary Cemetery—Los Angeles, California
Entered Service at: New York
Unit: U.S.S. *Kansas*
Battle or Place of Action: near Greytown, Nicaragua
Date of Action: 12 April 1872

G.O. Number, Date: 176, 9 July 1872
Citation: On board the U.S.S. *Kansas* near Greytown, Nicaragua, 12 April 1872. Displaying great coolness and self-possession at the time Comdr. A.F. Crosman and others were drowned, Denham, by heroism and personal exertion, prevented greater loss of life.

1996 ◆ EILERS, HENRY A.

Rank: Gunner's Mate (highest rank: Gunner)
Service: U.S. Navy
Birthday: 11 August 1870
Place of Birth: Newark, Essex County, New Jersey
Date of Death: 30 June 1901
Entered Service at: New Jersey
Unit: U.S.S. *Philadelphia*
Battle or Place of Action: Fort McHenry, Baltimore, Maryland
Date of Action: 17 September 1892
G.O. Number, Date: 404, 22 November 1892
Citation: On board the U.S.S. *Philadelphia* during the sham attack on Fort McHenry, Baltimore, Md., 17 September 1892. Displaying extraordinary heroism in the line of his profession on this occasion, Eilers remained at his post in the magazine and stamped out the burning particles of a prematurely exploded cartridge which had blown down the chute.

1997 ◆ ELMORE, WALTER

Rank: Landsman
Service: U.S. Navy
Birthday: 1857
Place of Birth: England
Entered Service at: Toulon, France
Unit: U.S.S. *Gettysburg*
Battle or Place of Action: Latitude 36 degrees 58 minutes north, longitude 3 degrees 44 minutes east.
Date of Action: 1 October 1878
Citation: On board the U.S.S. *Gettysburg*, for jumping overboard and saving from drowning Wallace Febrey, landsman, while that vessel was under way at sea in latitude 36 degrees 58 minutes north, longitude three degrees 44 minutes east, 1 October 1878.

1998 ◆ ENRIGHT, JOHN

Rank: Landsman
Service: U.S. Navy
Birthday: 2 July 1864
Place of Birth: Lynn, Essex County, Massachusetts
Date of Death: 19 February 1898
Place of Death: at Sea
Cemetery: Buried at sea
Entered Service at: Massachusetts
Unit: U.S.S. *Ranger*
Battle or Place of Action: off Ensenada, Mexico
Date of Action: 18 January 1886
Citation: On board the U.S.S. *Ranger* off Ensenada, Mexico, 18 January 1886. Jumping overboard from that ves-

sel, Enright rescued John Bell, ordinary seaman, and George Svensson, ordinary seaman, from drowning.

1999 ◆ EVERETTS, JOHN

Rank: Gunner's Mate Third Class
Service: U.S. Navy
Birthday: 25 August 1873
Place of Birth: Thorold, Canada
Date of Death: 12 September 1956
Cemetery: Long Island National Cemetery (DSS-36) (MH)—Farmingdale, New York
Entered Service at: New York
Unit: U.S.S. *Cushing*
Battle or Place of Action: at Sea
Date of Action: 11 February 1898
G.O. Number, Date: 489, 20 May 1898
Citation: Serving on board the U.S.S. *Cushing*, 11 February 1898, Everetts displayed gallant conduct in attempting to save the life of the late Ens. Joseph C. Breckenridge, U.S. Navy, who fell overboard at sea from that vessel.

2000 ◆ FASSEUR, ISAAC L.

Rank: Ordinary Seaman
Service: U.S. Navy
Birthday: 1860
Place of Birth: Flushing, Holland
Entered Service at: Valparaiso, Chile
Unit: U.S.S. *Lackawanna*
Battle or Place of Action: Callao, Peru
Date of Action: 13 June 1884
Citation: Serving on board the U.S.S. *Lackawanna*, 13 June 1884, at Callao, Peru, Fasseur rescued William Cruise, who had fallen overboard, from drowning.

2001 ◆ FLANNAGAN, JOHN

Rank: Boatswain's Mate
Service: U.S. Navy
Birthday: 1852
Place of Birth: Ireland
Entered Service at: New York
Unit: U.S.S. *Supply*
Battle or Place of Action: Le Havre, France
Date of Action: 26 October 1878
Citation: Serving on board the U.S.S. *Supply*, Flannagan rescued from drowning David Walsh, seaman, off Le Havre, France, 26 October 1878.

2002 ◆ FOWLER, CHRISTOPHER

Rank: Quartermaster
Service: U.S. Navy
Birthday: 1850
Place of Birth: New York
Entered Service at: New York
Unit: U.S.S. *Fortune*
Battle or Place of Action: off Point Zapotitlan, Mexico
Date of Action: 11 May 1874

Citation: Served on board the U.S.S. *Fortune* off Point Zapotitlan, Mexico, 11 May 1874. On the occasion of the capsizing of one of the boats of the *Fortune* and the drowning of a portion of the boat's crew, Fowler displayed gallant conduct.

2003 ◆ GIDDING, CHARLES

Rank: Seaman
Service: U.S. Navy
Birthday: 1853
Place of Birth: Bangor, Penobscot County, Maine
Entered Service at: Maine
Unit: U.S.S. *Plymouth*
Battle or Place of Action: Navy Yard, New York
Date of Action: 26 July 1876
G.O. Number, Date: 215, 9 August 1876
Citation: Serving on board the U.S.S. *Plymouth*, Gidding showed heroic conduct in trying to save the life of one of the crew of that ship, who had fallen overboard from aloft at the Navy Yard, New York, 26 July 1876.

2004 ◆ GILLICK, MATTHEW

Rank: Boatswain's Mate
Service: U.S. Navy
Birthday: 1852
Place of Birth: Providence, Providence County, Rhode Island
Entered Service at: Rhode Island
Unit: U.S.S. *Lancaster*
Battle or Place of Action: Marseille, France
Date of Action: 20 November 1883
G.O. Number, Date: 326, 18 October 1884
Citation: Serving on board the U.S.S. *Lancaster* at Marseille, France, 20 November 1883. Jumping overboard from the *Lancaster*, Gillick rescued from drowning a French lad who had fallen into the sea from a stone pier astern of the ship.

2005 ◆ HANDRAN, JOHN

Rank: Seaman
Service: U.S. Navy
Birthday: 1852
Place of Birth: Massachusetts
Entered Service at: Massachusetts
Unit: U.S.S. *Franklin*
Battle or Place of Action: Lisbon, Portugal
Date of Action: 9 January 1876
G.O. Number, Date: 206, 15 February 1876
Citation: For gallant conduct while serving on board the U.S.S. *Franklin* at Lisbon, Portugal, 9 January 1876. Jumping overboard, Handran rescued from drowning one of the crew of that vessel.

2006 ◆ HARRINGTON, DAVID

Rank: First Class Fireman
Service: U.S. Navy

Birthday: 4 April 1856
Place of Birth: Washington, D.C.
Date of Death: 20 September 1945
Cemetery: Arlington National Cemetery (17-23162-D) (MH)—Arlington, Virginia
Entered Service at: Washington, D.C.
Unit: U.S.S. *Tallapoosa*
Date of Action: 21 August 1884
G.O. Number, Date: 326, 18 October 1884
Citation: Served on board the U.S.S. *Tallapoosa* at the time of the sinking of that vessel, on the night of 21 August 1884. Remaining at his post of duty in the fireroom until the fires were put out by the rising waters, Harrington opened the safety valves when the water was up to his waist.

2007 ◆ HAYDEN, JOHN

Rank: Apprentice
Service: U.S. Navy
Birthday: 1863
Place of Birth: Washington, D.C.
Entered Service at: Washington, D.C.
Unit: U.S. Training Ship *Saratoga*
Battle or Place of Action: off The Battery, New York Harbor, New York
Date of Action: 15 July 1879
G.O. Number, Date: 246, 22 July 1879
Citation: On board the U.S. training ship *Saratoga*. On the morning of 15 July 1879, while the *Saratoga* was anchored off The Battery, in New York Harbor, R.L. Robey, apprentice, fell overboard. As the tide was running strong ebb, the man, not being an expert swimmer, was in danger of drowning. David M. Buchanan, apprentice, instantly, without removing any of his clothing, jumped after him. Stripping himself, Hayden stood coolly watching the two in the water, and when he thought his services were required, he made a dive from the rail and came up alongside them and rendered assistance until all three were picked up by a boat from the ship.

2008 ◆ HILL, GEORGE

Rank: Chief Quarter Gunner
Service: U.S. Navy
Birthday: 1844
Place of Birth: England
Entered Service at: New York, New York
Unit: U.S.S. *Kansas*
Battle or Place of Action: near Greytown, Nicaragua
Date of Action: 12 April 1872
G.O. Number, Date: 176, 9 July 1872
Citation: Serving on board the U.S.S. *Kansas*, Hill displayed great coolness and self-possession at the time Comdr. A.F. Crosman and others were drowned, near Greytown, Nicaragua, 12 April 1872, and by extraordinary heroism and personal exertion, prevented greater loss of life.

2009 ◆ HILL, WILLIAM LOWELL

Rank: Captain of the Top (highest rank: Chief Boatswain's Mate)

Service: U.S. Navy
Birthday: 12 October 1855
Place of Birth: Brooklyn, Kings County, New York
Date of Death: 2 August 1922
Cemetery: Lindenwood Cemetery (Lot 939 Gr.2) (MH)—Stoneham, Massachusetts
Entered Service at: New York
Unit: U.S. Training Ship *Minnesota*
Battle or Place of Action: Newport, Rhode Island
Date of Action: 22 June 1881
G.O. Number, Date: 326, 18 October 1884
Citation: Serving on board the U.S. training ship *Minnesota* at Newport, R.I., 22 June 1881, Hill jumped overboard and sustained William Mulcahy, third class boy, who had fallen overboard, until picked up by a steam launch.

2010 ◆ HOLT, GEORGE

Rank: Quarter Gunner
Service: U.S. Navy
Birthday: 1840
Place of Birth: Kentucky
Entered Service at: Kentucky
Unit: U.S.S. *Plymouth*
Battle or Place of Action: Hamburg Harbor, Germany
Date of Action: 3 July 1871
G.O. Number, Date: 180, 10 October 1872
Citation: On board the U.S.S. *Plymouth*, Hamburg Harbor, 3 July 1871. Jumping overboard at the imminent risk of his life, Holt, with a comrade, rescued from drowning one of a party who was thrown from a shore boat into a four-knot running tide while the boat was coming alongside the ship.

2011 ◆ HORTON, JAMES

Rank: Captain of the Top
Service: U.S. Navy
Birthday: 1850
Place of Birth: Boston, Suffolk County, Massachusetts
Entered Service at: Massachusetts
Unit: U.S.S. *Constitution*
Battle or Place of Action: at sea, northeast Atlantic, west of the English Channel
Date of Action: 13 February 1879
G.O. Number, Date: 326, 18 October 1884
Date of Presentation: 7 September 1879
Place of Presentation: On board the U.S.S. *Constitution* at the New York Navy Yard, presented by Lt. Commander Theodore F. Jewell, executive officer
Citation: Serving on board the U.S.S. *Constitution*, at sea, 13 February 1879, Horton showed courageous conduct in going over the stern during a heavy gale and cutting the fastenings of the ship's rudder chains.

2012 ◆ JARDINE, ALEXANDER

Rank: Fireman 1st Class
Service: U.S. Navy
Birthday: 19 March 1873
Place of Birth: Inverness, Scotland

Date of Death: 22 February 1949
Cemetery: Arlington National Cemetery (12-4280) (MH)—Arlington, Virginia
Entered Service at: Ohio
Unit: U.S.S. *Potomac*
Battle or Place of Action: at see between Cat Island and Nassau
Date of Action: 14 November 1898
G.O. Number, Date: 503, 13 December 1898
Citation: On board the U.S.S. *Potomac* during the passage of that vessel from Cat Island to Nassau, 14 November 1898. Volunteering to enter the fireroom, which was filled with steam, Jardine, after repeated attempts, succeeded in reaching the auxiliary valve and opening it, thereby relieving the vessel from further danger.

2013 ◆ JOHNSON, JOHN

Rank: Seaman
Service: U.S. Navy
Birthday: 1839
Place of Birth: Philadelphia, Philadelphia County, Pennsylvania
Entered Service at: Pennsylvania
Unit: U.S.S. *Kansas*
Battle or Place of Action: near Greytown, Nicaragua
Date of Action: 12 April 1872
G.O. Number, Date: 176, 9 July 1872
Citation: Serving on board the U.S.S. *Kansas*, near Greytown, Nicaragua, 12 April 1872, Johnson displayed great coolness and self-possession at the time Comdr. A.F. Crosman and others were drowned and, by extraordinary heroism and personal exertion, prevented greater loss of life.

2014 ◆ JOHNSON, WILLIAM

Rank: Cooper
Service: U.S. Navy
Birthday: 1855
Place of Birth: St. Vincent, West Indies
Date of Death: 20 May 1903
Cemetery: Arlington National Cemetery (23-16648-32) (MH)—Arlington, Virginia
Entered Service at: New York
Unit: U.S.S. *Adams*
Battle or Place of Action: Navy Yard, Mare Island, California
Date of Action: 14 November 1879
G.O. Number, Date: 326, 18 October 1884
Citation: Serving on board the U.S.S. *Adams* at the Navy Yard, Mare Island, Cal., 14 November 1879, Johnson rescued Daniel W. Kloppen, a workman, from drowning.

2015 ◆ KERSEY, THOMAS JOSEPH

Rank: Ordinary Seaman
Service: U.S. Navy
Birthday: 1847
Place of Birth: St. Johns, Newfoundland, Canada
Date of Death: 16 April 1888
Place of Death: Chelsea, Massachusetts

Cemetery: Woodlawn Cemetery—Everett, Massachusetts
Entered Service at: Massachusetts
Unit: U.S.S. *Plymouth*
Battle or Place of Action: Navy Yard, New York
Date of Action: 26 July 1876
G.O. Number, Date: 215, 9 August 1876
Citation: Serving on board the U.S.S. *Plymouth* at the Navy Yard, New York, 26 July 1876, Kersey displayed bravery and presence of mind in rescuing from drowning one of the crew of that vessel.

2016 ◆ KING, HUGH

Rank: Ordinary Seaman
Service: U.S. Navy
Birthday: 1845
Place of Birth: Ireland
Entered Service at: New York
Unit: U.S.S. *Iroquois*
Battle or Place of Action: Delaware River
Date of Action: 7 September 1871
G.O. Number, Date: 176, 9 July 1872
Citation: On board the U.S.S. *Iroquois*, Delaware River, 7 September 1871. Jumping overboard at the imminent risk of his life, King rescued one of the crew of that vessel from drowning.

2017 ◆ KYLE, PATRICK J.

Rank: Landsman
Service: U.S. Navy
Birthday: 4 November 1854
ace of Birth: Ireland
Date of Death: 28 October 1929
Place of Death: Charlestown, Massachusetts
Cemetery: Old Calvary Cemetery (MH)—Roslindas (Boston), Massachusetts
Entered Service at: Massachusetts
Unit: U.S.S. *Quinnebaug*
Battle or Place of Action: Port Mahon, Minorca, Spain
Date of Action: 13 March 1879
Citation: For rescuing from drowning a shipmate from the U.S.S. *Quinnebaug*, at Port Mahon, Minorca, 13 March 1879.

2018 ◆ LAKIN, THOMAS

Rank: Seaman
Service: U.S. Navy
Birthday: 1840
Place of Birth: New York
Entered Service at: New York
Unit: U.S.S. *Narragansett*
Battle or Place of Action: Navy Yard, Mare Island, California
Date of Action: November 1874
Citation: Serving on board the U.S.S. *Narragansett* at the Navy Yard, Mare Island, Cal., November 1874. Jumping overboard, Lakin displayed gallant conduct by rescuing two men of that ship from drowning.

2019 ◆ LAVERTY, JOHN✚

Rank: First Class Fireman
Service: U.S. Navy
Birthday: June 1845
Place of Birth: County Tyrone, Ireland
Date of Death: 13 November 1903
Place of Death: Philadelphia, Pennsylvania
Cemetery: Mount Moriah Cemetery (3-3-17 VA Plot)—Philadelphia, Pennsylvania
Entered Service at: California
Unit: U.S.S. *Alaska*
Battle or Place of Action: Callao Bay, Peru
Date of Action: 14 September 1881
G.O. Number, Date: 326, 18 October 1884
Citation: **Second Award** Serving on board the U.S.S. *Alaska* at Callao Bay, Peru, 14 September 1881. Following the rupture of the stop-valve chamber on that vessel, Laverty hauled the fires from under the boiler.
Notes: ✚Double Awardee: *see also* Civil War in which he served under the name John Lafferty

2020 ◆ LEJEUNE, EMILE

Rank: Seaman
Service: U.S. Navy
Birthday: 1853
Place of Birth: France
Entered Service at: New York
Unit: U.S.S. *Plymouth*
Battle or Place of Action: Port Royal, South Carolina
Date of Action: 6 June 1876
G.O. Number, Date: 212, 9 June 1876
Citation: Serving on board the U.S.S. *Plymouth*, Lejeune displayed gallant conduct in rescuing a citizen from drowning at Port Royal, S.C., 6 June 1876.

2021 ◆ LOW, GEORGE

True Name: Evatt, George L.
Rank: Seaman
Service: U.S. Navy
Birthday: 1847
Place of Birth: Canada
Entered Service at: New York
Unit: U.S.S. *Tennessee*
Battle or Place of Action: New Orleans, Louisiana
Date of Action: 15 February 1881
G.O. Number, Date: 326, 18 October 1884
Citation: For jumping overboard from the U.S.S. *Tennessee* at New Orleans, La., 15 February 1881, and sustaining, until picked up by a boat's crew, N.P. Petersen, gunner's mate, who had fallen overboard.

2022 ◆ LUCY, JOHN

Rank: Second Class Boy
Service: U.S. Navy
Birthday: 1859

Place of Birth: New York, New York
Entered Service at: New York
Unit: U.S. Training Ship *Minnesota*
Battle or Place of Action: Castle Garden, New York City, New York
Date of Action: 9 July 1876
G.O. Number, Date: 214, 27 July 1876
Citation: Displayed heroic conduct while serving on board the U.S. training ship *Minnesota* on the occasion of the burning of Castle Garden at New York, 9 July 1876.

2023 ◆ MADDIN, EDWARD

True Name: Madden, Edward
Rank: Ordinary Seaman
Service: U.S. Navy
Birthday: 15 May 1852
Place of Birth: Newfoundland, Canada
Entered Service at: Massachusetts
Unit: U.S.S. *Franklin*
Battle or Place of Action: Lisbon, Portugal
Date of Action: 9 January 1876
G.O. Number, Date: 206, 15 February 1876
Citation: Served on board the U.S.S. *Franklin* at Lisbon, Portugal, 9 January 1876. Displaying gallant conduct, Maddin jumped overboard and rescued one of the crew of that vessel from drowning.

2024 ◆ MAGEE, JOHN W.

Rank: Second Class Fireman
Service: U.S. Navy
Birthday: 1859
Place of Birth: Maryland
Entered Service at: Maryland
Unit: U.S.S. *Tallapoosa*
Date of Action: 21 August 1884
G.O. Number, Date: 326, 18 October 1884
Citation: Serving on board the U.S.S. *Tallapoosa* during the sinking of that vessel on the night of 21 August 1884. During this period, Magee remained at his post of duty in the fireroom until the fires were put out by the rising waters.

2025 ◆ MANNING, HENRY J.

Rank: Quartermaster
Service: U.S. Navy
Birthday: 1859
Place of Birth: New Haven, New Haven County, Connecticut
Entered Service at: Connecticut
Unit: U.S. Training Ship *New Hampshire*
Battle or Place of Action: off Coasters Harbor Island, Newport, Rhode Island
Date of Action: 4 January 1882
G.O. Number, Date: 326, 18 October 1884
Citation: Serving on board the U.S. training ship *New Hampshire*, off Newport, R.I., 4 January 1882. Jumping overboard, Manning endeavored to rescue Jabez Smith, second class musician, from drowning.

2026 ◆ MATTHEWS, JOSEPH

Rank: Captain of the Top
Service: U.S. Navy
Birthday: 1849
Place of Birth: Malta
Entered Service at: Pennsylvania
Unit: U.S.S. *Constitution*
Battle or Place of Action: at sea, northeast Atlantic, west of the English Channel
Date of Action: 13 February 1879
G.O. Number, Date: 326, 18 October 1884
Date of Presentation: 7 September 1879
Place of Presentation: On board the U.S.S. *Constitution* at the New York Navy Yard, presented by Lt. Commander Theodore F. Jewell, executive officer
Citation: For courageous conduct in going over the stern of the U.S.S. *Constitution* at sea, 13 February 1879, during a heavy gale, and cutting the fastenings of the ship's rudder chains.

2027 ◆ McCARTON, JOHN

Rank: Ship's Printer
Service: U.S. Navy
Birthday: 1847
Place of Birth: Brooklyn, Kings County, New York
Entered Service at: New York
Unit: U.S. Training Ship *New Hampshire*
Battle or Place of Action: off Coasters Harbor Island, Newport, Rhode Island
Date of Action: 4 January 1882
G.O. Number, Date: 326, 18 October 1884
Citation: For jumping overboard from the U.S. training ship *New Hampshire* off Coasters Harbor Island, near Newport, R.I., 4 January 1882, and endeavoring to rescue Jabez Smith, second class musician, from drowning.

2028 ◆ MILLER, HUGH

Rank: Boatswain's Mate
Service: U.S. Navy
Birthday: 1859
Place of Birth: Philadelphia, Philadelphia County, Pennsylvania
Entered Service at: Pennsylvania
Unit: U.S.S. *Quinnebaug*
Battle or Place of Action: Alexandria, Egypt
Date of Action: 21 November 1885
Citation: For jumping overboard from the U.S.S. *Quinnebaug*, at Alexandria, Egypt, on the morning of 21 November 1885 and assisting in saving a shipmate from drowning.

2029 ◆ MILLMORE, JOHN

Rank: Ordinary Seaman
Service: U.S. Navy

Birthday: 1860
Place of Birth: New York, New York
Entered Service at: New York
Unit: U.S.S. *Essex*
Battle or Place of Action: Monrovia, Liberia
Date of Action: 31 October 1877
G.O. Number, Date: 326, 18 October 1884
Citation: Serving on board the U.S.S. *Essex*, Millmore rescued from drowning John W. Powers, ordinary seaman, serving on the same vessel with him, at Monrovia, Liberia, 31 October 1877.

2030 ◆ MITCHELL, THOMAS

Rank: Landsman
Service: U.S. Navy
Birthday: 1857
Place of Birth: New York, New York
Date of Death: 18 July 1942
Cemetery: Long Island National Cemetery (M-27661)— Farmingdale, New York
Entered Service at: New York
Unit: U.S.S. *Richmond*
Battle or Place of Action: Shanghai, China
Date of Action: 17 November 1879
G.O. Number, Date: 326, 18 October 1884
Citation: Serving on board the U.S.S. *Richmond*, Mitchell rescued from drowning, M.F. Caulan, first class boy, serving with him on the same vessel, at Shanghai, China, 17 November 1879.

2031 ◆ MOORE, FRANCIS

Rank: Boatswain's Mate
Service: U.S. Navy
Birthday: 1858
Place of Birth: New York
Entered Service at: New York
Unit: U.S. Training Ship *Portsmouth*
Battle or Place of Action: Navy Yard, Washington, D.C.
Date of Action: 23 January 1882
G.O. Number, Date: 326, 18 October 1884
Citation: For jumping overboard from the U.S. training ship *Portsmouth*, at the Washington Navy Yard, 23 January 1882, and endeavoring to rescue Thomas Duncan, carpenter and caulker, who had fallen overboard.

2032 ◆ MOORE, PHILIP

Rank: Seaman
Service: U.S. Navy
Birthday: 1853
Place of Birth: Newfoundland, Canada
Entered Service at: Rhode Island
Unit: U.S.S. *Trenton*
Battle or Place of Action: Genoa, Italy
Date of Action: 21 September 1880
G.O. Number, Date: 326, 18 October 1884
Citation: For jumping overboard from the U.S.S. *Trenton*,

at Genoa, Italy, 21 September 1880, and rescuing from drowning Hans Paulsen, ordinary seaman.

2033 ◆ MORRIS, JOHN

Rank: Corporal
Service: U.S. Marine Corps
Birthday: 25 January 1855
Place of Birth: New York
Entered Service at: New York
Unit: U.S.S. *Lancaster*
Battle or Place of Action: Villefranche, France
Date of Action: 25 December 1881
G.O. Number, Date: 326, 18 October 1884
Citation: For leaping overboard from the U.S. flagship *Lancaster*, at Villefranche, France, 25 December 1881, and rescuing from drowning Robert Blizzard, ordinary seaman, a prisoner, who had jumped overboard.

2034 ◆ MORSE, WILLIAM

Rank: Seaman
Service: U.S. Navy
Birthday: 1852
Place of Birth: Germany
Entered Service at: New York
Unit: U.S.S. *Shenandoah*
Battle or Place of Action: Rio de Janeiro, Brazil
Date of Action: 19 September 1880
G.O. Number, Date: 326, 18 October 1884
Citation: For jumping overboard from the U.S.S. *Shenandoah* at Rio de Janeiro, Brazil, 19 September 1880, and rescuing from drowning James Grady, first class fireman.

2035 ◆ NOIL, JOSEPH B.

Rank: Seaman
Service: U.S. Navy
Birthday: 1841
Place of Birth: Nova Scotia, Canada
Entered Service at: New York
Unit: U.S.S. *Powhatan*
Battle or Place of Action: Norfolk, Virginia
Date of Action: 26 December 1872
Citation: Serving on board the U.S.S. *Powhatan* at Norfolk, 26 December 1872, Noil saved Boatswain J.C. Walton from drowning.

2036 ◆ NORRIS, J. W.

Rank: Landsman
Service: U.S. Navy
Birthday: 1862
Place of Birth: England
Entered Service at: New York
Unit: U.S.S. *Jamestown*
Battle or Place of Action: Navy Yard, New York
Date of Action: 20 December 1883
G.O. Number, Date: 326, 18 October 1884

Citation: Serving on board the U.S.S. *Jamestown*, New York Navy Yard, 20 December 1883, Norris rescued from drowning A.A. George, who had fallen overboard.

2037 ◆ O'CONNER, JAMES FRANCIS

True Name: O'Connor, James Francis
Rank: Landsman, Engineer's Force
Service: U.S. Navy
Birthday: 28 November 1861
Place of Birth: Portsmouth, Portsmouth County, Virginia
Date of Death: 17 September 1940
Place of Death: Portsmouth, Virginia
Cemetery: Oak Grove Cemetery (MH)—Portsmouth, Virginia
Entered Service at: Virginia
Unit: U.S.S. *Jean Sands*
Battle or Place of Action: opposite the Navy Yard, Norfolk, Virginia
Date of Action: 15 June 1880
G.O. Number, Date: 326, 18 October 1884
Citation: For jumping overboard from the U.S.S. *Jean Sands*, opposite the Norfolk Navy Yard, on the night of 15 June 1880, and rescuing from drowning a young girl who had fallen overboard.

2038 ◆ OHMSEN, AUGUST

Rank: Master-at-Arms (highest rank: Lieutenant)
Service: U.S. Navy
Birthday: 15 March 1854
Place of Birth: Lubeck, Germany
Date of Death: 13 February 1938
Place of Death: Portsmouth, Virginia
Cemetery: St. Paul's Catholic Cemetery (PM)—Portsmouth, Virginia
Entered Service at: New York
Unit: U.S.S. *Tallapoosa*
Battle or Place of Action: off Woods Hole, Massachusetts
Date of Action: 21 August 1884
G.O. Number, Date: 326, 18 October 1884
Citation: On board the U.S.S. *Tallapoosa* at the time of the sinking of that vessel, on the night of 21 August 1884. Clearing the berth deck, Ohmsen remained there until the water was waist deep, wading about with outstretched arms, rousing the men out of their hammocks. Then, going on deck, he assisted in lowering the first cutter and then the dinghy, of which he took charge.

2039 ◆ O'NEAL, JOHN

Rank: Boatswain's Mate
Service: U.S. Navy
Birthday: 1841
Place of Birth: Ireland
Entered Service at: Pennsylvania
Unit: U.S.S. *Kansas*
Battle or Place of Action: Greytown, Nicaragua
Date of Action: 12 April 1872

G.O. Number, Date: 179, 9 July 1872
Citation: Serving on board the U.S.S. *Kansas*, O'Neal displayed great coolness and self-possession at the time Comdr. A.F. Crosman and others were drowned near Greytown, Nicaragua, 12 April 1872, and by personal exertion prevented greater loss of life.

2040 ◆ OSBORNE, JOHN

Rank: Seaman
Service: U.S. Navy
Birthday: 1844
Place of Birth: New Orleans, Orleans County, Louisiana
Date of Death: 23 April 1920
Cemetery: Arlington National Cemetery (17-19689) (MH)—Arlington, Virginia
Entered Service at: Louisiana
Unit: U.S.S. *Juniata*
Battle or Place of Action: Philadelphia, Pennsylvania
Date of Action: 21 August 1876
G.O. Number, Date: 218, 24 August 1876
Citation: Serving on board the U.S.S. *Juniata*, Osborne displayed gallant conduct in rescuing from drowning an enlisted boy of that vessel, at Philadelphia, Pa., 21 August 1876.

2041 ◆ OSEPINS, CHRISTIAN

Rank: Seaman
Service: U.S. Navy
Birthday: 1858
Place of Birth: Holland
Entered Service at: New York
Unit: U.S. Tug *Fortune*
Battle or Place of Action: Hampton Roads, Virginia
Date of Action: 7 May 1882
G.O. Number, Date: 326, 18 October 1884
Citation: For jumping overboard from the U.S. Tug *Fortune*, 7 May 1882, at Hampton Roads, Va., and rescuing from drowning James Walters, gunner's mate.

2042 ◆ PARKER, ALEXANDER

Rank: Boatswain's Mate
Service: U.S. Navy
Birthday: 1832
Place of Birth: Kensington, New Jersey
Entered Service at: New Jersey
Battle or Place of Action: Mare Island Navy Yard, California
Date of Action: 25 July 1876
G.O. Number, Date: 215, 9 August 1876
Citation: For gallant conduct in attempting to save a shipmate from drowning at the Navy Yard, Mare Island, Cal., on 25 July 1876.

2043 ◆ PILE, RICHARD

Rank: Ordinary Seaman
Service: U.S. Navy

Birthday: 1849
Place of Birth: West Indies
Entered Service at: Massachusetts
Unit: U.S.S. *Kansas*
Battle or Place of Action: Greytown, Nicaragua
Date of Action: 12 April 1872
G.O. Number, Date: 179, 9 July 1872
Citation: Serving on board the U.S.S. *Kansas*, Pile displayed great coolness and self-possession at the time Comdr. A.F. Crosman and others were drowned near Greytown, Nicaragua, 12 April 1872, and by his extraordinary heroism and personal exertion prevented greater loss of life.

2044 ◆ REGAN, PATRICK

Rank: Ordinary Seaman
Service: U.S. Navy
Birthday: 1852
Place of Birth: Queenstown, County Cork, Ireland
Entered Service at: New York
Unit: U.S.S. *Pensacola*
Battle or Place of Action: in the harbor of Coquimbo, Chile
Date of Action: 30 July 1873
Citation: Serving on board the U.S.S. *Pensacola*, Regan displayed gallant conduct in the harbor of Coquimbo, Chile, 30 July 1873.

2045 ◆ ROUNING, JOHANNES

Rank: Ordinary Seaman
Service: U.S. Navy
Unit: U.S. Tug *Fortune*
Battle or Place of Action: Hampton Roads, Virginia
Date of Action: 7 May 1882
G.O. Number, Date: 326, 18 October 1884
Citation: For jumping overboard from the U.S. tug *Fortune*, 7 May 1882, at Hampton Roads, Va., and rescuing from drowning James Walters, gunner's mate.

2046 ◆ RUSSELL, JOHN

Rank: Seaman
Service: U.S. Navy
Birthday: 1852
Place of Birth: New York, New York
Entered Service at: New York
Unit: U.S.S. *Trenton*
Battle or Place of Action: Genoa, Italy
Date of Action: 21 September 1880
G.O. Number, Date: 326, 18 October 1884
Citation: For jumping overboard from the U.S.S. *Trenton*, at Genoa, Italy, 21 September 1880, and rescuing from drowning Hans Paulsen, ordinary seaman.

2047 ◆ RYAN, RICHARD

Rank: Ordinary Seaman
Service: U.S. Navy

Birthday: 1851
Place of Birth: Connecticut
Entered Service at: Connecticut
Unit: U.S.S. *Hartford*
Battle or Place of Action: Norfolk, Virginia
Date of Action: 4 March 1876
G.O. Number, Date: 207, 23 March 1876
Citation: Serving on board the U.S.S. *Hartford*, Ryan displayed gallant conduct in jumping overboard at Norfolk, Va., and rescuing from drowning one of the crew of that vessel, 4 March 1876.

2048 ◆ SADLER, WILLIAM

Rank: Captain of the Top
Service: U.S. Navy
Birthday: 1854
Place of Birth: Boston, Suffolk County, Massachusetts
Entered Service at: Massachusetts
Unit: U.S.S. *Saratoga*
Battle or Place of Action: off Coasters Harbor Island, Newport, Rhode Island
Date of Action: 25 June 1881
G.O. Number, Date: 326, 18 October 1884
Citation: For jumping overboard from the U.S.S. *Saratoga*, off Coasters Harbor Island, R.I., 25 June 1881, and sustaining until picked up by a boat from the ship, Frank Gallagher, second class boy, who had fallen overboard.

2049 ◆ SAPP, ISAAC

Rank: Seaman, Engineer's Force
Service: U.S. Navy
Birthday: 1844
Place of Birth: Philadelphia, Philadelphia County, Pennsylvania
Entered Service at: Pennsylvania
Unit: U.S.S. *Shenandoah*
Battle or Place of Action: Villefranche, France
Date of Action: 15 December 1871
G.O. Number, Date: 169, 8 February 1872
Citation: On board the U.S.S. *Shenandoah* during the rescue of a shipmate at Villefranche, 15 December 1871. Jumping overboard, Sapp gallantly assisted in saving Charles Prince, seaman, from drowning.

2050 ◆ SIMPSON, D. HENRY LAKIN

True Name: Simpson, Henry
Rank: Fireman First Class
Service: U.S. Navy
Birthday: 1859
Place of Birth: London, England
Entered Service at: New York
Unit: U.S.S. *Essex*
Battle or Place of Action: Monrovia, Liberia
Date of Action: 31 October 1877
G.O. Number, Date: 326, 18 October 1884
Citation: For rescuing from drowning John W. Powers,

ordinary seaman on board the U.S.S. *Essex*, at Monrovia, Liberia, 31 October 1877.

2051 ◆ SMITH, JAMES

Rank: Seaman
Service: U.S. Navy
Birthday: 1838
Place of Birth: Hawaiian Islands
Entered Service at: New York
Unit: U.S.S. *Kansas*
Battle or Place of Action: Greytown, Nicaragua
Date of Action: 12 April 1872
G.O. Number, Date: 176, 9 July 1872
Citation: Serving on board the U.S.S. *Kansas*, Smith displayed great coolness and self-possession at the time Comdr. A. F. Crosman and others were drowned near Greytown, Nicaragua, 12 April 1872, and by extraordinary heroism and personal exertion, prevented greater loss of life.

2052 ◆ SMITH, JOHN

Rank: Seaman
Service: U.S. Navy
Birthday: 1854
Place of Birth: Bermuda
Entered Service at: New York
Unit: U.S.S. *Shenandoah*
Battle or Place of Action: Rio de Janeiro, Brazil
Date of Action: 19 September 1880
G.O. Number, Date: 326, 18 October 1884
Citation: For jumping overboard from the U.S.S. *Shenandoah*, at Rio de Janeiro, Brazil, 19 September 1880, and rescuing from drowning James Grady, first class fireman.

2053 ◆ SMITH, THOMAS

Rank: Seaman
Service: U.S. Navy
Birthday: 1856
Place of Birth: Ireland
Entered Service at: Virginia
Unit: U.S.S. *Enterprise*
Battle or Place of Action: off Para, Brazil
Date of Action: 1 October 1878
Citation: For rescuing from drowning William Kent, coxswain of the U.S.S. *Enterprise*, off Para, Brazil, 1 October 1878.

2054 ◆ STEWART, JAMES A.

Rank: Corporal (highest rank: Sergeant)
Service: U.S. Marine Corps
Birthday: 1839
Place of Birth: Philadelphia, Philadelphia County, Pennsylvania
Entered Service at: Pennsylvania
Unit: U.S.S. *Plymouth*
Battle or Place of Action: Villefranche Harbor, France

Date of Action: 1 February 1872
G.O. Number, Date: 180, 10 October 1872
Citation: Serving on board the U.S.S. *Plymouth*, Stewart jumped overboard in the harbor of Villefranche, France, 1 February 1872 and saved Midshipman Osterhaus from drowning.

2055 ◆ SULLIVAN, JAMES F.

Rank: Boatswain's Mate
Service: U.S. Navy
Birthday: 1857
Place of Birth: Lowell, Middlesex County, Massachusetts
Entered Service at: Massachusetts
Unit: U.S. Training Ship *New Hampshire*
Battle or Place of Action: Newport, Rhode Island
Date of Action: 21 April 1882
G.O. Number, Date: 326, 18 October 1884
Citation: For jumping overboard from the U.S. training ship *New Hampshire*, at Newport, R.I., 21 April 1882, and rescuing from drowning Francis T. Price, third class boy.

2056 ◆ SWEENEY, ROBERT AUGUSTUS✣

Rank: Ordinary Seaman
Service: U.S. Navy
Birthday: 20 February 1853
Place of Birth: Montserrat, West Indies
Date of Death: 19 December 1890
Cemetery: Calvary Cemetery (unknown grave)—Woodside, New York
Entered Service at: New Jersey
Unit: U.S.S. *Kearsarge*—U.S.S. *Yantic*
Battle or Place of Action: Hampton Roads, Virginia & Navy Yard, New York
Date of Action: 26 October 1881 & 20 December 1883
G.O. Number, Date: 326, 18 October 1884
Citation: **First Award** Serving on board the U.S.S. *Kearsarge*, at Hampton Roads, Va., 26 October 1881, Sweeney jumped overboard and assisted in saving from drowning a shipmate who had fallen overboard into a strongly running tide. **Second Award** Serving on board the U.S.S. *Yantic*, at the Navy Yard, New York, 20 December 1883, Sweeney rescued from drowning A.A. George, who had fallen overboard from the U.S.S. *Jamestown*.
Notes: ✣Double Awardee

2057 ◆ SWEENEY, WILLIAM

Rank: Landsman, Engineer's Force
Service: U.S. Navy
Birthday: 1856
Place of Birth: Boston, Suffolk County, Massachusetts
Entered Service at: Massachusetts
Unit: U.S.S. *Jean Sands*
Battle or Place of Action: opposite the Navy Yard, Norfolk, Virginia
Date of Action: 15 June 1880
G.O. Number, Date: 326, 18 October 1884

Citation: For jumping overboard from the U.S.S. *Jean Sands*, opposite the Navy Yard, Norfolk, Va., on the night of 15 June 1880, and rescuing from drowning a young girl who had fallen overboard.

2058 ◆ TAYLOR, RICHARD HAMILTON

Rank: Quartermaster (highest rank: Schoolmaster)
Service: U.S. Navy
Birthday: 8 September 1870
Place of Birth: Staunton, Staunton County, Virginia
Date of Death: 24 March 1956
Place of Death: Holy Ghost Hospital, Cambridge, Massachusetts
Cemetery: Evergreen Cemetery—Boston, Massachusetts
Entered Service at: Virginia
Unit: U.S.S. *Nipsic*
Battle or Place of Action: Apia, Samoa
Date of Action: 19 March 1889
G.O. Number, Date: 157, 20 April 1904
Place of Presentation: The White House, presented by Pres. Theodore Roosevelt
Citation: Serving on board the U.S.S. *Nipsic*, Taylor displayed gallantry during the hurricane at Apia, Samoa, 16 March 1889.

2059 ◆ THAYER, JAMES

Rank: Ship's Corporal
Service: U.S. Navy
Birthday: 1853
Place of Birth: Ireland
Entered Service at: Pennsylvania
Unit: U.S.S. *Constitution*
Battle or Place of Action: Navy Yard, Norfolk, Virginia
Date of Action: 16 November 1879
G.O. Number, Date: 326, 18 October 1884
Citation: For rescuing from drowning a boy serving with him on the U.S.S. *Constitution*, at the Navy Yard, Norfolk, Va., 16 November 1879.

2060 ◆ THOMPSON, HENRY

Rank: Seaman
Service: U.S. Navy
Battle or Place of Action: Mare Island, California
Date of Action: 27 June 1878
Citation: For rescuing a man from drowning at Mare Island, Cal., 27 June 1878.

2061 ◆ THORNTON, MICHAEL

Rank: Seaman
Service: U.S. Navy
Birthday: 1856
Place of Birth: Ireland
Entered Service at: Pennsylvania
Unit: U.S. Tug *Leyden*
Battle or Place of Action: near Boston, Massachusetts

Date of Action: 26 August 1881
G.O. Number, Date: 326, 18 October 1884
Citation: For jumping overboard from the U.S. Tug *Leyden*, near Boston, Mass., 26 August 1881, and sustaining until picked up Michael Drennan, landsman, who had jumped overboard while temporarily insane.

2062 ◆ TOBIN, PAUL

Rank: Landsman
Service: U.S. Navy
Place of Birth: Plybin, France
Entered Service at: Brest, France
Unit: U.S.S. *Plymouth*
Battle or Place of Action: Hamburg Harbor, Germany
Date of Action: 3 July 1871
G.O. Number, Date: 180, 10 October 1872
Citation: On board the U.S.S. *Plymouth*, Hamburg Harbor, 3 July 1871. Jumping overboard at the imminent risk of his life, Tobin, with a comrade, rescued from drowning one of a party who was thrown from a shore boat into a four-knot running tide while the boat was coming alongside the ship.

2063 ◆ TROUT, JAMES M.

Rank: Fireman Second Class
Service: U.S. Navy
Birthday: 1850
Place of Birth: Philadelphia, Philadelphia County, Pennsylvania
Entered Service at: Pennsylvania
Unit: U.S.S. *Frolic*
Battle or Place of Action: Montevideo, Uruguay
Date of Action: 20 April 1877
Citation: Serving on board the U.S.S. *Frolic*, Trout displayed gallant conduct in endeavoring to save the life of one of the crew of that vessel who had fallen overboard at Montevideo, 20 April 1877.

2064 ◆ TROY, JEREMIAH

Rank: Chief Boatswain's Mate
Service: U.S. Navy
Birthday: 1845
Place of Birth: New York, New York
Entered Service at: New York
Unit: U.S. Training Ship *New Hampshire*
Battle or Place of Action: Newport, Rhode Island
Date of Action: 21 April 1882
G.O. Number, Date: 326, 18 October 1884
Citation: For jumping overboard from the U.S. training ship *New Hampshire*, at Newport, R.I., 21 April 1882, and rescuing from drowning Francis T. Price, third class boy.

2065 ◆ TURVELIN, ALEXANDER HAURE

Rank: Seaman
Service: U.S. Navy
Birthday: 1847

Place of Birth: Russia
Unit: U.S.S. *Trenton*
Battle or Place of Action: Toulon, France
Date of Action: February 1881
G.O. Number, Date: 326, 18 October 1884
Citation: For jumping overboard from the U.S.S. *Trenton*, at Toulon, France, February 1881, and rescuing from drowning Augustus Ohlensen, coxswain.

2066 ◆ WEISBOGEL, ALBERT✛

Rank: Captain of the Mizzen Top (highest rank: Petty Officer)
Service: U.S. Navy
Birthday: 1844
Place of Birth: New Orleans, Orleans County, Louisiana
Entered Service at: Louisiana
Unit: U.S.S. *Benicia*—U.S.S. *Plymouth*
Battle or Place of Action: at Sea
Date of Action: 11 January 1874 & 27 April 1876
G.O. Number, Date: 207, 23 March 1876 & 212, 9 June 1876
Citation: **First Award** For gallant conduct in jumping overboard from the U.S.S. *Benicia*, at sea, and rescuing from drowning one of the crew of that vessel, 11 January 1874. **Second Award** For gallant conduct in jumping overboard from the U.S.S. *Plymouth*, at sea, and rescuing from drowning one of the crew of that vessel on 27 April 1876.
Notes: ✛Double Awardee

2067 ◆ WEISSEL, ADAM

Rank: Ship's Cook
Service: U.S. Navy
Birthday: 1854
Place of Birth: Germany
Date of Death: 10 December 1928
Place of Death: Berkeley, California
Cemetery: Mountain View Cemetery—Oakland, California
Entered Service at: New York
Unit: U.S. Training Ship *Minnesota*
Battle or Place of Action: Newport, Rhode Island
Date of Action: 26 August 1881
G.O. Number, Date: 326, 18 October 1884
Citation: For jumping overboard from the U.S. training ship *Minnesota*, Newport, R.I., 26 August 1881, and sustaining until picked up by a boat from the ship, C. Lorenze, captain of the forecastle, who had fallen overboard.

2068 ◆ WILLIAMS, ANTONIO

Rank: Seaman
Service: U.S. Navy
Birthday: 1825
Place of Birth: Malta
Unit: U.S.S. *Huron*
Date of Action: 24 November 1877
Citation: For courage and fidelity displayed in the loss of the U.S.S. *Huron*, 24 November 1877.

2069 ◆ WILLIAMS, HENRY

Rank: Carpenter's Mate (highest rank: Carpenter)
Service: U.S. Navy
Birthday: 6 February 1834
Place of Birth: Canada
Date of Death: 17 October 1917
Place of Death: Wildwood Crest, New Jersey
Cemetery: West Laurel Cemetery—Bala-Cynwyd, Pennsylvania
Entered Service at: Pennsylvania
Unit: U.S.S. *Constitution*
Battle or Place of Action: at sea, northeast Atlantic, west of the English Channel
Date of Action: 13 February 1879
G.O. Number, Date: 326, 18 October 1884
Date of Presentation: 7 September 1879
Place of Presentation: On board the U.S.S. *Constitution* at the New York Navy Yard, presented by Lt. Commander Theodore F. Jewell, executive officer
Citation: For going over the stern of the U.S.S. *Constitution*, at sea, 13 February 1879, during a heavy gale, and performing important carpenter's work upon her rudder.

2070 ◆ WILLIAMS, LOUIS✛

True Name: Olsen, Ludwig Andreas
Rank: Captain of the Hold
Service: U.S. Navy
Birthday: 1845
Place of Birth: Christiana (now Oslo), Norway
Date of Death: 20 February 1886
Cemetery: Cypress Hills National Cemetery (G-42616) (MH)—Brooklyn, New York
Entered Service at: California
Unit: U.S.S. *Lackawanna*
Battle or Place of Action: Honolulu, Territory of Hawaii & Callao, Peru
Date of Action: 16 March 1883 & 13 June 1884

G.O. Number, Date: 326, 18 October 1884 (2nd award)
Citation: **First Award** For jumping overboard from the U.S.S. *Lackawanna*, 16 March 1883, at Honolulu, T.H., and rescuing from drowning Thomas Moran, landsman. **Second Award** Serving on board the U.S.S. *Lackawanna*, Williams rescued from drowning William Cruise, who had fallen overboard at Callao, Peru, 13 June 1884.
Notes: ✛Double Awardee

2071 ◆ WILLIS, GEORGE

Rank: Coxswain
Service: U.S. Navy
Birthday: 1839
Place of Birth: Boston, Suffolk County, Massachusetts
Entered Service at: Massachusetts
Unit: U.S.S. *Tigress*
Battle or Place of Action: off the coast of Greenland
Date of Action: 22 September 1873
Citation: Serving on board the U.S.S. *Tigress*, Willis displayed gallant and meritorious conduct on the night of 22 September 1873 off the coast of Greenland.

2072 ◆ WILSON, AUGUST

Rank: Boilermaker
Service: U.S. Navy
Birthday: 1864
Place of Birth: Danzig, Germany
Entered Service at: New York
Unit: U.S.S. *Puritan*
Date of Action: 1 July 1897
G.O. Number, Date: 482, 1 November 1897
Citation: For gallant conduct while serving on board the U.S.S. *Puritan* and at the time of the collapse of one of the crown sheets of boiler E on that vessel, 1 July 1897. Wrapping wet cloths about his face and arms, Wilson entered the fireroom and opened the safety valve, thus removing the danger of disabling the other boilers.

SPANISH-AMERICAN WAR

2073 ◆ BAKER, BENJAMIN F.

Rank: Coxswain (highest rank: Chief Master-at-Arms)
Service: U.S. Navy
Birthday: 12 March 1862
Place of Birth: Dennis Port, Barnstable County, Massachusetts
Date of Death: 19 May 1927
Place of Death: Dennisport, Massachusetts
Cemetery: Old Swan Lake Cemetery (MH)—Dennisport, Massachusetts
Unit: U.S.S. *Nashville*
Battle or Place of Action: Cienfuegos, Cuba
Date of Action: 11 May 1898
G.O. Number, Date: 521, 7 July 1899
Citation: On board the U.S.S. *Nashville* during the cutting of the cable leading from Cienfuegos, Cuba, 11 May 1898. Facing the heavy fire of the enemy, Baker set an example of extraordinary bravery and coolness throughout this action.

2074 ◆ BAKER JR., EDWARD LEE

Rank: Sergeant Major (highest rank: Captain)
Service: U.S. Army
Birthday: 28 December 1865
Place of Birth: Platte River, Laramie County, Wyoming
Date of Death: 26 August 1913
Place of Death: Presido of San Francisco, California
Cemetery: Rosedale Cemetery—Los Angeles, California
Entered Service at: Cincinnati, Hamilton County, Ohio
Unit: 10th U.S. Cavalry
Battle or Place of Action: Santiago, Cuba
Date of Action: 1 July 1898
Date of Issue: 3 July 1902
Citation: Left cover and, under fire, rescued a wounded comrade from drowning.

2075 ◆ BARROW, DAVID DUFFY

Rank: Seaman (highest rank: Coxswain)
Service: U.S. Navy
Birthday: 22 July 1876
Place of Birth: Reelsboro, North Carolina
Date of Death: 6 December 1948
Place of Death: Richmond, Virginia
Cemetery: Evergreen Memorial Cemetery (MH)—Portsmouth, Virginia
Entered Service at: Norfolk, Norfolk County, Virginia
Unit: U.S.S. *Nashville*

Battle or Place of Action: Cienfuegos, Cuba
Date of Action: 11 May 1898
G.O. Number, Date: 521, 7 July 1899
Citation: On board the U.S.S. *Nashville* during the cutting of the cable leading from Cienfuegos, Cuba, 11 May 1898. Facing the heavy fire of the enemy, Barrow set an example of extraordinary bravery and coolness throughout this action.

2076 ◆ BELL, DENNIS

Rank: Private
Service: U.S. Army
Birthday: 28 December 1866
Place of Birth: Washington, D.C.
Date of Death: 25 September 1953
Place of Death: Washington, D.C.
Cemetery: Arlington National Cemetery (31-349) (MH)—Arlington, Virginia
Entered Service at: Washington, D.C.
Unit: Troop H, 10th U.S. Cavalry
Battle or Place of Action: Tayabacoa, Cuba
Date of Action: 30 June 1898
Date of Issue: 23 June 1899
Citation: Voluntarily went ashore in the face of the enemy and aided in the rescue of his wounded comrades; this after several previous attempts at rescue had been frustrated.

2077 ◆ BENNETT, JAMES HARVEY

Rank: Chief Boatswain's Mate
Service: U.S. Navy
Birthday: 5 April 1851
Place of Birth: Haverstraw, Rockland County, New York
Entered Service at: New York
Unit: U.S.S. *Marblehead*
Battle or Place of Action: Cienfuegos, Cuba
Date of Action: 11 May 1898
G.O. Number, Date: 521, 7 July 1899
Citation: On board the U.S.S. *Marblehead* during the cutting of the cable leading from Cienfuegos, Cuba, 11 May 1898. Facing the heavy fire of the enemy, Bennett set an example of extraordinary bravery and coolness throughout this action.

2078 ◆ BERG, GEORGE FRANCIS

Rank: Private (highest rank: Master Sergeant Ret.)
Service: U.S. Army
Birthday: 2 December 1868

Place of Birth: Mount Erie, Wayne County, Illinois
Date of Death: 27 November 1945
Place of Death: Washington, D.C.
Cemetery: Mount Pleasant Cemetery (MH)—South Portland, Maine
Entered Service at: Fort Omaha, Douglas County, Nebraska
Unit: Company C, 17th U.S. Infantry
Battle or Place of Action: El Caney, Cuba
Date of Action: 1 July 1898
Date of Issue: 17 October 1927
Citation: Gallantly assisted in the rescue of the wounded from in front of the lines and while under heavy fire of the enemy.

2079 ◆ BEYER, ALBERT

Rank: Coxswain (highest rank: Chief Master-of-Arms)
Service: U.S. Navy
Birthday: 13 June 1859
Place of Birth: Hanover, Germany
Date of Death: 29 October 1929
Place of Death: Philadelphia, Pennsylvania
Cemetery: Mount Moriah Cemetery (VA Plot USN-1-9-2) (MH)—Philadelphia, Pennsylvania
Entered Service at: Boston, Suffolk County, Massachusetts
Unit: U.S.S. *Nashville*
Battle or Place of Action: Cienfuegos, Cuba
Date of Action: 11 May 1898
G.O. Number, Date: 521, 7 July 1899
Citation: On board the U.S.S. *Nashville* during the cutting of the cable leading from Cienfuegos, Cuba, 11 May 1898. Facing the heavy fire of the enemy, Beyer set an example of extraordinary bravery and coolness throughout this action.

2080 ◆ BLUME, ROBERT

Rank: Seaman (highest rank: Chief Boatswain's Mate)
Service: U.S. Navy
Birthday: 19 November 1868
Place of Birth: Pittsburgh, Allegheny County, Pennsylvania
Date of Death: 16 September 1937
Cemetery: Arlington National Cemetery (6-9752-SS) (MH)—Arlington, Virginia
Entered Service at: New Jersey
Unit: U.S.S. *Nashville*
Battle or Place of Action: Cienfuegos, Cuba
Date of Action: 11 May 1898
G.O. Number, Date: 521, 7 July 1899
Citation: On board the U.S.S. *Nashville* during the cutting of the cable leading from Cienfuegos, Cuba, 11 May 1898. Facing the heavy fire of the enemy, Blume set an example of extraordinary bravery and coolness throughout this action.

2081 ◆ BRADY, GEORGE F.

Rank: Chief Gunner's Mate
Service: U.S. Navy
Birthday: 7 September 1867
Place of Birth: Ireland

Entered Service at: New York
Unit: U.S.S. *Winslow*
Battle or Place of Action: Cardenas, Cuba
Date of Action: 11 May 1898
G.O. Number, Date: 497, 3 September 1899
Citation: On board the torpedo Boat *Winslow* during the actions at Cardenas, Cuba, 11 May 1989. Conspicuously gallant during this period, Brady, by his energy in assisting to sustain fire, his efforts to repair the steering gear and his promptness in maintaining watertight integrity, was largely instrumental in saving the vessel.

2082 ◆ BRIGHT, GEORGE WASHINGTON

Rank: Coal Passer
Service: U.S. Navy
Birthday: 27 December 1874
Place of Birth: Norfolk, Norfolk County, Virginia
Date of Death: 20 March 1949
Place of Death: Richmond, Virginia
Cemetery: Blanford Cemetery—Petersburg, Virginia
Entered Service at: Virginia
Unit: U.S.S. *Nashville*
Battle or Place of Action: Cienfuegos, Cuba
Date of Action: 11 May 1898
G.O. Number, Date: 521, 7 July 1899
Citation: On board the U.S.S. *Nashville* during the cutting of the cable leading from Cienfuegos, Cuba, 11 May 1898. Facing the heavy fire of the enemy, Bright set an example of extraordinary bravery and coolness throughout this action.

2083 ◆ BROOKIN, OSCAR

True Name: Brookins, Oscar
Rank: Private
Service: U.S. Army
Birthday: 19 July 1869
Place of Birth: Byron, Fond Du Lac County, Wisconsin
Date of Death: 18 August 1938
Cemetery: Sunset Cemetery (MH)—Galloway, Ohio
Entered Service at: Green County, Ohio
Unit: Company C, 17th U.S. Infantry
Battle or Place of Action: El Caney, Cuba
Date of Action: 1 July 1898
Date of Issue: 21 June 1899
Citation: Gallantly assisted in the rescue of the wounded from in front of the lines and under heavy fire from the enemy.

2084 ◆ BUZZARD, ULYSSES G.

Rank: Private (highest rank: Sergeant)
Service: U.S. Army
Birthday: 31 January 1865
Place of Birth: Armstrong, Pennsylvania
Date of Death: 2 August 1939
Place of Death: Philippine Islands
Cemetery: San Nicolas Cemetery American Lot—Cebu City, Philippine Islands

Entered Service at: Pittsburgh, Allegheny County, Pennsylvania
Unit: Company C, 17th U.S. Infantry
Battle or Place of Action: El Caney, Cuba
Date of Action: 1 July 1898
Date of Issue: 24 June 1899
Citation: Gallantly assisted in the rescue of the wounded from in front of the lines and under heavy fire from the enemy.

2085 ◆ CAMPBELL, DANIEL J.

Rank: Private
Service: U.S. Marine Corps
Birthday: 26 December 1874
Place of Birth: Prince Edward Island, Canada
Date of Death: 28 April 1955
Cemetery: Mount Hope Cemetery (MH)—Mattapan, Massachusetts
Entered Service at: Boston, Suffolk County, Massachusetts
Unit: U.S.S. *Marblehead*
Battle or Place of Action: Cienfuegos, Cuba
Date of Action: 11 May 1898
G.O. Number, Date: 521, 7 July 1899
Citation: On board the U.S.S. *Marblehead* during the cutting of the cable leading from Cienfuegos, Cuba, 11 May 1898. Facing the heavy fire of the enemy, Campbell set an example of extraordinary bravery and coolness throughout this action.

2086 ◆ CANTRELL, CHARLES P.

Rank: Private
Service: U.S. Army
Birthday: 13 February 1874
Place of Birth: Smithville, Dekalb County, Tennessee
Date of Death: 3 August 1948
Cemetery: Nashville National Cemetery (I-132) (MH)—Madison, Tennessee
Entered Service at: Nashville, Davidson County, Tennessee
Unit: Company F, 10th U.S. Infantry
Battle or Place of Action: Santiago, Cuba
Date of Action: 1 July 1898
Citation: Gallantly assisted in the rescue of the wounded from in front of the lines and under heavy fire from the enemy.

2087 ◆ CARTER, JOSEPH EDWARD

Rank: Blacksmith
Service: U.S. Navy
Birthday: 15 August 1875
Place of Birth: Manchester, Greater Manchester County, England
Date of Death: 19 June 1950
Cemetery: Arlington National Cemetery (34-2631-1) (MH)—Arlington, Virginia
Entered Service at: North Dakota
Unit: U.S.S. *Marblehead*
Battle or Place of Action: Cienfuegos, Cuba

Date of Action: 11 May 1898
G.O. Number, Date: 521, 7 July 1899
Citation: On board the U.S.S. *Marblehead* during the operation of cutting the cable leading from Cienfuegos, Cuba, 11 May 1898. Facing the heavy fire of the enemy, Carter set an example of extraordinary bravery and coolness throughout this action.

2088 ◆ CHADWICK, LEONARD B.

Rank: Apprentice First Class (highest rank: Gunner's Mate Third Class)
Service: U.S. Navy
Birthday: 24 November 1878
Place of Birth: Middletown, New Castle County, Delaware
Date of Death: 18 May 1940
Place of Death: Boston, Massachusetts
Cemetery: Mount Hope Cemetery (MH)—Mattapan, Massachusetts
Entered Service at: Delaware
Unit: U.S.S. *Marblehead*
Battle or Place of Action: Cienfuegos, Cuba
Date of Action: 11 May 1898
G.O. Number, Date: 521, 7 July 1899
Citation: On board the U.S.S. *Marblehead* during the operation of cutting the cable leading from Cienfuegos, Cuba, 11 May 1898. Facing the heavy fire of the enemy, Chadwick set an example of extraordinary bravery and coolness throughout this period.

2089 ◆ CHARETTE, GEORGE

Rank: Gunner's Mate First Class (highest rank: Lieutenant)
Service: U.S. Navy
Birthday: 6 June 1867
Place of Birth: Lowell, Middlesex County, Massachusetts
Date of Death: 7 February 1938
Cemetery: Arlington National Cemetery (7-10222)—Arlington, Virginia
Entered Service at: Lowell, Middlesex County, Massachusetts
Unit: U.S.S. *Merrimac*—assigned to the U.S.S. *New York*
Battle or Place of Action: harbor entrance, Santiago de Cuba, Cuba
Date of Action: 3 June 1898
G.O. Number, Date: 529, 2 November 1899
Citation: In connection with the sinking of the U.S.S. *Merrimac* at the entrance to the harbor of Santiago de Cuba, 2 June 1898. Despite heavy fire from the Spanish batteries, Charette displayed extraordinary heroism throughout this operation.
Notes: POW

2090 ◆ CHURCH, JAMES ROBB

Rank: Assistant Surgeon (highest rank: Colonel)
Service: U.S. Army
Birthday: 1866
Place of Birth: Chicago, Cook County, Illinois

Date of Death: 18 May 1923
Cemetery: Arlington National Cemetery (3-1409A)—Arlington, Virginia
Entered Service at: Washington, D.C.
Unit: 1st U.S. Volunteer Cavalry
Battle or Place of Action: Las Guasimas, Cuba
Date of Action: 24 June 1898
Date of Presentation: 10 January 1906
Place of Presentation: The White House, presented by Pres. Theodore Roosevelt
Citation: In addition to performing gallantly the duties pertaining to his position, voluntarily and unaided carried several seriously wounded men from the firing line to a secure position in the rear, in each instance being subjected to a very heavy fire and great exposure and danger.

2091 ◆ CLAUSEN, CLAUS KRISTIAN RANDOLPH

Rank: Coxswain (highest rank: Lieutenant)
Service: U.S. Navy
Birthday: 9 December 1869
Place of Birth: Denmark
Date of Death: 23 December 1958
Place of Death: St. Albans, New York
Cemetery: U.S. Columbarium—Middle Village, New York
Entered Service at: New York
Unit: U.S.S. *Merrimac*—assigned to the U.S.S. *New York*
Battle or Place of Action: harbor entrance, Santiago de Cuba, Cuba
Date of Action: 3 June 1898
G.O. Number, Date: 529, 2 November 1899
Citation: In connection with the sinking of the U.S.S. *Merrimac* at the entrance to the harbor of Santiago de Cuba, 2 June 1898. Despite heavy fire from the Spanish batteries, Clausen displayed extraordinary heroism throughout this operation.
Notes: POW

2092 ◆ COONEY, THOMAS C.

Rank: Chief Machinist (highest rank: Chief Carpenter)
Service: U.S. Navy
Birthday: 18 July 1853
Place of Birth: Westport, Nova Scotia, Canada
Date of Death: 8 January 1907
Place of Death: Norfolk, Virginia
Cemetery: U.S. Naval Academy Cemetery (Lot 254)—Annapolis, Maryland
Entered Service at: New Jersey
Unit: U.S. Torpedo Boat *Winslow*
Battle or Place of Action: Cardenas, Cuba
Date of Action: 11 May 1898
G.O. Number, Date: 497, 3 September 1898
Citation: On board the U.S. torpedo boat *Winslow* during the actions at Cardenas, Cuba, 11 May 1898. Following the piercing of the boiler by an enemy shell, Cooney, by his gallantry and promptness in extinguishing the resulting flames, saved the boiler tubes from burning out.

2093 ◆ CROUSE, WILLIAM ADOLPHUS

Rank: Watertender (highest rank: Chief Commissary Steward)
Service: U.S. Navy
Birthday: 22 October 1866
Place of Birth: Tannettsburg, Franklin County, Pennsylvania
Date of Death: 27 June 1941
Place of Death: Harrisburg, Pennsylvania
Cemetery: Arlington Cemetery—Drexel Hill, Pennsylvania
Entered Service at: Pennsylvania
Unit: U.S.S. *Concord*
Battle or Place of Action: off Cavite, Manila Bay, Philippine Islands
Date of Action: 21 May 1898
G.O. Number, Date: 502, 14 December 1898
Citation: On board the U.S.S. *Concord* off Cavite, Manila Bay, P.I., 21 May 1898. Following the blowing-out of a lower manhole plate joint on boiler B of that vessel, Crouse hauled the fires in the hot, vapor-filled atmosphere, which necessitated the playing of water into the fireroom from a hose.

2094 ◆ CUMMINS, ANDREW JOHNSON

Rank: Sergeant
Service: U.S. Army
Birthday: 1868
Place of Birth: Alexandria, Madison County, Indiana
Date of Death: 15 September 1923
Cemetery: Lewiston Cemetery—Lewiston, Montana
Entered Service at: Alexandria, Madison County, Indiana
Unit: Company F, 10th U.S. Infantry
Battle or Place of Action: Santiago, Cuba
Date of Action: 1 July 1898
Date of Issue: 22 June 1899
Citation: Gallantly assisted in the rescue of the wounded from in front of the lines and under heavy fire from the enemy.

2095 ◆ DAVIS, JOHN

Rank: Gunner's Mate Third Class (highest rank: Captain)
Service: U.S. Navy
Birthday: 28 October 1877
Place of Birth: Germany
Date of Death: 9 June 1970
Place of Death: St. Petersburg, Florida
Cemetery: Arlington National Cemetery (11-639-SS) (MH)—Arlington, Virginia
Entered Service at: New York, New York
Unit: U.S.S. *Marblehead*
Battle or Place of Action: Cienfuegos, Cuba
Date of Action: 11 May 1898
G.O. Number, Date: 521, 7 July 1899
Citation: On board the U.S.S. *Marblehead* during the operation of cutting the cable leading from Cienfuegos, Cuba, 11 May 1898. Facing the heavy fire of the enemy, Davis set an example of extraordinary bravery and coolness throughout this action.

2096 ◆ DEIGNAN, OSBORN WARREN

Rank: Coxswain (highest rank: Boatswain)
Service: U.S. Navy
Birthday: 24 February 1877
Place of Birth: Stuart, Guthrie County, Iowa
Date of Death: 16 April 1916
Place of Death: Cannon City, Colorado
Cemetery: Forest Lawn Memorial Park—Glendale, California
Entered Service at: Iowa
Unit: U.S.S. *Merrimac*
Battle or Place of Action: harbor entrance, Santiago de Cuba, Cuba
Date of Action: 3 June 1898
G.O. Number, Date: 529, 2 November 1899
Citation: In connection with the sinking of the U.S.S. *Merrimac* at the entrance to the harbor of Santiago de Cuba, 2 June 1898. Despite heavy fire from the Spanish batteries, Deignan displayed extraordinary heroism throughout this operation.
Notes: POW

2097 ◆ DESWAN, JOHN FRANCIS

Rank: Private
Service: U.S. Army
Birthday: 13 January 1876
Place of Birth: Philadelphia, Philadelphia County, Pennsylvania
Date of Death: 1 December 1956
Cemetery: Golden Gate National Cemetery (R-195-A)—San Bruno, California
Entered Service at: Philadelphia, Philadelphia County, Pennsylvania
Unit: Company H, 21st U.S. Infantry
Battle or Place of Action: Santiago, Cuba
Date of Action: 1 July 1898
Date of Issue: 22 June 1899
Citation: Gallantly assisted in the rescue of the wounded from in front of the lines and under heavy fire from the enemy.

2098 ◆ DOHERTY, THOMAS M.

Rank: Corporal (highest rank: Drum Major)
Service: U.S. Army
Birthday: 11 May 1869
Place of Birth: Mitchelstown, County Cork, Ireland
Date of Death: 21 September 1906
Place of Death: Fort Thomas, Kentucky
Cemetery: Evergreen Cemetery (U.S. Government Sec.)(MH)—Southgate, Kentucky
Entered Service at: Newcastle, Lincoln County, Maine
Unit: Company H, 21st U.S. Infantry
Battle or Place of Action: Santiago de Cuba, Cuba
Date of Action: 1 July 1898
Date of Issue: 22 June 1899
Citation: Gallantly assisted in the rescue of the wounded from in front of the lines and while under heavy fire from the enemy.

2099 ◆ DORAN, JOHN JAMES

Rank: Boatswain's Mate Second Class (highest rank: Chief Master-At-Arms)
Service: U.S. Navy
Birthday: 6 July 1864
Place of Birth: Boston, Suffolk County, Massachusetts
Date of Death: 16 February 1904
Place of Death: Santiago, Cuba
Cemetery: St. Patrick's Cemetery (MH)—Fall River, Massachusetts
Entered Service at: Massachusetts
Unit: U.S.S. *Marblehead*
Battle or Place of Action: Cienfuegos, Cuba
Date of Action: 11 May 1898
G.O. Number, Date: 521, 7 July 1899
Citation: On board the U.S.S. *Marblehead* during the operation of cutting the cable leading from Cienfuegos, Cuba, 11 May 1898. Facing the heavy fire of the enemy, Doran set an example of extraordinary bravery and coolness throughout this action.

2100 ◆ DURNEY, AUSTIN JOSEPH

Rank: Blacksmith
Service: U.S. Navy
Birthday: 26 November 1867
Place of Birth: Philadelphia, Philadelphia County, Pennsylvania
Date of Death: 17 November 1926
Place of Death: Ridgely, Maryland
Cemetery: St. Joseph's R.C. Cemetery—Cordova, Maryland
Entered Service at: Woodland, Maryland
Unit: U.S.S. *Nashville*
Battle or Place of Action: Cienfuegos, Cuba
Date of Action: 11 May 1898
G.O. Number, Date: 521, 7 July 1899
Citation: On board the U.S.S. *Nashville* during the operation of cutting the cable leading from Cienfuegos, Cuba, 11 May 1898. Facing the heavy fire of the enemy, Durney set an example of extraordinary bravery and coolness throughout this action.

2101 ◆ EGLIT, JOHN

Rank: Seaman
Service: U.S. Navy
Birthday: 17 October 1874
Place of Birth: Finland
Entered Service at: New York
Unit: U.S.S. *Nashville*
Battle or Place of Action: Cienfuegos, Cuba
Date of Action: 11 May 1898
G.O. Number, Date: 521, 7 July 1899
Citation: On board the U.S.S. *Nashville* during the operation of cutting the cable leading from Cienfuegos, Cuba, 11 May 1898. Facing the heavy fire of the enemy, Eglit set an example of extraordinary bravery and coolness throughout this action.

2102 ◆ EHLE, JOHN WALTER

Rank: Fireman First Class
Service: U.S. Navy
Birthday: 11 May 1873
Place of Birth: Kearney, Buffalo County, Nebraska
Date of Death: 25 July 1927
Place of Death: Presido of San Francisco, California
Cemetery: St. Mary's Cemetery—Oakland, California
Entered Service at: Nebraska
Unit: U.S.S. *Concord*
Battle or Place of Action: off Cavite, Manila Bay, Philippine Islands
Date of Action: 21 May 1898
G.O. Number, Date: 502, 14 December 1898
Citation: On board the U.S.S. *Concord* off Cavite, Manila Bay, P.I., 21 May 1898. Following the blowing-out of a lower manhole plate joint on boiler B of that vessel, Ehle assisted in hauling the fires in the hot, vapor-filled atmosphere, which necessitated the playing of water into the fireroom from a hose.

2103 ◆ ERICKSON, NICHOLAS

Rank: Coxswain
Service: U.S. Navy
Birthday: 18 July 1870
Place of Birth: Finland
Date of Death: 21 June 1931
Place of Death: New York, New York
Cemetery: Woodlawn Cemetery—Bronx, New York
Entered Service at: New York
Unit: U.S.S. *Marblehead*
Battle or Place of Action: Cienfuegos, Cuba
Date of Action: 11 May 1898
G.O. Number, Date: 521, 7 July 1899
Citation: On board the U.S.S. *Marblehead* during the operation of cutting the cable leading from Cienfuegos, Cuba, 11 May 1898. Facing the heavy fire of the enemy, Erickson set an example of extraordinary bravery and coolness throughout this action.

2104 ◆ FIELD, OSCAR WADSWORTH

Rank: Private (highest rank: Quartermaster Sergeant)
Service: U.S. Marine Corps
Birthday: 6 October 1873
Place of Birth: Jersey City, Hudson County, New Jersey
Date of Death: 5 January 1912
Cemetery: Dayton National Cemetery (0-Q-A9) (MH)—Dayton, Ohio
Entered Service at: New York
Unit: U.S.S. *Nashville*
Battle or Place of Action: Cienfuegos, Cuba
Date of Action: 11 May 1898
G.O. Number, Date: 521, 7 July 1899
Date of Issue: 19 August 1899
Citation: On board the U.S.S. *Nashville* during the operation of cutting the cable leading from Cienfuegos, Cuba, 11

May 1898. Facing the heavy fire of the enemy, Field set an example of extraordinary bravery and coolness throughout this action.

2105 ◆ FITZGERALD, JOHN

Rank: Private (highest rank: Gunnery Sergeant)
Service: U.S. Marine Corps
Birthday: 17 March 1873
Place of Birth: Limerick, Ireland
Date of Death: 19 April 1948
Cemetery: Holy Cross Cemetery—Brooklyn, New York
Entered Service at: New York
Battle or Place of Action: Cuzco, Cuba
Date of Action: 14 June 1898
G.O. Number, Date: 92, 8 December 1910
Citation: For heroism and gallantry in action at Cuzco, Cuba, 14 June 1898.

2106 ◆ FOSS, HERBERT LOUIS

Rank: Seaman
Service: U.S. Navy
Birthday: 12 October 1871
Place of Birth: Belfast, Waldo County, Maine
Date of Death: 1 September 1937
Cemetery: Forest Hill Cemetery (MH)—Hingman, Massachusetts
Entered Service at: Maine
Unit: U.S.S. *Marblehead*
Battle or Place of Action: Cienfuegos, Cuba
Date of Action: 11 May 1898
G.O. Number, Date: 521, 7 July 1899
Citation: On board the U.S.S. *Marblehead* during the operation of cutting the cable leading from Cienfuegos, Cuba, 11 May 1898. Facing the heavy fire of the enemy, Foss set an example of extraordinary bravery and coolness throughout this action.

2107 ◆ FOURNIA, FRANK OTTIS

Rank: Private
Service: U.S. Army
Birthday: January 1873
Place of Birth: Rome, Oneida County, New York
Entered Service at: Plattsburgh, Clinton County, New York
Unit: Company H, 21st U.S. Infantry
Battle or Place of Action: Santiago, Cuba
Date of Issue: 22 June 1899
Citation: Gallantly assisted in the rescue of the wounded from in front of the lines and while under heavy fire of the enemy.

2108 ◆ FRANKLIN, JOSEPH JOHN

Rank: Private (highest rank: Marine Gunner)
Service: U.S. Marine Corps
Birthday: 18 June 1870
Place of Birth: Buffalo, Erie County, New York

Date of Death: 28 April 1940
Place of Death: Philadelphia, Pennsylvania
Cemetery: Cypress Hills Cemetery—Brooklyn, New York
Entered Service at: New York
Unit: U.S.S. *Nashville*
Battle or Place of Action: Cienfuegos, Cuba
Date of Action: 11 May 1898
G.O. Number, Date: 521, 7 July 1899
Citation: On board the U.S.S. *Nashville* during the operation of cutting the cable leading from Cienfuegos, Cuba, 11 May 1898. Facing the heavy fire of the enemy, Franklin set an example of extraordinary bravery and coolness throughout this action.

2109   ◆   GAUGHAN, PHILIP

Rank: Sergeant (highest rank: First Sergeant)
Service: U.S. Marine Corps
Birthday: 17 March 1865
Place of Birth: Belmullet, County Mayo, Ireland
Date of Death: 31 December 1913
Place of Death: Philadelphia, Pennsylvania
Cemetery: Holy Cross Cemetery (MH)—Yeadon, Pennsylvania
Entered Service at: Pennsylvania
Unit: U.S.S. *Nashville*
Battle or Place of Action: Cienfuegos, Cuba
Date of Action: 11 May 1898
G.O. Number, Date: 521, 7 July 1899
Citation: On board the U.S.S. *Nashville* during the operation of cutting the cable leading from Cienfuegos, Cuba, 11 May 1898. Facing the heavy fire of the enemy, Gaughan set an example of extraordinary bravery and coolness throughout this action.

2110   ◆   GIBBONS, MICHAEL

Rank: Oiler (highest rank: Fireman First Class)
Service: U.S. Navy
Birthday: 15 November 1866
Place of Birth: Ireland
Date of Death: 27 February 1933
Place of Death: Rosow, Kilmeena, Westport, County Mayo, Ireland
Entered Service at: New York
Unit: U.S.S. *Nashville*
Battle or Place of Action: Cienfuegos, Cuba
Date of Action: 11 May 1898
G.O. Number, Date: 521, 7 July 1899
Citation: On board the U.S.S. *Nashville* during the operation of cutting the cable leading from Cienfuegos, Cuba, 11 May 1898. Facing the heavy fire of the enemy, Gibbons set an example of extraordinary bravery and coolness throughout this action.

2111   ◆   GILL, FREEMAN

Rank: Gunner's Mate First Class
Service: U.S. Navy

Birthday: 5 September 1851
Place of Birth: Boston, Suffolk County, Massachusetts
Date of Death: 8 April 1905
Place of Death: Chelsea, Massachusetts
Cemetery: Woodlawn Cemetery (MH)—Everett, Massachusetts
Entered Service at: Massachusetts
Unit: U.S.S. *Marblehead*
Battle or Place of Action: Cienfuegos, Cuba
Date of Action: 11 May 1898
G.O. Number, Date: 55, 19 July 1901
Citation: On board the U.S.S. *Marblehead* during the operation of cutting the cable leading from Cienfuegos, Cuba, 11 May 1898. Facing the heavy fire of the enemy, Gill set an example of extraordinary bravery and coolness throughout this action.

2112   ◆   GRAVES, THOMAS J.

Rank: Private (highest rank: Quartermaster Sergeant)
Service: U.S. Army
Birthday: 29 September 1866
Place of Birth: Milton, Wayne County, Indiana
Date of Death: 27 January 1944
Cemetery: Zion Lutheran Cemetery—Pershing, Indiana
Entered Service at: Millville, Indiana
Unit: Company C, 17th U.S. Infantry
Battle or Place of Action: El Caney, Cuba
Date of Action: 1 July 1898
Date of Issue: 22 June 1899
Citation: Gallantly assisted in the rescue of the wounded from in front of the lines and under heavy fire from the enemy.

2113   ◆   HARDAWAY, BENJAMIN FRANKLIN

Rank: First Lieutenant (highest rank: Colonel)
Service: U.S. Army
Birthday: 17 July 1865
Place of Birth: Benleyville, Kentucky
Date of Death: 9 July 1955
Cemetery: Arlington National Cemetery (2-1044-1)—Arlington, Virginia
Entered Service at: Fort Totten, Benson County, Dakota Territory
Unit: 17th U.S. Infantry
Battle or Place of Action: El Caney, Cuba
Date of Action: 1 July 1898
Date of Issue: 21 June 1899
Citation: Gallantly assisted in the rescue of the wounded from in front of the lines and under heavy fire from the enemy.

2114   ◆   HART, WILLIAM

Rank: Machinist First Class
Service: U.S. Navy
Birthday: 9 June 1866
Place of Birth: Massachusetts

Date of Death: 6 February 1899
Cemetery: The Green Wood Cemetery—Brooklyn, New York
Entered Service at: Massachusetts
Unit: U.S.S. *Marblehead*
Battle or Place of Action: Cienfuegos, Cuba
Date of Action: 11 May 1898
G.O. Number, Date: 521, 7 July 1899
Citation: On board the U.S.S. *Marblehead* during the operation of cutting the cable leading from Cienfuegos, Cuba, 11 May 1898. Facing the heavy fire of the enemy, Hart set an example of extraordinary bravery and coolness throughout this action.

2115   ◆   HEARD, JOHN WILLIAM

Rank: First Lieutenant (highest rank: Brigadier General)
Service: U.S. Army
Birthday: 27 March 1860
Place of Birth: Woodstock, Mississippi
Date of Death: 4 February 1922
Place of Death: New Orleans, Louisiana
Cemetery: U.S. Military Academy Cemetery (8-39)—West Point, New York
Entered Service at: Mississippi
Unit: 3d U.S. Cavalry
Battle or Place of Action: at mouth of Manimani River, west of Bahia Honda,Cuba
Date of Action: 23 July 1898
Date of Issue: 21 June 1899
Citation: After two men had been shot down by Spaniards while transmitting orders to the engine-room on the *Wanderer*, the ship having become disabled, this officer took the position held by them and personally transmitted the orders, remaining at his post until the ship was out of danger.

2116   ◆   HENDRICKSON, HENRY

Rank: Seaman
Service: U.S. Navy
Birthday: 12 March 1862
Place of Birth: Germany
Unit: U.S.S. *Marblehead*
Battle or Place of Action: Cienfuegos, Cuba
Date of Action: 11 May 1898
G.O. Number, Date: 521, 7 July 1899
Citation: On board the U.S.S. *Marblehead* during the operation of cutting the cable leading from Cienfuegos, Cuba, 11 May 1898. Facing the heavy fire of the enemy, Hendrickson displayed extraordinary bravery and coolness throughout this action.

2117   ◆   HILL, FRANK

Rank: Private
Service: U.S. Marine Corps
Birthday: 13 August 1864
Place of Birth: Hartford, Hartford County, Connecticut
Entered Service at: Connecticut

Unit: U.S.S. *Nashville*
Battle or Place of Action: Cienfuegos, Cuba
Date of Action: 11 May 1898
G.O. Number, Date: 521, 7 July 1899
Date of Issue: 15 August 1899
Citation: On board the U.S.S. *Nashville* during the operation of cutting the cable leading from Cienfuegos, Cuba, 11 May 1898. Facing the heavy fire of the enemy, Hill displayed extraordinary bravery and coolness throughout this action.

2118   ◆   HOBAN, THOMAS

Rank: Coxswain
Service: U.S. Navy
Birthday: 11 September 1872
Place of Birth: New York, New York
Entered Service at: New York
Unit: U.S.S. *Nashville*
Battle or Place of Action: Cienfuegos, Cuba
Date of Action: 11 May 1898
G.O. Number, Date: 521, 7 July 1899
Citation: On board the U.S.S. *Nashville* during the operation of cutting the cable leading from Cienfuegos, Cuba, 11 May 1898. Facing the heavy fire of the enemy, Hobin displayed extraordinary bravery and coolness throughout this action.

2119   ◆   HOBSON, RICHMOND PEARSON

Rank: Lieutenant (highest rank: Rear Admiral)
Service: U.S. Navy
Birthday: 17 August 1870
Place of Birth: Greensboro, Hale County, Alabama
Date of Death: 16 March 1937
Place of Death: New York, New York
Cemetery: Arlington National Cemetery (6-5014)—Arlington, Virginia
Entered Service at: New York
Unit: U.S.S. *Merrimac*
Battle or Place of Action: harbor entrance, Santiago de Cuba, Cuba
Date of Action: 3 June 1898
Date of Presentation: 29 April 1933
Place of Presentation: Presented by Pres. Franklin D. Roosevelt
Citation: In connection with the sinking of the U.S.S. *Merrimac* at the entrance to the fortified harbor of Santiago de Cuba, 3 June 1898. Despite persistent fire from the enemy fleet and fortifications onshore, Lt. Hobson distinguished himself by extraordinary courage and carried out this operation at the risk of his own personal safety.
Notes: POW

2120   ◆   HULL, JAMES LOTT

Rank: Fireman First Class
Service: U.S. Navy
Birthday: 27 November 1873
Place of Birth: Patoka, Marion County, Illinois

Date of Death: 25 July 1928
Cemetery: Haven Hill Cemetery—Olney, Illinois
Entered Service at: Illinois
Unit: U.S.S. *Concord*
Battle or Place of Action: off Cavite, Manila Bay, Philippine Islands
Date of Action: 21 May 1898
G.O. Number, Date: 502, 14 December 1898
Citation: On board the U.S.S. *Concord* off Cavite, Manila Bay, P.I., 21 May 1898. Following the blowing-out of a lower manhole plate joint on boiler B of that vessel, Hull assisted in hauling the fires in the hot, vapor-filled atmosphere, which necessitated the playing of water into the fireroom from a hose.

2121 ◆ ITRICH, FRANZ ANTON

Rank: Chief Carpenter's Mate (highest rank: Chief Gunner)
Service: U.S. Navy
Birthday: 26 November 1853
Place of Birth: Gross Katz, Germany
Date of Death: 11 June 1933
Cemetery: San Francisco National Cemetery (OSA-83-5)—San Francisco, California
Entered Service at: California
Unit: U.S.S. *Petrel*
Battle or Place of Action: Manila, Philippine Islands
Date of Action: 1 May 1898
G.O. Number, Date: 13, 5 December 1900
Citation: On board the U.S.S. *Petrel*, Manila, Philippine Islands, 1 May 1898. Serving in the presence of the enemy, Itrich displayed heroism during the action.

2122 ◆ JOHANSON, JOHN PETER

Rank: Seaman (highest rank: Chief Boatswain's Mate)
Service: U.S. Navy
Birthday: 22 January 1865
Place of Birth: Oskarshamn, Sweden
Date of Death: 14 December 1937
Cemetery: Arlington National Cemetery (6-9768) (MH)—Arlington, Virginia
Entered Service at: Maryland
Unit: U.S.S. *Marblehead*
Battle or Place of Action: Cienfuegos, Cuba
Date of Action: 11 May 1898
G.O. Number, Date: 529, 21 November 1899
Citation: On board the U.S.S. *Marblehead* during the operation of cutting the cable leading from Cienfuegos, Cuba, 11 May 1898. Facing the heavy fire of the enemy, Johanson set an example of extraordinary bravery and coolness throughout this action.

2123 ◆ JOHANSSON, JOHAN J.

Rank: Ordinary Seaman
Service: U.S. Navy
Birthday: 12 May 1870

Place of Birth: Sweden
Date of Death: 4 December 1948
Cemetery: Arlington National Cemetery (13-720) (MH)—Arlington, Virginia
Entered Service at: New York
Unit: U.S.S. *Nashville*
Battle or Place of Action: Cienfuegos, Cuba
Date of Action: 11 May 1898
G.O. Number, Date: 521, 7 July 1899
Citation: On board the U.S.S. *Nashville* during the operation of cutting the cable leading from Cienfuegos, Cuba, 11 May 1898. Facing the heavy fire of the enemy, Johansson set an example of extraordinary bravery and coolness throughout this action.

2124 ◆ JOHNSEN, HANS

Rank: Chief Machinist (highest rank: Lieutenant)
Service: U.S. Navy
Birthday: 3 January 1865
Place of Birth: Sandnes, Norway
Date of Death: 17 June 1920
Cemetery: Bayview Cemetery (MH)—Jersey City, New Jersey
Entered Service at: Pennsylvania
Unit: U.S. Torpedo Boat *Winslow*
Battle or Place of Action: Cardenas, Cuba
Date of Action: 11 May 1898
G.O. Number, Date: 497, 3 September 1899
Citation: On board the torpedo boat *Winslow* during the actions at Cardenas, Cuba, 11 May 1898. Showing great presence of mind, Johnsen turned off the steam from the engine which had been wrecked by a shell bursting in the cylinder.

2125 ◆ JOHNSON, PETER

Rank: Fireman First Class
Service: U.S. Navy
Birthday: 29 December 1857
Place of Birth: Sumerland, England
Entered Service at: Pennsylvania
Unit: U.S.S. *Vixen*
Date of Action: 28 May 1898
G.O. Number, Date: 167, 27 August 1904
Citation: On board the U.S.S. *Vixen* on the night of 28 May 1898. Following the explosion of the lower front manhole gasket of boiler A of the vessel, Johnson displayed great coolness and self-possession in entering the fireroom.

2126 ◆ KEARNEY, MICHAEL

Rank: Private (highest rank: Captain)
Service: U.S. Marine Corps
Birthday: 4 October 1874
Place of Birth: Newmarket, County Cork, Ireland
Date of Death: 31 October 1937
Place of Death: Brooklyn, New York
Cemetery: Holy Cross Cemetery—Brooklyn, New York

Entered Service at: Massachusetts
Unit: U.S.S. *Nashville*
Battle or Place of Action: Cienfuegos, Cuba
Date of Action: 11 May 1898
G.O. Number, Date: 521, 7 July 1899
Citation: On board the U.S.S. *Nashville* during the operation of cutting the cable leading from Cienfuegos, Cuba, 11 May 1898. Facing the heavy fire of the enemy, Kearney set an example of extraordinary bravery and coolness throughout this action.

2127 ◆ KEEFER, PHILIP BOGAN

Rank: Coppersmith
Service: U.S. Navy
Birthday: 4 September 1875
Place of Birth: Washington, D.C.
Date of Death: 15 January 1949
Cemetery: Arlington National Cemetery (11-527-SH) (MH)—Arlington, Virginia
Entered Service at: Washington, D.C.
Unit: U.S.S. *Iowa*
Battle or Place of Action: Santiago de Cuba, Cuba
Date of Action: 20 July 1898
G.O. Number, Date: 501, 14 December 1898
Citation: On board the U.S.S. *Iowa* off Santiago de Cuba, 20 July 1898. Following the blow-out of a manhole gasket of that vessel which caused the fireroom to be filled with live steam and the floor plates to be covered with boiling water, Keefer showed courageous and zealous conduct in hauling fires from two furnaces of boiler B.

2128 ◆ KELLER, WILLIAM G.

Rank: Private (highest rank: Corporal)
Service: U.S. Army
Birthday: 19 April 1876
Place of Birth: Buffalo, Erie County, New York
Date of Death: 20 September 1963
Place of Death: Sarasota, Florida
Cemetery: Lakeview Cemetery—Cleveland, Ohio
Entered Service at: Buffalo, Erie County, New York
Unit: Company F, 10th U.S. Infantry
Battle or Place of Action: Santiago de Cuba, Cuba
Date of Action: 1 July 1898
Date of Issue: 22 June 1899
Citation: Gallantly assisted in the rescue of the wounded from in front of the lines and under heavy fire of the enemy.

2129 ◆ KELLY, FRANCIS

Rank: Watertender (highest rank: Chief Machinist's Mate)
Service: U.S. Navy
Birthday: 5 July 1860
Place of Birth: Boston, Suffolk County, Massachusetts
Date of Death: 19 May 1938
Place of Death: Glasgow, Scotland
Cemetery: Sandymount Cemetery—Glasgow, Scotland
Entered Service at: Massachusetts

Unit: U.S.S. *Merrimac*
Battle or Place of Action: harbor entrance, Santiago de Cuba, Cuba
Date of Action: 3 June 1898
G.O. Number, Date: 529, 2 November 1899
Citation: In connection with the sinking of the U.S.S. *Merrimac* at the entrance to the harbor of Santiago de Cuba, 3 June 1898. Despite heavy fire from the Spanish batteries, Kelly displayed extraordinary heroism throughout this operation.
Notes: POW

2130 ◆ KELLY, THOMAS

Rank: Private
Service: U.S. Army
Place of Birth: Ireland
Date of Death: 17 December 1920
Cemetery: Post Barracks Cemetery (Q6) (MH)—Plattsburg, New York
Entered Service at: New York
Unit: Company H, 21st U.S. Infantry
Battle or Place of Action: Santiago de Cuba, Cuba
Date of Action: 1 July 1898
Date of Issue: 22 June 1899
Citation: Gallantly assisted in the rescue of the wounded from in front of the lines and while under heavy fire from the enemy.

2131 ◆ KRAMER, FRANZ

Rank: Seaman
Service: U.S. Navy
Birthday: 20 January 1865
Place of Birth: Nierstein, Germany
Date of Death: 18 April 1924
Place of Death: New York, New York
Cemetery: Calvary Cemetery—Woodside, New York
Entered Service at: Massachusetts
Unit: U.S.S. *Marblehead*
Battle or Place of Action: Cienfuegos, Cuba
Date of Action: 11 May 1898
G.O. Number, Date: 521, 7 July 1899
Citation: On board the U.S.S. *Marblehead* during the operation of cutting the cable leading from Cienfuegos, Cuba, 11 May 1898. Facing the heavy fire of the enemy, Kramer set an example of extraordinary bravery and coolness throughout this action.

2132 ◆ KRAUSE, ERNEST

Rank: Coxswain (highest rank: Gunner's Mate)
Service: U.S. Navy
Birthday: 3 July 1866
Place of Birth: Lubeck, Germany
Entered Service at: New York
Unit: U.S.S. *Nashville*
Battle or Place of Action: Cienfuegos, Cuba
Date of Action: 11 May 1898

G.O. Number, Date: 521, 7 July 1899
Citation: On board the U.S.S. *Nashville* during the operation of cutting the cable leading from Cienfuegos, Cuba, 11 May 1898. Facing the heavy fire of the enemy, Krause displayed extraordinary bravery and coolness throughout this action.

2133 ◆ KUCHNEISTER, HERMANN WILHELM

Rank: Private (highest rank: Corporal)
Service: U.S. Marine Corps
Birthday: 16 October 1877
Place of Birth: Hamburg, Germany
Date of Death: 1 February 1923
Cemetery: Winthrop Cemetery (MH)—Winthrop, Massachusetts
Entered Service at: New York
Unit: U.S.S. *Marblehead*
Battle or Place of Action: Cienfuegos, Cuba
Date of Action: 11 May 1898
G.O. Number, Date: 521, 7 July 1899
Citation: On board the U.S.S. *Marblehead* during the operation of cutting the cable leading from Cienfuegos, Cuba, 11 May 1898. Facing the heavy fire of the enemy, Kuchneister displayed extraordinary bravery and coolness throughout this action.

2134 ◆ LEE, FITZ

Rank: Private
Service: U.S. Army
Birthday: June 1866
Place of Birth: Dinwiddie County, Virginia
Date of Death: 14 September 1899
Place of Death: Leavenworth, Kansas
Cemetery: Leavenworth National Cemetery (G-3183) (MH)—Leavenworth, Kansas
Entered Service at: Philadelphia, Philadelphia County, Pennsylvania
Unit: Troop M, 10th U.S. Cavalry
Battle or Place of Action: Tayabacoa, Cuba
Date of Action: 30 June 1898
Date of Issue: 23 June 1899
Citation: Voluntarily went ashore in the face of the enemy and aided in the rescue of his wounded comrades; this after several previous attempts had been frustrated.

2135 ◆ LEVERY, WILLIAM

Rank: Apprentice First Class
Service: U.S. Navy
Birthday: 30 June 1879
Place of Birth: Philadelphia, Philadelphia County, Pennsylvania
Entered Service at: Pennsylvania
Unit: U.S.S. *Marblehead*
Battle or Place of Action: Cienfuegos, Cuba
Date of Action: 11 May 1898
G.O. Number, Date: 521, 7 July 1899

Citation: On board the U.S.S. *Marblehead* during the operation of cutting the cable leading from Cienfuegos, Cuba, 11 May 1989. Facing the heavy fire of the enemy, Levery displayed extraordinary bravery and coolness throughout this action.

2136 ◆ MACNEAL, HARRY LEWIS

Rank: Private (highest rank: Corporal)
Service: U.S. Marine Corps
Birthday: 22 March 1879
Place of Birth: Philadelphia, Philadelphia County, Pennsylvania
Date of Death: 13 March 1950
Cemetery: East Ridge Lawn Cemetery (MH)—Delawanna, New Jersey
Entered Service at: Pennsylvania
Unit: U.S.S. *Brooklyn*
Battle or Place of Action: Santiago de Cuba, Cuba
Date of Action: 3 July 1898
G.O. Number, Date: 526, 9 August 1899
Citation: On board the U.S.S. *Brooklyn* during action at the Battle of Santiago de Cuba, 3 July 1898. Braving the fire of the enemy, MacNeal displayed gallantry throughout this action.

2137 ◆ MAGER, GEORGE FREDERICK

Rank: Apprentice First Class
Service: U.S. Navy
Birthday: 23 February 1875
Place of Birth: Phillipsburg, Warren County, New Jersey
Date of Death: 12 April 1938
Cemetery: Greenwood Cemetery—Trenton, New Jersey
Entered Service at: New Jersey
Unit: U.S.S. *Marblehead*
Battle or Place of Action: Cienfuegos, Cuba
Date of Action: 11 May 1898
G.O. Number, Date: 529, 2 November 1899
Citation: On board the U.S.S. *Marblehead* during the operation of cutting the cable leading from Cienfuegos, Cuba, 11 May 1898. Facing the heavy fire of the enemy, Mager displayed extraordinary bravery and coolness throughout this action.

2138 ◆ MAHONEY, GEORGE

Rank: Fireman First Class
Service: U.S. Navy
Birthday: 15 January 1865
Place of Birth: Worcester, Worcester County, Massachusetts
Entered Service at: Pennsylvania
Unit: U.S.S. *Vixen*
Date of Action: 28 May 1898
G.O. Number, Date: 167, 27 August 1904
Citation: On board the U.S.S. *Vixen* on the night of 28 May 1898. Following the explosion of the lower front manhole gasket of boiler A of the vessel, Mahoney displayed great coolness and self-possession in entering the fireroom.

2139 ◆ MAXWELL, JOHN

Rank: Fireman Second Class (highest rank: Oiler)
Service: U.S. Navy
Birthday: 26 June 1874
Place of Birth: Brooklyn, Kings County, New York
Date of Death: 13 November 1931
Place of Death: Westbury, New York
Cemetery: Friends Cemetery—Westbury, New York
Entered Service at: New York
Unit: U.S.S. *Marblehead*
Battle or Place of Action: Cienfuegos, Cuba
Date of Action: 11 May 1898
G.O. Number, Date: 521, 7 July 1899
Citation: On board the U.S.S. *Marblehead* during the operation of cutting the cable leading from Cienfuegos, Cuba, 11 May 1898. Facing the heavy fire of the enemy, Maxwell displayed extraordinary bravery and coolness throughout this action.

2140 ◆ MEREDITH, JAMES

True Name: Ford Jr., Patrick F.
Rank: Private (highest rank: Sergeant)
Service: U.S. Marine Corps
Birthday: 11 April 1872
Place of Birth: Omaha, Douglas County, Nebraska
Date of Death: 18 January 1915
Cemetery: St. Mary's Cemetery—South Omaha, Nebraska
Entered Service at: Boston, Suffolk County, Massachusetts
Unit: U.S.S. *Marblehead*
Battle or Place of Action: Cienfuegos, Cuba
Date of Action: 11 May 1898
G.O. Number, Date: 521, 7 July 1899
Date of Issue: 15 August 1899
Citation: On board the U.S.S. *Marblehead* during the operation of cutting the cable leading from Cienfuegos, Cuba, 11 May 1898. Facing the heavy fire of the enemy, Meredith displayed extraordinary bravery and coolness throughout this action.

2141 ◆ MEYER, WILLIAM

Rank: Carpenter's Mate Third Class (highest rank: Carpenter Third Class)
Service: U.S. Navy
Birthday: 22 June 1863
Place of Birth: Germany
Date of Death: 6 September 1926
Place of Death: Chicago, Illinois
Cemetery: Forest Home Cemetery—Chicago, Illinois
Entered Service at: Illinois
Unit: U.S.S. *Nashville*
Battle or Place of Action: Cienfuegos, Cuba
Date of Action: 11 May 1898
G.O. Number, Date: 521, 7 July 1899
Citation: On board the U.S.S. *Nashville* during the operation of cutting the cable leading from Cienfuegos, Cuba, 11 May 1898. Facing the heavy fire of the enemy, Meyer displayed extraordinary bravery and coolness throughout this action.

2142 ◆ MILLER, HARRY HERBERT

Rank: Seaman (highest rank: Quartermaster Third Class)
Service: U.S. Navy
Birthday: 4 May 1879
Place of Birth: Noel Shore, Hants County, Nova Scotia, Canada
Date of Death: 12 March 1968
Place of Death: Costa Rica
Cemetery: Central Cemetery (MH)—Tres De Rios, Costa Rica
Entered Service at: Massachusetts
Unit: U.S.S. *Nashville*
Battle or Place of Action: Cienfuegos, Cuba
Date of Action: 11 May 1898
G.O. Number, Date: 521, 7 July 1899
Citation: On board the U.S.S. *Nashville* during the operation of cutting the cable leading from Cienfuegos, Cuba, 11 May 1898. Facing the heavy fire of the enemy, Miller displayed extraordinary bravery and coolness throughout this action.

2143 ◆ MILLER, WILLARD D.

Rank: Seaman
Service: U.S. Navy
Birthday: 5 June 1877
Place of Birth: Noel Shore, Hants County, Nova Scotia, Canada
Date of Death: 19 February 1959
Cemetery: Arlington National Cemetery (46-15) (MH)—Arlington, Virginia
Entered Service at: Massachusetts
Unit: U.S.S. *Nashville*
Battle or Place of Action: Cienfuegos, Cuba
Date of Action: 11 May 1898
G.O. Number, Date: 521, 7 July 1899
Citation: On board the U.S.S. *Nashville* during the operation of cutting the cable leading from Cienfuegos, Cuba, 11 May 1898. Facing the heavy fire of the enemy, Miller displayed extraordinary bravery and coolness throughout this action.

2144 ◆ MILLS, ALBERT LEOPOLD

Rank: Captain & Assistant Adjutant General (highest rank: Major General)
Service: U.S. Army
Birthday: 7 May 1854
Place of Birth: New York City (Washington Heights), New York
Date of Death: 18 September 1916
Place of Death: Washington, D.C.
Cemetery: U.S. Military Academy Cemetery (4-7)—West Point, New York
Entered Service at: New York, New York

Unit: U.S. Volunteers
Battle or Place of Action: near Santiago, Cuba
Date of Action: 1 July 1898
Date of Issue: 9 July 1902
Citation: Distinguished gallantry in encouraging those near him by his bravery and coolness after being shot though the head and entirely without sight.

2145 ◆ MONTAGUE, DANIEL

Rank: Chief Master-at-Arms (highest rank: Chief Boatswain)
Service: U.S. Navy
Birthday: 22 October 1867
Place of Birth: Wicklow, Ireland
Date of Death: 4 February 1912
Cemetery: U.S. Naval Academy Cemetery (275)—Annapolis, Maryland
Unit: U.S.S. *Merrimac*—assigned to the U.S.S. *New York*
Battle or Place of Action: harbor entrance, Santiago de Cuba, Cuba
Date of Action: 3 June 1898
G.O. Number, Date: 529, 2 November 1899
Citation: In connection with the sinking of the U.S.S. *Merrimac* at the entrance to the harbor of Santiago de Cuba, 3 June 1898. Despite heavy fire from the Spanish batteries, Montague displayed extraordinary heroism throughout this operation.
Notes: POW

2146 ◆ MORIN, WILLIAM HENRY

Rank: Boatswain's Mate Second Class (highest rank: Boatswain)
Service: U.S. Navy
Birthday: 23 May 1868
Place of Birth: Birmingham, West Midlands County, England
Date of Death: 29 August 1935
Place of Death: Staten Island, New York
Cemetery: St. John's Cemetery—Middle Village, New York
Entered Service at: New York
Unit: U.S.S. *Marblehead*
Battle or Place of Action: approaches to Caimanera, Guantanamo Bay, Cuba
Date of Action: 26-27 July 1898
G.O. Number, Date: 500, 14 December 1898
Citation: On board the U.S.S. *Marblehead* at the approaches to Caimanera, Guantanamo Bay, Cuba, 26 and 27 July 1898. Displaying heroism, Morin took part in the perilous work of sweeping for and disabling 27 contact mines during this period.

2147 ◆ MULLER, FREDERICK

Rank: Mate (highest rank: Lieutenant Commander)
Service: U.S. Navy
Birthday: 29 March 1861
Place of Birth: Copenhagen, Denmark
Date of Death: 9 June 1946

Cemetery: Arlington National Cemetery (8-6035)—Arlington, Virginia
Entered Service at: Massachusetts
Unit: U.S.S. *Wompatuck*
Battle or Place of Action: Manzanillo, Cuba
Date of Action: 30 June 1898
G.O. Number, Date: 45, 30 April 1901
Citation: On board the U.S.S. *Wompatuck*, Manzanillo, Cuba, 30 June 1898. Serving under the fire of the enemy, Muller displayed heroism and gallantry during this period.

2148 ◆ MURPHY, JOHN EDWARD

Rank: Coxswain
Service: U.S. Navy
Birthday: 3 May 1869
Place of Birth: Ireland
Date of Death: 9 April 1941
Cemetery: Fort Rosecrans National Cemetery (OS-363) (MH)—San Diego, California
Entered Service at: New York
Unit: U.S.S. *Merrimac*—assigned to the U.S.S. *Iowa*
Battle or Place of Action: harbor entrance, Santiago de Cuba, Cuba
Date of Action: 3 June 1898
G.O. Number, Date: 529, 2 November 1899
Citation: In connection with the sinking of the U.S.S. *Merrimac* at the entrance to the harbor of Santiago de Cuba, 3 June 1898. Despite heavy fire from the Spanish shore batteries, Murphy displayed extraordinary heroism throughout this operation.
Notes: POW

2149 ◆ NASH, JAMES J.

Rank: Private (highest rank: First Sergeant)
Service: U.S. Army
Birthday: 1875
Place of Birth: Louisville, Jefferson County, Kentucky
Date of Death: 11 June 1927
Cemetery: San Antonio National Cemetery (T-1461-A) (MH)—San Antonio, Texas
Entered Service at: Louisville, Jefferson County, Kentucky
Unit: Company F, 10th U.S. Infantry
Battle or Place of Action: Santiago, Cuba
Date of Action: 1 July 1898
Date of Issue: 22 June 1899
Citation: Gallantly assisted in the rescue of the wounded from in front of the lines and under heavy fire from the enemy.

2150 ◆ NEE, GEORGE HENRY

Rank: Private (highest rank: Sergeant)
Service: U.S. Army
Birthday: 12 March 1876
Place of Birth: Boston, Suffolk County, Massachusetts
Date of Death: 4 March 1952
Place of Death: Boston, Massachusetts

Cemetery: Forest Hills Cemetery—Boston, Massachusetts
Entered Service at: Boston, Suffolk County, Massachusetts
Unit: Company H, 21st U.S. Infantry
Battle or Place of Action: Santiago, Cuba
Date of Action: 1 July 1898
Date of Issue: 22 June 1899
Citation: Gallantly assisted in the rescue of the wounded from in front of the lines and under heavy fire from the enemy.

2151 ◆ NELSON, LAURITZ

Rank: Sailmaker's Mate (highest rank: Chief Boatswain's Mate)
Service: U.S. Navy
Birthday: 26 March 1860
Place of Birth: Norway
Date of Death: 19 September 1941
Cemetery: Long Island National Cemetery (DSS-2) (MH)—Farmingdale, New York
Unit: U.S.S. *Nashville*
Battle or Place of Action: Cienfuegos, Cuba
Date of Action: 11 May 1898
G.O. Number, Date: 521, 7 July 1899
Citation: On board the U.S.S. *Nashville* during the operation of cutting the cable leading from Cienfuegos, Cuba, 11 May 1898. Facing the heavy fire of the enemy, Nelson displayed extraordinary bravery and coolness throughout this action.

2152 ◆ OAKLEY, WILLIAM

Rank: Gunner's Mate Second Class
Service: U.S. Navy
Birthday: 25 August 1860
Place of Birth: Colchester, Essex County, England
Entered Service at: New York
Unit: U.S.S. *Marblehead*
Battle or Place of Action: Cienfuegos, Cuba
Date of Action: 11 May 1898
G.O. Number, Date: 521, 7 July 1899
Citation: On board the U.S.S. *Marblehead* during the operation of cutting the cable leading from Cienfuegos, Cuba, 11 May 1898. Facing the heavy fire of the enemy, Oakley displayed extraordinary bravery and coolness throughout this period.

2153 ◆ OLSEN, ANTON

Rank: Ordinary Seaman (highest rank: Quartermaster Third Class)
Service: U.S. Navy
Birthday: 13 July 1873
Place of Birth: Christiana (now Oslo), Norway
Date of Death: 23 June 1924
Cemetery: Cypress Hills National Cemetery (2-9158) (MH)—Brooklyn, New York
Entered Service at: Massachusetts
Unit: U.S.S. *Marblehead*
Battle or Place of Action: Cienfuegos, Cuba

Date of Action: 11 May 1898
G.O. Number, Date: 529, 2 November 1899
Citation: On board the U.S.S. *Marblehead* during the operation of cutting the cable leading from Cienfuegos, Cuba, 11 May 1898. Facing the heavy fire of the enemy, Olsen displayed extraordinary bravery and coolness throughout this period.

2154 ◆ PARKER, POMEROY

Rank: Private
Service: U.S. Marine Corps
Birthday: 17 March 1874
Place of Birth: Gates County, North Carolina
Date of Death: 30 December 1946
Place of Death: Savannah, Georgia
Cemetery: Roxobel-Kelford Cemetery (MH)—Bertie County, North Carolina
Entered Service at: North Carolina
Unit: U.S.S. *Nashville*
Battle or Place of Action: Cienfuegos, Cuba
Date of Action: 11 May 1898
G.O. Number, Date: 521, 7 July 1899
Citation: On board the U.S.S. *Nashville* during the operation of cutting the cable leading from Cienfuegos, Cuba, 11 May 1898. Facing the heavy fire of the enemy, Parker displayed extraordinary bravery and coolness throughout this action.

2155 ◆ PENN, ROBERT

Rank: Fireman First Class
Service: U.S. Navy
Birthday: 10 October 1872
Place of Birth: City Point, Virginia
Date of Death: 8 June 1912
Place of Death: Las Animas, Colorado
Cemetery: unknown cemetery—Philadelphia, Pennsylvania
Entered Service at: Virginia
Unit: U.S.S. *Iowa*
Battle or Place of Action: Santiago de Cuba, Cuba
Date of Action: 20 July 1898
G.O. Number, Date: 501, 14 December 1898
Citation: On board the U.S.S. *Iowa* off Santiago de Cuba, 20 July 1898. Performing his duty at the risk of serious scalding at the time of the blowing-out of the manhole gasket on board the vessel, Penn hauled the fire while standing on a board thrown across a coal bucket one foot above the boiling water which was still blowing from the boiler.

2156 ◆ PFISTERER, HERMAN

Rank: Musician
Service: U.S. Army
Birthday: 1 April 1866
Place of Birth: Brooklyn, Kings County, New York
Date of Death: 6 August 1905
Cemetery: Vancouver Barracks, Post Cemetery (4-E-448) (MH)—Vancouver, Washington

Entered Service at: New York, New York
Unit: Company H, 21st U.S. Infantry
Battle or Place of Action: Santiago, Cuba
Date of Action: 1 July 1898
Date of Issue: 22 June 1899
Citation: Gallantly assisted in the rescue of the wounded from in front of the lines and under heavy fire from the enemy.

2157 ◆ PHILLIPS, GEORGE FREDERICK

Rank: Machinist First Class (highest rank: Chief Machinist)
Service: U.S. Navy
Birthday: 8 March 1862
Place of Birth: St. John, New Brunswick, Canada
Date of Death: 4 June 1904
Place of Death: Cambridge, Massachusetts
Cemetery: Fernhill Cemetery (MH)—St. John, New Brunswick, Canada
Entered Service at: Galveston, Galveston County, Texas
Unit: U.S.S. *Merrimac*
Battle or Place of Action: harbor entrance, Santiago de Cuba, Cuba
Date of Action: 3 June 1898
G.O. Number, Date: 529, 2 November 1899
Citation: In connection with the sinking of the U.S.S. *Merrimac* at the entrance to the harbor of Santiago de Cuba, 3 June 1898. Despite heavy fire from the Spanish shore batteries, Phillips displayed extraordinary heroism throughout this operation.
Notes: POW

2158 ◆ POLOND, ALFRED

Rank: Private (highest rank: Sergeant)
Service: U.S. Army
Birthday: 29 February 1872
Place of Birth: Lapeer, Lapeer County, Michigan
Date of Death: 26 March 1956
Cemetery: Riverside Cemetery—Kalamazoo, Michigan
Entered Service at: Lapeer, Lapeer County, Michigan
Unit: Company F, 10th U.S. Infantry
Battle or Place of Action: Santiago, Cuba
Date of Action: 1 July 1898
Date of Issue: 22 June 1899
Citation: Gallantly assisted in the rescue of the wounded from in front of the lines and while under heavy fire from the enemy.

2159 ◆ QUICK, JOHN HENRY

Rank: Sergeant (highest rank: Sergeant Major)
Service: U.S. Marine Corps
Birthday: 20 June 1870
Place of Birth: Charleston, Kanawha County, West Virginia
Date of Death: 9 September 1922
Place of Death: St. Louis, Missouri
Cemetery: Memorial Park Cemetery (MH)—St. Louis, Missouri

Entered Service at: Pennsylvania
Battle or Place of Action: Cuzco, Cuba
Date of Action: 14 June 1898
G.O. Number, Date: 504, 13 December 1898
Citation: In action during the battle of Cuzco, Cuba, 14 June 1898. Distinguishing himself during this action, Quick signaled the U.S.S. *Dolphin* on three different occasions while exposed to a heavy fire from the enemy.

2160 ◆ QUINN, ALEXANDER M.

Rank: Sergeant (highest rank: Color Sergeant)
Service: U.S. Army
Birthday: 1866
Place of Birth: Passaic, Passaic County, New Jersey
Date of Death: 4 May 1906
Place of Death: Philippine Islands (Killed in Action)
Cemetery: Holy Sepulchre Cemetery (MH)—Totowa, New Jersey
Entered Service at: Philadelphia, Philadelphia County, Pennsylvania
Unit: Company A, 13th U.S. Infantry
Battle or Place of Action: Santiago, Cuba
Date of Action: 1 July 1898
Date of Issue: 22 June 1899
Citation: Gallantly assisted in the rescue of the wounded from in front of the lines and under heavy fire from the enemy.

2161 ◆ RESSLER, NORMAN W.

Rank: Corporal (highest rank: Master Gunner)
Service: U.S. Army
Birthday: 27 May 1873
Place of Birth: Dalmatia, Northumberland County, Pennsylvania
Date of Death: 29 September 1914
Cemetery: San Francisco National Cemetery (WS-134-A)—San Francisco, California
Entered Service at: Dalmatia, Northumberland County, Pennsylvania
Unit: Company D, 17th U.S. Infantry
Battle or Place of Action: El Caney, Cuba
Date of Action: 1 July 1898
Date of Issue: 21 August 1899
Citation: Gallantly assisted in the rescue of the wounded from in front of the lines and under heavy fire of the enemy.

2162 ◆ RILLEY, JOHN PHILLIP

Rank: Landsman
Service: U.S. Navy
Birthday: 22 January 1877
Place of Birth: Allentown, Lehigh County, Pennsylvania
Date of Death: 16 November 1950
Cemetery: Greenlawn Cemetery (MH)—Salem, Massachusetts
Entered Service at: Massachusetts
Unit: U.S.S. *Nashville*

Battle or Place of Action: Cienfuegos, Cuba
Date of Action: 11 May 1898
G.O. Number, Date: 521, 7 July 1899
Citation: On board the U.S.S. *Nashville* during the operation of cutting the cable leading from Cienfuegos, Cuba, 11 May 1898. Facing the heavy fire of the enemy, Rilley displayed extraordinary bravery and coolness throughout this action.

2163 ◆ ROBERTS, CHARLES DUVAL

Rank: Second Lieutenant (highest rank: Brigadier General)
Service: U.S. Army
Birthday: 18 June 1873
Place of Birth: Cheyenne Agency, Dakota
Date of Death: 24 October 1966
Place of Death: Silver Springs, Maryland
Cemetery: Arlington National Cemetery (2-3671)—Arlington, Virginia
Entered Service at: Fort D.A. Russell, Wyoming
Unit: 17th U.S. Infantry
Battle or Place of Action: El Caney, Cuba
Date of Action: 1 July 1898
Date of Issue: 21 June 1899
Citation: Gallantly assisted in the rescue of the wounded from in front of the lines under heavy fire of the enemy.

2164 ◆ RUSSELL, HENRY PETER

Rank: Landsman (highest rank: Captain U.S. Army Ret.)
Service: U.S. Navy
Birthday: 10 June 1878
Place of Birth: Quebec, Canada
Date of Death: 1 December 1956
Cemetery: Arlington National Cemetery (31-6377) (MH)—Arlington, Virginia
Entered Service at: New York
Unit: U.S.S. *Marblehead*
Battle or Place of Action: Cienfuegos, Cuba
Date of Action: 11 May 1898
G.O. Number, Date: 521, 7 July 1899
Citation: On board the U.S.S. *Marblehead* during the operation of cutting the cable leading from Cienfuegos, Cuba, 11 May 1898. Facing the heavy fire of the enemy, Russell displayed extraordinary bravery and coolness throughout this action.

2165 ◆ SCOTT, JOSEPH FRANCIS

Rank: Private (highest rank: Corporal)
Service: U.S. Marine Corps
Birthday: 4 June 1866
Place of Birth: Boston, Suffolk County, Massachusetts
Date of Death: 28 February 1941
Place of Death: Cambridge, Massachusetts
Cemetery: Cambridge Cemetery (MH)—Cambridge, Massachusetts
Entered Service at: Cambridge, Middlesex County, Massachusetts

Unit: U.S.S. *Nashville*
Battle or Place of Action: Cienfuegos, Cuba
Date of Action: 11 May 1898
G.O. Number, Date: 521, 7 July 1899
Citation: On board the U.S.S. *Nashville* during the operation of cutting the cable leading from Cienfuegos, Cuba, 11 May 1898. Facing the heavy fire of the enemy, Scott displayed extraordinary bravery and coolness throughout this action.

2166 ◆ SHEPHERD, WARREN JULIUS

Rank: Corporal
Service: U.S. Army
Birthday: 28 September 1871
Place of Birth: Cherry Tree, Indiana County, Pennsylvania
Date of Death: 24 April 1942
Cemetery: Inglewood Cemetery—Inglewood, California
Entered Service at: Westover, Clearfield County, Pennsylvania
Unit: Company D, 17th U.S. Infantry
Battle or Place of Action: El Caney, Cuba
Date of Action: 1 July 1898
Date of Issue: 21 August 1899
Citation: Gallantly assisted in the rescue of the wounded from in front of the lines under heavy fire from the enemy.

2167 ◆ SPICER, WILLIAM

Rank: Gunner's Mate First Class (highest rank: Chief Gunner's Mate)
Service: U.S. Navy
Birthday: 28 May 1864
Place of Birth: Liverpool, Merseyside County, England
Date of Death: 14 December 1949
Place of Death: Long Beach, California
Entered Service at: New York
Unit: U.S.S. *Marblehead*
Battle or Place of Action: approaches to Caimanera, Guantanamo Bay, Cuba
Date of Action: 26-27 July 1898
G.O. Number, Date: 500, 14 December 1898
Citation: On board the U.S.S. *Marblehead* at the approaches to Caimanera, Guantanamo Bay, Cuba, 26 and 27 July 1898. Displaying heroism, Spicer took part in the perilous work of sweeping for and disabling 27 contact mines during this period.

2168 ◆ SULLIVAN, EDWARD

Rank: Private (highest rank: Corporal)
Service: U.S. Marine Corps
Birthday: 16 May 1870
Place of Birth: Cork, Ireland
Date of Death: 11 March 1955
Place of Death: Grafton, Massachusetts
Cemetery: Prospect Hill Cemetery (MH)—Oxbridge, Massachusetts
Entered Service at: Massachusetts

Unit: U.S.S. *Marblehead*
Battle or Place of Action: Cienfuegos, Cuba
Date of Action: 11 May 1898
G.O. Number, Date: 521, 7 July 1899
Date of Issue: 15 August 1899
Citation: On board the U.S.S. *Marblehead* during the operation of cutting the cable leading from Cienfuegos, Cuba, 11 May 1898. Facing the heavy fire of the enemy, Sullivan displayed extraordinary bravery and coolness throughout this action.

2169 ◆ SUNDQUIST, AXEL LEOHARD

Rank: Chief Carpenter's Mate (highest rank: Carpenter)
Service: U.S. Navy
Birthday: 26 May 1867
Place of Birth: Finland
Date of Death: 22 December 1910
Place of Death: on board the U.S.S. *Alliance*, Culebra, Puerto Rico
Cemetery: Braman Cemetery—Newport, Rhode Island
Entered Service at: Pennsylvania
Unit: U.S.S. *Marblehead*
Battle or Place of Action: approaches to Caimanera, Guantanamo Bay, Cuba
Date of Action: 26-27 July 1898
G.O. Number, Date: 500, 14 December 1898
Citation: On board the U.S.S. *Marblehead* at the approaches to Caimanera, Guantanamo Bay, Cuba, 26 and 27 July 1898. Displaying heroism, Sundquist took part in the perilous work of sweeping for and disabling 27 contact mines during this period.

2170 ◆ SUNDQUIST, GUSTAV ADOLF

Rank: Ordinary Seaman (highest rank: Chief Special Mechanic)
Service: U.S. Navy
Birthday: 4 June 1879
Place of Birth: Sweden
Date of Death: 25 August 1918
Place of Death: Drowned at Cape Ferret, Gironne, France. Body not recovered.
Entered Service at: New York
Unit: U.S.S. *Nashville*
Battle or Place of Action: Cienfuegos, Cuba
Date of Action: 11 May 1898
G.O. Number, Date: 529, 2 November 1899
Citation: On board the U.S.S. *Nashville* during the operation of cutting the cable leading from Cienfuegos, Cuba, 11 May 1898. Facing the heavy fire of the enemy, Sundquist displayed extraordinary bravery and coolness throughout this action.

2171 ◆ THOMPKINS, WILLIAM H.

Rank: Private (highest rank: Sergeant)
Service: U.S. Army
Birthday: 3 October 1872

Place of Birth: Paterson, Passaic County, New Jersey
Date of Death: 24 September 1916
Cemetery: San Francisco National Cemetery (WS-1036-A Row 11) (MH)—San Francisco, California
Entered Service at: Paterson, Passaic County, New Jersey
Unit: Troop G, 10th U.S. Cavalry
Battle or Place of Action: Tayabacoa, Cuba
Date of Action: 30 June 1898
Date of Issue: 23 June 1899
Citation: Voluntarily went ashore in the face of the enemy and aided in the rescue of his wounded comrades; this after several previous attempts at rescue had been frustrated.

2172 ◆ TRIPLETT, SAMUEL S.

Rank: Ordinary Seaman (highest rank: Chief Gunner)
Service: U.S. Navy
Birthday: 18 December 1869
Place of Birth: Cherokee, Crawford County, Kansas
Date of Death: 25 August 1957
Cemetery: North Edna Cemetery (MH)—Edna, Kansas
Entered Service at: New York
Unit: U.S.S. *Marblehead*
Battle or Place of Action: approaches to Caimanera, Guantanamo Bay, Cuba
Date of Action: 26-27 July 1898
G.O. Number, Date: 500, 14 December 1898
Citation: On board the U.S.S. *Marblehead* at the approaches to Caimanera, Guantanamo Bay, Cuba, 26 and 27 July 1898. Displaying heroism, Triplett took part in the perilous work of sweeping for and disabling 27 contact mines during this period.

2173 ◆ VADAS, ALBERT

True Name: Wadas, Albert
Rank: Seaman
Service: U.S. Navy
Birthday: 26 March 1877
Place of Birth: Austria-Hungary
Date of Death: 3 October 1946
Place of Death: Camp Kilmer, New Jersey
Cemetery: Weehawken Cemetery (MH)—North Bergen, New Jersey
Entered Service at: New York
Unit: U.S.S. *Marblehead*
Battle or Place of Action: Cienfuegos, Cuba
Date of Action: 11 May 1898
G.O. Number, Date: 521, 7 July 1899
Citation: On board the U.S.S. *Marblehead* during the operation of cutting the cable leading from Cienfuegos, Cuba, 11 May 1898. Facing the heavy fire of the enemy, Vadas displayed extraordinary bravery and coolness throughout this period.

2174 ◆ VAN ETTEN, HUDSON

Rank: Seaman (highest rank: Chief Watertender)
Service: U.S. Navy

Birthday: 17 May 1874
Place of Birth: Port Jervis, Orange County, New York
Date of Death: 27 October 1941
Place of Death: Kittery, Maine
Cemetery: Prospect Cemetery (MH)—Greenland, New Hampshire
Entered Service at: New Jersey
Unit: U.S.S. *Nashville*
Battle or Place of Action: Cienfuegos, Cuba
Date of Action: 11 May 1898
G.O. Number, Date: 521, 7 July 1899
Citation: On board the U.S.S. *Nashville* during the operation of cutting the cable leading from Cienfuegos, Cuba, 11 May 1898. Facing the heavy fire of the enemy, Van Etten displayed extraordinary bravery and coolness throughout this period.

2175 ◆ VOLZ, ROBERT

Rank: Seaman (highest rank: Gunner's Mate First Class)
Service: U.S. Navy
Birthday: 31 January 1875
Place of Birth: San Francisco, San Francisco County, California
Entered Service at: Virginia
Unit: U.S.S. *Nashville*
Battle or Place of Action: Cienfuegos, Cuba
Date of Action: 11 May 1898
G.O. Number, Date: 521, 7 July 1899
Citation: On board the U.S.S. *Nashville* during the operation of cutting the cable leading from Cienfuegos, Cuba, 11 May 1989. Facing the heavy fire of the enemy, Volz displayed extraordinary bravery and coolness thoughout this period.

2176 ◆ WANTON, GEORGE HENRY

Rank: Private (highest rank: Master Sergeant)
Service: U.S. Army
Birthday: 15 May 1868
Place of Birth: Paterson, Passaic County, New Jersey
Date of Death: 27 November 1940
Place of Death: Washington, D.C.
Cemetery: Arlington National Cemetery (4-2749) (MH)—Arlington, Virginia
Entered Service at: Paterson, Passaic County, New Jersey
Unit: Troop M, 10th U.S. Cavalry
Battle or Place of Action: Tayabacoa, Cuba
Date of Action: 30 June 1898
Date of Issue: 23 June 1899
Citation: Voluntarily went ashore in the face of the enemy and aided in the rescue of his wounded comrades; this after several previous attempts at rescue had been frustrated.

2177 ◆ WELBORN, IRA CLINTON

Rank: Second Lieutenant (highest rank: Colonel)
Service: U.S. Army
Birthday: 13 February 1874
Place of Birth: Mico, Mississippi

Date of Death: 13 July 1956
Cemetery: Biloxi National Cemetery (12-4-12)—Biloxi, Mississippi
Entered Service at: Mico, Mississippi
Unit: 9th U.S. Infantry
Battle or Place of Action: Santiago, Cuba
Date of Action: 2 July 1898
Date of Issue: 21 June 1899
Citation: Voluntarily left shelter and went, under fire, to the aid of a private of his company who was wounded.

2178 ◆ WENDE, BRUNO

Rank: Private
Service: U.S. Army
Birthday: 17 April 1859
Place of Birth: Germany
Date of Death: 27 December 1929
Cemetery: Spring Grove Cemetery—Cincinnati, Ohio
Entered Service at: Canton, Stark County, Ohio
Unit: Company C, 17th U.S. Infantry
Battle or Place of Action: El Caney, Cuba
Date of Action: 1 July 1898
Date of Issue: 22 June 1899
Citation: Gallantly assisted in the rescue of the wounded from in front of the lines and under heavy fire from the enemy.

2179 ◆ WEST, WALTER SCOTT

Rank: Private
Service: U.S. Marine Corps
Birthday: 13 March 1872
Place of Birth: Bradford, Merrimack County, New Hampshire
Date of Death: 14 September 1943
Cemetery: Forest Hill Cemetery—Boston, Massachusetts
Entered Service at: New Hampshire
Unit: U.S.S. *Marblehead*
Battle or Place of Action: Cienfuegos, Cuba
Date of Action: 11 May 1898
G.O. Number, Date: 521, 7 July 1899
Citation: On board the U.S.S. *Marblehead* during the operation of cutting the cable leading from Cienfuegos, Cuba, 11 May 1898. Facing the heavy fire of the enemy, West displayed extraordinary bravery and coolness throughout this action.

2180 ◆ WILKE, JULIUS AUGUST ROBERT

Rank: Boatswain's Mate First Class
Service: U.S. Navy
Birthday: 14 November 1860
Place of Birth: Germany
Entered Service at: New York
Unit: U.S.S. *Marblehead*
Battle or Place of Action: Cienfuegos, Cuba
Date of Action: 11 May 1898
G.O. Number, Date: 521, 7 July 1899

Citation: On board the U.S.S. *Marblehead* during the operation of cutting the cable leading from Cienfuegos, Cuba, 11 May 1989. Facing the heavy fire of the enemy, Wilke displayed extraordinary bravery and coolness throughout this action.

2181 ◆ WILLIAMS, FRANK

Rank: Seaman
Service: U.S. Navy
Birthday: 19 October 1871

Place of Birth: Danzig, Germany
Entered Service at: New York
Unit: U.S.S. *Marblehead*
Battle or Place of Action: Cienfuegos, Cuba
Date of Action: 11 May 1898
G.O. Number, Date: 521, 7 July 1899
Citation: On board the U.S.S. *Marblehead* during the operation of cutting the cable leading from Cienfuegos, Cuba, 11 May 1989. Facing the heavy fire of the enemy, Williams displayed extraordinary bravery and coolness throughout this period.

2182 ◆ FISHER, FREDERICK THOMAS

Rank: Gunner's Mate First Class
Service: U.S. Navy
Birthday: 3 June 1872
Place of Birth: England
Date of Death: 15 April 1906
Cemetery: Naval Cemetery—Guantanamo Bay, Cuba
Entered Service at: California
Unit: U.S.S. *Philadelphia*
Battle or Place of Action: Samoa
Date of Action: 1 April 1899
G.O. Number, Date: 55, 19 July 1901
Citation: Served on board the U.S.S. *Philadelphia*, Samoa, 1 April 1899. Serving in the presence of the enemy on this date, Fisher distinguished himself by his conduct.

2183 ◆ FORSTERER, BRUNO ALBERT

Rank: Sergeant
Service: U.S. Marine Corps
Birthday: 14 July 1869
Place of Birth: Koenigsberg, Germany
Date of Death: 13 June 1957
Cemetery: Arlington National Cemetery (53-2757) (MH)—Arlington, Virginia
Entered Service at: Massachusetts
Battle or Place of Action: near Tagalli, Samoa
Date of Action: 1 April 1899
G.O. Number, Date: 55, 19 July 1901
Citation: For distinguished conduct in the presence of the enemy at Samoa, 1 April 1899.

2184 ◆ HULBERT, HENRY LEWIS

Rank: Private (highest rank: First Lieutenant)
Service: U.S. Marine Corps
Birthday: 12 January 1867
Place of Birth: Kingston upon Hull, Humberside County, England
Date of Death: 4 October 1918
Place of Death: near Mont Blanc, France (WWI)
Cemetery: Arlington National Cemetery (3-4309)—Arlington, Virginia
Entered Service at: California
Unit: Marine guard, U.S.S. *Philadelphia*
Battle or Place of Action: Samoa
Date of Action: 1 April 1899
G.O. Number, Date: 55, 19 July 1901
Citation: For distinguished conduct in the presence of the enemy at Samoa, 1 April 1899.

2185 ◆ McNALLY, MICHAEL JOSEPH

Rank: Sergeant
Service: U.S. Marine Corps
Birthday: 29 June 1860
Place of Birth: New York, New York
Entered Service at: California
Battle or Place of Action: Samoa
Date of Action: 1 April 1899
G.O. Number, Date: 55, 19 July 1901
Citation: For distinguished conduct in the presence of the enemy at Samoa, 1 April 1899.

PHILIPPINE INSURRECTION

2186 ◆ ANDERS, FRANK LAFAYETTE

Rank: Corporal (highest rank: Major)
Service: U.S. Army
Birthday: 10 November 1875
Place of Birth: Fort Lincoln, Dakota Territory
Date of Death: 20 January 1966
Cemetery: Hill Side Cemetery—Ripon, Wisconsin
Entered Service at: Fargo, Cass County, North Dakota
Unit: Company B, 1st North Dakota Volunteer Infantry
Battle or Place of Action: San Miguel de Mayumo, Luzon, Philippine Islands
Date of Action: 13 May 1899
Date of Issue: 3 March 1906
Citation: With 11 other scouts, without waiting for the supporting battalion to aid them or to get into a position to do so, charged over a distance of about 150 yards and completely routed about 300 of the enemy who were in line and in a position that could only be carried by a frontal attack.

2187 ◆ BATSON, MATTHEW ARLINGTON

Rank: First Lieutenant (highest rank: Captain)
Service: U.S. Army
Birthday: 24 April 1866
Place of Birth: Anna, Union County, Illinois
Date of Death: 13 January 1917
Cemetery: Arlington National Cemetery (2-3604-WS) (MH)—Arlington, Virginia
Entered Service at: Carbondale, Jackson County, Illinois
Unit: 4th U.S. Cavalry
Battle or Place of Action: Calamba, Luzon, Philippine Islands
Date of Action: 26 July 1899
Date of Issue: 8 March 1902
Citation: Swam the San Juan River in the face of the enemy's fire and drove him from his entrenchments.

2188 ◆ BEARSS, HIRAM IDDINGS

Rank: Colonel (highest rank: Brigadier General)
Service: U.S. Marine Corps
Birthday: 13 April 1875
Place of Birth: Peru, Miami County, Indiana
Date of Death: 26 August 1938
Place of Death: Peru, Indiana
Cemetery: Mount Hope Cemetery (MH)—Peru, Indiana
Entered Service at: Indiana
Unit: 1st Marine Brigade

Battle or Place of Action: Cadaean & Sohoton Rivers Junction, Samar, Philippine Islands
Date of Action: 17 November 1901
Date of Presentation: 5 April 1934
Place of Presentation: Presented by Pres. Franklin D. Roosevelt
Citation: For extraordinary heroism and eminent and conspicuous conduct in battle at the junction of the Cadacan and Sohoton Rivers, Samar, Philippine Islands, 17 November 1901. Col. Bearss (then Capt.), second in command of the columns upon their uniting ashore in the Sohoton River region, made a surprise attack on the fortified cliffs and completely routed the enemy, killing 30 and capturing and destroying the powder magazine, 40 lantacas (guns), rice, food and cuartels. Due to his courage, intelligence, discrimination, and zeal, he successfully led his men up the cliffs by means of bamboo ladders to a height of 200 feet. The cliffs were of soft stone of volcanic origin, in the nature of pumice, and were honeycombed with caves. Tons of rocks were suspended in platforms held in position by vine cables (known as bejuco) in readiness to be precipitated upon people below. After driving the insurgents from their position, which was almost impregnable, being covered with numerous trails lined with poison spears, pits, etc., he led his men across the river, scaled the cliffs on the opposite side, and destroyed the camps there. Col. Bearss and the men under his command overcame incredible difficulties and dangers in destroying positions which, according to reports from old prisoners, had taken three years to perfect, were held as a final rallying point, and were never before penetrated by white troops. Col. Bearss also rendered distinguished public service in the presence of the enemy at Quinapundan River, Samar, Philippine Islands, on 19 January 1902.

2189 ◆ BELL, HARRY

Rank: Captain
Service: U.S. Army
Birthday: 21 September 1860
Place of Birth: Milwaukee, Milwaukee County, Wisconsin
Date of Death: 10 November 1938
Cemetery: Fort Leavenworth National Cemetery (OFF-167) (MH)—Fort Leavenworth, Kansas
Entered Service at: Minneapolis, Hennepin County, Minnesota
Unit: 36th Infantry, U.S. Volunteers
Battle or Place of Action: near Porac, Luzon, Philippine Islands

Date of Action: 17 October 1899
Date of Issue: 8 March 1902
Citation: Led a successful charge against a superior force, capturing, and dispersing the enemy and relieving other members of his regiment from a perilous position.

2190 ◆ BELL, JAMES FRANKLIN

Rank: Colonel (highest rank: Major General)
Service: U.S. Army
Birthday: 9 January 1856
Place of Birth: Shelbyville, Shelby County, Kentucky
Date of Death: 8 January 1919
Place of Death: New York, New York
Cemetery: Arlington National Cemetery (3-1735-4)—Arlington, Virginia
Entered Service at: Shelbyville, Shelby County, Kentucky
Unit: 36th Infantry, U.S. Volunteers
Battle or Place of Action: near Porac, Luzon, Philippine Islands
Date of Action: 9 September 1899
Date of Issue: 11 December 1899
Citation: While in advance of his regiment, charged seven insurgents with his pistol and compelled the surrender of the captain and two privates under a close fire from the remaining insurgents concealed in a bamboo thicket.

2191 ◆ BICKHAM, CHARLES GOODWIN

Rank: First Lieutenant (highest rank: Captain)
Service: U.S. Army
Birthday: 12 August 1867
Place of Birth: Dayton, Montgomery County, Ohio
Date of Death: 14 December 1944
Cemetery: Woodlawn Cemetery (MH)—Dayton, Ohio
Entered Service at: Dayton, Montgomery County, Ohio
Unit: 27th U.S. Infantry
Battle or Place of Action: Bayong, near Lake Lanao, Mindanao, Philippine Islands
Date of Action: 2 May 1902
G.O. Number, Date: 165, W.D. 7 August 1909
Date of Issue: 29 April 1904
Citation: Crossed a fire-swept field, in close-range of the enemy, and brought a wounded soldier to a place of shelter.

2192 ◆ BIEGLER, GEORGE WESLEY

Rank: Captain (highest rank: Lieutenant Colonel)
Service: U.S. Army
Birthday: 31 May 1868
Place of Birth: Terre Haute, Vigo County, Indiana
Date of Death: 2 April 1929
Place of Death: Presidio of San Francisco, California
Cemetery: The Hollywood Cemetery—Hollywood, California
Entered Service at: Terre Haute, Vigo County, Indiana
Unit: 28th Infantry, U.S. Volunteers
Battle or Place of Action: near Loac, Luzon, Philippine Islands

Date of Action: 21 October 1900
Date of Issue: 11 March 1902
Citation: With but 19 men resisted and at close quarters defeated 300 of the enemy.

2193 ◆ BIRKHIMER, WILLIAM EDWARD

Rank: Captain (highest rank: Brigadier General U.S.A. Ret.)
Service: U.S. Army
Birthday: 1 March 1848
Place of Birth: Somerset, Perry County, Ohio
Date of Death: 10 June 1914
Place of Death: Washington, D.C.
Cemetery: Arlington National Cemetery (1-339-WD)—Arlington, Virginia
Entered Service at: Iowa
Unit: 3d U.S. Artillery
Battle or Place of Action: San Miguel de Mayumo, Luzon, Philippine Islands
Date of Action: 13 May 1899
Date of Issue: 15 July 1902
Citation: With 12 men charged and routed 300 of the enemy.

2194 ◆ BOEHLER, OTTO A.

Rank: Private
Service: U.S. Army
Birthday: 15 October 1873
Place of Birth: Germany
Date of Death: 15 October 1910
Cemetery: St. Mary's Catholic Cemetery (MH)—Breckenridge, Minnesota
Entered Service at: Wahpeton, Richland County, North Dakota
Unit: Company I, 1st North Dakota Volunteer Infantry
Battle or Place of Action: near San Isidro, Luzon, Philippine Islands
Date of Action: 16 May 1899
Date of Issue: 17 May 1906
Citation: With 21 other scouts charged across a burning bridge, under heavy fire, and completely routed 600 of the enemy who were entrenched in a strongly fortified position.

2195 ◆ BUCKLEY, HOWARD MAJOR

Rank: Private (highest rank: Gunnery Sergeant)
Service: U.S. Marine Corps
Birthday: 23 January 1862
Place of Birth: Croton Falls, Westchester County, New York
Date of Death: 2 July 1941
Place of Death: Bath, New York
Cemetery: Wheeler Cemetery—Wheeler, New York
Entered Service at: New York
Battle or Place of Action: with the Eighth Army Corps
Date of Action: 25, 27, 29 March 1899 & 4 April 1899
G.O. Number, Date: 55, 19 July 1901
Citation: For distinguished conduct in the presence of the

enemy in battle, while with the 8th Army Corps on 25, 27, 29 March, and 4 April 1899.

2196 ◆ BYRNE, BERNARD ALBERT

Rank: Captain (highest rank: Lieutenant Colonel)
Service: U.S. Army
Birthday: 19 October 1853
Place of Birth: Newport Barracks, Giles County, Virginia
Date of Death: 29 February 1910
Cemetery: Arlington National Cemetery (1-707)—Arlington, Virginia
Entered Service at: Washington, D.C.
Unit: 6th U.S. Infantry
Battle or Place of Action: Bobong, Negros, Philippine Islands
Date of Action: 19 July 1899
Date of Issue: 15 July 1902
Citation: Most distinguished gallantry in rallying his men on the bridge after the line had been broken and pushed back.

2197 ◆ CARSON, ANTHONY J.

Rank: Corporal
Service: U.S. Army
Birthday: 23 April 1869
Place of Birth: Boston, Suffolk County, Massachusetts
Date of Death: 25 April 1943
Place of Death: Dorchester, Massachusetts
Cemetery: Calvary Cemetery—Boston, Massachusetts
Entered Service at: Malden, Middlesex County, Massachusetts
Unit: Company H, 43d Infantry, U.S. Volunteers
Battle or Place of Action: Catubig, Samar, Philippine Islands
Date of Action: 15-19 April 1900
Date of Issue: 4 January 1906
Citation: Assumed command of a detachment of the company which had survived an overwhelming attack of the enemy, and by his bravery and untiring efforts and the exercise of extraordinary good judgment in the handling of his men, successfully withstood for two days the attacks of a large force of the enemy, thereby saving the lives of the survivors and protecting the wounded until relief came.

2198 ◆ CAWETZKA, CHARLES

Rank: Private
Service: U.S. Army
Birthday: 1 March 1877
Place of Birth: Detroit, Wayne County, Michigan
Date of Death: 23 October 1951
Cemetery: Romulus Cemetery—Romulus, Michigan
Entered Service at: Wayne, Wayne County, Michigan
Unit: Company F, 30th Infantry, U.S. Volunteers
Battle or Place of Action: near Sariaya, Luzon, Philippine Islands
Date of Action: 23 August 1900
Date of Issue: 14 March 1902

Citation: Singlehanded he defended a disabled comrade against a greatly superior force of the enemy.

2199 ◆ CECIL, JOSEPH SAMUEL

Rank: First Lieutenant (highest rank: Colonel)
Service: U.S. Army
Birthday: 11 January 1878
Place of Birth: New River, Tennessee
Date of Death: 20 August 1940
Cemetery: Arlington National Cemetery (6-5718)—Arlington, Virginia
Entered Service at: New River, Tennessee
Unit: 19th U.S. Infantry
Battle or Place of Action: Bud-Dajo, Jolo, Philippine Islands
Date of Action: 7 March 1906
G.O. Number, Date: 7, W.D. 3 February 1913
Date of Issue: 23 January 1913
Citation: While at the head of the column about to assault the first cotta under a superior fire at short-range, personally carried to a sheltered position a wounded man and the body of one who was killed beside him.

2200 ◆ CONDON, CLARENCE MILVILLE

Rank: Sergeant (highest rank: Lieutenant Colonel)
Service: U.S. Army
Birthday: 12 August 1875
Place of Birth: South Brooksville, Hancock County, Maine
Date of Death: 20 July 1916
Cemetery: Arlington National Cemetery (2-3834)—Arlington, Virginia
Entered Service at: St. Augustine, St. Johns County, Florida
Unit: Battery G, 3d U.S. Artillery
Battle or Place of Action: near Calulut, Luzon, Philippine Islands
Date of Action: 5 November 1899
Date of Issue: 11 March 1902
Citation: While in command of a detachment of four men, charged and routed 40 entrenched insurgents, inflicting on them heavy loss.

2201 ◆ DAVIS, CHARLES P.

Rank: Private
Service: U.S. Army
Birthday: 5 June 1872
Place of Birth: Long Prairie, Todd County, Minnesota
Date of Death: 28 May 1943
Cemetery: Hillside Cemetery (MH)—Valley City, North Dakota
Entered Service at: Valley City, Barnes County, North Dakota
Unit: Company G, 1st North Dakota Volunteer Infantry
Battle or Place of Action: near San Isidro, Luzon, Philippine Islands

Date of Action: 16 May 1899
Date of Issue: 28 April 1906
Citation: With 21 other scouts charged across a burning bridge, under heavy fire, and completely routed 600 of the enemy who were entrenched in a strongly fortified position.

2202 ◆ DOWNS, WILLIS H.

Rank: Private (highest rank: Wagoneer)
Service: U.S. Army
Birthday: 1 June 1870
Place of Birth: Mount Carmel, Connecticut
Date of Death: 15 September 1929
Cemetery: Highland Home Cemetery (MH)—Jamestown, North Dakota
Entered Service at: Jamestown, Stutsman County, North Dakota
Unit: Company H, 1st North Dakota Volunteer Infantry
Battle or Place of Action: San Miguel de Mayumo, Luzon, Philippine Islands
Date of Action: 13 May 1899
Date of Issue: 16 February 1906
Citation: With 11 other scouts, without waiting for the supporting battalion to aid them or to get into a position to do so, charged over a distance of about 150 yards and completely routed about 300 of the enemy who were in line and in a position that could only be carried by a frontal attack.

2203 ◆ EPPS, JOSEPH L.

Rank: Private
Service: U.S. Army
Birthday: 16 May 1870
Place of Birth: Jamestown, Moniteau County, Missouri
Date of Death: 20 June 1952
Cemetery: Green Hill Cemetery—Muskogee, Oklahoma
Entered Service at: Oklahoma Indian Territory
Unit: Company B, 33d Infantry, U.S. Volunteers
Battle or Place of Action: Vigan, Luzon, Philippine Islands
Date of Action: 4 December 1899
Date of Issue: 7 February 1902
Citation: Discovered a party of insurgents inside a wall, climbed to the top of the wall, covered them with his gun, and forced them to stack arms and surrender.

2204 ◆ FERGUSON, ARTHUR MEDWORTH

Rank: First Lieutenant (highest rank: Lieutenant Colonel)
Service: U.S. Army
Birthday: 11 December 1877
Place of Birth: Coffey County, Kansas
Date of Death: 20 February 1923
Cemetery: Arlington National Cemetery (3-4016)—Arlington, Virginia
Entered Service at: Burlington, Coffey County, Kansas
Unit: 36th Infantry, U.S. Volunteers
Battle or Place of Action: near Porac, Luzon, Philippine Islands
Date of Action: 28 September 1899
Date of Issue: 8 March 1902

Citation: Charged alone a body of the enemy and captured a captain.

2205 ◆ FITZ, JOSEPH

Rank: Ordinary Seaman
Service: U.S. Navy
Birthday: 24 May 1886
Place of Birth: Austria
Date of Death: 24 February 1945
Cemetery: Glendale Cemetery—Des Moines, Iowa
Entered Service at: Des Moines, Polk County, Iowa
Unit: U.S.S. *Pampanga*
Battle or Place of Action: Mount Dajo Jolo, Philippine Islands
Date of Action: 8 March 1906
G.O. Number, Date: 19, 1 May 1906
Citation: On board the U.S.S. *Pampanga*, Mount Dajo Jolo, Philippine Islands, 8 March 1906. Serving in the presence of the enemy on this date, Fitz displayed bravery and extraordinary heroism.

2206 ◆ FORBECK, ANDREW PETER

Rank: Seaman
Service: U.S. Navy
Birthday: 29 August 1881
Place of Birth: New York
Date of Death: 25 April 1924
Cemetery: Erie Cemetery—Erie, Pennsylvania
Entered Service at: New York
Unit: U.S.S. *Pampanga*
Battle or Place of Action: Katbalogan, Samar, Philippine Islands
Date of Action: 16 July 1900
G.O. Number, Date: 55, 19 July 1901
Citation: For distinguished conduct in the presence of the enemy during the battle of Katbalogan, Samar, Philippine Islands, 16 July 1900.

2207 ◆ FUNSTON SR., FREDERICK

Rank: Colonel (highest rank: Major General U.S.A.)
Service: U.S. Army
Birthday: 9 November 1865
Place of Birth: New Carlisle, Clark County, Ohio
Date of Death: 19 February 1917
Place of Death: Fort Sam Houston, Texas
Cemetery: San Francisco National Cemetery (OS-68-3) (MH)—San Francisco, California
Entered Service at: Iola, Allen County, Kansas
Unit: 20th Kansas Volunteer Infantry
Battle or Place of Action: Rio Grande de la Pampanga, Luzon, Philippine Islands
Date of Action: 27 April 1899
Date of Issue: 14 February 1900
Citation: Crossed the river on a raft and by his skill and daring enabled the general commanding to carry the enemy's entrenched position on the north bank of the river and to drive him with great loss from the important strategic position of Calumpit.

2208 ◆ GALBRAITH, ROBERT

Rank: Gunner's Mate Third Class
Service: U.S. Navy
Birthday: 18 February 1878
Place of Birth: Brooklyn, Kings County, New York
Date of Death: 13 May 1949
Cemetery: Long Island National Cemetery (DSS-17) (MH)—Farmingdale, New York
Entered Service at: New York
Battle or Place of Action: at El pardo, Cebu, Philippine Islands
Date of Action: 12-13 September 1899
G.O. Number, Date: 531, 21 November 1900r
Citation: For extraordinary heroism and gallantry while under fire of the enemy at El Pardo, Cebu, Philippine Islands, 12 and 13 September 1899.

2209 ◆ GALT, STERLING ARCHIBALD

Rank: Artificer (highest rank: Battalion Sergeant Major)
Service: U.S. Army
Birthday: October 1866
Place of Birth: Taneytown, Carroll County, Maryland
Date of Death: 21 October 1908
Place of Death: Kansas City, Missouri
Cemetery: Orient Cemetery (MH)—Harrisonville, Missouri
Entered Service at: Taneytown, Carroll County, Maryland
Unit: Company F, 36th Infantry, U.S. Volunteers
Battle or Place of Action: Bamban, Luzon, Philippine Islands
Date of Action: 9 November 1899
Date of Issue: 30 April 1902
Citation: Distinguished bravery and conspicuous gallantry in action against insurgents.

2210 ◆ GAUJOT, ANTOINE AUGUST

Rank: Corporal
Service: U.S. Army
Birthday: 1879
Place of Birth: Keweenaw, Baraga County, Michigan
Date of Death: 14 April 1936
Cemetery: Fairview Cemetery—Williamson, West Virginia
Entered Service at: Williamson, Mingo County, West Virginia
Unit: Company M, 27th Infantry, U.S. Volunteers
Battle or Place of Action: at San Mateo, Philippine Islands
Date of Action: 19 December 1899
Date of Presentation: 15 February 1911
Place of Presentation: The White House, presented by Pres. William H. Taft
Citation: Attempted under a heavy fire of the enemy to swim a river for the purpose of obtaining and returning with a canoe.

2211 ◆ GEDEON, LOUIS

Rank: Private (highest rank: Sergeant)
Service: U.S. Army
Birthday: 19 September 1878

Place of Birth: Pittsburgh, Allegheny County, Pennsylvania
Date of Death: 11 October 1950
Place of Death: Washington, D.C.
Cemetery: Soldier's Home National Cemetery (O-25) (MH)—Washington, D.C.
Entered Service at: Pittsburgh, Allegheny County, Pennsylvania
Unit: Company G, 19th U.S. Infantry
Battle or Place of Action: at Mount Amia, Cebu, Philippine Islands
Date of Action: 4 February 1900
Date of Issue: 10 March 1902
Citation: Singlehanded defended his mortally wounded captain from an overwhelming force of the enemy.

2212 ◆ GIBSON, EDWARD HERRICK

Rank: Sergeant
Service: U.S. Army
Birthday: 4 July 1872
Place of Birth: Boston, Suffolk County, Massachusetts
Date of Death: 25 April 1942
Cemetery: Golden Gate National Cemetery (L-5-7791)—San Bruno, California
Entered Service at: Boston, Suffolk County, Massachusetts
Unit: Company M, 27th Infantry, U.S. Volunteers
Battle or Place of Action: San Mateo, Philippine Islands
Date of Action: 19 December 1899
Date of Issue: 5 April 1911
Citation: Attempted under a heavy fire of the enemy to swim a river for the purpose of obtaining and returning with a canoe.

2213 ◆ GILLENWATER, JAMES ROBERT LEE

Rank: Corporal
Service: U.S. Army
Birthday: 28 October 1871
Place of Birth: Rye Cove, Virginia
Date of Death: 19 January 1946
Cemetery: Payne Cemetery (MH)—Rogersville, Tennessee
Entered Service at: Rye Cove, Virginia
Unit: Company A, 36th Infantry, U.S. Volunteers
Battle or Place of Action: near Porac, Luzon, Philippine Islands
Date of Action: 3 September 1899
Date of Issue: 15 March 1902
Citation: While on a scout drove off a superior force of insurgents and with the assistance of one comrade brought from the field of action the bodies of two comrades, one killed and the other severely wounded.

2214 ◆ GREER, ALLEN JAMES

Rank: Second Lieutenant (highest rank: Lieutenant Colonel)
Service: U.S. Army
Birthday: 11 August 1878

PHILIPPINE INSURRECTION

Place of Birth: Memphis, Shelby County, Tennessee
Date of Death: 16 March 1964
Cemetery: Arlington National Cemetery (1-701-B) (MH)—Arlington, Virginia
Entered Service at: Memphis, Shelby County, Tennessee
Unit: 4th U.S. Infantry
Battle or Place of Action: near Majada, Laguna Province, Philippine Islands
Date of Action: 2 July 1901
Date of Issue: 10 March 1902
Citation: Charged alone an insurgent outpost with his pistol, killing one, wounding two, and capturing three insurgents with their rifles and equipment.

2215 ◆ GROVE, WILLIAM REMSBURG

Rank: Lieutenant Colonel (highest rank: Colonel)
Service: U.S. Army
Birthday: 16 May 1872
Place of Birth: Montezuma, Poweshiek County, Iowa
Date of Death: 6 August 1952
Cemetery: Manasota Memorial Park—Sarasota, Florida
Entered Service at: Denver, Denver County, Colorado
Unit: 36th Infantry, U.S. Volunteers
Battle or Place of Action: near Porac, Luzon, Philippine Islands
Date of Action: 9 September 1899
Date of Issue: 16 July 1902
Citation: In advance of his regiment, rushed to the assistance of his colonel, charging, pistol in hand, seven insurgents, and compelling surrender of all not killed or wounded.

2216 ◆ HARVEY, HARRY

Rank: Sergeant
Service: U.S. Marine Corps
Birthday: 4 June 1873
Place of Birth: New York, New York
Date of Death: 5 April 1929
Cemetery: Los Angeles National Cemetery (60-E-4) (MH)—Los Angeles, California
Entered Service at: New Jersey
Battle or Place of Action: Benefictican, Philippine Islands
Date of Action: 16 February 1900
G.O. Number, Date: 55, 19 July 1901
Date of Issue: 24 January 1902
Citation: Served in battle against the enemy at Benefictican, 16 February 1900. Throughout this action and in the presence of the enemy, Harvey distinguished himself by meritorious conduct.

2217 ◆ HAYES, WEBB COOK

Rank: Lieutenant Colonel (highest rank: Colonel)
Service: U.S. Army
Birthday: 20 March 1856
Place of Birth: Cincinnati, Hamilton County, Ohio
Date of Death: 26 July 1934
Cemetery: Spiegal Grove Estate Park—Freemont, Ohio

Entered Service at: Fremont, Sandusky County, Ohio
Unit: 31st Infantry, U.S. Volunteers
Battle or Place of Action: Vigan, Luzon, Philippine Islands
Date of Action: 4 December 1899
Date of Issue: 17 December 1902
Citation: Pushed through the enemy's lines alone, during the night, from the beach to the beleaguered force at Vigan, and returned the following morning to report the condition of affairs to the Navy and secure assistance.

2218 ◆ HENDERSON, JOSEPH

Rank: Sergeant (highest rank: First Sergeant)
Service: U.S. Army
Birthday: December 1869
Place of Birth: Leavenworth, Leavenworth County, Kansas
Date of Death: 19 December 1938
Cemetery: Arlington National Cemetery (20-50042) (MH)—Arlington, Virginia
Entered Service at: Leavenworth, Leavenworth County, Kansas
Unit: Troop B, 6th U.S. Cavalry
Battle or Place of Action: Patian Island, Philippine Islands
Date of Action: 2 July 1909
Date of Presentation: 23 November 1912
Place of Presentation: Presented by Pres. William H. Taft
Citation: While in action against hostile Moros, voluntarily advanced alone, in the face of a heavy fire, to within about 15 yards of the hostile position and refastened to a tree a block and tackle used in checking the recoil of a mountian gun.

2219 ◆ HIGH, FRANK CHARLES

Rank: Private
Service: U.S. Army
Birthday: 7 June 1875
Place of Birth: Dunningham, Yolo County, California
Date of Death: 13 December 1966
Place of Death: Ashland, Oregon
Cemetery: Memory Gardens Cemetery—Medford, Oregon
Entered Service at: Ashland, Jackson County, Oregon
Unit: Company G, 2d Oregon Volunteer Infantry
Battle or Place of Action: near San Isidro, Luzon, Philippine Islands
Date of Action: 16 May 1899
Date of Issue: 4 April 1906
Citation: With 21 other scouts charged across a burning bridge, under heavy fire, and completely routed 600 of the enemy who were entrenched in a strongly fortified position.

2220 ◆ HUNTSMAN, JOHN A.

Rank: Sergeant (highest rank: Second Lieutenant)
Service: U.S. Army
Place of Birth: Oskaloosa, Mahaska County, Iowa
Entered Service at: Lawrence, Douglas County, Kansas
Unit: Company E, 36th Infantry, U.S. Volunteers
Battle or Place of Action: Bamban, Luzon, Philippine Islands

Date of Action: 9 November 1899
Date of Issue: 26 March 1902
Citation: For distinguished bravery and conspicuous gallantry in action against insurgents.

2221 ◆ JENSEN, GOTFRED

Rank: Private
Service: U.S. Army
Birthday: 20 November 1872
Place of Birth: Denmark
Date of Death: 26 December 1945
Cemetery: Washington Soldier's Home Cemetery (MH)—Retsil, Washington
Entered Service at: Devils Lake, Ramsey County, North Dakota
Unit: Company D, 1st North Dakota Volunteer Infantry
Battle or Place of Action: San Miguel de Mayumo, Luzon, Philippine Islands
Date of Action: 13 May 1899
Date of Issue: 6 June 1906
Citation: With 11 other scouts, without waiting for the supporting battalion to aid them or to get into a position to do so, charged over a distance of about 150 yards and completely routed about 300 of the enemy, who were in line and in a position that could only be carried by a frontal attack.

2222 ◆ JOHNSTON, GORDON

Rank: First Lieutenant (highest rank: Colonel)
Service: U.S. Army
Birthday: 25 May 1874
Place of Birth: Charlotte, Mecklenburg County, North Carolina
Date of Death: 8 March 1934
Cemetery: Arlington National Cemetery (7-10092)—Arlington, Virginia
Entered Service at: Birmingham, Jefferson County, Alabama
Unit: U.S. Signal Corps
Battle or Place of Action: Mount Bud Dajo, Jolo, Philippine Islands
Date of Action: 7 March 1906
G.O. Number, Date: 207
Date of Presentation: 7 November 1910
Place of Presentation: The White House, presented by Pres. William H. Taft
Citation: Voluntarily took part in and was dangerously wounded during an assault on the enemy's works.

2223 ◆ KENNEDY, JOHN THOMAS

Rank: Second Lieutenant (highest rank: Brigadier General)
Service: U.S. Army
Birthday: 22 July 1885
Place of Birth: Hendersonville, South Carolina
Date of Death: 26 September 1969
Place of Death: Columbia, South Carolina
Cemetery: Arlington National Cemetery (7-10076)—Arlington, Virginia

Entered Service at: Orangeburg, Orangeburg County, South Carolina
Unit: 6th U.S. Cavalry
Battle or Place of Action: at Patian Island, Philippine Islands
Date of Action: 4 July 1909
Date of Presentation: 23 November 1912
Place of Presentation: Presented by Pres. William H. Taft
Citation: While in action against hostile Moros, he entered with a few enlisted men the mouth of a cave occupied by a desperate enemy, this act having been ordered after he had volunteered several times. In this action 2d Lt. Kennedy was severely wounded.

2224 ◆ KILBOURNE JR., CHARLES EVANS

Rank: First Lieutenant (highest rank: Major General)
Service: U.S. Army
Birthday: 23 December 1872
Place of Birth: Fort Myer, Arlington County, Virginia
Date of Death: 12 November 1963
Cemetery: Arlington National Cemetery (3-1705)—Arlington, Virginia
Entered Service at: Portland, Multnomah County, Oregon
Unit: U.S. Volunteer Signal Corps
Battle or Place of Action: Paco Bridge, Philippine Islands
Date of Action: 5 February 1899
Date of Issue: 6 May 1905
Citation: Within a range of 250 yards of the enemy and in the face of a rapid fire climbed a telegraph pole at the east end of the bridge and in full view of the enemy coolly and carefully repaired a broken telegraph wire, thereby reestablishing telegraphic communication to the front.

2225 ◆ KINNE, JOHN BAXTER

Rank: Private (highest rank: Captain U.S. Medical Corps WWI)
Service: U.S. Army
Birthday: 3 October 1877
Place of Birth: Beloit, Rock County, Wisconsin
Date of Death: 19 June 1943
Cemetery: Fern Hill Cemetery—Aberdeen, Washington
Entered Service at: Fargo, Cass County, North Dakota
Unit: Company B, 1st North Dakota Volunteer Infantry
Battle or Place of Action: near San Isidro, Luzon, Philippine Islands
Date of Action: 16 May 1899
Date of Issue: 17 May 1906
Citation: With 21 other scouts charged across a burning bridge, under heavy fire, and completely routed 600 of the enemy who were entrenched in a strongly fortified position.

2226 ◆ *LEAHY, CORNELIUS J.

Rank: Private
Service: U.S. Army
Birthday: June 1872
Place of Birth: Limerick, Ireland

Date of Death: 1 December 1900
Place of Death: Philippine Islands (Killed in Action)
Cemetery: San Francisco National Cemetery (ADD-NA-970)—San Francisco, California
Entered Service at: San Francisco, San Francisco County, California
Unit: Company A, 36th Infantry, U.S. Volunteers
Battle or Place of Action: near Porac, Luzon, Philippine Islands
Date of Action: 3 September 1899
Date of Issue: 3 May 1902
Citation: Distinguished gallantry in action in driving off a superior force, and with the assistance of one comrade, brought from the field of action the bodies of two comrades, one killed and the other severely wounded, this while on a scout.

2227 ◆ LEONARD, JOSEPH H.

Rank: Private (highest rank: Sergeant)
Service: U.S. Marine Corps
Birthday: 28 August 1876
Place of Birth: Cohoes, Albany County, New York
Date of Death: 23 September 1946
Place of Death: Yountville, California
Cemetery: Veterans Home of California Cemetery (MH)—Yountville, California
Entered Service at: New York, New York
Battle or Place of Action: with the Eighth Army Corps
Date of Action: 25, 27, 29 March & 4 April 1899
G.O. Number, Date: 55, 19 July 1901
Citation: For distinguished conduct in the presence of the enemy in battles, while with the 8th Army Corps on 25, 27, 29 March, and 4 April 1899.

2228 ◆ *LOGAN JR., JOHN ALEXANDER

Rank: Major
Service: U.S. Army
Birthday: 24 July 1865
Place of Birth: Carbondale, Jackson County, Illinois
Date of Death: 11 November 1899
Place of Death: At San Jacinto, Philippine Islands
Cemetery: Oak Hill Cemetery (MH)—Youngstown, Ohio
Entered Service at: Youngstown, Mahoning County, Ohio
Unit: 33d Infantry, U.S. Volunteers
Battle or Place of Action: at San Jacinto, Philippine Islands
Date of Action: 11 November 1899
Date of Issue: 3 May 1902
Citation: For most distinguished gallantry in leading his battalion upon the entrenchments of the enemy, on which occasion he fell mortally wounded.

2229 ◆ LONGFELLOW, RICHARD MOSES

Rank: Private
Service: U.S. Army
Birthday: 24 June 1867
Place of Birth: Logan County, Illinois

Date of Death: 17 May 1951
Cemetery: Norman Hill Cemetery (MH)—Lewiston, Idaho
Entered Service at: Mandan, Morton County, North Dakota
Unit: Company A, 1st North Dakota Volunteer Infantry
Battle or Place of Action: near San Isidro, Luzon, Philippine Islands
Date of Action: 16 May 1899
Date of Issue: 4 April 1906
Citation: With 21 other scouts charged across a burning bridge, under heavy fire, and completely routed 600 of the enemy who were entrenched in a strongly fortified position.

2230 ◆ LYON, EDWARD EUGENE

Rank: Private
Service: U.S. Army
Birthday: 8 August 1871
Place of Birth: Hixton, Jackson County, Wisconsin
Date of Death: 18 November 1931
Place of Death: Los Angeles, California
Cemetery: Hollywood Cemetery—Hollywood, California
Entered Service at: Amboy, Clark County, Washington
Unit: Company B, 2d Oregon Volunteer Infantry
Battle or Place of Action: San Miguel de Mayumo, Luzon, Philippine Islands
Date of Action: 13 May 1899
Date of Issue: 24 January 1906
Citation: With 11 other scouts without waiting for the supporting battalion to aid them or to get into a position to do so, charged over a distance of about 150 yards and completely routed about 300 of the enemy, who were in line and in a position that could only be carried by a frontal attack.

2231 ◆ MACLAY, WILLIAM PALMER

Rank: Private (highest rank: First Lieutenant)
Service: U.S. Army
Birthday: 1877
Place of Birth: Spruce Creek, Huntingdon County, Pennsylvania
Date of Death: 31 July 1943
Cemetery: Arlington National Cemetery (7-9008-F) (MH)—Arlington, Virginia
Entered Service at: Altoona, Blair County, Pennsylvania
Unit: Company A, 43d Infantry, U.S. Volunteers
Battle or Place of Action: Hilongas, Leyte, Philippine Islands
Date of Action: 6 May 1900
Date of Issue: 11 March 1902
Citation: Charged an occupied bastion, saving the life of an officer in a hand-to-hand combat and destroying the enemy.

2232 ◆ MATHEWS, GEORGE WILLIAM

Rank: Captain Assistant Surgeon (highest rank: Major Surgeon)
Service: U.S. Army
Birthday: 1874

Place of Birth: Worcester, Worcester County, Massachusetts
Date of Death: 31 July 1943
Cemetery: St. John's Cemetery—Worcester, Massachusetts
Entered Service at: Worcester, Worcester County, Massachusetts
Unit: 36th Infantry, U.S. Volunteers
Battle or Place of Action: near Labo, Luzon, Philippine Islands
Date of Action: 29 October 1899
Date of Issue: 14 March 1902
Citation: While in attendance upon the wounded and under a severe fire from the enemy, seized a carbine and beat off an attack upon wounded officers and men under his charge.

2233 ◆ McCONNELL, JAMES

Rank: Private
Service: U.S. Army
Birthday: 1878
Place of Birth: Syracuse, Onondaga County, New York
Date of Death: 23 July 1918
Cemetery: Arlington National Cemetery (7-8317) (MH)—Arlington, Virginia
Entered Service at: Detroit, Wayne County, Michigan
Unit: Company B, 33d Infantry, U.S. Volunteers
Battle or Place of Action: Vigan, Luzon, Philippine Islands
Date of Action: 4 December 1899
Date of Issue: 1 October 1902
Citation: Fought for hours lying between two dead comrades, notwithstanding his hat was pierced, his clothing plowed through by bullets, and his face cut and bruised by flying gravel.

2234 ◆ *McGRATH, HUGH JOCELYN

Rank: Captain (highest rank: Major)
Service: U.S. Army
Birthday: 8 April 1856
Place of Birth: Fond Du Lac, Fond Du Lac County, Wisconsin
Date of Death: 7 November 1899
Place of Death: Philippine Islands
Cemetery: Arlington National Cemetery (1-315-ES)—Arlington, Virginia
Entered Service at: Eau Claire, Eau Claire County, Wisconsin
Unit: 4th U.S. Cavalry
Battle or Place of Action: Calamba, Luzon, Philippine Islands
Date of Action: 26 July 1899
Date of Issue: 29 April 1902
Citation: Swam the San Juan River in the face of the enemy's fire and drove him from his entrenchments.

2235 ◆ MILLER, ARCHIE

Rank: First Lieutenant (highest rank: Lieutenant Colonel)
Service: U.S. Army
Birthday: 1878

Place of Birth: Fort Sheridan, Lake County, Illinois
Date of Death: 28 May 1921
Cemetery: Arlington National Cemetery (1-300-A)—Arlington, Virginia
Entered Service at: St. Louis, St. Louis County, Missouri
Unit: 6th U.S. Cavalry
Battle or Place of Action: Patian Island, Philippine Islands
Date of Action: 2 July 1909
Date of Issue: 23 November 1912
Citation: While in action against hostile Moros, when the machine-gun detachment, having been driven from its position by a heavy fire, one member being killed, did, with the assistance of an enlisted man, place the machine gun in advance of its former position at a distance of about 20 yards from the enemy, in accomplishing which he was obliged to splice a piece of timber to one leg of the gun tripod, all the while being under a heavy fire, and the gun tripod being several times struck by bullets.

2236 ◆ MORAN, JOHN E.

Rank: Captain
Service: U.S. Army
Birthday: 13 August 1856
Place of Birth: Vernon, Windham County, Vermont
Date of Death: 7 November 1930
Cemetery: Highlands Cemetery (MH)—Great Falls, Montana
Entered Service at: Cascade County, Montana
Unit: Company L, 37th Infantry, U.S. Volunteers
Battle or Place of Action: near Mabitac, Laguna, Luzon, Philippine Islands
Date of Action: 17 September 1900
Date of Issue: 10 June 1910
Citation: After the attacking party had become demoralized, fearlessly led a small body of troops under a severe fire and through water waist deep in the attack against the enemy.

2237 ◆ MOSHER, LOUIS C.

Rank: Second Lieutenant (highest rank: First Lieutenant)
Service: U.S. Army
Birthday: 26 April 1880
Place of Birth: Westport, Bristol County, Massachusetts
Date of Death: 29 September 1958
Cemetery: San Francisco National Cemetery (NA-1408) (MH)—San Francisco, California
Entered Service at: Brockton, Plymouth County, Massachusetts
Unit: Philippine Scouts
Battle or Place of Action: Gagsak Mountain, Jolo, Philippine Islands
Date of Action: 11 June 1913
Date of Issue: 4 March 1914
Citation: Voluntarily entered a cleared space within about 20 yards of the Moro trenches under a furious fire from them and carried a wounded soldier of his company to safety at the risk of his own life.

2238 ◆ NOLAN, JOSEPH A.

Rank: Artificer
Service: U.S. Army
Birthday: 20 January 1857
Place of Birth: Elkhart, Elkhart County, Indiana
Date of Death: 19 August 1921
Cemetery: Silverbrook Cemetery (MH)—Niles, Michigan
Entered Service at: South Bend, St. Joseph County, Indiana
Unit: Company B, 45th Infantry, U.S. Volunteers
Battle or Place of Action: Labo, Luzon, Philippine Islands
Date of Action: 29 May 1900
Date of Issue: 14 March 1902
Citation: Voluntarily left shelter and at great personal risk passed the enemy's lines and brought relief to besieged comrades.

2239 ◆ PARKER, JAMES

Rank: Lieutenant Colonel (highest rank: Major General)
Service: U.S. Army
Birthday: 20 February 1854
Place of Birth: Newark, Essex County, New Jersey
Date of Death: 2 June 1934
Place of Death: New York, New York
Cemetery: St. Mary's Episcopal Cemetery—Portsmouth, Rhode Island
Entered Service at: Newark, Essex County, New Jersey
Unit: 45th Infantry, U.S. Volunteers
Battle or Place of Action: Vigan, Luzon, Philippine Islands
Date of Action: 4 December 1899
Date of Issue: 8 March 1902
Citation: While in command of a small garrison repulsed a savage night attack by overwhelming numbers of the enemy, fighting at close quarters in the dark for several hours.

2240 ◆ PIERCE, CHARLES H.

Rank: Private (highest rank: First Sergeant)
Service: U.S. Army
Birthday: 22 February 1875
Place of Birth: Cecil County, Maryland
Date of Death: 2 March 1944
Cemetery: Valhalla Memorial Park—North Hollywood, California
Entered Service at: Delaware City, New Castle County, Delaware
Unit: Company I, 22d U.S. Infantry
Battle or Place of Action: San Isidro, Luzon, Philippine Islands
Date of Action: 19 October 1899
Date of Issue: 10 March 1902
Citation: Held a bridge against a superior force of the enemy and fought, though severely wounded, until the main body came up to cross.

2241 ◆ PORTER, DAVID DIXON

Rank: Colonel (highest rank: Major General)
Service: U.S. Marine Corps

Birthday: 29 April 1877
Place of Birth: Washington, D.C.
Date of Death: 25 February 1944
Place of Death: Philadelphia, Pennsylvania
Cemetery: Arlington National Cemetery (2-3479) (MH)—Arlington, Virginia
Entered Service at: Washington, D.C.
Battle or Place of Action: Cadacan & Sohoton rivers junction, Samar, Philippine Islands
Date of Action: 17 November 1901
Date of Presentation: 25 April 1934
Place of Presentation: Presented by Pres. Franklin D. Roosevelt
Citation: For extraordinary heroism and eminent and conspicuous conduct in battle at the junction of the Cadacan and Sohoton Rivers, Samar, Philippine Islands, 17 November 1901. In command of the columns upon their uniting ashore in the Sohoton Region, Col. Porter (then Capt.) made a surprise attack on the fortified cliffs and completely routed the enemy, killing 30 and capturing and destroying the powder magazine, 40 lantacas (guns), rice, food and cuartels. Due to his courage, intelligence, discrimination, and zeal, he successfully led his men up the cliffs by means of bamboo ladders to a height of 200 feet. The cliffs were of soft stone of volcanic origin, in the nature of pumice, and were honeycombed with caves. Tons of rocks were suspended in platforms held in position by vine cables (known as bejuco) in readiness to be precipitated upon people below. After driving the insurgents from their position, which was almost impregnable, being covered with numerous trails lined with poison spears, pits, etc., Col. Porter led his men across the river, scaled the cliffs on the opposite side, and destroyed the camps there. He and the men under his command overcame incredible difficulties and dangers in destroying positions which, according to reports from old prisoners, had taken three years to perfect, were held as a final rallying post, and had never before been penetrated by white troops. Col. Porter also rendered distinguished public service in the presence of the enemy at Quinapundan River, Samar, Philippine Islands, 26 October 1901.

2242 ◆ PRENDERGAST, THOMAS FRANCIS

Rank: Corporal (highest rank: Sergeant)
Service: U.S. Marine Corps
Birthday: 2 April 1871
Place of Birth: Waterford, Ireland
Date of Death: 26 April 1913
Place of Death: Philadelphia, Pennsylvania
Cemetery: Greenwood Cemetery—Philadelphia, Pennsylvania
Entered Service at: Massachusetts
Battle or Place of Action: with the Eighth Army Corps
Date of Action: 25, 27, 29 March & 5 April 1899
Date of Issue: 19 July 1901
Citation: For distinguished conduct in the presence of the enemy in battle, while with the 8th Army Corps on 25, 27, 29 March, and 5 April 1899.

2243 ◆ QUINN, PETER H.

Rank: Private (highest rank: Trumpeter)
Service: U.S. Army
Birthday: May 1873
Place of Birth: San Francisco, San Francisco County, California
Date of Death: 19 April 1934
Cemetery: Arlington National Cemetery (6-9749-SH) (MH)—Arlington, Virginia
Entered Service at: San Francisco, San Francisco County, California
Unit: Company L, 4th U.S. Cavalry
Battle or Place of Action: San Miguel de Mayumo, Luzon, Philippine Islands
Date of Action: 13 May 1899
Date of Issue: 14 June 1906
Citation: With 11 other scouts, without waiting for the supporting battalion to aid them or to get into a position to do so, charged over a distance of about 150 yards and completely routed about 300 of the enemy, who were in line and in a position that could only be carried by a frontal attack.

2244 ◆ RAY, CHARLES W.

Rank: Sergeant
Service: U.S. Army
Birthday: 6 August 1872
Place of Birth: Pensacola, Yancey County, North Carolina
Date of Death: 23 March 1959
Place of Death: Grandfield, Oklahoma
Cemetery: Grandfield Memorial Cemetery—Grandfield, Oklahoma
Entered Service at: St. Louis, St. Louis County, Missouri
Unit: Company I, 22d U.S. Infantry
Battle or Place of Action: near San Isidro, Luzon, Philippine Islands
Date of Action: 19 October 1899
Date of Issue: 18 April 1902
Citation: Most distinguished gallantry in action. Captured a bridge with the detachment he commanded and held it against a superior force of the enemy, thereby enabling an army to come up and cross.

2245 ◆ ROBERTSON, MARCUS WILLIAM

Rank: Private
Service: U.S. Army
Birthday: 12 February 1870
Place of Birth: Flintville, Wisconsin
Date of Death: 24 May 1948
Place of Death: Portland, Oregon
Cemetery: Cremated at Lincoln Memorial Park—Portland, Oregon
Entered Service at: Hood River, Hood River County, Oregon
Unit: Company B, 2d Oregon Volunteer Infantry
Battle or Place of Action: near San Isidro, Luzon, Philippine Islands
Date of Action: 16 May 1899
Date of Issue: 28 April 1906
Citation: With 21 other scouts charged across a burning bridge, under heavy fire, and completely routed 600 of the enemy who were entrenched in a strongly fortified position.

2246 ◆ ROSS, FRANK FULTON

Rank: Private
Service: U.S. Army
Birthday: 2 December 1867
Place of Birth: Avon, Fulton County, Illinois
Date of Death: 29 January 1936
Place of Death: San Bernandino, California
Cemetery: Bellevue Cemetery—Ontario, California
Entered Service at: Langdon, Cavalier County, North Dakota
Unit: Company H, 1st North Dakota Volunteer Infantry
Battle or Place of Action: near San Isidro, Luzon, Philippine Islands
Date of Action: 16 May 1899
Date of Issue: 6 June 1906
Citation: With 21 other scouts charged across a burning bridge, under heavy fire, and completely routed 600 of the enemy who were entrenched in a strongly fortified position.

2247 ◆ SAGE, WILLIAM HAMPDEN

Rank: Captain (highest rank: Brigadier General)
Service: U.S. Army
Birthday: 6 April 1858
Place of Birth: Centerville, Allegany County, New York
Date of Death: 4 June 1922
Place of Death: Omaha, Nebraska
Cemetery: Arlington National Cemetery (2-913)—Arlington, Virginia
Entered Service at: Binghamton, Broome County, New York
Unit: 23d U.S. Infantry
Battle or Place of Action: near Zapote River, Luzon, Philippine Islands
Date of Action: 13 June 1899
Date of Issue: 24 July 1902
Citation: With nine men volunteered to hold an advanced position and held it against a terrific fire of the enemy estimated at 1,000 strong. Taking a rifle from a wounded man, and cartridges from the belts of others, Capt. Sage himself killed five of the enemy.

2248 ◆ SCHROEDER, HENRY FRANK

Rank: Sergeant (highest rank: Captain)
Service: U.S. Army
Birthday: 7 December 1874
Place of Birth: Chicago, Cook County, Illinois
Date of Death: 26 January 1959
Cemetery: Fort Rosecrans National Cemetery (S-854)—San Diego, California
Entered Service at: Chicago, Cook County, Illinois
Unit: Company L, 16th U.S. Infantry

Battle or Place of Action: Carig, Philippine Islands
Date of Action: 14 September 1900
Date of Issue: 10 March 1902
Citation: With 22 men defeated 400 insurgents, killing 36 and wounding 90.

2249 ◆ SHAW, GEORGE CLYMER

Rank: First Lieutenant (highest rank: Brigadier General)
Service: U.S. Army
Birthday: 6 March 1866
Place of Birth: Pontiac, Oakland County, Michigan
Date of Death: 10 February 1960
Cemetery: Arlington National Cemetery (3-4247)—Arlington, Virginia
Entered Service at: Washington, D.C.
Unit: Company C, 27th U.S. Infantry
Served as: Commanding Officer
Battle or Place of Action: Fort Pitacus, Lake Lanao, Mindanao, Philippine Islands
Date of Action: 4 May 1903
Date of Issue: 9 June 1904
Citation: For distinguished gallantry in leading the assault and, under a heavy fire from the enemy, maintaining alone his position on the parapet after the first three men who followed him there had been killed or wounded, until a foothold was gained by others and the capture of the place assured.

2250 ◆ SHELTON, GEORGE MATHEWS

Rank: Private (highest rank: Major)
Service: U.S. Army
Birthday: 23 December 1877
Place of Birth: Brownwood, Brown County, Texas
Date of Death: 18 January 1949
Place of Death: Presidio of San Francisco, California
Cemetery: San Francisco National Cemetery (OSD-799)—San Francisco, California
Entered Service at: Bellington, Texas
Unit: Company I, 23d U.S. Infantry
Battle or Place of Action: La Paz, Leyte, Philippine Islands
Date of Action: 26 April 1900
Date of Issue: 10 March 1902
Citation: Advanced alone under heavy fire of the enemy and rescued a wounded comrade.

2251 ◆ SHIELS, GEORGE FRANKLIN

Rank: Major Surgeon
Service: U.S. Army
Birthday: 13 April 1863
Place of Birth: California
Date of Death: 26 October 1943
Place of Death: Palo Alto, California
Cemetery: Cypress Lawn Cemetery—Colma, California
Entered Service at: California
Unit: U.S. Volunteers
Battle or Place of Action: at Tuliahan River, Philippine Islands

Date of Action: 25 March 1899
Date of Issue: 22 November 1906
Citation: Voluntarily exposed himself to the fire of the enemy and went with four men to the relief of two native Filipinos lying wounded about 150 yards in front of the lines and personally carried one of them to a place of safety.

2252 ◆ SLETTELAND, THOMAS

Rank: Private
Service: U.S. Army
Birthday: 1871
Place of Birth: Bergen, Norway
Date of Death: 1915
Cemetery: Evergreen Cemetery (MH)—Everett, Washington
Entered Service at: Grafton, Walsh County, North Dakota
Unit: Company C, 1st North Dakota Infantry
Battle or Place of Action: near Paete, Luzon, Philippine Islands
Date of Action: 12 April 1899
Date of Issue: 11 March 1902
Citation: Singlehanded and alone defended his dead and wounded comrades against a greatly superior force of the enemy.

2253 ◆ STEWART, GEORGE EVANS

Rank: Second Lieutenant (highest rank: Colonel)
Service: U.S. Army
Birthday: 2 August 1872
Place of Birth: New South Wales, Australia
Date of Death: 2 March 1946
Place of Death: Portland, Texas
Cemetery: Arlington National Cemetery (2-3408-A-RH)—Arlington, Virginia
Entered Service at: New York, New York
Unit: 19th U.S. Infantry
Battle or Place of Action: Passi, Island of Panay, Philippine Islands
Date of Action: 26 November 1899
Date of Issue: 26 June 1900
Citation: While crossing a river in the face of the enemy, this officer plunged in and at the imminent risk of his own life saved from drowning an enlisted man of his regiment.

2254 ◆ STOLTENBERG, ANDREW VINCENT

Rank: Gunner's Mate Second Class (highest rank: Chief Gunner's Mate)
Service: U.S. Navy
Birthday: 25 January 1866
Place of Birth: Bodo, Norway
Date of Death: 25 December 1941
Cemetery: San Francisco National Cemetery (A-242)—San Francisco, California
Entered Service at: California
Unit: U.S.S. *Panay*
Battle or Place of Action: Katbalogan, Samar, Philippine Islands

Date of Action: 16 July 1900
G.O. Number, Date: 55, 29 July 1899
Citation: For distinguished conduct in the presence of the enemy in battle at Katbalogan, Samar, Philippine Islands, 16 July 1900.

2255 ◆ STRAUB, PAUL FREDERICK

Rank: Major Surgeon
Service: U.S. Army
Birthday: 5 January 1865
Place of Birth: Baden, Germany
Date of Death: 25 November 1937
Cemetery: Forest Home Cemetery—Mount Pleasant, Iowa
Entered Service at: Mount Pleasant, Henry County, Iowa
Unit: 36th Infantry, U.S. Volunteers
Battle or Place of Action: at Alos Zambales, Luzon, Philippine Islands
Date of Action: 21 December 1899
Date of Issue: 3 October 1906
Citation: Voluntarily exposed himself to a hot fire from the enemy in repelling with pistol fire an insurgent attack and at great risk of his own life went under fire to the rescue of a wounded officer and carried him to a place of safety.

2256 ◆ THORDSEN, WILLIAM GEORGE

Rank: Coxswain (highest rank: Chief Gunner's Mate)
Service: U.S. Navy
Birthday: 2 April 1879
Place of Birth: Fredericstadt, Germany
Date of Death: 8 May 1932
Cemetery: Arlington National Cemetery (1-69-W) (MH)—Arlington, Virginia
Entered Service at: New York
Unit: U.S.S. *Pampanga*
Battle or Place of Action: Hilongas, Philippine Islands
Date of Action: 6 May 1900
G.O. Number, Date: 6, 15 August 1900
Citation: For heroism and gallantry under fire of the enemy at Hilongas, Philippine Islands, 6 May 1900.

2257 ◆ TREMBLEY, WILLIAM BEATTIE

Rank: Private
Service: U.S. Army
Birthday: 1877
Place of Birth: Johnson, Stanton County, Kansas
Date of Death: 13 January 1952
Place of Death: Pharr, Texas
Cemetery: Monticello Methodist Church Cemetery—Olathe, Kansas
Entered Service at: Kansas City, Wyandotte County, Kansas
Unit: Company B, 20th Kansas Volunteer Infantry
Battle or Place of Action: at Calumpit, Luzon, Philippine Islands
Date of Action: 27 April 1899
Date of Issue: 11 March 1902
Citation: Swam the Rio Grande de Pampanga in the face of

the enemy's fire and fastened a rope to the occupied trenches, thereby enabling the crossing of the river and the driving of the enemy from his fortified position.

2258 ◆ VAN SCHAICK, LOUIS JOSEPH

Rank: First Lieutenant (highest rank: Colonel)
Service: U.S. Army
Birthday: 1 July 1875
Place of Birth: Cobleskill, Schoharie County, New York
Date of Death: 14 February 1945
Place of Death: Philippine Islands
Cemetery: Santo Tomas Cemetery—Manila, Philippine Islands
Entered Service at: Cobleskill, Schoharie County, New York
Unit: 4th U.S. Infantry
Battle or Place of Action: near Nasugbu, Batangas, Philippine Islands
Date of Action: 23 November 1901
G.O. Number, Date: 33 1913
Date of Presentation: 19 May 1913
Place of Presentation: Presented by Pres. Woodrow Wilson
Citation: While in pursuit of a band of insurgents, was the first of his detachment to emerge from a canyon and, seeing a column of insurgents and fearing they might turn and dispatch his men as they emerged one by one from the canyon, galloped forward and closed with the insurgents, thereby throwing them into confusion until the arrival of others of the detachment.

2259 ◆ WALKER, FRANK T. O.

Rank: Private
Service: U.S. Army
Birthday: 6 October 1878
Place of Birth: South Boston, Suffolk County, Massachusetts
Date of Death: 29 October 1904
Cemetery: North Burial Cemetery (MH)—Bristol, Rhode Island
Entered Service at: Burlington, Middlesex County, Massachusetts
Unit: Company F, 46th Infantry, U.S. Volunteers
Battle or Place of Action: near Taal, Luzon, Philippine Islands
Date of Action: 18 January 1900
Date of Issue: 11 March 1902
Citation: Under heavy fire of the enemy he rescued a dying comrade who was sinking beneath the water.

2260 ◆ WALLACE, GEORGE WEED

Rank: Second Lieutenant (highest rank: Lieutenant Colonel)
Service: U.S. Army
Birthday: 25 May 1872
Place of Birth: Fort Riley, Geary County, Kansas
Date of Death: 22 May 1946
Cemetery: San Francisco National Cemetery (OS-319-A)—

San Francisco, California
Entered Service at: Denver, Denver County, Colorado
Unit: 9th U.S. Infantry
Battle or Place of Action: Tinuba, Luzon, Philippine Islands
Date of Action: 4 March 1900
Date of Issue: 25 June 1900
Citation: With another officer and a native Filipino, was shot at from an ambush, the other officer falling severely wounded. Second Lt. Wallace fired in the direction of the enemy, put them to rout, removed the wounded officer from the path, returned to the town, a mile distant, and summoned assistance from his command.

2261 ◆ WEAVER, AMOS

Rank: Sergeant
Service: U.S. Army
Birthday: 13 June 1869
Place of Birth: Niles Township, Delaware County, Indiana
Date of Death: 12 November 1937
Cemetery: Gaines Cemetery—Gaines, Michigan
Entered Service at: San Francisco, San Francisco County, California
Unit: Company F, 36th Infantry, U.S. Volunteers
Battle or Place of Action: Between Calubud & Malalong, Philippine Islands
Date of Action: 5 November 1899
Date of Issue: 15 March 1902
Citation: Alone and unaided, charged a body of 15 insurgents, dislodging them, killing four and wounding several.

2262 ◆ WELD, SETH LATHROP

Rank: Corporal (highest rank: Colonel)
Service: U.S. Army
Birthday: 19 February 1879
Place of Birth: Sandy Hook, Maryland
Date of Death: 20 December 1958
Cemetery: Fort Sam Houston National Cemetery (A-H-189) (MH)—San Antonio, Texas
Entered Service at: Altamont, Grundy County, Tennessee
Unit: Company L, 8th U.S. Infantry
Battle or Place of Action: La Paz, Leyte, Philippine Islands
Date of Action: 5 December 1906
Date of Issue: 10 October 1908
Citation: With his right arm cut open with a bolo, went to the assistance of a wounded constabulary officer and a fellow soldier who were surrounded by about 40 Pulajanes, and, using his disabled rifle as a club, beat back the assailants and rescued his party.

2263 ◆ *WETHERBY, JOHN C.

Rank: Private
Service: U.S. Army

Birthday: 2 July 1880
Place of Birth: Morgan County, Indiana
Date of Death: 29 November 1899
Place of Death: Luzon, Philippine Islands
Cemetery: Frye Cemetery—Martinsville, Indiana
Entered Service at: Martinsville, Morgan County, Indiana
Unit: Company L, 4th U.S. Infantry
Battle or Place of Action: near Imus, Luzon, Philippine Islands
Date of Action: 20 November 1899
Date of Issue: 25 April 1902
Citation: While carrying important orders on the battlefield, was desperately wounded and, being unable to walk, crawled far enough to deliver his orders.

2264 ◆ WHITE, EDWARD

Rank: Private
Service: U.S. Army
Birthday: 15 January 1877
Place of Birth: Seneca, Nemaha County, Kansas
Date of Death: 3 December 1908
Place of Death: Kansas City, Kansas
Cemetery: Mount Calvary Cemetery (MH)—Kansas City, Kansas
Entered Service at: Kansas City, Wyandotte County, Kansas
Unit: Company B, 20th Kansas Volunteer Infantry
Battle or Place of Action: at Calumpit, Luzon, Philippine Islands
Date of Action: 27 April 1899
Date of Issue: 11 March 1902
Citation: Swam the Rio Grande de Pampanga in the face of the enemy's fire and fastened a rope to the occupied trenches, thereby enabling the crossing of the river and the driving of the enemy from his fortified position.

2265 ◆ WILSON, ARTHUR HARRISON

Rank: Second Lieutenant (highest rank: Colonel)
Service: U.S. Army
Birthday: 17 August 1881
Place of Birth: Springfield, Sangamon County, Illinois
Date of Death: 15 December 1953
Place of Death: Port Isabel, Texas
Cemetery: Oakridge Cemetery—Springfield, Illinois
Entered Service at: Springfield, Sangamon County, Illinois
Unit: 6th U.S. Cavalry
Battle or Place of Action: Patian Island, Philippine Islands
Date of Action: 4 July 1909
Date of Issue: 23 November 1912
Citation: While in action against hostile Moros, when, it being necessary to secure a mountain gun in position by rope and tackle, voluntarily and with the assistance of an enlisted man, carried the rope forward and fastened it, being all the time under heavy fire of the enemy at short-range.

CHINA RELIEF EXPEDITION

2266 ◆ ADAMS, JOHN MAPES

Rank: Sergeant
Service: U.S. Marine Corps
Birthday: 11 October 1871
Place of Birth: Haverhill, Essex County, Massachusetts
Date of Death: 6 January 1921
Cemetery: Cypress Hills National Cemetery (2-8262) (MH)—Brooklyn, New York
Entered Service at: Massachusetts
Battle or Place of Action: Tientsin, China
Date of Action: 19 July 1900
G.O. Number, Date: 55, 19 July 1901
Citation: In the presence of the enemy during the battle near Tientsin, China, 13 July 1900, Adams distinguished himself by meritorious conduct.

2267 ◆ ADRIANCE, HARRY CHAPMAN

Rank: Corporal (highest rank: Sergeant)
Service: U.S. Marine Corps
Birthday: 27 October 1864
Place of Birth: Oswego, Oswego County, New York
Date of Death: 25 January 1934
Place of Death: Brooklyn, New York
Entered Service at: Massachusetts
Battle or Place of Action: Tientsin, China
Date of Action: 13 July 1900
G.O. Number, Date: 55, 19 July 1901
Citation: In the presence of the enemy during the battle near Tientsin, China, 13 July 1900, Adriance distinguished himself by meritorious conduct.

2268 ◆ ALLEN, EDWARD G.

Rank: Boatswain's Mate First Class (highest rank: Chief Boatswain)
Service: U.S. Navy
Birthday: 4 December 1859
Place of Birth: Amsterdam, Holland
Date of Death: 16 April 1917
Place of Death: Brooklyn, New York
Cemetery: The Evergreen Cemetery—Brooklyn, New York
Entered Service at: New York
Unit: U.S.S. *Newark*
Battle or Place of Action: China
Date of Action: 22 June 1900
G.O. Number, Date: 55, 19 July 1901
Citation: Fighting with the relief expedition of the Allied forces, 13, 20, 21, and 22 June 1900, Allen distinguished himself by meritorious conduct.

2269 ◆ APPLETON, EDWIN NELSON

Rank: Corporal (highest rank: Captain U.S.A.)
Service: U.S. Marine Corps
Birthday: 28 August 1877
Place of Birth: Brooklyn, Kings County, New York
Date of Death: 26 September 1937
Cemetery: The Green Wood Cemetery—Brooklyn, New York
Entered Service at: New York
Battle or Place of Action: Tientsin, China
Date of Action: 20 June 1900
G.O. Number, Date: 84, 22 March 1902
Citation: In action against the enemy at Tientsin, China, 20 June 1900. Crossing the river in a small boat while under heavy enemy fire, Appleton assisted in destroying buildings occupied by the enemy.

2270 ◆ BOYDSTON, ERWIN JAY

Rank: Private
Service: U.S. Marine Corps
Birthday: 22 April 1875
Place of Birth: Deer Creek, Colorado
Date of Death: 19 May 1957
Cemetery: National Memorial Cemetery of the Pacific (G-703) (MH)—Honolulu, Hawaii
Entered Service at: California
Battle or Place of Action: Peking, China
Date of Action: 19 July-17 August 1900
G.O. Number, Date: 55, 19 July 1901
Citation: In the presence of the enemy at Peking, China, 21 July to 17 August 1900. Under a heavy fire from the enemy during this period, Boydston assisted in the erection of barricades.

2271 ◆ BREWSTER, ANDRE WALKER

Rank: Captain (highest rank: Major General)
Service: U.S. Army
Birthday: 9 December 1862
Place of Birth: Hoboken, Hudson County, New Jersey
Date of Death: 27 March 1942
Cemetery: Arlington National Cemetery (2-1130) (MH)—Arlington, Virginia
Entered Service at: Philadelphia, Philadelphia County, Pennsylvania

Unit: 9th U.S. Infantry
Battle or Place of Action: Tientsin, China
Date of Action: 13 July 1900
Date of Issue: 15 September 1903
Citation: While under fire rescued two of his men from drowning.

2272 ◆ BURNES, JAMES

Rank: Private
Service: U.S. Marine Corps
Birthday: 14 January 1870
Place of Birth: Worcester, Worcester County, Massachusetts
Entered Service at: California
Battle or Place of Action: Tientsin, China
Date of Action: 20 June 1900
G.O. Number, Date: 84, 22 March 1902
Date of Issue: 21 April 1902
Citation: In action against the enemy at Tientsin, China, 20 June 1900. Crossing the river in a small boat with three other men while under a heavy fire from the enemy, Burnes assisted in destroying buildings occupied by hostile forces.

2273 ◆ CAMPBELL, ALBERT RALPH

Rank: Private (highest rank: Corporal)
Service: U.S. Marine Corps
Birthday: 8 April 1875
Place of Birth: Williamsport, Lycoming County, Pennsylvania
Date of Death: 4 December 1925
Cemetery: Forest Lawn Memorial Park—Glendale, California
Entered Service at: Pennsylvania
Battle or Place of Action: Tientsin, China
Date of Action: 21 June 1900
G.O. Number, Date: 55, 19 July 1901
Date of Issue: 24 March 1902
Citation: In action at Tientsin, China, 21 June 1900. During the advance on Tientsin, Campbell distinguished himself by his conduct.

2274 ◆ CARR, WILLIAM LOUIS

Rank: Private (highest rank: Corporal)
Service: U.S. Marine Corps
Birthday: 1 April 1878
Place of Birth: Peabody, Essex County, Massachusetts
Date of Death: 14 April 1921
Place of Death: Sandusky, Ohio
Cemetery: Ohio Veteran's Home Cemetery (MH)—Sandusky, Ohio
Entered Service at: Boston, Suffolk County, Massachusetts
Battle or Place of Action: Peking, China
Date of Action: 21 July-17 August 1900
G.O. Number, Date: 55, 19 July 1901
Date of Issue: 11 December 1901

Citation: In action at Peking, China, 21 July to 17 August 1900. Throughout this action and in the presence of the enemy, Carr distinguished himself by his conduct.

2275 ◆ CHATHAM, JOHN PURNESS

Rank: Gunner's Mate Second Class
Service: U.S. Navy
Birthday: 2 July 1872
Place of Birth: Warchester, Maryland
Date of Death: 3 October 1914
Place of Death: Salisbury, Maryland
Cemetery: Parsons Cemetery—Salisbury, Maryland
Entered Service at: Maryland
Unit: U.S.S. *Newark*
Battle or Place of Action: China
Date of Action: 13, 20-22 June 1900
G.O. Number, Date: 55, 19 July 1901
Citation: In action with the relief expedition of the Allied forces in China, 13, 20, 21, and 22 June 1900. During this period and in the presence of the enemy, Chatham distinguished himself by his conduct.

2276 ◆ CLANCY, JOSEPH

Rank: Chief Boatswain's Mate (highest rank: Lieutenant)
Service: U.S. Navy
Birthday: 29 September 1863
Place of Birth: New York, New York
Date of Death: 2 February 1929
Cemetery: Arlington National Cemetery (7-8145) (MH)—Arlington, Virginia
Unit: U.S.S. *Newark*
Battle or Place of Action: China
Date of Action: 13, 20-22 June 1900
G.O. Number, Date: 55, 19 July 1901
Citation: In action with the relief expedition of the Allied forces in China, 13, 20, 21, and 22 June 1900. During this period and in the presence of the enemy, Clancy distinguished himself by his conduct.

2277 ◆ COONEY, JAMES

Rank: Private (highest rank: Corporal)
Service: U.S. Marine Corps
Birthday: 27 July 1860
Place of Birth: Limerick, Ireland
Date of Death: 14 March 1903
Cemetery: Mare Island Cemetery (10-93) (MH)—Vallejo, California
Entered Service at: Massachusetts
Battle or Place of Action: Tientsin, China
Date of Action: 13 July 1900
G.O. Number, Date: 55, 19 July 1901
Date of Issue: 11 December 1901
Citation: In the presence of the enemy during the battle near Tientsin, China, 13 July 1900, Cooney distinguished himself by meritorious conduct.

2278 ◆ DAHLGREN, JOHN OLOF

Rank: Corporal
Service: U.S. Marine Corps
Birthday: 14 September 1872
Place of Birth: Kahliwar, Sweden
Date of Death: 11 February 1963
Cemetery: Golden Gate National Cemetery (Z-1950)—San Bruno, California
Entered Service at: California
Battle or Place of Action: Peking, China
Date of Action: 20 June & 16 July 1900
G.O. Number, Date: 55, 19 July 1901
Citation: In the presence of the enemy during the battle of Peking, China, 20 June to 16 July 1900, Dahlgren distinguished himself by meritorious conduct.

2279 ◆ DALY, DANIEL JOSEPH✛

Rank: Private (highest rank: Sergeant Major)
Service: U.S. Marine Corps
Birthday: 11 November 1873
Place of Birth: Glen Cove, Nassau County, New York
Date of Death: 27 April 1937
Place of Death: Glendale, New York
Cemetery: Cypress Hills National Cemetery (5-70) (MH)—Brooklyn, New York
Entered Service at: New York
Unit: Capt. Newt H. Hall's Marine Detachment, U.S.S. *Newark*
Battle or Place of Action: Peking, China
Date of Action: 14 August 1900
G.O. Number, Date: 55, 19 July 1901
Date of Issue: 11 December 1901
Citation: **First Award** In the presence of the enemy during the battle of Peking, China, 14 August 1900, Daly distinguished himself by meritorious conduct.
Notes: ✛Double Awardee: *see also* Haitian Campaign, 1915

2280 ◆ *FISHER, HARRY

True Name: Phillips, Franklin J.
Rank: Private
Service: U.S. Marine Corps
Birthday: 20 October 1874
Place of Birth: McKeesport, Allegheny County, Pennsylvania
Date of Death: 16 July 1900
Place of Death: Peking, China
Cemetery: Versailles Cemetery (MH)—McKeesport, Pennsylvania
Entered Service at: Pennsylvania
Battle or Place of Action: Peking, China
Date of Action: 20 June-16 July 1900
G.O. Number, Date: 55, 19 July 1901
Citation: Served in the presence of the enemy at the battle of Peking, China, 20 June to 16 July 1900. Assisting in the erection of barricades during the action, Fisher was killed by the heavy fire of the enemy.

2281 ◆ FOLEY, ALEXANDER JOSEPH

Rank: Sergeant (highest rank: First Sergeant)
Service: U.S. Marine Corps
Birthday: 19 February 1866
Place of Birth: Heckersville, Pennsylvania
Date of Death: 14 January 1910
Cemetery: Culebra Naval Station Cemetery—Culebra, Puerto Rico
Entered Service at: Pennsylvania
Unit: U.S.S. *Monadnock*
Battle or Place of Action: near Tientsin, China
Date of Action: 21 June 1900
G.O. Number, Date: 55, 19 July 1901
Citation: In the presence of the enemy during the battle near Tientsin, China, 13 July 1900, Foley distinguished himself by meritorious conduct.

2282 ◆ FRANCIS, CHARLES ROBERT

Rank: Private (highest rank: Second Lieutenant)
Service: U.S. Marine Corps
Birthday: 19 May 1875
Place of Birth: Doylestown, Bucks County, Pennsylvania
Date of Death: 15 July 1946
Place of Death: Santa Monica, California
Cemetery: Hollywood Cemetery—Hollywood, California
Entered Service at: Philadelphia, Philadelphia County, Pennsylvania
Battle or Place of Action: Tientsin, China
Date of Action: 21 June 1900
G.O. Number, Date: 55, 19 July 1901
Citation: In the presence of the enemy during the battle near Tientsin, China, 13 July 1900, Francis distinguished himself by meritorious conduct.

2283 ◆ GAIENNIE, LOUIS RENE

Rank: Private
Service: U.S. Marine Corps
Birthday: 9 June 1878
Place of Birth: St. Louis, St. Louis County, Missouri
Date of Death: 25 November 1942
Cemetery: Calvary Cemetery—St. Louis, Missouri
Entered Service at: St. Louis, St. Louis County, Missouri
Battle or Place of Action: Peking, China
Date of Action: 21 July-17 August 1900
G.O. Number, Date: 55, 19 July 1901
Date of Issue: 11 December 1901
Citation: In the presence of the enemy during the action at Peking, China, 21 July to 17 August 1900, Gaiennie distinguished himself by meritorious conduct.

2284 ◆ HAMBERGER, WILLIAM FRANCIS

Rank: Chief Carpenter's Mate (highest rank: Lieutenant Commander)
Service: U.S. Navy

Birthday: 5 January 1871
Place of Birth: Newark, Essex County, New Jersey
Date of Death: 1 September 1937
Cemetery: Arlington National Cemetery (6-9164)—Arlington, Virginia
Entered Service at: New Jersey
Unit: U.S.S. *Newark*
Battle or Place of Action: China
Date of Action: 13, 20-22 June 1900
G.O. Number, Date: 55, 19 July 1901
Citation: Fighting with the relief expedition of the Allied forces on 13, 20, 21, and 22 June 1900, Hamberger distinguished himself by meritorious conduct.

2285 ◆ HANFORD, BURKE

Rank: Machinist First Class (highest rank: Chief Machinist)
Service: U.S. Navy
Birthday: 17 December 1872
Place of Birth: Toledo, Lucas County, Ohio
Date of Death: 11 April 1928
Cemetery: Greenwood Memorial Park—San Diego, California
Entered Service at: Ohio
Unit: U.S.S. *Newark*
Battle or Place of Action: China
Date of Action: 13, 20-22 June 1900
G.O. Number, Date: 55, 19 July 1901
Citation: Served with the relief expedition of the Allied forces in China on 13, 20, 21, and 22 June 1900. In the presence of the enemy during this period, Hanford distinguished himself by meritorious conduct.

2286 ◆ HANSEN, HANS ANTON

Rank: Seaman
Service: U.S. Navy
Birthday: 16 April 1872
Place of Birth: Germany
Date of Death: 9 May 1915
Cemetery: Arlington National Cemetery (17-18576) (MH)—Arlington, Virginia
Entered Service at: California
Unit: U.S.S. *Newark*
Battle or Place of Action: China
Date of Action: 13, 20-22 June 1900
G.O. Number, Date: 55, 19 July 1901
Citation: Served with the relief expedition of the Allied forces in China on 13, 20, 21, and 22 June 1900. In the presence of the enemy during this period, Hansen distinguished himself by meritorious conduct.

2287 ◆ HEISCH, HENRY WILLIAM

Rank: Private
Service: U.S. Marine Corps
Birthday: 10 June 1872
Place of Birth: Latendorf, Germany

Date of Death: 10 July 1941
Place of Death: Napa, California
Cemetery: Tulocay Cemetery—Napa, California
Entered Service at: California
Battle or Place of Action: Tientsin, China
Date of Action: 20 June 1900
G.O. Number, Date: 84, 22 March 1902
Citation: In action against the enemy at Tientsin, China, 20 June 1900. Crossing the river in a small boat while under heavy fire, Heisch assisted in destroying buildings occupied by the enemy.

2288 ◆ HOLYOKE, WILLIAM EDWARD

Rank: Boatswain's Mate First Class
Service: U.S. Navy
Birthday: 13 March 1868
Place of Birth: Groveton, Coos County, New Hampshire
Date of Death: 3 April 1934
Cemetery: Charles Evans Cemetery (MH)—Reading, Pennsylvania
Entered Service at: Illinois
Unit: U.S.S. *Newark*
Battle or Place of Action: China
Date of Action: 13, 20-22 June 1900
G.O. Number, Date: 55, 19 July 1901
Citation: In action with the relief expedition of the Allied forces in China, 13, 20, 21, and 22 June 1900. During this period and in the presence of the enemy, Holyoke distinguished himself by meritorious conduct.

2289 ◆ HORTON, WILLIAM M. CHARLIE

Rank: Private (highest rank: Sergeant)
Service: U.S. Marine Corps
Birthday: 21 July 1876
Place of Birth: Chicago, Cook County, Illinois
Date of Death: 14 February 1969
Cemetery: Evergreen-Washelli Memorial Park—Seattle, Washington
Entered Service at: Philadelphia, Philadelphia County, Pennsylvania
Unit: U.S.S. *Oregon*
Battle or Place of Action: Peking, China
Date of Action: 21 July-17 August 1900
G.O. Number, Date: 55, 19 July 1901
Date of Issue: 5 January 1902
Citation: In action against the enemy at Peking, China, 21 July to 17 August 1900. Although under heavy fire from the enemy, Horton assisted in the erection of barricades.

2290 ◆ HUNT, MARTIN

Rank: Private (highest rank: Corporal)
Service: U.S. Marine Corps
Birthday: 9 July 1873
Place of Birth: County Mayo, Ireland
Date of Death: 22 July 1938

Place of Death: Pasay Rizal, Philippine Islands
Entered Service at: Boston, Suffolk County, Massachusetts
Battle or Place of Action: Peking, China
Date of Action: 20 June-16 July 1900
G.O. Number, Date: 55, 19 July 1901
Date of Issue: 2 July 1915
Citation: In the presence of the enemy during the battle of Peking, China, 20 June to 16 July 1900, Hunt distinguished himself by meritorious conduct.

2291 ◆ KATES, THOMAS WILBUR

Rank: Private (highest rank: Sergeant)
Service: U.S. Marine Corps
Birthday: 7 May 1865
Place of Birth: Shelby Center, New York
Entered Service at: New York
Battle or Place of Action: Tientsin, China
Date of Action: 21 June 1900
G.O. Number, Date: 55, 19 July 1901
Citation: In presence of the enemy during the advance on Tientsin, China, 21 June 1900, Kates distinguished himself by meritorious conduct.

2292 ◆ KILLACKEY, JOSEPH

Rank: Landsman (highest rank: Gunner's Mate Third Class)
Service: U.S. Navy
Birthday: 21 January 1879
Place of Birth: County Cork, Ireland
Date of Death: 8 September 1946
Cemetery: Mount Moriah VA plot (4-3-23) (MH)—Philadelphia, Pennsylvania
Entered Service at: Pennsylvania
Unit: U.S.S. *Newark*
Battle or Place of Action: China
Date of Action: 13, 20-22 June 1900
G.O. Number, Date: 55, 19 July 1901
Citation: In action with the relief expedition of the Allied forces in China, 13, 20, 21, and 22 June 1900. During this period and in the presence of the enemy, Killackey distinguished himself by meritorious conduct.

2293 ◆ LAWTON, LOUIS BOWEM

Rank: First Lieutenant (highest rank: Major)
Service: U.S. Army
Birthday: 1872
Place of Birth: Independence, Buchanan County, Iowa
Date of Death: 9 July 1949
Cemetery: Fort Hill Cemetery—Auburn, New York
Entered Service at: Auburn, Cayuga County, New York
Unit: 9th U.S. Infantry
Battle or Place of Action: Tientsin, China
Date of Action: 13 July 1900
Date of Issue: 11 March 1902
Citation: Carried a message and guided reinforcements

across a wide and fire-swept space, during which he was thrice wounded.

2294 ◆ MATHIAS, CLARENCE EDWARD

Rank: Private (highest rank: Sergeant Major)
Service: U.S. Marine Corps
Birthday: 12 December 1876
Place of Birth: Royalton, Dauphin County, Pennsylvania
Date of Death: 9 December 1935
Cemetery: Arlington National Cemetery (6-8681) (MH)—Arlington, Virginia
Entered Service at: Pennsylvania
Unit: U.S.S. *Solace*
Battle or Place of Action: Tientsin, China
Date of Action: 13 July 1900
G.O. Number, Date: 84, 22 March 1902
Citation: In the presence of the enemy during the advance on Tientsin, China, 13 July 1900, Mathias distinguished himself by meritorious conduct.

2295 ◆ McALLISTER, SAMUEL

Rank: Ordinary Seaman
Service: U.S. Navy
Birthday: 23 January 1869
Place of Birth: Belfast, County Antrim, Ireland
Date of Death: 13 December 1903
Place of Death: Died on active duty U.S.S. *Wisconsin*
Cemetery: Buried at sea between Japan and Hawaii
Entered Service at: California
Unit: U.S.S. *Newark*
Battle or Place of Action: Tientsin, China
Date of Action: 20 June 1900
G.O. Number, Date: 84, 22 March 1902
Citation: In action against the enemy at Tientsin, China, 20 June 1900. Crossing the river in a small boat while under heavy enemy fire, McAllister assisted in destroying buildings occupied by the enemy.

2296 ◆ McCLOY, JOHN✛

Rank: Coxswain (highest rank: Lieutenant Commander)
Service: U.S. Navy
Birthday: 3 January 1876
Place of Birth: Brewster, Putnam County, New York
Date of Death: 25 May 1945
Cemetery: Arlington National Cemetery (8-5246)—Arlington, Virginia
Entered Service at: New York
Unit: U.S.S. *Newark*
Battle or Place of Action: Wu-Tsing-Hune and near Peh-Tsang, China
Date of Action: 13, 20-22 June 1900
G.O. Number, Date: 55, 19 July 1901
Citation: **First Award** In action with the relief expedition of the Allied forces in China, 13, 20, 21 and 22 June 1900. During this period and in the presence of the enemy,

Coxswain McCloy distinguished himself by meritorious conduct.

Notes: ✛Double Awardee: *see also* Mexican Campaign (Vera Cruz)

2297 ◆ MITCHELL, JOSEPH ANDREW

Rank: Gunner's Mate First Class (highest rank: Lieutenant)
Service: U.S. Navy
Birthday: 27 November 1876
Place of Birth: Philadelphia, Philadelphia County, Pennsylvania
Date of Death: 9 June 1925
Place of Death: Philadelphia, Pennsylvania
Cemetery: St. Paul's Catholic Cemetery (MH)—Portsmouth, Virginia
Entered Service at: Pennsylvania
Unit: U.S.S. *Newark*
Battle or Place of Action: Peking, China
Date of Action: 12 July 1900
G.O. Number, Date: 55, 19 July 1901
Citation: In the presence of the enemy during the battle of Peking, China, 12 July 1900, Mitchell distinguished himself by meritorious conduct.

2298 ◆ MOORE, ALBERT

Rank: Private (highest rank: First Sergeant U.S. Army Retired)
Service: U.S. Marine Corps
Birthday: 25 December 1862
Place of Birth: Merced, Merced County, California
Date of Death: 14 September 1916
Place of Death: Port Mason, California
Cemetery: San Francisco National Cemetery (WS-1032-A)—San Francisco, California
Entered Service at: California
Battle or Place of Action: Peking, China
Date of Action: 21 July-17 August 1900
G.O. Number, Date: 55, 19 July 1901
Citation: In the presence of the enemy during the battle of Peking, China, 21 July to 17 August 1900. Although under a heavy fire from the enemy, Moore assisted in the erection of barricades.

2299 ◆ MURPHY, JOHN ALPHONSUS

Rank: Drummer
Service: U.S. Marine Corps
Birthday: 26 February 1881
Place of Birth: New York, New York
Date of Death: 29 November 1935
Place of Death: New York, New York
Entered Service at: Washington, D.C.
Battle or Place of Action: Peking, China
Date of Action: 21 July-17 August 1900
G.O. Number, Date: 55, 19 July 1901
Citation: In the presence of the enemy during the action at Peking, China, 21 July to 17 August 1900, Murphy distinguished himself by meritorious conduct.

2300 ◆ MURRAY, WILLIAM HENRY

True Name: Served as Davis, Henry W.
Rank: Private
Service: U.S. Marine Corps
Birthday: 3 June 1876
Place of Birth: Brooklyn, Kings County, New York
Date of Death: 12 October 1923
Place of Death: Rutland, Massachusetts
Cemetery: Oak Grove Cemetery (MH)—Medford, Massachusetts
Entered Service at: Brooklyn, Kings County, New York
Battle or Place of Action: Peking, China
Date of Action: 21 July-17 August 1900
G.O. Number, Date: 55, 19 July 1901
Citation: In the presence of the enemy during the action at Peking, China, 21 July to 17 August 1900. During this period, Murray distinguished himself by meritorious conduct.

2301 ◆ ORNDOFF, HARRY WESTLEY

True Name: Orndof, Harry Westley
Rank: Private
Service: U.S. Marine Corps
Birthday: 8 November 1875
Place of Birth: Sandusky, Erie County, Ohio
Date of Death: 14 July 1938
Cemetery: Highland Park Cemetery (MH)—Cleveland, Ohio
Entered Service at: California
Battle or Place of Action: China
Date of Action: 13, 20-22 June 1900
G.O. Number, Date: 55, 19 July 1901
Date of Issue: 10 December 1901
Citation: In action with the relief expedition of the Allied forces in China, 13, 20, 21, and 22 June 1900. During this period and in the presence of the enemy, Orndoff distinguished himself by meritorious conduct.

2302 ◆ PETERSEN, CARL EMIL

Rank: Chief Machinist
Service: U.S. Navy
Birthday: 24 August 1875
Place of Birth: Hamburg, Germany
Date of Death: 17 November 1971
Place of Death: Edison, New Jersey
Cemetery: Cloverleaf Park Cemetery (MH)—Woodbridge, New Jersey
Entered Service at: New Jersey
Unit: U.S.S. *Newark*
Battle or Place of Action: Peking, China
Date of Action: 28 June-17 August 1900
G.O. Number, Date: 55, 19 July 1901
Citation: In the presence of the enemy during the action at Peking, China, 28 June to 17 August 1900. During this peri-

od Chief Machinist Petersen distinguished himself by meritorious conduct.

2303 ◆ PHILLIPS, REUBEN JASPER

Rank: Corporal (highest rank: Sergeant)
Service: U.S. Marine Corps
Birthday: 28 July 1874
Place of Birth: Cambria, San Luis Obispo County, California
Date of Death: 8 February 1936
Cemetery: San Francisco National Cemetery (OS-D-3 Row 118) (MH)—San Francisco, California
Entered Service at: California
Battle or Place of Action: China
Date of Action: 13, 20-22 June 1900
G.O. Number, Date: 55, 19 July 1901
Citation: In action with the relief expedition of the Allied forces in China during the battles of 13, 20, 21, and 22 June 1900. Throughout this period and in the presence of the enemy, Phillips distinguished himself by meritorious conduct.

2304 ◆ PRESTON, HERBERT IRVING

Rank: Private
Service: U.S. Marine Corps
Birthday: 6 August 1876
Place of Birth: Berkeley, Union County, New Jersey
Entered Service at: New Jersey
Battle or Place of Action: Peking, China
Date of Action: 21 July-17 August 1900
G.O. Number, Date: 55, 19 July 1901
Citation: In the presence of the enemy during the action at Peking, China, 21 July to 17 August 1900. Throughout this period, Preston distinguished himself by meritorious conduct.

2305 ◆ ROSE, GEORGE HARRY

Rank: Seaman (highest rank: Lieutenant Commander)
Service: U.S. Navy
Birthday: 28 February 1880
Place of Birth: Stamford, Fairfield County, Connecticut
Date of Death: 7 December 1932
Place of Death: Newark, New Jersey
Cemetery: Arlington National Cemetery (7-9978-ES) (MH)—Arlington, Virginia
Entered Service at: Connecticut
Unit: U.S.S. *Newark*
Battle or Place of Action: Peking, China
Date of Action: 13, 20-22 June 1900
G.O. Number, Date: 55, 19 July 1901
Citation: In the presence of the enemy during the battles at Peking, China, 13, 20, 21, and 22 June 1900. Throughout this period, Rose distinguished himself by meritorious conduct. While stationed as a crewmember of the U.S.S. *Newark*, he was part of its landing force that went ashore off Taku, China. On 31 May 1900, he was in a party of six under John McCloy (MH) which took ammunition from the *Newark* to Tientsin. On 10 June 1900, he was one of a party that carried

dispatches from LaFa to Yongstsum at night. On the 13th, he was one of a few who fought off a large force of the enemy, saving the main baggage train from destruction. On the 20th and 21st he was engaged in heavy fighting against the Imperial Army, being always in the first rank. On the 22d he showed gallantry in the capture of the Siku Arsenal. He volunteered to go to the nearby village which was occupied by the enemy to secure medical supplies urgently required. The party brought back the supplies carried by newly taken prisoners

2306 ◆ RYAN, FRANCIS THOMAS

True Name: Gallagher, Frank
Rank: Coxswain (highest rank: Ship's Cook First Class Retired)
Service: U.S. Navy
Birthday: 6 April 1862
Place of Birth: Massachusetts
Date of Death: 14 June 1927
Place of Death: Philadelphia, Pennsylvania
Cemetery: Arlington National Cemetery (17-21008) (MH)—Arlington, Virginia
Entered Service at: Massachusetts
Unit: U.S.S. *Newark*
Battle or Place of Action: China
Date of Action: 13, 20-22 June 1900
G.O. Number, Date: 55, 19 July 1901
Citation: In action with the relief expediton of the Allied forces in China during the battles of 13, 20 21, and 22 June 1900. Throughout this period and in the presence of the enemy, Ryan distinguished himself by meritorious conduct.

2307 ◆ SCANNELL, DAVID JOHN

Rank: Private
Service: U.S. Marine Corps
Birthday: 30 March 1875
Place of Birth: Boston, Suffolk County, Massachusetts
Date of Death: 7 May 1923
Place of Death: Togus, Maine
Cemetery: Togus National Cemetery (3955-W-2-42) (MH)—Togus, Maine
Entered Service at: Boston, Suffolk County, Massachusetts
Battle or Place of Action: Peking, China
Date of Action: 21 July-17 August 1900
G.O. Number, Date: 55, 19 July 1901
Citation: In the presence of the enemy during the action at Peking, China, 21 July to 17 August 1900. Throughout this period, Scannell distinguished himself by meritorious conduct.

2308 ◆ SEACH, WILLIAM

Rank: Ordinary Seaman (highest rank: Lieutenant)
Service: U.S. Navy
Birthday: 23 May 1877
Place of Birth: London, England
Date of Death: 24 October 1978

Place of Death: Brockton, Massachusetts
Cemetery: Arlington National Cemetery (11-334-2) (MH)—Arlington, Virginia
Entered Service at: Massachusetts
Unit: U.S.S. *Newark*
Battle or Place of Action: China
Date of Action: 13, 20-22 June 1900
G.O. Number, Date: 55, 19 July 1901
Date of Issue: 1903
Citation: In action with the relief expedition of the Allied forces in China during the battles of 13, 20, 21, and 22 June 1900. June 13: Seach and six others were cited for their courage in repulsing an attack by 300 Chinese Imperialist soldiers and Boxer militants with a bayonet charge, thus thwarting a planned massive attack on the entire force. June 20: During a day-long battle, Seach ran across an open clearing, gained cover, and cleaned out nests of Chinese snipers. June 21: During a surprise saber attack by Chinese cavalrymen, Seach was cited for defending gun emplacements. June 22: Seach and others breached the wall of a Chinese fort, fought their way to the enemy's guns, and turned the cannon upon the defenders of the fort. Throughout this period and in the presence of the enemy, Seach distinguished himself by meritorious conduct.

2309 ◆ SILVA, FRANCE

Rank: Private
Service: U.S. Marine Corps
Birthday: 8 May 1876
Place of Birth: Hayward, Alameda County, California
Date of Death: 10 April 1951
Place of Death: Red Bluff, California
Cemetery: Sunset Hill Cemetery (MH)—Corning, California
Entered Service at: San Francisco, San Francisco County, California
Unit: U.S.S. *Newark*
Battle or Place of Action: Peking, China
Date of Action: 28 June-17 August 1900
G.O. Number, Date: 55, 19 July 1901
Citation: In the presence of the enemy during the action at Peking, China, 28 June to 17 August 1900. Throughout this period, Silva distinguished himself by meritorious conduct.

2310 ◆ SMITH, FRANK ELMER

Service: U.S. Navy
Birthday: 22 August 1864
Place of Birth: Boston, Suffolk County, Massachusetts
Entered Service at: Virginia
Unit: U.S.S. *Newark*
Battle or Place of Action: China
Date of Action: 13, 20-22 June 1900
G.O. Number, Date: 55, 19 July 1901
Citation: In action with the relief expedition of the Allied forces in China during the battles of 13, 20, 21, and 22 June 1900. Throughout this period and in the presence of the enemy, Smith distinguished himself by meritorious conduct.

2311 ◆ SMITH, JAMES A.

Rank: Landsman
Service: U.S. Navy
Birthday: 2 September 1880
Place of Birth: New York
Entered Service at: New York
Unit: U.S.S. *Newark*
Battle or Place of Action: near Tientsin, China
Date of Action: 13, 20-22 June 1900
G.O. Number, Date: 55, 19 July 1901
Citation: In action with the relief expedition of the Allied forces in China during the battles of 13, 20, 21, and 22 June 1900. Throughout this period and in the presence of the enemy, Smith distinguished himself by meritorious conduct.

2312 ◆ STANLEY, ROBERT HENRY

Rank: Hospital Apprentice (highest rank: Chief Pharmacist)
Service: U.S. Navy
Birthday: 2 May 1881
Place of Birth: Brooklyn, Kings County, New York
Date of Death: 15 July 1942
Place of Death: Pensacola, Florida
Cemetery: Arlington National Cemetery (7-8348)—Arlington, Virginia
Entered Service at: aboard U.S.S. *Vermont*
Unit: U.S.S. *Newark*
Battle or Place of Action: Peking, China
Date of Action: 13, 20-22 June 1900
G.O. Number, Date: 55, 19 July 1901
Place of Presentation: On board the U.S.S. *Brooklyn*
Citation: For distinguished conduct in the presence of the enemy in volunteering and carrying messages under fire at Peking, China, 12 July 1900.

2313 ◆ STEWART, PETER

Rank: Gunnery Sergeant
Service: U.S. Marine Corps
Birthday: 17 February 1858
Place of Birth: Airdrie, Scotland
Date of Death: 17 June 1914
Cemetery: Cypress Hills National Cemetery (2-7303) (MH)—Brooklyn, New York
Entered Service at: Washington, D.C.
Unit: Marine Guard, U.S.S. *Newark*
Battle or Place of Action: China
Date of Action: 13, 20-22 June 1900
G.O. Number, Date: 55, 19 July 1901
Citation: In action with the relief expedition of the Allied forces in China during the battles of 13, 20, 21, and 22 June 1900. Throughout this period and in the presence of the enemy, Stewart distinguished himself by meritorious conduct.

2314 ◆ SUTTON, CLARENCE EDWIN

Rank: Sergeant (highest rank: First Sergeant)
Service: U.S. Marine Corps

Birthday: 18 February 1871
Place of Birth: Urbanna, Middlesex County, Virginia
Date of Death: 9 October 1916
Cemetery: Arlington National Cemetery (17-18847) (MH)—Arlington, Virginia
Entered Service at: Washington, D.C.
Battle or Place of Action: Tientsin, China
Date of Action: 13 July 1900
G.O. Number, Date: 55, 19 July 1901
Citation: In action during the battle near Tientsin, China, 13 July 1900. Although under heavy fire from the enemy, Sutton assisted in carrying a wounded officer from the field of battle.

2315 ◆ THOMAS, KARL

Rank: Coxswain
Service: U.S. Navy
Birthday: 17 March 1871
Place of Birth: Germany
Entered Service at: New York
Unit: U.S.S. *Newark*
Battle or Place of Action: China
Date of Action: 13, 20-22 June 1900
G.O. Number, Date: 55, 19 July 1901
Citation: In action with the relief expedition of the Allied forces in China, 13, 20, 21, and 22 June 1900. During this period and in the presence of the enemy, Thomas distinguished himself by meritorious conduct.

2316 ◆ TITUS, CALVIN PEARL

Rank: Musician (highest rank: Lieutenant Colonel)
Service: U.S. Army
Birthday: 22 September 1879
Place of Birth: Vinton, Benton County, Iowa
Date of Death: 27 May 1966
Place of Death: San Fernando, California
Cemetery: Forest Lawn Memorial Park—Hollywood, California
Entered Service at: Iowa
Unit: Company E, 14th U.S. Infantry
Battle or Place of Action: Peking, China
Date of Action: 14 August 1900
Date of Issue: 11 March 1902
Citation: Gallant and daring conduct in the presence of his colonel and other officers and enlisted men of his regiment; was first to scale the wall of the city.

2317 ◆ TORGERSON, MARTIN TORINUS

Rank: Gunner's Mate Third Class
Service: U.S. Navy
Birthday: 7 November 1875
Place of Birth: Oleesen, Norway
Date of Death: 12 June 1935
Place of Death: Rosedale, New York
Cemetery: Arlington National Cemetery (6-8680)—Arlington, Virginia

Entered Service at: Virginia
Unit: U.S.S. *Newark*
Battle or Place of Action: China
Date of Action: 13, 20-22 June 1900
G.O. Number, Date: 55, 19 July 1901
Citation: In action with the relief expedition of the Allied forces in China, 13, 20, 21, and 22 June 1900. During this period and in the presence of the enemy, Torgerson distinguished himself by meritorious conduct.

2318 ◆ UPHAM, OSCAR JEFFERSON

Rank: Private
Service: U.S. Marine Corps
Birthday: 11 January 1871
Place of Birth: Toledo, Lucas County, Ohio
Date of Death: 18 February 1949
Place of Death: Guthrie, Oklahoma
Cemetery: Summit View Cemetery—Guthrie, Oklahoma
Entered Service at: Illinois
Unit: Marine Guard, U.S.S. *Oregon*
Battle or Place of Action: Peking, China
Date of Action: 21 July-17 August 1900
G.O. Number, Date: 55, 19 July 1901
Citation: In the presence of the enemy at Peking, China, 21 July to 17 August 1900. Although under a heavy fire from the enemy during this period, Upham assisted in the erection of barricades.

2319 ◆ VON SCHLICK, ROBERT H.

Rank: Private
Service: U.S. Army
Birthday: 2 January 1875
Place of Birth: Germany
Date of Death: 1 July 1941
Cemetery: Los Angeles National Cemetery (81-G-20) (MH)—Los Angeles, California
Entered Service at: San Francisco, San Francisco County, California
Unit: Company C, 9th U.S. Infantry
Battle or Place of Action: Tientsin, China
Date of Action: 13 July 1900
Date of Issue: 3 September 1903
Citation: Although previously wounded while carrying a wounded comrade to a place of safety, Von Schlick rejoined his command which partly occupied an exposed position upon a dike, remaining there after his command had been withdrawn, singly keeping up the fire, and obliviously presenting himself as a conspicuous target until he was literally shot off his position by the enemy.

2320 ◆ WALKER, EDWARD ALEXANDER

Rank: Sergeant
Service: U.S. Marine Corps
Birthday: 2 October 1864
Place of Birth: Huntley, Scotland
Date of Death: 24 October 1946

Cemetery: Oak Hill Mausoleum—San Jose, California
Entered Service at: Brooklyn, Kings County, New York
Battle or Place of Action: Peking, China
Date of Action: 20 June-16 July 1900
G.O. Number, Date: 55, 19 July 1901
Citation: In the presence of the enemy during the battle of Peking, China, 20 June to 16 July 1900. Throughout this period, Walker distinguished himself by meritorious conduct.

2321 ◆ WESTERMARK, AXEL

Rank: Seaman (highest rank: Gunner's Mate First Class)
Service: U.S. Navy
Birthday: 8 April 1875
Place of Birth: Bergo, Finland
Date of Death: 7 May 1911
Place of Death: Puget Sound, Washington
Cemetery: San Francisco National Cemetery (A-32)—San Francisco, California
Entered Service at: California
Unit: U.S.S. *Newark*
Battle or Place of Action: Peking, China
Date of Action: 28 June-17 August 1900
G.O. Number, Date: 55, 19 July 1901
Citation: In the presence of the enemy during the battle of Peking, China, 28 June to 17 August 1900. Throughout this period, Westermark distinguished himself by meritorious conduct.

2322 ◆ WILLIAMS, JAY P.

Rank: Coxswain
Service: U.S. Navy
Birthday: 23 September 1872
Place of Birth: Orland, Steuben County, Indiana
Date of Death: 4 July 1938
Cemetery: Woodlawn Cemetery (MH)—Norwalk, Ohio
Entered Service at: Ohio
Unit: U.S.S. *Newark*
Battle or Place of Action: China
Date of Action: 13, 20-22 June 1900

G.O. Number, Date: 55, 19 July 1901
Citation: In action with the relief expedition of the Allied forces in China, 13, 20, 21, and 22 June 1900. During this period and in the presence of the enemy, Williams distinguished himself by meritiorious conduct.

2323 ◆ YOUNG, FRANK ALBERT

Rank: Private (highest rank: Sergeant Major)
Service: U.S. Marine Corps
Birthday: 22 June 1876
Place of Birth: Milwaukee, Milwaukee County, Wisconsin
Date of Death: 3 April 1941
Place of Death: Mare Island Shipyard, California
Cemetery: Arlington National Cemetery (17-18979-D) (MH)—Arlington, Virginia
Entered Service at: Wisconsin
Battle or Place of Action: Peking, China
Date of Action: 20 June-16 July 1900
G.O. Number, Date: 55, 19 July 1901
Citation: In the presence of the enemy during the battle of Peking, China, 20 June to 16 July 1900. Throughout this period, Young distinguished himself by meritorious conduct.

2324 ◆ ZION, WILLIAM F.

Rank: Private (highest rank: First Lieutenant U.S. Army)
Service: U.S. Marine Corps
Birthday: 23 October 1872
Place of Birth: Knightstown, Henry County, Indiana
Date of Death: 25 March 1919
Cemetery: Chattanooga National Cemetery (U-40) (MH)—Chattanooga, Tennessee
Entered Service at: California
Battle or Place of Action: Peking, China
Date of Action: 21 July-17 August 1900
G.O. Number, Date: 55, 19 July 1901
Citation: In the presence of the enemy during the battle of Peking, China, 21 July to 17 August 1900. Throughout this period, Zion distinguished himself by meritorious conduct.

2325 ◆ BEHNE, FREDERICK

Rank: Fireman First Class
Service: U.S. Navy
Birthday: 3 October 1873
Place of Birth: Lodi, Bergen County, New Jersey
Date of Death: 11 February 1918
Entered Service at: New Jersey
Unit: U.S.S. *Iowa*
Battle or Place of Action: U.S.S. *Iowa*
Date of Action: 25 January 1905
G.O. Number, Date: 182, 20 March 1905
Citation: On board the U.S.S. *Iowa*, 25 January 1905. Following the blowing-out of the manhole plate of boiler D of that vessel, Behne displayed extraordinary heroism in the resulting action.

2326 ◆ BEHNKE, HEINRICH

Rank: Seaman First Class
Service: U.S. Navy
Birthday: 10 April 1882
Place of Birth: Germany
Date of Death: 19 June 1952
Cemetery: Long Island National Cemetery (DSS-20-A) (MH)—Farmingdale, New York
Entered Service at: Washington, D.C.
Unit: U.S.S. *Iowa*
Battle or Place of Action: U.S.S. *Iowa*
Date of Action: 25 January 1905
G.O. Number, Date: 182, 20 March 1905
Citation: While serving aboard the U.S.S. *Iowa*, Behnke displayed extraordinary heroism at the time of the blowing-out of the manhole plate of boiler D on board that vessel, 25 January 1905.

2327 ◆ BJORKMAN, ERNEST H.

Rank: Ordinary Seaman
Service: U.S. Navy
Birthday: 25 April 1881
Place of Birth: Malmo, Sweden
Date of Death: 16 September 1912
Place of Death: Edgewater, Colorado
Cemetery: Crown Hill Cemetery (MH)—Edgewater, Colorado
Entered Service at: New York
Unit: U.S.S. *Leyden*
Battle or Place of Action: on the rocks of Block Island, Rhode Island

Date of Action: 21 January 1903
G.O. Number, Date: 145, 26 December 1903
Citation: On board the U.S.S. *Leyden*, 21 January 1903, Bjorkman displayed heroism at the time of the wreck of that vessel.

2328 ◆ BOERS, EDWARD WILLIAM

Rank: Seaman
Service: U.S. Navy
Birthday: 10 March 1884
Place of Birth: Cincinnati, Hamilton County, Ohio
Date of Death: 2 April 1929
Place of Death: Cincinnati, Ohio
Cemetery: Vine Street Hill Cemetery—Cincinnati, Ohio
Entered Service at: Kentucky
Unit: U.S.S. *Bennington*
Battle or Place of Action: U.S.S. *Bennington*
Date of Action: 21 July 1905
G.O. Number, Date: 13, 5 January 1906
Citation: On board the U.S.S. *Bennington*, 21 July 1905. Following the explosion of a boiler of that vessel, Boers displayed extraordinary heroism in the resulting action.

2329 ◆ BONNEY, ROBERT EARL

Rank: Chief Watertender (highest rank: Chief Machinist–Warrant Officer)
Service: U.S. Navy
Birthday: 23 November 1882
Place of Birth: Maryville, Blount County, Tennessee
Date of Death: 22 November 1967
Cemetery: Acacia Memorial Park (MH)—Seattle, Washington
Entered Service at: Nashville, Davidson County, Tennessee
Unit: U.S.S. *Hopkins*
Battle or Place of Action: U.S.S. *Hopkins*
Date of Action: 14 February 1910
Citation: While serving on board the U.S.S. *Hopkins*, Bonney displayed extraordinary heroism in the line of his profession on the occasion of the accident to one of the boilers of that vessel, 14 February 1910.

2330 ◆ BREEMAN, GEORGE

Rank: Seaman (highest rank: Chief Turret Captain)
Service: U.S. Navy
Birthday: 15 September 1880
Place of Birth: Passaic, Passaic County, New Jersey
Date of Death: 10 April 1937

Place of Death: Passaic, New Jersey
Cemetery: Arlington National Cemetery (6-9743-SH)—Arlington, Virginia
Entered Service at: New Jersey
Unit: U.S.S. *Kearsarge*
Battle or Place of Action: U.S.S. *Kearsarge*
G.O. Number, Date: 21, 5 May 1906
Citation: Breeman displayed heroism in the line of his profession while serving on board the U.S.S. *Kearsarge* at the time of the accidental ignition of powder charges in the forward 13-inch turret.

2331 ◆ BRESNAHAN, PATRICK FRANCIS

Rank: Watertender
Service: U.S. Navy
Birthday: 1 May 1872
Place of Birth: Peabody, Essex County, Massachusetts
Date of Death: 29 January 1940
Cemetery: St. Mary's Cemetery (MH)—Salem, Massachusetts
Entered Service at: Vermont
Unit: U.S.S. *Iowa*
Battle or Place of Action: U.S.S. *Iowa*
Date of Action: 25 January 1905
G.O. Number, Date: 182, 20 March 1905
Citation: Serving on board the U.S.S. *Iowa* for extraordinary heroism at the time of the blowing-out of the manhole plate of boiler D on board that vessel, 25 January 1905.

2332 ◆ BROCK, GEORGE F.

Rank: Carpenter's Mate Second Class
Service: U.S. Navy
Birthday: 18 October 1872
Place of Birth: Cleveland, Montgomery County, Ohio
Entered Service at: California
Unit: U.S.S. *Bennington*
Battle or Place of Action: U.S.S. *Bennington*
Date of Action: 21 July 1905
G.O. Number, Date: 13, 5 January 1906
Citation: Serving on board the U.S.S. *Bennington* for extraordinary heroism displayed at the time of the explosion of that vessel at San Diego, Cal., 21 July 1905.

2333 ◆ CAHEY, THOMAS

Rank: Seaman (highest rank: Chief Gunner's Mate)
Service: U.S. Navy
Birthday: 13 April 1870
Place of Birth: Belfast, County Antrim, Ireland
Date of Death: 5 January 1935
Cemetery: Arlington National Cemetery (6-8667)—Arlington, Virginia
Entered Service at: New York
Unit: U.S.S. *Petrel*
Battle or Place of Action: U.S.S. *Petrel*
Date of Action: 31 March 1901
G.O. Number, Date: 59, 23 March 1910

Citation: On board the U.S.S. *Petrel* for heroism and gallantry, fearlessly exposing his own life to danger in saving others on the occasion of the fire on board that vessel, 31 March 1901.

2334 ◆ CLARY, EDWARD ALVIN

Rank: Watertender
Service: U.S. Navy
Birthday: 6 May 1883
Place of Birth: Foxport, Kentucky
Date of Death: 30 April 1939
Cemetery: Sante Fe National Cemetery (O-335)—Sante Fe, New Mexico
Entered Service at: Kentucky
Unit: U.S.S. *Hopkins*
Battle or Place of Action: U.S.S. *Hopkins*
Date of Action: 14 February 1910
G.O. Number, Date: 59, 23 March 1910
Citation: On board the U.S.S. *Hopkins* for extraordinary heroism in the line of his profession on the occasion of the accident to one of the boilers of that vessel, 14 February 1910.

2335 ◆ CLAUSEY, JOHN JOSEPH

Rank: Chief Gunner's Mate (highest rank: Lieutenant)
Service: U.S. Navy
Birthday: 16 May 1875
Place of Birth: San Francisco, San Francisco County, California
Date of Death: 9 September 1951
Cemetery: Golden Gate National Cemetery (C-121-B) (MH)—San Bruno, California
Entered Service at: California
Unit: U.S.S. *Bennington*
Battle or Place of Action: U.S.S. *Bennington*
Date of Action: 21 July 1905
G.O. Number, Date: 13, 5 January 1906
Citation: On board the U.S.S. *Bennington* for extraordinary heroism displayed at the time of the explosion of a boiler of that vessel at San Diego, Cal., 21 July 1905.

2336 ◆ CORAHORGI, DEMETRI

Rank: Fireman First Class
Service: U.S. Navy
Birthday: 3 January 1880
Place of Birth: Trieste, Austria
Date of Death: 15 October 1973
Cemetery: Mount Pleasant Cemetery—Seattle, Washington
Entered Service at: New York
Unit: U.S.S. *Iowa*
Battle or Place of Action: U.S.S. *Iowa*
Date of Action: 25 January 1905
G.O. Number, Date: 182, 20 March 1905
Citation: Serving on board the U.S.S. *Iowa* for extraordinary heroism at the time of the blowing-out of the manhole plate of boiler D on board that vessel, 25 January 1905.

2337 ◆ COX, ROBERT EDWARD

Rank: Chief Gunner
Service: U.S. Navy
Birthday: 22 December 1876
Place of Birth: St. Albans, Kanawha County, West Virginia
Date of Death: 24 April 1937
Place of Death: Philadelphia, Pennsylvania
Cemetery: Rose Hill Cemetery (MH)—Altoona, Pennsylvania
Entered Service at: West Virginia
Unit: U.S.S. *Missouri*
Battle or Place of Action: U.S.S. *Missouri*
Date of Action: 13 April 1904
G.O. Number, Date: 43, 14 April 1921
Place of Presentation: The White House, presented by Pres. Warren G. Harding
Citation: For extraordinary heroism on U.S.S. *Missouri* 13 April 1904. While at target practice off Pensacola, Fla., an accident occurred in the after turret of the *Missouri* whereby the lives of five officers and 28 men were lost. The ship was in imminent danger of destruction by explosion, and the prompt action of C.G. Cox and two gunners' mates caused the fire to be brought under control, and the loss of the *Missouri*, together with her crew, was averted.

2338 ◆ CRONAN, WILLIAM S. (WILLIE)

Rank: Boatswain's Mate
Service: U.S. Navy
Birthday: 18 October 1883
Place of Birth: Chicago, Cook County, Illinois
Date of Death: 22 October 1959
Cemetery: Fort Rosecrans National Cemetery (T-534) (MH)—San Diego, California
Entered Service at: Illinois
Unit: U.S.S. *Bennington*
Battle or Place of Action: U.S.S. *Bennington*
Date of Action: 21 July 1905
G.O. Number, Date: 13, 5 January 1906
Citation: Serving on board the U.S.S. *Bennington*, for extraordinary heroism displayed at the time of the explosion of a boiler of that vessel at San Diego, Cal., 21 July 1905.

2339 ◆ DAVIS, RAYMOND ERWIN

Rank: Quartermaster Third Class
Service: U.S. Navy
Birthday: 19 September 1885
Place of Birth: Mankato, Blue Earth County, Minnesota
Date of Death: 9 September 1965
Cemetery: Calvary Cemetery—Seattle, Washington
Entered Service at: Puget Sound, Washington
Unit: U.S.S. *Bennington*
Battle or Place of Action: U.S.S. *Bennington*
Date of Action: 21 July 1905
G.O. Number, Date: 13, 5 January 1906
Citation: Serving on board the U.S.S. *Bennington*, for extraordinary heroism displayed at the time of the explosion of a boiler of that vessel at San Diego, Cal., 21 July 1905.

2340 ◆ FADDEN, HARRY DELMAR

Rank: Coxswain
Service: U.S. Navy
Birthday: 17 September 1882
Place of Birth: The Dalles, Wasco County, Oregon
Date of Death: 2 February 1955
Cemetery: Evergreen-Washelli Memorial Park—Seattle, Washington
Entered Service at: Washington
Unit: U.S.S. *Adams*
Battle or Place of Action: off the California coast
Date of Action: 30 June 1903
G.O. Number, Date: 138, 31 July 1903
Citation: On board the U.S.S. *Adams*, for gallantry, rescuing O.C. Hawthorne, landsman for training, from drowning at sea, 30 June 1903.

2341 ◆ FLOYD, EDWARD

Rank: Boilermaker
Service: U.S. Navy
Birthday: 21 February 1850
Place of Birth: Ireland
Date of Death: 16 January 1923
Cemetery: St. Lawrence Cemetery (MH)—Charleston, South Carolina
Entered Service at: South Carolina
Unit: U.S.S. *Iowa*
Battle or Place of Action: U.S.S. *Iowa*
Date of Action: 25 January 1905
G.O. Number, Date: 182, 20 March 1905
Citation: Serving on board the U.S.S. *Iowa*, for extraordinary heroism at the time of the blowing-out of the manhole plate of boiler D on board that vessel, 25 January 1905.

2342 ◆ FREDERICKSEN, EMIL

Rank: Watertender
Service: U.S. Navy
Date of Death: 1960
Unit: U.S.S. *Bennington*
Battle or Place of Action: U.S.S. *Bennington*
Date of Action: 21 July 1905
G.O. Number, Date: 13, 5 January 1906
Citation: Serving on board the U.S.S. *Bennington*, for extraordinary heroism displayed at the time of the explosion of a boiler of that vessel at San Diego, Cal., 21 July 1905.

2343 ◆ GIRANDY, ALPHONSE

Rank: Seaman
Service: U.S. Navy
Birthday: 21 January 1868
Place of Birth: Guadaloupe, West Indies
Date of Death: 3 April 1941
Cemetery: Philadelphia National Cemetery (N-66) (MH)—Philadelphia, Pennsylvania

Entered Service at: Pennsylvania
Unit: U.S.S. *Petrel*
Battle or Place of Action: U.S.S. *Petrel*
Date of Action: 31 March 1901
G.O. Number, Date: 85, 22 March 1902
Citation: Serving on board the U.S.S. *Petrel*, for heroism and gallantry, fearlessly exposing his own life to danger for the saving of others, on the occasion of the fire on board that vessel, 31 March 1901.

2344 ◆ GOWAN, WILLIAM HENRY

Rank: Boatswain's Mate
Service: U.S. Navy
Birthday: 2 June 1884
Place of Birth: Rye, Westchester County, New York
Date of Death: 22 May 1957
Place of Death: Brooklyn, New York
Cemetery: Long Island National Cemetery (DSS-7) (MH)—Farmingdale, New York
Entered Service at: New York
Battle or Place of Action: Coquimbo, Chile
Date of Action: 20 January 1909
G.O. Number, Date: 18, 19 March 1909
Citation: For bravery and extraordinary heroism displayed by him during a conflagration in Coquimbo, Chile, 20 January 1909.

2345 ◆ GRBITCH, RADE

Rank: Seaman
Service: U.S. Navy
Birthday: 24 December 1870
Place of Birth: Austria
Date of Death: 5 March 1910
Cemetery: San Francisco National Cemetery (A-44)—San Francisco, California
Entered Service at: Illinois
Unit: U.S.S. *Bennington*
Battle or Place of Action: U.S.S. *Bennington*
Date of Action: 21 July 1905
G.O. Number, Date: 13, 5 January 1906
Citation: On board the U.S.S. *Bennington*, for extraordinary heroism displayed at the time of the explosion of a boiler of that vessel at San Diego, Cal., 21 July 1905.

2346 ◆ HALLING, LUOVI

Rank: Boatswain's Mate First Class
Service: U.S. Navy
Birthday: 7 August 1867
Place of Birth: Stockholm, Sweden
Date of Death: 22 March 1928
Cemetery: St. Michael's Cemetery—Astoria, New York
Entered Service at: New York
Unit: U.S.S. *Missouri*
Battle or Place of Action: off Martha's Vineyard, Massachusetts

Date of Action: 15 September 1904
G.O. Number, Date: 172, 4 October 1904
Citation: Serving on board the U.S.S. *Missouri*, for heroism in attempting to rescue from drowning Cecil C. Young, ordinary seaman, 15 September 1904.

2347 ◆ HELMS, JOHN HENRY

Rank: Sergeant
Service: U.S. Marine Corps
Birthday: 16 March 1874
Place of Birth: Chicago, Cook County, Illinois
Date of Death: 17 February 1919
Cemetery: Mound Grove Cemetery (MH)—Kankakee, Illinois
Entered Service at: Illinois
Unit: U.S.S. *Chicago*
Battle or Place of Action: Montevideo, Uruguay
Date of Action: 10 January 1901
G.O. Number, Date: 35, 23 March 1901
Citation: Serving on board the U.S.S. *Chicago*, for heroism in rescuing Ishi Tomizi, ship's cook, from drowning at Montevideo, Uruguay, 10 January 1901.

2348 ◆ HILL, FRANK EBENEZER

Rank: Ship's Cook First Class (highest rank: First Lieutenant U.S. Army WWI)
Service: U.S. Navy
Birthday: 31 July 1880
Place of Birth: La Grange, La Grange County, Indiana
Date of Death: 23 September 1932
Cemetery: unknown cemetery—St. Cloud, Florida
Entered Service at: Indiana
Unit: U.S.S. *Bennington*
Battle or Place of Action: San Diego, California
Date of Action: 21 July 1905
G.O. Number, Date: 13, 5 January 1906
Citation: On board the U.S.S. *Bennington*, for extraordinary heroism displayed at the time of the explosion of a boiler of that vessel at San Diego, Cal., 21 July 1905.

2349 ◆ HOLTZ, AUGUST

Rank: Chief Watertender
Service: U.S. Navy
Birthday: 12 February 1871
Place of Birth: St. Louis, St. Louis County, Missouri
Date of Death: 5 March 1938
Cemetery: Long Island National Cemetery (F-916) (MH)—Farmingdale, New York
Entered Service at: St. Louis, St. Louis County, Missouri
Unit: U.S.S. *North Dakota*
Battle or Place of Action: U.S.S. *North Dakota*
Date of Action: 8 September 1910
G.O. Number, Date: 83, 4 October 1910
Citation: On board the U.S.S. *North Dakota*, for extraordi-

nary heroism in the line of his profession during the fire on board that vessel, 8 September 1910.

2350 ◆ JOHANNESSEN, JOHANNES J.

Rank: Chief Watertender
Service: U.S. Navy
Birthday: 13 May 1872
Place of Birth: Bodo, Norway
Date of Death: 14 November 1915
Cemetery: Cypress Hills National Cemetery (2-7425) (MH)—Brooklyn, New York
Enlisted at: Yokohama, Japan
Unit: U.S.S. *Iowa*
Battle or Place of Action: U.S.S. *Iowa*
Date of Action: 25 January 1905
G.O. Number, Date: 182, 20 March 1905
Citation: Serving on board the U.S.S. *Iowa* for extraordinary heroism at the time of the blowing out of the manhole plate of Boiler D on board that vessel, 25 January 1905.

2351 ◆ KING, JOHN✛

Rank: Watertender (highest rank: Chief Watertender)
Service: U.S. Navy
Birthday: 7 February 1862
Place of Birth: County Mayo, Ireland
Date of Death: 20 May 1938
Cemetery: Calvary Cemetery (MH)—Hot Springs, Arkansas
Entered Service at: New York
Unit: U.S.S. *Vicksburg*; U.S.S. *Salem*
Served as: Watertender
Battle or Place of Action: U.S.S. *Vicksburg*; U.S.S. *Salem*
Date of Action: 29 May 1901; 13 September 1909
G.O. Number, Date: 72, 6 December 1901; 40, 19 October 1909
Citation: **First Award** On board the U.S.S. *Vicksburg*, for heroism in the line of his profession at the time of the accident to the boiler, 29 May 1901. **Second Award** Watertender, serving on board the U.S.S. *Salem*, for extraordinary heroism in the line of his profession on the occasion of the accident to one of the boilers of that vessel, 13 September 1909.
Notes: ✛Double Awardee

2352 ◆ KLEIN, ROBERT

Rank: Chief Carpenter's Mate
Service: U.S. Navy
Birthday: 11 November 1848
Place of Birth: Gerdonen, Germany
Date of Death: 29 November 1931
Place of Death: Shanghi, China
Cemetery: Bubbling Well Cemetery—Shanghi, China
Enlisted at: Marseilles, France
Unit: U.S.S. *Raleigh*
Battle or Place of Action: Olongapo, Philippine Island
Date of Action: 25 January 1904

G.O. Number, Date: 173, 6 October 1904
Citation: Serving on board the U.S.S. *Raleigh*, for heroism in rescuing shipmates overcome in double bottoms by fumes of turpentine, 25 January 1904.

2353 ◆ LIPSCOMB, HARRY

Rank: Watertender (highest rank: Chief Watertender)
Service: U.S. Navy
Birthday: 2 April 1878
Place of Birth: Washington, D.C.
Date of Death: 7 September 1926
Cemetery: Arlington National Cemetery (3-2481-WS)—Arlington, Virginia
Entered Service at: Washington, D.C.
Unit: U.S.S. *North Dakota*
Battle or Place of Action: U.S.S. *North Dakota*
Date of Action: 8 September 1910
G.O. Number, Date: 83, 4 October 1910
Citation: On board the U.S.S. *North Dakota*, for extraordinary heroism in the line of his profession during the fire on board that vessel, 8 September 1910.

2354 ◆ MONSSEN, MONS

Rank: Chief Gunner's Mate (highest rank: lieutenant)
Service: U.S. Navy
Birthday: 20 January 1867
Place of Birth: Bergen, Norway
Date of Death: 10 February 1930
Cemetery: Cypress Hills National Cemetery (OS-190) (MH)—Brooklyn, New York
Unit: U.S.S. *Missouri*
Battle or Place of Action: U.S.S. *Missouri*
Date of Action: 13 April 1904
G.O. Number, Date: 160, 26 May 1904
Citation: Serving on board the U.S.S. *Missouri*, for extraordinary heroism in entering a burning magazine through the scuttle and endeavoring to extinguish the fire by throwing water with his hands until a hose was passed to him, 13 April 1904.

2355 ◆ MULLIN, HUGH PATRICK

Rank: Seaman
Service: U.S. Navy
Birthday: 20 March 1878
Place of Birth: Richmond, McHenry County, Illinois
Date of Death: 9 June 1948
Cemetery: Golden Gate National Cemetery (A-2-294)—San Bruno, California
Entered Service at: Chicago, Cook County, Illinois
Unit: U.S.S. *Texas*
Battle or Place of Action: Hampton Roads, Virginia
Date of Action: 11 November 1899
G.O. Number, Date: 537, 8 January 1900
Citation: On board the U.S.S. *Texas* during the coaling of that vessel at Hampton Roads, Va., 11 November 1899. Jumping overboard while wearing a pair of heavy rubber

boots and at great risk to himself, Mullin rescued Alfred Kosminski, apprentice, second class, who fell overboard, by supporting him until he was safely hauled from the water.

2356 ◆ NELSON, OSCAR FREDERICK

Rank: Machinist's Mate First Class
Service: U.S. Navy
Birthday: 5 November 1881
Place of Birth: Minneapolis, Hennepin County, Minnesota
Date of Death: 26 September 1951
Cemetery: Fort Snelling National Cemetery (DS-64-N) (MH)—Minneapolis, Minnesota
Entered Service at: Minnesota
Unit: U.S.S. *Bennington*
Battle or Place of Action: U.S.S. *Bennington*
Date of Action: 21 July 1905
G.O. Number, Date: 13, 5 January 1906
Citation: Serving on board the U.S.S. *Bennington*, for extraordinary heroism displayed at the time of the explosion of a boiler of that vessel at San Diego, Cal., 21 July 1905.

2357 ◆ NORDSTROM, ISADOR A.

Rank: Chief Boatswain (highest rank: Lieutenant)
Service: U.S. Navy
Birthday: 24 May 1876
Place of Birth: Goteborg, Sweden
Date of Death: 6 March 1930
Cemetery: Arlington National Cemetery (7-8273)—Arlington, Virginia
Entered Service at: New York
Unit: U.S.S. *Kearsarge*
Battle or Place of Action: U.S.S. *Kearsarge*
Date of Action: 13 April 1906
G.O. Number, Date: 142, 4 December 1924
Citation: For gallant conduct upon the occasion of the disastrous fire of accidentally ignited powder charges, which occurred in the forward turret of the U.S.S. *Kearsarge* during target practice on 13 April 1906. Chief Boatswain Nordstrom, then chief boatswain's mate, was among the first to enter the turret in order to assist in bringing out the injured.

2358 ◆ PETERS, ALEXANDER

Rank: Boatswain's Mate First Class (highest rank: Chief Gunner's Mate)
Service: U.S. Navy
Birthday: 16 November 1869
Place of Birth: Russia
Date of Death: 11 June 1951
Place of Death: Martha's Vineyard, Massachusetts
Cemetery: Arlington National Cemetery (8-5300-A) (MH)—Arlington, Virginia
Entered Service at: Pennsylvania
Unit: U.S.S. *Missouri*
Battle or Place of Action: off Martha's Vineyard, Massachusetts
Date of Action: 15 September 1904

G.O. Number, Date: 172, 4 October 1904
Citation: For heroism in attempting to rescue from drowning Cecil C. Young, ordinary seaman, 15 September 1904, while serving on board the U.S.S. *Missouri*.

2359 ◆ PFEIFER, LOUIS FRED

Rank: Private
Service: U.S. Marine Corps
Birthday: 19 June 1876
Place of Birth: Philadelphia, Philadelphia County, Pennsylvania
Entered Service at: New Jersey
Unit: U.S.S. *Petrel*
Battle or Place of Action: U.S.S. *Petrel*
Date of Action: 31 March 1901
G.O. Number, Date: 85, 22 March 1902
Citation: Serving on board the U.S.S. *Petrel*; for heroism and gallantry, fearlessly exposing his own life to danger for the saving of the others on the occasion of the fire on board that vessel, 31 March 1901.

2360 ◆ QUICK, JOSEPH

Rank: Coxswain
Service: U.S. Navy
Birthday: 1877
Place of Birth: New York
Date of Death: 27 June 1969
Place of Death: Tampa, Florida
Cemetery: The Evergreen Cemetery—Brooklyn, New York
Entered Service at: New York
Unit: U.S.S. *Yorktown*
Battle or Place of Action: Yokohama, Japan
Date of Action: 27 April 1902
G.O. Number, Date: 93, 7 July 1902
Citation: For heroism in rescuing Walenty Wisnieroski, Machinist Second Class, from drowning at Yokohama, Japan, 27 April 1902, while serving on board the U.S.S. *Yorktown*.

2361 ◆ REID, PATRICK

Rank: Chief Watertender
Service: U.S. Navy
Birthday: 17 June 1875
Place of Birth: Dublin, Ireland
Entered Service at: New York
Unit: U.S.S. *North Dakota*
Battle or Place of Action: U.S.S. *North Dakota*
Date of Action: 8 September 1910
G.O. Number, Date: 83, 4 October 1910
Citation: For extraordinary heroism in the line of his profession during the fire on board the U.S.S. *North Dakota* where Reid was serving, 8 September 1910.

2362 ◆ ROBERTS, CHARLES CHURCH

Rank: Machinist's Mate First Class
Service: U.S. Navy

Birthday: 6 March 1882
Place of Birth: Newton, Middlesex County, Massachusetts
Date of Death: 8 March 1957
Cemetery: Prospect Hill Cemetery (MH)—Millis, Massachusetts
Entered Service at: Illinois
Unit: U.S.S. *North Dakota*
Battle or Place of Action: U.S.S. *North Dakota*
Date of Action: 8 September 1910
G.O. Number, Date: 83, 4 October 1910
Citation: Serving on board the U.S.S. *North Dakota*; for extraordinary heroism in the line of his profession during the fire on board that vessel, 8 September 1910.

2363 ◆ SCHEPKE, CHARLES STEPHEN

Rank: Gunner's Mate First Class (highest rank: Lieutenant)
Service: U.S. Navy
Birthday: 26 December 1878
Place of Birth: New York, New York
Date of Death: 27 February 1933
Place of Death: Brooklyn, New York
Cemetery: The Lutheran Cemetery—Middle Village, New York
Entered Service at: New York
Unit: U.S.S. *Missouri*
Battle or Place of Action: U.S.S. *Missouri*
Date of Action: 13 April 1904
G.O. Number, Date: 160, 26 May 1904
Citation: For extraordinary heroism while serving on the U.S.S. *Missouri* in remaining by a burning magazine and assisting in extinguishing the fire, 13 April 1904.

2364 ◆ SCHMIDT, OTTO DILLER

Rank: Seaman
Service: U.S. Navy
Birthday: 10 August 1883
Place of Birth: Blair, Washington County, Nebraska
Date of Death: 9 February 1963
Cemetery: Prospect Hill Cemetery (MH)—Norfolk, Nebraska
Entered Service at: Nebraska
Unit: U.S.S. *Bennington*
Battle or Place of Action: U.S.S. *Bennington*
Date of Action: 21 July 1905
G.O. Number, Date: 13, 5 January 1906
Citation: While serving on board the U.S.S. *Bennington* for extraordinary heroism displayed at the time of the explosion of a boiler of that vessel at San Diego, Cal., 21 July 1905.

2365 ◆ SHACKLETTE, WILLIAM SIDNEY

Rank: Hospital Steward
Service: U.S. Navy
Birthday: 17 May 1880
Place of Birth: Delaplane, Fauquier County, Virginia
Date of Death: 12 February 1945
Cemetery: Arlington National Cemetery (10-10688) (MH)—Arlington, Virginia

Entered Service at: Virginia
Unit: U.S.S. *Bennington*
Battle or Place of Action: U.S.S. *Bennington*
Date of Action: 21 July 1905
G.O. Number, Date: 13, 5 January 1906
Citation: For extraordinary heroism while serving on the U.S.S. *Bennington* at the time of the explosion of a boiler of that vessel at San Diego, Cal., 21 July 1905.

2366 ◆ SHANAHAN, PATRICK

Rank: Chief Boatswain's Mate (highest rank: Lieutenant)
Service: U.S. Navy
Birthday: 6 November 1867
Place of Birth: Shanat Castle, County Limerick, Ireland
Date of Death: 7 December 1937
Cemetery: Arlington National Cemetery (7-10295) (MH)—Arlington, Virginia
Entered Service at: New York
Unit: U.S. Training Ship *Alliance*
Battle or Place of Action: off Annapolis, Maryland
Date of Action: 28 May 1899
G.O. Number, Date: 534, 29 November 1899
Citation: On board the U.S.S. *Alliance*, 28 May 1899. Displaying heroism, Shanahan rescued William Steven, quartermaster first class, from drowning.

2367 ◆ SNYDER, WILLIAM ELLSWORTH

Rank: Chief Electrician (highest rank: Lieutenant Commander)
Service: U.S. Navy
Birthday: 24 February 1883
Place of Birth: South Bethlehem, Northampton County, Pennsylvania
Date of Death: 30 December 1944
Cemetery: Arlington National Cemetery (10-10636)—Arlington, Virginia
Entered Service at: Pennsylvania
Unit: U.S.S. *Birmingham*
Battle or Place of Action: U.S.S. *Birmingham*
Date of Action: 4 January 1910
G.O. Number, Date: 58, 2 March 1910
Citation: Serving on board the U.S.S. *Birmingham*, for extraordinary heroism, rescuing G.H. Kephart, seaman, from drowning at Hampton Roads, Va., 4 January 1910.

2368 ◆ STANTON, THOMAS

Rank: Chief Machinist's Mate
Service: U.S. Navy
Birthday: 11 August 1869
Place of Birth: Ireland
Date of Death: 7 May 1950
Cemetery: St. Columbia's Cemetery—Middleton, Rhode Island
Entered Service at: New York
Unit: U.S.S. *North Dakota*
Battle or Place of Action: U.S.S. *North Dakota*

Date of Action: 8 September 1910
G.O. Number, Date: 83, 4 October 1910
Citation: For extraordinary heroism in the line of his profession during the fire on board the U.S.S. *North Dakota*, 8 September 1910.

2369 ◆ STOKES, JOHN S.

Rank: Chief Master-of-Arms (highest rank: Boatswain)
Service: U.S. Navy
Birthday: 12 June 1871
Place of Birth: New York, New York
Date of Death: 14 February 1923
Cemetery: Arlington National Cemetery (17-20184) (MH)—Arlington, Virginia
Entered Service at: New York
Unit: U.S.S. *New York*
Battle or Place of Action: off the coast of Jamaica
Date of Action: 31 March 1899
G.O. Number, Date: 525, 29 July 1899
Citation: On board the U.S.S. *New York* off the coast of Jamaica, 31 March 1899. Showing gallant conduct, Stokes jumped overboard and assisted in the rescue of Peter Mahoney, watertender, U.S. Navy.

2370 ◆ STUPKA, LADDIE

Rank: Fireman First Class
Service: U.S. Navy
Birthday: 4 March 1878
Place of Birth: Cleveland, Cuyahoga County, Ohio
Date of Death: 20 February 1946
Cemetery: Baltimore National Cemetery (DS-1) (MH)—Baltimore, Maryland
Entered Service at: Ohio
Unit: U.S.S. *Leyden*
Battle or Place of Action: on the rocks of Block Island, Rhode Island
Date of Action: 21 January 1903
G.O. Number, Date: 145, 26 December 1903
Citation: Serving on board the U.S.S. *Leyden*; for heroism at the time of the wreck of that vessel, 21 January 1903.

2371 ◆ TEYTAND, AUGUST P.

True Name: Teytard, August P.
Rank: Quartermaster Third Class
Service: U.S. Navy
Birthday: 6 April 1878
Place of Birth: Santa Cruz, West Indies
Date of Death: 4 March 1956
Cemetery: Mount Moriah VA Plot (5-4-5) (MH)—Philadelphia, Pennsylvania
Entered Service at: New Jersey
Unit: U.S.S. *Leyden*
Battle or Place of Action: on the rocks of Block Island, Rhode Island
Date of Action: 21 January 1903

G.O. Number, Date: 145, 26 December 1903
Citation: For heroism while serving on board the U.S.S. *Leyden* at the time of the wreck of that vessel, 21 January 1903.

2372 ◆ WALSH, MICHAEL

Rank: Chief Machinist
Service: U.S. Navy
Birthday: 27 July 1858
Place of Birth: Newport, Newport County, Rhode Island
Date of Death: 29 June 1913
Cemetery: St. Columba's Cemetery (MH)—Middletown, Rhode Island
Entered Service at: Rhode Island
Unit: U.S.S. *Leyden*
Battle or Place of Action: on the rocks of Block Island, Rhode Island
Date of Action: 21 January 1903
G.O. Number, Date: 145, 26 December 1903
Citation: Serving on board the U.S.S. *Leyden*; for heroism at the time of the wreck of that vessel, 21 January 1903.

2373 ◆ WESTA, KARL

Rank: Chief Machinist's Mate
Service: U.S. Navy
Birthday: 8 April 1875
Place of Birth: Norway
Date of Death: 3 March 1949
Cemetery: Arlington National Cemetery (11-83-SH) (MH)—Arlington, Virginia
Entered Service at: New York
Unit: U.S.S. *North Dakota*
Battle or Place of Action: U.S.S. *North Dakota*
Date of Action: 8 September 1910
G.O. Number, Date: 83, 4 October 1910
Citation: On board the U.S.S. *North Dakota*; for extraordinary heroism in the line of his profession during the fire on board that vessel, 8 September 1910.

2374 ◆ WHEELER, GEORGE HUBER

Rank: Shipfitter First Class (highest rank: Lieutenant)
Service: U.S. Navy
Birthday: 26 September 1881
Place of Birth: Charleston, Charleston County, South Carolina
Date of Death: 20 January 1957
Place of Death: Bethesda, Maryland
Cemetery: Arlington National Cemetery (7-10040-EH)—Arlington, Virginia
Entered Service at: Washington, D.C.
Battle or Place of Action: Coquimbo, Chile
Date of Action: 20 January 1909
G.O. Number, Date: 18, 19 March 1909
Citation: For bravery and extraordinary heroism displayed by him during a conflagration in Coquimbo, Chile, 20 January 1909.

ACTION AGAINST OUTLAWS, PHILIPPINES 1911

2375 ◆ CATHERWOOD, JOHN HUGH

Rank: Ordinary Seaman
Service: U.S. Navy
Birthday: 7 August 1888
Place of Birth: Springfield, Sangamon County, Illinois
Date of Death: 18 December 1930
Cemetery: Camp Butler National Cemetery (MH)—Springfield, Illinois
Entered Service at: Illinois
Unit: U.S.S. *Pampang*
Battle or Place of Action: near the village of Mundang, Basilan Island, Philippine Islands
Date of Action: 24 September 1911
G.O. Number, Date: 138, 13 December 1911
Citation: While attached to the U.S.S. *Pampang*, Catherwood was one of a shore party moving in to capture Mundang, on the island of Basilan, P.I., on the morning of 24 September 1911. Advancing with the scout party to reconnoiter a group of nipa huts close to the trail, Catherwood unhesitatingly entered the open area before the huts, where his party was suddenly taken under point-blank fire and charged by approximately 20 enemy Moros coming out from inside the native huts and from other concealed positions. Struck down almost instantly by the outlaws' deadly fire, Catherwood, although unable to rise, rallied to the defense of his leader and fought desperately to beat off the hostile attack. By his valiant effort under fire and in the face of great odds, Catherwood contributed materially toward the destruction and rout of the enemy.

2376 ◆ HARRISON, BOLDEN REUSH

Rank: Seaman
Service: U.S. Navy
Birthday: 26 April 1886
Place of Birth: Savannah, Hardin County, Tennessee
Date of Death: 26 January 1952
Cemetery: Savannah Cemetery (MH)—Savannah, Tennessee
Entered Service at: Tennessee
Unit: U.S.S. *Pampang*
Battle or Place of Action: near the village of Mundang, Basilan Island, Philippine Islands
Date of Action: 24 September 1911
G.O. Number, Date: 138, 13 December 1911
Citation: While attached to the U.S.S. *Pampang*, Harrison was one of a shore party moving in to capture Mundang, on the island of Basilan, P.I., 24 September 1911. Harrison instantly responded to the calls for help when the advance scout party investigating a group of nipa huts close to the trail was suddenly taken under point-blank fire and rushed by approximately 20 enemy Moros attacking from inside the huts and from other concealed positions. Armed with a double-barreled shotgun, he concentrated his blasting fire on the outlaws, destroying three of the Moros and assisting in the rout of the remainder. By his aggressive charging of the enemy under heavy fire and in the face of great odds, Harrison contributed materially to the success of the engagement.

2377 ◆ HENRECHON, GEORGE FRANCIS

Rank: Machinist's Mate Second Class
Service: U.S. Navy
Birthday: 22 November 1885
Place of Birth: Hartford, Hartford County, Connecticut
Date of Death: 16 August 1929
Cemetery: Mount St. Benedict Cemetery (MH)—Bloomfield, Connecticut
Entered Service at: California
Unit: U.S.S. *Pampang*
Battle or Place of Action: near the village of Mundang, Basilan Island, Philippine Islands
Date of Action: 24 September 1911
G.O. Number, Date: 138, 13 December 1911
Citation: While attached to the U.S.S. *Pampang*, Henrechon was one of a shore party moving in to capture Mundang, on the island of Basilan, P.I., 24 September 1911. Ordered to take station within 100 yards of a group of nipa huts close to the trail, Henrechon advanced and stood guard as the leader, and his scout party first searched the surrounding deep grasses, then moved into the open area before the huts. Instantly enemy Moros opened point-blank fire on the exposed men and approximately 20 Moros rushed the small group from inside the huts and from other concealed positions. Henrechon, responding to the calls for help, was one of the first on the scene. With his rifle jammed after the first shot, he closed in with rifle, using it as a club to break the stock over the head of the nearest Moro and then, drawing his pistol, started in pursuit of the fleeing outlaws. Henrechon's aggressive charging of the enemy under heavy fire and in the face of great odds contributed materially to the success of the engagement.

2378 ◆ McGUIRE, FRED HENRY

Rank: Hospital Apprentice (highest rank: Chief Pharmacist)
Service: U.S. Navy

Birthday: 7 November 1890
Place of Birth: Gordonville, Cape Girardeau County, Missouri
Date of Death: 4 February 1958
Cemetery: Springfield National Cemetery (29-332) (MH)—Springfield, Missouri
Entered Service at: Gordonville, Cape Girardeau County, Missouri
Unit: U.S.S. *Pampanga*
Battle or Place of Action: near the village of Mundang, Basilan Island, Philippine Islands
Date of Action: 24 September 1911
G.O. Number, Date: 138, 13 December 1911
Citation: While attached to the U.S.S. *Pampang*, McGuire was one of a shore party moving in to capture Mundang, on the island of Basilan, P.I., 24 September 1911. Ordered to take station within 100 yards of a group of nipa huts close to the trail, McGuire advanced and stood guard as the leader and his scout party first searched the surrounding deep grasses, then moved into the open area before the huts. Instantly enemy Moros opened point-blank fire on the exposed men, and approximately 20 Moros charged the small group from inside the huts and from other concealed positions. McGuire, responding to the calls for help, was one of the first on the scene. After emptying his rifle into the attackers, he closed in with rifle, using it as a club to wage fierce battle until his comrades arrived on the field, when he rallied to the aid of his dying leader and other wounded. Although himself wounded, McGuire ministered tirelessly and efficiently to those who had been struck down, thereby saving the lives of two who otherwise might have succumbed to enemy-inflicted wounds.

2379 ◆ NISPEROS, JOSE B.

Rank: Private
Service: U.S. Army
Birthday: 30 December 1887
Place of Birth: San Fernandos Union, Philippine Islands
Date of Death: 1 September 1922
Place of Death: San Fernandos Union, Philippine Islands
Cemetery: New Municipal Cemetery—San Fernandos Union, Philippine Islands
Entered Service at: San Fernandos Union, Philippine Islands

Unit: 34th Company, Philippine Scouts
Battle or Place of Action: at Lapurap, Basilan Island, Philippine Islands
Date of Action: 24 September 1911
G.O. Number, Date: 64, 25 November 1912
Date of Presentation: 3 February 1913
Place of Presentation: Manila, Philippine Islands (Parade Grounds), presented by Mrs. J. Franklin Bell (wife of the commanding officer, Maj. Gen. Bell)
Citation: Having been badly wounded (his left arm was broken and lacerated and he had received several spear wounds in the body so he could not stand) continued to fire his rifle with one hand until the enemy was repulsed, thereby aiding materially in preventing the annihilation of his party and the mutilation of their bodies.

2380 ◆ VOLZ, JACOB

Rank: Carpenter's Mate Third Class
Service: U.S. Navy
Birthday: 23 June 1889
Place of Birth: Sutton, Clay County, Nebraska
Date of Death: 22 July 1965
Place of Death: Portland, Oregon
Cemetery: Lincoln Memorial Park—Portland, Oregon
Entered Service at: Nebraska
Unit: U.S.S. *Pampang*
Battle or Place of Action: near the village of Mundang, Basilan Island, Philippine Islands
Date of Action: 24 September 1911
G.O. Number, Date: 138, 13 December 1911
Citation: While attached to the U.S.S. *Pampang*, Volz was one of a shore party moving in to capture Mundang, on the island of Basilan, P.I., on 24 September 1911. Investigating a group of nipa huts close to the trail, the advanced scout party was suddenly taken under point-blank fire and rushed by approximately 20 enemy Moros attacking from inside the huts and from other concealed positions. Volz responded instantly to calls for help and, finding all members of the scout party writhing on the ground but still fighting, he blazed his rifle into the outlaws with telling effect, destroying several of the Moros and assisting in the rout of the remainder. By his aggressive charging of the enemy under heavy fire and in the face of great odds, Volz contributed materially to the success of the engagement.

MEXICAN CAMPAIGN (VERA CRUZ)

2381 ◆ ANDERSON, EDWIN ALEXANDER

Rank: Captain (highest rank: Admiral)
Service: U.S. Navy
Birthday: 16 July 1860
Place of Birth: Wilmington, New Hanover County, North Carolina
Date of Death: 23 September 1933
Cemetery: Arlington National Cemetery (2-3798)—Arlington, Virginia
Entered Service at: Wilmington, New Hanover County, North Carolina
Unit: 2d Regiment of Bluejackets
Served as: Commanding Officer
Battle or Place of Action: Vera Cruz, Mexico
Date of Action: 22 April 1914
G.O. Number, Date: 177, 4 December 1915
Citation: For extraordinary heroism in battle, engagement of Vera Cruz, 22 April 1914, in command of the 2d Seaman Regiment. Marching his regiment across the open space in front of the Naval Academy and other buildings, Capt. Anderson unexpectedly met a heavy fire from riflemen, machine guns and one-pounders, which caused part of his command to break and fall back, many casualties occurring amongst them at the time. His indifference to the heavy fire, to which he himself was exposed at the head of his regiment, showed him to be fearless and courageous in battle.

2382 ◆ BADGER, OSCAR CHARLES

Rank: Ensign (highest rank: Admiral)
Service: U.S. Navy
Birthday: 26 June 1890
Place of Birth: Washington, D.C.
Date of Death: 30 November 1958
Place of Death: Glen Cove, New York
Cemetery: Arlington National Cemetery (2-3760-WS)—Arlington, Virginia
Entered Service at: Washington, D.C.
Battle or Place of Action: Vera Cruz, Mexico
Date of Action: 21-22 April 1914
G.O. Number, Date: 177, 4 December 1915
Citation: For distinguished conduct in battle, engagements of Vera Cruz, 21–22 April 1914. Ens. Badger was in both days' fighting at the head of his company and was eminent and conspicuous in his conduct, leading his men with skill and courage.

2383 ◆ BEASLEY, HARRY C.

Rank: Seaman
Service: U.S. Navy
Birthday: 1 November 1889
Place of Birth: Ohio
Date of Death: 2 July 1931
Cemetery: Cedar Hill Cemetery (MH)—Newark, Ohio
Entered Service at: Ohio
Unit: U.S.S. *Florida*
Battle or Place of Action: Vera Cruz, Mexico
Date of Action: 21 April 1914
G.O. Number, Date: 101, 15 June 1914
Citation: On board the U.S.S. *Florida* for extraordinary heroism in the line of his profession during the seizure of Vera Cruz, Mexico, 21 April 1914.

2384 ◆ BERKELEY, RANDOLPH CARTER

Rank: Major (highest rank: Major General)
Service: U.S. Marine Corps
Birthday: 9 January 1875
Place of Birth: Staunton, Staunton County, Virginia
Date of Death: 31 January 1960
Place of Death: Beaufort, South Carolina
Cemetery: Arlington National Cemetery (3-1767-SH)—Arlington, Virginia
Appointed from: Washington, D.C
Unit: 1st Battalion, 2d Advanced Base Regiment
Served as: Commanding Officer
Battle or Place of Action: Vera Cruz, Mexico
Date of Action: 21-22 April 1914
G.O. Number, Date: 177, 4 December 1915
Citation: For distinguished conduct in battle, engagements of Vera Cruz, 21–22 April 1914. Maj. Berkeley was eminent and conspicuous in command of his battalion, was in the fighting of both days, and exhibited courage and skill in leading his men through action. His cool judgment and courage, and his skill in handling his men in encountering and overcoming the machine-gun and rifle fire down Cinco de Mayo and parallel streets account for the small percentage of the losses of marines under his command.

2385 ◆ BISHOP, CHARLES FRANCIS

Rank: Quartermaster Second Class (highest rank: Chief Quartermaster)
Service: U.S. Navy

Birthday: 2 August 1888
Place of Birth: Pittsburgh, Allegheny County, Pennsylvania
Date of Death: 1 February 1954
Cemetery: Fort Rosecrans National Cemetery (0-4562)—San Diego, California
Entered Service at: Pennsylvania
Unit: U.S.S. *Florida*
Battle or Place of Action: Vera Cruz, Mexico
Date of Action: 21 April 1914
G.O. Number, Date: 101, 15 June 1914
Citation: On board the U.S.S. *Florida* for extraordinary heroism in the line of his profession during the seizure of Vera Cruz, Mexico, 21 April 1914.

2386 ◆ BRADLEY, GEORGE

Rank: Chief Gunner's Mate (highest rank: Lieutenant)
Service: U.S. Navy
Birthday: 5 December 1881
Place of Birth: New York, New York
Date of Death: 9 June 1942
Cemetery: St. Columbia's Cemetery (MH)—Middletown, Rhode Island
Entered Service at: Rhode Island
Unit: U.S.S. *Utah*
Battle or Place of Action: Vera Cruz, Mexico
Date of Action: 21 April 1914
G.O. Number, Date: 117, 13 September 1923
Date of Presentation: 4 October 1923
Place of Presentation: The White House, presented by Pres. Calvin Coolidge
Citation: For meritorious service under fire on the occasion of the landing of the American naval forces at Vera Cruz in 1914. C.G. Bradley was then attached to the U.S.S. *Utah*, as a chief gunner's mate, and was in charge of the ammunition party and special details at Vera Cruz.

2387 ◆ BUCHANAN, ALLEN

Rank: Lieutenant Commander (highest rank: Captain)
Service: U.S. Navy
Birthday: 22 December 1876
Place of Birth: Evansville, Vanderburgh County, Indiana
Date of Death: 12 January 1940
Cemetery: Arlington National Cemetery (9-5845)—Arlington, Virginia
Entered Service at: Indiana
Battle or Place of Action: Vera Cruz, Mexico
Date of Action: 21-22 April 1914
G.O. Number, Date: 177, 4 December 1915
Citation: For distinguished conduct in battle, engagements of Vera Cruz, 21–22 April 1914. In command of the 1st Seaman Regiment, Lt. Comdr. Buchanan was in both days' fighting and almost continually under fire from soon after landing, about noon of the 21st, until we were in possession of the city, about noon of the 22d. His duties required him to be at points of great danger in directing his officers and men, and he exhibited conspicuous courage, coolness, and skill in his conduct of the fighting. Upon his courage and skill depended, in great measure, success or failure. His responsibilities were great, and he met them in a manner worthy of commendation.

2388 ◆ BUTLER, SMEDLEY DARLINGTON✛

Rank: Major (highest rank: Major General)
Service: U.S. Marine Corps
Birthday: 30 July 1881
Place of Birth: West Chester, Chester County, Pennsylvania
Date of Death: 21 June 1940
Place of Death: Philadelphia, Pennsylvania
Cemetery: Oakland Cemetery—West Chester, Pennsylvania
Entered Service at: Pennsylvania
Served as: Battalion Commander
Battle or Place of Action: Vera Cruz, Mexico
Date of Action: 22 April 1914
G.O. Number, Date: 177, 4 December 1915
Citation: **First Award** For distinguished conduct in battle, engagement of Vera Cruz, 22 April 1914. Maj. Butler was eminent and conspicuous in command of his battalion. He exhibited courage and skill in leading his men through the action of the 22d and in the final occupation of the city.
Notes: ✛Double Awardee: *see also* Haitian Campaign 1915

2389 ◆ CASTLE, GUY WILKINSON STUART

Rank: Lieutenant (highest rank: Commander)
Service: U.S. Navy
Birthday: 8 February 1879
Date of Death: 10 August 1919
Place of Death: Brest, France, on board the U.S.S. *Martha Washington*
Cemetery: Arlington National Cemetery (3-4345)—Arlington, Virginia
Appointed from: Wisconsin
Battle or Place of Action: Vera Cruz, Mexico
Date of Action: 21-22 April 1914
G.O. Number, Date: 177, 4 December 1915
Citation: For distinguished conduct in battle, engagements of Vera Cruz, 21–22 April 1914. Eminent and conspicuous in command of his battalion, Lt. Castle was in the fighting of both days, and exhibited courage and skill in leading his men through action. In seizing the customhouse, he encountered for many hours the heaviest and most pernicious concealed fire of the entire day, but his courage and coolness under trying conditions were marked.

2390 ◆ CATLIN, ALBERTUS WRIGHT

Rank: Major (highest rank: Brigadier General)
Service: U.S. Marine Corps
Birthday: 1 December 1868
Place of Birth: Gowanda, Cattaraugus County, New York
Date of Death: 31 May 1933
Place of Death: Culpeper, Virginia
Cemetery: Arlington National Cemetery (7-10038)—Arlington, Virginia
Appointed from: Minnesota

Unit: 3d Marines
Served as: Commanding Officer
Battle or Place of Action: Vera Cruz, Mexico
Date of Action: 22 April 1914
G.O. Number, Date: 177, 4 December 1915
Citation: For distinguished conduct in battle, engagement of Vera Cruz, 22 April 1914. Eminent and conspicuous in command of his battalion, Maj. Catlin exhibited courage and skill in leading his men through the action of the 22d and in the final occupation of the city.

2391 ◆ COURTS, GEORGE MCCALL

Rank: Lieutenant (j.g.) (highest rank: Commander)
Service: U.S. Navy
Birthday: 16 February 1888
Place of Birth: Washington, D.C.
Date of Death: 1 August 1932
Place of Death: Newport, Rhode Island
Cemetery: Arlington National Cemetery (7-9874)—Arlington, Virginia
Entered Service at: Washington, D.C.
Battle or Place of Action: Vera Cruz, Mexico
Date of Action: 21-22 April 1914
G.O. Number, Date: 177, 4 December 1915
Citation: For distinguished conduct in battle, engagements of Vera Cruz, 21–22 April 1914. Under fire, Lt. (j.g.) Courts was eminent and conspicuous in the performance of his duties. He had well qualified himself by thorough study during his years of duty in Mexico to deal with the conditions of this engagement, and his services were of great value. He twice volunteered and passed in an open boat through the zone of fire to convey important orders to the *Chester*, then under a severe fire.

2392 ◆ CREGAN, GEORGE

Rank: Coxswain (highest rank: Commander)
Service: U.S. Navy
Birthday: 11 December 1886
Place of Birth: New York, New York
Date of Death: 30 June 1969
Place of Death: Manasquan, New Jersey
Cemetery: Arlington National Cemetery (46-10666) (MH)—Arlington, Virginia
Entered Service at: New York
Unit: U.S.S. *Florida*
Battle or Place of Action: Vera Cruz, Mexico
Date of Action: 21 April 1914
G.O. Number, Date: 101, 15 June 1914
Citation: On board the U.S.S. *Florida*, for extraordinary heroism in the line of his profession during the seizure of Vera Cruz, Mexico, 21 April 1914. Cregan was ashore when he volunteered for an assault detail under Ens. George Maus Lowry on the Vera Cruz customhouse under enemy fire both in the alley between the customhouse and warehouse and the assault over the objective's walls. During the move up the alley, he tended a wounded comrade, J.F. Schumaker, holding a compress with one hand and firing with the other.

2393 ◆ DECKER, PERCY A.

Rank: Boatswain's Mate Second Class (highest rank: Lieutenant)
Service: U.S. Navy
Birthday: 4 August 1890
Place of Birth: New York, New York
Date of Death: 18 August 1936
Cemetery: Arlington National Cemetery (7-10302) (MH)—Arlington, Virginia
Entered Service at: New York
Unit: U.S.S. *Florida*
Battle or Place of Action: Vera Cruz, Mexico
Date of Action: 21 April 1914
G.O. Number, Date: 101, 15 June 1914
Citation: On board the U.S.S. *Florida* during the seizure of Vera Cruz, Mexico, 21 April 1914; for extraordinary heroism in the line of his profession during the seizure of Vera Cruz, Mexico.

2394 ◆ DESOMER, ABRAHAM

Rank: Lieutenant (highest rank: Lieutenant Commander, Ret.)
Service: U.S. Navy
Birthday: 29 December 1884
Place of Birth: Milwaukee, Milwaukee County, Wisconsin
Date of Death: 31 August 1974
Cemetery: San Francisco National Cemetery (MA-15)—San Francisco, California
Entered Service at: Wisconsin
Unit: U.S.S. *Utah*
Battle or Place of Action: U.S.S. *Utah* off the coast of Vera Cruz, Mexico
Date of Action: 21-22 April 1914
Place of Presentation: 8 January 1915
Citation: On board the U.S.S. *Utah*, for extraordinary heroism in the line of his profession during the seizure of Vera Cruz, Mexico, 21–22 April 1914.

2395 ◆ DRUSTRUP, NIELS

Rank: Lieutenant (highest rank: Lieutenant Commander)
Service: U.S. Navy
Birthday: 17 October 1876
Place of Birth: Denmark
Date of Death: 15 March 1957
Cemetery: Arlington National Cemetery (3-4378-RH) (MH)—Arlington, Virginia
Entered Service at: Pennsylvania
Unit: U.S.S. *Utah*
Battle or Place of Action: Vera Cruz, Mexico
Date of Action: 21 April 1914
G.O. Number, Date: 131, 17 July 1924
Citation: For meritorious service under fire on the occasion of the landing of the naval forces at Vera Cruz, Mexico, 21 April 1914. For several hours Lt. Drustrup was in charge of an advanced barricade under a heavy fire, and not only dis-

played utmost ability as a leader of men but also exerted a great steadying influence on the men around him. Lt. Drustrup was then attached to the U.S.S. *Utah* as a chief turret captain.

2396 ◆ DYER, JESSE FARLEY

Rank: Captain (highest rank: Brigadier General)
Service: U.S. Marine Corps
Birthday: 2 December 1877
Place of Birth: St. Paul, Ramsey County, Minnesota
Date of Death: 31 March 1955
Cemetery: Fort Rosecrans National Cemetery (P-1606)—San Diego, California
Appointed from: Minnesota
Served as: Company Commander
Battle or Place of Action: Vera Cruz, Mexico
Date of Action: 21-22 April 1914
G.O. Number, Date: 177, 4 December 1915
Citation: For distinguished conduct in battle, engagements of Vera Cruz, 21–22 April 1914; was in both days' fighting at the head of his company, and was eminent and conspicuous in his conduct, leading his men with skill and courage.

2397 ◆ ELLIOTT, MIDDLETON STUART

Rank: Surgeon
Service: U.S. Navy
Birthday: 16 October 1872
Place of Birth: Beauford, Beauford County, South Carolina
Date of Death: 29 October 1952
Place of Death: Long Beach, California
Cemetery: Fort Rosecrans National Cemetery (P-2628) (MH)—San Diego, California
Entered Service at: South Carolina
Served as: Surgeon
Battle or Place of Action: Vera Cruz, Mexico
Date of Action: 21-22 April 1914
G.O. Number, Date: 177, 4 December 1915
Citation: For distinguished conduct in battle, engagements of Vera Cruz, 21–22 April 1914. Surg. Elliott was eminent and conspicuous in the efficient establishment and operation of the base hospital, and in his cool judgment and courage in supervising first-aid stations on the firing line and removing the wounded.

2398 ◆ FLETCHER, FRANK FRIDAY

Rank: Rear Admiral
Service: U.S. Navy
Birthday: 23 November 1855
Place of Birth: Oskaloosa, Mahaska County, Iowa
Date of Death: 28 November 1928
Cemetery: Arlington National Cemetery (3-1933)—Arlington, Virginia
Entered Service at: Iowa
Battle or Place of Action: Vera Cruz, Mexico
Date of Action: 21-22 April 1914

G.O. Number, Date: 177, 4 December 1915
Citation: For distinguished conduct in battle, engagements of Vera Cruz, 21–22 April 1914. Under fire, Rear Adm. Fletcher was eminent and conspicuous in the performance of his duties; was senior officer present at Vera Cruz, and the landing and the operations of the landing force were carried out under his orders and directions. In connection with these operations, he was at times onshore and under fire.

2399 ◆ FLETCHER, FRANK JACK

Rank: Lieutenant (highest rank: Admiral)
Service: U.S. Navy
Birthday: 29 April 1885
Place of Birth: Marshalltown, Marshall County, Iowa
Date of Death: 25 April 1973
Place of Death: Bethesda, Maryland
Cemetery: Arlington National Cemetery (2-4736-E) (MH)—Arlington, Virginia
Entered Service at: Iowa
Battle or Place of Action: Vera Cruz, Mexico
Date of Action: 21-22 April 1914
G.O. Number, Date: 177, 4 December 1915
Citation: For distinguished conduct in battle, engagements of Vera Cruz, 21–22 April 1914. Under fire, Lt. Fletcher was eminent and conspicuous in performance of his duties. He was in charge of the *Esperanze* and succeeded in getting on board over 350 refugees, many of them after the conflict had commenced. Although the ship was under fire, being struck more than 30 times, he succeeded in getting all the refugees placed in safety. Lt. Fletcher was later placed in charge of the train conveying refugees under a flag of truce. This was hazardous duty, as it was believed that the track was mined, and a small error in dealing with the Mexican guard of soldiers might readily have caused a conflict, such a conflict at one time being narrowly averted. It was greatly due to his efforts in establishing friendly relations with the Mexican soldiers that so many refugees succeeded in reaching Vera Cruz from the interior.

2400 ◆ FOSTER, PAUL FREDERICK

Rank: Ensign (highest rank: Vice Admiral)
Service: U.S. Navy
Birthday: 25 March 1889
Place of Birth: Wichita, Sedgwick County, Kansas
Date of Death: 30 January 1972
Place of Death: Virginia Beach, Virginia
Cemetery: Arlington National Cemetery (5-106) (MH)—Arlington, Virginia
Entered Service at: Kansas
Battle or Place of Action: Vera Cruz, Mexico
Date of Action: 21-22 April 1914
G.O. Number, Date: 177, 4 December 1915
Citation: For distinguished conduct in battle, engagements of Vera Cruz, 21–22 April 1914. In both days' fighting at the head of his company, Ens. Foster was eminent and conspicuous in his conduct, leading his men with skill and courage.

2401 ◆ FRAZER, HUGH CARROLL

Rank: Ensign (highest rank: Commander)
Service: U.S. Navy
Birthday: 22 February 1891
Place of Birth: Martinsburg, Berkeley County, West Virginia
Date of Death: 9 July 1975
Place of Death: Washington, D.C.
Cemetery: Arlington National Cemetery (46-282) (MH)—Arlington, Virginia
Entered Service at: West Virginia
Battle or Place of Action: Vera Cruz, Mexico
Date of Action: 22 April 1914
G.O. Number, Date: 177, 4 December 1915
Citation: For extraordinary heroism in battle, engagement of Vera Cruz, 22 April 1914. During this engagement, Ens. Frazer ran forward to rescue a wounded man, exposing himself to hostile fire and that of his own men. Having accomplished the mission, he returned at once to his position in line.

2402 ◆ FRYER, ELI THOMPSON

Rank: Captain (highest rank: Brigadier General)
Service: U.S. Marine Corps
Birthday: 22 August 1878
Place of Birth: Hightstown, Mercer County, New Jersey
Date of Death: 6 June 1963
Cemetery: Arlington National Cemetery (34-102-A) (MH)—Arlington, Virginia
Appointed from: New Jersey
Unit: 2d Advanced Base Regiment
Battle or Place of Action: Vera Cruz, Mexico
Date of Action: 21-22 April 1914
G.O. Number, Date: 177, 4 December 1915
Citation: For distinguished conduct in battle, engagements of Vera Cruz, 21–22 April 1914. In both days' fighting at the head of his company, Capt. Fryer was eminent and conspicuous in his conduct, leading his men with skill and courage.

2403 ◆ GAUJOT, JULIEN EDMUND

Rank: Captain (highest rank: Colonel)
Service: U.S. Army
Birthday: 22 October 1874
Place of Birth: Keweenaw, Baraga County, Michigan
Date of Death: 7 April 1938
Cemetery: Arlington National Cemetery (6-8423-NH) (MH)—Arlington, Virginia
Entered Service at: Williamson, Mingo County, West Virginia
Unit: Troop K, 1st U.S. Cavalry
Battle or Place of Action: Aqua Prieta, Mexico
Date of Action: 13 April 1911
Date of Presentation: 23 November 1912
Place of Presentation: The White House, presented by Pres. William H. Taft
Citation: Crossed the field of fire to obtain the permission of the rebel commander to receive the surrender of the surrounded forces of Mexican Federals and escort such forces, together with five Americans held as prisoners, to the American line.
Notes: Pre-Vera Cruz

2404 ◆ GISBURNE, EDWARD ALLEN

Rank: Electrician Third Class (highest rank: Lieutenant)
Service: U.S. Navy
Birthday: 14 June 1892
Place of Birth: Providence, Providence County, Rhode Island
Date of Death: 29 June 1955
Cemetery: Milton Cemetery (MH)—Milton, Massachusetts
Entered Service at: Massachusetts
Unit: U.S.S. *Florida*
Battle or Place of Action: Vera Cruz, Mexico
Date of Action: 21-22 April 1914
G.O. Number, Date: 101, 15 June 1914
Citation: On board the U.S.S. *Florida* during the seizure of Vera Cruz, Mexico, 21–22 April 1914, and for extraordinary heroism in the line of his profession during this action.

2405 ◆ GRADY, JOHN

Rank: Lieutenant (highest rank: Captain)
Service: U.S. Navy
Birthday: 25 December 1872
Place of Birth: New Brunswick, Canada
Date of Death: 9 December 1956
Cemetery: Arlington National Cemetery (4-2723-2-RH)(MH)—Arlington, Virginia
Entered Service at: Massachusetts
Battle or Place of Action: Vera Cruz, Mexico
Date of Action: 22 April 1914
G.O. Number, Date: 177, 4 December 1915
Citation: For distinguished conduct in battle, engagement of Vera Cruz, 22 April 1914. During the second day's fighting, the service performed by Lt. Grady, in command of the 2d Regiment, Artillery, was eminent and conspicuous. From necessarily exposed positions, he shelled the enemy from the strongest position.

2406 ◆ HARNER, JOSEPH GABRIEL

Rank: Boatswain's Mate Second Class
Service: U.S. Navy
Birthday: 19 February 1889
Place of Birth: Louisville, Stark County, Ohio
Date of Death: 5 March 1958
Cemetery: Arlington National Cemetery (17-21199-B-2) (MH)—Arlington, Virginia
Entered Service at: Ohio
Unit: U.S.S. *Florida*
Battle or Place of Action: Vera Cruz, Mexico
Date of Action: 21 April 1914
G.O. Number, Date: 101, 15 June 1914
Citation: On board the U.S.S. *Florida*, for extraordinary heroism in the line of his profession during the seizure of Vera Cruz, Mexico, 21 April 1914.

2407 ◆ HARRISON, WILLIAM KELLY

Rank: Commander
Service: U.S. Navy
Birthday: 30 July 1870
Place of Birth: Waco, McLennan County, Texas
Date of Death: 15 August 1928
Cemetery: Arlington National Cemetery (2-1080)—Arlington, Virginia
Entered Service at: Texas
Unit: U.S.S. *Chester*
Battle or Place of Action: Vera Cruz, Mexico
Date of Action: 21-22 April 1914
G.O. Number, Date: 177, 4 December 1915
Citation: For distinguished conduct in battle, engagements of Vera Cruz, 21–22 April 1914. During this period, Comdr. Harrison brought his ship into the inner harbor during the nights of the 21st and 22d without the assistance of a pilot or navigational lights, and was in a position on the morning of the 22d to use his guns with telling effect at a critical time.

2408 ◆ HARTIGAN, CHARLES CONWAY

Rank: Lieutenant (highest rank: Rear Admiral)
Service: U.S. Navy
Birthday: 13 September 1882
Place of Birth: Middletown, Orange County, New York
Date of Death: 25 February 1944
Cemetery: Arlington National Cemetery (3-2194-B)—Arlington, Virginia
Entered Service at: Norwich, Chenango County, New York
Battle or Place of Action: Vera Cruz, Mexico
Date of Action: 22 April 1914
G.O. Number, Date: 177, 4 December 1915
Citation: For distinguished conduct in battle, engagement of Vera Cruz, 22 April 1914. During the second day's fighting the service performed by him was eminent and conspicuous. He was conspicuous for the skillful handling of his company under heavy rifle and machine-gun fire, for which conduct he was commended by his battalion commander.

2409 ◆ HILL, WALTER NEWELL

Rank: Captain (highest rank: Brigadier General)
Service: U.S. Marine Corps
Birthday: 29 September 1881
Place of Birth: Haverhill, Essex County, Massachusetts
Date of Death: 29 June 1955
Place of Death: St. Albans, New York
Cemetery: Arlington National Cemetery (6-9646-C)—Arlington, Virginia
Appointed from: Massachusetts
Served as: Company Commander
Battle or Place of Action: Vera Cruz, Mexico
Date of Action: 21-22 April 1914
G.O. Number, Date: 177, 4 December 1915
Citation: For distinguished conduct in battle, engagements of Vera Cruz, 21–22 April 1914. Capt. Hill was in both days' fighting at the head of his company, and was eminent and conspicuous in his conduct, leading his men with skill and courage.

2410 ◆ HUGHES, JOHN ARTHUR

Rank: Captain (highest rank: Colonel)
Service: U.S. Marine Corps
Birthday: 2 November 1880
Place of Birth: New York, New York
Date of Death: 25 May 1942
Place of Death: St. Petersburg, Florida
Cemetery: Arlington National Cemetery (8-5265)—Arlington, Virginia
Entered Service at: New York
Served as: Company Commander
Battle or Place of Action: Vera Cruz, Mexico
Date of Action: 21-22 April 1914
G.O. Number, Date: 177, 4 December 1915
Citation: For distinguished conduct in battle, engagements of Vera Cruz, 21–22 April 1914. Capt. Hughes was in both days' fighting at the head of his company, and was eminent and conspicuous in his conduct, leading his men with skill and courage.

2411 ◆ HUSE, HENRY MCLAREN PINCKNEY

Rank: Captain (highest rank: Vice Admiral)
Service: U.S. Navy
Birthday: 8 December 1858
Place of Birth: USMA, West Point, Orange County, New York
Date of Death: 14 May 1942
Place of Death: Bethesda, Maryland
Cemetery: Arlington National Cemetery (2-4889)—Arlington, Virginia
Appointed from: New York
Battle or Place of Action: Vera Cruz, Mexico
Date of Action: 21-22 April 1914
G.O. Number, Date: 177, 4 December 1915
Date of Issue: 24 January 1916
Citation: For distinguished conduct in battle, engagements of Vera Cruz, 21–22 April 1914. Under fire, Capt. Huse was eminent and conspicuous in the performance of his duties; was indefatigable in his labors of a most important character, both with the division commander in directing affairs and in his efforts onshore to get in communication with the Mexican authorities to avoid needlessly prolonging the conflict.

2412 ◆ INGRAM, JONAS HOWARD

Rank: Lieutenant (j.g.) (highest rank: Admiral)
Service: U.S. Navy
Birthday: 15 October 1887
Place of Birth: Jeffersonville, Clark County, Indiana
Date of Death: 10 September 1952
Cemetery: Arlington National Cemetery (30-643-RH)—Arlington, Virginia
Entered Service at: Indiana
Battle or Place of Action: Vera Cruz, Mexico

Date of Action: 22 April 1914
G.O. Number, Date: 177, 4 December 1915
Citation: For distinguished conduct in battle, engagement of Vera Cruz, 22 April 1914. During the second day's fighting the service performed by him was eminent and conspicuous. He was conspicuous for skillful and efficient handling of the artillery and machine guns of the Arkansas battalion, for which he was specially commended in reports.

2413 ◆ JARRETT, BERRIE HENRY

Rank: Seaman (highest rank: Gunner)
Service: U.S. Navy
Birthday: 10 June 1894
Place of Birth: Baltimore, Baltimore County, Maryland
Date of Death: 14 August 1927
Cemetery: Lorraine Park Cemetery—Baltimore, Maryland
Entered Service at: Maryland
Unit: U.S.S. *Florida*
Battle or Place of Action: Vera Cruz, Mexico
Date of Action: 21 April 1914
G.O. Number, Date: 116, 19 August 1914
Citation: On board the U.S.S. *Florida* Jarrett displayed extraordinary heroism in the line of his profession during the seizure of Vera Cruz, Mexico, 21 April 1914.

2414 ◆ JOHNSTON JR., RUFUS ZENAS

Rank: Lieutenant Commander (highest rank: Rear Admiral)
Service: U.S. Navy
Birthday: 7 June 1874
Place of Birth: Lincolnton, Lincoln County, North Carolina
Date of Death: 4 July 1959
Place of Death: Newport, Rhode Island
Cemetery: Arlington National Cemetery (2-3645-RH) (MH)—Arlington, Virginia
Entered Service at: North Carolina
Battle or Place of Action: Vera Cruz, Mexico
Date of Action: 22 April 1914
G.O. Number, Date: 177, 4 December 1915
Citation: For distinguished conduct in battle, engagement of Vera Cruz, 22 April 1914; was regimental adjutant, and eminent and conspicuous in his conduct. He exhibited courage and skill in leading his men through the action of the 22d and in the final occupation of the city.

2415 ◆ LANGHORNE, CARY DEVALL

Rank: Surgeon (highest rank: Commander)
Service: U.S. Navy
Birthday: 14 May 1873
Place of Birth: Lynchburg, Lynchburg County, Virginia
Date of Death: 25 April 1948
Cemetery: Arlington National Cemetery (11-868)—Arlington, Virginia
Entered Service at: Virginia
Battle or Place of Action: Vera Cruz, Mexico
Date of Action: 22 April 1914
G.O. Number, Date: 177, 4 December 1915

Citation: For extraordinary heroism in battle, engagement of Vera Cruz, 22 April 1914. Surg. Langhorne carried a wounded man from the front of the Naval Academy while under heavy fire.

2416 ◆ LANNON, JAMES PATRICK

Rank: Lieutenant (highest rank: Rear Admiral)
Service: U.S. Navy
Birthday: 12 October 1878
Place of Birth: Alexandria, Alexandria County, Virginia
Date of Death: 13 March 1953
Cemetery: Arlington National Cemetery (8-6410-B)—Arlington, Virginia
Entered Service at: Virginia
Battle or Place of Action: Vera Cruz, Mexico
Date of Action: 22 April 1914
G.O. Number, Date: 177, 4 December 1915
Citation: For extraordinary heroism in battle, engagement of Vera Cruz, 22 April 1914. Lt. Lannon assisted a wounded man under heavy fire, and after returning to his battalion, was himself desperately wounded.

2417 ◆ LOWRY, GEORGE MAUS

Rank: Ensign (highest rank: Rear Admiral)
Service: U.S. Navy
Birthday: 27 October 1889
Place of Birth: Erie, Erie County, Pennsylvania
Date of Death: 25 September 1981
Place of Death: Carmel, California
Cemetery: Ashes scattered at sea
Entered Service at: Pennsylvania
Battle or Place of Action: Vera Cruz, Mexico
Date of Action: 21-22 April 1914
G.O. Number, Date: 177, 4 December 1915
Citation: For distinguished conduct in battle, engagements of Vera Cruz, 21–22 April 1914; Ens. Lowry was in both days' fighting at the head of his company, and was eminent and conspicuous in his conduct, leading his men with skill and courage.

2418 ◆ McCLOY, JOHN✠

Rank: Chief Boatswain (highest rank: Lieutenant Commander)
Service: U.S. Navy
Birthday: 3 January 1876
Place of Birth: Brewster, Putnam County, New York
Date of Death: 25 May 1945
Cemetery: Arlington National Cemetery (8-5246)—Arlington, Virginia
Entered Service at: New York
Battle or Place of Action: Vera Cruz, Mexico
Date of Action: 22 April 1914
G.O. Number, Date: 177, 4 December 1915
Citation: **Second Award** For heroism in leading three picket launches along Vera Cruz sea front, drawing Mexican fire and enabling cruisers to save our men onshore, 22 April

1914. Though wounded, he gallantly remained at his post.

Notes: ✛Double Awardee: *see also* China Relief Expedition

2419 ◆ McDONNELL, EDWARD ORRICK

Rank: Ensign (highest rank: Vice Admiral)
Service: U.S. Navy
Birthday: 13 November 1891
Place of Birth: Baltimore, Baltimore County, Maryland
Date of Death: 6 January 1960
Place of Death: North Carolina
Cemetery: Arlington National Cemetery (2-4955-4)—Arlington, Virginia
Entered Service at: Maryland
Battle or Place of Action: Vera Cruz, Mexico
Date of Action: 21-22 April 1914
G.O. Number, Date: 177, 4 December 1915
Citation: For extraordinary heroism in battle, engagements of Vera Cruz, 21–22 April 1914. Posted on the roof of the Terminal Hotel and landing, Ens. McDonnell established a signal station there day and night, maintaining communication between troops and ships. At this exposed post he was continually under fire. One man was killed and three wounded at his side during the two days' fighting. He showed extraordinary heroism and striking courage and maintained his station in the highest degree of efficiency. All signals got through, largely due to his heroic devotion to duty.

2420 ◆ McNAIR JR., FREDERICK VALLETTE

Rank: Lieutenant (highest rank: Captain)
Service: U.S. Navy
Birthday: 13 March 1882
Place of Birth: Maryland
Date of Death: 2 September 1962
Cemetery: U.S. Naval Academy Cemetery (Lot 406)—Annapolis, Maryland
Appointed from: Appointed at large
Battle or Place of Action: Vera Cruz, Mexico
Date of Action: 22 April 1914
G.O. Number, Date: 177, 4 December 1915
Citation: For distinguished conduct in battle engagement of Vera Cruz, 22 April 1914. Lt. McNair was eminent and conspicuous in command of his battalion. He exhibited courage and skill in leading his men through the action of the 22d and in the final occupation of the city.

2421 ◆ MOFFETT, WILLIAM ADGER

Rank: Commander (highest rank: Rear Admiral)
Service: U.S. Navy
Birthday: 31 October 1869
Place of Birth: Charleston, Charleston County, South Carolina
Date of Death: 4 April 1933
Cemetery: Arlington National Cemetery (3-1655-A)—Arlington, Virginia
Entered Service at: Charleston, Charleston County, South Carolina

Unit: U.S.S. *Chester*
Battle or Place of Action: Vera Cruz, Mexico
Date of Action: 21-22 April 1914
G.O. Number, Date: 177, 4 December 1915
Citation: For distinguished conduct in battle, engagements of Vera Cruz, 21–22 April 1914. Comdr. Moffett brought his ship into the inner harbor during the nights of the 21st and 22d without the assistance of a pilot or navigational lights, and was in a position on the morning of the 22d to use his guns at a critical time with telling effect. His skill in mooring his ship at night was especially noticeable. He placed her nearest to the enemy and did most of the firing and received most of the hits.

2422 ◆ NEVILLE, WENDELL CUSHING

Rank: Lieutenant Colonel (highest rank: Major General)
Service: U.S. Marine Corps
Birthday: 12 May 1870
Place of Birth: Portsmouth, Portsmouth County, Virginia
Date of Death: 8 July 1930
Place of Death: Edgewater Beach, Maryland
Cemetery: Arlington National Cemetery (6-8409)—Arlington, Virginia
Appointed from: Virginia
Unit: 2d Marine Regiment
Served as: Commanding Officer
Battle or Place of Action: Vera Cruz, Mexico
Date of Action: 21-22 April 1914
G.O. Number, Date: 177, 4 December 1915
Citation: For distinguished conduct in battle engagements of Vera Cruz, 21–22 April 1914. In command of the 2d Regiment Marines, Lt. Col. Neville was in both days' fighting and almost continually under fire from soon after landing, about noon on the 21st, until we were in possession of the city, about noon of the 22d. His duties required him to be at points of great danger in directing his officers and men, and he exhibited conspicuous courage, coolness, and skill in his conduct of the fighting. Upon his courage and skill depended, in great measure, success or failure. His responsibilities were great, and he net them in a manner worthy of commendation.

2423 ◆ NICKERSON, HENRY NEHEMIAH

Rank: Boatswain's Mate Second Class
Service: U.S. Navy
Birthday: 2 December 1888
Place of Birth: Edgewood, West Virginia
Date of Death: 2 May 1979
Cemetery: Greenwood Cemetery (MH)—Wheeling, West Virginia
Entered Service at: West Virginia
Unit: U.S.S. *Utah*
Battle or Place of Action: Vera Cruz, Mexico
Date of Action: 21 April 1914
Citation: On board the U.S.S. *Utah*, Nickerson showed extraordinary heroism in the line of his profession during the seizure of Vera Cruz, Mexico, 21 April 1914.

2429 ◆ SINNETT, LAWRENCE CLINTON

2424 ◆ NORDSIEK, CHARLES LUERS

Rank: Ordinary Seaman (highest rank: lieutenant)
Service: U.S. Navy
Birthday: 19 April 1896
Place of Birth: New York, New York
Date of Death: 9 March 1937
Cemetery: Arlington National Cemetery (7-10230-SS) (MH)—Arlington, Virginia
Entered Service at: New York
Unit: U.S.S. *Florida*
Battle or Place of Action: Vera Cruz, Mexico
Date of Action: 21-22 April 1914
G.O. Number, Date: 101, 15 June 1914
Citation: On board the U.S.S. *Florida*, Nordsiek showed extraordinary heroism in the line of his profession during the seizure of Vera Cruz, Mexico, 21–22 April 1914.

2425 ◆ REID, GEORGE CROGHAN

Rank: Major (highest rank: Brigadier General)
Service: U.S. Marine Corps
Birthday: 9 December 1876
Place of Birth: Lorain, Lorain County, Ohio
Date of Death: 19 February 1961
Place of Death: Harlingen, Texas
Cemetery: Arlington National Cemetery (2-1096-A-LH)(MH)—Arlington, Virginia
Appointed from: Ohio
Served as: Division Marine Officer of the Atlantic Fleet
Battle or Place of Action: Vera Cruz, Mexico
Date of Action: 21-22 April 1914
G.O. Number, Date: 177, 4 December 1915
Citation: For distinguished conduct in battle, engagements of Vera Cruz, 21–22 April 1914; was eminent and conspicuous in command of his battalion; was in the fighting of both days and exhibited courage and skill in leading his men through action. His cool judgment and courage and his skill in handling his men in encountering and overcoming the machine-gun and rifle fire down Cinco de Mayo and parallel streets account for the small percentage of the losses of marines under his command.

2426 ◆ RUSH, WILLIAM REES

Rank: Captain
Service: U.S. Navy
Birthday: 19 September 1857
Place of Birth: Philadelphia, Philadelphia County, Pennsylvania
Date of Death: 2 August 1940
Place of Death: Pallanza, Italy
Cemetery: Arlington National Cemetery (3-3977)—Arlington, Virginia
Entered Service at: Pennsylvania
Battle or Place of Action: Vera Cruz, Mexico
Date of Action: 21-22 April 1914
G.O. Number, Date: 177, 4 December 1915
Citation: For distinguished conduct in battle, engagements of Vera Cruz, 21–22 April 1914. In command of the naval brigade, Capt. Rush was in both days' fighting and almost continually under fire from soon after landing, about noon on the 21st, until we were in possession of the city, about noon of the 22d. His duties required him to be at points of great danger in directing his officers and men, and he exhibited conspicuous courage, coolness and skill in his conduct of the fighting. Upon his courage and skill depended in great measure success or failure. His responsibilities were great, and he met them in a manner worthy of commendation.

2427 ◆ SCHNEPEL, FRED JURGEN

Rank: Ordinary Seaman (highest rank: Chief Quartermaster)
Service: U.S. Navy
Birthday: 24 February 1892
Place of Birth: New York, New York
Date of Death: 7 February 1948
Cemetery: Arlington National Cemetery (11-825) (MH)—Arlington, Virginia
Entered Service at: New York
Unit: U.S.S. *Florida*
Battle or Place of Action: Vera Cruz, Mexico
Date of Action: 21-22 April 1914
G.O. Number, Date: 101, 15 June 1914
Citation: On board the U.S.S. *Florida*, Schnepel showed extraordinary heroism in the line of his profession during the seizure of Vera Cruz, Mexico, 21–22 April 1914.

2428 ◆ SEMPLE, ROBERT

Rank: Chief Gunner (highest rank: Lieutenant Commander)
Service: U.S. Navy
Birthday: 18 August 1887
Place of Birth: Pittsburgh, Allegheny County, Pennsylvania
Date of Death: 13 May 1943
Cemetery: Fort Rosecrans National Cemetery (OS-A-192)—San Diego, California
Entered Service at: Pennsylvania
Unit: U.S.S. *Florida*
Battle or Place of Action: Vera Cruz, Mexico
Date of Action: 21 April 1914
G.O. Number, Date: 120, 10 January 1924
Citation: For meritorious service under fire on the occasion of the landing of the American naval forces at Vera Cruz on 21 April 1914. C.G. Semple was then attached to the U.S.S. *Florida* as a chief turret captain.

2429 ◆ SINNETT, LAWRENCE CLINTON

Rank: Seaman
Service: U.S. Navy
Birthday: 4 April 1888
Place of Birth: Burnt House, West Virginia
Date of Death: 11 June 1962
Cemetery: I.O.O.F. Cemetery—Harrisville, West Virginia
Entered Service at: Pennsylvania
Unit: U.S.S. *Florida*
Battle or Place of Action: Vera Cruz, Mexico

Date of Action: 21 April 1914
G.O. Number, Date: 101, 15 June 1914
Citation: On board the U.S.S. *Florida*, Sinnett showed extraordinary heroism in the line of his profession during the seizure of Vera Cruz, Mexico, 21 April 1914.

2430 ◆ STATON, ADOLPHUS

Rank: Lieutenant (highest rank: Rear Admiral)
Service: U.S. Navy
Birthday: 28 August 1879
Place of Birth: Tarboro, Edgecombe County, North Carolina
Date of Death: 4 June 1964
Cemetery: Arlington National Cemetery (4-280-A)—Arlington, Virginia
Entered Service at: North Carolina
Battle or Place of Action: Vera Cruz, Mexico
Date of Action: 22 April 1914
Date of Issue: 1915
Citation: For distinguished conduct in battle, engagement of Vera Cruz, 22 April 1914; was eminent and conspicuous in command of his battalion. He exhibited courage and skill in leading his men through the action of the 22d and in the final occupation of the city.

2431 ◆ STICKNEY, HERMAN OSMAN

Rank: Commander (highest rank: Rear Admiral)
Service: U.S. Navy
Birthday: 10 December 1867
Place of Birth: Pepperell, Middlesex County, Massachusetts
Date of Death: 13 September 1936
Cemetery: Arlington National Cemetery (3-1821)—Arlington, Virginia
Entered Service at: Massachusetts
Battle or Place of Action: Vera Cruz, Mexico
Date of Action: 21-22 April 1914
G.O. Number, Date: 177, 4 December 1915
Citation: For distinguished conduct in battle, engagements of Vera Cruz, 21–22 April 1914. Comdr. Stickney covered the landing of the 21st with the guns of the U.S.S. *Prairie*, and throughout the attack and occupation, rendered important assistance to our forces onshore with his 3-inch battery.

2432 ◆ TOWNSEND, JULIUS CURTIS

Rank: Lieutenant (highest rank: Rear Admiral)
Service: U.S. Navy
Birthday: 22 February 1881
Place of Birth: Athens, Missouri
Date of Death: 28 December 1939
Place of Death: Brooklyn, New York
Cemetery: Arlington National Cemetery (6-8590)—Arlington, Virginia
Entered Service at: Athens, Missouri
Battle or Place of Action: Vera Cruz, Mexico
Date of Action: 22 April 1914
G.O. Number, Date: 177, 4 December 1915

Citation: For distinguished conduct in battle, engagement of Vera Cruz, 22 April 1914. Lt. Townsend was eminent and conspicuous in command of his battalion. He exhibited courage and skill in leading his men through the action of the 22d and in the final occupation of the city.

2433 ◆ WAINWRIGHT JR., RICHARD

Rank: Lieutenant (highest rank: Lieutenant Commander)
Service: U.S. Navy
Birthday: 15 September 1881
Place of Birth: Washington, D.C.
Date of Death: 28 March 1944
Place of Death: Annapolis, Maryland
Cemetery: U.S. Naval Academy Cemetery—Annapolis, Maryland
Entered Service at: Washington, D.C.
Battle or Place of Action: Vera Cruz, Mexico
Date of Action: 21-22 April 1914
G.O. Number, Date: 177, 4 December 1915
Citation: For distinguished conduct in battle, engagements of Vera Cruz, 21–22 April 1914. Lt. Wainwright was eminent and conspicuous in command of his battalion; was in the fighting of both days, and exhibited courage and skill in leading his men through action. In seizing the customhouse, he encountered for many hours the heaviest and most pernicious concealed fire of the entire day, but his courage and coolness under trying conditions were marked.

2434 ◆ WALSH, JAMES ALOYSIUS

Rank: Seaman
Service: U.S. Navy
Birthday: 24 July 1897
Place of Birth: New York, New York
Date of Death: 29 May 1960
Cemetery: Long Island National Cemetery (DSS-47-A) (MH)—Farmingdale, New York
Entered Service at: New York, New York
Unit: U.S.S. *Florida*
Battle or Place of Action: Vera Cruz, Mexico
Date of Action: 21-22 April 1914
G.O. Number, Date: 101, 15 June 1914
Citation: On board the U.S.S. *Florida*; for extrordinary heroism in the line of his profession during the seizure of Vera Cruz, Mexico, 21 and 22 April 1914.

2435 ◆ WILKINSON JR., THEODORE STARK

Rank: Ensign (highest rank: Vice Admiral)
Service: U.S. Navy
Birthday: 22 December 1888
Place of Birth: Annapolis, Anne Arundel County, Maryland
Date of Death: 21 February 1946
Cemetery: Arlington National Cemetery (2-3645)—Arlington, Virginia
Appointed from: Louisiana
Unit: U.S.S. *Floria*
Battle or Place of Action: Vera Cruz, Mexico

Date of Action: 21-22 April 1914
G.O. Number, Date: 177, 4 December 1915
Citation: For distinguished conduct in battle, engagements of Vera Cruz, 21–22 April 1914. Ens. Wilkinson was in both days' fighting at the head of his company and was eminent and conspicuous in his conduct, leading his men with skill and courage.

2436 ◆ ZUIDERVELD, WILLIAM

Rank: Hospital Apprentice First Class (highest rank: Lieutenant)
Service: U.S. Navy

Birthday: 24 January 1888
Place of Birth: Michigan
Date of Death: 5 February 1978
Cemetery: Fort Rosecrans National Cemetery (A-1-9-13) (MH)—San Diego, California
Entered Service at: Michigan
Unit: U.S.S. *Florida*
Battle or Place of Action: Vera Cruz, Mexico
Date of Action: 21 April 1914
G.O. Number, Date: 116, 19 August 1914
Citation: On board the U.S.S. *Florida*, Zuiderveld showed extraordinary heroism in the line of his profession during the seizure of Vera Cruz, Mexico, 21 April 1914.

2437 ◆ BUTLER, SMEDLEY DARLINGTON✛

Rank: Major (highest rank: Major General)
Service: U.S. Marine Corps
Birthday: 30 July 1881
Place of Birth: West Chester, Chester County, Pennsylvania
Date of Death: 21 June 1940
Place of Death: Philadelphia, Pennsylvania
Cemetery: Oakland Cemetery—West Chester, Pennsylvania
Appointed from: Pennsylvania
Unit: U.S.S. *Connecticut*
Served as: Commanding Officer of Marines & Seaman
Battle or Place of Action: Fort Riviere, Haiti
Date of Action: 17 November 1915
Date of Issue: 1916
Citation: Second Award As commanding officer of detachments from the 5th, 13th, 23d Companies and the marine and sailor detachment from the U.S.S. *Connecticut*, Maj. Butler led the attack on Fort Riviere, Haiti, 17 November 1915. Following a concentrated drive, several different detachments of marines gradually closed in on the old French bastion fort in an effort to cut off all avenues of retreat for the Caco bandits. Reaching the fort on the southern side where there was a small opening in the wall, Maj. Butler gave the signal to attack and marines from the 15th Company poured through the breach, engaged the Cacos in hand-to-hand combat, took the bastion and crushed the Caco resistance. Throughout this perilous action, Maj. Butler was conspicuous for his bravery and forceful leadership.
Notes: ✛Double Awardee: *see also* Mexican Campaign (Vera Cruz)

2438 ◆ DALY, DANIEL JOSEPH✛

Rank: Gunnery Sergeant (highest rank: Sergeant Major)
Service: U.S. Marine Corps
Birthday: 11 November 1873
Place of Birth: Glen Cove, Nassau County, New York
Date of Death: 27 April 1937
Place of Death: Glendale, New York
Cemetery: Cypress Hills National Cemetery (5-70) (MH)—Brooklyn, New York
Entered Service at: New York
Unit: 15th Company, 2d Regiment
Battle or Place of Action: Fort Dipitie, Haiti
Date of Action: 24 October 1915
Citation: Second Award Serving with the 15th Company of Marines on 22 October 1915, G/Sgt. Daly was one of the company to leave Fort Liberte, Haiti, for a six-day reconnais-

sance. After dark on the evening of 24 October, while crossing the river in a deep ravine, the detachment was suddenly fired upon from three sides by about 400 Cacos concealed in bushes about 100 yards from the fort. The marine detachment fought its way forward to a good position, which it maintained during the night, although subjected to a continuous fire from the Cacos. At daybreak the marines, in three squads, advanced in three different directions, surprising and scattering the Cacos in all directions. G/Sgt. Daly fought with exceptional gallantry against heavy odds throughout this action.
Notes: ✛Double Awardee: *see also* China Relief Expedition

2439 ◆ GROSS, SAMUEL

True Name: Marguilies, Samuel
Rank: Private (highest rank: Corporal)
Service: U.S. Marine Corps
Birthday: 9 May 1891
Place of Birth: Philadelphia, Philadelphia County, Pennsylvania
Date of Death: 13 September 1934
Place of Death: Coatesville, Pennsylvania
Cemetery: Har-Nebo Jewish Cemetery (MH)—Philadelphia, Pennsylvania
Entered Service at: Pennsylvania
Unit: 23d Company
Battle or Place of Action: Fort Riviere, Haiti
Date of Action: 17 November 1915
Place of Presentation: Presented by Maj. Gen. George Barnett, Commandant U.S.M.C
Citation: In company with members of the 5th, 13th, 23d Companies and the marine and sailor detachment from the U.S.S. *Connecticut*, Gross participated in the attack on Fort Riviere, Haiti, 17 November 1915. Following a concentrated drive, several different detachments of marines gradually closed in on the old French bastion fort in an effort to cut off all avenues of retreat for the Caco bandits. Approaching a breach in the wall which was the only entrance to the fort, Gross was the second man to pass through the breach in the face of constant fire from the Cacos and, thereafter, for a 10-minute period, engaged the enemy in desperate hand-to-hand combat until the bastion was captured and Caco resistance neutralized.

2440 ◆ IAMS, ROSS LINDSEY

Rank: Sergeant
Service: U.S. Marine Corps

Birthday: 5 May 1881
Place of Birth: Graysville, Greene County, Pennsylvania
Date of Death: 29 March 1952
Cemetery: Fort Rosecrans National Cemetery (P-2930) (MH)—San Diego, California
Entered Service at: Pennsylvania
Unit: 5th Company
Battle or Place of Action: Fort Riviere, Haiti
Date of Action: 17 November 1915
Citation: In company with members of the 5th, 13th, and 23d Companies and marine and sailor detachment from the U.S.S. *Connecticut*, Sgt. Iams participated in the attack on Fort Riviere, Haiti, 17 November 1915. Following a concentrated drive, several different detachments of marines gradually closed in on the old French bastion fort in an effort to cut off all avenues of retreat for the Caco bandits. Approaching a breach in the wall which was the only entrance to the fort, Sgt. Iams unhesiatingly jumped through the breach despite constant fire from the Cacos and engaged the enemy in a desperate hand-to-hand combat until the bastion was captured and Caco resistance neutralized.

2441 ◆ OSTERMANN, EDWARD ALBERT

Rank: First Lieutenant (highest rank: Major General)
Service: U.S. Marine Corps
Birthday: 23 November 1882
Place of Birth: Columbus, Franklin County, Ohio
Date of Death: 18 May 1969
Place of Death: Fairfax, Virginia
Cemetery: Arlington National Cemetery (46-521) (MH)—Arlington, Virginia
Entered Service at: Ohio
Unit: 15th Company of Marines (Mounted)
Battle or Place of Action: Fort Dipitie, Haiti
Date of Action: 24 October 1915
Date of Issue: 1917
Citation: In company with members of the 15th Company of Marines, all mounted, 1st Lt. Ostermann left Fort Liberte, Haiti, for a six-day reconnaissance. After dark on the evening

of 24 October 1915, while crossing the river in a deep ravine, the detachment was suddenly fired upon from three sides by about 400 Cacos concealed in bushes about 100 yards from the fort. The marine detachment fought its way forward to a good position, which it maintained during the night, although subjected to a continuous fire from the Cacos. At daybreak, 1st Lt. Ostermann, in command of one of the three squads which advanced in three different directions, led his men forward, surprising and scattering the Cacos, and aiding in the capture of Fort Dipitie.

2442 ◆ UPSHUR, WILLIAM PETERKIN

Rank: Captain (highest rank: Major General)
Service: U.S. Marine Corps
Birthday: 28 October 1881
Place of Birth: Richmond, Richmond County, Virginia
Date of Death: 21 July 1943
Place of Death: Sitka, Alaska
Cemetery: U.S. Naval Academy Cemetery (Lot 250-A)—Annapolis, Maryland
Appointed from: Virginia
Unit: 15th Company, 2d Marine Regiment
Served as: Commanding Officer
Battle or Place of Action: Fort Dipitie, Haiti
Date of Action: 24 October 1915
Citation: In company with members of the 15th Company of Marines, all mounted, Capt. Upshur left Fort Liberte, Haiti, for a six-day reconnaissance. After dark on the evening of 24 October 1915, while crossing the river in a deep ravine, the detachment was suddenly fired upon from three sides by about 400 Cacos concealed in bushes about 100 yards from the fort. The marine detachment fought its way forward to a good position, which it maintained during the night, although subjected to a continuous fire from the Cacos. At daybreak, Capt. Upshur, in command of one of the three squads which advanced in three different directions, led his men forward, surprising and scattering the Cacos, and aiding in the capture of Fort Dipitie.

INTERIM 1915–1916

2443 ◆ CARY, ROBERT WEBSTER

Rank: Lieutenant Commander (highest rank: Rear Admiral)
Service: U.S. Navy
Birthday: 18 August 1890
Place of Birth: Kansas City, Clay County, Missouri
Date of Death: 15 July 1967
Place of Death: Toledo, Ohio
Cemetery: Arlington National Cemetery (6-5695-G)—Arlington, Virginia
Entered Service at: Bunceton, Cooper County, Missouri
Unit: U.S.S. *San Diego*
Battle or Place of Action: U.S.S. *San Diego*
Date of Action: 21 January 1915
Date of Issue: 23 May 1934
Citation: For extraordinary heroism in the line of his profession on the occasion of an explosion on board the U.S.S. *San Diego* 21 January 1915. Lt. Comdr. Cary (then Ens.), U.S. Navy, an observer on duty in the firerooms of the U.S.S. *San Diego*, commenced to take the half-hourly readings of the steam pressure at every boiler. He had read the steam and air pressure on No. 2 boiler and was just stepping through the electric watertight door into No. 1 fireroom when the boilers in No. 2 fireroom exploded. Ens. Cary stopped and held open the doors which were being closed electrically from the bridge, and yelled to the men in No. 2 fireroom to escape through these doors, which three of them did. Ens. Cary's action undoubtedly saved the lives of these men. He held the doors probably a minute with the escaping steam from the ruptured boilers around him. His example of coolness did much to keep the men in No. 1 fireroom at their posts hauling fires, although five boilers in their immediate vicinity had exploded and boilers Nos. 1 and 3 apparently had no water in them and were likely to explode any instant. When these fires were hauled under Nos. 1 and 3 boilers, Ens. Cary directed the men in this fireroom into the bunker, for they well knew the danger of these two boilers exploding. During the entire time Ens. Cary was cool and collected and showed an abundance of nerve under the most trying circumstances. His action on this occasion was above and beyond the call of duty.

2444 ◆ CRILLEY, FRANK WILLIAM

Rank: Chief Gunner's Mate (highest rank: Ensign)
Service: U.S. Navy
Birthday: 13 September 1883
Place of Birth: Trenton, Mercer County, New Jersey
Date of Death: 23 November 1947

Cemetery: Arlington National Cemetery (8-6430)—Arlington, Virginia
Entered Service at: Pennsylvania
Unit: Navy's Experimental Diving Team
Served as: Diver
Battle or Place of Action: off Honolulu, Territory of Hawaii
Date of Action: 17 April 1915
Date of Presentation: 15 February 1929
Citation: For display of extraordinary heroism in the line of his profession above and beyond the call of duty during the diving operations in connection with the sinking in a depth of water 304 feet of the U.S.S. *F-4* with all on board, as a result of loss of depth control, which occurred off Honolulu, T.H., 25 March 1915. On 17 April 1915, William F. Loughman, chief gunner's mate, U.S. Navy, who had descended to the wreck and had examined one of the wire hawsers attached to it, upon starting his ascent, and when at a depth of 250 feet beneath the surface of the water, had his lifeline and air hose so badly fouled by this hawser that he was unable to free himself; he could neither ascend nor descend. On account of the length of time that Loughman had already been subjected to the great pressure due to the depth of water, and of the uncertainty of the additional time he would have to be subjected to this pressure before he could be brought to the surface, it was imperative that steps be taken at once to clear him. Instantly, realizing the desperate case of his comrade, Crilley volunteered to go to his aid, immediately donned a diving suit and descended. After a lapse of time of two hours and 11 minutes, Crilley was brought to the surface, having by a superb exhibition of skill, coolness, endurance, and fortitude, untangled the snarl of lines and cleared his imperiled comrade, so that he was brought, still alive, to the surface.

2445 ◆ JONES, CLAUD ASHTON

Rank: Commander (rank at time of action: Lieutenant) (highest rank: Rear Admiral)
Service: U.S. Navy
Birthday: 7 October 1885
Place of Birth: Fire Creek, West Virginia
Date of Death: 8 August 1948
Cemetery: Arlington National Cemetery (11-546-SS)—Arlington, Virginia
Entered Service at: West Virginia
Unit: U.S.S. *Memphis*
Battle or Place of Action: off Santo Domingo City, Santo Domingo
Date of Action: 29 August 1916
Citation: For extraordinary heroism in the line of his profes-

sion as a senior engineer officer on board the U.S.S. *Memphis*, at a time when the vessel was suffering total destruction from a hurricane while anchored off Santo Domingo City, 29 August 1916. Lt. Jones did everything possible to get the engines and boilers ready, and if the elements that burst upon the vessel had delayed for a few minutes, the engines would have saved the vessel. With boilers and steampipes bursting about him in clouds of scalding steam, with thousands of tons of water coming down upon him and in almost complete darkness, Lt. Jones nobly remained at his post as long as the engines would turn over, exhibiting the most supreme unselfish heroism which inspired the officers and men who were with him. When the boilers exploded, Lt. Jones, accompanied by two of his shipmates, rushed into the firerooms and drove the men there out, dragging some, carrying others to the engineroom, where there was air to be breathed instead of steam. Lt. Jones' action on this occasion was above and beyond the call of duty.

2446 ◆ *RUD, GEORGE WILLIAM

Rank: Chief Machinist's Mate
Service: U.S. Navy
Birthday: 7 October 1883
Place of Birth: Minneapolis, Hennepin County, Minnesota
Date of Death: 29 August 1916
Cemetery: Crystal Lake Cemetery—Minneapolis, Minnesota
Entered Service at: Minnesota
Unit: U.S.S. *Memphis*
Battle or Place of Action: off Santo Domingo City, Santo Domingo
Date of Action: 29 August 1916
Citation: For extraordinary heroism in the line of his profession while attached to the U.S.S. *Memphis*, at a time when that vessel was suffering total destruction from a hurricane while anchored off Santo Domingo City, 29 August 1916. C.M.M. Rud took his station in the engineroom and remained at his post amidst scalding steam and the rushing of thousands of tons of water into his cepartment, receiving serious burns from which he immediately died.

2447 ◆ SMITH, EUGENE P.

Rank: Chief Watertender
Service: U.S. Navy
Birthday: 8 August 1871
Place of Birth: Illinois
Date of Death: 24 March 1918
Cemetery: Cypress Hills National Cemetery (2-7742) (MH)—Brooklyn, New York
Entered Service at: California
Unit: U.S.S. *Decatur*
Battle or Place of Action: U.S.S. *Decatur*
Date of Action: 9 September 1915
G.O. Number, Date: 189, 8 February 1916
Citation: Attached to U.S.S. *Decatur*; for several times entering compartments on board of *Decautur* immediately following an explosion on board that vessel, 9 September 1915, and locating and rescuing injured shipmates.

2448 ◆ SMITH, WILHELM

Rank: Gunner's Mate First Class
Service: U.S. Navy
Birthday: 10 April 1870
Place of Birth: Germany
Date of Death: 30 October 1925
Cemetery: Cypress Hills National Cemetery (2-9493) (MH)—Brooklyn, New York
Entered Service at: New York
Unit: U.S.S. *New York*
Battle or Place of Action: U.S.S. *New York*
Date of Action: 24 January 1916
G.O. Number, Date: 202, 6 April 1916
Citation: On board the U.S.S. *New York*; for entering a compartment filled with gases and rescuing a shipmate on 24 January 1916.

2449 ◆ TRINIDAD, TELESFORO DE LA CRUZ

Rank: Fireman Second Class
Service: U.S. Navy
Birthday: 25 November 1890
Place of Birth: New Washington, Capig, Philippine Islands
Date of Death: 8 May 1968
Place of Death: Cavite Navy Yard, Philippine Islands
Cemetery: Imus Cemetery—Imus, Cavite, Philippine Islands
Entered Service at: Philippine Islands
Unit: U.S.S. *San Diego*
Battle or Place of Action: U.S.S. *San Diego*
Date of Action: 21 January 1915
G.O. Number, Date: 142, 1 April 1915
Date of Issue: August 1915
Citation: For extraordinary heroism in the line of his profession at the time of the boiler explosion on board the U.S.S. *San Diego*, 21 January 1915. Trinidad was driven out of fireroom No. 2 by the explosion, but at once returned and picked up R.E. Daly, fireman second class, whom he saw injured, and proceeded to bring him out. While coming into No. 4 fireroom, Trinidad was just in time to catch the explosion in No. 3 fireroom, but without consideration for his own safety, passed Daly on and then assisted in rescuing another injured man from No. 3 fireroom. Trinidad was himself burned about the face by the blast from the explosion in No. 3 fireroom.

2450 ◆ WILLEY, CHARLES H.

Rank: Machinist
Service: U.S. Navy
Birthday: 31 March 1889
Place of Birth: East Boston, Suffolk County, Massachusetts
Date of Death: 11 September 1977
Place of Death: Manchester, New Hampshire
Cemetery: Blossom Hill Cemetery (MH)—Concord, New Hampshire
Entered Service at: Massachusetts
Unit: U.S.S. *Memphis*

Battle or Place of Action: off Santo Domingo City, Santo Domingo

Date of Action: 29 August 1916

G.O. Number, Date: 1 August 1932

Citation: For extraordinary heroism in the line of his profession while serving on board the U.S.S. *Memphis*, at a time when that vessel was suffering total destruction from a hurricane while anchored off Santo Domingo City, 29 August 1916. Machinist Willey took his station in the engineer's department and remained at his post of duty amidst scalding steam and the rush of thousands of tons of water into his department as long as the engines would turn, leaving only when ordered to leave. When the boilers exploded, he assisted in getting the men out of the fireroom and carrying them into the engineroom, where there was air instead of steam to breathe. Machinist Willey's conduct on this occasion was above and beyond the call of duty.

DOMINICAN CAMPAIGN

2451 ◆ GLOWIN, JOSEPH ANTHONY

Rank: Corporal
Service: U.S. Marine Corps
Birthday: 14 March 1892
Place of Birth: Detroit, Wayne County, Michigan
Date of Death: 23 August 1952
Cemetery: Mount Olivet Cemetery—Detroit, Michigan
Entered Service at: Michigan
Battle or Place of Action: Guayacanas, Dominican Republic
Date of Action: 3 July 1916
G.O. Number, Date: 244, 2 November 1916
Citation: During an engagement at Guayacanas on 3 July 1916, Cpl. Glowin participated in action against a considerable force of rebels on the line of march.

2452 ◆ WILLIAMS, ERNEST CALVIN

Rank: First Lieutenant (highest rank: Lieutenant Colonel)
Service: U.S. Marine Corps
Birthday: 2 August 1887
Place of Birth: Broadwell, Elkhart County, Illinois
Date of Death: 31 July 1940
Cemetery: Woodlawn Cemetery—Indianola, Illinois
Entered Service at: Illinois
Battle or Place of Action: San Francisco de Macoris, Dominican Republic
Date of Action: 29 November 1916
G.O. Number, Date: 289, 27 April 1917
Citation: In action against hostile forces at San Francisco de Macoris, Dominican Republic, 29 November 1916. With only a dozen men available, 1st Lt. Williams rushed the gate of the fortress. With eight of his party wounded by rifle fire of the defenders, he pressed on with the four remaining men, threw himself against the door just as it was being closed by the Dominicans, and forced an entry. Despite a narrow escape

from death at the hands of a rifleman, he and his men disposed of the guards and within a few minutes had gained control of the fort and the hundred prisoners confined there.

2453 ◆ WINANS, ROSWELL

Rank: First Sergeant (highest rank: Brigadier General)
Service: U.S. Marine Corps
Birthday: 9 December 1887
Place of Birth: Brookville, Franklin County, Indiana
Date of Death: 7 April 1968
Cemetery: Cypress View Mausoleum—San Diego, California
Entered Service at: Washington
Battle or Place of Action: Guayacanas, Dominican Republic
Date of Action: 3 July 1916
G.O. Number, Date: 244, 2 November 1916
Citation: During an engagement at Guayacanas on 3 July 1916, 1st Sgt. Winans participated in action against a considerable force of rebels on the line of march. During a running fight of 1,200 yards, our forces reached the enemy entrenchments and Cpl. Joseph A. Gowin, USMC, placed the machine gun, of which he had charge, behind a large log across the road and immediately opened fire on the trenches. He was struck once but continued firing his gun, but a moment later he was again struck and had to be dragged out of the position into cover. First Sgt. Winans, USMC, then arrived with a Colt's gun which he placed in a most exposed position, coolly opened fire on the trenches and when the gun jammed, stood up and repaired it under fire. All the time Glowin and Winans were handling their guns they were exposed to a very heavy fire which was striking into the logs and around the men, seven men being wounded and one killed within 20 feet. First Sgt. Winans continued firing his gun until the enemy had abandoned the trenches.

WORLD WAR I

2454 ◆ ADKINSON, JOSEPH B.

Rank: Sergeant
Service: U.S. Army
Birthday: 4 January 1892
Place of Birth: Egypt, Tennessee
Date of Death: 23 May 1965
Cemetery: Salem Cemetery—Atoka, Tennessee
Entered Service at: Memphis, Shelby County, Tennessee
Unit: Company C, 119th Infantry, 30th Division
Battle or Place of Action: near Bellicourt, France
Date of Action: 29 September 1918
G.O. Number, Date: 59, W.D. 3 May 1919
Citation: When murderous machine-gun fire at a range of 50 yards had made it impossible for his platoon to advance and had caused the platoon to take cover, Sgt. Adkinson alone, with the greatest intrepidity, rushed across the 50 yards of open ground directly into the face of the hostile machine gun, kicked the gun from the parapet into the enemy trench, and at the point of the bayonet captured the three men manning the gun. The gallantry and quick decision of this soldier enabled the platoon to resume its advance.

2455 ◆ ALLEX, JAKE

True Name: Mandushich, Jake Allex
Rank: Corporal
Service: U.S. Army
Birthday: 13 July 1887
Place of Birth: Streska, near Prizren, Serbia
Date of Death: 28 August 1959
Place of Death: Chicago, Illinois
Cemetery: St. Sava Cemetery—Libertyville, Illinois
Entered Service at: Chicago, Cook County, Illinois
Unit: Company H, 131st Infantry, 33d Division
Battle or Place of Action: at Chipilly Ridge, France
Date of Action: 9 August 1918
G.O. Number, Date: 44, W.D. 2 April 1919
Citation: At a critical point in the action, when all the officers of his platoon had become casualties, Cpl. Allex took command of the platoon and led it forward until the advance was stopped by fire from a machine-gun nest. He then advanced alone for about 30 yards in the face of intense fire and attacked the nest. With his bayonet he killed five of the enemy, and when it was broken, used the butt of his rifle, capturing 15 prisoners.

2456 ◆ ALLWORTH, EDWARD C.

Rank: Captain
Service: U.S. Army
Birthday: 6 July 1887
Place of Birth: Crawford, Washington
Date of Death: 25 June 1966
Cemetery: Crystal Lake Cemetery—Corvallis, Oregon
Entered Service at: Corvallis, Benton County, Oregon
Unit: 60th Infantry, 5th Division
Battle or Place of Action: at Clery-le-Petit, France
Date of Action: 5 November 1918
G.O. Number, Date: 16, W.D. 22 January 1919
Citation: While his company was crossing the Meuse River and canal at a bridgehead opposite Clery-le-Petit, the bridge over the canal was destroyed by shell fire and Capt. Allworth's command became separated, part of it being on the east bank of the canal and the remainder on the west bank. Seeing his advance units making slow headway up the steep slope ahead, this officer mounted the canal bank and called for his men to follow. Plunging in he swam across the canal under fire from the enemy, followed by his men. Inspiring his men by his example of gallantry, he led them up the slope, joining his hard-pressed platoons in front. By his personal leadership he forced the enemy back for more than a kilometer, overcoming machine-gun nests and capturing 100 prisoners, whose number exceeded that of the men in his command. The exceptional courage and leadership displayed by Capt. Allworth made possible the reestablishment of a bridgehead over the canal and the successful advance of other troops.

2457 ◆ ANDERSON, JOHANNES SEIGFRIED

Rank: First Sergeant
Service: U.S. Army
Birthday: 20 July 1887
Place of Birth: Bjoroky, Finland
Date of Death: 3 April 1950
Cemetery: Acacia Cemetery—Chicago, Illinois
Entered Service at: Chicago, Cook County, Illinois
Unit: Company B, 132d Infantry, 33d Infantry Division
Battle or Place of Action: at Consenvoye, France
Date of Action: 8 October 1918
G.O. Number, Date: 16, W.D. 22 January 1919
Date of Presentation: 17 February 1919
Place of Presentation: Chaumont, France, presented by Gen. John J. Pershing
Citation: While his company was being held up by intense

artillery and machine-gun fire, 1st Sgt. Anderson, without aid, voluntarily left the company and worked his way to the rear of the nest that was offering the most stubborn resistance. His advance was made through an open area and under constant hostile fire, but the mission was successfully accomplished, and he not only silenced the gun and captured it, but also brought back with him 23 prisoners.

2458 ◆ *BAESEL, ALBERT E.

Rank: Second Lieutenant
Service: U.S. Army
Birthday: 21 March 1890
Place of Birth: Berea, Cuyahoga County, Ohio
Date of Death: 27 September 1918
Cemetery: Woodvale Union Cemetery (MH)—Cleveland, Ohio
Entered Service at: Berea, Cuyahoga County, Ohio
Unit: Company B, 148th Infantry, 37th Division
Battle or Place of Action: near Ivry, France
Date of Action: 27 September 1918
G.O. Number, Date: 43, W.D. 23 October 1922
Citation: Upon hearing that a squad leader of his platoon had been severely wounded while attempting to capture an enemy machine-gun nest about 200 yards in advance of the assault line and somewhat to the right, 2d Lt. Baesel requested permission to go to the rescue of the wounded corporal. After thrice repeating his request and permission having been reluctantly given, due to the heavy artillery, rifle, and machine-gun fire, and heavy deluge of gas in which the company was at the time, accompanied by a volunteer, he worked his way forward, and reaching the wounded man, placed him upon his shoulders and was instantly killed by enemy fire.

2459 ◆ BALCH, JOHN HENRY

Rank: Pharmacist's Mate First Class (highest rank: Commander)
Service: U.S. Navy
Birthday: 2 January 1896
Place of Birth: Edgerton, Johnson County, Kansas
Date of Death: 15 October 1980
Place of Death: Sun City, California
Cemetery: Riverside National Cemetery (2-1925) (MH)—Riverside, California
Entered Service at: Kansas City, Clay County, Missouri
Unit: 6th Regiment, U.S. Marines
Battle or Place of Action: Vierzy & Somme-Py, France
Date of Action: 19 July & 5 October 1918
Date of Presentation: September 1919
Place of Presentation: Great Lakes Naval Station, presented by Adm. William A. Moffett
Citation: For gallantry and intrepidity at the risk of his life above and beyond the call of duty, with the 6th Regiment, U.S. Marines, in action at Vierzy, on 19 July 1918. Balch unhesitatingly and fearlessly exposed himself to terrific machine-gun and high-explosive fire to succor the wounded as they fell in the attack, leaving his dressing station voluntari-ly and keeping up the work all day and late into the night unceasingly for 16 hours. Also in the action at Somme-Py on 5 October 1918, he exhibited exceptional bravery in establishing an advanced dressing station under heavy shellfire.

2460 ◆ BARGER, CHARLES DENVER

Rank: Private First Class
Service: U.S. Army
Birthday: 1892
Place of Birth: Mount Vernon, Lawrence County, Missouri
Date of Death: 25 November 1936
Place of Death: Kansas City, Missouri
Cemetery: Blue Springs Cemetery (MH)—Blue Springs, Missouri
Entered Service at: Stotts City, Lawrence County, Missouri
Unit: Company L, 354th Infantry, 89th Division
Battle or Place of Action: near Bois-de-Bantheville, France
Date of Action: 31 October 1918
G.O. Number, Date: 20, W.D. 30 January 1919
Citation: Learning that two daylight patrols had been caught out in No Man's Land and were unable to return, Pfc. Barger and another stretcher bearer upon their own initiative made two trips 500 yards beyond our lines, under constant machine-gun fire, and rescued two wounded officers.

2461 ◆ *BARKELEY, DAVID B.

True Name: Barkley, David Bennes
Rank: Private
Service: U.S. Army
Birthday: 31 March 1899
Place of Birth: Laredo, Webb County, Texas
Date of Death: 9 November 1918
Cemetery: San Antonio National Cemetery (G-1302) (MH)—San Antonio, Texas
Entered Service at: San Antonio, Bexar County, Texas
Unit: Company A, 356th Infantry, 89th Division
Battle or Place of Action: near Pouilly, France
Date of Action: 9 November 1918
G.O. Number, Date: 20, W.D. 30 January 1919
Date of Presentation: 1919
Place of Presentation: San Antonio, presented to his Mother at her home
Citation: When information was desired as to the enemy's position on the opposite side of the Meuse River, Pvt. Barkeley, with another soldier, volunteered without hesitation and swam the river to reconnoiter the exact location. He succeeded in reaching the opposite bank, despite the evident determination of the enemy to prevent a crossing. Having obtained his information, he again entered the water for his return, but before his goal was reached, he was seized with cramps and drowned.

2462 ◆ BARKLEY, JOHN LEWIS

Rank: Private First Class
Service: U.S. Army

Birthday: 28 August 1895
Place of Birth: Blairstown, Henry County, Missouri
Date of Death: 14 April 1966
Cemetery: Forest Hills Cemetery—Kansas City, Missouri
Entered Service at: Blairstown, Henry County, Missouri
Unit: Company K, 4th Infantry, 3d Division
Battle or Place of Action: near Cunel, France
Date of Action: 7 October 1918
G.O. Number, Date: 44, W.D. 2 April 1919
Citation: Pfc. Barkley, who was stationed in an observation post half a kilometer from the German line, on his own initiative repaired a captured enemy machine gun and mounted it in a disabled French tank near his post. Shortly afterward, when the enemy launched a counterattack against our forces, Pfc. Barkley got into the tank, waited under the hostile barrage until the enemy line was abreast of him and then opened fire, completely breaking up the counterattack and killing and wounding a large number of the enemy. Five minutes later an enemy 77-millimeter gun opened fire on the tank point-blank. One shell struck the drive wheel of the tank, but this soldier nevertheless remained in the tank and after the barrage ceased broke up a second enemy counterattack, thereby enabling our forces to gain and hold Hill 25.

2463 ◆ BART, FRANK J.

Rank: Private
Service: U.S. Army
Birthday: 15 April 1883
Place of Birth: New York, New York
Date of Death: 31 March 1961
Cemetery: Flower Hill Cemetery (MH)—North Bergen, New Jersey
Entered Service at: Newark, Essex County, New Jersey
Unit: Company C, 9th Infantry, 2d Division
Battle or Place of Action: near Medeah Ferme, France
Date of Action: 3 October 1918
G.O. Number, Date: 16, W.D. 22 January 1919
Citation: Pvt. Bart, being on duty as a company runner, when the advance was held up by machine-gun fire voluntarily picked up an automatic rifle, ran out ahead of the line, and silenced a hostile machine-gun nest, killing the German gunners. The advance then continued, and when it was again hindered shortly afterward by another machine-gun nest this courageous soldier repeated his bold exploit by putting the second machine gun out of action.

2464 ◆ *BLACKWELL, ROBERT LESTER

Rank: Private
Service: U.S. Army
Birthday: 4 October 1895
Place of Birth: Person County, North Carolina
Date of Death: 11 October 1918
Cemetery: Somme Cemetery (D-20-2) (MH)—Bony Aisne, France
Entered Service at: Hurdle Mills, Person County, North Carolina
Unit: Company K, 119th Infantry, 30th Division

Battle or Place of Action: near St. Souplet, France
Date of Action: 11 October 1918
G.O. Number, Date: 13, W.D. 18 January 1919
Citation: When his platoon was almost surrounded by the enemy and his platoon commander asked for volunteers to carry a message calling for reinforcements, Pvt. Blackwell volunteered for this mission, well knowing the extreme danger connected with it. In attempting to get through the heavy shell and machine-gun fire this gallant soldier was killed.

2465 ◆ *BLECKLEY, ERWIN RUSSELL

Rank: Second Lieutenant
Service: U.S. Army Air Service
Birthday: 30 December 1894
Place of Birth: Wichita, Sedgwick County, Kansas
Date of Death: 6 October 1918
Cemetery: Meuse-Argonne Cemetery (F-25-33) (MH)—Romagne Meuse, France
Entered Service at: Wichita, Sedgwick County, Kansas
Unit: 50th Aero Squadron, 130th Field Artillery, Air Service
Served as: DH-4 Observer
Battle or Place of Action: near Binarville, France
Date of Action: 6 October 1918
G.O. Number, Date: 56, W.D. 30 December 1922
Citation: Second Lt. Bleckley, with his pilot, 1st Lt. Harold E. Goettler, Air Service, left the airdrome late in the afternoon on their second trip to drop supplies to a battalion of the 77th Division, which had been cut off by the enemy in the Argonne Forest. Having been subjected on the first trip to violent fire from the enemy, they attempted on the second trip to come still lower in order to get the packages even more precisely on the designated spot. In the course of his mission the plane was brought down by enemy rifle and machine-gun fire from the ground, resulting in fatal wounds to 2d Lt. Bleckley, who died before he could be taken to a hospital. In attempting and performing this mission 2d Lt. Bleckley showed the highest possible contempt of personal danger, devotion to duty, courage, and valor.

2466 ◆ BOONE, JOEL THOMPSON

Rank: Lieutenant (highest rank: Vice Admiral)
Service: U.S. Navy
Birthday: 29 August 1889
Place of Birth: St. Clair, Schuylkill County, Pennsylvania
Date of Death: 2 April 1974
Place of Death: Bethesda, Maryland
Cemetery: Arlington National Cemetery (11-137-2)—Arlington, Virginia
Entered Service at: St. Clair, Schuylkill County, Pennsylvania
Unit: 6th Regiment, U.S. Marines
Served as: Surgeon (Medical Corps)
Battle or Place of Action: vicinity of Vierzy, France
Date of Action: 19 July 1918
Citation: For extraordinary heroism, conspicuous gallantry, and intrepidity while serving with the 6th Regiment, U.S. Marines, in actual conflict with the enemy. With absolute dis-

regard for personal safety, ever conscious and mindful of the suffering fallen, Surg. Boone, leaving the shelter of a ravine, went forward onto the open field where there was no protection and despite the extreme enemy fire of all calibers, through a heavy mist of gas, applied dressings and first aid to wounded marines. This occurred southeast of Vierzy, near the cemetery, and on the road south from the town. When the dressings and supplies had been exhausted, he went through a heavy barrage of large-caliber shells, both high-explosive and gas, to replenish these supplies, returning quickly with a side-car load, and administered them in saving the lives of the wounded. A second trip, under the same conditions and for the same purpose, was made by Surg. Boone later that day.

2467 ◆ BRADLEY JR., WILLIS WINTER

Rank: Commander (highest rank: Captain)
Service: U.S. Navy
Birthday: 28 June 1884
Place of Birth: Ransomville, Niagara County, New York
Date of Death: 27 August 1954
Cemetery: Fort Rosecrans National Cemetery (0-2925) (MH)—San Diego, California
Entered Service at: North Dakota
Unit: U.S.S. *Pittsburgh*
Battle or Place of Action: U.S.S. *Pittsburgh*
Date of Action: 23 June 1917
Citation: For extraordinary heroism and devotion to duty while serving on the U.S.S. *Pittsburgh*, at the time of an accidental explosion of ammunition on that vessel. On 23 July 1917, some saluting cartridge cases were being reloaded in the after casemate: through an accident an explosion occurred. Comdr. Bradley (then lieutenant), who was about to enter the casemate, was blown back by the explosion and rendered momentarily unconscious, but while still dazed, crawled into the casemate to extinguish burning materials in dangerous proximity to a considerable amount of powder, thus preventing further explosions.

2468 ◆ BRONSON, DEMING

Rank: First Lieutenant
Service: U.S. Army
Birthday: 8 July 1894
Place of Birth: Rhinelander, Oneida County, Wisconsin
Date of Death: 29 May 1957
Place of Death: Roseburg, Oregon
Cemetery: Arlington National Cemetery (30-500-2) (MH)—Arlington, Virginia
Entered Service at: Seattle, King County, Washington
Unit: Company H, 364th Infantry, 91st Division
Battle or Place of Action: near Eclisfontaine, France
Date of Action: 26-27 September 1918
G.O. Number, Date: 12, W.D. 27 June 1929
Date of Presentation: 1929
Place of Presentation: Presented by Pres. Herbert Hoover
Citation: For conspicuous gallantry and intrepidity above and beyond the call of duty in action with the enemy. On the morning of 26 September, during the advance of the 364th Infantry, 1st Lt. Bronson was struck by an exploding enemy hand grenade, receiving deep cuts on his face and back of his head. He nevertheless participated in the action which resulted in the capture of an enemy dugout from which a great number of prisoners were taken. This was effected with difficulty and under extremely hazardous conditions because it was necessary to advance without the advantage of cover and, from an exposed position, throw hand grenades and phosphorous bombs to compel the enemy to surrender. On the afternoon of the same day he was painfully wounded in the left arm by an enemy rifle bullet, and after receiving first-aid treatment he was directed to the rear. Disregarding these instructions, 1st Lt. Bronson remained on duty with his company through the night although suffering from severe pain and shock. On the morning of the 27 September, his regiment resumed its attack, the object being the village of Eclisfontaine. Company H, to which 1st Lt. Bronson was assigned, was left in support of the attacking line, Company E being in the line. He gallantly joined that company in spite of his wounds and engaged with it in the capture of the village. After the capture he remained with Company E and participated with it in the capture of an enemy machine gun, he himself killing the enemy gunner. Shortly after this encounter the company was compelled to retire due to the heavy enemy artillery barrage. During this retirement 1st Lt. Bronson, who was the last man to leave the advanced position, was again wounded in both arms by an enemy high-explosive shell. He was then assisted to cover by another officer who applied first aid. Although bleeding profusely and faint from loss of blood, 1st Lt. Bronson remained with the survivors of the company throughout the night of the second day, refusin g to go to the rear for treatment. His conspicuous gallantry and spirit of self-sacrifice were a source of great inspiration to the members of the entire command.

2469 ◆ CALL, DONALD MARSHALL

Rank: Corporal
Service: U.S. Army
Birthday: 29 November 1892
Place of Birth: New York, New York
Date of Death: 19 March 1984
Place of Death: Bethesda, Maryland
Cemetery: Cremated Ashes in Flower Garden—Bethesda, Maryland
Entered Service at: France
Unit: 344th Battalion, Tank Corps
Battle or Place of Action: near Varennes, France
Date of Action: 26 September 1918
G.O. Number, Date: 13, W.D. 18 January 1919
Citation: During an operation against enemy machine-gun nests west of Varennes, Cpl. Call was in a tank with an officer when half of the turret was knocked off by a direct artillery hit. Choked by gas from the high-explosive shell, he left the tank and took cover in a shellhole 30 yards away. Seeing that the officer did not follow, and thinking that he might be alive, Cpl. Call returned to the tank under intense machine-gun and shell fire and carried the officer over a mile under machine-gun and sniper fire to safety.

2470 ◆ CANN, TEDFORD HARRIS

Rank: Seaman (highest rank: Ensign)
Service: U.S. Navy
Birthday: 3 September 1897
Place of Birth: Bridgeport, Fairfield County, Connecticut
Date of Death: 26 January 1963
Place of Death: Port Chester, New York
Cemetery: Arlington National Cemetery (7-10118-SS) (MH)—Arlington, Virginia
Entered Service at: New York
Unit: U.S.S. *May*
Battle or Place of Action: between Bermuda & the Azores
Date of Action: 5 November 1917
G.O. Number, Date: 366, W.D. 1918
Place of Presentation: Brest, France, presented by Adm. Newton A. McCully
Citation: For courageous conduct while serving on board the U.S.S. *May*, 5 November 1917. Cann found a leak in a flooded compartment and closed it at the peril of his life, thereby unquestionably saving the ship.

2471 ◆ *CHILES, MARCELLUS HOLMES

Rank: Captain
Service: U.S. Army
Birthday: 5 February 1895
Place of Birth: Eureka Springs, Carroll County, Arkansas
Date of Death: 5 November 1918
Cemetery: Meuse-Argonne Cemetery (C-31-23) (MH)—Romagne Meuse, France
Entered Service at: Denver, Denver County, Colorado
Unit: Company A, 356th Infantry, 89th Division
Served as: Battalion Commander
Battle or Place of Action: near Le Champy Bas, France
Date of Action: 3 November 1918
G.O. Number, Date: 20, W.D. 30 January 1919
Date of Issue: 15 April 1919
Citation: When his battalion, of which he had just taken command, was halted by machine-gun fire from the front and left flank, he picked up the rifle of a dead soldier and, calling on his men to follow, led the advance across a stream, waist deep, in the face of the machine-gun fire. Upon reaching the opposite bank this gallant officer was seriously wounded in the abdomen by a sniper, but before permitting himself to be evacuated he made complete arrangements for turning over his command to the next senior officer, and under the inspiration of his fearless leadership, his battalion reached its objective. Capt. Chiles died shortly after reaching the hospital.

2472 ◆ *COLYER, WILBUR E.

Rank: Sergeant
Service: U.S. Army
Birthday: 5 March 1898
Place of Birth: Brooklyn, Kings County, New York
Date of Death: 10 October 1918
Cemetery: Cypress Hills National Cemetery (2-8588)—Brooklyn, New York

Entered Service at: South Ozone, Queens County, New York
Unit: Company A, 1st Engineers, 1st Division
Battle or Place of Action: near Verdun, France
Date of Action: 9 October 1918
G.O. Number, Date: 20, W.D. 30 January 1919
Citation: Volunteering with two other soldiers to locate machine-gun nests, Sgt. Colyer advanced on the hostile positions to a point where he was half surrounded by the nests, which were in ambush. He killed the gunner of one gun with a captured German grenade and then turned this gun on the other nests, silencing all of them before he returned to his platoon. He was later killed in action.

2473 ◆ *COSTIN, HENRY G.

Rank: Private
Service: U.S. Army
Birthday: 15 June 1898
Place of Birth: Baltimore, Baltimore County, Maryland
Date of Death: 8 October 1918
Cemetery: Loudon Park National Cemetery (B-460)—Baltimore, Maryland
Entered Service at: Baltimore, Baltimore County, Maryland
Unit: Company H, 115th Infantry, 29th Division
Battle or Place of Action: near Bois-de-Consenvoye, France
Date of Action: 8 October 1918
G.O. Number, Date: 34, W.D. 7 March 1919
Citation: When the advance of his platoon had been held up by machine-gun fire and a request was made for an automatic rifle team to charge the nest, Pvt. Costin was the first to volunteer. Advancing with his team, under terrific fire of enemy artillery, machine guns, and trench mortars, he continued after all his comrades had become casualties and he himself had been seriously wounded. He operated his rifle until he collapsed. His act resulted in the capture of about 100 prisoners and several machine guns. He succumbed to the effects of his wounds shortly after the accomplishment of his heroic deed.

2474 ◆ COVINGTON, JESSE WHITFIELD

Rank: Ship's Cook Third Class (highest rank: Chief Steward)
Service: U.S. Navy
Birthday: 16 September 1889
Place of Birth: Haywood, Tennessee
Date of Death: 21 November 1966
Place of Death: Richmond, Virginia
Cemetery: Oak Grove Cemetery (PM)—Portsmouth, Virginia
Entered Service at: California
Unit: U.S.S. *Stewart*
Battle or Place of Action: at Sea
Date of Action: 17 April 1918
G.O. Number, Date: 403, W.D. 1918
Date of Issue: 1919
Citation: For extraordinary heroism following internal explosion of the *Florence H.* The sea in the vicinity of wreck-

age was covered by a mass of boxes of smokeless powder, which were repeatedly exploding. Jesse W. Covington, of the U.S.S. *Stewart*, plunged overboard to rescue a survivor who was surrounded by powder boxes and too exhausted to help himself, fully realizing that similar powder boxes in the vicinity were continually exploding and that he was thereby risking his life in saving the life of this man.

2475 ◆ CUKELA, LOUIS ✚

Rank: Sergeant (highest rank: Major)
Service: U.S. Marine Corps
Birthday: 1 May 1888
Place of Birth: Spalato, Yugoslavia
Date of Death: 19 March 1956
Place of Death: Bethesda, Maryland
Cemetery: Arlington National Cemetery (1-427-A)—Arlington, Virginia
Entered Service at: Minneapolis, Hennepin County, Minnesota
Unit: 66th Rifle Company, 5th Regiment, 2d Division
Battle or Place of Action: near Villers-Cotterets, France
Date of Action: 18 July 1918
G.O. Number, Date: 34, W.D. 7 March 1919
Citation: **Army Medal of Honor** When his company, advancing through a wood, met with strong resistance from an enemy strong point, Sgt. Cukela crawled out from the flank and made his way toward the German lines in the face of heavy fire, disregarding the warnings of his comrades. He succeeded in getting behind the enemy position and rushed a machine-gun emplacement, killing or driving off the crew with his bayonet. With German hand grenades he then bombed out the remaining portion of the strong point, capturing four men and two damaged machine guns. **Navy Medal of Honor** For extraordinary heroism while serving with the 66th Company, 5th Regiment, during action in the Forest de Retz, near Viller-Cottertes, France, 18 July 1918. Sgt. Cukela advanced alone against an enemy strong point that was holding up his line. Disregarding the warnings of his comrades, he crawled out from the flank in the face of heavy fire and worked his way to the rear of the enemy position. Rushing a machine-gun emplacement, he killed or drove off the crew with his bayonet, bombed out the remaining part of the strong point with German hand grenades, and captured two machine guns and four men.
Notes: Received both the Army and Navy Medal of Honor for the same deed.

2476 ◆ *DILBOY, GEORGE

Rank: Private First Class
Service: U.S. Army
Birthday: 5 February 1896
Place of Birth: Greece
Date of Death: 18 July 1918
Cemetery: Arlington National Cemetery (18-4574) (MH)—Arlington, Virginia
Entered Service at: Keene, Cheshire County, New Hampshire

Unit: Company H, 103d Infantry, 26th Division
Battle or Place of Action: near Belleau, France
Date of Action: 18 July 1918
G.O. Number, Date: 13, W.D. 18 January 1919
Citation: After his platoon had gained its objective along a railroad embankment, Pfc. Dilboy, accompanying his platoon leader to reconnoiter the ground beyond, was suddenly fired upon by an enemy machine gun from 100 yards. From a standing position on the railroad track, fully exposed to view, he opened fire at once, but failing to silence the gun, rushed forward with his bayonet fixed, through a wheat field toward the gun emplacement, falling within 25 yards of the gun with his right leg nearly severed above the knee and with several bullet holes in his body. With undaunted courage he continued to fire into the emplacement from a prone position, killing two of the enemy and dispersing the rest of the crew.

2477 ◆ DONALDSON, MICHAEL ALOYISIUS

Rank: Sergeant
Service: U.S. Army
Birthday: 16 January 1887
Place of Birth: Haverstraw, Rockland County, New York
Date of Death: 12 April 1970
Place of Death: Montrose, New York
Cemetery: St. Peter's Cemetery (MH)—Haverstraw, New York
Entered Service at: Haverstraw, Rockland County, New York
Unit: Company I, 165th Infantry, 42d Division
Battle or Place of Action: road between Sommerance and Landres-et St. Georges, France
Date of Action: 14 October 1918
G.O. Number, Date: 9, W.D. 23 March 1923
Citation: The advance of his regiment having been checked by intense machine-gun fire of the enemy, who were entrenched on the crest of a hill before Landres-et-St.-Georges, his company retired to a sunken road to reorganize their position, leaving several of their number wounded near the enemy lines. Of his own volition, in broad daylight and under direct observation of the enemy and with utter disregard for his own safety, he advanced to the crest of the hill, rescued one of his wounded comrades, and returned under withering fire to his own lines, repeating his splendidly heroic act until he had brought in all the men, six in number.

2478 ◆ DONOVAN, WILLIAM JOSEPH "WILD BILL"

Rank: Lieutenant Colonel (highest rank: Major General)
Service: U.S. Army
Birthday: 1 January 1883
Place of Birth: Buffalo, Erie County, New York
Date of Death: 8 February 1959
Place of Death: Washington, D.C.
Cemetery: Arlington National Cemetery (2-4874) (MH)—Arlington, Virginia
Entered Service at: Buffalo, Erie County, New York
Unit: 165th Infantry, 42d Division

Battle or Place of Action: near Landres-et-St. Georges, France
Date of Action: 14-15 October 1918
G.O. Number, Date: 56, W.D. 30 December 1922
Citation: Lt. Col. Donovan personally led the assaulting wave in an attack upon a very strongly organized position, and when our troops were suffering heavy casualties he encouraged all near him by his example, moving among his men in exposed positions, reorganizing decimated platoons, and accompanying them forward in attacks. When he was wounded in the leg by machine-gun bullets, he refused to be evacuated and continued with his unit until it withdrew to a less exposed position.

2479 ◆ DOZIER, JAMES C.

Rank: First Lieutenant (highest rank: Lieutenant General SCARNG)
Service: U.S. Army
Birthday: 17 February 1885
Place of Birth: Galivants Ferry, Horry County, South Carolina
Date of Death: 24 October 1974
Cemetery: Elmwood Cemetery (MH)—Columbia, South Carolina
Entered Service at: Rock Hill, York County, South Carolina
Unit: Company G, 118th Infantry, 30th Division
Battle or Place of Action: near Montbrehain, France
Date of Action: 8 October 1918
G.O. Number, Date: 16, W.D. 22 January 1919
Date of Presentation: 21 January 1919
Place of Presentation: Southwest of Teille, France, presented By Gen. John J. Pershing
Citation: In command of two platoons, 1st Lt. Dozier was painfully wounded in the shoulder early in the attack, but he continued to lead his men, displaying the highest bravery and skill. When his command was held up by heavy machine-gun fire, he disposed his men in the best cover available and with a soldier continued forward to attack a machine-gun nest. Creeping up to the position in the face of intense fire, he killed the entire crew with hand grenades and his pistol and a little later captured a number of Germans who had taken refuge in a dugout nearby.

2480 ◆ *DUNN, PARKER F.

Rank: Private First Class
Service: U.S. Army
Place of Birth: Albany, Albany County, New York
Date of Death: 23 October 1918
Cemetery: St. Agnes Cemetery—Albany, New York
Entered Service at: Albany, Albany County, New York
Unit: Company A, 312th Infantry, 78th Division
Battle or Place of Action: near Grand-Pre, France
Date of Action: 23 October 1918
G.O. Number, Date: 49, W.D. 25 November 1922
Citation: When his battalion commander found it necessary to send a message to a company in the attacking line and hesitated to order a runner to make the trip because of the extreme danger involved, Pfc. Dunn, a member of the intelligence section, volunteered for the mission. After advancing but a short distance across a field swept by artillery and machine-gun fire, he was wounded, but continued on and fell wounded a second time. Still undaunted, he persistently attempted to carry out his mission until he was killed by a machine-gun bullet before reaching the advance line.

2481 ◆ EDWARDS, DANIEL RICHMOND

Rank: Private First Class (highest rank: Major)
Service: U.S. Army
Birthday: 9 April 1888
Place of Birth: Mooreville, Texas
Date of Death: 21 October 1967
Cemetery: Cunningham Cemetery (MH)—Hot Springs, Arkansas
Entered Service at: Bruceville, McLennan County, Texas
Unit: Company C, 3d Machine Gun Battalion, 1st Division
Battle or Place of Action: near Soissons, France
Date of Action: 18 July 1918
G.O. Number, Date: 14, W.D. 4 April 1923
Citation: Reporting for duty from the hospital where he had been for several weeks under treatment for numerous and serious wounds and although suffering intense pain from a shattered arm, he crawled alone into an enemy trench for the purpose of capturing or killing enemy soldiers known to be concealed therein. He killed four of the men and took the remaining four men prisoners; while conducting them to the rear, one of the enemy was killed by a high-explosive enemy shell which also completely shattered one of Pfc. Edwards' legs, causing him to be immediately evacuated to the hospital. The bravery of Pfc. Edwards, now a tradition in his battalion because of his previous gallant acts, again caused the morale of his comrades to be raised to high pitch.

2482 ◆ EGGERS, ALAN LOUIS

Rank: Sergeant
Service: U.S. Army
Birthday: 2 November 1895
Place of Birth: Saranac Lake, Franklin County, New York
Date of Death: 3 October 1968
Cemetery: Arlington National Cemetery (2-3389-A) (MH)—Arlington, Virginia
Entered Service at: Summit, Union County, New Jersey
Unit: 3d Platoon, Machine Gun Company, 107th Infantry, 27th Division
Battle or Place of Action: near Le Catelet, France
Date of Action: 29 September 1918
G.O. Number, Date: 20, W.D. 30 January 1919
Date of Presentation: 4 February 1919
Place of Presentation: Chaumont, France, presented by Gen. John J. Pershing
Citation: Becoming separated from their platoon by a smoke barrage, Sgt. Eggers, Sgt. John C. Latham and Cpl. Thomas E. O'Shea took cover in a shell hole well within the enemy's lines. Upon hearing a call for help from an American tank, which had become disabled 30 yards from them, the

three soldiers left their shelter and started towards the tank, under heavy fire from German machine guns and trench mortars. In crossing the fire-swept area Cpl. O'Shea was mortally wounded, but his companions, undeterred, proceeded to the tank, rescued a wounded officer, and assisted two wounded soldiers to cover in a sap of a nearby trench. Sgt. Eggers and Sgt. Latham then returned to the tank in the face of the violent fire, dismounted a Hotchkiss gun, and took it back to where the wounded men were, keeping off the enemy all day by effective use of the gun and later bringing it, with the wounded men, back to our lines under cover of darkness.

2483 ◆ ELLIS, MICHAEL B.

Rank: Sergeant
Service: U.S. Army
Birthday: 28 October 1894
Place of Birth: St. Louis, St. Louis County, Missouri
Date of Death: 9 December 1937
Place of Death: Chicago, Illinois
Cemetery: Arlington National Cemetery (6-9520) (MH)—Arlington, Virginia
Entered Service at: East St. Louis, St. Clair County, Illinois
Unit: Company C, 28th Infantry, 1st Division
Battle or Place of Action: near Exermont, France
Date of Action: 5 October 1918
G.O. Number, Date: 74, W.D. 7 June 1919
Citation: During the entire day's engagement he operated far in advance of the first wave of his company, voluntarily undertaking most dangerous missions and singlehandedly attacking and reducing machine-gun nests. Flanking one emplacement, he killed two of the enemy with rifle fire and captured 17 others. Later he singlehandedly advanced under heavy fire and captured 27 prisoners, including two officers and six machine guns, which had been holding up the advance of the company. The captured officers indicated the locations of four other machine guns, and he in turn captured these, together with their crews, at all times showing marked heroism and fearlessness.

2484 ◆ FORREST, ARTHUR J.

Rank: Sergeant
Service: U.S. Army
Birthday: 1896
Place of Birth: St. Louis, St. Louis County, Missouri
Date of Death: 30 November 1964
Place of Death: St. Louis, Missouri
Cemetery: Grand View Burial Park (MH)—Hannibal, Missouri
Entered Service at: Hannibal, Marion County, Missouri
Unit: Company D, 354th Infantry, 89th Division
Battle or Place of Action: near Remonville, France
Date of Action: 1 November 1919
G.O. Number, Date: 50, W.D. 12 April 1919
Citation: When the advance of his company was stopped by bursts of fire from a nest of six enemy machine guns, without being discovered, he worked his way singlehandedly to a point within 50 yards of the machine-gun nest. Charging, sin-

glehandedly, he drove out the enemy in disorder, thereby protecting the advance platoon from annihilating fire, and permitting the resumption of the advance of his company.

2485 ◆ FOSTER, GARY EVANS

Rank: Sergeant
Service: U.S. Army
Birthday: 6 November 1894
Place of Birth: Spartanburg, Spartanburg County, South Carolina
Date of Death: 22 July 1951
Cemetery: New Prospect Cemetery—Boiling Springs, South Carolina
Entered Service at: Inman, Spartanburg County, South Carolina
Unit: Company F, 118th Infantry, 30th Division
Battle or Place of Action: near Montbrehain, France
Date of Action: 8 October 1918
G.O. Number, Date: 16, W.D. 22 January 1919
Citation: When his company was held up by violent machine-gun fire from a sunken road, Sgt. Foster with an officer went forward to attack the hostile machine-gun nests. The officer was wounded, but Sgt. Foster continued on alone in the face of the heavy fire and by effective use of hand grenades and his pistol killed several of the enemy and captured 18.

2486 ◆ FUNK, JESSE N.

Rank: Private First Class
Service: U.S. Army
Birthday: 20 August 1888
Place of Birth: New Hampton, Harrison County, Missouri
Date of Death: 21 March 1933
Cemetery: Calhan Cemetery (MH)—Calhan, Colorado
Entered Service at: Calhan, El Paso County, Colorado
Unit: Company L, 354th Infantry, 89th Division
Battle or Place of Action: near Bois-de-Bantheville, France
Date of Action: 31 October 1918
G.O. Number, Date: 20, W.D. 30 January 1919
Citation: Learning that two daylight patrols had been caught out in No Man's Land and were unable to return, Pfc. Funk and another stretcher bearer, upon their own initiative, made two trips 500 yards beyond our lines, under constant machine-gun fire, and rescued two wounded officers.

2487 ◆ FURLONG, HAROLD ARTHUR

Rank: First Lieutenant (highest rank: Colonel)
Service: U.S. Army
Birthday: 1 August 1895
Place of Birth: Pontiac, Oakland County, Michigan
Date of Death: 27 July 1987
Cemetery: Oak Hill Cemetery—Pontiac, Michigan
Entered Service at: Detroit, Wayne County, Michigan
Unit: Company M, 353d Infantry, 89th Division
Battle or Place of Action: near Bantheville, France
Date of Action: 1 November 1918

G.O. Number, Date: 16, W.D. 22 January 1919
Date of Presentation: 9 February 1919
Place of Presentation: Chaumont, France, presented by Gen.John J. Pershing
Citation: Immediately after the opening of the attack in the Bois-de-Bantheville, when his company was held up by severe machine-gun fire from the front, which killed his company commander and several soldiers, 1st Lt. Furlong moved out in advance of the line with great courage and coolness, crossing an open space several hundred yards wide. Taking up a position behind the line of the machine guns, he closed in on them, one at a time, killing a number of the enemy with his rifle, putting four machine-gun nests out of action, and driving 20 German prisoners into our lines.

2488 ◆ GAFFNEY, FRANK J.

Rank: Private First Class
Service: U.S. Army
Birthday: 16 December 1883
Place of Birth: Buffalo, Erie County, New York
Date of Death: 25 May 1948
Place of Death: Niagara Falls, New York
Cemetery: United German & French RC Cemetery (MH)—Buffalo, New York
Entered Service at: Niagara Falls, Niagara County, New York
Unit: Company G, 108th Infantry, 27th Division
Served as: Automatic Rifleman
Battle or Place of Action: near Ronssoy, France
Date of Action: 29 September 1918
G.O. Number, Date: 20, W.D. 30 January 1919
Citation: Pfc. Gaffney, an automatic rifleman, pushing forward alone, after all the other members of his squad had been killed, discovered several Germans placing a heavy machine gun in position. He killed the crew, captured the gun, bombed several dugouts, and, after killing four more of the enemy with his pistol, held the position until reinforcements came up, when 80 prisoners were captured.

2489 ◆ *GOETTLER, HAROLD ERNEST

Rank: First Lieutenant
Service: U.S. Army Air Service
Birthday: 21 July 1890
Place of Birth: Chicago, Cook County, Illinois
Date of Death: 6 October 1918
Cemetery: Graceland Cemetery—Chicago, Illinois
Entered Service at: Chicago, Cook County, Illinois
Unit: 50th Aero Squadron, Air Service
Served as: DH-4 Pilot
Battle or Place of Action: near Binarville, France
Date of Action: 6 October 1918
G.O. Number, Date: 56, W.D. 1922
Citation: First Lt. Harold E. Goettler, with his observer, 2d Lt. Erwin R. Bleckley, 130th Field Artillery, left the airdrome late in the afternoon on their second trip to drop supplies to a battalion of the 77th Division which had been cut off by the enemy in the Argonne Forest. Having been subjected on the

first trip to violent fire from the enemy, they attempted on the second trip to come still lower in order to get the packages even more precisely on the designated spot. In the course of his mission the plane was brought down by enemy rifle and machine-gun fire from the ground, resulting in the instant death of 1st Lt. Goettler. In attempting and performing this mission 1st Lt. Goettler showed the highest possible contempt of personal danger, devotion to duty, courage, and valor.

2490 ◆ GRAVES, ORA

Rank: Seaman
Service: U.S. Navy
Birthday: 26 July 1896
Place of Birth: Las Animas, Bent County, Colorado
Date of Death: 28 September 1961
Cemetery: Fort Rosecrans National Cemetery (W-1208)—San Diego, California
Entered Service at: Nebraska
Unit: U.S.S. *Pittsburgh*
Battle or Place of Action: at Sea aboard the U.S.S. *Pittsburgh*
Date of Action: 23 July 1917
G.O. Number, Date: 366, W.D. 1918
Citation: For extraordinary heroism on 23 July 1917, while the U.S.S. *Pittsburgh* was proceeding to Buenos Aires, Argentina. A 3-inch saluting charge exploded, causing the death of C.T. Lyles, seaman. Upon the explosion, Graves was blown to the deck, but soon recovered and discovered burning waste on the deck. He put out the burning waste while the casemate was filled with clouds of smoke, knowing that there was more powder there which might explode.

2491 ◆ GREGORY, EARL D.

Rank: Sergeant
Service: U.S. Army
Birthday: 18 October 1897
Place of Birth: Chase City, Mecklenburg County, Virginia
Date of Death: 6 January 1972
Place of Death: Birmingham, Alabama
Cemetery: Tuscaloosa Memorial Park Corp.—Tuscaloosa, Alabama
Entered Service at: Chase City, Mecklenburg County, Virginia
Unit: Headquarters Company, 116th Infantry, 29th Division
Battle or Place of Action: at Bois-de-Consenvoye, France
Date of Action: 8 October 1918
G.O. Number, Date: 34, W.D. 7 March 1919
Citation: With the remark "I will get them," Sgt. Gregory seized a rifle and a trench mortar shell, which he used as a hand grenade, left his detachment of the trench-mortar platoon, and advancing ahead of the infantry, captured a machine gun and three of the enemy. Advancing still farther from the machine-gun nest, he captured a 7.5 centimeter mountain howitzer and, entering a dugout in the immediate vicinity, singlehandedly captured 19 of the enemy.

2492 ◆ GUMPERTZ, SYDNEY G.

Rank: First Sergeant (highest rank: Captain)
Service: U.S. Army
Birthday: 24 October 1879
Place of Birth: San Raphael, Marin County, California
Date of Death: 16 February 1971
Cemetery: Long Island National Cemetery (DSS-65)
(MH)—Farmingdale, New York
Entered Service at: Chicago, Cook County, Illinois
Unit: Company E, 132d Infantry, 33d Division
Battle or Place of Action: in the Bois-de-Forges, France
Date of Action: 29 September 1918
G.O. Number, Date: 16, W.D. 22 January 1919
Citation: When the advancing line was held up by machine-gun fire, 1st Sgt. Gumpertz left the platoon of which he was in command and started with two other soldiers through a heavy barrage toward the machine-gun nest. His two companions soon became casualties from bursting shells, but 1st Sgt. Gumpertz continued on alone in the face of direct fire from the machine gun, jumped into the nest, and silenced the gun, capturing nine of the crew.

2493 ◆ *HALL, THOMAS LEE

Rank: Sergeant
Service: U.S. Army
Place of Birth: Fort Mill, York County, South Carolina
Date of Death: 8 October 1918
Cemetery: Unity Cemetery (MH)—Fort Mill, South Carolina
Entered Service at: Fort Mill, York County, South Carolina
Unit: Company G, 118th Infantry, 30th Division
Battle or Place of Action: near Montbrehain, France
Date of Action: 8 October 1918
G.O. Number, Date: 50, W.D. 12 April 1919
Citation: Having overcome two machine-gun nests under his skillful leadership, Sgt. Hall's platoon was stopped 800 yards from its final objective by machine-gun fire of particular intensity. Ordering his men to take cover in a sunken road, he advanced alone on the enemy machine-gun post and killed five members of the crew with his bayonet and thereby made possible the further advance of the line. While attacking another machine-gun nest later in the day this gallant soldier was mortally wounded.

2494 ◆ HAMMANN, CHARLES HAZELTINE

Rank: Ensign
Service: U.S. Naval Reserve Fleet
Birthday: 16 March 1892
Place of Birth: Baltimore, Baltimore County, Maryland
Date of Death: 14 June 1919
Place of Death: Hampton, Virginia
Cemetery: Oak Lawn Cemetery (MH)—Baltimore, Maryland
Entered Service at: Maryland
Served as: Pilot (Seaplane)
Battle or Place of Action: off Pola, Austria
Date of Action: 21 August 1918

Citation: For extraordinary heroism as a pilot of a seaplane on 21 August 1918, when with three other planes Ens. Hammann took part in a patrol and attacked a superior force of enemy land planes. In the course of the engagement which followed, the plane of Ens. George M. Ludlow was shot down and fell in the water five miles off Pola. Ens. Hammann immediately dived down and landed on the water close alongside the disabled machine, where he took Ludlow on board. Although his machine was not designed for the double load to which it was subjected, and although there was danger of attack by Austrian planes, he made his way to Porto Corsini.

2495 ◆ HATLER, M. WALDO

Rank: Sergeant
Service: U.S. Army
Birthday: 6 January 1894
Place of Birth: Bolivar, Polk County, Missouri
Date of Death: 31 August 1967
Cemetery: Grand Army of the Republic Cemetery—Sulphur Springs, Arkansas
Entered Service at: Neosho, Newton County, Missouri
Unit: Company B, 356th Infantry, 89th Division
Battle or Place of Action: near Pouilly, France
Date of Action: 8 November 1918
G.O. Number, Date: 74, W.D. 7 June 1919
Citation: When volunteers were called for to secure information as to the enemy's position on the opposite bank of the Meuse River, Sgt. Hatler was the first to offer his services for the dangerous mission. Swimming across the river, he succeeded in reaching the German lines after another soldier, who had started with him, had been seized with cramps and drowned in midstream. Alone he carefully and courageously reconnoitered the enemy's positions, which were held in force, and again successfully swam the river, bringing back information of great value.

2496 ◆ HAYDEN, DAVID EPHRAIM

Rank: Hospital Apprentice First Class (highest rank: Pharmacist's Mate Third Class)
Service: U.S. Navy
Birthday: 2 October 1897
Place of Birth: Florence, Williamson County, Texas
Date of Death: 18 March 1974
Cemetery: Arlington National Cemetery (35-1864)
(MH)—Arlington, Virginia
Entered Service at: Texas
Unit: 2d Battalion, 6th Regiment, U.S. Marines
Battle or Place of Action: Thiaucourt, France
Date of Action: 15 September 1918
Citation: For gallantry and intrepidity at the risk of his life above and beyond the call of duty. During the advance, when Cpl. Creed was mortally wounded while crossing an open field swept by machine-gun fire, Hayden unhesitatingly ran to his assistance and, finding him so severely wounded as to require immediate attention, disregarded his own personal safety to dress the wound under intense machine-gun fire, and then carried the wounded man back to a place of safety.

2497 ◆ HAYS, GEORGE PRICE

Rank: First Lieutenant (highest rank: Lieutenant General)
Service: U.S. Army
Birthday: 27 September 1892
Place of Birth: Chee Foo, China
Date of Death: 7 September 1978
Place of Death: Pinehurst, North Carolina
Cemetery: Arlington National Cemetery (11-540-2) (MH)—Arlington, Virginia
Entered Service at: Okarche, Kingfisher County, Oklahoma
Unit: 10th Field Artillery, 3d Division
Battle or Place of Action: near Greves Farm, France
Date of Action: 14-15 July 1918
G.O. Number, Date: 34, W.D. 7 March 1919
Date of Issue: 17 March 1919
Citation: At the very onset of the unprecedented artillery bombardment by the enemy, his line of communication was destroyed beyond repair. Despite the hazard attached to the mission of runner, he immediately set out to establish contact with the neighboring post of command and further establish liaison with French batteries, visiting their position so frequently that he was mainly responsible for the accurate fire therefrom. While thus engaged, seven horses were shot under him and he was severely wounded. His activity under most severe fire was an important factor in checking the advance of the enemy.

2498 ◆ *HERIOT, JAMES DAVIDSON

Rank: Corporal
Service: U.S. Army
Birthday: 2 November 1890
Place of Birth: Providence, South Carolina
Date of Death: 12 October 1918
Place of Death: France
Cemetery: Rembert Church Cemetery—Rembert, South Carolina
Entered Service at: Providence, South Carolina
Unit: Company I, 118th Infantry, 30th Division
Battle or Place of Action: at Vaux-Andigny, France
Date of Action: 12 October 1918
G.O. Number, Date: 13, W.D. 18 January 1919
Citation: Cpl. Heriot, with four other soldiers, organized a combat group and attacked an enemy machine-gun nest which had been inflicting heavy casualties on his company. In the advance two of his men were killed, and because of the heavy fire from all sides the remaining two sought shelter. Unmindful of the hazard attached to his mission, Cpl. Heriot, with fixed bayonet, alone charged the machine gun, making his way through the fire for a distance of 30 yards and forcing the enemy to surrender. During this exploit he received several wounds in the arm, and later in the same day, while charging another nest, he was killed.

2499 ◆ HILL, RALYN M.

Rank: Corporal
Service: U.S. Army
Birthday: 6 May 1899
Place of Birth: Lindenwood, Ogle County, Illinois
Date of Death: 25 March 1977
Cemetery: Abilene Cemetery (MH)—Abilene, Kansas
Entered Service at: Oregon, Ogle County, Illinois
Unit: Company H, 129th Infantry, 33d Division
Battle or Place of Action: near Donnevoux, France
Date of Action: 7 October 1918
G.O. Number, Date: 34, W.D. 7 March 1919
Citation: Seeing a French airplane fall out of control on the enemy side of the Meuse River with its pilot injured, Cpl. Hill voluntarily dashed across the footbridge to the side of the wounded man and, taking him on his back, started back to his lines. During the entire exploit he was subjected to murderous fire of enemy machine guns and artillery, but he successfully accomplished his mission and brought his man to a place of safety, a distance of several hundred yards.

2500 ◆ HILTON, RICHMOND HOBSON

Rank: Sergeant
Service: U.S. Army
Birthday: 8 October 1898
Place of Birth: Westville, Kershaw County, South Carolina
Date of Death: 13 August 1933
Cemetery: Quaker Cemetery—Camden, South Carolina
Entered Service at: Westville, Kershaw County, South Carolina
Unit: Company M, 118th Infantry, 30th Division
Battle or Place of Action: at Brancourt, France
Date of Action: 11 October 1918
G.O. Number, Date: 16, W.D. 22 January 1919
Citation: While Sgt. Hilton's company was advancing through the village of Brancourt it was held up by intense enfilading fire from a machine gun. Discovering that this fire came from a machine-gun nest among shell holes at the edge of the town, Sgt. Hilton, accompanied by a few other soldiers, but well in advance of them, pressed on toward this position, firing with his rifle until his ammunition was exhausted, and then with his pistol, killing six of the enemy and capturing 10. In the course of this daring exploit he received a wound from a bursting shell, which resulted in the loss of his arm.

2501 ◆ HOFFMAN, CHARLES F.✚

True Name: Janson, Ernest August
Rank: Gunnery Sergeant (highest rank: Sergeant Major)
Service: U.S. Marine Corps
Birthday: 17 August 1878
Place of Birth: New York, New York
Date of Death: 14 May 1940
Cemetery: Evergreen Cemetery—Brooklyn, New York
Entered Service at: Brooklyn, Kings County, New York
Unit: 49th Company, 5th Regiment, 2d Division
Battle or Place of Action: near Chateau-Thierry, France
Date of Action: 6 June 1918
G.O. Number, Date: 34, W.D. 7 March 1919
Citation: **Army Medal of Honor:** Immediately after the

company to which he belonged had reached its objective on Hill 142, several hostile counterattacks were launched against the line before the new position had been consolidated. G/Sgt. Hoffman was attempting to organize a position on the north slope of the hill when he saw 12 of the enemy, armed with five light machine guns, crawling toward his group. Giving the alarm, he rushed the hostile detachment, bayoneted the two leaders, and forced the others to flee, abandoning their guns. His quick action, initiative, and courage drove the enemy from a position from which they could have swept the hill with machine-gun fire and forced the withdrawal of our troops. **Navy Medal of Honor**: For conspicuous gallantry and intrepidity above and beyond the call of duty in action with the enemy near Chateau-Thierry, France, 6 June 1918. Immediately after the company to which G/Sgt. Janson belonged had reached its objective on Hill 142, several hostile counterattacks were launched against the line before the new position had been consolidated. G/Sgt. Janson was attempting to organize a position on the north slope of the hill when he saw 12 of the enemy, armed with five light machine guns, crawling toward his group. Giving the alarm, he rushed the hostile detachment, bayoneted the two leaders, and forced the others to flee, abandoning their guns. His quick action, initiative, and courage drove the enemy from a position from which they could have swept the hill with machine-gun fire and forced the withdrawal of our troops.
Notes: ✝Received both the Army and Navy Medal of Honor for the same deed.

2502 ◆ HOLDERMAN, NELSON MILES

Rank: Captain (highest rank: Colonel)
Service: U.S. Army
Birthday: 10 November 1885
Place of Birth: Trumbull, Clay County, Nebraska
Date of Death: 3 September 1953
Cemetery: Golden Gate National Cemetery (R-17)—San Bruno, California
Entered Service at: Santa Ana, Orange County, California
Unit: 307th Infantry, 77th Division
Battle or Place of Action: northeast of Binarville, in the Argonne Forest, France
Date of Action: 2-8 October 1918
G.O. Number, Date: 11, W.D. 12 March 1921
Citation: Capt. Holderman commanded a company of a battalion which was cut off and surrounded by the enemy. He was wounded on 4, 5, and 7 October, but throughout the entire period, suffering great pain and subjected to fire of every character, he continued personally to lead and encourage the officers and men under his command with unflinching courage and with distinguished success. On 6 October, in a wounded condition, he rushed through enemy machine-gun and shell fire and carried two wounded men to a place of safety.

2503 ◆ *INGRAM, OSMOND KELLY

Rank: Gunner's Mate First Class
Service: U.S. Navy
Birthday: 4 August 1887
Place of Birth: Alabama
Date of Death: 15 October 1917
Place of Death: at Sea
Cemetery: A.B.M.C. Wall of the Missing—Brookwood, Surrey, England
Entered Service at: Alabama
Unit: U.S.S. *Cassin*
Battle or Place of Action: at sea 20 miles south of Mind Head, Ireland
Date of Action: 15 October 1917
Citation: For extraordinary heroism in the presence of the enemy on the occasion of the torpedoing of the *Cassin*, 15 October 1917. While the Cassin was searching for the submarine, Ingram sighted the torpedo coming, and realizing that it might strike the ship aft in the vicinity of the depth charges, ran aft with the intention of releasing the depth charges before the torpedo could reach the *Cassin*. The torpedo struck the ship before he could accomplish his purpose, and Ingram was killed by the explosion. The depth charges exploded immediately afterward. His life was sacrificed in an attempt to save the ship and his shipmates, as the damage to the ship would have been much less if he had been able to release the depth charges.

2504 ◆ IZAC, EDOUARD VICTOR MICHEL

Rank: Lieutenant
Service: U.S. Navy
Birthday: 18 December 1889
Place of Birth: Cresco, Howard County, Iowa
Date of Death: 18 January 1990
Cemetery: Arlington National Cemetery (3-4222-16 (MH)—Arlington, Virginia
Entered Service at: Illinois
Unit: U.S.S. *President Lincoln*
Battle or Place of Action: aboard German submarine U-90 as prisoner of war
Date of Action: 21 May 1918
Date of Presentation: 11 November 1920
Place of Presentation: The Washington Navy Yard, presented by Under Secretary of the Navy Franklin D. Roosevelt
Citation: When the U.S.S. *President Lincoln* was attacked and sunk by the German submarine *U-90*, 21 May 1918, Lt. Izac was captured and held as a prisoner on board the *U-90* until the return of the submarine to Germany, when he was confined in the prison camp. During his stay on the *U-90* he obtained information of the movements of German submarines which was so important that he determined to escape, with a view to making this information available to the U.S. and Allied Naval authorities. In attempting to carry out this plan, he jumped through the window of a rapidly moving train at the imminent risk of death, not only from the nature of the act itself but from the fire of the armed German soldiers who were guarding him. Having been recaptured and reconfined, Lt. Izac made a second and successful attempt to escape, breaking his way through barbed-wire fences and deliberately drawing the fire of the armed guards in the hope of permitting others to escape during the confusion. He made

his way through the mountains of southwestern Germany, having only raw vegetables for food, and at the end, swam the river Rhine during the night in the immediate vicinity of German sentries.

2505 ◆ JOHNSTON, HAROLD IRVING

Rank: Sergeant (rank at time of action: Private First Class) (highest rank: Major A.A.C. WWII)
Service: U.S. Army
Birthday: 9 March 1892
Place of Birth: Kendall, Hamilton County, Kansas
Date of Death: 28 August 1949
Cemetery: Fairmount Cemetery (MH)—Denver, Colorado
Entered Service at: Chicago, Cook County, Illinois
Unit: Company A, 356th Infantry, 89th Division
Battle or Place of Action: near Pouilly, France
Date of Action: 9 November 1918
G.O. Number, Date: 20, W.D. 30 January 1919
Citation: When information was desired as to the enemy's position on the opposite side of the Meuse River, Sgt. Johnston, with another soldier, volunteered without hesitation and swam the river to reconnoiter the exact location of the enemy. He succeeded in reaching the opposite bank, despite the evident determination of the enemy to prevent a crossing. Having obtained his information, he again entered the water for his return. This was accomplished after a severe struggle which so exhausted him that he had to be assisted from the water, after which he rendered his report of the exploit.

2506 ◆ KARNES, JAMES ERNEST

Rank: Sergeant
Service: U.S. Army
Birthday: 20 July 1889
Place of Birth: Arlington, Shelby County, Tennessee
Date of Death: 8 July 1966
Cemetery: Greenwood Cemetery—Knoxville, Tennessee
Entered Service at: Knoxville, Knox County, Tennessee
Unit: Company D, 117th Infantry, 30th Division
Battle or Place of Action: near Estrees, France
Date of Action: 8 October 1918
G.O. Number, Date: 50, W.D. 12 April 1919
Citation: During the advance, his company was held up by a machine gun, which was enfilading the line. Accompanied by another soldier, he advanced against this position and succeeded in reducing the nest by killing three and capturing seven of the enemy and their guns.

2507 ◆ KATZ, PHILLIP CARL

Rank: Sergeant
Service: U.S. Army
Birthday: 12 December 1889
Place of Birth: San Francisco, San Francisco County, California
Date of Death: 29 October 1987
Place of Death: San Francisco, California

Cemetery: Cypress Lawn Cemetery—Colma, California
Entered Service at: San Francisco, San Francisco County, California
Unit: Company C, 363d Infantry, 91st Division
Battle or Place of Action: near Eclisfontaine, France
Date of Action: 26 September 1918
G.O. Number, Date: 16, W.D. 22 January 1919
Citation: After his company had withdrawn for a distance of 200 yards on a line with the units on its flanks, Sgt. Katz learned that one of his comrades had been left wounded in an exposed position at the point from which the withdrawal had taken place. Voluntarily crossing an area swept by heavy machine-gun fire, he advanced to where the wounded soldier lay and carried him to a place of safety.

2508 ◆ KAUFMAN, BENJAMIN

Rank: First Sergeant
Service: U.S. Army
Birthday: 10 March 1894
Place of Birth: Buffalo, Erie County, New York
Date of Death: 5 February 1981
Cemetery: Fountain Lawn Memorial Park (MH)—Trenton, New Jersey
Entered Service at: Brooklyn, Kings County, New York
Unit: Company K, 308th Infantry, 77th Division
Battle or Place of Action: in Argonne Forest, France
Date of Action: 4 October 1918
G.O. Number, Date: 50, W.D. 12 April 1919
Citation: He took out a patrol for the purpose of attacking an enemy machine gun which had checked the advance of his company. Before reaching the gun he became separated from his patrol and a machine-gun bullet shattered his right arm. Without hesitation he advanced on the gun alone, throwing grenades with his left hand and charging with an empty pistol, taking one prisoner and scattering the crew, bringing the gun and prisoner back to the first-aid station.

2509 ◆ KELLY, JOHN JOSEPH✣

Rank: Private
Service: U.S. Marine Corps
Birthday: 24 June 1898
Place of Birth: Chicago, Cook County, Illinois
Date of Death: 20 November 1957
Place of Death: Florida
Cemetery: All Saints Cemetery—Des Plaines, Illinois
Entered Service at: Chicago, Cook County, Illinois
Unit: 78th Company, 6th Regiment, 2d Division
Battle or Place of Action: at Blanc Mont Ridge, France
Date of Action: 3 October 1918
G.O. Number, Date: 16, W.D. 22 January 1919
Date of Presentation: 17 March 1919
Place of Presentation: Coblenz, France, presented by Gen. John J. Pershing
Citation: **Army Medal of Honor** Pvt. Kelly ran through our own barrage 100 yards in advance of the front line and attacked an enemy machine-gun nest, killing the gunner with a grenade, shooting another member of the crew with his pis-

tol, and returning through the barrage with eight prisoners.
Navy Medal of Honor For conspicuous gallantry and intrepidity above and beyond the call of duty while serving with the 78th Company, 6th Regiment, 2d Division, in action with the enemy at Blanc Mont Ridge, France, 3 October 1918. Pvt. Kelly ran through our own barrage a hundred yards in advance of the front line and attacked an enemy machine-gun nest, killing the gunner with a grenade, shooting another member of the crew with his pistol, and returning through the barrage with eight prisoners.
Notes: ✛Double Awardee: received both the Army and Navy Medal of Honor for the same deed

2510 ◆ *KOCAK, MATEJ✛

Rank: Sergeant
Service: U.S. Marine Corps
Birthday: 31 December 1882
Place of Birth: Gbely (Slovakia), Austria
Date of Death: 4 October 1918
Place of Death: Blanc Mont Ridge, France
Cemetery: Meuse Argonne Cemetery (D-41-32) (MH)—Romagne Meuse, France
Entered Service at: New York, New York
Unit: 66th Company, 5th Regiment, 2d Division
Battle or Place of Action: Soissons, France
Date of Action: 18 July 1918
G.O. Number, Date: 34, W.D. 7 March 1919
Date of Issue: Army: 18 February 1919 Navy: 11 November 1920
Citation: **Army Medal of Honor** When the advance of his battalion was checked by a hidden machine-gun nest, he went forward alone, unprotected by covering fire from his own men, and worked in between the German positions in the face of fire from enemy covering detachments. Locating the machine-gun nest, he rushed it and with his bayonet and drove off the crew. Shortly after this he orgnized 25 French colonial soldiers who had become separated from their company and led them in attacking another machine-gun nest, which was also put out of action. **Navy Medal of Honor** For extraordinary heroism while serving with the 66th Company, 5th Regiment, 2d Division, in action in the Viller-Cottertes section, south of Soissons, France, 18 July 1918. When a hidden machine-gun nest halted the advance of his battalion, Sgt. Kocak went forward alone unprotected by covering fire and worked his way in between the German positions in the face of heavy enemy fire. Rushing the enemy position with his bayonet, he drove off the crew. Later the same day, Sgt. Kocak organized French colonial soldiers who had become separated from their company and led them in an attack on another machine-gun nest which was also put out of action.
Notes: ✛Double Awardee: received both the Army and Navy Medal of Honor for the same deed

2511 ◆ LATHAM, JOHN CRIDLAND

Rank: Sergeant [highest rank: Warrant Officer (j.g.)]
Service: U.S. Army
Birthday: 3 March 1888

Place of Birth: Windemere, Cumbria County, England
Date of Death: 2 November 1975
Place of Death: Stanford, Connecticut
Cemetery: Arlington National Cemetery (35-1127) (MH)—Arlington, Virginia
Entered Service at: Rutherford, Bergen County, New Jersey
Unit: 3d Platoon, Machine Gun Company, 107th Infantry, 27th Division
Battle or Place of Action: near Le Catelet, France
Date of Action: 29 September 1918
G.O. Number, Date: 20, W.D. 30 January 1919
Date of Presentation: 4 February 1919
Place of Presentation: Chaumont, France, presented by Gen. John J. Pershing
Citation: Becoming separated from their platoon by a smoke barrage, Sgt. Latham, Sgt. Alan L. Eggers, and Cpl. Thomas E. O'shea took cover in a shellhole well within the enemy lines. Upon hearing a call for help from an American tank which had became disabled 30 yards from them, the three soldiers left their shelter and started toward the tank under heavy fire from German machine guns and trench mortars. In crossing the fire-swept area, Cpl. O'Shea was mortally wounded, but his companions, undeterred, proceeded to the tank, rescued a wounded officer, and assisted two wounded soldiers to cover in the sap of a trench nearby. Sgts. Latham and Eggers then returned to the tank in the face of violent fire, dismounted a Hotchkiss gun, and took it back where the wounded men were, keeping off the enemy all day by effective use of the gun, and later bringing it with the wounded men back to our lines under cover of darkness.

2512 ◆ *LEMERT, MILO

Rank: First Sergeant
Service: U.S. Army
Birthday: 25 March 1890
Place of Birth: Marshalltown, Marshall County, Iowa
Date of Death: 29 September 1918
Place of Death: France
Cemetery: Crossville City Cemetery (MH)—Crossville, Tennessee
Entered Service at: Crossville, Cumberland County, Tennessee
Unit: Company G, 119th Infantry, 30th Division
Battle or Place of Action: near Bellicourt, France
Date of Action: 29 September 1918
G.O. Number, Date: 59, W.D. 3 May 1919
Citation: Seeing that the left flank of his company was held up, he located the enemy machine-gun emplacement, which had been causing heavy casualties. In the face of heavy fire he rushed it singlehandedly, killing the entire crew with grenades. Continuing along the enemy trench in advance of the company, he reached another emplacement, which he also charged, silencing the gun with grenades. A third machine-gun emplacement opened up on him from the left and with similar skill and bravery he destroyed this also. Later, in company with another sergeant, he attacked a fourth machine-gun nest, being killed as he reached the parapet of the emplace-

ment. His courageous action in destroying in turn four enemy machine-gun nests prevented many casualties among his company and very materially aided in achieving the objective.

2513 ◆ LOMAN, BERGER HOLTON

Rank: Private (highest rank: Corporal)
Service: U.S. Army
Birthday: 24 August 1886
Place of Birth: Bergen, Norway
Date of Death: 9 May 1968
Cemetery: Arlington National Cemetery (37-4909) (MH)—Arlington, Virginia
Entered Service at: Chicago, Cook County, Illinois
Unit: Company H, 132d Infantry, 33d Division
Battle or Place of Action: near Consenvoye, France
Date of Action: 9 October 1918
G.O. Number, Date: 16, W.D. 22 January 1919
Citation: When his company had reached a point within 100 yards of its objective, to which it was advancing under terrific machine-gun fire, Pvt. Loman voluntarily and unaided made his way forward after all others had taken shelter from the direct fire of an enemy machine gun. He crawled to a flank position of the gun and, after killing or capturing the entire crew, turned the machine gun on the retreating enemy.

2514 ◆ *LUKE JR., FRANK

Rank: Second Lieutenant
Service: U.S. Army Air Service
Birthday: 19 May 1897
Place of Birth: Phoenix, Maricopa County, Arizona
Date of Death: 29 September 1918
Place of Death: near Murvaux, France
Cemetery: Meuse-Argonne Cemetery (A-26-13) (MH)—Romagne Meuse, France
Entered Service at: Phoenix, Maricopa County, Arizona
Unit: 27th Aero Squadron, 1st Pursuit Group, Air Service
Served as: Pilot of a SPAD
Battle or Place of Action: near Murvaux, France
Date of Action: 29 September 1918
G.O. Number, Date: 59, W.D. 3 May 1919
Date of Presentation: 29 May 1919
Place of Presentation: Phoenix, Arizona, presented by Brig. Gen. Howard R. Hickok to his Father
Citation: After having previously destroyed a number of enemy aircraft within 17 days, he voluntarily started on a patrol after German observation balloons. Though pursued by eight German planes which were protecting the enemy balloon line, he unhesitatingly attacked and shot down in flames three German balloons, being himself under heavy fire from ground batteries and the hostile planes. Severely wounded, he descended to within 50 meters of the ground, and flying at this low altitude near the town of Murvaux opened fire upon enemy troops, killing six and wounding as many more. Forced to make a landing and surrounded on all sides by the enemy, who called upon him to surrender, he drew his automatic pistol and defended himself gallantly until he fell dead from a wound in the chest.

2515 ◆ LYLE, ALEXANDER GORDON

Rank: Lieutenant Commander (highest rank: Vice Admiral)
Service: U.S. Navy
Birthday: 12 November 1889
Place of Birth: Gloucester, Essex County, Massachusetts
Date of Death: 15 July 1955
Cemetery: Arlington National Cemetery (2-1114-1)—Arlington, Virginia
Entered Service at: Massachusetts
Unit: Dental Corps serving with the 5th Regiment U.S.M.C.
Battle or Place of Action: the French Front, France
Date of Action: 23 April 1919
Date of Issue: 11 December 1919
Citation: For extraordinary heroism and devotion to duty while serving with the 5th Regiment, U.S. Marine Corps. Under heavy shellfire, 23 April 1918, on the French front, Lt. Comdr. Lyle rushed to the assistance of Cpl. Thomas Regan, who was seriously wounded, and administered such effective surgical aid while bombardment was still continuing as to save the life of Cpl. Regan.

2516 ◆ MacKENZIE, JOHN

Rank: Chief Boatswain's Mate
Service: U.S. Navy
Birthday: 7 July 1886
Place of Birth: Bridgeport, Fairfield County, Connecticut
Date of Death: 26 December 1933
Cemetery: Foresdale Cemetery (MH)—Holyoke, Massachusetts
Entered Service at: Massachusetts
Unit: U.S.S. *Remlik*
Battle or Place of Action: at Sea
Date of Action: 17 December 1917
G.O. Number, Date: 391, W.D. 1918
Citation: For extraordinary heroism while serving on board the U.S.S. *Remlik*, on the morning of 17 December 1917, when the *Remlik* encountered a heavy gale. During this gale, there was a heavy sea running. The depth charge box on the taffrail aft, containing a Sperry depth charge, was washed overboard, the depth charge itself falling inboard and remaining on deck. MacKenzie, on his own initiative, went aft and sat down on the depth charge, as it was impracticable to carry it to safety until the ship was headed up into the sea. In acting as he did, MacKenzie exposed his life and prevented a serious accident to the ship and probable loss of the ship and the entire crew.

2517 ◆ MADISON, JAMES JONAS

Rank: Lieutenant Commander
Service: U.S. Naval Reserve Force
Birthday: 20 May 1884
Place of Birth: Jersey City, Hudson County, New Jersey
Date of Death: 25 December 1922
Cemetery: Fairview Cemetery—Fairview, New Jersey
Entered Service at: Mississippi
Unit: U.S.S. *Ticonderoga*
Served as: Commanding Officer

Battle or Place of Action: at Sea
Date of Action: 4 October 1918
Citation: For exceptionally heroic service in a position of great responsibility as commanding officer of the U.S.S. *Ticonderoga*, when, on 4 October 1918, that vessel was attacked by an enemy submarine and was sunk after a prolonged and gallant resistance. The submarine opened fire at a range of 500 yards, the first shots taking effect on the bridge and forecastle, one of the two forward guns of the *Ticonderoga* being disabled by the second shot. The fire was returned and the fight continued for nearly two hours. Lt. Comdr. Madison was severely wounded early in the fight, but caused himself to be placed in a chair on the bridge and continued to direct the fire and to maneuver the ship. When the order was finally given to abandon the sinking ship, he became unconscious from loss of blood, but was lowered into a lifeboat and was saved, with 31 others, out of a total number of 236 on board.

2518 ◆ MALLON, GEORGE H.

Rank: Captain
Service: U.S. Army
Birthday: 15 June 1877
Place of Birth: Ogden, Riley County, Kansas
Date of Death: 2 August 1934
Place of Death: St. Cloud, Minnesota
Cemetery: Fort Snelling National Cemetery (DS-1-S) (MH)—St. Paul, Minnesota
Entered Service at: Minneapolis, Hennepin County, Minnesota
Unit: Company E, 132d Infantry Regiment, 33d Division
Served as: Company Commander
Battle or Place of Action: in the Bois-de-Forges, France
Date of Action: 26 September 1918
G.O. Number, Date: 16, W.D. 22 January 1919
Date of Presentation: 9 February 1919
Place of Presentation: Chaumont, France, presented by Gen. John J. Pershing
Citation: Becoming separated from the balance of his company because of fog, Capt. Mallon, with nine soldiers, pushed forward and attacked nine active and hostile machine guns, capturing all of them without the loss of a man. Continuing on through the woods, he led his men in attacking a battery of four 155-millimeter howitzers, which were in action, rushing the position and capturing the battery and its crews. In this encounter Capt. Mallon personally attacked one of the enemy with his fists. Later, when the party came upon two more machine guns, this officer sent men to the flanks while he rushed forward directly in the face of the fire and silenced the guns, being the first one of the party to reach the nest. The exceptional gallantry and determination displayed by Capt. Mallon resulted in the capture of 100 prisoners, 11 machine guns, four 155-millimeter howitzers, and one antiaircraft gun.

2519 ◆ MANNING, SIDNEY E.

Rank: Corporal
Service: U.S. Army
Birthday: 17 July 1892

Place of Birth: Butler County, Alabama
Date of Death: 15 December 1960
Cemetery: Little Escombia Cemetery (MH)—Flomaton, Alabama
Entered Service at: Flomaton, Escambia County, Alabama
Unit: Company G, 167th Infantry, 42d Division
Battle or Place of Action: near Breuvannes, France
Date of Action: 28 July 1918
G.O. Number, Date: 44, W.D. 2 April 1919
Citation: When his platoon commander and platoon sergeant had both become casualties soon after the beginning of an assault on strongly fortified heights overlooking the Ourcq River, Cpl. Manning took command of his platoon, which was near the center of the attacking line. Though himself severely wounded he led forward the 35 men remaining in the platoon and finally succeeded in gaining a foothold on the enemy's position, during which time he had received more wounds and all but seven of his men had fallen. Directing the consolidation of the position, he held off a large body of the enemy only 50 yards away by fire from his automatic rifle. He declined to take cover until his line had been entirely consolidated with the line of the platoon on the front when he dragged himself to shelter, suffering from nine wounds in all parts of the body.

2520 ◆ McGUNIGAL, PATRICK

Rank: Shipfitter First Class (highest rank: Carpenter)
Service: U.S. Navy
Birthday: 30 May 1876
Place of Birth: Hubbard, Trumbull County, Ohio
Date of Death: 19 January 1936
Cemetery: Arlington National Cemetery (6-8674) (MH)—Arlington, Virginia
Entered Service at: Ohio
Unit: U.S.S. *Huntington*
Battle or Place of Action: at Sea
Date of Action: 17 September 1917
G.O. Number, Date: 341, W.D. 7 November 1917
Citation: For extraordinary heroism while attached to the U.S.S. *Huntington*. On the morning of 17 September 1917, while the U.S.S. *Huntington* was passing through the war zone, a kite balloon was sent up with Lt. (j.g.) H.W. Hoyt, U.S. Navy, as observer. When the balloon was about 400 feet in the air, the temperature suddenly dropped, causing the balloon to descend about 200 feet, when it was struck by a squall. The balloon was hauled to the ship's side, but the basket trailed in the water and the pilot was submerged. McGunigal, with great daring, climbed down the side of the ship, jumped to the ropes leading to the basket, and cleared the tangle enough to get the pilot out of them. He then helped the pilot to get clear, put a bowline around him, and enabled him to be hauled to the deck. A bowline was lowered to McGunigal and he was taken safely aboard.

2521 ◆ McMURTRY, GEORGE G.

Rank: Captain (highest rank: Major)
Service: U.S. Army
Birthday: 6 November 1876

Place of Birth: Pittsburgh, Allegheny County, Pennsylvania
Date of Death: 22 November 1958
Place of Death: New York, New York
Cemetery: Ledge Lawn Cemetery—Bar Harbor, Maine
Entered Service at: New York, New York
Unit: 308th Infantry, 77th Division
Battle or Place of Action: in the Argonne Forest, at Charlevaux, France
Date of Action: 2-8 October 1918
G.O. Number, Date: 118, W.D. 2 December 1918
Citation: Commanded a battalion which was cut off and surrounded by the enemy and although wounded in the knee by shrapnel on 4 October and suffering great pain, he continued throughout the entire period to encourage his officers and men with a resistless optimism that contributed largely toward preventing panic and disorder among the troops, who were without food, cut off from communication with our lines. On 4 October during a heavy barrage, he personally directed and supervised the moving of the wounded to shelter before himself seeking shelter. On 6 October he was again wounded in the shoulder by a German grenade, but continued personally to organize and direct the defense against the German attack on the position until the attack was defeated. He continued to direct and command his troops, refusing relief, and personally led his men out of the position after assistance arrived before permitting himself to be taken to the hospital on 8 October. During this period the successful defense of the position was due largely to his efforts.

2522 ◆ *MESTROVITCH, JAMES I.

Rank: Sergeant
Service: U.S. Army
Birthday: 22 May 1894
Place of Birth: Crna Cora, Yugoslavia
Date of Death: 4 November 1918
Place of Death: France
Cemetery: Cemetery near Sveti Jovan Church—Crna Gora, Yugoslavia
Entered Service at: Pittsburgh, Allegheny County, Pennsylvania
Unit: Company C, 111th Infantry, 28th Division
Battle or Place of Action: at Fismette, France
Date of Action: 10 August 1918
G.O. Number, Date: 20, W.D. 30 January 1919
Date of Issue: 1922
Citation: Seeing his company commander lying wounded 30 yards in front of the line after his company had withdrawn to a sheltered position behind a stone wall, Sgt. Mestrovitch voluntarily left cover and crawled through heavy machine-gun and shell fire to where the officer lay. He took the officer upon his back and crawled to a place of safety, where he administered first-aid treatment, his exceptional heroism saving the officer's life.

2523 ◆ MILES, LOUIS WARDLAW

Rank: Captain
Service: U.S. Army

Birthday: 23 March 1873
Place of Birth: Baltimore, Baltimore County, Maryland
Date of Death: 27 June 1944
Cemetery: Greenmount Cemetery—Baltimore, Maryland
Entered Service at: Princeton, Mercer County, New Jersey
Unit: 308th Infantry, 77th Division
Battle or Place of Action: near Revillon, France
Date of Action: 14 September 1918
G.O. Number, Date: 44, W.D. 2 April 1919
Citation: Volunteered to lead his company in a hazardous attack on a commanding trench position near the Aisne Canal, which other troops had previously attempted to take without success. His company immediately met with intense machine-gun fire, against which it had no artillery assistance, but Capt. Miles preceded the first wave and assisted in cutting a passage through the enemy's wire entanglements. In so doing he was wounded five times by machine-gun bullets, both legs and one arm being fractured, whereupon he ordered himself placed on a stretcher and had himself carried forward to the enemy trench in order that he might encourage and direct his company, which by this time had suffered numerous casualties. Under the inspiration of this officer's indomitable spirit his men held the hostile position and consolidated the front line after an action lasting two hours, at the conclusion of which Capt. Miles was carried to the aid station against his will.

2524 ◆ *MILLER, OSCAR F.

Rank: Major
Service: U.S. Army
Place of Birth: Franklin County, Arkansas
Date of Death: 30 September 1918
Place of Death: France
Cemetery: Meuse-Argonne Cemetery (F-10-36) (MH)—Romagne Meuse, France
Entered Service at: Los Angeles, Los Angeles County, California
Unit: 361st Infantry, 91st Division
Battle or Place of Action: near Gesnes, France
Date of Action: 28 September 1918
G.O. Number, Date: 16, W.D. 22 January 1919
Citation: After two days of intense physical and mental strain, during which Maj. Miller had led his battalion in the front line of the advance through the Argonne Forest, the enemy was met in a prepared position south of Gesnes. Though almost exhausted, he energetically reorganized his battalion and ordered an attack. Upon reaching open ground the advancing line began to waver in the face of machine-gun fire from the front and flanks and direct artillery fire. Personally leading his command group forward between his front-line companies, Maj. Miller inspired his men by his personal courage, and they again pressed on toward the hostile position. As this officer led the renewed attack he was shot in the right leg, but he nevertheless staggered forward at the head of his command. Soon afterwards he was again shot in the right arm, but he continued the charge, personally cheering his troops on through the heavy machine-gun fire. Just before the objective was reached he received a wound in the

abdomen, which forced him to the ground, but he continued to urge his men on, telling them to push on to the next ridge and leave him where he lay. He died from his wounds a few days later.

2525 ◆ MORELOCK, STERLING LEWIS

Rank: Private
Service: U.S. Army
Birthday: 5 June 1890
Place of Birth: Silver Run, Maryland
Date of Death: 1 September 1964
Cemetery: Arlington National Cemetery (35-1824) (MH)—Arlington, Virginia
Entered Service at: Oquawka, Henderson County, Illinois
Unit: Company M, 28th Infantry, 1st Division
Battle or Place of Action: near Exermont, France
Date of Action: 4 October 1918
G.O. Number, Date: 43, W.D. 23 October 1919
Citation: While his company was being held up by heavy enemy fire, Pvt. Morelock, with three other men who were acting as runners at company headquarters, voluntarily led them as a patrol in advance of his company's front line through intense rifle, artillery, and machine-gun fire and penetrated a woods which formed the German front line. Encountering a series of five hostile machine-gun nests, containing from one to five machine guns each, with his patrol he cleaned them all out, gained and held complete mastery of the situation until the arrival of his company commander with reinforcements, even though his entire party had become casualties. He rendered first aid to the injured and evacuated them by using stretcher bearers 10 German prisoners whom he had captured. Soon thereafter his company commander was wounded and while dressing his wound Pvt. Morelock was very seriously wounded in the hip, which forced his evacuation. His heroic action and devotion to duty were an inspiration to the entire regiment.

2526 ◆ NEIBAUR, THOMAS CROFT

Rank: Private (highest rank: Private First Class)
Service: U.S. Army
Birthday: 17 May 1898
Place of Birth: Sharon, Idaho
Date of Death: 23 December 1942
Cemetery: Sugar City Cemetery (MH)—Sugar City, Idaho
Entered Service at: Sugar City, Madison County, Idaho
Unit: Company M, 107th Infantry, 42d Division
Battle or Place of Action: near Landres-et-St. Georges, France
Date of Action: 16 October 1918
G.O. Number, Date: 118, W.D. 2 December 1919
Citation: On the afternoon of 16 October 1918, when the Cote-de-Chatillion had just been gained after bitter fighting and the summit of the strong bulwark in the *Kriemhilde Stellung* was being organized, Pvt. Neibaur was sent out on patrol with his automatic rifle squad to enfilade enemy machine-gun nests. As he gained the ridge, he set up his automatic rifle and was directly thereafter wounded in both

legs by fire from a hostile machine gun on his flank. The advance wave of the enemy troops, counterattacking, had about gained the ridge, and although practically cut off and surrounded, the remainder of his detachment being killed or wounded, this gallant soldier kept his automatic rifle in operation to such effect that by his own efforts and by fire from the skirmish line of his company, at least 100 yards in his rear, the attack was checked. The enemy wave being halted and lying prone, four of the enemy attacked Pvt. Neibaur at close quarters. These he killed. He then moved alone among the enemy lying on the ground about him, in the midst of the fire from his own lines, and by coolness and gallantry captured 11 prisoners at the point of his pistol and, although painfully wounded, brought them back to our lines. The counterattack in full force was arrested to a large extent by the single efforts of this soldier, whose heroic exploits took place against the skyline in full view of his entire battalion.

2527 ◆ O'NEILL, RICHARD WILLIAM

Rank: Sergeant (highest rank: First Lieutenant)
Service: U.S. Army
Birthday: 28 August 1898
Place of Birth: New York, New York
Date of Death: 9 April 1982
Place of Death: Hawthorne, New York
Cemetery: Gate of Heaven Cemetery—Hawthorne, New York
Entered Service at: New York, New York
Unit: Company D, 165th Infantry, 42d Division
Battle or Place of Action: on the Ourcq River, France
Date of Action: 30 July 1918
G.O. Number, Date: 30, W.D. 15 July 1921
Citation: In advance of an assaulting line, he attacked a detachment of about 25 of the enemy. In the ensuing hand-to-hand encounter he sustained pistol wounds, but heroically continued in the advance, during which he received additional wounds; but, with great physical effort, he remained in active command of his detachment. Being again wounded, he was forced by weakness and loss of blood to be evacuated, but insisted upon being taken first to the battalion commander in order to transmit to him valuable information relative to enemy positions and the disposition of our men.

2528 ◆ ORMSBEE JR., FRANCIS EDWARD

Rank: Chief Machinist's Mate (highest rank: Chief Aviation Pilot)
Service: U.S. Navy
Birthday: 30 April 1892
Place of Birth: Providence, Providence County, Rhode Island
Date of Death: 24 October 1936
Place of Death: Ardmore, Oklahoma
Cemetery: St. Francis Cemetery—Newport, Rhode Island
Entered Service at: Florida
Battle or Place of Action: Pensacola, Florida
Date of Action: 25 September 1918
G.O. Number, Date: 436, W.D. 1918

Citation: For extraordinary heroism while attached to the Naval Air Station, Pensacola, Fla., 25 September 1918. While flying with Ens. J.A. Jova, Ormsbee saw a plane go into a tailspin and crash about three-quarters of a mile to the right. Having landed nearby, Ormsbee lost no time in going overboard and made for the wreck, which was all under water except the two wing tips. He succeeded in partially extricating the gunner so that his head was out of the water, and held him in this position until the speedboat arrived. Ormsbee then made a number of desperate attempts to rescue the pilot, diving into the midst of the tangled wreckage although cut about the hands, but was too late to save his life.

2529 ◆ *OSBORNE, WEEDON EDWARD

Rank: Lieutenant (j.g.)
Service: U.S. Navy
Birthday: 13 November 1892
Place of Birth: Chicago, Cook County, Illinois
Date of Death: 6 June 1918
Place of Death: France
Cemetery: Aisne-Marne Cemetery (A-3-39) (MH)—Belleau Aisne, France
Entered Service at: Illinois
Unit: Dental Corps, attached to U.S. Marines, 6th Regiment
Battle or Place of Action: Bouresche, France
Date of Action: 6 June 1918
Citation: For extraordinary heroism while attached to the 6th Regiment, U.S. Marines, in actual conflict with the enemy and under fire during the advance on Bouresche, France, on 6 June 1918. In the hottest of the fighting when the marines made their famous advance on Bouresche at the southern edge of Belleau Wood, Lt. (j.g.) Osborne threw himself zealously into the work of rescuing the wounded. Extremely courageous in the performance of this perilous task, he was killed while carrying a wounded officer to a place of safety.

2530 ◆ *O'SHEA, THOMAS E.

Rank: Corporal
Service: U.S. Army
Birthday: 18 April 1895
Place of Birth: New York, New York
Date of Death: 29 September 1918
Place of Death: France
Cemetery: Somme Cemetery (B-16-14) (MH)—Bony Aisne, France
Entered Service at: Summit, Union County, New Jersey
Unit: 3d Platoon, Machine Gun Company, 107th Infantry, 27th Division
Battle or Place of Action: near Le Catelet, France
Date of Action: 29 September 1918
G.O. Number, Date: 20, W.D. 30 January 1919
Citation: Becoming separated from their platoon by a smoke barrage, Cpl. O'Shea, with two other soldiers, took cover in a shell hole well within the enemy's lines. Upon hearing a call for help from an American tank, which had become disabled 30 yards from them, the three soldiers left their shelter and started toward the tank under heavy fire

from German machine guns and trench mortars. In crossing the fire-swept area Cpl. O'Shea was mortally wounded and died of his wounds shortly afterwards.

2531 ◆ PARKER, SAMUEL IREDELL

Rank: Second Lieutenant
Service: U.S. Army
Birthday: 17 October 1891
Place of Birth: Monroe, Union County, North Carolina
Date of Death: 1 December 1975
Cemetery: Oakwood Cemetery (MH)—Concord, North Carolina
Entered Service at: Monroe, Union County, North Carolina
Unit: Company K, 28th Infantry, 1st Division
Served as: Platoon Leader
Battle or Place of Action: near Soissons, France
Date of Action: 18-19 July 1918
G.O. Number, Date: 1, W.D. 1937
Place of Presentation: The White House, presented by Pres. Franklin D. Roosevelt
Citation: For conspicuous gallantry and intrepidity above and beyond the call of duty. During the attack the 2d and 3d Battalions of the 28th Infantry were merged, and after several hours of severe fighting, successfully established a frontline position. In so doing, a gap was left between the right flank of the French 153d Division on their left and the left flank of the 28th Infantry, exposing the left flank to a terrific enfilade fire from several enemy machine guns located in a rock quarry on high ground. Second Lt. Parker, observing this serious situation, ordered his depleted platoon to follow him in an attack upon the strong point. Meeting a disorganized group of French Colonials wandering leaderlessly about, he persuaded them to join his platoon. This consolidated group followed 2d Lt. Parker through direct enemy rifle and machine-gun fire to the crest of the hill, and rushing forward, took the quarry by storm, capturing six machine guns and about 40 prisoners. The next day when the assault was continued, 2d Lt. Parker in command of the merged 2d and 3d Battalions was in support of the 1st Battalion. Although painfully wounded in the foot, he refused to be evacuated and continued to lead his command until the objective was reached. Seeing that the assault battalion was subjected to heavy enfilade fire due to a gap between it and the French on its left, 2d Lt. Parker led his battalion through this heavy fire up on the line to the left of the 1st Battalion and thereby closed the gap, remaining in command of his battalion until the newly established lines of the 28th Infantry were thoroughly consolidated. In supervising the consolidation of the new position, 2d Lt. Parker was compelled to crawl about on his hands and knees on account of his painful wound. His conspicuous gallantry and spirit of self-sacrifice were a source of great inspiration to the members of the entire command.

2532 ◆ PECK, ARCHIE A.

Rank: Private (highest rank: First Sergeant)
Service: U.S. Army

Birthday: 22 November 1894
Place of Birth: Tyrone, Schuyler County, New York
Date of Death: 15 September 1978
Place of Death: Jamestown, New York
Cemetery: Evergreen Cemetery (MH)—Sinclairville, New York
Entered Service at: Hornell, Steuben County, New York
Unit: Company A, 307th Infantry, 77th Division
Served as: Rifleman
Battle or Place of Action: in the Argonne Forest, France
Date of Action: 6 October 1918
G.O. Number, Date: 16, W.D. 22 January 1919
Date of Presentation: 9 February 1919
Place of Presentation: Chaumont, France, presented by Gen. John J. Pershing
Citation: While engaged with two other soldiers on patrol duty, he and his comrades were subjected to the direct fire of an enemy machine gun, at which time both his companions were wounded. Returning to his company, he obtained another soldier to accompany him to assist in bringing in the wounded men. His assistant was killed in the exploit, but he continued on, twice returning safely, bringing in both men, being under terrific machine-gun fire during the entire journey.

2533 ◆ *PERKINS, MICHAEL J.

Rank: Private First Class
Service: U.S. Army
Birthday: 1899
Place of Birth: Boston, Suffolk County, Massachusetts
Date of Death: 28 October 1918
Place of Death: France
Cemetery: New Calvary Cemetery (MH)—Mattapan, Massachusetts
Entered Service at: Boston, Suffolk County, Massachusetts
Unit: Company D, 101st Infantry, 26th Division
Battle or Place of Action: at Belieu Bois, France
Date of Action: 27 October 1918
G.O. Number, Date: 34, W.D. 7 March 1919
Citation: He, voluntarily and alone, crawled to a German "pill box" machine-gun emplacement, from which grenades were being thrown at his platoon. Awaiting his opportunity, when the door was again opened and another grenade thrown, he threw a bomb inside, bursting the door open, and then, drawing his trench knife, rushed into the emplacement. In a hand-to-hand struggle he killed or wounded several of the occupants and captured about 25 prisoners, at the same time silencing seven machine guns.

2534 ◆ PETTY, ORLANDO HENDERSON

Rank: Lieutenant
Service: U.S. Naval Reserve Forces
Birthday: 20 February 1874
Place of Birth: Harrison, Hamilton County, Ohio
Date of Death: 2 June 1932
Cemetery: St. Timothy's Church Yard Cemetery—Roxborough, Pennsylvania

Entered Service at: Pennsylvania
Unit: Medical Corps, attached to the 5th Regiment, U.S. Marines
Battle or Place of Action: Boise de Belleau, France
Date of Action: 11 June 1918
Citation: For extraordinary heroism while serving with 5th Regiment, U.S. Marines, in France during the attack in the Bois de Belleau, 11 June 1918. While under heavy fire of high-explosive and gas shells in the town of Lucy, where his dressing station was located, Lt. Petty attended to and evacuated the wounded under most trying conditions. Having been knocked to the ground by an exploding gas shell which tore his mask, Lt. Petty discarded the mask and courageously continued his work. His dressing station being hit and demolished, he personally helped carry Capt. Williams, wounded, through the shellfire to a place of safety.

2535 ◆ *PIKE, EMORY JENISON

Rank: Lieutenant Colonel
Service: U.S. Army
Birthday: 17 December 1876
Place of Birth: Columbus City, Louisa County, Iowa
Date of Death: 16 September 1918
Place of Death: France
Cemetery: Woodland Cemetery—Des Moines, Iowa
Entered Service at: Sigourney, Keokuk County, Iowa
Unit: Division Machine-gun Officer, 82d Division
Battle or Place of Action: near Vandieres, France
Date of Action: 15 September 1918
G.O. Number, Date: 16, W.D. 22 January 1919
Citation: Having gone forward to reconnoiter new machine-gun positions, Lt. Col. Pike offered his assistance in reorganizing advanced infantry units which had become disorganized during a heavy artillery shelling. He succeeded in locating only about 20 men, but these he advanced and when later joined by several infantry platoons rendered inestimable service in establishing outposts, encouraging all by his cheeriness, in spite of the extreme danger of the situation. When a shell had wounded one of the men in the outpost, Lt. Col. Pike immediately went to his aid and was severely wounded himself when another shell burst in the same place. While waiting to be brought to the rear, Lt. Col. Pike continued in command, still retaining his jovial manner of encouragement, directing the reorganization until the position could be held. The entire operation was carried on under terrific bombardment, and the example of courage and devotion to duty, as set by Lt. Col. Pike, established the highest standard of morale and confidence to all under his charge. The wounds he received were the cause of his death.

2536 ◆ POPE, THOMAS A.

Rank: Corporal
Service: U.S. Army
Birthday: 15 December 1894
Place of Birth: Chicago, Cook County, Illinois
Date of Death: 14 June 1989
Place of Death: Maywood, Illinois

Cemetery: Arlington National Cemetery (35-3157) (MH)—Arlington, Virginia
Entered Service at: Chicago, Cook County, Illinois
Unit: 1st Platoon, Company E, 131st Infantry, 33d Division
Battle or Place of Action: at Hamel, France
Date of Action: 4 July 1918
G.O. Number, Date: 44, W.D. 2 April 1919
Date of Presentation: 22 April 1919
Place of Presentation: Chaumont, France, presented by Gen. John J. Pershing
Citation: His company was advancing behind the tanks when it was halted by hostile machine-gun fire. Going forward alone, he rushed a machine-gun nest, killed several of the crew with his bayonet, and, standing astride his gun, held off the others until reinforcements arrived and captured them.

2537 ◆ *PRUITT, JOHN HENRY✤

Rank: Corporal
Service: U.S. Marine Corps
Birthday: 4 October 1896
Place of Birth: Fayetteville, Washington County, Arkansas
Date of Death: 4 October 1918
Place of Death: France
Cemetery: Arlington National Cemetery (18-2453) (MH)—Arlington, Virginia
Entered Service at: Phoenix, Maricopa County, Arizona
Unit: 78th Company, 6th Regiment, 2d Division
Battle or Place of Action: at Blanc Mont Ridge, France
Date of Action: 3 October 1918
G.O. Number, Date: 62, W.D. 10 May 1919
Citation: Army Medal of Honor Cpl. Pruitt singlehandedly attacked two machine guns, capturing them and killing two of the enemy. He then captured 40 prisoners in a dugout nearby. This gallant soldier was killed soon afterwards by shellfire while he was sniping at the enemy. **Navy Medal of Honor** For extraordinary gallantry and intrepidity above and beyond the call of duty while serving with the 78th Company, 6th Regiment, 2d Division, in action with the enemy at Blanc Mont Ridge, France, 3 October 1918. Cpl. Pruitt, singlehandedly attacked two machine guns, capturing them and killing two of the enemy. He then captured 40 prisoners in a dugout nearby. This gallant soldier was killed soon afterward by shellfire while he was sniping at the enemy.
Notes: ✤Double Awardee: received both the Army and Navy Medal of Honor for the same deed

2538 ◆ REGAN, PATRICK J.

Rank: Second Lieutenant
Service: U.S. Army
Birthday: 25 March 1882
Place of Birth: Middleboro, Plymouth County, Massachusetts
Date of Death: 30 October 1943
Cemetery: Mount Olivet Cemetery (MH)—Bloomfield, New Jersey
Entered Service at: Los Angeles, Los Angeles County, California

Unit: 115th Infantry, 29th Division
Battle or Place of Action: at the Bois-de-Consenvoye, France
Date of Action: 8 October 1918
G.O. Number, Date: 50, W.D. 12 April 1919
Citation: While leading his platoon against a strong enemy machine-gun nest which had held up the advance of two companies, 2d Lt. Regan divided his men into three groups, sending one group to either flank, and he himself attacking with an automatic rifle team from the front. Two of the team were killed outright, while 2d Lt. Regan and the third man were seriously wounded, the latter unable to advance. Although seriously wounded, 2d Lt. Regan dashed with empty pistol into the machine-gun nest, capturing 30 Austrian gunners and four machine guns. This gallant deed permitted the companies to advance, avoiding a terrific enemy fire. Despite his wounds, he continued to lead his platoon forward until ordered to the rear by his commanding officer.

2539 ◆ RICKENBACKER, EDWARD VERNON

Rank: First Lieutenant (highest rank: Captain)
Service: U.S. Army Air Service
Birthday: 8 October 1890
Place of Birth: Columbus, Franklin County, Ohio
Date of Death: 23 July 1973
Place of Death: Zurich, Switzerland
Cemetery: Greenlawn Cemetery—Columbus, Ohio
Entered Service at: Columbus, Franklin County, Ohio
Unit: 94th Aero Squadron, Air Service
Served as: Commanding Officer/Pilot of a SPAD
Battle or Place of Action: near Billy, France
Date of Action: 25 September 1918
G.O. Number, Date: 2, W.D. 23 January 1931
Date of Presentation: 6 November 1930
Place of Presentation: Bolling Field near Washington, D.C., presented by Pres. Herbert Hoover
Citation: For conspicuous gallantry and intrepidity above and beyond the call of duty in action against the enemy near Billy, France, 25 September 1918. While on a voluntary patrol over the lines, 1st Lt. Rickenbacker attacked seven enemy planes (five type Fokker, protecting two type Halberstadt). Disregarding the odds against him, he dived on them and shot down one of the Fokkers out of control. He then attacked one of the Halberstadts and sent it down also.

2540 ◆ ROBB, GEORGE SEANOR

Rank: First Lieutenant
Service: U.S. Army
Birthday: 18 May 1887
Place of Birth: Assaria, Saline County, Kansas
Date of Death: 14 May 1972
Place of Death: Topeka, Kansas
Cemetery: Gypsum Hill Cemetery—Salina, Kansas
Entered Service at: Salina, Saline County, Kansas
Unit: 369th Infantry, 93d Division
Battle or Place of Action: near Sechault, France
Date of Action: 29-30 September 1918

G.O. Number, Date: 16, W.D. 22 January 1919
Citation: While leading his platoon in the assault, 1st Lt. Robb was severely wounded by machine-gun fire, but rather than go to the rear for proper treatment he remained with his platoon until ordered to the dressing station by his commanding officer. Returning within 45 minutes, he remained on duty throughout the entire night, inspecting his lines and establishing outposts. Early the next morning he was again wounded, once again displaying his remarkable devotion to duty by remaining in command of his platoon. Later the same day a bursting shell added two more wounds, the same shell killing his commanding officer and two officers of his company. He then assumed command of the company and organized its position in the trenches. Displaying wonderful courage and tenacity at the critical times, he was the only officer of his battalion who advanced beyond the town, and by clearing machine-gun and sniping posts contributed largely to the aid of his battalion in holding their objective. His example of bravery and fortitude and his eagerness to continue with his mission despite severe wounds set before the enlisted men of his command a most wonderful standard of morale and self-sacrifice.

2541 ◆ *ROBERTS, HAROLD W.

Rank: Corporal
Service: U.S. Army
Place of Birth: San Francisco, San Francisco County, California
Date of Death: 4 October 1918
Place of Death: France
Cemetery: Meuse-Argonne Cemetery (B-45-36) (MH)—Romagne Meuse, France
Entered Service at: San Francisco, San Francisco County, California
Unit: Company A, 344th Battalion, Tank Corps
Served as: Tank Driver
Battle or Place of Action: in the Montrebeau Woods, France
Date of Action: 4 October 1918
G.O. Number, Date: 16, W.D. 22 January 1919
Citation: Cpl. Roberts, a tank driver, was moving his tank into a clump of bushes to afford protection to another tank which had become disabled. The tank slid into a shell hole, 10 feet deep, filled with water, and was immediately submerged. Knowing that only one of the two men in the tank could escape, Cpl. Roberts said to the gunner, "Well only one of us can get out, and out you go," whereupon he pushed his companion through the back door of the tank and was himself drowned.

2542 ◆ ROBINSON, ROBERT GUY

Rank: Gunnery Sergeant (highest rank: First Lieutenant)
Service: U.S. Marine Corps
Birthday: 30 April 1896
Place of Birth: New York, New York
Date of Death: 5 October 1974
Cemetery: Arlington National Cemetery (46-390) (MH)—Arlington, Virginia

Entered Service at: Chicago, Cook County, Illinois
Unit: 1st Marine Aviation Force
Served as: Observer/Gunner
Battle or Place of Action: Pittham, Belgium
Date of Action: 14 October 1918
Citation: For extraordinary heroism as observer in the 1st Marine Aviation Force at the front in France. In company with planes from Squadron 218, Royal Air Force, conducting an air raid on 8 October 1918, G/Sgt. Robinson's plane was attacked by nine enemy scouts. In the fight which followed, he shot down one of the enemy planes. In a later air raid over Pittham, Belgium, on 14 October 1918, his plane and one other became separated from their formation on account of motor trouble and were attacked by 12 enemy scouts. Acting with conspicuous gallantry and intrepidity in the fight which ensued, G/Sgt. Robinson, after shooting down one of the enemy planes, was struck by a bullet which carried away most of his elbow. At the same time his gun jammed. While his pilot maneuvered for position, he cleared the jam with one hand and returned to the fight. Although his left arm was useless, he fought off the enemy scouts until he collapsed after receiving two more bullet wounds, one in the stomach and one in the thigh.

2543 ◆ SAMPLER, SAMUEL M.

Rank: Corporal
Service: U.S. Army
Birthday: 27 January 1895
Place of Birth: Decatur, Wise County, Texas
Date of Death: 19 November 1979
Cemetery: Memorial Gardens Cemetery—Fort Myers, Florida
Entered Service at: Altus, Jackson County, Oklahoma
Unit: Company H, 142d Infantry, 36th Division
Battle or Place of Action: near St. Etienne, France
Date of Action: 8 October 1918
G.O. Number, Date: 59, W.D. 3 May 1919
Citation: His company, having suffered severe casualties during an advance under machine-gun fire, was finally stopped. Cpl. Sampler detected the position of the enemy machine guns on an elevation. Armed with German hand grenades, which he had picked up, he left the line and rushed forward in the face of heavy fire until he was near the hostile nest, where he grenaded the position. His third grenade landed among the enemy, killing two, silencing the machine guns, and causing the surrender of 28 Germans, whom he sent to the rear as prisoners. As a result of his act the company was immediately enabled to resume the advance.

2544 ◆ SANDLIN, WILLIE

Rank: Sergeant
Service: U.S. Army
Birthday: 1 January 1890
Place of Birth: Jackson, Breathitt County, Kentucky
Date of Death: 29 May 1949
Cemetery: Zachary Taylor National Cemetery (E-10-A) (MH)—Louisville, Kentucky

Entered Service at: Hyden, Leslie County, Kentucky
Unit: Company A, 132d Infantry, 33d Division
Battle or Place of Action: at Bois-de-Forges, France
Date of Action: 26 September 1918
G.O. Number, Date: 16, W.D. 22 January 1919
Citation: He showed conspicuous gallantry in action by advancing alone directly on a machine-gun nest which was holding up the line with its fire. He killed the crew with a grenade and enabled the line to advance. Later in the day he attacked alone and put out of action two other machine-gun nests, setting a splendid example of bravery and coolness to his men.

2545 ◆ *SAWELSON, WILLIAM

Rank: Sergeant
Service: U.S. Army
Birthday: 5 August 1895
Place of Birth: Newark, Essex County, New Jersey
Date of Death: 26 October 1918
Place of Death: France
Cemetery: Meuse-Argonne Cemetery (C-9-33) (MH)—Romagne Meuse, France
Entered Service at: Harrison, Hudson County, New Jersey
Unit: Company M, 312th Infantry, 78th Division
Battle or Place of Action: at Grand-Pre, France
Date of Action: 26 October 1918
G.O. Number, Date: 16, W.D. 22 January 1919
Citation: Hearing a wounded man in a shell hole some distance away calling for water, Sgt. Sawelson, upon his own initiative, left shelter and crawled through heavy machine-gun fire to where the man lay, giving him what water he had in his canteen. He then went back to his own shell hole, obtained more water, and was returning to the wounded man when he was killed by a machine-gun bullet.

2546 ◆ SCHAFFNER, DWITE H.

Rank: First Lieutenant
Service: U.S. Army
Birthday: 5 November 1889
Place of Birth: Arroya, Pennsylvania
Date of Death: 22 November 1955
Cemetery: Rose Hill Cemetery—Akron, Ohio
Entered Service at: Falls Creek, Jefferson County, Pennsylvania
Unit: Company K, 306th Infantry, 77th Division
Served as: Company Commander
Battle or Place of Action: near St. Hubert's Pavillion, Boureuilles, France
Date of Action: 28 September 1918
G.O. Number, Date: 15, W.D. 5 April 1923
Citation: He led his men in an attack on St. Hubert's Pavillion through terrific enemy machine-gun, rifle, and artillery fire and drove the enemy from a strongly held entrenched position after hand-to-hand fighting. His bravery and contempt for danger inspired his men, enabling them to hold fast in the face of three determined enemy counterattacks. His company's position being exposed to enemy fire from both flanks, he made three efforts to locate an enemy machine gun which had caused heavy casualties. On his third reconnaissance he discovered the gun position and personally silenced the gun, killing or wounding the crew. The third counterattack made by the enemy was initiated by the appearance of a small detachment in advance of the enemy attacking wave. When almost within reach of the American front line, the enemy appeared behind them, attacking vigorously with pistols, rifles, and hand grenades, causing heavy casualties in the American platoon. First Lt. Schaffner mounted the parapet of the trench and used his pistol and grenades, killing a number of the enemy soldiers, finally reaching the enemy officer leading the attack forces, a captain, shooting and mortally wounding the latter with his pistol, and dragging the captured officer back to the company's trench, securing from him valuable information as to the enemy's strength and position. The information enabled 1st Lt. Schaffner to maintain for five hours the advanced position of his company despite the fact that it was surrounded on three sides by strong enemy forces. The undaunted bravery, gallant soldierly conduct, and leadership displayed by 1st Lt. Schaffner undoubtedly saved the survivors of the company from death or capture.

2547 ◆ SCHMIDT JR., OSCAR

Rank: Chief Gunner's Mate
Service: U.S. Navy
Birthday: 25 March 1896
Place of Birth: Philadelphia, Philadelphia County, Pennsylvania
Date of Death: 24 March 1973
Place of Death: Sommers Point, New Jersey
Cemetery: Arlington National Cemetery (11-116-LH) (MH)—Arlington, Virginia
Entered Service at: Pennsylvania
Unit: U.S.S. *Chestnut Hill*
Battle or Place of Action: at Sea
Date of Action: 9 October 1918
G.O. Number, Date: 450, W.D. 1919
Citation: For gallant conduct and extraordinary heroism while attached to the U.S.S. *Chestnut Hill*, on the occasion of the explosion and subsequent fire on board the U.S. submarine chaser *219*. Schmidt, seeing a man, whose legs were partly blown off, hanging on a line from the bow of the *219*, jumped overboard, swam to the sub chaser and carried him from the bow to the stern where a member of the *219*'s crew helped him land the man on the afterdeck of the submarine. Schmidt then endeavored to pass through the flames amidships to get another man who was seriously burned. This he was unable to do, but when the injured man fell overboard and drifted to the stern of the chaser Schmidt helped him aboard.

2548 ◆ SEIBERT, LLOYD MARTIN

Rank: Sergeant (highest rank: Chief Warrant Officer)
Service: U.S. Army
Birthday: 23 May 1889

Place of Birth: Caledonia, Kent County, Michigan
Date of Death: 15 October 1972
Cemetery: San Francisco National Cemetery (OS-10-128-31) (MH)—San Francisco, California
Entered Service at: Salinas, Monterey County, California
Unit: Company F, 364th Infantry, 91st Division
Battle or Place of Action: near Epinonville, France
Date of Action: 26 September 1918
G.O. Number, Date: 445, W.D. 1919
Citation: Suffering from illness, Sgt. Seibert remained with his platoon and lead his men with the highest courage and leadership under heavy shell and machine-gun fire. With two other soldiers he charged a machine-gun emplacement in advance of their company, he himself killing one of the enemy with a shotgun and capturing two others. In this encounter he was wounded, but he nevertheless continued in action, and when a withdrawal was ordered he returned with the last unit, assisting a wounded comrade. Later in the evening he volunteered and carried in wounded until he fainted from exhaustion.

2549 ◆ SIEGEL, JOHN OTTO

Rank: Boatswain's Mate Second Class
Service: U.S. Navy
Birthday: 21 April 1890
Place of Birth: Milwaukee, Milwaukee County, Wisconsin
Entered Service at: New Jersey
Unit: U.S.S. *Mohawk*
Date of Action: 1 November 1918
Citation: For extraordinary heroism while serving on board the *Mohawk* in performing a rescue mission aboard the schooner *Hjeltenaes* which was in flames on 1 November 1918. Going aboard the blazing vessel, Siegel rescued two men from the crew's quarters and went back the third time. Immediately after he had entered the crew's quarters, a steam pipe over the door burst, making it impossible for him to escape. Siegel was overcome with smoke and fell to the deck, being finally rescued by some of the crew of the *Mohawk* who carried him out and rendered first aid.

2550 ◆ *SKINKER, ALEXANDER RIVES

Rank: Captain
Service: U.S. Army
Birthday: 13 October 1883
Place of Birth: St. Louis, St. Louis County, Missouri
Date of Death: 26 September 1918
Place of Death: Cheppy, France
Cemetery: Bellafontaine Cemetery—St. Louis, Missouri
Entered Service at: St. Louis, St. Louis County, Missouri
Unit: Company I, 138th Infantry, 35th Division
Served as: Company Commander
Battle or Place of Action: at Cheppy, France
Date of Action: 26 September 1918
G.O. Number, Date: 13, W.D. 18 January 1919
Citation: Unwilling to sacrifice his men when his company was held up by terrific machine-gun fire from iron pill boxes in the Hindenburg Line, Capt. Skinker personally led an auto-

matic rifleman and a carrier in an attack on the machine guns. The carrier was killed instantly, but Capt. Skinker seized the ammunition and continued through an opening in the barbed wire, feeding the automatic rifle until he too, was killed.

2551 ◆ SLACK, CLAYTON KIRK

Rank: Private
Service: U.S. Army
Birthday: 23 February 1896
Place of Birth: Plover, Portage County, Wisconsin
Date of Death: 1 March 1976
Cemetery: Arlington National Cemetery (34-59) (MH)—Arlington, Virginia
Entered Service at: Madison, Dane County, Wisconsin
Unit: Company D, 124th Machine Gun Battalion, 33d Division
Battle or Place of Action: near Consenvoye, France
Date of Action: 8 October 1918
G.O. Number, Date: 16, W.D. 22 January 1919
Citation: Observing German soldiers under cover 50 yards away on the left flank, Pvt. Slack, upon his own initiative, rushed them with his rifle and, singlehandedly, captured 10 prisoners and two heavy-type machine guns, thus saving his company and neighboring organizations from heavy casualties.

2552 ◆ *SMITH, FRED E.

Rank: Lieutenant Colonel
Service: U.S. Army
Birthday: 29 March 1873
Place of Birth: Rockford, Winnebago County, Illinois
Date of Death: 29 September 1918
Place of Death: France
Cemetery: Meuse-Argonne Cemetery (A-7-18) (MH)—Romagne Meuse, France
Entered Service at: Bartlett, North Dakota
Unit: 308th Infantry, 77th Division
Battle or Place of Action: near Binarville, France
Date of Action: 29 September 1918
G.O. Number, Date: 49, W.D. 25 November 1922
Citation: When communication from the forward regimental post of command to the battalion leading the advance had been interrupted temporarily by the infiltration of small parties of the enemy armed with machine guns, Lt. Col. Smith personally led a party of two other officers and 10 soldiers, and went forward to reestablish runner posts and carry ammunition to the front line. The guide became confused and the party strayed to the left flank beyond the outposts of supporting troops, suddenly coming under fire from a group of enemy machine guns only 50 yards away. Shouting to the other members of his party to take cover, this officer, in disregard of his danger, drew his pistol and opened fire on the German gun crew. About this time he fell, severely wounded in the side, but regaining his footing, he continued to fire on the enemy until most of the men in his party were out of danger. Refusing first-aid treatment, he then made his way in plain view of the enemy to a hand grenade dump and returned under continued heavy machine-gun fire for the pur-

pose of making another attack on enemy emplacements. As he was attempting to ascertain the exact location of the nearest nest, he again fell, mortally wounded.

2553 ◆ *STOCKHAM, FRED WILLIAM

Rank: Gunnery Sergeant
Service: U.S. Marine Corps
Birthday: 16 March 1881
Place of Birth: Detroit, Wayne County, Michigan
Date of Death: 22 June 1918
Place of Death: France
Cemetery: Hollywood Cemetery (MH)—Union, New Jersey
Entered Service at: New York, New York
Unit: 96th Company, 2d Battalion, 6th Regiment, 4th Brigade, 2d Division
Battle or Place of Action: in Bois-de-Belleau, France
Date of Action: 13-14 June 1918
G.O. Number, Date: W.D. 15 July 1939
Date of Presentation: 21 December 1939
Place of Presentation: Smithsonian Institute, Washington, D.C., later presented to American Legion Post named in his honor in St. Louis, Mo
Citation: **Army Medal of Honor** During an intense enemy bombardment with high-explosive and gas shells which wounded or killed many members of the company, G/Sgt. Stockham, upon noticing that the gas mask of a wounded comrade was shot away, without hesitation, removed his own gas mask and insisted upon giving it to the wounded man, well knowing that the effects of the gas would be fatal to himself. He continued with undaunted courage and valor to direct and assist in the evacuation of the wounded, until he himself collapsed from the effects of gas, dying as a result thereof a few days later. His courageous conduct undoubtedly saved the lives of many of his wounded comrades, and his conspicuous gallantry and spirit of self-sacrifice were a source of great inspiration to all who served with him.
Notes: This marine received only the Army Medal of Honor, whereas five other Marines in the 2d Division who received the Medal received both the Army and Navy Medal of Honor

2554 ◆ *STOWERS, FREDDIE

Rank: Corporal
Service: U.S. Army
Birthday: 1896
Place of Birth: Sandy Springs, Anderson County, South Carolina
Date of Death: 28 September 1918
Place of Death: Champagne Marne Sector, France
Cemetery: A.B.M.C. Meuse-Argonne Cemetery—Meuse, France
Entered Service at: Anderson County, South Carolina
Unit: Company C, 371st Infantry Regiment, 93d Division
Served as: Squad Leader
Battle or Place of Action: Hill 188, Champagne Marne Sector, France

Date of Action: 28 September 1918
Date of Presentation: 24 April 1991
Place of Presentation: The White House, presented by Pres. George Bush to his sisters
Citation: Cpl. Freddie Stowers distinguished himself by exceptional heroism on 28 September 1918 while serving as a squad leader in Company C, 371st Infantry Regiment, 93d Infantry Division. His company was the lead company during the attack on Hill 188, Champagne Marne Sector, France, during World War I. A few minutes after the attack began, the enemy ceased firing and began climbing up onto the parapets of the trenches, holding up their arms as if wishing to surrender. The enemy's actions caused the American forces to cease fire and to come out into the open. As the company started forward and when within about 100 meters of the trench line, the enemy jumped back into their trenches and greeted Cpl. Stowers' company with interlocking bands of machine-gun fire and mortar fire causing well over fifty percent casualties. Faced with incredible enemy resistance, Cpl. Stowers took charge, setting such a courageous example of personal bravery and leadership that he inspired his men to follow him in the attack. With extraordinary heroism and complete disregard of personal danger under devastating fire, he crawled forward, leading his squad toward an enemy machine-gun nest which was causing heavy casualties to his company. After fierce fighting, the machine-gun position was destroyed and the enemy soldiers were killed. Displaying great courage and intrepidity Cpl. Stowers continued to press the attack against a determined enemy. While crawling forward and urging his men to continue the attack on a second trench line, he was gravely wounded by machine-gun fire. Although Cpl. Stowers was mortally wounded, he pressed forward, urging on the members of his squad, until he died. Inspired by the heroism and display of bravery of Cpl. Stowers, his company continued the attack against incredible odds, contributing to the capture of Hill 188 and causing heavy enemy casualties. Cpl. Stowers' conspicuous gallantry, extraordinary heroism, and supreme devotion to his men were well above and beyond the call of duty, follow the finest traditions of military service, and reflect the utmost credit on him and the United States Army.

2555 ◆ SULLIVAN, DANIEL AUGUSTUS JOSEPH

Rank: Ensign (highest rank: lieutenant Commander)
Service: U.S. Naval Reserve Force
Birthday: 31 July 1884
Place of Birth: Charleston, Charleston County, South Carolina
Date of Death: 27 January 1941
Cemetery: Arlington National Cemetery (8-5327-A)—Arlington, Virginia
Entered Service at: South Carolina
Unit: U.S.S. *Cristabel*
Battle or Place of Action: at Sea
Date of Action: 21 May 1918
Citation: For extraordinary heroism as an officer of the U.S.S. *Christabel* in conflict with an enemy submarine on 21

May 1918. As a result of the explosion of a depth bomb dropped near the submarine, the *Christabel* was so badly shaken that a number of depth charges which had been set for firing were thrown about the deck and there was imminent danger that they would explode. Ens. Sullivan immediately fell on the depth charges and succeeded in securing them, thus saving the ship from disaster, which would inevitably have caused great loss of life.

2556 ◆ *TALBOT, RALPH

Rank: Second Lieutenant
Service: U.S. Marine Corps
Birthday: 6 January 1897
Place of Birth: South Weymouth, Norfolk County, Massachusetts
Date of Death: 25 October 1918
Cemetery: Mount Wollaston Cemetery (MH)—Quincy, Massachusetts
Entered Service at: Connecticut
Unit: Squadron C, 1st Marine Aviation Force
Battle or Place of Action: France
Date of Action: 8, 14 October 1918
Citation: For exceptionally meritorious service and extraordinary heroism while attached to Squadron C, 1st Marine Aviation Force, in France. Second Lt. Talbot participated in numerous air raids into enemy territory. On 8 October 1918, while on such a raid, he was attacked by nine enemy scouts, and in the fight that followed shot down an enemy plane. Also, on 14 October 1918, while on a raid over Pittham, Belgium, 2d Lt. Talbot and another plane became detached from the formation on account of motor trouble and were attacked by 12 enemy scouts. During the severe fight that followed, his plane shot down one of the enemy scouts. His observer was shot through the elbow and his gun jammed. Second Lt. Talbot maneuvered to gain time for his observer to clear the jam with one hand, and then returned to the fight. The observer fought until shot twice, once in the stomach and once in the hip, and then collapsed. Second Lt. Talbot attacked the nearest enemy scout with his front guns and shot him down. With his observer unconscious and his motor failing, he dived to escape the balance of the enemy and crossed the German trenches at an altitude of 50 feet, landing at the nearest hospital to leave his observer, and then returning to his aerodrome.

2557 ◆ TALLEY, EDWARD R.

Rank: Sergeant
Service: U.S. Army
Birthday: 6 September 1890
Place of Birth: Russellville, Hamblen County, Tennessee
Date of Death: 14 December 1950
Cemetery: Bent Creek Cemetery—Whitesburg, Tennessee
Entered Service at: Russellville, Hamblen County, Tennessee
Unit: Company L, 117th Infantry, 30th Division
Battle or Place of Action: near Ponchaux, France
Date of Action: 7 October 1918

G.O. Number, Date: 50, W.D. 12 April 1919
Citation: Undeterred by seeing several comrades killed in attempting to put a hostile machine-gun nest out of action, Sgt. Talley attacked the position singlehandedly. Armed only with a rifle, he rushed the nest in the face of intense enemy fire, killed or wounded at least six of the crew, and silenced the gun. When the enemy attempted to bring forward another gun and ammunition he drove them back by effective fire from his rifle.

2558 ◆ THOMPSON, JOSEPH HENRY

Rank: Major (highest rank: Colonel)
Service: U.S. Army
Birthday: 26 September 1871
Place of Birth: Kilkeel, County Down, Ireland
Date of Death: 1 February 1928
Cemetery: Beaver Falls Cemetery & Memorial Park (MH)—Beaver Falls, Pennsylvania
Entered Service at: Beaver Falls, Beaver County, Pennsylvania
Unit: 110th Infantry, 28th Division
Battle or Place of Action: near Apremont, France
Date of Action: 1 October 1918
G.O. Number, Date: 21, W.D. 5 October 1925
Citation: Counterattacked by two regiments of the enemy, Maj. Thompson encouraged his battalion in the front line by constantly braving the hazardous fire of machine guns and artillery. His courage was mainly responsible for the heavy repulse of the enemy. Later in the action, when the advance of his assaulting companies was held up by fire from a hostile machine-gun nest and all but one of the six assaulting tanks were disabled, Maj. Thompson, with great gallantry and coolness, rushed forward on foot three separate times in advance of the assaulting line, under heavy machine-gun and antitank-gun fire, and led the one remaining tank to within a few yards of the enemy machine-gun nest, which it succeeded in reducing, thereby making it possible for the infantry to advance.

2559 ◆ TURNER, HAROLD LEO

Rank: Corporal (highest rank: Second Lieutenant)
Service: U.S. Army
Birthday: 5 May 1898
Place of Birth: Aurora, Lawrence County, Missouri
Date of Death: 12 March 1933
Place of Death: Caddo Lake, Texas
Cemetery: Little Cemetery (MH)—Little, Oklahoma
Entered Service at: Seminole, Seminole County, Oklahoma
Unit: Company F, 142d Infantry, 36th Division
Battle or Place of Action: near St. Etienne, France
Date of Action: 8 October 1918
G.O. Number, Date: 59, W.D. 3 May 1919
Date of Presentation: 2 May 1919
Place of Presentation: Cheney, France, presented by Gen. William R. Smith
Citation: After his platoon had started the attack, Cpl. Turner assisted in organizing a platoon consisting of the battalion scouts, runners, and a detachment of Signal Corps. As

second in command of this platoon he fearlessly led them forward through heavy enemy fire, continually encouraging the men. Later he encountered deadly machine-gun fire which reduced the strength of his command to but four men, and these were obliged to take shelter. The enemy machine-gun emplacement, 25 yards distant, kept up a continual fire from four machine guns. After the fire had shifted momentarily, Cpl. Turner rushed forward with fixed bayonet and charged the position alone, capturing the strong point with a complement of 50 Germans and four machine guns. His remarkable display of courage and fearlessness was instrumental in destroying the strong point, the fire from which had blocked the advance of his company.

2560 ◆ *TURNER, WILLIAM BRADFORD

Rank: First Lieutenant
Service: U.S. Army
Birthday: 1892
Place of Birth: Dorchester, Suffolk County, Massachusetts
Date of Death: 27 September 1918
Place of Death: Near Ronssoy, France
Cemetery: Somme Cemetery (B-13-1) (MH)—Bony, Aisne, France
Entered Service at: Garden City, Nassau County, New York
Unit: Company M, 105th Infantry, 27th Division
Battle or Place of Action: near Ronssoy, France
Date of Action: 27 September 1918
G.O. Number, Date: 81, W.D. 26 June 1919
Citation: He led a small group of men to the attack, under terrific artillery and machine-gun fire, after they had become separated from the rest of the company in the darkness. Singlehandedly he rushed an enemy machine gun which had suddenly opened fire on his group and killed the crew with his pistol. He then pressed forward to another machine-gun post 25 yards away and had killed one gunner himself by the time the remainder of his detachment arrived and put the gun out of action. With the utmost bravery he continued to lead his men over three lines of hostile trenches, cleaning up each one as they advanced, regardless of the fact that he had been wounded three times, and killed several of the enemy in hand-to-hand encounters. After his pistol ammunition was exhausted, this gallant officer seized the rifle of a dead soldier, bayoneted several members of a machine-gun crew, and shot the other. Upon reaching the fourth-line trench, which was his objective, 1st Lt. Turner captured it with the nine men remaining in his group and resisted a hostile counterattack until he was finally surrounded and killed.

2561 ◆ UPTON, FRANK MONROE

Rank: Quartermaster (highest rank: Ensign)
Service: U.S. Navy
Birthday: 29 April 1896
Place of Birth: Loveland, Larimer County, Colorado
Date of Death: 25 June 1962
Cemetery: Arlington National Cemetery (8-55-A) (MH)—Arlington, Virginia
Entered Service at: Colorado

Unit: U.S.S. *Stewart*
Battle or Place of Action: at Sea
Date of Action: 17 April 1918
G.O. Number, Date: 403, W.D. 1918
Citation: For extraordinary heroism following internal explosion of the *Florence H*, on 17 April 1918. The sea in the vicinity of wreckage was covered by a mass of boxes of smokeless powder, which were repeatedly exploding. Frank M. Upton, of the U.S.S. *Stewart*, plunged overboard to rescue a survivor who was surrounded by powder boxes and too exhausted to help himself. Fully realizing the danger from continual explosion of similar powder boxes in the vicinity, he risked his life to save the life of this man.

2562 ◆ VALENTE, MICHAEL

Rank: Private
Service: U.S. Army
Birthday: 5 February 1895
Place of Birth: Cassino, Italy
Date of Death: 10 January 1976
Place of Death: Long Beach, New York
Cemetery: Long Island National Cemetery (DSS-60-A) (MH)—Farmingdale, New York
Entered Service at: Ogdensburg, St. Lawrence County, New York
Unit: Company D, 107th Infantry, 27th Division
Battle or Place of Action: Hindenburg Line, east of Ronssoy, France
Date of Action: 29 September 1918
G.O. Number, Date: 16, W.D. 26 September 1919
Date of Presentation: 27 September 1929
Place of Presentation: The White House (lawn), presented by Pres. Herbert Hoover
Citation: For conspicuous gallantry and intrepidity above and beyond the call of duty in action with the enemy during the operations against the Hindenburg line, east of Ronssoy, France, 29 September 1918. Finding the advance of his organization held up by a withering enemy machine-gun fire, Pvt. Valente volunteered to go forward. With utter disregard of his own personal danger, accompanied by another soldier, Pvt. Valente rushed forward through an intense machine-gun fire directly upon the enemy nest, killing two and capturing five of the enemy and silencing the gun. Discovering another machine-gun nest close by which was pouring a deadly fire on the American forces, preventing their advance, Pvt. Valente and his companion charged upon this strong point, killing the gunner and putting this machine gun out of action. Without hesitation they jumped into the enemy's trench, killed two and captured 16 German soldiers. Pvt. Valente was later wounded and sent to the rear.

2563 ◆ VAN IERSEL, LUDOVICUS M.M.

True Name: Changed name to: Van Iersel, Louis M.M.
Rank: Sergeant
Service: U.S. Army
Birthday: 19 October 1893
Place of Birth: Dussen, Holland

Date of Death: 9 June 1987
Place of Death: Roseburg, Oregon
Cemetery: Arlington National Cemetery (42-1770) (MH)—Arlington, Virginia
Entered Service at: Glen Rock, Bergen County, New Jersey
Unit: Company M, 9th Infantry, 2d Division
Battle or Place of Action: at Mouzon, France
Date of Action: 9 November 1918
G.O. Number, Date: 34, W.D. 7 March 1919
Citation: While a member of a reconnaissance patrol, sent out at night to ascertain the condition of a damaged bridge, Sgt. Van Iersel volunteered to lead a party across the bridge in the face of heavy machine-gun and rifle fire from a range of only 75 yards. Crawling alone along the debris of the ruined bridge, he came upon a trap, which gave way and precipitated him into the water. In spite of the swift current he succeeded in swimming across the stream and found a lodging place among the timbers on the opposite bank. Disregarding the enemy fire, he made a careful investigation of the hostile position by which the bridge was defended and then returned to the other bank of the river, reporting this valuable information to the battalion commander.

2564 ◆ VILLEPIGUE, JOHN CANTEY

Rank: Corporal
Service: U.S. Army
Birthday: 29 March 1896
Place of Birth: Camden, Kershaw County, South Carolina
Date of Death: 18 April 1943
Cemetery: Quaker Cemetery—Camden, South Carolina
Entered Service at: Camden, Kershaw County, South Carolina
Unit: Company M, 118th Infantry, 30th Division
Battle or Place of Action: at Vaux-Andigny, France
Date of Action: 15 October 1918
G.O. Number, Date: 16, W.D. 22 January 1919
Citation: Having been sent out with two other soldiers to scout through the village of Vaux-Andigny, he met with strong resistance from enemy machine-gun fire, which killed one of his men and wounded the other. Continuing his advance without aid 500 yards in advance of his platoon and in the face of machine-gun and artillery fire, he encountered four of the enemy in a dugout, whom he attacked and killed with a hand grenade. Crawling forward to a point 150 yards in advance of his first encounter, he rushed a machine-gun nest, killing four and capturing six of the enemy and taking two light machine guns. After being joined by his platoon he was severely wounded in the arm.

2565 ◆ WAALER, REIDAR

Rank: Sergeant
Service: U.S. Army
Birthday: 12 February 1894
Place of Birth: Christiana, now Oslo, Norway
Date of Death: 5 February 1979
Cemetery: Forest Hills Memorial Park—Palm City, Florida

Entered Service at: New York, New York
Unit: Company A, 105th Machine-Gun Battalion, 27th Division
Battle or Place of Action: near Ronssoy, France
Date of Action: 27 September 1918
G.O. Number, Date: 20, W.D. 30 January 1919
Date of Presentation: 4 February 1919
Place of Presentation: Chaumont, France, presented by Gen. John J. Pershing
Citation: In the face of heavy artillery and machine-gun fire, he crawled forward to a burning British tank, in which some of the crew were imprisoned, and succeeded in rescuing two men. Although the tank was then burning fiercely and contained ammunition which was likely to explode at any time, this soldier immediately returned to the tank and, entering it, made a search for the other occupants, remaining until he satisfied himself that there were no more living men in the tank.

2566 ◆ WARD, CALVIN JOHN

Rank: Private (highest rank: Private First Class)
Service: U.S. Army
Birthday: 30 October 1899
Place of Birth: Green County, Tennessee
Date of Death: 15 December 1967
Place of Death: Morristown, Tennessee
Cemetery: Glenwood Cemetery—Bristol, Tennessee
Entered Service at: Morristown, Hamblen County, Tennessee
Unit: Company D, 117th Infantry, 30th Division
Battle or Place of Action: near Estrees, France
Date of Action: 8 October 1918
G.O. Number, Date: 16, W.D. 22 January 1919
Citation: During an advance, Pvt. Ward's company was held up by a machine gun, which was enfilading the line. Accompanied by a noncommissioned officer, he advanced against this post and succeeded in reducing the nest by killing three and capturing seven of the enemy and their guns.

2567 ◆ WEST, CHESTER HOWARD

Rank: First Sergeant
Service: U.S. Army
Birthday: 3 January 1888
Place of Birth: Fort Collins, Larimer County, Colorado
Date of Death: 20 May 1935
Place of Death: Gallipolis, Ohio
Cemetery: Pine Grove Cemetery—Pliny, West Virginia
Entered Service at: Los Banos, Merced County, California
Unit: Company D, 363d Infantry, 91st Division
Battle or Place of Action: near Bois-de-Cheppy, France
Date of Action: 26 September 1918
G.O. Number, Date: 34, W.D. 7 March 1919
Citation: While making his way through a thick fog with his automatic rifle section, his advance was halted by direct and unusual machine-gun fire from two guns. Without aid, he at once dashed through the fire and, attacking the nest, killed two of the gunners, one of whom was an officer. This prompt

and decisive hand-to-hand encounter on his part enabled his company to advance farther without the loss of a man.

2568 ◆ WHITTLESEY, CHARLES WHITE

Rank: Major (highest rank: Lieutenant Colonel
Service: U.S. Army
Birthday: 20 January 1884
Place of Birth: Florence, Florence County, Wisconsin
Date of Death: 27 November 1921
Place of Death: at sea between New York & Cuba
Cemetery: Atlantic Ocean (lost at sea)
Entered Service at: Pittsfield, Berkshire County, Massachusetts
Unit: 1st Battalion, 308th Infantry, 77th Division
Served as: Battalion Commander
Battle or Place of Action: northeast of Binarville, in the Argonne Forest, France
Date of Action: 2-7 October 1918
G.O. Number, Date: 118, W.D. 2 December 1918
Date of Presentation: 25 December 1918
Place of Presentation: Boston Common, Massachusetts
Citation: Although cut off for five days from the remainder of his division, Maj. Whittlesey maintained his position, which he had reached under orders received for an advance, and held his command, consisting originally of 46 officers and men of the 308th Infantry and of Company K, of the 307th Infantry, together in the face of superior numbers of the enemy during the five days. Maj. Whittlesey and his command were cut off, and no rations or other supplies reached him, in spite of determined efforts which were made by his division. On the fourth day Maj. Whittlesey received from the enemy a written proposition to surrender, which he treated with contempt, although he was at the time out of rations and had suffered a loss of about 50 percent in killed and wounded of his command and was surrounded by the enemy.

2569 ◆ *WICKERSHAM, J. HUNTER

Rank: Second Lieutenant
Service: U.S. Army
Place of Birth: New York, New York
Date of Death: 12 September 1918
Place of Death: France
Cemetery: St. Mihiel Cemetery (B-19-12) (MH)—Thiaucourt, France
Entered Service at: Denver, Denver County, Colorado
Unit: 353d Infantry, 89th Division
Battle or Place of Action: near Limey, France
Date of Action: 12 September 1918
G.O. Number, Date: 16, W.D. 22 January 1919
Citation: Advancing with his platoon during the St. Mihiel offensive, he was severely wounded in four places by the bursting of a high-explosive shell. Before receiving any aid for himself, he dressed the wounds of his orderly, who was wounded at the same time. He then ordered and accompanied the further advance of his platoon, although weakened by the loss of blood. His right hand and arm being disabled by wounds, he continued to fire his revolver with his left

hand until, exhausted by loss of blood, he fell and died from his wounds before aid could be administered.

2570 ◆ *WOLD, NELS T.

Rank: Private
Service: U.S. Army
Birthday: 24 December 1895
Place of Birth: Winger, Polk County, Minnesota
Date of Death: 26 September 1918
Place of Death: France
Cemetery: Elim Cemetery (MH)—Winger, Minnesota
Entered Service at: Minnewaukan, Benson County, North Dakota
Unit: Company I, 138th Infantry, 35th Division
Battle or Place of Action: near Cheppy, France
Date of Action: 26 September 1918
G.O. Number, Date: 16, W.D. 22 January 1919
Citation: He rendered most gallant service in aiding the advance of his company, which had been held up by machine-gun nests, advancing, with one other soldier, and silencing the guns, bringing with him, upon his return, 11 prisoners. Later the same day he jumped from a trench and rescued a comrade who was about to be shot by a German officer, killing the officer during the exploit. His actions were entirely voluntary, and it was while attempting to rush a fifth machine-gun nest that he was killed. The advance of his company was mainly due to his great courage and devotion to duty.

2571 ◆ WOODFILL, SAMUEL

Rank: First Lieutenant (highest rank: Major)
Service: U.S. Army
Birthday: 6 January 1883
Place of Birth: Jefferson County, Indiana
Date of Death: 10 August 1951
Cemetery: Arlington National Cemetery (34-642-A) (MH)—Arlington, Virginia
Entered Service at: Bryantsburg, Indiana
Unit: Company M, 60th Infantry, 5th Division
Served as: Company Commander
Battle or Place of Action: at Cunel, France
Date of Action: 12 October 1918
G.O. Number, Date: 16, W.D. 22 January 1919
Citation: While he was leading his company against the enemy, his line came under heavy machine-gun fire, which threatened to hold up the advance. Followed by two soldiers at 25 yards, this officer went out ahead of his first line toward a machine-gun nest and worked his way around its flank, leaving the two soldiers in front. When he got within 10 yards of the gun it ceased firing, and four of the enemy appeared, three of whom were shot by 1st Lt. Woodfill. The fourth, an officer, rushed at 1st Lt. Woodfill, who attempted to club the officer with his rifle. After a hand-to-hand struggle, 1st Lt. Woodfill killed the officer with his pistol. His company thereupon continued to advance, until shortly afterwards another machine-gun nest was encountered. Calling on his men to follow, 1st Lt. Woodfill rushed ahead of his line in the face of

heavy fire from the nest, and when several of the enemy appeared above the nest, he shot them, capturing three other members of the crew and silencing the gun. A few minutes later this officer for a third time demonstrated conspicuous daring by charging another machine-gun position, killing five men in one machine-gun pit with his rifle. He then drew his revolver and started to jump into the pit, when two other gunners only a few yards away turned their guns on him. Failing to kill them with his revolver, he grabbed a pick lying nearby and killed both of them. Inspired by the exceptional courage displayed by this officer, his men pressed on to their objective under severe shell and machine-gun fire.

2572 ◆ YORK, ALVIN CULLIUM

Rank: Corporal (highest rank: Sergeant)
Service: U.S. Army
Birthday: 13 December 1887
Place of Birth: Fentress County, Tennessee

Date of Death: 2 September 1964
Place of Death: Nashville, Tennessee
Cemetery: Wolf River Cemetery—Jamestown, Tennessee
Entered Service at: Pall Mall, Fentress County, Tennessee
Unit: Company G, 2d Battalion, 328th Infantry, 82d Division
Served as: Squad Leader
Battle or Place of Action: near Chatel-Chehery, France
Date of Action: 8 October 1918
G.O. Number, Date: 59, W.D. 3 May 1919
Place of Presentation: France, presented by Maj. Gen. Duncan, commanding general 82nd Division
Citation: After his platoon had suffered heavy casualties and three other noncommissioned officers had become casualties, Cpl. York assumed command. Fearlessly leading seven men, he charged with great daring a machine-gun nest which was pouring deadly and incessant fire upon his platoon. In his heroic feat the machine-gun nest was taken, together with four officers and 128 men and several guns.

HAITIAN CAMPAIGN
1919–1920

2573 ◆ BUTTON, WILLIAM ROBERT

Rank: Corporal
Service: U.S. Marine Corps
Birthday: 3 December 1895
Place of Birth: St. Louis, St. Louis County, Missouri
Date of Death: 15 April 1921
Place of Death: Cape Haitien, Haiti
Cemetery: Valhalla Cemetery—St. Louis, Missouri
Entered Service at: St. Louis, St. Louis County, Missouri
Unit: Gendarmerie d'Haiti
Battle or Place of Action: near Grande Riviere, Republic of Haiti
Date of Action: 31 October-1 November 1919
G.O. Number, Date: 536, 10 June 1920
Date of Presentation: 1 July 1920
Place of Presentation: Washington, D.C., presented by Gen. John A. Lejeune
Citation: For extraordinary heroism and conspicuous gallantry and intrepidity in actual conflict with the enemy near Grande Riviere, Republic of Haiti, on the night from 31 October to 1 November 1919, resulting in the death of Charlemagne Peralte, the supreme bandit chief in the Republic of Haiti, and the killing, capture, and dispersal of about 1,200 of his outlaw followers. Cpl. William R. Button not only distinguished himself by his excellent judgment and leadership but also unhesitatingly exposed himself to great personal danger when the slightest error would have forfeited not only his life but the lives of the detachments of Gendarmerie under his command. The successful termination of his mission will undoubtedly prove of untold value to the Republic of Haiti.

2574 ◆ HANNEKEN, HERMAN HENRY

Rank: Second Lieutenant (highest rank: Brigadier General)
Service: U.S. Marine Corps

Birthday: 23 June 1893
Place of Birth: St. Louis, St. Louis County, Missouri
Date of Death: 23 August 1986
Place of Death: Lanolla, California
Cemetery: Fort Rosecrans National Cemetery (C-1166-D)—San Diego, California
Entered Service at: St. Louis, St. Louis County, Missouri
Unit: Gendarmerie d'Haiti
Battle or Place of Action: near Grande Riviere, Republic of Haiti
Date of Action: 31 October-1 November 1919
G.O. Number, Date: 536, 10 June 1920
Date of Presentation: 1 July 1920
Place of Presentation: Washington, D.C., presented by Gen. John A. Lejeune
Citation: For extraordinary heroism and conspicuous gallantry and intrepidity in actual conflict with the enemy near Grande Riviere, Republic of Haiti, on the night from 31 October to 1 November 1919, resulting in the death of Charlemagne Peralte, the supreme bandit chief in the Republic of Haiti, and the killing, capture, and dispersal of about 1,200 of his outlaw followers. Second Lt. Hanneken not only distinguished himself by his excellent judgment and leadership but also unhesitatingly exposed himself to great personal danger when the slightest error would have forfeited not only his life but the lives of the detachments of Gendarmerie under his command. The successful termination of his mission will undoubtedly prove of untold value to the Republic of Haiti.

SECOND NICARAGUAN CAMPAIGN

2575 ◆ SCHILT, CHRISTIAN FRANKLIN

Rank: First Lieutenant (highest rank: General)
Service: U.S. Marine Corps
Birthday: 18 March 1895
Place of Birth: Richland County, Illinois
Date of Death: 8 January 1987
Place of Death: Norfolk, Virginia
Cemetery: Arlington National Cemetery (2E-151-2) (MH)—Arlington, Virginia
Entered Service at: Illinois
Unit: Observation Squadron 7-M
Battle or Place of Action: Quilali, Nicaragua
Date of Action: 6-8 January 1928
Citation: During the progress of an insurrection at Quilali, Nicaragua, 6, 7, and 8 January 1928, 1st Lt. Schilt, then a member of a Marine expedition which had suffered severe losses in killed and wounded, volunteered under almost impossible conditions to evacuate the wounded by air and to transport a relief commanding officer to assume charge of a very serious situation. First Lt. Schilt bravely undertook this dangerous and important task and, by taking off a total of ten times in the rough, rolling street of a partially burning village, under hostile infantry fire on each occasion, succeeded in accomplishing his mission, thereby actually saving three lives and bringing supplies and aid to others in desperate need.

2576 ◆ TRUESDELL, DONALD LEROY

True Name: Name Changed to: Truesdale, Donald Leroy
Rank: Corporal (highest rank: Chief Warrant Officer 2)
Service: U.S. Marine Corps
Birthday: 8 August 1906
Place of Birth: Lugoff, Kershaw County, South Carolina
Date of Death: 21 September 1993
Place of Death: Lugoff, South Carolina
Entered Service at: South Carolina
Battle or Place of Action: vicinity of Constancia, near Coco River, northern Nicaragua
Date of Action: 24 April 1932
Place of Presentation: Presented by Brig. Gen. Randolph C. Berkeley
Citation: Cpl. Truesdale was second in command of a Guardia Nacional Patrol in active operations against armed bandit forces in the vicinity of Constancia, near Coco River, northern Nicaragua, on 24 April 1932. While the patrol was in formation on the trail searching for a bandit group with which contact had just previously been made, a rifle grenade fell from its carrier and struck a rock, igniting the detonator. Several men close to the grenade at the time were in danger. Cpl. Truesdale, who was several yards away, could easily have sought cover and safety for himself. Knowing full well the grenade would explode within two or three seconds, he rushed for the grenade, grasped it in his right hand, and attempted to throw it away from the patrol. The grenade exploded in his hand, blowing it off and inflicting serious multiple wounds about his body. Cpl. Truesdale, in taking the full shock of the explosion himself, saved the members of the patrol from loss of life or serious injury.

INTERIM 1920–1940

2577 ◆ BADDERS, WILLIAM

Rank: Chief Machinist's Mate
Service: U.S. Navy
Birthday: 15 September 1900
Place of Birth: Harrisburg, Saline County, Illinois
Date of Death: 23 November 1986
Cemetery: San Francisco National Cemetery (A-788A)
(MH)—San Francisco, California
Entered Service at: Indianapolis, Marion County, Indiana
Unit: Submarine Rescue & Salvage Unit, U.S.S. *Falcon*
Battle or Place of Action: Portsmouth, southeast off the Isle
of Shoals, New Hampshire
Date of Action: 23 May 1939
Date of Presentation: 19 January 1940
Place of Presentation: Washington, D.C., presented by Sec.
of the Navy Charles Edison
Citation: For extraordinary heroism in the line of his profession during the rescue and salvage operations following the sinking of the U.S.S. *Squalus* on 23 May 1939. During the rescue operations, Badders, as senior member of the rescue chamber crew, made the last extremely hazardous trip of the rescue chamber to attempt to rescue any possible survivors in the flooded afterportion of the *Squalus*. He was fully aware of the great danger involved in that if he and his assistant became incapacitated, there was no way in which either could be rescued. During the salvage operations, Badders made important and difficult dives under the most hazardous conditions. His outstanding performance of duty contributed much to the success of the operations and characterizes conduct far above and beyond the ordinary call of duty.

2578 ◆ BENNETT, FLOYD

Rank: Machinist (highest rank: Chief Aviation Machinist
Mate)
Service: U.S. Navy
Birthday: 25 October 1890
Place of Birth: Warrensburg, Warren County, New York
Date of Death: 25 April 1928
Place of Death: Quebec, Canada
Cemetery: Arlington National Cemetery (3-1852-B)—
Arlington, Virginia
Entered Service at: New York
Served as: Co-Pilot/Radio Operator
Battle or Place of Action: Spitsbergen, Norway to the
North Pole
Date of Action: 9 May 1926
Date of Presentation: 25 February 1927

Place of Presentation: The White House, presented by Pres.
Calvin Coolidge
Citation: For distinguishing himself conspicuously by courage and intrepidity at the risk of his life as a member of the Byrd Arctic Expedition and thus contributing largely to the success of the first heavier-than-air flight to the North Pole and return.

2579 ◆ BREAULT, HENRY

Rank: Torpedoman Second Class
Service: U.S. Navy
Birthday: 14 October 1900
Place of Birth: Putnam, Windham County, Connecticut
Date of Death: 5 December 1941
Place of Death: Newport, Rhode Island
Cemetery: St. Mary's Cemetery (MH)—Putnam,
Connecticut
Entered Service at: Vermont
Unit: U.S. Submarine *O-5*
Battle or Place of Action: Limon Bay, Canal Zone, Panama
Date of Action: 28 October 1923
G.O. Number, Date: 125, 20 February 1924
Date of Presentation: 8 March 1924
Place of Presentation: The White House, presented by Pres.
Calvin Coolidge
Citation: For heroism and devotion to duty while serving on board the U.S. submarine *O-5* at the time of the sinking of that vessel. On the morning of 28 October 1923, the *O-5* collided with the steamship *Abangarez* and sank in less than a minute. When the collision occurred, Breault was in the torpedo room. Upon reaching the hatch, he saw that the boat was rapidly sinking. Instead of jumping overboard to save his own life, he returned to the torpedo room to the rescue of a shipmate who he knew was trapped in the boat, closing the torpedo room hatch on himself. Breault and Brown remained trapped in this compartment until rescued by the salvage party 31 hours later.

2580 ◆ BYRD JR., RICHARD EVELYN

Rank: Commander (highest rank: Rear Admiral)
Service: U.S. Navy
Birthday: 25 October 1888
Place of Birth: Winchester, Frederick County, Virginia
Date of Death: 11 March 1957
Place of Death: Boston, Massachusetts
Cemetery: Arlington National Cemetery (2-4969-1)
(MH)—Arlington, Virginia

Entered Service at: Virginia
Served as: Pilot
Battle or Place of Action: Spitsbergen, Norway to the North Pole
 of Action: 9 May 1926
Date of Presentation: 25 February 1927
Place of Presentation: The White House, presented by Pres. Calvin Coolidge
Citation: For distinguishing himself conspicuously by courage and intrepidity at the risk of his life, in demonstrating that it is possible for aircraft to travel in continuous flight from a now inhabited portion of the earth over the North Pole and return.

2581 ◆ *CHOLISTER, GEORGE ROBERT

Rank: Boatswain's Mate First Class
Service: U.S. Navy
Birthday: 18 December 1898
Place of Birth: Camden, Camden County, New Jersey
Date of Death: 21 October 1924
Cemetery: Colestown Cemetery—Cherry Hill, New Jersey
Entered Service at: New Jersey
Unit: U.S.S. *Trenton*
Battle or Place of Action: U.S.S. *Trenton*
Date of Action: 20 October 1924
Date of Issue: 3 February 1933
Citation: For extraordinary heroism in the line of his profession on the occasion of a fire on board the U.S.S. *Trenton*. At 3:35 on the afternoon of 20 October 1924, while the *Trenton* was preparing to fire trial installation shots from the two 6-inch guns in the forward twin mount of that vessel, two charges of powder ignited. Twenty men were trapped in the twin mount. Four died almost immediately and 10 later from burns and inhalation of flames and gases. The six others were severely injured. Cholister, without thought of his own safety, on seeing that the charge of powder from the left gun was ignited, jumped for the right charge and endeavored to put it in the immersion tank. The left charge burst into flame and ignited the right charge before Cholister could accomplish his purpose. He fell unconscious while making a supreme effort to save his shipmates and died the following day.

2582 ◆ *CORRY JR., WILLIAM MERRILL

Rank: Lieutenant Commander
Service: U.S. Navy
Birthday: 5 October 1889
Place of Birth: Quincy, Gadsden County, Florida
Date of Death: 6 October 1920
Place of Death: Hartford, Connecticut
Cemetery: Eastern Cemetery—Quincy, Florida
Entered Service at: Florida
Battle or Place of Action: near Hartford, Connecticut
Date of Action: 2 October 1920
Citation: For heroic service in attempting to rescue a brother officer from a flame-enveloped airplane. On 2 October 1920, an airplane in which Lt. Comdr. Corry was a passenger crashed and burst into flames. He was thrown 30 feet clear of the plane and, though injured, rushed back to the burning machine and endeavored to release the pilot. In so doing he sustained serious burns, from which he died four days later.

2583 ◆ CRANDALL, ORSON LEON

Rank: Chief Boatswain's Mate (highest rank: Lieutenant)
Service: U.S. Navy
Birthday: 2 February 1903
Place of Birth: St. Joseph, Buchanan County, Missouri
Date of Death: 10 May 1960
Place of Death: St. Petersburg, Florida
Cemetery: Arlington National Cemetery (48-2004) (MH)—Arlington, Virginia
Entered Service at: Connecticut
Unit: Submarine Rescue & Salvage Unit, U.S.S. *Falcon*
Served as: Master Diver
Battle or Place of Action: Portsmouth, southeast off the Isle of Shoals, New Hampshire
Date of Action: 23 May 1939
Date of Presentation: 19 January 1940
Place of Presentation: Washington, D.C., presented by Sec. of the Navy Charles Edison
Citation: For extraordinary heroism in the line of his profession as a master diver throughout the rescue and salvage operations following the sinking of the U.S.S. *Squalus* on 23 May 1939. His leadership and devotion to duty in directing diving operations and in making important and difficult dives under the most hazardous conditions characterize conduct far above and beyond the ordinary call of duty.

2584 ◆ *DREXLER, HENRY CLAY

Rank: Ensign
Service: U.S. Navy
Birthday: 7 August 1901
Place of Birth: Braddock, Allegheny County, Pennsylvania
Date of Death: 20 October 1924
Place of Death: on board U.S.S. Trenton
Cemetery: Arlington National Cemetery (4-3051)—Arlington, Virginia
Entered Service at: Pennsylvania
Unit: U.S.S. *Trenton*
Battle or Place of Action: U.S.S. *Trenton*
Date of Action: 20 October 1924
Date of Issue: 3 February 1933
Citation: For extraordinary heroism in the line of his profession on the occasion of a fire on board the U.S.S. *Trenton*. At 3:35 on the afternoon of 20 October 1924, while the Trenton was preparing to fire trial installation shots from the two 6-inch guns in the forward twin mount of that vessel, two charges of powder ignited. Twenty men were trapped in the twin mount. Four died almost immediately and 10 later from burns and inhalation of flames and gases. The six others were severely injured. Ens. Drexler, without thought of his own safety, on seeing that the charge of powder from the left gun was ignited, jumped for the right charge and endeavored to put it in the immersion tank. The left charge burst into

flame and ignited the right charge before Ens. Drexler could accomplish his purpose. He met his death while making a supreme effort to save his shipmates.

2585 ◆ EADIE, THOMAS

Rank: Chief Gunner's Mate
Service: U.S. Navy
Birthday: 7 April 1887
Place of Birth: Scotland
Date of Death: 14 November 1974
Place of Death: Brockton, Massachusetts
Cemetery: Island Cemetery Annex—Newport, Rhode Island
Entered Service at: Newport, Newport County, Rhode Island
Served as: Diver
Battle or Place of Action: off Provincetown, Massachusetts
Date of Action: 18 December 1927
Place of Presentation: Presented by Pres. Calvin Coolidge
Citation: For display of extraordinary heroism in the line of his profession above and beyond the call of duty on 18 December 1927, during the diving operations in connection with the sinking of the U.S.S. *S-4* with all on board, as a result of a collision off Provincetown, Mass. On this occasion when Michels, chief torpedoman, U.S. Navy, while attempting to connect an air line to the submarine at a depth of 102 feet became seriously fouled, Eadie, under the most adverse diving conditions, deliberately, knowingly, and willingly took his own life in his hands by promptly descending to the rescue in response to the desperate need of his companion diver. After two hours of extremely dangerous and heartbreaking work, by his cool, calculating, and skillful labors, he succeeded in his mission and brought Michels safely to the surface.

2586 ◆ EDWARDS, WALTER ATLEE

Rank: Lieutenant Commander
Service: U.S. Navy
Birthday: 8 November 1886
Place of Birth: Philadelphia, Philadelphia County, Pennsylvania
Date of Death: 15 January 1928
Cemetery: Arlington National Cemetery (4-3183)—Arlington, Virginia
Entered Service at: Pennsylvania
Unit: U.S.S. *Bainbridge*
Battle or Place of Action: Sea of Marmora, Turkey
Date of Action: 16 December 1922
G.O. Number, Date: 123, 4 February 1924
Date of Presentation: 2 February 1924
Place of Presentation: The White House, presented by Pres. Calvin Coolidge
Citation: For heroism in rescuing 482 men, women, and children from the French military transport *Vinh-Long*, destroyed by fire in the Sea of Marmora, Turkey, on 16 December 1922. Lt. Comdr. Edwards, commanding the U.S.S. *Bainbridge*, placed his vessel alongside the bow of the transport and, in spite of several violent explosions which

occurred on the burning vessel, maintained his ship in that position until all who were alive were taken on board. Of a total of 495 on board, 482 were rescued by his coolness, judgment, and professional skill, which were combined with a degree of heroism that must reflect new glory on the U.S. Navy.

2587 ◆ GREELY, ADOLPHUS WASHINGTON

Rank: Major General
Service: U.S. Army Ret.
Birthday: 27 March 1844
Place of Birth: Newburyport, Essex County, Massachusetts
Date of Death: 20 October 1935
Place of Death: Washington, D.C.
Cemetery: Arlington National Cemetery (1-129)—Arlington, Virginia
Entered Service at: Louisiana
Served as: Commander
Date of Action: 26 July 1861-10 February 1906
G.O. Number, Date: 3 W.D. 1935 Act of Congress, 21 March 1935
Date of Issue: 27 March 1935
Citation: For his life of splendid public service, begun on 27 March 1844, having enlisted as a private in the U.S. Army on 26 July 1861, and by successive promotions was commissioned as major general 10 February 1906, and retired by operation of the law on his 64th birthday.

2588 ◆ HUBER, WILLIAM RUSSELL

Rank: Machinist's Mate (highest rank: Lieutenant)
Service: U.S. Navy
Birthday: 16 July 1902
Place of Birth: Harrisburg, Dauphin County, Pennsylvania
Date of Death: 25 January 1982
Place of Death: San Mateo, California
Cemetery: Golden Gate National Cemetery (2-B-4085)—San Bruno, California
Entered Service at: Pennsylvania
Unit: U.S.S. *Bruce*
Battle or Place of Action: Navy Yard, Norfolk, Virginia
Date of Action: 11 June 1928
Date of Presentation: 15 December 1928
Place of Presentation: The White House, presented by Pres. Calvin Coolidge
Citation: For display of extraordinary heroism in the line of his profession on 11 June 1928, after a boiler accident on the U.S.S. *Bruce*, then at the Naval Shipyard, Norfolk, Va. Immediately on becoming aware of the accident, Huber without hesitation and in complete disregard of his own safety, entered the steam-filled fireroom and at grave risk to his life succeeded by almost superhuman efforts in carrying Charles H. Byran to safety. Although having received severe and dangerous burns about the arms and neck, he descended with a view toward rendering further assistance. The great courage,

grit, and determination displayed by Huber on this occasion characterized conduct far above and beyond the call of duty.

2589 ◆ *HUTCHINS, CARLTON BARMORE

Rank: Lieutenant
Service: U.S. Navy
Birthday: 12 September 1904
Place of Birth: Albany, Albany County, New York
Date of Death: 2 February 1938
Place of Death: at Sea Pacific Ocean
Cemetery: Remains not recovered.
Entered Service at: New York
Unit: U.S. Navy Seaplane PBY-2 No. 0463 (11-P-3)
Battle or Place of Action: off California Coast
Date of Action: 2 February 1938
Citation: For extraordinary heroism as the pilot of the U.S. Navy seaplane PBY-2 No.0463 (11-P-3) while engaged in tactical exercises with the U.S. Fleet on 2 February 1938. Although his plane was badly damaged, Lt. Hutchins remained at the controls endeavoring to bring the damaged plane to a safe landing and to afford an opportunity for his crew to escape by parachutes. His cool, calculated conduct contributed principally to the saving of the lives of all who survived. His conduct on this occasion was above and beyond the call of duty.

2590 ◆ LINDBERGH JR., CHARLES AUGUSTUS

Rank: Captain (highest rank: Brigadier General)
Service: U.S. Army Air Corps Reserve
Birthday: 4 February 1902
Place of Birth: Detroit, Wayne County, Michigan
Date of Death: 26 August 1974
Cemetery: Kipahulu Church Cemetery—Maui, Hawaii
Entered Service at: Little Falls, Morrison County, Minnesota
Served as: Pilot, Navigator
Battle or Place of Action: from New York City to Paris, France
Date of Action: 20-21 May 1927
G.O. Number, Date: 5, W.D. 1928; Act of Congress: 14 December 1927
Citation: For displaying heroic courage and skill as a navigator, at the risk of his life, by his nonstop flight in his airplane, the *Spirit of St. Louis*, from New York City to Paris, France, 20–21 May 1927, by which Capt. Lindbergh not only achieved the greatest individual triumph of any American citizen but demonstrated that travel across the ocean by aircraft was possible.

2591 ◆ McDONALD, JAMES HARPER

Rank: Chief Metalsmith (highest rank: Lieutenant)
Service: U.S. Navy
Birthday: 15 July 1900
Place of Birth: near Newmand, Scotland
Date of Death: 29 December 1973

Cemetery: Fishing Creek Cemetery—Roulette, Pennsylvania
Entered Service at: Washington, D.C.
Served as: Master Diver
Battle or Place of Action: Portsmouth, southeast off the Isle of Shoals, New Hampshire
Date of Action: 23 May 1939
Date of Presentation: 19 January 1940
Place of Presentation: Washington, D.C., presented by Sec. of the Navy Charles Edison
Citation: For extraordinary heroism in the line of his profession as a master diver throughout the rescue and salvage operations following the sinking of the U.S.S. *Squalus* on 23 May 1939. His leadership, masterly skill, general efficiency, and untiring devotion to duty in directing diving operations and in making important and difficult dives under the most hazardous conditions, characterize conduct far above and beyond the ordinary call of duty.

2592 ◆ MIHALOWSKI, JOHN

Rank: Torpedoman First Class (highest rank: Lieutenant Commander)
Service: U.S. Navy
Birthday: 12 August 1910
Place of Birth: Worcester, Worcester County, Massachusetts
Date of Death: 29 October 1993
Place of Death: Largo, Florida
Cemetery: Serenity Gardens Memorial Park (MH)—Largo, Florida
Entered Service at: Massachusetts
Unit: Submarine Rescue & Salvage Unit, U.S.S. *Falcon*
Served as: Diver
Battle or Place of Action: Portsmouth, southeast off the Isle of Shoals, New Hampshire
Date of Action: 23 May 1939
Date of Presentation: 19 January 1940
Place of Presentation: Washington, D.C., presented by Sec. of the Navy Charles Edison
Citation: For extraordinary heroism in the line of his profession during the rescue and salvage operations following the sinking of the U.S.S. *Squalus* on 23 May 1939. Mihalowski, as a member of the rescue chamber crew, made the last extremely hazardous trip of the rescue chamber to attempt the rescue of any possible survivors in the flooded afterportion of the *Squalus*. He was fully aware of the great danger involved, in that, if he and the other member of the crew became incapacitated, there was no way in which either could be rescued. During the salvage operations Mihalowski made important and difficult dives under the most hazardous conditions. His outstanding performance of duty contributed much to the success of the operations and characterizes conduct far above and beyond the ordinary call of duty.

2593 ◆ RYAN JR., THOMAS JOHN

Rank: Ensign (highest rank: Rear Admiral)
Service: U.S. Navy

Birthday: 5 August 1901
Place of Birth: New Orleans, Orleans County, Louisiana
Date of Death: 28 January 1970
Place of Death: New Orleans, Louisiana
Cemetery: Arlington National Cemetery (34-80-A-1) (MH)—Arlington, Virginia
Entered Service at: Louisiana
Battle or Place of Action: Yokohama, Japan
Date of Action: 1 September 1923
Date of Presentation: 15 March 1924
Place of Presentation: The White House, by Pres. Calvin Coolidge
Citation: For heroism in effecting the rescue of a woman from the burning Grand Hotel, Yokohama, Japan, on 1 September 1923. Following the earthquake and fire which occurred in Yokohama on 1 September, Ens. Ryan, with complete disregard for his own life, extricated a woman from the Grand Hotel, thus saving her life. His heroic conduct upon this occasion reflects the greatest credit on himself and on the U.S. Navy, of which he is part.

2594 ◆ SMITH, ALBERT JOSEPH

Rank: Private (highest rank: Sergeant)
Service: U.S. Marine Corps

Birthday: 31 July 1898
Place of Birth: Calumet, Houghton County, Michigan
Date of Death: 27 March 1973
Cemetery: Grand Lawn Cemetery—Detroit, Michigan
Entered Service at: Michigan
Served as: Sentry
Battle or Place of Action: Marine Barracks, Naval Air Station, Pensacola, Florida
Date of Action: 11 February 1921
G.O. Number, Date: 72, 29 September 1921
Date of Presentation: 17 October 1921
Place of Presentation: Santo Domingo, Dominican Republic, presented by Brig. Gen. Harry Lee
Citation: At about 7:30 A.M. on the morning of 11 February 1921, Pvt. Smith, while on duty as a sentry, rescued Plen M. Phelps, late machinist's mate second class, U.S. Navy, from a burning seaplane which had fallen near his post, gate No. 1, Marine Barracks, Naval Air Station, Pensacola, Fla. Despite the explosion of the gravity gasoline tank, with total disregard of personal safety, he pushed himself to a position where he could reach Phelps, who was pinned beneath the burning wreckage, and rescued him from the burning plane, in the performance of which he sustained painful burns about the head, neck, and both hands.